Ben Hodges / Scott Denny

THEATRE WORLD®

THEATRE WORLD®
Volume 67
Copyright © 2012 by Ben Hodges

Published in 2012 by Theatre World Media
Distributed by Applause Theatre & Cinema Books
An Imprint of Hal Leonard Corporation
7777 West Bluemound Road
Milwaukee, WI 53213

Trade Book Division Editorial Offices
33 Plymouth Street, Montclair, NJ 07042

Printed in the United States of America
Book design by Tony Meisel

ISBN 978–1-55783-840-7
ISSN 1088–4564
www.applausebooks.com

To Tovah Feldshuh

Whose incredible diversity and success onstage is matched only by her philanthropy offstage. Her steadfast support of this publication and the Theatre World Awards will forever be appreciated by its editors.

PAST EDITORS	Daniel Blum (1945–1963)
	John Willis (1963–2007)
EDITOR IN CHIEF	Ben Hodges (1998–present)
COEDITOR	Scott Denny (2005-present)
ASSOCIATE OFF-OFF BROADWAY EDITOR	Shay Gines
ASSOCIATE REGIONAL EDITOR	Rommel "Raj" Autencio
ASSOCIATE EDITOR	Heath McCormack
ASSISTANT EDITOR	Kelley Murphy Perlstein
CONTRIBUTING BROADWAY EDITOR	Adam Feldman
CONTRIBUTING OFF-BROADWAY EDITOR	Linda Buchwald
CONTRIBUTING REGIONAL EDITOR	Rob Weinert-Kendt
STAFF PHOTOGRAPHERS	Rommel "Raj" Autencio, Konrad Brattke, Bruce Glikas, Walter McBride, Laura and Michael Viade

Acknowledgements

Theatre World would like to extend a very special thank you to all the New York and regional press agents, theatre marketing departments, and theatre photographers for their constant and steadfast support of this publication as well as for the endless resources that they provide to the editorial staff.

Our gratitude is eternally extended to our contributing photographers: Joan Marcus, Carol Rosegg, Paul Kolnik, Richard Termine, Gerry Goodstein, T. Charles Erickson, Monique Carboni, Dixie Sheridan, Paula Court, Michal Daniel, Robert J. Saferstein, Peter James Zielinski, David Alkire, Richard Anderson, Pavel Antonov, Miranda Arden, Catherine Ashmore, Pier Baccaro, Jim Baldassare, Erin Balino, SuzAnne Barabas, Armin Bardel, Brian Barenio, Stan Barouh, Rachelle Beckerman, Derrick Belcham, Chris Bennion, Stephanie Berger, Kevin Berne, Rick Berubé, Rose Billings, Marc Bovino, Jay Brady, Michael Brosilow, Harry Butler, Nino Fernando Campagna, Owen Carey, Roy Chicas, Jonathan Christman, Meagan Cignoli, Bradley Clements, Larry Cobra, Peter Coombs, Arthur Cornelius, Gregory Costanzo, Sandra Coudert, Lindsey Crane, Amanda Culp, Julie Curry, Whitney Curtis, Ellie D'Eustachio, Blaine Davis, Robert Day, Manuel Navarro de la Fuente, Joe del Tufo, Phile Deprez, Jeff Derose, Henry DiRocco, Lisa Dozier, Erik Ekroth, Aaron Epstein, Eric Y. Exit, Felix Photography, Benoit Fontaine, Joshua Frachisseur, Tim Fuller, Marc Garvin, Drew Geraci, Gili Getz, Gion, Ronald L. Glassman, Jenny Graham, Larry Gumpel, Aric Gunter, Steven Gunther, Raymond Haddad, Sabrina Hamilton, Jeremy Handelman, John Haynes, Murray Head, Susan Helbock, Michael Henninger, Ben Hider, Albert Hirshon, Justin Hoch, Nikola Horejs, Ken Howard, Lyn Hughes, Ken Huth, James David Jackson, Ken Jacques, Ryan Jensen, Rafael Jordan, Kristie Kahns, Thom Kaine, Jon Kandel, Dermot Kelly, Jennifer Maufrais Kelly, Sue Kessler, Ben King, Johnny Knight, Alex Koch, Ed Kreiger, Stephen Kunken, Michael Kwlechinski, Michael Lamont, Liz Lauren, Chang W. Lee, Corky Lee, Kantu Lentz, Stuart Levine, Geraint Lewis, James Leynse, Alexandria Marlin, Roger Mastroianni, Douglas McBride, Dave McCracken, Jeff McCrum, Steve McNicholas, Ari Mintz, Gustavo Monroy, Meghan Moore, Jerry Naunheim Jr., Doug Nuttelman, Erik Pearson, Ry Pepper, Johan Persson, Pierre, Ves Pitts, Eduardo Placer, Stephen Poff, Michael Portantiere, Leah Prater, Jaime Quinoñes, Patrick Redmond, Justin Richardson, Alyssa Ringler, John Roese, Mark Rohna, Suzi Sadler, Craig Schwartz, Darron Setlow, The Shaltzes, Kim T. Sharp, Bev Sheehan, Steve Shevett, Erika Sidor, Michelle Sims, Jonathan Slaff, Richard Hubert Smith, Gil Smith, Owen Smith, Diane Sobolewski, Hong Sooyeon, Squid Ink Creative, Theresa Squire, Marcus Stern, Noah Strone, Ben Strothmann, Scott Suchman, Stephen Sunderlin, Evan Sung, Daniel Talbott, Steve Tanner, Eran Tari, Brandon Thibodeaux, Ned Thorne, Stephen B. Thornton, Shirin Tinat, Ali Tollervey, Dominick Totino, Mark Turek, Sandy Underwood, Goran Veljic, Pascal Victor, Levi Walker, Bree Michael Warner, Sturgis Warner, Jon Wasserman, Lee Wexler, Drew Wingert, Nicholas Woods, Scott Wynn, Jordana Zeldin, and Tom Zuback.

Equally, we are extrememly grateful for our New York press agents: *The Acting Company*: Paula Raymond; Janet Appel; Jim Baldassare; *Boneau/Bryan-Brown*: Chris Boneau, Adrian Bryan-Brown, Jim Byk, Jackie Green, Kelly Guiod, Linnae Hodzic, Jessica Johnson, Kevin Jones, Amy Kass, Holly Kinney, Emily Meagher, Aaron Meier, Christine Olver, Joe Perrotta, Matt Polk, Amanda Sales, Heath Schwartz, Michael Strassheim, Susanne Tighe; Jill Bowman; John Capo; Bruce Cohen; *Cohn Dutcher*: Dan Dutcher, Candace Newson; Peter Cromarty; *DARR Publicity*: David Gibbs, *David Gersten and Associates*: David Gersten, Shane Marshall Brown, Bill Evans, Jim Randolph; Helene Davis; Lauren Fitzgerald; Merle Frimark; Karen Greco; *The Hartman Group*: Michael Hartman, Leslie Baden Papa, Nicole Capatasto, Tom D'Ambrosio, Juliana Hannett, Alyssa Hart, Bethany Larsen, Matt Ross, Frances White, Wayne Wolfe; Ellen Jacobs; Judy Jacksina; *The Karpel Group*: Bridget Kaplinski; *Keith Sherman and Associates*: Keith Sherman, Scott Klein, Bret Oberman, Glenna Freedman, Dan Demello, Logan Metzler; *Jeffrey Richards and Associates*: Irene Gandy, Elon Rutberg, Alana Karpoff, Diana Rissetto; Ryan Hallett; Beck Lee; Jenny Lerner; *Lincoln Center Theater*: Philip Rinaldi, Barbara Carroll, Amanda Dekker; Kevin McAnarney; *Miller Wright and Associates*: Miller Wright, Dan Fortune, Danielle Grabianowski; *Maya PR*: Penny Landau; Emily Owens; *O + M Company*: Rick Miramontez, Dusty Bennett, Molly Barnett, Philip Carrubba, Jaron Caldwell, Sam Corbett, Jon Dimond, Richard Hillman, Yufen Kung, Jillian Lawton, Chelsea Nachman, Patrick O'Neil, Felicia Pollack, Alexandra Rubin, Andy Snyder, Elizabeth Wagner; *Paper Mill Playhouse*: Shayne Austin Miller; Patrick Paris; *Pearl Theatre Company*: Aaron Schwartzbord; *The Public Theater*: Candi Adams, Sam Neuman, Josh Ferri, Julie Danni; *The Publicity Office*: Marc Thibodeau, Michael Borowski, Jeremy Shaffer, Matt Fasano; Scotti Rhodes; Katie Rosin; Audrey Ross; *Richard Kornberg and Associates*: Richard Kornberg, Don Summa, Billy Zavelson, Danielle McGarry; *Rubenstein Communications Inc.*: Howard Rubenstein, Amy Jacobs, Tom Keaney, Elyse Weissman; *Sam Rudy Media Relations*: Sam Rudy, Robert Lasko, Dale Heller; Pete Sanders; Susan L. Schulman; Brett Singer; Jonathan Slaff; *Spin Cycle*: Ron Lasko; *Springer Associates*: Gary Springer, Joe Trentacosta; *Sun Productions*: Stephen Sunderlin; *Type A Marketing*: DJ Martin; *Walt Disney Theatricals*: Adrianna Douzous, Dennis Crowley, Michelle Bergmann; *The Wooster Group*: Clay Hapaz; Blake Zidell; and Lanie Zipoy.

Our gratitude is also eternally extended to our contributing regional theatre staff and press personnel who have contributed time and efforts for their company's listing: Becky Lathrop, Clayton Weller (ACT- A Contemporary Theatre); Kirsty Gaukel, Melinda Beck (Actors Theatre of Louisville); Meg Lewis (Alabama Shakespeare Festival); Lauren Pelletier (Alley Theatre); Kathleen Covington (Alliance Theatre Company); Evren Odcikin (American Conservatory Theater); Katalin Mitchell (American Repertory Theatre); Leigh Goldenberg (Arden Theatre Company); Greta Hays (Arena Stage at the Mead Center for American Theater); Jami Kozemczak, Jonathan Crider (Arizona Theatre Company), Ashley Pettit (Arkansas Repertory Theatre); Charlie Siedenburg (Barrington Stage Company); Danielle Goodrich (Barter Theatre); Terence Keane (Berkeley Repertory Theatre); Rebecca Brighenti, Colleen Hughes (Berkshire Theatre Festival); Marilyn Langbehn (California Shakespeare Theater); Darcy Koch (Casa Mañana Theatre); T.J. Gerckens (CATCO); Nancy Hereford, Shannon Smith (Center Theatre Group); Heather Jackson (CENTERSTAGE); Connie Yeager (Cincinnati Playhouse in the Park); Lisa Craig (Cleveland Play House); Kelsey Guy (Dallas Theatre Center); Amy Bish (Delaware Theatre Company); Jane Mcdonald (Denver Center Theatre Company); Bridget Summers (The 5th Avenue Theatre); Allison Rawlings (Geffen Playhouse); Heidi Blackwell (Georgia Shakespeare Festival); Dawn Kellogg (Geva Theatre Center); Denise Schneider (Goodman Theatre); Elisa Hale (Goodspeed Musicals); Todd Krispinsky (Great Lakes Theater); Seena Hodges (Guthrie Theater); Rebecca Curtiss

(Huntington Theatre Company); Jon Billig (Illinois Theatre Center); Richard Roberts (Indiana Repertory Theatre); Laura Muir (Kansas City Repertory Theatre); Deanna Chew (La Jolla Playhouse); Steven Scarpa (Long Wharf Theatre); Dan Bauer (McCarter Theatre); Ryan Axford (Merrimack Repertory Theatre); Wayne Bryan, Michael Kline (Music Theatre of Wichita); Kristin Buie (North Carolina Theatre); Heather Latiri (Olney Theatre Center); Amy Richard (Oregon Shakespeare Festival); Shayne Austin Miller (Paper Mill Playhouse); Deborah K. Fleischman, Stephanie Dennis (Philadelphia Theatre Company); Margie Romero (Pittsburgh Public Theater); Connie Mahan, Tim Scales (PlayMakers Repertory Company); Cynthia Fuhrman, Kinsley Suer (Portland Center Stage); Katie Puglisi (Repertory Theatre of St. Louis); Laura Saldivar (San Jose Repertory Theatre); Joanna Harowitz, Danielle Girard (Seattle Repertory Theatre); Peter Eramo, Jr. (Signature Theatre); Beth George (South Coast Repertory); Eric Pugh (Stages St. Louis); Linda Garrison, David Rosenberg, Cassidi Stuckman (Steppenwolf Theatre); Patrick Finlon (Syracuse Stage); Pat Patrick (Tennessee Rep); Marilyn Busch, Stephanie Schwartz (Trinity Repertory Company); Morgan Vaughan (Virginia Stage Company); Patricia Blaufuss (Westport Country Playhouse); Noel Edwards (Woolly Mammoth Theatre Company); and Stephen Padla (Yale Repertory).

The editors of *Theatre World* would also like give very special thanks to: John Cerullo (Group Publisher, Hal Leonard Performing Arts Publishing Group), the staff at Hal Leonard Performing Arts Publishing Group: Jamie Nelson (Publicity and Marketing Assistant), Carol Flannery (Editorial Director), Clare Cerullo (Production Manager), Marybeth Keating, (Associate Editor); the staff of Ouest restaurant; Gerard Alessandrini; Beth Allen, Bob Anderson; Epitacio Arganza; Elvira, Kenneth, Bryan, J.R., Arlene, Daryl, and Kayden Autencio; Feliciano Baltazar; Joel Banuelos; Jason Baruch and Sendroff and Baruch LLP; Seth Barrish, Lee Brock, Eric Paeper, and The Barrow Group Theater Company/The Barrow Group School; Jed Bernstein and the Commercial Theater Institute; Wayne Besen and Truth Wins Out; Micah-Shane Brewer and Drew Ogle; Fred Cantor; Fred Caruso; Jason Cicci, Monday Morning Productions, and Summer Stage New York; June Clark; Richard Cohen; Sue Cosson; Susan Cosson; Kimberly Courtney Esq.; Robert Dean Davis; Carol and Nick Dawson; Bob and Brenda Denny; Jamie deRoy; Tim Deak; Diane Dixon; Jetaun Dobbs; Eleanor Speert, Allan Hubby, and the staff of the Drama Book Shop; Craig Dudley; the staff of the Duplex Cabaret and Piano Bar; Sherry Eaker; Ben Feldman Esq. and Beigelman, Feiner, and Feldman, P.C.; Emily Feldman; David Fritz; Christine and David Grimsby; the Estates of the late Charles J. Grant Jr. and Zan Van Antwerp; Helen Guditis and the Broadway Theater Museum; Brenda Saunders-Hampden Esq.; Brad Hampton; Laura Hagan; Al and Sherry Hodges; Michael Humphreys Esq.; Charlie and Phyllis Hurt; Gretchen, Aaron, Eli, and Max Kerr; Sofia Khalid; Jane, Lynn, Kris, and Leslie Kircher; the staff of Macy's Parade and Entertainment Group; Andrew Kirtzman, Luke Escamilla, and The Madison Fire Island Pines; Bob Levine; David Lowry; Stuart Marshall; Kenneth Marzin; Joaquin Matias Esq.; Heath McCormack; Michael Messina; Barry Monush and Screen World; Ted Chapin, Howard Sherman; Jason Bowcutt, Shay Gines, Nick Micozzi, and the staff and respective voting committees of the New York Innovative Theatre Awards; Barbara O'Malley; Petie Dodrill, Craig Johnson, Rob Johnson, Dennis Romer, Katie Robbins, Dean Jo Ann VanSant, Ed Vaughan, the late Dr. Charles O. Dodrill and the staff of Otterbein College/Otterbein College Department of Theatre and Dance, P.J. Owen; William Craver and Paradigm; Bernadette Peters; John Philip Esq. and Andrew Resto; Frank Politano Esq.; Angie and Drew Powell; Kay Radtke; Carolyn, David, Glenna, and Jonas Rapp; Charlotte St. Martin and the League of American Theatres and Producers; Andrea Evans Young and the SFX Archive; P.J. McAteer, Mario Priola, and the staff of the Sip-n-Twirl; Susan Stoller; Henry Grossman, Michael Riordan, John Sala, Mark Snyder, Martha Swope; Renée Isely Tobin and Bob, Kate, Eric, Laura, and Anna, Tobin; Bob Ost and Theater Resources Unlimited Inc.; Tom Lynch, Kati Meister, Erin Oestreich, Steven Bloom, Mary Botosan, Randall Hemming, Barry Keating, Jane Stuart, and the board of directors of The Theatre World Awards Inc.; Peter Filichia, Harry Haun, Howard Kissel, Matthew Murray, Frank Scheck, Michael Sommers, Linda Winer, and the voting committee of The Theatre World Awards Inc.; Jack Williams, Steven Smith, and the staff of the University of Tennessee at Knoxville; Hugo Uys; Wilson Valentin; Laura and Michael Viade; Kathie Packer and the Estate of the late Frederic B. Vogel; Sarah and Bill Willis; the Estate of John A. Willis; George Wilson; Seth and Wolkofsky and Adeena Gabriel; Shane Frampton; and Doug Wright.

Contents

Editor's Note

This is the sixty-seventh consecutive year that this book has been published. It is unlikely that *Theatre World* would have survived this long, because for over a half a century the responsibility for churning out this publication has rested in the hands of precious few. But it also has been likely that it would continue, because those hands have always proven, and continue to prove, so very capable.

This is the first volume that was created—from beginning to end—without the supervision of our longtime editor, John Willis, who guided this publication, as well as the Theatre World Awards for Outstanding Broadway Debuts, for over forty years. His devotion to theatre is by now legendary and the number of lives he touched, including mine, legion.

This is also the first volume published by the newly formed Theatre World Media imprint, for which I am proud to serve as president. Theatre World Media also now publishes our companion volume *Screen World*, which, at sixty-two, is the oldest pictorial and statistical record of the American foreign and domestic film seasons, admirably edited by seasoned author and film aficionado, Barry Monush. *Screen World Volume 62: The Films of 2010* debuted under the Theatre World Media imprint in November 2011, and just this past February received a rave review by *Library Journal*.

Both publications continue to be admirably distributed by Applause Theatre and Cinema Books, an imprint of the Hal Leonard Corporation. But this new relationship means that the compilation, design, layout, and all other aspects of both publications will now be supervised entirely by our own editorial staffs, yet still guarantees that both volumes will be accessible to the industry professionals, students, historians, and theatre fans worldwide who have come to rely on them year after year.

This volume, as always, continues to be the most complete annual pictorial and statistical record of the entire American theatre season. I am particularly proud of the new overall design of the past few volumes by our estimable designing partner, Tony Meisel, who has worked with us to ensure the inclusion of the voluminous material involved in pursuing our mission to include as many productions as possible, which includes Broadway, Off-Broadway, Off-Off-Broadway, as well as regional theatre. And our editorial staff constantly strives to include as many productions from all of those venues as possible, and in the case of regional theatres, as many as respond to our requests for information.

These past few volumes have also showcased—more thoroughly than ever before—the venues in which theatre is performed all across the nation, seen through the eyes of preeminent journalists and innovators in the theatre who know those venues best, by way of detailed overviews that introduce each respective section.

Many aspects of this newly excellent design and content are also due in large part due to the tireless work of my coeditor, Scott Denny, whose devotion to this publication is matched only by his devotion to the theatre itself. His attention to the detail included within these pages has allowed me to focus on the larger picture of the incorporation of Theatre World Media and ensuring the continuation of both *Theatre World* and *Screen World* well into the future.

While there is no predicting the various media transitions through which the printed word will traverse in the future, our editorial staff greets the challenges of the digital media age with enthusiasm at the opportunities that lie ahead in expanding our work to a broader audience. There is still, after all, more information on the annual American theatre season between these covers than is currently available in print, on the Internet, or anywhere else and we remain committed to making that information available annually in whatever form it may eventually take.

I would like to think that John Willis, and *Theatre World*'s founder before him, Daniel Blum, would be proud of the tradition that we continue with this, the sixty-seventh volume of this book, exploring and expanding the productions throughout America that define theatre in our time. We do this all the while remaining true to the vision that resulted in the very first volume of *Theatre World*, which was merely one man's personal love letter to Broadway.

While this letter is now authored by many men and women, it is our collective hope that it will be received in the loving spirit with which it has been sent.

—Ben Hodges
New York City

Also by Ben Hodges

The Commercial Theater Institute Guide to Producing Plays and Musicals
(Applause Theatre and Cinema Books)

Forbidden Acts: Pioneering Gay and Lesbian Plays of the Twentieth Century
(Applause Theatre and Cinema Books)

The American Theatre Wing Presents The Play That Changed My Life: America's Foremost Playwrights on the Plays That Influenced Them
(Applause Theatre and Cinema Books)

Outplays: Landmark Gay and Lesbian Plays of the Twentieth Century
(Alyson Books)

Also by Theatre World Media

Screen World Volume 62: The Films of 2010

BROADWAY
June 1, 2010–May 31, 2011

Top: *Brian Cox, Jason Patric, Jim Gaffigan, Chris Noth, and Kiefer Sutherland in* That Championship Season. *Opened at the Bernard B. Jacobs Theatre March 6, 2011 (photo by Joan Marcus)*

Center: *Jeffrey Wright (seated center) and the Company of Lincoln Center Theater production of* A Free Man of Color. *Opened at the Vivian Beaumont Theater November 18, 2010 (photo by T. Charles Erickson)*

Bottom: *John Leguizamo in* Ghetto Klown. *Opened at the Lyceum Theatre March 22, 2011 (photo by Carol Rosegg)*

Left: *Hannah Yelland and Tristan Sturrock in the Roundabout Theatre Company production of* Brief Encounter. *Opened at Studio 54 September 28, 2010* (photo by Joan Marcus)

Bottom left: *Christopher Connel, Brian Lonsdale, Deka Walmsley, Michael Hodgson, and David Whitaker in the Manhattan Theatre Club production of* The Pitmen Painters. *Opened at the Samuel J. Friedman Theatre September 30, 2010* (photo by Joan Marcus)

Bottom right: *Cherry Jones and Edward Hibbert in the Roundabout Theatre Company production of* Mrs. Warren's Profession. *Opened at the American Airlines Theatre October 3, 2010* (photo by Joan Marcus)

Benjamin Walker and the Company of Bloody Bloody Andrew Jackson. *Opened at the Bernard B. Jacobs Theatre October 13, 2010 (photo by Joan Marcus)*

Mark Rylance and David Hyde Pierce in La Bête. *Opened at the Music Box Theatre October 14, 2010 (photo by Joan Marcus)*

Vanessa Redgrave and James Earl Jones in Driving Miss Daisy. *Opened at the John Golden Theatre October 25, 2010* (photo by Carol Rosegg)

Kendrick Jones, Julius Thomas II, James T. Lane, Rodney Hicks, John Cullum, Christian Dante White, Jeremy Gumbs, Derrick Cobey, and Josh Breckenridge in The Scottsboro Boys. *Opened at the Lyceum Theatre October 31, 2010* (photo by Paul Kolnik)

Vivian Nixon, Laura Benanti, and Yanira Marin in the Lincoln Center Theater production of Women on the Verge of a Nervous Breakdown. *Opened at the Belasco Theatre November 4, 2010 (photo by Paul Kolnik)*

Sebastian Arcelus, Amy Spanger, and the Company of Elf. *Opened at the Al Hirschfeld Theatre November 14, 2010 (photo by Joan Marcus)*

Sara Topam, David Furr, and Brian Bedford in the Roundabout Theatre Company production of The Importance of Being Earnest. *Opened at the American Airlines Theatre January 13, 2011 (photo by Joan Marcus)*

Becky Ann Baker, Estelle Parsons, and Frances McDormand in the Manhattan Theatre Club production of Good People. *Opened at the Samuel J. Friedman Theatre March 3, 2011 (photo by Joan Marcus)*

Billy Crudup, Lea Williams, Raúl Esparza, and Grace Gummer in Arcadia. Opened at the Ethel Barrymore Theatre March 17, 2011 (photo by Carol Rosegg)

Will Swenson, Tony Seldon, and Nick Adams and the Company of Priscilla Queen of the Desert. Opened at the Palace Theatre March 20, 2011 (photo by Joan Marcus)

Left: *Rema Webb, Andrew Rannells, and Josh Gad in* The Book of Mormon. *Opened at the Eugene O'Neill Theatre March 24, 2011 (photo by Joan Marcus)*

Bottom left: *Robin Williams in* Bengal Tiger at the Baghdad Zoo. *Opened at the Richard Rodgers Theatre March 31, 2011 (photo by Carol Rosegg)*

Bottom right: *Rose Hemingway, Daniel Radcliffe, and the Company of* How to Succeed in Business Without Really Trying. *Opened at the Al Hirschfeld Theatre March 27, 2011 (photo by Ari Mintz)*

Top: *Bobby Cannavale and Chris Rock in* The Motherf**ker with the Hat. *Opened at the Gerald Schoenfeld Theatre April 11, 2011* (photo by Joan Marcus)

Bottom: *Aaron Tveit and the Company of* Catch Me If You Can. *Opened at the Neil Simon Theatre April 10, 2011* (photo by Joan Marcus)

Laura Osnes and Collin Donnell in the Roundabout Theatre Company production of Anything Goes. *Opened at the Stephen Sondheim Theatre April 7, 2011 (photo by Joan Marcus)*

The Company of the National Theatre of Great Britain and Lincoln Center Theater production of War Horse. *Opened at the Vivian Beaumont Theatre April 14, 2011 (photo by Paul Kolnik)*

Karen Mason and the Company of Wonderland. *Opened at the Marquis Theatre April 17, 2011 (photo by Paul Kolnik)*

Patina Miller, Victoria Clark, and the Company of Sister Act. *Opened at the Broadway Theatre April 20, 2011 (photo by Joan Marcus)*

Mark Rylance in Jerusalem. Opened at the Music Box Theatre
April 21, 2011 (photo by Simon Annand)

Jim Belushi and Nina Arianda in Born Yesterday. *Opened at the Cort Theatre April 24, 2011 (photo by Carol Rosegg)*

Al Pacino in the Public Theater production of The Merchant of Venice. *Opened at the Broadhurst Theatre November 13, 2010 (photo by Joan Marcus)*

Top: *Bill Dawes, Chris Sullivan, Robert Christopher Riley, Dan Lauria, Judith Light, and Keith Nobbs in* Lombardi. *Opened at the Circle in the Square Theatre October 21, 2010 (photo by Joan Marcus)*

Left: *Crystal Starr, Christina Sajous, Beth Leavel, Erica Ash, and Kyra DeCosta in* Baby It's You! *Opened at the Broadhurst Theatre April 27, 2011 (photo by Ari Mintz)*

Ben Stiller and Edie Falco in The House of Blue Leaves. *Opened at the Walter Kerr Theatre April 25, 2011 (photo by Joan Marcus)*

Alexander Gemignani, Chip Zien, Donna Murphy, Joyce Van Patten, and Lewis J. Stadlen in the Roundabout Theatre Company production of The People in the Picture. *Opened at Studio 54 April 28, 2011 (photo by Joan Marcus)*

Ellen Barkin in The Normal Heart. *Opened at the John Golden Theatre April 27, 2011 (photo by Joan Marcus)*

Oh, What a Tangled Web

Adam Feldman, Associate Theatre Editor/Cabaret Editor,
Time Out New York

Whatever else one might think about the 2010-2011 Broadway season, this much is true: It did not lack drama, either on stage or off. Two original musicals made national headlines—the first as a disaster waiting to happen, the second as a triumph on arrival. Meanwhile, with less hullabaloo, Broadway offered its richest slate of serious new plays in years.

Even more than usual, most of the season's biggest critical and commercial successes were crammed into a crowded final stretch in March and April. The first ten months of the season, by contrast, were overshadowed by a single show that loomed in seemingly eternal suspension: the superhero mega-musical *Spider-Man: Turn Off the Dark*, a collaboration between the visionary director Julie Taymor (of *The Lion King*) and rock royals Bono and the Edge (of U2).

Touted as the most expensive show in Broadway history, *Spider-Man* had already been pushed back from a scheduled opening in the spring of 2010. But its troubles began in earnest during the show's October rehearsal period, when several cast members were injured while executing complicated aerial stunts; each misfortune came under a microscope of media scrutiny as the production scrambled to right itself.

For months, *Spider-Man* dangled above Broadway like a sword of Damocles; journalists, gossips, and late-night comedians circled it eagerly, scissors at the ready, eager to snip its wires. Instead of lasting a few weeks, as is normal, the show's preview period stretched on for months, as the official opening date was pushed back from December to January, then February, then March. Critics debated whether to write about the show before it was officially offered for review.

When the *New York Times* broke its silence in February, most of the other major publications followed suit, directing a volley of flaming arrows at the already troubled production. Most of the reviews faulted Taymor for *Spider-Man*'s innovative but incoherent second act, in which the hero faced off against a spider-woman from Greek mythology. In March, Taymor was fired from the show, whose opening date was again rescheduled, this time to June—making it the first show of the 2011-2012 season.

By then, the press had moved on to a happier musical-theater story: the smash success of *The Book of Mormon*, which opened to universal raves in March and promptly became Broadway's hottest ticket since the heyday of *The Producers* ten years earlier. At the end of the season, the show swept up awards like a tornado, winning nine Tony Awards among other accolades. Andrew Rannells and Josh Gad played mismatched missionaries—one an uptight egotist, the other a well-meaning spaz—in Uganda on behalf of the Church of the Latter-Day Saints; the charming Nikki M. James played a local woman who embraces their hopelessly mangled message of love.

But the real star of *The Book of Mormon* was the writing. The brainchild of Trey Parker and Matt Stone (the duo behind TV's animated hit *South Park*) and Robert Lopez (one of the creators of Broadway's *Avenue Q*), *The Book of Mormon* put its authors' celebrated penchant for irreverent humor in the service of a plot that transcended snark. Behind its potty mouth and larkish swipes at Mormon beliefs were an old-fashioned love story and a good-faith take on the value of religion. (The show's heart, wrote Ben Brantley in the *New York Times*, was "as pure as that of a Rodgers and Hammerstein show.")

Original musical-theater writing staged a significant comeback throughout the season. Of the dozen tuners that opened on Broadway, nine had original scores—a huge increase from the 2009 2010 season, when just two new musicals could boast new music. And only one show in 2010-2011 did not have a story-oriented book: *Rain*, a tourist-friendly Beatles tribute concert that landed with minimal splash at the Neil Simon Theatre in October, then transferred to the smaller Brooks Atkinson in February, where it continued for six modest months.

Aside from *The Book of Mormon* and Taymor's aborted *Spider-Man*, the two most interesting new musicals of the season were also its first. *Bloody Bloody Andrew Jackson* and *The Scottsboro Boys* had a good deal in common: Both had begun Off-Broadway (*BBAJ* at the Public Theater, *Scottsboro* at the Vineyard); both viewed tragic episodes of American history (the forced relocation of Native Americans and the legal railroading of African-Americans, respectively) through the ironic lenses of particular genres (modern emo rock and old-fashioned minstrel shows, respectively). And both, despite fervent admirers, closed after fewer than 100 performances.

Written and directed by Off-Broadway wunderkind Alex Timbers, of the brainy-prankish troupe Les Freres Corbusier, *Bloody Bloody Andrew Jackson* starred the charismatic Benjamin Walker—in body-groping rock-star pants—as America's populist seventh president. After luring the audience in with sketch-comedy humor and a rollicking post-punk score (by composer Michael Friedman), the show sobered up in its second half, which took stock of policies that some consider genocidal. But despite mostly positive reviews, and a gorgeous Dada-Americana junk shop of a set, the musical could not find a Broadway audience.

A similar fate befell *The Scottsboro Boys,* which arrived with a more traditional pedigree. One of the final collaborations between the great Broadway songwriting team of John Kander and the late Fred Ebb—who had died six years earlier—the musical tried to use the minstrel format at a jaunty off-angle from the dark story it told, as *Cabaret* and *Chicago* had used Weimar and vaudeville tropes. Directed by Susan Stroman, *The Scottsboro Boys* took on charged material with commendable force, and though it closed in less than a month, it was remembered with an impressive eleven Tony nominations at the end of the season.

The Scottsboro Boys's Tony bounty was due in part to the lukewarm critical and popular reception afforded to most of the potential rivals that followed it. Prominent among that group were five shows that, in keeping with recent trends in musical theater, were adapted from movies. Two had only brief runs in the fall. David Yazbek and Jeffrey Lane's *Women on the Verge of a Nervous Breakdown* was adapted from Pedro Almodóvar's colorful cult film; despite lively supporting turns by the 2008 *Gypsy* team of Patti LuPone and Laura Benanti, it was widely dismissed as jumbled. The Christmas trifle *Elf*, adapted from the Will Ferrell holiday comedy, was pleasant seasonal fare that shuttered, as scheduled, after the holidays.

Priscilla Queen of the Desert, which opened in March following runs in Australia and England, tucked a catalog of beloved pop songs from the 1970s and 1980s (including "It's Raining Men" and "MacArthur Park") into a story about three drag queens traveling through hostile rural territory en route to a gig. Veteran Aussie actor Tony Sheldon gave a soulful turn as the eldest of the trio; if the production otherwise struck some viewers as busy and hollow, the costumes were undeniably fabulous—and netted a Tony for their designers, who had also won an Oscar for the 1994 film version.

Another campy film adaptation was *Sister Act*, which transferred from London in April with its Alan Menken–Glenn Slater score largely intact but with a new director (Broadway veteran Jerry Zaks) and an almost entirely new book by *Xanadu* wit Douglas Carter Beane. Based on the 1992 Whoopi Goldberg flick about a nightclub singer forced to hole up in a convent—with Patina Miller in the lead role (and Goldberg on board as a producer)—this adaptation reset the action to 1970s Philadelphia. Critical reaction was mixed, describing the show as capable but uninspired.

Less charitable was the April response to *Catch Me If You Can,* adapted from the 2002 con-boy movie, with songs by the *Hairspray* team of Marc Shaiman and Scott Wittman. Despite a smashing (and Tony-winning) performance by Broadway funnyman Norbert Leo Butz as an FBI man on the trail of a slick teenage fraud played by Aaron Tveit, the musical did not catch fire; many reviewers found fault with the show's TV-variety-special framing device.

The season of new musicals ended with a trio of loud thuds. *Wonderland,* the latest effort from serial flop composer Frank Wildhorn, offered a loud modern riff on Lewis Carroll's Alice books; the reception was withering—*Time Out New*

York's review bashed it in "Jabberwocky"-style verse—and the show quickly folded. The sentimental *The People in the Picture* (which starred Donna Murphy as a Holocaust survivor recalling her past) and *Baby It's You!* (which imagined Beth Leavel as the New Jersey housewife who discovered the Shirelles) proved only slightly more successful. All three were roundly panned, and none lasted more than 150 performances.

The season's accent on original material was even more pronounced in light of the relative paucity of musical revivals: Just two opened in 2010-2011, the lowest since 2001-2002. The boyish Daniel Radcliffe, famous from his films as teen wizard Harry Potter, starred as J. Pierrepont Finch in director-choreographer Rob Ashford's bustling, athletic revival of Frank Loesser's 1961 business-world satire *How to Succeed in Business Without Really Trying*. Eager and hard-working— notwithstanding the show's title—Radcliffe was paired to amusing effect with the much taller sitcom veteran John Larroquette, and Tammy Blanchard earned laughs as a sexy ditz.

It was Roundabout Theatre Company's ship-shape production of Cole Porter's maritime farce *Anything Goes*, however, that took the Tony for Best Revival of a Musical. Directed and choreographed by Kathleen Marshall, the show tapped— literally—into the madcap spirit of 1930s Broadway. Sutton Foster picked up a second Best Actress Tony for her winsome and pert portrayal of nightclub singer Reno Sweeney; veteran showman Joel Grey made less of an impression as a harmless gangster.

Though not technically a musical or a revival, *Brief Encounter*—the first straight play to open in the 2010-2011 season—often seemed like both. Directed and adapted by Emma Rice from a 1945 Noël Coward noble-weepie screenplay, the play was created by England's Kneehigh Theatre and mounted by the Roundabout at Broadway's Studio 54 (after a hit 2009 run at St. Ann's Warehouse in Brooklyn). A whimsical blend of multimedia stagecraft and interstitial songs from the Coward catalog, *Brief Encounter* was an elegantly reserved crowd-pleaser. It was also typical of the faint fog of Anglophilia that permeated Broadway for the most of the season. Nearly every straight play or revival that opened before March, in fact, either starred or was written by English or Irish artists.

Brief Encounter was immediately followed by Manhattan Theatre Club's *The Pitmen Painters,* imported from its production at London's National Theatre earlier in the year. Lee Hall's group portrait of the Ashington Group—working-class artists who rose to notoriety in the 1940s—was reviewed respectfully but unexcitedly, as was the Roundabout's next offering: a revival of George Bernard Shaw's *Mrs. Warren's Profession,* featuring theater eminence Cherry Jones as a woman whose fortune is based in a secret line of brothels. Simon Bent's off-kilter comedy *Elling* had been a 2007 hit in London's West End; on Broadway, where it paired Denis O'Hare and Brendan Fraser as mentally deranged roommates, it was considered too quirky, and imploded after just nine performances.

Two classic plays from the British Isles illustrated the continuing firepower of the canon. Director Daniel Sullivan's intelligent, delicately balanced take on Shakespeare's Jew-baiting *The Merchant of Venice* opened at the Broadhurst Theatre for a limited run in November, with most of the cast that had made it a sensation in Central Park over the summer. Heading the ensemble again were Al Pacino (forcefully vengeful as Shylock) and Lily Rabe (witty and nuanced as Portia). The Roundabout struck a lighter comedic note in January with the first Broadway revival in decades of Oscar Wilde's dazzlingly epigrammatic *The Importance of Being Earnest*. The venerable English actor Brian Bedford directed the production and also donned elaborate gowns to drip venom as the dragonish Lady Bracknell, for which he received a Tony nomination (as he had for all six of his Broadway plays in the previous twenty years).

Even revivals of American plays had British names above the title in the fall. Patrick Stewart played an aging actor (opposite T.R. Knight as an up-and-comer) in a short-lived production of David Mamet's slender, episodic *A Life in the Theater*. Vanessa Redgrave played the titular Southern fussbudget in a mild, popular restaging of Alfred Uhry's 1987 Pulitzer Prize winner, *Driving Miss Daisy*, costarring American stage vets James Earl Jones and Boyd Gaines. And Mark

Rylance painted the Great White Way red in a revival of David Hirson's 1991 verse comedy *La Bête,* which transferred from London with costars David Hyde Pierce and Joanna Lumley. Although the show ran for just three months, Rylance made his turn as a doltish French playwright into a volcanic comedic tour de force.

Not quite everything in the fall had British lineage, of course. In *Lombardi,* a rare Broadway drama pitched to straight male sports lovers—the National Football League was one of its producers—Dan Lauria played the legendary Green Bay Packers coach Vince Lombardi, with Judith Light as his tippling wife. (The show scored a solid seven-month run at Circle in the Square.) The gruff comedian and *Saturday Night Live* alum Colin Quinn offered a wisecracking tour of world history in a well-received one-man show, *Colin Quinn: Long Story Short,* directed by stand-up and sitcom king Jerry Seinfeld. And Paul Reubens rejuvenated his 1980s kiddie-show persona, an irrepressibly imaginative man-child, in *The Pee-Wee Herman Show,* a colorful blast of Generation X nostalgia.

John Guare's *A Free Man of Color,* which opened at Lincoln Center in November, was the most ambitious new play of the season to date: an ornate and sprawling fantasia, partially rhymed, that starred Jeffrey Wright as a rich mulatto sybarite in nineteenth-century New Orleans. (Secondary characters included Napoleon Bonaparte and Thomas Jefferson.) Critics and audiences alike seemed confused by Guare's epic gilt trip, which ran just two months but was a surprise finalist for the 2011 Pulitzer Prize for Drama.

It is a sign of the season's remarkable dramatic strength that *A Free Man of Color* was not the only Pulitzer finalist to be left out of the running when the Tony nominations for Best Play were announced in May. Sharing that unlikely distinction was Rajiv Joseph's haunted *Bengal Tiger at the Baghdad Zoo,* a 2010 Pulitzer finalist whose Broadway incarnation (which opened in March) starred Robin Williams as a jungle cat with existential angst triggered by the U.S. occupation of Iraq.

Duking it out for the Best Play Tony were four very different shows—two American, two English—that rushed out of the gate in March and April. The first to open was David Lindsay-Abaire's *Good People,* a timely look at luck, responsibility and class mobility in America. Frances McDormand won a Tony for her unsentimental performance as a mouthy South Boston woman who bears her burdens with mulish pride, and Lindsay-Abaire won the New York Drama Critics' Circle Award for Best Play.

The NYDCC's prize for Best Foreign Play went to *Jerusalem,* Jez Butterworth's drama about a decrepit modern Falstaff named Johnny "Rooster" Byron, who sells drugs out of a trailer and spins tall tales about encounters with giants. Mark Rylance, just three months after *La Bête,* got even better notices here, driving reviewers to superlatives. The *Times'* Brantley described his work as "a performance for the ages" to be recalled "with glassy-eyed rapture"; the Drama Critics' Circle gave Rylance a Special Citation for his double accomplishment, and he won the Tony for Best Actor as well, in the category's highest-level field in recent memory.

Also in contention for the Best Play Tony was Stephen Adly Guirgis' loud, vivid, and funny dramedy about users of various kinds, *The Motherf**ker with the Hat,* which starred Bobby Cannavale as a recovering addict and comedian Chris Rock as his Alcoholics Anonymous sponsor. (Elizabeth Rodriguez and Yul Vazquez were acclaimed for their supporting roles.) But the winner, ultimately, was *War Horse,* a ravishing pageant about an English lad separated from his equine buddy during World War I. Imported from London's National Theatre and tightened for Lincoln Center, the production rendered its animal characters through complex, beautiful puppetry. Given *War Horse's* massive appeal, its Tony win was no surprise, but the victory of a spectacle-based show did occasion some hand-wringing given the literary merits of its competitors. (Although there are separate categories for Best Book and Best Score in addition to the prize for Best Musical, the Tonys make no distinction between the writing and overall production of straight plays.)

Two other new plays that opened in the spring were left out of Tony consideration entirely. In a less jam-packed season, the charismatic comic monologist John Leguizamo's fourth Broadway solo show, *Ghetto Klown*—in which he reflected on his uneven showbiz career—might have gotten more recognition. But *High,* a clumsy melodrama starring Kathleen Turner as a tough-talking nun and rehab counselor, was a low point of the dramatic season by any standard; it closed after just seven performances.

The spring lineup of play revivals paled somewhat in comparison with the original work. A star-studded but earthbound production of Jason Miller's 1972 team-reunion drama, *That Championship Season* (with a cast that included Kiefer Sutherland and Miller's son Jason Patric) made the play seem past its prime. A new staging of the 1946 Garson Kanin comedy *Born Yesterday* showcased the prodigious talents of actress Nina Arianda (in the Judy Holiday role) as she continued her meteoric rise, but was not a financial success. And the general reaction was cool to director David Cromer's dour revival of John Guare's *The House of Blue Leaves,* starring Ben Stiller (who made his Broadway debut in the 1986 revival), Edie Falco, and Jennifer Jason Leigh.

A revival of Tom Stoppard's intellectual puzzle play *Arcadia,* featuring a blended cast of American and English actors—including Billy Crudup, who had played a different role in *Arcadia*'s 1995 Broadway premiere—was greeted with cordial praise and interest. But the season went out with a blast of passion in its final dramatic production: George C. Wolfe's extraordinary staging of *The Normal Heart,* Larry Kramer's Ibsenian 1985 jeremiad about AIDS and gay pride. Broadway director Joe Mantello, who had not acted in nearly twenty years, returned to the boards in a searing lead performance; John Benjamin Hickey and Ellen Barkin both won Tonys for their featured work, and the production took the award for Best Revival. Lest anyone think that the famously ornery playwright had gone soft, Kramer could often be found at the exit of the John Golden Theatre after performances of the show, handing out pamphlets and urging shaken audiences to action.

No season's summary would be complete without remembering some of the major talents that left us along the way. The lights on Broadway's marquees were dimmed twelve times during the season to honor members of the theater community who had died. These included: actors Elizabeth Taylor, Patricia Neal, and Jill Clayburgh; playwrights Arthur Laurents, Joseph Stein, Romulus Linney, and Lanford Wilson; composer Jerry Bock; costume designer Theoni V. Aldredge; stage manager Beverley Randolph; Off-Off-Broadway force of culture Ellen Stewart; and *Theater World*'s own longtime editor, John Willis. (Among many others lost this year were Tom Bosley, Betty Garrett, Pam Gems, Farley Granger, Jill Haworth, Larry Keith, Marcia Lewis, Marian Mercer, Arthur Penn, Helen Stenborg, Sada Thompson, Doric Wilson, and Norman Wisdom.)

Neither these losses nor the various confusions and disappointments of the season, however, could dim the sense that 2010-2011 was—in the end—a very good year for Broadway indeed, especially in the beleaguered arena of straight plays. And there is something oddly cheering about the fact that most of the season's best news did happen *in the end*: in a final burst of achievement that followed months of griping, sniping, and middling work. Who doesn't like a plot twist? Count Broadway out at your own risk, the season seemed to say; the old girl still has surprises up her sleeve.

A scene from Spider-Man: Turn Off the Dark *(photo by Jacob Cohl)*

Harry Connick Jr. in Concert on Broadway

Neil Simon Theatre; Opened: July 15, 2010; Closed July 31, 2010; 15 performances

Presented by James L. Nederlander and Broadway Across America (John Gore, CEO; Thomas McGrath, Chairman); Music arranged and orchestrated by Harry Connick Jr.; General Management, Richards/Climan (David R. Richards and Tamar Haimes); Publicist, Kristen Foster, PMK*BNC; Artist Manager, Ann Marie Wilkins; Management Associate, Maria Betro; Tour Manager, Brendan Goedde; Tour Coordinator, Ben Willmott; Management Assistant, Ruth Stefanides; Assistant to Mr. Connick, Melissa Mittereder; HCJ Fan Club Manager, Ellen O'Neill; Production Manager, Ted Jonas; Stage Manager, Adam Parks; Front of House Sound Engineer, Josh Sprague; Lighting Design, Ted Wells; Lighting Director, Tom Halpain; Audio Monitor Systems Technician, Dave Sockrider; Set Carpenter, Jeff Bray; Head Carpenter, George "Chip" Davis; Electrician, John Robison; Merchandising, JSR Merchansing; Booking, Mitch Rose/CAA; Record Company, Columbia Records; Sound Company, Jonas Productions; Lighting Company, Mas Lighting; Associate General Managers, Michael Sag, Jeromy Smith; General Management Assistants, Kyle Bonder, Cesar Hawas, Erica Rothstein; House Carpenter, John Gordon; House Electrician, James Travers Sr.; House Props, Danny Viscardo; House Flyman, Douglas McNeill; Advertising, SpotCo (Drew Hodges, Jim Edwards, Tom Greenwald, Kyle Hall, Cory Spinney, Matt Wilstein, Stephen Santore); Technical Supervision, Juniper Street Productions (Hillary Blanken, Guy Kwan, Kevin Broomell, Ana Rose Greene); Press, The Hartman Group, Michael Hartman, Wayne Wolfe, Matt Ross

Piano/Vocals **Harry Connick Jr.**

MUSICIANS Alto Saxophone **Geoff Burke**; Tenor Saxophone **Jerry Weldon**; Trumpet **Kevin Bryan**, **Mark Braud**; Trombone **Lucien Barbarin**, **Dion Tucker**; Bass Trombone **Joe Barati**; Concertmaster **Sylvia D'Avano**; 1st Violin **Kristina Musser**, **Louise Owen**, **Antoine Silverman**; 2nd Violin **Jonathan Dinklage**, **Philip Payton**, **Hiroko Taguchi**; Viola **Todd Low**, **Orlando Wells**; Cello **Amy Ralske**, **Anja Wood**; Bass **Neal Caine**; Drums **Arthur Latin**

MUSICAL NUMBERS We Are in Love, The Way You Look Tonight, Bésame Mucho, The Other Hours (from *Thou Shalt Not*), Nowhere with Love, How Insensitive, Come by Me, Medley: My Time of Day / I've Never Been in Love Before, All the Way, Bayou Maharajah, Hear Me in the Harmony, Light the Way (from *Thou Shalt Not*), St. James Infirmary Blues, Take Her to the Mardi Gras (from *Thou Shalt Not*), Bourbon Street Parade, Mardi Gras in New Orleans

A concert of Broadway and pop tunes presented in two acts.

SYNOPSIS Crooner Harry Connick Jr. returns to Broadway after his 2006 acting debut in the Roundabout Theatre Company's production of *The Pajama Game* (and twenty years after his first Broadway concert) and presents an evening of Broadway and pop standards with his big band and twelve-piece string section in his token New Orleans style.

Harry Connick Jr. (photo by Bruce Glikas)

Harry Connick Jr. (photo by Palma Kolansky)

Harry Connick Jr. (photo by Bruce Glikas)

Tristan Sturrock and Hannah Yelland

Annette McLaughlin and Joseph Alessi (photos by Joan Marcus)

Brief Encounter

Studio 54; First Preview: September 10, 2010; Opening Night: September 28, 2010; Closed January 2, 2011; 21 previews, 111 performances

Written by Noel Coward; Adapted and Directed by Emma Rice from the play *Still Life* and the screenplay of *Brief Encounter*; Produced by the Roundabout Theatre Company (Todd Haimes, Artistic Director; Harold Wolpert, Managing Director; Julia C. Levy, Executive Director) in association with David Pugh, Dafydd Rogers, and Cineworld; Originally produced by The Kneehigh Theatre (Cornwall, U.K.; Emma Rice, Artistic Director); Set & Costumes, Neil Murray; Lighting, Malcolm Rippeth; Sound, Simon Baker; Projections, Gemma Carrington and Jon Driscoll; Original Music, Stu Barker; Production Stage Manager, Peter Hanson; Technical Supervisor, Steve Beers; U.K. Casting, Sam Jones; U.S. Casting, Jim Carnahan, Stephen Kopel; General Manager, Sydney Beers; Director of Marketing/Sales, David B. Steffen; Founding Director, Gene Feist; Associate Artistic Director, Scott Ellis; Company Manager, Denise Cooper; Stage Manager, Jon Krause; Associate Director, Wes Grantom; U.K. Set/Costume Assistant, Imogen Clöet; Associate Design, Michael Clark; Associate Lighting, Daniel Walker; Video Programmer, Eric Norris; Prod. Carpenter, Dan Hoffman; Flyman, Steve Jones; Prod. Electrician, John Wooding; Lighting Programmer, Marc Polimeni; Spot Op, Paul Coltoff; U.K. Sound Associate, Andy Graham; Prod. Sound Engineer, Wallace Flores; Deck Sound, T.J. McEvoy; House Props, Lawrence Jennino; Wardrobe Supervisor, Nadine Hettel; Dresser, Stephanie Sleeper; Ms. Yelland's Hair, John Barrett Salon; Dialect Coach, Stephen Gabis; U.S. Musical Director, Andy Einhorn; U.K. Stage Managers, Steph Curtis, Karen Habens; U.K. Musical Coordinator, Pete Judge; U.K. Production Manager, Dom Fraser; U.K. Deputy Production Manager, Cath Bathes; Roundabout Staff: Director of Artistic Development/Casting, Jim Carnahan; Director of Education, Greg McCaslin; Director of Finance, Susan Neiman; Director of Development, Lynne Gugenheim Gregory; IT Director, Antonio Palumbo; Director of Ticketing Sales, Charlie Garbowski Jr.; Press, Boneau/Bryan-Brown, Adrian Bryan-Brown, Matt Polk, Jessica Johnson, Amy Kass

CAST Laura **Hannah Yelland**; Alec **Tristan Sturrock**; Fred/Albert **Joseph Alessi**; Deryl **Dorothy Atkinson**; Myrtle **Annette McLaughlin**; Stanley **Gabriel Ebert**; Musicians **Edward Jay, Adam Pleeth**; Bill/Ensemble **Damon Daunno**

UNDERSTUDIES Damon Daunno (Fred/Albert, Stanley); Gabriel Ebert (Alec)

SONG LIST Any Little Fish, No Good at Love, Mad About the Boy, Wide Lagoon, Go Slow Johnny, Romantic Fool, So Good at Love, A Room with a View, Always

2010-2011 AWARDS Outer Critics Circle Award: Outstanding Set Design (Neil Murray)

Broadway premiere of a new adaptation of a 1936 one-act play and 1945 screenplay with music presented without intermission. Originally presented at the Kneehigh Theatre (Cornwall) in 2008, the show subsequently toured the United States, playing San Francisco, Minneapolis, and Brooklyn's St. Ann's Warehouse last season (see *Theatre World* Vol. 66, page 154.)

SYNOPSIS Switching seamlessly between live theater and remade film footage, *Brief Encounter* takes audiences back to a bygone age of romance and the silver screen. The production careens around varying moods of clipped, clenched passion heaving under the middle-class restraint of the duty-bound Alec and Laura, and the wild music-hall exuberance of the slap-and-tickle high-jinks of two other clandestine couples among the railway station staff. The lives and loves of the three couples are played out in the train station tearoom as a grand entertainment, using the words (some newly set to original music) and familiar songs of Noël Coward to create a breathtaking, funny, and tear-inducing show with live musicians on stage, characters jumping in and out of film screens, and a couple in love floating in mid-air.

Standing): David Whitaker, Michael Hodgson, Ian Kelly (background), Deka Walmsley, Christopher Connel (sitting); Phillippa Wilson, Brian Lonsdale

Christopher Connel, David Whitaker, Deka Walmsley, Michael Hodson, Ian Kelly

Christopher Connel, Michael Hodson, Deka Walmsley, David Whitaker (photos by Joan Marcus)

The Pitmen Painters

Samuel J. Friedman Theatre; First Preview: September 14, 2010; Opening Night: September 30, 2010; Closed December 12, 2010; 18 previews, 86 performances

Written by Lee Hall, inspired by a book by William Feaver; Produced by Manhattan Theatre Club (Lynne Meadow, Artistic Director; Barry Grove, Executive Producer) by special arrangement with Bob Boyett; Originally presented by Live Theatre, Newcastle/National Theatre of Great Britain; Director, Max Roberts; Set & Costumes, Gary McCann; Lighting, Douglas Kuhrt; Sound, Martin Hodgson; Production Stage Manager, Charles Means; Company Manager, Seth Shepsle; Stage Manager, Elizabeth Maloney; Dialect Consultant, Kate Wilson; Assistant Director, David F. Chapman; Associate Lighting, Zach Murphy; Assistant Costumes, Gabriella Ingram; Assistant Sound, Asa Wember; Hair/Makeup Supervisors , Natasha Steinhagen, Robin Baxter; Lightboard Programmer, Jessica Morton; Video Technician, Brandon Epperson; For MTC: General Manager, Florie Seery; Associate Artistic Director, Mandy Greenfield; Director of Artistic Development, Jerry Patch; Marketing, Debra Waxman-Pilla; Production Manager, Kurt Gardner; Director of Casting, Nancy Piccione; Artistic Line Producer, Lisa McNulty; Development, Lynne Randall; Artistic Consultant, Daniel Sullivan; Artistic Operations, Amy Gilkes Loe; Finance, Jeffrey Bledsoe; Associate General Manager, Lindsey Brooks Sag; Subscriber Services, Robert Allenberg; Telesales, George Tetlow; Education, David Shookhoff; Associate Production Manager, Philip Naudé; Prop Supervisor, Scott Laule; Costume Supervisor, Erin Hennessy Dean; For Live Theatre: Chairman of the Board, Paul Callaghan; CEO, Jim Beirne; Artistic Director, Max Roberts; Operations Director, Wendy Barnfather; For the National Theatre: Chairman of the Board, Sir Hayden Phillips; Chairman Elect, John Markinson; Director of the National, Nicholas Hytner; Executive Director, Nick Starr; Finance Director, Lisa Burger; Associate Producer, Pádraig Cusack; Advertising, SpotCo; Press, Boneau/Bryan-Brown, Chris Boneau, Aaron Meier, Christine Olver, Emily Meagher

CAST Oliver Kilbourn **Christopher Connel**; Harry Wilson **Michael Hodgson**; Robert Lyon **Ian Kelly**; Young Lad/Ben Nicholson **Brian Lonsdale**; Susan Parks **Lisa McGrillis**; George Brown **Deka Walmsley**; Jimmy Floyd **David Whitaker**; Helen Sutherland **Phillipa Wilson**

UNDERSTUDIES Trevor Fox (Oliver Kilbourn/Harry Wilson/Young Lad/George Brown/Jimmy Floyd), Jack Koenig (Robert Lyon/Ben Nicholson), Christa Scott-Reed (Susan Parks/Helen Sutherland), John Curless (Oliver Kilbourn/Young Lad)

SETTING Ashington, Northumberland, Newcastle upon Tyne, London and Edinburgh between 1934 and 1947. American premiere of a new play presented in two acts. World premiere at Live Theatre (Newcastle U.K.) in 2007. Subsequently produced by the National Theatre of Great Britain with this cast in 2008 and 2009.

SYNOPSIS *The Pitman Painters* is a humorous, deeply moving, and timely look at art, class, and politics. In 1934, a group of Ashington miners hired a professor to teach an art appreciation evening class. Rapidly abandoning theory in favor of practice, the pitmen began to paint. Within a few years the most avant-garde artists became their friends and their work was acquired by prestigious collections; but every day they worked, as before, down the mine.

Mrs. Warren's Profession

American Airlines Theatre; First Preview: September 3, 2010; Opening Night: October 3, 2010; Closed November 28, 2010; 35 previews, 65 performances

Written by George Bernard Shaw; Produced by the Roundabout Theatre Company (Todd Haimes, Artistic Director; Harold Wolpert, Managing Director; Julia C. Levy, Executive Director); Director, Doug Hughes; Sets, Scott Pask; Costumes, Catherine Zuber; Lighting, Kenneth Posner; Original Music & Sound, David Van Tieghem; Hair & Wigs, Tom Watson; Dialect Consultant, Elizabeth Smith; Production Stage Manager, James FitzSimmons; Production Management, Aurora Productions; Casting, Jim Carnahan & Carrie Gardner; General Manager, Rebecca Habel; Director of Marketing & Sales Promotion, David B. Steffen; Director of Development, Lynne Gugenheim Gregory; Founding Director, Gene Feist; Associate Artistic Director, Scott Ellis; Company Manager, Carly DiFulvio; Stage Manager, Bryce McDonald; Assistant Director, Alexander Greenfield; Associate Design: Frank McCullough (set), Brandon Wolcott (sound); Assistant Design: Lauren Alvarez, Jeff Hinchee (set), Nicole Moody (costumes), Peter Hoerburger (lighting); Assistant to Ms. Zuber, Ryan Park; Additional Dialect Coaching, Deborah Hecht; Prod. Props Supervisor, Peter Sarafin; Prod. Carpenter, Glenn Merwede; Prod. Electrician, Brian Maiuri; Running Props, Robert W. Dowling II; Sound Operator, Dann Wojnar; Flymen, Mike Allen; Automation Operator, Richard Holst; Stagehand/Props, Jennifer Fagant; Wardrobe Superisor, Susan J. Fallon; Dressers, Cathy Cline, Kat Martin; Hair and Wig Supervisor, Manuela Laporte; Fight Consultant, TomSchall; Wardrobe Dayworker, Lauren Gallitelli; Production Assistants, Morgan R. Holbrook, James Steele; Roundabout Staff: Director of Artistic Development/Casting, Jim Carnahan; Director of Education, Greg McCaslin; General Manager, Sydney Beers; Director of Finance, Susan Neiman; IT Director, Antonio Palumbo; Director of Ticketing Sales, Charlie Garbowski Jr.; Press, Boneau/Bryan-Brown, Adrian Bryan-Brown, Matt Polk, Jessica Johnson, Amy Kass

CAST Vivie Warren **Sally Hawkins**; Mr. Praed **Edward Hibbert**; Mrs. Kitty Warren **Cherry Jones**; Sir George Crofts **Mark Harelik**; Frank Gardiner **Adam Driver**; Reverend Samuel Gardner **Michael Siberry**

UNDERSTUDIES Stephenie Janssen (Vivie Warren), Charlotte Maier (Mrs. Warren), Peter Bradbury (Mr. Praed, Sir George Crofts, Reverend Samuel Gardner), Cary Donaldson (Frank Gardner)

SETTING Time: Late Summer. Place: England. Act I: Wednesday afternoon in a cottage garden near Haslemere, Surrey. Act II: Inside the cottage around night. Act III: Late next morning in a rectory garden nearby. Act IV: Two days later in Honoraria Fraser's chambers, Chancery Lane, London. Revival of a classic play presented in four acts with one intermission and two brief pauses.

SYNOPSIS George Bernard Shaw's scorching tour de force *Mrs. Warren's Profession* tells the story of Kitty Warren, a mother who makes a terrible sacrifice for her daughter Vivie's independence. The clash of these two strong-willed but culturally constrained women is the spark that ignites the ironic wit of one of Shaw's greatest plays.

Edward Hibbert and Mark Harelik

Cherry Jones and Sally Hawkins (photos by Joan Marcus)

Cherry Jones and Adam Driver

Time Stands Still

Cort Theatre; First Preview: September 23, 2010; Opening Night: October 7, 2010; Closed January 30, 2011; 16 previews, 126 performances

Written by Donald Margulies; Produced by Manhattan Theatre Club Productions (Lynne Meadow, Artistic Director; Barry Grove, Executive Producer), Nelle Nugent, Bud Martin, Wendy Federman, Ted Snowdon, Max Cooper, Susan Adamski, Mari Nakachi, Elisabeth Morten/Sharon A. Carr, in association with Jack M. Dalgleish and Joseph Sirola; Director, Daniel Sullivan; Set, John Lee Beatty; Costumes, Rita Ryack; Lighting, Peter Kaczorowski; Sound, Darron L West; Original Music, Peter Golub; Makeup, Mindy Hall; Stunt Coordinator, Thomas Schall; Production Stage Manager, Robert Bennett; Associate Producer, Kenneth Teaton; Marketing, aka & Debra Waxman-Pilla; Casting, Nancy Piccione; MTC Associate Artistic Director, Mandy Greenfield; Technical Supervisor, Larry Morley; General Manager, Peter Bogyo; Company Manager, Chris Morey; Stage Manager, Denise Yaney; Associate Sound, Charles Coes; Assistant Design: Katie Hultgren (set), Richard Schurkamp (costumes), Jake DeGroot (lighting); Prod. Electrician, Shannon January; Prod. Props, Paul Trapani; Prod. Sound Engineer, Jens McVoy; House Electrician, Scott DeVerna; House Props, Lonnie Gaddy; Wardrobe Supervisor, Growler; Dresser, Derek Moreno; Hair and Makeup Supervisor, Natasha Steinhagen; Production Assistant, Lauren Klein; Assistant to the Technical Supervisor, Amanda Raymond; Website, Art Meets Commerce; Advertising, SpotCo; For MTC: General Manager, Florie Seery; Director of Artistic Development, Jerry Patch; Production Manager, Kurt Gardner; Director of Casting, Nancy Piccione; Development, Jill Turner Lloyd; Artistic Consultant, Daniel Sullivan; Artistic Administration/Assistant to Artistic Director, Amy Gilkes Loe; Finance, Jeffrey Bledsoe; Associate General Manager, Lindsey Brooks Sag; Subscriber Services, Robert Allenberg; Telesales, George Tetlow; Education, David Shookhoff; Press, Boneau/Bryan-Brown, Chris Boneau, Aaron Meier, Christine Olver, Emily Meagher

CAST Richard Ehrlich **Eric Bogosian**; James Dodd **Brian d'Arcy James**; Sarah Goodwin **Laura Linney**; Mandy Bloom **Christina Ricci**

UNDERSTUDIES Heidi Armbruster (Sarah, Mandy), Tony Carlin (Richard, James)

SETTING A loft in Williamsburg, Brooklyn. Recently. Commercial extension of a new drama presented in two acts. Originally commissioned and produced at the Geffen Playhouse (Gil Cates, Producing Director; Randall Arney, Artistic Director) February 3–March 11, 2009 (see *Theatre World* Vol. 65, page 322). This production ran last season at the Samuel J. Friedman Theatre January 5–March 23, 2010, playing 28 previews and 67 performances (see *Theatre World* Vol. 66, page 55). Ms. Ricci replaced Alicia Silverstone from that production.

SYNOPSIS *Time Stands Still* is about two journalists who return home after covering war—only to investigate their own conflicting feelings about life and work. Sarah and James, a photographer and a journalist, have been together for nine years and share a passion for documenting the realities of war. When injuries force them to return home to New York, the adventurous couple confronts the prospect of a more conventional life.

Christina Ricci and Eric Bogosian (photos by Joan Marcus)

Laura Linney and Brian d'Arcy James

Laura Linney, Brian d'Arcy James, Eric Bogosian, and Christina Ricci

Patrick Stewart and T.R. Knight (pahotos by Carol Rosegg)

Patrick Stewart

A Life in the Theatre

Gerald Schoenfeld Theatre; First Preview: September 21, 2010; Opening Night: October 12, 2010; Closed November 28, 2010; 24 previews, 56 performances

Written by David Mamet; Produced by Jeffrey Richards, Jerry Frankel, Jam Theatricals (Steve Traxler and Arny Granat), Debbie Bisno, Eva Price, Larry Magid, Kathleen K. Johnson, Herbert Goldsmith Productions Inc., Roger Kass, Barry Cole & Carole Kaye, Kelpie Arts, Black-Pereira, Freedberg-Dale/Dombrowski-Manuel, Kathleen Seidel; Director, Neil Pepe; Set, Santo Loquasto, Costumes, Laura Bauer; Lighting, Kenneth Posner; Wigs, Charles LaPointe; Casting, Telsey + Company; Fight Choreographer, J. David Brimmer; Production Stage Manager, Matthew Silver; Technical Supervision, Hudson Theatrical Associates (Neil Mazella, Sam Ellis, Irene Wang); Associate Producers, Jeremy Scott Blaustein, Shane Marshall Brown, Matthew Salloway; Company Manager, Mary Miller; General Management, Richards/Climan Inc. (David R. Richards, Tamar Haimes, Michael Sag, Kyle Bonder, Cesar Hawas, Julianna Slaten); Stage Manager, Jillian M. Oliver; Orignal Music, Obadiah Eaves; Assistant Director, Cat Williams; Associate Design, Jenny Sawyors (set), Bobby Tilley (costumes), John Viesta (lighting); Movement/Dance Consultant, Kelly Maurer; Fight Choreography Assistants, Dan O'Driscoll, John Robichau, Michael Yahn; Dialect Coach, Deborah Hecht, Prod. Assistant, Catherine Lynch; Prod. Carpenters, Chad Hershey, Scott Monroe; Prod. Electrician, Justin Freeman; Prod. Props, Kathy Fabian/Propstar; Head Props, Laura McGarty; Wardrobe Supervisor, Sandy Binion; Hair Supervisor, Jason P. Hayes; Dressers, Moira Conrad, Julien Havard; Assistant Set, Antje Ellerman; Associate Props Coordinator, Carrie Mossman; Props Assistants, Tim Ferro, Sarah Bird; Assistant Producer, Michael Crea; Assistants to the Producers, Brandi Preston, Will Trice; Advertising, Serino Coyne Inc; Interactive Marketing, Situation Marketing; Press, Jeffrey Richards Associates, Irene Gandy, Alana Karpoff, Elon Rutberg, Diana Rissetto

CAST Robert **Patrick Stewart**; John **T.R. Knight**

UNDERSTUDIES Conan McCarty (Robert), Sean McNall (John)

Broadway debut of a revival of an Off-Broadway play presented without intermission. Orignially produced at the Goodman Theatre in Chicago in February 1977. The play premiered Off-Broadway at Theatre De Lys (now the Lucille Lortel) October 20, 1977–July 9, 1978 playing 288 performances (see *Theatre World* Vol. 34, page 68.)

SYNOPSIS *A Life in the Theatre* follows two actors in a repertory company: Robert, an older, experienced performer and John, a newcomer to the stage. John at first welcomes Robert's guidance, but soon overshadows his mentor. From rehearsals to reprisals, from ego trips to acting tips, the play gives a glimpse into the complex relationship that develops as the torch is passed from one generation to the next—a passing that wavers from love and mutual respect to impatience and resentment.

T.R. Knight anad Patrick Stewart

T.R. Knight and Patrick Stewart

Bloody Bloody Andrew Jackson

Bernard B. Jacobs Theatre; First Preview: September 30, 2010; Opening Night: October 13, 2010; Closed January 2, 2011; 26 previews, 94 performances

Book by Alex Timbers, music and lyrics by Michael Friedman; Produced by The Public Theater (Oskar Eustis: Artistic Director; Andrew D. Hamingson: Executive Director), Jeffrey Richards, Jerry Frankel, Norton Herrick & Herrick Entertainment, Stewart Lane & Bonnie Comley, Susan Quint Gallin/Mary Lu Roffe/Jennifer Manocherian, Nancy C. Paduano/Harold Thau, Joey Parnes (Executive Producer), Center Theatre Group (Michael Ritchie, Artistic Director; Charles Dillingham, Managing Director); Associate Producer: Mandy Hackett, Jeremy Scott Blaustein, Michael Crea, S.D. Wagner, John Johnson; Director, Alex Timbers; Choreography, Danny Mefford; Set, Donyale Werle; Costumes, Emily Rebholz; Lighting, Justin Townsend; Sound, Bart Fasbender; Music Director, Justin Levine; Music Coordinator, Seymore Red Press; Fight Director, Jacob Griglia-Rosenbaum; Broadway Casting, Carrie Gardner; Production Stage Manager, Arthur Gaffin; Dramaturgs, Anne Davison & Mike Sablone; General Management, Joey Parnes, John Johnson, S.D. Wagner, Kim Selton; Company Manager, David van Zyll de Jong; Stage Manager, Jamie Greathouse; Assistant Stage Manager, Alaina Taylor; Assistant Company Manager, Madeline Felix; Management Associates, Kristen Luciani, Nate Koch; Assistant Director, Andrew Scoville; Dance Captain, Greg Hildreth; Fight Captain, Ben Steinfeld; Associate Design: Michael Carnahan (set), Sarah Laux (costumes), David Sanderson (sound); Assistant Design, Jon Collins (set), Greg Bloxham (1st lighting), Carl Faber (2nd lighting), Emma Wilk (sound); Scenic Supervisors, Larry Morley, Sam Ellis; Assistant to the Scenic Supervisor, Amanda Raymond; Prod. Carpenter, Todd Frank; Prod. Electrician, Richie Mortell; Moving Light Programmer, Jay Penfield; Prod. Prop Supervisor, Mike Smanko; Head Props, Dylan Foley; Advance Props, Neil Rosenberg; Outside Prop Associate, James Keane; Lead Prop Sculptor, Kenneth Grady Barker; Assistant Prop Sculpter, Justin Couchara; Prop Craft Artists, Meghan Buchana, Joshua Hackett, Richard DiBella, Meredith Ries, Heather Dunbar; Prod. Sound Engineer, JJ Hillman; Wardrobe Supervisro, Dave Olin Rogers; Dressers, Sis Obidowski, Clarion Overmoyer, Chip White; Production Assistant, Jenny Kennedy; Child Supervisor, Amy Groeschel; Advertising & Interactive Marketing/Web Design, SpotCo; Press, Jeffrey Richards Associates, Irene Gandy, Alana Karpoff, Elon Rutberg, Diana Risetto; Cast recording (Off-Broadway Cast): Sh-K-Boom/Ghostlight Records/Razor & Tie Music 844432

CAST Andrew Jackson **Benjamin Walker**; The Storyteller **Kristine Nielsen**; Elizabeth, Erica **Kate Cullen Roberts**; Andrew Sr., Calhoun **Darren Goldstein**; Cobbler, Messenger, John Quincy Adams, Tour Guide, Florida Man **Jeff Hiller**; Toula, Female Ensemble **Nadia Quinn**; Female Soloist, Announcer, Naomi **Emily Young**; Monroe **Ben Steinfeld**; Rachel, Florida Woman **Maria Elena Ramirez**; Black Fox, Clay **Bryce Pinkham**; Male Soloist, Citizen, Phil **James Barry**; Red Eagle, University President **Greg Hildreth**; Keokuk, Van Buren **Lucas Near-Verbrugghe**; Lyncoya **Cameron Ocasio**; Swings **Heath Calvert, Erin Felgar, Eli James, Joe Jung, Maria-Christina Oliveras**

UNDERSTUDIES Heath Calvert (Andrew Jackson), Bryce Pinkham (Andrew Jackson), Aiden Eyrick (Lyncoya), Nadia Quinn (The Storyteller), Erin Felgar (The Storyteller)

ORCHESTRA Justin Levine (Piano/Guitar/Conductor), Charlie Rosen (Bass/Associate Conductor), Kevin Garcia (Drums)

MUSICAL NUMBERS Populism, Yea, Yea!; I'm Not That Guy; Oh, Andrew Jackson; Illness As Metaphor; I'm So That Guy; Ten Little Indians; The Corrupt Bargain; Rock Star; The Great Compromise; Public Life; Crisis Averted; The Saddest Song; Second Nature; The Hunters of Kentucky

Broadway premiere of a new musical presented without intermission. Produced Off-Broadway last season at the Public Theater's Newman Theater March 23–June 27, 2010 (Opened April 6), playing 15 previews and 96 performances (see *Theatre World* Vol. 66, page 242). The musical was presented May 5–24, 2009 as part of the Public LAB series (see *Theatre World* Vol. 65, page 231). World premiere

presented by Center Theatre Group at the Kirk Douglas Theatre January 2008 (see *Theatre World* Vol. 64, page 298). Developed in association with Les Freres Corbusier.

SYNOPSIS *Bloody Bloody Andrew* Jackson, an audacious mix of historical fact and fiction, redefines America's controversial seventh president—the man who invented the Democratic Party, drove the Indians west, and ultimately doubled the size of our nation—with a raucous blend of outrageous comedy, anarchic theatricality and an infectious emo rock score.

The Company (photos by Joan Marcus)

Maria Elena Ramirez and Benjamin Walker

Benjamin Walker (center) and the Company

Greg Hildreth, Benjamin Walker, Nadia Quinn, and the Company

Benjamin Walker

Ben Steinfeld and Benjamin Walker

Darren Goldstein, Bryce Pinkham, Ben Steinfeld, Jeff Hiller, and Lucas Near-Verbrugghe

Mark Rylance, Joanna Lumley, and David Hyde Pierce

La Bête

Music Box Theatre; First Preview: September 23, 2010; Opening Night: October 14, 2010; Closed January 9, 2011; 24 previews, 101 performances

Written by David Hirson; Produced by Scott Landis & Sonia Friedman Productions, Roger Berlind, Bob Bartner/Norman Tulchin, Bob Boyett/Tim Levy, Roy Furman, Max Cooper, Dan Frishwasser, Bud Martin, Philip Morgaman/Frankie J. Grande and Stephanie P. McClelland/Hageman-Rosenthal in association with 1001 Nights and Richard Winkler; Director, Matthew Warchus; Set & Costumes, Mark Thompson; Lighting, Hugh Vanstone; Composer, Claire van Kampen; Sound, Simon Baker; Hair/Makeup, Campbell Young; U.S. Casting, Jim Carnahan; U.K. Casting, Lisa Makin; Production Stage Manager, Ira Mont; Technical Supervisor, Aurora Productions; Associate Director, Beatrice Terry; Advertising, SpotCo; Marketing, Type A/Anne Rippey; U.K. General Management, Sonia Friedman Productions; U.S. General Management, Richards/Climan Inc.; Company Manager, John E. Gerndron; Stage Manager, Matthew Lacey; Associate Design: Nancy Thun (set), Barry Doss (costumes), Ted Mather (lighting), Chris Cronin (sound); Assistant Design, Ben Davies, James Humbphrey (set), Josh Lieber (sound); Moving Lights Programmer, Michael Hill; Prod. Assistant, Jason Pelusio; Prod. Carpenter, Mike Martinez; Prod. Props, Christopher Pantuso (U.S.), Marcus Hall Props-Chris Marcus & Jonathan Hall (U.K.); Prod. Electrician, Dan Coey; Prod. Sound, Wiliam Lewis; Wardrobe Supervisor, Kay Grunder; Dresser, Jennie Naughton; Hair Supervisor, Carmel Vargyas; Hair Assistant, Emilia Martin; Vocalist,William Purefoy; Fight Supervisor, Terry King; Choreographer, Sian Williams; Mask Work, Roddy Maude-Roxby; Press, The Hartman Group, Michael Hartman, Matt Ross, Nicole Capataso

CAST Elomire **David Hyde Pierce**; Bejart **Stephen Ouimette**; Valere **Mark Rylance**; Dorine **Greta Lee**; The Princess **Joanna Lumley**; Madeleine Bejart **Sally Wingert**; Rene Du Parc **Robert Lonsdale**; Marquise-Theresa Du Parc **Lisa Joyce**; De Brie **Michael Milligan**; Catherine De Brie **Liza Sadovy**

UNDERSTUDIES Lisa Joyce (Dorine), Robert Lonsdale (Valere), Deanne Lorette (Catherine De Brie, Madeleine Bejart, Marquise - Theresa Du Parc, The Princess), Michael Milligan (Elomire), Steve Routman (Bejart, De Brie, Rene Du Parc, Valere), Liza Sadovy (The Princess)

2010-2011 AWARDS New York Drama Critics Circle Award: Special Citation (Mark Rylance); Drama League Award: Distinguished Performance (Mark Rylance)

SETTING France, 1654. Revival of a play presented in two acts. Originally produced at the Eugene O'Neill Theatre Janurary 29–March 2, 1991, playing 25 performances (see *Theatre World* Vol. 47, page 22). This revival played in London at the Comedy Theatre June 26–September 4, 2010 with this cast prior to coming to Broadway.

SYNOPSIS *La Bête* is a comic tour de force about Elomire, a high-minded classical dramatist who loves only the theater, and Valere, a low-brow street clown who loves only himself. When the fickle princess decides she's grown weary of Elomire's royal theatre troupe, he and Valere are left fighting for survival as art squares off with ego in a literary showdown for the ages.

Mark Rylance (photos by Joan Marcus)

David Hyde Pierce and Joanna Lumley

Lombardi

Circle in the Square Theatre; First Preview: September 23, 2010; Opening Night: October 21, 2010; Closed May 22, 2011; 31 previews, 244 performances

Written by Eric Simonson; Based on the book *When Pride Still Mattered: A Life of Vince Lombardi* by David Maraniss; Produced by Fran Kirmser, Tony Ponturo, Friends of Lombardi, in association with The National Football League; Director, Thomas Kail; Set, David Korins; Costumes, Paul Tazewell; Lighting, Howell Binkley; Sound, Acme Sound Partners; Projections, Zachary Borovay; Hair, Charles LaPointe; Dialect Coach, Stephen Gabis; Casting, Laura Stanczyk; Technical Supervisor, Peter Fulbright; Production Stage Manager, Tripp Philllips; Marketing, HHC Marketing; General Management, 101 Productions (Wendy Orshan, Jeffrey M. Wilson, David Auster, Elie Landua); Executive Producer, Red Awning/Nicole Kastrinos; Associate Producers, Joseph Favorito, Andrew Frank & John Mara Jr., Rebecca Gold; Al Kahn, Myla Lerner, Lauren Stevens, S.D. Wagner & John Johnson; Company Manager, Barbara Crompton; Makeup, Marilyn Jordan; Associate Director, David Ruttura; Stage Manager, Diane DiVita; Associate Design: Rod Lemmond (set), Valerie Marcus Ramshur (costumes), Mark Simpson, Ryan O'Gara (lighting), Jason Crystal (sound), Daniel Brodie (projections); Assistant to Mr. Korins, Sarah Miles, Amanda Stephens; Assistant Costumes, Daryl Stone; Moving Light Programmer, Sean Beach; Projection Editing Assistant, Hannelore Williams; Assistant to Mr. LaPointe, Leah Loukas; Casting Assistant, Anika Chapin; Music Consultants, Jesse Lagrazie, Debbie Markowitz; Prod. Carpenter, Anthony Menditto; Prod. Electrician, Thomas Lawrey; Prod. Sound Engineer, Jim Bay; Prod. Props Supervisor, Robert Presley; Deck Props, Rob Dayna, Wardrobe Supervisor, Eileen Miller; Hair & Makeup Supervisor, Katie Beatty; Dressers, Charles Catanese, Maura Clifford, Kelly Saxon; Advertising, Art Meets Commerce; Press, Boneau/Bryan-Brown, Chris Boneau, Jackie Green, Kelly Guiod

CAST Vincent Lombardi **Dan Lauria**; Michael McCormick **Keith Nobbs**; Marie Lombardi **Judith Light**; Dave Robinson **Robert Christopher Riley**; Paul Hornung **Bill Dawes**; Jim Taylor **Chris Sullivan**

UNDERSTUDIES Jeff Still (Vincent Lombardi), Henny Russell (Marie Lombardi), Brad Schmidt (Michael McCormick, Paul Hornung, Jim Taylor), Javon Johnson (Dave Robinson)

SETTING The Time: Mostly November 1965, but also 1958, 1959, and 1964. The Place: Various locations in Green Bay, Wisconson and Englewood, New Jersey. New York premiere of a new play presented without intermission. World premiere at the Mahaiwe Performing Arts Center in Great Barrington, Massachusetts July 22–28, 2010.

SYNOPSIS *Lombardi* brings the audience into the life and times of legendary Hall of Fame football coach Vince Lombardi, one of America's most inspirational and mercurial personalities. This production marked the NFL's first foray into live theatrical production.

Dan Lauria (photos by Joan Marcus)

Judith Light and Dan Lauria

Robert Christopher Riley, Chris Sullivan, and Bill Dawes

Keith Nobbs and Dan Lauria

Driving Miss Daisy

John Golden Theatre; First Preview: October 7, 2010; Opening Night: October 25, 2010; Closed April 9, 2011; 20 previews, 180 performances

Written by Alfred Uhry; Produced by Jed Bernstein, Adam Zotovich, Elizabeth Ireland McCann, Roger Berlind, Beth Kloiber, Albert Nocciolino, Jon B. Platt, StylesFour Productions, Ruth Hendel/Shawn Emamjomeh, Larry Hirschhorn/ Spring Sirkin, Carl Moellenberg/Wendy Federman, Daryl Roth/Jane Bergère in association with Michael Filerman; Director, David Esbjornson; Set, John Lee Beatty; Costumes, Jane Greenwood; Lighting, Peter Kaczorowski; Projections, Wendall K. Harrington; Music, Mark Bennett; Sound, Christopher Cronin; Casting, Dave Clemmons; Production Stage Manager, Karen Armstrong; Technical Supervisor, Larry Morley; Company Manager, Bruce Klinger; General Manager, Richards/Climan Inc.; Stage Manager, Matthew Farrell; Dialect Coaches, Deborah Hecht and Kate Wilson; Assistant Technical Supervisor, Amanda Raymond; Associate Composer, Matthew Henning; Associate Design: Kacie Hultgren (set), Moria Clinton (cosutmes); Assistant Design: Yoshinori Tanokura (set), Keri Thibodeau (lighting), Alex Neumann (sound), Tim Brown (projections); Production Assistants, Deanna Weiner, Jojo Karlin; Casting Assistant, Alan Lane; Prod. Carpenter, Jordan Gable; Prod. Electrician, Brian GF McGarity; Lighting Programmer, Josh Weitzman; Projection Programmer, Paul Vershbow; Prod. Props, Neil Rosenberg; Wardrobe Supervisor, John Robelen; Dressers, Amelia R. Heywood (Mr. Jones), Laura Beattie (Ms. Redgrave); Hair Supervisor, Nathaniel Hathaway; Head Carpenter, Terry McGarty; Head Electrician, Sylvia Yashioka; Head Props, Steve McDonald; Head Sound, Brien Brannigan; Marketing, Above The Title Entertainment; Advertising, SPOTCo, Inc.; Press Representative: O&M Company, Rick Miramontez, Molly Barnett, Elizabeth Wagner

CAST Boolie Werthan **Boyd Gaines**; Hoke Coleburn **James Earl Jones**; Daisy Werthan **Vanessa Redgrave**

UNDERSTUDIES Maureen Anderman (Daisy), Allen Fitzpatrick (Boolie), Count Stovall (Hoke)

SETTING Atlanta, Georgia, in the 1950s and 1960s at the height of the Civil Rights Movement. Broadway debut of a revival of an Off-Broadway play presented without intermission. Originally produced at Playwrights Horizons April 15, 1987 and later transferred to the John Houseman Theatre where it closed June 3, 1990 after 1,195 performances (see *Theatre World* Vol. 43, page 127).

SYNOPSIS When Daisy Werthan, a widowed, 72-year-old Jewish woman living in midcentury Atlanta, is deemed too old to drive, her son Boolie hires Hoke Coleburn, an African American man, to serve as her chauffeur. What begins as a troubled and hostile pairing, soon blossoms into a profound, life-altering friendship that transcends all the societal boundaries placed between them. From its landmark Off-Broadway production in 1987 to the remarkable success of the Oscar-winning film version (4 Academy Awards, including Best Picture), and now its celebrated Broadway debut, *Driving Miss Daisy* has become one of the most beloved American stories of the late twentieth century.

Vanessa Redgrave (photos by Carol Rosegg)

James Earl Jones and Vanessa Redgrave

Vanessa Redgrave and Boyd Gaines

Boyd Gaines and James Earl Jones

Steve Landes (photos by Cylla von Tiedemann)

Joe Bithorn, Joey Curatolo, Steve Landes, and Ralph Castelli

Joey Curatolo, Joe Bithorn, Ralph Castelli, and Steve Landes

Rain: A Tribute to The Beatles on Broadway

Neil Simon Theatre⁺; First Preview: October 19, 2010; Opening Night: October 26, 2010; 8 previews, 229 performances as of May 31, 2011

Produced by Annerin Production, Magic Arts & Entertainment/NewSpace/Tix Productions, Nederlander Presentations Inc., and RAIN; Set, Scott Christensen, Todd Skinner; Video, Darren McCaulley, Mathieu St-Arnaud; Lighting, Stephan Gotschel; Sound, Abe Jacob; General Management, NIKO Companies and Steve Boulay; Band Management, Mark Lewis; Production Supervisor, Theatrical Services Inc., Arthur Siccardi, Pat Sullivan; Marketing, Bruce Granath; For NIKO: Manny Kladitis, David Loughner, Jason T. Vanderwoude; Marketing & Original Press, Merle Frimark Associates; Production Manager, Scott Christensen; Company Manager, Jesse White/Robert Tevyaw; Production Stage Manager, Lurie Horns Pfeffer; Costume Coordinators, Robin Robinson, Russ Lease; Sound Assistant, Joshua D. Reid; Prod. Sound Operator, Jim vanBergen; Monitor Mixer, Craig Van Tassel; Sound System Consultants, Acme Sound Partners; Video Technician, Brandon Epperson; Show Electrician/Board Op, Michael Cornell; Electric Advisor, Jimmy Fedigan; Wardrobe Supervisor, Allison Goodsell; Backline, Ted Pallas; Graphics, Gary Hewitt, Wedge.a&d; Media Design, Paul J. Toth; AdvanceHD.com; Press Associates, Amy Katz, Twilla Duncan; Advertising, SpotCo; Tour Direction, The Road Company; For Annerin Productions: Jeff Parry (CEO/Producer), Ralph Schmidtke (COO), Stu Peterson (CFO), Jenna DeBoice (Prod. Assistant), Kate McConney (Administration); Magic Arts & Entertainment/NewSpace/Tix Productions: John W. Ballard (President), Lee D. Marshall (Producer), Joe Marsh (Producer), Steve Boulay (COO), Bruce Granath (Marketing), Mary Ann Porcaro (Operations Manager); Press, The Hartman Group

CAST Joe Bithorn (Vocals, Lead Guitar, Guitar Synth, Sitar), **Ralph Castelli** (Drums, Percussion, Vocals), **Joey Curatolo** (Vocals, Bass, Piano, Guitar), **Steve Landes** (Vocals, Rhythm Guitar, Piano, Harmonica)

ALTERNATES Mark Beyer (Keyboard, Percussion), Graham Alexander (Vocals, Bass, Piano, Guitar), Joe Bologna (Drums, Percussion, Vocals), Douglas Cox (Drums, Percussion, Vocals), Jim Irizarry (Vocals, Rhythm Guitar, Piano, Harmonica), David Leon (Vocals, Rhythm Guitar, Piano, Harmonica), Mark Lewis (Keyboard, Percussion), Jimmy Pou (Vocals, Lead Guitar, Guitar Synth), Mac Ruffing (Vocals, Bass, Piano, Guitar), Chris Smallwood (Keyboard, Percussion), Tom Teeley (Vocals, Lead Guitar, Guitar Synth, Sitar)

MUSICAL NUMBERS Across The Universe, All My Loving, All You Need Is Love, And I Love Her, Blackbird, Come Together, A Day In The Life, Day Tripper, Eleanor Rigby, The End, Get Back, Girl, Give Peace A Chance, A Hard Day's Night, Hello Goodbye, Hey Jude, I Am The Walrus, I Feel Fine, I Saw Her Standing There, I Want To Hold Your Hand, I'm Happy Just To Dance With You, I've Just Seen A Face, Let It Be, Mother Nature's Son, Norwegian Wood (This Bird Has Flown), Revolution, Rocky Raccoon, Sgt. Pepper's Lonely Hearts Club Band, Strawberry Fields Forever, This Boy (Ringo's Theme), Till There Was You, Twist And Shout, Two Of Us, We Can Work It Out, With A Little Help From My Friends, Yesterday

2010-2011 AWARDS Drama Desk Award: Outstanding Revue

Broadway premiere of a revue/concert presented in two acts.

SYNOPSIS With the goal of delivering a perfect note-for-note performance, *Rain* performs the music of the Beatles live, with the same respect a classical musician treats Mozart. The show covers songs ranging from the early days of the band's appearances on The Ed Sullivan Show through the Abbey Road years, including historical film footage and television commercials, plus live cameras zooming in for close-ups of the band.

+ The production ran at the Neil Simon through January 15, 2011, went on haitus for three weeks, and reopened at the Brooks Atkinson Theatre February 8, 2011.

The Scottsboro Boys

Lyceum Theatre; First Preview: October 7, 2010; Opening Night: October 31, 2010; Closed December 12, 2010; 29 previews, 49 performances

Music by John Kander, lyrics by Fred Ebb, book by David Thompson; Produced by Barry & Fran Weissler, Jacki Barlia Florin, Janet Pailet/Sharon Carr/Patricia R. Klausner, Nederlander Presentations Inc., The Shubert Organization (Phillip J. Smith: Chairman; Robert E. Wankel: President), Beechwood Entertainment, Broadway Across America, Mark Zimmerman, Adam Blanshay/R2D2 Productions, Rick Danzansky/Barry Tatelman, Bruce Robert Harris/Jack W. Batman, Allen Spivak/Jerry Frankel, Bard Theatricals/Probo Productions/Randy Donaldson, Catherine Schreiber/Michael Palitz/Patti Laskawy, Vineyard Theatre; Director & Choreographer, Susan Stroman; Music Direction & Vocal Arrangements, David Loud; Sets, Beowulf Boritt; Costumes, Toni-Leslie James; Lighting, Ken Billington; Sound, Peter Hylenski; Orchestrations, Larry Hochman; Music Arrangements, Glen Kelly; Music Coordinator, John Monaco; Conductor, Paul Masse; Production Stage Manager, Joshua Halperin; Casting, Jim Carnahan, Stephen Kopel; Fight Director, Rick Sordelet; Production Manager, Aurora Productions; Associate Producers, Carlos Arana, Ruth Eckerd Hall and Brett England; Associate Director/Choreographer, Jeff Whiting; Executive Producer, Alecia Parker; General Manager, Richards/Climan Inc; Company Manager, Kathy Lowe; Stage Manager, Alex Lyu Volckhausen; Assistant Stage Manager, Cherene Snow/Robin S. Walker; Assistant Director/Choreographer, Eric Santagata; Dance Captain, Josh Breckenridge; Fight Captain, Rodney Hicks; Music Copying, Kaye Houseton Music (Anne Kaye & Doug Houston); Additional Percussion Arrangements, Bruce Doctor; Associate Design: Jo Winiarski (set), John Demous (lighting), Nicky Tobolski (cosutmes), Keith Caggiano (sound); Assistant Design: Alesxis Distler (set), James Milkey (lighting); Hair, Wigs & Makeup, Wendy Parson; General Management Associate, Elizabeth Talmadge; Prod. Electrician, James Fedigan; Head Electrician, Christopher Moeller; Moving Lights, Tim Rogers, David Arch; Prod. Props, Chris Pantuso; Prod. Sound Engineers, Phil Logo, Paul Delcioppo; Head Sound Engineer, Cassy Givens; Wardrobe Supervisor, Barry Doss; Dressers, Gayle Palmieri, Cailin Anderson; Hair & Makeup Supervisor, Joel Mendenhall; Child Wrangler, Alissa Zulvergold; Prod. Assistant/Sub Stage Manager, Ryan Durham; Advertising, SpotCo; VP of Marketing, Marci Kaufman; Director of Marketing, Ken Sperr; Multicultural Marketing, Full House – FHTT Inc.; Press, Boneau/Bryan-Brown, Chris Boneau, Jim Byk, Michael Strassheim; Cast recording (Off-Broadway): Jay Records 1421

CAST Interlocutor **John Cullum**; Mr. Bones **Colman Domingo**; Mr. Tambo **Forrest McClendon**; The Lady **Sharon Washington**; *The Scottsboro Boys*: Olen Montgomery **Josh Breckenridge**; Andy Wight **Derrick Cobey**; Eugene William **Jeremy Gumbs**; Haywood Patterson **Joshua Henry**; Clarence Norris **Rodney Hicks**; Willie Roberson **Kendrick Jones**; Ozie Powell **James T. Lane**; Roy Wright **Julius Thomas III**; Charles Weems **Christian Dante White**; *Playing various other characters*: Sherrif Bones/Lawyer Bones/Guard Bones/Attorney General/Clerk **Colman Domingo**; Deputy Tambo/Lawyer Tambo/Guard Tambo/Samuel Leibowitz **Forrest McClendon**; Victoria Price **Christian Dante White**; Ruby Bates **James T. Lane**; Judge/Govenor of Alabama **John Cullum**; Electrified Charlie **Kendrick Jones**; Electrified Isaac/Billy **Julius Thomas III**; Preacher **Rodney Hicks**; Little George **Jeremy Gumbs**; Swings **E. Clayton Cornelious**, **JC Montgomery**, **Clinton Roane**

UNDERSTUDIES Josh Breckenridge (Charles Weems, Electrified Charlie, Electrified Isaac, Mr. Tambo, Ozie Powell, Ruby Bates, Samuel Leibowitz, Victoria Price), E. Clayton Cornelious (Andy Wright, Billy, Charles Weems, Clarence Norris, Electrified Charlie, Electrified Isaac, Eugene Williams, Little George, Olen Montgomery, Ozie Powell, Preacher, Roy Wright, Ruby Bates, The Lady, Victoria Price, Willie Roberson), Rodney Hicks (Haywood Patterson), JC Montgomery (Attorney General, Clarence Norris, Governor of Alabama, Mr. Bones, Mr. Tambo, Preacher, Samuel Leibowitz, The Interlocutor), Clinton Roane (Andy Wright, Billy, Electrified Charlie, Electrified Isaac, Eugene Williams, Little George, Olen Montgomery, Ozie Powell, Roy Wright, Ruby Bates, Victoria Price, Willie Roberson), Cherene Snow/Roin S. Walker (The Lady)

ORCHESTRA Paul Masse (Conductor/Piano, Harmonium), Wayne duMaine (Associate Conductor/Trumpet, Cornet, Flugel Horn), Charles Gordon (Contractor/Tenor Trombone), Andrew Sterman (Clarinet, Bass Clarinet, Flute, Piccolo), Justin Smith (Violin), Ernie Collins (Upright Bass, Tuba), Bruce Doctor (Drums, Percussion), Greg Utzig (Banjo, Guitar, Mandolin, Ukulele, Harmonica)

MUSICAL NUMBERS Minstrel March, Hey, Hey, Hey, Hey!, Commencing in Chattanooga, Alabama Ladies, Nothin', Electric Chair, Go Back Home, Shout!, Make Friends With the Truth, That's Not the Way We Do Things, Never Too Late, Financial Advice, Southern Days, Chain Gang, Alabama Ladies (reprise), Zat So?, You Can't Do Me, The Scottsboro Boys, Minstrel March (reprise)

2010-2011 AWARDS Drama League Award: Julia Hansen Award for Excellence in Directing (Susan Stroman); Fred & Adele Astaire Award: Best Choreographer on Broadway (Susan Stroman)

SETTING Scottsboro, Alabama; 1931–1937. Transfer of the Off-Broadway musical presented without intermission. World premiere at the Vineyard Theatre February 12–April 18, 2010; the production subsequently ran at the Guthrie Theatre July 31–September 25, 2010 prior to its Broadway engagement (see *Theatre World* Vol. 66, pages 254 and 371).

SYNOPSIS *The Scottsboro Boys* takes the ratially insensitive minstrel show form of yore to explore the infamous 1930s Scottsboro Case, in which nine young black men were falsely accused of a raping two white women. They spent years in jail for crimes they did not commit, and ultimately provoked national outrage that sparked the American Civil Rights movement. Complete with sentimental songs, a tap specialty, a cakewalk, low comedy, and three stock characters, the musical conjures the defunct, highly theatrical minstrel form but puts a fierce spin on it.

Forrest McClendon and the Company

Jeremy Gumbs, Rodney Hicks, Josh Breckenridge, Derrick Cobey, Kendrick Jones, Julius Thomas III, Joshua Henry, Christian Dante White, and James T. Lane

Rodney Hicks and Joshua Henry

John Cullum

Sharon Washington (photos by Paul Kolnik)

Colman Domingo, Forrest McClendon with John Cullum (center, background), and the Company

James T. Lane, Derrick Cobey, Julius Thomas III, Joshua Henry (standing), Josh Breckenridge, Kendrick Jones, and Rodney Hicks

Nikka Graff Lanzarone, Laura Benanti, and Justin Guarini

Patti LuPone and de'Adre Aziza

Sherie Rene Scott and Danny Burstein

Sherie Rene Scott and Brian Stokes Mitchell

Vivian Nixon, Brian Stokes Mitchell, Nina Lafarga, and Justin Guarini

Laura Benanti, Luis Salgado, Justin Guarini, Nikka Graff Lanzarone
and the Company

Women on the Verge of a Nervous Breakdown

Belasco Theatre; First Preview: October 8, 2010; Opening Night: November 4, 2010; Closed January 2, 2011; 30 previews, 69 performances

Book by Jeffrey Lane, music & lyrics by David Yazbek; Based on the film by Pedro Almodóvar; Produced by Lincoln Center Theater (André Bishop, Artistic Director; Bernard Gersten, Executive Producer) in association with Bob Boyett; Director, Bartlett Sher; Choreography, Christopher Gattelli; Music Director, Jim Abbott; Sets, Michael Yeargan; Costumes, Catherine Zuber; Lighting, Brian MacDevitt; Sound, Scott Lehrer; Projections, Sven Ortel; Aerial Design, The Sky Box; Special Effects, Gregory Meeh; Wigs and Hair, Charles LaPointe; Casting, Telsey + Company; Production Stage Manager, Rolt Smith; Musical Theatre Associate Producer, Ira Weitzman; General Manager, Adam Siegel; Production Manager, Jeff Hamlin; Development, Hattie K. Jutagir; Marketing, Linda Mason Ross; Finance, David S. Brown; Education, Kati Koerner; Dramaturg, Anne Cattaneo; 1st Assistant Stage Manager, Andrea O. Saraffian; 2nd Assistant Stage Manager, Jennifer Rae Moore; Dance Captain, John Carroll; Assistant Dance Captain, Samantha Shafer; Company Manager, Matthew Markoff; Associate Company Manager, Josh Lowenthal; Associate Director, Sarna Lapine; Associate Choreographer, Lou Castro; Assistant Choreographers, Rebecca Tomas, Mark Stuart Eckstein; Dialect Coach, Deborah Hecht; Technical Supervision, Bill Nagle, Patrick Merryman; Associate Design: Mikiko Suzuki MacAdams (set), Jennifer Schriever (lighting), Drew Levy (sound), S. Katy Tucker (projections), Jeremy Chernick (special effects); Assistant Design: David Newell (costumes), Benjamin C. Travis (lighting); Projections Programmer, Michael Kohler; Projections Assistant, Lucy Mackinnon; Incidental Music/Vocal & Dance Arrangements, Jim Abbott; Music Coordinator, Dean Sharenow; Music Copying, Emily Grishman, Katharine Edmonds; Synthesizer Programmer, Randy Cohen; Assistant Synthesizer Programmer, Bryan Cox; Props Coordinator, Kathy Fabian/Propstar; Props Associates, Carrie Mossman, Timothy Ferro; Props Artisans, Mary Wilson, Catherine Small, Eric Berninghausen, Rebecca Perrenod; Show Carpenter, Kevin McNeill; Prod. Carpenter, John Weingart; Prod. Electrician, David Karlson; Prod. Propertyman, Mark Dignam; Prod. Sound, Scott Sanders; Automated Lights, Victor Seastone; Wardrobe Supervisor, Tom Bertsch; Dressers, Alice Bee, Steve Chazaro, Laura Ellington, Kathleen Gallagher, Mel Hansen, Geoffrey Polischuk, Leah Redmond, Tree Sarvay, Mark Trezza, Claire Verlaet, Patricia White; Hair Supervisor, Amy Nexwald; Assistant Hair Supervisor, Rick Caroto; Hair Assistant, Vanessa Anderson; Ms. LuPone's Wig, Paul Huntley; Mus. LuPones's Makeup, Angelina Avallone; Prod. Assistant, Lisa Chernoff; Music Production Assistant, Will Reynolds; Rehearsal Pianist, Adam Ben-David; Shoppers, Ryan Park, Nicole Moody; Advertising, Serino Coyne;Press, Philip Rinaldi, Barbara Carroll, Amanda Dekker; Cast recording: Sh-K-Boom/Ghostlight Records/Record & Tie Music 84447

CAST Pepa **Sherie Rene Scott**; Ivan **Brian Stokes Mitchell**; Taxi Driver **Danny Burstein**; Cristina **Jennifer Sanchez**; Hector, TV Husband, Magistrate, Chief Inspector **Murphy Guyer**; Man in Film, Telephone Repairman **Charlie Sutton**; Woman in Film, Ana **Nina LaFarga**; Doctor, Detective **Sean McCourt**; Candela **Laura Benanti**; Malik **Luis Salgado**; Carlos **Justin Guarini**; Marisa **Nikka Graff Lanzarone**; Ivan's Concierge, Magistrate 2 **Alma Cuervo**; Lucia **Patti LuPone**; Paulina **De'Adre Aziza**; Pepa's Concierge **Mary Beth Peil**; Ambite **Julio Agustin**; Ensemble **Julio Agustin, Alma Cuervo, Murphy Guyer, Nina LaFarga, Yanira Marin, Sean McCourt, Vivian Nixon, Luis Salgado, Jennifer Sanchez, Phillip Spaeth, Matthew Steffens, Charlie Sutton, Candace Marie Woods**; Swings **John Carroll, Rachel Bay Jones, John Schiappa, Samantha Shafer**

UNDERSTUDIES Julio Agustin (Malik), De'Adre Aziza (Pepa), John Carroll (Malik, Man at Train, Telephone Repairman), Alma Cuervo (Lucia, Pepa's Concierge), Rachel Bay Jones (Ivan's Concierge, Lucia, Magistrate 2, Pepa's Concierge, Woman in Cinema), Nina Lafarga (Marisa, Paulina), Yanira Marin (Ana, Cristina, Marisa), Sean McCourt (Chief Inspector, Ivan, Taxi Driver), Vivian Nixon (Candela, Paulina), Luis Salgado (Ambite, Detective), Jennifer Sanchez (Candela), John Schiappa (Chief Inspector, Doctor, Hector, Ivan, Magistrate, Man in Cinema, Taxi Driver), Samantha Shafer (Ana, Cristina, Pepa, Woman at Train), Phillip Spaeth (Carlos, Telephone Repairman), Matthew Steffens (Ambite), Charlie Sutton (Carlos, Detective)

ORCHESTRA Marco Paguia (Associate Conductor/Keyboard 1), Dean Sharenow (Drums), Brian Hamm (Bass), Erik Della Penna (Guitar), Javier Diaz (Percussion), CJ Camerieri (Trumpet), Tim Albright (Trombone), R.J. Kelley (French Horn), Todd Groves (Reed 1), Dan Willis (Reed 2), Alden Banta (Reed 3), Lori Miller (Violin 1/Concertmaster), Entcho Todorov (Violin 2), Jonathan Dinklage (Viola), Anik Oulianine (Cello)

MUSICAL NUMBERS Madrid; Lie to Me; Lovesick; Time Stood Still; My Crazy Heart; Model Behavior; Island; The Microphone; On the Verge; Mother's Day; Yesterday, Tomorrow and Today; Tangled; Invisible; Island (reprise); Marisa/The Chase; Talk to Me

2010-2011 AWARDS Drama Desk Award: Outstanding Featured Actress in a Musical (Laura Benanti); Outer Critics Circle Award: Outstanding Featured Actress in a Musical (Laura Benanti)

SETTING Madrid, 1987. World premiere of a new musical presented in two acts.

SYNOPSIS *Women on the Verge of a Nervous Breakdown* is a story about women and the men who pursue them... finding them, losing them, needing them, and rejecting them. At the center is Pepa whose friends and lovers are blazing a trail through 1980s Madrid. And why do they all keep showing up at her high-rise apartment? Is it her gazpacho? Along with Pepa, there's her missing (possibly philandering) lover, Ivan; his ex-wife of questionable sanity, Lucia; Pepa's friend, Candela, and her terrorist boyfriend; a power-suited lawyer plus a taxi driver who dispenses tissues, mints and advice in equal proportion. Mayhem and comic madness abound, balanced by the empathy and heart that are trademarks of Almodóvar's work.

Sherie Rene Scott (photos by Paul Kolnik)

Colin Quinn: Long Story Short

Helen Hayes Theatre; First Preview: October 22, 2010; Opening Night: November 9, 2010; Closed March 5, 2011; 21 previews, 135 performances

Written by Colin Quinn; Produced by Eva Price, Richard Martini, Bruston Kade Manuel & Will Dombrowski, Richard Winkler, George Shapiro, Matthew Salloway, Jack Thomas, Bisno/Frankel/Fireman, Dan Frishwasser, Avram Freedberg & Mary Beth Dale and Allen Spivak; Director, Jerry Seinfled; Sets and Projections, David Gallo; Lighting, Howell Binkley; Sound, Christopher "Kit" Bond; Original Compositions, Scott Elmegreen; Production Stage Manager, Daniel J. Kells; Creative Consultant, Hal Brooks; Advertising, Hofstetter+Partners/Agency 212; Marketing, HHC Marketing; Website & Social Media, Bay Bridge Productions; General Management, Cesa Entertainment (Jamie Cesa, Diane Alianiello), KL Management (Richard Martini, Elinor Prince, Sharon T. Pratt, Christy Ellingsworth), and Maximum Entertainment (Avram Freedberg, Mary Beth Dale, Eva Price, Holly Sutton, Taylor James); Company Manager, Holly Sutton; Associate Scenic Design, Steven C. Kemp; Animator/Associate Projections Design/Projection Assistant, Steve Channon; Projection Assistant Design, Caite Hevner; Design Studio Manager, Sarah Zeitler; Associate Lighting, Ryan O'Gara; Light Board Programmer, Sean Beach; Assistant Lighting, Amanda Zleve; Spot Op, Brendan Keane; Master Electrician, Joe Beck; Sound Technician, Bob Etter; Interns: Ashely Cavadas (scenic), Michael Rummage (lighting), Crystal Lee (projections); Creative Directors, Jules Evenson, Erin McParland; Marketing Team, Hugh Hysell, Michael Redman, Todd Brtiscoe, Kiara Kincheloe, Christopher Rosenow; Advertising Team, Bill Hofstetter, Jennifer Katz; For Bay Bridge: Laura Wagner, Adam Magazine; Dramaturg, Dani Vetere; Assitant to Mr. Quinn, Claire Gilbertsen; Assistant to Mr. Seinfeld, Melissa Gastgarber; Press, Rubenstein Communications, Tom Keaney, Amy Jacobs, Elyse Weissman, Rachel Silverman

Performed by **Colin Quinn**

Transfer of the Off-Broadway solo performance play presented without intermission. World premiere at the Bleecker Street Theatre June 19–September 4, 2010 (see Off-Broadway listings in this volume)

SYNOPSIS Comically channeling the demise of great world empires, Colin Quinn uses his articulate brand of comedy in taking audiences through an uproarious history of the world in 75 minutes. From his personification of Caesar as the original Italian mobster to his complaints about Ancient Greece and Antigone giving way to Costco and Snooki, Quinn is at his satirical best, taking on the attitudes, appetites and bad habits that toppled the world's most powerful nations. *Colin Quinn: Long Story Short* proves that throughout human history, the joke has always been on us.

Colin Quinn

Colin Quinn (photos by Carol Rosegg)

Colin Quinn

Paul Rebuens and Lynn Marie Stewart

Paul Reubens (photos by Jeff Vespa)

Paul Reubens

The Pee-wee Herman Show

Stephen Sondheim Theatre; First Preview: October 26, 2010; Opening Night: November 11, 2010; Closed January 2, 2011; 18 previews, 62 performances

Written by Paul Reubens and Bill Steinkellner, additional material by John Paragon; Based on the original *The Pee-wee Herman Show* by Paul Reubens, Bill Steinkellner, Phil Hartman, John Paragon, Edi McClurg, John Moody, Lynne Marie Stewart, Ivan Flores, Brian Seff, Monica Ganas, Tito Larriva; Original *Pee-wee's Playhouse* production design by Gary Panter; Music by Jay Cotton; Produced by Scott Sanders Productions, Adam S. Gordon, Allan S. Gordon; Élan V. McCallister, Roy Miller, Carol Fineman, Scott Zeilinger Productions/ Radio Mouse Entertainment, StylesFour Productions/Randy Donaldson/Tim Laczynski; Associate Prouder, Kelly Bush; Director, Alex Timbers; Set, David Korins; Costumes, Ann Closs-Farley; Lighting, Jeff Croiter; Sound, M.L. Dogg; Puppetry, Basil Twist; Projections, Jake Pinholster; Technical Supervision, Larry Morley/Sam Ellis; Design Consultant, Jimmy Cuomo; Cartoon & Film Consultant, Prudence Fenton; Makeup/Hair & Wigs, Ve Neill; Marketing/Promotions, TEAM Services, Bonnie Werth, James McCune; Key Art, Mixed Business Group (Marc Balet, Mark Cline, Ryan Cox); Advertising, SpotCo; Associate Producers, Jared Geller, David Foster, Anne Caruso; Production Stage Manager, Lois L. Griffing; General Management, Richards/Climan Inc.; Company Manager, Doug Gaeta; Stage Manager, James D. Latus; Puppet Captain, Adam Pagdon; Choreography, Wendy Seyb; L.A. Production Casting, Bruce H. Heuberg; N.Y. Casting, Ian Unterman; Associate Director, Ian Unterman; Assistant Director, Jeremy Bloom; Associate Design: Rod Lemmond (set), Grant W.S. Yaeger (lighting), Daniel Brodie (projections); Assistant Design: Kharen Zeunert (costumes), Price Johnston, Michah Stieglitz (projections); Sound System Design, Cody Spencer; Prod. Sound Engineer, Francis Elers; Deck Sound, Jocelyn Smith; Prod. Carpenter, John J. Tutalo; Prod. Electrician, Cletus Karamon; Prod. Props, Neil Rosenberg; Audio Effects Operator, Joshua Maszle; Puppet Consultant, Sean Johnson, Swazzle Inc.; Miss Yvonne Wig Design, Steven Perfidia; Wardrobe Supervisor, Melissa Crawford; Dresser, Lauren Oppelt; Makeup/Hair & Wig Supervisor, Cristina Waltz; Assistants to Mr. Reubens, Allison Berry, Sarah Sahin; Mr. Reubens Management, Kelly Bush & Kristina Sorensen, Vic Entertainment; Prod. Assistants, Megan J. Alvord, Stephanie Ward, Alex Hilhorst; Assistant to Mr. Sanders, Jason Grossman; Press, The Hartman Group (Michael Hartman, Tom D'Ambosio, Michelle Bergmann) & ID (Carrie Byalick, Lia Mahoney, Molly Kawachi, Natalie Lent)

CAST Pee-wee Herman **Paul Reubens**; Mailman Mike **John Moody**; Bear/ Voice **Drew Powell**; Jambi/Voice **John Paragon**; Sergio **Jesse Garcia**; Cowboy Curtis **Phil LaMarr**; Miss Yvonne **Lynne Marie Stewart**; King of Cartoons/Voice **Lance Roberts**; Firefighter/Voice **Josh Meyers**; Voice **Lexy Fridell**; Puppeteers **Oliver Dalzell, Haley Jenkins, Matt Leabo, Eric Novak, Adam Pagdon, Jessica Scott, Amanda Villalobos, Chris de Ville**

UNDERSTUDIES Lexy Fridell (Miss Yvonne), Drew Powell (Firefighter, Jambi, Mailman Mike), Caesar Samayoa (Bear, Cowboy Curtis, King of Cartoons, Sergio, Voice)

New York premiere of a variety show with music, magic, animation, and puppetry presented without intermission. Previously played a sold-out engagement in Los Angeles at Club Nokia @ L.A. Live January 12–February 7, 2010

SYNOPSIS *The Pee-wee Herman Show* reunites the one-and-only Pee-wee Herman (the alter ego of Paul Reubens) with many of the original Playhouse cast of characters, including Miss Yvonne, Cowboy Curtis, Pterri the Pterodactyl, Jambi the Genie, and Chairry, for an all new celebration of sophisticated silliness. Based on the original show created at the Groundlings in 1981 and the children's television series from the 1980s, *The Pee-wee Herman Show* is an eye-popping ninety minutes of subversive humor and childlike wonder that charts a day in the life of our bow tied hero, one of the most inspired comic personas of our time.

The Merchant of Venice

Broadhurst Theatre; First Preview: October 19, 2010; Opening Night: November 13, 2010; Closed February 20, 2011; 26 previews, 73 performances

Written by William Shakespeare; Produced by The Public Theater (Oskar Eustis, Artistic Director; Andrew D. Hamingson, Executive Director), Jeffrey Richards, Jerry Frankel, Debbie Bisno & Eva Price, Amy Nederlander, Jonathan First, Stewart F. Lane & Bonnie Comley, Universal Pictures Stage Productions, Merritt Forrest Baer, The Araca Group, Broadway Across America, Joseph & Matthew Deitch, JK Productions, Terry Allen Kramer, Cathy Chernoff/Jay & Cindy Gutterman, Mallory Factor/Cheryl Lachowicz and The Shubert Organization (Phillip J. Smith, Chairman; Robert E. Wankel, President); Executive Producer, Joey Parnes; Associate Producers, Joy Newman, David Schumeister, Barry Edelstein, Jeremy Scott Blaustein, Elon Rutberg, S.D. Wagner, John Johnson; Director, Daniel Sullivan; Set, Mark Wendland; Costumes, Jess Goldstein; Lighting, Kenneth Posner; Sound, Acme Sound Partners; Hair & Wigs, Charles LaPointe; Original Music, Dan Moses Schreier; Fight Director, Thomas Schall; Choreographer, Mimi Lieber; Production Stage Manager, Stephen M. Kaus; Casting, Jordan Thaler, Heidi Griffiths; Associate Producers, Joy Newman, David Schumeister; General Management, Joey Parnes, John Johnson, S.D. Wagner; Company Manager, Kim Sellon; Public Theater: Madny Hackett (Associate Artistic Director), Andrea Nellis (General Manager), Maria Goyanes (Associate Producer), Ruth Sternberg (Director of Production), Barry Edelstein (Director of Shakespeare Initiative), Nella Vera (Director of Marketing); Stage Manager, David Sugarman; Assistant Company Manager, Christina Huschle; Management Associates, Kristen Luciani, Nate Koch; Assistant Director, Laura Savia; Dialect Coach, Kate Wilson; Dramaturgy, Barry Edelstein; Associate Design: John Viesta (lighting), Nick Borisjuk (sound); Assistant Design: Rachel Nemec & Jon Collins (set), China Lee & Tristan Scott Barton Raines (costumes); Wig Assistant, Leah Loukas; Prod. Carpenter, Larry Morley; Prod. Electrician, Richard Mortell; Head Electrician, Jeff Turner; Prod. Prop Supervisor, Mike Smanko; Head Props, Faye Armon; Head Sound, Mike Farfalla; Wardrobe Supervisor, Rick Kelly; Mr. Pacino's Dresser, Emily Merriweather; Dressers, Gary Biangone, Cat Dee, Mary Ann Lewis-Oberpriller, Hair Supervisor, Erick Medinilla; Assistant Hair, Carole Morales; Music Contractor, Seymour Red Press; Advertising, Serino Coyne; Website/New Media Marketing, Art Meets Commerce; Press, Candi Adams, Josh Ferri, Julie Danni

CAST Antonio, *a Venetian merchant* **Byron Jennings**; Salerio, *his friend* **Peter Francis James**; Solanio, *his friend* **Matthew Rauch**; Bassanio, *a lord, Antonio's friend* **David Harbour**; Lorenzo, *a gentleman of Venice* **Seth Numrich** [1]; Gratiano, *a gentleman of Venice* **Jesse L. Martin** [2]; Portia, *an heiress in Belmont* **Lily Rabe**; Nerissa, *her lady* **Marsha Stephanie Blake**; Balthasar, *servant to Portia* **Herb Foster** [3]; Shylock, *a Jewish moneylender* **Al Pacino**; Prince of Morocco, *suitor to Portia* **Isaiah Johnson**; Launcelot Gobbo, *servant to Shylock* **Christopher Fitzgerald**; Jessica, *Shylock's daughter* **Heather Lind**; Prince of Arragon, *suitor to Portia* **Charles Kimbrough** [4]; Antonio's Man **Glenn Fleshler**; Tubal, *an associate of Shylock's* **Richard Topol**; Duke of Venice **Gerry Bamman**; Priest **Baylen Thomas**; Stephano, *servant to Portia* **Curt Hostetter**; Ensemble **Happy Anderson, Liza J. Bennett, Glenn Fleshler, Luke Forbes, Herb Foster, Jade Hawk, Bethany Heinrich, Curt Hostetter, Tia James, Kelsey Kurz, Brian Keith MacDonald, Dorien Makhloghi, Baylen Thomas**

*The production went on hiatus January 10–February 1. Cast replacements for the extention were: 1. Thomas Michael Hammond 2. David Aaron Baker 3. George Bartenieff 4. Herb Foster 5. Brian Sgambati

UNDERSTUDIES Glenn Fleshler (Gratiano, Launcelot Gobbo), Luke Forbes (Prince of Morocco), Herb Foster (Duke of Venice, Prince of Arragon), Bryce Gill (Antonio's Man), Curt Hostetter (Antonio, Tubal), Liza J. Bennett (Jessica), Tia James (Nerissa), Thomas Michael Hammond [5] (Bassanio, Lorenzo), Dorien Makhloghi (Solanio), Kim Martin-Cotten (Portia), Baylen Thomas (Salerio), Richard Topol (Shylock)

RECORDED MUSICIANS Rob Berman (Conductor/Piano), Suzanne Ornstein (Violin), Richard Brice (Viola), Roger Shell (Cello), Lino Gomez (Clairnet), Melanie Feld (English Horn), Ronald Jannelli (Bassoon)

2010-2011 AWARDS *Theatre World Award:* Heather Lind; Equity Awards: Extraordinary Excellence in Diversity on Broadway; Joseph A. Callaway Award (Lily Rabe, best performance in a classic play in New York area); St. Clair Bayfield Award (Charles Kimbrough, best supporting performance by an actor in a Shakespearean play in the New York area)

SETTING Venice and on The Belmont. Transfer of the Off-Broadway revival of a classical play with original music presented in two acts. Previously presented at the Public Theater's Shakespeare in the Park June 2010 (see Off-Broadway Company Series in this volume). This production marked the fiftieth major New York presentation of the play since the eighteenth century.

SYNOPSIS *The Merchant of Venice* is one of Shakespeare's most thrilling and controversial plays, rich with love and betrayal, forgiveness and revenge. The Jewish moneylender Shylock makes a loan to Antonio, a Christian merchant. Their loan contract, steeped in prejudice and centered on the play's infamous "pound of flesh," sweeps the two men and everyone in their worlds into chaos. Only the insightful Portia can imagine a way forward, but for her and those she loves, even "the quality of mercy" has its limits.

Al Pacino and Byron Jennings

Seth Numrich and Heather Lind (photos by Joan Marcus)

Elf

Al Hirschfeld Theatre; First Preview: November 2, 2010; Opening Night: November 14, 2010; Closed January 2, 2011; 15 previews, 57 performances

Book by Thomas Meehan and Bob Martin, music by Matthew Sklar, lyrics by Chad Beguelin; Based on the New Line Cinema film written by David Berenbaum; Produced by Warner Brothers Theatre Ventures Inc. (Gregg Maday, Executive Vice President; Raymond Wu, SVP/Development/Head of Operations; Laura Valan, CFO; Mark Coker, SVP Finance) in association with Unique Features; Director and Choreography, Casey Nicholaw; Music Direction and Vocal Arrangements, Phil Reno; Orchestrations, Doug Besterman; Sets, David Rockwell; Costumes, Gregg Barnes; Lighting, Natasha Katz; Sound, Peter Hylenski; Casting, Telsey + Company; Projections, Zacharay Borovay; Hair, Josh Marquette; Dance Arrangements, David Chase; Production Stage Manager, Karen Moore; Associate Director, Casey Hushion; Music Coordinator, John Miller; Technical Supervisor, Chris Smith/Smitty; Executive Producer, Mark Kaufman; Marketing, aka; General Manager Charlotte Wilcox Company (Charlotte Wilcox, Seth Marquette); For Warner Brothers: Barry Meyer (Chairman & CEO), Alan Horn (President & COO); For Unique Features: Michael Lynne & Bob Shaye (Principal), Mark Kaufman, Dylan Sellers, Julie Crowne, Christina Delgado, Jonna Smith, Leah Holzer; Keyboard Programmer, Randy Cohen; Company Manager, Heidi Nen; Associate Company Manager, Michael Bolgar; Stage Manager, Rachel S. McCutchen; Assistant Stage Manager, Brian Bogin; Associate Choreographer, Brian J. Marcum; Dance Captain, Callie Carter; Assistant Dance Captain, Marc Kessler; Associate Design: Richard Jaris (set), Matthew Pachtman (costumes), Peter Hoerburger (lighting), Keith Caggiano (sound), Driscoll Otto (projections); Assistant Design: Ann Bartok, Charles Corcoran, Christine Peters (set), Sarah Sophia Lidz, Sky Switser (costumes), Kathleen Dobbins (lighting); Assistant to Mr. Rockwell, TJ Greenway; Makeup Consultant, Joe Dulude II; Skating Coach, Marni Halasa; Prod. Electrician, James Fedigan; Prod. Props Supervisor, Emiliano Pares; Advance Sound, Jason Strangeld; Prod. Carpenter, Patrick Shea; Automation Carpenter, Mike Norris; Head Electrician, Brian Dawson; Assistant Electrician, Chris Robinson; Head Sound, Jesse Stevens; Head Props, Peter Drummond; Assistant Props, Peter Drummond; Wardrobe Supervisor, James Hall; Assistant Wardrobe Supervisor, Franklin Hollenbach; Dressers, Joshua Burns, Suzanne Delahunt, Kristin Farley, Dan Foss, Kaye Gowenlock, Jennifer Griggs, Anthony Hoffman, Kate Sorg; Hair Supervisor, Richard Orton; Hair Dressers, Elisa Acevedo, Monica Costea, Joel Hawkins; Assistant to Mr. Miller, Nicole Jennino; Advertising, Serino Coyne; Website & Online Marketing, Art Meets Commerce; Press, The Hartman Group, Michael Hartman, Juliana Hannett, Frances White; Cast recording: Sh-K-Boom/Ghostlight Records 84453

CAST Santa **George Wendt**; Mrs. Claus **Nancy Johnston**; Buddy **Sebastian Arcelus**; Charlie **Noah Weisberg**; Shawanda **Asmeret Ghebremichael**; Walter Hobbs **Mark Jacoby**; Sam **Noah Weisberg**; Matthews **Matt Loehr**; Chadwick **Blake Hammond**; Emily **Beth Leavel**; Michael **Matthew Gumley**; Deb **Valerie Wright**; Macy's Manager **Michael Mandell**; Jovie **Amy Spanger**; Fake Santa **Timothy J. Alex**; Policemen **Noah Weisberg, Lee A. Wilkins**; Mr. Greenway **Michael McCormick**; Charlotte Dennon **Emily Hsu**; Ensemble **Timothy J. Alex, Lisa Gajda, Asmeret Ghebremichael, Blake Hammond, Jenny Hill, Emily Hsu, Nancy Johnston, Matt Loehr, Michael James Scott, Noah Weisberg, Lee A. Wilkins, Kirsten Wyatt**; Swings **Callie Carter, Cara Cooper, Stacey Todd Holt, Marc Kessler**; Standby for Michael **Matthew Schechter**

UNDERSTUDIES Timothy J. Alex (Mr. Greenway, Walter Hobbs), Cara Cooper (Emily, Jovie), Blake Hammond (Macy's Manager, Santa), Jenny Hill (Deb), Stacey Todd Holt (Walter Hobbs), Nancy Johnston (Emily), Matt Loehr (Buddy), Michael James Scott (Macy's Manager), Noah Weisberg (Buddy), Kirsten Wyatt (Deb, Jovie)

ORCHESTRA Phil Reno (Conductor/Keyboard), Mat Eisenstein (Associate Conductor/Keyboard), Rick Dolan (Concert Master), Belinda Whitney (Violin), Sarah Hewitt Roth (Cello), Michael Kuennen (Bass), Tom Murray, Rick Heckman, Mark Thrasher (Woodwinds), Craig Johnson, Scott Harrell (Trumpets), Alan Ferber, Jeff Nelson (Trombones), Charles Descarfino (Percussion), Perry Cavari (Drums), Mark C. Mitchell (Keyboards)

MUSICAL NUMBERS Christmastown, World's Greatest Dad, In the Way, Sparklejollytwinklejingley, I'll Believe in You, In the Way (reprise), Just Like Him, A Christmas Song, I'll Believe in You (reprise), Nobody Cares About Santa, Never Fall in Love, There Is a Santa Claus, The Story of Buddy the Elf, Nobody Cares About Santa (reprise), A Christmas Song (reprise), Finale

SETTING The North Pole and New York City. World premiere of a new musical preseted in two acts.

SYNOPSIS Based on the 2003 hit Warner Brothers' film starring Will Farrell, *Elf* is the hilarious tale of Buddy, a young orphan child who mistakenly crawls into Santa's bag of gifts and is transported back to the North Pole. Buddy is raised unaware that he is actually a human, until his enormous size and poor toy-making abilities cause him to face the truth. With Santa's permission, Buddy embarks on a journey to New York City to find his birth father and discover his true identity. Faced with the harsh reality that his father is on the naughty list and his step-brother doesn't even believe in Santa, Buddy is determined to win over his new family and help New York remember the true meaning of Christmas.

Sebastian Arcelus

Sebastian Arcelus and Amy Spanger

The Company (photos by Joan Marcus)

Mark Jacoby and Sebastian Arcelus

Matthew Gumley and Sebastian Arcelus

Beth Leavel and Matthew Gumley

George Wendt

A Free Man of Color

Vivian Beaumont Theatre; First Preview: October 23, 2010; Opening Night: November 18, 2010; Closed January 9, 2011; 29 previews, 61 performances

Written by John Guare; Produced by Lincoln Center Theater (André Bishop, Artistic Director; Bernard Gersten, Executive Producer); Director, George C. Wolfe; Sets, David Rockwell; Costumes, Ann Hould-Ward; Lighting, Jules Fisher & Peggy Eisenhauer; Original Music, Jeanine Tesori; Sound, Scott Stauffer; Choreography, Hope Clarke; Stage Manager, Gwendolyn M. Gilliam; Casting, Daniel Swee; General Manager, Adam Siegel; Production Manager, Jeff Hamlin; Development, Hattie K. Jutagir; Marketing, Linda Mason Ross; Company Manager, Jessica Perlmeter Cochrane; Associate Company Manager, Daniel Hoyos; Assistant Stage Manager, Kevin Bertolacci; Assistant Director, Saheem Ali; Mr. Guare's Assistant, Stella Powell Jones; Associate Set, Richard Jaris; Assistant Design: T.J. Greenway, Gaetane Bertol, Ann Bartok, Christine Peters, Todd Potter (set), Christopher Vergara (costumes), Tricia Nicholas, Dan Ozminkowski (lighting), Benjamin Furiga, Bridget O'Connor (sound); Assistant to Ms. Hould-Ward, Robin McGee; Assitant to Ms. Tesori, Peter Lerman; Automated Light Programmer, Timothy F. Rogers; Props, Scott Laule; Prop Assistant, Julie Sandy; Wardrobe Supervisor, Lynn Bowling; Hair Supervisor, Carrie Lynn Rohm; Makeup, Cynthia Demand; Prod. Carpenter, William Nagle; Prod. Electrician, Patrick Merryman; Prod. Props, Karl Rausenberger; Prod. Flyman, John Weingart; House Technician, Linda Heard; Dressers, Adam Adelman, Richard Gross, Donna Holland, Peggy Danz Kazdan, Shannon Koger, Patti Luther, James Nadeaux, Chuck ReCar, Sarah Rochford, Melinda Suarez-White, Rosie Wells; Hair Assistants, Erin Hicks, John McNulty, Tim Miller, Chelsea Roth, April Schuller; Prod. Assistants, Cliff Moller, Laura Wilson; For LCT: Finance, David S. Brown; Education, Kati Koerner; Resident Director, Bartlett Sher; Dramaturg/LCT Directors Lab, Anne Cattaneo; Musical Theatre Associate Producer, Ira Weitzman; LCT3 Artistic Director, Paige Evans; Poster Art, James McMullan; Advertising, Serino Coyne; Press, Philip Rinaldi, Barbara Carroll, Amanda Dekker

CAST Jacques Cornet **Jeffrey Wright**; Cupidon Murmur, *his slave* **Mos**; Zeus-Marie Pincepoosse, *his half-brother* **Reg Rogers**; Margery Jolicoeur, *a country wife* **Nicole Beharie**; *Citizens of New Orleans*: Dr. Toubib **Joseph Marcell**; Intendante Juan Ventura Morales **Triney Sandoval**; Doña Smeralda, *Toubib's wife* **Justina Machado**; Orphee and Leda, *Toubib's slaves* **Esau Pritchett** and **Teyonnah Parris**; Doña Athene, *Cornet's wife* **Sara Gettelfinger**; Remy Dorilante **Arnie Burton**; Mme. Dorilante, *his wife* **Teyonnah Parris**; Jonathan Sparks **Brian Reddy**; Mrs. Sparks, *his wife* **Rosal Colón**; Lord Harcourt **Robert Stanton**; Lady Harcourt, *his wife* **Wendy Rich Stetson**; Alcibiade **David Emerson Toney**; Pythagore **Nick Mennell**; Mercure **Peter Bartlett**; Mme. Mandragola **Veanne Cox**; Melpomene **Teyonnah Parris**; Euterpe **Wendy Rich Stetson**; Calliope **Sara Gettelfinger**; Terpsichore **Rosal Colón**; *Citizens of Sante Domingue*: Count Achille Creux **Peter Bartlett**; Doña Polissena, *his wife, a scientist* **Veanne Cox**; Toussaint Louverture, *Haitian revolutionary* **Mos**; *The Americans*: Thomas Jefferson **John McMartin**; Meriwether Lewis, *his secretary* **Paul F. Dano**; Robert Livingston, *Minister to France* **Veanne Cox**; James Monroe, *future President* **Arnie Burton**; Major Walter Reed **Brian Reddy**; *The French*: Napoleon Bonaparte **Triney Sandoval**; Josephine, *his wife* **Justina Machado**; Tallyrand, *his foreign minister* **Reg Rogers**; General LeClerc, *his brother-in-law* **Nick Mennell**; LeClerc's Captain **Robert Stanton**; Georges Feydeau, *Playwright* **Robert Stanton**; *The Spanish*: King Carlos Cuarto **Nick Mennell**; The Infanta **Rosal Colón**; Slaves of New Orleans **Yao Ababio**, **Derric Harris**, **Postell Pringle**, **Jerome Stigler**, **Senfaub Stoney**

UNDERSTUDIES Ashley Bryant (Leda, Melpomene, Mme. Dorilante), Rosal Colón (Smeralda, Josephine), Stephanie DiMaggio (Calliope, Athene, Euterpe, Lady Harcourt, Mrs. Sparks, Terpsichore, The Infanta), Kyle Fabel (Morales, Sparks, Reed, Bonaparte, Dorilante), Derric Harris (Alcibiade, Orphee), David Graham Jones (LeClerc, Feydeau, Monroe, King Carlos Cuarto, LeClerc's Captain, Harcourt, Lewis, Pythagore), David Manis (Creux, Mercure, Jefferson), Howard

W. Overshown (Cornet), Teyonnah Parris (Jolicoeur), Postell Pringle (Murmur, Louverture), Wendy Rich Stetson (Polissena, Mme. Mandragola, Livingston), David Emerson Toney (Toubib)

SETTING Time: 1801-1806. Place: New Orleans and other locations in Europe and America. World premiere of a new play presented in two acts.

SYNOPSIS *A Free Man of Color* is a freewheeling epic set in 1801 New Orleans. Jacques Cornet, the title character, is a new world Don Juan and the wealthiest inhabitant of this sexually charged and racially progressive city. Jacques thinks all is well in his paradise until history intervenes, setting off a chain of events which no one, much less this free man of color, realizes is about to splinter the world.

Robert Stanton, Arnie Burton, Brian Reddy, Reg Rogers, Mos, and Jeffrey Wright

Veanne Cox and Jeffrey Wright (photos by T. Charles Erickson)

Elling

Ethel Barrymore Theatre; First Preview: November 2, 2011; Opening Night: November 21, 2010; Closed November 28, 2010; 22 previews, 9 performances

Based on the novels by Ingvar Ambjørnsen; New English adaptaion by Simon Bent; Stage and Film Adaptation by Axel Hellsteinius in collaboration with Petter Næss; Produced by Howard Panter for Ambassador Theatre Group, Robert G. Bartner, Bill Kenwright, John O'Boyle, Deborah Taylor, Burnt Umber, Finola Dwyer, Elling Ellingsen and Magnus Karlsen, Bill Ballard/David Mirvish, Ronnie Planalp, Toledo Productions, Lorenzo Thione, Jay Kuo, Harris Karma Productions, Jayne Baron Sherman, Robert Driemeyer, Scott Cameron/Dan Mathieu, and Dodger Theatricals (Michael David, Edward Strong, Rocco Landesman), in association with Bob Boyett; Director, Doug Hughs; Set, Scott Pask; Costumes, Catherine Zuber; Lighting, Kenneth Posner; Original Music & Sound, David Van Tieghem; Hair & Wigs, Tom Watson; Casting, Jim Carnahan; Production Stage Manager, Barclay Stiff; Production Management, Aurora Productions; Associate Producer, Tali Pelman; General Management, Stuart Thompson Productions/Marshall B. Purdy; Executive Producer, David Lazar; Company Manager, Adam J. Miller; Stage Manager, Kelly Beaulieu; Assistant Director, Alexander Greenfield; Associate Design: Christine Peters (set), Nichole Moody, Ryan Park (costumes), Justin Partier (lighting), David Sanderson (sound); Prod. Carpenter, Mike Martinez; Prod. Electrician, Dan Coey; Prod. Sound Engineer, Phil Lojo/Paul Delcioppo; Electrician, Stephen Allain; Properties Coordinator, Pete Sarafin; Wardrobe Supervisor, Kathleen Gallagher; Hair Supervisor, Lisa Weiss; Dressers, Paul Rinner, Katt Masterson; Makeup Consultants, Dick Page, Ashley Ryan; Production Assistant, Michael Padden; Advertising/Marketing, SpotCo; Press, Boneau/Bryan-Brown, Adrian Bryan-Brown, Susanne Tighe, Kelly Guiod

CAST Kjell Bjarne **Brendan Fraser**; Elling **Denis O'Hare**; Ridum Nordsletten, Gunn, Johanne, Poet **Jennifer Coolidge**; Frank Asli, Poet **Jeremy Shamos**; Alfons Jorgensen **Richard Easton**

STANDBYS Ted Koch (Kjell Bjarne, Frank Asli), Robert Emmet Lunney (Elling, Alfons Jorgensen), Lusia Strus (Reidum Nordsletten)

SETTING Oslo, Norway. The present. New York premiere of a new comedy presented in two acts. Originally presented at the Bush Theatre in London where it transferred to the West End.

SYNOPSIS Set in the current day, *Elling* is a comedy about a wildly mismatched pair of roommates trying to embrace life, love, friendship, pizza, poetry, and women.

Denis O'Hare, Brendan Fraser, and Jennifer Coolidge

Denis O'Hare and Brendan Fraser (photos by Joan Marcus)

Denis O'Hare, Jennifer Coolidge, and Brendan Fraser

Donny and Marie Osmond

Marie Osmond (photos by Kim Goodwin)

Donny & Marie: A Broadway Christmas

Marquis Theatre; Opening Night: December 9, 2010; Closed January 2, 2011; 20 performances

Produced by Gregory Young–The Production Office, Jon B. Platt–On the Line Company,Magic Arts & Entertainment, NewSpace Entertainment, in association with Greg Sperry and Eric Gardner; Director and Choreography, Barry Lather; Musical Director, Jerry Williams; Production Design, Perry "Butch" Allen & Peter Morse; Set and Video, Perry "Butch" Allen; Costumes, Kirstin Gallo; Lighting, Peter Morse; General Management, Alchemy Production Group LLC, Carl Pasbjerg, Frank Scardino; Production Management, Eberg Stage Solutions, Steven Ehrenberg; Production Coordinator, David Novich; Marketing, Bruce Granath; Dance Captain, Jaymz Tuaileva; Company Manager, Erik Birkeland; Executive Assistant to Marie Osmond, Darla Speery; Assistants to Marie Osmond, Rachel Lauren, Kim Goodwin; Managerial Associate, Tegan Meyer; Assistant to the General Managers, Amanda Coleman; Head Writer, Marcia Wilkie; Video Director, Simon Greaves; Assistant Choreographer, Bryan Anthony; Assistant to Eric Gardner, Lynn Robnett; Production Monitor Engineer, Joe Webster; Lighting Programmer, Joseph Eddy; Backline Technician, Michael "Micro" Shaw; Video Shader, Jesus "Chuy" Guerrero; Head Wardrobe, Maria Gomez; Dressers, Moira Conrad, Julien Havard, Daryl Stone; Prod. Audio Engineer, David Bullard; Prod. Carpenter, Joseph P. Valentino; Sound Engineer, Lucas "Rico" Corrubia Jr.; Prod. Props, Scott Mecionis; General Manager for On the Line, Terrie Lootens Hyde; For Magic Arts & Entertainment/NewSpace Entertainment: Lee D. Marshall & Joe Marsh (Co-CEOs), Steve Boulay (COO), John W. Ballard (President), Michael Braxton (Sales Director), Mary Ann Porcaro (Operations Manager), Patty Vartenuk (Controller), Dave Stinson (General Manager), Tracie Yagi (Ticketing), Cate Kizerian (Production Manager), Sandy Winchester (Accounting); Advertising, Serino Coyne; Press, The Hartman Group, Michael Hartman, Wayne Wolfe, Matt Ross

CAST **Donny Osmond** and **Marie Osmond**; Dancers **Matthew Fish**, **Karl Hendrickson**, **Jermaine Johnson**, **Kelene Johnson**, **Makinzee Love**, **Richard McAmish**, **Jessie Thacker**, **Jaymz Tuaileva**, **Ashley Williams**, **Ivy Michelle Williams**

MUSICIANS Jerry Williams (Musical Director), Joey Finger (Drums), Steven Lee (Guitar), Gabriel Falcon (Percussion), Rocco Barbato (Saxaphone), Robert Mader (Saxaphone), Mike Turnbull (Trombone), Gil Kaupp (Trumpet), Rochon Westmoreland (Bass)

Broadway premiere of a concert/variety show presented without intermission.

SYNOPSIS In the holiday tradition of the *Osmond Family Christmas* television specials, Donny & Marie celebrate the joy of the season in true Osmond fashion, in person, as the pair share a Broadway stage for the first time. With their trademark show-stopping Christmas production numbers, *Donny & Marie: A Broadway Christmas* features their favorite hits mixed with the irresistible chemistry that made them international stars.

Marie and Donny Osmond and the Company

Brian Bedford and Charlotte Parry

David Furr and Santino Fontana

Dana Ivey and Paxton Whitehead (photos by Joan Marcus)

The Importance of Being Earnest

American Airlines Theatre; First Preview: December 17, 2010; Opening Night: January 13, 2011; 30 previews, 158 performances as of May 31, 2011

Written by Oscar Wilde; Presented by the Roundabout Theatre Company (Todd Haimes, Artistic Director; Harold Wolpert, Managing Director; Julia C. Levy, Executive Director); Director, Brian Bedford; Set & Costumes, Desmond Heeley; Lighting, uane Schuler; Sound, Drew Levy; Original Music, Berthold Carrière; Hair & Wigs, Paul Huntley; Dialect Consultant, Elizabeth Smith; Production Stage Manager, Robyn Henry; Production Management, Aurora Productions; Casting, Jim Carnahan, Carrie Gardner, Kate Boka; General Manager, Rebecca Habel; Director of Development, Lynne Gugenheim Gregory; Founding Director, Gene Feist; Associate Artistic Director; Company Manager, Carly DiFulvio; Stage Manager, Bryce McDonald; Assistant Director, Robert Beard; Makeup, Angelina Avallone; Associate Design: Michael Carnahan (set), Devon Painter (costumes), Justin Partier (lighting), Will Pickens (sound); Assistant Set Design, Rachel Nemec, Shana Burns; Assistant Makeup Artist, Jorge Vargas; Assistant to Mr. Heeley, Ren LaDassor; Prod. Props Supervisor, Peter Sarafin; Prod. Consultant, Campbell Baird; Period Movement Consultant, Frank Ventura; Prod. Carpenter, Glenn Merwede; Prod. Electrician, Brian Maiuri; Running Properties, Robert W. Dowling II; Sound Operator, Dann Wojnar; Flyman, Mike Allen; Wardrobe Supervisor, Susan J. Fallon; Dressers, Lauren Gallitelli, Kat Martin; Wardrobe Dayworker, Dale Carman; Hair & Wig Supervisor, Manuela Laporte; Hair & Wig Assistant, Yolanda Ramsay; Prod. Assistant, Sara Cox Bradley; Roundabout Staff: Director of Artistic Development/Casting, Jim Carnahan; Director of Education, Greg McCaslin; Associate Managing Director, Greg Backstrom; General Manager, Sydney Beers; Director of Finance, Susan Neiman; IT Director, Antonio Palumbo; Director of Marketing and Sales Promotion, David B. Steffen; Director of Ticketing Sales, Charlie Garbowski Jr.; Press, Boneau/Bryan-Brown, Adrian Bryan-Brown, Matt Polk, Jessica Johnson, Amy Kass

CAST Lane **Paul O'Brien**; Algernon Moncreiff **Santino Fontana**; John Worthing **David Furr**; Lady Bracknell **Brain Bedford**; Gwendolen Fairfax **Sara Topham**[*1]; Cecily Cardew **Charlotte Parry**; Miss Prism **Dana Ivey**[*2]; Rev. Canon Chasuble **Paxton Whitehead**[*3]; Merriman **Tim MacDonald**; Servant **Amanda Lee Cobb**

UNDERSTUDIES Sean Arbuckle (John Worthing, Algernon Moncrief), Amanda Lee Cobb (Gwendolyn Fairfax, Cecily Cardew), Colin McPhillamy (Merriman, Lane, Servant), Paul O'Brien (Rev. Canon Chasuble), Sandra Shipley (Lady Bracknell, Miss Prism); Replacements during the run: Richard Gallagher (John Worthing, Algernon Moncrief, Servant), Jefrey Heyenga (Rev. Canon Chausuble, Merriman, Lane)

*Succeeded by: 1. Jessie Austrian (3/22/11) 2. Jayne Houdyshell (3/22/11) 3. Brian Murray (3/22/11)

2010-2011 AWARDS Tony Award: Best Costume Design of a Play (Desmond Heeley); Drama Desk Award and Outer Critics Circle Award: Outstanding Featured Actor in a Play (Brian Bedford); Clarence Derwent Award: Most promising male performer on the New York stage (Santino Fontana)

SETTING Algernon Moncrieff's rooms in Picadilly. The garden at the Manor House, Wooton. Morning room at the Manor House, Woolton. Late nineteenth century. Revival of a play presented in three acts with two intermissions. The Stratford Shakespeare Festival presented Mr. Bedford's acclaimed production May 9–October 30, 2009. This production marked the 8th major New York revival since the plays Broadway debut in 1895.

SYNOPSIS One of the funniest comedies in the English language–and a critique of the conventions and hypocrisies of so-called polite society that remains stingingly pertinent even today–*The Importance of Being Earnest* centers on dashing men-about-town John Worthing and Algernon Moncrieff, who pursue fair ladies Gwendolen Fairfax and Cecily Cardew. Matters are complicated by the imaginary characters invented by both men to cover their on-the-sly activities–not to mention the disapproval of Gwendolen's mother, the formidable Lady Bracknell.

Good People

Samuel J. Friedman Theatre; First Preview: February 8, 2011; Opening Night: March 3, 2011; Closed May 29, 2011; 27 previews, 101 performances

Written by David Linday-Abaire; Produced by Manhattan Theatre Club (Lynne Meadow, Artistic Director; Barry Grove, Executive Producer); Director, Daniel Sulivan; Sets, John Lee Beatty; Costumes, David Zinn; Lighting, Pat Collins; Sound, Jill BC DuBoff; Dialect Coach, Charlotte Fleck; Casting, David Caparelliotis; Production Stage Manager, Roy Harris; Associate Producer/ Associate Artistic Director, Mandy Greenfied; General Manager, Florie Seery; Director of Artistic Development, Jerry Patch; Marketing, Debra Waxman-Pilla; MTC Casting, Nancy Piccione; Development, Lynne Randall; Company Manager, Seth Shepsle; Stage Manager, Denise Yaney; Assistant Director, Rachel Slaven; Associate Design: Kacie Hultgren (set), Gordon Olson (lighting), David Sanderson (sound); Assistant Design, Nick Koster (set), Jacob A. Climer (costumes); Makeup, Angelina Avallone; Lightboard Programmer, Jae Day; Automation Operator, Vaughn Preston; Hair/Makeup Supervisor, Natasha Steinhagen; Dresser, Savan Leveille; Prod. Assistant, Alex Mark; Voice of Ali, Emma Lyle; For MTC: Production Manager, Kurt Gardner; Artistic Line Producer, Lisa McNulty; Development, Lynne Randall; Artistic Consultant, Daniel Sullivan; Artistic Operations, Amy Gilkes Loe; Finance, Jeffrey Bledsoe; Associate General Manager, Lindsey Brooks Sag; Subscriber Services, Robert Allenberg; Telesales, George Tetlow; Education, David Shookhoff; Associate Production Manager, Philip Naudé; Prop Supervisor, Scott Laule; Costume Supervisor, Erin Hennessy Dean; Press, Boncau/Bryan-Brown, Chris Boneau, Aaron Meier, Christine Olver, Emily Meagher

CAST Jean **Becky Ann Baker**; Stevie **Patrick Carroll**; Mike **Tate Donovan**; Kate **Renée Elise Goldsberry**; Margaret **Frances McDormand**; Dottie **Estelle Parsons**

UNDERSTUDIES Tony Carlin (Mike), Tasha Lawrence (Jean, Margaret, Dottie), Garrett Neergaard (Steve), Karen Pittman (Kate)

2010-2011 AWARDS Tony Award: Best Performance by an Actress in a Leading Role in a Play (Frances McDormand); Drama Desk Award: Outstanding Actress in a Play (Frances McDormand); New York Drama Critics' Circle Award: Best Play; Outer Critics Circle Award: Outstanding Actress in a Play (Frances McDormand)

SETTING Time: The present. Place: South Boston's Lower End and Chestnut Hill, Massachusetts. World premiere of a new play presented in two acts.

SYNOPSIS Welcome to Southie, a Boston neighborhood where a night on the town means a few rounds of bingo… where this month's paycheck covers last month's bills… and where Margie Walsh has just been let go from yet another job. Facing eviction and scrambling to catch a break, Margie thinks an old fling who has made it out of Southie might be her ticket to a fresh new start. But is this apparently self-made man secure enough to face his humble beginnings? Margie is about to risk what little she has left to find out.

Frances McDormand and Renée Elise Goldsberry

Patrick Carroll (photos by Joan Marcus)

Tate Donovan and Frances McDormand

Becky Ann Baker, Frances McDormand, and Estelle Parsons

That Championship Season

Bernard B. Jacobs Theatre; First Preview: February 9, 2011; Opening Night: March 6, 2011; Closed May 29, 2011; 28 previews, 97 performances

Written by Jason Miller; Presented by Robert Cole, Frederick Zollo, Shelter Island Enterprises, The Shubert Organization (Phillip J. Smith, Chairman; Robert E. Wankel, President), James MacGilvray, Orin Wolf, The Weinstein Company, Second Chance Productions, Brannon Wiles, Scott M. Delman/Lucky VIII; Director, Gregory Mosher; Set, Michael Yeargan; Costumes, Jane Greenwood; Lighting, Peter Kaczorowski; Sound, Scott Lehrer; Original Music, Michael Barrett; Casting, Cindy Tolan; Fight Director, Rick Sordelet; Production Stage Manager, Jane Grey; Production Management, Aurora Productions; Advertising, SpotCo; General Management, Robert Cole Productions, Lisa M. Poyer; Aurora Productions: Gene O'Donovan, Ben Heller, Stephanie Sherline, Jarid Sumner, Liza Luxenberg, Jason Margolis, Ryan Stanisz, Melissa Mazdra; Stage Manager, Cambra Overend; Associate Design: Wade Laboissonniere (costumes), Drew Levy (sound); Assistant Design: Mikiko Suzuki MacAdams, Wilson Chin (set), Keri L. Thibodeau (lighting), Will Pickens (sound); Assistant to the Director, Otoja Abit; Assistant to the Stage Managers, Bryn Magnus; Assistant to the General Manager, Lucius Robinson; Advance Carpenter, Brian Munroe; Prod. Electrician, Brian GF McGarity; Light Board Programmer, Jessica Morton; Sound Operator, Scott Sanders; Advance Props, Christopher Pantuso; Wardrobe Supervisor, Dave Olin Rogers; Dressers, Mickey Abbate, Jenn Maolloy; Assistants to the Producers, Michael Shapiro; Avertising Team, Drew Hodges, Jim Edwards, Tom Greenwald, Stephen Sosnowski, Meghan Ownbey; Inertactive Marketing, Situtation Interactive, Davian Bazadona, John Lanasa, Brian Hawe, Victoria Gettler; Press, Boneau/Bryan-Brow, Chris Boneau, Matt Polk, Amy Kass

CAST Tom Daley **Jason Patric**; George Silkowski **Jim Gaffigan**; James Daley **Kiefer Sutherland**; Phil Romano **Chris Noth**; Coach **Brian Cox**; Voice of Announcer **David Garrison**

UNDERSTUDIES Peter Bradbury (Tom Daley, James Daley), Don Harvey, (George Sikowski, Phil Romano), Stephen Rowe (Coach)

SETTING 1972. The Coach's house, somewhere in the Lackawana Valley. Revival of a play presented in two acts. Originally presented on Broadway at the Booth Theatre September 14, 1972–April 21, 1974 playing 700 performances (see *Theatre World* Vol. 29, page 10).

SYNOPSIS On the anniversary of their victory in the Pennsylvania state championship game, four members of the starting lineup of a small-town Catholic high school basketball team gather with their coach to re-live their youthful glory. As the night progresses, the long buried grudges and secrets of the once-confident players surface, threatening not just their solidarity, but the meaning of their victory. With savage humor, *That Championship Season* probes the darkest aspects of the American dream of success at all costs.

Kiefer Sutherland, Jim Gaffigan, Chris Noth, Jason Patric, Brian Cox

Brian Cox, Jason Patric, Jim Gaffigan, Chris Noth, Kiefer Sutherland

Jim Gaffigan, Brian Cox, Jason Patric, Kiefer Sutherland, Chris Noth (photos by Joan Marcus)

Jason Patric, Chris Noth, Kiefer Sutherland, Brian Cox, Jim Gaffigan

Kathy Griffin (photo by Mike Ruiz)

Kathy Griffin Wants a Tony

Belasco Theatre; Opening Night: March 11, 2011; Closed March 19, 2011; 10 performances

Written and directed by Kathy Griffin; Produced by Robert Ahrens, Eva Price, Manny Kladitis; Lighting, Matt Berman; Sound, Matt Kraus; General Manager, Niko Companies, Manny Kladitis, Jeffrey Chrzczon; Press, Sunshine Sachs & Associates, Whitney Tancred; Booking Agency, International Creative Management (ICM), Steve Levine, Katherine Gatenby; Production Manager, Jason T. Vanderwoude; Assitant to Mr. Ahrens, Diana Davidson; Assistant to Ms. Price, Taylor James; Associate General Manager, Holly Sutton; Advertising, Serino Coyne, Ryan Cunningham, Joaquin Esteva, Nehanda Loiseau; Digital Outreach, Art Meets Commerce/Jim Gluab, Chip Meyrelles, Laurie Connor, Ryan Greer, Crystal Chase; Ms. Griffin's Assistant, Tiffany Rinehart

CAST Kathy Griffin **Kathy Griffin**

UNDERSTUDIES Maggie Griffin (Kathy Griffin)

Broadway debut of a solo stand-up comedy show presented without intermission.

SYNOPSIS Double Emmy winner, Grammy nominee, and *New York Times* Best Selling author Kathy Griffin takes her new stand-up comedy show to the Great White Way for a limited engagement, delighting audiences with her outrageous candor and rapid-fire wit. Dishing on all pop culture and shinig a light on inappropriate water cooler talk, *Kathy Griffin Wants a Tony* features all new material about her hilarious observations and run-ins with celebrities. Let's just say Broadway will never be the same again!

Kathy Griffin (photo by Walter McBride)

Kathy Griffin (photo by Walter McBride)

Arcadia

Ethel Barrymore Theatre; First Preview: February 26, 2011; Opening Night: March 17, 2011; 20 previews, 85 performances as of May 31, 2011

Written by Tom Stoppard; Produced by Sonia Friedman Productions, Roger Berlind, Stephanie P. McClelland, Scott M. Delman, Nicholas Quinn Rosenkranz, Disney Theatrical Group, Robert G. Bartner, Olympus Theatricals, Douglas Smith, in association with Janine Safer Whitney; Director, David Levaux; Set, Hildegard Bechtler; Costumes, Gregory Gale; Lighting, Donald Holder; Sound, David Van Tieghem; Hair, David Bryan Brown; Music, Corin Buckeridge; Casting, Jim Carnahan; Advertising and Marketing, aka; U.S. General Management, 101 Productions Ltd.; U.K. General Management, Sonia Friedman Productions; Production Stage Manager, Ira Mont; Technical Supervisro, Peter Fulbright; Dialect Consultant, Elizabeth Smith; Choreographer, Jodi Moccia; Company Manager, David van Zyll de Jong; Makeup, Naomi Donne; Stage Manager, Matthew Lacey; Assistant Director, Jawson Lawson; Associate Design, Colleen Kesterson (costumes), John Viesta (lighting), David Sanderson (sound); Assistant Design: Luke Smith (U.K. set), Evan Adamson & Frank McCullough (U.S. set), Caroline Chao & Michael P. Jones (lighting); Assistants to Mr. Gale, Julia Broer, Jennifer A. Jacob; Assistant to Mr. Holder, Anna Cecilia Martin; Prod. Carpenter, Rich Cocchiara; Prod. Electrician, Michael LoBue; Prod. Sound, Darin Stillman; Advance Props, Dylan Foley, Robert Presley; Wardrobe Supervisor, Robert Guy; Dressers, Renee Borys, Kevin O'Brien; Wig and Hair Supervisor, Rick Caroto; Production Assistant, Jason Pelusio; Press, Boneau/Bryan-Brown, Adrian Bryan-Brown, Aaron Meier, Emily Meagher

CAST Thomasina Coverly **Bel Powley**; Septimus Hodge **Tom Riley**; Jellaby **Edward James Hyland**; Ezra Chater **David Turner**; Richard Noakes **Byron Jennings**; Lady Croom **Margaret Colin**; Captain Brice, RN **Glenn Fleshler**; Hannah Jarvis **Lia Williams**; Chloë Coverly **Grace Gummer**; Bernard Nightingale **Billy Crudup**; Valentine Coverly **Raúl Esparza**; Gus Coverly/ Augustus Coverly **Noah Robbins**

UNDERSTUDIES Bianca Amato (Hannah Jarvis, Lady Croom), Jack Cutmore-Scott (Augustus Coverly, Gus Coverly, Septimus Hodge), Alyssa May Gold (Chloë Coverly, Thomasina Coverly), Baylen Thomas (Bernard Nightingale, Valentine Coverly), Ray Virta (Captain Brice, RN, Ezra Chater, Jellaby, Richard Noakes)

2010-2011 AWARDS *Theatre World Award*: Grace Gummer

SETTING The room on the garden front of a very large country house in Derbyshire, England; 1809 and the present day. Revival of a play presented in two acts. Mr. Levaux's production previously played the West End prior to this Broadway engagement. World premiere produced at the Royal National Theatre in London April 13, 1993. Lincoln Center Theater produced the New York premiere at the Vivian Beaumont Theater March 31–August 27, 1995 playing 173 performances (see *Theatre World* Vol. 51, page 47). Mr. Crudup appeared as "Septimus" in that production, and won a 1995 Theatre World Award for his Broadway debut.

SYNOPSIS Thomasina, a gifted pupil, proposes a startling theory, beyond her comprehension. All around her, the adults, including her tutor Septimus, are preoccupied with secret desires, illicit passions, and professional rivalries. Two hundred years later, academic adversaries Hannah and Bernard are piecing together puzzling clues, curiously recalling those events of 1809, in their quest for an increasingly elusive truth.

Tom Riley and Bel Powley (photos by Carol Rosegg)

Billy Crudup, Lia Williams, and Raúl Esparza

Lia Williams and Billy Crudup

Priscilla Queen of the Desert

Palace Theatre; First Preview: February 28, 2011; Opening Night: March 20, 2011; 23 previews, 84 performances as of May 31, 2011

Book by Stephan Elliott and Alan Scott, based on the Latent Image/Specific Films motion picture distributed by Metro-Godwyn-Mayer Inc.; Produced by Bette Midler, James L. Nederlander, Garry McQuinn, Liz Koops, Michael Hamlyn, Allan Scott, Roy Furman/Richard Willis, Terry Allen Kramer, Terri and Timothy Childs, Ken Greiner, Ruth Hendel, Chugg Entertainment, Michael Buckley, Stewart F. Lane/Bonnie Comley, Bruce Davey, Thierry Suc/TS3, Bartner/Jenkins, Broadway Across America/Heni Koenigsberg, Myla Lerner/Debbie Bisno/Kit Seidel/Rebecca Gold, Paul Boskind and Martian Entertainment/Kevin Spirtas-Scott Mauro Productions/MAS Music Arts & Show, David Mirvish; Produced in association with MGM On Stage, Darcie Denkert and Dean Stolber; Associate Producer, Ken Sunshine; Executive Producer, Aleica Parker; Director/Development for the Stage, Simon Phillips; Choreography, Ross Coleman; Music Supervision & Arrangements, Stephen "Spud" Murphy; Production Supervision, Jerry Mitchell; Bus Concept & Production Design, Brian Thompson; Costumes, Tim Chappel & Lizzy Gardiner; Lighting, Nick Schlieper; Sound, Jonathan Deans & Peter Fitzgerald; Orchestratrions, Stephen "Spud" Murphy & Charlie Hull; Music Director, Jeffrey Klitz; Musical Coordinator, John Miller; Casting, Telsey + Company; Associate Director, Dean Bryant; Associate Choreographer, Andrew Hallsworth; Advertising, SpotCo; Marketing, Nick Pramik; Technical Supervisor, David Benken; Production Stage Manager, David Hyslop; Flying, Flying by Foy; Makeup, Cassie Hanlon; General Manager, B.J. Holt; Company Manager, Thom Clay; North America-International Associate Producer, Clare Rainbow; International Associate Producer, Kristen Hann; Associate Technical Supervisor, Rose Palombo; Stage Manager, Mahlon Kruse; Assistant Stage Manager, Megan Schneid; Associate General Manager, Hilary Hamilton; General Management Associate, Stephen Spadaro; Assistant Company Manager, Tammie Ward; Dance Captain, Eric Sciotto; Assistant Dance Captain, Joshua Buscher; Assistant to Ms. Parker, Marilyn Stout; Assistant to Mr. Holt, Katharine Hayes; Associate Design: Bryan Johnson (set), Brian J. Bustos (costumes), Michael P. Jones (lighting), Richard Mawbey (wigs); Assistant Design: Katie Irish, Mike Floyd (costumes), Carolyn Wong (lighting), Benjamin Moir (makeup); Bus Visual Animation Sequences Design, Brian Thomson; Animators, Jamie Clennett, Kenji Oates; Photoshoppers, Pip Runciman, Micka Agosta; LED Web Content, Chris Twyman; Head Carpenter, Patrick Eviston; Automation, Michael Shepp Jr.; Assistant Carpenter, Jeff Zink; Prod. Electrician, Jon Lawson; Head Electrician, Patrick Ainge; Assistant Electrician, Jesse Hancox; Moving Lights and Video Programmer, Chris Herman; Prod. Sound, Garth Helm; Head Sound, Steve Henshaw; Additional Synthesizer Programming, Jeff Marder; Prod. Props, Jerry Marshall; Assistant Props, James Cariot; Wardrobe Supervisor, Meghan Carsella; Assistant Wardrobe Supervisor, Meghan Bowers; Australian Sound Design, Michael Waters; Hair & Makeup Supervisor, Justen Brosnan; Prod. Assistants, Nathan K. Claus, Amanda Gwin, Kevin MacLeod, Carly J. Price, Willie Ruiz; Music Copying, Martine Monroe; Advertising/Website/Online Marketing, SpotCo; Dialect Coach, Gillian Lane-Plescia; Press, Boneau/Bryan-Brown, Adrian Bryan-Brown, Joe Perrotta, Michael Strassheim; Cast recording: Rhino Records 081227977733

CAST Divas **Jacqueline B. Arnold, Anastacia McCleskey, Ashley Spencer**; Tick (Mitzi) **Will Swenson**; Miss Understanding **Nathan Lee Graham**; Marion **Jessica Phillips**; Benji **Luke Mannikus** or **Ahston Woerz**; Farrah/Young Bernadette **Steve Schepis**; Bernadette **Tony Sheldon**; Adam (Felicia) **Nick Adams**; Shirley **Keala Settle**; Jimmy **James Brown III**; Bob **C. David Johnson**; Cynthia **J. Elaine Marcos**; Frank **Mike McGowan**; Ensemble **Thom Allison, Jacqueline B. Arnold, James Brown III, Kyle Brown, Nathan Lee Graham, Gavin Lodge, J. Elaine Marcos, Anastacia McCleskey, Mike McGowan, Jeff Metzler, Jessica Phillips, Steve Shepis, Keala Settle, Ashley Spencer, Bryan West, Tad Wilson**; Swings **Joshua Buscher, Ellyn Marie Marsh, Eric Sciotto, Amaker Smith, Esther Stillwell**

UNDERSTUDIES Thom Allison (Bernadette, Jimmy, Miss Understanding), James Brown III (Miss Understanding), Kyle Brown (Frank), Joshua Buscher (Farrah, Young Bernadette), Gavin Lodge (Bernadette, Frank, Tick [Mitzi]), Luke Mannikus (Benji), Ellyn Marie Marsh (Cynthia, Diva, Marion, Shirley), Mike McGowan (Bob), Jeff Metzler (Young Bernadette), Steve Schepis (Adam (Felicia)), Eric Sciotto (Tick [Mitzi]), Amaker Smith (Jimmy), Esther Stilwell (Cynthia, Diva, Marion, Shirley), Bryan West (Adam [Felicia]), Tad Wilson (Bob), Ashton Woerz (Benji)

ORCHESTRA Jeffrey Klitz (Conductor), Jeff Marder (Associate Conductor), David Mann (Woodwinds), Ed Hamilton (Guitar), Barry Danielian (Trumpet), Michael Davis (Trombone), Luico Hopper (Bass), Warren Odze (Drums), Roger Squitero (Percussion)

MUSICAL NUMBERS It's Raining Men, What's Love Got to Do With It?, I Say a Little Prayer, Don't Leave Me This Way, Material Girl, Go West, Holiday, Like a Virgin, I Say a Little Prayer (reprise), I Love the Nightlife, True Colors, Sempre Libre, Color My World, I Will Survive, Thank God I'm a Country Boy, A Fine Romance, Thank God I'm a Country Boy (reprise), Shake Your Groove Thing, Pop Muzik, A Fine Romance (reprise), Girls Just Wanna Have Fun, Hot Stuff, MacArthur Park, Boogie Wonderland, The Floor Show, Always on My Mind, Like a Prayer, We Belong, Finally Medley

2010-2011 AWARDS Tony Award: Best Costume Design of a Musical (Tim Chappel and Lizzie Gardiner); Drama Desk Award: Outstanding Costume Design (Tim Chappel and Lizzie Gardiner); *Theatre World Award*: Tony Sheldon

SETTING Sydney and Alice Springs, Australia, and the roads between. U.S. premiere of a new musical presented in two acts. World premiere in Sydney in 2006, and subsequently in Melbourne, New Zealand, and London (where it continues to play at the Palace Theatre in the West End. Mr. Sheldon starred in the production in Sydney, Melbourne, and London. Most of this cast performed the show in Toronto at the Princess of Wales Theatre October 12, 2010–January 2, 2011 as a pre-Broadway tryout.

SYNOPSIS Based on the Academy Award-winning film, *Priscilla Queen of the Desert* follows a trio of friends (who happen to be drag queens) as they hop aboard a battered old bus searching for love and friendship in the middle of the Austrailian outback and end up finding more than they could ever have dreamed. The musical features a score of pop and dance music favorites.

Will Swenson, Tony Sheldon, and Nick Adams

Tad Wilson, Will Swenson, Tony Sheldon, Keala Settle, Nick Adams, Mike McGowan, and the Company

Jacqueline B. Arnold, Ashley Spencer, and Anastacia Mcleskey (top); Tony Sheldon, Nick Adams, C. David Johnson, and Will Swenson (in bus)

Will Swenson and the Company (photos by Joan Marcus)

J. Elaine Marcos, Will Swenson, C. David Johnson, and Tony Sheldon

Tony Sheldon

Luke Mannikus and Jessica Phillips

Ghetto Klown

Lyceum Theatre; First Preview: February 21, 2011; Opening Night: March 22, 2011; 25 previews, 61 performances as of May 31, 2011

Written by John Leguizamo; Produced by WestBeth Entertainment (Arnold Engelman, Camron Cooke, Juliana Slaton, Jenni Muller), Daveed D. Frazier, and Nelle Nugent; Executive Producer, Arnold Engleman; Associate Producers, Insurgent Media, Camron Cooke, Kenneth Treaton; Director, Fisher Stevens; Set, Happy Massee; Lighting, Jen Schriever; Sound, Peter Fitzgerald; Projecctions, Aaron Gonzalez; Technical Supervision, Hudson Theatrical Associates; Production Consultant, Christopher Cronin; Movement Consultant, Marlyn Ortiz; Publicity, Blanca Lasalle, Creative Link; Online Marketing, Bay Bridge Productions; Advertising, Neil Turton; Production Stage Manager, Arabella Powell; Company Manager, John E. Gendron; Stage Manager, Chelsea Antrim; Associate Lighting, Peter Hoerburger; Assistant to Ms. Schriever, John Wilder; Moving Light Programmer, Sean Beach; Assistant Sound, Megan Henninger; Assistant Projections, Eric T. Sutton; Wardrobe Stylist, Young-Ah Kim; Prod. Carpenter, Adam Braunstein; Prod. Electrician, Jonathan Cohen; Advance Electrician, James Maloney; Prod. Sound, Wallace Flores; Props Coordinator, Kathy Fabian/Propstar; Associate Props Coordinator, Tim Ferro/Propstar; Prod. Properties, Leah Nelson; Wardrobe Supervisor, Danny Paul; Assistant Director, Micha Frank; Assistant to Mr. Stevens, Zara Duffy; Graphic Design, KRL Creative/Kim Lyle; Key Art, Billi Kid; Press, Boneau/Bryan-Brown, Jackie Green, Kelly Guiod

Performed by **John Leguizamo**

2010-2011 AWARDS Drama Desk Award: Outstanding Solo Performance; Outer Critics Circle: Outstanding Solo Performance

New York premiere of a solo performance play presented in two acts. *Ghetto Klown* was showcased in earlier incarnations in Philadelphia, New Haven, Santa Fe, Louisville, La Jolla, Toronto, and Montreal; an "unplugged" version of the show played at the Royal George Theatre in Chicago under the title *John Leguizmo Warms Up* prior to his Broadway engagement.

SYNOPSIS *Ghetto Klown* is the next chapter in John Leguizamo's popular personal and professional story. It is his fifth one man play, his third on Broadway, and follows in the uninhibited tradition of his *Mambo Mouth, Spic-O-Rama, Freak,* and *Sexaholix…a Love Story*. In Leguizamo's trademark style, the piece explodes with energy, heating up the stage with vivid accounts of the colorful characters who have populated his life. He takes audiences from his adolescent memories in Queens to the early days of his acting career and on to the sets of major motion pictures and his roles opposite some of Hollywood's biggest stars.

John Leguizamo

John Leguizamo

John Leguizamo

John Leguizamo (photos by Carol Rosegg)

The Book of Mormon

Eugene O'Neill Theatre; First Preview: February 24, 2011; Opening Night: March 24, 2011; 28 previews, 78 performances as of May 31, 2011

Book, music, and lyrics by Trey Parker, Robert Lopez, and Matt Stone; Produced by Anne Garefino, Scott Rudin, Roger Berlind, Scott M. Delman, Jean Doumanian, Roy Furman, Important Musicals LLC, Stephanie P. McClelland, Kevin Morris, Jon B. Platt, Sonia Friedman Productions; Executive Producer, Stuart Thompson; Directors, Casey Nicholaw and Trey Parker; Choreography, Casey Nicholaw; Music Direction/Vocal Arrangements, Stephen Oremus; Sets, Scott Pask; Costumes, Ann Roth; Lighting, Brian MacDevitt; Sound, Brian Ronin; Hair, Josh Marquette, Casting, Carrie Gardner; Production Stage Manager, Karen Moore; Orchestrations, Larry Hochman & Stephen Oremus; Dance Music Arrangements, Glen Kelly; Music Coordinator, Michael Keller; Production Management, Aurora Productions; General Mangement, Stuart Thompson Productions/David Turner; Company Manager, Adam J. Miller; Makeup, Randy Houston Mercer; Associate Director, Jennifer Werner; Associate Choreographer, John MacInnis; For Scott Rudin Productions: Eli Bush, Steven Cardwell, Max Grossman, Adam Klaff, Joshua Mehr, Allie Moore, Matt Nemeth, Jill Simon, Nora Skinner; Stage Manager, Rachel S. McCutchen; Assistant Stage Manager, Michael P. Zaleski; Assistant Company Manager, Megan Curren; Dance Captain, Graham Bowen; Assistant Dance Captain, Asmeret Ghebremichael; Associate Design: Frank McCullough (set), Matthew Pachtman, Michelle Matland (costumes), Benjamin C. Travis (lighting), Asley Hanson (sound); Assistant Design: Lauren Alvarez, Christine Peters (set), Carl Faber (lighting); Costume Design Assistant, Irma Escobar; Associate Music Director, Adam Ben-David; Keyboard Programmer, Randy Cohen; Drum Programmer, Sean McDaniel; Rehearsal Pianist, Brian Usifer; Music Copying, Emily Grishman Music Preparation, Katharine Edmonds; Prod. Carpenter, Mike Martinez; Prod. Electrician, Dan Coey; Head Electrician, Drayton Allison; Prod. Sound Engineer, Chris Sloan; Moving Light Programmer, David John Arch; Lead Front Electrics, Damian Caza-Cleypool; Sound Engineer, Jason McKenna; Deck Automation, Andrew Lanzarotta; Fly Automation, Scott Dixon; Prod. Props, Ken Keneally; Props Coordinator, Pete Sarafin; Wardrobe Supervisor, Dolly Williams; Assistant Wardrobe Supervisor, Fred Castner; Hair Supervisor, Tod L. McKim; Dressers, D'Ambrose Boyd, Micheal Harrell, Eugene Nicks, Melanie McClintock, Jeff McGovney, Virginia Neinenger, Veneda Treusdale; Hair Dressers, Joel Hawkins, Mathew Wilson; Prod Assistants, Sara Cox Bradley, Derek DiGregorio; Music Department Assistant, Matthew Aument; Costume Shoppers, Brenda Abbandandolo, Kate Friedberg; Assistant to Ms. Roth, Jonathan Schwartz; Research Assistant to Ms. Roth, Debbe DuPerrieu; Assistants to Mr. MacDevitt, Ariel Benjamin, Jonathan Dillard; Prop Shopper, Buist Bickley; Casting Associate, Jillian Cimini; For Stuart Thompson: Stuart Thompson, David Turner, Marshall B. Purdy, Cassidy Briggs, Kevin Emrick, Geo Karapetyan, Brittany Levasseur, Andrew Lowy, Christpher Taggart; For Aurora Productions: Gene O'Donovan, W. Benjamin Heller II, Stephanie Sherline, Jarid Sumner, Liza Luxenberg, Jason Margolis, Ryan Stanisz, Melissa Mazdra; Advertising, Serino Coyne/Greg Coradetti, Sandy Block, Scott Johnson, Lauren Pressman, Sarah Miller; Marketing/Web Interactive, aka/Elizabeth Furze, Scott A. Moore, Andrew Damer, Terry Goldman, Adam Jay, Janette Roush, Meghan Bartley; Website, South Park Digital Studios/aka; General Management Interns, Rikki Bahar, Liz Shumate; Press, Boneau/Bryan-Brown, Chris Boneau, Jim Byk, Christine Olver; Cast recording: Sh-K-Boom/Ghostlight Records 84446

CAST Mormon **Jason Michael Snow**; Moroni **Rory O'Malley**; Elder Price **Andrew Rannells**; Elder Cunningham **Josh Gad**; Price's Dad **Lewis Cleale**; Cunningham's Dad **Kevin Duda**; Mrs. Brown **Rema Webb**; Guards **John Eric Parker, Tommar Wilson**; Mafala Hatimbi **Michael Potts**; Nabulungi **Nikki M. James**; Elder McKinley **Rory O'Malley**; General **Brian Tyree Henry**; Doctor **Michael James Scott**; Mission President **Lewis Cleale**; Ensemble **Scott Barnhardt, Justin Bohon, Darlesia Cearcy, Kevin Duda, Asmeret Ghebremichael, Brian Tyree Henry, Clark Johnson, John Eric Parker, Benjamin Schrader, Michael James Scott, Brian Sears, Jason Michael Snow, Lawrence Stallings, Rema Webb, Maia Nkenge**

Wilson, Tommar Wilson; Swings **Graham Bowen, Ta'rae Campbell, Tyson Jennette, Nick Spangler**

UNDERSTUDIES Scott Barnhardt (Elder McKinley), Ta'Rea Campbell (Nabulungi), Kevin Duda (Elder Price, Mission President, Price's Dad), Asmeret Ghebremichael (Nabulungi), Tyson Jennette (Mafala Hatimbi), John Eric Parker (Mafala Hatimbi), Benjamin Schrader (Elder Cunningham, Mission President, Price's Dad), Brian Sears (Elder McKinley), Nick Spangler (Elder Price); Standby for Elder Cunningham: Jared Gertner

ORCHESTRA Stephen Oremus (Conductor/Keyboard), Adam Ben-David (Associate Conductor/Keyboard), Jake Schwartz (Guitars), Dave Phillips (Bass), Sean McDaniel (Drums/Percussion), Bryan Cook (Reeds), Raul Agraz (Trumpet), Randy Andos (Trombone), Entcho Todorov (Violin/Viola)

MUSICAL NUMBERS Hello!, Two By Two, You And Me (But Mostly Me), Hasa Diga Eebowai, Turn It Off, I Am Here For You, All American Prophet, Sal Tlay Ka Siti, Man Up, Song List, Making Things Up Again, Spooky Mormon Hell Dream, I Believe, Baptize Me, I Am Africa, Joseph Smith American Moses, Tomorrow Is a Latter Day

2010-2011 AWARDS Tony Awards: Best Musical, Best Book of a Musical (Robert Lopez, Trey Parker, Matt Stone), Best Original Score Written for the Theatre (Robert Lopez, Trey Parker, Matt Stone), Best Performance by an Actress in a Featured Role in a Musical (Nikki M. James), Best Direction of a Musical (Casey Nicholaw, Trey Parker), Best Orchestrations (Stephen Oremus, Larry Hochman), Best Scenic Design of a Musical (Scott Pask), Best Lighting Design of a Musical (Brian MacDevitt), Best Sound Design of a Musical (Brian Ronan); Drama Desk Awards: Outstanding Orchestrations (Stephen Oremus, Larry Hochman), Outstanding Lyrics (Robert Lopez, Trey Parker, Matt Stone), Outstanding Music (Robert Lopez, Trey Parker, Matt Stone), Outstanding Director of a Musical (Casey Nicholaw, Trey Parker); Outer Critics Circle Award: Outstanding New Broadway Musical, Outstanding Director of a Musical (Casey Nicholaw, Trey Parker), Outstanding Actor in a Musical (Josh Gad); New York Drama Critics' Circle Award: Best Musical; Drama League Award: Best Musical

World premiere of a new musical presented in two acts.

SYNOPSIS Created by the writers of *South Park* and the composer of *Avenue Q, The Book of Morman* tells the tale of an unlikely pair of Mormon missionaries who have their faith and their sanity tested when they venture from Salt Lake City to AIDS-ravaged Uganda in the hopes of converting villagers with the story of Joseph Smith and the founding of the Mormon Church. The problem is, only one of them has actually read the book.

Michael James Scott, Asmeret Ghebremichael, Rema Webb, Lawrence Stallings, Maia Nkenge Wilson (sitting), Darlesia Cearcy, and Josh Gad

Nikki M. James, Andrew Rannells, Josh Gad, and the Company

Rema Webb, Andrew Rannells, and Josh Gad

Andrew Rannells (photos by Joan Marcus)

How to Succeed in Business Without Really Trying

Al Hirschfeld Theatre; First Preview: February 26, 2011; Opening Night: March 27, 2011; 30 previews, 74 performances as of May 31, 2011

Music & lyrics by Frank Loesser, book by Abe Burrows, Jack Weinstock, & Willie Gilbert; Based on the book by Shepherd Mead; Produced by Broadway Across America, Craig Zadan, Neil Meron, Joseph Smith, Michael McCabe, Candy Spelling, Takonkiet Viravan/Scenario Thailand, Hilary A. Williams, Jen Namoff/Fakston Productions, Two Left Feet Productions/Power Arts, Hop Theatricals, LLC/PaulChau/Daniel Frishwasser/Michael Jackowitz and Michael Speyer-Bernie Abrams/Jacki Barlia Florin-Adam Blanshay/Arlene Scanlan/TBS Service; Director & Choreographer, Rob Ashford; Music Director/Arrangements, David Chase; Set, Derek McLane; Costumes, Catherine Zuber; Lighting, Howell Binkley; Sound, Jon Weston; Hair & Wigs, Tom Watson; Orchestrations, Doug Besterman; Music Coordinator, Howard Joines; Production Stage Manager, Michael J. Passaro; Associate Director, Stephen Sposito; Associate Choreographer, Christopher Bailey; Assistant Choreographers, Sarah O'Gleby, Charlie Williams; Casting, Tara Rubin; Production Manager, Juniper Street Productions; Marketing, Type A Marketing, Anne Rippey; General Management, Alan Wasser, Allan Williams, Mark Shacket; Associate Producers, Stage Ventures, 2010 Limited Partnership; Executive Producer, Beth Williams; Company Manager, Penelope Dalton; Stage Manager, Pat Sosnow; Assistant Stage Manager, Jim Athens; Assistant Company Manager, Cathy Kwon; Dance Captain, Sarah O'Bleby; Assistant Dance Captain, Matt Wall; SDC Traube Fellow, Sara-Ahsley Bischoff; Associate Design: Shoko Kambara (set), Ryan O'Gara (lighting), Jason Strangfeld (sound); Assistant Design: Brett Banakis (set), Sean Beach, Amanda Zieve (lighting), Michael Eisenberg (sound); Scenic Design Assistant, Paul Depoo; Costume Design Intern, Peter Dolhas; Moving Lights Programmer, Eric Norris; Makeup Design, Ahsley Ryan; Aerial Design, Sonja Rzepski; Stunt Coordinator, Mike Russo; Prod. Carpenter, Erik Hansen; Automation Carpenter, Scott "Gus" Poitras; Prod. Electricians, James J. Fedigan, Randall Zaibek; Head Electrician, Brian Dawson; Prod. Props Supervisor, Christopher Pantuso; Assistant Props Supervisor, Jim Cane; Prod. Sound Engineers, Paul Delcioppo, Phil Lojo; Deck Audio,. Charles Grieco; Wardrobe Supervisor, Debbie Cheretun; Assistant Wardrobe Supervisor, Brendan Cooper; Mr. Radcliffe's Dresser, Sandy Binion; Mr. Larroquette's Dresser, Barry Hoff; Dressers, Shana Albery, Joshua Burns, Kristin Farley, Anthony Hoffman, Jeffrey Johnson, Nesreen Mahmoud, Icey Parks; Hair Supervisor, Katie Beatty; Hair Dressers, Carla Muniz, Brendan O'Neal; Keyboard Programmer, Randy Cohen; Music Preparation, Anixter Rice Music Service; Advertising, Serino Coyne/Nancy Coyne, Sandy Block, Greg Corradetti, Robert Jones, Danielle Boyle; For Alan Wasser: Mark Shacket, Aaron Lustbader; For Type A: Michael Porto, Elyce Henkin, Sarah Ziering; For Juniper Street: Hilary Blanken, Guy Kwan, Joseph DeLuise, Kevin Broomell, Ana Rose Grene; For Mr. Radcliffe: Mark Meylan (Vocal Coach), Spencer Soloman (Dance Tutor), Barbara Houseman (Voice Work), Penny Dyer (Dialect Coach); General Management Associates, Lane Marsh, Steve Greer; Prod. Assistants, Shannon Bonds, Steve Chazaro, Melissa Hansen, Morgan Holbrook, Jeff Siebert; Press, The Hartman Group, Michael Hartman, Wayne Wolfe, Matt Ross, Nicole Capataso; Cast recording: Decca Broadway DCAUB001564502

CAST The Voice of the Narrator **Anderson Cooper**; J. Pierpont Finch **Daniel Radcliffe**; Mr. Gatch **Nick Mayo**; Mr. Jenkins **Charlie Williams**; Mr. Johnson/TV Announcer **Kevin Covert**; Mr. Matthews **Ryan Watkinson**; Mr. Peterson **Marty Lawson**; Mr. Tackaberry **Joey Sorge**; Mr. Toynbee **David Hull**; Mr. Andrews **Barrett Martin**; J.B. Biggley **John Larroquette**; Rosemary Pilkington **Rose Hemingway**; Mr. Bratt **Michael Park**; Smitty **Mary Faber**; Miss Jones **Ellen Harvey**; Miss Krumholtz **Megan Sikora**; Bud Frump **Christopher J. Hanke**; Mr. Twimble/Wally Womper **Rob Bartlett**; Hedy LaRue **Tammy Blanchard**; Mr. Davis **Justin Keyes**; Meredith **Stephanie Rothenberg**; Kathy/Scrub Woman **Cameron Adams**; Miss Grabowski/Scrub Woman **Paige Faure**; Nancy **Tanya Birl**; Lily **Samantha Zack**; Mr. Ovington **Cleve Asbury**; Swings **Erica Mansfield, Sarah O'Gleby, Michaeljon Slinger, Matt Wall**

UNDERSTUDIES Cameron Adams (Rosemary Pillkington), Cleve Asbury (Mr. Twimble, Wally Womper), Rob Bartlett (J.B. Biggley), Kevin Covert (Mr. Twimble, Wally Womper), Paige Faure (Hedy La Rue, Smitty), Dave Hull (J. Pierrepont Finch), Justin Keyes (Bud Frump, J. Pierrepont Finch), Erica Mansfield (Miss Jones), Nick Mayo (Bert Bratt), Michael Park (J.B. Biggley), Stephanie Rothenberg (Rosemary Pillkington), Megan Sikora (Hedy La Rue, Miss Jones, Smitty), Joey Sorge (Bert Bratt), Charlie Williams (Bud Frump)

ORCHESTRA David Chase (Conductor), Matt Perri (Associate Conductor/Keyboard/Piano), Steve Kenyon, Lawrence Feldman, Mark Thrasher (Reeds), Nicholas Marchione, Scott Wendholt (Trumpets), John Allred, George Flynn (Trombones), David Peel (Horn), Paul Pizzuti (Drums), Neal Caine (Bass), Scott Kuney (Guitars), Erik Charlston (Percussion), Grace Paradise (Harp)

MUSICAL NUMBERS Overture, How to Succeed, Happy To Keep His Dinner Warm, Coffee Break, Company Way, Company Way (reprise), Rosemary's Philosophy, A Secretary Is Not a Toy, Been a Long Day, Been a Long Day (reprise), Grand Old Ivy, Paris Original, Rosemary, Act I Finale, Cinderella Darling, Happy To Keep His Dinner Warm (reprise), Love From a Heart of Gold, I Believe in You, Pirate Dance, I Believe in You (reprise), Brotherhood of Man, Finale

2010-2011 AWARDS Tony Award: Best Performance by an Actor in a Featured Role in a Musical (John Larroquette); Drama Desk Award: Outstanding Featured Actor in a Musical (John Larroquette); *Theatre World Awards*: Rose Hemingway, John Larroquette

SETTING The new Park Avenue office building of The World Wide Wicket Company in New York City; 1961. Revival of a musical presented in two acts. Originally produced on Broadway at the 46th Street (Richard Rodgers) Theatre starring Robert Morse October 14, 1961–March 6, 1965 playing 1,417 performances (see *Theatre World* Vol. 18, page 26). The musical was revived at the Richard Rodgers Theatre starring Matthew Broderick March 23, 1996–July 14, 1996 playing 548 performances (see *Theatre World* Vol. 54, page 42).

SYNOPSIS The 1961 Tony and Pulitzer Prize-winning musical comedy satire about the world of big business returns to Broadway in this 50th Anniversary revival. Daniel Radcliffe stars as J. Pierpont Finch, a young window washer, who with the help of the titular book, rises to the top of the World Wide Wicket Company in New York City.

Rose Hemingway (photos by Ari Mintz)

Daniel Radcliffe and John Larroquette

Christopher J. Hanke, Mary Faber, and the Company

The Company

Daniel Radcliffe and the Company

Daniel Radcliffe and Tammy Blanchard

The Company

Bengal Tiger at the Baghdad Zoo

Richard Rodgers Theatre; First Preview: March 11, 2011; Opening Night: March 31, 2011; 23 previews, 70 performances as of May 31, 2011

Written by Rajiv Joseph; Produced by Robyn Goodman, Kevin McCollum, Jeffrey Seller, Sander Jacobs, Ruth Hendel/Burnt Umber, Scott Zeilinger, Brian Zeilinger, Center Theatre Group, Stephen Kocis/Walt Grossman; Director, Moisés Kaufman; Sets, Derek McLane; Costumes, David Zinn; Lighting, David Lander; Sound, Acme Sound Partners and Cricket S. Myers; Music, Kathryn Bostic; Casting Bonnie Grisan & MelCap Casting; Production Stage Manager, Beverly Jenkins; Original Fight Director, Bobby C. King; Technical Supervisor, Brian Lynch; General Management, Richards/Climan Inc.; Company Manager, Lizbeth Cone; Stage Manager, Alex Lyu Volckhausen; Production Assistants, Erica Christensen, Dwayne K. Mann, Johnny A. Milani; Assistant Director, Timothy Koch; Arabic Coach, Fajer Al-Kaisi; Translations/Cultural Consultants, Raida Fahmi, Ammar Ramzi; Associate Design: Brett Banakis (set) Jacob Climer (costumes), Heather Graf (lighting), Jason Crystal (sound); Assistant Lighting, Ben Pilat; Head Carpenter/Automation, McBrien Dunbar; Head Electrician, Cletus Karamon; Head Sound Operator, Justin Rathbun; Moving Light Programmer, Jay Pennfield; Properties Supervisor, George Wagner; Head Properties, Ron Groomes; Wardrobe Supervisor, Moira MacGregor-Conrad; Dresser, Tree Sarvay; Additional Fight Director, Ron Piretti; Fight Captain, Brad Fleischer; Gunshot Blood Effects, Hero Props/Seán McArdle; Hair & Makeup Supervisor-Special Effects, Adam Bailey; Assistant to Mr Williams, Rebecca Erwin Spencer; Advertising, SpotCo; Press, Sam Rudy Media Relations, Sam Rudy, Dale Heller

CAST Tiger **Robin Williams**; Tom **Glenn Davis**; Kev **Brad Fleischer**; Musa **Arian Moayed**; Iraqi Teenager, Hadia **Sheila Vand**; Iraqi Man, Uday **Hrach Titizian**; Iraqi Woman, Leper, Arabic Vocals **Necar Zadegan**

UNDERSTUDIES Understudies: Hend Ayoub (Hadia, Iraqi Teenager, Iraqi Woman, Leper), Corey Brill (Kev, Tom), Daoud Heidami (Iraqi Man, Musa, Uday), Sherman Howard (Tiger)

2010-2011 AWARDS Drama Desk Awards: Outstanding Sound Design in a Play (Acme Sound Partners and Cricket S. Myers), Outstanding Lighting Design (David Lander); *Theatre World Award*: Arian Moayed

SETTING Baghdad; 2003. New York premiere of a new play presented in two acts. World Premiere produced by Center Theatre Group Mark Taper Forum in Los Angeles (Michael Ritchie, Artistic Director; Charles Dillingham, Managing Director) April 14–May 30, 2010 (see *Theatre World* Vol. 66, page 356). Developed at the Lark Play Development Center in New York City.

SYNOPSIS In *Bengal Tiger At The Baghdad Zoo*, a tiger haunts the streets of present day Baghdad seeking the meaning of life. As he witnesses the puzzling absurdities of war, the tiger encounters Americans and Iraqis who are searching for friendship, redemption, and a toilet seat made of gold.

Arian Moayed and Robin Williams

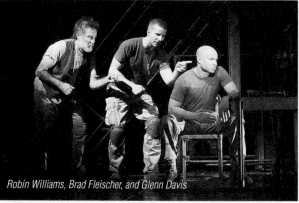
Robin Williams, Brad Fleischer, and Glenn Davis

Arian Moayed and Sheila Vand
(photos by Carol Rosegg)

Brad Fleischer and Arian Moayed

Anything Goes

Stephen Sondheim Theatre; First Preview: March 10, 2011; Opening Night: April 7, 2011; 32 previews, 62 performances as of May 31, 2011

Music and lyrics by Cole Porter, original book by P.G. Wodehouse, Guy Bolton, Howard Lindsay and Russell Crouse; Revised book by Timothy Crouse and John Weidman; Produced by the Roundabout Theatre Company (Todd Haimes, Artistic Director; Harold Wolpert, Managing Director; Julia C. Levy, Executive Director) Director and Choreographer, Kathleen Marshall; Musical Supervisor/Vocal Arrangements, Rob Fisher; Sets, Derek McLane; Costumes, Martin Pakledinaz; Lighting, Peter Kaczorowski; Sound, Brian Ronan; Additional Orchestrations, Bill Elliott; Original Orchestrations, Michael Gibson; Dance Arrangements, David Chase; Music Director, James Lowe; Music Coordinator, Seymour Red Press; Hair & Wigs, Paul Huntley; Makeup, Angelina Avallone; Production Stage Manager, Peter Hanson; Casting, Jim Carnahan & Stephen Kopel; Associate Director, Marc Bruni; Associate Choreographer, Vince Pesce; Technical Supervisor, Steve Beers; Executive Producer, Sydney Beers; Director of Marketing & Sales Promotion, David B. Steffen; Director of Development, Lynne Gugenheim Gregory; Founding Director, Gene Feist; Associate Artistic Director, Scott Ellis; Company Manager, Doug Gaeta; Assistant Company Manager, David Solomon; Stage Manager, Jon Krause; Dance Captain, Jennifer Savelli; Assistant Dance Captain, Justin Greer; Assistant Choreographer, David Eggers; Music Preparation, Emily Grishman, Katharine Edmonds; Synthesizer Programer, Bruce Samuels; Associate Design: Sara Jean Tosetti (costumes), Paul Toben (lighting), Giovanna Calabretta (hair & wigs); Assistant Design, Erica Hemminger (set), John Emmett O'Brien (sound); Costume Design Assistant, Carisa Kelly; Assistant to the Costume Designer, Justin Hall; Costume Interns, Hannah Kittel, Shannon Smith, Heather Mathiesen; Prod. Sound Engineer/Mixer, Shannon Slaton; Music Department Interns, Molly Gachignard, Ian Weinberger; Automation Operator, Paul Ashton; Flyman, William Craven; Prod. Electrician/Moving Light Programmer, Josh Weitzman; Assistant Production Electricians, John Wooding, Jocelyn Smith; Followspots, Dorian Fuchs, Erika Warmbrunn, Jessica Morton; Deck Electricians, Jocelyn Smith, Francis Elers; House Props, Andrew Forste; Props Running Crew, Dan Mendeloff, Nelson Vaughn; Associate Prod. Props, Carrie Mossman, Prop Artisans, Mike Billings, Tim Ferro, Cathy Small, Mary Wilson; Wardrobe Supervisor, Nadine Hettel; Dressers, Suzanne Delahunt, Tara Delahunt, Kevin Mark Harris, Julien Havard, Emily Meriweather, Pamela Pierzina, Stacy Sarmiento; Hair & Wig Supervisor, Nathaniel Hathaway; Hair Assistants, Monica Costea, Heather Wright; SDC Oberver, Adam Cates; Prod. Assistants, Rachel Baudner, Hannah Dorfman; Advertising, SpotCo; Interactive Marketing, Situation Interactive; Roundabout Staff: Director of Artistic Development/Casting, Jim Carnahan; Director of Education, Greg McCaslin; Director of Finance, Susan Neiman; IT Director, Antonio Palumbo; Director of Ticketing Sales, Charlie Garbowski Jr.; Press, Boneau/Bryan-Brown, Adrian Bryan-Brown, Matt Polk, Jessica Johnson, Amy Kass; Cast recording: Sh-K-Boom/Ghostlight Records 84452

CAST Elisha J. Whitney **John McMartin**; Fred, *a bartender* **Josh Franklin**; Billy Crocker **Colin Donnell**; Reno Sweeney **Sutton Foster**; Captain **Walter Charles**; Ship's Purser **Robert Creighton**; Crew **Clyde Alves, Ward Billeisen, Daniel J. Edwards, Josh Franklin, Kevin Munhall, Adam Perry, William Ryall, Anthony Wayne**; A Reporter **Anthony Wayne**; A Photographer **Clyde Alves**; Henry T. Dobson, *a minister* **William Ryall**; Luke **Andrew** Cao; John **Raymond J. Lee**; *Angels*: Purity **Shina Ann Morris**; Chastity **Kimberly Fauré**; Charity **Jennifer Savelli**; Virtue **Joyce Chittick**; Hope Harcourt **Laura Osnes**; Mrs. Evangeline Harcourt **Jessica Walter**; Lord Evelyn Oakleigh **Adam Godley**; Erma **Jessica Stone**; Moonface Martin **Joel Grey**; Old Lady in Wheelchair **Linda Muggleston**; Quartet **Ward Billeisen, Josh Franklin, Daniel J. Edwards, William Ryall**; Ship's Passengers **Clyde Alves, Ward Billeisen, Nikki Renée Daniels, Daniel J. Edwards, Josh Franklin, Tari Kelly, Linda Mugleston, Kevin Munhall, Adam Perry, William Ryall, Anthony Wayne, Kristen Beth Williams**; Swings **Margot de la Barre, Justin Greer**

UNDERSTUDIES Clyde Alves (Purser), Joyce Chittick (Erma), Robert Creighton (Moonface Martin), Nikki Renée Daniels (Hope Harcourt), Daniel J. Edwards (John, Luke), Josh Franklin (Billy Crocker, Lord Evelyn Oakleigh), Tari Kelly (Reno Sweeney), Linda Mugleston (Mrs. Evangeline Harcourt), William Ryall (Captain, Elisha J. Whitney)

ORCHESTRA James Lowe (Conductor), David Gursky (Associate Conductor/ Piano), James Ercole, Ronald Jannelli, Ralph Olsen, David Young (Reeds), Earl Gardner, Ken Rampton, Stu Satalof (Trumpets), Larry Ferrell, Robert Fornier, Wayne Goodman (Trombones), Jeffrey Carney (Bass), John Redsecker (Drums), Bill Hayes (Percussion), Eric Davis (Guitar)

MUSICAL NUMBERS I Get a Kick Out of You; There's No Cure Like Travel; Bon Voyage; You're the Top; Easy to Love; Easy to Love (reprise); The Crew Song; Friendship; There'll Always Be A Lady Fair (Sailor's Chantey); Friendship (reprise); It's De-lovely; Anything Goes; Public Enemy #1; Blow, Gabriel, Blow; Goodbye, Little Dream, Goodbye; Be Like the Bluebird; All Through the Night; The Gypsy in Me; Buddie, Beware; Finale

2010-2011 AWARDS Tony Awards: Best Revival of a Musical, Best Perfomance by a Leading Actress in a Musical (Sutton Foster); Best Choreography (Kathleen Marshall); Drama Desk Award: Outstanding Revival of a Musical, Outstanding Actress in a Musical (Sutton Foster), Outstanding Choreography (Kathleen Marshall), Outstanding Scenic Design (Derek McLane), Outstanding Sound Design in a Musical (Brian Ronan); Outer Critics Circle Award: Outstanding Revival of a Musical, Outstanding Choreography (Kathleen Marshall), Outstanding Actress in Musical (Sutton Foster), Outstanding Featured Actor in a Musical (Adam Godley); Drama League Award: Outstanding Revival of a Musical

SETTING A smoky Manhattan bar and onboard a luxury ocean liner; 1930s. Revival of a musical presented in two acts. The original Broadway production was presented at the Alvin (Neil Simon) Theatre and the 46th Street (Richard Rodgers) Theatre November 21, 1934–November 16, 1935 (starring Ethyl Merman). The musical was first revived Off-Broadway at the Orpheum Theatre May 15– December 9, 1962 and incorporated songs from the film version and songs from other Cole Porter musicals (see *Theatre World* Vol. 18, page 164). Lincoln Center Theater revived and revised the musical at the Vivian Beaumont Theater October 19, 1987–September 3, 1989 (starring Patti LuPone), playing 784 performances (see *Theatre World* Vol. 44, page 92). This new revival is based on the Lincoln Center revival version.

SYNOPSIS Cole Porter's classic musical *Anything Goes* returns to Broadway for its second major revival. When the S.S. American heads out to sea, etiquette and convention head out the portholes as two unlikely pairs set off on the course to true love... proving that sometimes destiny needs a little help from a crew of singing sailors, an exotic disguise, and some good old-fashioned blackmail.

Collin Donell and Sutton Foster

Adam Godley, Laura Osnes, Jessica Walter, John McMartin, and Colin Donnell

Sutton Foster and the Company

Sutton Foster and the Company

Shina Ann Morris, Joyce Chittick, Collin Donnell, Sutton Foster, Joel Grey, Kimberly Fauré, and Jennifer Savelli

Sutton Foster and the Company

Joel Grey and Sutton Foster (photos by Joan Marcus)

Catch Me If You Can

Neil Simon Theatre; First Preview: March 11, 2011; Opening Night: April 10, 2011; 32 previews, 59 performances as of May 31, 2011

Book by Terrence McNally, music by Marc Shaiman, lyrics by Scott Wittman & Marc Shaiman; Based on the DreamWorks Motion Picture; Produced by Margo Lion, Hal Luftig, Stacey Mindich, Yasuhiro Kawana, Scott and Brian Zeilinger, The Rialto Group, The Araca Group, Michael Watt, Barbara and Buddy Freitag, Jay & Cindy Gutterman/Pittsburgh CLO, Elizabeth Williams, Johnny Roscoe Productions/Van Dean, Fakston Productions/Solshay Productions, Patty Baker/Richard Winkler, Nederlander Presentations, Inc. and Warren Trepp; Produced in association with Remmel T. Dickinson, Paula Herold/Kate Lear, Stephanie P. McClelland, Jamie deRoy, Barry Feirstein, Rainerio J. Reyes, Rodney Rigby, Loraine Boyle, Amuse Inc., Joseph & Matthew Deitch/Cathy Chernoff, Joan Stein/Jon Murray and The 5th Avenue Theatre; Director, Jack O'Brien; Choreography, Jerry Mitchell; Music Director, John McDaniel; Arrangements, Marc Shaiman; Orchestrations, Marc Shaiman & Larry Blank; Set, David Rockwell; Costumes, William Ivey Long; Lighting, Kenneth Posner; Sound, Steve Canyon Kennedy; Casting, Telsey + Company; Wigs & Hair, Paul Huntley; Associate Director, Matt Lenz; Associate Choreographers, Joey Pizzi, Nick Kenkel; Production Stage Manager, Rolt Smith; Music Coordinator, John Miller; Technical Supervisor, Chris Smith/Smitty; Associate Producers, Brian Smith, T. Rick Hayashi; General Manager, The Charlotte Wilcox Company; Keyboard Programmer, Synthlink LLC, Jim Harp; Company Manager, James Lawson; Assistant Company Manager, Katrina Elliott; Stage Manager, Andrea O. Saraffian; Assistant Stage Manager, Lisa Ann Chernoff; Dance Captain, Nick Kenkel; Associate Design: Michael Todd Potter (set), Martha Bromelmeier (costumes), Aaron Spivey (lighting), Andrew Keister, Walter Trabach (sound), Giovanna Calabretta, Edward J. Wilson (hair & wig); Assistant Design: Ann Bartek, Charles Corcoran, Todd Edward Ivins, Dick Jaris (set), Rachel Attridge (costumes), Kathleen Dobbins (lighting); Assistant to Mr. Rockwell, Anne Colice; Rockwell Studio Leader, Barry Richards; Rockwell Studio Support, T.J. Greenway; William Ivey Long Studio Director, Donald Sanders; Moving Light Programmer, Paul J. Sonnleitner; Makeup Consultant, Joseph Dulude II; Prod. Electricians, Randall Zaibek, James Fedigan; Prod. Props Supervisor, Mike Pilipski; Prod. Carpenter, Donald J. Oberpriller; Head Electrician, Michael Cornell; Assistant Electrician, Sandy Paradise; Sound Engineer/Board Op, Daniel Tramontozzi; Assistant Sound Engineer, Brett Bingman; Head Props, Peter Drummond; Assistant Props, Jacob White; Wardrobe Supervisor, Douglas Petitjean; Assistant Wardrobe Supervisor, Deirdre LaBarre; Dressers, Scotty Cain, Tracey Diebold, Adam Giradet, Tanya Guercy-Blue, Samantha Lawrence, Jeanine Naughton, John Rinaldi, Julie Tobia, Lolly Totero, Mark Trezza; Hair Supervisor, Edward J. Wilson; Assistant Hair Supervisor, Steven Kirkham; Hair Dressers, Jeanette Harrington, Anna Hoffman; Music Tech Associate, Scott Riessett; Music Preparation, Joann Kane Music Service/Russ Bartmus, Mark Graham; Rehearsal Pianists, Jason Sherbundy, Seth Farber; Assistants to the Composer & Lyricist, Richard Read; Assistant to John Miller, Nichole Jennino; Prod. Assistants, Holly Coombs, Carly J. Price; For Charlotte Wilcox: Seth Markette, Matthew w. Krawiec, Dina S. Friedler, Regina Mancha, Steve Supeck, Margaret Wilcox, Ryan Smilie, Stephen Donovan; Advertising, SpotCo; Online Marketing, Situation Interactive; Press, The Hartman Group, Michael Hartman, Leslie Papa, Alyssa Hart; Cast recording: Sh-K-Boom/Ghostlight Records 84449

CAST Frank Abagnale Jr. **Aaron Tveit**; Agen Branton **Joe Cassidy**; Agent Dollar **Brandon Wardell**; Agent Carl Hanratty **Norbert Leo Butz**; Agent Cod **Timothy McCuen Piggee**; Frank Abagnale Sr. **Tom Wopat**; Paula Abagnale **Rachel de Benedet**; Cheryl Ann **Rachelle Rak**; Brenda Strong **Kerry Butler**; Roger Strong **Nick Wyman**; Carol Strong **Linda Hart**; The Frank Abagnale Jr. Players **Joe Cassidy, Alex Ellis, Jennifer Frankel, Lisa Gajda, Bob Gaynor, Kearran Giovanni, Grasan Kingsberry, Michael X. Martin, Aleks Pevec, Timothy McCuen Piggee, Rachelle Rak, Joe Aaron Reid, Angie Schworer, Sabrina Sloan, Sarrah Strimel, Charlie Sutton, Brandon Wardell, Katie Webber, Candice Marie Woods**; Standby for Frank Abagnale Jr. **Jay Armstrong Johnson**; Swings **Sara Andreas, Will Erat, Nick Kenkel, Kristin Piro**

UNDERSTUDIES Joe Cassidy (Agent Carl Hanratty), Alex Ellis (Brenda Strong), Will Erat (Agent Carl Hanratty, Roger Strong), Jennifer Frankel (Carol Strong), Lisa Gajda (Carol Strong), Bob Gaynor (Frank Abagnale Sr.), Michael X. Martin (Frank Abagnale Sr., Roger Strong), Rachelle Rak (Paula Abagnale), Angie Schworer (Paula Abagnale), Brandon Wardell (Frank Abagnale Jr.), Katie Webber (Brenda Strong)

ORCHESTRA John McDaniel (Conductor), Lon Hoyt (Associate Conductor/Keyboard), Todd Groves, Rick Heckman, Alden Banta (Woodwinds), Dave Trigg, Trevor Neumann (Trumpets), Alan Ferber (Trombone), Larry Saltzman (Guitar), Vincent Fay (Bass), Clint de Ganon (Drums), Joseph Passaro (Percussion), Jason Sherbundy (Keyboards), Brian Koonin (Keyboard/Guitar), Rick Dolan (Concert Master), Belinda Whitney (Violin), Clay Reude (Cello)

MUSICAL NUMBERS Live in Living Color; The Pinstripes Are All That They See; Someone Else's Skin; Jet Set; Live in Living Color (reprise); Don't Break the Rules; The Pinstripes Are All That They See (reprise); Butter Outta Cream; The Man Inside the Clues; Christmas Is My Favorite Time of Year; My Favorite Time of Year; Doctor's Orders; Live in Living Color (reprise); Don't Be a Stranger; Little Boy, Be a Man; Seven Wonders; (Our) Family Tree; Fly, Fly Away; Good-Bye; Strange But True

2010-2011 AWARDS Tony Award: Best Performance by a Leading Actor in a Musical (Norbert Leo Butz); Drama Desk Award: Outstanding Actor in a Musical (Norbert Leo Butz); Fred and Estelle Astaire Award: Best Dancer in a Musical (Norbert Leo Butz)

New York premiere of a new musical presented in two acts. World premiere at the 5th Avenue Theatre in Seattle, Washington (David Armstrong, Executive Producer and Artistic Director; Bernadine Griffin, Managing Director; Bill Berry, Producing Director) July 23–August 16, 2009 (see *Theatre World* Vol. 66, page 363).

SYNOPSIS *Catch Me If You Can* captures the astonishing true story of Frank Abagnale Jr., a world-class con artist who passed himself off as a doctor, a lawyer, and a jet pilot–all before the age of 21. With straight-arrow FBI agent Carl Hanratty on Frank's trail, we're off on a jet-setting, cat-and-mouse chase, as a jazzy, swinging-sixties score keeps this adventure in constant motion. In the end, Agent Hanratty learns he and Frank aren't so very different after all, and Frank finds out what happens when love catches up to a man on the run.

Rachel de Benedet (photos by Joan Marcus)

Norbert Leo Butz

Aaron Tveit and Kerry Butler

Aaron Tveit and the Company

Aaron Tveit and Norbert Leo Butz

Aaron Tveit and Tom Wopat

Aaron Tveit and the Company

The Motherf**ker with the Hat

Gerald Schoenfeld Theatre; First Preview: March 15, 2011; Opening Night: April 11, 2011; 28 previews, 58 performances as of May 31, 2011

Written by Stephen Adly Guirgus; Produced by Scott Rudin, Stuart Thompson, Public Theater Productions, LAByrinth Theater Company, Fabula Media Partners LLC, Jean Doumanian, Ruth Hendel, Carl Moellenberg, Jon B. Platt, Tulchin Bartner/Jamie deRoy; Director, Anna D. Shapiro; Sets, Todd Rosenthal; Costumes, Mimi O'Donnell; Lighting, Donald Holder; Sound, Acme Sound Partners; Original Music, Terence Blanchard; Casting, Jordan Thaler & Heidi Griffiths; Production Stage Manager, Charles Means; Production Management, Aurora Productions; General Management, Stuart Thompson Productions/Marshall B. Purdy; Company Manager, Kathy Lowe; Stage Manager, Antonia Gianino; Fight Choreographer, Steve Arboleda; Assistant Director, Cat Miller; Assistant to Mr. Guirgis, Japhet Balaban; Associate Design, Valerie Ramshur (costumes), Caroline Chao (lighting), David Thomas (sound); Assistants to Mr. Rosenthal, Kevin Depinet, Shaun Renfro; Assistant Lighting, Michael P. Jones; Makeup, Cookie Jordan; Prod. Carpenter, Todd Frank; House Carpenter, Timothy McWilliams; Automation, Glenn Ingram; Prod. Electrician, James Maloney; Head Electrician, Justin Freeman; House Electrician, Leslie Ann Kilian; Sound Engineer, Michael Farfalla; Head Props, John Tutalo; House Props, Heidi L. Brown; Prop Shopper, Sarah Bird; Wardrobe Supervisor, Susan Checklick; Dresser, Paul Ludick; Production Assistant, Jule DeVore; Advertising & Marketing, aka; Press, Boneau/Bryan-Brown, Chris Boneau, Heath Schwartz, Kelly Guiod

CAST Veronica **Elizabeth Rodriguez**; Jackie **Bobby Cannavale**; Ralph D. **Chris Rock**; Victoria **Annabella Sciorra**; Cousin Julio **Yul Vázquez**

UNDERSTUDIES Rosál Colon (Veronica, Victoria), Ron Cephas Jones (Ralph D.), Alfredo Narciso (Jackie, Cousin Julio)

2010-2011 AWARDS Drama Desk Award: Outstanding Actor in a Play (Bobby Cannavale); Outer Critics Circle Award: Outstanding Featured Actress in a Play (Elizabeth Rodriguez); *Theatre World Award*: Lunt-Fontanne Award for Ensemble Excellence (The Cast)

SETTING New York City, present day. World premiere of a new play presented in two acts. Developed at Ojai Playwrights Conference and at LAByrinth Theatre Company.

SYNOPSIS *The Motherfucker with the Hat* is a new high-octane, verbal cage match about love, fidelity, and misplaced haberdashery from playwright Stephen Adly Guirgis. Jackie and Veronica have been in love since the 8th grade. But now, Jackie is on parole and living clean and sober under the guidance of his sponsor, Ralph D, while still living and loving with his volatile soul mate Veronica who is fiercely loving, but far from sober. Still, their love is pure. And true. Nothing can come between them – except a hat.

Bobby Cannavale and Elizabeth Rodriguez

Bobby Cannavale, Yul Vázquez, and Chris Rock

Bobby Cannavale
(photos by Joan Marcus)

Annabella Sciorra

War Horse

Vivian Beaumont Theatre; First Preview: March 15, 2011; Opening Night: April 14, 2011; 33 previews, 54 performances as of May 31, 2011

Based on the novel by Michael Morpurgo, adapted by Nick Stafford, in association with Handspring Puppet Company; Produced by Lincoln Center Theater (André Bishop, Artistic Director; Bernard Gersten, Executive Producer) and the National Theatre of Great Britain (Nicholas Hytner, Director of the National; Nick Star, Executive Director) in association with Bob Boyett and War Horse LP; Presented by the National Theatre of Great Britain; Directors, Marianne Elliott & Tom Morris; Sets, Costumes, and Drawings, Rae Smith; Puppet Design, Fabrication, and Direction, Adrian Kohler with Basil Jones for Handspring Puppet Company; Lighting, Paule Constable; Director of Movement & Horse Sequences, Toby Sedwick; Animation & Projection Design, 59 Productions; Music, Adrian Sutton; Songmaker, John Tams; Sound, Christopher Shutt; Music Pliska; Associate Puppetry Director, Mervyn Millar; Stage Manager, Rick Steiger; Casting, Daniel Swee; NT Technical Producer, Katrina Gilroy; NT Producer, Chris Harper; NT Associate Producer, Robin Hawkes; NT Marketing, Alex Bayley; Boyett Theatricals Producer, Tim Levy; Fight Director, Thomas Schall; Dialect Coach, Gillian Lane-Plescia; Vocal Coach, Kate Wilson; Hair & Wigs, Paul Huntley; General Manager, Adam Siegel; Production Manager, Jeff Hamlin; Development, Hattie K. Jutagir; Marketing, Linda Mason Ross; Musical Theatre Associate Producer, Ira Weitzman;Finance, David S. Brown; Education, Kati Koerner; LCT Directors Lab/Dramaturg, Anne Cattaneo; LCT3 Artistic Director, Paige Evans; House Manager, Rheba Flegelman; Company Manager, Matthew Markoff; Associate Company Manager, Jessica Perlmeter Cochrane; Associate Director, Drew Barr; Puppetry Associate, Matt Acheson; Movement Associate, Adrienne Kapstein; Assistant Stage Managers, Lisa Iacucci, Amy Marsico; Associate Design: Frank McCullough (U.S. set), Johanna Coe (U.K. costumes), Sarah Laux (U.S. costumes), Nick Simmons (U.K. lighting), Karen Spahn (U.S. lighting), John Owens (U.K. sound); U.S. Assistant Sound, Bridget O'Connor; U.K. Puppetry Technician, Ed Dimbleby; Automated Light Programmer, Benjamin Pearcy; Props, Faye Armon; Fight Captain, Ian Lassiter; Makeup, Cynthia Demand; Prod. Carpenter, William Nagle; Prod. Electrician, Patrick Merryman; Prod. Soundman, Marc Salzberg; Prod. Propertyman, Karl Rausenberger; Prod. FLyman, John Weingart; House Technician, Linda Heard; Wardrobe Supervisor, Lynn Bowling; Dressers, Adam Adelman, Peggy Danz, Richard Gross, Donna Holland, Shannon Koger, Patti Luther, Erick Medinilla, James Nadeaux, Sarah Rochford, Rosie Wells, Kristi Wood; Hair Supervisor, Cynthia Demand; Prod. Assistants, Christopher R. Munnell, Deanna Weiner; Guardian, John Mara; Incidental Music: Gary Maurer (Engineer), Steve Cohen (Copyist), Jim Lake (Trumpet/Coronet), Angela Gosse (Trumpet/Coronet), Judy Yin-Chi Lee (Horn/Alto Horn), Hitomi Yakata (Trombone/Euphonium), Richard Heckman (Clarinet/Flute); Advertising, Serino Coyne; Press, Philip Rinaldi, Barbara Carroll, Amanda Dekker

CAST *The Horses*: Joey as a foal **Stephen James Anthony, David Pegram, Leenya Rideout**; Joey **Joby Earle, Ariel Heller, Alex Hoeffler, Jeslyn Kelly, Jonathan David Martin, Prentice Onayemi, Jude Sandy, Zach Villa,** or **Enrico D. Wey**; Topthorn **Joby Earle, Joel Reuben Ganz, Ariel Heller, Alex Hoeffler, Tom Lee, Jonathan Christopher MacMillan, Jude Sandy, Zach Villa,** or **Enrico D. Wey**; Coco **Joby Earle, Joel Reuben Ganz, Alex Hoeffler, Jeslyn Kelly, Tom Lee, Jonathan David Martin, Zach Villa,** or **Enrico D. Wey**; Coco **Joby Earle, Joel Reuben Ganz, Alex Hoeffler, Jeslyn Kelly, Tom Lee, Jonathan David Martin, Zach Villa,** or **Enrico D. Wey**; Heine **Sanjit De Silva, Bhavesh Patel**; *The People*: Song Woman **Kate Pfaffl**; Song Man **Liam Robinson**; Lieutenant James Nicholls **Stephen Plunkett**; Arthur Narracott **T. Ryder Smith**; Billy Narracott **Matt Doyle**; Albert Narracott **Seth Numrich**; Ted Narracott **Boris McGiver**; Chapman Carter **Austin Durant**; Allan **Elliot Villar**; John Greig **Joby Earle, Joel Reuben Ganz, Alex Hoeffler,** or **Jonathan David Martin**; Rose Narracott **Alyssa Breshnahan**; Priest **Peter Hermann**; Captain Charles Stewart **Brian Lee Huynh**; Seargeant Thunder **Richard Crawford**; Private David Taylor **David Pegram**; Paulette **Cat Walleck**; Soldat Schnabel **Zach**

Appelman; Hauptmann Friedrich Müller **Peter Hermann**; Soldat Klausen **Elliot Villar**; Doctor Schweyk **Sanjit De Silva**; Oberst Strauss **Bhavesh Patel**; Sergeant Fine **Zach Appelman**; Unteroffizier Klebb **Stephen Plunkett**; Emilie **Madeleine Rose Yen**; Taff **Sanjit De Silva**; Manfred **Austin Durant**; Matron Callaghan **Leenya Rideout**; Annie Gilbert **Hannah Sloat**; Veterinary Officer Martin **Ian Lassiter**; Goose **Joby Earle, Jonathan Christopher MacMillan** or **Jude Sandy**

UNDERSTUDIES Stephen James Anthony (Albert Narracott, Billy Narracott, Private David Taylor), Zach Appelman (Captain Charles Stewart, Lieutenant James Nicholls, Private David Taylor), Alyssa Bresnahan (Matron Callaghan), Richard Crawford (Arthur Narracott, Unteroffizier Klebb), Matt Doyle (Albert Narracott), Austin Durant (Arthur Narracott, Sergeant Thunder, Ted Narracott), Peter Hermann (Allan, Chapman Carter), Brian Lee Huynh (Joey as a Foal, Sergeant Fine), Ian Lassiter (Allan, Doctor Schweyk, Oberst Strauss, Soldat Klausen, Taff, Thomas Bone), Boris McGiver (Manfred, Oberst Strauss, Sergeant Thunder), Bhavesh Patel (Doctor Schweyk, Sergeant Fine, Soldat Schnabel, Taff, Ted Narracott), David Pegram (Billy Narracott, Thomas Bone), Kate Pfaffl (Annie Gilbert), Stephen Plunkett (Soldat Klausen, Veterinary Officer Martin), Leenya Rideout (Paulette, Rose Narracott, Song Man, Song Woman), Liam Robinson (Soldat Schnabel), Sanit de Silva (Captain Charles Stewart, Lieutenant James Nicholls, Priest, Unteroffizier Klebb), Hannah Sloat (Emilie, Joey as a Foal, Paulette), T. Ryder Smith (Hauptmann Friedrich Muller, Manfred), Elliot Villar (Chapman Carter, Hauptmann Friedrich Muller, Priest, Veterinary Officer Martin), Cat Walleck (Annie Gilbert, Joey as a Foal, Matron Callaghan, Rose Narracott).

2010-2011 AWARDS Tony Awards: Best Play, Best Direction of a Play (Marianne Elliott and Tom Morris), Best Scenic Design of a Play (Rae Smith), Best Lighting Design of a Play (Paule Constable), Best Sound Design of a Play (Christopher Shutt), Special award for Adrian Kohler and Basil Jones of Handspring Puppet Company; Drama Desk Awards: Outstanding Play, Special Award for the Creative Team (Paule Constable, Marianne Elliott, 59 Productions, Adrian Kohler with Basil Jones for Handspring Puppet Company, Tom Morris, Rae Smith, Christopher Shutt, Toby Sedgwick, Adrian Sutton and John Tams); Outer Critics Circle Awards: Outstanding New Broadway Play, Outstanding Director of a Play (Marianne Elliott and Tom Morris), Outstanding Lighting Design (Paule Constable), Special Citation (Adrian Kohler with Basil Jones for Handspring Puppet Company for puppet design, fabrication and direction); New York Drama Critics' Circle Award: Special Citation; Drama League Award: Distinguished Production of a Play; *Theatre World Award*: Dorothy Loudon Award for Excellence in the Theatre (Seth Numrich)

SETTING Devon, England and France, 1914. U.S. premiere of a play with music presented in two acts. World premiere at the National Theatre's Olivier Theatre in South Bank, London October 17, 2007–February 14, 2008 and a second run September 10, 2008–March 18, 2009. The production transferred to the West End at the New London Theatre April 3, 2009 where it continues to run.

SYNOPSIS In Devon at the outbreak of World War I, Joey, young Albert Narracott's beloved horse, is sold to the cavalry and shipped to France. Joey serves in the British and German armies, befriends Topthorn (another army horse), and gets caught up in enemy fire. Death, disease, and fate take him on an extraordinary odyssey, serving on both sides before finding himself alone in a no man's land. But Albert cannot forget Joey, and, still not old enough to enlist in the army, he embarks on a dangerous mission to find and bring him back to Devon.

The Company (photos by Paul Kolnik)

Jude Sandy and Prentice Onayemi

Jude Sandy, Madeleine Rose Yen, Peter Hermann, and Cat Walleck

David Pegram, Seth Numrich, Ariel Heller, Madeleine Rose Yen, and Peter Hermann

The Company

Seth Numrich and the Company

Jose Llana, Janet Dacal, and the Company

Stefan Raulston, Julius Anthony Rubio, Darren Ritchie, Joey Calveri, Derek Ferguson

Wonderland

Marquis Theatre; First Preview: March 21, 2011; Opening Night: April 17, 2011; Closed May 15, 2011; 30 previews, 33 performances

Book by Gregory Boyd and Jack Murphy, music by Frank Wildhorn, lyrics by Jack Murphy; Produced by David A. Straz Jr. Center for the Performing Arts (Judy Lisi, President and CEO), Franzblau Media Inc., Nederlander Presentations, Inc., The Knights of Tampa Bay (David Scher and Hinks Shimberg), Michael Speyer & Bernie Abrams, Jay H. Harris, Larry & Kay Payton, June & Tom Simpson, Independent Presenters Network, Sonny Everett Productions; Associate Producers, Judy Joseph, StageVentures 2010 Limited Partnership; Executive Producer, William Franzblau; Director, Gregory Boyd; Choreography, Marguerite Derricks; Music Director/Incidental & Dance Music Arrangements, Jason Howland; Set, Neil Patel; Costumes, Susan Hilferty; Lighting, Paul Gallo; Sound, Peter Hylenski; Video & Projections, Sven Ortel; Hair & Wigs, Tom Watson; Music Supervisor & Orchestrations, Kim Scharnberg; Vocal Arrangements, Ron Melrose & Jason Howland; Casting, Dave Clemmons, Joe Dewing Casting; Fight Director, Rick Sordelet; Associate Director, Kenneth Ferrone; Associate Choreographer, Michelle Elkin; Musical Coordinator, David Lai; Technical Supervisor, Chris Smith/Smitty; Production Stage Manager, David O'Brien; General Manager, The Charlotte Wilcox Company; Company Manager, Alexandra Agosta; Stage Manager, Stephen R. Gruse; Assistant Company Manager, Sherra Johnston; Assistant Stage Manager, Colleen Danaher; Associate Design: Caleb Levengood (set), Tricia Barsamian (costumes), Craig Stelzenmuller (lighting), Tony Smolenski IV and Keith Caggiano (sound), S. Katy Tucker (video), Tony Smolenski, Keith Caggiano (sound); Assistant Design, Michael Carnahan, Stephen Dobay (set), Becky Lasky, Marina Reti (costumes), Joel Shier (lighting), Lucy Mackinnon (video); Assistant to Frank Wildhorn, Nicholas Cheng; Assistant Fight Director, Christian Kelly-Sordelet; Video/Projections Programmer, Peter Vincent Acken; Additional Programming, Cory FitzGerald; Special Effects, Chic Silber; Magic Consultant, Matthew Holtzclaw; Synthesizer Programmer, Randy Cohen; Assistant Synthesizer Programmers, Bryan Crook, Tim Crook; Prod. Electrician, Michael Ward; Prod. Prop Master, Neil Rosenberg; Prod. Sound Engineer, Philip Lojo/Paul Delcioppo; Head Carpenter, Jason Clark; Flyman, David Elmer; Head Electrician, Evan Vorono; Tampa Moving Light Programmer, David Arch; N.Y. Moving Light Programmer, Thomas Hague; Spotlight, June Abernathy; Assistant Prop Master, Trevor Ricci; Sound Operator, William Ruger; Assistant Sound Operator, Jesse Stevens; Wardrobe Supervisor, Scott Westervelt; Associate Wardrobe Supervisor, Kelly Saxon; Dressers, Douglas Earl, Lillian Colon-Jaramillo, Jake Fry, Suli Hilda-Garcia, Hector Lugo, Evelina Norvil, Allison Rogers, Roy Seiler, Jay Woods; Hair Supervisor, Thomas Augustine; Assistant Hair Supervisor, Joshua D. First; Makeup Consultant, Ashley Ryan; Prod. Assistant, Aaron Elgart; Dance Captain, Mallauri Esquibel; Assistant Dance Captain, Lauren Lim Jackson; Fight Captain, Stefan Raulston; Marketing, aka; Advertising, SpotCo, Press, Boneau/Bryan-Brown, Adrian Bryan-Brown, Susanne Tighe, Kelly Guiod; Cast recording: Masterworks Broadway 88697 88669 2

CAST Edwina **Karen Mason**; Chloe **Carly Rose Sonenclar**; Alice **Janet Dacal**; The White Rabbit **Edward Staudenmayer**; Caterpillar **E. Clayton Cornelious**; El Gato **Jose Llana**; Jack the White Knight **Darren Ritchie**; Morris the March Hare **Danny Stiles**; The Mad Hatter **Kate Shindle**; The Queen of Hearts **Karen Mason**; The Victorian Gentleman **Darren Ritchie**; Ensemble **April Berry, Joey Calveri, Sae La Chin, Mallauri Esquibel, Derek Ferguson, Wilkie Ferguson III, Laura Hall, Natalie Hill, Lauren Lim Jackson, Morgan James, Ryan Link, Kate Loprest, Heather Parcells, Stefan Raulston, Julius Anthony Rubio, Tanairi Sade Vazquez** Swings **Grady McLeod Bowman, Renee Marino**

UNDERSTUDIES April Berry (Chloe), Joey Calveri (El Gato, Jack the White Knight), Mallauri Esquibel (Chloe), Wilkie Ferguson III (Caterpillar, Morris the March Hare), Natalie Hill (Edwina, Queen of Hearts), Morgan James (Alice), Ryan Link (Jack the White Knight, The White Rabbit), Kate Loprest (Alice), Heather Parcells (Edwina, Mad Hatter, Queen of Hearts), Danny Stiles (The White Rabbit)

ORCHESTRA Jason Howland (Conductor), Jeff Lams (Associate Conductor/Keyboard), Katherine Livolsi-Landau (Concert Master), Lisa Matricardi, Jennifer Choi, Roger Mahadeen (Violins), David Blinn (Viola), CJ Camerieri (Trumpets) Mairi Dorman-Phaneuf (Cello),: Jennifer Wharton (Trombones/Tuba), R.J. Kelley (French Horn/Alto Horn), Kurt Bacher, Daniel Willis (Woodwinds), Marc Copely (Guitars), (Chris Lightcap Acoustic/Electric Bass), Nicholas Cheng, Kirsten Agresta Copely (Keyboards), Bill Lanham (Percussion), Adam Wolfe (Drums)

MUSICAL NUMBERS Worst Day of My Life, Down the Rabbit Hole, Welcome to Wonderland, Drink Me, Advice From a Caterpillar, Go With the Flow, One Knight, The Tea Party, The Mad Hatter, Hail the Queen, Home, A Nice Little Walk, Through the Looking Glass, I Will Prevail, I Am My Own Invention, Off With Their Heads, Once More I Can See, Together, Home (reprise), Finding Wonderland

SETTING Chloe's Bedroom, and various places in Wonderland and Looking Glass Land. World premiere of a new musical presented in two acts in sixteen scenes.

SYNOPSIS Wonderland is a new spin on the classic story of Alice and her Looking-Glass world, inspired by the tales of Lewis Carroll. This time, Alice is a modern-day woman who goes on a life-changing adventure far below the streets of New York City, where a colorful cast of strange but familiar characters help her rediscover what's really important.

Janet Dacal

Kate Shindle, Carly Rose Sonenclar, and Danny Stiles

Kate Shindle (photos by Paul Kolnik)

The Company

*Kathleen Turner
(photos by Joan Marcus)*

Stephen Kunken

High

Booth Theatre; First Preview: March 25, 2011; Opening Night: April 19, 2011; Closed April 24, 2011; 29 previews, 7 performances

Written by Matthew Lombardo; Produced by Leonard J. Soloway, Chase Mishkin, Terry Schnuck, Ann Cady Scott, Timothy J. Hampton, James and Catherine Berges, Craig D. Schnuck, Barbara and Buddy Breitag, Lauren Class Schneider, David Mirvish, Gene Fisch Jr./Stu Sternback, David Fagin/Rosalind Resnick, Jacki Barlia Florin/Michael A. Alden and Lizabeth Zindel, The Shubert Organization and the Repertory Theatre of St. Louis; Director, Rob Ruggiero; Sets, David Gallo; Costumes, Jess Goldstein; Lighting, John Lasiter; Sound & Original Composition, Vincent Olivieri; Special Makeup, Joe Rossi; Production Supervisor, Arthur Siccardi & Patrick Sullivan; Casting, Pat McCorkle; Production Stage Manager, Bess Marie Glorioso; Company Manager, Jennifer Hindman Kemp; Marketing & Advertising, aka (Elizabeth Furze, Scott A. Moore, Clint Bond Jr., Andrew Damer, Richard Arnold, Adam Jay, Janette Roush); Associate Producer, Lawrence J. Moss; General Manager, Loenard Soloway; Stage Manager, Ana M. Garcia; Assistant Director, Nick Eilerman; Associate Design: Steven C. Kemp (set), China Lee (costumes), Christopher Cronin (sound); Assistant Design: Thomas George (set), Keri Thibodeau (lighting); Design Interns: Brian Dudkiewicz (set), Jeffrey Small (lighting); Production Properties Supervisor, Mike Pilpski; Automation, Chad Hershey; Production Electrician, Neil McShane; Wardrobe Supervisor, Jesse Galvin; Dresser, Dawn Marcoccia; Press, Boneau/Bryan-Brown, Chris Boneau, Jessica Johnson, Amada de Souza

CAST Sister Jamison Connelly **Kathleen Turner**; Father Michael Delpapp **Stephen Kunken**; Cody Randall **Evan Jonigkeit**

UNDERSTUDIES Elizabeth Norment (Sister Jamison Connelly), Tim Altemeyer (Father Michael Delpapp), Jeff Cuttler (Cody Randall)

SETTING A Catholic rehabilitation center. New York premiere of a new play presented in two acts. World premiere produced by Hartford, Connecticut's TheatreWorks (Steve Campo, Executive Director), Cincinatti Playhouse in the Park (Edward Stern, Producing Artistic Director; Buzz Ward, Executive Director), and the Repertory Theatre of St. Louis (Steven Woolf, Artistic Director; Mark D. Bernstein, Managing Director).

SYNOPSIS When Sister Jamison Connelly agrees to sponsor a 19 year-old drug user in an effort to help him combat his addiction, her own faith is ultimately tested. Struggling between the knowledge she possesses as a rehabilitation counselor and a woman of religious conviction, she begins to question her belief in miracles and whether people can find the courage to change. *High* explores the universal themes of truth, forgiveness, redemption, and human fallibility.

Kathleen Turner and Evan Jonigkeit

Sister Act

Broadway Theatre; First Preview: March 24, 2011; Opening Night: April 20, 2011; 28 previews, 42 performances as of May 31, 2011

Music by Alan Menken, lyrics by Glenn Slater, book by Cheri Steinkellner & Bill Steinkellner; Additional Book Material by Douglas Carter Beane; Based on the Touchstone Pictures Motion Picture written by Joseph Howard; Presented by Whoopi Goldberg & Stage Entertainment in association with the Shubert Organization and Disney Theatrical Productions; Producers, Whoopi Goldberg, Joop Van Den Ende, Bill Taylor, Rebecca Quigley; Director, Jerry Zaks; Choreography, Anthony Vna Laast; Set, Klara Zieglerova; Costumes, Lez Brotherston; Lighting, Natasha Katz; Sound, John Shivers; Casting, Telsey + Company; Wigs and Hair, David Brian Brown; Production Management, Aurora Productions; Production Supervisor, Steven Beckler; Orchestrations, Doug Besterman; Dance Arrangements, Mark Hummel; Music Director, Brent-Alan Huffman; Music Coordinator, John Miller; Music Supervisor, Vocal & Incidental Music Arrangements, Michael Kosarin; Original Production Depeveloped in Association with Peter Schneider & Michael Reno; Associate Producer for Whoop Inc., Tom Leonardis; Director of Creative Development, Ulrike Burger-Brujis; General Manager, 321 Theatricals; Executive Producer, Beverley D. Mac Keen; For 321: Nina Essman, Nancy Nagel Gibbs, Marcia Goldberg; For Aurora: Gene O'Donovan, W. Benjamin Heller II, Stephanie Sherline, Jarid Sumner, Liza Luxenberg, Jason Margolis, Ryan Stanisz, Melissa Mazdra; Company Manager, Roeya Banuazizi; Associate Company Manager, Eric Cornell; Production Stage Manager, Steven Beckler; Stage Manager, Jason Trubitt; Assistant Stage Manager, Mar MacLeod; Associate Director, Steve Bebout; Assistant Director, Stephen Edlund; Script Assistant, Paul Downs Colaizzo; Associate Choreographer, Ben Clare; U.S. Associate Choreographer, Janet Rothermel; Associate Design: Andrew D. Edwards (set), Diane Williams (costumes – U.K), Amy Clark (costumes – U.S.), Yael Lubetzky (lighting), David Patridge (sound); Assistant Design, Marina Reti (costumes), Jonathan Spencer (lighting); Moving Light Programmer, Hilary Knox; Makeup Consultant, Milagros Medina-Cerdeira; Prod. Carpenter, Fran Rapp; Deck Automation, Patrick Shea; Fly Automation, Steve Schroettnig; Production Electrician, J. Michael Pitzer; Head Electrician, Jeremy Wahlers; Follow Spot, Justin McClintock; Prod. Props, Emiliano Pares; Prop Master, Brian Schweppe; Assistant Prop Master, Anmaree Rodibaugh; Prod. Sound, Kevin Kennedy; Sound Engineer, George Huckins; Assistant Sound Engineer, Pitsch Karrer; Wardrobe Supervisor, Eddie Harrison; Wardrobe Assistant, Jennifer Griggs-Cennamo; Hair Supervisor, Wanda Gregory; Hair Assistant, Ashley Leitzel-Reichenbach; Dressers, Maeve Fiona Butler, Cat Dee, Kathleen Gallagher, Viictoria Grecki, Tim Greer, Sue Hamilton, Gayle Palmieri, Geoffrey Polischuk, Erin Brooke Roth, Chris Sanders; House Crew: Charles Rasmussen (carpenter), George D. Milne (electrician), Rick DalCortivo (properties), Thomas Cole Jr (flyman); Music Preparation, Russell Anixter, Donald Rice; Electronic Music Design, Andrew Barrett/Lionella Productions LLC; Rehearsal Musicians, Aron Accurso (piano), Steven Malone (piano), Richard Mercurio (drums); Music Interns, Adam Overett, Brendan Whiting; Prod. Assistants, Kathryn Ambrose, Chirstopher Michael Borg, Rebecca Peterson, Jamie Ware; Assistant to John Miller, Jennifer Coolbaugh; Advertising/Website/Interactive Media, SpotCo; Marketing, aka; For Stage Entertainment: Bill Taylor (CEO), Rebecca Quigley (Executive Producer), Beverley D. MacKeen (Executive Director); Press, The Hartman Group, Michael Hartman, Tom D'Ambrosio, Michelle Bergmann; Cast recording (London): Sh-K-Boom/Ghostlight Records 84446

CAST Deloris Van Cartier **Patina Miller**; Tina **Aléna Watters**; Michelle **Rashidra Scott**; Curtis Jackson **Kingsley Leggs**; Joey **John Treacy Egan**; Pablo **Caesar Samayoa**; TJ **Desmond Green**; Eddie Souther **Chester Gregory**; Mother Superior **Victoria Clark**; Monsignor O' Hara **Fred Applegate**; Mary Robert **Marla Mindelle**; Mary Patrick **Sarah Bolt**; Mary Lazarus **Audrie Neenan**; Ensemble **Jennifer Allen, Charl Brown, Holly Davis, Christina DeCicco, Madeleine Doherty, Alan H. Green, Blake Hammond, Wendy James, Kevin Ligon, Marissa Perry, Corbin Reid, Rashidra Scott, Jennifer Simard, Lael Van Keuren, Roberta B. Wall,**

Aléna Watters; Swings **Natalie Bradshaw, Carrie A. Johnson, Louise Madison, Ernie Pruneda, Lance Roberts**

UNDERSTUDIES Jennifer Allen (Mary Lazarus, Mother Superior), Charl Brown (Eddie Souther, Pablo, TJ), Holly Davis (Mary Patrick), Christina DeCicco (Mary Robert), Alan H. Green (Curtis Jackson, Eddie Souther), Blake Hammond (Joey, Monsignor O' Hara), Wendy James (Mother Superior), Kevin Ligon (Joey, Monsignor O' Hara), Marissa Perry (Mary Patrick), Ernie Pruneda (Pablo, TJ), Corbin Reid (Deloris Van Cartier, Michelle, Tina), Lance Roberts (Curtis Jackson), Rashidra Scott (Deloris Van Cartier), Lael Van Keuren (Mary Robert, Michelle, Tina), Roberta B. Wall (Mary Lazarus)

ORCHESTRA Michael Kosarin (Conductor), Brent-Alan Huffman (Associate Conductor/Keyboards), Aron Accurso (Assistant Conductor/Keyboards), Suzanne Ornstein (Concert Master), Mineko Yajima, Eric DeGioia, Kristina Musser (Violins), Roger Shell (Cello), Andrew Sterman, Marc Phaneuf, Jacqueline Henderson (Woodwinds), Craig Johnson, Scott Harrell (Trumpets), Gary Grimaldi, Jeff Nelson (Trombones), John Benthal (Guitar), Dick Sarpola (Bass), Rich Mercurio (Drums), Michael Englander (Percussion)

MUSICAL NUMBERS Take Me to Heaven; Fabulous, Baby!; Here Within These Walls; It's Good to Be a Nun; When I Find My Baby; I Could Be That Guy; Raise Your Voice; Take Me to Heaven (reprise); Sunday Morning Fever; Lady in the Long Black Dress; Haven't Got a Prayer; Bless Our Show; The Life I Never Led; Fabulous, Baby! (reprise); Sister Act; When I Find My Baby (reprise); The Life I Never Led (reprise); Sister Act (reprise); Spread the Love Around

2010-2011 AWARDS *Theatre World Award*: Patina Miller

SETTING Philadelphia; 1978. New York premiere of a new musical presented in two acts. Originally produced by Pasadena Playhouse (Pasadena, California) October 24–December 23, 2006 and subsequently at the Alliance Theatre (Atlanta, Georgia) January 17–February 25, 2007 (see *Theatre World* Vol. 63, page 305). The London production opened on the West End at the London Palladium June 2, 2009–October 30, 2010 starring Ms. Miller.

SYNOPSIS When disco diva Deloris Van Cartier witnesses a murder, she is put in protective custody in the one place cops are sure she won't be found—a convent! Disguised as a nun, she finds herself at odds with both the rigid lifestyle and an uptight Mother Superior. Using her unique disco moves and singing talent to inspire the choir, Deloris breathes new life into the church and community, but in doing so blows her cover. Soon the gang are giving chase, only to find themselves up against Deloris and the power of her new found Sister Hood.

Alena Watters, Rashidra Scott, and Patina Miller

Sarah Bolt, Marla Mindelle, and Patina Miller

Victoria Clark and Patina Miller

Demond Green, Caesar Samayoa, Kingsley Leggs, and John Treacy Egan

Chester Gregory and Patina Miller

Fred Applegate, Victoria Clark, Chester Gregory, and Patina Miller

Patina Miller and the Company (photos by Joan Marcus)

Mark Rylance (photos by Simon Annand)

Aimeé-Ffion Edwards

Mackenzie Crook (photos by Joan Marcus))

Jerusalem

Music Box Theatre; First Preview: April 2, 2011; Opening Night: April 21, 2011; 21 previews, 46 performances as of May 31, 2011

Written by Jez Butterworth; Produced by Sonia Friedman Productions, Stuart Thompson, Scott Rudin, Roger Berlind, Royal Court Theatre Productions, Beverly Bartner/Alice Tulchin, Dede Harris/Rupert Gavin, Broadway Across America, Jon B. Platt, 1001 Nights/Stephanie P. McClelland, Carole L. Haber/Richard Willis, Jacki Baria Florin/Adam Blanshay; Presented by The Royal Court Theatre; Director, Ian Rickson; Sets & Costumes, Ultz; Lighting, Mimi Jordan Sherin; Sound, Ian Dickinson (Autograph); Original Music, Stephen Warbeck; U.K. Casting, Amy Ball; U.S. Casting, Jim Carnahan; Production Stage Manager, Jill Cordle; Production Management, Aurora Productions; General Management, Stuart Thompson Productions/David Turner; U.K. General Management, Sonia Friedman Productions; Company Manager, Christopher D'Angelo; Stage Manager, Kenneth McGee; U.K Stage Managers, Cath Bates, Maddy Grant; Associate Design: Josh Zangen, Ryan Trupp (set); Katie Irish (costumes); Steve Andrews [U.K], D.M. Wood [U.S] (lighting); Joanna Lynne Staub (sound); Assistant Lighting [U.S.], Gordon Olson; U.K. Production Management, Paul Handley; U.K. Costume Supervisors, Iona Kenrick, Rana Fowler; Prod. Carpenter, Jim Fossi; Prod. Electrician, Brendan Quigley; Light Board Programmer, Eric Norris; Prod. Props, Scott Monroe; Prod. Sound, Beth Berkeley; House Carpenter, Dennis Maher; House Props, Kim Garnett; House Electrician, William K. Rowland; Wardrobe Supervisor, Kay Grunder; Dressers, Kimberly Prentice, Chip White; Production Assistants, Hannah Gore, Jason Pelusio; Dialect Coach, Charmian Hoare; U.S. Vocal Coach, Andrew Wade; Advertising, aka; Press, Boneau/Bryan-Brown, Chris Boneau, Jim Byk, Christine Olver

CAST Phaedra **Aimeé-Ffion Edwards**; Ms. Fawcett **Sarah Moyle**; Mr. Parsons **Harvey Robinson**; Johnny 'Rooster' Byron **Mark Rylance**; Ginger **Mackenzie Crook**; The Professor **Alan David**; Lee **John Gallagher Jr.**; Davey **Danny Kirrane**; Pea **Molly Ranson**; Tanya **Charlotte Mills**; Wesley **Max Baker**; Marky **Aiden Eyrick** or **Mark Page**; Dawn **Geraldine Hughes**; Troy Whitworth **Barry Sloane**; Frank Whitworth **Jay Sullivan**; Danny Whitworth **Richard Short**

UNDERSTUDIES Frances Mercanti-Anthony (Dawn, Ms. Fawcett), James Riordan (The Professor, Wesley), Harvey Robinson (Ginger), Richard Short (Davey, Troy Whitworth), Jay Sullivan (Lee, Mr. Parsons), Libby Woodbridge (Pea, Phaedra, Tanya)

2010-2011 AWARDS Tony Award: Best Performance by a Leading Actor in a Play (Mark Rylance); New York Drama Critics' Circle: Best Foreign Play; Best Actor (Mark Rylance); Drama League: Distinguished Performance (Mark Rylance); Outer Critic Circle: Best Actor in a Play (Mark Rylance)

SETTING Flintrock, Wiltshire, England 2011. American premiere of a new play presented in three acts with one intermission after Act 1 and a short pause between Acts 2 & 3. Originally presented at the Royal Court Theatre (London) July 13–August 22, 2009 and transferred to the Apollo Theatre January 28–April 24, 2010.

SYNOPSIS In the woods of South West England, Johnny 'Rooster' Byron, former daredevil motorcyclist and modern-day Pied Piper, is a wanted man. The council officials want to serve him an eviction notice, his son wants to be taken to the country fair, a stepfather wants to give him a serious kicking, and a motley crew of friends wants his ample supply of drugs and alcohol.

Born Yesterday

Cort Theatre; First Preview: March 31, 2011; Opening Night: April 24, 2011; 28 previews, 42 performances as of May 31, 2011

Written by Garson Kanin; Produced by Philip Morgaman, Anne Caruso, Vincent Caruso, Frankie J. Grande, James P. MacGilvray, Brian Kapetanis, Robert S. Basso, in association with Peter J. Puleo; Director, Doug Hughes; Set, John Lee Beatty; Costumes, Catherine Zuber; Lighting, Peter Kaczorowski; Original Music/Sound, David Van Tieghem; Hair/Wigs, Tom Watson; Casting, Jay Binder; Fight Director, J. David Brimmer; Production Stage Manager, Tripp Phillips; Technical Supervisor, Larry Morley; Company Manager, Brig Berney; General Management, Richards/Climan Inc.; Press, Stage Manager, Jason Hindelang; Assistant Director, Alexander Greenfield; Fight Captain, Fred Arsenault; Associate Design: Kacie Hultgren (set), David Sanderson (sound); Assistant Design: Patrick Bevilacqua, Nicole Moody, Ryan Park (costumes); Jake DeGroot (lighting); Lighting Programmer, David Sanderson; Assistant Fight Director, Turner Smith; Prod. Carpenter, Edward Diaz; Prod. Electrician, Shannon M.M. January; Prod. Sound, Jens McVoy; Head Electrician, Scott DeVerna; Head Props, Lonnie Gaddy; Props Coordinators, Scott Laule, Buist Bickley; Props Supervisor, David Levenberg; Wardrobe Supervisor, Patrick Bevilacqua; Hair Supervisor, Carmel A. Vargyas; Makeup Design, Ashley Ryan; Dressers, Erin Byrne, Ste e Chazaro, Claire Verlaet; Production Assistants, Robbie Peters, John Bantal; Assistant to Mr. Belushi, Laura Marriott; Advertising, Serino Coyne; Marketing, Type A; Press, Richard Kornberg & Associates, Don Summa, Billy Zavelson, Danielle McGarry

CAST Helen, *a maid* **Jennifer Regan**; Paul Verrall **Robert Sean Leonard**; Eddie Brock **Michael McGrath**; Bellhop **Fred Arsenault**; Another Bellhop/Bootblack **Danny Rutigliano**; A Third Bellhop/Barber **Bill Christ**; Harry Brock **Jim Belushi**; Assistant Manager **Andrew Weems**; Billie Dawn **Nina Arianda**; Ed Devery **Frank Wood**; Manicurist **Liv Rooth**; Senator Norval Hedges **Terry Beaver**; Mrs. Hedges **Patricia Hodges**

UNDERSTUDIES Liv Rooth (Billie Dawn), Bill Christ (Harry Brock), Fred Arsenault (Paul Verrall), Robert Emmet Lunney (Ed Devery, Assistant Manager, Bellhops, Barber, Bootblack), Danny Rutigliano (Eddie Brock), Andrew Weems (Senator Hedges), Jennifer Regan (Mrs. Hedges)

SETTING Washington D.C.; 1946. Act I: September; Act II: About two months later; Act III: Later that night. Revival of a play presented in three acts with one intermission and one brief pause between Acts II & III. Originally produced on Broadway at the Lyceum Theatre and subsequently Henry Miller's Theatre February 4, 1946–December 31, 1949 (starring Judy Holliday and Paul Douglas) playing 1,642 performances (see *Theatre World* Vol. 2, page 66). The show had a previous revival at the 46th Street (Richard Rodgers) Theatre January 18–June 11, 1989 (starring Ed Asner and Madeline Kahn) playing 153 performances (see *Theatre World* Vol. 45, page 23).

SYNOPSIS *Born Yesterday* is the timeless and timely story of a not-so-dumb-blonde, her less-than-honest brute of a boyfriend, and the no-nonsense reporter who helps her uncover some of the dirtiest little secrets in Washington.

Robert Sean Leonard and Nina Arianda

Nina Arianda and Patricia Hodges (photos by Carol Rosegg)

Jim Belushi, Robert Sean Leonard, Nina Arianda, and Michael McGrath

Jim Belushi, Terry Beaver, and Frank Wood

Ben Stiller, Edie Falco, and Jennifer Jason Leigh (photos by Joan Marcus)

Ben Stiller and Alison Pill (photos by Joan Marcus)

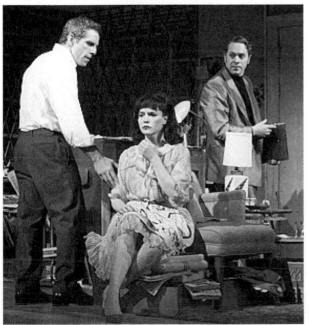

Ben Stiller, Jennifer Jason Leigh, and Thomas Sadoski

The House of Blue Leaves

Walter Kerr Theatre; First Preview: April 4, 2011; Opening Night: April 25, 2011; 21 previews, 42 performances as of May 31, 2011

Written by John Guare; Produced by Scott Rudin, Stuart Thompson, Jean Doumanian, Mary Lu Roffe/Susan Gallin/Rodger Hess, The Araca Group, Scott M. Delman, Roy Furman, Ruth Hendel, Jon B. Platt, Sonia Friedman Productions/Scott Landis; Director, David Cromer; Original Songs, John Guare; Set, Scott Pask; Costumes, Jane Greenwood; Lighting, Brian Macdevvitt; Sound, Fitz Patton & Josh Schmidt; Hair/Wigs, Tom Watson; Casting, MelCap Casting; Fight Direction, Thomas Schall; Production Stage Manager, Barclay Stiff; Production Management, Aurora Productions; General Management, Stuart Thompson Productions/Marshall B. Purdy; Company Manager, Chris Morey; Stage Manager, Kelly Beaulieu; Assistant Director, Michael Padden; Associate Design: Christine Peters, Lauren Alvarez (set), Moria Clinton (costumes), Jennifer Schriever (lighting), Joshua Reid, Joanna Lynne Staub (sound); Hair Stylist for Mr. Stiller, Lori Guidroz; Makeup Consultants, Naomi Donne, Alicce Lane; Prod. Carpenter, Brian Munroe; Prod. Electrician, Dan Coey; Head Electrician, Will King; Moving Lights, Timothy Rogers; Prod. Props Coordinator, Kathy Fabian/Propstar; Advance Props, Andrew Meeker; Head Sound Engineer, David Stollings; Wardrobe Supervisor, John A. Robelen III; Dresers, Amelia Haywood, Jill Heller, Daniel Eaton, Jennifer Hohn; Hair Supervisor, Joshua First; Hairdresser, April Schuller; Dialect Coach, Howerd Samuelson; Piano Coaches, Gerard D'Angelo, Garry Dial; Music Coach, Richard Carsey; Production Assistant, Davin DeSantis; Marketing, aka; Advertising, Serino Coyne Inc.; Press, Boneau/Bryan-Brown, Chris Boneau, Heath Schwarth, Michael Strassheim

CAST Artie Shaughnessy **Ben Stiller**; Ronnie Shaughnessy **Christopher Abbot**; Bunny Flingus **Jennifer Jason Lee**; Bananas Shaughnessy **Edie Falco**; Corrina Stroller **Alison Pill**; Head Nun **Mary Beth Hurt**; Second Nun **Susan Bennett**; Little Nun **Halley Feiffer**; Policeman **Jimmy Davis**; White Man **Tally Sessions**; Billy Einhorn **Thomas Sadoski**

UNDERSTUDIES Jim Bracchitta (Artie), Katie Kreisler (Bananas, Head Nun, Second Nun), Susan Bennett (Bunny), Tally Sessions (Billy), Amelia McClain (Corrinna, Little Nun), Jimmy Davis (Ronnie)

2010-2011 AWARDS Drama Desk Award: Outstanding Featured Actress in a Play (Edie Falco); *Theatre World Award*: Halley Feiffer

SETTING A cold apartment in Sunnyside, Queen, New York City. October 4, 1965. Revival of a black comedy presented in two acts. Originally presented at the Eugene O'Neill Theater Center in 1966. The original New York production opened Off-Broadway at the Truck and Warehouse Theatre on February 10, 1971 (featuring Mr. Stiller's mother Anne Meara as "Bunny") playing 337 perfomances (see *Theatre World* Vol. 27, page 98). In the spring of 1986 Jerry Zak's Off-Broadway revival (which featured Mr. Stiller as "Ronnie" in his New York theatre debut) at Lincoln Center's Mitzi E. Newhouse Theater transferred to Broadway on April 29 at the Vivian Beaumont, then transferred to the Plymouth Theatre October 14, where it closed March 15, 1987 after playing a total of 398 performances (see *Theatre World* Vol 42, pages 43 & 97). The revival starred John Mahoney, Swoosie Kurtz, Stockard Channing, Julie Haggerty, and subsequently Christine Baranski and Patricia Clarkson.

SYNOPSIS Set on the day of Pope Paul VI's visit to New York City, Artie Shaughnessy, a Central Park zookeeper, is trying to cope with a schizophrenic wife, an impatient girlfriend, and a bomb-making son who is AWOL from the Army, all the while dreaming of getting a blessing from the Pope to escape his lower-middle class existence and pursue his dream of becoming a popular singer and songwriter. *The House of Blue Leaves* is a satirical take on celebrity, religion, and the frequent merging of the two.

Christina Sajous, Erica Ash, Kyra DaCosta, Crystal Starr, Brandon Uranowitz, and Beth Leavel

Baby It's You!

Broadhurst Theatre; First Preview: March 26, 2011; Opening Night: April 27, 2011; 33 previews, 39 performances as of May 31, 2011

Book by Floyd Mutrux & Colin Escott, conceived by Floyd Mutrux; Produced by Warner Brothers Theatre Ventures (Gregg Maday, Executive Vice President/ Lead Producer) and American Pop Anthology (Jonathan Sanger, Producer) in association with Universal Music Group and Pasadena Playhouse (Sheldon Epps, Artistic Director; Stephen Eich, Executive Director); Directors, Floyd Mutrux & Sheldon Epps; Choreography, Birgitte Mutrux; Music Director, Shelton Becton; Set, Anna Louizos; Costumes, Lizz Wolff; Lighting, Howell Binkley; Sound, Carl Casella; Projections, Jason H. Thompson; Hair & Wigs, David H. Lawrence; Casting, Telsey + Company; Production Stage Manager, Joshua Halperin; Music Supervisor & Arrangements, Rahn Coleman; Orchestrations, Don Sebesky; Music Coordinator, John Miller; Marketing, Type A Marketing, Anne Rippey; Advertising, SpotCo; Technical Director/Production Management, Brian Lynch; General Management, Alan Wasser, Allan Williams, Aaron Lustbader; Consulting Producer, Richard Perry; For Warner Brothers: Barry Meyer (Chairman & CEO), Alan Horn (President & COO); For Warner Theatre Ventures: Raymond Wu (SVP/Development/Operations; Laura Valan (CFO), Mark Coker (SVP Finance); For American Pop Anthology: Gerald Katell (Executive Producer), Artie Ripp (Historical Consultant); Company Manager, Matthew Sher; Casting, Telsey + Company; Stage Manager, Matthew Aron Stern; Assistant Stage Manager, Jason Brouillard; Assistant Company Manager, Maia Sutton; Assistant Choreographer, Tyrone A. Jackson; Associate Design: Aimee B. Dombo, Jeremy W. Foil (Set), Sarah Sophia Lidz (costumes), Ryan O'Gara (lighting), Wallace Flores (sound), Oslyn Holder (makeup); Assistant Design: Melissa Shakun (set), Amanda Bujak (costumes), Josh Liebert, Robert Hanlon (sound), Jeff Teeter, Resa Deverich (projections), Linda Rice (hair); Costume Design Assistant, Elizabeth Van Buren; Assistant to Mr. Binkley, Michael Rummage; Automated Lighting/Moving Lighting Programmer, David Arch; Music Copying, Emily Grishman, Katharine Edmonds; Synthesizer Programmer, Karl Mansfied; Music Clearances, Jill Myers Music, Projection Image Clearances, Jay Floyd; House Carpenter, Brian McGarty; Prod. Carpenter, Chris Kluth; Automation, Robert Hentze; Flyman, Brian Bullard; House Electrician, Charlie DeVerna; Prod. Electrician, Keith Buchanan; Spotlight Op, Patrick Harrington; Projection Programming, Matthew Mellinger; House Props, Ronnie Vitelli; Prod. Props, George Wagner; Prod. Sound Supervisor, James Wilinson; Prod. Sound Engineer, Ty Lackey; Wardrobe Supervisor, James Hall; Hair Supervisor, Renee Kelly; Dressers, Jason Blair, Kay Gowenlock, Franklin Hollenbeck, Ginny Housel, Susan Kroeter, Ylena Nunez, Kathreine Sorg; Hairstylists, Patrica Marcus, Richard Fabris; Assitant to John Miller, Jennifer Coolbaugh; Assistant to Mr. Epps, Courtney Harper; Assistant to Mr. Mutrux, Ashley Mutrux; Press, The Hartman Group, Michael Hartman, Wayne Wolfe, Nicole Capatasto; Cast recording: Universal/Verve Music Group VRVB001570402

CAST Florence Greenberg **Beth Leavel**; Luther Dixon **Allan Louis**; Jocko, Chuck Jackson, Ronald Isley, Gene Chandler **Geno Henderson**; Micki, Romantic, Dionne Warwick **Erica Ash**; Mary Jane Greenberg, Lesley Gore **Kelli Barrett**; Beverly, Ruby **Kyra Da Costa**; Millie **Erica Dorfler**; Street Singer **Jahi A. Kearse**; Doris, Romantic **Crystal Starr**; Bernie Greenberg, Milt Gabler **Barry Pearl**; Shirley **Christina Sajous**; Stanley Greenberg, Murray Schwartz, Kingsman **Brandon Uranowitz**

STANDBYS Erica Ash (Shirley), Alison Cimmet (Florence), Erica Dorfler (Beverly/Ruby, Doris/Romantic, Shirley), Berlando Drake (Beverly/Ruby, Micki/Romantic/Dionne Warwick, Shirley), Adam Heller (Bernie/Milt), Jahi A. Kearse (Jocko/Jacskon/Isley/Chandler), Annette Moore (Millie, Beverly/Ruby, Micki/Romantic/Warwick, Doris/Romantic), Zachary Prince (Stanley/Scwartz/Kingsman), Ken Robinson (Jocko/Jackson, Isley/Chandler, Luther), Chelsea Morgan Stock (Lesley Gore, Mary Jane)

ORCHESTRA Shelton Becton (Coductor/Synth 1), Joel Scott (Associate Conductor/Synth 2), Tom Murray (Reeds), Ravi Best (Trumpet/Flugel), Raymond Pounds (Drums), Francisco Centeno (Electric Bass), Michael Aarons (Guitar), Charlie Descarfino (Percussion)

Beth Leavel and Allan Louis

MUSICAL NUMBERS Mr. Lee; Book of Love; Rockin' Robin; Dance With Me; Mama Said; Yakety Yak; Get a Job; The Stroll; I Met Him on a Sunday; Dedicated to the One I Love; Sixteen Candles; Tonight's the Night; Dedicated to the One I Love (reprise); Since I Don't Have You; Big John; He's So Fine; Soldier Boy; Shout; Twist And Shout; Mama Said; Mr. Bassman; Duke of Earl; Foolish Little Girl; It's My Party; Our Day Will Come; The Dark End of the Street; Rhythm of the Rain; You're So Fine; Hey Paula; Louie, Louie; You Really Got a Hold on Me; Baby It's You; Any Day Now; A Thing of the Past; Don't Make Me Over; Walk on By; Baby It's You (reprise); Tonight's the Night (reprise); Dedicated to the One I Love (reprise); I Say a Little Prayer; Shout (reprise); Twist and Shout

SETTING 1958-1965. Passaic, New Jersey and New York City. New York premiere of a new musical presented in two acts. World premiere produced at Pasadena Playhouse November 13–December 20, 2009.

SYNOPSIS *Baby It's You!* Is inspired by the true story of Florence Greenberg, the woman who changed the recording world forever. Before Motown and the British Invasion, Greenberg took the male-dominated music industry by storm, revolutionizing pop music and becoming the most influential and successful female record company president ever. After discovering one of the greatest girl-groups of all time, The Shirelles, at her daughter's high school, Greenberg packed the girls in her car, drove across the George Washington Bridge to New York City, and embarked on a trailblazing journey from New Jersey housewife to record mogul, creating the independent house of hits that was Scepter Records.

Crystal Starr, Christina Sajous, Beth Leavel, Erica Ash, and Kyra DeCosta

Crystal Starr, Erica Ash, Kyra DaCosta, Geno Henderson, and Christine Sajous

Christina Sajous and Geno Henderson

Crystal Starr (photos by Ari Mintz)

The Normal Heart

John Golden Theatre; First Preview: April 19, 2011; Opening Night: April 27, 2011; 10 previews, 40 performances as of May 31, 2011

Written by Larry Kramer; Produced by Daryl Roth, Paul Boskind and Martian Entertainment in association with Gregory Rae and Jayne Baron Sherman/ Alexander Fraser; Directors, Joel Grey & George C. Wolfe; Set, David Rockwell; Costumes, Martin Pakledinaz; Lighting, David Weiner; Projections, Batwin + Robin Productions Inc.; Original Music & Sound, David Van Tieghem; Casting, Telsey + Company; Technical Supervisor, Tech Production Services, Peter Fulbright, Mary Duffe, Colleen Houlehen, Kaitlyn Anderson; Production Stage Manager, Karen Armstrong; Marketing, Serino Coyne/Leslie Barrett; General Management, 101 Productions Ltd (Wendy Orshan, Jeffrey M. Wilson, David Auster, Elie Landau); Company Manager, Ron Gubin; Stage Manager, Matthew Farrell; Associate Design: Richard Jaris (set) David J. Kaley (costumes), Michael P. Jones (lighting), David Sanderson (sound), Bob Peterson (projections); Moving Light Programmer, Marc Polimeni; Video Programmer, Paul Vershbow; Makeup, Joseph Dulude II; Prod. Carpenter, Peter Malbuisson; Prod. Electrician, Michale S. LoBue; Prod. Props Supervisor, Kathy Fabian; Head Props, Andrew Meeker; Head Sound Operator, Nick Borisjuk; Wardrobe Supervisor, Barry Doss; Dressers, Jamie Engelhart, Bryen Shannon; Prod. Assistants, David Cohen, Brian Gold; Advertising and New Media Marketing, Serino Coyne (Nancy Coyne, Gregt Coradetti, Joaquin Esteve, Jim Glaub, Whitney Manalio Creighton, Mark Seeley); Assistants to Ms. Roth, Greg Raby, Megan Smith; Press, O+M Company, Rick Miramontez, Molly Barnett, Andy Snyder, Sam Corbett

CAST Craig Donner/Grady **Luke MacFarlane**; Mickey Marcus **Patrick Breen**; Ned Weeks **Joe Mantello**; David **Wayne Alan Wilcox**; Dr. Emma Brookner **Ellen Barkin**; Bruce Niles **Lee Pace**; Felix Turner **John Benjamin Hickey**; Ben Weeks **Mark Harelik**; Tommy Boatwright **Jim Parsons**; Hiram Keeble/Examining Doctor **Richard Topol**

UNDERSTUDIES Jordan Baker (Dr. Emma Brookner), Jon Levenson (Ben Weeks, Examining Doctor, Hiram Keebler, Mickey Marcus, Ned Weeks), Lee Aaron Rosen (Bruce Niles, Craig Donner, David, Grady, Tommy Boatwright)

2010-2011 AWARDS Tony Awards: Best Revival of a Play, Best Performance by a Featured Actress in a Play (Ellen Barkin), Best Performance by a Featured Actor in a Play (John Benjamin Hickey); Drama Desk Awards: Outstanding Revival of a Play, Outstanding Director of a Play (George C. Wolfe and Joel Grey), Outstanding Ensemble; Outer Critics Circle Award: Best Revivial of a Play, Special Achievement Award (Ellen Barkin); New York Drama Critics Circle: Special Citation; Drama League Award: Distinguised Revival of a Play; *Theatre World Awards*: Ellen Barkin and Jim Parsons

SETTING Between July 1981 and May 1984 in New York City. Broadway premiere of the revival of an Off-Broadway play presented in two acts. Originally presented at The Public Theater April 21, 1985–January 5, 1986 playing 294 performances (see *Theatre World* Vol. 41, page 114). The Worth Street Theatre revived the play at the Public Theater (in Anspacher Hall where the original production performed in 1985) April 21–June 29, 2004 (see *Theatre Word* Vol. 60, page 123). This production was inspired by a one-night only benefit reading of the play for the Actors Fund and Friends in Deed at the Walter Kerr Theatre on October 18, 2010, produced by Daryl Roth and directed by Joel Grey, starring Glenn Close, Victor Garber, Jason Butler Harner, John Benjamin Hickey, Joe Mantello, Jack McBrayer, Michael Stuhlbarg, and Patrick Wilson.

SYNOPSIS Twenty-six years after its Off-Broadway debut, *The Normal Heart* finally arrives on Broadway. The bruising story, set in the early '80s, dramatizes the outbreak of the AIDS crisis in New York and one group of gay men's fight to win recognition of their plight from a seemingly indifferent media and mayor. The action, centered on the irascible, enemy-making firebrand Ned Weeks, is largely drawn from Larry Kramer's own experiences founding—and eventually losing control of—the Gay Mens' Health Crisis, now the world's largest private organization assisting people living with AIDS.

Joel Mantello and John Benjamin Hickey

Jim Parsons and Lee Pace (photos by Joan Marcus)

Lee Pace, Jim Parsons, Joe Mantello, and Patrick Breen

The People in the Picture

Studio 54; First Preview: April 1, 2011; Opening Night: April 28, 2011; 30 previews, 37 performances as of May 31, 2011

Book and lyrics by Iris Rainer Dart, music by Mike Stoller and Artie Butler; Additional music and lyrics by Mark Warshavsky; Produced by the Roundabout Theatre Company (Todd Haimes, Artistic Director; Harold Wolpert, Managing Director; Julia C. Levy, Executive Director) in association with Tracy Aron, Al Parinello and Stefany Bergson; Director, Leonard Foglia; Musical Staging, Andy Blanenbuehler; Music Director, Paul Gemignani; Set, Riccardo Hernandez; Costumes, Ann Hould-Ward; Lighting, Howell Binkley and James F. Ingalls; Sound, Dan Moses Schreier; Projections, Elaine J. McCarthy; Hair and Wigs, Paul Huntley; Makeup, Angelina Avallone; Orchestrations, Michael Starobin; Dance Arrangements, Alex Lacamoire; Dialect Coach, Kate Wilson; Fight Director, Rick Sordelet; Production Stage Manager, Peter Wolf; Production Manager, Aurora Productions; Casting, Jim Carnahan & Stephen Kopel; General Manager, Rebecca Habel; Executive Producer, Sydney Beers; Director of Marketing and Sales Promotion, David B. Steffen; Director of Development, Lynne Gugenheim Gregory; Founding Director, Gene Feist; Associate Artistic Director, Scott Ellis; Company Manager, Karl Baudendistel; Stage Manager, Brian Bogin; Assistant Company Manager, Laura Stuart; Assistant Director, Cat Williams; Associate Musical Stager/Dance Captain, Rachel Bress; Fight Captain, Brad Bradley; Peter West (lighting), Giovanna Calabretta (wigs and hair), Shawn E. Boyle (projections), David Bullard (sound); Assistant Design: Andrew Boyce, Maruti Evans, Jenny Sawyers (set), Christopher Vergara (costumes), Sooyeon Hong, Stephen Terry (lighting), Jorge Vargas (makeup), Richard Latta, Caitlin O'Connor, Austin Switser, Vita Tzykun (projections); Foy Flying Supersior, Tim MacKay; Music Copying, Emily Grishman, Katharine Edmonds; Music Contractor: Bruce Eidem; Synthesizer Programmer, Randy Cohen; Prod. Props Supervisor, Peter Sarafin; Associate Prod. Props, Shana Burns; Props Shopper, Jen Dunlap; Moving Lights Programmer, Paul Vershbow, Austin Switser; Prod. Carpenter, Dan Hoffman; Automation, Rebecca O'Neill; Flyman, Steve Jones; Carpenters, Cory Verkuilen, Mike Widmer; Prod. Electrician, John Wooding; Deck Electrician, Paul Coltoff; Spot Ops, Barb Bartel, Peter Guernsey; Prod. Sound Engineer, Scott Anderson; House Props, Lawrence Jennino; Props Run Crew, Erin Mary Delaney, Susanne Poulin; Wardrobe Supervisor, Rick Kelly; Dressers, Melanie Hanson (Ms. Murphy), Gary Biangone, Cecilia Cruz, Becky Judd, Mary Ann Lewis-Oberpriller; Hair and Wig Supervisor, Carrie Rohm; Ms. Murphy's Hairdresser, Ruth Carsh; Hair Assistant, John McNulty; Child Wrangler, Felica Velasco; Roundabout Staff: Director of Artistic Development/Casting, Jim Carnahan; Director of Education, Greg McCaslin; Director of Finance, Susan Neiman; IT Director, Antonio Palumbo; Director of Ticketing Sales, Charlie Garbowski Jr.; Advertising, SpotCo; Press, Boneau/Bryan-Brown, Adrian Bryan-Brown, Matt Polk, Jessica Johnson, Amy Kass; Cast recording: Kritzerland Records

CAST Doovie Feldman **Hal Robinson**; Moishe Rosenwald **Alexander Gemignani**; Chayesel Fisher **Joyce Van Patten**; Yossie Pinsker **Chip Zien**; Avram Krinsky **Lewis J. Stadlen**; Chaim Bradovsky **Christopher Innvar**; Jenny **Rachel Resheff**; Bubbie/Raisel **Donna Murphy**; Red **Nicole Parker**; Hoodlums **Jeremy Davis, Jeffrey Schecter**; Hollywood Girls **Emilee Dupré, Shannon Lewis, Jessica Lea Patty, Megan Reinking**; Rabbi Velvel **Hal Robinson**; Dobrisch **Megan Reinking**; Dr. Godblum **Louis Hobson**; Young Red **Andie Mechanic**; Jerzy **Paul Anthony Stewart**; Rachel **Maya Goldman**; Swings **Brad Bradley, Rachel Bress**

UNDERSTUDIES Brad Bradley (Dr. Goldblum, Jerzy), Emilee Dupré (Dobrisch), Maya Goldman (Jenny, Young Red), Louis Hobson (Moishe Rosenwald), Andie Mechanic (Rachel), Jessica Lea Patty (Red), Jeffrey Howard Schecter (Yossie Pinsker), Lori Wilner (Bubbie/Raisel, Chayesel Fisher), Stuart Zagnit (Avram Krinsky, Doovie Feldman, Rabbi Velvel)

ORCHESTRA Paul Gemignani (Musical Director); Mark Mitchell (Associate Conductor/Keyboard); Larry Lelli (2nd Associate Conductor/Drummer, Small Percussion); Sylvia D'Avanzo (Concert Master/1st Violin); Deborah Assael (Cello); Steven Lyons (Oboe, EH, FL, Clarinet, Tenor); Don McGeen (Clarinet, Bass Clarinet, Bassoon, Baritone); Greg Thymius (Flute, Piccolo, Alto Sax, Soprano Sax); Dominic Derasse (Trumpet 1, Flugal Horn, Cornet); Bruce Eidem (Trombone, Euphonium); Phil Granger (Trumpet 2, Flugal Horn, Librarian); Randy Cohen (Synthesizer, Accordion); John Beal (Bass)

MUSICAL NUMBERS Prologue; Bread and Theatre; Matryoshka; A Workin' Mama (cut in previews); Before We Lose the Light/The Dybbuk; Remember Who You Are; Hollywood Girls; Remember Who You Are (reprise); And God Laughs; Oyfen Pripitchik; Red's Dilemma; For This; Oyfen Pripitchik (reprise); Prologue, We Were Here; Now and Then; Ich, Uch, Feh; Selective Memory; Saying Goodbye; Child of My Child; Remember Who You Are (reprise); Bread and Theatre (reprise)/We Were Here (finale)

SETTING New York City 1977 and Warsaw, Poland 1935-1946. World premiere of a new musical presented in two acts.

SYNOPSIS Once the darling of the Yiddish Theatre in pre-war Poland, now a grandmother in New York City, Bubbie has had quite a life. But what will it all mean if she can't pass on her stories to the next generation? Though her granddaughter is enchanted by her tales, her daughter Red will do anything to keep from looking back. A fiercely funny and deeply moving new musical that spans three generations, *The People in The Picture* celebrates the importance of learning from our past, and the power of laughter.

Donna Murphy and Christopher Innvar

Donna Murphy and Rachel Resheff (photos by Joan Marcus)

Spider-Man Turn Off the Dark (Still in Previews)

Foxwoods Theatre; First Previews: November 28, 2010; 167 previews as of May 31, 2011 (The production went on hiatus April 19–May 11 for creative changes)

Music & lyrics by Bono and The Edge, book by Julie Taymor & Glen Berger; Produced by Michael Cohl & Jeremiah J. Harris, Land Line Productions, Hello Entertainment/David Garfinkle/Tony Adams, Sony Pictures Entertainment, Norton Herrick & Herrick Entertainment, Billy Rovzar & Fernando Rovzar, Stephen Bronfman, Jeffrey B. Hecktman, Omneity Entertainment/Richard G. Weinberg, James L. Nederlander, Terry Allen Kramer, S2BN Entertainment, Jam Theatricals, Mayerson/Gould/Hauser/Tysoe Group, Patricia Lambrecht, Paul McGuinness in arrangement with Marvel Entertainment; Director, Julie Taymor; Choreography & Ariel Choreography, Daniel Ezralow; Sets, George Tsypin; Lighting, Donald Holder; Costumes, Eiko Ishioka; Sound, Jonathan Deans; Projections, Kyle Cooper; Masks, Julie Taymor; Hair, Campbell Young Associates, Luc Verschueren; Makeup, Judy Chin; Aeria Design, Scott Rogers; Aerial Rigging, Jaque Paquin; Projection Coordinator/Additional Content Design, Howard Werner; Arrangements & Orchestrations, David Campbell; Music Supervision, Teese Gohl; Music Director, Kim Grigsby; Music Coordinator, Antoine Silverman; Vocal Arrangements, David Campbell, Teese Gohl, Kimberly Grigsby; Additional Arrangements/Vocal Arrangements, Dawn Kenny, Rori Coleman; Associate Set Design, Rob Bissinger; Resident Director, Keith Batten; Resident Choreographer, Cherice Barton; Production Stage Managers, C. Randall White & Kathleen E. Purvis; Casting, Telsey + Company; Marketing Director, Len Gill; Marketing, Keith Hurd; Associate Producer, Anne Tanaka; Production Management, Juniper Street Productions & MB Productions; General Management, Alan Wasser, Allan Williams, Aaron Lustbader; Executive Producers, Glenn Orsher, Martin McCallum, Adam Silberman; Consulting Executive Producer, Stephen Howard; Technical Director, Fred Gallo; Company Manager, Marc Borsak; Advertising, Serino Coyne; Press, O+M Company, Rick Miramontez, Andy Snyder, Jaron Caldwell, Elizabeth Wagner, Sam Corbett; Production Credits Post-Hiatus: Additional Book, Roberto Aguirre-Sacasa; Creative Consultant, Philip Wm. McKinley; Additional Choreography, Chase Brock; Resident Choreographer, Jason Snow; Music Producer, Paul Bogaev; Prosthetics, Louie Zakarian.

CAST * Mary Jane Watson **Jennifer Damiano**; Peter Parker/Spider-Man **Reeve Carney**; Jimmy-6 (*Geek Chorus*) **Gideon Glick**; Professor Cobwell (*Geek Chorus*) **Jonathan Schwartz**; Grim Hunter (*Geek Chorus*) **Mat Devine**; Miss Arrow (*Geek Chorus*) **Alice Lee**; Arachne **T.V. Carpio**; Classics Teacher **Isabel Keating**; Flash (*A Bully*) **Matt Caplan**; Boyle (*A Bully*) **Dwayne Clark**; Kong (*A Bully*) **Luther Creek**; Meeks (*A Bully*) **Joshua Kobak**; Uncle Ben **Ken Marks**; Aunt May **Isabel Keating**; MJ's Father **Patrick Page**; Normon Osborn/The Green Goblin **Patrick Page**; Emily Osborn **Laura Beth Wells**; J. Jonah Jameson **Michael Mulheren**; Hero Flyer **Joshua Kobak**; Green Goblin Flyer **Collin Baja**; Swarm Exterminator Flyer **Craig Henningsen**; Purse Snatcher **Sean Samuels**; Busker **Dwayne Clark**; *The Sinister Six*: Carnage **Collin Baja**; Kraven the Hunter **Joshua Kobak**; The Lizard **Brandon Rubendall**; Electro **Emmanuel Brown**; Swiss Miss **Sean Samuels**; Swarm **Gerald Avery**; Citizens, Weavers, Students, Lab Assistants, Reporters, Generals, Spider-Men, Secretaries, Soldiers, Furies, and Aerialists **Gerald Avery, Collin Baja, Marcus Bellamy, Emmanuel Brown, Jeb Brown, Matt Caplan, Dwayne Clark, Luther Creek, Craig Henningsen, Dana Marie Ingraham, Ayo Jackson, Isabel Keating, Joshua Kobak, Heather Lang, Natalie Lomonte, Ken Marks, Kristen Martin, Jodi McFadden, Kristen Faith Oei, Jennifer Christine Perry, Brandon Rubendall, Sean Samuels, Dollar Tan, Christopher W. Tierney, Laura Beth Wells**; Swings **Kevin Aubin, Daniel Case, Daniel Curry, Erin Elliott, Ari Loeb, Kevin C. Loomis, América Olivo, Kyle Post;** Peter Parker/Spider-Man at certain performances **Matthew James Thomas**

*Natalie Mendoza was originally cast as "Arachne" but had to depart the show in the first weeks of previews after sustaining an injury. The "Geek Chorus" was eliminated in the revamped version, and several roles changed as the structure of the show changed. Natalie Lomonte and Bethany Moore were added to the ensemble; Jessica Leigh Brown and Joey Taranto were additional swings. *Theatre World* Volume 68 will list the updated cast credits as well as full production credits for the show's eventual opening night of June 14, 2011.

ORCHESTRA Kimberly Grigsby (Conductor); Charles duChateau (Associate Conductor/Keyboard); Zane Carney, Matt Beck, Ben Butler (Guitar); Aiden Moore, Richard Hammond (Bass); Jon Epcar (Drums); Billy Jay Stein (Keyboard); John Clancy (Percussion);: Bill Ruyle (Hammered Dulcimer/Percussion); Antoine Silverman (Concert Master); Christopher Cardona (Viola/Violin); Anja Wood (Cello); Don Downs, Tony Kadleck (Trumpets); Theresa MacDonnell (French Horn); Marcus Rojas (Trombone/Tuba) Aaron Heick (Reeds)

MUSICAL NUMBERS *Initial Previews*: Splash Page, Behold and Wonder, Bullying By Numbers, No More, D.I.Y. World, Bouncing Off the Walls, Rise Above, Pull the Trigger, Picture This, I'll Take Manhattan, Spider-Man Rising, Turn Off the Dark, Walk Away, Think Again, Sinistereo, Deeply Furious, If the World Should End, The Boy Falls From the Sky, Love Me Or Kill Me; *Added Songs*: The Myth of Arachne, A Freak Like Me, Spider-Man!, I Just Can't Walk Away, Finale – A New Dawn

World premiere of a new musical presented in two acts.

SYNOPSIS Drawing from more than 40 years of Marvel comic books for inspiration, *Spider-Man Turn Off the Dark* spins a new take on the mythic tale of Peter Parker, a teenager whose unremarkable life is turned upside-down when he's bitten by a genetically-altered spider and wakes up the next morning clinging to the ceiling. As he discovers he has been endowed with astonishing powers, and also great responsibility, Peter learns to navigate the perilous and peculiar demands of being a web-slinging superhero.

Editor's Note: *Spider-Man Turn Of f the Dark* was originally slated to bow December 21, 2010, but was postponed three times (January 11, February 7, then to March 15, 2011. On March 11, after encountering weeks of technical challenges, safety problems, and cast injuries, the producers decided to close the production April 18–May 11 and open June 14, 2011 to allow rehearsal time to re-tool the show and add new creative staff. The headline-making 68 million dollar production broke the record for playing the most previews of any Broadway show in history. Previously the record had been held by Jackie Mason and Mike Mortmon's 1969 play, *A Teaspoon Every Four Hours*, which played 97 previews and 1 performance. The 1976 musical revue *Let My People Come* played 128 previews but never had an official opening night.

Reeve Carney (photo by Jacob Cohl)

PLAYED THROUGH/CLOSED THIS SEASON

The Addams Family

Lunt-Fontanne Theatre; First Preview: March 8, 2010; Opening Night: April 8, 2010; 35 previews, 475 performances as of May 31, 2011

Book by Marshall Brickman & Rick Elice, music by Andrew Lippa; Based on characters created by Charles Addams; Produced by Stuart Oken, Roy Furman, Michael Leavitt, Five Cent Productions, Stephen Schuler, Decca Theatricals, Scott M. Delman, Stuart Ditsky, Terry Allen Kramer, Stephanie P. McClelland, James L. Nederlander, Eva Price, Jam Theatricals (Arny Granat, Jerry Mickelson, Steve Traxler)/Mary Lu Roffe, Pittsburgh CLO/Jay & Cindy Gutterman/Mort Swinsky, Vivek Tiwary/Gary Kaplan, The Weinstein Company/Clarence LLC, Adam Zotovich/Tribe Theatricals (Carl Moellenberg, Wendy Federman, Jamie deRoy, Larry Hirschhorn) in special arrangement with Elephant Eye Theatrical; Direction/Design, Phelim McDermott & Julian Crouch; Choreography, Sergio Trujillo; Creative Consultant, Jerry Zaks; Lighting, Natasha Katz; Sound, Acme Sound Partners, Puppetry, Basil Twist; Hair, Tom Watson; Makeup, Angelina Avallone; Special Effects, Gregory Meeh; Orchestrations, Larry Hochman; Music Director, Mary-Mitchell Campbell; Dance Arrangements, August Eriksmoen; Vocal Arrangements & Incidental Music, Andrew Lippa; Casting, Telsey + Company; Marketing, Type A Marketing; Music Coordinator, Michael Keller; Production Supervisor, Beverley Randolph; Production Management, Aurora Productions; General Management, 101 Productions Ltd.; Company Manager, Sean Free; Stage Manager, Scott Taylor Rollison; Assistant Stage Manager, Allison A. Lee; Associate Directors, Heidi Miami Marshal, Steve Bebout; Associate Choreographer, Dontee Kiehn; Associate Company Manager, Chris D'Angelo; Associate Design: Frank McCullough (set), MaryAnn D. Smith, David Kaley (costumes), Yael Lubetzky (lighting), Jason Crystal (sound), Jeremy Chernick (special effects), Ceili Clemens (puppets); Automated Lighting, Aland Henderson; Assistant Design: Lauren Alvarez, Jeffrey Hinchee, Christine Peters (set), Sarah Laux (costumes), Joel Shier (lighting), Jorge Vargas (makeup); Costume Assistant, Jennifer A. Jacob; Assistant in Puppetry, Meredith Miller; Music Preparation, Kaye-Houston Music Inc.; Electronic Music Programmer, James Abbott; Additional Orchestrations, August Eriksmoen, Danny Troob; Additional Drum & Percussion Arrangements, Damien Bassman; Advertising, Serino Coyne, Sandy Block, Angelo Desimini; Interactive Marketing, Situation Interactive; Press, The Publicity Office, Marc Thibodeau, Jeremy Shaffer, Michael S. Borowski, Matthew Fasano; Cast recording: Decca 001428002

CAST *The Addams Family:* Gomez Addams **Nathan Lane**[*1]; Morticia Addams **Bebe Neuwirth**; Uncle Fester **Kevin Chamberlin**[*2]; Grandma **Jackie Hoffman**; Wednesday Addams **Krysta Rodriguez**[*3]; Pugsley Addams **Adam Riegler**[*4]; Lurch **Zachary James**; *The Beineke Family:* Mal Beineke **Terrence Mann**[*5]; Alice Beineke **Carolee Carmello**[*6]; Lucas Beineke **Wesley Taylor**[*7]; *The Addams Ancestors*[*8]: **Erick Buckley, Rachel de Benedet, Matthew Gumley, Fred Inkley, Morgan James, Clark Johnson, Barrett Martin, Jessica Lea Patty, Liz Ramos, Charlie Sutton, Aléna Watters**; Standby for Gomez Addams and Mal Beineke **Merwin Foard**; Swings[*9] **Jim Borstelmann, Colin Cunliffe, Valerie Fagan, Samantha Sturm**

UNDERSTUDIES For Gomez: Jim Borstelmann; For Morticia: Rachel deBenedet, Jessica Lea Patty/Stephanie Gibson, Becca Ayers; For Uncle Fester: Jim Borstelmann, Erick Buckley, For Wednesday: Morgan James, Jessica Lea Patty/Lisa Karlin, Courtney Wolfson; For Grandma: Valerie Fagan, Becca Ayers; For Pugsley: Matthew Gumley/Logan Rowland; For Lurch: Fred Inkley, Barrett Martin/Tom Berklund; For Mal: Fred Inkley; For Alice: Valerie Fagan, Morgan James/Becca Ayers; For Lucas: Colin Cunliffe, Clark Johnsen/Mo Brady

*Succeeded by: 1. Roger Rees (3/22/11) 2. Brad Oscar (3/8/11) 3. Rachel Potter (3/8/11) 4. Matthew Gumley, Adam Riegler 5. Adam Grupper (3/8/11) 6. Heidi Blickenstaff (3/8/11) 7. Jesse Swenson (3/8/11) 8. Ancestor Replacements:

Becca Ayers, Tom Berklund, Mo Brady, Erick Buckley, Stephanie Gibson, Curtis Holbrook, Lisa Karlin, Reed Kelly, Allison Thomas Lee, Logan Rowland, Courtney Wolfson 9. Added Swings: Michael Buchanan, Mike Cannon, Dontee Kiehn

ORCHESTRA Mary Mitchell Campbell (Conductor), Chris Fenwick/Marco Paguia (Associate Conductor/keyboard 1), Victoria Paterson (Concert Master/Violin), Sean Carney (Violin), Hiroko Taguchi (Viola), Allison Seidner (Cello), Tony Kadleck (Lead Trumpet), Bud Burridge (Trumpet), Randy Andos (Trombones/Tuba), Erica Von Kleist (Reed 1), Charles Pillow (Reed 2), Mark Thrasher (Reed 3), Zohar Schondorf (French Horn), Damien Bassman (Drums), Dave Kuhn (Bass), Will Van Dyke (Keyboard 2), Jim Hershman (Guitars), Billy Miller (Percussion)

MUSICAL NUMBERS Overture, When You're an Addams, Pulled, Where Did We Go Wrong, One Normal Night, Morticia, What If, Full Disclosure, Waiting, Full Disclosure – Part 2, Entr'acte, Just Around the Corner, The Moon and Me, Happy/Sad, Crazier Than You, Let's Not Talk About Anything Else But Love, In the Arms, Live Before We Die, Tango de Amor, Move Toward the Darkness

SETTING The Addams Family mansion in Central Park, New York City. New York premiere of a new musical presented in two acts. World premiere (out-of-town tryout) at the Ford Center for the Performing Arts Oriental Theatre in Chicago, Illinois, November 13, 2009–January 10, 2010.

SYNOPSIS Based on the beloved *The New Yorker* cartoon characters created by American cartoonist Charles Addams, *The Addams Family* is a new musical comedy about the ghoulish clan that lives by its own rules in a haunted mansion. The macabre family is put to the test when daughter Wednesday falls for the normal "boy next door," Lucas Beineke. When the Beineke family comes to dinner, Gomez, Morticia, Wednesday, Pugsley, Fester, Grandma, and Lurch are sent headlong into a night that will change the family forever.

Heidi Blickenstaff, Zachary James, and Adam Grupper

Kevin Chamberlin, Jackie Hoffman, and Roger Rees (photos by Jeremy Daniel)

American Idiot

St. James Theatre; First Preview: March 24, 2010; Opening Night: April 20, 2010; Closed April 24, 2011; 26 previews, 422 performances

Music by Green Day (Billie Joe Armstrong, Mike Dirnt, Tré Cool), lyrics by Billie Joe Armstrong, book by Billie Joe Armstrong and Michael Mayer; Produced by Tom Hulce, Ira Pittelman, Ruth and Stephen Hendel, Vivek J. Tiwary and Gary Kaplan, Aged in Wood and Burnt Umber, Scott M. Delman, Latitude Link, HOP Theatricals and Jeffrey Finn, Larry Welk, Chris Bensinger/Michael Filerman and Carl Moellenberg/Deborah Taylor, Allan S. Gordon and Élan V. McAllister, Berkeley Repertory Theatre, in association with Awaken Entertainment (Jennifer Maloney and Steve Kantor), John Pinckard and John Domo; Director, Michael Mayer; Choreographer, Steven Hoggett; Musical Supervision, Arrangements, and Orchestrations, Tom Kitt; Additional Lyrics, Mike Dirnt & Tré Cool, Set, Christine Jones; Costumes, Andrea Lauer; Lighting, Kevin Adams; Sound, Brian Ronan; Video/Projections, Darrel Maloney; Casting, Jim Carnahan, Carrie Gardner; Production Stage Manager, James Harker; Technical Supervisor, Hudson Theatrical Associates, Neil A. Mazzella, Sam Ellis, Irene Wang; Music Coordinator, Michael Keller; General Management, Abbie M. Strassler; Marketing, Type A Marketing (Anne Rippey, Nick Pramik, Janette Rouch); Music Director, Carmel Dean; Associate Choreographer, Lorin Latarro; Associate Director, Johanna McKeon; Associate Producers, SenovvA (K Lee Harvey, Arianna Knapp, Jon Kimbell), Tix Productions, Tracy Straus and Barney Straus, Lorenzo Thione and Jay Kuo, Pat Magnarella, Christopher Maring; Company Manager, Kimberly Helms; Production Vocal Supervisor, Liz Caplan Vocal Studios LLC; Stage Manager, Freda Farrell; Assistant Stage Manager, Bethany Russell; Assistant Company Manager, Rachel Scheer; Dance Captain, Lorin Latarro; Assistant Dance Captain, Ben Thompson; Assistant Director, Austin Regan; Hair Design, Brandon Dailey; Wigs, Leah Loukas; Makeup, Amy Jean Wright; Flying, Flying by Foy; Associate Design: Edward Coco (set), Chloe Chapin (costumes), Aaron Sporer (lighting), Ashley Hanson (sound), Dan Scully (video/projections); Assistant Design: Damon Pelletier (set), Janice Lopez (costumes), Benjamin Travis (lighting); Moving Light Programmer, Victor Seastone; Video/Projections, SenovvA (Jeff Cady, Programmer; Alex Marshall, Assistant); Craft Artisan, Jennilee Houghton; Music Preparation, Colleen Darnall; Management Associate, Scott Armstrong; Advertising, Serino Coyne Inc., Press, The Hartman Group, Michael Hartman, Leslie Baden, Alyssa Hart; Cast recording: Reprise Records 523724

CAST Johnny **John Gallagher Jr.** [*1]; Will **Michael Esper** [*2]; Tunny **Stark Sands** [*3]; Heather **Mary Faber** [*4]; Whatsername **Rebecca Naomi Jones**; St. Jimmy **Tony Vincent** [*5]; The Extraordinary Girl **Christina Sajous** [*6]; Ensemble [*7] **Declan Bennett, Andrew Call, Gerard Canonico, Miguel Cervantes, Joshua Henry** [*7], **Brian Charles Johnson, Leslie McDonel, Chase Peacock, Theo Stockman, Ben Thompson, Alysha Umphress, Libby Winters**; Standby for Johnny, Will, Tunny **Van Hughes** [*8]; Swings [*8] **Joshua Kobak, Lorin Latarro, Omar Lopez-Cepero, Aspen Vincent**

UNDERSTUDIES Declan Bennett (Will), Andrew C. Call (St. Jimmy), Joshua Kobak (St. Jimmy), Leslie McDonel (Heather, Whatsername), Chase Peacock (Johnny), Christina Sajous (Whatsername), Ben Thompson (Tunny), Aspen Vincent (The Extraordinary Girl), Libby Winters (Heather, The Extraordinary Girl)

*Succeeded by: 1. Van Hughes 2. Justin Guarini (3/1/11) 3. David Larsen (3/1/11) 4. Jenna de Waal 5. Billie Joe Armstrong (10/27/11) Tony Vincent (10/29), Billie Joe Armstrong (1/1/11), Melissa Etheridge (2/1/11), Billie Joe Armstrong (2/8/11), Davey Havok (3/1/11), Billie Joe Armstrong (3/15/11) 6. Libby Winters (2/27/11) 7. Wallace Smith; Additional Ensemble: Krystina Alabado, Sean Wing, Jason Kappus 8. Additional and Replacements: Sydney Harcourt, Corbin Reid, P.J. Griffith, Jennifer Bowles, Mikey Winslow

BAND Carmel Dean (Conductor/Keyboard/Accordion), Trey Files (Drums/Percussion), Michael Aarons (Guitar 1), Alec Berlin (Guitar 2), Dan Grennes (Bass), Cenovia Cummins (Violin), Alissa Smith (Viola), Amy Ralske (Cello), Jared Stein (Associate Conductor)

MUSICAL NUMBERS American Idiot, Jesus of Suburbia, City of the Damned, I Don't Care, Dearly Beloved, Tales of Another Broken Home, Holiday, Boulevard of Broken Dreams, Favorite Son, Are We the Waiting, St. Jimmy, Give Me Novacaine, Last of the American Girls/She's a Rebel, Last Night on Earth, Too Much Too Soon, Before the Lobotomy, Extraordinary Girl, Before the Lobotomy (reprise), When It's Time, Know Your Enemy, 21 Guns, Letterbomb, Wake Me Up When September Ends, Homecoming, The Death of St. Jimmy, East 12th Street, Nobody Likes You, Rock and Roll Girlfriend, We're Coming Home Again, Whatsername

SETTING Time: The Recent Past. Place: Jingletown, U.S.A. New York premiere of a new musical presented without intermission. Developed at Berkeley Repertory Theatre November–December 2008 and New York Stage and Film and the Powerhouse Theater at Vassar, July 2009. World premiere at Berkeley Repertory's Roda Theatre (Tony Taccone, Artistic Director; Susan Medak, Managing Director) September 4–November 15, 2009 prior to its Broadway engagement.

SYNOPSIS Based on Green Day's Grammy® Award-winning rock opera album of the same name, American Idiot follows the exhilarating journey of a new generation of young Americans as they strive to find meaning in a post 9/11 world, borne along by Green Day's electrifying score. The musical includes every song from the acclaimed album as well as several songs from the band's Grammy® Award-winning new release, 21st Century Breakdown.

Christina Sajous and Stark Sands

Tony Vincent and John Gallagher Jr (photos by Paul Kolnik)

Christopher Walken, Anthony Mackie, and Zoe Kazan

Christopher Walken (photos by Joan Marcus)

Christopher Walken and Sam Rockwell

A Behanding in Spokane

Gerald Schoenfeld Theatre; First Preview: February 15, 2010; Opening Night: March 4, 2010; Closed June 6, 2010; 20 previews, 108 performances

Written by Martin McDonagh; Produced by Robert Fox, Carole Shorenstein Hays, Debra Black, Stephanie P. McClelland, Ostar, Roger Berlind, Scott Rudin, Shubert Organization (Philip J. Smith, Chairman; Robert E. Wankel, President) in association with Robert G. Bartner, Lorraine Kirke, Jamie deRoy/Rachel Neubuger; Presented in association with the Atlantic Theater Company (Neil Pepe, Artistic Director; Jeffory Lawson, Managing Director); Director, John Crowley; Sets & Costumes, Scott Pask; Lighting, Brian MacDevitt; Original Music & Sound, David Van Tieghem; Casting, Jim Carnahan; Technical Supervisor, Theatersmith Inc.; General Management, Nina Lannan Associates, Maggie Brohn; Production Stage Manager, Frank Lombardi; Associate Producers, Erich Jungwirth, Richard Jordan; Company Manager, Beverly Edwards; Stage Manager, Lisa Buxbaum; Associate Company Manager, Steve Dow; Assistant Director, JV Mercanti; Production Assistant, Timothy Eaker; Associate Design: Antje Ellerman (set), Valerie Ramshur (costumes), Jennifer Schriever (lighting), David Sanderson (sound); Assistant Set, Lauren Alvarez; Assistant to Mr. Pask, Warren Stiles; Automated Lighting Programmer, Timothy F. Rogers; Makeup, Angelina Avallone; Prosthetic Effects Design, Prosthetic Renaissance Inc., Mike Marino, Hayes Vilandry, Chris Kelly; Production Properties, Kathy Fabian/Propstar; Specialty Prop Artisan, Craig Grigg; Propstar Assistants, Tim Ferro, Carrie Mossman; Advertising, SpotCo; Press, Boneau/Bryan-Brown, Chris Boneau, Susanne Tighe, Christine Olver

CAST Carmichael **Christopher Walken**; Mervyn **Sam Rockwell**; Marilyn **Zoe Kazan**; Toby **Anthony Mackie**

UNDERSTUDIES Glenn Fleshler (Carmichael), Dashiell Eaves (Mervyn), Meredith Forlenza (Marilyn), Tory Kittles (Toby)

SETTING A hotel room in Spokane, Washington; the present. World premiere of a new play presented without intermission.

SYNOPSIS In Irish playwright Martin McDonagh's new dark comedy (and his first set in America) *A Behanding in Spokane*, the title is just the starting point. Take a man searching for his missing hand (Walken), two con artists out to make a few hundred bucks (Mackie and Kazan), and an overly curious hotel clerk (Rockwell), and the rest is up for grabs.

Christopher Walken and Sam Rock

Billy Elliot

Imperial Theatre; First Preview: October 1, 2008; Opening Night: November 13, 2008; 40 previews, 1,061 performances as of May 31, 2011

Music by Elton John, book and lyrics by Lee Hall; based on the Universal Pictures/Studio Canal film *Billy Elliot* with screenplay by Lee Hall and direction by Stephen Daldry; Produced by Universal Pictures Stage Productions, Working Title Films, Old Vic Productions, in association with Weinstein Live Entertainment & Fidelity Investments; Director, Stephen Daldry; Choreography, Peter Darling; Associate Director, Julian Webber; Sets, Ian MacNeil; Costumes, Nicky Gillibrand; Lighting, Rick Fisher; Sound, Paul Arditti; Producers, Tim Bevan, Eric Fellner, Jon Fin, Sally Greene; Executive Producers, David Furnish, Angela Morrison; Musical Supervision and Orchestrations, Martin Koch; Music Director, David Chase; Associate Choreographer, Kathryn Dunn; Assistant Choreographer, Nikki Belsher; Hair/Wigs/Makeup, Campbell Young; U.K. Associate Design: Paul Atkinson (set), Claire Murphy (costumes), Vic Smerdon (lighting/programmer), John Owens (sound); Adult Casting, Tara Rubin; Children's Casting, Nora Brennan; Resident Director, B.T. McNicholl; Production Stage Manager, Bonnie L. Becker; Music Contractor, Michael Keller; Production Supervisors, Arthur Siccardi, Patrick Sullivan; General Management, Nina Lannan Associates/Devin Keudell; U.K. Casting, Pippa Ailion; Company Manager, Greg Arst; Associate Company Manager, Carol. M. Oune; Assistant Company Manager, Ashley Berman; Stage Manager, Charles Underhill; Assistant Stage Managers, Scott Rowen, Mary Kathryn Flynt; Supervising Dialect Coach (U.K.), William Conacher; Resident Dialect Coach, Ben Furey; Fight Director, David S. Leong; Dance Captains, Greg Graham & Cara Kjellman; Fight Captain, Grady McLeod Bowman; Choreographic Supervision, Ellen Kane; Staging and Dance Assistant, Lee Proud; Associate Music Director/Conductor, Shawn Gough; U.S. Associate Design: Brian Russman (costumes), Daniel Walker (lighting), Tony Smolenski IV (sound); Moving Lights, David Arch; Music Copying, Emily Grishman Music Preparation; Ballet Instructors, Finis Jhung, Francois Perron; Acrobat Instructor, Hector Salazar; Marketing, Allied Live; Advertising, SpotCo; Press, The Hartman Group; London Cast recording: Decca Broadway B0006 130-72

CAST Billy[*1] **Alex Ko** or **Jacob Clemente** or **Michael Dameski** or **Liam Redhead** or **Dayton Tavares**; Mrs. Wilkinson **Kate Hennig**[*2]; Dad **Gregory Jbara**; Grandma **Carole Shelley**[*3]; Tony **Jeff Kready**[*3]; George **Joel Hatch**; Michael **Jake Evan Schwencke**[*4]; Debbie **Izzy Hanson-Johnston**[*5]; Small Boy[*6] **Seth Fromowitz** or **Luke Trevisan**; Big Davey **Rick Hilsabeck**[*7]; Lesley **Amber Stone**[*8]; Scab/Posh Dad **Donnie Kehr**[*9]; Mum **Stephanie Kurtzuba**[*10]; Mr. Braithwaite **Thommie Retter**; Tracey Atkinson **Ruby Rakos**; Older Billy/Scottish Dancer **Stephen Hanna**; Mr. Wilkerson **David Hibbard**[*11]; Pit Supervisor **J. Austin Eyer**[*12]; Tall Boy/Posh Boy **Kylend Hetherington**[*13]; Clipboard Woman **Liz Pearce**; "Expressing Yourself" Dancers[*14] **Grady McLeod Bowman, Brad Bradley, C.K. Edwards, J. Austin Eyer, David Hibbard, David Larsen, Amber Stone, Grant Turner**; Ensemble[*15] **Grady McLeod Bowman, Brad Bradley, C.K. Edwards, J. Austin Eyer, Eric Gunhus, Stephen Hanna, David Hibbard, Rick Hilsabeck, Aaron Kaburick, Donnie Kehr, Stephanie Kurtzuba, David Larsen, Merle Louise, Liz Pearce, Thommie Retter, Amber Stone, Grant Turner**; Ballet Girls[*16] **Ava DeMary, Eboni Edwards, Georgi James, Marina Micalizzi, Tessa Netting, Maddy Novak, Kara Oates, Ruby Rakos, Kendra Tate, Holly Taylor**; Swings[*17] **Kyle DesChamps, David Eggers, Brianna Fragomeni, Chelsea Galembo, Cara Kjellman, David Koch, Robbie Roby, Heather Tepe, Natalie Wisdom**

*Succeeded by: 1. Liam Redhead and Michael Dameski departed 8/29/10 and 9/5/10, respectively; Peter Mazurowski joined the cast 8/29/10; Joseph Harrington began performances 10/24/10; Dayton Tavares departed 10/12/10; Tade Biesinger began performances 5/17/11 2. Emily Skinner (10/2/11) 3. Will Chase (9/1/10) 4. David Bologna returned to the show 6/16/10–8/8/10 and alternated the role with Jake Evan Schwenke; Mr. Schwenke took a leave 8/1/10–10/21/10 then departed the show 1/30/11; Gabriel Rush alternated 8/8/10–3/6/11; Neil McCaffrey joined

as an alternate 8/14/10; Cameron Clifford joined as an alternate 3/10/11 5. Georgi James (6/28/10), Lilla Crawford (3/8/11) 6. Alex Dreier (6/27/11) or Zachary Maitlin (11/2010) 7. Brad Nacht 8. Stephanie Kurtzuba (Feb. 2011) 9. Drew McVety (Aug. 2010) 10. Laura Marie Duncan (10/5/10) 11. Kevin Bernard, Brad Bradley 12. Austin Lesch 13. Ben Cook 14. Michael Arnold, Austin Lesch, Eugene Fleming, Jason Babinsky, Kevin Bernard 15. Eugene Fleming, Kevin Bernard, Laura Marie Duncan, Christopher Brian Williams, Thad Turner Wilson 16. Aly Brier, Makenzi Rae Fischbach, Annabelle Kempf, Kayla Vanderbilt 17. Stephen Carrasco, Jeremy Davis, Alison Levenberg, Michaeljon Slinger, Ryan Steele, Caroline Workman

ORCHESTRA David Chase (Conductor); Shawn Gough (Associate Conductor/Keyboards); Ed Salkin, Rick Heckman, Mike Migliore, Jay Brandford (Reeds); James Dela Garza, John Dent, Alex Holton (Trumpets); Dick Clark, Jack Schatz (Trombones); Roger Wendt, Eva Conti (French Horns); Joseph Joubert (Assistant Conductor/Keyboards); JJ McGeehan (Guitar); Randy Landau (Bass); Gary Seligson (Drums); Howard Joines (Percussion/Assistant Conductor)

MUSICAL NUMBERS The Stars Look Down, Shine, We'd Go Dancing, Solidarity, Expressing Yourself, Dear Billy (Mum's Letter), Born to Boogie, Angry Dance, Merry Christmas Maggie Thatcher, Deep Into the Ground, He Could Go and He Could Shine, Electricity, Once We Were Kings, Dear Billy (Billy's Reply), Company Celebration

Neil McCaffrey

SETTING A small mining town in County Durham, Northeast England, 1984–1985. Act 1: The eve of the Miner's Strike. Act 2: Six months later. American premiere of a musical presented in two acts. World premiere at the Victoria Palace Theatre (London), March 31, 2005 where it is still running.

SYNOPSIS Set behind the political backdrop of England's coal miner strike, *Billy Elliot The Musical* is a funny, heart-warming and feel-good celebration of one young boy's dream to break free from the expectations of his middle class roots. Based on the enormously popular film, this powerful new musical is the story of a boy who discovers he has a special talent for dance.

Tade Biesinger and the Company (photos by Carol Rosegg)

Chicago

Ambassador Theatre; First Preview: October 23, 1996; Opening Night: November 14, 1996; 25 previews, 6,040 performances as of May 31, 2011

Lyrics by Fred Ebb, music by John Kander, book by Fred Ebb and Bob Fosse; based on the play by Maurine Dallas Watkins; Production based on the 1996 City Center *Encores!* production; Original production directed and choreographed by Bob Fosse; Produced by Barry & Fran Weissler/Kardana/Hart Sharp Productions, in association with Live Nation; Director, Walter Bobbie; Choreography, Ann Reinking in the style of Bob Fosse; Supervising Music Director, Rob Fisher; Music Director, Leslie Stifelman; Set, John Lee Beatty; Costumes, William Ivey Long; Lighting, Ken Billington; Sound, Scott Lehrer; Orchestrations, Ralph Burns; Dance Arrangements, Peter Howard; Adaptation, David Thompson; Musical Coordinator, Seymour Red Press; Hair/Wigs, David Brian Brown; Casting, James Calleri/Duncan Stewart (current), Jay Binder (original); Technical Supervisor, Arthur P. Siccardi; Dance Supervisor, Gary Chryst; Production Stage Manager, David Hyslop; Associate Producer, Alecia Parker; General Manager, B.J. Holt; Company Manager, Jean Haring; Stage Managers, Terrence J. Witter, Mindy Farbrother; Assistant Choreographer, Debra McWaters; Dance Captains, Gregory Butler, Bernard Dotson, Gabriela Garcia; Associate General Manager, Hilary Hamilton; General Manager Associate, Stephen Spadaro; Assistant Director, Jonathan Bernstein; Press, The Publicity Office, Jeremy Shaffer; Cast recording: RCA 68727-2

CAST Velma Kelly **Terra C. MacLeod**[1]; Roxie Hart **Ruthie Henshall**[2]; Amos Hart **Raymond Bokhour**[3]; Matron "Mama" Morton **Terri White**[4]; Billy Flynn **Matthew Settle**[5]; Mary Sunshine **D. Vogel**[6]; Fred Casely **Dan LoBuono**[7]; Sergeant Fogarty **Adam Zotovitch**; Liz **Nicole Bridgewater**; Annie **Solange Sandy**; June **Donna Marie Asbury**; Hunyak **Nili Bassman**; Mona **Dylis Croman**[8]; Go-To-Hell-Kitty **Melissa Rae Mahon**; Harry/The Jury **Shawn Emanjomeh**[9]; Aaron/"Me and My Baby" Specialty **James T. Lane**[10]; Doctor/Judge **Jason Patrick Sands**; Martin Harrison/"Me and My Baby" Specialty **Michael Cusumano**[11]; Bailiff/Court Clerk **Greg Reuter**[12]

UNDERSTUDIES Melissa Rae Mahon (Roxie/Velma), Jill Nicklaus (Roxie), Donna Marie Asbury (Velma, "Mama" Morton), Jason Patrick Sands (Billy), James T. Lane (Amos), Adam Zotovich (Amos), Nicole Bridgewater ("Mama" Morton), David Kent/Brian Spitulnik (Fred Casely, "Me and My Baby"), J. Loeffelholtz (Mary Sunshine); Gabriela Garcia, David Kent, Sharon Moore, Brian Spitulnik (All other roles); Eddie Bennett, Jennifer Dunne (Swings)

*Succeeded by: 1. Amra-Faye Wright (7/13/10), Leigh Zimmerman (10/8/10), Amra-Faye Wright (April 2011) 2. Charlotte d'Amboise (8/30/10), Bianca Marroquin (12/20/10), Christie Brinkley (4/8/11) 3. Tom Riis Farrell, Raymond Bokhour (8/30/10), Robert Creighton (11/29/10), Raymond Bokhour (2/24/11) 4. Carol Woods (7/13/10), Roz Ryan (9/2/10), LaVon Fisher-Wilson (11/29/10), Roz Ryan (2/28/11), Carol Woods 5. Colman Domingo (6/14/10), John O'Hurley (7/20/10), Tom Hewitt (9/13/10), Brett Barrett (10/11/10), Tom Hewitt (11/22/10), Colman Domingo (1/10/11), Brett Barrett (2/7/11), Jeff McCarthy (3/8/11), Brent Barret (3/26/11) 6. R. Lowe, D. Micciche, R. Lowe 7. James Patric Moran (July-Sept 2010), James Harkness (Oct 2010) 8. Jill Nicklaus, Jennifer Dunne, Dylis Croman 9. Dan LoBuono, Peter Nelson 10. Ryan Worsing 11. Peter Nelson, Michael Cusumano 12. Brian O'Brien, Greg Reuter

ORCHESTRA Leslie Stifelman (Conductor); Scott Cady (Associate Conductor/Piano); Seymour Red Press, Jack Stuckey, Richard Centalonza (Woodwinds); John Frosk, Darryl Shaw (Trumpets); Dave Bargeron, Bruce Bonvissuto (Trombones); John Johnson (Piano/Accordion); Jay Berliner (Banjo); Ronald Raffio (Bass/Tuba); Marshall Coid (Violin); Ronald Zito (Drums/Percussion)

MUSICAL NUMBERS All That Jazz, Funny Honey, Cell Block Tango, When You're Good to Mama, Tap Dance, All I Care About, A Little Bit of Good, We Both Reached for the Gun, Roxie, I Can't Do It Alone, My Own Best Friend, Entr'acte, I Know a Girl, Me and My Baby, Mister Cellophane, When Velma Takes the Stand, Razzle Dazzle, Class, Nowadays, Hot Honey Rag, Finale

SETTING Chicago, Illinois. The late 1920s. A musical vaudeville presented in two acts. This production originally opened at the Richard Rodgers Theatre; transferred to the Shubert on February 12, 1997; and transferred to the Ambassador on January 29, 2003. For original production credits see *Theatre World* Vol. 53, page 14. The original Broadway production ran June 3, 1975–August 27, 1977 at the 46th Street Theatre (now the Richard Rodgers Theatre where this revival first played) playing 936 performances (see *Theatre World* Vol. 32, Page 8). On March 25, 2011, the production became the fifth-longest running production in Broadway history.

SYNOPSIS Murder, media circus, vaudeville, and celebrity meet in this 1920s tale of two of the Windy City's most celebrated felons and their rise to fame amidst a razzle dazzle trial.

Michelle DeJean and the Company (photo by Paul Kolnik)

Ryan Worsing, Charlotte d'Amboise, and Michael Cusumano (photo by Jeremy Daniel)

Collected Stories

Samuel J. Friedman Theatre; First Preview: April 6, 2010; Opening Night: April 28, 2010; Closed June 13, 2010; 22 previews, 54 performances

Written by Donald Margulies; Produced by Manhattan Theatre Club (Lynne Meadow, Artistic Director; Barry Grove, Executive Producer); Director, Lynne Meadow; Set, Santo Loquasto; Costumes, Jane Greenwood; Lighting, Natasha Katz; Original Music & Sound, Obadiah Eaves; Wigs, Paul Huntley; Casting, David Caparelliotis; Production Stage Manager, Laurie Goldfeder; General Manager, Florie Seery; Associate Artistic Director, Mandy Greenfield; Director of Artistic Development, Jerry Patch; Marketing, Debra Waxman-Pilla; Production Manager, Kurt Gardner; Director of Casting, Nancy Piccione; Development, Jill Turner Lloyd; Artistic Consultant, Daniel Sullivan; Artistic Administration/Assistant to Artistic Director, Amy Gilkes Loe; Finance, Jeffrey Bledsoe; Associate General Manager, Lindsey Brooks Sag; Subscriber Services, Robert Allenberg; Telesales, George Tetlow; Education, David Shookhoff; Associate Production Manager, Philip Naudé; Prop Supervisor, Scott Laule; Costume Supervisor, Erin Hennessy Dean; Company Manager, Seth Shepsle; Stage Manager, Timothy R. Semon; Assistant Director, Hilary Adams; Associate Design: Jenny B. Sawyers (set), Wade Laboissonniere (costumes), Aaron Spivey (lighting), Brandon Wolcott (sound); Assistant Set, Yoki Lai; Makeup Angelina Avallone; Video Design, Rocco DiSanti; Lightboard Programmer, Mark Davidson; Advertising, SpotCo; Press, Boneau/Bryan-Brown, Chris Boneau, Aaron Meier, Christine Olver, Emily Meagher

CAST Ruth Steiner **Linda Lavin**; Lisa Morrison **Sarah Paulson**

UNDERSTUDIES Anne Bowles (Lisa Morrison), Kit Flanagan (Ruth Steiner)

SETTING Time: Act 1 – Scene One: September 1990; Scene Two: May 1991; Scene Three: August 1992. Act II– Scene One: December 1994; Scene Two: October 1996; Scene Three: Later that night. Place: The Greenwich Village apartment of Ruth Steiner. Broadway premiere and revival of an Off-Broadway play presented in six scenes in two acts. World premiere at South Coast Repertory in 1996 (see *Theatre World* Vol. 53, page 206). Manhattan Theatre Club produced the original Off-Broadway production at City Center Stage I, starring Maria Tucci and Debra Messing, April 30–July 27, 1997 (see *Theatre World* Vol. 53, page 94). The play was revived at the Lucille Lortel Theatre, starring Uta Hagen and Lorca Simons, July 28, 1998–February 28 1999 (see *Theatre World* Vol. 55, page 138).

SYNOPSIS *Collected Stories* chronicles the relationship between two female writers–Ruth Steiner, a celebrated New York author and her young protégé, Lisa Morrison. As their fascinating story evolves, and the line between fact and fiction blurs, the twists and turns of this complex relationship weave a play that's as smart and witty as it is powerful.

Sarah Paulson (photos by Joan Marcus)

Linda Lavin and Sarah Paulson

Linda Lavin and Sarah Paulson

Come Fly Away

Marquis Theatre; First Preview: March 1, 2010; Opening Night: March 25, 2010; Closed September 5, 2010; 26 previews, 188 performances

Concept, book, direction, and choreography by Twyla Tharp, music by various, vocals by Frank Sinatra; Presented by special arrangement with the Frank Sinatra family and Frank Sinatra Enterprises; Produced by James L. Nederlander, Nicholas Howey, W.A.T. Ltd., Terry Allen Kramer, Patrick Catullo/Jon B. Platt, Jerry Frankel, Ronald Frankel/Marc Frankel, Roy Furman, Allan S. Gordon/Élan McAllister, Jam Theatricals, Stewart F. Lane /Bonnie Comley, Margo Lion/Daryl Roth, Hal Luftig/Yasuhiro Kawana, Pittsburgh CLO/GSFD, Spark Productions, The Weinstein Company and Barry & Fran Weissler; Sets, James Youmans; Costumes, Katherine Roth; Lighting, Donald Holder; Sound, Peter McBoyle; Original Sinatra Arrangements, Nelson Riddle, Don Costa, Gordon Jenkins, Quincy Jones, Johnny Mandel, Neal Hefti, Torrie Zito, Sam Nestico, Emuir Deodato, Ernie Freeman; Additional Orchestrations & Arrangements, Don Sebesky, Dave Pierce; Original Music Supervisor, Sam Lutfiyya; Musical Supervisor & Coordinator, Patrick Vaccariello; Conductor/Pianist, Russ Kassoff; Casting, Stuart Howard, Amy Schecter, Paul Hardt; Marketing, Scott A. Moore; Creative Consultant, Charles Pignone; Production Executive, Randall A. Buck; Resident Director, Kim Craven; Production Stage Manager, Rick Steiger; Technical Supervisor, David Benken; General Management, The Charlotte Wilcox Company (Seth Marquette, Matthew W. Krawiec, Dina S. Friedler, Steve Supeck, Margaret Wilcox); Company Manager, Heidi Neven; Assistant Company Manager, Michael Bolgar; Stage Manager, Lisa Dawn Cave; Assistant Stage Manager, Kevin Bertolacci; Dance Captain, Alexander Brady; Assistant Dance Captain, Colin Bradbury; Associate Director of W.A.T. Ltd, Ann Tuomey DePiro; Assistant to Ms. Tharp, Roy Chicas; Associate Design: Jerome Martin (set), Amy Clark (costumes), Jeanne Koenig, Caroline Chao (lighting), David Patridge (sound); Assistants to Costume Designer, Mike Floyd, Caitlin Hunt; Assistant Sound, Daniel Fiandaca; Assistant Production Manager, Canara Price; Rehearsal Programmer, Joe DeVico; Rehearsal Pianist, Jim Laev; Music Copying, Emily Grishman, Katharine Edmonds; Advertising, SpotCo; Press, The Hartman Group, Michael Hartman, Tom D'Ambrosio, Michelle Bergmann; Additional Press, Ellen Jacobs Company; Cast recording. Reprise Records

CAST *Evening performances:* Betsy **Laura Mead**; Marty **Charlie Neshyba-Hodges**; Vico **Alexander Brady**; Sid **John Selya**; Kate **Karine Plantadit**; Slim **Rika Okamoto**; Hank **Keith Roberts**; Chanos **Matthew Stockwell Dibble**; Babe **Holley Farmer**; Featured Vocalist **Hilary Gardner**; *Matinee performances:* Betsy **Ashley Tuttle**; Marty **Jeremy Cox**; Vico **Alexander Brady**; Sid **Cody Green**; Kate **Marielys Molina**; Slim **Kristine Bendul**; Hank **Joel Prouty**; Chanos **Ron Todorowski**; Babe **Laurie Kanok**; Featured Vocalist **Rosena M. Hill**; Ensemble **Todd Burnsed**, **Carolyn Doherty**, **Heather Hamilton**, **Meredith Miles**, **Eric Michael Otto**, **Justin Peck**

ALTERNATES/SWINGS Kristine Bendul, Colin Bradbury, Jeremy Cox, Amanda Edge, Cody Green, Laurie Kanyok, Marielys Molina, Joel Prouty, Ron Todorowski, Ashley Tuttle

ORCHESTRA Russ Kassoff (Conductor/Piano); Jerry Dodgion, Jimmy Cozier, P.J. Perry, Dave Noland, Frank Basile (Reeds); Dave Stahl, Earl Gardner, Larry Moses, Richie Vitale (Trumpets); John Mosca, Mark Miller, Clarence Banks, Jeff Nelson (Trombones); Jay Anderson (Bass); James Chirillo (Guitar); Warren Odze (Drums); Hilary Gardner/Rosena M. Hil (Percussion)

MUSICAL NUMBERS Moonlight Becomes You, Come Fly With Me, I've Got the World on a String, Let's Fall in Love, I've Got You Under My Skin, Summer Wind, Fly Me to the Moon, I've Got a Crush On You, Body and Soul, It's Alright With Me, You Make Me Feel So Young, September of My Years, Witchcraft, Yes Sir, That's My Baby, Learnin' the Blues, That's Life, Nice 'n' Easy, Makin Whoopee, Jumpin' at the Woodside, Saturday Night Is the Loneliest Night, I'm Gonna Live 'Til I Die, Pick Yourself Up, Wave, Let's Face the Music and Dance, Teach Me Tonight, Take Five, Just Friends, Lean Baby, Makin' Whoopee (reprise), One for My Baby, My Funny Valentine, Air Mail Special, My Way, New York, New York, All the Way

New York premiere of a new dance musical presented in two acts. World premiere (under the title *Come Fly With Me*) at the Alliance Theatre, Atlanta, Georgia (Susan V. Booth, Artistic Director; Thomas Pechar, Managing Director) September 15–October 11, 2009 (see "Regional Theatre" listings in this volume).

SYNOPSIS Based on the songs of Frank Sinatra, *Come Fly Away* follows four couples as they fall in and out of love during one song and dance filled evening at a crowded nightclub. Blending Sinatra's legendary vocals with a live on-stage big band and the world's finest dancers, *Come Fly Away* weaves an unparalleled hit parade of classics into a soaring musical fantasy of romance and seduction.

John Selya, Holley Farmer, Matthew Stockwell Dibble, and the Company

The Company (photos by Joan Marcus)

Sherrie Rene Scott (photos by Carol Rosegg)

Lindsay Mendez, Sherrie Rene Scott, and Betsy Wolfe

Everyday Rapture

American Airlines Theatre; First Preview: April 19, 2010; Opening Night: April 29, 2010; Closed July 11, 2010; 11 previews, 85 performances

Written by Dick Scanlan and Sherie Rene Scott; Produced by the Roundabout Theatre Company (Todd Haimes, Artistic Director; Harold Wolpert, Managing Director; Julia C. Levy, Executive Director); Originally presented by Second Stage (Carole Rothman, Artistic Director; Ellen Richard, Executive Director) Director, Michael Mayer; Choreography, Michele Lynch; Set, Christine Jones; Costumes, Tom Broecker; Lighting, Kevin Adams; Sound, Ashley Hanson, Kurt Eric Fischer, Brian Ronan; Projections, Darrel Maloney; Orchestrations/Arrangements, Tom Kitt; Music Supervisor, Michael Rafter; Musical Director, Marco Paguia; Music Coordinator, Michael Keller; Production Stage Manager, Richard C. Rauscher; Production Management, Aurora Productions (Gene O'Donovan, W. Benjamin Heller II, Rachel Sherbill, Jarid Sumner, Steve Rosenberg, Melissa Mazdra, Amy Merlino Coey, Amanda Raymond, Graham Forden, Liza Luxenberg); Original Casting, MelCap Casting; Additional Casting, Jim Carnahan; General Manager, Rebecca Habel; Marketing/Sales Promotion, David B. Steffen; Founding Director, Gene Feist; Associate Artistic Director, Scott Ellis; Director of Artistic Development and Casting, Jim Carnahan; Finance, Susan Neiman; Education, Greg McCaslin; General Manager, Sydney Beers; Telesales, Marco Frezza; IT Director, Antonio Palumbo; Development Directors, Julie K. D'Andrea, Steve Schaeffer, Joy Pak, Amber Jo Manuel; Sales Operations, Charlie Garbowski Jr.; Company Manager, Carly DiFulvio; Stage Manager, Bryce McDonald; Hair, John Barrett/John Barrett Salon; Makeup, Tiffany Hicks; Assistant Director, Austin Regan; Associate Choreographer, Eric Sean Fogel; Associate Design: John C. Collings (set), David Withrow (costumes), Aaron Sporer, Paul Toben (lighting), Drew Levy (sound), Dan Scully (projections); Dance Captain, Lindsay Mendez; Magic Consultant, Steve Cuiffo; Synthesizer Programmer, Randy Cohen; Music Copying, Colleen Darnall; Music Search Supervisor, Hank Aberle; Advertising, SpotCo; Press, Boneau/Bryan-Brown, Adrian Bryan-Brown, Matt Polk, Jessica Johnson, Amy Kass, Emily Meagher; Cast recording: Sh-K-Boom Records/Ghostlight 82010

CAST **Sherie Rene Scott**, **Lindsay Mendez**, **Betsy Wolfe**, **Eamon Foley**

UNDERSTUDIES Riley Costello, Natalie Weiss

MUSICIANS Marco Paguia (Conductor/piano), Clint De Ganon (drums), Brian Hamm (bass), John Benthall (guitar), Joe Brent (violin/guitar)

MUSICAL NUMBERS The Other Side of This Life (Overture); Got a Thing on My Mind; Elevation; On the Atchison, Topeka, and Santa Fe; Get Happy; You Made Me Love You; Mr. Rodgers Medley (It's Such a Good Feeling, Everybody's Fancy, & I Like to Be Told); It's You I Like; I Guess the Lord Must Be in New York City; Life Line; The Weight; Rainbow Sleeves; Why; Won't You Be My Neighbor; Up the Ladder to the Roof

SETTING Topeka, Kansas and New York City; the past and present. Transfer of the Off-Broadway musical presented without intermission. Originally presented at Second Stage April 7–June 14, 2009 (see *Theatre World* Vol. 64, page 236). A previous version of the show entitled *You May Worship Me Now* was presented as a benefit concert for the Actors Fund Phyllis Newman Women's Health Initiative on March 31, 2008.

SYNOPSIS *Everyday Rapture* tells the true-ish story of a young woman's journey from Mennonite to Manhattanite and from bedroom lip-syncher to Broadway semi-star! Featuring songs by David Byrne, Elton John, Mister Rogers, The Supremes, Tom Waits, U2 and Judy Garland, *Everyday Rapture* is an uplifting and uproarious new musical that asks, is it better to worship...or BE worshipped?

Fela!

Eugene O'Neill Theatre; First Preview: October 19, 2009; Opening Night: November 23, 2009; Closed January 2, 2011; 34 previews, 463 performances

Book by Jim Lewis & Bill T. Jones, music and lyrics by Fela Anikulapo-Kuti, book, additional lyrics by Jim Lewis, additional music by Aaron Johnson & Jordan McLean; Based on the life of Fela Anikulapo; Conceived by Bill T. Jones, Jim Lewis, & Stephen Hendel; Produced by Shawn "Jay-Z" Carter, Will Smith and Jada Pinkett Smith, Ruth & Stephen Hendel, Roy Gabay, Sony Pictures Entertainment, Edward Tyler Nahem, Salva Smolokowski, Chip Meyrelles/Ken Greiner, Douglas G. Smith, Steve Semlitz/Cathy Glaser, Daryl Roth/True Love Productions, Susan Dietz/Mort Swinsky, Knitting Factory Entertainment; Director/Choreographer, Bill T. Jones; Music Director & Supervision/Orchestrations/Arrangements, Aaron Johnson; Sets/Costumes, Marina Draghici; Lighting, Robert Wierzel; Sound, Robert Kaplowitz; Projections, Peter Nigrini; Wigs, Hair, & Makeup, Cookie Jordan; Production Stage Manager, Jon Goldman; Casting, Mungioli Theatricals, Arnold J. Mungioli; Advertising & New Media Services, Art Meets Commerce; Marketing, HHC Marketing–Hugh Hysell, Walk Tall Girl Productions–Marcia Pendleton; Technical Supervision, Hudson Theatrical Associates, Neil A. Mazzella; Associate Technical Supervision, Jay Janicki, John Tiggeloven, Aduro Productions, Caitlin McInerney; General Manager, Roy Gabay; Music Coordinator, Michael Keller; Associate Producer, Ahmir "Questlove" Thompson; Associate Musical Director & Arranger, Jordan McLean; Music Consultant, Antibalas; Associate Director, Niegel Smith; Associate Choreographer, Maija Garcia; Company Management, Daniel Kuney, Chris Aniello; Stage Manager, Linda Marvel; Assistant Stage Manager, Hilary Austin; Associate Design: Timothy R. Mackabee, Wilson Chin, Katheryn Monthei (set), Amy Clark (costumes), Paul Hackenmueller (lighting), Jessica Paz (sound); Original Mural/Scenic Art, IRLO, Omar and Nuclear Fairy; Assistant Design: Mike Floyd (costumes), G. Benjamin Swope (lighting), John Emmett O'Brien (sound); Assistant to Lighting Designer, Xavier Pierce; Associate Projection Designers, C. Andrew Bauer (content), Dan Scully (system); Additional Projection Content and Editing, Mirit Tal; Props Master, Kathy Fabian/Propstar; Associate Props, Jennifer Breen, Sid King; Props Artisans, Sarah Bird, Corey Shipler, Hanna Davis, Martin Izquierdo Studio, Arianna Zindler, Emily Walsh; Flame Treatment, Turning Star Inc.; General Management Staff, Chris Aniello, Bobby Driggers, Daniel Kuney, Jennifer Pluff, Mandy Tate; Casting Associates, Alex Hanna, Melanie Lockyer; Production Assistants, Melanie Ganim, Leslie Grisdale, Colleen M. Sherry; Artistic Assistant, Radha Blank; Press, Richard Kornberg & Associates, Billy Zavelson, Don Summa, Tommy Wesely; Off-Broadway Cast recording: Knitting Factory 1103

CAST Fela Anikulapo-Kuti **Kevin Mambo** or **Sahr Ngaujah**; Funmilayo Anikulapo-Kuti **Lillias White**[*1]; Sandra Isadore **Saycon Sengbloh**; Ismael/Geraldo Piño/Orisha/Ensemble **Ismael Kouyaté**; J.K. Brahman (Tap Dancer)/Egungun/Ensemble **Gelan Lambert**; Ensemble **Corey Baker, Hettie Barnhill, Lauren De Veaux, Nicole Chantal de Weever, Elasea Douglas, Rujeko Dumbutshena, Catherine Foster Talu Green, Shaneeka Harrell, Abena Koomson, Gelan Lambert, Shakira Marshall, Afi McClendon, Adesola Osakalumi, Jeffrey Page, Daniel Soto, Iris Wilson, Aimee Graham Wodobode**; Swings **Chanon Judson, Farai M. Malianga, Oneika Phillips, Justin Prescott, Ryan Rankine, Jill M. Valler, J.L. Williams**

UNDERSTUDIES Adesola Osakalumi (Fela), Abena Koomso & Oneika Phillips (Funmilayo), Elasea Douglas & Oneika Phillips (Sandra)

*Succeeded by: 1. Patti LaBelle

BAND Aaron Johnson (Conductor/trombone), Greg Gonzalez (Assistant Conductor/drums/percussion), Jordan McLean (trumpet), Jeremy Wilms (bass/keyboards/percussion), Oren Bloedow (guitar/percussion), Ricardo Quinones (guitar/percussion), Yoshihiro Takemasa (percussion), Alex Harding (baritone saxophone/percussion), Stuart Bogie (tenor saxophone/percussion/featured saxophone soloist), Dylan Fusillo (percussion)

MUSICAL NUMBERS Everything Scatter, Iba Orisa, Hymn, Medzi Medzi, Mr. Syms, Manteca, I Got the Feeling, Originality/Yellow Fever, Trouble Sleep, Teacher Don't Teach Me Nonsense, Lover, Upside Down, Expensive Shit, Pipeline/I.T.T. (International Thief Thief), Kere Kay, Water No Get Enemy, Egbe Mio, Zombie, Trouble Sleep (reprise), Na Poi, Sorrow Tears and Blood, Iba Orisa/Shakara, Rain, Coffin for Head of State, Kere Kay (reprise)

SETTING Fela's final concert at the Shrine in Lagos, Nigeria; the summer of 1978, six months after the death of Funmilayo, Fela's mother. Transfer of the Off-Broadway musical presented in two acts. The show had its world premiere at 37 Arts Theatre B August 5–October 5, 2008 (see *Theatre World* Vol. 65, page 146).

SYNOPSIS His story inspired a nation. His music inspires the world. *Fela!* tells the true story of the legendary Nigerian musician Fela Kuti, whose soulful Afrobeat rhythms ignited a generation. Motivated by his mother, a civil rights champion, he defied a corrupt and oppressive military government and devoted his life and music to the struggle for freedom and human dignity. *Fela!* is a triumphant tale of courage, passion, and love, featuring Fela Kuti's captivating music (a blend of jazz, funk and African rhythm and harmonies) and Bill T. Jones's imaginative staging.

Patti Labelle and Sahr Ngaujah (photo by Tristam Kenton)

Fences

Cort Theatre; First Preview: April 14, 2010; Opening Night: April 26, 2010; Closed July 11, 2010; 13 previews, 88 performances

Written by August Wilson; Produced by Carole Shorenstein Hays and Scott Rudin; Director, Kenny Leon; Original Music, Brandford Marsalis; Sets, Santo Loquasto; Costumes, Constanza Romero; Lighting, Brian MacDevitt; Sound, Acme Sound Partners; Production Stage Manager, Narda E. Alcorn; Casting, MelCap Casting, Mele Nagler, David Caparelliotis; Production Management, Aurora Productions, Gene O'Donovan, Ben Heller, Jarid Sumner, Rachel Sherbill, Melissa Mazdra, Amanda Raymond, Graham Forden, Liza Luxenberg; General Management, Stuart Thompson Productions, David Turner, James Triner; Associate Producer, Constanza Romero; Company Manager, Chris Morey; Fight Director, Rick Sordelet; Wigs, Charles LaPointe; Stage Manager, Michael P. Zaleski; Associate Director, Todd Kreidler; Associate Design: Jenny Sawyers (set), Katie Irish (costumes), Jennifer Schriever (lighting), Nick Borisjuk (sound); Assistant Design: Antje Ellerman, Yoki Lai (set), Aaron Parsekian (lighting); Production Props Coordinator, Kathy Fabian/Propstar; Propstar Associates, Carrie Mossman, Timothy Ferro; Fight Captain, Chris Chalk; Advertising, SpotCo; Marketing, Walk Tall Girl Productions, Marcia Pendleton, Jesse Wooden Jr., Kojo Ade, Sharif Colon, Merielin Lopez; Press, Boneau/Bryan-Brown, Chris Boneau, Heath Schwartz, Kelly Guiod

CAST Troy Maxon **Denzel Washington**; Jim Bono, *Troy's friend* **Stephen McKinley Henderson**; Rose, *Troy's wife* **Viola Davis**; Lyons, *Troy's oldest son by a previous marriage* **Russell Hornsby**; Gabriel, *Troy's brother* **Mykelti Williamson**; Cory, *Troy and Rose's son* **Chris Chalk**; Raynell, *Troy's daughter* **Eden Duncan-Smith** or **SaCha Stewart-Coleman**

STANDBYS Jason Dirden (Corey, Lyons), Michael Genet (Gabriel, Jim Bono), Roslyn Ruff (Rose), Keith Randolph Smith (Troy Maxson)

SETTING Pittsburg, 1957. Revival of a play presented in two acts. World premiere at Yale Repertory Theatre in 1985. Originally produced on Broadway at the 46th Street (now the Richard Rodgers) Theatre March 17, 1987–June 26, 1988 playing 525 performances (see *Theatre World* Vol. 43, page 35).

SYNOPSIS Both a monumental drama and an intimate family portrait, *Fences* tells the story of Troy Maxson, a man torn between the glory of his past and the uncertainty of his future. Emboldened by pride and embittered by sacrifice, Troy is determined to make life better for future generations, even as he struggles to embrace the dreams of his own son.

Dylan Baker, Lucy Liu, Janet McTeer, and Jeff Daniels (photo by Joan Marcus)

God of Carnage

Bernard B. Jacobs Theatre; First Preview: February 28, 2009 Opening Night: March 22, 2009; Closed June 6, 2010; 24 previews, 452 performances

Written by Yasmina Reza, translated by Christopher Hampton; Produced by Robert Fox, David Pugh & Dafydd Rogers, Stuart Thompson, Scott Rudin, Jon B. Platt, The Weinstein Company, and The Shubert Organization; Director, Matthew Warchus; Set and Costumes, Mark Thompson; Lighting, Hugh Vanstone; Music, Gary Yershon; Sound, Simon Baker/Christopher Cronin; Casting, Daniel Swee; Production Stage Manager, Jill Cordle; Production Management, Aurora Productions (Gene O'Donovan, W. Benjamin Heller II, Bethany Weinstein, Melissa Mazdra, Amy Merlino Coey, Laura Archer, Dana Hesch); General Management, Stuart Thompson Productions/David Turner; Company Manager, Chris Morey; Stage Manager, Kenneth J. McGee; Associate Director, Beatrice Terry; Associate Design: Nancy Thun (set), Daryl A. Stone (costumes), Ted Mather (lighting); Vocal Coach, Deborah Hecht; Makeup Consultant, Judy Chin; Advertising, Serino Coyne Inc.; Press, Boneau/Bryan-Brown, Chris Boneau, Susanne Tighe, Christine Olver, Kelly Guiod

CAST Alan **Dylan Baker**; Annette **Lucy Liu**; Michael **Jeff Daniels**; Veronica **Janet McTeer**

STANDBYS Bruce McCarty (Alan, Michael), Charlotte Maier (Annette, Veronica)

SETTING Michael and Veronica's living room; the present. American premiere of a new play presented without intermission. Mr. Warchus directed the English language premiere at the Gielgud Theatre (London) starring Janet McTeer and Ralph Fiennes March 25–June 14, 2008. World premiere in Zurich, Switzerland December 8, 2006.

SYNOPSIS *God of Carnage* is a comedy of manners (without the manners) the deals with the aftermath of a playground altercation between two boys and what happens when their parents meet to talk about it. A calm and rational debate between grown-ups about the need to teach kids how to behave properly? Or a hysterical night of name-calling, tantrums and tears before bedtime? Boys will be boys... but the adults are usually worse... much worse...

Viola Davis and Denzel Washington (photo by Joan Marcus)

Hair, The American Tribal Love-Rock Musical

Al Hirschfeld Theatre; First Preview: March 6, 2009 Opening Night: March 31, 2009; Closed June 27, 2010; 29 previews, 519 performances

Book and lyrics by Gerome Ragni & James Rado, music and orchestrations by Galt MacDermot; Produced by The Public Theater (Oskar Eustis, Artistic Director; Andrew D. Hamingson, Executive Director); Jeffrey Richards, Jerry Frankel, Gary Goddard Entertainment, Kathleen K. Johnson, Nederlander Productions Inc., Fran Kirmser Productions/Jed Bernstein, Marc Frankel, Broadway Across America, Barbara Manocherian/WenCarLar Productions, JK Productions/Terry Schnuck, Andy Sandberg, Jam Theatricals, The Weinstein Company/Norton Herrick, Jujamcyn Theaters, Joey Parnes, and by special arrangement with Elizabeth Ireland McCann; Director, Diane Polis; Choreography, Karole Armitage; Music Director, Nadia Digiallonardo; Associate Producers, Arielle Tepper Madover, Debbie Bisno/Rebecca Gold, Christopher Hart, Apples and Oranges, Tony & Ruthe Ponturo, Joseph Traina; Sets, Scott Pask; Costumes, Michael McDonald; Lighting, Kevin Adams; Sound, Acme Sound Partners; Music Coordinator, Seymour Red Press; Casting, Jordan Thaler & Heidi Griffiths; Production Stage Manager, Nancy Harrington; Wigs, Gerard Kelly; Associate Producer (The Public Theater), Jenny Gersten; Marketing, Allied Live Inc.; Sponsorship, Rose Polidoro; General Management, Joey Parnes, John Johnson, S.D. Wagner; Company Manager, Kim Sellon; Stage Manager, Julie Baldauff; Assistant Stage Manager, Elizabeth Miller; Associate Company Manager, Leslie A. Glassburn; Assistant Company Manager, Kit Ingui; Assistant Directors, Allegra Libonati, Shira Milikowsky; Assistant Choreographer, Christine O'Grady; Dance Captain, Tommar Wilson; Associate Design: Orit Jacoby Carroll (set), Aaron Sporer (lighting), Lisa Zinni (costumes); Assistant Design: Jeffrey Hinchee & Lauren Alvarez (set), Joel Silver (lighting), Chloe Chapin (costumes), Alex Hawthorn (sound); Assistants to Designers: Warren Stiles (set), David Mendizabal (costumes); Costume Assistant, Sydney Ledger; Mural Illustration, Scott Pask with Amy Guip; Music Consultant, Tom Kitt; Music Copyist, Rob Baumgardner; Management Associate, Madeline Felix; Director of Communications (The Public Theater), Candi Adams; Director of Marketing (The Public Theater), Ilene Rosen; Advertising, SpotCo; Interactive Marketing, Situation Interactive; Press, O+M Co.; Cast recording: Sh-K-Boom/Ghostlight Records 4467

CAST Dionne **Jeannette Bayardelle**; Berger **Ace Young**; Woof **Jason Wooten**; Hud **Wallace Smith**; Claude **Kyle Riabko**; Sheila **Diana DeGarmo**; Jeanie **Annaleigh Ashford**; Crissy **Vanessa Ray**; Mother/Buddhadalirama **Rachel Bay Jones**; Dad/Margaret Mead **Josh Lamon**; Hubert **Lee Zarrett**; Abraham Lincoln **Anastacia McCleskey**; Tribe **Justin Badger, Larkin Bogan, Natalie Bradshaw, Catherine Brookman, Ericka Jerry, Jay Armstrong Johnson, Mykal Kilgore, Josh Lamon, Anastacia McClesky, Paris Remillard, Arbender J. Robinson, Kate Rockwell, Cailan Rosenthal, Rashidra Scott, Jen Sese, Lawrence Stallings, Terrance Thomas, Emma Zaks, Lee Zarrett**; Tribe Swings **Nicholas Belton, Matt DeAngelis, Briana Carlson-Goodman, Antwayn Hopper, Nicole Lewis, Arbender J. Robinson**

MUSICIANS Nadia Digiallonardo (Conductor/Keyboard), Lon Hoyt (Assistant Conductor/Keyboard), Steve Bargonetti & Andrew Schwartz (Guitar), Wilbur Bascomb (Bass), Allen Won (Woodwinds), Elaine Burt, Ronald Buttacavoli & Christian Jaudes (Trumpets), Vincent MacDermot (Trombone), Joe Cardello (Percussion), Bernard Purdie (Drums)

MUSICAL NUMBERS Aquarius, Donna, Hashish, Sodomy, Colored Spade, Manchester England, I'm Black, Ain't Got No, Sheila Franklin, I Believe in Love, Ain't Got No (reprise), Air, The Stone Age, I Got Life, Initials, Going Down, Hair, My Conviction, Easy to Be Hard, Don't Put It Down, Frank Mills, Hare Krishna, Where Do I Go, Electric Blues, Oh Great God of Power, Black Boys, White Boys, Walking in Space, Minuet, Yes I's Finished on Y'alls Farmlands, Four Score and Seven Years Ago/Abie Baby, Give Up All Desires, Three-Five-Zero-Zero, What a Piece of Work Is Man, How Dare They Try, Good Morning Starshine, Ain't Got No (reprise), The Flesh Failures, Eyes Look Your Last, Let the Sun Shine In

SETTING New York City, the late 1960s. Revival of the rock musical presented in two acts. This production was previously presented at the Delacorte Theater July 22–September 14, 2008, and as part of Joe's Pub in the Park September 22-24, 2007 (see *Theatre World* Vol. 64, page 186). Originally produced Off-Broadway at the Public Theater October 17–December 10, 1967; reopened at the midtown discothèque Cheetah December 22, 1968–January 28, 1968. After extensive rewrites and recasting, it transferred to the Biltmore Theatre April 29, 1968, closing July 1, 1972 after 1,750 performances (see *Theatre World* Vol. 24, pages 59 and 11). Briefly revived at the Biltmore August 3–November 6, 1977 (see *Theatre World* Vol. 34, page 14).

SYNOPSIS *Hair* depicts the birth of a cultural movement in the '60s and '70s that changed America forever. The musical follows a group of hopeful, free-spirited young people who advocate a lifestyle of pacifism and free-love in a society riddled with intolerance and brutality during the Vietnam War. As they explore sexual identity, challenge racism, experiment with drugs and burn draft cards, the tribe in *Hair* creates an irresistible message of hope that continues to resonate with audiences 40 years later.

The Tribe (photo by Joan Marcus)

In the Heights

Richard Rodgers Theatre; First Preview: February 14, 2008; Opening Night: March 9, 2008; Closed January 9, 2011; 29 previews, 1,184 performances

Concept, music and lyrics by Lin-Manuel Miranda, book by Quiara Alegría Hudes; Produced by Kevin McCollum, Jeffrey Seller, Jill Furman, Sander Jacobs, Goodman/Grossman, Peter Fine, Everett/Skipper; Director, Thomas Kail; Choreographer, Andy Blankenbuehler; Music Director, Alex Lacamoire; Sets, Anna Louizos; Costumes, Paul Tazewell; Lighting, Howell Binkley; Sound, Acme Sound Partners; Arrangements and Orchestrations, Alex Lacamoire & Bill Sherman; Music Coordinator, Michael Keller; Casting, Telsey + Company; Marketing, Scott A. Moore; Company Manager, Brig Berney; General Manager, John S. Corker, Lizbeth Cone; Technical Supervisor, Brian Lynch; Production Stage Manager, J. Philip Bassett; Associate Producers, Ruth Hendel, Harold Newman; Wigs, Charles LaPointe; Assistant Director, Casey Hushion; Assistant Choreographer, Joey Dowling; Fight Director, Ron Piretti; Latin Assistant Choreographer, Luis Salgado; Fight/Dance Captain, Michael Balderrama; Stage Manager, Amber Wedin; Assistant Stage Manager, Heather Hogan; Associate Design: Donyale Werle, Todd Potter (set), Michael Zecker (costumes), Mark Simpson (lighting), Sten Severson (sound); Assistant Design: Hilary Noxon, Heather Dunbar (set), Caitlin Hunt (costumes), Greg Bloxham, Ryan O'Gara (lighting); Moving Lights, David Arch; Music Copying, Emily Grishman; Rehearsal Pianist, Zachary Dietz; Keyboard Programming, Randy Cohen; Advertising, SpotCo; Press, The Hartman Group; Cast recording: Sh-K-Boom/Ghostlight Records 4428

CAST Graffiti Pete **William B. Wingfield**[1]; Usnavi **Corbin Bleu**[2]; Piragua Guy **Eliseo Román**[3]; Abuela Claudia **Olga Merediz**; Carla **Courtney Reed**; Daniela **Andréa Burns**[4]; Kevin **Rick Negron**[5]; Camila **Priscilla Lopez**; Sonny **David Del Rio**[6]; Benny **Christopher Jackson**[7]; Vanessa **Marcy Harriell**; Nina **Janet Dacal**[8]; Ensemble[9] **Danny Bolero, Tony Chiroldes, Dwayne Clark, Rosie Lani Fiedelman, Ruben Flores, Marcus Paul James, Jennifer Locke, Nina Lafarga, Doreen Montalvo, Gabrielle Ruiz, Eliseo Román, Luis Salgado, Noah Rivera, Rickey Tripp, Willis White**; Swings **Michael Balderrama, Blanca Camacho, Antuan Raimone, Alejandra Reyes, Jon Rua, Allison Thomas Lee, Daniel J. Watts, Sandy Alvarez, Kristina Fernandez, Michael Fielder, Afra Hines, Nancy Ticotin, Alicia Taylor**

UNDERSTUDIES Michael Balderrama (Usnavi, Graffiti Pete, Piragua Guy), Blanca Camacho (Abuela Claudia, Camila, Daniela), Tony Chiroldes (Kevin, Piragua Guy), Janet Dacal (Vanessa, Nina), Dwayne Clark (Benny), Marcus Paul James (Benny), Allison Thomas Lee (Carla), Nina Lafarga (Nina), Doreen Montalvo (Abuela Claudia, Camila, Daniela), Gabrielle Ruiz (Nina, Carla, Vanessa), Eliseo Román (Kevin), Shaun Taylor-Corbett (Usnavi, Sonny, Piragua Guy), Rickey Tripp (Graffiti Pete)

*Succeeded by: 1. John Rua, Seth Stewart 2. Kyle Beltran (8/19/11), Lin Manuel Miranda (12/25/10) 3. Tony Chiroldes 4. Bianca Marroquin (6/12/11), Andréa Burns (8/17/11) 5. Danny Bolero, Rick Negron 6. Noah Rivera, Shaun Taylor-Corbett 7. Clifton Oliver, Christopher Jackson 8. Jordin Sparks (8/19/11), Arielle Jacobs 9. Sharona D'Ornellas, Marcos Santana

ORCHESTRA Zachary Dietz (Conductor/Keyboard 1); Joseph Church (Associate Conductor/Keyboard 2); Raul Agraz (Lead Trumpet); Scott Wendholt (Trumpet); Joe Fiedler, Ryan Keberle (Trombones); Dave Richards, Kristy Norter (Reeds); Andres Forero (Drums); Doug Hinrichs, Wilson Torres (Percussion); Irio O'Farrill (Bass); Manny Moreira (Guitars)

MUSICAL NUMBERS In the Heights, Breathe, Benny's Dispatch, It Won't Be Long Now, Inútil (Useless), No Me Diga, 96,000, Paciencia Y Fe (Patience and Faith), When You're Home, Piragua, Siempre (Always), The Club/Fireworks, Sunrise, Hundreds of Stories, Enough, Carnaval del Barrio, Atencíon, Alabanza, Everything I Know, No Me Diga (reprise), Champagne, When the Sun Goes Down, Finale

SETTING Washington Heights, Manhattan. Fourth of July weekend, the present. A new musical presented in two acts. For original production credits see *Theatre World* Volume 64, page 46. Previously presented Off-Broadway at 37 Arts, February 8–July 15, 2007 (see *Theatre World* Vol. 63, page 162).

SYNOPSIS *In the Heights* follows two days in Washington Heights, a vibrant immigrant neighborhood at the top of Manhattan. From the vantage point of Usnavi's corner bodega, we experience the joys, heartbreaks and bonds of a Latino community struggling to redefine home. This original musical features a mix of hip-hop, salsa and meringue music.

The Company (photos by Joan Marcus)

Lin-Manuel Miranda

Jersey Boys

August Wilson Theatre; First Preview: October 4, 2005; Opening Night: November 6, 2005; 38 previews, 2,299 performances as of May 31, 2011

Book by Marshall Brickman and Rick Elice, music by Bob Gaudio, lyrics by Bob Crewe; Produced by Dodger Theatricals (Michael David, Edward Strong, Rocco Landesman, Des McAnuff), Joseph J. Grano, Pelican Group, Tamara Kinsella and Kevin Kinsella, in association with Latitude Link, Rick Steiner and Osher/Staton/Bell/ Mayerson Group; Director, Des McAnuff; Choreography, Sergio Trujillo; Musical Director, Vocal Arrangements/Incidental Music, Ron Melrose; Sets, Klara Zieglerova; Costumes, Jess Goldstein; Lighting, Howell Binkley; Sound, Steve Canyon Kennedy; Projections, Michael Clark; Hair/Wigs, Charles LaPointe; Fight Director, Steve Rankin; Assistant Director, West Hyler; Production Supervisor, Richard Hester; Production Stage Manager, Michelle Bosch; Orchestrations, Steve Orich; Music Coordinator, John Miller; Technical Supervisor, Peter Fulbright; Casting, Tara Rubin (East), Sharon Bialy, Sherry Thomas (West); Company Manager, Sandra Carlson; Associate Company Manager, Tim Sulka; Associate Producers, Lauren Mitchell and Rhoda Mayerson; Executive Producer, Sally Campbell Morse; Promotions, HHC Marketing; Stage Manager, Michael T. Clarkston/Jason Brouillard/Michelle Reupert; Assistant Stage Manager, Rachel Wolff/Michelle Reupert/Brendan M. Fay; Dialect Coach, Stephen Gabis; Dance and Fight Captain, Peter Gregus; Music Technical Design, Deborah Hurwitz; Associate General Manager, Jennifer F. Vaughan; Marketing, Dodger Marketing; Advertising, Serino-Coyne; Press, Boneau/Bryan-Brown, Susanne Tighe, Heath Schwartz; Cast recording: Rhino R2 73271

CAST French Rap Star/Detective #1/Hal Miller/Barry Belson/Police Officer/Davis **Kris Coleman**; Stanley/Hank Majewski/Crewe's PA/Joe Long **Erik Bates**; Bob Crewe/others **Peter Gregus**; Tommy DeVito **Dominic Nolfi**; Nick DeVito/Stosh/Billy Dixon/Norman Waxman/Charlie Calello/others **Miles Aubrey**; Joey/Recording Studio Engineer/others **Russell Fischer**; Gyp De Carlo/others **Mark Lotito**; Mary Delgado/Angel/others **Bridget Berger**[1]; Church Lady/Miss Frankie Nolan/Rob's Party Girl/Angel/Lorraine/others **Heather Ferguson**[2]; Bob Gaudio **Sebastian Arcelus**[3]; Frankie's Mother/Nick's Date/Angel/Francine/others **Sara Schmidt**; Nick Massi **Matt Bogart**; Frankie Valli **Jarrod Spector** (evenings)/**Cory Grant**[4] (matinees); Thugs **Ken Dow, Joe Payne**; Swings[5] **Michelle Aravena, John Hickman, Katie O'Toole, Jake Speck, Taylor Sternberg**

UNDERSTUDIES Eric Bates (DeVito, Crewe), Russell Fischer (Valli), Miles Aubrey (Massi, Gyp), John Hickman (Gaudio, Massi, Gyp, Crewe), Taylor Sternberg, (Valli), Jake Speck (Gaudio, Massi, DeVito)

*Succeeded by: 1. Merissa Haddad, Cara Cooper (Jan 2011) 2. Jessica Rush 3. Ryan Jesse (10/12/11) 4. Dominic Scaglione Jr (9/29/11) 5. Scott Campbell, Jared Bradshaw, Lauren Tartaglia, Brad Bass, Nathan Scherich

MUSICIANS Andrew Wilder (Conductor/Keyboards); Deborah Hurwitz (Associate Conductor/Keyboards); Stephen "Hoops" Snyder (Keyboards); Joe Payne (Guitars); Ken Dow (Bass); Kevin Dow (Drums); Matt Hong, Ben Kono (Reeds); David Spier (Trumpet)

MUSICAL NUMBERS Ces Soirées-La (Oh What a Night), Silhouettes, You're the Apple of My Eye, I Can't Give You Anything But Love, Earth Angel, Sunday Kind of Love, My Mother's Eyes, I Go Ape, (Who Wears) Short Shorts, I'm in the Mood for Love/Moody's Mood for Love, Cry for Me, An Angel Cried, I Still Care, Trance, Sherry, Big Girls Don't Cry, Walk Like a Man, December, 1963 (Oh What a Night), My Boyfriend's Back, My Eyes Adored You, Dawn (Go Away), Walk Like a Man (reprise), Big Man in Town, Beggin', Stay, Let's Hang On (To What We've Got), Opus 17 (Don't You Worry 'Bout Me), Bye Bye Baby, C'mon Marianne, Can't Take My Eyes Off of You, Working My Way Back to You, Fallen Angel, Rag Doll, Who Loves You

SETTING New Jersey, New York, and across the U.S., 1950s–now. A new musical presented in two acts. For original production credits see *Theatre World* Vol. 62, page 34. World Premiere produced by La Jolla Playhouse, October 5, 2004.

SYNOPSIS "How did four blue-collar kids become one of the greatest successes in pop music history? You ask four guys, you get four different answers." *Jersey Boys* is the story of the legendary Four Seasons, blue-collar boys who formed a singing group and reached the heights of rock 'n' roll stardom.

Katie O'Toole, Sara Schmidt, Jessica Rush, and the Company

Matt Bogart (photos by Joan Marcus)

La Cage aux Folles

Longacre Theatre; First Preview: April 6, 2010; Opening Night: April 18, 2010; Closed May 1, 2011; 15 previews, 433 performances

Music and lyrics by Jerry Herman, book by Harvey Fierstein; Based on the play *La Cage aux Folles* by Jean Poiret; Presented by the Menier Chocolate Factory; Produced by Sonia Friedman Productions, David Babani, Barry and Fran Weissler, Edwin W. Schloss, Bob Bartner/Norman Tulchin, Broadway Across America (John Gore, CEO; Thomas B. McGrath, Chairman; Beth Williams, COO & Head of Production), Matthew Mitchell, Raise the Roof 4 (Harriet Newman Leve, Jennifer Manocherian, Elaine Krauss), Richard Winkler/Chris Bensinger/Deborah Taylor/Pam Laudenslager/Jane Bergère, Arlene Scanlan/John O'Boyle, Independent Presenters Network, Olympus Theatricals (Liz Timperman, Executive Director), Allen Spivak, Jerry Frankel/Bat-Barry Productions (Robert Masterson & Barry Weisbord), Nederlander Presentations Inc., INC/Harvey Weinstein; Director, Terry Johnson; Choreography, Lynne Page; Music Supervision, Orchestrations, & Dance Arrangements, Jason Carr; Set, Tim Shortall; Costumes, Matthew Wright; Lighting, Nick Richings; Sound, Jonathan Deans; Wigs & Makeup, Richard Mawbey; Associate Choreographer, Nicholas Cunningham; Technical Supervision, Arthur Siccardi & Patrick Sullivan; Production Stage Manager, Kristen Harris; Associate Producers, Carlos Arana, Robert Driemeyer; Music Director, Todd Ellison; Music Coordinator, John Miller; Casting, Duncan Stewart; U.K. General Management, Diane Benjamin, Pam Skinner, Tom Siracusa; General Manager, B.J. Holt; Executive Producer, Alecia Parker; Company Manager, Kimberly Kelly; Stage Manager, Glynn David Turner; Assistant Stage Manager, Neveen Mahmoud; Associate General Manager, Hilary Hamilton; General Management Associates, Dana Sherman, Stephen Spadaro; Assistant Company Manager, Dominic Shiach; Original Set Design, David Farley; Associate Design: Bryan Johnson (set), Vivien Leone (lighting); Assistant Lighting Design, Michael Hill; U.K. Production Consultant, Kristen Turner; Casting Associate, Benton Whitley; Vice President of Marketing, Todd Stuart; Director of Marketing, Ken Sperr; Advertising, SpotCo; Press, Boneau/Bryan-Brown, Adrian Bryan-Brown, Jim Byk, Michael Strassheim; Cast recording: PS Classics

CAST Georges **Kelsey Grammer**[1]; Angelique (Les Cagelles) **Nick Adams**[2]; Bitelle (Les Cagelles) **Logan Keslar**; Chantal (Les Cagelles) **Sean Patrick Doyle**; Hanna (Les Cagelles) **Nicholas Cunningham**[3]; Mercedes (Les Cagelles) **Terry Lavell**; Phaedra (Les Cagelles) **Sean A. Carmon**[4]; Francis **Chris Hoch**; Babette **Cheryl Stern**; Jacob **Robin De Jesús**[5]; Albin **Douglas Hodge**[6]; Jean-Michel **A.J. Shively**; Anne **Elena Shaddow**[7]; Colette **Heather Lindell**[8]; Etienne **David Nathan Perlow**[9]; Tabarro **Bill Nolte**[10]; Jacqueline **Christine Andreas**; M. Renaud/M. Dindon **Fred Applegate**[11]; Mme. Renaud/Mme. Dindon **Veanne Cox**[12]; Waiter **Dale Hensley**; Swings[13] **Christophe Caballero, Todd Lattimore, Caitlin Mundth**

UNDERSTUDIES Nick Adams (Jean-Michel), Christophe Caballero (Francis, Jacob), Sean Patrick Doyle (Jacob), Dale Hensley (Albin, Edouard Dindon, Francis, M. Renaud), Chris Hoch (Albin, Georges), Heather Lindell (Anne, Jacqueline, Mme. Dindon, Mme. Renaud), Caitlin Mundth (Anne), Bill Nolte (Edouard Dindon, Georges, M. Renaud), David Nathan Perlow (Jean-Michel), Cheryl Stern (Jacqueline, Mme. Dindon, Mme. Renaud)

*Succeeded by: 1. Jeffrey Tambor (2/15/11-2/24/11), Chris Hoch (2/25/11), Christopher Sieber (3/11/11) 2. Matt Ancil (8/24/10) 3. Karl Warden 4. Yurel Echezarreta 5. Wilson Jermaine Heredia (2/15/11) 6. Harvey Fierstein (2/15/11) 7. Heather Lindell (4/5/11) 8. Ashley Cate Adams (4/5/11) 9. Michael Lowney 10. Bruce Winant 11. Mike McShane (2/15/11) 12. Allyce Beasley (9/14/10), Veanne Cox (4/5/11) 13. Sean A. Carmon

ORCHESTRA Todd Ellison (Conductor/Keyboards), Antony Geralis (Associate Conductor/Keyboards), Steve Kenyon and Roger Rosenberg (Woodwinds), Don Downs (Trumpet), Keith O'Quinn (Trombone), Marc Schmied (Acoustic Bass), Sean McDaniel (Drums/Percussion)

MUSICAL NUMBERS We Are What We Are, A Little More Mascara, With Anne on My Arm, With You on My Arm, Song on the Sand, La Cage aux Folles, I Am What I Am, Song on the Sand (reprise), Masculinity, Look Over There, Cocktail Counterpoint, The Best of Times, Look Over There (reprise), Finale

SETTING Summer, St. Tropez, France; in and around the La Cage aux Folles nightclub. Revival of a musical presented in fourteen scenes in two acts. Originally presented on Broadway at the Palace Theatre August 21, 1983–November 15, 1987, playing 1,761 performances (see *Theatre World* Vol. 40, page 10). The first Broadway revival played the Marquis Theatre December 9, 2004–June 26, 2005, playing 229 performances (see *Theatre World* Vol. 61, page 44). This production premiered at London's Menier Chocolate Factory (David Babani, Artistic Director), starring Mr. Hodge, November 23, 2007–March 8, 2008 and transferred to the Playhouse Theatre October 30, 2008.

SYNOPSIS Jerry Herman and Harvey Fierstein's hilarious musical comedy *La Cage aux Folles* returns to Broadway in this production presented by London's Menier Chocolate Factory. Georges is the owner of a glitzy nightclub in Saint-Tropez, and his partner Albin moonlights as the glamorous chanteuse "Zaza." When Georges' son Jean-Michele brings his fiancée's conservative parents home to meet the flashy pair, the bonds of family are put to the test and the feather boas fly!

Terry Lavell, Nick Adams, Logan Keslar, Sean Patrick Doyle, Nicholas Cunningham, and Sean A. Carmon

Harvey Fierstein and Christopher Sieber (photos by Joan Marcus)

Anthony LaPaglia, Tony Shalhoub, and Justin Bartha

Mary Catherine Garrison and Justin Bartha

Brooke Adams and Tony Shalhoub

Lend Me a Tenor

Music Box Theatre; First Preview: March 12, 2010; Opening Night: April 4, 2010; Closed August 15, 2010; 25 previews, 153 performances

Written by Ken Ludwig; Produced by The Araca Group (Matthew Rego, Michael Rego, Hank Unger), Stuart Thompson, Carl Moellenberg, Rodney Rigby, Olympus Theatricals, Broadway Across America (John Gore, CEO; Thomas B. McGrath, Chairman; Beth Williams, COO & Head of Production), The Shubert Organization (Phillip J. Smith, Chairman; Robert E. Wankel, President) in association with Wendy Federman/Jamie deRoy/Richard Winkler, Lisa Cartwright, Spring Sirkin, Scott and Brian Zeilinger; Director, Stanley Tucci; Set, John Lee Beatty; Costumes, Martin Pakledinaz; Lighting, Kenneth Posner; Sound, Peter Hylenski; Wigs & Hair, Paul Huntley; Casting, MelCap/David Caparelliotis, Mele Nagler; Dialect Coach, Stephen Gabis; Production Stage Manager, David O'Brien; Production Management, Juniper Street Productions, Kevin Broomell, Hilary Blanken, Guy Kwan, Ana-Rose Greene, Sue Semaan; General Management, Stuart Thompson Productions, David Turner, James Triner; Executive Producer, Amanda Watkins; Company Manager, Adam J. Miller; Musical Supervisor, Patrick Vaccariello; Makeup, Joe Dulude II; Marketing Direction, Type A Marketing, Anne Rippey, Nick Pramik, Elyce Henkin; Internet Marketing/Merchandising, The Araca Group; Stage Manager Rachel E. Wolff; Assistant Director, Kristin McLaughlin; Associate Design: Kacie Hultgren (set), Sarah Sophia Lidz (costumes), Aaron Spivey (lighting), Keith Caggiano (sound); Costume Assistant, Tescia Seufferlein; Assistant to Mr. Pakledinaz, Inca Kangal; Production Management Assistants, Alexandra Paull; Assistant to Mr. Zeilinger, Robert Wachsberger; Costume Interns, Carly Bradt, Jaime Torres; Advertising, Serino Coyne, Greg Corradetti, Sandy Block, Joaquin Esteve, Lauren D'Elia Pressman; Press, Boneau-Bryan/Brown, Adrian Bryan-Brown, Jackie Green, Emily Meagher

CAST Maggie **Mary Catherine Garrison**; Max **Justin Bartha**; Saunders **Tony Shalhoub**; Tito Merelli **Anthony LaPaglia**; Maria **Jan Maxwell**; Bellhop **Jay Klaitz**; Diana **Jennifer Laura Thompson**; Julia **Brooke Adams**

UNDERSTUDIES Jessie Austrian (Diana, Maggie), Tony Carlin (Saunders, Tito Merelli), Donna English (Julia, Maria), Brian Sears (Bellhop, Max)

SETTING A hotel suite in Cleveland, in 1934, an afternoon and evening on a Saturday in September. Revival of a play presented in four scenes in two acts with one intermission. Originally produced on Broadway at the Royale Theatre (now the Bernard B. Jacobs Theatre) February 17, 1989–April 22, 1990, playing 18 previews and 476 performances (see *Theatre World* Vol. 45, page 26). World premiere at the Globe Theatre in London in 1986.

SYNOPSIS *Lend Me a Tenor* is a madcap screwball comedy that takes place when Tito Merelli, the fiery-tempered and world famous Italian superstar, arrives in Cleveland, Ohio to make his debut with the local opera and promptly goes missing. As Saunders, the show's presenter, conspires to cover for Tito's absence, placate his hot-blooded wife, and distract his most passionate fans, chaos on a truly operatic level ensues.

Anthony LaPaglia and Justin Bartha

The Lion King

Minskoff Theatre; First Preview: October 15, 1997; Opening Night: November 13, 1997; 33 previews, 5,672 performances as of May 31, 2011

Music by Elton John, lyrics by Tim Rice, additional music and lyrics by Lebo M, Mark Mancina, Jay Rifkin, Julie Taymor, Hans Zimmer; book by Roger Allers and Irene Mecchi, adapted from screenplay by Ms. Mecchi, Jonathan Roberts and Linda Woolverton; Produced by Walt Disney Theatrical Productions (Peter Schneider, President; Thomas Schumacher, Executive VP); Director, Julie Taymor; Choreography, Garth Fagan; Orchestrations, Robert Elhai, David Metzger, Bruce Fowler; Music Director/Conductor, Karl Jurman; Original Music Director, Joseph Church; Sets, Richard Hudson; Costumes/Masks/Puppets, Julie Taymor; Lighting, Donald Holder; Masks/Puppets, Michael Curry; Sound, Tony Meola/Steve Canyon Kennedy; Hair/Makeup, Michael Ward; Projections, Geoff Puckett; Technical Director, David Benken; Casting, Jay Binder; General Manager, Alan Levey; Company Manager, Thomas Schlenk; Assistant Company Manager, Fred Hemminger; Associate Producer, Anne Quart; Project Manager, Nina Essman; Production Stage Manager, Ron Vodicka; Stage Manager, Carmen I Abrazado, Antonia Gianino, Narda Alcorn, Tom Reynolds; Associate Director, Jeff Lee; Resident Director, Darren Katz; Resident Dance Supervisor, Ruthlyn Salomons; Associate Design: Peter Eastman (set), Mary Nemecek Peterson (costumes), Louis Troisi (mask & puppets), John Shivers (sound), Carole Hancock (hair & wigs), Jeanne Koenig (lighting); Assistant Design: Marty Vreeland (lighting), Shane Cook (sound); Executive Music Producer, Chris Montan; Vocal Arrangements, Lebo M; Music Coordinator, Michael Keller; Dance Captains, Garland Days, Willa Noel-Montague; Fight Captain, Ray Mercer; Assistant Choreographers, Norwood J. Pennewell, Natalie Rogers; South African Dialect Coach, Ron Kunene; For *The Lion King* Worldwide: Doc Zorthian (Production Supervisor), Myriah Perkins (Production Manager), John Stefaniuk (Associate Director), Marey Griffith (Associate Choreographer), Clement Ishmael (Music Supervisor), Celise Hicks (Dance Supervisor), Jay Alger (Associate Music Supervisor), Aland Henderson (Automated Lighting), Tara Engler (Production Coordinator), Elizabeth Fine (Management Assistant); Advertising, Serino Coyne Inc.; Interactive Marketing, Situation Marketing, Damian Bazadonna, Lisa Cecchini, Miriam Gardin; Press, Disney Theatricals, Dennis Crowley, Adriana Douzos, Lindsay Braverman; Cast recording: Walt Disney 60802-7

CAST Rafiki **Tshidi Manye**; Mufasa **Nathaniel Stampley**[*1]; Sarabi **Jean Michelle Grier**; Zazu **Jeff Binder**[*2]; Scar **Derek Smith**[*3]; Young Simba **Joshua J. Jackson**[*4] or **Alphonso Romero Jones II**[*5]; Young Nala **Jade Milan**[*6] or **Khail Toi Bryant**; Shenzi **Bonita J. Hamilton**; Banzai **James Brown-Orleans**; Ed **Enrique Segura**; Timon **Robert Creighton**[*7]; Pumbaa **Tom Alan Robbins**[*8]; Simba **Dashaun Young**[*9]; Nala **Ta'Rea Campbell**[*10]; Ensemble Singers[*11]: **Alvin Crawford, Lindiwe Dlamini, Bongi Duma, Jean Michelle Grier, Joel Karie, Ron Kunene, Sheryl McCallum, Brenda Mhlongo, S'bu Ngema, Nteliseng Nkhela, Selloane Albertina Nkhela, L. Steven Taylor, Rema Webb, Kenny Redell Williams**; Dancers[*12]: **Sant'gria Bello, Camille M. Brown, Michelle Brugal, Gabriel Croom, Christopher Freeman, Nicole Adell Johnson, Lisa Lewis, Charity De Loera, Ray Mercer, Brandon Christopher O'Neal, Kellen Stancil, Phillip W. Turner, Camille Workman**; Swings[*13] **Sean Bradford, Garland Days, Angelica Edwards, Kenny Ingram, Brian M. Love, Dennis Johnston, Willa-Noel Montague, James A. Pierce III, Jacqueline René, Natalie Turner, Lisa Nicole Wilkerson**; Standbys **John E. Brady**[*14] (Timon, Pumbaa, Zazu), **Thom Christopher Warren** (Scar, Pumbaa, Zazu)

*Succeeded by: 1 Alton Fitzgerald White (6/15/10) 2. Cameron Pow (6/15/10) 3. Gareth Saxe (6/15/10) 4. Judah Bellamy (3/29/11) 5. Aubrey Omari Joseph 6. Eden Sanaa Duncan-Smith, Shaylin Becton (3/29/11) 7. Fred Berman (6/15/10), Damian Baldet, Fred Berman 8. Ben Jeffrey (6/15/10), Tom Alan Robbins 9. Clifton Oliver (5/13/11) 10. Chaunteé Schuler (6/15/10) 11. Moya Angela, Trista Dollison, Andrea Jones, Cornelius Jones Jr., Vusi Sondiyazi, Lisa Nicole

Wilkerson 12. Jennifer Harrison Newman, Izell O. Blunt, Charlaine Katsuyoshi, Kristina Bethel-Blunt, Jaysin McCollum, Torya 13. Keisha Lauren Clarke 14. Jim Ferris

MUSICIANS Karl Jurman (Conductor); Cherie Rosen (Associate Conductor/Keyboard Synthesizer); Ted Baker, Paul Ascenzo (Synthesizers); David Weis (Wood Flute/Flute/Piccolo); Francisca Mendoza (Concertmaster/Violin); Krystof Witek, Avril Brown (Violins); Ralph Farris (Violin/Viola); Eliana Mendozza, Bruce Wang (Cellos); Robert DeBellis (Flute/Clarinet/Bass Clarinet); Patrick Milando, Alexandra Cook, Greg Smith (French Horns); Rock Ciccarone (Trombone); Moris Kainuma (Bass Trombone/Tuba); Tom Barney (Upright & Electric Bass); Tommy Igoe (Assistant Conductor/Drums); Kevin Kuhn (Guitar); Rolando Morales-Mantos (Assistant Conductor/Percussion); Valerie Dee Naranjo, Tom Brett (Percussion/Mallets); Junior "Gabu" Wedderburn (Percussion)

MUSICAL NUMBERS Circle of Life, Morning Report, I Just Can't Wait to Be King, Chow Down, They Live in You, Be Prepared, Hakuna Matata, One by One, Madness of King Scar, Shadowland, Endless Night, Can You Feel the Love Tonight, King of Pride Rock/Finale

A musical presented in two acts. For original production credits see *Theatre World* Vol. 54, page 20. Originally opened at the New Amsterdam Theatre and transferred to the Minskoff Theatre June 13, 2006.

SYNOPSIS Based on the 1994 Disney animated feature film, *The Lion King* tells the story of the adventures of Simba, a young lion cub, as he struggles to accept the responsibilities of adulthood and his destined role as king.

Tshidi Manye (photo by Joan Marcus)

A Little Night Music

Walter Kerr Theatre; First Preview: November 24, 2009; Opening Night: December 13, 2009; Closed January 9, 2011; 20 previews, 425 performances

Music and lyrics by Stephen Sondheim; book by Hugh Wheeler; Suggested by a film by Ingmar Bergman; Originally produced and directed on Broadway by Harold Prince; Produced by Tom Viertel, Steven Baruch, Marc Routh, Richard Frankel, The Menier Chocolate Factory, Roger Berlind, David Babani, Sonia Friedman Productions, Andrew Fell, Daryl Roth/Jane Bergère, Harvey Weinstein/Raise the Roof 3, Beverly Bartner/Dancap Productions Inc., Nica Burns/Max Weitzenhoffer, Erik Falkenstein/Anna Czekaj, Jerry Frankel/Ronald Frankel, James D. Stern/Douglas L. Meyer; Director, Trevor Nunn; Choreography, Lynne Page; Music Supervision, Caroline Humphris; Sets & Costumes, David Farley; Lighting, Hartley T.A. Kemp; Sound, Dan Moses Schreier, Gareth Owen; Wigs & Hair, Paul Huntley; Makeup, Angelina Avallone; Casting, Tara Rubin Casting; Production Stage Manager, Ira Mont; Associate Director, Seth Sklar-Heyn; Associate Choreographer, Scott Taylor; Music Direction, Tom Murray; Orchestrations, Jason Carr; Music Coordinator, John Miller; General Management, Frankel Green Theatrical Management, Richard Frankel, Laura Green, Joe Watson, Leslie Ledbetter; Technical Supervision, Aurora Productions (Gene O'Donovan, Ben Heller, Rachel Sherbill, Jarid Sumner, Melissa Mazdra, Amy Merlino Coey, Amanda Raymond, Graham Forden, Liza Luxenberg); Associate Producers, Broadway Across America, Dan Frishwasser, Jam Theatricals, Richard Winkler; Company Manager, Sammy Ledbetter; Associate Company Manager, Grant A. Rice; Stage Manager, Julia P. Jones; Assistant Stage Manager/Dance Captain, Mary MacLeod; U.K. Stage Management Consultant, Ciara Fanning; Associate Design: Josh Zangen (U.K. set), Tracy Christensen (U.S. costumes), Poppy Hall (U.K. costumes), Vivien Leone (lighting), David Bullard (sound); Assistant Design: Machiko Hombu, Cara Newman (U.K. set), Ellan Perry (U.K. costumes), Ben Hagen (lighting); U.K. Set Intern, Vicki Stevenson; U.K Costume Supervisor, Binnie Bowerman; Assistant to the Wig Designer, Giovanna Calabretta; Company Management Assistant, Travis Ferguson; Dialect Coach, Deborah Hecht; Music Consultant, Kristen Blodgette; Music Preparation, Emily Grishman (U.S.), Colin Rae (U.K.); Synthesizer Programmer, Bruce Samuels; Music Copying, Katharine Edmonds; Rehearsal Pianists, Paul Staroba, Mathew Eisenstein; Assistant to Mr. Sondheim, Steven Clar; Advertising, Serino Coyne Inc., Sandy Block, Scott Johnson, Robert Jones; Online Advertising & Marketing, Art Meets Commerce; Press, Boneau/Bryan-Brown, Chris Boneau, Heath Schwartz, Michael Strassheim; Cast recording: PS Classics 523488

CAST Henrik Egerman **Hunter Ryan Herdlicka**; Mr. Lindquist **Stephen R. Buntrock**[*1]; Mrs. Nordstrom **Jayne Paterson**[*2]; Mrs. Anderssen **Marissa McGowan**[*3]; Mr. Erlanson **Kevin David Thomas**; Mrs. Segstrom **Betsy Morgan**[*4]; Fredrika Armfeldt **Katherine McNamara** (Tues., Wed. mat, Fri., Sat. mat); **Keaton Whittaker** (Wed. eve., Thurs., Sat. eve., Sun.); Madame Armfeldt **Angela Lansbury**[*5]; Frid **Bradley Dean**[*6]; Anne Egerman **Ramona Mallory**; Petra **Leigh Ann Larkin**; Desirée Armfeldt **Catherine Zeta-Jones**[*7]; Fredrik Egerman **Alexander Hanson**[*8]; Count Carl-Magnus Malcolm **Aaron Lazar**[*9]; Countess Charlotte Malcolm **Erin Davie**; Swings[*10] **Karen Murphy**, **Erin Stewart**, **Kevin Vortmann**

UNDERSTUDIES Stephen R. Buntrock[*1] (Fredrik Egerman, Frid), Bradley Dean[*6] (Count Carl-Magnus Malcolm), Marissa McGowan[*3] (Anne Egerman, Petra), Betsy Morgan[*4] (Countess Charlotte Malcolm), Karen Murphy (Madame Armfeldt), Jayne Paterson[*2] (Desiree Armfeldt), Erin Stewart (Anne Egerman, Countess Charlotte Malcolm, Petra), Kevin David Thomas (Henrik Egerman), Kevin Vortmann (Frid)

*Succeeded by: 1. Ben Davis (8/31/10) 2. Erin Stewart 3. Sara Jean Ford, Jessica Grové (8/31/10) 4. Gina Lamparella 5. Elaine Stritch (7/13/10) 6. Stephen R. Buntrock (8/31/10), Ron Bohmer (9/28/10) 7. Bernadette Peters (7/13/10) 8. Stephen R. Buntrock (9/28/10) 9. Bradley Dean (8/31/10) 10. Matt Dengler, Heather Ayers, Justin Patterson

ORCHESTRA Tom Murray (Conductor/keyboard), Paul Staroba (Associate Conductor), Matthew Lehmann (Concert Master), David Blinn (Viola), Mairi Dorman-Phaneuf (Cello), David Young (Woodwind), Thomas Sefcovic (Bassoon), Susan Jolles (Harp), Dick Sarpola (Bass)

MUSICAL NUMBERS Overture, Night Waltz, Now, Later, Soon, The Glamorous Life, Remember?, You Must Meet My Wife, Liaisons, In Praise of Women, Every Day a Little Death, A Weekend in the Country, The Sun Won't Set, It Would Have Been Wonderful, Night Waltz II, Perpetual Anticipation, Send in the Clowns, The Miller's Son, Finale

SETTING Time: Turn of the last century. Place: Sweden. Revival of a musical presented in two acts. Originally opened on Broadway at the Shubert Theatre February 25, 1973, transferred to the Majestic Theatre September 17, 1973, and closed August 3, 1974 after 601 performances (see *Theatre World* Vol. 29, page 56). This version of the show originally played at the London's Menier Chocolate Factory (David Babani, Artistic Director), featuring Mr. Hanson as "Fredrick", November 22, 2008–March 8, 2009. The show transferred to the Garrick Theatre in the West End from March 28–July 25, 2009 for a limited commercial run.

SYNOPSIS *A Little Night Music* is set in a weekend country house in turn of the century Sweden, bringing together surprising liaisons, long simmering passions, and a taste of love's endless possibilities. Hailed as witty and wildly romantic, the story centers on the elegant actress Desirée Armfeldt and the spider's web of sensuality intrigue and desire that surrounds her.

Elaine Stritch and Bernadette Peters (photos by Joan Marcus)

Alexander Hanson, Bernadette Peters, and Aaron Lazar

Mamma Mia!

Winter Garden Theatre; First Preview: October 5, 2001: Opening Night: October 18, 2001; 14 previews, 4,000 performances as of May 31, 2011

Book by Catherine Johnson, music, lyrics, and orchestrations by Benny Andersson, Björn Ulvaeus, some songs with Stig Anderson; Produced by Judy Craymer, Richard East and Björn Ulvaeus for Littlestar Services Limited, in association with Universal; Director, Phyllida Lloyd; Sets and Costumes, Mark Thompson; Lighting, Howard Harrison; Sound, Andrew Bruce & Bobby Aitken; Wigs, Paul Huntley; Choreography, Anthony Van Laast; Musical Supervision/Orchestrations, Martin Koch; Associate Musical Director, David Holcenberg; Musical Coordination, Michael Keller; Associate Director, Robert McQueen; Associate Choreographer, Nichola Treherne; Technical Supervisor, Arthur Siccardi; General Manager, Nina Lannan; Associate General Manager/Company Manager, Rina L. Saltzman; Production Stage Manager, Andrew Fenton; Stage Managers, Sherry Cohen, Dean R. Greer; Dance Captain, Janet Rothermel; Resident Director, Martha Banta; Casting, Tara Rubin; Music Coordinator, Michael Keller; Synthesizer Programmer, Nicholas Gilpin; Press, Boneau/Bryan-Brown; London Cast recording: Polydor 543 115 2

CAST Sophie Sheridan **Alyse Alan Louis**[1]; Ali **Traci Victoria**[2]; Lisa **Halle Morris**; Tanya **Judy McLane**; Rosie **Gina Ferrall**[3]; Donna Sheridan **Beth Leavel**[4]; Sky **Corey Greenan**; Pepper **Michael Mindlin**[5]; Eddie **Raymond J. Lee**[6]; Harry Bright **David Andrew Macdonald**[7]; Bill Austin **Patrick Boll**; Sam Carmichael **John Dossett**; Father Alexandrios **Bryan Scott Johnson**; Ensemble[8] **Brent Black**, **Timothy Booth**, **Allyson Carr**, **Felicity Claire**, **Mark Dancewicz**, **Stacia Fernandez**, **Natalie Gallo**, **Heidi Godt**, **Albert Guerzon**, **Bryan Scott Johnson**, **Monica Kapoor**, **Monette McKay**, **Corinne Melançon**, **Ian Paget**, **Gerard Salvador**, **Sharone Sayegh**, **Laurie Wells**, **Blake White**; Swings[9] **Matthew Farver**, **Rachel Frankenthal**, **Eric Giancola**, **Jon-Erik Goldberg**, **Tony Gonzales**, **Joi Danielle Price**, **Janet Rothermel**, **Ryan Sander**, **Collette Simmons**

UNDERSTUDIES Brent Black (Bill, Sam, Father Alexandrios), Timothy Booth (Harry, Bill, Sam), Fleicity Claire (Lisa, Sophie), Stacia Fernandez (Tanya, Rosie), Natalie Gallo (Ali), Heidi Godt (Donna, Tanya, Rosie), Tony Gonzalez (Sky, Eddie, Father Alexandrios), Albert Guerzon (Eddie), Bryan Scott Johnson (Harry, Bill), Monica Kapoor (Lisa), Corinne Melançon (Donna, Tanya), Ian Paget (Pepper), Ryan Sander (Sky, Eddie), Gerard Salvador (Pepper), Sharone Saygh (Lisa), Laurie Wells (Blake White) (Sky)

*Succeeded by: 1. Liana Hunt (10/22/10) 2. Catherine Ricafort 3. Jennifer Perry 4. Lisa Brescia (10/22/10) 5. Mark Dancewicz 6. Matthew J. Farver, Andrew Chappelle 7. Clarke Thorell (10/22/10) 8. Meredith Akins, Michelle Dawson, Todd Galantich, Annie Edgerton, Catherine Ricafort, Allison Strong, Leah Zepel 9. Adrienne Jean Fisher

ORCHESTRA Wendy Bobbitt Cavett (Conductor/Keyboard); Rob Preuss (Associate Conductor/Keyboard 3); Steve Marzullo (Keyboard 2); Myles Chase (Keyboard 4); Doug Quinn, Jeff Campbell (Guitars); Paul Adamy (Bass); Gary Tillman (Drums); David Nyberg (Percussion)

MUSICAL NUMBERS Chiquitita; Dancing Queen; Does Your Mother Know?; Gimme! Gimmie! Gimmie!; Honey, Honey; I Do, I Do, I Do, I Do; I Have a Dream; Knowing Me Knowing You; Lay All Your Love on Me; Mamma Mia; Money Money Money; One of Us; Our Last Summer; Slipping Through My Fingers; S.O.S.; Super Trouper; Take a Chance on Me; Thank You For the Music; The Name of the Game; The Winner Takes All; Under Attack; Voulez-Vous

SETTING Time: A wedding weekend. Place: A tiny Greek island. A musical presented in two acts. For original production credits see *Theatre World* Vol. 58, Page 27.

SYNOPSIS *Mamma Mia!* collects a group of hit songs by the Swedish pop group ABBA and shapes them around the story of a single mother coping with her young daughter's marriage on a picturesque Greek isle. While the daughter plans her future with the love of her life, her mother is haunted by three different men who may or may not be her daughter's father.

Jennifer Perry and Patrick Boll (photos by Joan Marcus)

Judy McLane, Lisa Brescia, and Jennifer Perry

Mary Poppins

New Amsterdam Theatre; First Preview: October 14, 2006; Opening Night: November 16, 2006; 30 previews, 1,889 performances as of May 31, 2011

Music and lyrics by Richard M. Sherman and Robert B. Sherman, book by Julian Fellowes, new songs and additional music/lyrics by George Stiles and Anthony Drewe; based on the stories of P.L. Travers and the 1964 Walt Disney Film; Produced and co-created by Cameron Mackintosh; Produced for Disney Theatrical Productions by Thomas Schumacher; Associate Producers, Todd Lacy, James Thane; Director, Richard Eyre; Co-Direction/Choreography, Matthew Bourne; Sets/Costumes, Bob Crowley; Lighting, Howard Harrison; Co-choreographer, Stephen Mear; Music Supervisor, David Caddick; Music Director, Brad Haak; Orchestrations, William David Brohn; Sound, Steve Canyon Kennedy; Dance/Vocal Arrangements, George Stiles; Associate Director, Anthony Lyn; Associate Choreographer, Geoffrey Garratt;; Makeup, Naomi Donne; Casting, Tara Rubin; Technical Director, David Benken; Production Stage Manager, Mark Dobrow; Resident Choreographer, Tom Kosis; Company Manager, Dave Ehle; Assistant Company Manager, Laura Eichholz; Associate GM, Alan Wasser; Stage Manager, Jason Trubitt; Assistant Stage Managers, Valerie Lau-Kee Lai, Michael Wilhoite, Terence Orleans Alexander; Dance Captain, Brian Collier, Suzanne Hylenski; Dialect/Vocal Coach, Deborah Hecht; Wigs, Angela Cobbin; Illusions, Jim Steinmeyer; Technical Director, David Benken; Production Supervisor, Patrick Eviston; Production Manager, Jane Abramson; Flying, Raymond King; Automation, Steve Stackle, David Helk; Properties, Victor Amerling, Tim Abel, Joe Bivone, John Saye; Keyboard Programming, Stuart Andrews; Music Contractor, David Lai; Advertising, Serino-Coyne; Music Copyist, Emily Grisham Music Preparation; Press, Disney Theatricals, Dennis Crowley, Adriana Douzos, Lindsay Braverman; London Cast recording: Disney Theatricals 61391-7

CAST Bert **Christian Borle**[*1]; George Banks **Karl Kenzler**[*2]; Winifred Banks **Megan Osterhaus**; Jane Banks[*3] **Kelsey Fowler** or **Juliette Allen Angelo** or **Cassady Leonard**; Michael Banks[*4] **Jeremiah Kissane** or **Matthew Schecter** or **Andrew Shipman**; Katie Nanna/Annie **Kristine Carbone**; Policeman **Corey Skaggs**; Miss Lark **Jessica Sheridan**[*5]; Admiral Boom/Bank Chairman **Jonathan Freeman**; Mrs. Brill **Valerie Boyle**; Robertson Ay **Mark Price**[*6]; Mary Poppins **Laura Michelle Kelly**[*7]; Park Keeper/Mr. Punch **James Hindman**; Neleus **Nick Kepley**; Queen Victoria/Miss Smythe/Miss Andrew **Ruth Gottschall**; Von Hussler/Jack-In-A-Box **Sean McCourt**[*8]; Northbrook **Sam Strasfeld**; Bird Woman **Ann Arvia**; Mrs. Corry **Janelle Anne Robinson**; Fannie **Amber Owens**; Annie **Catherine Brunell**; Valentine **Aaron J. Albano**; William **T. Oliver Reid**; Glamorous Doll **Elizabeth DeRosa**; Ensemble[*9] **Aaron J. Albano, David Baum, Brandon Bieber, Catherine Brunell, Kristin Carbone, Elizabeth DeRosa, James Hindman, Nick Kepley, Mark Ledbetter, Melissa Lone, Sean McCourt, Jeff Metzler, Kathleen Nanni, Amber Owens, T. Oliver Reid, Janelle Anne Robinson, Laura Schutter, Chad Seib, Jessica Sheridan, Corey Skaggs, Sam Strasfeld, Catherine Walker**; Swings[*10] **Pam Bradley, Kathy Calahan, Brian Collier, Barrett Davis, Suzanne Hylenski, Rommy Sandhu, James Tabeek**

*Succeeded by: 1. Nicholas Dromard (7/16/10), Gavin Lee (8/24/10) 2. Laird Mackintosh, Karl Kenzler 3. Rozi Baker, Catherine Missal, Rachel Resheff, Brigid Harrington, Kara Oates, Sadie Seelert 4. Christopher Flaim, Ethan Haberfield, David Gabriel Lerner, Lewis Grosso, Anthony Scarpone-Lambert 5. Kate Chapman 6. Andrew Keenan-Bolger (10/12/10), Shua Potter, Andrew Keenan-Bolger 7. Ashley Brown (3/8/11) 8. Tom Souhrada 9. Tia Altinay, Nick Corley, Justin Keyes, Brian Letendre, Michelle Lookadoo, Tom Souhrada, Case Dillard, Garett Hawe, Kelly Jacobs, Regan Kays, Tyler Maynard, Kevin Samuel Yee, Brian Ogilvie 10. Julie Barnes

ORCHESTRA Brad Haak (Conductor); Dale Rieling (Associate Conductor/2nd Keyboard); Milton Granger (Assistant Conductor/Piano); Peter Donovan (Bass); Dave Ratajczak (Drums); Daniel Haskins (Percussion), Nate Brown (Guitar/Banjo/E-Bow); Russell Rizner, Lawrence DiBello (Horns); John Sheppard, Jason Covey (Trumpets); Marc Donatelle (Trombone/Euphonium); Randy Andos (Bass trombone/Tuba); Paul Garment (Clarinet); Alexandra Knoll (Oboe/English Horn); Brian Miller (Flutes); Stephanie Cummins (Cello)

MUSICAL NUMBERS Chim Chim Cher-ee, Cherry Tree Lane (Part 1), The Perfect Nanny, Cherry Tree Lane (Part 2), Practically Perfect, Jolly Holiday, Cherry Tree Lane (reprise), Being Mrs. Banks, Jolly Holiday (reprise), A Spoonful of Sugar, Precision and Order, A Man Has Dreams, Feed the Birds, Supercalifragilisticexpialidocious, Temper, Temper, Chim, Chim, Cher-ee (reprise), Cherry Tree Lane (reprise), Brimstone and Treacle (Part 1), Let's Go Fly A Kite, Good For Nothing, Being Mrs. Banks (reprise), Brimstone and Treacle (Part 2), Practically Perfect (reprise), Chim Chim Cher-ee (reprise), Step in Time, A Man Has Dreams, A Spoonful of Sugar (reprise), Anything Can Happen, A Spoonful of Sugar (reprise), A Shooting Star

SETTING In and around the Banks' household somewhere in London at the turn of the last century. American premiere of a new musical presented in two acts. For original production credits, see *Theatre World* Vol. 63, page 41. Originally opened in London at the Prince Edward Theatre on December 15, 2004.

SYNOPSIS Based on the Walt Disney classic film and the novels by P.L. Travers, *Mary Poppins* is the story of the Banks family and how their lives change after the arrival of nanny Mary Poppins at their home at 17 Cherry Tree Lane in London.

Laura Michelle Kelly and Christian Borle

Laura Michelle Kelly and Christian Borle (photos by Joan Marcus)

Memphis

Shubert Theatre; First Preview: September 23, 2009; Opening Night: October 19, 2009; 30 previews, 675 performances as of May 31, 2011

Book and lyrics by Joe DiPietro, music and lyrics by David Bryan; Based on a concept by George W. George; Produced by Junkyard Dog Productions (Randy Adams, Kenny Alhadeff, Sue Frost), Barbara and Buddy Freitag, Marleen and Kenny Alhadeff, Latitude Link, Jim and Susan Blair, Demos Bizar Entertainment (Nick Demos & Francine Bizar), Land Line Productions, Apples and Oranges Productions, Dave Copley, Dancap Productions Inc., Alex and Katya Lukianov, Tony Ponturo, 2 Guys Productions, Richard Winkler, in association with Lauren Doll, Eric and Marsi Gardiner, Linda and Bill Potter, Broadway Across America (John Gore, CEO; Thomas B. McGrath, Chairman; Beth Williams, COO & Head of Production), Jocko Productions, Patty Baker, Dan Frishwasser, Bob Bartner/Scott and Kaylin Union, Loraine Boyle/Chase Mishkin, Remmel T. Dickinson/Memphis Orpheum Group (Pat Halloran), ShadowCatcher Entertainment/Vijay and Sita Vashee; Director, Christopher Ashley; Choreographer, Sergio Trujillo; Music Producer/Music Supervisor, Christopher Jahnke; Associate Producers, Emily and Aaron Alhadeff, Alison and Andi Alhadeff, Ken Clay, Joseph Craig, Ron and Marjorie Danz, Cyrena Esposito, Bruce and Joanne Glant, Matt Murphy; Sets, David Gallo; Costumes, Paul Tazewell; Lighting, Howell Binkley; Sound, Ken Travis; Projections, David Gallo & Sandy Sagady; Hair & Wigs, Charles G. LaPointe; Fight Director, Steve Rankin; Casting, Telsey + Company; Associate Choreographer, Kelly Devine; Orchestrations, Daryl Waters & David Bryan; Musical Director, Kenny J. Seymour; Dance Arrangements, August Eriksmoen; Music Contractor, Michael Keller; Production Stage Manager, Arturo E. Porazzi; General Manager, Alchemy Production Group, Carl Pasbjerg & Frank Scardino; Production Management, Juniper Street Productions, Hilary Blanken, Guy Kwan, Kevin Broomell, Ana Rose Greene; Marketing Direction, Type A Marketing, Anne Rippey, Nick Pramik, Janette Roush, Nina Bergelson; Company Manager, Jim Brandeberry; Associate Director, Beatrice Terry; Associate Choreographer, Edgar Godineaux; Stage Manager, Gary Mickelson; Assistant Stage Manager, Monica A Cuoco; Assistant Company Manager, Tegan Meyer; Junkyard Dog Associate, Carolyn D. Miller; Associate to the General Managers, Sherra Johnston; Dance/Fight Captain, Jermaine R. Rembert; Assistant Dance Captain, Dionne Figgins; Assistant Fight Director, Shad Ramsey; Dramaturg, Gabriel Greene; Dialect Coach, Stephen Gabis; Makeup, Angelina Avellone; Associate Design: Steven C. Kemp (set), Rory Powers (costumes), Mark Simpson (lighting), Leah Loukas (hair); Assistant Design: Maria Zamansky (costumes), Alex Hawthorn (sound), Steve Channon (projections); Assistants to Desginers: Kara Harmon (costumes), Amanda Zieve (lighting); Moving Light Programmer, David Arch; Projection Programmer, Florian Mosleh; Music Copying, Christopher Deschene; Keyboard Programmer, Kenny J. Seymoure; Scenic/Projection Studio Manager, Sarah Zeitler; Advertising, SpotCo; Press, The Hartman Group, Michael Hartman, Juliana Hannett, Frances White; Cast recording: Rhino 523944

CAST White DJ/Mr. Collins/Gordon Grant **John Jellison**[1]; Black DJ **Rhett George**; Delray **J. Bernard Calloway**; Bobby **Derrick Baskin**; Wailin' Joe/Reverend Hobson **John Eric Parker**[2] Ethel **LaQuet Sharnell**[3]; Felicia **Montego Glover**; Huey **Chad Kimball**; Mr. Simmons **Michael McGrath**[4]; Clara **Jennifer Allen**[5]; Buck Wiley/Martin Holton **Kevin Covert**[6]; Perry Como/Frank Dryer **Brad Bass**[7]; Mama **Cass Morgan**[8]; Ensemble[9] **John Jellison, Rhett George, John Eric Parker, Tracee Beazer, Dionne Figgins, Vivian Nixon, LaQuet Sharnell, Ephraim M. Sykes, Danny Tidwell, Daniel J. Watts, Dan'yelle Williamson, Jennifer Allen, Kevin Covert, Hilary Elk, Bryan Fenkart, Cary Tedder, Katie Webber, Charlie Williams, Brad Bass**; Swings[10] **Candice Monet McCall, Sydney Morton, Jermaine R. Rembert**

UNDERSTUDIES Jennifer Allen (Mama), Brad Bass (Huey), Tracee Beazer (Felicia), Bryan Fenkart (Huey), Rhett G. George (Bobby, Delray), John Jellison (Mr. Simmons), John Eric Parker (Bobby, Delray), Jermaine R. Rembert (Gator), Ephraim M. Sykes (Gator), Dan'yelle Williamson (Felicia)

*Succeeded by: 1. David McDonald (3/15/11) 2. Robert Hartwell 3. Monette McKay 4. Allen Fitzpatrick, Michael McGrath, John Jellison (3/15/11) 5. Elizabeth Ward Land 6. Justin Patterson 7. Jamison Scott 8. Nancy Opel (3/15/11) 9. James Brown III, Tanya Birl, Todrick Hall, Sam J. Cahn, Preston Dugger III, Bahiyah Sayyed Gaines, Betsy Struxness, Paul McGill, Andy Mills, Bryan Langlitz, Darius Barnes, Ashley Blanchet, Felicia Boswell, Erica Dorfler, Gregory Haney, Robert Hartwell, Tiffany Janene Howard, Elizabeth Ward Land, Lyle Leland, Kevin Massey, David McDonald, Monette McKay, Justin Patterson, Jamison Scott, Ephraim Sykes 10. Tyrone A. Jackson, Jill Morrison, Daniel J. Watts

THE MEMPHIS BAND Kenny J. Seymour (Conductor/Keyboard 1), Shelton Becton (Associate Conductor/Keyboard 2), Michael Aarons (Guitars), George Farmer (Bass), Clayton Craddock (Drums), Nicholas Marchione (Trumpet), Mike Davis (Trombone), Tom Murray & Ken Hitchcock (Reeds)

MUSICAL NUMBERS Underground; The Music of My Soul; Scratch My Itch; Ain't Nothin' But a Kiss; Hello, My Name is Huey; Everybody Wants to Be Black on a Saturday Night; Make Me Stronger; Colored Woman; Someday; She's My Sister; Radio; Say a Prayer; Crazy Little Huey; Big Love; Love Will Stand When All Else Falls; Stand Up; Change Don't Come Easy; Tear the House Down; Love Will Stand/Ain't Nothin' But a Kiss (reprise); Memphis Lives in Me; Steal Your Rock 'n' Roll

SETTING Time: The 1950s. Place: Memphis, Tennessee and New York City. New York premiere of a new musical presented in two acts. World premiere produced as a joint venture at North Shore Music Theatre in Beverly, Massachusetts September 23–October 12, 2003 and at TheatreWorks in Palo Alto, California January 24–February 15, 2004. The show played LaJolla Playhouse August 19–September 28, 2008 and at 5th Avenue Theatre in Seattle January 27–February 15, 2009 prior to its Broadway debut (see Theatre World Vol. 65, pages 319 and 330).

SYNOPSIS Inspired by actual events, Memphis takes place in the smoky halls and underground clubs of the segregated 1950s. A young white DJ named Huey Calhoun who wants to change the world falls in love with everything he shouldn't: rock and roll and an electrifying black club singer who is ready for her big break. Memphis is an original story about the cultural revolution that erupted when his vision met her voice, and the music changed forever.

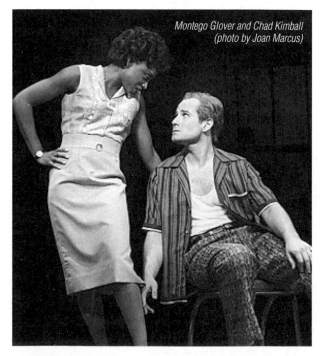

Montego Glover and Chad Kimball
(photo by Joan Marcus)

Million Dollar Quartet

Nederlander Theatre; First Preview: March 13, 2010; Opening Night: April 11, 2010; 34 previews, 474 performances as of May 31, 2011

Book by Colin Escott & Floyd Mutrux; Original concept and direction by Floyd Mutrux; Inspired by Elvis Presley, Johnny Cash, Jerry Lee Lewis, and Carl Perkins; Produced by Relevant Theatricals (Gigi Pritzker and Ted Rawlins), John Cossette Productions, American Pop Anthology, Broadway Across America (John Gore, CEO; Thomas B. McGrath, Chairman; Jennifer Costello, Associate Producer; Sara Skolnick, Associate Producer), James L. Nederlander; Director, Eric Schaeffer; Musical Arrangements/Supervisor, Chuck Mead; Set, Derek McLane; Costumes, Jane Greenwood; Lighting, Howell Binkley; Sound, Kai Harada; Hair & Wigs, Tom Watson; Associate Music Supervisor, August Eriksmoen; Casting, Telsey + Company; Marketing Director, Carol Chiavetta; Marketing, Allied Live LLC; Production Stage Manager, Robert Witherow; Production Manager, Juniper Street Productions, Hilary Blanken, Kevin Broomell, Guy Kwan, Ana Rose Greene, Sue Semaan; General Management, Alan Wasser, Allan Williams, Mark Shacket, Dawn Kusinski; Company Manager, Jolie Gabler; Assistant Director, David Ruttura; U.K. Consulting Producers, Joseph Smith, Michael McCabe; Japan Consulting Producer, TBS Services Inc.; Stage Manager, Carolyn Kelson; Assistant Stage Manager, Erik Hayden; Associate Design: Shoko Kambara (set), Moria Clinton (costumes), Ryan O'Gara (lighting); Assistant Lighting Designers, Amanda Zieve, Sean Beach; Music Contractor, Michael Keller; Additional Arrangements, Levi Kreis; Advertising, SpotCo; Press, Boneau/Bryan-Brown, Adrian Bryan-Brown, Aaron Meier, Amy Kass

CAST Carl Perkins **Robert Britton Lyons**; Johnny Cash **Lance Guest**; Jerry Lee Lewis **Levi Kreis**; Elvis Presley **Eddie Clendening**; Jay Perkins (Bass Player) **Corey Kaiser**; Fluke (Drummer) **Larry Lelli**; Sam Phillips **Hunter Foster**; Dyanne **Elizabeth Stanley**

UNDERSTUDIES Christopher Ryan Grant (Johnny), Erik Hayden (Elvis, Carl), Jared Mason (Jerry Lee, Carl), Victoria Matlock (Dyanne), James Moye (Sam); Steve Benoit (Elvis), Nicolette Hart (Dyanne), Dan Mills (Carl), Randy Redd (Jerry Lee), Billy Woodward (Elvis, Johnny)

MUSICAL NUMBERS Blue Suede Shoes, Real Wild Child, Matchbox, Who Do You Love? Folsom Prison Blues, Fever, Memories Are Made of This, That's All Right, Brown Eyed Handsome Man, Down By the Riverside, Sixteen Tons, My Babe, Long Tall Sally, Peace in the Valley, I Walk the Line, I Hear You Knocking, Party, Great Balls of Fire, Down By the Riverside (reprise), Hound Dog, Riders in the Sky, See You Later Alligator, Whole Lotta Shakin' Goin On

SETTING Time: December 4, 1956. Place: Sun Records, Memphis, Tennessee. New York premiere of a new musical presented without intermission.

SYNOPSIS On December 4, 1956, an auspicious twist of fate brought Johnny Cash, Jerry Lee Lewis, Carl Perkins, and Elvis Presley together. The place was Sun Records' storefront studio in Memphis. The man who made it happen was Sam Phillips, the "Father of Rock and Roll," who discovered them all. The four young musicians united for the only time in their careers for an impromptu recording that has come to be known as one of the greatest rock jam sessions of all time.

Levi Kreis, Elizabeth Stanley, Eddie clendening, Hunter Foster, Lance Guest, and Robert Britton Lyons (photo by Joan Marcus)

Patrick Heusinger and Patrick Breen (photo by Carol Rosegg)

Next Fall

Helen Hayes Theatre; First Preview: February 16, 2010; Opening Night: March 11, 2010; Closed July 4, 2010; 26 previews, 132 performances

Written by Geoffrey Nauffts; Produced by Elton John and David Furnish, Barbara Manocherian, Richard Willis, Tom Smedes, Carole L. Haber/Chase Mishkin, Ostar, Anthony Barrile, Michael Palitz, Bob Boyett, James Spry/Catherine Schreiber, Probo Productions, Roy Furman in association with Naked Angels (Geoffrey Nauffts, Artistic Director; John Alexander, Managing Director; Andy Donald, Associate Artistic Director; Brittany O'Neill, Producer); Director, Sheryl Kaller; Set, Wilson Chin; Costumes, Jess Goldstein; Lighting, Jeff Croiter; Original Music and Sound, John Gromada; Casting, Howie Cherpakov; Production Stage Manager, Charles Means; Marketing, Promotional and Digital Services, Allied Live; Production Management, Aurora Productions; Executive Producer, Susan Mindell; General Management, Stuart Thompson Productions, David Turner, James Triner; Company Manager, Bobby Driggers; Fight Director, Drew Leary; Stage Manager, Elizabeth Moloney; Associate Director, Joe Langworth; Associate Design: Mikiko Suzuki MacAdams (set), China Lee (costumes), Grant W.S. Yeager (lighting), Christopher Cronin (sound); Assistant Sound Design, Alex Neumann; Advertising, SpotCo. (Drew Hodges, Jim Edwards, Tom Greenwald, Beth Watson, Tim Falotico); Press, Boneau/Bryan-Brown

CAST Holly **Maddie Corman**; Brandon **Sean Dugan**; Arlene **Connie Ray**; Adam **Patrick Breen**; Butch **Cotter Smith**; Luke **Patrick Heusinger**

STANDBYS David Adkins (Adam, Butch), Clayton Apgar (Brandon, Luke), Kristie Dale Sanders (Arlene, Holly)

SETTING A hospital waiting room, an apartment, and various locations in and around New York City and Washington D.C. over the course of five years. Transfer of the Off-Broadway play presented in two acts.

SYNOPSIS *Next Fall* takes a witty and provocative look at faith, commitment and unconditional love, and forces us all to examine what it means to "believe" and what it might cost us not to. Luke believes in God. Adam believes in everything else. *Next Fall* portrays the ups and downs of this unlikely couple's five-year relationship with sharp humor and unflinching honesty. And when an accident changes everything, Adam must turn to Luke's family and friends for support… and answers. *Next Fall* goes beyond a typical love story and paints a beautiful and funny portrait of modern romance.

Next to Normal

Booth Theatre; First Preview: March 27, 2009 Opening Night: April 15, 2009; Closed January 16, 2011; 20 previews, 733 performances

Music by Tom Kitt, book and lyrics by Brian Yorkey; Produced by David Stone, James L. Nederlander, Barbara Whitman, Patrick Catullo, Second Stage (Carole Rothman, Artistic Director; Ellen Richard, Executive Director); Director, Michael Greif; Musical Staging, Sergio Trujillo; Set, Mark Wendland; Costumes, Jeff Mahshie; Lighting, Kevin Adams; Sound, Brian Ronan; Orchestrations, Michael Starobin & Tom Kitt; Vocal Arrangements, AnnMarie Milazzo; Music Director, Charlie Alterman; Music Coordinator, Michael Keller; Casting, Telsey + Company; Production Stage Manager, Judith Schoenfeld; Company Manager, Marc Borsak; Technical Supervisor, Larry Morley; General Management, 321 Theatrical Management (Nina Essman, Nancy Nagel Gibbs, Marcia Goldberg); Stage Manager, Martha Donaldson; Assistant Stage Manager, Sally E. Sibson; Assistant Director, Laura Pietropinto; Associate Choreographer, Dontee Kiehn; Assistant Music Director, Mat Eisenstein; Associate Design: Joel E. Silver (lighting), David Stollings (sound); Assistant Design: Rachel Nemec (set), Paul Toben, Aaron Sporer (lighting), Jon Collin & Shoko Kambara (scenic design assistants); Associate Technical Supervisor, Bradley Thompson; Dance Captain, Jessica Phillips; Writers' Assistant, Brandon Ivie; Production: Bill Craven (production carpenter), Richard Mortell (production electrician), Mike Farfalla (production electrician), Kenneth McDonough (carpenter), Ed White (flyman), Susan Goulet (electrician), James Keane (props), Chris Sloan (sound engineer), Elizabeth Berkeley (assistant sound engineer), Kyle LaColla (wardrobe supervisor), Sara Jane Darneille & Vangeli Kaseluris (dressers); Music Preparation, Emily Grishman; Drum and Percussion Arrangements, Damien Bassman; Additional Guitar Arrangements, Michael Aarons; Assistants: Aaron Glick (to Mr. Stone), Tara Geesaman, Jeanette Norton (to general managers), Stuart Shefter (production); Advertising, Serino Coyne Inc.; Press, The Hartman Group, Michael Hartman, Tom D'Ambrosio, Michelle Bergmann; Cast recording: Sh-K-Boom/Ghostlight Records 4433

CAST Henry **Adam Chanler-Berat**; Natalie **Jennifer Damiano**[1]; Dr. Madden/Dr. Fine **Louis Hobson**; Diana **Alice Ripley**[2]; Dan **Brian d'Arcy James**[3]; Gabe **Kyle Dean Massey**

UNDERSTUDIES AND STANDBYS Michael Berry (Standby for Dan, u.s. Dr. Madden/Dr. Fine), Jessica Phillips[4] (Standby for Diana), Meghann Fahy[5] (u.s. Natalie), Tim Young (u.s Gabe, Henry)[6]

*Succeeded by: 1. Meghann Fahy (7/19/10) 2. Marin Mazzie (7/19/10) 3. Jason Danieley (7/19/10) 4. Kathy Voytko 5. Emma Hunton & MacKenzie Mauzy 6. Brian Crum. Additional Standbys/Understudies: Curt Hanson (Gabe), Adam Kantor (Henry), Michael McElroy (Dr. Madden/Dr. Fine), Asa Sommers (Dan, Dr. Madden/Dr. Fine), Catherine Porter (Standby for Diana)

***NEXT TO NORMAL* BAND** Charlie Alterman (Conductor/Piano), Yuiko Kamakari (Piano/Violin), Benjamin Kalb/Alisa Horn (Cello), Eric Davis (Guitars), Michael Blanco (Bass), Damien Bassman (Drums/Percussion)

MUSICAL NUMBERS Prelude, Just Another Day, Everything Else, Whos Crazy/ My Psychopharmacologist and I, Perfect for You, I Miss the Mountains, Its Gonna Be Good, He's Not Here, You Don't Know, I Am the One, Superboy and the Invisible Girl, I'm Alive, Make Up Your Mind/Catch Me I'm Falling, I Dreamed a Dance, There's a World, I've Been, Didn't I See This Movie?, A Light in the Dark, Wish I Were Here, Song of Forgetting, Hey #1, Seconds and Years, Better Than Before, Aftershocks, Hey #2, You Don't Know (reprise), How Could I Ever Forget?, It's Gonna Be Good (reprise), Why Stay?/A Promise, I'm Alive (reprise), The Break, Make Up Your Mind/Catch Me Im Falling (reprise), Maybe (Next to Normal), Hey #3/Perfect for You (reprise), So Anyway, I Am the One (reprise), Light

SETTING A suburban household; the present. A new musical presented in two acts. World premiere presented at Second Stage February 13–March 16, 2008 (see *Theatre World* Vol. 64, page 190) and subsequently presented at Arena Stage (Molly Smith, Artistic Director), November 21, 2008–January 18, 2009 (see *Theatre World* Vol. 65, page 308). Originally presented and workshopped (under the title *Feeling Electric*) at the New York Musical Theatre Festival, September 2005, and the Village Theatre (Issaquah Washington), June 21-23, 2005.

SYNOPSIS *Next to Normal* explores how one suburban household copes with its past and future. How does an almost average family navigate today's over-stimulated and over medicated world? This groundbreaking new musical takes a close look at contemporary mental illness and treatment as it shows how far two parents will go to keep themselves sane and their family's world intact.

Kyle Dean Massey, Jennifer Damiano, and Adam Chanler-Berat

Kyle Dean Massey, Marin Mazzie, and Jason Danieley (photos by Joan Marcus)

The Phantom of the Opera

Majestic Theatre; First Preview: January 9, 1988. Opening Night: January 26, 1988; 16 previews, 9,723 performances as of May 31, 2011

Music and book by Andrew Lloyd Webber, lyrics by Charles Hart; additional lyrics and book by Richard Stilgoe; based on the novel by Gaston Leroux; Produced by Cameron Mackintosh and The Really Useful Theatre Company; Director, Harold Prince; Musical Staging/Choreography, Gillian Lynne; Orchestrations, David Cullen, Mr. Lloyd Webber; Design, Maria Björnson; Lighting, Andrew Bridge; Sound, Martin Levan; Original Musical Director and Supervisor, David Caddick; Musical Director, David Lai; Production Supervisor, Peter von Mayrhauser; Casting, Tara Rubin; Original Casting, Johnson-Liff Associates; General Manager, Alan Wasser; Production Dance Supervisor, Denny Berry; Associate Musical Supervisor, Kristen Blodgette; Associate General Manager, Allan Williams; Technical Production Managers, John H. Paull III, Jake Bell; Company Manager, Steve Greer; Stage Managers, Craig Jacobs, Bethe Ward, Brendan Smith; Assistant Company Manager, Cathy Kwon; Press, The Publicity Office, Marc Thibodeau, Michael S. Borowski, Jeremy Shaffer; London Cast recording: Polydor 831273

CAST The Phantom of the Opera **John Cudia**[1]; Christine Daae **Jennifer Hope Wills**[2]; Christine Daae (alt.) **Marni Rabb**; Raoul, Vicomte de Chagny **Ryan Silverman**[3]; Carlotta Giudicelli **Patricia Phillips**[4]; Monsieur André **George Lee Andrews**; Monsieur Firmin **David Cryer**; Madame Giry **Cristin J. Hubbard**; Ubaldo Piangi **Evan Harrington**; Meg Giry **Heather McFadden**; Monsieur Reyer/Hairdresser **Jim Weitzer**[5]; Auctioneer **John Kuether**; Jeweler (Il Muto) **Frank Mastrone**; Monsieur Lefevre/Firechief **Kenneth Kantor**; Joseph Buquet **Richard Poole**; Don Attilio **John Kuether**; Passarino **Jeremy Stolle**; Slave Master & Solo Dancer/Flunky/Stagehand (roles rotate weekly) **Mykal D. Laury II** or **James Zander**; Page **Kimilee Bryant**; Porter/Fireman **Chris Bohannon**; Spanish Lady **Melanie Field**; Wardrobe Mistress/Confidante **Michele McConnell**; Princess **Julie Hanson**[6]; Madame Firmin **Kris Koop**; Innkeeper's Wife **Mary Illes**; Marksman **Paul A. Schaefer**; Ballet Chorus of the Opera Populaire[7] **Emily Adonna, Polly Baird, Kara Klein, Jessy Hendrickson, Gianna Loungway, Mabel Modrono, Jessica Radetsky, Carly Blake Sebouhian, Dianna Warren**; Ballet Swing **Laurie V. Langdon**[8]; Swings **Scott Mikita, James Romick, Janet Saia, Jim Weitzer, Stephen Tewksbury**

*Succeeded by: 1. Hugh Panaro (9/7/10) 2. Sara Jean Ford (9/7/10) 3. Sean MacLaughlin (12/6/10) 4. Liz McCartney (12/6/10) 5. Greg Mills, Carrington Vilmont, Ted Keegan, Kyle Barrish 6. Susan Owen, Elizabeth Welch 7. Paloma Garcia-Lee, Erin Brooke-Burton 8. Joelle Gates, Dara Adler. Other cast subs: Harlan Bengel (Slave Master), Sean A. Carmon (Solo Dancer), Marilyn Caskey (Madame Giry at certain performances), Kelly Jeanne Grant (Innkeeper's Wife, Spanish Lady, Swing, Wardrobe Mistress/Confidante), Nancy Hess (Madame Giry), Satomi Hofman (Carlotta, Spanish Lady), Rebecca Judd (Madame Firman), Peter Lockyer (Jeweler), Elizaberh Welch (Christine Daaé at certain performances).

ORCHESTRA David Caddick, Kristen Blodgette, David Lai, Tim Stella, Norman Weiss (Conductors); Joyce Hammann (Concert Master), Alvin E. Rogers, Gayle Dixon, Kurt Coble, Jan Mullen, Karen Milne (Violins); Stephanie Fricker, Veronica Salas (Violas); Ted Ackerman, Karl Bennion (Cellos); Melissa Slocum (Bass); Henry Fanelli (Harp); Sheryl Henze, Ed Matthew, Melanie Feld, Matthew Goodman, Atsuko Sato (Woodwinds); Lowell Hershey, Francis Bonny (Trumpets); William Whitaker (Trombone); Daniel Culpepper, Peter Reit, David Smith (French Horn); Eric Cohen, Jan Hagiwara (Percussion); Tim Stella, Norman Weiss (Keyboards)

MUSICAL NUMBERS Think of Me, Angel of Music, Little Lotte/The Mirror, Phantom of the Opera, Music of the Night, I Remember/Stranger Than You Dreamt It, Magical Lasso, Notes/Prima Donna, Poor Fool He Makes Me Laugh, Why Have You Brought Me Here?/Raoul I've Been There, All I Ask of You, Masquerade/Why So Silent?, Twisted Every Way, Wishing You Were Somehow Here Again, Wandering Child/Bravo Bravo, Point of No Return, Down Once More/Track Down This Murderer, Finale

SETTING In and around the Paris Opera House, 1881–1911. A musical presented in two acts with nineteen scenes and a prologue. For original production credits see *Theatre World* Vol. 44, page 20. The show became the longest running show in Broadway history on January 9, 2006.

SYNOPSIS A disfigured musical genius haunts the catacombs beneath the Paris Opera and exerts strange control over a lovely young soprano.

Hugh Panaro and Sara Jean Ford

Evan Harrington (photos by Joan Marcus)

Promises, Promises

Broadway Theatre; First Preview: March 28, 2010; Opening Night: April 25, 2010; Closed January 2, 2011; 30 previews, 289 performances

Book by Neil Simon, music by Burt Bacharach, lyrics by Hal David; Based on the screenplay *The Apartment* by Billy Wilder and I.A.L. Diamond; By arrangement with MGM On Stage; Produced by Broadway Across America (John Gore, CEO; Thomas B. McGrath, Chairman; Beth Williams, COO & Head of Production), Craig Zadan, Neil Meron, The Weinstein Company/Terry Allen Kramer, Candy Spelling, Pat Addiss, Bernie Abrams/Michael Speyer, Takonkiet Viravan/Scenario Thailand, Norton Herrick/Barry & Fran Weissler/TBS Service/Laurel Oztemel; Director/Choreographer, Rob Ashford; Orchestrations, Jonathan Tunick; Music Director, Phil Reno; Set, Scott Pask; Costumes, Bruce Pask; Lighting, Donald Holder; Sound, Brian Ronan; Hair and Wigs, Tom Watson; Musical Coordinator, Howard Joines; Dance Music Arrangements, David Chase; Casting, Tara Rubin Casting; Production Stage Manager, Michael J. Passaro; Associate Director/Choreographer, Christopher Bailey; Production Manager, Juniper Street Productions (Hilary Blanken, Guy Kwan, Kevin Broomell, Ana Rose Green; Marketing, Type A Marketing, Anne Rippey; General Manager, Alan Wasser, Allan Williams, Mark D. Shacket; Associate Producers, Michael McCabe/Joseph Smith, Stage Ventures 2009, No. 2 Limited Partnership; Executive Producer, Beth Williams; Company Manager, Penelope Daulton; Fight Director, Thomas Schall; Stage Manager, Pat Sosnow; Assistant Director, Stephen Sposito; SDC Directing Fellow, Gregg Wiggans; Dance Captain, Sarah O'Gleby; Assistant Dance Captain, Matt Wall; Associate Design: Orit Jacoby Carroll (set), Matthew Pachtman (costumes), Karen Spahn, Carolyn Wong (lighting), Joanna Lynne Staub (sound); Assistant Design: Lauren Alvarez (set) Katie Irish, Jessica Pabst (costumes); Assistants to Designers: G. Warren Stiles (set), R. Christopher Stokes (lighting); Makeup, Ashley Ryan; Technical Director, Fred Gallo; Moving Lights Programmer, Richard Tyndall; Music Copying, Emily Grishman, Katherine Edmonds; Synthesizer Programmer, Bruce Samuels; Advertising, Serino Coyne Inc.; Website and Internet Marketing, Art Meets Commerce; Press, The Hartman Group; Cast recording: Masterworks Broadway 773495

CAST Chuck Baxter **Sean Hayes**; J.D. Sheldrake **Tony Goldwyn**; Fran Kubelik **Kristin Chenoweth**; Eddie Roth **Keith Kühl**; Mr. Dobitch **Brooks Ashmanskas**; Sylvia Gilhooley, Miss Polanski **Megan Sikora**; Mike Kirkeby **Peter Benson**; Ginger, Miss Della Hoya, Lum Ding Hostess **Cameron Adams**; Mr. Eichelberger **Seán Martin Hingston**; Vivien, Miss Wong **Mayumi Miguel**; Dr. Dreyfuss **Dick Latessa**; Jesse Vanderhof **Ken Land**; Miss Kreplinski, Helen Sheldrake **Ashley Amber**; Company Doctor, Karl Kubelik **Brian O'Brien**; Miss Olson **Helen Anker**[1]; Kathy, Orchestra Voice **Sarah Jane Everman**; Patsy, Orchestra Voice **Kristen Beth Williams**; Barbara, Orchestra Voice **Nikki Renée Daniels**; Sharon, Orchestra Voice **Chelsea Krombach**; Night Watchman, New Young Executive **Ryan Watkinson**[2]; Lum Ding Waiter **Matt Loehr**[3]; Eugene **Adam Perry**; Marge MacDougall **Katie Finneran**[4]; Swings[5] **Nathan Balser, Wendi Bergamini, Sarah O'Gleby, Matt Wall**

UNDERSTUDIES Ashley Amber (Miss Olson, Miss Polanski), Nathan Balser (Eugene, Jesse Vanderhof, Karl Kubelik, Lum Ding Waiter, Mike Kirkeby, Mr. Dobitch, Mr. Eichelberger, Night Watchman), Wendi Bergamini (Ginger, Helen Sheldrake, Miss Della Hoya, Miss Kreplinski, Miss Olson, Miss Polanski, Miss Wong, Orchestra Voice, Sylvia Gilhooley, Vivien), Sarah Jane Everman (Fran Kubelik), Ken Land (Dr. Dreyfuss, J.D. Sheldrake), Matt Loehr (Chuck Baxter, Mike Kirkeby), Sarah O'Gleby (Ginger, Helen Sheldrake, Miss Della Hoya, Miss Kreplinski, Miss Olson, Miss Polanski, Miss Wong, Orchestra Voice, Sylvia Gilhooley, Vivien), Brian O'Brien (J.D. Sheldrake, Jesse Vanderhof, Mr. Dobitch, Mr. Eichelberger, Night Watchman), Megan Sikora (Fran Kubelik, Marge MacDougall), Matt Wall (Eugene, Jesse Vanderhof, Karl Kubelik, Lum Ding Waiter, Mike Kirkeby, Mr. Dobitch, Mr. Eichelberger, Night Watchman), Ryan Watkinson (Karl Kubelik), Kristen Beth Williams (Marge MacDougall)

*Succeeded by : 1. Wendi Bergamini (12/15/10) 2. Marty Lawson (Night Watchman track only) 3. Ryan Watkinson (also remained as Young Executive) 4. Molly Shannon (10/12/10) 5. Simone De La Rue, Matthew Steffens, Ian Liberto

ORCHESTRA Phil Reno (Conductor); Mat Eisenstein (Associate Conductor/Keyboard 2); Les Scott, James Ercole, Kenneth Dybisz, Jacqueline Henderson (Reeds); Barry Danielian, David Trigg, Dan Urness (Trumpets); Jason Jackson Trombone; Perry Cavari (Drums); Michael Kuennen (Bass), Ed Hamilton (Guitar), Bill Hayes (Percussion); Rick Dolan (Concert Master/Violin); Elizabeth Lim-Dutton (Violin), Liuh-Wen Ting (Viola), Laura Bontrager (Cello), Matthew Perri (Keyboard 1)

MUSICAL NUMBERS Half As Big As Life, Grapes of Roth, Upstairs, You'll Think of Someone, Our Little Secret, I Say a Little Prayer, She Likes Basketball, Knowing When to Leave, Where Can You Take a Girl?, Wanting Things, Turkey Lurkey Time, A House Is Not a Home, A Fact Can Be a Beautiful Thing, Whoever You Are, Christmas Day, A House Is Not a Home (reprise), A Young Pretty Girl Like You, I'll Never Fall in Love Again, Promises, Promises, I'll Never Fall in Love Again (reprise)

SETTING Manhattan, 1962. Revival of a musical presented in two acts. Originally presented on Broadway at the Shubert Theatre December 1, 1968–January 1, 1972 playing 1,281 performances (see *Theatre World* Vol. 25, page 32). While this production marked the first Broadway revival, New York City Center *Encores!* presented a staged concert of the show March 20-23, 1997 (see *Theatre World* Vol. 53, page 53).

SYNOPSIS Based on the 1960 Academy Award-winning Billy Wilder film *The Apartment, Promises, Promises* tells the story of the Consolidated Life Insurance Company and Chuck Baxter, one of its charming young employees. In an effort to advance at the company, Chuck lends executives his apartment for their extramarital romantic trysts. But things become slightly complicated when Fran Kubelik, the object of Chuck's affection, becomes the mistress of one of his executives.

Sean Hayes and Kristin Chenoweth (photos by Joan Marcus)

James Spader, Kerry Washington, and Richard Thomas (photo by Robert J. Saferstein)

Race

Ethel Barrymore Theatre; First Preview: November 17, 2009; Opening Night: December 6, 2009; Closed August 21, 2010; 23 previews, 297 performances

Written and Directed by David Mamet; Produced by Jeffrey Richards, Jerry Frankel, Jam Theatricals, JK Productions, Peggy Hill & Nicholas Quinn Rosenkranz, Scott M. Delman, Terry Allen Kramer/James L. Nederlander, Mort Swinsky/Joseph Deitch, Bat-Barry Productions, Ronald Frankel, James Fuld Jr., Kathleen K. Johnson, Terry Schnuck, The Weinstein Company, Marc Frankel, Jay & Cindy Gutterman/Stewart Mercer; Associate Producer, Jeremy Scott Blaustein; Set, Santo Loquasto; Costumes, Tom Broecker; Lighting, Brian MacDevitt; Production Stage Manager, Matthew Silver; Casting, Telsey + Company; Technical Supervision, Hudson Theatrical Associates; Company Manager, Bruce Klinger; General Management, Richards/Climan Inc.(David R. Richards and Tamar Haimes); West Coast Casting, Sharon Bialy & Sherry Thomas; Stage Manager, Jillian M. Oliver; Technical Supervisor, Neil A. Mazzella/Hudson Theatrical Associates; Assistant to the Director, Justin Fair; Associate Design, Jenny Sawyers (set), David Withrow (costumes), Driscoll Otto (lighting); Associate General Manager, Michael Sag; General Management Associate, Jeromy Smith; Advertising, Serino Coyne Inc; Press, Jeffrey Richards Associates, Irene Gandy, Alana Karpoff, Elon Rutberg, Diana Rissetto

CAST Jack Lawson **James Spader**[*1]; Henry Brown **David Alan Grier**[*2]; Susan **Kerry Washington**[*3]; Charles Strickland **Richard Thomas**

UNDERSTUDIES Jordan Lage (Jack Lawson, Charles Strickland), Ray Anthony Thomas (Henry Brown), Afton C. Williamson[*4] (Susan)

*Suceeded by: 1. Eddie Izzard (6/21/11) 2. Dennis Haysbert (6/21/11) 3. Afton C. Williamson (6/21/11) 4. Kari Nicolle

SETTING The law office of Jack Lawson and Henry Brown. World premiere of a new play presented in two acts.

SYNOPSIS *Race*, a play about lies, centers on three attorneys, two black and one white, who are offered a chance to defend a white man charged with a crime against a black woman.

Red

John Golden Theatre; First Preview: March 11, 2010; Opening Night: April 1, 2010; Closed June 27, 2010; 22 previews, 101 performances

Written by John Logan; Produced by Arielle Tepper Madover, Stephanie P. McClelland, Matthew Byam Shaw, Neal Street Productions, Fox Theatricals, Ruth Hendel/Barbara Whitman, Philip Hagemann/Murray Rosenthal, The Donmar Warehouse; Presented by the Donmar Warehouse; Director, Michael Grandage; Set/Costumes, Christopher Oram; Lighting, Neil Austin; Composer & Sound, Adam Cork; Donmar Warehouse Executive Producer, James Bierman; Casting, Annie McNulty; Marketing Director, Eric Schnall; General Management, 101 Productions Ltd. (Wendy Orshan, Jeffrey M. Wilson, David Auster, Elie Landau); Production Stage Manager, Arthur Gaffin; Production Management, Aurora Productions (Gene O'Donovan, W. Benjamin Heller II, Rachel Sherbill, Jarid Sumner, Steve Rosenberg, Jarid Sumner, Melissa Mazdra, Amy Merlino Coey, Amanda Raymond, Graham Forden, Liza Luxenberg); Company Manager, Barbara Crompton; Stage Manager, Jamie Greathouse; Associate Director, Paul Hart; U.K. Scenic Associate, Richard Kent; Associate Costumes, Barry Doss; Associate Lighting, Rob Halliday (U.K.), Pamela Kupper (U.S); Associate Sound, Chris Cronin; Dialect Coach, Kate Wilson; For Donmar Warehouse: Michael Grandage (Artistic Director), Jo Danvers (General Manager); Press, Boneau/Bryan-Brown, Adrian Bryan-Brown, Jim Byk, Christine Olver

CAST Mark Rothko **Alfred Molina**; Ken **Eddie Redmayne**

UNDERSTUDIES Gabriel Ebert (Ken), Stephen Rowe (Mark Rothko)

SETTING A New York art studio in the Bowery, 1958. New York premiere of a new play presented without intermission. *Red* had its world premiere at the Donmar Warehouse December 8, 2009–February 6, 2010 prior to its Broadway run.

SYNOPSIS New York artist Mark Rothko has received the art world's largest commission to create a series of murals for The Four Seasons restaurant in the new Seagram building on Park Avenue. Under the watchful gaze of his young assistant, Ken, and the threatening presence of a new generation of artists, Rothko faces his greatest challenge yet: to create a definitive work for an extraordinary setting. *Red* is a moving and compelling account of one of the greatest artists of the twentieth century, whose struggle to accept his growing riches and praise became his ultimate undoing.

Alfred Molina and Eddie Redmayne (photo by Johan Persson)

Rock of Ages

Brooks Atkinson Theatre+; First Preview: March 20, 2009 Opening Night: April 7, 2009; 22 previews, 948 performances as of May 31, 2011

Book by Chris D'Arienzo; Produced by Matthew Weaver, Carl Levin, Barry Habib, Scott Prisand, Corner Store Fund, in association with Janet Billig Rich, Hillary Weaver, Toni Habib, Paula Davis, Simon & Stefany Bergson/Jennifer Maloney, Charles Rolecek, Susanne Brook, Israel Wolfson, Sara Katz/Jayson Raitt, Max Gottlieb/John Butler, David Kaufman/Jay Franks, Michael Wittlin, Prospect Pictures, Laura Smith/Bill Bodnar; Director, Kristin Hanggi; Choreography, Kelly Devine; Music Supervision, Arrangements & Orchestrations, Ethan Popp; Music Director, Henry Aronson; Music Coordinator, John Miller; Original Arrangements, David Gibbs; Set, Beowulf Boritt; Costumes, Gregory Gale; Lighting, Jason Lyons; Sound, Peter Hylenski; Projections, Zak Borovay; Hair & Wigs, Tom Watson; Makeup, Angelina Avallone; Casting, Telsey + Company; Production Stage Manager, Claudia Lynch; Vocal Coach, Liz Caplan Vocal Studios; Associate Choreographer, Robert Tatad; Associate Director/Stage Manager, Adam John Hunter; Associate Producer, David Gibbs; General Management, Frankel Green Theatrical Management (Richard Frankel, Laura Green, Joe Watson, Leslie Ledbetter); Technical Supervisor, Peter Fulbright/Tech Production Services Inc. (Colleen Houlehen, Mary Duffe, Miranda Wigginton); Company Management, Tracy Geltman (Manager), Susan Keappock (Assistant); Associate General Manager, Aliza Wassner; Assistant Stage Managers, Marisha Ploski & Matthew Dicarlo; Associate Design, Jo Winiarski (set), Karl Ruckdeschel (costumes), Austin Switzer (projections & programming); Assistant Design: Julia Broer & Colleen Kesterson (costumes), Driscoll Otto (lighting), Barbara Samuels (assistant to lighting designer), Keith Caggiano (sound), Daniel Brodie (projections); Creative Advisor, Wendy Goldberg; Production: Brian Munroe, Ray Harold, Mike LoBue, Brent Oakley, Phillip Lojo, Jesse Stevens, Mike Pilipski, Jacob White, Buist Bickly, Robert Guy, Joshua Speed Schwartz, Renee Borys, Michael Louis, Danny Mura, Arlene Watson, Susan Cook, Marisa Lerette; Production Assistant, Samantha Saltzman; Script Supervisor, Justin Mabardi; Synthesizer Programmer, Randy Cohen; Music Copying/Preparation, Firefly Music Service/Brian Hobbs; Rehearsal Pianist, Keith Cotton; Dance Captain, Bahiyah Sayyed Gaines; Advertising, Serino Coyne Inc.; Marketing, Leanne Schanzer Promotions & The Pekoe Group; Internet Marketing, Art Meets Commerce; Press, The Hartman Group; Cast recording: New Line Records

CAST Lonny/Record Company Man **Mitchell Jarvis**[*1]; Justice/Mother **Michele Mais**; Dennis/Record Company Man **Adam Dannheisser**[*2]; Drew **Constantine Maroulis**[*3]; Sherrie **Emily Padgett**[*4]; Father/Stacee Jaxx **James Carpinello**[*5]; Regina/Candi **Lauren Molina**[*6]; Mayor/Ja'Keith Gill/ Ensemble **André Ward**; Hertz **Paul Schoeffler**; Franz **Derek St. Pierre**[*7]; Waitress/Ensemble **Katie Webber**[*8]; Reporter/Ensemble **Katherine Tokarz**[*9]; Sleazy Producer/Joey Primo/Ensemble **Jeremy Woodard**; Young Groupie/ Ensemble **Angel Reed**[*10]; Offstage Voices **Ericka Hunter**[*11], **Matthew Stocke**[*12]; Swings[*13] **Jennifer Foote**, **Geoff Packard**, **Becca Tobin**, **Jeremy Jordan**, **Michael Minarik**

UNDERSTUDIES Ericka Hunter (Sherrie), Jeremy Jordan (Drew, Franz, Stacee Jaxx), Michael Minarik (Dennis, Hertz, Lonny, Stacee Jaxx), Katherine Tokarz (Justice, Regina), Matthew Stocke (Dennis, Hertz, Lonny), Katie Webber (Sherrie), Jeremy Woodard (Drew, Franz, Stacee Jaxx), Jennifer Foote (Justice, Regina), Geoff Packard (Drew)

*Succeeded by: 1. Jay Klaitz (9/6/10), Mitchell Jarvis (3/24/11) 2. Dee Snider (10/11/10), Adam Dannheiser (12/26/10) 3. Joey Taranto (9/10/10), Dan Domenech (3/24/11) 4. Rebecca Faulkenberry (3/24/11) 5. Mitchell Jarvis (9/13/10), MiG Ayesa (3/24/11) 6. Josephine Rose Roberts (8/2/10) 7. Cody Scott Lancaster (3/24/11) 8. Erika Hunter (3/24/11) 9. Sarah Strimmel, Emily Williams (3/24/11) 10. Julie Nelson, Tessa Alves (3/24/11) 11. Cassie Silva 12. Tony LePage 13. Ralph Meitzler, Justin Matthew Sargent, Valerie Stanois

ROCK OF AGES BAND Henry Aronson (Conductor/Keyboard), Joel Hoekstra (Guitar 1), David Gibbs or Tommy Kessler (Guitar 2), Jon Weber (Drums), Winston Roye (Bass)

MUSICAL NUMBERS We Built This City, Nothin' but a Good Time, Keep on Loving You, Just Like Paradise, I Wanna Rock, Too Much Time on My Hands, Renegade, I Hate Myself for Loving You, Oh Sherrie, Waiting for a Girl Like You, Shadows of the Night, Don't Stop Believing, Heaven, The Search is Over, We're Not Gonna Take It, High Enough, The Final Countdown, I Want to Know What Love Is, Harden My Heart, Here I Go Again, To Be With You, Every Rose Has Its Thorn, Hit Me With Your Best Shot, Can't Fight This Feeling, Wanted Dead or Alive, Cum on Feel the Noize, Any Way You Want It, Heat of the Moment, Sister Christian, More Than Words

SETTING Los Angeles and Hollywood, 1987. Transfer of the Off-Broadway musical presented in two acts. Previously presented at New World Stages October 1, 2008–January 4, 2009. World premiere at the Vanguard Hollywood January 26–February 18, 2006.

SYNOPSIS *Rock of Ages* is an explosive new musical with a heart as big as 80's rock hair. In 1987 on the Sunset Strip, as a legendary rock club faces its demise at the hands of eager developers, a young rocker hoping for his big break falls for a small town girl chasing big dreams of her own, and they fall in love to the greatest songs of the era. An arena-rock love story, *Rock of Ages* is told through the hits of some of the '80's greatest rockers including Journey, Bon Jovi, Styx, Reo Speedwagon, Pat Benatar, Joan Jett, Warrant, Night Ranger, Extreme, Foreigner, Survivor, Quarterflash, Damn Yankees, Twisted Sister, Poison, Asia, and Whitesnake.

+The show temporarily closed January 9, 2011, went on a ten week hiatus, and reopened at the Helen Hayes Theatre March 24, 2011.

The Company (photo by Paul Kolnik)

Sondheim on Sondheim

Studio 54; First Preview: March 19, 2010; Opening Night: April 22, 2010; Closed June 27, 2010; 37 previews, 76 performances

Music and lyrics by Stephen Sondheim; Conceived and directed by James Lapine; Produced by the Roundabout Theatre Company (Todd Haimes, Artistic Director; Harold Wolpert, Managing Director; Julia C. Levy, Executive Director); Musical Staging, Dan Knechtges; Music Direction/Arrangements, David Loud; Sets, Beowulf Boritt; Costumes, Susan Hilferty; Lighting, Ken Billington; Sound, Dan Moses Schreier; Video & Projections, Peter Flaherty; Orchestrations, Michael Starobin; Music Coordinator, John Miller; Conductor/Rehearsal Pianist, Andy Einhorn; Production Stage Manager, Peter Hanson; Casting, Jim Carnahan; Technical Supervisor, Steve Beers; Executive Producer/General Manager, Sydney Beers; Marketing/Sales Promotion, David B. Steffen; Founding Director, Gene Feist; Associate Artistic Director, Scott Ellis; Director of Artistic Development & Casting, Jim Carnahan; Education, Greg McCaslin; Finance, Susan Neiman; Telesales, Marco Frezza; Sales Operations, Charlie Garbowski Jr.; Concept Inspiration, David Kernan; Company Manager, Denise Cooper; Stage Manager, Shawn Pennington; Wigs, Tom Watson; Hair, John Barrett; Company Manager Assistant, David Solomon; Assistant Director; Sarna Lapine; Assistant Musical Stager, DJ Gray; Assistant to Mr. Sondheim, Steve Clar; Assistant Technical Supervisor, Chad Woerner; Associate Design: Jo Winiarski (set), Tricia Barsamian (costumes), John Demous (lighting), David Bullard (sound), Austin Switser (video/video programmer), Joshua Higgason (video); Assistant Design: Jason Lajka, Maiko Chii (set), Jeremy Cunningham (lighting), Daniel Brodie (video); Assistant to Costume Designer, Becky Lasky; Costume Shopper, Brooke Cohen; Production Sound Engineer, Scott Anderson; Lead Video Animator, Michael Bell-Smith; Musical Assistant, David Ben Dabbon; Assistant to John Miller, Nichole Jennino; Synthesizer Programmer, Randy Cohen; Music Copying, Emily Grishman, Katharine Edmonds; Advertising, SpotCo; Press, Boneau/Bryan-Brown, Adrian Bryan-Brown, Matt Polk, Jessica Johnson, Amy Kass; Cast recording: PS Classics 1083

CAST Barbara Cook, Leslie Kritzer, Norm Lewis, Erin Mackey, Euan Morton, Matthew Scott, Vanessa Williams, Tom Wopat

UNDERSTUDIES Kyle Harris (Euan Morton, Matthew Scott), N'Kenge (Vanessa Williams, Leslie Kritzer, Erin Mackey)

ORCHESTRA Andy Einhorn (Conductor/Piano), Mark Hartman (Assistant Conductor/Keyboard), Christian Hebel (Concert Master/Violin), Sarah Seiver (Cello), Rick Heckman & Alden Banta (Woodwinds), R.J. Kelly (French Horn), Bill Ellison (Bass)

MUSICAL CHRONOLOGY I'll Meet You at the Donut (*By George*); So Many People (*Saturday Night*); Something's Coming (*West Side Story*), Smile, Girls (*Gypsy*); Invocation/Forget War, Love Is in the Air, Comedy Tonight (*A Funny Thing Happened on the Way to the Forum*); Anyone Can Whistle (*Anyone Can Whistle*); Do I Hear a Waltz? (*Do I Hear a Waltz?*); Take Me to the World (*Evening Primrose*); You Could Drive a Person Crazy, The Wedding Is Off, Multitudes of Amys, Happily Ever After, Being Alive, Company (*Company*); Ah, But Underneath, Waiting for the Girls Upstairs, In Buddy's Eyes (*Follies*); Send in the Clowns, A Weekend in the Country (*A Little Night Music*); Entr'acte (*Pacific Overtures*); Epiphany (*Sweeney Todd*); Now You Know, Franklin Shepard Inc., Good Thing Going, Opening Doors, Not a Day Goes By, Old Friends (*Merrily We Roll Along*); Finishing the Hat, Sunday, Beautiful (*Sunday in the Park With George*); Children Will Listen, Ever After (*Into the Woods*); Something Just Broke, The Gun Song (*Assassins*); Fosca's Entrance (I Read), Is This What You Call Love?, Loving You, Happiness (*Passion*); The Best Thing That Ever Has Happened (*Road Show* formerly titled *Bounce*); God (original number for *Sondheim on Sondheim*)

World premiere of a new musical revue with video presented in two acts.

SYNOPSIS He brought us *Into The Woods*, *Company*, *Sweeney Todd*, *A Little Night Music*, *Sunday in the Park with George*, *A Funny Thing Happened On The Way To The Forum*, *West Side Story* and *Gypsy* (to name a few). By writing songs that reflect the complexity of his characters, he has changed the way we define a great musical. But even though millions of fans know his songs by heart, few know much about Stephen Sondheim himself. Until now. *Sondheim on Sondheim* offers an intimate portrait of the famed composer in his *own* words... and music. Through the use of exclusive interview footage, the revue takes an inside look at Sondheim's personal life and artistic process. With brand-new arrangements of over two dozen Sondheim tunes, ranging from the beloved to the obscure, and helmed by frequent Sondheim collaborator James Lapine, this unique experience takes audiences inside the life and mind of an ordinary New Yorker... with an extraordinary talent.

Barbara Cook and Vanessa Williams (photos by Richard Termine)

Vanessa Williams, Tom Wopat, Matthew Scott, Erin Mackey, Barbara Cook, Euan Morton, Norm Lewis, and Leslie Kritzer

South Pacific

Vivian Beaumont Theatre; First Preview: March 1, 2008; Opening Night: April 3, 2008; Closed August 22, 2010; 37 previews, 996 performances

Music by Richard Rodgers, lyrics and book by Oscar Hammerstein II, book and original staging by Joshua Logan, adapted from the novel "Tales of the South Pacific" by James A. Michener; Produced by Lincoln Center Theater (André Bishop, Artistic Director; Bernard Gersten, Executive Producer) in association with Bob Boyett; Director, Bartlett Sher; Musical Staging, Christopher Gattelli; Music Director, Ted Sperling; Sets, Michael Yeargan; Costumes, Catherine Zuber; Lighting, Donald Holder; Sound, Scott Lehrer; Orchestrations, Robert Russell Bennett; Dance & Incidental Music Arrangements, Trude Rittmann; Casting, Telsey + Company; Production Stage Manager, Michael Brunner; Musical Theatre Associate Producer, Ira Weitzman; General Manager, Adam Siegel; Production Manager, Jeff Hamlin/Rolt Smith; Development, Hattie K. Jutagir; Marketing, Linda Mason Ross; Finance, David S. Brown; Education, Kati Koerner; Dramaturg, Anne Cattaneo; Vocal Coach, Deborah Hecht; Company Manager, Matthew Markoff, Jessica Perlmeter Cochrane/Josh Lowenthal; Assistant Company Manager, Daniel Hoyos; Assistant Stage Managers, David Sugarman, Samantha Greene, Dana Williams; Dance Captain, Wendy Bergamini/George Psomas; Assistant Dance Captain, George Psomas/Margot de la Barre; Assistant Director, Sarna Lapine; Associate Choreographer, Joe Langworth; Associate Design: Lawrence King (sets), Karen Spahn (lighting), Leon Rothenberg (sound); Assistant Design: Mikiko Suzuki (sets), Holly Cain, David Newell, Court Watson (costumes), Caroline Chao (lighting); Rehearsal Pianist, Jonathan Rose; Wigs and Hair, Tom Watson; Makeup, Cookie Jordan; Properties Coordinator, Kathy Fabian; Music Coordinator, David Lai; Press, Philip Rinaldi, Barbara Carroll; Cast recording: Sony BMG – Masterworks Broadway 88697-30457-2

CAST Ensign Nellie Forbush **Laura Osnes**[*1]; Emile de Becque **Paulo Szot**; Ngana **Laurissa Romain**; Jerome **Luka Kain**; Henry **Helmar Augustus Cooper**; Bloody Mary **Loretta Ables Sayre**; Liat **Li Jun Li**; Bloody Mary's Assistants **MaryAnn Hu, Debra Lew**[*2], **Kimber Monroe**; Luther Billis **Danny Burstein**; Stewpot **Eric Anderson**; Professor **Christian Delcroix**; Lt. Joseph Cable, USMC **Andrew Samonsky**; Capt. George Bracket, USN **Skipp Sudduth**; Cmdr. William Harbison, USN **Sean Cullen**; Lt. Buzz Adams **George Merrick**; Yeoman Herbert Quale **Jason Michael Snow**; Radio Operator Bob McCaffrey **Peter Lockyer**; Seabee Morton Wise **Todd Cerveris**; Seabee Richard West **Nick Mayo**; Seabee Johnny Noonan **Michael Arnold**; Seabee Billy Whitmore **Robert Lenzi**; Sailor Tom O'Brien **Alfie Parker Jr.**; Sailor James Hayes **Jerold E. Solomon**; Sailor Kenneth Johnson **Christian Carter**; Petty Officer Hamilton Steeves **Taylor Frey**; Seaman Thomas Hassinger **Craig Bennett**; Shore Patrolman Lt. Eustis Carmichael **Rob Gallagher**; Lead Nurse Lt. Genevieve Marshall **Liz McCartney**; Ensign Dinah Murphy **Laura Marie Duncan**; Ensign Janet MacGregor **Samantha Shafer**; Ensign Connie Walewska **Margot de la Barre**; Ensign Sue Yaeger **Garrett Long**; Ensign Cora MacRae **Marla Mindelle**; Islanders, Sailors, Seabees, Party Guests: **Michael Arnold, Craig Bennett, Christian Carter, Todd Cerveris, Helmar Augustus Cooper, Margot de la Barre, Laura Marie Duncan, Taylor Frey, Rob Gallagher, MaryAnn Hu, Robert Lenzi, Deborah Lew**[*2], **Garrett Long, Nick Mayo, Liz McCartney, George Merrick, Kimber Monroe, Alfie Parker Jr., Samantha Shafer, Jason Michael Snow, Jerold E. Solomon**; Swings **Julie Foldesi, Greg Roderick, Correy West, George Psomas**

*Succeeded by: 1. Kelli O'Hara (8/10/11) 2. Lamae. Additional understudies: Becca Ayers, Christopher Carl

ORCHESTRA Ted Sperling/James Moore (Conductor); Fred Lassen (Associate Conductor); Belinda Whitney (Concertmistress); Antoine Silverman, Karl Kawahara, Katherine Livolsi-Landau, Lisa Matricardi, Jim Tsao, Michael Nicholas, Rena Isbin, Louise Owen (Violins); David Blinn, David Creswell (Violas); Peter Sachon, Caryl Paisner (Celli); Charles du Chateau (Assistant Conductor/Cello); Lisa Stokes-Chin (Bass); Liz Mann (Flute/Piccolo); Todd Palmer, Shari Hoffman (Clarinet); Matt Dine/Kelly Perai (Oboe/English Horn); Damian Primis (Bassoon); Robert Carlisle, Chris Komer, Shelagh Abate, Daniel Grabois (French Horns); Dominic Derasse, Gareth Flowers, Wayne Dumaine (Trumpets); Mark Patterson, Mike Boschen, Nate Mayland (Trombones); Marcus Rojas/Andrew Rodgers (Tuba); Grace Paradise (Harp); Bill Lanham (Drums/Percussion)

MUSICAL NUMBERS Overture, Dites-Moi, A Cockeyed Optimist, Twin Soliloquies, Some Enchanted Evening, Dites-Moi (reprise), Bloody Mary, There Is Nothin' Like a Dame, Bali Ha'i, My Girl Back Home, I'm Gonna Wash That Man Right Outa My Hair, Some Enchanted Evening (reprise), A Wonderful Guy, Bali Ha'i (reprise), Younger Than Springtime, Finale Act I, Entr'acte, Happy Talk, Honey Bun, You've Got to Be Carefully Taught; This Nearly Was Mine, Some Enchanted Evening (reprise), Finale Ultimo

SETTING The action takes place on two islands in the South Pacific during World War II. Revival of a musical presented in two acts.

SYNOPSIS Rodgers and Hammerstein's classic receives its first major New York revival, almost sixty years after its debut. The story centers on the romance between a southern nurse and a French planter who find love on a small tropical island amidst a backdrop of war and racism.

Laura Osnes, Danny Burstein, and the Company (photos by Joan Marcus)

Paulo Szot, Laurissa Romain, Luka Kain, and Laura Osnes

West Side Story

Palace Theatre; First Preview: February 23, 2009 Opening Night: March 19, 2009; Closed January 2, 2011; 27 previews, 748 performances

Book and direction by Arthur Laurents, music by Leonard Bernstein, lyrics by Stephen Sondheim; Conception and original direction and choreography by Jerome Robbins; Produced by Kevin McCollum, James L. Nederlander, Jeffrey Seller, Terry Allen Kramer, Sander Jacobs, Roy Furman/Jill Furman Willis, Freddy DeMann, Robyn Goodman/Walt Grossman, Hal Luftig, Roy Miller, The Weinstein Company, and Broadway Across America; Choreography Reproduction, Joey McKneely; Music Supervisor/Music Director, Patrick Vaccariello; Set, James Youmans; Costumes, David C. Woolard; Lighting, Howell Binkley; Sound, Dan Moses Schreier; Wigs & Hair, Mark Adam Rampmeyer; Makeup, Angelina Avallone; Casting, Stuart Howard, Amy Schecter, Paul Hardt; Associate Director, David Saint; Associate Choreographer, Lori Werner; Associate Producer, LAMS Productions; Translations, Lin-Manuel Miranda; Orchestrations, Leonard Bernstein with Sid Ramin and Irwin Kostal; Music Coordinator, Michael Keller; Production Stage Manager, Joshua Halperin; Original Broadway Production Co-Choreography, Peter Gennaro; Technical Supervisor, Brian Lynch; Marketing, Scott A. Moore; General Management, The Charlotte Wilcox Company (Seth Marquette, Matthew W. Krawiec, Dina S. Friedler, Margaret Wilcox); Company Manager, James Lawson; Assistant Company Manager, Erica Ezold; Stage Manager, Lisa Dawn Cave; Assistant Stage Manager, Jason Brouillard; Assistant to the Director, Isaac Klein; Fight Director, Ron Piretti; Dance Captain, Marina Lazzaretto; Assistant Dance Captain, Michaeljon Slinger; Fight Captain, Joshua Buscher; Keyboard Programmer, Randy Cohen; Associate Design: Jerome Martin (set), Ryan O'Gara (lighting), David Bullard (sound); Assistant Design: Robert Martin, Daryl A. Stone, Maria Zamansky (costumes), Carrie Wood (lighting); Assistants to Designers: Sara James, Yuri Cataldo, Angela Harner (costume), Lazaro Arencibia (makeup); Moving Light Programmer, David Arch; Assistant Keyboard Programmers, Bryan Cook, Jim Mironchik; Production Assistants, Rachel E. Miller, Zac Chandler; Advertising/Website, SpotCo; Press, The Hartman Group; Cast recording: Sony Masterworks 88697-52391-2

CAST *The Jets:* Action **Wes Hart**; Anybodys **Sara Dobbs**; A-Rab **Kyle Coffman**; Baby John **Ryan Steele**; Big Deal **Mikey Winslow**; Diesel **Joshua Buscher**[1]; Graziella **Pamela Otterson**; Hotsie **Marina Lazzaretto**; Kiddo **Michael Kleeman** or **Kyle Brenn/Nathan Brenn**; Mugsy **Amy Ryerson**[2]; Riff **John Arthur Greene**; Snowboy **Mike Cannon**; Tony **Matthew Hydzik** or **Jeremy Jordan**; Velma **Jessica Bishop**[3]; Zaza **Kaitlin Mesh**; 4H **Sam Rogers**; *The Sharks:* Alicia **Yanira Marin**[4]; Anita **Karen Olivo**[5]; Bebecita **Mileyka Mateo**; Bernardo **George Akram**; Bolo **Stephen Diaz**; Chino **Michael Rosen**[6]; Consuela **Shina Ann Morris**; Federico **Phillip Spaeth**[7]; Fernanda **Kat Nejat**; Inca **Isaac Calpito**; Indio **Manuel Santos**[8]; Lupe **Tanairi Sade Vazquez**; Maria **Josefina Scaglione**[9]; Pepe **Sean Ewing**[10]; Rosalia **Jennifer Sanchez**[11]; Tio **Jace Coronado**; *The Adults:* Doc **Greg Vinkler**; Glad Hand **Michael Mastro**[12]; Krupke **Lee Sellars**[13]; Lt. Schrank **Steve Bassett**; Swings **Deanna Aguinaga, Jessica Bishop, Shawn Burgess, Angelica Burgos, Haley Carlucci, Desirée Davar, Sean Ewing, Karla Puno Garcia, Tim

Hausemann, Michael D. Jablonski, Matthew Marks, Angelina Mullins, Alex Ringler, Alex Michael Stoll, Brendon Stimson; Standby for Adults **Mark Zimmerman**; Standby for Tony **Matt Shingledecker**

*Succeeded by: 1. Colt Prattes 2. Skye Mattox 3. Lindsay Dunn 4. Kristine Covillo 5. Natalie Cortez 6. Manuel Santos 7. Waldemar Quinones-Villanueva 8. Patrick Ortiz 9. Sarah Amengual 10. Michael Williams 11. Renée Marino 12. Greg Vinkler 13. Ron Piretti

ORCHESTRA   Patrick Vaccariello (Conductor); Maggie Torre (Associate Conductor/Piano); Martin Agee (Concertmaster/Violin); Paul Woodiel, Robert Shaw, Victoria Paterson, Fritz Krakowski, Dana Ianculovici, Philip Payton (Violins); Peter Prosser, Vivian Israel, Diane Barere, Jennifer Lang (Celli); Bill Sloat (Bass); Lawrence Feldman, Lino Gomez, Dan Willis, Adam Kolker, Gilbert DeJean (Reeds); John Chudoba [lead], Trevor Neumann, Matthew Peterson (Trumpets); Tim Albright (Trombone); Jeff Nelson (Bass Trombone); Chris Komer, Theresa MacDonnell (French Horns); Jim Laev (Keyboard); Eric Poland (Drums); Dan McMilla, Pablo Rieppi (Percussion)

MUSICAL NUMBERS Prologue; Jet Song; Something's Coming; Dance at the Gym; Maria; Tonight; America; Cool; One Hand, One Heart; Tonight (Quintet); The Rumble; Me Siento Hermosa (I Feel Pretty); Somewhere; Gee, Officer Krupke; Un Hombre Asi (A Boy Like That)/I Have a Love

SETTING   Upper West Side of New York City during the last days of summer, 1957. Revival of the musical presented in fifteen scenes in two acts. This production played a pre-Broadway engagement December 15, 2008–January 17, 2009 at Washington, DC's National Theatre, where the musical made its world premiere in 1957. Originally presented on Broadway at the Winter Garden Theatre September 26, 1957–June 27, 1959, playing 732 performances (see *Theatre World* Vol. 14, page 11).

SYNOPSIS   *West Side Story* transports the achingly beautiful tale of Shakespeare's *Romeo and Juliet* to the turbulent streets of the Upper West Side in 1950s New York City. Two star-crossed lovers, Tony and Maria, find themselves caught between the rival street gangs of different ethnic backgrounds, the "'Jets'" and the "Sharks." Their struggle to exist together in a world of violence, hate and prejudice is one of the most heart-breaking, relevant and innovative musical masterpieces of our time.

The Company (photo by Joan Marcus)

Wicked

Gershwin Theatre; First Preview: October 8, 2003; Opening Night: October 30, 2003; 25 previews, 3,154 performances as May 31, 2011

Book by Winnie Holzman, music and lyrics by Stephen Schwartz; based on the novel by Gregory Maguire; Produced by Marc Platt, Universal Pictures, The Araca Group, Jon B. Platt and David Stone; Director, Joe Mantello; Musical Staging, Wayne Cilento; Music Supervisor, Stephen Oremus; Orchestrations, William David Brohn; Sets, Eugene Lee; Costumes, Susan Hilferty; Lighting, Kenneth Posner; Sound, Tony Meola; Projections, Elanie J. McCarthy; Wigs/Hair, Tom Watson; Technical Supervisor, Jake Bell; Arrangements, Alex Lacamoire, Stephen Oremus; Dance Arrangements, James Lynn Abbott; Music Coordinator, Michael Keller; Special Effects, Chic Silber; Production Supervisor, Thom Widmann; Dance Supervisor, Mark Myars; Associate Director, Lisa Leguillou; Casting, Bernard Telsey; Production Stage Manager, Marybeth Abel; Stage Manager, Jennifer Marik; Assistant Stage Managers, Christy Ney, J. Jason Daunter; General Management, 321 Theatrical Management; Executive Producers, Marcia Goldberg and Nina Essman; Company Management, Susan Sampliner, Robert Brinkerhoff; Fight Director, Tom Schall; Flying, Paul Rubin/ZFX Inc.; Dressing/Properties, Kristie Thompson; Makeup, Joe Dulude II; Assistant Choreography, Corinne McFadden-Herrera; Music Preparation, Peter R. Miller; Synthesizer Programming, Andrew Barrett; Advertising, Serino-Coyne; Press, The Hartman Group; Cast recording: Decca B 0001 682-02

CAST Glinda **Katie Rose Clarke**; Witch's Father/Ozian Official **Michael DeVries**; Witch's Mother **Kristen Leigh Gorski**; Midwife **Kathy Santen**; Elphaba **Mandy Gonzalez**[*1]; Nessarose **Jenny Fellner**; Boq **Alex Brightman**[*2]; Madame Morrible **Rondi Reed**[*3]; Doctor Dillamond **Timothy Britten Parker**[*4]; Fiyero **Andy Karl**[*5]; The Wonderful Wizard of Oz **P.J. Benjamin**[*6]; Chistery **Mark Shunkey**[*7]; Ensemble[*8] **Nova Bergeron, Sarah Bolt, Jerad Bortz, Michael DeVries, Maia Evwaraye-Griffin, Kristina Fernandez, Adam Fleming, Kristen Leigh Gorski, Kenway Hon Wai K. Kua, Jonathan McGill, Lindsay K. Northen, Eddie Pendergraft, Alexander Quiroga, Kathy Santen, Heather Spore, Brian Wanee, Robin Wilner, David Hull, Manuel Herrera, Rhea Patterson, Nathan Peck, Mark Shunkey, Stephanie Torns, Bryan West**; Standbys **Jennifer Dinoia** (Elphaba), **Laura Woyasz** (Glinda); Swings[*9] **Anthony Galde, Brenda Hamilton, Lindsay Janisse, Amanda Rose, Jonathan Warren, Briana Yacavone, Brian Munn, Samantha Zack**

*Succeeded by: 1. Teal Wicks (2/1/11) 2. Etai BenShlomo (11/2/10) 3. Kathy Fitzgerald (6/29/11) 4. Tom Flynn (11/2/10) 5. Kyle Dean Massey (1/25/11), Richard H. Blake (3/29/11) 6. Tom McGowan (5/3/11) 7. Todd Anderson, Mark Shunkey 8. Lori Holmes, Eric Jon Mahlum, Josh Rouah, Blake Whyte, Aaron J. Albano, Betsy Webel 9. Ryan Patrick Kelly, Robert Pendilla, Kristina Fernandez, Tiffany Haas, Kevin Jordan, Libby Servais

ORCHESTRA Dominick Amendum (Conductor); David Evans (Associate Conductor/Keyboards); Ben Cohn (Assistant Conductor/Keyboards); Christian Hebel (Concertmaster); Victor Schultz (Violin); Kevin Roy (Viola); Dan Miller (Cello); Konrad Adderly (Bass); John Moses, John Campo, Tuck Lee, Helen Campo (Woodwinds); Jon Owens, Tom Hoyt (Trumpets); Dale Kirkland, Douglas Purviance (Trombones); Theo Primis, Chad Yarbrough (French Horn); Paul Loesel (Keyboards); Ric Molina, Greg Skaff (Guitars); Andy Jones (Percussion); Matt VanderEnde (Drums); Laura Sherman (Harp)

MUSICAL NUMBERS No One Mourns the Wicked, Dear Old Shiz, The Wizard and I, What Is This Feeling?, Something Bad, Dancing Through Life, Popular, I'm Not That Girl, One Short Day, A Sentimental Man, Defying Gravity, No One Mourns the Wicked (Reprise), Thank Goodness, The Wicked Witch of the East, Wonderful, I'm Not That Girl (Reprise), As Long as You're Mine, No Good Deed, March of the Witch Hunters, For Good, Finale

SETTING The Land of Oz. A musical presented in two acts. World premiere presented in San Francisco at the Curran Theatre May 28–June 29, 2003. For original production credits see *Theatre World* Vol. 60, page 34.

SYNOPSIS *Wicked* explores the early life of the witches of Oz, Glinda and Elphaba, who meet at Shiz University. Glinda is madly popular and Elphaba is green. After an initial period of mutual loathing, the roommates begin to learn something about each other. Their life paths continue to intersect, and eventually their choices and convictions take them on widely different paths.

Katie Rose Clarke and Teal Wicks

Kathy Fitzgerald (photos by Joan Marcus)

SPECIAL EVENTS

Brigadoon

Shubert Theatre; June 14, 2010

Book & lyrics by Alan Jay Lerner, music by Frederick Loewe; Adapted and directed by Charlotte Moore; Original Dances, Agnes DeMille; Produced by the Irish Repertory Theatre (Charlotte Moore, Artistic Director; Ciarán O'Reilly, Producing Director); Music Director and Conductor, Mark Hartman; Choreography, Barry McNabb; Lighting, Howell Binkley; Stage Managers, Pamela Brusoski, Christine Lemme, Rebecca C. Monroe; Hosts: Matthew Broderick and Jonathan Cake

CAST Narrator **Ciaráran O'Reilly**; Tommy Albright **Jason Danieley**; Jeff Douglas **Don Stephenson**; Harry Beaton **Ciaran Sheehan**; Meg Brockie **Christine Ebersole**; Andrew McLaren **Gordon Stanley**; Andrew McLaren **Jim Brochu**Fiona McLaren **Melissa Errico**; Jean McLaren **Bonnie Fraser**; Angus McGuffie **Christopher Lynn**; Charlie Dalrymple **A.J. Shively**; Mr. Lundie **Len Cariou**; Jane Ashton **Kerry Conte**; Dancers **Karl Maier**, **Morgan McEwen**; Bagpiper **Jock Nisbet**; Towsfolk of Brigadoon **Michael Alden, Anthony Aloise, Sean Bernardi, Brad Bradley, Bill Brooks, Dewey Caddell, Matt Castle, Elizabeth Cherry, Dashira Cortes, Dan Debenport, Scott Denny, Natalie Douglas, Beth Eunice, Katie Fabel, Frank Galgano, Shawna Hamic, Rita Harvey, A.J. Irvin, Danny Katz, Daniel Frank Kelly, Matt Leahy, Robyn Lee, David Levinson, Harold Lewter, Elizabeth Lucas, Michael Mahoney, Gregory McDonald, Jake Liam McGuire, Helen McTernan, Brian Nash, Mary Orzano, Georgia Osborne, Marcie Passley, Robyn Payne, Kate Postotnik, Steve Schalchlin, Becca Shimkin, Seth Sikes, Emily Skeggs, Tom Stajmiger, Peter Tinaglia, Sorab Wadia, Jim Williams, Darryl Winslow, Jennifer Wren**

ORCHESTRA Mark Hartman (Conductor), Jeff Schiller (Flute/Piccolo), Steven Lyon (Oboe), Joseph D'Auguste (Clarinet 1), Ed Nishimura (Clarinet 2), Anny Lyle (Bassoon), Benjamin Brody (Horn), Timothy Wendt (Trumpet 1), Colin Brigstocke (Trumpet 2), Jason Wiseman (Trumpet 3), Kevin Birk (Trombone), Michael Croiter (Percussion), Chris Haberl (Piano/Celeste), Blair Lawhead (Violin/Concertmaster), Martha Mott-Gale, Antonia Nelson (Violin 1), Kiku Enomoto Vonnie Quinn(Violin 2), Karlos Rodruguez (Cello), Steve Millhouse (Bass)

MUSICAL NUMBERS Prologue, Brigadoon, Down on MacConnachy Square, Waitin' For My Dearie, I'll Go Home With Bonnie Jean, The Heather on the Hill, Come To Me Bend To Me, Come To Me Bend To Me (reprise), Pas de Deux, Almost Like Bein' In Love; End of Lundie Scene, Chase Interlude, There But For You Go I, My Mother's Weddin' Day, Reprises, Brigadoon, Finale

Concert version of a revival of a musical presented without intermission. The original production opened on Broadway at the Ziegfeld Theatre March 13, 1947 playing 581 performances (see *Theatre World* Vol. 2, page 94).

SYNOPSIS The Irish Repertory produces a ninety-minute concert version of the Lerner and Loewe classic musical for their annual Gala Benefit. In *Brigadoon*, Tommy and Jeff, two American tourists traveling in the Scottish Highlands, stumble upon the mystical village of Brigadoon, a town that only appears every 100 years. When Tommy falls in love with Fiona, one of the local lasses, he must decide if he will stay in the town as it disappears in the mist or return to his life in New York City and never see her again. He decides to return home, and finds himself lost and in misery. He returns to Scotland in hopes of finding Fiona, and the power of his love reawakens the slumbering town just long enough for him join her.

Broadway Bares XX: Strip-opoly

Roseland Ballroom; June 20, 2010

Produced by Broadway Cares/Equity Fights AIDS, Michael Graziano, Scott Tucker; Executive Producer, Jerry Mitchell; Director, Josh Rhodes; Lighting, Paul Miller; Set, Mary Houston; Production Design, Michael Clark; Costume Coordination, Elizabeth Dellario; Hair & Wig Coordination, Danny Koye; Makeup Design and Coordination, The M•A•C Pro Team; Sound, Acme Sound Partners; Production Manager, Nathan Hurlin; Production Stage Manager, Jennifer Rogers; Presenting Sponsor, M•A•C Viva; Sponsors, 1-800-Postcards, Absolut Vodka, Actors Connection, aussieBum, CAA, Club H Fitness, Continental Airlines, Harrah's, New York Marriott Marquis, Next Magazine, Showtime, Zarley Family Fondation; Choreographers, Enrique Brown, Tammy Colucci, Josh Dean, Armado Farfan Jr., Nick Kenkel, Larry Keigwin, Dontee Kiehn, Steve Konopelski, Stephanie Lang, Lorin Latarro, Melissa Rae Mahon, Sean McKnight, Barry Morgan, Josh Rhodes, Lee Wilkins; Associate Producers, Trisha Doss, Colyn Fiendel; Associate Production Manager and Props, Michael Palm; Associate Director, Lee Wilkins; Assistant to the Director, Christopher Berens; Stage Managers, Alix Claps, Zac Chandler, Kimothy Cruise, Aurora De Lucia, Christopher Economakos, Colyn Fiendel, Theresa Flanagan, Melanie Ganim, Bess Marie Glorioso, Marci Glotzer, Michaeil Haynes, Cynthia M. Hennon, Kelly Ice, Trey Johnson, Samuel-Moses Jones, Terri K. Kohler, Talia Krispel, Jerry Dee Lame, Melissa Magliula, Rachel Maier, Kelly McGrath, Johnny Milani, Francis Eric Montesa, John Murdock, Shawn Pennington, Jason Quinn, Brian Rardin, Lisa Schwartz, Justin Scribner, Daniel Seth, David Sugarman, Ron Tal, Jason Trubitt, Alex Lyu Volckhausen; Rotation Masters, Christopher Sleber, Jen Cody; Scenes written by Mark Waldrop, Eric Kornfeld; Opening Number Music, David Nehls; Press, Boneau/Bryan-Brown

The Company of the Irish Repertory Theatre Brigadoon *Concert (photo by James Higgins)*

THE COMPANY Euan Morton, Kristin Chenoweth, Vanessa Williams, Felicia Finely, Rachelle Rak, Lucy Liu, Reichen Lehmkuhl, Alysha Umphress, John Carroll, Jackie Hoffman, Katie Finneran, Diana DiGarmo, Rosie Colosi, Danny Calvert, Scott Guthrie, Rachel Potter, Marty Thomas, Nick Adams, Heidi Blickenstaff, Kevin Burrows, Charles Busch, Kevin Chamberlin, Jennifer Cody, Alan Cumming, Lea DeLaria, Barrett Foa, Julie Halston, Cheynee Jakcson, Denis Jones, Julia Murney, Christopher Sieber, Andrew Rannells, Bruce Vilanch, Lillias White, Jerry Mitchell; DANCERS: Cesar Abreu, Cameron Adams, Scott Ahearn, Monique Alhaddad, John Alix, Matt Anctil, Beckley Andrews, Sara Antkowiak-Maier, Ashley Arcement, Allyson Carr Arena, Dave August, Jolynn Baca, Sol Baird, Matthew Baker, Steven Boyd Baker, Hettie Barnhill, Sant'gria Bello, Daniel Bentley, John Berno, Brandon Bieber, Ward Billeisen, Michael Blatt, Nathaniel Braga, Scott Brateng, Steve Bratton, Nancy Renée Braun, Amy Brewer, Jessica Leigh Brown, James Brown III, Lawrence M. Bullock, Joshua Buscher, Tym Byerz, Daniel Byrd, Christophe Caballero, Michelle Aguilar-Camaya, LaMae Caparas, Sean Carmon, Aaron Carr, John Carroll, Adam Cassel, Andrew Cheng, Lindsey Clayton, Jennifer Cody, Shaun Colledge, Lani Corson, Gabriel Croom, Holly Cruz, Colin Cunliffe, Nicholas Cunningham, Michael Cusumano, Jason Davies, Barrett Davis, Kristin Rose DeCesare, Antonio deMarco, Kyle DesChamps, Michelle Dowdy, Sean Patrick Doyle, Sara Edwards, Trevor Efinger, Hillary Elk, Hillary Elliott, Lynann Escatel, Daniel Lynn Evans, Sean Ewing, Armando Farfan Jr., Felicia Finley, Russell Fischer, Adam Fleming, Kenny Frisby, Andrew Glaszek, Duane Gosa, Jonathon Grant, Alyssa Gray, David Gray, Jessica Green, Latrice M. Gregory, Jenny Gruby, Tony Guerrero, Autumn Guzzardi, Aaron Hamilton, Ellie Harrison, Adam Michael Hart, Mair Heller, Nam Holtz, Rory Hughes, Tyrone A. Jackson, Danielle Jordan, Naomi Kakuk, Rachel Kelley, Reed Kelly, Mike Kelton, Logan Keslar, Freddie Kimmel, Kyle Kleiboeker, Caitlin Krause, Kenway Kua, Brent D. Kuenning, Sebastian LaCause, Nina Lafarga, Leah Landau, Nikka Graff Lanzarone, John Paul LaPorte, Todd Lattimore, Marina Lazzaretto, Kenny Lear, Adam Lendermon, Aaron J. Libby, Giselle Lorenz-Brock, Jonathan D. Lovitz, Craig Lowry, Christopher Mai, Karl Maier, Timothy John Mandala, Nalina Mann, Sarah Kay Marchetti, Renée Marino, Danny Marr, Jon-Paul Mateo, Gina Mazzarella, Candice Monet McCall, Tim McGarrigal, Michael McGurk, Stephanie Janette Meade, Kaitlin Mesh, Christopher Messina, Brant Michaels, Denise M. Miller, Jacob Moody, Shina Ann Morris, Halle Morse, Sydney Morton, Caitlin Mundth, Tony Neidenbach, Vince Nelson, Brandon O'Neal, Diana Obradovich, Ian Paget, Alfie Parker Jr., Brandon Perayda, Giovanni Perez, William Michael Peters, Annie Petersmeyer, Michael SpencerPhillips, Robert Piper, Tera-Lee Pollin, Nicholas Porche, Rachel Potter, Jessica Press, Eddie Rabon, Rachelle Rak, John Raterman, Madeline Reed, Jermaine R. Rembert, Ian M. Richardson, Paul Riner, Alex Ringler, Arbender Robinson, Greg Roderick, Sam Rogers, Ryan Rubek, Brandon Rubendall, Celia Mei Rubin, Naomi Rusalka, Ben Ryan, Amy Ryerson, Valerie Salgado, Gerard Salvador, Manuel Santos, Kimberly Schafer, Gary Schaufeld, John Selya, Samantha Shafer, Micah Shepard, Laurie Sheppard, Robb Sherman, Evan D. Siegel, Joseph J. Simeone, Matthew Skrincosky, Alexandra C. Smith, Dani Spieler, Adair Springfield, Derek St. Pierre, Taylor Sternberg, Gregory D. Stockbridge, Dennis Stowe, Sam Strasfeld, Lauren Strigari, Betsy Struxness, Mark Stuart, Charlie Sutton, Ephraim M. Sykes, James Tabeek, Tim Taylor, Casey Leigh Thompson, Rickey Tripp, Phillip W. Turner, Richard E. Waits, Seth Watsky, Derek Allen Watson, Aléna Watters, Daniel T. Watts, Correy West, Tracy J. Wholf, Charlie Williams, Kristen Beth Williams, Jake Wilson, Jacob Wood, Jody Cole Wood, Sidney Erik Wright, James Zander, Adam Zelasko

THE PROGRAM The Best Game In Town, The Bank, Connecticut Avenue, Electric Company, Pass Go, Railroads, Orient Avenue, Boardwalk, Hotels, Go to Jail, Waterworks, Luxury Tax, Finale

FUNDRAISING Event Total: **$1,015,985**; Strip-a-thon Team Winner: "Boardwalk" number ($50,740); Strip-a-thon Individual Winner: Reed Kelly ($42,395); Male Runners-up: Ben Ryan ($12,045), Steve Bratton ($10,348); Female Runners-up: Nikka Lanzarone ($4,135), Amy Brewer ($3,329)

SYNOPSIS A variety burlesque show presented without intermission. Since its inception in 1992, choreographer and director Jerry Mitchell – then in the ensemble of The Will Rogers Follies – put six of his fellow dancers up on the bar at an infamous "watering hole" in New York City's Chelsea district and raised $8,000 for Broadway Cares, the 20 editions of Broadway Bares have grown beyond all expectations, raising more than $7.5 million for Broadway Cares/Equity Fights AIDS. In January, Mitchell announced the goal of $1 million for the 20th edition, throwing his support and personal fundraising muscle behind a series of "Solo Strips" events (held at the site of the original BROADWAY BARES during the Spring of 2011) and even returning to the stage to shed some layers in a new routine on June 6 entitled "Classic Strips," which brought back some of the most titillating numbers from past editions.

Sebastian LeCause at Broadway Bares (photo by Peter James Zielinski)

Broadway Flea Market and Grand Auction

Shubert Alley; September 26, 2010

Produced by Broadway Cares/Equity Fights AIDS (Tom Viola, Executive Director); Celebrity Autograph Table and Photo Booth: Bebe Neuwirth, Sean Hayes, Cherry Jones, Patrick Wilson, Donna Murphy, Susan Blackwell, Heidi Blickenstaff, Denis O'Hare, Kathleen Chalfant, Mario Cantone, Patrick Page, Jordan Sparks, Jason Danieley, Marin Mazzie, Malcolm Gets, Montego Glover, Chad Kimball, Alice Ripley, Julie Halston, Anthony Rapp, Donna McKechnie, Ann Harada, Jessica Hecht, Hunter Ryan Herdlicka, Gregory Jbara, Carol Shelley, Levi Kreis, Judith Light and Dan Lauria, Kelli O'Hara, Bobby Steggert, John Tartaglia, Julie White, PJ Benjamin, Stephanie D'Abruzzo, Andy Karl, Orfeh, Jerry Mitchell, Matthew Hydzik, Robert Britton Lyons, Phyllis Newman, Elizabeth Stanley, Terri Colombino, Ellen Dolan, David Andrew MacDonald, Austin Peck, Vanessa Ray, Colleen Zenk

Kristin Chenoweth at the 24th Annual Broadway Flea Market (photo by Linda Lenzi)

FUNDRAISING TOTAL $476,917

TOP FUNDRAISING TABLES *Wicked* ($19,834), Broadway Beat ($12,171), TDF ($11,314), *American Idiot* ($10,164), *The Phantom of the Opera* ($6,660), (United Scenic Artists Local 829 ($6,626), Kristin Chenoweth & Maddie's Corner ($6,458), *Next to Normal* ($6,367), *The Addams Family* ($5,883), Triton Gallery ($5,616), *Billy Elliot* ($5,313)

SYNOPSIS Twenty-fourth annual flea market and auction benefit for Broadway Cares/Equity Fights AIDS. This free event open to the public offers a chance for fans to purchase autographed show memorabilia, posters, playbills, rare costume sketches, and several other show related items, as well as a live auction that includes walk-on roles in such hits as *Promises, Promises*, *Rock of Ages*, *In the Heights*, and *Wicked*, as well as other special autographed and celebrity items from Broadway's top stars. One of the most popular events at the Flea Market includes the Celebrity Autograph Table and Photo booth, where fans can meet the celebrities in exchange for contributions. Since its debut in 1987, twenty-four editions of this event have raised $8,638,669 for the social services provided by The Actors Fund and hundreds of AIDS and family service organizations BC/EFA supports each year.

Gypsy of the Year

New Amsterdam Theatre; December 6 & 7, 2010

Presented by Broadway Cares/Equity Fights AIDS; Producers, Michael Graziano, Kimberly Russell, Tom Viola; Director, Kristin Newhouse; Lighting, Philip Rosenberg; Sound, Kurt Fischer, Marie Renee Foucher; Production Manager, Nathan Hurlin; Production Stage Manager, Jason Trubitt; Associate Producers, Trisha Doss, Colyn Fiendel; Script, Eric Kornfeld; Stage Managers, Terry Alexander, Michael Rico Cohen, Bess Marie Glorioso, Samuel Moses Jones, Bart Kahn, Valerie Lau Kee Lai, Johnny Milani, Joshua Pilote, Alexis Prussack, Jennifer Rogers, David Sugarman; Assistant Director, Alex Lyu Volckhausen; Host, Seth Rudetsky; Special Guest, Carol Channing; Opening Number Created by Ben Cohn, Rob Krausz, Melissa Mahon, Sean McKnight; Presenters, Cherry Jones, T.R. Knight, Judith Light, Billy Porter, Hunter Ryan Herdlicka, Elizabeth Stanley, Colin Quinn, Bernadette Peters, David Hyde Pierce; Final Presenters, Bernadette Peters, Kristin Chenoweth, Sean Hayes; Judges, Jason Danieley, Alison Fraser, Boyd Gaines, Marin Mazzie, Bebe Neuwirth, Eve Plumb, Patricia White, Nick Wyman; Opening Number Associate Musical Director, Chris Haberl; Opening Number Stage Managers, Colyn W. Fiendel, Johnny Milani, Veronica Falhorn; Opening Number Costumes, Brian Hemesath; Press, Boneau/Bryan-Brown

HIGHLIGHTS Opening Number "Carol for a Cure" featuring Carol Channing, Lee Roy Reams, Tyne Daly, and members of the 1995 revival of *Hello, Dolly*; The National Tour of *Jersey Boys* ("The Movie Medley"); *Mary Poppins* ("Say"); *My Big Gay Italian Wedding* ("Drive by Comments"); *Wicked* ("When the River Meets the Sea"); *Rock of Ages* ("The Puppet Master"), *The Addams Family* ("...After these messages we'll be right back..."), *Fela!* ("Sector 65131"); *Bloody Bloody Andrew Jackson* ("We're Much More Like Broadway Than You Think"); The Gypsy Robe – Celebrating 60 Years of the Gypsy Robe (conceived by Pamela Remler and Shea Sullivan); *La Cage aux Folles* (untitled presentation); *The Lion King* ("Mele Ohana" in memory of former cast member Shannon Skye Tavarez, a "Young Nala" from last season who tragically passed away November 1, 2010 from myeloid leukemia and dedicated to cast member Lisa-Marie Lewis and her fight against breast cancer); *Mamma Mia!* ("Another Winter [Garden]"); *Chicago* ("The Name on Everybody's Lips is Gonna be Olya!"), The National Tour of *Mary Poppins* ("Here We Go"); *Billy Elliot the Musical* ("Don't Stop the Music"); *Promises, Promises* ("I'm Here for the Audition"); *Women on the Verge of a Nervous Breakdown* ("On the Verge"); *In the Heights* (untitled presentation)

COMPETETION Winner: *Rock of Ages* ("The Puppet Master" created and performed by Julie Nelson and Rudi Macaggi); First Runner-up: *The Addams Family* ("...After these messages we'll be right back..." written and created by Nathan Lane, Alena Watters, and Kevin Phillips, performed by Adam Riegler)

FUNDRAISING Total for 63 participating Broadway, Off-Broadway, and National Touring Companies: **$3,776,720**; Top Fundraisers: Broadway Musicals: *Promises, Promises* (Top Fundraiser: $195,011); *Wicked* (1st Runner-up: $181,609), *Billy Elliot* (2nd Runner-up $152,268), *The Addams Family* (3rd Runner-up: $150,000); Broadway Plays: *Driving Miss Daisy* (Top Fundraiser: $94,044), *A Life in the Theatre* (1st Runner-up: $72,452); Off-Broadway: *Avenue Q* (Top Fundraiser: $26,831), *The Divine Sister* (First Runner-up: $24,444); National Tours: *Jersey Boys* (Top Fundraiser: $285,398), *Wicked* Emerald City Company (1st Runner-up: $247,571), *Wicked* Munchkinland Company (2nd Runner-up: $236,352), *Shrek the Musical* (3rd Runner-up: $137,888)

SYNOPSIS Twenty-second annual talent and variety show presented without intermission. The *Gypsy of the Year Competition* is the culmination of a period of intensive fundraising where New York's most talented "gypsies," chorus members from Broadway and Off-Broadway shows, join in a competition variety show as six weeks of intensive fundraising by the community comes to a close. Since 1989, 22 editions of the *Gypsy of the Year* have raised a combined total of $44,136,720 for Broadway Cares/Equity Fights AIDS.

The Company of Women on the Verge of a Nervous Breakdown *at the* 2010 Gypsy of the Year *(photo by Peter James Zielinski)*

Broadway Backwards 6

Longacre Theatre; February 7, 2011

Created, written, and directed by Robert Bartley, special material by Danny Whitman; Produced by The Lesbian, Gay, Bisexual & Transgender Community Center and Broadway Cares/Equity Fight AIDS: Executive Producer, Tom Viola; Producers, Michael Graziano, Danny Whitman; Music Direction, Chris Haberl; Arrangements/Orchestrations, Matt Aument, Josh Clayton, Ben Cohn, Sam Davis, Oran Eldor, August Eriksmoen, Chris Haberl, Karlan Judd; Co-Choreographer/Assiociate Director, Kathryn Kendall; Sound, David Gotwald; Costumes, Philip Heckman; Lighting, Paul D. Miller; Production Manager, Nathan Hurlin; Production Stage Manager, Matthew DiCarlo; Music Supervisor, Patrick Vaccariello; Producer, Kimberly Russel; Associate Producer, Trisha Doss; Associate Production Manager, Michael Palm; Stage Managers, Colyn Fiendel & David Sugarman; Assistant Stage Managers, Michael Alifanz, Nathan K. Claus, Susan Davison, Ryan Gibbs, Heather Hogan, Ellie MacPherson, Andrew Jo Martin, Kenneth McGee, Kelly McGrath, Johnny Milani, Liz Reddick, Jennifer Rogers, Anna Tractman, Heather Weiss; Sound Stage Managers, Valerie Lau-Kee Lai, Alexis Prussack-Martin; Company Manager, Scott T. Stevens; Dance Captains, Barbara Angeline, Kurt Domoney, Patrick O'Neill; Moving Lights, Victor

Seastone; Music Copying/Preparation, Kaye/Houston Music; "You Could Drive a Person Crazy" Choreography, Penny Ann Maas; Re-creation of Ann Reinking's choreography for "All I Care About is Love", Melissa Rae Mahon; Re-creation of Michael Bennet's choreography for "Music and the Mirror", Michael Gorman; Hair & Makeup, Shannon Harrington, Danny Koye; Wardrobe Supervisor, Barbara Berman; Special Events Officer for the Center, Amanda DeMeester

CAST *Hosts* Dan Butler, Kristen Wyatt; *Starring* F. Murray Abraham, Clay Aiken, Farah Alvin, Brooks Ashmanskas, Hinton Battle, Ward Billeisen, Tituss Burgess, Len Cariou, Alan Cumming, Robin de Jesús, Colman Domingo, Mandy Gonzalez, Derek Hanson, Jose Llana, Jan Maxwell, Debra Monk, Bebe Neuwirth, Denis O'Hare, Karen Olivo, Mo Rocca, Brian Charles Rooney, Bobby Steggert, Jason Tam, Lillias White, Tony Yazbeck; *Ensemble* Barbara Angeline, Paul Blankenship, Joshua Cruz, Brendan Cyrus, Amy Decker, Kurt Domoney, Valerie Dowd, Jennifer Dunne, Kelli Gautreau, Matt Gibson, Jennifer Leah Gottlieb, Joe Grandy, Scott McLean Harrison, Robyn Hurder, Suzanne Hylenski, Reed Kelly, Kathryn Kendall, Kenway Hon Wai K. Kua, Charis Leos, Kevin Loreque, Kristin Maloney, Tim McGarrigal, Michael-Kennen Miller, Pilar Millhollen, Dana Moore, Patrick O'Neill, Masaya Palmer, Alfie Parker Jr., Jody Reynard, Danielle Erin Rhodes, Chris-Ian Sanchez, Matt Steffens, Mark Richard Taylor, Tonya Wathen, Shonté Walker, Jeannine Elizabeth Yoder

ORCHESTRA Chris Haberl (Conductor), Adam Kolker, Dave Noland, David Young (Reeds), Matthew Peterson, Jeff Wilfore (Trumpet), David Nelson, Robert Fournier (Trombone), Robert Meffe (Piano), Jack Morer (Guitar), David Phillips (Bass), Gary Seligson (Drums), Martin Agee (Violin), Summer Boggess (Cello)

MUSICAL NUMBERS "Extra! Extra!" (*Gypsy*):; Paul Blankenship, Amy Decker, Danielle Erin Rhodes & Chris-Ian Sanchez; "Don't Tell Mama" (*Cabaret*): Alan Cumming with Reed Kelly, Alfie Parker Jr., Jody Reynard & Matt Steffens; "You Could Drive A Person Crazy" (*Company*): Ward Billeisen, Colman Domingo & Jose Llana; "When You're Home" (*In the Heights*): Mandy Gonzalez & Karen Olivo; "Summer Nights" (*Grease*): Farah Alvin & Jason Tam with Jan Maxwell & Amy Decker, Kurt Domoney, Jennifer Leah Gottlieb, Joe Grandy, Tim McGarrigal, Michael-Kennen Miller, Masaya Palmer, Danielle Erin Rhodes & Jeannine Elizabeth Yoder; "Lida Rose/Will I Ever Tell You?" (*The Music Man*): Hinton Battle with Valerie Dowd, Kathryn Kendall, Charis Leos & Kristin Maloney; "On the Street Where You Live" (*My Fair Lady*): Debra Monk; "Cell Block Tango (*Chicago*): Reed Kelly, Kenway Hon Wai K. Kua, Patrick O'Neill, Alfie Parker Jr., Jody Reynard & Matt Steffens; "I'll Never Be Jealous Again" (*The Pajama Game*): Dan Butler & Kirsten Wyatt; "Some Enchanted Evening" (*South Pacific*): Lillias White; "One Halloween" & "But Alive" (*Applause*): Brian Charles Rooney & Ensemble; "The Trolley Song" (*Meet Me In St. Louis*): Robin De Jesús & Bobby Steggert with Mo Rocca & Ensemble; "Bewitched, Bothered and Bewildered" (*Pal Joey*): Len Cariou; "Stars and the Moon" (*Songs For A New World*): Tituss Burgess; "All I Care About Is Love" (*Chicago*): Bebe Neuwirth with Jennifer Dunne, Robyn Hurder, Suzanne Hylenski, Pilar Millhollen, Dana Moore & Tonya Wathen; "The Music and the Mirror" (*A Chorus Line*): Tony Yazbeck with Derek Hanson; "Marry the Man Today (*Guys and Dolls*): Brooks Ashmanskas & Denis O'Hare; "Home" (*The Wiz*): Clay Aiken; "Hello, Young Lovers" (*The King and I*): F. Murray Abraham with JoJo Edward & Ensemble

SYNOPSIS Sixth annual benefit concert presented in two acts. *Broadway Backwards* reinterprets the songs of musical theater by featuring women singing songs originally written for men and men singing songs written for women. By keeping the lyrics intact, including the pronouns, each song takes on an entirely new dimension. It's Broadway in a whole new key. This year's concert raised a record-breaking total of $281,243 for both Broadway Cares and the LGBT Center.

Alan Cumming with Reed Kelly, Alfie Parker Jr., Jody Reynard, and Matt Steffens in Broadway Backwards 6 *(photo by Peter James Zielinski)*

Easter Bonnet Competition

Minskoff Theatre; April 25 & 26, 2011

Written by Eric Kornfeld, Dan Perry, and Danny Whitman; Presented by Broadway Cares/Equity Fights AIDS; Producers, Michael Graziano, Kimberly Russell, and Tom Viola; Director, Kristin Newhouse; Sound, Alain Van Achte; Lighting, Martin E. Vreeland; Production Manager, Nathan Hurlin; Production Stage Manager, Valerie Lau-Kee Lai; Stage Managers, Lisa Dawn Cave, Bess Marie Glorioso, Bart Kahn, Lucy Kennedy, Johnny Milani, Melanie Morgan, Jason Quinn, Jennifer Rogers, Brooke Rowzee, Jason Trubitt, Nancy Wernick; Associate Producers, Trisha Doss, Colyn Fiendel; Associate Production Manager, Michael Palm; Assistant Director, Alex Lyu Volckhausen; Assistant Lighting, Eli Polofsky; Hosts: Robin Williams, Judith Light, Jose Llana, Dan Lauria, Heidi Blickenstaff, Roger Rees, Josh Gad, Andrew Ranells, Maxwell Caulfield, Renée Elise Goldsberry, Jayne Houdyshell, Tshidi Manye, Ron Kunene, with Kerry Butler; Special Guests/ Award Presentations: Harvey Fierstein, Sutton Foster, Daniel Radcliffe; Judges: Nick Adams, Montego Glover, Bobby Lopez, Mary McColl, Casey Nicholaw, Martin Pakledinaz, Estelle Parsons, Kate Shindle; Judge Introductions: Rob Bartlett and John Leguizamo; Sponsors, *The New York Times* and United Airlines; Additional Guest Appearance: Jen Cody and Don Richard as "Little Sally" and "Officer Lockstock"

HIGHLIGHTS Opening Number (inspired by "*Glee*"): Director/Choreographer, Shea Sullivan; Associate Director/Choreographer, Lori Barber; Music Direction/ Arrangements/Orchestrations, Ben Cohn; Lyrics, Jordan Mann; Additional Material, Jeff Thompson; *Bengal Tiger at the Bagdad Zoo* Bonnet Presentation; *Avenue Q* ("*Avenue Q* Goes Green"): Writer/Director, James Darrah; Music Director, Andrew Graham; Dancers Respoding to AIDS ("Another Parade" excerpt): Choreography, Monica Bill Barnes; *Freud's Last Session* ("*Freud's Last Session:* The Musical"): Writer/Director, Mark St. Germain; Choreography, David Rossetti; Music Direction/Accompaniment, John T. Prestianni; *The Phantom of the Opera* ("Heal the World"): Concept/Director, Kris Koop Ouellette; Music Director/Accompaniment, Tim Welch; *The Lion King* ("Drag Race"): Writers, Jim Ferris, Erin Maguire; Director/Choreography, Alvin Crawford; Music Director, Jim Ferris; *The Addams Family* ("Me and My Shadow") Director, Bebe Neuwirth; Choreography, Tom Berklund, Stephanie Gibson Chase; R.evolución Latina ("The Passion of a Dream"): Director, Luis Salgado; Choreography, Rebecca Tomas; National Tour Bonnets (*Blossoming Kalinka Snowball Bush*); Director, Melissa Mahon; Choreography, Olga Vaghinavah; Bonnets from *Les Misérables*, *The Lion King* – Gazelle Company, *Wicked* – Emerald City Company; *Mamma Mia!* ("You Get What You Give"): Director, Stacia Fernandez; Choreography, Rachel

Frankenthal, Monica Kapoor, AJ Fisher, Allyson Carr; Music Director, Wendy Bobbit Cavett; Doris Eaton Travis – A Fond Remembrance: Concept, Christopher Gattelli; Music Direction, Rick Hip-Flores; *Priscilla Queen of the Desert* ("Priscilla Queens of Burlesque"): Director, James Brown III; Choreography, James Brown III & Brandon Rubendall; *Chicago* ("If Looks Could Kill"): Writers/Directors, Melissa Mahon, Brian O'Brien; Choreography, Melissa Mahon; *Billy Elliot* ("Express Yourself"): Writer/Director, David Koch; Choreography, Rachel Nelson; *La Cage Aux Folles* ("25 Years of Easter Bonnet"): Writers, Tony Spinosa, Cheryl Stern; Concept, Sean Patrick Doyle; Director, Tony Spinosa; Choreography, Nicholas Cunningham; Music Direction/Arrangements, Matt Aument; Closing Number/ Finale ("Help Is On the Way" – the official anthem of BC/EFA): Music Director, Mary-Mitchell Campbell; Sung by Kerry Butler

BONNET PRESENTATION Winner: *La Cage aux Folles*; First Runner-up: *The Addams Family*

BONNET DESIGN AWARD *Bengal Tiger at the Baghdad Zoo* (Created by Moira MacGregor-Conrad and Tree Sarvay)

FUNDRAISING Total for 52 participating Broadway, Off-Braodway, and National Touring Companies: **$3,706,085**; Top Fundraising Award (Overall): *Wicked* – Munchkinlad Tour ($360,021); Broadway Musical: *How to Succeed in Business Without Really Trying* (Top Fundraiser: $271,916), *Wicked* (First Runner-up: $165,979), *Billy Elliot* (Second Runner-up: $131,363), *The Phantom of the Opera* (Third Runner-up: $149,194); Broadway Play: *That Championship Season* (Top Fundraiser: $163,532), *Lombardi* (First Runner-up: $86,099); National Touring Shows: *Wicked* – Emerald City Company (Top Fundraiser: $242,212), *Mary Poppins* (First Runner-up: $150,472), *Les Misérables* (Second Runner-up: $124,019), *Billy Elliot* (Third Runner-up: $116,384); Off-Broadway: *Avenue Q* (Top Fundraiser: $44,072), *Freud's Last Session* (First Runner-up: $24,500)

SYNOPSIS Twenty-fifth annual talent and variety show presented without intermission. The *Easter Bonnet Competition* is the two-day spectacular that features the companies of more than 20 Broadway, Off-Broadway, and touring productions singing, dancing, performing comedic sketches, and donning hand-crafted original Easter bonnets. This Broadway tradtion is the culmination of six intensive weeks of fundraising efforts by Broadway, Off-Broadway, and national touring companies. Since 1987, the 25 editions of the *Easter Bonnet Competition* have raised over $46 million for Broadway Cares/Equity Fights AIDS, which in turn has supported programs at the Actors Fund including the AIDS Initiative, The Phyllis Newman Women's Heath Initiative, The Al Hirschfeld Free Heath-Clinic, as well as over 400 AIDS and family service organizations across the country.

The Phantom of the Opera *Company and their family members participate in the* Easter Bonnet Competition *(photo by Peter James Zielinski)*

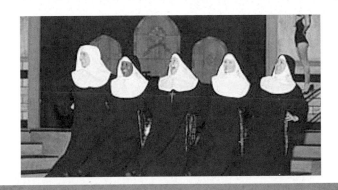

OFF-BROADWAY

Top: *Stephanie Wahl, Bambi Jones, Bonnie Lee, Jeanne Tinker, and Marie Montana in the 25th Anniversary production of* Nunsense. *Opened at the Cherry Lane Theatre June 20, 2010 (photo by Michael Feldser)*

Center: *Daniel Beaty in* Through the Night. *Opened at Union Square Theatre September 26, 2010 (photo by Carol Rosegg)*

Bottom: *Maxwell Caulfield and Lois Robbins in* Cactus Flower. *Opened at the Westside Theatre March 10, 2011 (photo by Carol Rosegg)*

Colin Quinn in Long Story Short. *Opened at the Bleecker Street Theatre June 19, 2010 (photo by Carol Rosegg)*

Charles Busch and Jennifer Van Dyck in The Divine Sister. *Opened at Soho Playhouse September 22, 2010 (photo by David Rodgers)*

Mark H. Dold and Martin Rayner in Freud's Last Session. *Opened at the Marjorie S. Deane Little Theater July 22, 2010 (photo by Carol Rosegg)*

Eve Plumb and Mauricio Perez in Miss Abigail's Guide to Dating, Mating, and Marriage! *Opened at the Downstairs Cabaret Theatre at Sofia's October 24, 2010 (photo by Jeremy Daniel)*

A scene from Sleep No More. *Opened at the McKittrick Hotel April 13, 2011 (photo by Yaniv Schulman)*

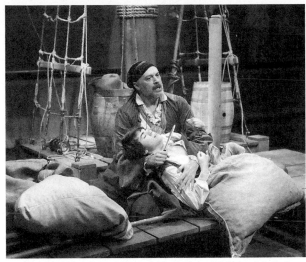

Tom Hewitt and Noah Galvin in Treasure Island. *Opened at the Irondale Center March 5, 2011 (photo by Ken Howard)*

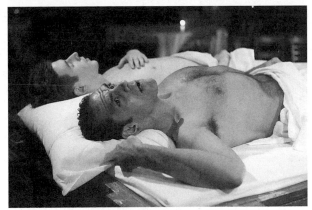

Jonathan Hammond and Blake Daniel in the Transport Group's Hello Again. *Opened at 52 Mercer March 20, 2011 (photo by Carol Rosegg)*

Elizabeth Loyacano and Jim Stanek in the Peccadillo Theater Company's A Tree Grows in Brooklyn. *Opened at the Theatre at St. Clements March 20, 2011 (photo by Carol Rosegg)*

Michael Shannon in Mistakes Were Made. *Opened at the Barrow Street Theatre November 14, 2010 (photo by Ari Mintz)*

Lilias White, David Burnham, Sally Mayes, Billy Stritch on piano, Howard McGillin, and Rachel York in The Best Is Yet to Come: The Music of Cy Coleman. *Opened at 59E59 May 25, 2011 (photo by Carol Rosegg)*

The Off-Broadway Season:
Thinking Outside The Box

Linda Buchwald, Contributing Editor, *TDF Stages* and *StageGrade*

The most anticipated show of the 2010-2011 Off-Broadway season was arguably the first New York revival of Tony Kushner's *Angels in America*—1993's Pulitzer Prize winner for drama. Both parts—*Millennium Approaches* and *Perestroika*—were directed by Michael Greif and performed in repertory at Signature Theatre Company. The initial run, during which tickets were just $20 thanks to the Signature Ticket Initiative (ticket prices increased to $75 for the rest of the run), sold out within hours of going on sale and the plays were extended four times. Such was the demand that on the day tickets went on sale, the phone lines and Web site were jammed.

Angels in America began previews on September 14 and officially opened on October 28 to extremely positive reviews. John Lahr wrote in his review for *The New Yorker*, "Eighteen years later, *Angels in America* (in a Signature Theatre Company revival at the Peter Norton Space, under the splendid direction of Michael Greif) is as majestic and luminous as ever—a kind of brainstorm; with the passage of time, however, its music strikes different dominant chords. Now the play's most visionary element is not what it has to say about the homosexual struggle but what it has to say about the grinding undertow of reactionary and progressive historical forces."

The initial cast included Christian Borle as Prior Walter, Zachary Quinto (who received a Theatre World Award for his performance) as Louis Ironson, Frank Wood as Roy Cohn, Bill Heck as Joe Pitt, Zoe Kazan as Harper Pitt, Robin Bartlett as Hannah Pitt, Billy Porter as Belize, and Robin Weigert as the Angel. The initial run was set to close on December 19, but it ran through April 24. Heck and Porter stayed throughout the run and the rest of the cast, due to prior commitments, was replaced with Michael Urie (Prior), Adam Driver (Louis), Jonathan Hadary (Roy Cohn), Keira Keeley (Harper), Lynne McCollough (Hannah), and Sofia Jean Gomez (the Angel).

Signature, which usually devotes each season to one playwright, finished its Kushner season with one of his early plays, 1988's rarely performed *The Illusion* based on Pierre Corneille's *L'Illusion Comique*. In the play, a lawyer (David Margulies) enlists a wizard (Lois Smith) to help him find out what happened to his son (Finn Wittrock) since being expelled from home. Directed by Michael Mayer, *The Illusion* received mostly warm reviews, especially for the design elements (set by Christine Jones, lighting by Kevin Adams, costumes by Susan Hilferty), but did not have the same popularity as *Angels in America*, and ran from May 17 through July 17.

Signature joined with the Public Theater and the Guthrie Theatre in Minneapolis to present a new work by Kushner—*The Intelligent Homosexual's Guide to Capitalism and Socialism with a Key to the Scriptures*. In most circles, the unwieldy title was shortened to *iHo*. The play about a retired longshoreman (Michael Cristofer) who gathers his family to vote on whether or not he should commit suicide premiered at the Guthrie in 2009 and opened at The Public on May 5, 2011 to mixed reviews. In Ben Brantley's *New York Times* review, he wrote, "*Angels in America* established that Mr. Kushner is a great playwright. In *Guide* he registers mainly as a great conversationalist who keeps talking well after he has made his essential points." Brenda Wehle won an Obie Award for her performance as the patriarch's sister Clio. The rest of the cast included *Angels in America*'s original Prior Stephen Spinella, Steven Pasquale, and Linda Emond.

To sum up the 2010-2011 season with a trend, it might be "the longer the better." Each part of *Angels in America* clocked in at about three-and-a-half hours. *iHo* was nearly four hours long. The Public Theater's hottest ticket was the eight-hours long (including the intermission and dinner break) Elevator Repair Service's *Gatz*, in which an office drone (played by Scott Sheperd) finds a copy of F. Scott Fitzgerald's *The Great Gatsby* at his desk and reads it from cover to cover. The show, directed by John Collins, ran from September 26 to November 28 to mostly

sold-out audiences, officially opening on October 6 to rave reviews. Shepherd won an Obie Award for his performance.

Joining *Gatz* in the unconventional-theater-creating-a-ticket-fervor category was Punchdrunk's *Sleep No More*, a site-specific theater experience based on *Macbeth* at the McKittrick Hotel. The production, directed by Felix Barrett and Maxine Doyle, began previews on March 7 and opened on April 13. There are five arrival times through the night and audience members, each donning a requisite mask, can stay for as long or as little as they like until the end (the whole experience lasts up to three hours). The show won a Drama Desk Award for unique theatrical experience. Rapturous reviews and positive word of mouth (even celebrities, including Neil Patrick Harris and Anderson Cooper were taking to Twitter to recommend the show) led to sell outs and multiple extensions. At the time of writing, tickets were on sale through January 21, 2012.

Shows like *Gatz* and *Sleep No More* would be hard/impossible to transfer to Broadway due to their length and nature, but several other successful Off-Broadway shows are being transferred to Broadway in the 2011-2012 season. A hit Off-Broadway is not always able to find an audience on Broadway, as was the case with both *Bloody Bloody Andrew Jackson* and *The Scottsboro Boys* last season (both runs were cut abruptly short), but time will tell whether these transfers will prove profitable.

A play from the 2009-2010 season is due for Broadway in the spring. *Clybourne Park*—Bruce Norris's take on *A Raisin in the Sun*—premiered in February 2010 at Playwrights Horizons and won the 2011 Pulitzer Prize in drama. The Center Theatre Group/Mark Taper Forum is presenting the play in January 2012 and that production will move to Broadway.

A Broadway run of the *Peter Pan*-prequel *Peter and the Starcatcher* was also announced for the spring of 2012. The New York Theatre Workshop production, which began previews on February 18 and opened on March 9, was notable for its staging, in which actors became the props and sets. Directors Roger Rees and Alex Timbers received an Obie for their efforts, and Wayne Barker won a Drama Desk for outstanding music in a play. Christian Borle went from his much-praised turn in *Angels* to more rave reviews as the pirate Black Stache. The reviews were actually fairly mixed, with some critics not falling for the self-indulgent humor, but there were enough glowing reviews—especially Ben Brantley's rave in which he wrote, "All sinking sensations should feel this sensational"—to lead to several extensions.

Lysistrata Jones, a hit for the Transport Group in late spring/early summer, is another show making the transition from small, intimate space to a large Broadway stage. It opened on Broadway in the fall of 2011 at the Walter Kerr Theatre. A modern take on the Greek play *Lysistrata* by Aristophanes, the musical is about a college basketball team on a losing streak. The players' girlfriends withhold sex until the team wins. The show has a score by Lewis Flinn and a book by Douglas Carter Beane and is directed/choreographed by Dan Knechtges. The Transport Group production was performed in an actual gym and the young up-and-comers in that cast all made the transfer.

Also in the fall of 2011, Lincoln Center Theatre transferred its production of *Other Desert Cities*—directed by Joe Mantello—to Broadway's Booth Theatre. Jon Robin Baitz's political family drama had a successful run at Lincoln Center Theatre's Off-Broadway space, the Mitzi E. Newhouse Stage in January 2011. Ben Brantley called it "the most richly enjoyable new play for grown-ups that New York has known in many a season." The play received the 2011 Outer Critics Circle Award for outstanding new Off-Broadway play as well as a Drama Desk nomination for outstanding play. It starred Stockard Channing, Stacy Keach, Linda Lavin (replaced by Judith Light), Elizabeth Marvel (replaced by Rachel Griffiths), and Thomas Sadoski. Sadoski won an Obie Award for his performance.

Another Obie went to F. Murray Abraham for sustained excellence of performance. In March, he played Shylock in a Theater for a New Audience production of *The Merchant of Venice* at the Michael Schimmel Center for the Arts at Pace University. This production, directed by Darko Tresnjak, opened just weeks after the Broadway version starring Al Pacino (a transfer of the Shakespeare in the Park production from the summer of 2010) closed. The memory of Pacino did not stop critics from embracing Abraham's performance.

Some other powerful performances this season came from Reed Birney, who won a Special Drama Desk for his roles in *Tigers Be Still*, *The Dream of the Burning Boy* (both at Roundabout Underground), and *A Small Fire* at Playwrights Horizons. In Adam Bock's well-received *A Small Fire*, which opened on January 6, 2011, Birney played the husband of a middle-aged contractor who is losing each of her senses in turn.

Roundabout Underground produces new work by emerging artists. *Tigers Be Still* by Kim Rosenstock and directed by Sam Gold starred Halley Feiffer as an unemployed woman living at home with her mother (who does not appear in the play) and sister (Natasha Lyonne). In David West Read's *The Dream of the Burning Boy* directed by Evan Cabnet, Birney played Larry Morrow, a teacher whose favorite student died suddenly. Both Rosenstock and Read received encouragement from critics.

Another new playwright who received attention was Matthew Lopez who wrote *The Whipping Man*, which opened at Manhattan Theatre Club's Stage I at New York City Center on February 1, 2011. The play takes place after the Civil War as a Jewish Confederate soldier returns from the war to find only two former slaves—also raised as Jews—left in his home and the three men celebrate the Passover Seder together. Andre Braugher won an Obie Award for his performance as one of the slaves. Even though Lopez had a few detractors in the critics, who were turned off by the melodramatic tendencies of the writing, the play did get three extensions and stayed open through April 10.

For all the new plays, new musicals were not as visible on the Off-Broadway scene—a contrast to the fruitful year for new musicals on Broadway—but one musical had a surprising success story. Primary Stages' *In Transit*, an a cappella musical about life on the subway with book, music, and lyrics by Kristen Anderson-Lopez, James-Allen Ford, Russ Kaplan, and Sara Wordsworth, ran from September 21 through October 30 at 59E59. Reviews were lukewarm and the show came and went quietly, but it was remembered come award season, nominated for five Drama Desks, one Outer Critics Award, one Drama League Award, and four Lucille Lortel Awards.

While non-profit houses thrived, commercial Off-Broadway had a few setbacks. A revival of Abe Burrow's *Cactus Flower*—a '60s farce in which a bachelor pretends to be married to his secretary—starring Maxwell Caulfield opened at the Westside Theatre on March 10 (previews began on February 24). What was supposed to be an open run ended on April 24 after critics panned the revival for being dated and unfunny. On the main floor of that same space, *Love, Loss, and What I Wore* continues to thrive after two years on constantly rotating casts.

Freckleface Strawberry, based on the children's book by Julianne Moore, started previews at New World Stages on September 9 and opened on October 1. The musical about a seven-year-old girl who gets made fun of for her red hair and freckles with music and lyrics by Gary Kupper and a book by Kupper and Rose Caiola seemed to be off to a promising start with positive reviews and attracting family audiences, but it closed on April 24. It reopened at the MMAC Theatre, a new 199-seat theatre as part of the Manhattan Movement and Arts Center on the Upper West Side on November 8 (the original re-opening date was supposed to be August 3).

Perhaps the biggest blow to commercial Off-Broadway was the new country musical *Lucky Guy* written, directed, and composed by Willard Beckham, starring Leslie Jordan and Varla Jean Merman. It closed on May 29, just ten days after opening. Though *Lucky Guy* had quite a few admirers amidst the mixed reviews, the show was expensive to run and producers could not keep the show going at the 499-seat Little Shubert Theatre.

That is not to say there were no success stories. The longest running Off-Broadway show of the 2010-2011 season was *Freud's Last Session* by Mark St. Germain. The two-hander, directed by Tyler Marchant, imagines a meeting between Sigmund Freud (Martin Rayner) and C.S. Lewis (Mark H. Dold) on the eve of W.W. II. It opened on July 22 at the Marjorie S. Deane Little Theatre. Critics and audiences embraced the intellectual debate. The play had to close on November 28 due to a prior booked show, but it reopened on January 14. The show played its final performance at the Marjorie S. Deane Little Theatre on October 2 and reopened on October 7 at New World Stages, where it continues to run, joining the recent revival of *Rent* and the Broadway to Off-Broadway transfers of *Avenue Q* and *Million Dollar Quartet*.

Varla Joan Merman (aka Jeffrey Roberson) and the Cast of Lucky Guy
(photo by Joan Marcus)

The Cast of Freckleface Strawberry: The Musical (photo by Carol Rosegg)

This Wide Night

Peter Jay Sharp Theater; First Preview: May 8, 2010; Opening Night: May 16, 2010*; Closed June 28, 2010

Written by Chloë Moss; Produced by the Naked Angels (Andy Donald, Artistic Director; Renee Blinkwolt, Managing Director; Richie Jackson, and Highbrow; Director, Anne Kauffman; Set, Rachel Hauck; Costumes, Emily Rebholz; Lighting, Matthew Frey; Sound and Composition, Robert Kaplowitz; Video and Media, Richard DiBella; Dialect and Vocal Coach, Deborah Hecht; Props, Desiree Maurer; Production Stage Manager, April A. Kline; Production Manager, Dave Nelson; Assistant Stage Manager, Lyndsey A. Goode; Press, Boneau/Bryan-Brown, Michael Strassheim

CAST Lorraine **Edie Falco**; Marie **Alison Pill**

New York premiere of a new play presented without intermission. Originally produced by Clean Break (London) and premiered July 2008 at the Soho Theatre (London). The play won the 2009 Blackburn Prize.

SYNOPSIS A prison sentence isn't over once you leave jail. Having just begun to rebuild a life on the outside, Marie is confronted with her past when former cellmate Lorraine shows up unannounced on her doorstep. The two outcasts, once so close on the inside, struggle to navigate a friendship beyond the prison walls — which may threaten their prospects to start over.

*This listing was inadvertently omitted in last year's volume.

Edie Falco and Alison Pill in This Wide Night *(photo by Carol Rosegg)*

Adventures of Hershele Ostropolyer

Baruch Performing Arts Center–Rose Nagelberg Theatre; First Preview: May 25, 2010; Opening Night: June 3, 2010; Closed June 27, 2010; 11 previews, 27 performances; Return engagement May 15, 2011–June 26, 2011; 37 performances

Adapted, directed, and choreographed by Eleanor Reissa; Based on the play *Hershele Ostropolyer* by Moyshe Gershenson, later adapted by Joseph Glickson; Presented by the National Yiddish Theatre Folksbiene (Zalmen Mlotek, Artistic Director; Georgia Buchanan, Managing Director); Musical Score, Chana Mlotek with Zalmen Mlotek and Eleanor Reissa; Set, Roger Hanna; Lighting, Kirk Bookman; Costumes, Gail Cooper Hecht; Sound, Bruce Ellman; Supertitles, Motl Didner; PSM, Marci Skolnik; ASM/Associate Choreography, Penny Ayn Maas; Music Director, Dmitri Slepovitch; Music Supervision, Zalmen Mlotek; Supertitles, Motl Didner; Production Manager, Ken Larson; Russian Translator, Dmitri "Zisl" Slepovitch; Press, Beck Lee

Mike Burstyn and the Company of The Adventures of Hershele Ostropolyer *(photo by Michael Priest)*

CAST Berele **Nimmy Weisbrod** (return engagement: **Ari Jacobson**); Tsipke **Dani Marcus**; Grandma/Genendl **Lori Wilner** (return engagement: **Joanne Borts**); Hershele **Mike Burstyn**; Dvoshe **Daniella Rabbani** (return engagement: **Rebecca Lawrence**);Kalmen **I.W. "Itzy" Firestone**; Bunim **Shane Bertram Baker**; Stanavoy **Edward Furs**; Zaydl **Steve Sterner**

MUSICIANS Dmitri "Zisl" Slepovitch (Music Director/Pianist), Taylor Bergren-Chrisman (Double Bass/Guitar), Suzie Perelman/Rima Fand (Violin), Carl Reihl (Accordion)

MUSICAL NUMBERS Prologue Nigun, Oy A Nakht A Sheyne (A Beautiful Night), Du Shaynst Vi Di Zun (You Shine Like the Sun), A Gutn Ovnt (A Good Evening), Bin Ikh Mir a Soykherl (I Am a Business Man), Haynt Hob Ikh a Vetchere (Today I Have a Meal), Dos Dinst Lid (The Maid's Song), Ale Vegn Ful Mit Shteyner (All Roads are Filled With Stones), Oy Vi Nemt Men Aza Mazl? (Where Can You Get Such Luck?), Vi Makht Men Im Shoyn Khasene? (How Do We Get Him Married?), Meshuge (Crazy), Koynim (Customers), Di Oreme Kapote (My Poor Coat), Di Negidim (The Rich Folk), Raz Dva Tri (The Policeman's Song), Lomir Zikh Iberbetn (Let us Make Up), Hershele Ostropolyer

Revival of a musical presented in Yiddish with English and Russian supertitles without intermission.

SYNOPSIS Before the Marx Brothers, there was "Hershele", a beloved folk hero and compassionate jester who battles injustice armed only with his wits. In this comic tale full of song, Hershele mobilizes a community to overcome the greedy desires of a villain who stands in the way of young love.

Prophecy

4th Street Theatre; First Preview: May 27, 2010; Opening Night: June 4, 2010; Closed June 20, 2010

Written and directed by Karen Malpede; Produced by Theater Three Collaborative in association with New York Theatre Workshop; Set, Maxine Willi Klein; Lighting, Tony Giovannetti; Costumes, Sally Ann Parsons; Music/Sound, Arthur Rosen; PSM, Jonathan Donahue; ASM, Jessa Nicole Pollack; Production Manager, Lisa Jacobson

CAST Sarah Golden **Kathleen Chalfant**; Alan Golden **George Bartenieff**; Miranda Cruz/Hala Jabar/Mariam Jabar **Najla Said**; Dean Charles Muffler **Peter Francis James**; Jeremy Thrasher/Lukas Brightman **Brendand Donaldson**

Brendan Donaldson and Kathleen Chalfant in Prophecy *(photo by Ari Mintz)*

U.S. premiere of a new play presented in two acts. World premiere at the New End Theatre (Hampsted, London) September 2008.

SYNOPSIS A play about the far-reaching effects of both the Iraq and Vietnam wars on those who served on the battlefield and those who served in protests, *Prophecy* is also the story of a marriage: Alan Golden, a Jew whose past includes an affair with an Arab co-worker that results in the birth of a child, and his wife Sarah, an actress and acting teacher, whose intense bond with one of her students -- a talented and vulnerable Iraq War veteran -- triggers memories of a young man from her past.

A Night in Vegas

Bleecker Street Theatre; First Preview: May 27, 2010; Opening Night: June 5, 2010; Closed June 20, 2010

Written and directed by Joe Marshall; Presented by the Alternative Theatre Company; Set/Lighting, Casper De la Torre; Costumes, Seth Gamble; Stage Manager, Anthony Fusco; Press, Springer Associates, Joe Trentacosta

CAST Daniel Bak, Jonathan Craig, Edy Escamilla, Joe Fanelli, Ali Grieb, Denis Hawkins, Scott Lilly, Nicholas Pierro, Gerald Prosser Jr., Bill Purdy, Kelly Riley, Jason Romas, Drew Stark, Chris von Hoffmann

World premiere of a new play presented in six scenes without intermission.

SYNOPSIS Set in the gayest hotel on the Vegas strip, *A Night in Vegas* is a raucous comedy that features six vignettes that covers everything from male prostitutes to anonymous sex, to gay marriage and everything in between.

Joe Fanelli, Denis Hawkins, Kelly Riley, Nicholas Pierro and Edy Escamilla in A Night in Vegas *(photo by Paul Crispin Quitoriano)*

Amerissiah

Theatre 80 St. Marks; First Preview: June 3, 2010; Opening Night: June 5, 2010; Closed June 28, 2010

Written and directed by Derek Ahonen; Presented by The Amoralists (James Kautz, Derek Ahonen, Matthew Pilieci, Co-Artistic Directors; Kelcie Beene, Managing Director); Set Design/Fight Director, Alfred Schatz; Lighting/Assistant Director, Jeremy Pape; Stage Manager, Dan Stern; Costumes, Ricky Lang; Spritual Advisor, Larry Cobra; Sound, Brian Lazarus; Makeup, Lisa K. Hokans; Production Assistant, Kelly Swindall; Press, David Gibbs

CAST Ricky Ricewater **William Apps**; Loni **Selene Beretta**; Carrie Murphy **Jennifer Fouche**; Bernie the Attorney **James Kautz**; Terry Murphy **Nick Lawson**; Holly Ricewater **Sarah Lemp**; Barry Ricewater **Matthew Pilieci**; Margie Ricewater **Aysha Quinn**; Johnny Ricewater **George Walsh**

SETTING One night in Barry and Margi Ricewater's newly borrowed two-room apartment in Marble Hill, Bronx. Off-Broadway premiere of a new play presented without intermission. Previously presented at the Gene Frankel Theatre November 2008.

SYNOPSIS Barry Ricewater is dying of cancer. He also claims to be the Messiah. His older, hippie wife and his recovering drug-addict brother believe him, but the rest of the family harbors doubts. Barry's sister and father are preoccupied dodging jail sentences for fraud, and their lawyer is ready to send them to the big house. When an aspiring rapper and his seemingly psychic wife show up looking for the Amerissiah, the family is forced to confront their sins and seek redemption- but are they worshiping a false idol?

Matthew Pilieci, William Apps, and Sarah Lemp in Amerissiah *(photo by Larry Cobra)*

Another Part of the Forest

Theatre at St. Clements; First Preview: June 3, 2010; Opening Night: June 7, 2010; Closed July 11, 2010; 4 previews, 28 performances

Written by Lillian Hellman; Presented by the Peccadillo Theater Company; Director, Dan Wackerman; Set, Joseph Spirito; Costumes, Amy C. Bradshaw; Lighting, Kate Ashton; Dramaturg, Rick McKay; Dialect Coach, Lester Thomas Shane; PSM, Evan Hernandez; ASM, Mitch Kelly; Wardrobe, Mary Wilson; Press, Peter Cromarty

CAST Harold Penniman **Oliver Buckingham**; Oscar Hubbard **Ben Curtis**; Coralee **Perri Gaffney**; Marcus Hubbard **Sherman Howard**; Captain John Bagtry **Christopher Kelly**; Colonel Isham/Gilbert Jugger **Christopher Lukas**; Benjamin Hubbard **Matthew Floyd Miller**; Laurette Sincee **Ryah Nixon**; Lavinia Hubbard **Elizabeth Norment**; Birdie Bagtry **Kendall Rileigh**; Regina Hubbard **Stephanie Wright Thompson**; Jake **Anthony Wills Jr.**

SETTING June 1880. The Alabama town of Snowden. The Side terrace and the living room of the Hubbard house. Revival of a play presented in two acts. Originally presented on Broadway at the Fulton Theatre November 26, 1946–April 26, 1947 (see *Theatre World* Vol. 2, page 48).

SYNOPSIS A rarely seen "prequal" to her play *The Little Foxes*, Hellman's *Another Part of the Forest* tells the story of the most "dysfunctional" family in all of American drama, the notorious Hubbards — wealthy, ruthless, and immoral — and their rise to prominence.

Alysia Reiner and Stacey Linnartz in Modotti *(photo by Joan Marcus)*

World premiere of a new play presented in two acts.

SYNOPSIS *Modotti* is the story of sleek and sesuous photographer, silent film actress, activist, and communist subversive Tina Modotti, who fled to Mexico, lured by the revolution and artistic excitement, where she tore through the male dominated political forums almost as fast as she tore through her lovers. Accompanied by her lover, American photographer, Edward Weston, she took on the challenge of a culture undergoing rapid change.

Freed

59E59 Theater A; First Preview: June 11, 2010; Opening Night: June 16, 2010; Closed July 3, 2010

Written by Charles Smith; Produced by Chase Mishkin; Presented by the Penguin Rep Theatre (Joe Brancato, Artistic Director; Andrew W. Horn, Executive Director) as part of the Americas Off Broadway Festival; Director, Joe Brancato; Set/Props, Joseph J. Egan; Costumes, Patricia E. Doherty; Lighting, Martin E. Vreeland; Sound, Chris Rummel; Casting, Cindi Rush; Assistant Director, Anya Saffir; Stage Manager, C. Renee Alexander; Production Manager, Zachary Spitzer; Literary Manager, Samantha Carlin; ASM, Maggie Sinak; Master Electrician, Lloyd Rothschild; Light/Sound Operator, D. Alex Bright; Crew,Shannon Sass; Press, Karen Greco

CAST Robert Wilson **Christopher McCann**; John Newton Templeton **Sheldon Best**; Jane Wilson **Emma O'Donnell**

SETTING 1824-1828; Athens, Ohio. New York City premiere of a new play presented in two acts. Originally produced under the title *Free Man of Color* at Victory Gardens Theater (Chicago) in January 2004, and by Penguin Rep Theatre (Stony Point, NY), October 2009.

SYNOPSIS In 1824, on the edge of the frontier, a college president, his wife, and a former slave explore the limits of their freedom. Based on the true story, *Freed* tells the story of John Newton Templeton, the first African-American to attend college in the Midwest — 40 years before the Emancipation Proclamation.

Sherman Howard and Stephanie Wright Thompson in Another Part of the Forest *(photo by Dick Larson)*

Modotti

Acorn Theatre on Theatre Row; First Preview: June 9, 2010; Opening Night: June 11, 2010; Closed July 3, 2010

Written and directed by Wendy Beckett; Presented by Pascal Productions; Set, John McDermott; Costumes, Theresa Squire; Lighting, Lauren Phillips; Sound, Ray Thomas; Projections; Brett Heath; PSM, William Land; Press, Katie Rosin

CAST Tina Modotti **Alysia Reiner**; Edward Weston **Jack Gwaltney**; Diego Rivera **Marco Greco**; Robo/Mella **Andy Paris**; Young Woman/Patron/Susan **Stacey Linnartz**; Ella Wolfe **Dee Pelletier**; Vidali **Mark Zeisler**; Musician **Josh Tyson**

Sheldon Best and Emma O'Donnell in Freed *(photo by John Quilty)*

When We Go Upon the Sea

59E59 Theater B; First Preview: June 10, 2010; Opening Night: June 17, 2010; Closed July 3, 2010

Written by Lee Blessing; Presented by InterAct Theatre Company (Seth Rozin, Artistic Director) as part of the Americas Off Broadway Festival; Director, Paul Meshejian; Set, Meghan Jones; Costumes, Rosemarie McKelvey; Sound, Christopher Colucci; Lighting, Thom Weaver; Technical Director, Britt Plunkett; Stage Manager, Amy Kaskeski; ASM, Glenn R. Grieves; Props, Avista Custom Theatrical Services; Dramaturg, Rebecca Wright; Casting Consultant, Judy Bowman; Managing Director, David Brown; Marketing, David Golston; Press, Karen Greco

CAST George **Conan McCarty**; Piet **Peter Schmitz**; Anna-Lisa **Kim Carson**

SETTING A posh hotel room in the Hague, Netherlands. New York premiere of a new play presented without intermission. Previously presented at InterAct Theatre Company (Philadelphia).

SYNOPSIS *When We Go Upon the Sea* imagines former President George W. Bush on the eve of his trial for international war crimes. Tended to by an inscrutable Dutch butler and an alluring masseuse, the President embarks on a long night of drinking, joking and ruminating, taking the audience through a deep exploration of how we regard our leaders - loving them, fearing them, unintentionally deifying them. The play exposes one of the world's most intriguing and influential conflicts: the battle between the elected leader of the free world and a democracy of millions.

Conan McCarty and Peter Schmitz in When We Go Upon the Sea *(photo by Seth Rozin)*

Colin Quinn: Long Story Short

Bleecker Street Theatre; Opening Night: June 19, 2010; Closed September 4, 2010

Written by Colin Quinn; Produced by Columbus 81 Productions; Presented by CQE Live Inc.; Director, Jerry Seinfeld; Sets/Video, Aaron Rhyne; Lighting, Perchik Kreiman-Miller; Sound, Scott Elmegreen; General Manager, Eva Price, Maximum Entertainment Productions

Performed by **Colin Quinn**

World premiere of a new solo performance play presented without intermission. This production transferred to the Helen Hayes Theatre later this season (see page 44 in this volume for full production credits and photos).

SYNOPSIS Covering more than 2000 years in 75 minutes, *Long Story Short* is Colin Quinn's hilarious look at the ups and downs of great civilizations gone wrong. In this one-man sendup, Quinn channels comedic personalities of nations past, offering satirical takes on the attitudes, appetites and habits that toppled powerful empires.

Dietrich & Chevalier: The Musical

St. Luke's Theatre; First Preview: June 5, 2010; Opening Night: June 20, 2010; Closed December 11, 2010

Written by Jerry Mayer; Produced by Edmund Gaynes in association with Emily Bettman; Director, Pamela Hall; Music Direction/Pianist, Ken Lundie; Musical Staging, Gene Castle; Set, Josh Iacovelli & Scott Heineman; Costumes, Karen Flood; Lighting, Graham Kindred; Media Design, Chris Jensen; PSM, Josh Iacovelli; Casting, Moss Kale Anastasi; General Manager, Jessimeg Productions; ASM, Luca Pierucci; Props Master, Dustin Cross; Wardrobe, Sandy Sardar; Press, David Gerten

Robert Cuccioli and Jodi Stevens in Dietrich & Chevalier: The Musical
(photo by Carol Rosegg)

CAST Maurice Chevalier **Robert Cuccioli**; Marlene Dietrich **Jodi Stevens**; Eight Fascinating Characters **Donald Corren**

World premiere of a new play with musical numbers presented in two acts.

SYNOPSIS *Dietrich & Chevalier* tells the story of real life film stars of Hollywood's Golden Age, Marlene Dietrich and Maurice Chevalier. These two famous lovers were separated by World War II, but when Chevalier was wrongfully accused of treason, Dietrich rushed to his side to defend him. This musical portraying their epic love story features 15 of their signature songs from their films.

Nunsense

Cherry Lane Theatre; First Preview: June 13, 2010; Opening Night: June 20, 2010; Closed July 18, 2010

Written and directed by Dan Goggin; Produced by Cherry Lane Theatre (Angelina Fiordellisi, Artistic Director; James King, Executive Director); Musical Staging and Chroeography, Teri Gibson; Set, Barry Axtell; Lighting, Paul Miller; Music Direction, Leo P. Carusone; Orchestrations, Michael Rice; Production Manager, Michael Catalan; PSM, J.P. Elins; ASM, Nancy WErnick; Marketing, Steam, Elizabeth Findlay; Development Consultant, James McNeel; Development Associate, Colleen O'Shea; Program Associate, Seri Lawrence; Business Management, Friedman & LaRosa Inc., Joyce Friedman; Technical Director, Janio Marrero; Company Coordinator, Alexander Orbovich; Press, Sam Rudy Media Relations

CAST Reverend Mother Mary Regina **Bonnie Lee**; Sister Mary Hubert **Bambi Jones**; Sister Robert Anne **Maria Montana**; Sister Mary Amnesia **Jeanne M. Tinker**; Sister Mary Leo **Stephanie Wahl**

THE BAND Leo P. Carusone (Conductor/Keyboard), Patrick Kelly (Synthesizers)

MUSICAL NUMBERS Overture, Nunsense is Habit Forming, A Difficult Transition, Benedicte (Morning at the Convent), The Biggest Ain't the Best, Playing Second Fiddle, So You Want to Be a Nun, Turn Up the Spotlight, Lilacs Bring Back Memories, Tackle That Temptation with a Time-Step, Growing Up Catholic, Clean Out the Freezer, Just a Coupl'a Sisters, Soup's On (The Dying Nun Ballet)), Playing Second Fiddle (reprise), I Just Want to Be a Star, The Drive-In, I Could've Gone to Nashville, Holier Than Thou, Finale

SETTING Mount Saint Helen's School Auditorium; the present. 25th Anniversary revival of a musical presented in two acts. The original production of *Nunsense* opened at the Cherry Lane Theatre December 12, 1985, moved to Sheridan Square Playhouse/Circle Repertory Theatre February 27, 1986, then to the Douglas Fairbanks Theatre September 8, 1986 where it concluded its run there October 16, 1994 after playing 3,672 performances (see *Theatre World* Vol. 42, page 68 for original production credits.)

SYNOPSIS *Nunsense* celebrates its 25th Anniversary with this revival at its original home. *Nunsense* follows the riotous escapades of five nuns from the Little Sisters of Hoboken who realize that one of their own, Sister Julia, Child of God, has accidentally poisoned to death 52 fellow nuns in the convent while the quintet was off playing Bingo.

Jeanne Tinker, Bonnie Lee, and Bambi Jones in Nunsense
(photo by Michael Feldser)

PTP/NYC (Potomac Theatre Project)

Atlantic Stage 2; First Preview: July 6, 2010; Opening Night: July 11 (*A Question of Mercy*), July 12 (*Plevna* and *Gary the Thief*), July 13 (*Lovesong of the Electric Bear*); Closed August 1, 2010; 8 previews, 31 performances (3 previews, 10 performances for *Lovesong* and *Mercy*; 2 previews, 11 performances for *Plevna* and *Gary the Thief*)

Four plays in Repertory: *A Question of Mercy* by David Rabe; Director, Jim Petosa; *Plevna: Meditations on Hatred* and *Gary the Thief* by Howard Barker; Director, Richard Romagnoli; *Lovesong of the Electric Bear* by Snoo Wilson; Director, Cheryl Faraone; Produced PTP (Cheryl Faraone, Jim Petosa, Richard Romagnoli, Co-Artistic Directors); Sets, Christina Galvez; Furniture (*Mercy*), Eleanor Kahn; Lighting, Hallie Zieselman; Costumes, Emma Ermotti (*Mercy*), Danelle Nieves (*Lovesong*); Projections, Ross Bell, Hallie Zieselman; Sound, Jimmy Wong (*Lovesong*), Andrew Duncan Will (*Mercy*); Production Manager, Hallie Zieselman; PSMs, Alex Mark, Lisa McGinn; Choreography (*Lovesong*), Peter B. Schmitz; Additional Music (*Lovesong*), Lilli Stein; ASMs, Lauren Fondren, Stephanie Spencer, Michael Block; Assistants to the Directors, Emily Rosenkrantz, Catherine Lidstone, Claire Graves; Assistants to the Producers, Matha Newman, Lilli Stein, Cassidy Boys; Costume Oversite, Jule Emerson, Marcia Provoncha; Press, David Gibbs

CAST *A Question of Mercy*: Dr. Chapman **Paula Langton**; Anthony **Tim Spears**; Thomas **Alex Cranmer**; Susanah **Martha Newman**; Eddie Ruggero **Mathew Nakitare**; *Gary the Thief*: Gary the Thief **Robert Emmet Lunney**; *PLEVNA: Meditations on Hatred*: Plevna **Alex Draper**; *Lovesong of the Electric*

Bear: Alan Turning **Alex Draper**; Porgy Bear **Tara Giordano**; Blackwood/Turing Sr/Cornish/Sergeant **Alex Cranmer**; Churchill/Davis/Barman/Greenbaum/Dilly Knox **Peter B. Schmitz**; Clemmie/Mother/Judge **Nina Silver**; Christopher Morcom/Joan **Cassidy Boyd**; Kjell/Undergrad 1/Rejewski/Arnold **Willie McKay**; Nurse/Fortune Teller/Undergrad 2/Ylena **Claire Graves**; Bronwyn/Varia **Lilli Stein**; Old Southern Woman/Hallam/Man **Martina Bonolis**

UNDERSTUDIES *Lovesong*: Lilli Stein, Martina Bonolis, Stephanie Spencer, Mathew Nakitare, Claire Graves, Cassidy Boyd; *Mercy*: Martha Newman, Willy McKay, Catherine Lidstone; *Plevna*: Matthew Nakitare; *Gary the Thief*: Willy McKay

SETTING Three evenings of plays and poems presented in repertory. *Lovesong*: June 1912 to June 1954. New York premiere of a new play presented in two acts. *A Question of Mercy*: Revival of a play presented in two acts; *Plevna* and *Gary the Thief*: New York premiere and World premiere, respectively, of two solo performance poems presented without intermission.

SYNOPSIS PTP/NYC, formerly known as The Potomac Theatre Project, in association with Middlebury College, proudly presents its 24th repertory season, its fourth consecutive in New York, continuing to redefine political theatre for the 21st century. Howard Barker's two poems for the stage examine human polarization, cruelty and self-determination. *Lovesong of the Electric Bear* centers on the life and times of Alan Turing - mathematician, WWII code-breaker and father of computer science. In *A Question Of Mercy*, David Rabe explores the controversial and emotional issue of euthanasia.

Tara Giordano and Alex Draper in Lovesong of the Electric Bear *(photo by Stan Barouh)*

Marc Wolf in Another American: Asking and Telling

Another American: Asking and Telling

DR2; Opening Night: July 12, 2010; Closed October 4, 2010; 12 performances (Monday evenings)

Written by Marc Wolf; Produced by Daryl Roth; Original Direction, Joe Mantello

Performed by **Marc Wolf**

Revival of a solo performance play presented without intermission. Originally presented at the New Group December 7, 1999–February 6, 2000. (See *Theatre World* Vol. 56, page 92).

SYNOPSIS *Another American: Asking and Telling* takes the audience on a national tour of sexual politics, the American military, sanctioned discrimination, and its human fallout. Distilled from over one hundred and fifty interviews with straight, gay and lesbian military personnel (from World War II veterans to anonymous service members serving today), in addition to civil rights lawyers, federal judges, professors and politicians, Wolf portrays a community of characters struggling with the government's ban on gays and lesbians in the armed forces.

With Glee

Kirk Theatre on Theatre Row; First Preview: July 10, 2010; Opening Night: July 13, 2010; Closed August 29, 2010; 2 previews, 43 performances

Book, music, and lyrics by John Gregor; Presented by Prospect Theater Company (Cara Reichel, Artistic Director; Melissa Huber, Managing Director; Peter Mills, Associate Artist/Resident Writer); Director, Igor Goldin; Music Director, Daniel Feyer; Choreography, Antoinette Di Pietropolo; Set, Jen Price Fick; Costumes, Tricia Barsamian; Lighting, Cory Pattak; PSM, Emily Paige Ballou; ASM, Katy Moore; Orchestrations, Rob Hartmann; Assistant Director, Shane Bland; Associate Producer, Jaki Silver; Production Manager, Mary E. Leach; Assistant Costumes, Brooke Cohen; Technical Director, Michael Riff; Press, Corinne Zadik; Cast Recording: Brimmer Street Productions

CAST Scott **Zach Bandler**; Nathanial **Christopher Davis Carlisle**; Kip **Jason Edward Cook**; Clay **Dan Lawler**; Sam **Max Spitulnik**; Dads/Professors/Headmaster **Greg Horton**; Moms/Dr. Whitehead **Erin Jerozal**

BAND Daniel Feyer (Piano/Conductor), Rob Ouellette (Keyboard 2), Dennis Michael Keefe (Bass), Jessie Nelson (Drums)

MUSICAL NUMBERS Bad Kid School; Gaul Was Divided Into Three Parts; Clay's Song; If You Want to Be a Vanderberg; Back to Mom's; Normal; Christmas Cheer; Amanda; We're Going to Worcester; That Boat; Tomas, A One Act Musical; Home; Co-ed Dorms

Off-Broadway premiere of a new musical presented without intermission. Previously presented at in a workshop at the NYU's Skirball Center and at the 2007 New York Musical Theatre Festival.

SYNOPSIS *With Glee* is a new, old-fashioned musical comedy about five wayward, eccentric, isolated, awkward, sweet, naive, nerdy teenage boys who are sent away to a boarding school in Maine. As they revel in the trials of their freshman year-striving for acceptance, friendship, and normalcy-we are reminded that every life must be lived to its fullest, every song sung with glee.

Jason Edward Cook, Zach Bandler, Christopher Davis Carlisle, Dan Lawler, and Max Spitulnik in With Glee *(photo by Gerry Goodstein)*

We the People: America Rocks!

Lucille Lortel Theatre; First Preview: July 8, 2010; Opening Night: July 14, 2010; Closed August 13, 2010

Book by Joe Iconis, songs by Brad Alexander & Kevin Del Aguila, Eli Bolin & Sam Forman, Joe Iconis, Tommy Newman, Ryan Scott Oliver, Adam Overett, Erik Weiner, Mark Weiner & Jordan Alen-Dutton; Presented by Theatreworks USA (Barbara Pasternack, Artistic Director; Ken Arthur, Producing Director) by special arrangement with Lucille Lortel Foundation; Director, Gordon Greenberg; Choreography, Michele Lynch; Set, Adam Koch; Costumes, Lora LaVon; Lighting, Jeff Croiter; Sound, Michael S. Eisenberg; Music Director/Arrangements, J. Oconer Navarro; Orchestrations, Greg Pliska; PSM, Carly J. Price; Associate Director, Wes Grantom; Associate Choreographer, Tony Vierling; Production Manager, Bob Daley; Associate Sound, T.J. Pallas; Associate Lighting, Grant Yeager; Press, The Publicity Office, Jeremy Shaffer

CAST Washington **Colin Campbell McAdoo**; Adams **F. Michael Haynie**; Jefferson **Jamie LaVerdiere**; Franklin **Abe Goldfarb**; Dawn **Badia Farha**; Understudies **Justin Flagg**, **Brittany N. Williams**

MUSICAL NUMBERS The Road to Democracy, We the People, The First Amendment, We in the House, It's My Air Too, Dawn's President, King of the Ring, We the People (reprise), We Got the Power

World premiere of a new musical for young audiences presented without intermission.

SYNOPSIS On a quest to win her school election, Dawn cares more about padding her college applications than making her school a better place. With the help of the American Revolution Fab Four, she discovers that 'We the People' have the power to raise a patriotic ruckus and make a difference.

Jamie LaVerdiere, Abe Goldgarb, F. Michael Haynie, and Colin Campbell McAdoo in We the People: America Rocks! *(photo by Joan Marcus)*

In God's Hat

Peter Jay Sharp Theater; First Preview: July 14, 2010; Opening Night: July 18, 2010; Closed August 7, 2010; 3 previews, 16 performances

Written by Richard Taylor; Presented by the Apothecary Theatre Company (Shawn Renfro, Artistic Director; Dennis Flanagan, Executive Director); Director, Kevin Kittle; Set, Michael Reese; Lighting, Jerome J. Hoppe Jr.; Costumes, Victoria Depew; Sound/Tech Director, Lou Albruzzese; Fight Choreography, Rick Sordelet; Stage Manager, Chris Rinaldi

CAST Roy **Tom Pelphrey**; Mitch **Rhett Rossi**; Arthur Cruter **Dennis Flanagan**; Early Boyle **Gary Francis Hope**; Corrections Officer **Mike Mihm**

SETTING A motel on a desolate highway leading away from a penitentiary. World premiere of a new play presented in two acts.

SYNOPSIS *In God's Hat* involves two brothers who haven't seen each other for a bit more than the decade. Mitch has been locked up for pedophilia. When Roy, the younger of the two, implies that his brother's payment of his debt to society still leaves an unpaid balance to the family, a feeling of double jeopardy is seeping under the door. As two Aryan skinheads butt in to add their own crude indictments, Mitch's punishment is starting to look a lot worse than the crime.

Dennis Flanagan, Rhett Rossi, and Tom Pelphrey in In God's Hat *(photo by Dale Jabagat)*

Viagara Falls

Little Shubert Theatre; First Preview: July 5, 2010; Opening Night: July 21, 2010; Closed August 29, 2010

Written by Lou Cutell and Joao Machado; Produced by SJ Productions, Stanley Browne, John Finocchio, and Robert Nederlander Jr. in association with Richard George, Michael Carazza and J.J.J.; Director, Don Cricton; Set, Sydne Litwack; Costumes, Bob Mackie; Lighting, Joshua Scherr; Sound, Peter Fitzgerald; General Manager, John Lowe; PSM, William Gilinsky; Press, Keith Sherman and Associates

CAST Moe Crubbs **Bernie Kopell**; Charlie Milhouse **Lou Cutell**; Jacqueline Tempest **Teresa Ganzel**

SETTING Charlie's apartment in Sunnyside, Queens; the present. New York premiere of a new play presented without intermission.

SYNOPSIS Charley and Moe are widowers, war buddies and life-long pals. For his 77th birthday, rather than sitting around listening to old records, Charley decides that he and Moe need one more crack at sowing some wild oats. Moe is wary, but with the help of one loopy lady of the evening and some black market blue pills, Charley and Moe are in for the birthday party of their lives.

Bernie Kopell, Teresa Ganzel, and Lou Cutell in Viagara Falls
(photo by Carol Rosegg)

Freud's Last Session

Marjorie S. Deane Little Theatre; First Preview: July 9, 2010; Opening Night: July 22, 2010; 15 previews, 305 performances as of May 31, 2011 (Hiaitus November 29, 2010–January 13, 2011)

Written by Mark St. Germain, suggested by "The Question of God" by Dr. Armand M. Nicholi Jr.; Produced by Carolyn Rossi Copeland, Robert Stillman, and Jack Thomas; Presented by Barrington Stage Company (Julianne Boyd, Artistic Director; Richard M. Parison Jr., Producing Director); Director, Tyler Marchant; Set, Brian Prather; Costumes, Mark Mariani; Lighting, Clifton Taylor; Sound, Beth Lake; Advertising/Marketing, The Pekoe Group; Casting, Pat McCorkle; PSM, Kate J. Cudworth; Production Managers, Wheeler Kincaid, Cedric Hill; General Management, CRC Productions; Company Manager, Robert E. Schneider; Assistant Set, Alexander Woodward; Assistant Lighting, Greg Guarnaccia; Press, Jim Randolph

CAST Sigmund Freud **Martin Rayner**; C.S. Lewis **Mark H. Dold**; Standby **Tuck Milligan**

Martin Rayner and Mark H. Dold in Freud's Last Session
(photo by Carol Rosegg)

SETTING September 3, 1939; Freud's Study at 20 Maresfield Gardens, Hampstead, NW London. New York premiere of a new play presented without intermission. Originally produced at Barrington Stage Company (Sheffield, Massachusettes) June 2009.

SYNOPSIS *Freud's Last Session* centers on legendary psychoanalyst Dr. Sigmund Freud, who invites the young, rising academic star C.S. Lewis to his home in London. Lewis, expecting to be called on the carpet for satirizing Freud in a recent book, soon realizes Freud has a much more significant agenda. On the day England enters World War II, Freud and Lewis clash on the existence of God, the joy of love, the purpose of sex, and the meaning of life – just a few weeks before Freud's own death.

The Shoemaker

Acorn Theatre on Theatre Row; First Preview: July 14, 2010; Opening Night: July 24, 2010; Closed August 14, 2010; 11 previews, 16 performances

Written by Susan Charlotte; Producers, Danny Aiello and Susan Charlotte; Co-Producers, Louis Baldonieri and Mary Davis; Presented by Cause Celebrè; Director, Antony Marsellis; Set, Ray Klausen; Costumes, Theresa Squire; Lighting/Sound, Bernie Dove; Wardrobe, David Toser; PSM, Anita Ross; Stage Manager, C. Renee Alexander; Marketing, Tracey Miller & Associates; Assistant to the Producer, Brendan Hill; Press, Springer Associates

Danny Aiello and Alma Cuervo in The Shoemaker *(photo by Ben Hider)*

CAST Guiseppe **Danny Aiello**; Hilary **Alma Cuervo**; Louise **Lucy DeVito**; Offstage Voices **Michael Twaine**

SETTING Hell's Kitchen, New York. World premiere of a new play presented in two acts. A one-act version of the show was produced in 2001.

SYNOPSIS *The Shoemaker* is a compelling drama that focuses on a shoemaker, an Italian Jew, on a devastating day that has become a turning point in American history. As each hour passes he confronts yet another part of his past, present and an uncertain future.

See Rock City & Other Destinations

Duke on 42nd Street; First Preview: July 17, 2010; Opening Night: July 25, 2010; Closed August 14, 2010

Music by Brad Alexander, book & lyrics by Adam Mathias; Presented by the Transport Group (Jack Cummings III, Artistic Director; Lori Fineman, Executive Director); Director, Jack Cummings III; Music Director/Orchestrations/Vocal Arrangements, Justin Hatchimonji; Set & Costumes, Dane Laffrey; Lighting, R. Lee Kennedy; Casting, Alan Filderman; PSM, Theresa Flanagan; ASM, Michelle Beige; Production Manager, Wendy Patten; Managing Producer, Michelle Ellis; Dramaturg, Krista Williams; Music Coordinator, Christine Kim; Master Electrician, Adam B. Orseck; Press, Richard Kornberg & Associates, Don Summa

CAST Evan/Rick **Stanley Bahorek**; Claire/Kate **Donna Lynne Champlin**; Dempsey/Tour Guide **Jonathan Hammond**; Grampy/Carney **Ryan Hilliard**; Dodi/Lily **Mamie Parris**; Jess/Cotter **Bryce Ryness**; Lauren/Judy **Sally Wilfert**

MUSICIANS Justin Hatchimoni (Piano), Steve Count (Bass), Craig Magnano (Guitar), Christine Kim (Cello)

MUSICAL NUMBERS Rock City, I Can Tell, Mile After Mile, We Are Not Alone, All There Is to Say, Grampy's Song, We Are Not Alone (reprise), Three Fair Queens, Here, Q Train to Coney Island, You Are My Bitch, Dark Ride, Niagra Falls The Tour, What Am I Afraid Of?, Some People Do/Finale

SETTING Off-Broadway premiere of a new musical presented without intermission. Originally presented as part of the Raw Impressions Music Theatre Festival in 2007, and as part of William Finn's Musical Theatre Lab at Barrington Stage in the summer of 2008. Transport Group workshopped the show in June 2009.

Bryce Ryness and Stanley Bahorek in See Rock City & Other Destinations *(photo by Carol Rosegg)*

SYNOPSIS *See Rock City & Other Destinations* is a contemporary musical about connections missed and made at tourist destinations across America. A wanderer believes his destiny is written on rooftops along the North Carolina Interstate. A young man yearns to connect with intelligent life in Roswell, New Mexico. A woman at the Alamo steps out of the shadow of her grandparents' idealized romance to take a chance on love. Three estranged sisters cruise to Glacier Bay to scatter their father's ashes. Two high school boys face unexpected fears in the Coney Island Spook House. A terrified bride-to-be ponders taking the leap...over Niagara Falls.

Tales from the Tunnel

Bleecker Street Theatre; First Preview: July 10, 2010; Opening Night: July 25, 2010; Closed October 3, 2010

Written and directed by Troy Diana and James Valletti; Produced by Adam Blanshay and Stephenie Overton; Associate Producers/Set, Brad Zizomor and Dag Folger (a+i design corp.); Lighting, Paul Miller; Sound, Jess Bauer; Casting, Daryl Eisenberg; Associate Producer/General Manager, Brierpatch Productions; Associate Producers, Nathan Burgess, Deborah Reda/Jill Steinberg, Lori Zlotoff; PSM, Byron F. Abens; ASM, Jamie Rog; Press, Keith Sherman and Associates

CAST **Farah Bala**, **Geri Brown**, **Carla Corvo**, **Wilson Jermaine Heredia**, **Brandon Jones**, **Vayu O'Donnell**, **Sam Rosenberg**, **Maria Silverman**

Off-Broadway premiere of a new play without intermission. Previously presented at the 2009 New York International Fringe Festival.

SYNOPSIS *Tales from the Tunnel* highlights six actors playing nearly 100 characters in a series of humorous, heartbreaking, and insightful accounts of true New York City Subway experiences, woven together into an entertaining ride. It's a trip you won't forget.

Wilson Jermaine Heredia, Brandon Jones, Vayu O'Donnell, and Farah Bala in Tales from the Tunnel *(photo by Aaron Epstein)*

The Flying Karamazov Brothers: 4play

Minetta Lane Theatre; First Preview: July 22, 2010; Opening Night: August 9, 2010; Closed April 3, 2011

Book by Paul Magid & The Flying Karamazov Brothers; Presented by The Flying Karamazov Brothers; Original Music, Mark Ettinger, Doug Wieselman, Howard Patterson; Music Director, Mark Ettinger; Juggling Czar, Rod Kimball;

Choreography, Doug Elkins; Set, The Flying Karamazov Brothers; Costumes, Susan Hilferty; Lighting, David Huston; PSM, Emily Cornelius; Assistant Musical Director, Stephen Bent; General Management, Two Step Productions, Cris Buchner, Kate Mott, Amy Dalba, Rachel Merrill Moss; Associate Producer, Highbrow Entertainment; Advertising, Eliran Murphy Group; Marketing, HHC Marketing; Press, Richard Kornberg & Associates, Tommy Wesely

CAST Dmitri **Paul Magid**; Alexei **Mark Ettinger**; Pavel **Roderick Kimball**; Zossima **Stephen Bent**

Commercial extension of a new theatrical juggling/physical comedy experience with music presented in two acts. The show had its World Premiere at the Minetta Lane February 8–March 7, 2010 (see *Theatre World* Vol. 66, page 161).

SYNOPSIS A unique blend of music, comedy, dance, theater, and juggling, *4Play* features The Flying Karamazov Brothers, New York's favorite multi-faceted new-vaudevillians at the apex of their ambidextrous and alliterative ability. The Flying K's prove with each performance that chaos and unexpected events in our lives are the best part of being human.

Paul Magid, Rod Kimball, Stephen Brent, and Mark Ettinger in
The Flying Karamazov Brothers *(photo by Carol Rosegg)*

Abraham Lincoln's Big, Gay Dance Party

Acorn Theatre on Theatre Row; First Preview: July 27, 2010; Opening Night: August 11, 2010; Closed September 5, 2010

Written by Aaron Loeb; Produced by BlueRare Productions in association with Aaron Glick and Deborah Taylor; Director, Chris Smith; Choreography, Vince Pesce; Set, Bill English; Lighting, Jeff Croiter, Grant Yeager; Costumes, Rebecca Lustig; Sound, Kim Furh-Carbone; Original Music, Rick Burkhardt and Rick Hip-Flores; Production Manager, James Cleveland; Casting, Howard Cherpakov; Associate Set, Mike Billings; PSM, Christine Catti; Press, O+M Company

CAST Tina, Violet, George Washington, and Abe **Lisa Birnbaum**; Anton, Judge, and Abe **Arnie Burton**; Regina, Esmerelda and Abe **Stephanie Pope Caffey**; Tom, Walter and Abe **Robert Hogan**; Lloyd, Timmy, Principal and Abe **Ted Koch**; Harmony, Mom and Abe **Pippa Pearthree**; Jerry, Bailiff, Sparky, Thomas Jefferson and Abe **Ben Roberts**

Off-Broadway premiere of a new play with dance presented in three acts. World Premiere at San Francisco Playhouse December 13, 2008–January 17, 2009. Previously presented at the 2009 New York International Fringe Festival.

SYNOPSIS In *Abraham Lincoln's Big, Gay Dance Party*, a fourth-grade Christmas pageant in Lincoln's rural Illinois hometown sets off a firestorm of controversy when it calls into question Honest Abe's sexuality. A thought-provoking, laugh-out-loud funny, and uniquely American story unfolds, offering surprises at every turn. Each of the three acts lets the audience see the story from a different character's viewpoint – and at each performance the audience decides in which order the acts are performed, creating a Rubik's Cube-like theatrical event. A truly democratic theatergoing experience!

The cast of Abraham Lincoln's Big, Gay Dance Party *(photo by Carol Rosegg)*

Power Balladz

Midtow Theatre at Ha!; First Preview: August 5, 2010; Opening Night: August 19, 2010; Closed October 23, 2010; 13 previews, 37 performances

Created and written by Dan Nycklemoe and Mike Todaro with Peter Rothstein; Presented by Bruce Johnson, Mike Todaro, and Dan Nycklemoe; Director, Mike Todaro; Set, Hilary Noxon; Lighting, Bradley Clements; Sound, Alex Ritter; Costumes, Abbi Stern; Projections, Dan Nyclemoe; Associate Producer, Michael Skipper; General Management, Davenport Theatrical Enterprises; Advertising and Marketing, Davenport Media Enterprises; Casting, Adam Caldwell; Music Director, Karen Dryer; PSM, Jermiah Peah; Arrangements/Orchestrations, Jason Loffredo & Karl Mansfield; Music Supervisor, Jason Loffredo; Company Manager, Kimberly Shaw; ASM, Brad Resnick; Press, Sam Rudy Media Relations

CAST **Dieter Bierbrauer**, **Scott Richard Foster**, **Mary Mossberg**; Understudies **Melanie Kann**, **Peter James Zielinski**

BAND Karen Dryer (Conductor/Keyboard), Jason Bozzi & Sean Driscoll (Guitars), Mark Vanderpoel (Bass), Brad Carbone (Drums)

New York premiere of a new musical presented without intermission. World premiere at the LAB Theatre (Minneapolis).

SYNOPSIS *Power Balladz* celebrates the best music of the 70's 80's and 90's and liberates the rock star inside of you. Start with some blood-pumping arena rock songs by Motley Crue, Poison, Guns 'N' Roses, Journey, and other kick-ass arena bands, add some talented rock singers, give them a full band, lights, a fog machine, a video projection screen, plenty of leather and long hair, and you've got a concert. And while the *Power Balladz* band knows how to rock, the show takes an unexpected turn when the high school sweetheart of one of the musicians stumbles into the show after ten years apart, raising the question — will he be man enough to finally score the girl of his dreams?

The cast of Power Balladz *(photo by Carol Rosegg)*

All-American Girls

Actors Temple Theatre; First Preview: August 4, 2010; Opening Night: August 25, 2010; Closed October 27, 2010

Written and directed by Layon Gray; Produced by Edmund Gaynes, The Black Gents, and The Layon Gray Experience; Sets, Josh Iacovelli; Costumes, Farelle Kiya; Lighting, David W. Boykins; Sound, Aidan Cole; Movement, Layon Gray; PSM, Bonnie Hilton; Press, David Gersten and Associates

CAST Betty Thibideaux **Daphanee Duplaix**; Laura James **Mari White**; Coach Hicks **Arlene McGruder**; Ester **Antoinette Robertson**; Mattie Jackson **Setor E. Attipoe**; Sara Jenkins **Yasha Jackson**; Charley **Ashley Jeffrey**; Jonnetta Burns **Chantal Nchako;** Eddie Coleman **Catherine Peoples**; Mr. West **Steve Brustein**

SETTING Chicago; 1945. Off-Broadway premiere of a new play presented in two acts in repertory with *Black Angels Over Tuskegee*. A previous version of the play entitled *The Girls of Summer* played the Midtown International Theatre Festival in 2006.

SYNOPSIS *All-American Girls* is a tale of racism, deceit and betrayal after the coach of an all-Negro female baseball team goes missing. The drama captures an era in American history when women were called on to keep baseball alive as the men went off to fight in World War II.

The cast of All-American Girls *(photo by Mark Glenn Studios)*

An Error of the Moon

30, 2010; Closed October 10, 2010; 18 previews, 42 performances

Written by Luigi Creatore; Presented by Theater 21 and Carolyn Rossi Copeland Productions; Director, Kim Weild; Set, Steven Capone; Costumes, Alixandra Englund; Lighting, Charles Foster; Sound, Christain Frederickson; Projections, C. Andrew Bauer; Fight Director, Rick Sordelet; Casting, Pat McCorkle; PSM, Donald William Myers; ASM, Taylor Michael; Production Manager, Scott H. Schneider; General Management, CRC Productions, Robert E. Schneider; Company Manager, Ben Bartolone; Assistant Director, Jeremiah M. Davis; Advertising/Marketing, The Pekoe Group; Press, Jim Randolph

CAST Mary Devlin Booth **Margaret Copeland**; Edwin Booth **Erik Heger**; John Wilkes Booth **Andrew Veenstra**; The Player **Brian Wallace**; Understudy **Donovan Patton**

SETTING A backstage dressing room of a theater in the 1860s perhaps. Off-Broadway premiere of a new play presented without intermission.

SYNOPSIS An Error of the Moon is a fictional portrait of the brothers Edwin and John Wilkes Booth, the rock star actors of their day. Edwin tells his tale of a man consumed by jealousy, of bitter sibling rivalry, and the mad obsession that sparked the assassination of Abraham Lincoln.

Margaret Copeland, Andrew Veenstra and Erik Heger in An Error of the Moon *(photo by Carol Rosegg)*

It Must Be Him

Peter Jay Sharp Theater; First Preview: August 24, 2010; Opening Night: September 1, 2010; Closed September 26, 2010

Written by Lenny Solms; Presented by Orin Wolf and Off the Aisle Productions; Director, Daniel Kutner; Choreography, Wendy Seyb; Special Music Material, Larry Grossman (music) and Ryan Cunningham (lyrics); Sets, Court Watson; Costumes, Laurie Churba; Lighting, Joel E. Silver; Sound, Duncan Edwards; PSM, Tom Taylor; ASM, Vanessa Poggioli; Production Manager, Robert G. Mahon III; Orchestrations, Ned Paul Ginsburg; General Manager, Snug Harbor Productions; Casting, Mark Simon; Vocal Coach, Susan Schuld; Dance Captain, Jessica Tyler Wright; Assistant Design: Brian Kalin (set), Chris Kohn (costumes), Andy Fritsch (lighting), Jana Hogland (sound); Press, O+M Company

CAST Ana **Liz Torres**; Louie **Peter Scolari**; Scott **Patrick Cummings**; Leo **Bob Ari**; Rose **Alice Playten**; Myles **Harris Doran**; Ross **John Treacy Egan**; Mark/Eddie **Jonathan C. Kaplan**; Pete **Ryan Duncan**; Joan **Stephanie D'Abruzzo**; Brenda/Hildy **Jessica Tyler Wright**;Ty/Emcee **Edward Staudenmayer**; Understudies: **Christina Biano** (Ana/Joan/Hildy), **Patrick Richwood** (Louie/Ross/Ty)

SETTING Beverly Hills; The present. World premiere of a new play with music presented without intermission.

SYNOPSIS In *It Must Be Him*, Louie Wexler, a whiz kid comedy writer from the heyday of variety television, is now down on his luck. With his devoted agent , and his considerably less devoted housekeeper by his side, Louie finds himself broke, lonely, and on the wrong side of middle age. Desperate to rekindle his fading career, save his posh Beverly Hills home and find the man of his dreams, Louie searches high and low for one last shot at his own real-life happy ending.

Jonathan C. Kaplan, Edward Staudenmayer, and Ryan Duncan in It Must Be Him *(photo by Carol Rosegg)*

Oresteia

Kirk Theatre; Opening Night: September 8, 2010; Closed September 19, 2010, Encored November 23–December 8, 2011

Written by Aeschylus, adapted by Marika Thomadaki; Presented by Ethos Performing Arts in association with Leonidas Loizidis Theatre Group; Director, Leonidas Loizidis; Music, Elena-Fedra; Lyrics, Kate Nikolopoulou; Sets, Nasos Gurov; Music Director, Christos Alexandrou; Choreography, Cindi Trent & Betty Vytinarou; English Translation, Depoina Kontaxis; English Consultant & Editor, Louis Markos; Assistant Directors, Haris Georgiadis & Alexander Leontaritis; Photography, Christos Tourlakis; Masks and Weapons, Haris Georgiadis

CAST Orestis/Aigisthos/Agamemnon/Herald **Philippos Constantine** and **Tasos Lamakis**; Klytaimnistra **Dimitra Limniou**; Apollo **Christos Alexandrou**; Ilektra/Kassandra/Athena **Eftychia Papadopoulou**; Pythia/Nurse/Chorus **Veronica Iliopoulou**; Lead Chorus **Georgia Baka**; Chorus **Sofia Kominea, Tina Gavasiades;** Suppliant/Music Coordination-Improvisation **Elena Faidra**

Revival of a trilogy of classic plays presented in Greek with English titles with two intermissions.

SYNOPSIS *Oresteia* is a trilogy of Greek tragedies that concerns the end of the curse on the House of Atreus. *Agamemnon* details the homecoming of Agamemnon, King of Argos, from the Trojan War and his wife, Clytemnestra, who has been planning his murder. *The Libation Bearers* deals with the reunion of Agamemnon's children, Electra and Orestes, and their revenge on Clytemnestra. In *The Eumenides*, Orestes, Apollo, and the Erinyes go before Athena and a jury consisting of the Athenians at the Areopagus to decide whether Orestes' murder of his mother, Clytemnestra, makes him worthy of the torment they have inflicted upon him.

The Leonidas Loizides Theatrical Group in the Oresteia

Penny Penniworth

TADA! Theatre; First Preview: September 8, 2010; Opening Night: September 13, 2010; Closed October 3, 2010

Adapted by Chris Weikel from the story by Charles Dickens; Presented by Emerging Artists Theatre (Paul Adams, Artistic Director); Director, Mark Finely; Set, Tim McMath; Costumes, House of Goody; Lighting, Jennifer Granrund; Original Music, Peter Saxe; Sound, Aaron Blank; Set Assistant Helen Jun; Costumer/Wardrobe Mistress, Kate Jansyn Thaw; Costume Assistant, Meredith Neal; Production Manager/Managing Director, Deb Guston; PSM, Terra Vetter; Production Assistant, Alison Jane Carroll; Graphics, Tzipora Kaplan; Associate Artistic Director, Derek Jamison; Literary Manager, Kevin Brofsky; Actors Company Manager, Ron Bopst; Press, Ron Lasko/Spin Cycle

CAST Hotchkiss Spit & Others **Christopher Borg**; Rupert Stryfe, Heir to the House of Stryfe & Others **Jason O'Connell**; Miss Havasnort & Others **Ellen Reilly**; Penny Penniworth & Others **Jamie Heinlein**; Understudies **Lee Kaplan, Karen Stanion**

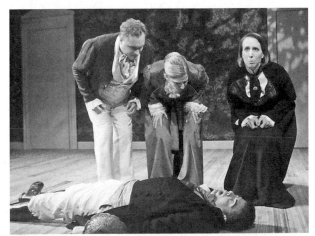

Christopher Borg, Jamie Heinlein, Jason O'Connell (on floor), and Ellen Reilly in Penny Penniworth *(photo by Ned Thorne)*

SETTING The present, but invoking a time early in the reign of Queen Victoria; Place: A stage, but meant to signify Merrie Olde Englande. Revival of a play presented without intermission. Previously presented by Emerging Artists in 2002, and subsequently presented by TOSOSII in the 2003 New York International Fringe Festival. The play was also presented last season October 1–November 8, 2009 (see *Theatre World* Vol. 66 page 139).

SYNOPSIS *Penny Penniworth* is Charles Dickens' "lost" epic as mounted by a short-staffed theatre troupe with Royal Shakespeare Company aspirations. The play tells the story of young Penny Penniworth whose childhood love is driven out of town after nearly killing a wealthy businessman. Soon, Penny finds herself penniless, left alone to make her way through a convoluted maze of strange relationships, anonymous benefactors and ultimate justice.

The Sensational Josephine Baker

TADA! Theatre; First Preview: September 7, 2010; Opening Night: September 14, 2010; Closed October 3, 2010

Written by Cheryl Howard; Presented by Emerging Artists Theatre (Paul Adams, Artistic Director); Director, Ian Streicher; Set, Tim McMath; Lighting, G. Ben Swope; Costumes, Nichole Wee; Sound, Aaron Blank; Music, Peter Saxe; Projections, David Bengali; PSM, Alison Jane Carroll; Press, Gonzalez Public Relations

Performed by **Cheryl Howard**

Off-Broadway premiere of a new play presented without intermission. Previously developed at EAT's One Woman Standing Series last season.

SYNOPSIS *The Sensational Josephine Baker* follows Josephine on her journey from conservative St. Louis to the risqué cabarets of France, from little girl to showgirl. Howard gives voice to an array of fascinating female characters: Josephine's domineering mother, fellow chorus girl Lydia Jones, Ada "Bricktop" Smith, and a raw, fearless portrayal of Ms. Baker herself in a series of defining moments – from the hilarious antics which rescued her from the obscurity of the chorus, to the humiliation of being shunned by a narrow-minded American public, to her life-long search for unconditional love... compelled throughout it all by an enduring passion to live life to the fullest.

Cheryl Howard in The Sensational Josephine Baker *(photo by Ned Thorne)*

The cast of Down There *(photo by Dixie Sheridan)*

Down There

Axis Theatre; First Preview: September 9, 2010; Opening Night: September 18, 2010; Closed October 30, 2010; 5 previews, 19 performances

Written by Randy Sharp, based on an original script by Randy Sharp and Michael Gump; Presented by Axis Company (Randy Sharp, Artistic Director; Brian Barnhart, Producing Director; Jeffrey Resnick, Executive Producer); Director, Randy Sharp; Assistant Director, Marc Palmieri; Lighting, David Zeffren; Sound, Steve Fontaine; Costumes, Elisa Santiago; Stage Manager, Edward Terhune; ASM, Marc Palmieri; Dramaturges, Christopher Swift, Marc Palmieri; Assistant Lighting, Amy Harper; Carpenters, Chad Yarborough, Carlo Adinolfi, Jackie McCarthey; Scene Painter, Jackie McCarthey; Prop Master, Lynn Mancinelli; Costume Construction, Aughra Moon; Cosutme Assistant, Britt Genelin; Wigs & Hair, Regina Betancourt; Website and Graphics, Ethan Crenson; Press, Blake Zidell & Associates

CAST Casey Kindens **Lynn Mancinelli**; Pat Menckl **Laurie Kilmartin**; Frank **Jim Sterling**; Jim **George Demas**; Paula **Britt Genelin**; Rickie **David Crabb**; John **Brian Barnhart**; Joyce **Regina Betancourt**

SETTING Indianapolis, Indiana; 1965. World premiere of a new play presented without intermission.

SYNOPSIS *Down There* tells the true story of Sylivia Likens, a 16-year old girl who was tortured and killed in the Indiana home of the Menckl family. The play explores who this could have happened and what it might have felt like to the perpetrators as well as the victim.

The Divine Sister

SoHo Playhouse; First Preview: September 12, 2010; Opening Night: September 22, 2010; Closed May 1, 2011; 9 previews, 253 performances

Written by Charles Busch; Produced by Daryl Roth and Bob Boyett; Director, Carl Andress; Set/Graphics, Brian T. Whitehall; Costumes, Fabio Toblini; Lighting, Kirk Bookman; Sound, Jill BC DuBoff; Wigs, Katherine Carr; Original Music, Lewis Flinn; PSM, Angela Allen; ASM, Trisha Henson; Assistant Director, James Valletti; Associate Producers, Alexander Fraser, Tim Levy, Land Line Productions; General Manager, Adam Hess; Company Manager, Danielle Karliner; Marketing, aka; Online Marketing, Situation Interactive; Press, Boneau/Bryan-Brown

CAST Mother Superior **Charles Busch**; Sister Walburga/Mrs. Macduffie **Alison Fraser***; Agnes **Amy Rutberg**; Mrs. Levinson/Timothy **Jennifer Van Dyk**; Jeremy/Brother Venerius **Jonathan Walker**; Sister Acacius **Julie Halston**

*Succeeded by Marcy McGuigan (4/9/11)

SETTING St. Veronica's Convent in Pittsburgh. Off-Broadway premiere of a new play presented without intermission. The play had a developmental run at Theater for the New City February 6–March 7, 2010 (see *Theater World* Vol. 66, page 326).

SYNOPSIS *The Divine Sister* is an outrageous comic homage to nearly every Hollywood film involving nuns, from *The Song of Bernadette* and *The Bells of St. Mary's* to *The Singing Nun* and *Agnes of God*. The play tells the story of St. Veronica's indomitable Mother Superior, who is determined to build a new school for her Pittsburgh convent. Along the way, she has to deal with a young postulant who is experiencing "visions," sexual hysteria among her nuns, a sensitive schoolboy in need of mentoring, a mysterious nun visiting from the Mother House in Berlin and a former suitor intent on luring her away from her vows.

Amy Rutberg, Charles Busch, Alison Fraser, and Julie Halston in
The Divine Sister *(photo by David Rodgers)*

Through the Night

Union Square Theatre; First Preview: September 10, 2010; Opening Night: September 26, 2010; Closed December 5, 2010; Westside Theatre (Monday evenings) January 24–March 28, 2011

Written by Daniel Beaty; Produced by Daryl Roth; Director, Charles Randolph-Wright; Set/Projections/Lighting, Alexander V. Nichols; Original Music/Sound, Lindsay Jones; PSM, Bess Marie Glorioso; General Manager, Adam Hess; Company Manager, Kyle Provost; Production Manager, Gregg Bellón; Marketing, aka, Donna Walker-Kuhne; Online Marketing, Pit Bull Interactive; Co-Producer, Jana Robbins; Associate Producer, Alexander Fraser, Marcia Pendelton; Artistic Ambassadors, Bill Cosby, Ruby Dee, Brian Stokes Mitchell, Phylicia Rashad; Press, O+M Company

Performed by **Daniel Beaty**

New York premiere of a new solo performance play presented without intermission. Originally presented at the Crossroads Theatre and the Geffen Playhouse in Los Angeles.

SYNOPSIS Six characters. Three generations. One unforgettable performance. Mr. Beaty portrays an entire cast of characters, from inquisitive boy to elder preacher, spinning a tale in which lives collide to show how hope, faith and love can pull anyone *Through the Night*.

Daniel Beaty in Through the Night *(photo by Carol Rosegg)*

Freckleface Strawberry: The Musical

New World Stages; First Preview: September 9, 2010; Opening Night: October 1, 2010; Closed April 24, 2011

Book by Gary Kupper and Rose Caiola, music and lyrics by Gary Kupper; Based on the children's book *Freckleface Strawberry* by Julianne Moore; Presented by Manhattan Movement and Arts Center Productions; Director, Buddy Crutchfield; Choreography, Gail Pennington Crutchfield; Music Director/Additional Arrangements, Dave Keyes; Set, Beowulf Boritt; Costumes, Fabio Toblini and Holly Cain; Lighting, Jason Kantrowitz; Sound, Peter Fitzgerald and Christopher Cronin; General Manager, Laura Heller; Company Manager, Rick Shulman/Bobby Driggers; PSM, Pamela Edington/Brian Meister; Stage Manager, Jana Llynn/Jeff Davolt; Production Manager, Brian White; Associate Production Manager/Technical Director, Jason McCullough; Production Associate, Sean Barrett; Assistant Director, Abigail Crutchfield; Associate Choreograhy, Allison Plamondon; Dance Captain, Morgan Smith; Associate Set, Alexis Distler; Associate Sound, Adam Rigby; Assistant Costumes, Loren Shaw; Assistant Lighting, Matthew Taylor; Hair Design, Charles G. LaPointe; Hair/Makeup, Dave Bova; Props, Buist Bickley; Casting, Mark Simon; Music Arrangements, Gary Kupper, Chris Hajian; Music Coordinator, John Miller; Advertising/Marketing, Davenport Media Enterprises; Press, Pete Sanders/JS2 Communications, Jessica Goon/5W Public Relations; Cast recording: MMAC Records

CAST Strawberry **Hayley Podschun**[1]; Ballet Girl **Jessica Bishop**[2]; Jake **Andrew Cristi**; Mother/Teacher/Jane **Linda Gabler**; Emily **Kimiko Glenn**; Henry **Mykal Kilgore**; Danny/Little Brother **Joey Haro**[3]

UNDERSTUDIES Morgan Smith (Strawberry/Female Roles), Eric Nelsen[4] (Male Roles), Kimiko Glenn (Strawberry)

*Succeeded by: 1. Remy Zaken (2/4/11) 2. Julia Bray 3. Xavier Cano, Sanjaya Malakar (2/23/11) 4. Christopher Brian Williams

MUSICIANS Dave Keyes (Conductor/Keyboards), Eric Halvorson (Drums)

MUSICAL NUMBERS Opening, Look At Me, Little Freckleface Strawberry, I Like Danny, I Hate Freckles, Freckleface Gangster Vaudeville, Perfect, Lonely Girl, I Can Be Anything, We Wanna Be Like Them, Kid In the Mask, Creative Minds, Be Yourself, Basketball, Lonely Girl (reprise), Hey It's Me, Once Upon A Time, When You Got Friends, Different, Happily Ever After

World premiere of a new musical for young audiences presented without intermission.

SYNOPSIS *Freckleface Strawberry* chronicles the life of seven-year-old Strawberry being teased by her schoolmates for having bright red hair and freckles. She feels different from everyone else and does anything to get rid of them — from scrubbing them with soap and even wearing a ski mask to school. Strawberry goes on a journey and discovers that all people are different. She ultimately learns to accept herself for all of who she is, freckles and all.

The cast of Freckleface Strawberry *(photo by Carol Rosegg)*

A Season in the Congo

Lion Theatre; First Preview: September 30, 2010; Opening Night: October 2, 2010; Closed October 17, 2010

Written by Aimé Césaire; Presented by Rico Workshop Productions; Produced by Jackie Jeffries and A. Rico Speight; Director, A. Rico Speight; Set, Patrice Andrew Davidson; Lighting, James "Prez" Carter; Costumes, Zenola Norwood; Technical Director, Bill Glover; Lighting Technician, Haywood Nelson; Sound and Video, Bill Toles; Stage Manager, Fulton C. Hodges; Wardrobe, Anna-Marie Lawrence; Production Assistants, Alvin Jowers, Chuck Lander

CAST Patrice Lumumba **Ezra Mabengeza**; Pauline **Althea Alexis**; Hammarskjold **Mark Lang**; General Massens **Sam Van Chama**; Mercenary **Brandon Despain**; Kala Lubu **Julius Hollingsworth**; Mama Makosi **Jennifer Joseph**; Mokutu **Lee Marvin Sabastiany**; Ensemble **David Arkema**, **Greg Bastien**, **Chiquita Camille**, **Albert Eggleston**, **Quatis Tarkington**, **Adrain Washington**

Revival of a play presented without intermission.

SYNOPSIS *A Season in the Congo* is a tale of passion and peril, leadership and betrayal, and devoted love of nation. Although written over five decades ago, this timely revisiting of *A SeasonIn the Congo* sheds light on important issues and incidents in the Congo's history relevant to the chaos in the region today.

Ezra Mabengeza in A Season in the Congo *(photo by courtesy of A. Rico Speight)*

Once Upon a Time in New Jersey

Hudson Guild Theatre; First Preview: October 2, 2010; Opening Night: October 4, 2010; Closed October 31, 2010; 2 previews, 18 performances

Book and lyrics by Susan DiLallo, music by Stephen Weiner; Presented by Prospect Theater Company (Cara Reichel, Artistic Director; Melissa Huber, Managing Director; Peter Mills, Artistic Associate/Resident Writer) in association with the New York Music Theatre Festival; Director, Cara Reichel; Choreography, Christine O'Grady; Music Director, Remy Kurs; Set, Jen Price Fick; Costumes, Sidney Shannon; Lighting, Isabella F. Byrd; Sound, Asa F. Wember; Stage Manager, Lisa McGinn; Orchestrations/Vocal Arrangements, Dimitri Nakhamkin; ASM, Hannah Fogler; Dance Captain, Jason Kappus; Props, Clifton Chadick; Assistant Costumes, Travis Chinick; Production Manager, David Scobble; Casting, Diana Glazer; Press, John Capo

CAST Rocco **Jeremy Cohen**; Narrator/Ed/Announcer **Jason Collins**; Millie **Denise DeMirjian**; Etta **Mishaela Faucher**; Billy **Jonathan Gregg**; Angie Moscato **Briga Heelan**; Ensemble/Delivery Man/Artie **Jason Kappus**; Ensemble/Princess/Gorgonzola **Theresa Kloos**; Ensemble/Luigi/Shoe Salesman **Alex Krasser**; Celeste **Catherine LeFrere**; Tony **John Mervini**; Loretta **Samia Mounts**; Vinnie LoBianco **David Pelman**; Conchetta **Darcy Yellin**; Buddy **Noah Zachary**

MUSICIANS Remy Kurs (Conductor/Piano), Jeremy Clayton (Reeds), Chris Allen (Violin), Dan Erben (Guitar/Mandolin), Julie Danielson (Bass), Matt Ritter (Drums/Percussion)

MUSICAL NUMBERS Once Upon A Time In New Jersey; Rocco; A Girl Like Her; Quiet Little Dinner; Someone That I Hate; Kiss Your Ass Goodbye; How'd Ya Like To Be Me?; God Knows, Mrs. LoBianco; Montage; Rocco (reprise); One of A Kind; Once Upon A Time In New Jersey (reprise); Little Girl, Beware; Quando Scungilli; Tango; Married to a Thug; Mama; A Good Job; I Always Knew It Was You; Sandwiches to Make; In the Deli; Finale

SETTING 1956; Hoboken. New York premiere of a new musical presented in two acts. Originally presented at Marriott's Lincolnshire Theatre (Terry James, Executive Producer).

SYNOPSIS *Once Upon a Time in New Jersey* is an Italian-American fairy tale about Vinnie LoBianco, an unassuming sandwich-maker, is in love with counter girl Angie Moscato. But Angie's got it bad for Rocco, the local hunk, whose sights are set on sexy dance teacher Celeste. When Rocco runs afoul of Celeste's husband Billy, the result is a series of hilarious misunderstandings and madcap misadventure.

Dramatis Personae

Cherry Lane Studio Theatre; First Preview: October 1, 2010; Opening Night: October 7, 2010; Closed October 23, 2010; 5 previews, 14 performances

Written by Gonzalo Rodriguez Risco; Presented by The Playwrights Realm (Katherine Kovner, Artistic Director); Director, Erik Pearson; Producing Director, Stephanie Ybarra; Set, Michael Locher; Costumes, Amy Clar; Lighting, Burke Brown; Composer/Sound, Nathan A. Roberts; Props, Katherine Akiko Day; PSM, Joanne E. McInerney; ASM, Jessica Barker; Casting, Paul Davis, Calleri Casting; Production Manager, Kellen McNally; Producing Assistant, Alyssa Anderson; Technical Director, Janio Marrero; Assistant Director, Joshua Feder; Fall Consultant, Fabio Tavares; Production Assistant/Wardrobe, Cynthia Jankowski; Light Board, Allison Carney; Graphics, Maggie Elliott

CAST Lucas **Felix Solis**; Ben **Gerardo Rodriguez**; Marla **Liza Fernandez**; Squiggles/Anton/Marc **Bobby Moreno**; Woman/Prostitute/Wife **Laura Esposito**

SETTING Lima, Peru. Early 1990s. U.S. premiere of a new play presented without intermission. World premiere at Casa Espacio Libre (Lima, Peru) in 2008.

SYNOPSIS In *Dramatis Personae*, Peruvian playwright Gonzalo Rodriguez Risco delves into the intersecting lives and minds of three authors searching for inspirational triggers amid the trigger-happy environment of Peru's political coup in the early nineties. When the writers' demons emerge, the lines between fiction and reality blur in this dark and wickedly witty play that forever changes what it means to be based on a true story.

Felix Solis in Dramatis Personae *(photo by Richard Termine)*

Love Divided By/Times Three

Kirk Theatre; Opening Night: October 7, 2010; Closed October 31, 2010

Three plays *Folded Hands, Love Divided By,* and *Tango Finish* written by Susan Charlotte; Presented by Cause Celebrè; Director, Antony Marsellis; Choreography, Gene Castle; Music, Billy Goldenberg; Set, Roy Klausen; Lighting and Sound, Matt Berman; Music Production, Paul Rolnick; PSM, Anita Ross; Stage Manager, C. Renee Alexander; Co-Producers, Billy Goldenberg, Nancy Jackman; Company Manager, Deb Hackenberry; Assistant Company Manager, Brendan Hill

CAST Sheila at 10 **Fatima Ptacek**; Mary **Loni Ackerman**; Sheila as Adult **Lisa Bostnar**; Rose **Marilyn Sokol**; David **Kevin Stapleton**

World premiere of three one-act plays presented without intermission.

SYNOPSIS Mary, a former dancer, is losing her memory but never forgets a dance step. She is befriended by Rose, a mother who has psychologically blocked out parts of her past. Through the dance of tango Mary teaches Rose the importance of trust and enables her to come to terms with painful memories of her children in the past and move into the present.

The Deep Throat Sex Scandal

Bleecker Street Theatre; First Preview: September 17, 2010; Opening Night: October 10, 2010; Closed October 10, 2010; 25 previews, 1 performance

Written by David Bertolino; Presented by When Harry Met Linda; Director, Jerry Douglas; Set, Josh Iacovelli; Lighting, Graham Kindred; Costumes Jeffrey Wallach; Projections, 2K Productions LLC; Sound, Phillip Rudy; PSM, Ernie Fimbres; ASM, Jeremy Neal; Production Manager, Greg Hirsch; General Manager, Foster Entertainment; Social Media, Carrie Siegel Sheerin; Creative Consultant, Ron Jeremy; Press, David Gersten and Associates

CAST Linda Lovelace **Lori Gardner**; Harry Reems **Malcolm Madera**; Tim/D.A./FBI Man #1/Kramer **Graham Stuart Allen**; Larry Parrish/Makeup Man/Cop/Memphis Reporter **Frank Blocker**; Keating/Vito/Judge/Memphis Reporter **Stephen Hope**; Gerard Damiano/Cop/Allen Ginsburg/Memphis Reporter **John-Charles Kelly**; Shana Babcock/Mona/Woman in Audience/Cashier/Memphis Reporter **Rita Rehn**; Chuck Traynor/Cop #1/FBI #2/Tony Dill **Zach Wegner**; Understudy **Chelsea Cipolla**

Lori Gardner, Malcolm Madera, John-Charles Kelly, Frank Blocker, and Stephen Hope in The Deep Throat Sex Scandal *(photo by Carol Rosegg)*

World premiere of a new play presented in two acts. The production was forced to shut down after the Bleecker Street Theatre abruptly closed on October 12 due to the theatre's dispute with the landlord.

SYNOPSIS In 1972, a hairdresser from the Bronx made a little movie that grossed over $600 million and ignited the sexual revolution. *The Deep Throat Sex Scandal* takes you behind the scenes into the secret world of adult filmmaking, introduces you to the legendary Linda Lovelace and Harry Reems, and follows the bizarre journey from the creation of the movie, through the raids, arrests and the banning of the film, to the political fallout of the ensuing courtroom drama, which launched the career of Allen Dershowitz.

Three Women

59E59 Theater B; First Preview: October 5, 2010; Opening Night: October 12, 2010; Closed October 31, 2010

Written by Sylvia Plath; Produced by 59E59 (Elizabeth Kleinhans, Artistic Director; Peter Tear, Executive Producer); Presented by Inside Intelligence (London); Director, Robert Shaw; Design, Lucy Reed; Lighting, Maruti Evans; Press, Karen Greco

CAST The Wife **Francis Benhamou**; The Student **Kina Bermudez**; The Secretary **Angela Church**

U.S. premiere of a play presented without intermission. This production was presented at Inside Intelligence at the Jermyn Street Theatre (London) in January 2009.

SYNOPSIS Three diverse women reveal what every woman knows about having a child, seeking a greater universal truth about the human condition. Fascinating, frank and powerful, *Three Women* was originally written as a radio play, which Plath wrote one year before her death.

Francis Benhamou, Angela Chruch, and Kina Bermudez in Three Women *(photo by Ari Mintz)*

Swan Lake

New York City Center; Opening Night: October 13, 2010; Closed November 7, 2010

Music by Peter IlyichTchikovsky; Presented by New York City Center, Sadler's Wells Theater London, Back Row Productions, and New Adventures (Matthew Bourne, Artistic Director); Director & Choreographer, Matthew Boune; Set/Costumes, Lez Brotherston; Lighting, Rick Fisher; Associate Directors, Scott Ambler, Etta Murfitt; Resident Tour Director, Steve Kirkham; Reheasal Director, Pia Driver; New Adventures Director, Robert Noble; Company Manager, Ian Wheatstone; Stage Manager, Laura Ann Booth; Technial Stage Manager, Chris Tonini; ASM, Kate John; General Manager, Jennie Green and Gemma Kicks/Great Leap Forward; Marketing, Kinsley Jayasekera; Production Manager, David Evans; Associate Lighting, Andy Murrell; Back Row Productions Managing Directors, Liz Koops and Garry McQuinn; Press, Boneau/Bryan-Brown

CAST The Swan/Stranger **Richard Winsor** or **Jonathan Ollivier**; The Queen **Nina Goldman** or **Madelaine Brennan**; The Prince **Dominic North** or **Simon Williams;** The Prince's Girlfriend **Madelaine Brennan** or **Shelby Williams**; The Private Secretary **Ashley Bain** or **Steve Kirkham** or **Scott Ambler**; The Company **Ashley Bain, Tim Bartlett, Tom Clark, Travis Clausen-Knight, Cindy Ciunfini, James Cousins, Pia Driver, Tom Davies, Gavin Eden, Ross Fountain, Phil Jack Gardner, Scott Jennings, Jack Jones, Mari Kamata, Nicole Kabera, Simon Karaiskos, Daisy May Kemp, Franklyn Lee, Katy Lowenhoff, Katie Lusby, Jamie McDonald, Luke Murphy, Ashley Orwin, Gemma Payne, Samuel Plant, Alastair Postlethwaite, Danny Reubens, Anwar Russell, Chris Trenfield, Vince Virr, Lewis Wilkins**

SETTING The Palace, An Opera House, The Prince's Private Quarters, The Street, A Seedy Club, A City Park, The Royal Ball, The Princes Bedroom. A new version of the 1895 ballet presented in five acts with one intermission. Previously presented on Broadway at the Neil Simon Theatre September 26, 1998–January 23, 1999 (see *Theatre World* Vol. 55, page 16).

SYNOPSIS Twelve years after it's succesful run on Broadway, Bourne's New Adventures Company produciton of *Swan Lake* returns to New York for a limited engament. Bourne blends dance, style, humor, spectacle, character, comedy, and mime to create a provocative interpretation of the classic, and replaces the traditional female corps de ballet with a menacing male ensemble.

The Company of Swan Lake *(photo by Bill Cooper)*

Friends

Theatre Three (Mint Theatre Space); First Preview: October 7, 2010; Opening Night: October 14, 2010; Closed October 31, 2010; 6 previews, 14 performances

Written by Peter L. Levy; Presented by The Donis Group; Director, Jerry Donis; Set, Eric Steding & Jacques Rosas; Lighting, Steve O'Shea; Original Music, Chris Sobol; PSM, April Ann Kline; Graphics, Joseph S. Marcou; Makeup, Stephen Dupuis; Lighting and Audio, Michael Watkins; Crew, Katie Ferguson and Mikey Denis; Press, Kevin P. McAnarney

CAST Ruth Appfelbuam **Judy Spiegel**; Max Horowitz **Harlan Tuckman**

SETTING Central Park and Ruth's Apartment; The Present. New York premiere of a new play presented in two acts.

SYNOPSIS Ruth Appfelbaum and Max Horowitz, both in their seventies, meet on a bench in Central Park. Max, a widower, an intellectual, who used to devise crossword puzzles for a living, is existing on the edge because of his limited finances; and, Ruth, is a dreamer who never experienced true love. Their chance encounter gets off to a rocky start. Ruth finally condescends to allow Max to temporarily stay in her apartment, but as friends. As certain revelations are disclosed one can only wonder whether this relationship will survive.

Judy Spiegel and Harlan Tuckman in Friends *(photo by Richard Termine))*

Pinocchio: The Italian Musical

Kaye Playhouse; Opening Night: October 19, 2010; Closed October 23, 2010; 6 performances

Created and directed by Saverio Marconi; Music by Dodi Battaglia, Red Canzian, Roby Facchinetti; Lyrics by Stefano D'Orazio, Valerio Negroni; Book by Pierluigi Ronchetti, Saverio Marconi; Based on the story by Carlo Collodi; Presented by Compagnia della Rancia in association with Incanto Productions LLC and the Kaye Playhouse;

CAST Pinocchio **Manuel Frattini**; Geppetto **Pierpaolo Lopatriello**; Angela **Simona Rodano**; The Fox **Via Di Stefano**; Lucignolo **Mauro Simone**; The Cat **Luca Arrigoni**; The Fairy with Turquoise Hair **Daniela Pobega**; The Cricket **Andrea Verzicco**; Mangiafuoco/Director of the Circus **Raffaele Latagliata**; Lucignolo's Mother **Silvia Querci**; Owl/Columbina **Ilaria Suss**; Ensemble **Filippo Randisi, Paola Ciccarelli, Lello Busiello, Eugenio Contenti, Andrea De Santis, Arianna Luzi, Andrea Marchetti, Luca Spadaro, Daniele Volpin**

U.S. debut of a musical presented in Italian with English titles in two acts.

SYNOPSIS Based on the classic Italian fairytale *The Adventures of Pinocchio* written in 1881, *Pinocchio: The Italian Musical* is a modern musical adaptation that features a diverse genre of music, including rock ballads, operetta, canzone, hip-hop, and Latin, ideal for children and adults of all ages.

The Company of Pinocchio: The Italian Musical

Fyvush Finkel Live

Baruch Performing Arts Center–Rose Nagelberg Theatre; First Preview: October 17, 2010; Opening Night: October 21, 2010; Closed November 7, 2010

Conceived by Fyvush Finkel; Presented by the National Yiddish Theatre Folksbiene (Zalmen Mlotek, Artistic Director; Georgia Buchanan, Managing Director); Director, Motl Didner; Choreography, Shorey Walker; Music Direction/Arrangements/Special Material, Elliot Finkel; Music Supervision/Orchestrations/Special Material, Ian Finkel; Additional Lyrics, Phillip Namanworth; Sets, Roger Hanna; Costumes, Izzy Fields; Lighting, Natalie Robin; Sound, Bruce Ellman; Projections, Rory Dale; Supertitles, Motl Didner; PSM, Marci Skolnick; Marketing & Promotions, Ashley Bundis, Rock the Stage Inc.; Group Sales, I.W. (Itzy) Firestone; ASM, Sevek Majors-Peer; Company Manager, Bradley A. Cherna; Production Manager, Pam Traynor; Press, Beck Lee

CAST Fyvush Finkel, **Merwin Goldsmith, June Gable, Ian Finkel, Elliot Finkel**

BAND Elliot Finkel (Piano/Conductor), Ian Finkel (Xylophone), Andrea Andros (Violin), Martin Fischer (Drums), Ed Sterbenz (Bass), Ralph Olsen (Clarinet/Sax), Lisa Pike (French Horn)

World premiere of a new musical entertainment with comedy sketches and dance presented in two acts.

SYNOPSIS Fyvush Finkel offers a first-hand account of an incredible career spanning English and Yiddish roles, from Second Avenue to modern-day television stardom. A musical celebration of a life on stage, *Fyvush Finkel Live!* is chock-a-block with songs, stories, jokes and ample evidence of Finkel's undiminished mastery, at 88, of showbusiness razzle dazzle.

Penelope

St. Ann's Warehouse; Opening Night: October 23, 2010; Closed November 14, 2010; 26 performances

Written by Enda Walsh; Presented by Druid Theatre Company and St. Ann's Warehouse; Director, Mikel Murfi; Set/Costumes, Sabine Dargent; Lighting, Paul Keogan; Sound, Gregory Clarke; Casting, Maureen Hughes; Production Manager, Eamonn Fox; Company Stage Manager, Lee Davis; ASM/Props, Danny Erskine; ASM, Joshua Hoglund; Costume Supervisor, Doreen McKenna; Wigs and Makeup, Val Sherlock; Scenic Artist, Sandra Butler; Special Effects, Black Powder Monkeys; Special Effects Supervisor, Fusion Special Effects LLC; Magic Consultants, Keelan Leyser, Charlotte Marie; Press, Blake Zidell and Associates

CAST Fitz **Niall Buggy**; Dunne **Denis Conway**; Burns **Tadhg Murphy**; Quinn **Karl Shiels**; Penelope **Olga Wehrly**

U.S. premiere of a new play presented without intermission. Originally presented at Druid Lane Theatre (Galway, Ireland) July 8–24, 2010.

SYNOPSIS In *Penelope*, based on the final chapter of Homer's "The Odyssey", four ridiculous men meet daily at the bottom of a drained swimming pool and take turns attempting to woo Ulysses' wife. On this particular day, they all sense that Ulysses will return, find them pursuing her, and kill them. In this iteration of Walsh's ongoing exploration of Beckettian existential entrapment, unwinnable love leaves men in speedos staring down the inevitability of death.

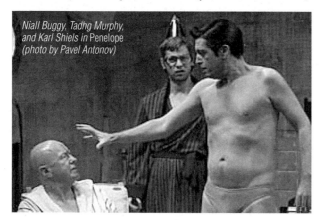

Niall Buggy, Tadhg Murphy, and Karl Shiels in Penelope *(photo by Pavel Antonov)*

Miss Abigail's Guide to Dating, Mating and Marriage!

Theatre at Sofia's; First Preview: October 7, 2010; Opening Night: October 24, 2010; 22 previews, 248 performances as of May 31, 2011

Written by Ken Davenport and Sarah Saltzberg; Inspired by the book by Abigail Grotke; Presented by Ken Davenport; Director, Ken Davenport; Set, Hilary Noxon; Lighting, Graham Kindred; Costumes, Abbi Stern; Production Manager, Jeremiah Peay; Associate Producers, Lily M. Fan, Todd Miller; General Management, Davenport Theatrical Enterprises/Matt Kovich; Casting, Daryl Eisenberg; PSM, Carlos Maisonet; Theme Song, Matt Kovich (music and lyrics), Doug Katsaros (orchestrations); Company Manager, Melissa Heller; Production Supervisor/ Technical Director, Katie Takacs; Marketing & Advertising, Davenport Media Enterprises; Assistant Company Manager, Lindsey Freeman; Press, The Morris + King Company

CAST Miss Abigail **Eve Plumb**; Paco **Manuel Herrera***

* Succeeded by Mauricio Perez (2/2/11)

New York premiere of a new play presented without intermission. World premiere developmental production at the David A Strasz Jr. Performing Arts Center (Tampa, Florida) June 9–July 3, 2010.

SYNOPSIS *Miss Abigail's Guide to Dating, Mating, & Marriage* is the story of Miss Abigail, the most sought-after relationship expert to the stars (think Dr. Ruth meets Emily Post), and her sexy sidekick Paco, as they travel the world teaching Miss Abigail's outrageously funny "how-to's" on dating, mating, and marriage! Let Miss Abigail take you back to a simpler time, before booty calls and before speed-dating . . . back when the divorce rate wasn't 50% and when 'fidelity' was more than an investment firm!

Manuel Herrara and Eve Plumb in Miss Abigail's Guide to Dating, Mating, and Marriage! *(photo by Jeremy Daniel)*

Futura

TBG Theatre; First Preview: October 23, 2010; Opening Night: October 26, 2010; Closed November 13, 2010

Written by Jordan Harrison; Presented by the National Asian American Theatre Company; Director, Liz Diamond; Set, David Evans Morris; Costumes, Olivera Gajic; Lighting, Raquel Davis; Sound, Matt Hubbs; Projections, Tal Yarden; Dramaturg, Vanessa Banta; Stage Manager, Irena Cumbow

CAST Edward **Edward Hajj**; The Professor **Mia Katigbak**; Grace **Angela Lin**; Gash **Christopher Larkin**

World premiere of a new play presented without intermission.

SYNOPSIS *Futura* ponders, among other things, whether a font can change the future. On her first day back at the University, a rogue Professor sets out to avenge her missing husband — and the lost art of ink on paper — by conducting a dangerous lesson on typography. When the Professor's lecture jumps the rails, we peer into a near future where desperate people search for the tangible in an ever more virtual age.

Angela I in and Christopher Larkin in Futura *(photo by William P. Steele)*

Perfect Harmony

Acorn Theatre on Theatre Row; First Preview: October 21, 2010; Opening Night: October 27, 2010; Closed November 13, 2010; 11 previews,, 19 performances*

Written by Andrew Grosso and The Essentials; Produced by Michael Musto and Joshua P. Weiss; Director, Andrew Grosso; Set, Nick Francone; Lighting, Brian Jones; Costumes, Becky Lasky; Music Directors/Arrangements, Ray Bailey, Adam Wachter; Casting, Geof Josselson; PSM, Erin Maureen Koster; PSM at 45 Bleecker, William E. Cruttenden III; Advertising and Marketing, The Pekoe Group; Line Producer, Steve Werner; ASM, Nathan K. Claus; Props, Emily Nichols; Associate Lighting, Seth Reiser; Assistant Costumes, Lisa Loen; Technical Production Manager, Elle Sunman; Wardrobe, Veronica Jay Clay; Press, Jim Baldassare

CAST Melody McDaniels **Dana Acheson**; Valerie Smooter **Faryl Amadeus**; Jasper Mergh/Dr. Larry Mergh **Clayton Apgar**; Kerri Taylor/Tobi McClintoch **Marie-France Arcilla**; Simon Depardieu/Goran Dhiardeaubovic **David Barlow**; Michaela "Mickey D" Dhiardeaubovic/Kiki Tune **Kate Morgan Chadwick**; JB Smooter/Jesus **Jarid Faubel**; Philip Fellowes V **Kobi Libii**; Meghan Beans **Kelly McCreary**; Lassiter A. Jayson III **Robbie Collier Sublett**; Understudies **Tate Evans**, **Marshall York**

Off-Broadway premiere of a play with music presented without intermission. Created as a workshop at NYU Graduate Acting Studio Tisch program. Originally presented at the 2006 New York International Fringe Festival and an Off-Off Broadway run at the Clurman Theatre in 2008. Prior to this engagement, the show had an out-of-town run at Stoneham Theatre (Stoneham, MA; Weylin Symes, Producing Artistic Director; Matt Chapuran, General Manager).

SYNOPSIS *Perfect Harmony* is a comedy about the greatest singing group in high school history, seventeen-time national champions, The Acafellas. It's also about their classmates and female counterpart, perennial runners up, The Ladies in Red. Through song and story, we see these students grapple with the weighty issues of truth, love, what constitutes appropriate choreography for Nationals — and ultimately we learn not just about these students but also about the true nature of harmony.

* *Perfect Harmony* was slated to run at the Bleecker Street Theatre and played five preview performance there from October 8–October 12, before the theatre was abruptly closed due to a landlord dispute.

Kate Morgan and David Barlow in Perfect Harmony *(photo by Jim Baldassare)*

The Merry Wives of Windsor

Michael Schimmel Center for the Arts; Opening Night: October 28, 2010; Closed November 7, 2010

Written by William Shakespeare; Presented by Shakespeare's Globe Theatre (Dominic Dromgoole, Artistic Director; Conrad Lynch, Executive Producer); Director, Christopher Luscombe; Sets/Costumes, Janet Bird; Music, Nigel Hess; Choreography, Jenny Arnold; Lighting, Jason Taylor; Associate Director, Sarah Norman; U.S. General Management, 2Luck Concepts, Eleanor Oldham, John Luckacovic; U.K. General Management, Lotte Buchan; Casting, Charlotte Bevan; Fight Director, Malcolm Ranson; Production Manager, Paul Russell; Press, Richard Kornberg and Associates

CAST Peter Simple **Nathan Amzi**; Sir Hugh Evans **Gareth Armstrong**; Master Abraham Slender **William Belchambers**; Sir John Falstaff **Christopher Benjamin**; Dr. Caius **Philip Bird**; Anne Page **Ceri-Lyn Cissone**; John Rugby **Barnaby Edwards**; Mistress Meg Page **Serena Evans**; Justice Shallow **Peter Gale**; George Page **Michael Garner**; Nym/Robert **Gregory Gudgeon**; Robin **Edward Holtom**; Master Ford **Andrew Havill**; Fenton **Gerard McCarthy**; Host of the Garter Inn **Jonty Stephens**; Mistress Quickly **Sue Wallace**; Pistol/John **Paul Woodson**; Mistress Ford **Sarah Woodward**

SETTING Windsor in Berkshire County, England during the Elizabethan Age. New York premiere of a revival of a classic play presented in two acts. This acclaimed production played at Shakespeare's Globe in 2008 and began an international tour at the Eli and Edythe Broad Stage in Los Angeles prior to it's New York run.

SYNOPSIS *The Merry Wives of Windsor*, one of the great comedies by William Shakespeare, is a hilarious tale of love and marriage, jealousy and revenge, class and wealth, and is Shakespeare's only play to deal with the contemporary Elizabethan era English middle class life. It was first published in 1602, although it was believed to have been written prior to 1597.

Serena Evans, Christopher Benjamin, and Sarah Woodward in The Merry Wives of Windsor *(photo by John Tramper)*

Photograph 51

Ensemble Studio Theatre; First Preview: October 27, 2010; Opening Night: November 1, 2010; Closed November 21, 2010

Written by Anna Ziegler; Presented by Ensemble Studio Theatre (William Carden, Artistic Director; Paul Alexander Slee, Executive Director) with the Alfred P. Sloan Foundation Science & Technology Project (Doron Weber, Vice President, Programs); Producer, Annie Trizna; Director, Linsay Firman; Costumes, Suzanne Chesney; Set, Nick Francone; Lighting, Led Dickert; Props, Caitlin Fergus; Original Music/Sound, Shane Rettig; Dialects, Erik Singer; PSM, Danielle Buccino; Production Manager/Technical Director, Daniel Thomas; Associate Producer, Web Begole; Casting, Kelly Gillespie; ASM, Olga Kreimer; Science Advisors, Stuart Firestein, Darcy Kelley; Marketing/Box Office, Tim Scales; Hair, Jon Jordan; Press, Bruce Cohen, Rich Kelley

CAST Rosalind Franklin **Kristen Bush**; Maurice Wilkins **Kevin Collins**; Ray Gosling **David Gelles**; James Watson **Haskell King**; Don Caspar **Benjamin Pelteson**; Francis Crick **Jeremy Webb**

SETTING London, 1951-1953. New York premiere of a new play presented without intermission. Commissioned and first presented at Active Cultures Theatre (Maryland) February 10, 2008. Subsequently produced at the Fountain Theatre (Los Angeles).

SYNOPSIS Scientists are on the brink of discovering what is called the secret of life: the DNA double helix. Ahead of them all is a brilliant and passionate scientist, Rosalind Franklin, whose greatest strength – her uncompromising independence – leads to her undoing. When her competitors find out about her "photograph 51" – the first recorded image of the double helix – her work is suddenly not her own. In 1962, the Nobel Prize for one of the greatest scientific breakthroughs is awarded to James Watson, Francis Crick, and Maurice Wilkins. Rosalind Franklin was never even nominated.

Imagining Herschel

Cherry Lane Theatre; First Preview: November 4, 2010; Opening Night: November 8, 2010; Closed November 28, 2010; 4 previews, 17 performances

Written by Colin Greer; Presented by the Culture Project (Allan Buchman, Artistic Director; Nan Richardson, Executive Director); Director, Larry Moss; Lighting, Jake Platt; Production Supervisor/PSM, Jonathon Golman; ASM, Kathleen E.G. Munroe; Assistant Director/Company Manager, Noelle Ghoussaini; Managing Director Culture Project, Vanessa Sparling; Marketing, Elisa Lavery; Development, Jennifer Joyce; Press, O+M Company

CAST Rabbi Abraham Joshua **Richard Dreyfuss**; Cardinal Augustin Bea **Rinde Eckert**

SETTING 1962-1973. World premiere of a new play concert reading presented without intermission.

SYNOPSIS *Imagining Herschel* brings to light the imagined private conversations between Cardinal Augustin Bea and Rabbi Abraham Joshua Heschel as the two men attempt to resolve the Vatican's formal exoneration of the Jewish people for the death of Christ. This drama explores the issues of faith, violence, and forgiveness in the Jewish and Catholic spheres.

Pieces

59E59 Theater C; First Preview: November 3, 2010; Opening Night: November 9, 2010; Closed November 21, 2010; 6 previews, 16 performances

Written by Hywel John; Presented by Clwyd Theatr Cymru, Wales, as part of the 2010 Brits Off Broadway; Director, Kate Wasserberg; Original Set Design/Costumes, Mark Bailey; Sound, Andrea J. Cox; Producer, Emma Lucia; Company Stage Manager, Nicola Ireland; Production Management, Hannah Lobb, Jim Davis, Chris Skinner; AEA Stage Manager, Jess Johnston; Press, Karen Greco

CAST Beatrice **Louise Collins**; Sophie **Jennifer Kidd**; Jack **Steven Meo**

U.S. Premiere of a new play presented in two acts.

SYNOPSIS Jack and Beatrice are twins. They have no cousins, uncles, aunties, and no grandparents. And now they have no Mum and Dad. The one person who can look after them is their godmother Sophie, who arrives shocked and unprepared at their remote family home in the Welsh borders. Sophie has not seen the children since they were tiny: too tiny for them to remember her - and too tiny to remember what caused her long, enforced absence.

Haskell King, Jeremy Webb, Kristen Bush, David Gelles, and Kevin Collins in Photograph 51 *(photo by Gerry Goodstein)*

Joanne King, Mark Oosterveen, and Peter Clapp in Personal Enemy
(photo by Ari Mintz)

Louise Collins and Steven Meo in Pieces *(photo by Nobby Clark)*

Personal Enemy

59E59 Theater B; First Preview: November 4, 2010; Opening Night: November 10, 2010; Closed November 28, 2010; 6 previews, 22 performances

Written by John Osborne and Anthony Creighton; Presented by FallOut Theatre, London (Ollie Jordan and Hanna Osmolska) as part of the 2010 Brits Off Broadway; Director, David Aula; Design, Anna Hourriere; Lighting, James Baggaley; Sound, Edward Lewis; Original Music, Luke Rosier; London Stage Manager, Cosmo Cooper; AEA Stage Manager, Cheryl D. Olszowka; Dialect Coach, Sally Hague; Video Editor, Charles Arrowsmith; Animation, Jon Goodman; Press, Karen Greco

CAST Mrs. Constant **Karen Lewis**; Mr. Constant **Tony Turner**; Caryl Kessler **Joanne King**; Sam Kessler **Mark Oosterveen**; Arnie Constant **Peter Clapp**; Mrs. Slifer **Genevieve Allenbury**; Ward Perry/The Investigator/Reverend Merrick **Steven Clark**

SETTING August, 1953; The home of the Constant family in Langley Springs, United States. U.S. premiere of a lost play presented in three acts with one intermission. An earlier version of play was censored in 1955 in Harrogate, Yorkshire. The White Bear Theatre in London presented the world premiere of the full production June 17–July 11, 2010, shortly after the play had been rediscovered.

SYNOPSIS *Personal Enemy* is a vivid depiction of the political and sexual paranoia that gripped America in the 1950s at the height of McCarthyism, and explores a time when the public enemy suddenly became a lot more personal. Written years before *Look Back in Anger*, *Personal Enemy* is a sharp interrogation of small-town thinking and the tyranny of familial love.

Play Dead

Players Theatre; First Preview: October 21, 2010; Opening Night: November 10, 2010; Closed July 24, 2011

Written by Teller and Todd Robbins; Produced by Alan Schuster, Cheryl Wiesenfeld, Fran Gero, Jono Gero, Pat Blake, Ethan Silverman; Director, Teller; Set, David Korins; Lighting, Thom Weaver; Sound, Leon Rothberg; Original Music, Gary Stockdale; Magic Consultant, Johnny Thompson; Associate Director, Jim Millan; PSM, Maggie Sinak; Sound Engineer, Reece Nunez; ASM, Amanda Sheets; Press, Richard Kornberg and Associates

CAST Narrator **Todd Robbins**; Margery Crandon **Charlotte Pines**; Eusapia Palladino **Geri Berman**; Albert Fish **Don Meehan**; Girl **Drea Lorraine**

New York premiere of a new thriller presented without intermission.

SYNOPSIS Teller and Todd Robbins invite Death out to play in *Play Dead*, a new spirit-shaking show that explores themes of death, darkness and deception. Robbins draws audiences into an unknown haunted world full of frightful surprises and diabolical laughter. Although very much a theatrical work, it is hardly a typical "play," but rather a dramatic, unnerving thriller - here and now in an "abandoned" theater, illuminated by a single ghostlight - in which audiences test their nerves and face their fears as they are surrounded by ethereal sights, sounds and even touches of the returning dead - all achieved by wry, suspenseful storytelling and uncanny stage illusions.

Charlotte Pines and Todd Robbins in Play Dead *(photo by Thom Kaine)*

Devil Boys from Beyond

New World Stages; First Preview: November 3, 2010; Opening Night: November 13, 2010; Closed December 4, 2010

Written by Buddy Thomas; Produced by David Foster in association with MadCap Productions; Director, Kenneth Elliott; Set & Graphic Designer, Brian T. Whitehill; Lighting, Vivien Leone; Costumes, Gail Baldoni; Sound & Original Score, Drew Fornarola; Co-Sound Design and Producer, John Fontein; Wigs and Hair, Gerard Kelly; General Manager, Foster Entertainment/Jennie Connery; Production Manager, Malinda Sorci; PSM, Eileen Arnold; ASM, Richard Duffy; Company Manager, Deana Marie Kirsch; Associate Lighting, Ben Hagen; Master Carpenter, Derek Cecil; Master Electrician, Tom Dyer; Carpenter, Josh Iacovelli; Running Crew, Frank Boccia; Wardrobe Supervisor, Derek Lockwood; Marketing, HHC Marketing; Advertising, The Pekoe Group; Press, O+M Company

CAST Dotty Primrose **Andy Halliday**; Florence Wexler **Everett Quinton**; Gilbert Wiatt **Peter Cormican**; Gregory Graham **Robert Berliner**; Harry Wexler **Jeff Riberdy**; Jack Primrose **Jacques Mitchell**; Lucinda Marsh **Chris Dell'Armo**; Mattie Van Buren **Paul Pecorino**

SETTING 1957; Lizard Lick, Florida. Off-Broadway premiere of a new play presented without intermission. Originally presented at the 2009 New York International Fringe Festival.

SYNOPSIS Summer of 1957 is a scorcher and something strange is going on in the swamps of Lizard Lick, Florida. With rumors of missing people and giant spaceships running rampant, star NYC reporter Mattie Van Buren races down in search of her next Pulitzer, her booze-hound ex-husband, Gregory Graham in tow, and her arch-enemy, Lucinda Marsh hot on her heels to scoop her story. Flying saucers! Backstabbing bitches! Muscle hunks and men in pumps!

Jeff Riberdy, Paul Pecorino and Jacques Mitchell in Devil Boys from Beyond *(photo by Carol Rosegg)*

Ghosts in the Cottonwoods

Theatre 80 St. Marks; First Preview: November 11, 2010; Opening Night: November 13, 2010; Closed December 12, 2010

Written and directed by Adam Rapp; Presented by The Amoralists (James Kautz, Derek Ahonen, Matthew Pilieci, Co-Artistic Directors; Kelcie Beene, Managing Director); Set, Alfred Schatz; Costumes, Jessica Pabst; Lighting, Keith Parham; Sound, Eric Shimelonis; Sculpture Design, Jenna Levine; Assistant Director, Gretchen Hollis; Stage Manager, Judy Merrick; Makeup, Erin Kennedy Lunsford; Production Assistant, Jan Rosenberg; Press, David Gibbs

CAST Bean Scully **Sarah Lemp**; Pointer Scully **Nick Lawson**; Newton Yardly **Willam Apps**; Shirley Judyhouse **Mandy Nicole Moore**; Jeff Scully **James Kautz**; The Man **Matthew Pilieci**

World premiere of a new play presented without intermission.

SYNOPSIS On the night of a terrible storm, a single mother and her younger son await the arrival of the older son, who has broken out of prison. Two others arrive before him: a stranger with a wounded leg and a girl with a suitcase. Nothing will ever be the same.

Mandy Nicole Moore, Nick Lawson, and Sarah Lemp in Ghosts in the Cottonwoods *(photo by Annie Parisse)*

Mistakes Were Made

Barrow Street Theatre; First Preview: November 5, 2010; Opening Night: November 14, 2010; Closed February 27, 2011; 12 previews, 113 performances

Written by Craig Wright; Presented by Scot Morfee, Jean Doumanian, Tom Wirtshafter with Marc Biales, Rebecca Gold, Christian Chadd Taylor, The Weinstein Company; Produced in association with the Red Orchid Theatre; Director, Dexter Bullard; Set, Tom Burch; Costumes, Tif Bullard; Lighting, Keith Parham; Sound, Joseph Fosco; Props/Set Dressing, Michele Spadaro; Hair/Makeup, Nan Zabriskie; PSM, Richard A. Hodge; ASM/Understudy, Kate McDoniel; Puppeteer, Sam Deutsch; Associate Producers, Starry Night Entertainment, Patrick Daly; Associate Partners, Mickey Murray, Cathy Nathan; Assistant Director, Duncan Riddell; Production Supervisor, James E. Cleveland/La Vie Productions; Production Manager, Katy Ross; General Management, Barrow Street Theatre; Technical Director, Pete Fry; Carpenter, Austin Tidwell; Scenic Artist, Daphne Hayner; Master Electrician, Michael McGee; Sound Head, Alex Jepson; Production Assistant, Laura Archer; Website, Steve Dilewski; Artwork, Frank Verlizzo; Technical Consultant, Brian Duea; Management Consultant, Two Step Productions; Advertising, SteamCo Inc.; Press, O+M Company

CAST Felix Artifex **Michael Shannon**; Esther **Mierka Girten**

SETTING The midtown office of Felix Artifex. New York premiere of a new play presented without intermission. World premiere at the Red Orchid Theatre (Chicago) September 8, 2009 starring Mr. Shannon and Ms. Girten.

SYNOPSIS *Mistakes Were Made* is an hilarious, deeply moving character study of a man seeking redemption, but inescapably creating destruction. Felix Artifex, a B-list Off-Broadway producer, gets in way over his fast-talking head when he takes on a gargantuan epic about the French Revolution which he thinks is going to be his ticket to professional and personal reclamation. While trying to land a big star for the lead role, he uses all his powers of persuasion, seduction and intimidation to strong-arm the writer into massively rewriting his play. At the same time, he attempts to reconnect with his estranged wife and untangle himself from a mess involving sheep in a distant war-torn country.

Michael Shannon in Mistakes Were Made *(photo by Ari Mintz)*

New Worlds: A Celebration of I.L. Peretz

Baruch Performing Arts Center–Rose Nagelberg Theatre; First Preview: November 11, 2011; Opening Night: November 14, 2010; Closed November 21, 2010; 12 performances

Two short plays: *Di Tsvey Brider (The Two Brothers)* and *A Gilgl Fun A Nign (The Metamorphosis of a Melody)* by I.L. Peretz; Presented by the National Yiddish Theatre Folksbiene (Zalmen Mlotek, Artistic Director; Georgia Buchanan, Managing Director); Directors, Motl Didner (*Di Tsvey Brider*), Pascal Holtzer (*A Gilgl Fun A Nighn*); Choreography (*Di Tsvey Brider*), Rebecca Warner; Musical Scores, Dmitri "Zisl-Yesef" Slepovitch (*Di Tsvey Brider*), Jean-Raymond Gelis (*A Gilgl Fun A Nighn*); Set, Roger Hanna; Costumes, Izzy Fields; Lighting, Natalie Robin; Sound, Bruce Ellman; Video, Marlette Feltin and Patrick Floch; Supertitles, Rory Dale, Motl Didner; PSM, Marci Skolnick; Marketing, Ashley Bundis, Rock the Stage Inc.; Production Manager, Sara Friedman, Kelvin Productions LLC; ASM, Shevek Majors-Peer; Company Manager, Bradley A. Cherna; Press, Beck Lee

CAST *Di Tsvey Brider:* Dancers **Colette Krogol, Matthew Reeves, Brandon Washington**; Musicicans **Dmitri "Zisl-Yeysef" Slepovitch, Matt Temkin**; Voices **Shane Baker, Mikhl Baran**; *A Gilgl Fun A Nign:* **Rafael Godwaser**

An evening of two one-one act pieces presented without intermission.

SYNOPSIS *New Worlds: A Celebration of I.L. Peretz* is an evening dedicated to the writings of the great Yiddish writer I.L. Peretz. A world premiere, *Di Tsvey Brider* reinvests a classic folk tale about greed and exploitation with a timely energy derived from the mixing of dance, music, video, and performance elements. *A Gigl Fun A Nign*, a virtuosic solo, multi-media performance conceived and performed by Goldwaser (seen at the 2010 New York International Fringe Festival) traces the strange and beautiful evolution and migration of a favorite nigun melody across geographies and generations.

Lingua Franca

59E59 Theater A; First Preview: November 9, 2010; Opening Night: November 16, 2010; Closed November 28, 2010; 8 previews, 15 performances

Written by Peter Nichols; Presented by the Cherub Company, London, as part of the 2010 Brits Off Broadway; Producer, Will Wrightson; Director, Michael Gieleta; Design, James MacNamara; Lighting, James Smith; Sound, Will Jackson; Costumes, Emily Stuart; Casting, Jim Arnold; Company Stage Manager, Sophie Cable; Associate Lighting, Chris Withes; AEA Stage Manager, Amy Kaskeski;

Projections, Radoslaw Konopka; Italian Accent Coach, Ceclila Gragnani; German Accent Coach, Christina Honigs; Fight Director, Bret Yount; U.K. Press, Sue Hyman Associates; U.S. Press, Karen Greco

CAST Irena Brentano **Anna Carteret**; Gennaro Manetti **Enzo Cilenti**; Jestin Overton **Ian Gelder**; Madge Fox **Abigail McKern**; Steven Flowers **Chris New**; Peggy Carmichael **Charlotte Randle**; Heidi Schumann **Natalie Walter**

U.S. premiere of a new play presented in two acts. Orignally presented by the Cherub Company at the Finborough Theatre July 13, 2010.

SYNOPSIS *Lingua Franca* follows innocent abroad, Steven Flowers, as he travels from National Service in South-East Asia to 1950's Florence. He soon finds himself working for a chaotically-run language school, together with a cosmopolitan muddle of six foreign misfits killing their post-war nihilism in the cafés of Florence, the cradle of Renaissance high culture.

Charlotte Randle and Natalie Walter in Lingua Franca *(photo by Ari Mintz)*

Edgewise

Walkerspace; First Preview: November 9, 2010; Opening Night: November 17, 2010; Closed December 4, 2010

Written by Eliza Clark; Presented by The Play Company (Kate Loewald, Founding Producer; Lauren Weigel, Executive Producer) and Page 73 Productions (Liz Jones & Asher Richelli, Executive Directors); Director, Trip Cullman; Set, Andromache Chalfant; Costumes, Nicole Pearce; Sound/Original Music, Bart Fasbender; Special Effects, Jeremy Chernick; Fight Choreography, Thomas Schall; PSM, Kelly Glasgow; Production Management, La Vie Productions/James E. Cleveland; Casting, Jack Doulin and Jenn Haltman; Press, Sam Rudy Media Relations

CAST Paul **Brandon Dirden**; Louis **Philip Ettinger**; Emma **Aja Naomi King**; Louis **Alfredo Narciso**; Marco **Tobias Segal**

World premiere of a new play presented without intermission.

SYNOPSIS War sucks. Flipping burgers sucks harder. In *Edgewise*, a suspenseful drama, it's just another morning at the suburban burger joint where Ruckus, Marco and Emma smoke up, talk smack, and - oh yeah - work. But when a bloodied stranger staggers in, the three teens are forced to choose sides in the grueling war advancing just outside the door.

Tobias Segal and Philip Ettinger in Edgewise *(photo by Carol Rosegg)*

The Red Shoes

St. Ann's Warehouse; Opening Night: November 19, 2010; Closed December 12, 2010; 28 performances

Based on the fairy tale by Hans Christian Andersen; Adapted and directed by Emma Rice; Presented by Kneehigh Theatre in association with Piece by Piece Productions; Producer, Paul Crewes; Assistant Director, Simon Harvey; Poems, Anna Maria Murphy; Design, Bill Mitchell; Music, Stu Barker; Film, Mark Jenkin; Lighting, Malcolm Rippeth; Sound, Simon Baker; Additional Text, Mike Shepherd; Design Associate, Sarah Wright; Production/Stage Manager, Steph Curtis; Sound Operator, Andy Graham; Lighting Operator, Ben Nichols; Press, Blake Zidell and Associates

CAST The Girl **Patrycja Kujawska**; Lady Lydia **Giles King**; The Old Lady/The Preachers Wife **Dave Mynne**; The Soldier/The Shoemaker **Robert Luckay**; The Preacher/The Angel/The Butcher **Mike Shepherd**; Musicians **Stu Barker/Ian Ross**

American premiere of a new play with music based on a classic fairy tale presented without intermission. Originally presented at Kneehigh Theatre in 2003.

A scene from Kneehigh Theatre's The Red Shoes *(photo by Pavel Antonov)*

SYNOPSIS Our girl can't resist her red shoes. They make her dance with delight, spin with possibilities. But what happens when she can't get them off? What happens when she can't stop dancing? Surreal and sensuous, quirky and profound, bloody and bare – Kneehigh brings a menacing cabaret where anything is possible and nothing is probable. With music to make your toes twitch, images to make your mouth water and a story to make your heart pound, the menacing world of the fairy story is revealed.

In the Footprint: The Battle Over Atlantic Yards

Irondale Center; First Preview: November 12, 2010; Opening Night: November 22, 2010; Closed December 11, 2010

Written by Steven Cosson and Jocelyn Clarke; Created and presented by The Civilians (Steve Cosson, Artistic Director; Marion Friedman, Managing Director) in association with the Irondale Center; Based on interviews conducted by Marsha Stephanie Blake, Greg McFadden, Melanie Nicholls-King, Michael Premo, Alex Rosenthal, Joaquin Torres, and Colleen Werthmann; Produced in association with Exchange NYC; Director, Steven Cosson; Music and Lyrics, Michael Friedman; Set, Andromache Chalfant; Costumes, Chloe Chapin; Lighting, Lucrecia Briceno; Sound, Shane Rettig; Video and Projections, Jeanette Yew; Music Director, Kris Kukul; PSM, Terri K. Kohler

CAST Ken Fisher/Sal Zarzana/Scott Turner **Matthew Dellapina**; Bertha Lewis/Shabnam Merchant/Esther Kelly **Donnetta Lavinia Grays**; James Caldwell/Jerry Campbell/Tracy Collins **Billy Eugene Jones**; Jim Vogel/Daniel Goldstein/Jonathan Lethem **Greg McFadden**; Tish James/Kyiesha Kelly **Simone Moore**; Patti Hagan/Jerza Kaye **Colleen Werthmann**

World premiere of a new play with music presented without intermission. The initial presentation of the Atlantic Yards project, entitled *Brooklyn at Eye Level* was produced by The Civilians in December 2008 at the Brooklyn Lyceum.

SYNOPSIS *In the Footprint* chronicles the conflicts surrounding the largest land development project in Brooklyn's history. This lively theatrical production is inspired by interviews with the real-life players in the controversy, representing many different perspectives: residents of Prospect Heights and Fort Greene, political leaders such as Letitia James and Marty Markowitz, members of Develop Don't Destroy Brooklyn, union members, and project supporters such as ACORN's Bertha Lewis.

The Civilians in In the Footprint: The Battle Over Atlantic Yards *(photo by Carol Rosegg)*

Being Sellers

59E59 Theater C; First Preview: November 23, 2010; Opening Night: November 28, 2010; Closed December 12, 2010; 7 previews, 16 performances

Written by Carl Caulfield; Presented by Waterloo East Theatre, London, as part of the 2010 Brits Off Broadway; Director, Simon Green; Assistant Director, Evan Pappas; Lighting, Allan Ramsay; Costumes and Props, Caroline Howard; AEA Stage Manager, Jess Johnston; Press, Karen Greco

CAST Peter Sellers **David Boyle**

U.S. premiere of a new solo performance play presented without intermission. Prior to this engagement the show premiered at Waterloo East Theatre, a new Off West End venue, November 2-19, 2010

SYNOPSIS Peter Sellers was celebrated for his ability to transform himself completely into his characters-from Chief Inspector Clouseau to Doctor Strangelove-but who was he and what was the personal cost of his comic genius? Marking the 30th anniversary of Sellers' death, Carl Caulfield's poignant comedy is an endearing portrait of one of the 20th Century's most iconic, admired and adored actor/comedians.

David Boyle in Being Sellers *(photo by Oscar Blustin)*

An Audience with Mrs Moneypenny

59E59 Theater B; First Preview: November 30, 2010; Opening Night: December 1, 2010; Closed December 5, 2010; 1 previews, 7 performances

Written by Heather McGregor and Robert McGregor; Presented as part of the 2010 Brits Off Broadway; Director, Owen Lewis; Press, Karen Greco

Performed by **Mrs Moneypenny** (Heather McGregor)

U.S. premiere of a solo performance piece presented without intermission. The show previously played the Edinburgh Fringe Festival to sold out houses.

SYNOPSIS The former investment banker, university professor, entrepreneur, ultimate working mother and popular Financial Times Weekend columnist, avidly read each week by over 725,000 people worldwide, descends upon New York with extraordinary tales of banking, business, bonuses and her three sons - better known to loyal readers as Cost Centers One, Two and Three!

Soledad Barrio y Noche Flamenca

Cherry Lane Theatre; Opening Night: December 1, 2010; Closed January 13, 2011

Created and presented by Noche Flamenca (Martin Santangelo, Artistic Director and Producer); Director, Martin Santangelo; Choreography, Soledad Barrio; Lighting, S. Benjamin Farrar; Technical Director, Christopher Thielking; Production Manager, Maria de la O Rodriguez Fernandez; Company Manager, Michelle Coe

CAST Dancers **Solodad Barrio, Juan Ogalla, Antonio Jimenez**; Singers **Emilio Florido, Manuel Gago, Miguel Rosendo**; Guitar **Salva de Maria, Eugenio Iglesias**

A theatrical evening of flamenca presented without intermission.

SYNOPSIS Hailed for its transcendent and deeply emotional performances, Noche Flamenca is recognized as the most authentic flamenco touring company in the field today. Santangelo has successfully brought to the stage the essence, purity, and integrity of one of the world's most complex and mysterious art forms without the use of tricks or gimmicks. All aspects of flamenco – dance, song, and music – are interrelated and given equal weight, creating a true communal spirit within the company - the very heart and soul of flamenco.

Soledad Barrio y Noche Flamenca *(photo by Andrea Mohin)*

Blind Date

Ars Nova; First Preview: December 2, 2010; Opening Night: December 6, 2010; Closed December 20, 2010; 22 performances

Created by Rebecca Northan; Produced by Kevin McCullom; Lighting, Richard DiBella; Set and Props, Jeramiah Peay; Stage Manager/Sound, Sean Bowie; Company Manager, Kimberly Shaw; General Management, Davenport Theatrical Enterprises, Ken Davenport, Ryan Lympus, Matt Kovich, Blair Ingenthron; Marketing and Advertising, Davenport Media Enterprises, Ken Davenport, Kristin Johnson, Jamie Lynn Ballard, Steve Tartick, Jody Bell, Jennifer Ashley Tepper, Jackie Ionin, Jenni Marks; Press, Sam Rudy Media Relations

CAST Mimi **Rebecca Northan**; Supporting Roles **Jamie Northan, Bruce Horak**

US. premiere of a new improviastional play presented without intermission. World premiere in Toronto at World Stage at Harbourfront Centre.

SYNOPSIS There's nothing like the thrill of a first date...anything can happen! In the new play Blind Date, Mimi - a Parisian temptress - goes on a blind date with a different man each and every night - in fact; Mimi's *Blind Date* is selected directly from the audience. Hilarious and touching, Blind Date takes the audience - and Mimi and her date - through the unforgettable stages of romance, from courtship to commitment, all in 90 minutes.

Rebecca Nortan in Blind Date *(photo by Greg Tjepkema)*

GOLF: The Musical

Midtown Theatre at HA! Comedy Club; First Preview: November 20, 2010; Opening Night: December 6, 2010; Closed January 16, 2011

Book, music, and lyrics by Michael Roberts; Based on a concept and produced by Eric Krebs; Director, Christopher Scott; Music Director, Ken Lundie; Set, James Joughin; Costumes, Bernard Grenier; Lighting, Aaron Spivey; Stage Manager, Brian Westmoreland; Casting, Stephanie Klapper; General Manager, Geoff Cohen; Press, David Gersten

CAST Tom Gamblin, Lyn Philistine, Brian Runbeck, Christopher Sutton; Replacement **Aaron Davis**

MUSICIANS Ken Lundie, Rachel Kaufman (Piano)

MUSICAL NUMBERS Life's Unanswerable Questions; That's How You Play Golf; Scratch Golfer; Plaid; The Golfer's Psalm; A Great Lady Golfer; Let's Bring Golf to the Gulf; My Husband Is Playing Around; Golfing Museum; The Road to Heaven; No Blacks, No Chicks, No Jews; Big Bertha; Golf's Such a Naughty Game; Presidents and Golf; The Beautiful Time; I'm Going Golfing Tomorrow

Revival of a musical revue presented in two acts. Originally presented at The John Houseman Theatre November 19, 2003–April 4, 2004 (see *Theatre World* Vol. 60, page 107).

SYNOPSIS *GOLF: The Musical* returns to New York City after having played throughout the United States and in 50 countries around the world, including a run in Saint Andrews, Scotland, the home of the game of golf, during the 2005 British Open. As a sport, golf may be exasperating for some and exciting for others; but in the world of *GOLF: The Musical*, a hugely talented quartet of actors celebrates the fun, frustration and elation of this popular sport in a manner that makes it funny and fun for the whole foursome.

Haunted

59E59 Theater A; First Preview: December 1, 2010; Opening Night: December 8, 2010; Closed January 2, 2011; 8 previews, 28 performances

Written by Edna O'Brien; Presented by Royal Exchange Theatre, Manchester, in association with Karl Sydow as part of the 2010 Brits Off Broadway; Director, Braham Murray; Design, Simon Higlett; Lighting, Johanna Town; Sound, Pete Rice; Video, Jack James; Composer, Akintayo Akinbode; Fight Director, Renny

Brian Runbeck, Christopher Sutton, Lyn Philistine, and Tom Gamblin in GOLF: The Musical *(photo by Gerry Goodstein)*

Krupinski; Company Manager, Lee Drinkwater; Deputy Stage Manager, Tracey Fleet; Costume Supervisor, Lucy Woodcock; Production Manager, Simon Curtis; AEA Stage Manager, Amy Kaskeski; Producer, Richard Morgan; Press, Karen Greco

CAST Mrs. Berry **Brenda Blethyn**; Mr. Berry **Niall Buggy**; Hazel **Beth Cooke**

U.S. premiere of a new play presented in two acts. Originally presented at the Royal Exchange Theatre, Manchester, U.K., May 13, 2009.

SYNOPSIS When a captivating young woman enters the life of the quixotic Mr. Berry, his desperation to ensure her return causes him to declare his wife dead and give away her clothes in exchange for elocution lessons. But as the very much alive Mrs. Berry searches for a reason for her rapidly diminishing wardrobe, Mr. Berry finds both his relationships under threat.

Brenda Blethyn in Haunted *(photo by Jonathan Keenan)*

Black Nativity Now

Theatre at St. Clements; First Preview: December 3, 2010; Opening Night: December 9, 2010; Closed January 2, 2011; 7 previews, 37 performances

Written by Alfred Preisser and Tracy Jack; Music and lyrics by Kelvyn Bell; Produced by Jeffrey Glaser, Christopher McElroen, Alfred Preisser, Dana Watkins, Kingsize-USA, and 9One Productions/Lawrence Winslow; Director, Alfred Preisser; Choreography, Tracy Jack; Set, Evan Collier; Costumes, Mia Bienovich; Lighting, Kate Ashton; Sound, Janie Bullard; Music Director, Kelvyn Bell; Stage Manager, Katie Hong; Press, Lia Chang

CAST Pastor **Nikkieli DeMone**; Chorus Leader/Pastor **Jeff Bolding**; Joseph **Jarvis Manning Jr.**; Mary **Breanna Bartley**; Angel **Naja Jack**; Chorus **Melanie Charles, Tracy Jack, Vincent Leggett, Brittney Mack, Amma Osei, Stephen Scott Wormley**

MUSICIANS Kelvyn Bell (Guitar), David "Red" Harrington (Bass), Chris Eddelton (Drums); Guest Choirs: The Harlem Japanese Gospel Choir (12/4, 12/11, 12/18), The Inspirational Ensemble of Convent Avenue Baptist Church (12/10)

Off-Broadway premiere of a holiday gospel pageant with music presented without intermission.

SYNOPSIS Set in a present day urban setting that could be the city where you live, *Black Nativity Now* tells the story of the birth of Christ from a fresh and wholly original perspective. The contemporary setting provides a heartfelt reference point for an evening of exuberant music and dance that celebrates humanity's need for hope and grace. The show unfolds within an intimate and passionate church presided over by a pastor heavily influenced by Broadway show-biz. Supported by a choir of singers and dancers who perform musical sets infused with gospel, pop, funk, and soul, *Black Nativity Now* is the universal story of mankind's search for salvation and peace on earth.

The cast of Black Nativity Now *(photo by Lia Chang)*

Ben Lewis, Lucinka Eisler, and Giulia Innocenti in Hysteria
(photo by Joseph Alford)

Hysteria

59E59 Theater B; First Preview: December 7, 2010; Opening Night: December 12, 2010; Closed December 26, 2010; 7 previews, 7 performances

Created by Inspector Sands (Ben Lewis, Giulia Innocenti, and Lucinka Eisler); Produced in Association with Stamping Ground; Developed at Battersea Arts Centre and the Nightingale Theatre (Brighton); Supported by Arts Council England and Awards For All; Presented as part of the 2010 Brits Off Broadway; Associate Director, Joseph Alford; Set, Yukiko Tsukamoto; Lighting, Katherine Williams; Sound, Carolyn Downing and Adrienne Quartly; Costumes, Suncana Dulic; Dramagturgy, Jonathan Young; Set Construction, Yukiko Tsukamoto and Stuart Heyes; Relights, Jack Knowles; AEA Stage Manager, Cheryl D. Olszowsky; Press, Karen Greco

CAST Waiter **Lucinka Eisler**; Man **Ben Lewis**; Woman **Giulia Innocenti**

U.S. premiere of a new play presented without intermission; in repertory with *If That's All There Is*. World premiere at Aurora Nova at the Edinburgh Fringe Festival in 2006. *Hysteria* was the company's first production.

SYNOPSIS Inspired by T.S. Eliot's poem of the same name, *Hysteria* is an award-winning play about panic, the apocalypse and table manners. A man and a woman are on the most awkward dinner date of their lives. Caught in the middle is their mortified waiter, haunted by visions of global catastrophe.

Dear Edwina

DR2; Opening Night: December 17, 2010; Closed February 25, 2011; 83 performances

Book and lyrics by Marcy Heisler, music by Zina Goldrich; Presented by Daryl Roth; Director, Timothy A. McDonald; Choreography, Steven G. Kennedy; Sets, Court Watson; Costumes, Theresa Squire; Lighting, Kathryn Furst; Music Director, Joe Kinosian; Orchestrations, Zina Goldrich, Michael Croiter; General Manager, Adam Hess; Casting, Dave Clemmons; Cast recording: PS Classics

CAST Bobby Newsome **Jared Picone**; Edwina Spoonapple **Beth Cheryl Tarnow**; Scott **Noah Zachary**; Billy Vanderploonk **David McDaniel**; Annie Smith **Judith Dry**; Kelli Poshkonozovich **Katie Whetsell**; Swings **Brad Giovanine, Katy Vaughn**

MUSICAL NUMBERS Paw Paw Michigan; Up on the Fridge; Dear Edwina; Here Comes a Letter; Hephaestus; Say No Thank You; Another Letter!; Abigail; Frankenguest; Carrie; Fork, Knife, Spoon; Time for Intermission; Periwinkel; Hola, Lola; Ziggy; Put It in the Piggy; Thanks for Coming; Fridge Breakdown; Sing Your Own Song; Fridge Reprise; Hola, Lola Encore

SETTING The Spoonaple Family Garage, Paw Paw Michigan, U.S.A.; the present. Revival of a musical presented without intermission. Originally presented at DR2 November 14, 2008–April 19, 2009, playing 197 performances (see *Theatre World* Vol. 65, page 158). The show returned last season from December 11, 2009–February 15, 2010.

SYNOPSIS In the time-honored tradition of "Let's put on a show," Edwina Spoonapple, decides that she and her pals will do just that. Edwina's special talent is giving advice, and she would do almost anything to be a part of the Kalamazoo Advice-a-palooza Festival. When a talent scout visits her hometown of Paw Paw, Michigan, Edwina, assisted by a host of quirky friends and neighbors, enthusiastically sings out her musical advice in hilarious and endearing songs about everything from party etiquette to the proper way to set a table.

Judith Dry, David McDaniel, Jared Picone, Beth Cheryl Tarno, Noah Zachary, and Katie Whetsell in Dear Edwina *(photo by Carol Rosegg)*

If That's All There Is

59E59 Theater B; First Preview: December 14, 2010; Opening Night: December 19, 2010; Closed January 2, 2011; 7 previews, 8 performances

Created by Inspector Sands (Ben Lewis, Giulia Innocenti, and Lucinka Eisler); Commissioned by The Lyric Hammersmith; Co-Developed at South Street (Reading) and The Nightingale Theatre (Brighton); Supported by Arts Council Englad, Battersea Arts Centre, and Alleyn's School; Presented as part of the 2010 Brits Off Broadway; Associate Director, Lu Kemp; Set/Costumes, Yukiko Tsukamoto; Lighting, Jack Knowles; Sound, Carolyn Downing; Assoicate Set/Costumes, Gabriella Gerdelcs; Associate Sound, Elena Peña; Choreography, Miranda Henderson; Tour Booking, Mark Makin; Associate Producers, Artsagenda; AEA Stage Manager, Cheryl D. Olszowka; Press, Karen Greco

CAST Frances **Lucinka Eisler**; Daniel **Ben Lewis**; Therapist/Christina **Giulia Innocenti**

U.S. premiere of a new play presented without intermission in repertory with *Hysteria*. Originally presented at the Transverse Theatre in the 2009 Edinburgh Fringe Festival as part of the British Council Showcase.

SYNOPSIS In *If That's All There Is*, a couple teeter on the brink of marriage. As the happiest day of their lives approaches, the panic begins to rise. And everyone's watching. Inspired by Peggy Lee's version of Lieber and Stoller's "Is That All There Is?," this award-winning play dissects our obsession with finding fulfillment at any cost.

Licinka Eisler in If That's All There Is *(photo by Ed Collier)*

Mummenschanz

Skirball Center; Opening Night: December 21, 2010; Closed January 8, 2011; 22 performances

Presented by Mummenschanz Foundation (Floriana Frassetto and Bernie Schürch, Artistic Directors); Technical Director/Lighting Design, Jan Maria Lukas; Tour Manager, Diego Schürch; Publicity, Dera, Roslan & Campion; Marketing, HHC Marketing; Social Media, Bay Bridge Productions; Advertising, Elizabeth Findlay; North America Representation, Laura Colby/Elsie Management

CAST **Floriana Frassetto**, **Bernie Schürch**, **Raffaella Mattioli**, **Pietro Montandon**

A non-verbal mime/performance piece presented without intermission. Mummenschanz opened at the Bijou Theatre March 30, 1977–April 30, 1980 playing 1,326 performances (see *Theatre World* Vol. 33, page 62).

SYNOPSIS Currenty in its fourth decade, Mummenscahnz returns to the U.S. for the first time since 2003 with a new program that showcases the incredible humor, versatility, and pure imagination of the Swiss performance troupe. Mummenschanz remains one of the most successful theatre groups in the world. Formed in 1972 by Bernie Schürch and Andrew Bossard with Swiss-American artist Floriana Frassetto, the pioneering troupe created a non-verbal theatrical language that transcends traditional barriers of nationality and culture, and never before or since has a show without words or music succeeded on Broadway for three consecutive years.

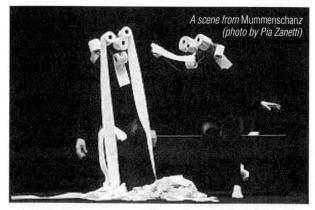

A scene from Mummenschan*z* *(photo by Pia Zanetti)*

Dracula

Little Shubert Theatre; First Preview: December 14, 2010; Opening Night: January 5, 2011; Closed January 9, 2011; 25 previews, 7 performances

Written by John L. Balderston and Hamilton Deane, based on the novel by Bram Stoker; Produced by Bram Stoker's Dracula LLC, Tony Travis, George Shipley, Dona Shipley, Leslie Evers, Ed Bankole, Megan Barnett, Carolyn Bechtel, and Michael Alden in association with Bob Kale, John Manley, and Barry Moss; Director, Paul Alexander; Set, Dana Kenn; Costumes, Willa Kim; Lighting, Brian Nason; Sound, Chris DelVecchio; Fight Director Rick Sordelet and Mike Rossmy; Special Effects, Flying by Foy, Greg Mee, Mike Rossmy, Rick Sordelet; Casting, MKA Casting; Associate Set, Christopher Nowak; Assistant Costumes, Leanne Mahoney; Assistant Lighting, Ken Elliot; Hair, Paul Huntley; Dialect Coach, Louis Colaianni; PSM, Brian Meister; ASM, Stacey Zaloga; General Manager, Alexander Morr; Press, Shirley Herz Associates

CAST Count Dracula **Michel Altieri**; Lucy Seward **Emily Bridges**; Professor Van Helsing **George Hearn**; Dr. Seward **Timothy Jerome**; Miss Wells/Woman in White **Katharine Luckinbill**; Renfield **John Buffalo Mailer**; Butterworth **Rob O'Hare**; Jonathan Harker **Jake Silbermann**

UNDERSTUDIES Malcolm Madera (Dracula/Butterworth), Rob O'Hare (Jonathan Harker/Renfield), Nicholas Stannard (Dr. Seward/Van Helsing)

SETTING Purley, England. The 1920s. Revival of a play presented in three acts with one intermission. Originally presented in New York at the Fulton Theatre October 5, 1927–May 1928 starring Bela Lugosi as "Dracula." The play had a brief revival at the Royale Theatre for a week in April 1931. The last revival played the Martin Beck Theatre (now the Al Hirschfeld Theatre) October 13, 1977–January 6, 1980 starring Frank Langella, playing 925 performances (see *Theatre World* Vol. 34, page 17.)

SYNOPSIS *Dracula* is the classic Gothic drama about the power of seduction and the nature of true love. When the mysterious Count Dracula takes an interest in the beautiful, young Lucy, who suffers from horrific dreams and a strange illness, he arouses the suspicions of her fiancé, Jonathan Harker, and Professor Abraham van Helsing. Following a series of grisly murders and unexplained occurrences, the men fear Dracula may be an undead creature who prowls the darkness and preys upon innocent souls.

George Hearn, Jake Silberman, and John Buffalo Mailer in Dracula *(photo by Carol Rosegg)*

Abbie

West End Theatre; Opening Night: January 6, 2011; Closed January 29, 2011

Adapted by Bern Cohen, based on writings and speeches of Abbie Hoffman; Produced by Bern Cohen and Jason Scheff; Director, Thomas Caruso; Projections/Sound, Morgan Paul Freeman; Lighting, Zachary Spitzer; Production Manager, Wendy Czerwinski; Technical Director, Sean Ryan; Production Coordinator, Brittany Gischner; Production Assistant, Patrick Scheid; Assistant Producer, Penny Bittone; Light Board, Tim Guccione

CAST Abbie Hoffman **Bern Cohen**

World premiere of a new solo performance play presented without intermission.

SYNOPSIS *Abbie* is a politically charged exploration into the life of Abbie Hoffman, the Sixties activist who was a member of the infamous 'Chicago Eight' and known to many as 'The Clown Prince of the Revolution.' This one-man show will give audiences a compelling inside look of what life was like as a leader of the anti-establishment, revealing the emotional stress caused by his underground hiding, the effects of beatings at the hands of hateful police, and other conflicts which eventually overwhelmed him, resulting in his suicide over two decades ago.

Bern Cohen in Abbie *(photo by Sam Morris)*

The Interminable Suicide of Gregory Church

St. Ann's Warehouse; Opening Night: January 6, 2011; Closed January 30, 2011; 22 performances

Written by Daniel Kitson; Presented by St. Ann's Warehouse (Susan Feldman, Artistic Director) as part of the 2011 Under the Radar Festival; Lighting, Heather Sparling; Sound, Kristyn R. Smith; Press, Blake Zidell

Performed by **Daniel Kitson**

American premiere of a new solo performance play presented without intermission. Previously presented at the 2009 Edinburgh Fringe Festival.

SYNOPSIS In this singular 90-minute monologue, the celebrated comedian and theatrical storyteller tells the tale of a man whose suicide is perpetually deferred by all the goodbye letters he must write-and the responses some of them provoke. A story of death postponed by life.

(leave about 3 lines of extra room in this listing – I am waiting for correct cast

Daniel Kitson in
The Interminable Suicide of
Gregory Church
(photo by Pavel Antonov)

Angelina Ballerina the Musical

Union Square Theatre; Opening Night: January 8, 2011; Closed March 13, 2011; 30 performances

Book and lyrics by Susan DiLallo, music by Ben Morss, based on the the books and characters created by Katharine Holabird, with illustrations by Helen Craig; Produced by Vital Theatre Company in association with HIT Entertainment; Director/Choreographer, Sam Viverito; Music Director, Michael Borth; Set, Kyle Dixon; Costumes, Elisabeth Vastola; Lighting, Josh Bradford; Sound, Martin Peacock; PSM, Shani Colleen Murfin; Assistant Director, Shani Colleen Murfin; Press, Stephen Sunderlin

CAST Gracie **Carole Ashley** or **Amanda Yachechak**; Dad **Ronn Burton** or **Kevin Michael Wade**; Viki **Amber Coartney** or **Tiffany Wiesend**; Miss Mimi **Alexis Field**; Serena **Jessica Freitas** or **Amy White**; Alice **Maggie Gomes Madonia** or **Cassie Okenka**; Angelina **Whitney Meyer** or **Kara Jones**; AZ **Wesley Tunison** or **Jake Weinstein**

Amber Coartney, Amanda Yachechak, Eric Rstivo, Whitney Meyer, and Amy White in Angelina Ballerina the Musical *(photo by Sun Productions)*

Off-Broadway transfer of a musical for young audiences presented without intermission. Previously played at Vital Theatre October 2, 2010–January 2, 2011.

SYNOPSIS Angelina and her friends, Alice, Gracie, AZ, Viki and even their teacher, Ms. Mimi, are all aflutter because a special guest is coming to visit Camembert Academy! Angelina and her friends will perform all types of dance, including hip-hop, modern dance, the Irish jig and of course, ballet and they are excited to show off their skills to their famous visitor. Angelina is the most excited of all, but will she get the starring moment she hopes for?

Girl Talk: The Musical

Midtown Theatre at HA! Comedy Club*; First Preview: November 3, 2010; Opening Night: January 9, 2011; Closed July 1, 2011

Written by Louise Roche, Sonya Carter, and Tim Flaherty; Additional Book, Betsy Kelso; Conceived by Tim Flaherty; Produced by Robert Dragotta, Tim Flaherty and Entertainment Events; Directors, Sonya Carter and Tim Flaherty; Choreography/Music Director, Amy Jones; Press, David Gersten

CAST Barbara **Tina Jensen**; Dr. Laura **Priscilla Fernandez**; Janice **Sonya Carter**

World premiere of a new interactive play with music presented without intermission.

SYNOPSIS *Girl Talk* focuses on the final live studio broadcast of the hit radio show GIRL TALK on WPMS after a wild ten year run. The two top radio hosts and their most popular regular guest are going out in style! The ladies love to dish about life, love, sex, marriage, relationships, friendships, motherhood, careers, food, alcohol, and yes, men in any capacity. When it's time for music, these talented ladies bust out to hits by diverse artists such as The Pointer Sisters, Jennifer Lopez, Carrie Underwood, Aretha Franklin, and many more!

*The production began the first week of previews at the Times Square Arts Center.

Tina Jensen, Proscilla Fernandez, and Sonya Carter in Girl Talk: The Musical *(photo by Ken Flaherty)*

NEWSical the Musical: Full Spin Ahead

Krik Theatre; First Preview: December 13, 2010; Opening Night: January 9, 2011; Still running as of May 31, 2011

Created and written by Rick Crom; Produced by Elyse Pasquale and Tom D'Angora in association with Annette Niemtzow and Adam Weinstock, Director, Mark Waldrop; Music Director/Arrangements/Accompanist, Ed Goldsheider; Set/Projections, Jason Courson; Costumes, Davdi Kaley; Lighting, Josh Starr; Wigs, J. Jared Janas and Rob Greene; PSM/General Manager, Scott F. Delacruz; Production Assistant/Board Op, Ryan Obermeier; Wardrobe, Christine Massoud; Marketing, Meri Krassner/S.R.O. Marketing; Graphics/Web Design, Michael Duling; Press, John Capo

CAST Christina Bianco, Christine Pedi, John Walton West, Michael West; Understudies **Amy Griffin, Tommy Walker**

New edition of a musical revue presented in two acts. Originally presented at the John Houseman Studio January 9, 2004 for an eight-week limited engagment. The show re-opened as an Off-Broadway at Upstairs at Studio 54 September 17, 2004–April 17, 2005 playing 215 performances (see *Theatre World* Vol. 61, page 125). The show returned last season at the 47th Street Theatre December 9, 2009–March 21, 2010 playing 121 performances (see *Theatre World* Vol. 66, page 155.)

SYNOPSIS The Drama Desk nominated NEWSical the Musical is back again lampooning current events, headlines, newsmakers, celebrities, and politicians. With songs and material being updated on a regular basis, composer-lyricist Rick Crom's topical musical comedy is an ever-evolving mockery of all the news that is fit to spoof!

Pants on Fire's Metamorphoses

Flea Theater; First Preview: January 5, 2011; Opening Night: January 9, 2011; Closed January 30, 2011; 5 previews, 21, performances

Conceived and adapted by Peter Bramley after Ovid, devised by Pants on Fire (Peter Bramley, Artistic Director; Mabel Jones, Company Manager); Presented by The Carol Tambor Theatrical Foundation and The Flea Theater (Jim Simpson, Artistic Director; Carol Ostrow, Producing Director); Director, Peter Bramley; Original Songs, Lucy Egger; Lighting, Ralph Stokeld; Projections/Film Edit, Johnathan Davenport; Sound, Alex Packer; Puppets/Illustrator, Samuel Wyer; Additional Songs, Harry Akst and Grant Clarke

CAST Jupiter/Daedalus/Perseus **Jonathan Davenport**; Juno/Salmacis/Nurse **Jo Dockery**; Cupid/Io/Nurse/Semele **Mabel Jones**; Apollo/Narcissus/Icarus **Tom McCall**; Tiresias/Hermaphroditus/Atlas/Theseus **Alex Packer**; Echo/Tiresias (as female)/Andromeda/Nurse **Hannah Pierce**; Daphne/Mercury/Medusa/Ariadne **Eloise Secker**

U.S. premiere of a play presented without intermission. Originally opened at the Pleasance Theatre, Edinburgh August 6, 2006.

SYNOPSIS Pants on Fire's *Metamorphoses* presents ancient myths as you've never seen them before! This swell party fuses live original music and song, magical stagecraft and breathtaking imagery relocating Ovid's epic tales of fantastical transformation to WWII Britain. Cupid is an evacuee with a catapult. Narcissus, an iconic Hollywood heartthrob drooling over his own cinematic image, and The Chorus – Andrews-like sisters finding close harmony amid cosmic chaos. Tales of love, gods, heroics and monsters are retold by blending gas masks, gramophones, puppetry, film and live original music.

Hannah Pierce, Eloise Secker, and Mabel Jones in Pant On Fire's Metamorphoses *(photo by Tom Packer)*

ScreenPlay

59E59 Theater B; First Preview: January 12, 2011; Opening Night: January 16, 2011; Closed February 6, 2011

Created by Scott Brooks; Presented by Badlands Theater Company; Director, Jenny Greeman; Design, Lex Liang; Lighting, Ian Wehrle; Fight Director, Paul C. Molnar; Stage Manager, Stephany Ward; Press, Karen Greco

CAST Graham **Scott Brooks**; Suzie **Heather Dilly**; Lisa **Diana DeLaCruz**; Dean **Jonathan Sale**

Off-Broadway premiere of a new play presented without intermission. Previously presented at the 2010 Midtown International Theatre Festival.

SYNOPSIS Dean is a failed screenwriter. Graham is a dot com millionaire who wants to produce movies. These former college friends reunite when Dean's Oscar-bait screenplay captures Graham's imagination. How much is Dean willing to compromise to get the picture made? A biting Hollywood satire that examines friendship, rivalry and ambition, *ScreenPlay* traces the explosive journey of a film on its way to Oscar night.

Jonathan Sale and Scott Brooks in ScreenPlay *(photo by Jesse Teeters)*

Flipzoids

Peter Jay Sharp Theater; First Preview: January 11, 2011; Opening Night: January 18, 2011; Closed February 6, 2011

Written by Ralph B. Peña; Presented by the Ma-Yi Theater Company (Ralph B. Peña, Artistic Director; Jorge Z. Ortoll, Executive Director); Director/Set Design, Loy Arcenas; Lighting, James Vermeulen; Sound, Fabian Obispo and Chris Schardin; PSM, Danielle Buccion; Associate Director, Suzette Porte; Literary Manager, Joi Barrios; Marketing/Development, Luke Harlan; Press, Sam Rudy Media Relations

CAST Aying **Ching Valdes-Aran**; Redford **Carlo Alban**; Vangie **Tina Chilip**

SETTING A deserted beach in Southern California. Off-Broadway premier of a play resented without intermission. Previously presented by Ma-Yi in 1996.

SYNOPSIS In *Flipzoids*, a 70-year-old woman – a recent immigrant from the Philippines – crosses paths with a young Filipino man on a deserted beach. Far from their native land, a cautious friendship ensues as they attempt to reconcile their very different understandings of their old home, and try to fit in to their new one.

The Witch of Edmonton

Theatre at St. Clements; First Preview: January 25, 2011; Opening Night: February 3, 2011; Closed February 20, 2011

Written by Thomas Dekker, John Ford, and William Rowley; Produced by Red Bull Theater (Jesse Berger, Artistic Director); Director, Jesse Berger; Set, Anka Lupes; Costumes, Cait O'Connor; Sound, Elizabeth Rhodes; Lighting, Peter West; Original Music, Daniel Levy; Hair and Makeup, Erin Kennedy Lunsford; Special Effects/Costume Effects, Jessica Scott; Properties, Deb Gauoette; Projections, Dan Scully; Casting, Stuart Howard; Voice and Text, Dan Pardo; Choreography, Tracy Bersley; Aerial Effects, Paul Rubin; Fight Director, Rick Sordelet; Stage Manager, Damon Arrington; Production Supervisor, James E. Cleveland; Associate Producers, Renee Blinkwold; Press, David Gersten

CAST Warbeck/Countryman **Craig Baldwin**; Frank **Justin Blanchard**; Old Banks **Andre De Shields**; Cuddy Banks **Adam Green**; Sir Arthur Clarington **Christopher Innvar**; Somerton/Countryman **Carman Lacivita**; Thorney **Christopher McCann**; Susan Carter **Christina Pumariega**; Katherine Carter **Amanda Quaid**; Old Ratcliffe/Anne Ratcliffe **Everett Quinton**; Winifred **Miriam Silverman**; Dog **Derek Smith**; Justice **Raphael Nash Thompson**; Carter **Sam Tsoutsouvas**; Elizabeth Sawyer **Charlayne Woodard**

Off-Broadway premiere of a classic play presented in two acts.

SYNOPSIS A witch, a fool, a young man, his two wives, an angry mob, and one very devilish dog takes the stage in the first major Off-Broadway production of this fantastical tragicomedy. In a new adaptation of the original Jacobean play, this rarely-performed classic rips open the dark underbelly of a small town with humor and pathos. As the lives of its inhabitants intersect in spellbinding ways, the power of a community for both good and evil is revealed.

Kid Shamrock

Atlantic Stage 2; Opening Night: February 8, 2011; Closed February 13, 2011; 7 performances

Written by Bobby Cassidy Jr.; Produced by Faz In Ate Films, Imelda O'Reilly; Director, Jimmy Smallhourn

CAST Narrator **Bobby Cassidy Sr**; Young Bobby Cassidy Sr. **John Duddy**; Older Bobby Cassidy Sr **Seamus McDonagh**; Rodrigo Valdes **Nick Roman**; Paddy Floyd **Gary Hope**; Referee **Wayne Kelly**; Thomas Connor **Patrick Joseph Connolly**

Off-Broadway premiere of a new play with boxing presented without intermission. An earlier version of the show played at the Producers Club in 2007.

SYNOPSIS Recreating the fight between Bobby Cassidy (Kid Shamrock) and Rodrigo Valdez at Madison Square Garden on St. Patrick's Day in 1971, a fight that ultimately led to Bobby's retirement from boxing and enlightenment as a human being. The play, written by Cassidy's son, is a homage to the vibrant blue-collar tradition of Irish American boxing.

Nick Roman, Wayne Kelly, and John Duddy in Kid Shamrock
(photo by Guy Warren)

A Perfect Future

Cherry Lane Theatre; First Preview: February 4, 2011; Opening Night: February 17, 2011; Closed March 6, 2011; 13 previews, 22 performances

Written by David Hay; Presented by Andy Sandberg, Whitney Hoagland Edwards, Neal-Rose Creations in association with the Cherry Lane Theatre (Angelina Fiordellisi, Executive Director); Director, Wilson Milam; Set, Charles Corcoran; Costumes, Michael McDonald; Lighting, Ben Stanton; Sound, Daniel Kluger; Casting, Pat McCorkle; Marketing, The Pekoe Group; PSM, Donald Fried; Production Supervisor, PRF Productions/Peter R. Feuchtwanger; General Management, Denise Cooper; ASM, Melissa Jernigan; Assistant to the Producer, Colin O'Rourke; Assistant Costumes, Abby Hahn; Properties, Kathy Fabian/Propstar; Press, O+M Company, Rick Miramontez, Philip Carrubba

CAST Elliot Murphy **Daniel Oreskes**; Natalie Schiff-Hudson **Donna Bullock**; John Hudson **Michael T. Weiss**; Mark Colvin **Scott Drummond**

UNDERSTUDIES Conan McCarty (John, Elliot), Nicole Orth-Pallavicini (Natalie), Markus Potter (Mark)

SETTING Natalie and John's Manhattan apartment. Fall 2005. World premiere of a new play presented in two acts.

SYNOPSIS *A Perfect Future* explores whether people can be married and truly love each other when their political persuasions are diametrically opposed. New York power-couple John and Natalie are hosting a dinner for Elliot, a friend from their days as college radicals. Also invited is Mark, a straight-laced young man from John's risk management firm. With the help of a few too many expensive bottles of wine, the group's past and their long buried secrets resurface. Over the course of this raucous evening, their basic belief systems are upended, as the four must come to terms with each other's true politics and behavior.

Donna Bullock, Scott Drummond, Michael T. Weiss, and Daniel Oreskes in Perfect Future *(photo by Richard Termine)*

La Barbería

New World Stages; First Preview: February 3, 2011; Opening Night: February 17, 2011; Closed June 12, 2011

Written by David Maldonado and Ari Maniel Cruz; Presented by David Maldonado and Juan Toro; Director, Waddys Jacquez; Set, Raul Abrego; Lighting, Sarah Sidman; Costumes, Hochi Asiatico; Sound, Abe Viera; Production Supervisor, James Cleveland; Production Manager, Josh Scherr; General Management, Cesa Entertainment/Jamie Cesa, Diane Alianiello; PSM, Jeff Rodriguez; ASM, Paul Brewster; Props, Michelle Spadaro; Advertising/Press/Marketing, Debbie Medina

CAST Benny **Manny Perez**; Cheo **Mateo Gomez**; Bachatero/Policeman **Ruperto Vanderpool**; Correo **Modesto Lacen**; Nurys **Sunilda Caraballo**; Sandy **Ivan Camilo**; Jeffrey/Banquero **Graciany Miranda**; Swings **Juan Carlo Diaz, Emme Bonilla**

Off-Broadway premiere of a new play primarily in Spanish presented in two acts.

SYNOPSIS When Beny Acevedo, landlord and proprietor of a bustling Washington Heights barbershop, gets a multi-million dollar offer to sell his building, he faces the toughest decision of his life. Set against a score of original contemporary Latin music emanating from the airwaves, *La Barbería* is a comedic and wistful portrait of a neighborhood in flux and a tribute to the strength of a community.

The cast of **La Barbería** *(photo by Carol Rosegg)*

The Body Politic

59E59 Theater B; First Preview: February 10, 2011; Opening Night: February 20, 2011; Closed March 6, 2011

Written by Richard Abrons; and Margarett Perry; Presented by At Hand Theatre Company (Dan Horrigan, Artistic Director; Justin Scribner, Executive Director); Director, Margarett Perry; Set, Timothy R. Mackabee; Costumes, Nicole Wee; Lighting, Jesse Belsky; Sound, Daniel Kluger; Managing Director, Matthew DiCarlo; Associate Producer, Laura A. Wright; Stage Manager, Paige Van Den Burg; Press, Ron Lasko, Spin Cycle

CAST Spencer Davis **Matthew Boston**; Trish Rubinstein **Eve Danzeisen**; Granville Parker **Brian Dykstra**; Brunhilde Logan **Leslie Hendrix**; Harley Grant **Daren Kelly**; Viktor Spasky **Michael Puzzo**

U.S. premiere of a new play presented in two acts.

SYNOPSIS Two opposing political operators find themselves falling in love behind party lines. Can this high-voltage political odd couple navigate a bipartisan romance? A heartfelt and hilarious look at love on the campaign trail, *The Body Politic* is an old fashioned romantic comedy that reaches across the aisle with 21st century sex appeal.

Brian Dykstra, Michael Puzzo, and Eve Danzeisen in The Body Politic *(photo by Carol Rosegg)*

Invasion!

Walkerspace; First Preview: February 9, 2011; Opening Night: February 21, 2011; Closed March 12, 2011

Written by Jonas Hassen Khemiri; Presented by The Play Company (Kate Loewald, Founding Producer; Lauren Weigel, Executive Producer); Director, Erica Schmidt; Translator, Rachel Wilson-Broyles; Set, Antje Ellerman; Costumes, Oana Botez Ban; Lighting, Mattew Richards; Sound, Bart Fasbender; PSM, April Ann Kline; Fight Choreography, J. Steven White; Press, Sam Rudy Media Relations

CAST **Francis Benhamou, Andrew Guilarte,Bobby Moreno, Debargo Sanyal**

U.S. premiere of a new Swedish play presented without intermission.

SYNOPSIS *Invasion!* is a subversive comedy that centers on 'Abulkasem,' a name that bears seemingly magical powers, and a series of characters who assume the name for their own reasons. Who is 'Abulkasem'? Is he a character in a fairy tale, or an international super-spy? Is she a renowned auteur director? Does he/she pose a clear and present danger? And is there more than one? That all depends on who you ask.

Andrew Guilarte and Francis Benhamou in Invasion! *(photo by Carol Rosegg)*

White People

Ensemble Studio Theatre; First Preview: February 16, 2011; Opening Night: February 21, 2011; Closed March 13, 2011

Written by Neil Cuthbert; Presented by Ensemble Studio Theatre (William Carden, Artistic Director; Paul Alexander Slee, Executive Director); Prodcuer, Annie Trizna; Director, Michael Barakiva; Set, Maiko Chii; Costumes, Suzanne Chesney; Lighting, Cat Tate Starmer; Props, Sound, Matt Sherwin; Fight Choreographer, Maggie MacDonald; Production Manager, Joshua Scherr; PSM, Samone B. Weissman; Technical Director, Michael Hetzer; Assistant Director, Jason Bruffy; ASM, Beth Stegman; Marketing/Box Office, Ryan Hugh McWilliams; Casting, Tom Rowan; Assistant Set/Props, Yoshiko Asai; Movement Consultant, Mimi Quillen; Magic Consultant, Kern McFadden; Graphics, Chrissie Lein; Press, Bruce Cohen

CAST Hal **James DeMarse**; Mag **Cecilia deWolf**; Kate **Jennifer Joan Thompson**; Jeff **David Gelles**; Bear **Matthew Minor**; Gramma **Delphi Harrington**; Boo Boo **Mickey Solis**

SETTING A Saturday in October, 1975. A house in suburban New Jersey. World premiere of a new play presented in two acts.

SYNOPSIS *White People* is a bruising family comedy in which the long repressed conflicts of a middle class WASP family finally explode. The father is drinking again; the son has moved home to write an epic science fiction novel; the daughter receives a visit from a mysterious stranger; and the domineering racist grandmother comes for lunch on the wrong day.

Front: James DeMarse, Cecilia deWolf; Back: Delphi Harrington, David Gelles, Matthew Minor, and Mickey Solis in White People *(photo by Natalia Vergara/ Gerry Goodstein)*

Vieux Carré

Baryshnikov Arts Center; First Preview: February 2, 2011; Opening Night: February 22, 2011; Closed March 13, 2011

Written by Tennesse Williams; Presented by The Wooster Group and Théâtre National de Strasbourg, Les Spectacles Vivants-Centre Pompidou, Festival d'Automne à Paris; Director, Elizabeth LeCompte; Associate Director, Kate Valk; Lighting, Jennifer Tipton; Sound, Matt Schloss, Omar Zubair; Video, Bozkurt Karasu; Stage Manager, Teresa Hartmann; Technical Director/Additional Video, Aron Deyo; Master Electrician, Kent Barrett; Technical Assistant, Daniel Jackson; Wardrobe, Enver Chakartash; Sound Consultant, Jamie McElhinney; Special Advisor, Casey Spooner; Cineturg, Dennis Dermody; Producer, Cynthia Hedstrom; General Manager, Edward McKeany; Archivist, Clay Hapaz; Media Projects, Geoff Abbas; Arts Education Manager, Kaneza Schaal; Adminsitrator, Jason Gray Platt; Strategic Consultant, Joel Bassin

CAST The Writer **Ari Fliakos**; Photographer/Sky **Daniel Pettrow**; Mrs. Wire/ Jane Sparks **Kate Valk**; Nursie **Kaneza Schaal**; Nightingale/Ty McCool **Scott Shepherd**; The Pickup **Daniel Jackson**; Mary Maude/Miss Carrie (on video) **Alan Boyd Kleiman**; Avatar **Andrew Schneider**; Dancer (on video) **Casey Spooner**; The Judge (voiceover) **Ben Williams**

New York premiere of a new revival of a play with multimedia presented without intermission. The Wooster Group premiered this piece initially at Festival d'Automne at Centre Pomidou (Paris) November 19-23, 2009. The U.S. premiere played REDCAT in Los Angeles December 1-10, 2010 prior to the New York engagement.

SYNOPSIS Like Williams' first big success *The Glass Menagerie*, *Vieux Carré* is a "memory play," set in the boarding house in New Orleans where Williams himself stayed as a young man during the Depression. The young writer, as narrator, remembers his artistic and sexual awakening there. Inhabitants of the house swirl up out of the writer's mind as archetypal Williams characters, longing for release and haunted by thwarted dreams. In The Wooster Group's version of *Vieux Carré*, the Group experiments with new modes of expression for Williams' lyric voice.

Kate Valk and Scott Shepherd in the Wooster Group's Vieux Carré *(photo by Franck Beloncle)*

Musical Legends

Urban Stages; Opening Night: February 24, 2011; Closed March 13, 2011; 33 performances

Presented by Urban Stages (Frances Hill, Artistic Director; Founding Artistic Director); Program Director, Rachel Sullivan; Company Manager, Olga Devyatisilnaya; Development/Marketing, Antoinette Mullins; Producing Associate, Peter Napolitano; Directors: Lee Summers (*Nat 'King' Cole*), Peter Napolitano (*Grand Illusions*), Barry Kleinbort (*Special Kaye*), Tom Jones (*Pearl Bailey*); Music Directors: Tony Romano (*Nat 'King' Cole*), Paul Trueblood (*Grand Illusions*), David Gaines (*Special Kaye*), William A. Knowles (*Pearl Bailey*); Press, Springer Associates, Joe Trentacosta

CAST **Cleve Douglass** in *Nat 'King' Cole: Unforgettable Smooth Grooves*; **Janice Hall** in *Grand Illusions: The Music of Marlene Dietrich*; **Gretchen Reinhagen** in *Special Kaye: A Tribute to the Incomparable Kaye Ballard*; **Roz White** in *Pearl Bailey...By Request*

MUSICIANS *Nat 'King' Cole*: Tony Romano (Guitar), Phil Palombi (Bass), Matt Kane (Percussion); *Grand Illusions*: Paul Trueblood (Piano), Ritt Henn (Bass); *Special Kaye*: David Gaines (Piano), Tom Hubbard (Bass), Donna Kelly (Percussion); *Pearl Bailey*: Mike Mitchell (Piano)

A series of four theatrical tribute performances presented in repertory, each presented without intermission.

SYNOPSIS Urban Stages presents four unique, self-contained theatrical tributes, each celebrating the music and lives of four sensational entertainers: Pearl Bailey, Kaye Ballard, Marlene Dietrich, and Nat 'King' Cole, as performed by Roz White, Janice Hall, Gretchen Reinhagen, and Cleve Douglass.

Beautiful Burnout

St. Ann's Warehouse; Opening Night: February 25, 2011; Closed March 27, 2011; 31 performances

Written by Bryony Lavery; Presented by Frantic Assembly (Scott Graham and Steven Hoggett, Artistic Directors) and National Theatre of Scotland in association with St. Ann's Warehouse; (Susan Feldman, Artistic Director); Director/Choreography, Scott Graham and Steven Hoggett; Additional Choreography by the Company; Featuring the music of Underworld; Design, Laura Hopkins; Lighting, Andy Purves; Sound, Carolyn Downing; Video, Ian William Galloway; Casting, Anne Henderson; Stage Manager, Joni Carter; Technical Stage Manager, Nick Hill; Sound/Video Supervisor, Andrew Elliott; Wardrobe, Kat Smith; Light Board, Celeste White; Press, Blake Zidell

CAST Carlotta Burns **Blythe Duff**; Cameron Burns **Ryan Fletcher**; Steve George/Neil Neill **Eddie Kay**; Dina Massie **Vicki Manderson**; Ajay Chopra **Taqi Nazeer**; Ainsley Binney **Henry Pettigrew**; Bobby Burgess **Ewan Stewart**

SETTING A boxing ring in Glasgow, Scotland. American premiere of a new play presented without intermission. World premiere at the 2010 Edinburgh Fringe Festival.

SYNOPSIS *Beautiful Burnout* is about the soul sapping three-minute rounds that determine which young men become gods and which gods become mortal. *Beautiful Burnout* was instigated by Hoggett's observations of young boxers in training at Brooklyn's famous Gleason's Gym, where he became intrigued with both the beauty and brutality in the movement and distress of the live boxers. It resonated with the authentic drilling and soldiering he explored so brilliantly as choreographer of *Black Watch*, coupled with similar issues among working class youth seeking transcendent ways to escape, in this case, through amateur fighting.

Eddie Kay, Ryan Fletcher, and Taqi Nazeer in Beautiful Burnout (photo by Richard Termine)

Treasure Island

Irondale Center; First Preview: February 15, 2011; Opening Night: March 5, 2011; Closed March 26, 2011

Adapted for the stage by Vernon Morris and B.H. Barry from the novel by Robert Louis Stevenson; Presented by Golden Rivet Productions and Irondale Ensemble (Terry Greiss, Executive Director; Jim Niesen, Artistic Director); Producer/Director/Fight Director, B.H. Barry; Set, Tony Straiges; Costumes, Luke Brown; Lighting, Stewart Wagner; Sound, Will Pickens; Effects, Gregory Meeh; Set Decorator/Props, Jim Balzaretti; Production Manager, Jeff Benish; Assistant Fight Director, Brad Lemons; Music Director, Ken Schatz; PSM, J.P. Elkins; Stage Manager, Nancy Wernick; Graphics, Five Zoo Concepts & Design; Advertising/Marketing, The Pekoe Group; Casting, Pat McCorkle; General Manager, Cheryl Dennis; Company Manager, Dan Gallagher; Press, Springer Associates

CAST Billy Bones/Morgan **John Ahlin**; Blind Pew/Ben Gunn **Tom Beckett**; Captain Smollett **Steve Blanchard**; Captain Flint/Israel Hands **Rod Brogan**; Mr. Arrow/Tom Hunter/Hoot/Jake **Josh Clayton**; Jim Hawkins **Noah E. Galvin**; Black Dog/George Merry **Michael Gabriel Goodfriend**; Long John Silver **Tom Hewitt**; Chanteyman/Mrs. Hawkins/Redruth/Parrot **Ken Schatz**; Dr. Livesey **Rocco Sisto**; Allerdyce/O'Brien **Lindsay Smiling**; Squire Trelawney **Kenneth Tigar**; Dirk **Philip Willingham**; Understudies **Ryan Barry**, **Jonathan Judge-Russo**

Off-Broadway premiere of a new play presented in two acts.

SYNOPSIS *Treasure Island* is a spine-tingling adventure about treachery, treasure and a young man's rite of passage. The enthralling classic tale of Jim Hawkins, Long John Silver and swashbuckling pirates is brought to life by B.H. Barry. Surrounded by elements of wind and water, swords and sea chanteys, and old ropes and rowboats, the audience is swept away to the South Seas for an infinitely sensational, intimate and nostalgic experience.

The cast of Treasure Island (photo by Ken Howard)

Cactus Flower

Westside Theatre – Upstairs; First Preview: February 24, 2011; Opening Night: March 10, 2011; Closed April 24, 2011; 17 previews, 52 performances

Written by Abe Burrows; Based on a play by Pierre Barileet and Jean Pierre Gredy; Presented by Daryl Roth and Stonemill Productions; Director, Michael Bush; Sets, Anna Louizos; Costumes, Karen Ann Ledger; Lighting, Philip Rosenberg; Sound, Brad Berridge; Wigs, Edward J. Wilson; Casting, Stephanie Klapper; General Manager, DR Theatrical Management; Production Manager, Greg Bellon/Production Consilidated; PSM, Rebecca Goldstein-Glaze; Stage Manger, Julie DeRossi; Marketing/Advertising, aka; Associate Producer, Alexander Fraser; Assistant Design: Melissa Shakun (set), Emily deAngelis (costumes), Brandon Mitchell (lighting), Emma Wilk (sound); Technical Director, John Trevilini; Props, Deb Gaouette; Wardrobe, Laura Bowman; Press, O+M Company

CAST Dr. Julian Winston **Maxwell Caulfield**; Stephanic Dixon Durant **Lois Robbins**; Toni Simmons **Jenni Barber**; Igor Sullivan **Jeremy Bobb**; Senor Arturo Sanchez **John Herrera**; Harvey Greenfield **Anthony Reimer**; Mrs. Dixon Durant **Robin Skye**; Botticelli's Springtime **Emily Walton**

UNDERSTUDIES Jay Sullivan (Igor), Chris Vettel (Harvey/Sanchez/Julian), Brigitte Villieu-Davis (Stephanie, Mrs. Durant), Emily Walton (Toni)

SETTING Mid 1960s; Uptown and downtown Manhattan. Revival of a play presented in fifteen scenes in two acts. Originally presented on Broadway at the Royale Theatre (and later the Longacre Theatre) December 8, 1965–November 23, 1968 playing 1,234 performances (see *Theatre World* Vol. 22, page 42).

SYNOPSIS *Cactus Flower* tells the story of Julian Winston, a handsome, middle-aged Park Avenue dentist and bachelor, who, to evade commitment, tells his much younger girlfriend Toni that he is married. When Toni demands to meet his fictional wife, hilarity ensues.

Maxwell Caulfield, Jenni Barber, Lois Robbins, and Anthony Reimer in Cactus Flower *(photo by Carol Rosegg)*

Play Nice!

59E59 Theater B; First Preview: March 8, 2011; Opening Night: March 15, 2011; Closed March 28, 2011

Written by Robin Rice Lichtig, based on Jean Genet's *The Maids*; Presented by Ego Actus Design; Director, Joan Kane; Set, Jason Simms; Lighting, Bruce Al Kraemer; Costumes, Cat Fisher; Sound, Ryan Kilcourse; PSM, Caitlyn Lyons; Press, Karen Greco

CAST Matilda **Lauren Roth**; Luce **Andrew Broussard**; Isabelle **Laura Hankin**; Joanie **Debby Brand**

SETTING Ridgewood, New Jersey. The present. New York premiere of a new play presented without intermission.

SYNOPSIS *Play Nice!* is a gothic fairy tale. Isabelle, Luce and Matilda live in a perfect home in an idyllic suburb. But when the front door closes, their home is far from ideal, and they spend most of their days hiding from their abusive mother in the attic. On Thanksgiving, Mother was poisoned. She is now on her way home from the hospital, and the children fear her wrath as she determines which child tried to kill her. Will their power of imagination, the most valuable weapon in their arsenal, be enough to cope with the Dragon Queen?

Lauren Roth and Laura Hankin in Play Nice! *(photo by Richard Termine)*

A Number

Cherry Lane Studio Theatre; First Preview: March 12, 2011; Opening Night: March 17, 2011; Closed April 3, 2011

Written by Caryl Churchill; Presented by National Asian America Theatre Company (NAATCO) (Mia Katigbak, Artistic Producing Director; Chrisoph Hahner, Co-Producer); Director/Costumes, Maureen Payne-Hahner; Set, Czerrton Lim; Lighting, D. Alex Bright; Sound, Kate Brown; Graphic Design, Matthew Grayson; Stage Manager, Clara Dalzell; Press, Sam Rudy Media Relations

CAST Salter **James Saito;** Bernard 1/Bernard 2/Michael Black **Joel de la Fuente**

Revival of a play presented without intermission. Originally presented at the Royal Court Theatre September 23, 2002. U.S. premiere of the play was presented at New York Theatre Workshop December 7, 2004 (see *Theatre World* Vol. 61, page 188.)

SYNOPSIS In *A Number*, Caryl Churchill explores the human experience, the essence of personality, and the nature verses nurture as a man confronts his father after discovering that he has several siblings – each one of his clones.

James Saito and Joel de la Fuenta in A Number *(photo by William P. Steele)*

A Tree Grows in Brooklyn

Theatre at St. Clements; First Preview: March 12, 2011; Opening Night: March 20, 2011; Closed April 10, 2011

Book by George Abbott and Betty Smith (based on her novel), revised book by Elinor Renfield, music by Arthur Scwartz, lryics by Dorothy Fields; New book revisions by Susan DiLallo; Presented by the Peccadillo Theatre Company (Dan Wakerman, Artistic Director; Kevin Kennedy, Managing Director; Sarahbeth Grossman, Executive Producer); Director, Dan Wackerman; Music Director, Kristen Blodgette; Choreography, Richard Stafford; Original Orchestrations, Joe Glover, Robert Russell Bennett; Set, Joseph Spirito; Lighting, Kate Ashton; Costumes, Amy C. Bradshaw; Sound, Jeremy Wilson; Graphic Design, Frank Dain; Dialects, David Wells; Dramaturg, Rick McKay; Associate Music Director, William Waldrop; Associate Choreography, Jonathan Stahl; General Manager, Tim Hurley; Production Manager, Greg Hirsch; PSM, Ernie Fimbres; ASM, Jeremy Neal; Casting, Jay Binder, Nikole Vallins; Wigs and Makeup, Sarah Levine; Properties, Paul Bourgeois; Press, Richard Kornberg & Associates

CAST Francie Nolan **Keaton Whittaker** Petey, Promenade Gentleman **Matthew Bauman**; Willie, Promenade Gentleman **Freddie Kimmel**; Allie, Promenade Gentleman **Johnny Stellard**; Hildy O'Dair **Lianne Marie Dobbs**; Katie Rommelly **Elizabeth Loycano**; Johnny Nolan **Jim Stanek**; Aloysius, Watermelon Peddler **Jason Simon**; Cissy Rommelly **Klea Blackhurst**; Oscar **Timothy Shew**; Nellie **Thursday Farrar**; Moriarty, Clothes Peddler, Priest, Neighborhood Man **Jack Doyle**; Mickey, Neighborhood Man, Promenade Lady **Christopher Kauffmann**; Max, Phineas White, Harry **John Weigand**; Neighborhood Woman, Gwen **Toni Elizabeth White**; Neighborhood Woman, Meg, Promenade Lady **Lauren Blackman**; Neighborhood Woman, Jill, Promenade Lady **Leah Landau**

MUSICIANS William Waldrop (Conductor/Piano), David Robison (Piano), Suzy Perleman (Violin/Viola), David Mancusso (Drums)

Jim Stanek (center), Michael McGurk, Johnny Stellard, and Matthew Bauman in A Tree Grows in Brooklyn (photo by Carol Rosegg)

MUSICAL NUMBERS Overture, Payday, Mine Till Monday, I'll Buy You a Star, Make the Man Love Me, Love Is the Reason, I'm Like a New Broom, Look Who's Dancing, If You Haven't Got a Sweetheart, Don't Be Afraid, I'll Buy You a Star (reprise), That's How It Goes, He Had Refinement, Growing Pains, Good Time Charley, If You Haven't Got a Sweetheart (reprise), Is That My Prince?, Make the Man Love Me (reprise), Good Time Charley (reprise), Nightmare Interlude, Love Is the Reason (reprise), Proud of You, Don't Be Afraid (reprise)

SETTING Williamsburg, Brooklyn; 1902 and 1914. Revival of a musical presented in fourteen scenes in two acts. Originally produced on Broadway at the Alvin Theatre (now the Neil Simon Theatre) in April 19–December 8, 1951 playing 267 performances (see *Theatre World* Vol. 7, page 109.)

SYNOPSIS For the first time in sixty years, the Peccadillo Theater presents a fully staged revival of *A Tree Grows in Brooklyn*, the poignant story of the Irish-American Nolan family. There's Johnny Nolan, a ne'er do well singer with dreams of Broadway glory, his wife, Katie, struggling to make a better life for her family, and twelve year-old Francie, an aspiring writer who relies on her imagination and her love of reading to get through hard times.

Between Worlds

New World Stages; First Preview: March 4, 2011; Opening Night: March 20, 2011; Closed May 22, 2011; 16 previews, 83 performances

Created, directed, and produced by Pablo Croce; Original Music, Diego Franco, Ernesto Briceno, Roberto Castillo; Additional Music, Pepe Perez, DJ Leo Castillo; Additional Choreography, Jesus Orto, Roberto Castillo, Brian Abadia; Dance Consultant, Candy Machado; Set, Neil Patel; Lighting, Jeff Croiter and Grant Yeager; Projections, Jan Hartley; Sound, Marcelo Anez; Flamenco Costume Designs, Siudy & Suidy Quintero; Urban Costume Design, Veronica Porras and Joey Rolon; Hair/Makeup, Javier Martinez; General Manager, Cesa Entertainment; Computer Animation, Esteban Mora; Production Supervisor, Production Core; PSM, Christine Catti; Production Supervisor, James E. Cleveland; Production Manager, Joshua Scherr; Associate General Manager, Diane Alianiello; ASM, Michael Hetzer; Advertising, Elizabeth Findlay; Marketing, HHC Marketing; Website and Social Media, Bay Bridge Productions; Press, O+M Company

CAST Starring **Siudy**; Featuring **Roberto Castillo, Adolpho Herrera, Joaquin Gomez, Michael Feigenbaum**; Flamenco Tribe **Anali Alcantara, Patricia Cinquemani, Claudia Gonzalez, Patricia Morean, Adriana Olivares, Natalia Novela, Daniela Rosi, Samantha Zerpa**; Urban Tribe **Brian Abadia, Aquiles Acosta, Omar Amado, Celina Beach, Tomas Ruiz, Melissa Sadler**

Off-Broadway engagement of a flemenco dance theatre piece presented in two acts.

SYNOPSIS *Between Worlds* bursts through artistic and cultural boundaries, transporting us to a future where water has all but disappeared and desperate tribes war with each other and the elements for survival. Only one force is powerful enough to save humanity from itself — love. Twenty-two performers from around the globe drum and dance in a kinetic and provocative blend of Flamenco, urban dance and percussion to create a multi-sensory theatrical experience for the whole family.

Siudy Garrido and the Company of Between Worlds (photo by Carol Rosegg)

Hello Again

52 Mercer; First Preview: March 4, 2011; Opening Night: March 20, 2011; Closed April 3, 2011

Words and Music by Michael John LaChiusa; Suggested by the play *La Ronde* by Arthur Schnitzler; Presented by The Transport Group (Jack Cummings III, Artistic Director; Lori Fineman, Executive Director) in association with Sarah Ackerman; Director, Jack Cummings III; Choreography, Scott Rink; Music Supervisor, Chris Fenwick; Music Director, Chris Harberl; Orchestrations, Mary-Mitchell Campbell; Drum/Percussion Arrangements, Damien Bassman; Set, Sandra Goldmark; Lighting, R. Lee Kennedy; Costumes, Kathryn Rohe; Sound, Michael Rasbury; Casting, Nora Brennan; Dramaturg, Kristina Corcoran Williams; PSM, Wendy Patten; Stage Manager, Donald Butchko; Production Manager, James Weinman; Assistant Director, Adam Blanshay; Dance Captain, Nikka Graff Lanzarone; Managing Producer, Michele Ellis; Associate Managing Producer, Greg Santos; Technical Director, Kyle Crose; Props, Ryan Morrison; Press, Richard Kornberg and Associates, Don Summa

CAST The Senator **Alan Campbell**; The Young Thing **Blake Daniel**; The Writer **Jonathan Hammond**; The Actress **Rachel Bay Jones**; The Whore **Nikka Graff Lanzarone**; The College Boy **Robert Lenzi**; The Young Wife **Alexandra Silber**; The Nurse **Elizabeth Stanley**; The Husband **Bob Stillman/Bruce Sabath**; The Soldier **Max von Essen**

ORCHESTRA Brett Macias (Music Prep Supervisor), Jeff Barone (Guitar), Summer Boggess (Cello), Chris Harberl (Piano), Harry Hassell (Reed), Brad Russell (Bass), David Vincola (Percussion

SCENES AND MUSICAL NUMBERS *The Whore and the Soldier:* Hello Again; *The Soldier and the Nurse:* Zei Gezent, I Gotta Little Time, We Kiss; *The Nurse and the College Boy:* In Some Other Life; *The College Boy and the Young Wife:* Story of My Life; *The Young Wife and the Husband:* At the Prom, Ah Maein Zeit, Tom; *The Husband and the Young Thing:* Listen to the Music; *The Young Thing and the Writer:* Montage, Safe, The One I Love; *The Writer and the Actress:* Silent Movie; *The Actress and the Senator:* Rock With Rock, Angel of Mercy, Mistress of the Senator; *The Senator and the Whore:* The Bed Was Not My Own, Hello Again (Reprise)

Revival of a musical presented in ten scenes without intermission. Originally presented at Lincoln Center Theater's Mitzi E. Newhouse Theater December 20, 1993–March 27, 1994 (see *Theatre World* Vol. 50, page 132).

SYNOPSIS 20 Lovers. 10 Affairs. 1 Century. Hello Again explores the passion, sex, and power of 10 love affairs, one from each decade of the 20th Century. Witness The Whore, The Young Thing, The Senator, The Soldier and others as they navigate each new sexual entanglement. Love and desire clash as each character seeks elusive connections. Inspired by Schnitzler's controversial 1897 play, *La Ronde*, LaChiusa brings Schnitzler's love stories to life with musical and lyrical styles of each decade, ranging from opera to jazz to disco. Transport Group's production, the first New York City revival is staged non-traditionally in a raw space in SoHo.

Laughing Liberally: This Ain't No Tea Party

Midtown Theatre at HA! Comedy Club; First Preview: March 14, 2011; Opening Night: March 24, 2011; Closed July 28, 2011

Created by David Alpert, Katie Halper, and Justin Krebs; Presented by Living Liberally; Director, Justin Krebs; Original Music, Jamie Jackson; Press, David Gersten

ROTATING CAST James Adomian, Scott Blakeman, Lee Camp, Rick Crom, Jim David, Will Durst, Brian Dykstra, Negin Farsad, John Fugelsang, Julie Goldman, Jamie Jackson, Katie Halper, Myq Kaplan, Jamie Kilstein, Dean Obeidallah, Harry Terjanian, Baratunde Thurston, Elon James White

Off-Broadway premiere of a comedy, multi-media, and musical show presented without intermission. Originally presented at The Tank in 2005.

SYNOPSIS *Laughing Liberally: This Ain't No Tea Party* is a comedy extravaganza, which mixes humor, musical numbers, video, and political satire to spread understanding of liberal ideas and advance progressive values. eaturing performers from Comedy Central, HBO, The Onion, The Huffington Post, and MTV, *Laughing Liberally: This Ain't No Tea Party* will save democracy one laugh at a time!

My Girlfriend's Boyfriend

Barrow Street Theatre; First Preview: March 18, 2011; Opening Night: March 31, 2011; Closed June 25, 2011; 6 previews, 75 performances

Written by Mike Birbiglia; Produced by Mike Berkowitz, Joseph Birbiglia, Mike Lavoie; Director, Seth Barrish; Set, Beowulf Boritt; Lighting, Aaron Copp; Lighting, Jim Corona; Board Operator, James Fauvell; Barrow Street Producers, Scott Morfee, Tom Wirtshafter; Marketing, Live Nation Entertainment; Press, Keith Sherman and Associates

Performed by **Mike Birbiglia**

World premiere of a new solo performance play presented without intermission.

SYNOPSIS On the heels of his succesful previous Off-Broadway show *Sleepwalk With Me* which played two seasons ago, Mike Birbiglia returns with his newest show, *My Girlfriend's Boyfriend*. Mike shares a lifetime of romantic blunders and miscues that most adults would spend a lifetime trying to forget. On this painfully honest journey, Mike struggles to find reason in an area where it may be impossible to find – love.

Elizabeth Stanley and Max Von Essen in Hello Again *(photo by Carol Rosegg)*

Mara Lilieas, Anna Stromberg (standing), Sarah Roy, and Jordan Tisdale in Bring Us the Head of Your Daughter *(photo by Larry Cobra)*

Mike Birbiglia in My Girlfriend's Boyfriend *(photo by Joan Marcus)*

Bring Us the Head of Your Daughter

PS 122; First Preview: March 31, 2011; Opening Night: April 2, 2011; Closed April 24, 2011

Written and directed by Derek Ahonen; Presented by The Amoralists (James Kautz, Derek Ahonen, Matthew Pilieci, Co-Artistic Directors; Kelcie Beene, Managing Director); Director of Production, Matthew Fraley; Set, Alfred Schatz; Lighting, Jeremy Pape; Costumes, Ricky Lang; Sound, The Hernandez Brother; Stage Manager, Lauren Jane Brown; Assistant Director, Christopher Wharton; Artwork, Alfred Schatz; Graphic Design, Brooke Aldrich; Crew Master, Sean Bauer; Spritual Advisor, Larry Cobra; Press, David Gibbs

CAST Contessa **Mara Lileas**; Jackie **Anna Stromberg**; Garance **Sarah Roy**; Drexel **Jordan Tisdale**

SETTING Jackie and Contessa's Grammercy Park apartment, NYC. World premiere of a new play presented

SYNOPSIS Jackie and Contessa are far from the typical American family. One black, one Jewish, and both women, they have overcome years of alcoholism and self-doubt to remain loving partners. But when their absent daughter Garance is accused of cannibalism, their apartment becomes a center of chaos. The phone rings relentlessly, Contessa's long-lost brother mysteriously reappears, and to top it all off, the alleged cannibal makes a grand entrance. *Bring Us the Head of Your Daughter* is a biting examination of an unconventional family and the outermost limits of familial love.

One Night with Fanny Brice

St. Luke's Theatre; First Preview: March 16, 2011; Opening Night: April 3, 2011; Closed August 20, 2011; 10, previews, 58 performances

Written, arranged, and directed by Chip Deffaa; Presented by Edmund Gaynes; Choreography, Justin Boccitto; Music Director, Richard Danley; Set, Josh Iacovelli; Costumes, Renee Purdy; Lighting, Graham Kindred; Press, David Gersten

Performed by **Kimberly Faye Greenberg**

MUSICIANS Richard Danley (Piano), Jonathan Russell (Violin)

MUSICAL NUMBERS That Mysterious Rag, I'm Always Chasing Rainbows, Bill Bailey Won't You Please Come Home?, Will You Love Me in December as You Do in May?, I'm Sorry I Made You Cry, When You Know You're Not Forgotten by the Girl You Can't Forget; Be My Little Baby Bumble Bee; Grizzly Bear, Lovie Joe, Rose of Washington Square, You Made Me Love You, I'm an Indian; Oh! How I Hate That Fellow Nathan, Second Hand Rose, Baby Won't You Please Come Home, A Pretty Girl Is Like a Melody, Ja-Da, My Man, After You've Gone

Off-Broadway premiere of a solo performance musical presented in two acts.

SYNOPSIS *One Night With Fanny Brice* chronicles Fanny Brice's rise from rather humble origins to become an internationally popular entertainer and the highest paid American singing comedienne - a Ziegfeld star equally effective whether putting over a broadly comic number or a dramatic torch song. A strong, intuitive, street-smart woman, Fanny Brice's life story provided the inspiration for the musical *Funny Girl*.

Kimberly Faye Greenberg in One Night with Fanny Brice *(photo by Carol Rosegg)*

The Promise

59E59 Theater B; First Preview: March 29, 2011; Opening Night: April 3, 2011; Closed April 17, 2011

Written by Douglas Maxwell; Presented by Random Accomplice and the Scottish Government; Director, Johnny McKnight; Set/Costumes, Lisa Sangster; Lighting, Dave Shea; Original Music/Sound, Karen MacIver; Projections, Tim Reid; Production Manager, Dave Shea; Stage Managers, Kay Hesford, Gary Morgan; Producer, Julie Brown; Press, Karen Greco

CAST Maggie Brodie **Joanna Tope**

U.S. premiere of a new solo performance play presented without intermission.

SYNOPSIS Maggie Brodie is a retired teacher who has been dragged back to her local primary school for a reluctant day of substitute teaching. Her craving for alcohol is strong and her opinion of her colleagues is rock bottom, so it's going to be a tough day. Then there's Rosie, a six year old Somalian girl who refuses to speak. Community leaders believe she is possessed and are on their way to start her 'treatment.' But Maggie, surprised by her connection to this girl, knows they are wrong. So wrong, that she is going to have to take drastic action.

Joanna Tope in The Promise *(photo by Niall Walker)*

Janie Condon: Raw & Unchained!

St. Luke's Theatre; First Preview: April 4, 2011; Opening Night: April 5, 2011; Closed May 17, 2011

Written by Janie Condon; Produced by Kim Vasquez/Gray Lady Entertainment; Director, Gus Kaikkonen; Sets, Josh Iacovelli; Costumes, Lisa Zinni; Lighting, Valentina Migoulia; Sound, Nick Borisjuk; Production Manager, Kelly Stillwell; Graphics, Doug Barron; Artwork, Klaus Steinkuhl; General Management, Gray Lady Entertainment; Press, Sam Rudy Media Relations, Bob Lasko

Performed by **Janie Condon**

Return engagement of a solo performance play presented without intermission. The show was workshopped at Ensemble Studio Theatre and was performed at Theatre 3 (Mint Space) May 2010 for four performances.

SYNOPSIS *Janie Condon: Raw & Unchained!* is the hilarious and moving account of Jane's journey through comedy and a family life that was, by turns, colorful and complex. And there are many reasons why Jane has been a storyteller and comedian all her life: wanting attention as the youngest of four in an Irish Catholic brood, a father in the FBI, not being voted funniest in high school and the real reason - a long-held family secret. She learned comedy at the knees of the masters: her fellow students at Cardinal Spellman High School in Brockton, Massachusetts.

Janie Condon (photo by Josh Manning)

Love Song

59E59 Theater A; First Preview: April 5, 2011; Opening Night: April 13, 2011; Closed May 8, 2011

Written and directed by John Kolvenbach; Produced by Jaimie Mayer Phinney/ Don't Eat The Pictures Productions in association with Wellfleet Harbor Actors Theater as part of the 2011 Americas Off Broadway; Set/Lighting, Ji-Youn Chang; Costumes, Deborah Newhall; Sound, Colin Whitely; Props, Mary Fritz; Original Music, Jonathan Bell; Press, Karen Greco

CAST Beane **Andrew Pastides**; Harry **Ian Barford**; Joan **Laura Latreille**; Molly **Zoe Winters**

New York premiere of a new play presented without intermission.

SYNOPSIS Beane is an exile from life — an oddball. His well-meaning sister, Joan, and brother-in- law, Harry, try and make time for him in their busy lives, but no one can get through. Following a burglary on Beane's apartment, Joan is baffled to find her brother blissfully happy and tries to unravel the story behind his mysterious new love, Molly.

Andrew Pastides, Ian Barford, and Laura Latreille in Love Song *(photo by Jeff Larkin)*

Nicholas Bruder and Sophie Bortolussi in Sleep No More *(photo by Yaniv Schulman)*

Sleep No More

McKittrick Hotel; First Preview: March 7, 2011; Opening Night: April 13, 2011; Still playing as of May 31, 2011

Created by Punchdrunk; Produced by Emursive (Randy Weiner, Arthur Karpati, and Jonathan Hochwald) in association and Rebecca Gold Productions and Douglas G. Smith; Directors, Felix Barrett and Maxine Doyle; Design, Felix Barrett, Livi Vaughan, Beatrice Minns; Choreography, Maxine Doyle; Sound, Stephen Dobie; Lighting, Felix Barrett, Euan Maybank, Austin R. Smith; Costumes, David Israel Reynoso, Becka Landau; Assistant Designers, Zoe Franklin, Lucia Rosenwald; Associate Choreographer, Conor Doyle; Senior Event Manager, Carolyn Rae Boyd; Production Consultant, Colin Nightingale; Supervising Producer, Vance Garrett

CAST Macbeth/Porter **Eric Jackson Bradley** or **Nicholas Bruder**; Macduff/Bellhop/Mr. Bargarran **Luke Murphy** or **John Sorensen-Jolink**; Lady Macbeth/Agnes Naismith **Sophie Bortolussi** or **Tori Sparks**, Lady Macduff/Matron **Isadora Wolfe** or **Lucy York** or **Alli Ross**; Banquo/J. Fulton **Gabriel Forestieri** or **Jeffery Lyon**; Bald Witch/Catherine Campbell **Kelly Bartnik** or **Hope T. Davis**; Boy Witch/Speakeasy Barman **Jordan Morley** or **Paul Singh**; Constance DeWinter/Matron/Hecate (swing) **Maya Lubinsky**; Malcolm **Rob Najarian** or **Adam Scher** or **Benjamin Thys**; Duncan **Phil Atkins**; Maximilian Martell **Nicholas Atkinson** or **Alexander Silverman**; Hecate **Careena Melia**; Porter/Orderly/Malcolm/Macduff/Speakeasy Barman **Matthew Oaks**; Sexy Witch/Nurse Shaw **Ching-I Chang**; Sexy Witch/Nurse Shaw/Lady Macbeth **Stephanie Eaton**; Violet **Elizabeth Romanski**; Swings **Natalie Thomas** (Lady Macbeth, Bald Witch, Agnes Naismith), **Marla Phelan** (Sexy Witch/Matron/Agnes Naismith/Catherine Campbell), **Ted Johnson** (J. Fulton/Speakeasy Barman/Bellhop/Mr. Bargarran/Orderly/Porter), **Conor Doyle** (Boy Witch)

*Nearly the entire company performs every performance, but all alternate roles. Listed here are the actors who most often play the specific role, though many have played other roles as well.

New York premiere of an immersive theatre and performance installation. Originally presented in London at the Beaufoy Building in 2003 and in 2009 in collaboration with American Repertory Theatre in Boston at the Old Lincoln School in Brookline.

SYNOPSIS London's Punchdrunk expands their 2003 film noir-inspired *Sleep No More*, based on *Macbeth*, and creates a unique theatrical experience in three former Chelsea Warehouses which have been converted into the fictional "McKittrick Hotel." *Sleep No More* takes a non-linear approach to its storytelling, allowing theatergoers to freely explore the environment, where scenes, tableaux and scenarios play out, conjuring the world and themes of Shakespeare's bloody tale. The audience, in mask, moves at their own pace, creating a unique journey for each theatre goer, as they navigate up and down stairs, through dimly lit furniture cluttered rooms and corridors, and dim passages.

Black Watch

St. Ann's Warehouse; Opening Night: April 14, 2011; Closed May 8, 2011; 24 performances

Written by Gregory Burke; Presented by the National Theatre of Scotland (Vicky Featherstone, Artistic Director) and St. Ann's Warehouse (Susan Feldman, Artistic Director) in association with Affinity Company Theater; Director, John Tiffany; Associate Directors, Steven Hoggett (movement), Davey Anderson (music); Sets, Laura Hopkins; Costumes, Jessica Brettle; Lighting, Colin Grenfell; Video, Leo Warner and Mark Grimmer for Fifty Nine Prods.; Company Stage Manager, Carrie Hutcheon; Deputy Stage Manager, Sarah Alford-Smith; ASM, Fiona Kennedy; Casting, Anne Henderson; Production Manager, Owen Hughes; Company Manager, Keren-Or Reiss; Technical Director, Bill Kennedy; Production Coordinator, Aaron Rosenblum; Press, Blake Zidell & Associates

CAST Macca **Cameron Barnes**; Stewarty **Chris Starkie**; Fraz **Jamie Quinn**; Kenzie **Scott Fletcher**; Lord Elgin/The Officer **Ian Pirie**; Writer/Sergeant **Adam McNamara**; Rossco **Ross Anderson**; Nabsy **Stuart Martin**; Cammy **Jack Lowden**; Granty **Richard Rankin**; Understudy **Paul Tinto**

Second return engagement of a play presented without intermission. Previously presented at St. Ann's October 20–November 11, 2007 (see *Theatre World* Vol. 64, page 118) and October 9–December 21, 2008 (see *Theatre World* Vol. 65, page 149).

SYNOPSIS *Black Watch* follows the disassembling of Scotland's most esteemed regiment over the course of its final tour in Iraq, written from the personal testimonies of ten men on the ground. *Black Watch* reveals what it really means to be part of the War on Terror and what it means to make the journey home again. Lyrical and loaded with testosterone, the production makes powerful and inventive use of movement, music and song to create a visceral, complex and urgent piece of theater.

The cast of Black Watch *(photo by Manuel Harlan)*

Reading Under the Influence:
The "Real" Westchester Women's Book Club

DR2; First Preview: April 6, 2011; Opening Night: April 16, 2011; Closed May 29, 2011

Written by Tony Glazer; Produced by Choice Theatricals; Director, Wendy C. Goldberg; Sets, Alexander Dodge; Lighting, Raquel Davis; Costumes, Anne Kennedy; Sound, Matt Hubbs; Props, Barb Kielhofer; Production Manager, Jeff Benish; PSM, Meredith Dixon; ASM, Fran Rubenstein; Casting, Judy Bowman; General Manager, Cheyl Dennis; Company Manager, Dan Gallagher; Advertising, The Pekoe Group; Press, Springer Associates

CAST Jocelyn Anders **Joanna Bayless**; Sara Chambers **Summer Crockett Moore**; Kerry **Ashley Austin Morris**; Margrit Somosa-Williams **Maria-Christina Oliveras**; Megan Goldstein **Barbara Walsh**; Carson Todlene **Jeremy Webb**

UNDERSTUDIES Harris Doran (Carson), Julie Leedes (Sara, Kerry, Margrit), Pat Patterson (Jocelyn, Megan)

SETTING The Westchester home of Jcelyn Anders. World premiere of a new play presented in two acts.

Ashley Austin Morris, Barbara Walsh, and Summer Crockett Moore
in Reading Under the Influence: The "Real" Westchester Women's Book Club
(photo by Orlando Behar)

SYNOPSIS In *Reading Under the Influence*, the wine hits the fan as the women of the Westchester Book Club gather to discuss their current required reading, *The Homeless Dogs of Egypt*. During their chardonnay-fueled discussion, they find out that the rights to their book club have been sold to a reality TV production company. It's the "The Real Housewives" meets "Oprah." Don't judge a book club by its cover... you never know how the pages will turn!

Triangle

59E59 Theater C; First Preview: April 14, 2011; Opening Night: April 20, 2011; Closed May 1, 2011

Written by Jack Gilhooley and Daniel Czitrom; Presented by Big Tim Productions in association with The Great American Play Series as part of the 2011 Americas Off Broadway; Director, Stephen Morrow; Press, Karen Greco

CAST Esther/Flossie **Ruba Audeh**; Cathleen Murphy **Donna Davis**; Izzy Weissman **Dennis Wit**; Margaret Holland **Ashley C. Williams**; "Big Tim" Sullivan **Joe Gately**; Mary Catherine **Michaela McPherson**

New York City and Albany, New York; 1900-1913. New York premiere of a new play presented in two acts.

SYNOPSIS Turn-of-the-century New York's political underworld and immigrant energy come to life in this new play focused on the tumultuous love affair between the legendary political boss 'Big Tim' Sullivan, roguish and colorful 'King of the Bowery,' and the beautiful actress and reformer Margaret Holland. After years of an adulterous affair that produced a daughter, the notorious Tammany Hall power broker and the Seven Sisters' graduate find themselves inextricably bound by the Triangle Shirtwaist Factory fire of 1911.

Ashley C. Williams, Joe Gately, and Donna Davis in Triangle
(photo by Carol Rosegg)

Under Construction

Dance Theatre Workshop; First Preview: April 21, 2011; Opening Night: April 23, 2011; Closed May 7, 2011; 2 previews, 13 performances

Written by Charles Mee; Created, presented, and performed by SITI Company; Director, Anne Bogart; Set, Neil Patel; Costumes, James Schuette; Lighting/Video, Brian H. Scott; Soundscape, Darron L West; PSM, Kris Longley-Postema; Production Manager, Megan Caplan; Production Assistant, Dave Sleswick; Music Director, Eben Hoffer; Associate Producers, Roberta Pereira, David Roberts; Executive Director, Megan Wanlass Szalla

CAST **Akiko Aizawa, J. Ed Araiza, Leon Ingulsrud, Ellen Lauren, Tom Nelis, Barney O'Hanlon, Makela Spielman, Samuel Stricklen, Stephen Duff Webber**

SETTING America in the 50s and the present., the red states and blue states, where we grew up and where we live today. New York premiere of new play presented without intermission.

SYNOPSIS Juxtaposing the fifties and the present, the *Under Construction* retraces the historical move from Noman Rockwell to installation artist Jason Rhoades while offering a portrait of a nation that is constantly reinventing itself – or permanently 'under construction.' A meta-collection of scenes from America, it interpolates image and ideas of past generations – from Rockwell's nostalgic Thanksgiving dinner and barbershop scenes to 1950s lessons in etiquette dating – with blogging and postmodern art. Throughout the play, actors build rickety constructions out of found objects to create a physical artistic installation piece which by the end incorporates all the props on stage.

Justin Preston and Marley McClean in Julia *(photo by Alex Moy)*

The SITI Company in Under Construction *(photo by Michael Brosilow)*

Julia

59E59 Theater B; First Preview: April 21, 2011; Opening Night: April 27, 2011; Closed May 15, 2011

Written by Vince Melocchi; Presented by Pacific Resident Theatre (California) as part of the 2011 Americas Off Broadway; Director, Guillermo Cienfuegos; Set, Norman Scott; Lighting, William Wilday; Sound, Keith Stevenson and Guillermo Cienfuegos; PSM, Angela Fong; Associate Producers, Dan Cole, Melody Fernandez; Press, Karen Greco

CAST Lou **Richard Fancy**; Steve **Keith Stevenson**; Frank **Haskell Vaughn Anderson III**; Young Julia **Marley McClean**; Young Lou **Justin Preston**; Julia **Roses Prichard**

SETTING McKeesport, Pennsylvania; the present and 50 years earlier. New York premiere of a new play presented without intermission. World premiere at Pacific Resident Theatre December 4, 2010–April 10, 2011 prior to this engagement.

SYNOPSIS *Julia* is a touching and tender examination of a 50-year-old-love lost and reclaimed. After years of self-exile in Detroit, Lou Perino returns to his hometown in Pennsylvania to right a wrong he did 50 years ago to Julia, the girl he loved. Once, the Korean War stood in their way. Now it's something entirely different. This beautiful love story delicately explores the nature of forgiveness, grief and redemption.

Be a Good Little Widow

Ars Nova; First Preview: April 20, 2011; Opening Night: May 2, 2011; Closed May 14, 2011; 9 previews, 10 performances

Written by Bekah Brunstetter; Presented by Ars Nova (Jason Eagan, Artistic Director; Jeremy Blocker, Managing Director); Director, Stephen Brackett; Set, Daniel Zimmerman; Costume, Jessica Pabst; Lighting, Burke Brown; Sound, Bart Fasbender; PSM, Bryan Bradford; ASM, Catherine Anne Tucker; Casting, MelCap Casting; Associate Artistic Director, Emily Shooltz; General Manager, Ann Marshall; Production Manager, Joshua Kohler; Marketing, Claire Graves; Development, Cameron Kroll; Artistic Coordinator, Jocelyn Florence; Production Associate, Jon Rubin; Props, Jon Knust; Assistant Director, Reed Whitney; Technical Director, Joel Howell; Press, Bridget Kaplinski

CAST Hope **Jill Eikenberry**; Craig **Chad Hoeppner**; Brad **Jonny Orsini**; Melody **Wrenn Schmidt**

World premiere of a new play presented without intermission.

SYNOPSIS Melody thought being a young wife was hard, until she became a widow. Luckily her mother-in-law is a professional – mourner, that is. As Melody navigates the prickly terrain of pressed black dresses, well-meant advice and inappropriate outbursts, she stumbles toward understanding what it means to find someone through losing them. *Be a Good Little Widow* is a sad comedy about handling loss like a grownup.

Chad Hoeppner, Wrenn Schmidt, and Jill Eikenberry in Be a Good Little Widow *(photo by Ben Arons)*

Little Black Dress

Theatre at St. Clements; First Preview: May 1, 2011; Opening Night: May 5, 2011; Closed May 28, 2011

Written by Ronan Noone; Presented by The Exchange; Producer, Kelcie Beene; Director, Ari Edelson; Set/Costumes, Dane Laffrey; Lighting, Christopher Studley; Sound, Bart Fasbender; Associate Producer, David Paarlberg; Stage Manager, Michael Alifanz

CAST Amy Beaudreaux **Nina Hellman**; Jimmy Beaudreaux **Daniel Oreskes**; Jimmy Beaudreaux Jr. **Tobias Segal**; Charley Prescott **Brian J. Smith**

SETTING Blue River, Kansas. New York premiere of a new play presented without intermission.

SYNOPSIS *Little Black Dress* is a funny, dark and poignant look at the sacrifices one makes when one leaves behind all that is familiar. Set in a rural Kansas home, the story centers on frustrated waitress, Amy Beaudreaux, who lives with her boorish husband, their slacker pot-smoking son and his buddy, a gigolo.

Brian J. Smith and Nina Hellman in Little Black Dress *(photo by Kerry Long)*

City Love Song

59E59 Theater C; First Preview: May 3, 2011; Opening Night: May 6, 2011; Closed May 15, 2011

Written and created by Jack Finnegan; Presented by Four Fins Ink as part of the 2011 Americas Off Broadway; Director, Tralen Doler; Press, Karen Greco

Performed by **Jack Finnegan**

Parts One (New York) and Two (America) of a theatrical cycle on travel and storytelling presented without intermission. The second cycle had its world premiere at 59E59 in the summer of 2010 as part of the East to Edinburgh Festival. Part One, previously presented in 2009.

SYNOPSIS *City Love Song* is traveler's tale of America, a story drawn from 13 weeks of railroad track and city sidewalks. Jack Finnegan presents a portrait of our country, constructed from the character of 24 American cities and the land and waters between them.

Jack Finnegan in City Love Song *(photo by Carol Rosegg)*

Murrow's Boys

Irondale Center; First Preview: April 27, 2011; Opening Night: May 6, 2011; Closed June 3, 2011

Written and directed by Jim Niesen; Presented by Irondale Ensemble (Terry Greiss, Executive Director; Jim Niesen, Artistic Director); Set, Ken Rothchild; Lighting, Randy Glickman; Technical Director, Michael DeSerio; PSM, Maria Knapp; Assistant Design, Steve Brenman; Electrics, Brian Ireland, John H. Kirman, Ariel Pierce, Amy Singerman

CAST **Scarlet Maressa Rivera**, **Michael-David Gordon**, **Terry Greiss**, **Patrina Murray**, **Kate Garfield**, **Gabriel King**, **Paul Leopold**, **Alex Miyashiro**

World premiere of a new theatrical piece presented in two acts.

SYNOPSIS Edward R. Murrow and the 'boys' (which included one girl) created the field of broadcast journalism as we know it today by bringing the story of WW II home to Americans. The Irondale Ensemble's new devised theater piece uses the words and deeds of these intrepid reporters to investigate the questions: Is news important today, where do we get it and why should it matter? This is the story of Murrow, Shirer, Collingwood, Sevareid, Hottelet, Smith and others like them for whom the need to get intelligent information and analysis of world events was not just a career, it was an adventure.

Paul Leopold in Murrow's Boys
(photo by Gerry Goodstein)

Channeling Kevin Spacey

St. Luke's Theatre; First Preview: April 17, 2011; Opening Night: May 15, 2011; 8 previews, 5 performances as of May 31, 2011

Written by Elan Wolf Farbiarz and Cory Terry; Presented by Wolf & William Productions; Director, Elan Wolf Farbiarz; General Manager, Jessimeg Productions; Stage Manager/Technical Director, Josh Iacovelli; Graphics, Micah Logsdon; Press, John Capo

CAST Charlie **Justin R.G. Holcomb**; Multiple Characters **Jamil Chokachi**

Off-Broadway premiere of a new play presented without intermission. World premiere at the 2008 Winnipeg Fringe Festival. U.S. premiere at Broward Center for the Performing Arts (Ft. Lauderdale) in 2010.

SYNOPSIS In *Channeling Kevin Spacey* we meet Charlie, a meek pushover stuck in a dead end job and a loveless relationship. After a particularly soul-squashing day at work, Charlie has an epiphany and resolves to change his life. Fans of Kevin Spacey and Al Pacino are in for a treat as Charlie's adventure channels the characters of both actors, triggering devastating and hilarious confrontations.

Jamil Chokachi and Justin R.G. Holcomb in Channeling Kevin Spacey *(photo by Warren Chow)*

The Sphinx Winx

Beckett Theatre on Theatre Row; First Preview: May 3, 2011; Opening Night: May 18, 2011; Closed June 19, 2011; 15 previews, 35 performances

Book by Philip Capice, Robert Keuch, and Anne Hitchner; Music by Kenneth Hitchner Jr; Lyrics by Philip Capice, Kenneth Hitchner Jr, and Robert Keuch; Presented by Tifft Productions; Executive Producer, R. Erin Craig; Director, Matthew Hamel; Choreographer, Tara Jeanne Vallee; Music Director/Arrangements, Jeffrey Lodin; Sets, Robert Andrew Kovach; Costumes, Gail Baldoni; Lighting, Annmarie Duggan; Sound, David Margolin Lawson; Stage Manager, Heather Hogan; ASM, Amanda Susan Johnson; Orchestrations, Doug Katsaros; Dramaturg, Eric C. Webb; Casting, Clemmons/Dewing Casting; Marketing/Advertising, The Pekoe Group; Production Supervisor, Production Core; General Manager, La Vie Productions; Press, Sam Rudy Media Relations

CAST Cleopatra **Erika Amato**; Crecia/Enobarbus **Rebecca Riker**; Julius Caesar/Doctor **Bruce Sabath**; Marc Antony/Guard/Doctor **Bret Shuford**; Lunia/Laurel/Judge **Beth Cheryl Tarnow**; Soothsayer/Marius/Emtius/Etc. **Ryan Williams**

MUSICAL NUMBERS Prologue, Queen of Today, Always Get It Right, Count the Ways, Hail to Thee, Did You Ever, Must Be Falling in Love, Farewell Ladies, One of These Days, Act Yourself, I Sail For Home, Always Get It Right (reprise), There's Gonna Be a Trial, Goodbye Julius, Goodbye Julius (reprise), Epilogue

Off-Broadway premiere of a new musical presented without intermission. An earlier version of the show played in 1952 at Dickinson College in Carlisle, Pennsylvania. The show was reworked in 2006 and had a showcase production in 2008 at the Algonquin Theatre, and two staged readings in March 2010 and January 2011.

SYNOPSIS A hilarious romp through history, *The Sphinx Winx* is a musical comedy misinterpretation of the classic love triangle among Julius Caesar, Cleopatra and Marc Antony. With the kingdom of Egypt horribly in arrears to the Roman government because of Caesar's frivolous spending on lavish gifts for his Queen of the Nile, Marc Antony is brought in to ascertain the cause and mete out justice. When the court's Soothsayer mistakenly forecasts that Antony will fall in love with Cleopatra, he unwittingly sets into motion a series of events the likes of which won't be found in any history books!

The cast of The Sphinx Winx *(photo by Peter James Zielinski)*

Lucky Guy

Little Shubert Theatre; First Preview: April 29, 2011; Opening Night: May 19, 2011; Closed May 29, 2011; 23 previews, 14 performances

Book, music, and lyrics by Williard Beckham; Produced by L. Glenn Poppleton; Director, Williard Beckham; Choreography, A.C. Ciulla; Music Superision/Orchestrations/Vocal Arrangements, Todd Ellison; Set, Rob Bissinger; Costumes, William Ivey Long; Lighting, Paul Miller; Sound, Kurt Fischer; Hair/Wigs, Paul Huntley; Casting, Janet Foster; Dance Music Arrangements, Mark Hummel; Music Director, Paul Staroba; Music Contractor/Coordinator, John Miller; General Manager, Alchemy Production Group, Carl Pasbjerg, and Frank Scardion; PSM, Bonnie Panson; Production Management, Juniper Street Productions; Stage Manager, Ryan J. Bell; Assistant Director, Jenn Rapp; Associate Choreographer, Sean Havens; Dance Captain, Wes Hart; Makeup Consultant, Angelina Avallone; Marketing Director, Leanne Schanzer; Advertising, Art Meets Commerce; Press, O+M Company

CAST The Buckaroos **Callan Bergmann, Xavier Cano, Wes Hart, Joshua Woodie**; Big Al Wright **Leslie Jordan**; Wanda Clark **Savannah Wise**; Chicky Lay **Jenn Collela**; Billy Ray Jackson **Kyle Dean Massey**; G.C. Wright **Jim Newman**; Miss Jeannie Jeannine **Varla Jean Merman**

UNDERSTUDIES Meggie Cansler (Wanda, Chicky), Zak Resnick (Billy Ray, G.C), Ryan Koss (Swing)

MUSICIANS Paul Staroba (Conductor/Keyboards), Maggie Torre (Associate Conductor/Keyboards), Bobby Baxmeyer & Nicholas DiFabbio (Guitars), Justin Smith (Fiddle/Mandolin), Ray Kilday (Bass), Frank Pagano (Drums/Percussion), Dave Noland (Woodwinds)

MUSICAL NUMBERS Overture, Nashville, Big Al, I'm Doin' Hair Today, Osage County Line, Lucky Guy, Folks Makin' Money, Blue Jean Blues, Folks Makin' Money (reprise #1), Queen of Country Music, Queen of Country Music (reprise), Needle in a Haystack, Folks Makin' Money (reprise #2), Do What You Can Do, Nashville (reprise), Louis From Kahului, Yo' A Little Lady, Find Him and Bring Him Home, Make Up His Mind, Rememberin' You, Trailer Park Romance, Chicky, My Ole Friend, Lucky Guy (reprise), My Lucky Guy, The Big Finale

SETTING Place: Nashville; Time: Not too long ago, back when the hits were big and the hairdos were bigger. New York premiere of a new musical presented in two acts. Developmental production at Goodspeed Musicals–Norma Terris Theatre in May 14, 2009 (see *Theatre World* Vol. 65, page 325).

SYNOPSIS Welcome to Nashville, a town full of colorful characters all chasing after the very same dream: a smash hit record. To beat the odds and strike gold (or, better yet, platinum), it takes one great song, serious talent, or lots of luck – and preferably all three. Featuring an array of musical styles with salutes to Country, Broadway, Vaudeville, Bluegrass, Pop, and even Hawaiian, *Lucky Guy* weaves a tale of down-home dreamers and low-down schemers all willing to do whatever it takes to come out on top in the cut-throat world of Music City, USA.

Leslie Jordan and Varla Jean Merman (aka Jeffrey Roberson) in Lucky Guy *(photo by Joan Marcus)*

I Married Wyatt Earp

59E59 Theater B; First Preview: May 20, 2011; Opening Night: May 24, 2011; Closed June 12, 2011; 3 previews, 18 performances

Book by Thomas Edward West and Sheilah Rae, lyrics by Sheilah Rae, music by Michael Brourman; Suggested in part by *I Married Wyatt Earp* edited and collected by Glenn G. Boyer; Presented by Prospect Theatre Company (Cara Reichel, Artistic Director; Melissa Huber, Managing Director; Peter Mills, Associate Artist/Resident Writer) and the New York Theatre Barn (Joe Barros, Producing Artistic Director; Julianne Alberty, Executive Director) as part of the 2011 Americas Off Broadway; Director, Cara Reichel; Choreography, Joe Barros; Set, Ann Bartek; Lighting, Jorge Arroyo; Costumes, Ryan J. Miller; Sound, Andy Leviss; Music Director, Remy Kurs; Stage Manager, Naomi Anhorn; Orchestrations, Bruce Coughlin; Production Manager, Jason Najjoum; Props, Elyse Handelman; Technical Director, Jak Prince; Assistant Director, Nick Brennan; Assistant Choreography, Laura Brandel; ASM, Caitlin Lyons; Press, Karen Greco

CAST Josie Earp **Carolyn Mignini**; Allie Earp **Heather Mac Rae**; Young Josie **Mishaela Faucher**; Mattie Earp **Anastasia Barzee**; Young Allie **Stephanie Paulumbo**; Bess Earp **Carol Linnea Johnson**; Hattie Earp **Laura Hankin**; Kate Haroney **Ariela Morgenstern**; Pauline Rackham **Tina Stafford**; Maude **Cara Massey**; Cora **Karla Mosley**; Penelope **Ariela Morgenstern**

MUSICAL NUMBERS Prologue, Don't Blame Me for That, Unpacking Dreams, Nothing Like the Girsl at Home, When a Maiden Makes a Promise, I Ain't Goin' Back, High Class Attraction, Mama Oh Mama, They Got Snakes Out Here, Pins and Needles, Don't Blame Me for That (reprise), Didya Hear?, Little Black Sheep, Mama Oh Mama (reprise), It's Different This Time, Pins and Needles (reprise), Don't Blame Me for That (reprise), In the Cards, Room to Breathe, The Dust, Games Are Everywhere, I'd Do It All Again, Stand Your Ground, Pins and Needles/Shootout, All These Years

BAND Remy Kurs (Conductor/Piano), Adam Waddell (Violin/Viola), Dan Erben (Guitar/Mandolin), Matt Scharfglass (Bass), Jeff Roberts (Percussion)

SETTING Los Angeles, Cailifornia, 1944; Tombstone, Arizona, 1879-1881. New York premiere of a new musical presnted in two acts. World premiere at Bristol Riverside Theatre (Pakeith Baker, Artistic Director; Susan D. Atkinson, Founding Producing Director). Developed by New York Theatre Barn in 2007.

SYNOPSIS Young Josie Marcus is nothing like the girls back home. Passionate and fearless, she leaves behind her upper class Jewish family for the adventure of Tombstone, Arizona—home of legendary lawman Wyatt Earp. Eleven gutsy women give voice to the untold story of the American frontier in this compelling new musical.

Carol Linnea Johnson, Stepanie Palumbo, and Anatasia Barzee in I Married Wyatt Earp *(photo by Gerry Goodstein)*

WTC View

59E59 Theater C; First Preview: May 19, 2011; Opening Night: May 24, 2011; Closed June 5, 2011

Written by Brian Sloan; Produced by WTC View Onstage, Brian Sloan, and 59E59 as part of the 2011 Americas Off Broadway; Director, Andrew Volkoff; Set, Brian Prather; Lighting, Jeff Davis; Costumes, Jacob Climer; Sound, David M. Lawson; Company Manager, George Heslin; Stage Manager, Carol Sullivan; Press, Karen Greco

CAST Kevin **Michael Carlsen**; Max **Martin Edward Cohen**; Josie **Leah Curney**; Jeff **Torsten Hillhouse**; Eric **Nick Lewis**; Alex **Patrick Edward O'Brien**; Jeremy **Bob Braswell**; *Voice Roles*: Will **Jay Gaussoin**; Carlos **Jorge Cordova**; Lorenzo **Nick Potenzieri**; Victor **Brian Prather**; Joey **Chad Miller**

SETTING New York City, September, 2011. Off-Broadway premiere of a new play presented without intermission. Originally presented at the 2003 New York International Fringe Festival.

SYNOPSIS On the night before 9/11, a young man living in SoHo places an ad for a roommate online. Then, the world changes. In his debut play, writer/filmmaker Brian Sloan gives a surprising and intimate glimpse of life in lower Manhattan during the strange days of September 2001.

The Best Is Yet to Come: The Music of Cy Coleman

59E59 Theater A; First Preview: May 18, 2011; Opening Night: May 25, 2011; Closed July 3, 2011

Music by Cy Coleman, lyrics by Alan and Marilyn Bergman, Betty Comden and Adolph Green, Dorothy Fields, Ira Gasman, Carolyn, Leigh, Michael Stewart and David Zippel; Devised and directed by David Zippel; Produced by the Rubicon Theatre Company (Karyl Lynn Burns and James O'Neil, Artistic Directors; Michael Jackowitz, Executive Producer) in association with David Elzer, Barbara Meister, Dottie and Bernie Novatt, Charles Hughen–Stage Too, Marvin Kahan, Normand Kurtz, and Dale Joan Young; Presented by 59E59 (Elysabeth Kleinhaus, Artistic Director; Peter Tear, Executive Director) as part of the 2011 Americas Off Broadway; Sets, Douglas W. Schmidt; Lighting, Michael Gilliam; Sound, Costumes, William Ivey Long; Sound, Jonathan Burke; Music Director/Arrangements, Billy Stritch; Orchestrations, Don Sebesky; Choreography, Lorin Latarro; PSM, Christina M. Burck; Press, Karen Greco

CAST **David Burnham**, **Sally Mayes**, **Howard McGillin**, **Billy Stritch**, **Lillias White**, **Rachel York**; Sub for Ms. Mayes **Natascia Diaz** (June 16-19)

THE BAND Billy Stritch (Conductor/Piano); Chuck Wilson, Nathan Childers, Frank Basile (Woodwinds); Ross Konikoff (Trumpet); Dan Levine (Trombone), Bob Renino (Bass); Scott Neuman (Drums)

New York premiere of a new musical revue presented without intermission. Originally presented at Ventura, California's Rubicon Theatre Company July 9–August 2, 2009.

SYNOPSIS The music of legendary Broadway composer Cy Coleman (who passed away in 2004) comes alive in this newly devised revue conceived by his *City of Angles* friend and collaboratoer, David Zippel. *The Best Is Yet to Come* dipped into the deep well of Coleman's catalog, offering classic and obscure numbers he wrote with a variety of lyricists. Coleman composed the scores of some of Broadway's best-loved shows, including *City of Angels*, *Sweet Charity*, *Barnum*, *The Life*, *The Will Rogers Follies*, and *Little Me*.

Billy Stritch (on piano), Lillias White, Howard McGillin, Sally Mayes, David Burnham, and Rachel York in The Best Is Yet to Come: The Music of Cy Coleman *(photo by Carol Rosegg)*

Nick Lewis and Patrick Edward O'Brien in WTC View *(photo by Carol Rosegg)*

PLAYED THROUGH / CLOSED THIS SEASON

The 39 Steps

New World Stages; First Preview: March 25, 2010; Opening Night: April 15, 2010; Closed January 16, 2011; 23, previews, 318 performances

Adapted by Patrick Barlow from the film by Alfred Hitchcock and the book by John Buchan; based on an original concept by Simon Corble and Nobby Dimon; Produced by Bob Boyett, Harriet Newman Leve, Richard Winkler/Dan Frishwasser, Pamela Laudenslager/Douglas Denoff, Jane Dubin, Olympus Theatricals, Tim Levy/Jennifer Isaacson, Manocherian Productions, Stewart F. Lane/Bonnie Comely, Remmel T. Dickinson, True Love Productions, Kevin Lyle, John Retsios, Marek J. Cantor/Probo Productions, Lary Brandt/Meredith Lucio in association with the Roundabout Theatre Company (Todd Haimes, Artistic Director; Harold Wolpert, Managing Director; Julia C. Levy, Executive Director), Huntington Theatre Company (Nicholas Martin, Artistic Director; Michael Maso, Managing Director), and Edward Snape for Fiery Angel Ltd.; Director, Maria Aitken; Set/Costumes, Peter McKintosh; Lighting, Kevin Adams; Sound, Mic Pool; Dialect Coach, Stephen Gabis; Original Movement, Toby Sedgewick; Additional Movement, Christopher Bays; Production Manager, Aurora Productions; PSM/Resident Director, Nevin Hedley; Casting, Jay Binder/Jack Bowdan; Marketing, HHC Marketing; Associate Producers, Emily Genduso, Howard Tilkin; General Manager, Roy Gabay; Stage Manager, Rosy Garner; Company Manager, Jennifer Pluff; Assistant Director, Kevin Bigger; Associate Design: Josh Zangen (set), Joel Silver (lighting), Drew Levy (sound); Advertising, SpotCo; Press, Boneau/Bryan-Brown, Adrian Bryan-Brown, Jessica Johnson, Jim Byk, Emily Meagher

CAST Man #1 **Jamie Jackson**; Man #2 **Cameron Folmar**; Richard Hannay **John Behlmann**; Annabella Schmidt/Pamela/Margaret **Kate MacCluggage**

UNDERSTUDIES Greg Jackson (Man #1, Man #2, Richard Hannay), Jane Pfitsch (Annabella Schmidt/Pamela/Margaret)

SETTING Scotland and London. Transfer of the Broadway comedy/thriller presented in two acts. Originally presented at the Tricycle Theatre in London in August 2006, and at Boston's Huntington Theatre Company September 14, 2007 prior its New York engagement. The show played a total of 771 performances on Broadway at the American Airlines Theatre (January 4–March 29, 2008) and a commercial run at the Cort Theatre and eventually the Helen Hayes Theatre (April 29, 2008–January 10, 2010) prior to this Off-Broadway transfer (see *Theatre World* Vol. 64, page 38 for original production credits).

Jamie Jackson, Cameron Folmar and John Behlmann in Alfred Hitchcock's The 39 Steps (photo by Carol Rosegg)

SYNOPSIS Four cast members play over 150 roles in this hilarious whodunit, part espionage thriller and part slapstick comedy. The story revolves around an innocent man who learns too much about a dangerous spy ring and is then pursued across Scotland and to London. *The 39 Steps* contains every legendary scene from the award-winning movie—the chase on the Flying Scotsman, the escape on the Forth Bridge, the first theatrical bi-plane crash ever staged, and the sensational death-defying finale in the London Palladium.

The Accidental Pervert

Players Theatre; First Preview: December 4, 2009; Opening Night: January 23, 2010; 13 previews, 178 performances as of May 31, 2011 (limited performance schedule)

Written by Andrew Goffman; Director, Charles Messina; Choreography, Sherri Norige; Audio/Visual Design, Andrew Wingert; Dramaturg, Liza Lentina; Production Coordinator, Gina Ferranti; Lighting, Shannon Epstein; Set/Technical Director, Anthony Augello; Graphic Design, Robert Tallon; Dialogue Coach, Stanley Harrison; Creative Assistant, Christy Benati; House Manager, Carlo Rivieccio; Press, Judy Jacksina

Performed by **Andrew Goffman**

Off-Broadway debut of a solo performance play presented without intermission. Originally workshopped at the 45th Street Theatre and eventually played Off-Off-Broadway at the Triad Theatre.

SYNOPSIS *The Accidental Pervert* is the true accounting of one boy's odyssey to manhood via a childhood dominated by pornography, an addiction accumulated after the boy happens upon his father's collection of XXX-Rated video tapes in a bedroom closet. Goffman takes his audience on a hilarious and self-deprecating journey into a world of his addiction to pornography until the age of 26, when he met his wife.

Andrew Goffman in The Accidental Pervert (photo by Drew Wingert)

Avenue Q

New World Stages; First Preview: October 9, 2009; Opening Night: October 21, 2010; 14, previews, 672 performances as of May 31, 2011

Music and lyrics by Robert Lopez and Jeff Marx, book by Jeff Whitty; Produced by Kevin McCollum, Robyn Goodman, Jeffrey Seller, Vineyard Theatre & The New Group; Director, Jason Moore; Choreography, Ken Roberson; Music Supervision/Orchestrations/Arrangements, Stephen Oremus; Music Director, Andrew Graham; Puppets Conception/Design, Rick Lyon; Set, Anna Louizos; Costumes, Mirena Rada; Lighting, Howell Binkley; Sound, Acme Sound Partners; Animation, Robert Lopez; Incidental Music, Gary Adler; Casting, Cindy Tolan; General Manager, Davenport Theatrical Enterprises; Production Manager, Travis Walker, Autonomous Production Services; PSM, Christine M. Daly; Marketing, Scott A. Moore; Stage Manager, James Darrah; ASM, Rob Morrison; Company Manager, Ryan Lympus; Resident Director, Evan Ensign; Dance Captain/Puppet Captain, Seth Rettberg; Associate Design: Todd Potter (set), Ryan O'Gara (lighting), Karl Ruckdeschel (costumes); Music Copying, Emily Grishman/Alex Lacamoire; Animation/Video Production, Sound Associates Inc., Sound & Video Design Effects, Brett Jarvis; Advertising, SpotCo; Press, Sam Rudy Media Relations; Broadway Cast recording: RCA 82876-55923-2

CAST Princeton/Rod **Seth Rettberg**[1]; Brian **Nicholas Kohn**; Kate Monster/Lucy the Slut & others **Sarah Stiles**[2]; Nicky/Trekkie Monster/Bad Idea Bear & others **Cullen Titmas**[3]; Christmas Eve **Ann Sanders**[4]; Gary Coleman **Haneefah Wood**; Mrs. T./Bad Idea Bear & others **Jennifer Barnhart**[5]; Ensemble **Katie Boren**[6], **Jed Resnick**; Swings **Erica Dorfler**[7], **Rob Morrison**[8]

*Succeeded by: 1. Adam Kantor (7/9/10) 2. Veronica Kuhn (7/20/10) 3. Rob Morrison 4. Hazel Ann Raymundo 5. Lexie Fridell, Ruthie Ann Miles 6. Ruthie Ann Miles, Kate Lippstreu (11/29/10) 7. Jasmin Walker 8. Michael Liscio

ORCHESTRA Andrew Graham (Conductor/keyboard); Randy Cohen (Associate Conductor/keyboard); Patience Higgins (reeds); Joe Choroszewski (drums)

MUSICAL NUMBERS Avenue Q Theme, What Do You Do With a BA in English?/It Sucks to be Me, If You Were Gay, Purpose, Everyone's a Little Bit Racist, The Internet Is for Porn, Mix Tape, I'm Not Wearing Underwear Today, Special, You Can Be as Loud as the Hell You Want (When You're Making Love), Fantasies Come True, My Girlfriend, Who Lives in Canada, There's a Fine, Fine Line, There Is Life Outside Your Apartment, The More You Ruv Someone, Schadenfreude, I Wish I Could Go Back to College, The Money Song, For Now

SETTING An outer borough of New York City; the present. A musical presented in two acts. Originally presented Off-Broadway March 19, 2003 at the Vineyard Theatre (see *Theatre World* Vol. 59, page 179). Transferred to Broadway at the John Golden Theatre July 10, 2003–September 13, 2010, playing 2,534 performances (see *Theatre World* Vol. 60, page 25 for original Broadway credits). This unprecedented transfer back to Off-Broadway marked the first time a Broadway musical has moved to an Off-Broadway theatre.

SYNOPSIS *Avenue Q* is about real life: finding a job, losing a job, learning about racism, getting an apartment, getting kicked out of your apartment, being different, falling in love, promiscuity, avoiding commitment, and internet porn. Twenty and thirty-something puppets and humans survive life in the big city and search for their purpose in this naughty but timely musical that features "full puppet nudity!"

The Awesome 80s Prom

Webster Hall; First Preview: July 23, 2004 (Friday evenings only); Opening Night: September 10, 2004 (Fridays and Saturdays); 369 performances as of May 31, 2011 (Saturdays only)

Written and produced by Ken Davenport; Co-Authored by The Class of '89 (Sheila Berzan, Alex Black, Adam Bloom, Anne Bobby, Courtney Balan, Mary Faber, Emily McNamara, Troy Metcalf, Jenna Pace, Amanda Ryan Paige, Mark Shunock, Josh Walden, Noah Weisberg, Brandon Williams, Simon Wong and Fletcher Young); Director, Ken Davenport; Choreography, Drew Geraci; Costumes, Randall E. Klein; Lighting, Martin Postma; Production Stage Manager, Carlos Maisonet; Associate Producers, Amanda Dubois, Jennifer Manocherian; Company Manager, Matt Kovich; ASM, Kathryn Galloway; Casting, Daryl Eisenberg; Press, David Gersten & Associates

CAST Johnny Hughes – The DJ **Dillon Porter**; Lloyd Parker – The Photographer **Daryl Embry**[1]; Dickie Harrington – The Drama Queen **Bennett Leak**; Michael Jay – The Class President **Craig Jorczak**; Mr. Snelgrove – The Principal **Thomas Poarch**; Molly Parker – The Freshman **Lauren Schafler**[2]; Inga Swanson – The Swedish Exchange Student **Lindsay Ryan**; Joshua "Beef" Beefarowski – A Football Player **Michael Barra**; Whitley Whitiker – The Head Cheerleader **Jessica West Regan**; Nick Fender – The Rebel **Brandon Marotta**; Heather #1 – A Cheerleader **Jenny Peters**[3]; Heather #2 – The Other Cheerleader **Kate Wood Riley**; Kerrie Kowalski – The Spaz **Missy Diaz**; Melissa Ann Martin – Head of the Prom Committee **Angie Blocher**[4]; Louis Fensterpock – The Nerd **Nick Austin**[5]; Blake Williams – Captain of the Football Team **Jason Carden**[6]; Mrs. Lascalzo – The Drama Teacher **Andrea Biggs**; Feung Schwey – The Asian Exchange Student **Anderson Lim**; The Mystery Guest **CP Lacey**

*Succeeded by: 1. Alex Fast 2. Pamela Macey 3. Joanne Nosuchinsky 4. Lauren Schafler 5. Daryl Embry 6. Chris Cafero

SETTING Wanaget High's Senior Prom, 1989. An interactive theatrical experience presented without intermission

SYNOPSIS The Captain of the Football Team, the Asian Exchange Student, the Geek, and the Head Cheerleader are all competing for Prom King and Queen. The audience decides who wins while moonwalking to retro hits from the decade.

Lucy the Slut and Sarah Stiles in Avenue Q (photo by Carol Rosegg)

Black Angels Over Tuskegee

Actors Temple Theatre[+]; First Preview: January 29, 2010; Opening Night: February 15, 2010; Closed open; 6 previews, 178 performances as of May 31, 2011 (limited schedule)

Written and directed by Layon Gray; Produced by The Black Gents of Hollywood, Edmund Gaynes, and The Layon Gray Experience; Set, Josh Iacovelli; Costumes, Jason McGee; Lighting, David Boykins & Graham Kindred; Sound, Aidan Cole; General Management, Jessimeg Productions, Julia Beardsley; PSM, Bonnie Hilton; Technical Operator, Jonathon Santos; Choreography/Movement, Layon Gray; Set Dressing/Props, Gayle Lowe; Assistant to Writer, Jackie Coleman; Assistant to Director, Maria Canidy; Casting, Karrie Moore; Advertising, Epstein-Obrien; Press, David Gersten & Associates, Jim Randolph

CAST Man **Thaddeus Daniels**; Quenten Dorsey **Layon Gray**; Abraham Dorsey **Thom Scott II**; Theodore Franks **David Wendell Boykins** or **Anaias Dixon**; Elijah Sams **Lamman Rucker** or **Lawrence Saint-Victor** or **Jay Jones**; Jerimah Jones **Melvin Huffnagle**; Percival Nash **David Roberts** or **Tobias Truvillion**; Sgt. Roberts **Steve Brustein**

UNDERSTUDIES Stephon Pettyway (Quenten), Reggie Barnes (Jerimah), Jeantique Oriol (Elijah), Rob Morgan (Man), David Roberts (Abe), Annanias Dixon (Theodore), Craig Colasanti, Reginald Wilson, Greg Casimir, Andrew Mathews, Tobias Truvillion, Reginald L. Barnes

New York premiere of a new play presented in two acts. World premiere presented at the Whitmore Lindley Theatre Center in North Hollywood October 10–19, 2008 and January 31–March 1, 2009.

SYNOPSIS In *Black Angels Over Tuskegee*, which is based on true events, six men explore their collective struggle with Jim Crow, their intelligence, patriotism, dreams of an inclusive fair society, and brotherhood as they become the first African American fighter pilots in the U.S. Army Air Forces.

+ The production originally opened at the Theatre at St. Luke's and transferred to the Actors Temple Theater on June 5, 2011.

Blue Man Group

Astor Place Theatre; Opening Night: November 7, 1991; Closed open; 10 previews, 10,600 performances as of May 31, 2011

Created and written by Matt Goldman, Phil Stanton, Chris Wink; Produced by Blue Man Productions; Director, Marlene Swartz and Blue Man Group; Artistic Directors, Caryl Glaab, Michael Quinn; Artistic/Musical Collaborators, Larry Heinemann, Ian Pai; Set, Kevin Joseph Roach; Costumes, Lydia Tanji, Patricia Murphy; Lighting, Brian Aldous, Matthew McCarthy; Sound, Raymond Schilke, Jon Weston; Computer Graphics, Kurisu-Chan; Video, Caryl Glaab, Dennis Diamond; PSM, Patti McCabe; Company Manager, Akia Squitieri; Stage Managers, Bernadette Castro, Jenny Lynch; Resident General Manager, Leslie Witthohn; General Manager of North American Productions, Alison Schwartz; Performing Director, Chris Bowen; Performing Directors, Chris Bowen, Michael Dahlen, Randall Jaynes, Jeffrey Doornbos, Brian Scott; Original Executive Producer, Maria Di Dia; Casting, Deb Burton; Press, Tahra Milan

CAST (rotating) **Kalen Allmandinger**, **Gideon Banner**, **Collin Batten**, **Chris Bowen**, **Wes Day**, **Michael Dahlen**, **Isaac Eddy**, **Josh Elrod**, **Matt Goldman**, **Randall Jaynes**, **General Judd**, **Peter Musante**, **Matt Ramsey**, **Pete Simpson**, **Scott Speiser**, **Phil Stanton**, **Chris Wink**

MUSICIANS (rotating) Tom Shad, Geoff Gersh, Clem Waldmann, Dan Dobson, Jeff Lipstein, Byron Estep, Matt Hankle, Tommy Kessler, Jerry Kops, Josh Matthews, Jordan Perlson, Jano Rix, Clifton Hyde, Dave Steele

An evening of performance art presented without intermission. For original production credits see *Theatre World* Volume 48, Page 90.

SYNOPSIS The three-man new-vaudeville Blue Man Group combines comedy, music, art, and multimedia to produce a unique form of entertainment.

The Complete Performer

SoHo Playhouse Huron Club; Opening Night: December 19, 2009; Closed open; 72 performances as of May 31, 2011 (Saturday evenings)

Written by Ted Greenberg, and Mike Motz; Presented by Matt Wayne; Director/Writing Consultant, Steve Rosenfield; Lighting/Stage Manager, Kate August; Production Design, Bestar Mujaj and Matt Wayne; Choreographer, Mike Motz; Website, Stephen Bittrich; Graphics, Jessica Disbrow Talley, Wade Dansby; Technical Director, Bestar Mujaj; Props, Saz Freymann, Ien Denio; Press, Lanie Zipoy

CAST The Complete Performer **Ted Greenberg**; Guest Mascot **Matt Wayne**; Mascot Trainer **Mike Motz**; Audience **Olga Wood**, **Samantha Chapman**

Return engagement of a mostly one-man comedy presented without intermission. Previously presented at the 2008 New York International Fringe Festival and November 8–December 27, 2008 at Soho Playhouse (see *Theatre World* Vol. 65, page 155.)

SYNOPSIS *The Complete Performer* is a mostly one-man comedy show, featuring The Late Show with David Letterman's Emmy Award-winning writer Ted Greenberg and his crowd-rousing mascot. The show combines stand-up, mind reading, magic, a half-time show and full-frontal nudity. *The Complete Performer* is a quintessential New York theatre experience.

Danny and Sylvia: The Danny Kaye Musical

St. Luke's Theatre; First Preview: May 6, 2009; Opening Night: May 13, 2009; Closed open; 5 previews, 303 performances as of May 31, 2011 (limited schedule)

Book and lyrics by Robert McElwaine, music by Bob Bain; Presented by Hy Juter and Edmund Gaynes; Director, Pamela Hall; Choreographer, Gene Castle; Sets, Josh Iacovelli; Lighting, Garaham Kindred; Costumes, Elizabeth Flores; Music Director, David Fiorello; General Manager, Jessimeg Productions; PSM, Josh Iacovelli; Associate General Manager, Julia Beardsley; Props, Robert Pemberton; Press, Susan L. Schulman

CAST Danny Kaye **Brian Childers**; Sylvia Fine **Kimberly Faye Greenberg**

MUSICIAN David Fiorello (piano)

MUSICAL NUMBERS Another Summer, At Liberty, at the Club Versailles, At the London Palladium, Can't Get That Man Off My Mind, Danny Kaminsky, I Can't Live Without You, If I Knew Then, If I Needed a Guy, I'm a Star, Just one Girl, La Vie Paree, Now Look What You Made Me Do, Requiem for Danny Kaminsky, She's Got a Fine Head on My Shoulders, Sylvia's Song, Tummler, We've Closed On Opening Night, We Make a Wonderful Team, What Shall We Say, You Got A Problem With That, Anatole of Paris, The Maladjusted jester, Melody in 4F, One Life to Live, Tchaikovsky, Dinah, Minnie the Moocher, Ballin' the Jack, P.S. One Four Nine

SETTING 1936 to 1948 in New York, Hollywood and London. Off-Broadway premiere of a musical presented in two acts.

SYNOPSIS *Danny and Sylvia* takes a look at the famous couple from the time the young undisciplined comic Danny Kaminsky meets aspiring songwriter Sylvia Fine at an audition in the 1930s. Under Sylvia's guidance as mentor, manager, and eventually, wife, Kaye rises from improvisational comic to international film star. The musical explores their inspired collaboration and the romance and conflict that made them such a volatile and successful couple.

Brian Childers and Kimberly Faye Greenberg in Danny and Sylvia: The Danny Kaye Musical *(photo by Carol Rosegg)*

The Fantasticks

Snapple Theatre Center; First Preview: July 28, 2006; Opening Night: August 23, 2006; 27 previews, 1,888 performances as of May 31, 2011

Book and lyrics by Tom Jones, music by Harvey Schmidt, suggested by the play *Les Romanesques* by Edmond Rostand; Produced by Terzetto LLC, Pat Flicker Addiss, and MARS Theatricals (Amy Danis/Mark Johanness); Director, Tom Jones; Original Staging, Word Baker; Sets and Costumes, Ed Wittstein; Lighting, Mary Jo Dondlinger; Sound, Dominic Sack; Casting, Terzetto LLC; Musical Director, Robert Felstein; Choreography/Musical Staging, Janet Watson; Production Stage Manager, Shanna Spinello/Paul Blankenship; ASMs, Michael Krug, Brandon Kahn, Paul Blankenship; Associate Director, Kim Moore; Associate Producers, Carter-Parke Productions and Patrick Robustelli; Production Supervisor, Dan Shaheen; Press, John Capo–DBS Press; Cast recording: Sh-K-Boom/Ghostlight 84415

CAST The Narrator (El Gallo) **Edward Watts**; The Boy (Matt) **Erik Altemus**[1]; The Girl (Luisa) **Kimberly Whalen**[2]; The Boy's Father (Hucklebee) **Gene Jones**; The Girl's Father (Bellomy) **Steve Routman**[3]; The Old Actor (Henry) **MacIntyre Dixon**; The Man Who Dies (Mortimer) **Michael Nostrand**; The Mute **Matt Leisy**[4]; At the Piano **Robert Felstein**; At the Harp **Jacqueline Kerrod**

STANDBYS Tom Flagg (Hucklebee/Henry/Mortimer), Scott Willis[5] (El Gallo/Hucklebee/Bellomy), Evy Ortiz[6] (The Mute/Luisa), Matt Leisy[4] (Matt)

*Succeeded by: 1. Matt Leisey (12/6/10) 2. Juliette Trafton (6/28/10) 3. Bill Bateman (6/28/10) 4. Matt Dengler (12/6/10) 5. Charles West (6/28/10) 6. Ann Markt (9/27/10)

MUSICAL NUMBERS Overture, Try to Remember, Much More, Metaphor, Never Say No, It Depends on What You Pay, Soon It's Gonna Rain, Abduction Ballet, Happy Ending, This Plum is Too Ripe, I Can See It, Plant a Radish, Round and Round, They Were You, Try to Remember (reprise)

Revival of the musical presented in two acts. *The Fantasticks* is the world's longest running musical and the longest running Off-Broadway production ever. The original production opened at the Sullivan Street Playhouse on May 3, 1960– January 13, 2002, playing over 17,000 performances (see *Theatre World* Volume 16 page 167 for original cast credits).

SYNOPSIS *The Fantasticks* tells the story of a young boy and girl who fall madly in love at the hands of their meddling fathers, but soon grow restless and stray from one another. The audience uses its imagination to follow El Gallo as he creates a world of moonlight and magic, then pain and disillusionment, until the boy and girl find their way back to one another.

JT Waite and Michael Nostrand in The Fantasticks *(photo by Joan Marcus)*

Fuerza Bruta: Look Up

Daryl Roth Theatre; First Preview: October 11, 2007; Opening Night: October 24, 2007; 14 previews, 1,269 performances as of May 31, 2011

Created and directed by Diqui James; Produced by Live Nation Artists Events Group, Fuerzabruta, Ozono, and Stephen Shaw; Executive Producer, Steve Howard; Composer/Musical Director, Gaby Kerpel; Lighting, Edi Pampin; Sound, Hernan Nupieri; Costumes, Andrea Mattio; Automation, Alberto Figueiras; General Coordinator, Fabio D'Aquila; Production, Agustina James; Technical Director, Alejandro Garcia; Marketing, Eric Schnall; Casting, James Calleri; Set-up Technical Supervisor, Bradley Thompson; General Manager, Laura Kirspel; PSM, Jeff Benish; Production Coordinator/ASM, E. Cameron Holsinger; Special Effects, Rick Sordelet; Press, Rogers & Cohen, Lauren Wilsman

CAST **Freddy Bosche**, **Hallie Bulleit**, **Daniel Case**, **Dusty Giamanco**, **John Hartzell**, **Michael Hollick**, **Joshua Kobak**, **Angelica Kushi**, **Gwyneth Larsen**, **Tamara Levinson**, **Rose Mallare**, **Brooke Miyasaki**, **Jon Morris**, **Marlyn Ortiz**, **Kepani Salgado-Ramos**; Swings **Jason Novak**, **Kira Morris**, **Andy Pellick**, **Jeslyn Kelly**, **Ilia Castro**

U.S. premiere of a theatrical experience piece with music presented without intermission. Originally presented in Buenos Aries, and subsequently in Lisbon, London, and Bogata. Since 2005, Fuerza Bruta has played over 2,500 shows in over 20 cities worldwide.

SYNOPSIS The creators of the long running hit *De La Guarda* push the boundaries of theatrical creativity, motivation, and innovation in their new work featuring a non-stop collision of dynamic music, visceral emotion, and kinetic aerial imagery. *Fuerza Bruta: Look Up* breaks free from the confines of spoken language and theatrical convention as both performers and audience are immersed in an environment that floods the senses, evoking pure visceral emotion in a place where individual imagination soars.

A scene from Fuerza Bruta: Look Up *(photo by courtesy of Fuerza Bruta)*

Gazillion Bubble Show

New World Stages; First Preview: January 17, 2007; Opening Night: February 15, 2007; 1,700 performances as of May 31, 2011

Created and staged by Fan Yang; Produced and Set Design by Fan Yang and Neodus Company, Ltd.; Artistic Director, Jamie Jan; Show Director, Steve Lee; Lighting, Jin Ho Kim; Sound, Joon Lee; Gazilllion Bubbles FX, Special Effects, Alex Cheung; Theatrical Special Effects, CITC/Gary and Stephanie Crawford; Original Music, Workspace Co, Ltd.; Laser Design, Abhilash George; Lumalaser, Tim Ziegenbein; Lighting Effects, David Lau; Special Effects Inventor, Dragan Maricic; Production Stage Manager, Yeung Jin Son; Stage Manager, Min Song; Technical Director, Alan Kho; General Manager, New World Stages; Marketing, HHC Marketing; Marketing Director, Chermaine Cho; Press, Springer Associates, Joe Trentacosta, Gary Springer

Performed by **Ana Yang**, **Fan Yang**, **Jano Yang**, **Deni Yang**, or **Melody Yang**

New York premiere of an interactive theatrical event presented without intermission. Fan Yang's son Deni joined the show September 24 (with an official opening night of October 29) and the show was subtitled *The Next Generation*. Later in the year, Fan's daughter joined the rotating cast of family performers.

SYNOPSIS The first interactive stage production of its kind, complete with fantastic light effects and lasers, Fan Yang blends art and science to dazzle audiences with his jaw-dropping masterpieces of bubble artistry that defy gravity and logic as we know it.

ImaginOcean

New World Stages; First Preview: March 17, 2010; Opening Night: March 31, 2010; 11 previews, 398 performances as of May 31, 2011

Book by John Tartaglia, music & lyrics by William Wade; Presented by Philip Katz, Michael Shawn Lewis, and John Tartaglia; Director/Musical Staging, Donna Drake; Set, Robert Andrew Kovach; Puppet Design & Fabrication, The Puppet Kitchen; Music Recording, Yellow Sound Lab/Matthias Winter & Michael

Croiter; Recording Engineer, Matthias Winter; Advertising, Hofstetter+Partners/Agency 212; Marketing, HHC Marketing; Casting, Melanie Lockyer; Development Consultant, Georgianna Young; PSM, Emilie Bray Schoenfeld; General Manager, The Splinter Group (Seth A. Goldstein, Heather Schings, William Goldstein); Production Assistant, Beth Rolfs); Creative and Website, Michael Naylor; Assistant to the Director/Producers, Daniel Seth; Study Guide/Educational Outreach, Thru the Stage Door; Press, Betsy Braun

CAST *Puppeteers*: Tank **James W. Wojtal Jr.**; Bubbles **Stacey Weingarten**; Dorsel **Ryan Dillon**; Ripple/Leonard **Lara Maclean**; Baby Jellyfish/Arrows/Others **Carole D'Agostino**; Spirit of Friendship/Jellyfish/Arrow/Others **Nate Begle**; Spirit of Friendship/Jellyfish/Arrows/Others **Jonathan Carlucci**; Puppet Wrangler/Swing **Brian T. Carson**; *Voice*: Tank/Dorsel/Leonard **John Tartaglia**; Bubbles/Arrow **Donna Drake**; Ripple/Baby Jellyfish **Michael Shawn Lewis**; Spirit of Friendship **Meladi Montano** (speaking), **Cathlene Grant** (singing)

RECORDING MUSICIANS Randy Andos (trombone), Michael Croiter (drums), Joe Fiedler (trombone), Brian Koonin (guitar), MaryAnn McSweeney (acoustic/electric bass), Kristy Norter (reeds/winds), Clay Ruede (cello), Denise Stillwell (violin/viola), William Wade (piano/orchestrations); Back-up Vocals: Camilo Castro, Heather Curran, Gavin Esham, Nick Gaswirth, Samantha Grenell-Zaidman, Amy Jones, Tyrick Jones, Ruperta Nelson, Krista Severeid, Michael Yeshion; Children's Chorus: Willow Bennison, Allegra Berman, Nadia Filanovsky, Cathlene Grant, Savannah Henry, Ashley Laird, Meldi Montano, Delainah Perkins, Miranda Powell, Lila Smith-Marooney; "Which Way to Turn" Soloist: Nick Gaswirth

MUSICAL NUMBERS On Our Way, Jellyfish Jive, On Our Way (reprise), Which Way to Turn, Imagination, Just a Stone's Throw Away, The Treasure, Finale

SETTING The Ocean Floor. New York premiere of a puppet theatre musical presented without intermission. A previous version debuted November 20, 2009 on Royal Caribbean International's newest and most revolutionary cruise ship, *Oasis of the Seas*.

SYNOPSIS A one-of-a-kind live black-light puppet show, John Tartaglia's *ImaginOcean* is a magical undersea adventure for kids of all ages. Tank, Bubbles and Dorsel are three best friends who just happen to be fish, and they're about to set out on a remarkable journey of discovery. And it all starts with a treasure map. As they swim off in search of clues, they'll sing, dance, and make new friends, including everyone in the audience. Ultimately they discover the greatest treasure of all: friendship.

Love, Loss, and What I Wore

Westside Theatre; First Preview: September 21, 2009; Opening Night: October 1, 2009; 11 previews, 681 performances as of May 31, 2011

Written by Nora Ephron and Delia Ephron, based on the book by Ilene Beckerman; Produced by Daryl Roth; Director, Karen Carpenter; Sets, Jo Winiarski; Costumes, Jessica Jahn; Lighting, Jeff Croiter; Sound, Walter Trarbach; Casting, Tara Rubin; Makeup, Maria Verel; PSM, Zoya Kachadurian; ASM, Nancy Elizabeth Vest; Production Manager, Shannon Case; General Manager, Adam Hess; Associate Producer, Alexander Fraser; Associate General Manager, Jodi Schoenbrun Carter; Advertising, Eliran Murphy Group; Marketing, Leanne Schanzer Promotions; Assistant Design: Carla Cruz (set), Sarah James (costumes), Grant Yeager (lighting); Propmaster, Buist Bickley; Wardrobe Supervisor, Ren LaDassor; Production Carpenter, Colin McNamara; Press, O+M Company, Rick Miramontez, Molly Barnett, Andy Snyder

CAST *June 1-27*: **Penny Fuller**, **Rachel Harris**, **Diane Neal**, **Sherri Shepherd**, **Cobie Smulders**; *June 30-July 27*: **Haylie Duff**, **Penny Fuller**, **Sharon Lawrence**, **Ashley Austin Morris**, **Myra Lucretia Taylor**; *July 28-August 29*: **Jayne Houdyshell**, **Adriane Lenox**, **Alison Mack**, **Kate Mulgrew**, **Kristine Nielsen**; *September 1-October 3*: **Helen Carey**, **Victoria**

Clark, Nancy Giles, Stacy London, Jamie-Lynn Sigler (to 9/19)/**Ashley Austin Morris** (9/21-10/3); *October 6-31:* Aisha de Haas, Erin Dilly, Barbara Feldon, Tovah Feldshuh, Ashley Austin Morris; *November 3-December 5:* Tichina Arnold, Margaret Colin, Alicia Goranson, Ann Harada, Maria Tucci; *December 8-January 9:* Brenda Braxton, Didi Conn, Kate Flannery, Loretta Swit, Mary Testa; *January 12-February 13:* Alexis Bledel, Nikki Blonsky, Anita Gillette, Judy Gold, Pauletta Washington; *February 16-March 20:* Katrina Bowden, Sabrina Le Beauf, Orfeh, Barbara Rhoades, Kim Zimmer; *March 23-April 24:* Sonia Manzano, Donna McKechnie, Annie Starke, Fredi Walker-Browne, Rumer Willis; *April 27-May 29:* Conchata Ferrell, Minka Kelly, AnnaLynne McCord, Anne Meara, B. Smith.

Off-Broadway commercial transfer of a collection of monologues and scenes presented without intermission. Previously presented last season at the DR2 Theatre. A portion of ticket sales benefit Dress for Success.

SYNOPSIS This collection of vignettes and monologues by Nora and Delia Ephron is based on the best-selling book by Ilene Beckerman, as well as on the recollections of the Ephrons' friends. The production features a five- member all-star rotating cast who will perform the piece in four-week cycles. Like the book it's based on, *Love, Loss, and What I Wore* uses clothing and accessories and the memories they trigger to tell funny and often poignant stories that all women can relate to.

Penny Fuller, Rachel Harris, Cobie Smulders, Sherri Shepherd, and Diane Neal in Love, Loss, and What I Wore *(photo by Carol Rosegg)*

My Big Gay Italian Wedding

St. Luke's Theatre; First Preview: May 5, 2010; Opening Night: May 22, 2010; 11 previews, 183 performances as of May 31, 2011 (limited performance schedule)

Written by Anthony J. Wilkinson; Produced by Dina Manzo & Sonia Blangiardo in association with Anndee Productions; Director, Teresa A. Cicala; Choreography, J. Austin Eyer; Original Music, David Boyd; Sets, Rob Santeramo; Costumes, Philip Heckman; Lighting, Graham Kindred; General Manager, Davenport Theatrical Enterprises, Matt Kovich; Marketing, HHC Marketing; Production Manager, Jeramiah Peay; Casting, Daryl Eisnberg; PSM, C.J. Thom III; ASM, Kelly Ice; Wardrobe Supervisor, Megan Opalinski; Press, Keith Sherman & Associates, Brett Oberman

CAST Anthony **Anthony Wilkinson**; Andrew **Reichen Lehmkuhl**[*1]; Lucia **Liz Gerecitano**; Angela **Randi Kaplan**; Rodney **Erik Ransom**; Father Rosalia **Chad Kessler**; ToniAnn **Carla-Marie Mercun**[*2]; Gregorio **Fabio Taliercio**; Connie **Meagan Robar**; Joseph **Joe Scanio**; Mario **Adam Zelasko**; Frankie **Bryan Anthony**[*3]; Maria **Tricia Burns**[*4]; Maurizio **Brett Douglas**; Ensemble/

Male Understudy **Kevin McIntyre**[*5]; Ensemble/Female Understudy **Leah Gerstel**

*Succeeded by: 1. Daniel Robinson (7/2010), David Moretti (11/18/10), Marty Thomas (1/2011) 2. Ilene Kristen (1/2011), Kim Sozzi (3/31/11) 3. Billy Yoder 4. Marissa Rosen 5. Joey Murray; Guest cast members this season: Teresa Giudice, Caroline Manzo, Lauren Manzo, Jacqueline Laurita (from television's *The Real Housewives of New Jersey*) (9/1-9/4; 10/20-10/23), Dr. Joy Browne (9/30-10/2), Ilene Kristen and Claire Buffie (11/18), Tabatha Coffey (12/2-12/4; 3/3-3/5), Lance Bass (12/2010), Vincent Pastore (12/2010), Ellen Dolan, Brittany Underwood, Kristin Alderson, and Marie Schulenberg (3/17-19)

SETTING Revised version of a play presented in two acts. Originally presented at the Actors Playhouse November 14, 2003 (see *Theatre World* Vol. 60, page 107).

SYNOPSIS Planning a wedding can be hell… or a hell of a lot of fun! Two handsome grooms, one overbearing Italian mother, a jealous ex-boyfriend, the wedding planner from Hell, and an assortment of kooky family and friends all gather together for Off-Broadway's newest laugh-out-loud comedy with a heart.

Reichen Lehmkuhl, Fabio Taliercio (background), and Anthony Wilkinson in My Big Gay Italian Wedding *(photo by Carol Rosegg)*

Naked Boys Singing

New World Stages; First Preview: July 2, 1999; Opening Night: July 22, 1999; 3,000 performances as of May 31, 2011 (weekends only)

Written by Stephen Bates, Marie Cain, Perry Hart, Shelly Markham, Jim Morgan, David Pevsner, Rayme Sciaroni, Mark Savage, Ben Schaechter, Robert Schrock, Trance Thompson, Bruce Vilanch, Mark Winkler; Conceived and directed by Robert Schrock; Produced by Jamie Cesa, Carl D. White, Hugh Hayes, Tom Smedes, Jennifer Dumas; Choreography, Jeffry Denman; Music Director, Jeffrey Biering; Original Musical Director and Arrangements, Stephen Bates; Set/Costumes, Carl D. White; Lighting, Aaron Copp; Production Stage Manager, Heather Weiss/Scott DelaCruz; Assistant Stage Manager, Mike Kirsch/Dave August; Dance Captain, Craig Lowry; Press, David Gersten; Original Press, Peter Cromarty; L.A. Cast recording: Café Pacific Records

CAST Naked Maid **Gregory Stockbridge**; Radio **Eric Dean Davis**[*1]; Robert Mitchum **Nimmy Weisbrod**; Entertainer **Russell Saylor**; Bris **Matt Burrow**[*2]; Porn Star **Tony Neidenbach**[*3]; Muscle Addiction **Trevor Efinger**[*4]; Window **Dave August**; Swings[*5] **Craig Lowry**, **Melvin Bell III**; Piano: **Jeffrey Biering**

*Succeeded by: 1. Aubrey Grant (11/2010) 2. Zachary Clause (7/2010) 3. Anthony Romero (09/2010), Chris Layton (11/2010), Tony Neidenbach (1/2011) 4. Michael Munoz (9/2010) 5. Garret D. Smith (11/2010)

MUSICAL NUMBERS Gratuitous Nudity, Naked Maid, The Bliss of a Bris, Window to Window, Fight the Urge, Robert Mitchum, Jack's Song, Members Only, Perky Little Porn Star, Kris Look What You've Missed, Muscle Addiction, Nothin' But the Radio On, The Entertainer, Window to the Soul, Finale/Naked Boys Singing!

A musical revue presented in two acts. For original production credits see *Theatre World* Volume 56, page 114. Originally opened at The Actors' Playhouse; transferred to Theatre Four March 17, 2004; transferred to the John Houseman Theater September 17, 2004; transferred to the 47th Street Theatre November 12, 2004; transferred to the Julia Miles Theatre May 6, 2005; transferred to New World Stages October 14, 2005.

SYNOPSIS The title says it all! Caution and costumes are thrown to the wind in this all-new musical revue featuring an original score and a handful of hunks displaying their special charms as they celebrate the splendors of male nudity in comedy, song and dance.

Our Town

Barrow Street Theatre; First Preview: February 17, 2009; Opening Night: February 26, 2009; Closed September 12, 2010; 10 previews, 644 performances

Written by Thornton Wilder; Presented by Scott Morfee, Jean Doumanian, Tom Wirtshafter, Ted Snowdon, Eagle Productions, Dena Hammerstein/Pam Pariseau, The Weinstein Company, Burnt Umber Productions; Director, David Cromer; Sets, Michele Spadaro; Costumes, Alison Siple; Lighting, Heather Gilbert; Original Music/Music Director, Jonathan Mastro; Production Manager, B.D. White; PSM, Richard A. Hodge; ASM, Kate McDoniel; Associate Producers, Patrick Daly & Marc Biales; Assistant Director, Michael Page; General Management, Two Step Productions; Advertising, Eliran Murphy Group; Casting, Pat McCorkle, Joe Lopick, Assistant Director, Michael Page; Press, O+M Company

CAST Stage Manager **Michael Shannon***; Mrs. Gibbs **Donna Jay Fulks**; Mrs. Webb **Kati Brazda**; Dr. Gibbs **Ben Livingston**; Joe Crowell Jr. **Will Brill**; Howie Newsome **Robert Beitzel**; George Gibbs **James McMenamin**; Rebecca Gibbs **Emma Galvin**; Emily Webb **Jennifer Grace**; Wally Webb **Seamus Mulcahy**; Professor Willard **Edwin Henry**; Mr. Webb **David Manis**; Simon Stimson **Jonathan Mastro**; Mrs. Soames **Elizabeth Audley**; Constable Warren **Mark Hattan**; Si Crowell **Jason Yachanin**; Joe Stoddard **Roger DeWitt**; Sam Craig **Nathan Dame**; Irma **Dana Jacks**; Citizen **Lynn Lawrence**; Farmer McCarty **Keith Perry**; Citizen **Kathleen Pierce**; Citizen **Mark Shock**

*Succeeded by: Michael McKean (6/12/10), Helen Hunt (7/6/10), David Cromer (8/24/10)

SETTING 1901. Grover's Corners, New Hampshire. Revival of a play presented in three acts with two intermissions. This production was originally presented by The Hypocrites (Chicago) May 1, 2008. On December 17, 2009, this engagement became the longest-running production of the play in its 72-year history with its 337th performance, surpassing the original Broadway run.

David Cromer in Our Town *(photo by Carol Rosegg)*

Perfect Crime

Snapple Theatre Center; First Preview: April 18, 1987; Opening Night: 9,865 performances as of May 31, 2011

By Warren Manzi; Presented by The Actors Collective in association with the Methuen Company; Director, Jeffrey Hyatt; Set, Jay Stone, Warren Manzi; Costumes, Nancy Bush; Lighting, Jeff Fontaine; Sound, David Lawson; PSM, Brian Meister; Press, John Capo–DBS Press

CAST Margaret Thorne Brent **Catherine Russell**; Inspector James Ascher **Richard Shoberg**; W. Harrison Brent **John Hillner**; Lionel McAuley **George McDaniel**; David Breuer **Patrick Robustelli**; Understudies **Andrea Leigh**, **Don Noble**

SETTING Windsor Locks, Connecticut. A mystery presented in two acts. For original production credits see *Theatre World* Volume 43, page 96. Catherine Russell has only missed four performances since the show opened in 1987, and on April 18, 2009, she was inducted into the Guinness Book of Records for "Most Performances by a Theater Actor in the Same Role" for not missing a day of work in twenty-two years. The show originally opened at the Courtyard Playhouse (39 Grove Street); transferred to: Second Stage Uptown (now the McGinn-Cazale Theatre) August–October 1987; 47th Street Theatre: October–December 1987; Intar 53 Theater on 42nd Street (now demolished): January–April 1988; Harold Clurman Theatre (now demolished): May 1988–August 1990; 47th Street Theatre: August–December 1990; Theatre Four (now the Julia Miles Theatre): January 1991–September 1993; 47th Street Theatre: September 1993–January 1994; The Duffy Theatre at Broadway and 46th (now demolished): February 1994–May 2006; Snapple Theatre Center–Duffy Theatre: May 22, 2006–present. *Perfect Crime* is the longest running play in the history of New York theatre.

SYNOPSIS Margaret Brent is an accomplished Connecticut psychiatrist and potential cold-blooded killer. When her wealthy husband turns up dead, she gets caught in the middle of a terrifying game of cat and mouse with a deranged patient and the handsome but duplicitous investigator assigned to the case.

Pinkalicious, The Musical

Bleecker Street Theatre[+]; Opening Day: November 1, 2008; 285 performances as of May 31, 2011 (weekend performances)

Book and lyrics by Elizabeth Kann & Victoria Kann, music & lyrics by John Gregor; Produced by Vital Theatre Company (Stephen Sunderlin, Artistic Director; Linda Ames Key, Education Director; Mary Kate Burke, Associate Producer); Director, Teresa K. Pond; Original Director, Suzu McConnell-Wood; Choreography, Dax Valdes; Music Director, Jad Bernardo; Set, Mary Hamrick; Costumes, Colleen Kesterson & Randi Fowler; Props, Dan Jagendorf & Kerry McGuire; PSM, Kara M. Teolis; Stage Managers, Nataliya Vasilyeva and Katie Gorman; Casting, Bob Cline; Company Manager, Cadien Dumas; Press, Stephen Sunderlin

CAST Peter Pinkerton **Marc De La Conca**[*1] or **Eric Restivo**[*2]; Pinkalicious **Kristin Parker**[*3] or **Bridget Riley**[*4]; Dr. Wink/Alison **Rori Nogee** or **Molly Gilman** or **Kyla Schoer**; Mr. Pinkerton **John Galas**[*5] or **John Bauchman** or **Ryan Speakman**; Mrs. Pinkerton **Claire McClanahan**[*6] or **Chloe Sabin**[*7]; Understudy **Holly Buczek**

*Succeeded by: 1. Johnny Beauchamp 2. Adam Spiegel, Travis Nunes 3. Cara Fish, Megan MacPhee 4. Amber Dickerson 5. Ryan Albers 6. Joanna Hernandez 7. Melanie Dusel

A musical for young audiences presented without intermission. Previously played at New World Stages January 12–May 25, 2008 (see *Theatre World* Vol. 64, page 268) and encored there August 2–September 21, 2008. Originally presented at the McGinn Cazale Theatre January 13–February 25, 2007, and extended at Soho Playhouse March 3–May 25, 2007 (see *Theatre World* Vol. 63, page 291).

SYNOPSIS Pinkalicious can't stop eating pink cupcakes despite warnings from her parents. Her pink indulgence lands her at the doctor's office with Pinkititis, an affliction that turns her pink from head to toe - a dream come true for this pink loving enthusiast. But when her hue goes too far, only Pinkalicious can figure out a way to get out of this predicament.

+After the abrupt closing of Bleecker Street Theatre on October 14, 2010, the show played the Cherry Lane Theatre October 16-23, the Theatre at St. Peter's to November 6–December 5, the Vineyard Theatre December 11, 2010–March 11, 2011, and eventually to Manhattan Movement & Arts Center on April 2.

Ryan Albers, Joanna Hernandez, Amber Dickerson, and Travis Nunes in Pinkalicious, The Musical *(photo by Sun Productions Inc.)*

Quantum Eye: Magic and Mentalism

Bleecker Street Theatre[+]; Opening Night: February 9, 2007; 545 performances as of May 31, 2011 (limited performances)

Created by Sam Eaton; Produced and directed by Samuel Rosenthal; Original Music, Scott O'Brien; Art Design, Fearless Design; Assistant Producer, Mimi Rosenthal; Artwork, Glenn Hidlago; House Manger, Janet Oldenbrook; Wardrobe, Larry the Tailer

Performed by **Sam Eaton**

Programme: A Guilty Conscience, One Card, Fourth Dimension, Reading Minds, Animal Instinct, Digimancy, Mental Sketch, Transmission, An Unusual Talent, Mnemoncis, Strange News

A mentalist/magic show presented in 90 minutes without intermission. The show was workshopped and made open to the public from August 2006 through its opening at the WorkShop Theatre's Jewel Box Theatre on January 5, 2007. The show transferred to Soho Playhouse Huron Club on June 15, 2007, then to the Duffy Theatre on November 24, 2007, and then transferred to the Bleecker Street Theatre Downstairs on February 14, 2009, performing on Saturday twilights and Tuesday evenings.

SYNOPSIS *The Quantum Eye* is Sam Eaton's entertaining and fascinating exploration of mentalism, magic, perception and deception, where extraordinary ability and humor blend with the audience to make for a unique performance every time. His masterful use of prediction, manipulation, memorization and calculation will amaze and entertain audiences. It is an extraordinary blend of 21st Century mentalism and Victorian-era mystery. Join Sam on a journey past the limits of possibility in a show that you will never forget.

+After the abrupt closing of the Bleecker Street Theatre on October 14, the show relocated to various venues before moving to Theatre 80 on January 15, 2011.

The Screwtape Letters

Westside Theatre; First Preview: April 15, 2010; Opening Night: May 3, 2010; Closed January 9, 2011; 30 previews, 309 performances

Adapted and directed for the stage by Jeffrey Fiske and Max McLean from the story by C.S. Lewis; Produced by Fellowship for the Performing Arts (Max McLean, President and Artistic Director) and William & Bridget Coughran and Walt & Anne Waldie; Executive Producer, Ken Denison; Set, Cameron Anderson; Costumes, Michael Bevins; Lighting, Jesse Klug; Original Music & Sound, John Gromada; Sound Supervisor, Lew Mead; Production Supervisor, Bill Castellino; Production Manager, Technical Theater Solutions, Rys Williams; General Management, Aruba Productions, Ken Denison, Samantha Schuster, Eddie Williams; Advertising Manager, Aruba Advertising, Robyn Sunderland; PSM, Jane Grey; Casting, Carol Hanzel, Colleen Piquette; Company Manager, Michael Altbaum; Technical Director, Michael East; Marketing & Press, Noreen Heron & Associates

CAST His Abysmal Sublimity Screwtape **Max McLean**; Toadpipe, *Screwtape's personal secretary* **Elise Giradin**

STANDBYS Steven Hauck (Screwtape), Beckley Andrews (Toadpipe)

SETTING A Dining Hall in Hell; The Graduation Banquet at the Tempters' Training College for Young Devils; Screwtape's Office in Hell. New York. Commercial revival of a play presented without intermission. Previously presented at Theatre at St. Clements October 18–December 19, 2007 (see *Theatre World* Vol. 64, page 122).

SYNOPSIS In this inverted and moral universe set in an office in hell, God is called the "Enemy" and the devil is referred to as "Our Father Below." *The Screwtape Letters* follows the clever scheming a high level demon employs to entice a human toward damnation. At his feet is the creature-demon Toadpipe, who transforms into paragons of vice that Screwtape conjures with a flick of his fingers.

Max McLean in The Screwtape Letters *(photo by Johnny Knight)*

Stomp

Orpheum; First Preview: February 18, 1994; Opening Night: February 27, 1994; 7,284 performances as of May 31, 2011

Created/Directed by Luke Cresswell and Steve McNicholas; Produced by Columbia Artists Management, Harriet Newman Leve, James D. Stern, Morton Wolkowitz, Schuster/Maxwell, Galin/Sandler, and Markley/Manocherian; Lighting, Mr. McNicholas, Neil Tiplady; Casting, Vince Liebhart/Scot Willingham; Executive Producers, Richard Frankel Productions/Marc Routh; Associate Producer, Fred Bracken; General Manager, Richard Frankel Productions/Joe Watson; PSM, Paul Botchis; ASM, Elizabeth Grunewald; Technical Director, Joseph Robinson; Company Manager, Tim Grassel; Assistant Company Manager, Maia Watson; Press, Boneau/Bryan-Brown, Jackie Green, Joe Perrotta

CAST (rotating) **Alan Asuncion, Michelle Dorrance, Dustin Elsea, Fritzlyn Hector, Brad Holland, Lance Liles, Stephanie Middleton, Keith Middleton, Jason Mills, Joeseph Russomano, Marivaldo Dos Santos, Carlos Thomas, Fiona Wilkes, Nicholas V. Young**

A percussive performance art piece presented with an intermission. For original production credits see *Theatre World* Vol. 50, page 113.

SYNOPSIS *Stomp* is a high-energy, percussive symphony, coupled with dance, played entirely on non-traditional instruments, such as garbage can lids, buckets, brooms and sticks.

The cast of Stomp *(photo by Steve McNicholas)*

Tony and Tina's Wedding

Sweet Carolines; Opening Night: February 6, 1988; Closed June 2, 2011; 5,901 performances

Written by Artificial Intelligence; Conceived by Nancy Cassaro; Originally created by Thomas Allen, James Altuner, Mark Campbell, Nancy Cassaro, Patricia Cregan, Elizabeth Dennehy, Chris Fracchiolla, Jack Fris, Kevin Alexander, Mark Nassar, Larry Pellegrini, Susan Varon, Moira Wilson; Produced by Big Apple Entertainment, Raphael Berko, Jeff Gitlin, Sonny Ricciardi, Kim Ricciardi; Director, Larry Pelligrini; Choreography, Hal Simons; Costumes/Hair/Makeup, Juan DeArmas; Stage Manager, Ryan DeLorge; Assistant Stage Manager, Derek Barbara; Wardrobe and Hair, Concetta Rella; Senior Production Coordinator, Drew Seltzer; Production Coordinator, Evan Weinstein; Marketing, Gary Shaffer; Promotions, DeMarcus Reed

CAST Valentina Lynne Vitale Nunzio **Joli Tribuzio**; Anthony Angelo Nunzio Jr. **Craig Thomas Rivela**; Connie Mocogni **Dina Rizzo**i; Barry Wheeler **Gregory Allen Bock**; Donna Marsala **Jessica Aquino**; Dominick Fabrizzi **Anthony Augello**; Marina Gulino **Dawn Luebbe**; Johnny Nunzio **Matthew Cassaro**; Josephine Vitale **Anita Salvate**; Joseph Vitale **Rhett Kalman**; Sister Albert Maria **Daniela Genoble**; Anthony Angelo Nunzio, Sr. **John DiBenedetto**; Madeline Monore **Emily Rome Mudd**; Michael Just **Matthew Knowland**; Father Mark **Craig Clary**; Vinnie Black **Henry Caplan**; Loretta Black **Cindi Kostello**; Sal Antonucci **Joe Leone**; Donny Dolce **Johnny Tammaro**; Celeste Romano **Sharon Kenny**; Carlo Cannoli **Anthony Ventura**; Rocco Caruso **Ray Grappone**

SETTING Tony and Tina's wedding and reception. An interactive environmental theatre production. For original production credits see *Theatre World* Volume 44, page 63. Originally played at Washington Square Church and Carmelita's; transferred to St. John's Church (wedding ceremony) and Vinnie Black's Coliseum (reception) until August, 1988; transferred to St. Luke's Church and Vinnie Black's Vegas Room Coliseum in the Edison Hotel. The production closed May 18, 2003, then reopened on October 3, 2003. It closed again May 1, 2004, reopened under new co-producers (Raphael Berko and Jeff Gitlin) on May 15th, 2004. The show was performed on the Circle Line Cruises during the summer of 2009, and returned to the Edison Hotel, and transferred to Sweet Caroline's April 10, 2010, and alternate Friday performances at Il Cortile restaurant in Little Italy.

SYNOPSIS Tony and Tina are getting hitched. Audience members become part of the exuberant Italian family—attending the ceremony, mingling with relatives and friends, eating, drinking and dancing to the band.

Zero Hour

Actors Temple Theatre; First Preview: November 14, 2009; Opening Night: November 22, 2009; Closed January 9, 2011; 9 previews, 238 performances

Written by Jim Brochu; Presented by Kurt Peterson & Edmund Gaines in association with the Peccadillo Theater Company (Dan Wackerman, Artistic Director; Abigail Rose Solomon, Producing Director; Kevin Kennedy, Managing Director); Director, Piper Laurie; Associate Producer, Richard I. Bloch; Artistic Associate, Steve Schalchlin; Set, Josh Iacovelli; Lighting, Jason Arnold; PSM, Donald William Myers; Marketing, Leanne Schanzer Promotions; General Management, Jessimeg Productions, Edmund Gaynes, Julia Beardsley; Press, David Gersten and Associates

CAST "The Artist" **Jim Brochu**

SETTING An Artist's Studio on West 28th Street, New York City; July 1977. New York premiere of a solo performance play presented in two acts. This production originally started at the Theatre at St. Clements until January 31, 2010, transferred to the DR2 for a commercial run on February 23 (opening night March 7) and ended its run there May 30, 2010 before resuming performances at the Actors Temple on June 19, 2011.

SYNOPSIS In *Zero Hour*, a naïve reporter attempts to interview the famously volatile actor, prompting an explosion of memory, humor, outrage, and juicy backstage lore. The play traces Mostel's early days growing up on the Lower East Side as the son of Orthodox Jewish immigrant parents, through his rise as a stand-up comedian, from the Borscht Belt to Manhattan's most exclusive supper clubs, and from the devastation of the blacklist to his greatest Broadway triumphs, most notably as Tevye in *Fiddler on the Roof* and working through his love-hate relationship with Jerome Robbins. This final interview was made before Mostel left for the pre-Broadway tryout of *The Merchant of Venice* in Philadelphia. Mostel only played one performance as Shylock before his sudden death at the age of 62.

Jim Brochu in Zero Hour *(photo by Stan Barouh)*

SPECIAL EVENTS / PRODUCTIONS

Broadway Barks 12

Shubert Alley; June 10, 2010

Written by Julie Halston and Richard Hester; Presented by Shubert Alley and Broadway Cares/Equity Fights AIDS; Produced by Richard Hester, Patty Saccente, and Scott T. Stevens; Executive Producers/Hosts, Mary Tyler Moore and Bernadette Peters; Stage Managers, Brian Bogin, Monica Cuoco, Meg Friedman, Bess Marie Glorioso, Ken McGee, Kim Russell, Sarah Safer, Nancy Wernick, Rachel Wolff; Shelter Coordinator, Barbara Tolan; Sound Equipment, John Grasso; Sound Design and Engineer, Lucas Rico Corrubia; Graphic Design, Carol A. Ingram; Website, David Risley; Program Design, Tracy Lynn Putman; Press, Judy Katz & Associates

GUEST STARS Brooke Adams, Jan Maxwell, Tony Shalhoub, George Akram, Karen Olivo, Michael Mastro, Fred Applegate, Robin De Jesús and Veanne Cox, Sean Hayes, Katie Finneran, Tony Goldwyn, Brooks Ashmanskas, Corbin Bleu, Kevin Chamberlin, Jackie Hoffman, Alexander Hanson, Erin Davie, Hunter Ryan Herdlicka, Ramona Mallory, Leigh Ann Larkin, Aaron Lazar, Beth Leavel, Judy McLane, John Dossett, Gina Ferrall, Ruthie Henshall, Cheyenne Jackson, Karl Kenzler, Chad Kimball, Loretta Ables Sayre, Richard Thomas, Bill Berloni

A theatrical animal adoption marathon with entertainment.

SYNOPSIS A star-studded dog and cat adopt-a-thon benefiting New York City animal shelters and adoption agencies. The event, produced by Broadway Cares/Equity Fights AIDS and sponsored by the ASPCA and PEDIGREE with additional sponsorship by the New York Times, helps many of New York City's shelter animals find permanent homes by informing New Yorkers about the plight of the thousands of homeless dogs and cats in the metropolitan area.

Chad Kimball at Broadway Barks 12 (photo by Peter James Zielinski)

Lincoln Center Festival – Theater Events

July 7-25, 2010

Nigel Redden, Director

Musashi Written by Hisashi Inoue; Presented by Ninagawa Company; Director, Yukio Ninagawa; Composer, Akira Miyagawa; Set, Tsukasa Nakagoshi; Lighting, Jiro Katsushiba; Costumes, Lily Komine; Sound, Mashiro Inoue; Hair, Yuichi Akiba; Fight Choreography, Masahiro Kunii; Choreography, Uran Hirosaki, Juraku Hanayagi; Noh Superviosr, Yoshiki Honda; Kyogen Supervisor, Mansai Nomura; Assistant Directors, Sonsho Inoue, Naoko Okouchi; Stage Manager, Kiyotaka Kobayashi; Production Manager, Yuichiro Kanai; Cast: Tatsuya Fujiwara (Musashi Miyamoto), Ryo Katsuji (Kojiro Sasaki), Anne Suzuki (Otome Fudeya), Naomasa Musaka (Soho Takuan), Kayoko Shiraishi (Mai Kiya), Keita Oishi (Heishin), Yukio Tsukamoto (Chusuke), Kunihiro Iida (Jinbei Asakawa), Fumiaki Hori (Kanbei Asakawa), Takeshi Inomo (Yuzen Tadan); North American premiere of a play presented in Japanese with English titles in two acts; David H. Koch Theater; July 7-10

The Demons Based on the novel by Fyodor Dostoyevsky; Directed and adapted by Peter Stein; Composer, Arturo Annecchino; Set, Ferdinand Wogerbauer; Costumes, Anna Maria Heinreich; Lighting, Joachim Barth; English Titles, Rosanna Giammanco Frongia, Jonathan T. Hine; Producer, Emilo Russo; Associate Producer, Valentina Cimino; Tour Manager, Patrizia Capellari; Cast: Andrea Nicolini (Anton Lavrentyevich Grigoreiev), Elia Schilton (Stepan Trofimovich Verkhovensky), Maddalena Crippa (Varvara Petrovna Stavrogina), Maria Grazia Mandruzzato (Praskovya Ivanovna Drozdova), Ivan Alovisio (Nikolay Vsevolodovich Stavrogin), Alessandro Averone (Pyotr Stepanovich Verkhovensky), Rosario Lisma (Ivan Pavlovich Shatov), Fausto Russo Alesi (Alexey Nilych Kirillov/Father Tikhon), Irene Vecchio (Lizaveta Nikolayevna Drozdova), Franca Penone (Marya Ignatyevna Shatova/Darya Pavlovna Shatova [Dasha]), Pia Lanciotti (Arina Pròchorovna Virginskaya/Marya Timofeyevna Lebyadkina), Franco Ravera (Captain Ignat Timofeyevich Lebyadkin), Paolo Mazzarelli (Mavriky Nikolayevich/Chief of Militia), Paola Benocci (Yuliya Mikhaylovna von Lembke), Graziano Piazza (Andrey Antonovich von Lembke), Giovanni Visentin (Liputin), Carlo Bellamio (Virginsky), Fulvio Pepe (Shigalyov), Luca Iervolino (Lyamshin), Riccardo Ripani (Erkel), Armando De Ceccon (Gaganov/Limping Teacher/Prince), Matteo Romoli (Fedka/Student from the Gymnasium), Nanni Tormen (Alexey/Professor/Chief of the Militia), Federica Stefanelli (A Student), Antonia Renzella (A Girl/The Slim Lady); North American premiere of a new play presented in Russian with English titles in a 12 hour marathon with four intermissions and 2 meal breaks; Governors Island; July 10-11

A Disappearing Number Conceived and directed by Simon McBurney; Devised and presented by Complicite; Original Music, Nitin Sawhney; Design, Michael Levine; Lighting, Paul Anderson; Sound, Christopher Shutt; Projections, Sven Ortel; Costumes, Christina Cunningham; Associate Director, Douglas Rintoul; Production Manager, Jamie Maisey; Company Stage Manager, Cath Binks; Technical Stage Manager, Rod Wilson; Stage Managers, Emma Cameron, Ian Andlaw; Producer, Judith Dimant; Cast: David Annen (G.H. Hardy), Firdous Bamji (Al Cooper), Paul Bhattacharjee (Aninda Rao), Hiren Chate (Tabla Player), Divya Kasturi (Mother/University Cleaner/Dancer), Chetna Pandya (Surita Bhogarita/Barbara Jones), Saskia Reeves (Ruth Minnen), Shane Shambhu (Srinivasa Ramanujan/Dancer); New York premiere of a new play presented without intermission; David H. Koch Theater; July 15-18

Teorema Adapted by Ivo van Hove and Willem Bruls from the film and novel by Pier Paolo Pasolini; Presented and performed by Toneelgroep Amsterdam; Director, Ivo van Hove; Dramaturg, Willem Burls; Set/Lighting, Jan Versweyveld; Cosutmes, An d'Huys; Composer, Eric Sleichim; Music, Bl!ndman [new strings]—Jennifer de Keersmaecker, Joyce Kuipers, Ine Kuypers, Floris Uytterhoeven; Technical and Production Manager, Gotz Schworer; Stage Manager, Reyer Meeter; Cast: Chico Kenzari (The Guest), Jacob Derwig (Paolo, the father), Chris Nietvelt (Lucia, the mother), Hadewych Minis (Odetta, the daughter), Eelco Smits (Pietro, the son), Frieda Pittoors (Emilia, the housekeeper); North American premiere of a new play with music presented in Dutch with English titles without intermission; Governors Island; July 15-19

The Battle of Stalingrad Conceived, designed, and directed by Rezo Gabriadze; Presented by Mr. Gabriadze's Tbilisi Municipal Theatre Studio; Lighting, Mamuka Bakradse; Sound, Zurabi Nadaraia; Puppeteers, Tamara Amiredjibi, Badri Gvazava, Vladimer Meltser, Anna Nijaradze, Irakli Sharashidze; Voices, Lia Akhidjakova, Valeriy Basel, Evgeny Buler, Oleg Fendura, Tatiane Kuznecova, Uri Loparev, Igor Luchinkin, Tatiana Minkina, Anatoyl Paduka, Uri Plashkov, Inessa Pomanoff, Oleg Shkolnkik, Hatalya Smirnova, Igor Tiltikov, Vasiliy Vakovec, Svetlana Vinogradova, Uri Votaikov; Revival of a puppet-theatre production presented in Russian with English titles without intermission; Clark Studio Theater; July 20-25

Recipe For Life Part 2

Acorn Theatre; July 12-13, 2010

Written by A.R. Gurney, Christopher Durang, and Tennessee Williams; Presented by Cause Cèlébre/Part Time Productions (Susan Charlotte, Artistic/Executive Director) and Tina's Wish in association with The New Group; Directors, Christopher Hart and Antony Marsellis; Set, Ray Klausen; Lighting, Lee Terry; PSM, Anita Ross; Stage Manager, Bernita Robinson; Company Manager, Deb Hackenberry; Assistant Company Manager, Brendan Hill; Accounting, Ira Schall; Legal, Nan Bases; Public Relations, Barbara Graham

CAST July 12: *Mrs. Sorken* (by Christopher Durang): Mrs. Sorken **Marian Seldes**; *Adam and Eve on a Ferry* (by Tennessee Williams): Adam **Len Cariou**; Eve **Penny Fuller**; *The Pretty Trap* (by Tennessee Williams): Amanda Wingfield **Elaine Stritch**; Laura Wingfield **Tasha Lawrence**; Tom Wingfield **Michael Riedel**; Jim O'Conner **Jake Robards**; July 13: *The Pretty Trap*: Amanda Wingfield **Frances Sternhagen**; Amanda Wingfield **Tasha Lawrence**; Tom Wingfield **P.J. Sosko**; Jim O'Conner **Jake Robards**; *Interior: Panic* (by Tennessee Williams): Blanch Shannon **Johanna Day**; Grace Kiefaber **Tasha Lawrence**; Jack Kiefaber **Jake Robards**; George **Michael Citriniti**

An evening of short plays presented in two acts. Preview performances of *The Shoemaker* (with Danny Aiello) from July 14-18 were also presented in conjunction with *Recipe for Life*. (see production credits in this section).

SYNOPSIS Cause Cèlébre/Part Time Productions present their fourth Off-Broadway production (and second in this series) with short plays that explore the Recipe for Life, including two Tennessee Williams one-act plays that would eventually become *The Glass Menagerie* and *A Streetcar Named Desire*. Presented as a benefit for Tina's Wish, a non-profit organization supporting research to create an early and effective test for ovarian cancer and education for diagnosis and treatment.

They're Playing Our Song

Gerald W. Lynch Theatre; August 30, 2010

Book by Neil Simon, music by Marvin Hamlisch, lyrics by Carol Bayer Sager; Presented by The Actors Fund; Director/Choreography, Denis Jones; Music Director, Steve Freeman; Set, Paul Weimer; Lighting, Jeff Croiter; Sound, Patrick Weaver; Costume Supervisor, Michael Growler; Event Marketing, Adam Jay; PSM, Lisa Iacucci; Technical Producer, Stephen Yuhasz; Producer, Tim Pinckney; Stage Manager, Marisa Merrigan; ASM/Props, Angela Allen; Assistants to Mr. Jones, Peter Gregus, Dontee Kiehn; Press, The Publicity Office, Jeremy Shaffer

CAST Vernon Gersch **Seth Rudetsky**; Sonia Walsk **Sutton Foster**; Voices of Vernon Gersch **Tyler Maynard**, **Matt Loehr**, **Jesse Nager**; Voices of Sonia Walsk **Amber Efé**, **Kaitlyn Davidson**, **Alex Ellis**

MUSICIANS Steven Freeman (Conductor); Scott Cady, Steve Marzullo (Piano); Greg Utzig, Kevin Kuhn (Guitars); Marc Schmied (Electric Bass); Rick Dolan, Avril Brown, Kiku Enomoto, Philip Payton, Blair Lawhead, Shi-Hung Young (Violins); Todd Sullivan, David Fallo (Viola); Mairi Dorman-Phaneuf, Summer Boggess (Cello); Barbara Biggers (Harp); Steve Greenfield, Julie Ferrara, Marc Phaneuf (Wodwinds); Jon Owens, Ronald Buttacavoli (Trumpets); Charles Gordon, Chris Olness (Trombones); Billy Miller (Drums); Kerry Meads (Percussion)

MUSICAL NUMBERS Fallin', Workin' It Out, If He Really Knew Me, They're Playing My Song (His), They're Playing My Song (Hers), Right, Just For Tonight, Entr'acte-They're Playing Our Song, When You're In My Arms, If He Really Knew Me (reprise), I Still Believe In Love, Fill In The Words, They're Playing Our Song (The Bows)

SETTING New York City; late 1970s. One night only benefit concert revival of a musical presented in two acts. The musical was originally presented at the Imperial Theatre February 11, 1979–September 6, 1981 playing 1,082 performances (see *Theatre World* Vol. 35, page 28).

SYNOPSIS When Vernon Gersch, an established and wisecracking composer, takes on the kooky and offbeat lyricist Sonia Walsk (Sutton Foster) as his new collaborator, their initial match is a professional success but a personal disaster. Together, the two undergo a series of trials and overcome a number of hurdles before finding true love by the final curtain.

Sutton Foster and Seth Rudetsky in They're Playing Our Song *(photo by Krissie Fullerton/The Actors Fund)*

Swimming Upstream

Apollo Theatre; September 13, 2010

Written by Carol Bebelle, Troi Bechet, Reverend Lois Dejean, Asali DeVan Ecclesiastes, Anne-Liese Juge Fox, Adella Gautier, Briceshanay Gresham, Herreast Harrison, Karen-kaia Livers, Tommye Myrick, Cherice Harrison Nelson, Kathy Randels, Dollie Rivas, Dina Roudeze, Karel Sloane-Boekbinder, Carol Sutton; Presented by V-Day (Eve Ensler, Founder) and Ashe' Cultural Arts Center (Carol Bebelle, Executive Director/Co-founder) with support from Open Society Foundation; Director, Eve Ensler

CAST **Shirley Knight**, **LaChanze**, **Troi Bechet**, **Asali Njeri DeVan Ecclesiastes**, **Anne-Liese Juge Fox**, **Karen-kaia Livers**, **Michaela A. Harrison**, **Leslie Blackshear Smith**

Benefit performance of a theatrical produciton containing stories and songs presented without intermission.

SYNOPSIS Written by 16 New Orleans' women, *Swimming Upstream* is a powerful theatrical production that tells the raw and soulful stories of women who lived through Hurricanes Rita and Katrina with grace, rage and great resiliency, punctuated by a flair for story telling, humor and music that comes from being New Orleanian. Proceeds from the event benefit women of the Gulf and New Orleans who continue to struggle five years after the hurricanes.

Radio Macbeth and War of The Worlds– The Radio Play

Dance Theatre Workshop; October 5-16, 2010; 11 performances/4 performances

Two radio plays created and presented by SITI Company; *Radio Macbeth*: Directed by Anne Bogart and Darron L West, adapted from the play by William Shakespeare; Set/Costumes, James Schuette; Lighting, Brian H. Scott; Soundscape, Darron L West; Dramaturgy, J. Ed Araiza; PSM, Melissa Miller; *War of the Worlds–The Radio Play*: Written by Howard Koch; Directors, Anne Bogart and Darron L West

CAST Akiko Aizawa, Will Bond, Gian Murray Gianino, Leon Ingulsrud, Ellen Lauren, Kelly Maurer, Barney O'Hanlon, Stephen Duff Webber

Revival of two radio plays presented in one act. On the four nights of the double bill, they were presented with intermission.

SYNOPSIS SITI Company presents two of their works, *Radio Macbeth* (created in 2007) and *War of the Worlds-A Radio Play* (created in 1999), which have been performed all around the world. *Radio Macbeth* takes place late at night in the guts of an abandoned theater. Actors circle restlessly around the common shared warmth of a rehearsal table, moving through the bullet of Shakespeare's play. Around them, in the perimeter of the space, the ghosts of all previous productions hover and encroach. *War of the Worlds* was originally presented by Orson Welles' Mercury Theater on October 30, 1938 as a Halloween thriller, but many who tuned in became terrified as they believed the country was being attacked by aliens from Mars.

Stephen Duff Webber and Ellen Lauren in Radio Macbeth
(photo by Michael Brosilow)

The Boys

Baryshnikov Arts Center; October 6-10, 2010

Adapted and directed by Sergey Zhenovach from nine chapters of *The Brothers Karamazov* by Fyodor Dostoevsky; Presented by Moscow's Studio Art Theatre; Set, Maria Utrobina; Lighting, Evgeny Vinogradov; Composer, Grigory Gobernik

CAST Alexey Karamzov **Alexandr Koruchekov**; Nikolay Krasotkin **Andrey Shibarshin**; Ilyusha Snegiryov **Sergey Pirnyak**; Nikolay Ilyitch Snegiryov **Alexey Vertkov**; Ariana Petrovna **Anna Rud** or **Maria Shashlova**; Vavara Nikolaevna **Maria Shaslova** or **Tatyana Volkova**; Nina **Olga Kalashnikov** or **Miriam Sekhon** or **Maria Shashlova**; Smurov **Alexandr Proshin**; Katashov **Alexnadr Lutoshkin** or **Andrey Nazimov**; Bulkin **Nikita Moskovoy**; Bulkin **Nikita Moskovoy**; Borovikov **Gregory Sloujitel**; Tuzikov **Alexandr Oblasov**; Doctor **Sergey Kachanov**; Perezvon **Sergey Abroskin**

U.S. Premiere of a new adaptation of a Russian novel presented in Russian with English titles without intermission.

SYNOPSIS Winner of the Crystal Turandot Moscow Theater Award for directing, this powerful production in the best tradition of Russian theater is an adaptation of Fyodor Dostoevsky's *The Brothers Karamazov. The Boys* focuses on nine chapters of the Dostoevsky novel: a sub-plot in which Alexei Karamazov befriends a group of schoolboys and convinces them to stop bullying their dying peer, Ilyusha Snegiryov.

Christmas Eve with Christmas Eve

Midtown Theatre at HA! Comedy Club; November 29, 2010

Conceived and written by Gary Adler, Ann Harada, and Alan Muraoka; Presented by Broadway Cares/Equity Fights AIDS; Director, Alan Muraoka; Choreography, Michael Mindlin; Music Director, Gary Adler

CAST Christmas Eve **Ann Harada**; Brian **Jordan Gelber**; As Themselves **Paul Castree, Michel Mindlin, Jason Tam, Jose Llana, John Tartaglia, Christopher Sieber, Willy Falk, Howard McGillin, Stephen Bogardus, Marc Kudisch, Ryan Watkinson**

Second edition of a musical revue benefit performance presented without intermission. Presented as a benefit for Broadway Cares/Equity Fights AIDS. Originally presented in 2009, this benefit raised more than $7,000.

SYNOPSIS Christmas Eve, the beloved, opinionated, heavily-accented therapist from *Avenue Q*, makes her holiday fantasies come true in this evening of song and comedy. Christmas Eve and her guests both skewer and pay tribute to great romantic duets and iconic moments of Broadway. No lyricist will be spared as Harada reinterprets the Broadway songbook with the help of talented, hilarious and gorgeous leading men.

Ann Harada and Christopher Sieber in Christmas Eve with Christmas Eve
(photo by Peter James Zielinski)

The Idealist

The Times Center; February 23, 2011

Written by Jennifer Strome; Presented by the Spellbound Development Company, Kathryn Appleton, and Gatewave Inc.; Director, Lee Sankowich

CAST Alison Pill, Tony Roberts, Samantha Soule, Martin Vidnovic, Brandon Ladd Burkey, Lauren English, Clancy O'Connor, Andy Prosky

A staged reading of a play presented as a benefit for the Anne Frank Foundation.

SYNOPSIS *The Idealist* divulges the infamous, behind-the-scenes saga of author Meyer Levin (1905-1981), in a fact-based account of his role as the original dramatist of *The Diary of Anne Frank*, the most famous diary to have emerged from the 20th century.

Broadway Bears XIV

B.B. Kings; March 6, 2011

Presented by Scott T. Stevens for Broadway Cares/Equity Fights AIDS; Production Manager, Michael Palm; Music Director, Michael Lavine; Opening Number Lyrics, Douglas Braverman; Stage Manager, Bess Marie Glorioso; Program/Poster, Carol A. Ingram; Press, Boneau/Bryan-Brown

TALENT Host **Bryan Batt**; Auctioneer **Lorna Kelly**; Performers and Special Guest Stars **Crista Moore, George Dvorsky, Veanne Cox, Annie Golden, Anthony Hollock, Hunter Ryan Herdlicka, Elizabeth Welch, David Garrison, Trevor Braun, Paul Canaan, Harvey Evans, Jeremy Gumbs, Lexi Fridell, Reeve Carney, Chrisopher Sieber**

Reeve Carney at Broadway Bears XIV (photo by Peter James Zielinski)

HIGHEST BIDS Eliza Doolittle from *My Fair Lady* ($14,000), designed by Richard St. Clair and autographed by Julie Andrews; **Witch** from *Into The Woods* ($6,500), designed by Ariel Pellman and signed by Bernadette Peters and Stephen Sondheim; **Drew** from *Rock of Ages*, ($6.000), designed by Karl Ruckdeschel and autographed by Constantine Maroulis; **Link Larkin** from *Hairspray* ($5,500), designed by Susan Bolt and signed by Matthew Morrison; **Peter Parker/Spider-Man** from *Spider-Man: Turn Off the Dark* ($5,200), designed by Katie Falk and autographed by Reeve Carney; **Shylock** from *The Merchant of Venice* ($5,000), designed by Matthew Hemesath and autographed by Al Pacino; **Sir Lancelot** from *Spamalot* ($5,000), designed by Amy Milcallef and autographed by Hank Azaria; **Jennyanydots** from *Cats* ($4,500), designed by Therese Stadelmeier-Tresco, autographed by Anna McNeely

A Grand Audtion of Broadway inspired teddy bears presented with special entertainment.

SYNOPSIS A total of 42 teddy bears, donated by the North American Bear Company and transformed into uniquely costumed, handmade, one-of-a-kind, collectibles, raised $103,095 through online bids, telephone bids, and, of course, live bids. Proceeds went to Broadway Cares/Equity Fights AIDS. $1,843,977 has been raised so far from fourteen editions of this favorite event.

Michael Cusumano, Matt Anctil, Ray Lee, James Tabeek, anmd Brandon Rubendall in the Broadway Beauty Pageant

The Broadway Beauty Pageant

Symphony Space; March 21, 2011

Conceived by Jeffery Self and Ryan J. Davis; Produced by the Ali Forney Center, Ryan J. Davis, Jeffrey Self, Wil Fisher, and Matthew Oberstein; Director, Ryan J. Davis; Opening Number "Beautiful Boys" created by Gerard Alessandrini, performed by Lee Roy Reams; Musical Director, Christopher Denny; Choreography, Erin Porvaznika; Host: Tovah Feldshuh; Judges: Bruce Vilanch, Rachel Dratch, Carson Kressley; Press, O+M Company, Jaron Caldwell

CONTESTANTS Matt Anctil (Mr. *La Cage aux Folles*), **Michael Cusuman** (Mr. *Chicago*–WINNER), **Raymond J. Lee** (Mr. *Anything Goes*), **Brandon Rubendall** (Mr. *Spider-Man: Turn Off the Dark*), **James Tabeek** (Mr. *Mary Poppins*)

SYNOPSIS The fifth annual *Broadway Beauty Pageant*, formerly titled *Mr. Broadway*, features male cast members representing their respective Broadway shows, competing for the title crown through talent, interview, and swimsuit competitions. The contestants go head to head in front of a panel of celebrity judges, but the final vote is in the audience's hands. Presented as a benefit for the Ali Forney Center, the nation's largest and most comprehensive organization dedicated to LGBT youth.

Company

Avery Fisher Hall; April 7-9, 2011; 4 performances

Music and lyrics by Stephen Sondheim, book by George Furth; Presented by the New York Philharmonic; Director/Producer, Lonny Price; Co-Producer, Matt Cowart; Choreography, Josh Rhodes; Music Director/Conductor; Orchestrations, Jonathan Tunick

CAST Robert **Neil Patrick Harris**; Harry **Stephen Colbert**; Sarah **Martha Plimpton**; Marta **Anika Noni Rose**; Larry **Jim Walton**; David **Jon Cryer**; Peter **Craig Bierko**; Amy **Katie Finneran**; April **Christina Hendricks**; Paul **Aaron Lazar**; Susan **Jill Paice**; Jenny **Jennifer Laura Thompson**; Kathy **Chryssie Whitehead**; Joanne **Patti LuPone**; Vocal Minority **Alexa Green, Fred Inkley, Rob Lorey, Jessica Vosk**; Ensemble **Callie Carter, Ariana DeBose, Sean Eweing, Ashley Fitgerald, Lorin Latarro, Lee Wilkins**

Concert version of a revial of a musical presented in two acts.

SYNOPSIS *Company* follows five married, once-married, and soon-to-be married couples and their mutual friend, Robert, a bachelor who has been unable to connect in a long-term relationship. The relationships are presented in a series of vignettes, primarily through Robert's eyes.

Aquila Theatre Touring Productions

Skirball Center; April 20-23, 2011; 4 performances

Two plays presented by Aquila Theatre (Peter Meineck, Artistic Director); *Six Characters in Search of an Author* by Luigi Pirandello, translated by Carl R. Mueller; Director/Design, Desiree Sanchez; Masks, David Knezz; Lighting, Kevin Shaw; Design, Peter Meineck and Kenn Sabberton; Lighting, Peter Meineck and Kevin Shaw; Costumes, Heidi Buckingham and Louise Handford; For both productions: Production Manager, Nate Terracio; Company Technical Director, Kevin Shaw; Assistant Company Stage Manager, Chantel King

CAST **Sarah Amankwah, Matthew Clancy, Howard Crossley, Andrew French, Jessica Tomchak, Alinka Wright, Owen Young**

Tourning presentations of two classic plays, each presented without intermission.

SYNOPSIS In its twentieth season, the Aquila Theatre brings their 2010-2011 touring shows home to New York for a limited engagement. *Six Characters in Search of an Author* dares to ask fundamental questions about the very nature of art and entertainment, blurring the line between reality and artifice. Set against an Athenian backdrop, *A Midsummer Night's Dream* examines the universal theme of love and its attendant complications: passion, lust, frustration, depression, confusion and marriage. Known for their imaginative stagings, Aquila Theatre strives to create bold reinterpretations of classical plays for contemporary audiences, and to free the spirit of the original work and recreate the excitement of the live performance that made it become a classic play.

The Aquila Theater in A Midsummer Night's Dream *(photo by Renato Rotolo)*

Uncle Vanya

Tribeca Performing Arts Center; May 14-15, 2011; 3 performances

Written by Anton Chekov; Presented by Moscow State Mossovet Theatre and A & Y Productions; Producer, Andrei Konchalovsky; Stage Director, Rustam Khamdamov; Composer, Eduard Artemiev

CAST Aleksandr Vladimirovich Serebryakov **Alexander Filippenko**; Elena Andreevna Serebryakova **Natalia Vdovina**; Sonya Alexandrovna Serebyakova **Julia Vysotskaya**; Maria Vasilevna Voinitskaya **Irina Kartasheva**; Ivan Petrovich Vointsky (Uncle Vanya) **Pavel Derevyanko**; Mikhail Lvovich Astrov **Alexander Domogarov**; Ilya Ilich Telegin **Alexander Bobrovsky**; Marina Timofeevna **Larisa Kuznetsova**

SETTING U.S. engagement of a revival of a classic play presented in Russian with English translation with intermission. This production celebrates the 150th anniversary of the birth of Anton Checkov.

SYNOPSIS Uncle Vanya centers on an aging caretaker of a country estate owned by his wealthy brother-in-law, a renowned professor. Vanya's constricted life as a bumbling farm manager contrasts with the professor's cosmopolitan world and second marriage to a beautiful, much-younger woman. As their extended family and neighbors circle around the two aging men, once friends, now antagonists, Chekhov portrays the cultural and emotional dynamics of youth and age, ambition and disappointment, town and country, and love and loss in late 19th century Russian society.

_____OFF-BROADWAY Company Series

Top: Jay Wilkison and André Braugher in Manhattan Theatre Club's The Whipping Man. *Opened at City Center Stage I February 1, 2011 (photo by Joan Marcus)*

Center: Gordon Clapp, Ethan Hawke, and Ann Dowd in the New Group production of Blood From a Stone. *Opened at the Acorn Theatre on Theatre Row January 12, 2011 (photo by Monique Carboni)*

Bottom: Peter Friedman, Sarah Sokolovic, Kevin Cahoon, and Jamey Hood in the Playwrights Horizons/ New York Theatre Workshop co-production of The Shaggs: Philosophy of the World. *Opened at Playwrights Horizons June 7, 2011 (photo by Joan Marcus)*

Matt McGrath, Darren Pettie, and Larry Bryggman in the Atlantic Theater Company production of The Collection. *Opened at the East 13th Street Theater (Classic Stage Company) November 22, 2010 (photo by Ari Mintz)*

Linda Lavin and Stockard Channing in Lincoln Center Theater's Other Desert Cities. *Opened at the Mitzi E. Newhouse Theater January 13, 2011 (photo by Joan Marcus)*

Kelli O'Hara in the City Center Encores production of Bells Are Ringing. *Opened at New York City Center November 18, 2010 (photo by Joan Marcus)*

The Cast of Mint Theatre's A Little Journey. *Opened at the Mint Theatre June 6, 2011 (photo by Richard Termine)*

David Duchovny and Amanda Peet in Manhattan Class Company's The Break of Noon. *Opened at the Lucille Lortel Theatre November 22, 2010 (photo by Joan Marcus)*

Michael Warner, Jan Maxwell, and Adam Heller in the Second Stage production of Wings. Opened at Second Stage October 24, 2010 (photo by Joan Marcus)

Adam Chanler-Berat and Christian Borle in New York Theatre Workshop's Peter and the Starcatcher. Opened at NYTW March 9, 2011 (photo by Joan Marcus)

Jim Fletcher and Scott Shepherd in Elevator Repair Service/Public Theater co-production of Gatz. Opened at Martinson Hall October 3, 2010 (photo by Joan Marcus)

Olympia Dukakis and Darren Pettie in the Roundabout Theatre Company production of The Milk Train Doesn't Stop Here Anymore. Opened at the Laura Pels Theatre January 30, 2011 (photo by Joan Marcus)

Billy Porter, Robin Weigert, and Christian Borle in the Signature Theatre Company's production of Angels in America: A Gay Fantasia on National Themes, Part 2: Perestroika. Opened at Peter Norton Space October 28, 2010 (photo by Richard Termine)

Abingdon Theatre Company

Eighteenth Season

Artistic Director, Jan Buttram; Managing Director, Samuel J. Bellinger; Associate Artistic Director & Literary Manager, Kim T. Sharp; General Manager and Marketing, Amanda Kate Joshi; Technical Director, John Trevellini; Casting, William Schill; Playwright Outreach Coordinator, Bara Swain; Playwright Group Coordinator, Frank Tangredi; Rental Facilities Associate, Jerry Bradley; Sunday Series Coordinator, David Flora; Artistic Director Emeritus, Pamela Paul; Development Intern, Jacqueline Maddox; Literary Itern, Nathan Dick, Keith Filangieri; Press, Bob Lasko

Studio Productions

Nanjing Race by Reggie Cheong-Leen; Director, Brian Tom; Set and Lighting, Andrew Lu; Costumes, Pam Prior; Sound, David Margolin Lawson; Fight Choreography, Rick Sordelet; PSM, Genevieve Ortiz; ASM, Christine Kwon; Production Manager, John Trevellini; Graphic Design, Doug DeVita, Nicole Yang; House Manager, Patricia Croew; **Cast:** James Chen (Bao), Marcus Ho (Philip), Ian Wen (Yu Ahn)

Dorothy Strelsin Theatre; First Preview: October 29, 2010; Opening Night: November 7, 2010; Closed November 21, 2010; 22 performances. Setting: 1988; A Hotel in Nanjing, China. New York premiere of a new play presented without in two acts.

How I Fell in Love by Joel Fields; Director, Jules Ochoa; Set, Wilson Chin and David Arsenault; Costumes, Kimberly Matela; Lighting, Travis McHale; Sound, Ian Wehrle; PSM, Genevieve Ortiz; Production Manager, John Trevellini; Assistant Director, Benji Shaw; ASM, Sarah Livant; Graphic Design, Doug DeVita, Joseph Riccio; **Cast:** Mark Doherty (Eric), Polly Lee (Nessa), Tommy Schrider (Todd), Roya Shanks (Crystal/Louise)

Dorothy Strelsin Theatre; First Preview: January 21, 2011; Opening Night: January 30, 2011; Closed February 13, 2011; 22 performances. New York premiere of a new play presented without intermission.

Summer in Sanctuary by Al Letson; Director, Rob Urbinati; Costumes, Karen Anselm; Lighting, Andrew Lu; Sound, David Margolin Lawson; PSM, Mark Hoffner; Production Manager, John Trevellini; Assistant Director, Steve Werner; ASM, Sarah Livant; Grapic Design, Victoria Bukowski, Joseph Riccio; **Cast:** Al Letson (Performer), Willie Evans Jr (Musician)

Dorothy Strelsin Theatre; First Preview: March 25, 2011; Opening Night: April 3, 2011; Closed April 17, 2011; 22 performances. Setting: 2006; The Sanctuary in Jacksonville, Florida. New York premiere of a new solo performance play with music, multimedia, and poetry presented without intermission.

Ian Wren and James Chen in Nanjing Race *(photo by Kim T. Sharp)*

Al Letson in Summer in Sanctuary *(photo by Kim T. Sharp)*

Tommy Schneider and Polly Lee in How I Fell in Love *(photo by Kim T. Sharp)*

The Actors Company Theatre (TACT)

Eighteenth Season

Co-Artistic Directors, Scott Alan Evans, Cynthia Harris, & Simon Jones; Executive Director, Scott Alan Evans; General Manager, Cathy Bencivenga; Associate Producer, Jenn Thompson; Development, Anna Hayman; Resident Casting Director, Kelly Gillespie; Dramaturg, Stephanie Vella; Press, O+M Company, Richard Hilman

The Memorandum by Vaclav Havel; Director, Jenn Thompson; Set, Adrian W. Jones; Lighting, Philip S. Rosenberg; Costumes, David Toser; Sound and Projections, Stephen Kunken; Music, Joseph Trapanese; PSM, Meredith Dixon; ASM, Megan E. Coutts; Marketing Assistant, Brian M. Flanagan; Production Manager, Matt McAdon; Props, Lily Fairbanks; Technical Director, Patrick Cecala; Production Electrician, John Anselmo; Light Programmer, Stuart Burgess; Wardrobe, Christine Massoud; Production Assistants, Daniel Hainsworth, Korrie Strodel; **Cast:** Simon Jones (Josef Gross), Mark Alhadeff (Jan Ballas), Jeffrey C. Hawkins (Pillar/Thumb/George/Column), Lynn Wright (Hana), Joel Leffert (Mark Lear), John Plumpis (Otto Stroll), Trent Dawson (Alex Savant), Kate Levy (Helena), Nilanjana Bose (Maria)

Beckett Theatre on Theatre Row; First Preview: October 25, 2010; Opening Night: November 4, 2010; Closed April 17, 2011; 9 previews, 31 performances. Setting: A large organization within three offices over the course of two days. Revival of a play presented in twelve scenes in two acts.

Three Men on a Horse by John Cecil Holm and George Abbott; Director, Scott Alan Evans; Brett J. Banakis; Lighting, Mary Louise Geiger; Costumes, Martha Hally; Sound, Daryl Bornstein; Original Music, Joseph Trapanese; Props, Lauren Madden; Production Manager, Matt McAdon; PSM, E. Sara Barnes; ASM, Kristen Vaphides; Wardrobe, Jillian Tully; Production Assistant, Michael Friedlander; Assistant to the Director, Lauren Miller; **Cast:** Becky Baumwoll (Audrey Trowbridge), Geoffrey Molloy (Erwin Trowbridge), Scott Schafer (Clarence Dobbins), Ron McClary (Harry), Jeffrey C. Hawkins (Charlie), Don Burroughs (Frankie), Gregory Salata (Patsy), Julianna Zinkel (Mabel), Kristen Vaphides (Maid), James Murtaugh (Mr. Carver), Dave Johnson (Race Track Announcer)

Beckett Theatre on Theatre Row; First Preview: March 14, 2011; Opening Night: March 24, 2011; Closed April 23, 2011; 9 previews, 32 performances. Setting: In and around Ozone Heights, New Jersey and the Lavillere Hotel in New York City; 1935. Revival of a play presented in two acts.

Salon Series – Staged Readings at TACT Studio

Olympia by Ferenc Molnar; Director, Stuart Ross; Music, Wally Gunn; PSM, Megan E. Coutts; Pianist, Chia-En Hsie; **Cast:** Cynthia Harris (Countess Lina), Evan Thompson (Count Albert), Lauren English (Olympia), Delphi Harrington (Princess Eugenie Plata-Ettingen), Joel Rooks (Colonel Krehl), Gene Gillette (Captain Kovacs), James Prendergast (Prince Plata-Ettingen); September 24-26, 2010

I Am a Camera by John Van Druten; Director, Drew Barr; Composer, Amir Khosropour; PSM, Katie Kavett; ASM, Lauren Williams; **Cast:** Jeremy Beck (Christopher Isherwood), Nora Chester (Fraulein Schneider), Todd Gearhart (Fritz Wendell), Amelia Pedlow (Sally Bowles), Christopher Burns (Clive Mortimer), Victoria Mack (Natalia Landauer), Delphi Harrington (Mrs. Watson-Courneidge); December 10-13, 2010

Uncle Harry by Thomas Job; Director, Henry Wishcamper; Music, Ayanna Witter-Johnson; PSM, Susan Manikas; **Cast:** Eve Bianco (Miss Phipps), Sam Breslin Wright (Mr. Jenkins/Ben), Scott Schafer (Uncle Harry), Cynthia Harris (Hester), Nora Chester (Lettie), Mary Bacon (Lucy), Francesca Di Mauro (Nona/Matron), Jeffrey M. Bender (George Waddy/Albert), James Prendergast (D'Arcy/Mr. Burton), Wilbur Edwin Henry (Blake/The Governor); January 21-24, 2011

Two Dozen Red Roses by Aldo de Benedetti; Director, Kenneth Horne; Music, Jack Ramsey; PSM, Susan Manikas; **Cast:** Matt Faucher (Bernardo), Mackenzie Meehan (Rosina), Scott Schafer (Tomasso), Francesca DiMauro (Marina), John Plumpis (Alberto); May 20-23, 2011

Special Events and Readings

The Triangle Factory Fire Project by Christopher Piehler and Scott Alan Evans; Director, Scott Alan Evans; Music, Colin McGrath; Sound, Daryl Bornstein; Lighting, Mary Louise Geiger; PSM, Meredith Dixon; ASM, Megan E. Coutts; **Cast**: Cynthia Harris, Jamie Bennett, Nora Chester, Francesca Di Mauro, Timothy McCracken, James Murtaugh, Scott Schafer, Victoria Mack, Jeff Talbott. Theatre 80 St. Marks; February 7, 2011; staged reading of TACT's 2004 Off-Broadway production presented as a benefit in commemoration of the centenary of the Triangle Shirtwaist Company fire that killed 146 people on March 25, 1911.

newTACTics New Play Festival Producing Director, Barry Satchwell Smith; Associate Producer, Lauren Miller; Original Music, Jack Ramsey; Included: *The Queen of Spades* by Joel Gross, directed by Robert Kalfin; *Sia* by Matthew Mackenzie, directed by Jenn Thompson; *You Are Here* by Zakiyyah Alexander, directed by Barry Satchwell Smith; *Spy: The Betrayal of Mata Hari* by Bart Midwood, directed by Barry Satchwell Smith; Readings of four new plays presented over four weeks, June 2011.

Trent Dawson, Katie Levy, John Plumpis, and Mark Alhadeff in The Memorandum *(photo by Stephen Kunken)*

Julianna Zinkel, Don Burroughs, Gregory Salata, Geoffrey Molloy, and Jeffrey C. Hawkins in Three Men on a Horse *(photo by Stephen Kunken)*

Atlantic Theater Company

Twenty-fifth Season

Artistic Director, Neil Pepe; Managing Director, Jeffory Lawson; General Manager, Jamie Tyrol; Associate Artistic Director, Christian Parker; School Executive Director, Mary McCann; Development Director, Cynthia Flowers; Institutional Giving/Speical Events, Chloe Hughes; Institutional Giving, Nick Luckenbaugh; Production Managers, Michael Wade and Gabriel Evansohn; Marketing, Ryan Pointer; Business Manager, Chris Kam; Artistic Leadership Associate, Jaime Castañeda; Audience Services, Sara Montgomery; Operations, Ian Crawford; Company Manager, Teresa Gozzo; Literary Associate, Abigail Katz; School Associate Director, Lorielle Mallue; Student Affairs, Clayton Early; School Artistic Director, Allison Beatty; Education and Recruitment, Heather Baird; Box Office, Frances Tarr; Casting, Telsey + Company; Press, Boneau/Bryan-Brown, Chris Boneau, Joe Perrotta, Kelly Guiod

Bottom of the World by Lucy Thurber; Director, Caitriona McLaughlin; Set, Walt Spangler; Costumes, Emily Rebholz; Lighting, Matthew Richards; Sound/Original Music, Robert Kaplowitz; Original Music/Musicians, Robert Kaplowitz, Alexander Sovronsky (Fiddle), Bennett Sullivan (Banjo/Mandolin); PSM, Eileen Ryan Kelly; Assistant Director, Jenna Worsham; ASM, Emily E. Levin; **Cast:** Crystal A. Dicinson (Abigail), Jessica Love (Kate), Aubrey Dollar (Susan/Dana), Peter Maloney (Marshall/Paul), Kristin Griffith (Louise/Christine), Brendan Griffin (Josh), Brandon J. Dirden (Ely), K.K. Moggie (Gina/Sally)

Atlantic Stage 2; First Preview: September 3, 2010; Opening Night: September 14, 2010; Closed October 3, 2010; 11 previews, 21 performances. Setting: Contemporary; NYC and a fictional past in western Massachusettes. World premiere of a new play presented without intermission.

The Collection and **A Kind of Alaska** by Harold Pinter; Director, Karen Kohlhaas; Sets, Walt Spangler; Costumes, Bobby Frederick Tilley II; Lighting, Jason Lyons; Sound, Obadiah Eaves; Fight Consultant, Rick Sordelet; Dialect Coach, Stephen Gabis; PSM, David H. Lurie; ASM, Paige D. Causey; Technical Director, Brian Kalin; **Cast:** *The Collection*: Larry Bryggman (Harry), Darren Pettie (James), Rebecca Henderson (Stella), Matt McGrath (Bill); *A Kind of Alaska*: Lisa Emery (Deborah), Larry Bryggman (Hornby), Rebecca Henderson (Pauline)

East 13th Street Theatre (Classic Stage Company); First Preview: November 3, 2010; Opening Night: November 21, 2010; Closed December 24, 2010; 22 previews, 38 performances. Revivals of two one-act plays presented with intermission. This season Atlantic Theater's mainstage (the Linda Gross Theater) was under renovation, so the company produced mainstage productions at alternative spaces.

The New York Idea Adapted by David Auburn from the original script by Langdon Mitchell; Director, Mark Brokaw; Sets, Allen Moyer; Costumes, Michael Krass; Lighting, Mary Louise Geiger; Original Music, Lewis Flinn; Period Etiqutte and Style, Frank Ventura; Dialect Coach, Ben Furey; PSM, Jenna Woods; ASM, Jessica Barker; Technical Director, Brian Kalin; Props, Desiree Maurer; **Cast:** Patricia O'Connell (Mrs. Philimore), Patricia Conolly (Miss Henage), Tom Patrick Stephens (Thomas), Peter Maloney (Sudley), Jaime Ray Newman (Cynthia Karslake), Michael Countryman (Philip Philimore), Joey Slotnick (Matthew Philimore), John Keating (Fiddler), Jeremy Shamos (John Karslake), Rick Holmes (Wilfred Cates-Darby), Francesca Faridany (Vida Philimore), Mikaela Feely-Lehmann (Jacqueline)

Lucille Lortel Theatre; First Preview: January 6, 2011; Opening Night: January 26, 2011; Closed February 26, 2011; 22 previews, 39 performances. Setting: 1906, Washington Square, Greenwich Village. World premiere of a new adaption of a 1906 play presented in two acts.

10x25 Twenty-five ten minute plays; Sets, Riccardo Hernandez; Costumes, Katja Andreiev; Lighting, Eric Southern; Sound, Tony Smolenski IV; Casting, MelCap Casting; PSM, Kyle Gates; ASM, Hilary Austin; **Series A** (May 18-29): *The Redeemers* by Ethan Coen; directed by Neil Pepe, with Michael Chernus, Tim Blake Nelson, Greg Stuhr; *Posh Pill* by Kia Corthron, directed by Karen Kohlhaas, with Lisa Gorlitsky, Kristin Griffith, Michelle Hurst, Peter Maloney, Christa Scott-Reed; *In a Linguistics Class* by David Mamet, directed by Jaime Cataneda, with Zackary Grady, Jordan Lage; *Master Class with Cassiopeia O'Hara* by Kate Moira Ryan, directed by Christian Parker, with Kristen Johnston; *Elzbieta* by John Guare, directed by Neil Pepe, with Glenn Fitzgerald, Omar Sangare; *Various Rigors* by Stephen Belber, directed by Lucie Tiberghien, with Michael Chernus and Mary McCann; *Marriage* by Lucy Thurber, directed by Hilary Hinckle, with Mikaela Feely-Lehmann, Kristin Griffith, Peter Maloney, Ben McKenzie; *Jacob Sterling, Distinguished Alumnus* by David Pittu and Randy Redd, directed by David Pittu, with Aaron Farenback-Brateman, David Pittu; **Series B** (June 1-12): *Practice* written and directed by Annie Baker, with Susan Pourfar, Danielle Slavick, Michael Chernus, Mary McCann, Reed Birney, Nick Choksi; *The New Paradigm* by Keith Reddin, directed by Neil Pepe, with Stephen Park, Larry Bryggman, Rod McLachlan; *The Naked Eye* by Jez Butterworth, directed by Neil Pepe, with Zosia Mamet; *Caution, This Bus Kneels. Stand Clear.* by Tina Howe, directed by Christian Parker, with David Fonteno, Larry Bryggman, Kate Blumberg, Joey Slotnick, Susan Pourfar, Mary Beth Peil; *The Sell* by Craig Lucas, directed by Neil Pepe, with Mary McCann and Talia Balsam; *Smiling* by Edwin Sanchez, directed by Jaime Castaneda, with Michael Chernus and Reed Birney; *There You Are* written and directed by Leslie Ayvazian, with Maria Tucci, Mary Beth Peil; *This Backstage Life* by Bill Wrubel, directed by Todd Weeks, with Rick Holmes, Kate Blumberg, Joey Slotnick, John Early, Rod McLachlan, Mary Beth Peil, Larry Bryggman, Matthew Montelongo; **Series C** (June 15-26): *Run* by Bekah Brunstetter, directed by Jackson Gay, with Michael Countryman, Syndey Matthews; *Two Dads* by David Auburn, directed by Hilary Hinckle, with Zach Grenier, Ray Anthony Thomas; *Dada Woof Papa Hot* by Peter Parnell, directed by Jackson Gay, with Brad Heberlee, Rick Holmes; *I Need a Quote* by Tom Donaghy, directed by Anya Saffir, with Kate Blumberg, Eddie Cahill; *Evanescence* by Sam Shepard, directed by Neil Pepe, with Kathryn Erbe, Nic Novicki; *Sold* by Moira Buffini, directed by Scott Zigler, with Kathryn Erbe, T.R. Knight; *Inside Play* by Kate Robin, directed by Anya Saffir, with Anthony Arkin, Ilana Levine; *As Himself* by Kevin Heelan, directed by Christian Parker, with Marcia DeBonis, Kari Nicolle, Chris Myers, Ray Anthony Thomas; *In Which I Tender My Resignation* by Jeff Whitty, directed by Matt McGrath, with Anthony Arkin, Kate Gersten, Jeff Whitey

Atlantic Stage 2; Opening Night: May 18, 2011; Closed June 26, 2011; 42 performances (14 of each series). Three evenings of short plays written by Atlantic Theater Company alumni and company members.

Through a Glass Darkly Adapted from Ingmar Bergman's film by Jenny Worton; Presented in association with Andrew Higgie, Garry McQuinn, Debbie Bisno, and Bruce Davey; Director, David Leveaux; Sets, Takeshi Kata; Costumes, Jess Goldstein; Lighting, David Weiner; Original Music & Sound, David Van Tieghem; Dialect Coach, Stephen Gabis; PSM, Jenna Woods; ASM, Joanne E. McInerney; Assistant Director, Jason Lawson; Technical Director, Chris Soley; Props, Susan Barras; **Cast:** Chris Sarandon (David), Ben Rosenfield (Max), Carey Mulligan (Karin), Jason Butler Harner (Martin)

East 4th Street Theatre (New York Theatre Workshop); First Preview: May 13, 2011; Opening Night: June 6, 2011; Closed July 3, 2011; 28 previews, 32 performances. Setting: 1960, an island off the coast of Sweden. U.S premiere of a new play based on the 1961 Swedish film presented without intermission. World premiere presented June 10, 2010 at the Almeida Theatre (London).

Atlantic for Kids

Miss Nelson Is Missing! Based on the books by Harry Allard and James Marshall; Book, music, and lyrics by Joan Cushing; Director/Choreography, Alison Beatty; Music Director, Nate Weida; Set/Lighting, Gabe Evansohn; Costumes, Katja Adreiev; Orchestrations, Deborah Wicks LaPuma; **Cast:** Jann Emig (Miss Nelson/Viola Swamp), Andy Schneeflock (Pop Hanson/Detective McSmogg), Brad Mielke (Mr. Blandworth/Al Catraz), Seth Clayton, Kelsey Glasser,

Ben Katz, Kate Manfre, Brian Maxsween, Arielle Siegel (The Kids of Room 207); a new musical for young audiences presented without intermission; Lucille Lortel Theatre; January 29-February 20, 2011.

Revolting Rhymes Based on poems and books by Roald Dahl; Presented with Tisch Drama Stage Works; Director/Composer, Elizabeth Swados; Music Director, Kris Kukul; Lighting, Gabe Evansohn; Costumes, Molly Deale; Puppets, Federico Restrepo; Artistic Direction, Alison Beatty; **Cast:** Travis Artz, Stephanie Hsu, Rachel McGarry, Eli Palzkill, Jeanna Phillips, Megan Putnam, Anthony Ritosa, Alex Romania, Patricia Sabulis, Trevor Salter, Jacob Samuels, Elise Sokolow, Jonathan Sokolow, Hannah Solow; a series of new mini-musicals for young audiences presented without intermission; Lucille Lortel Theatre; April 3-30, 2011.

Lisa Emery and Rebecca Henderson in A Kind of Alaska *(photo by Ari Mintz)*

Brendan Griffin, Aubrey Dollar, Peter Maloney, Kristin Griffith, and Brandon J. Dirden in Bottom of the World *(photo by Ari Mintz)*

Joey Slotnick, Francesca Faridany, and David Auburn in The New York Idea *(photo by Ari Mintz)*

Carey Mulligan and Jason Butler Harner in Through a Glass Darkly *(photo by Ari Mintz)*

Brooklyn Academy of Music

Founded in 1861

Alan H. Fishman, Chairman of the Board; Karen Brooks Hopkins, President; William I. Campbell, Vice Chairman of the Board; Joseph V. Melillo, Executive Producer

2010 Next Wave Festival (28ᵗʰ Annual)

Delusion Music, text, and visual design by Laurie Anderson; Commissioned by Vancouver 2010 Cultural Olympiad (Vancouver) and Barbicanbite10 (London); Video Design and Live Mix, Amy Khoshbin; Lighting/Production Manager, Rus Snelling; House Audio, Dave Cook; Audio Rig Design, Shane Koss; Audio Software Design, Konrad Kaczmarek; Violin Design, Ned Steinberger; Story Team, Bob Currie, Rande Brown; Tour Manager, Brad Hampton; Tour Representation, Pomegranate Arts/Linda Brumbach; PSM, Brian Scott; Performed by Laurie Anderson (Violin/Vocals) with Eyvind Kang (Viola), Colin Stetson (Horns)

Harvey Theater; September 21–October 3, 2010; 12 performances. New York premiere of a theatrical piece with music, poetry, puppetry, and visuals presented without intermission.

Laurie Anderson in Delusion *(photo by Rahev Segev)*

Vollmond Directed and choreographed by Pina Bausch; Presented by Tanztheater Wuppertal Pina Bausch; Music, René Aubry, Alexander Balanescu with the Balanescu Quartet and Steve Arguelles, Carl Craig, Siegfried Ganhör and to rococo rot, Nenad Jelić, Leftfield, Marasma, Jun Miyake and Sublime, Magyar Posse, Cat Power, Amon Tobin, Tom Waits; Set, Peter Pabst; Costumes, Marion Cit; Music Collaboration, Mattias Burkert and Andreas Eisenschneider; Collaborators, Marion Cito, Daphnis Kokkinos, Robert Sturm; Reheasal Directors, Daphnis Kokkinos, Dominque Merscy, Robert Sturm; Ballet Master, Ernesta Corvino; Technical Director, Jorg Ramershoven; Lighting, Fernando Jacon; Sound, Andreas Eisenschneider; Stage Manager, Felicitas Willems; Properties, Arnulf Eichholz; Technicians, Dietrich Roder, Martin Winterscheidt; **Cast:** Pablo Aran Gimeno, Rainer Behr, Ditta Miranda Jasjfi, Dominique Mercy, Nazareth Panader, Helena Pikon, Jorge Puerta Armenta, Azusa Seyama, Julie Anne Stanzak, Michael Strecker, Fernando Suels Mendoza,Tsai-Chin Yu

Howard Gilman Opera House; September 29–October 9, 2010; 9 performances. U.S. premiere of a theatrical dance piece presented in two acts.

The Deer House Text, direction, and set by Jans Lauwers; Presented by Needcompany in association with Salzburger Festspiele, Schauspielhaus Zurich, PACT Zollverein, with the collaboration of deSingel (Antwerp), Kaaitheater (Brussels); Music, Hans Petter Dahl, Maarteen Seghers, Jan Lauwers; Choreography, The Company; Costumes, Lot Lemm; Lighting, Ken Hioco, Koen Raes; Sound, Dré Schneider; Production Manager Luc Galle; Assistant to the

Director/Surtitles; Translations, Gregory Ball (English), Olivier Taymans (French); Language Coaches, Louise Chamberlain, Helen McNamara, Anny Czupper; **Cast:** Viviane De Muynck, Grace Ellen Barkey, Hans Petter Dahl,Anneke Bonnema, Misha Downey, Maarten Seghers, Julien Faure,Yumiko Funaya, Benoît Gob, Inge Van Bruystegem, Eléonore Valère

Harvey Theater; October 5-9, 2010; 4 performances. U.S. premiere of a theatrical piece presented in French and English without intermission.

How Can You Stay in the House All Day and Not Go Anywhere? Conceived, choreographed, and directed by Ralph Lemon; Created by the Company; Co-produced by Cross Performance Inc and MAPP International Productions; Dramaturg, Katherine Profeta; Lighting, Roderick Murray; Video, Jim Findlay; *Sunshine Room* film editor, Mike Taylor; Sound, Ralph Lemon; Sound Consultant, Doc Davis; Costumes, Anne de Velder; Lighting Director/ Production Manager, Christopher Kuhl; Videographer, Shoko Letton; Stage Manager/Company Manager, Kate Danziger; Editing Assistant, Josh Higgason; **Cast:** Djédjé Djédjé Gervais, Darrell Jones,Ralph Lemon, Gesel Mason, Okwui Okpokwasili, Omagbitse Omagbemi, David Thomson, and Walter Carter, Edna Carter

Harvey Theater; October 13-16, 2010; 4 performances. New York premiere of a multimedia dance piece presented in three parts without intermission. World premiere at the Krannert Center at the University of Illinois September 10, 2010.

A House in Bali Presented by Bang on a Can All-Stars (Kenny Savelson, Producer) and Gamelan Salukat (Dewa Ketut Alit, Director) in association with Asia Society; Director, Jay Scheib; Music, Evan Ziporyn; Choreography, Kadek Dewi Aryani and I Nyoman Catra; Libretto, Paul Schick (after Colin McPhee's *A House in Bali* and texts by Margaret Mead and Walter Spies); Additional Dialogue and Lyrics, Evan Ziporyn; Set, Sara Brown; Lighting, Peter Ksander; Costumes, Oana Botez-Ban; Sound, Andrew Cotton; Video, Jay Scheib and Noah Feehan; Assistant Director, Laine Rettmer; Stage Manager, Jenni Bowman; Company Manager/ASM, Susan Wilson; Associate Video, Alex Koch; Assistant Music Director, Thomas Carr; **Cast:** Peter Tantsits (Colin McPhee), Kadek Dewi Aryani (Penari [Dancer]), Rantun, Camplung, Lèyak), Desak Madé Suarti Laksmi (Penari, Ibu [Mother], Penyanyi Kekawin [Kekawin Singer]), I Nyoman Catra (Kesyur, Bapak [Father], Kalèr Sagami, Dutch Poiceman), Tumur Bekbosunov (Walter Spies), Anne Harley (Margaret Mead), Nyoman Triyana Usadhi (Sampih); Orchestra: Ashley Bathgate (Cello), Robert Black (Bass), Vicky Chow (Piano/ Keyboards), Andrew Cotton (Engineer), Derek Johnson (Guitar), Eduardo Leandro (Percussion), Todd Reynolds (Violin)

Howard Gilman Opera House; October 14-16, 2010; 3 performances. New York premiere of an opera presented in two parts without intermission.

A scene from in A House in Bali *(photo by Christine Southworth)*

Brooklyn Omnibus Songs and Notions by Stew and Heidi Rodewald; Presented by BAM; Performed by The Negro Problem; Sound, Tom Morse; Projections, Jim Findlay and Jeff Sugg; Lighting, KJ Hardy; Wardrobe Styling, Elizabeth Hope Clancy; PSM, Rachel Motz; Sound Engineer, Jamie McElhinney; Guitar Tech, Kelly Macaulay; **Cast:** Brian Drye (Trombone), Jacob Garchik (Tuba, Accordion), Jeff Hermanson (Trumpet, Flugelhorn), Greg Joseph (Drums), Michael McGinnis (Woodwinds), Joe McGinty (Keyboards), Chivas Michael (Vocals), Sonja Perryman (Vocals), Heidi Rodewald (Bass, Vocals, Flip cam), Urbano Sanchez (Percussion), Stew (Flip cam, Guitar, Ringmaster), Eisa Davis (Guest Star)

Harvey Theater; October 20-23, 2010; 4 performances. World premiere of a new theatrical song cycle presented without intermission.

Persephone Music by Ben Neill and Mimi Goese, lyrics by Mimi Goese, book by Warren Leight; Produced by Kenny Savelson; Presented by Ridge Theatre; Co-commisioned by Virgina Tech Department of Theatre and Cinema; Director, Bob McGrath; Choreography, Dan Safer; Sets, Jim Findlay; Lighting, John Ambrosone; Costumes, Jane Alois Stein; Sound, Jamie McElhiney; Dramaturg, Daniel Zippi and Karl Precoda; PSM, Sarah Elizabeth Ford; Associate Producer/First Assistant Director, Hunter Parker; Production Manager, Bill Barksdale; Stage Manager, Ryan Parow; Assistant Production Manager, Caitlin Merryman; Props, Kristen Morgan; ASMs, Laura Baugh, Jackie Mullen; Makeup, Kelley Coleman; Vocal Coach, Brandy Buckles Baxter; **Cast:** Julia Stiles (Clara/Persephone), Mimi Goese (Grace/Demeter), Sean Haberle (Jules/Zeus), Michael Anthony Williams (Nicholas/Hades), Ben Neill (Mercury), Alexis Demetra Baker (Iris, a siren), Amy Cammel (Siren), Bryanna Demerly (Eve, a siren), Kara Drechsel (Siren), Kristin Macomber (Siren), Sarah Wylie (Myrtle, a siren); Understudies: Jordan Goldston (Jules/Zeus), Carly Erickson (Grace/Demeter), Kara Drechel (Persephone), Marlo Clingman (Siren)

Harvey Theater; October 26-30, 2010; 5 performances. New York premiere of a theatrical musical multimedia production presented without intermission.

Empty moves (parts I & II) Presented by Ballet Preljocaj; Chorography, Angelin Preljocaj; Music, John Cage; Associate Artistic Director, Youri Van den Bosch; Choreologist, Dany Levêque; Technical Director, Luc Corazz; Sound Manager, Martin Lecarme; Dancers: Fabrizio Clemente, Gaëlle Chappaz, Julien Thibault, Yurie Tsugawa; Alternates: Charlotte Siepiora, Baptiste Coissieu

Howard Gilman Opera House; October 27-30, 2010; 3 performances. Revival (Part I) and New York premiere (Part II) of a theatrical dance piece presented in two parts without intermission.

Gezeiten Directed and choreographed by Sasha Waltz; Presented by Sasha Waltz & Guests; Produced in association with Schaubühne am Lehniner Platz, Berlin; Music, Jonathan Bepler and Johann Sebastian Bach; Stage Design, Thomas Schenk, Sasha Waltz; Costumes, Beate Borrmann; Lighting, Martin Hauk; Props, Brad Hwang; Light Technician, Martin Hauk; Stage Technician, Daniel Herrmann; Sound Technician, Lutz Nerger; Technical Director, Reinhard Wizisla; Assistant Technical Director, Carsten Grigo; Hair/Makeup, Kati Heimann; Assistant Directors, Steffen Döring, Francesca Noia; **Cast:** Liza Alpízar Aguilar, Davide Camplani, Juan Kruz Diaz de Garaio Esnaola, Matija Ferlin, Gabriel Galindez Cruz, Maria Öhman, Pinar Ömerbeyoglu, Friederike Plafki, Koen De Preter, Virgis Puodziunas, Sasa Queliz, Maria Eugenia Rivas Medina, Mata Sakka, Claudia de Serpa Soares, Xuan Shi, Davide Sportelli

Howard Gilman Opera House; November 3-6, 2010; 3 performances. U.S. premiere of a theatrical dance piece presented without intermission.

Raoul Concept, scenography, and performance by James Thiérrée; Presented by Compagnie du Hanneton; Costume/Animal Design and Fabrication, Victoria Thiérrée; Sound, Thomas Delot; Lighting, Jerome Sabre; Scenic Assistant, Mehdi Duman; Stage Managers, Guillaume Pissembon, Anthony Nicholas; Lighting Manager, Bastein Courthieu; Costume Dresser/Set Maker, Daniele Gagliardo; Assistant Directors, Laetitia Hélin, Disonie Pigeon; Artistic Consultants, Kaori Ito, Magnus Jakobsson, Bruno Fontaine; Electric Guitar Recording, Matthieu Chedid; Company Manager, Emmanuelle Taccard

Harvey Theater; November 5-14, 2010; 8 performances. U.S. premiere of a solo physical theater performance piece presented without intermission.

James Thiérrée in Raoul *(photo by Richard Termine)*

Throne of Blood Adapted and directed by Ping Chong; Based on the film directed by Akira Kurosawa; Presented by the Oregon Shakepeare Festival (Bill Rauch, Artistic Director; Paul Nicholson, Executive Director); Developed in association with Ping Chong & Company (Bruce Allardice, Managing Director); Set, Christopher Acebo; Costumes, Stefani Mar; Original Lightign, Darren McCroom; Lighting Design Transfer, Noah Beauregard and Michael Maag; Video and Projections, Maya Ciarrocchi; Composer/Sound, Todd Barton; Dramaturgs, Lue Morgan Douthit, Gina Pisasale; Original Screenplay, Akira Kurosawa, Hideo Oguni, Shinobu Hashimoto, Ryuzo Kikushima; Voice and Text Director, Sara Becker; Movement/Fight Director, John Sipes; Stage Manager, Amy Miranda Warner; ASM, Mandy Younger; Production Manager, Tom Knapp; **Cast:** Kevin Kenerly (Washizu), Ako (Lady Asaji), Danforth Comins (Yoshiako Miki/Third Forest Spirit), Jonathan Haugen (Lord Kuniharu/Soldier), JaMario Stills (Prince Kunimaru/Koken), Richard Howard (Noriyasu Odagura/Second Forest Spirit), Michael Winters (Old General), Cristofer Jean (Forest Spirit/Soldier), Gregory Linington (First Quartet/First Retainer), Peter Macon (Second General/Second Quartet), James Newcomb (Third General/Third Quartet), U. Jonathan Toppo (First General/Fourth Quartet), Elijah Alexander (Fourth General/Second Retainer), Kacy-Earl David (First Soldier/First Messenger/Second Retainer), Emily Sophia Knapp (Koken/Old Woman), Eddie Lopez (Koken), Alonzo Lee Moore IV (Koken), Daniel Marmion (Yoshiteru/Second Messenger), Kacy-Earl David, Jonathan Haugen, Gregory Linington, Eddie Lopez, Daniel Marmion, Alonzo Lee Moore IV, JaMario Stills (Ensemble)

Howard Gilman Opera House; November 10-13, 2010; 3 performances. Setting: 17th Century feudal Japan. New York premiere of a theatrical stage adaptation of a film presented without intermission.

The Marriage of Maria Braun Screenplay by Rainer Werner Fassbinder, playscript by Peter Märthesheimer, Pea Fröhlich; Presented by Schaubühne am Lehniner Platz; Director, Thomas Ostermeier; Design, Nina Wetzel; Costumes, Ulrike Gutbrod; Lighting, Max Keller; Music, Nils Ostendorf; Video, Sebastien Dupouey; Dramaturgy, Julia Lochte; General Management, Jürgen Schitthelm; Technical Director, Heinrich Pfeilschifter; **Cast:** Jean-Pierre Cornu, Brigitte Hobmeier, Hans Kremer, Bernd Moss, Steven Scharf

Harvey Theater; November 17-21, 2010; 6 performances. U.S. premiere of a theatrical stage version of a film presented without intermission.

Metamorphosis Adapted and directed by David Farr and Gísli Örn Gardarsson from the novel by Franz Kafka; Music, Nick Cave and Warren Ellis; Presented by Vesturport Theatre/Lyric Hammersmith; Set, Börkur Jónsson; Lighting,

Björn Helgason; Costumes, Brenda Murphy; Sound, Nick Manning; Stage Manager, Gunnar Gunnsteinsson; ASM, Haradur Björn Haraldsson; Company/Tour Manager, Gunnhildur H. Gunnars; Producer, Dyri Jonsson; American Stage Manager, R. Michael Blanco; **Cast:** Gísli Örn Gardarsson (Gregor Samsa), Nína Dögg Filippusdóttir (Greta Samsa), Ingvar E. Sigurdsson (Hermann Samsa), Kelly Hunter (Lucy Samsa), Jonathan McGuinness (Herr Stietl/Herr Fischer)

Harvey Theater; November 30–December 5, 2010; 6 performances. U.S. premiere of a play presented without intermission.

Invar E. Sigurdsson, Jonathan McGuinness, and Gisli Orn Gardarsson in Metamorphosis

Red Hot + New Orleans Presented by BAM & Paul Heck/Red Hot Organization; Music Director, Trombone Shorty (Troy Andrews); Video, Yuki Nakajima; Design, Alex Delaunay; PSM, Sarah Ford; **Cast:** Trombone Shorty and Orleans Avenue, Dr. John aka Malcolm Rebnnack, Irma Thomas, Kermit Ruffins, Ledisi, Marc Broussard, Ivan Neville, Partners-N-Crime, Mannie Fresh, Roger Lewis (Dirty Dozen Brass Band), Phil and Keith Frazier(Rebirth Brass Band)

Howard Gilman Opera House; December 3-4, 2010; 2 performances. World premiere of a theatrical concert with multimedia presented without intermission.

Gravity Radio Conceived, written, and directed by Mikel Rouse; Produced by BAM; Set/Video, Jeffery Sugg; Sound, Christopher Ericson; Lighting, Hideaki Tsutsui; Music Director, Matthew Gandolfo; Film Editor, Jeff Carpenter; Production Manager, William Knapp; **Cast:** Mikel Rouse (Guitars and vocals), Claire Kenny (Newsreader), Matthew Gandolfo (Conductor/newsreader assistant/vocals), Kristi Helberg (Violin), Nanae Iwata (Violin), Kyle Armbrust (Viola), Julia Maclaine (Cello), Sarah Emley (Vocals), Eryn Murman (Vocals)

Harvey Theater; December 7-11, 2010; 4 performances. New York premiere of a theatrical song cycle with multimedia presented without intermission.

The Hard Nut Based on the work of Charles Burns and the *The Nutcracker and the Mouse King* by E.T.A. Hoffman; Choreography by Mark Morris; Presented by BAM and the Mark Morris Dance Group (Mark Morris, Artistic Director; Nancy Umanoff, Executive Director); Music, Pyotr Ilyich Tchaikovsky; Set, Adrianne Lobel; Costumes, Martin Pakledinaz; Lighting, James F. Ingalls; Conductor MMDG Music Ensemble, Robert Cole; Technical Director, Johan Henckens; **Cast:** Lauren Grant (Marie), Mark Morris (Dr. Stahlbaum/King), Kraig Patterson (Housekeeper/Nurse), John Heginbotham (Mrs. Stahlbaum/Queen), William Smith III (Drosselmeier), David Leventhal (Nutcracker/Young Drosselmeier), Aaron Loux (G.I Joe Soldier, Arabian, Flower, Snow), Amber Star Merkens (Flower, Party Guest, Arabian, Snow), Bradley Shelver (Changer), Brian Lawson (Arabian, G.I. Joe Soldier, Snow, Suitor), Claudia MacPherson (Russian, Rat Soldier, Snow), Dallas McMurray (Russian, Party Guest, Snow, Flower), Domingo Estrada Jr. (Party Guest, Spanish, Flower, Snow), Elisa Clark (Barbie Doll, Snow, French, Flower), Jenn Weddel (Rat Soldier, Rat Queen, Russian, Snow), Jennifer Jones (Flower, Rat Soldier, Snow, Party Guest), Joe Bowie (Party Guest), Julie Fiorenza (Rat Soldier, Snow, Chinese), Julie Worden (Louise/Princess Pirlpat, Snow),

June Omura (Fritz, Flower), Justin D. Melvin (G.I. Joe Soldier, Arabian, Snow), Kanji Segawa (Suitor, G.I. Joe Soldier, Chinese, Snow), Laurel Lynch (Rat Soldier, Flower, Snow, Arabian), Lesley Garrison (Flower, Rat Soldier, Snow, Russian), Maile Okamura (Flower, Party Guest, French, Snow), Michelle Yard (Party Guest, Snow, Spanish, Flower), Noah Vinson (Party Guest, Flower, Snow, French), Rita Donahue (Party Guest, Flower, Snow, Russian), Samuel Black (G.I. Joe Soldier, Snow, Russian, Flower), Shawn Gannon (Dentist/Party Guest), Spencer Ramirez (Robot, Changer, Snow, French), Utafumi Takemura (Rat King, Chinese, Snow)

Howard Gilman Opera House; November 10-13, 2010; 3 performances. Revival of a modern adaptation of a ballet presented in two acts.

Spring Season

John Gabriel Borkman by Henrik Ibsen in a new version by Frank McGuinness; Presented by the Abbey Theatre (Ireland); Director, James Macdonald; Set, Tom Pye; Lighting, Jean Kalman; Costumes, Joan Bergin; Sound, Ian Dickinson; American Stage Manager, Bonnie Panson; Assistant Director, Sophie Motley; Casting, Holly Ní Chiardha; Company Stage Mangaer, Anne Kyle; Deputy Stage Manager, Tara Furlong; Sound Assistant, Ben Delaney; Electrician, Kevin McFadden; Voice Director, Andrea Ainsworht; International Touring Producer, Pádraig Cusack; **Cast:** Fiona Shaw (Mrs. Gunhild Borkman), Joan Sheehy (Malene), Lindsay Duncan (Miss Ella Rentheim), Cathy Belton (Mrs. Fanny Wilton), Marty Rea (Erhart Borkman), Amy Molloy (Frida Foldal), Alan Rickman (John Gabriel Borkman), John Kavanagh (Vilhelm Foldal)

Harvey Theater; Opening Night: January 7, 2011; Closed February 6, 2011; 32 performances. Setting: A winter evening at the REntheim family estate outside the capital. U.S. premire of a foreign revival of a classic play presented in two acts. This production premiered at the Abbey Theatre October 13, 2010.

Alan Rickman, Lindsay Duncan, and Fiona Shaw in John Gabriel Borkman *(photo by Richard Termine)*

The Diary of a Madman by Nilolai Gogol; Adapted by David Holman with Neil Armfield and Geoffrey Rush; Presented by Belvoir (Surry Hills, New South Wales, Austrailia; Ralph Myers, Artistic Director; Brenna Hobson, General Manager); Director, Neil Armfield; Set, Catherine Martin; Costumes, Tess Schofield; Lighting, Mark Shelton; Sound, Paul Charlier; Music, Alan John (after Mussorgsky); Set Design Assistant, Chris Tangney; Company Manager, Annelies Crowe; Stage Manager, Mark Lowrey; Assistant Stage Manager, Mel Dyer; American Stage Manager, R. Michael Blanco; Dialect Coach, Billie Sarho; **Cast:** Geoffrey Rush (Aksentii Poprishchin), Yael Stone (Tuovi/Sophia/Tatiana), Paul Cutlan, Erkki Veltheim (Musicians)

Harvey Theater; Opening Night: February 11, 2011; Closed March 12, 2011; 28 performances. Setting: St. Petersburg Russia, during the first half of the 19th century. U.S. premiere of a play presented in two acts. This production began at Belvoir Street Theatre December 8, 2010.

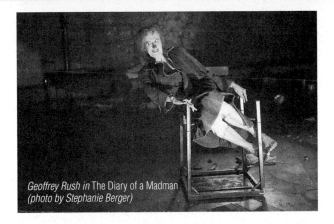

Geoffrey Rush in The Diary of a Madman
(photo by Stephanie Berger)

The Comedy of Errors by William Shakespeare, adapted by Edward Hall and Roger Warren; Presented by Propeller and The Touring Partnersnhip; Director, Edward Hall; Design, Michael Pavelka; Lighting, Ben Ormerod; Original Music/Additional Arrangements, Jon Trenchard; American Stage Manager, R. Michael Blanco; Sound, David Gregory; Tour Re-lighting, Andy Purves; Associate Director, Paul Hart; Company Manager, Nick Chesterfield; Production Manager, Nick Ferguson; Deputy Stage Manager, Laura Routledge; ASMs, Bryony Rutter, Charley Sargant; Executive Producer, Caro MacKay; Executive Producer for The Touring Partnership, Geoffrey Rowe; Education Consultant, William Wollen; **Cast:** Richard Clothier (The Duke of Ephesus), John Dougall (Aegeon), Dugald Bruce-Lockhart (Atipholus of Syracuse), Sam Swainsbury (Antipholus of Ephesus), Richard Frame (Dromio of Syracuse), Jon Trenchard (Dromio of Ephesus), Robert Hands (Adriana), David Newman (Luciana), Wayne Cater (Balthasar), Thomas Padden (Angelo), Officer (Dominic Tighe), Kelsey Brookfield (Courtesan), Tony Bell (Pinch), Chris Myles (Aemilia)

Harvey Theater; Opening Night: March 16, 2011; Closed March 27, 2011; 11 performances. U.S. premire of a foreign revival of a classic play presented in two acts. The production was first presented at Sheffield, U.K.'s Lyceum Tehatre January 19, 2011.

David Newman and Robert Hands in The Comedy of Errors
(photo by Manuel Harlan)

Macbeth by William Shakespeare; Presented by Cheek by Jowl; Director, Declan Donnellan; Design, Nick Ormerod; Associate Director/Movement, Jane Gibson; Lighting, Jane Greenwood; Music, Catherine Jayes; Sound, Helen Atkinson; American Stage Manager, R. Michael Blanco; Assistant Director, Owen Horsley; Company Voice Work, Patsy Rodenburg, Emma Woodvine; Fight Director, Jonathan Walker; Casting, Siobhan Bracke; Technical Director, Simon Bourne; Technical Stage Manager, Dougie Wilson; Costume Supervisor, Angie Burns; Company Stage Manager, Richard Llewelyn; Deputy Stage Manager, Clare Loxley; Executive Director, Griselda Yorke; Tour Producer, Anna Schmitz; Assistant Producer, Hannah Proctor; **Cast:** Will Keen (Macbeth), Anastasia Hille (Lady Macbeth), David Caves (Macduff), David Collings (Duncan/Scottish Doctor), Kelly Hotten (Porter/Lady Macduff), Orlando James (Malcolm), Ryan Kiggell (Banquo), Phillip Cairns, Vincent Enderby, Nicholas Goode, Greg Kolpakchi, Edmund Wiseman (Thanes)

Harvey Theater; Opening Night: April 5, 2011; Closed April 17, 2011; 13 performances. U.S. premire of a foreign revival of a classic play presented without intermission. This production was originally presented at Théâtre de Namur, Belgium September 22, 2009.

King Lear by William Shakespeare; Presented by the Donmar Warehouse (Micheal Grandage, Artistic Director, Nick Giles, Executive Director; Jo Danvers, General Manager); Director, Michael Grandage; Set/Costumes, Christopher Oram; Lighting, Neil Austin; Composer & Original Sound, Adam Cork; Casting, Anne McNulty; Associate Director, Titas Halder; Associate Design, Richard Kent; Associate Lighting, Richard Howell; Associate Sound, Sebastian Frost; Production Manager, Patrick Molony; American Stage Manager, Arthur Gaffin; Deputy Stage Manager, Mary O'Hanlon; ASM, Rhiannon Harper; Costume Supervisor, Stephanie Arditti; Fight Director, Terry King; Text Consultant, Russell Jackson; **Cast:** Michael Hadley (Earl of Kent), Paul Jesson (Earl of Gloucester), Alec Newman (Edmund), Derek Jacobi (King Lear), Gina McKee (Goneril), Justine Mitchell (Regan), Pippa Bennett-Warner (Cordelia), Tom Beard (Duke of Albany), Gideon Turner (Duke of Cornwall), Stefano Braschi (Duke of Burgundy), Ashley Zhangazha (King of France), Gwilym Lee (Edgar), Amit Shah (Oswald), Ron Cook (The Fool), Harry Attwell (Gentleman), Derek Hutchinson (Old Servant)

Harvey Theater; Opening Night: April 28, 2011; Closed June 5, 2011; 35 performances. U.S. premiere of a foreign revival of a classic play presented in two acts. This production was originally presented at London's Donmar Warehouse December 3, 2010–February 5, 2011.

Derek Jacobi in King Lear *(photo by Johan Persson)*

City Center *Encores!*

Eighteenth Season

Artistic Director, Jack Viertel; President & CEO of City Center, Arlene Shuler; Senior Vice President & Managing Director, Mark Litvin; *Encores!* General Manager, Stephanie Overton; Season Music Director, Rob Berman; Concert Adaptation, David Ives; Scenic Consultant, John Lee Beatty; Music Coordinator, Seymour Red Press; Company Manager, Michael Zande; Casting; Jay Binder, Jack Bowdan; Press, Helene Davis; Encores Artistic Associates: John Lee Beatty, Jay Binder, Walter Bobbie, David Ives, Kathleen Marshall

Bells Are Ringing Book and lyrics by Betty Comden and Adolph Green, music by Jule Styne; Director, Kathleen Marshall; Music Director, Rob Berman; Original Production Directed by Jerome Robbins; Dance Musical Numbers of Original Production Staged by Jerome Robbins and Bob Fosse; Costume Consultant, Martin Pakledinaz; Lighting, Peter Kaczorowksi; Sound, Scott Lehrer; Original Orchestrations, Robert Russell Bennett; PSM, Rick Steiger; Associate Choreographer, Rommy Sandhu; General Management, Gretchen Margaroli; Stage Manager, Lisa Iacucci; Associate Director, Eric Sean Fogel; Associate Music Director, David Gurskey; Assistant Scenic Consultants, Hannah Davis; Kacie Hultgren; Assistant Costume Consultant, Amanda Seymour; Costume Assistant, Luke Brown; Ms. O'Hara's Wig, Paul Huntley; **Cast:** David Hyde Pierce (Announcer), Judy Kaye (Sue Summers), Leah Edwards (Miss Stevens), Kelli O'Hara (Ella Peterson), Jack Doyle (Morty Hopper), Rachel Coloff (Mme. Grimaldi), Meggie Cansler (Olga), Niffer Clarke (Mrs. Mallet), Alyse Alan Louis (Jimmy), Jeffrey Schecter (Carl), Will Chase (Jeffrey Moss), Dylan Baker (Inspector Barnes), Danny Rutigliano (Francis), David Pittu (J. Sandor Prantz), Bobby Cannavale (Blake Barton), William Ryall (Ludwig Smiley/Man from Corvello Mob), Brad Oscar (Dr. Kitchell), Michael Halling (Paul Arnold/Man from Corvello Mob), Andrew Cao (Butler), J.D. Webster (Pyramid Club Slnger); *Telephone Girls, New Yorkers, Party Guests, and Pyramid Club Performers*: Clyde Alves, Meggie Cansler, Andrew Cao, Niffer Clarke, Rachel Coloff, Jack Doyle, Leah Edwards, Kimberly Fauré, Marya Grandy, Michael Halling, Max Kumangai, Alyse Alan Louis, Michael Marcotte, Shina Ann Morris, Kevin Munhall, William Ryall, Jennifer Savelli, Anthony Wayne, J.D. Webster, Anna Aimee White; Orchestra: Conductor: Rob Berman; Associate Music Director: David Gursky; Music Associate: Josh Clayton; Violins: Suzanne Ornstein (Concertmistress), Mineko Yajima, Eric DeGioia, Maura Giannini, Kristina Musser, Christoph Franzgrote, Lisa Matricardi, Fritz Krakowski, Lorra Bayliss; Violas: Richard Brice, David Blinn, Shelly Holland-Moritz; Celli: Roger Shell, Deborah Assael; Double Bass: John Beal; Piano/Celeste: Jeffrey Saver; Harp: Susan Jolles; Woodwinds: Steven Kenyon, James Ercole, Dennis Anderson, Lino Gomez, John Winder; French Horns: David Byrd-Marrow, Chad Yarbrough; Trumpets: James De La Garza, Glenn Drewes, Stu Satalof; Trombones: Bruce Bonvissuto, Randy Andos; Drums/Percussion: Richard Rosenzweig; Guitar: Jay Berliner

Musical Numbers: Overture; Bells Are Ringing; It's a Perfect Relationship; Independent (On My Own), You've Got to Do It; It's a Simple Little System; Is It a Crime?; Better Than a Dream; Hello, Hello There!; I Met a Girl; Long Before I Knew You; Entr'acte; Mu-Cha-Cha; Just in Time; Drop That Name; The Party's Over; Salzburg; The Midas Touch; Long Before I Knew You (reprise); I'm Goin' Back; Finale

New York City Center; Opening Night: November 18, 2010; Closed November 21, 2010; 5 performances. Setting: 1950s, New York City. Revival of a music in staged concert format presented in twenty-one scenes in two acts. The original production of *Bells Are Ringing* opened at the Shubert Theatre November 20, 1956 playing 924 performances. The musical was revived at the Plymouth Theatre April 12, 2001 playing 68 performances (see *Theatre World* Vol. 13, page 53; Vol. 57, page 38).

Kelli O'Hara and Will Chase in Bells Are Ringing *(photo by Joan Marcus)*

Lost in the Stars Music by Kurt Weill, book and lyrics by Maxwell Anderson; Based on the novel *Cry, The Beloved Country* by Alan Paton; Director, Gary Griffin; Music Director, Rob Berman; Choreography, Chase Brock; Costume Consultant, Paul Tazewell; Lighting, Paul Miller; Sound, Scott Lehrer; Original Orchestrations, Kurt Weill; PSM, Tripp Phillips; General Management Associate, Gretchen Margaroli; Stage Manager, Jason Hindelang; Associate Director, Jasper Grant; Associate Choreography, Jason Snow; Associate Music Director, Mark Mitchell; Assistant Scenic Consultant, Emily Walsh; Assistant Costume Consultant, Valerie Marcus Ramshur; Assistant Lighting, Cory Pattak; Assistant Sound, Kurt Fischer; **Cast:** Quentin Earl Darrington (Leader), Joy Lynn Matthews (Answerer), Sharon Washington (Grace Kumalo), Chuck Cooper (Stephen Kumalo), Eric Van Hoven (Stationmaster), Christian Dante White (Young Man), Lindsay Roberts (Young Woman), Daniel Gerroll (James Jarvis), Kieran Campion (Arthur Jarvis), Ted Sutherland (Edward Jarvis), John Douglas Thompson (John Kumalo), André Garner (Paulus), Jeremy Gumbs (Alex), Adam Alexander (Factory Foreman), Rosena M. Hill (Mrs. Mkize), Nathaniel Stampley (Hlabeni), Stephen Kunken (Mark Eland), Patina Miller (Linda), Clifton Duncan (Matthew Kumalo), Chiké Johnson (Johannes Pafuri), Daniel Breaker (Absalom Kumalo), Sherry Boone (Irina), J.D. Webster (Servant), Eric Van Hoven (Prison Guard), Kevin Vortmann (Burton), James Rebhorn (The Judge), Jorell Williams (Villager), Amy McClendon (Dancer), Justin Prescott (Dancer); *Chorus*: Adam Alexander, Sumayya Ali, Alvin Crawford, André Garner, Rosena M. Hill, Mary Illes, Emily Jenda, Amy Justman, Joy Lynn Matthews, André McRae, Patricia Phillips, Devin Richards, Lindsay Roberts, Nathaniel Stampley, Eric van Hoven, Kevin Vortmann,

J.D. Webster, Christian Dante White, Jorell Williams; Orchestra: Conductor: Rob Berman; Associate Music Director: Mark Mitchell; Music Associate: Josh Clayton; Violas: Richard Brice, David Blinn; Celli: Roger Shell, Deborah Assael; Double Bass: John Beal; Piano/Accordion/Harmonium: Josh Rosenblum; Harp: Susan Jolles; Woodwinds: Steven Kenyon, Richard Heckman, John Winder; Trumpet: John Dent; Drums/Percussion: Erik Charlston

Musical Numbers: The Hills of Ixopo; Thousands of Miles, Train to Johannesburg; The Search; The Little Grey House, Who'll Buy?; Trouble Man; Murder in Parkwold; Fear!; Lost in the Stars; The Wild Justice; O Tixo, Tixo, Help Me!; Stay Well, The Wild Justice (reprise); Cry, the Beloved Country; Big Mole; A Bird of Passage; Four O'Clock; Thousands of Miles (reprise)

New York City Center; Opening Night: February 3, 2011; Closed February 6, 2011; 5 performances. Setting: Ndotsheni, a small village in South Africa, and Johannesburg; 1949. Revival of a musical in stage concert format presented in nineteen scenes in two acts. The original production of *Lost in the Stars* opened at the Music Box Theatre on October 30, 1949 playing 281 performances. The show was revived at the Imperial Theatre April 18, 1972 playing 39 performances (see *Theatre World* Vol. 6, page 30; Vol. 28, page 48).

Chuck Cooper and Sharon Washington in Lost in the Stars
(photo by Joan Marcus)

Where's Charley Book by George Abbott, music and lyrics by Frank Loesser; Based on *Charley's Aunt* by Brandon Thomas; Director, John Doyle; Music Director, Rob Berman; Choreography, Alex Sanchez; Costume Consultant, Ann-Hould Ward; Lighting, Paul Miller; Sound, Scott Lehrer; Concert Adaptation, John Doyle; Original Orchestrations, Ted Royal, Hans Spialek, Philip J. Lang; PSM, Peter Lawrence; General Management Associate, Gretchen Margaroli; Stage Manager, Lisa Bixbaum; Associate Choreograper, Lanie Sakakura; Associate Music Director, Ben Whiteley; Assistant Scenic Consultant, Hannah Davis; Assistant Costume Consultant, Abigail D. Hahn; Assistant Lighting, Cory Pattak; Wig Design, David Lawrence; Music Consultant, Larry Moore; **Cast:** Jeff Brooks (Brassett), Sebastian Arcelus (Jack Chesney), Rob McClure (Charley Wykeham), Jill Paice (Kitty Verdun), Lauren Worsham (Amy Spettigue), Dan Callaway

(Wilkinson), Howard McGillin (Sir Francis Chesney), Dakin Matthews (Stephen Spettigue), Rebecca Luker (Donna Lucia D'Alvadorez); *Boys and Girls:* Elliott Bradley, Dan Callaway, Meggie Cansler, Hannah Chin, Nick Cosgrove, Desireé Davar, Ashlee Dupré, Leah Edwards, Drew Franklin, Arlo Hill, Leah Horowitz, Jordan Fife Hunt, Amy Justman, Max Kumangai, Analisa Leaming, Angelina Mullins, Patricia Noonan, Weston Wells Olson, Lainie Sakakura, Tommy Scrivens, Kendal Sparks, Brendon Stimson, Amos Wolff; Orchestra: Conductor: Rob Berman; Associate Music Director: Ben Whiteley; Music Associate: Josh Clayton; Violins: Christophe Franzgrote (Concertmaster), Martin Agee, Cenovia Cummins, Maura Giannini, Robert Zubrycki, Lorra Bayliss, James Tsao, Fritz Krakowski, Laura Seaton; Violas: Richard Brice, Shelly Holland-Moritz; Celli: Deborah Assael, Diane Barere; Double Bass: John Beal; Piano: Milton Granger; Harp: Susan Jolles; Woodwinds: David Weiss, Matthew Dine, Lino Gomez, Scott Schacter, John Winder; French Horns: Russ Rizner, Chad Yarbrough; Trumpets: James De La Garza, Glenn Drewes, Jeremy Miloszewicz; Trombone: Bruce Bonvissuto; Drums/Percussion: Rich Rosenzweig

Musical Numbers: Overture; The Years Before Us; Better Get Out of Here; The New Ashmolean Marching Society and Students' Conservatory Band; My Darling, My Darling; Make a Miracle; Serenade With Asides; Lovelier Than Ever; The Woman in His Room; Pernambuco; Entr'acte; Where's Charley; Once in Love With Amy; The Gossips; The Years Before Us (reprise); At the Red Rose Cotillion; Finale

New York City Center; Opening Night: March 17, 2011; Closed March 20, 2011; 5 performances. Setting: Oxford University; 1892. Revival of a musical in stage concert format presented in seven scenes in two acts. The original production of *Where's Charley* opened at the St. James Theatre on October 11, 1948 playing 792 performances (see *Theatre World* Vol. 5).

Lauren Worsham and Rob McClure in Where's Charley? *(photo by Joan Marcus)*

Classic Stage Company

Forty-fourth Season

Artistic Director, Brian Kulick; Executive Director, Jessica R. Jenen; General Manager, Jeff Griffin; Development, Audrey Carmeli; Associate Artistic Director, Tony Speciale; Audience Services, John C. Hume; Marketing and Communcations, Meghan Zaneski; Education and Development Assistant, Kathleen Dorman; Casting, James Calleri; General Management Assistant, Jeff Feola; Production Manager, James E. Cleveland/La Vie Productions/Production Core; Press, The Publicity Office, Marc Thibodeau

Orlando Adapted by Sarah Ruhl from the novel by Virginia Woolf; Director, Rebecca Taichman; Choreography, Annie-B Parson; Set, Allen Moyer; Lighting, Christopher Akerlind; Costumes, Anita Yavich; Original Music/Sound, Christian Frederickson and Ryan Rumery; PSM, Erin Maureen Koster; ASM, Molly Minor Eustis; **Cast:** David Greenspan (Ensemble), Tom Nelis (Ensemble), Howard Overshown (Ensemble), Francesca Faridany (Orlando), Annika Boras (Sasha)

East 13th Street Theatre; First Preview: September 8, 2010; Opening Night: September 23, 2010; Closed October 17, 2010; 15 previews, 25 performances. World premiere of a new play presented in two acts.

Francesca Faridany and Tom Nelis in Orlando *(photo by Joan Marcus)*

Three Sisters by Anton Chekhov, translated by Paul Schmidt; Director, Austin Pendleton; Set, Walt Spangler; Lighting, Keith Parham; Costumes, Marco Piemontese; Original Music/Sound, Christian Frederickson and Ryan Rumery; Hair, Paul Huntley; PSM, Timothy R. Semon; ASM, Raynelle Wright; Assistant Production Manager, Jared Goldstein; Assistant Production Manager, Adrian White; Assistant Director, Stephen Kaliski; Assistant Design: Jisun Kim (set), Dan Dansby (lighting), Michelle Bohn (costume); Technical Director, Jack Blacketer; Assistant Technical Director, Tim Jones; **Cast:** Jessica Hecht (Olga Prozorov), Juliet Rylance (Irina Prozorov), Louis Zorich (Chebutykin), Ebon Moss-Bachrach (Baron Tuzenbach), Maggie Gyllenhaal (Masha Prozorov), Anson Mount (Solyony), Roberta Maxwell (Anfisa), George Morfogen (Ferapont), Peter Sarsgaard (Vershinin), Josh Hamilton (Andrey Prozorov), Paul Lazar (Kulygin), Marin Ireland (Natasha), James Patrick Nelson (Fedotik), Gabe Bettio (Rohde)

East 13th Street Theatre; First Preview: January 12, 2011; Opening Night: February 3, 2011; Closed March 6, 2011; 22 previews, 32 performances. Revival of a classic play presented in three acts with two intermissions.

Maggie Gyllenhaal, Juliet Rylance, and Jessica Hecht in The Three Sisters *(photo by Joan Marcus)*

Double Falsehood by William Shakespeare and John Fletcher, adapted by Lewis Theobald; Director, Brian Kulick; Set/Costumes, Oana Botez-Ban; Lighting, Brian H. Scott; Original Music/Sound, Christian Frederickson; PSM, Andrea Wales; ASM, Kelly Ice; Assistant Production Manager, Ron Grimshan; Technical Director, Megan Caplan; Production Assistant, Zack Moody; Assistant Director, Alicia House; Dramaturg, Joseph P. Cermatori; Assistant Set, Brian Ireland; Assistant Costumes, Brieanna Lewis; **Cast:** Bryce Gill (Roderick/Citizen/Shepherd), Philip Goodwin (Duke/Camillo/Shepherd), Clayton Apgar (Julio), Hayle Treider (Leonora), Jon DeVries (Don Bernardo), Slate Holmgren (Henriquez), Mackenzie Meehan (Violante)

East 13th Street Theatre; First Preview: March 12, 2011; Opening Night: March 22, 2011; Closed April 3, 2011; 9 previews, 13 performances. Off-Broadway premiere of an eighteenth century reworking of a forgotten classic play presented in two acts. Prior to this production, the play had not been presented in over 250 years.

Clayton Apgar and Hayley Treider in Double Falsehood *(photo by Joan Marcus)*

The School for Lies Adapted from Molière's *The Misanthrope* by David Ives; Director, Walter Bobbie; Set, John Lee Beatty; Costumes, William Ivey Long; Lighting, Peter Kaczorowski; Sound, Acme Sound Partners; Hair, Paul Huntley; PSM, Terri K. Kohler; ASM, Lauren Kurinskas; Props, Mary Houston; Fight Director, Adam Rihacek; Associate Production Manager, Adrian White; Assistant Production Manager, Maggie Davis; Assistant Set, Kacie Hultgren; Assistant to Costume Designer, Donald Sanders; Assistant Lighting, Laura Schoch; Assistant Sound, David Sanderson; **Cast:** Hoon Lee (Philante), Mamie Gummer (Celimene), Alison Fraser, (Arsinoé), Hamish Linklater (Frank), Rick Holmes (Oronte), Jenn Gambatese (Elainte), Steven Boyer (Dubois/Basque), Matthew Maher (Acaste), Frank Harts (Clitander)

East 13th Street Theatre; First Preview: April 13, 2011; Opening Night: May 1, 2011; Closed May 29, 2011; 15 previews, 32 performances. World premiere of a new adaptation of a classic play presented in two acts.

Hamish Linklater and Mamie Gummer in (photo by Joan Marcus)

Additional Events

Books on Stage Third installment of a new series of staged readings of adaptations of the novels; Included: *Jacques and His Master* adapted by Milan Kundare (September 27, 2010); *Haroun and the Sea of Stories* by Salman Rushdie (October 4, 2010).

The Young Company: As You Like It by William Shakespeare; Presented in association with the Graduate Acting Program of Columbia School for the Arts; Director, James Rutherford; March 17–April 1, 2011.

First Look Festival: Molière Staged readings series; Included: *School for Wives* and *Tartuffe*; May 2 & 16, 2011.

Unnatural Acts Written by members of the Plastic Theatre, conceived and directed by Tony Speciale; Sets, Walt Spangler; Costumes, Andrea Lauer; Lighting, Justin Townsend; Original Music/Sound, Christian Frederickson; PSM, Charles M. Turner III; Marketing, HHC Marketing; ASM, Courtney James; Production Manager, Adrian White; Assistant Production Manager, Nicholas Aliff; Production Assistants, Sven Nelson, Catherine Lynch; Associate Director/Co-Author, Catherine Barricklow; Dramaturg/Co-Author, Heather Denyer; Props, Zach Roland; Script Supervisor, Nicholas Norman; Assistant Set, Stephen Kolack; Assistant Costumes, Ky Harder; Assistant Lighting, Christopher Thielking; Technical Director, Joshua Scherr; **Cast:** Brad Koed (Eugene Cummings), Roe Hartrampf (Kenneth Day), Nick Westrate (Ernest Roberts), Jess Burkle (Edward Say), Will Rogers (Joseph Lumbard), Jerry Marsini (Donald Clark), Max Jenkins (Stanley Gilkey), Frank De Julio (Keith Smerage), Roderick Hill (Lester Wilcox), Devin Norik (Harold Saxton), Joe Curnutte (Nathaniel Wollf)

East 13th Street Theatre; First Preview: June 14, 2011; Opening Night: June 23, 2011; Closed July 31, 2011; 8 previews, 39 performances. Setting: Harvard University; 1920s. World premiere of a new play presented in two acts.

The Cast of Unnatural Acts *(photo by Joan Marcus)*

Irish Repertory Theatre

Twenty-third Season

Artistic Director, Charlotte Moore; Producing Director, Ciarán O'Reilly; Audience Services, Jared Dawson; Business Manager, Dave Friedman; Development, Patrick A. Kelsey/Maureen Cavanaugh; Membership Manager, Abigail Lynn; Literary Manager, Kara Manning; Marketing, Melissa L. Pelkey; Box Office Manager, Jeffrey Wingfield; Casting, Deborah Brown; Press, Shirley Herz Associates, Dan Demello

Banished Children of Eve by Kelly Younger, adapted from the novel by Peter Quinn; Director, Ciarán O'Reilly; Choreography, Barry McNabb; Set, Charlie Corcoran; Costumes, Martha Hally; Lighting, Brian Nason; Music and Sound, Christopher Frederickson and Ryan Rumery; Hair and Wigs, Robert-Charles Vallance; Songs Arrangements, Malcolm Gets; Fight Director, Rick Sordelet; Specialty Props, Den Design Studio; Props, Deirdre Brennan; PSM, Pamela Brusoski; ASM, Rebecca C. Monroe; Production Coordinator, Cynthia Jankowski; Poster/Scenic Art, Matt Allamon; Design Assistants: Luamar Ciervejeira (lighting), Karle J. Meyers (costumes), Sara Bender (wigs); **Cast:** Malcolm Gets (Stephen Collins Foster), Patrice Johnson (Euphemia Blanchard), Christopher Borger (Squirt), David Lansbury (Jack Mulcahey), Jonny Orsini (Jimmy Dunne), Rory Duffy (Mike Manning/Ensemble), Amanda Quaid (Margaret O'Driscoll), Graeme Malcolm (Waldo Capshaw), Amber Gray (Eliza), Kern McFadden (Mr. Miller/Ensemble)

Francis J. Greenberger Mainstage; First Preview: October 13, 2010; Opening Night: October 24, 2010; Closed December 5, 2010. Setting: New York City, July 1863. World premiere of a new play presented in two acts.

Christopher Borger (background), David Lansbury, Amber Gray, Patrice Johnson in Banished Children of Eve *(photo by Carol Rosegg)*

St. Nicholas by Conor McPherson; Director, Alex Dmitriev; Lighting, Mary Jo Dondlinger; PSM, Michael Palmer; Production Coordinator, Cynthia Jankowski; Wardrobe, Deirdre Higgings; Carpenter, Donal O'Reilly; **Cast:** John Martello (A Man)

W. Scott McLucas Studio; First Preview: October 15, 2010; Opening Night: October 20, 2010; Closed No November 28, 2010. Setting: Now; Here. Revival of a solo performance play presented in two acts. Originally presented at the Bush Theatre (London) February 19, 1997. U.S. premiere at Primary Stages March 17, 1988 (see *Theatre World* Vol. 54, page 102).

John Martello in St. Nicholas *(photo by Carol Rosegg)*

A Child's Christmas in Wales in Concert by Dylan Thomas, arranged and directed by Charlotte Moore; Music Director, John Bell; Costumes, David Toser; Lighting, Mary Jo Dondlinger; PSM, April Ann Kline; ASM, Naomi Anhorn; Production Coordinator, Cynthia Jankowski; Carpenter, Donal O'Reilly; Electrician, Tom Dyer; Wardrobe, Deirdre Higgins; **Cast:** John Bell (Piano), Kerry Conte, Simon Jones, Victoria Mallory, Ashley Robinson, Martin Vidnovic (Ensemble)

W. Scott McLucas Studio; First Preview: December 8, 2010; Opening Night: December 12, 2010; Closed January 2, 2011. A theatrical concert with text and music presented without intermission. The Irish Rep first produced *A Child's Christmas in Wales* in December 2000, and revived the production in 2007 and 2008. This version contained revised musical material.

Molly Sweeney by Brian Friel; Director, Charlotte Moore; Set, James Morgan; Costumes, Linda Fisher; Lighting, Richard Pilbrow and Michael Gottlieb; Sound, Zachary Williamson; PSM, Pamela Brusoski; ASM, Rebecca C. Monroe; Production Coordinator, Cynthia Jankowsko; Carpenter, Donal O'Reilly; Electrician, Tom Dyer; Lighting Programmer, Megan L. Peti; Wardrobe, Deirdre Higgins; **Cast:** Geraldine Hughes (Molly), Jonathan Hogan (Mr. Rice), Ciarán O'Reilly (Frank)

Francis J. Greenberger Mainstage; First Preview: January 19, 2011; Opening Night: January 30, 2011; Closed April 10, 2011. Setting: Donegal, Ireland. Revival of a play presented in two acts. World premiere at the Gate Theatre (Dublin) August 9, 1994. U.S. premiere at the Roundabout Theatre's Criterion Center December 26, 1995–May 12, 1996 playing 145 performances (see *Theatre World* Vol. 52, page 102).

Jonathan Hogan, Geraldine Hughes, and Ciaran O'Reilly in Molly Sweeney
(photo by Carol Rosegg)

My Scandalous Life by Thomas Kilroy; Director, John Going; Set, Charlie Corcoran; Costumes, David Toser; Lighting, Michael O'Connor; Sound, Zachary Williamson; PSM, Michael Palmer; Production Coordinator, Cynthia Jankowski; Carpenter, Donal O'Reilly; Set Construction, Ken Larson; Wardrobe, Deirdre Higgins; **Cast:** Des Keogh (Lord Alfred Douglas), Fiana Toibin (Eileen)

W. Scott McLucas Studio; First Preview: February 2, 2011; Opening Night: February 6, 2011; Closed March 6, 2011. Setting: 1944; Hove, England. World premiere of a new play presented without intermission.

Des Keogh and Fiana Toibin in My Scandalous Life *(photo by Carol Rosegg)*

The Shaugraun by Dion Boucicault; Director, Charlotte Moore; Set, Klara Zieglcrova; Costumes, Linda Fisher and Jessica Barrios Wright; Lighting, Brian Nason; Sound, Zachary Williamson; Associate Set, Sonoka Fukuma Guzelski; Hair and Wigs, Robert-Charles Vallance; Dialect Coach, Stephen Gabis; Choreography, Barry McNabb; PSM, Elis C. Arroyo; ASM, Arthur Atkinson; Associate Producer, Alexis Doyle; Production Coordinator, Cynthia Jankowski; Carpenter, Donal

O'Reilly; Set Construction, Ken Larson; Scenic Artist, Matt Allamon; Electrician, Tom Dyer; Assistant Lighting, Luamar Cervejeira; Assistant to Mr. Vallance, Sara Bender; Wardrobe, Deirdre Higgins; Production Assistant, Jason Brubaker; **Cast:** Patrick Fitzgerald (Conn, The Shaughgraun), Terry Donnelly (Mrs. O'Kelly), Rory Duffy (Prison Officer/Sullivan), Katie Fabel (Arte O'Neal), Sean Gormley (Corry Kincela), Scott Kerns (Robert Ffolliott), Laurence Lowry (Reilly), Emma O'Donnell (Moya Dolan), Tim Ruddy (Harvey Duff), Mark Shanahan (Captain Harry Molineaux), Geddeth Smith (Father Dolan), Gwenfair Vaughan (Bridget Madigan), Allison Jean White (Claire Ffolliott), Jake Zachry (Sergeant Jones/Mangan)

Francis J. Greenberger Mainstage; First Preview: April 21, 2011; Opening Night: May 1, 2011; Closed June 12, 2011. Setting: 1867; County Sligo, Ireland. Revival of a classic play presented in sixteen scenes in two acts. New York premiere at Wallack's Theatre in 1874. The Irish Repertory previously produced this play October 30, 1998–January 30, 1999 (see *Theatre World* Vol. 55, page 98).

Geddeth Smith, Katie Fabel, Mark Shanahan, Allison Jean White, Patrick Fitzgerald, and Jake Zachry (background) in The Shaugraun
(photo by Carol Rosegg)

Tryst by Karoline Leach; Director, Joe Brancato; Set, Michael Schweikardt; Costumes, Alejo Vietti; Lighting, Martin Vreeland; Sound, Johnna Doty; PSM, Michael Palmer; ASM, Arthur Atkinson; Dialect Coach, Stephen Gabis; Production Coordinator, Cynthia Jankowski; Carpenter, Donal O'Reilly; Set Construction, Ken Larson; Scenic Artist, Sarah Brown; Props, Sven Nelson; Electrician, Tom Dyer; Assistant Lighting, Eli Polofsky; Costume Associate, Tricia Barsamian; Wardrobe, Deirdre Higgins; **Cast:** Andrea Maulella (Adelaide Pinchin), Mark Shanahan (George Love)

Francis J. Greenberger Mainstage; First Preview: July 1, 2011; Opening Night: July 7, 2011; Closed August 21, 2011. Setting: London and Weston Super Mare; 1910. Revival of a play presented in two acts. World premiere at the Promenade Theatre April 6, 2006 (see *Theatre World* Vol. 62, page 126).

Andrea Maulella and Mark Shanahan in Tryst
(photo by Carol Rosegg)

Keen Company

Eleventh Season

Artistic Director, Carl Forsman; Executive Director, Wayne Kelton; Education Director, Blake Lawrence; Resident Director, Jonathan Silverstein; Marketing Director, Abigail Rose Solomon; Company Manager, Laura Braza; Production Manager, Josh Bradford; Casting, Judy Bowman; Press, David Gersten and Associates

Alphabetical Order by Michael Frayn; Director, Carl Forsman; Set, Nathan Heverin; Costumes, Jennifer Paar; Lighting, Josh Bradford; Sound, Jill BC DuBoff; Technical Director, Marshall Miller; Stage Manager, Justin Scribner; Associate Lighting, Stephen Sakowski; **Cast:** Audrey Lynn Weston (Lesley), John Windsor-Cunningham (Geoffrey), Brad Bellamy (Arnold), William Connell (John), Angela Reed (Lucy), Margaret Daly (Nora), Paul Molnar (Wally)

Clurman Theatre on Theatre Row; First Preview: September 14, 2010; Opening Night: September 26, 2010; Closed October 23, 2010; 13 previews, 28 performances. U.S. premiere of a revised edition of a play presented in two acts. The original version was first produced at the Hampstead Theatre (London) in 1975. This revised version is based on their 2009 revival of the production.

Benefactors by Michael Frayn; Director, Carl Forsman; Set, Dane Laffrey; Costumes, Jennifer Paar; Lighting, Josh Bradford; Sound, Will Pickens; Stage Manager, Jeff Meyers; **Cast:** Vivienne Benesch (Jane), Daniel Jenkins (David), Deanne Lorette (Sheila), Stephen Barker Turner (Kevin)

Clurman Theatre on Theatre Row; First Preview: March 22, 2011; Opening Night: April 5, 2011; Closed May 7, 2011; 13 previews, 34 performances. Setting: London, over the course of several years in the 1960s. Twenty-fifth anniversary revival of a play presented in two acts. World premiere at the Vaudeville Theatre (London) on April 4, 1984. First presented in New York at the Brooks Atkinson Theatre December 22, 1985–June 29, 1986 playing 217 performances (see *Theatre World* Vol. 42, page 27).

Daniel Jenkins, Vivienne Benesch, Deanne Lroette, and Stephen Barker Turner in Benefactors *(photo by Richard Termine)*

LAByrinth Theater

Nineteenth Season

Artistic Directors, Stephen Adly Guirgis, Mimi O'Donnell, and Yul Vázquez; Managing Director, Danny Feldman; General Manager, Robert Sherrill; Development Consultant, Yasmine Falk; Communications Manager, Willie Orbison; Education, Monique Carboni; Founding Artistic Directors, John Ortiz, Philip Seymour Hoffman; Press, O+M Company, Rick Miramontez, Philip Carrubba

Thinner Than Water by Melissa Ross; Director, Mimi O'Donnell; Set, Lee Savage; Costumes, Bobby Frederick Tilley II; Lighting, Japhy Weideman; Sound, Jeremy Lee; PSM, Pamela Salling; **Cast:** Elizabeth Canavan (Renee), Stephen Ellis (Benjy), Lisa Joyce (Cassie), Megan Mostyn-Brown (Angela), Alfredo Narciso (Gary), Deirdre O'Connell (Gwen), Aaron Roman Weiner (Henry), David Zayas (Mark)

The Cherry Pit; First Preview: February 8, 2011; Opening Night: February 15, 2011; Closed March 6, 2011; 6 previews, 18 performances. World premiere of a new play presented in two acts.

Alfredo Narciso, Lisa Joyce, and Elizabeth Canavan in Thinner Than Water *(photos by Monique Carboni)*

Readings

Barn Series 2010 Eleventh annual reading series; The Cherry Pit; November 29–December 21, 2010; Included: *Channel* by John Jiler, directed by Brian Roff, with Charles Goforth, Ron Cephas Jones; *Marcy Comes Home* by Adam Bock, directed by Trip Cullman, with Vanessa Aspillaga, Quincy Tyler Bernstine, Zack Booth, Ari Graynor, Jason Butler Harner, Linda Larkin, Maulik Pancholy; *If You Love Me* by Lyle Kessler, directed by Lola Glaudini, with Elizabeth Rodriguez, Yul Vazquez; *You Are Here* by Melissa Ross, directed by Mimi O'Donnell, with Max Casella, Sarah Nina Hayon, Jennifer Mudge, Amanda Perez; *The Bends* by Megan Mostyn-Brown, directed by Josh Hecht, with Jeff Biehl, Caitlin Fitzgerald, Michael Gladis, Sarah Nina Hayon, Greg Keller*, Alexa Scott-Flaherty; *Oh, the Power* by David Bar Katz, directed by Philip Seymour Hoffman, with Tina Benko, Saidah Arrika Ekulona, Jeffrey Horwitz, Joseph Parks, Ed Vassallo, Yul Vazquez; *Rivers of January* by Ben Snyder, directed by Stephen Adly Guirgis; *Heal Me Television* by Martha Wollner, directed by Kevin Geer, with Japhet Balaban, Elizabeth Canavan, Scout Cook, Andrea Haring, Scott Hudson, Russell G. Jones, Florencia Lozano, Kelley Rae O'Donnell, Richard Petrocelli, Yolonda Ross, Finnerty Steeves, Sidney Williams; *The Walking Game* by Daniel Harnett, directed by Padraic Lillis, with Scout Cook, Kevin Geer, Charles Goforth, Marshall Sharer; *Utilities* by Jonathan Marc Sherman, directed by David Bar Katz, Didi O'Connell, Annie Parisse, Yul Vazquez, Frank Whaley; *New Short Plays: Just The Way You Are, Inconsolable, The Vote In Orange, Beirut Rocks,* and *What Strong Fences Make* by Israel Horovitz, directed by Israel Horovitz and Scott Illingworth, with Scout Cook, Jeremy Sisto, Fracisco Solorzano; *They Killed Boo Boo?* by Maggie Bofill, directed by Jill DeArmon, with Carlo Alban, Raul Castillo, Adam Cohen, Angela Lewis, Paula Pizzi, Yolanda Ross; *A Family For All Occassions* by Bob Glaudini, directed by Philip Seymour Hoffman, with Lex Friedman, Craig "muMs" Grant, Didi O'Connell, Charlie Saxton, David Strathairn; *Untitled Works in Progress* by Stephen Adly Guirgis

Lincoln Center Theater

Twenty-sixth Season

Artistic Director, André Bishop; Executive Producer, Bernard Gersten; General Manager, Adam Siegel; Production Manager, Jeff Hamlin; Development, Hattie K. Jutagir; Finance, David S. Brown; Marketing, Linda Mason Ross; Education, Kati Koerner; Associate Directors, Graciela Danielle, Nicholas Hytner, Jack O'Brien, Susan Stroman, Daniel Sullivan; Resident Director, Bartlett Sher; Dramaturg and Director of Director of LCT Directors Lab, Anne Cattaneo; Musical Theatre Associate Producer, Ira Weitzman; LCT3 Director, Paige Evans; Casting, Daniel Swee; House Manager, William Cannon; Advertising, Serino Coyne; Principal Poster Art, James McMullen; Press, Philip Rinaldi, Barbara Carroll

Other Desert Cities by Jon Robin Baitz; Director, Joe Mantello; Sets, John Lee Beatty; Costumes, David Zinn; Lighting, Kenneth Posner; Sound, Jill BC DuBoff; Original Music, Justin Ellington; Stage Manager, James FitzSimmons; ASM, Neil Krassnow; Company Manager, Jessica Perlmeter Cochrane; Associate Company Manager, Daniel Hoyos; Assistant Director, Nicolas Townsend; Assistant Design: Kacie Hultgren (set), Jacob Climer (costumes), Christian Deangelis (lighting), Brandon Wolcott and Dave Sanderson (sound); Props, Buist Bickley; Makeup, Angelina Avallone; Wigs, Paul Huntley; **Cast:** Stockard Channing (Polly Wyeth), Elizabeth Marvel (Brooke Wyeth), Stacy Keach (Lyman Wyeth), Thomas Sadoski (Trip Wyeth), Linda Lavin (Silda Grauman); Understudies: Jack Davidson (Lyman Wyeth), Lauren Klein (Polly Wyeth, Silda Grauman), Liz Wisan (Brooke Wyeth)

Mitzi E. Newhouse Theater; First Preview: December 16, 2010; Opening Night: January 13, 2011; Closed February 27, 2011; 31 previews, 53 performances. Setting: Christmas 2004 and March 2010, the Wyeth home in Palm Springs, California. World premiere of a new play presented in two acts.

Stockard Channing and Stacy Keach in Other Desert Cities
(photo by Joan Marcus)

A Minister's Wife Book by Austin Pendleton, music by Joshua Schmidt, lyrics by Jan Levy Tranen; Based on the play *Candida* by George Bernard Shaw; Director/Conciever, Michael Halberstram; Sets, Alan Moyer; Costumes, David Zinn; Lighting, Keith Parham; Sound, Scott Stauffer; Orchestrations, Joshua Schmidt; Music Supervisor, Richard Carsey; Conductor, Timothy Splain; Casting, Tara Rubin; Stage Manager, Jennifer Rae Moore; ASM, Emily Glinick; Company Manager, Matthew Markoff; Associate Company Manager, Josh Lowenthal; Assistant Director, David F. Chapman; Assistant Design: Warren Karp (set), Jacob A. Climer (costumes), Adam Greene (lighting); Props Coordinator, Sarah Bird; Music Copyist, Timothy Splain; Makeup, Cynthia Demand; Dialect Coach, Stephen Gabis; Wigs/Hair, Paul Huntley; **Cast:** Liz Baltes (Miss Proserpine Garnett), Marc Kudisch (The Reverand James Mavor Morell), Drew Gehling (The Reverand Alexander Mill), Kate Fry (Candida), Bobby Steggert (Eugene

Marchbanks); Orchestra: Timothy Splain (Conductor/Piano), Pasquale Laurino (Violin), Laura Bontrager (Cello), Jonathan Levine (Bass Clarinet); Understudies: Graham Rowat (Rev. Morell), Abby Mueller (Miss Garnett, Candida), Joseph Medeiros (Rev. Mill, Eugene)

Musical Numbers: Sermon; Candida's Coming Home; Enchantment; In Response; The Love of a Fool; Kingdom of Heaven; Is It Like This for Her Here Always?; Shy, Shy Shy; Isn't He Foolish?; Shallops and Scrubbing Brushes; Off to the Guild of St. Matthew; At the Gate of Heaven; Candida, Candida!; The Second Preaching Match, Champagne, Spoiled From the Cradle; Into the Night

Mitzi E. Newhouse Theatre; First Preview: April 7, 2011; Opening Night: May 8, 2011; Closed June 12, 2011; 45 previews, 41 performances. Setting: A fine October morning, 1898, the East End of London. New York premiere of a new musical presented without intermission. World premiere presented by Writers' Theatre (Glencoe, Illinois) June 4–July 19, 2009.

Drew Gehling, Marc Kudisch, and Liz Baltes in A Minister's Wife
(photo by Paul Kolnik)

LCT3 Series – The Steinberg New Works Program

The Coward by Nick Jones; Director, Sam Gold; Sets, David Zinn; Costumes, Gabriel Berry; Lighting, Ben Stanton; Sound, Jane Shaw; Fight Director, J. David Brimmer; Special Effects, Waldo Warshaw; Stage Manager, Megan Schwarz Dickert; ASM, Erica S. Holz; Company Manager, Josh Lowenthal; Assistant Director, Peter James Cook; Assistant Design: Tim McMath (set), Justin Hall (costumes), Nicholas Houfek (lighting), Kim Fuhr (sound); Technical Director, Adam Shive; Props, Faye Armon; Fight Captain, John Patrick Doherty; Dialect Coach, Deborah Hecht; **Cast:** Steven Boyer (Robert Blythe), Jarlath Conroy (Old Man/Egbert/Freiedmont/Sir Derek Lanley), John Patrick Doherty (Gavin Klaff), Richard Poe (Nathaniel Culling), Kristen Schaal (Isabelle Dupree), Jeremy Strong (Lucidus Culling), Christopher Evan Welch (Henry Blaine)

Duke on 42nd Street; First Preview: November 8, 2010; Opening Night: November 22, 2010; Closed December 4, 2010; 15 previews, 16 performances; Setting: England – Late 18th Century. World premiere of a new play presented in two acts.

Stephen Ellis, Steven Boyer, and Jeremy Strong in The Coward
(photo by Erin Baiano)

When I Come to Die by Nathan Louis Jackson; Director, Thomas Kail; Sets, Robin Vest; Costumes, Emily Rebholz; Lighting, Betsy Adams; Sound, Jill BC DuBoff; Stage Manager, Emily Glinick; ASM, Jenny Kennedy; Company Manager, Josh Lowenthal; Assistant Director, Anika Chapin; Assistant Design: Jisun Kim (set), Mira Veikley (costumes), Paul Hudson (lighting), Brandon Wolcott (sound); Script Assistant, Matt Ocks; Technical Director, Adam Shive; Props, Marina Guzman; **Cast:** Michael Balderama (Officer Cooper), Chris Chalk (Damon Robinson), Neal Huff (Adrian Crouse), David Patrick Kelly (James "Roach" Teagle), Amada Mason Warren (Chantel Robinson)

Duke on 42nd Street; First Preview: January 31, 2011; Opening Night: February 10, 2011; Closed February 26, 2011; 11 previews, 20 performances; Setting: Indiana State Prison. World premiere of a new play presented without intermission.

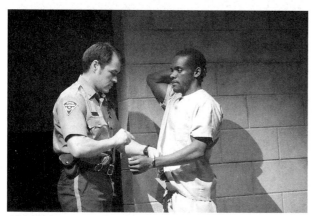

Michael Balderrama and Chris Chalk in When I Come to Die
(photo by Erin Baiano)

4000 Miles by Amy Herzog; Director, Daniel Aukin; Sets, Lauren Helpern; Costumes, Kaye Voyce; Lighting, Japhy Weideman; Sound, Ryan Rummery; Stage Manager, Kasey Ostopchuck; ASM, Kelly Stillwell; Company Manager, Josh Lowenthal; Assistant Director, Judy Merrick; Assistant Design: Brian Ireland (set), Sarah Gosnell (costumes), atalie Robin (lighting), Matt Otto (sound); Prop Coordinator, Faye Armon; Technical Director, Ernie Johns; **Cast:** Gabriel Ebert (Leo), Mary Louise Wilson (Vera Joseph), Zoë Winters (Bec), Greta Lee (Amanda)

Duke on 42nd Street; First Preview: June 6, 2011; Opening Night: June 20, 2011; Closed July 9, 2011; 14 previews, 23 performances. Setting: A few years ago, September; Greenwich Village. World premiere of a new play presented without intermission. Originally written in the Soho Rep Writer/Director Lab.

Gabriel Ebert and Mary Louise Wilson in 4000 Miles *(photo by Erin Baiano)*

MCC Theater (Manhattan Class Company)

Twenty-fifth Season

Artistic Directors, Robert LuPone & Bernard Telsey; Associate Artistic Director, William Cantler; Executive Director, Blake West; General Manager, Ted Rounsaville; Company Manager/Assistant General Manager, Jenna Lauren Freed; Literary Manager/Dramaturg, Stephen Willems; Development, Erica Lynn Schwartz; Development Associate, Glenn Grieves; Marketing, Ian Allen; Marketing Associate, Sarah Rushakoff; Education/Outreach, Alex Sarian; Youth Company Acting Lab Director, Jennifer Shirley; Youth Company Playwriting Diector, Lucy Thurber; Production Manager, B.D. White; Resident Playwright, Neil LaBute; Producing Special Arrangements, The Lucille Lortel Theatre Foundation; Casting, Telsey + Company; Press, O+M Company, Rick Miramontez, Jon Dimond

The Break of Noon by Neil LaBute; Co-produced with the Geffen Playhouse (Gil Cates, Producing Director; Randall Arney, Artistic Director; Ken Novice, Managing Director); Director, Jo Bonney; Original Music, Justin Ellington; Set, Neil Patel; Lighting, David Weiner; Costumes, Emilio Sosa; Sound, Darron L West; Fight Director, Thomas Schall; Assistant Design: Stephen K. Dobay (set), Ashley Farra (costumes), David Sexton (lighting), M. Florian Staab (sound); Wigs, Rob Greene, J. Jared Janas; Special Effects, Matthew Holtzclaw; PSM, Christina Lowe; ASM, Katherine Wallace; Props, Michelle Spadaro; Dialect Coach, Stephen Gabis; Assistant Director, Tyrone Brown; Technical Director, Jason McCullough; Assistant Technical Director, Nicholas Warren Gray; **Cast:** Tracee Chimo (Jenny/Gigi), David Duchovny (John Smith), John Earl Jelks (Lawyer/Detective), Amanda Peet (Ginger/Jesse)

Lucille Lortel Theatre; First Preview: October 28, 2010; Opening Night: November 22, 2010; Closed December 22, 2010. Setting: Now; in and around a big city. World premiere of a new play presented without intermission.

Tracee Chimo and David Duchovny in The Break of Noon *(photo by Joan Marcus)*

The Other Place by Sharr White; Presented in associaition with Marc Platt; Director, Joe Mantello; Sets, Eugene Lee; Costumes, Dane Laffrey; Lighting, Justin Townsend; Sound, Fitz Patton; Projections/Video, William Cusick; PSM, Linda Marvel; ASM, Hilary Austin; Technical Director, Jason McCullough; Assistant Technical Director, Nicholas Warren Gray; Sound Supervisor, Bill Grady; Associate Set, Edward Pierce; Associate Sound, Joshua Reid; Assistant Design: Alex Michaels (costumes), Christopher Thielking (lighting), Joe Cantalup (projections); Props, Mary Houston; **Cast:** Dennis Boutsikaris (Ian), Aya Cash (The Woman), Laurie Metcalf (Juliana), John Schiappa (The Man)

Lucille Lortel Theatre; First Preview: March 11, 2011; Opening Night: March 28, 2011; Closed May 1, 2011. Setting: The Present Cape Cod; Ten Years Ago, and the present. World premiere of a new play presented without intermission.

Dennis Boutsikaris, Aya Cash, and Laurie Metcalf in The Other Place *(photo by Joan Marcus)*

Side Effects by Michael Weller; Director, David Auburn; Set, Beowulf Boritt; Costumes, Wade Laboissonniere; Lighting, Jeff Croiter; Original Music & Sound, Scott Killian; Fight Director, Thomas Schall; PSM, Kelly Glasgow; Stage Manager, Rachel Motz; Technical Director, Nicholas Warren Gray; Assistant Technical Director, Fred Potter; Props, Buist Bickley; Assistant Design: Alexis Distler (set), Cory Pattak (lighting), Christopher Peifer (sound); Assistant Director, Sherri Eden Barber; Production Assistant, Angela F. Kiessel; **Cast:** Joely Richardson (Melinda Metz), Cotter Smith (Hugh Metz)

Lucille Lortel Theatre; First Preview: June 2, 2011; Opening Night: June 19, 2011; Closed July 3, 2011. Setting: A city in the Midwest; nowl. World premiere of a new play presented without intermission.

Cotter Smith and Joely Richardson in Side Effects *(photo by Joan Marcus)*

Manhattan Theatre Club

Thirty-ninth Season

Artistic Director Lynne Meadow; Executive Producer, Barry Grove; General Manager, Florie Seery; Associate Artistic Director, Mandy Greenfield; Director of Artistic Development, Jerry Patch; Director of Artistic Operations, Amy Gilkes Loe; Artistic Line Producer, Lisa McNulty; Director of Casting, Nancy Piccione; Development, Lynne Randall; Marketing, Debra Waxman-Pilla; Finance, Jeffrey Bledsoe; Associate General Manager, Lindsey Brooks Sag; Subscriber Services, Robert Allenberg; Telesales, George Tetlow; Education, David Shookhoff; Production Manager, Kurt Gardner/Joshua Helman; Company Manager, Erin Moeller; Properties Supervisor, Scott Laule; Costume Supervisor, Erin Hennessy Dean; Press, Boneau/Bryan-Brown, Chris Boneau, Aaron Meier, Christine Olver

Spirit Control by Beau Willimon; Director, Henry Wishcamper; Set, Robin Vest; Costumes, Jenny Manis; Lighting, Natasah Katz; Sound, Broken Chord; Projections, Aaron Rhyne; Original Music, Chas Willimon; PSM, Alison DeSantis; Casting, Dave Caparelliotis; Company Manager, ErinMoeller; Stage Manager, Johnny Milani; Hair/Wigs, Charles LaPointe; Makeup, Cookie Jordan; Dialects, Charlotte Fleck; Movement Consultant, Thomas Schall; Associate Design: Charles Coes (sound), Ned Stesen-Reuter (projections); Assistant Design: Kina Park (set), Tilly Grimes (costumes), Grant Wilcoxen (lighting); Light Board Progamming, Jane Masterson; Projection Programming, Tim Clark; **Cast:** Mia Barron (Maxine/Girl at the bar), Charles Borland (FAA Official/Bill), Aaron Michael Davies (Tommy Wyatt), Brian Hutchison (Karl Jensen), Maggie Lacey (Jess Wyatt), Jeremy Sisto (Adam Wyatt); Understudies: Ryan McCarthy (Adam Wyatt, FAA Offical/Bill, Karl Jensen), Blaine Miller (Tommy Wyatt), Lisa Velten Smith (Jess Wyatt, Maxine/Girl at the bar)

City Center Stage I; First Preview: October 7, 2010; Opening Night: October 26, 2010; Closed December 5 2010; 21 previews, 48 performances. Setting: Summer 1985; Fall 1997; Winter 2010; In and around St. Louis, Missouri. World premiere of a new play presented in two acts.

Brian Hutchison and Jeremy Sisto in Spirit Control *(photo by Joan Marcus)*

The Whipping Man by Matthew Lopez; Director, Doug Hughes; Set, John Lee Beatty; Costumes, Catherine Zuber; Lighting, Ben Stanton; Sound, Jill BC DuBoff; Hair/Wigs, Tom Watson; Fight Director, J. David Brimmer; PSM, Winnie Y. Lok; Stage Manager, Carlos Maisonet; Company Manager, Julia Baldwin; Associate Design: Kacie Hultgren (set), Dave Sanderson (sound); Assistant Design: Phillip Tokarsky (set), Nicole Moody (costumes), Ken Elliot (lighting); Makeup Consultant, Ashley Ryan; Dialect Consultant, Kate Wilson; Head Fight Assistant Director, Turner Smith; Assistant Fight Directors, James Hutchison, Dan O'Driscoll; **Cast:** André Braugher (Simon), André Holland (John), Jay Wilkison (Caleb)

Greg Keller and Maria Dizzia in Cradle and All *(photo by Joan Marcus)*

Jay Wilkison, André Braugher, and André Holland in The Whipping Man *(photo by Joan Marcus)*

City Center Stage I; First Preview: January 13, 2011; Opening Night: February 1, 2011; Closed April 10, 2011; 21 previews, 80 performances. Setting: April 1865; Richmond Virginia. New York premiere of a new play presented in two acts. World premiere at Luna Stage (Montclair, New Jersey; Jane Mandel, Artistic Director) April 27–May 21, 2006. Subsequently produced in 2009 at Penumbra (Saint Paul, MN) and in 2010 at The Old Globe (San Diego) and Barrington Stage (Pittsfield, MA).

Cradle and All by Daniel Goldfarb; Director, Sam Buntrock; Set, Neil Patel; Costumes, Mattie Ullrich; Lighting, Ken Billington; Sound, Jill BC DuBoff; PSM, Hannah Cohen; Stage Manager, Jillian M. Oliver; Movie Poster Design, Michael Brunsfeld; Associate Design, John Demous (lighting), David Sanderson (sound); Assistant Design: Yoon Young Choi (set), Heather Lockard (costumes); Light Board Programmer, Jane Masterson; **Cast:** Act I: Infantry: Maria Dizzia (Claire DeRosier), Greg Keller (Luke Sean Joy); Act II: The Extinction Method: Maria Dizzia (Annie Saxe), Greg Keller (Nate Hamburger)

City Center Stage I; First Preview: May 10, 2011; Opening Night: May 25, 2010; Closed June 19, 2011; 17 previews, 31 performances. Setting: The present; adjacent apartments in Brooklyn Heights, NY. World premiere of a new play presented in two acts.

Mint Theater Company

Nineteenth Season

Artistic Director, Jonathan Bank; General Manager, Sherri Kotimsky; Marketing Associate, Sherri Kronfeld; Development Associate/Dramaturg, Heather J. Violanti; Box Office Manager, Adrienne Scott; Development Consultant, Ellen Mittenthal; Casting, Stuart Howard, Amy Schecter, and Paul Hardt; Press, David Gersten & Associates

Wife to James Whelan by Teresa Deevy; Director, Jonathan Bank; Set, Vicki R. Davis; Costumes, Martha Hally; Lighting, Nicole Pearce; Sound, Jane Shaw; Properties, Deborah Gaouette; Dialects/Dramaturgy, Amy Stoller; PSM, Samone B. Weissman; ASM, Lauren McArthur; Assistant to the Director, Arielle Lipshaw; Assistant Costumes, Karle J. Meyers; Production Manager, Sherri Kotimsky; Illustration, Stefano Imbert; Graphics, Hunter Kaczorowski; Assistant Producion Manager, Wayne Yeager; Fight Director, Alexandra Hastings; En Garde Entertainment; Lighting Assistant, Kate Ashton; Lighting Programmer, Kia Rogers; **Cast:** Aidan Redmond (Tom Carey), Jeremy S. Holm (Bill McGafferty), Janie Brookshire (Nan Bowers), Rosie Benton (Kate Moran), Shawn Fagan (James Whelan), Thomas Matthew Kelley (Jack McClinsey), Jon Fletcher (Apollo Moran), Liv Rooth (Nora Keane)

Mint Theatre; First Preview: July 29, 2010; Opening Night: August 23, 2010; Closed September 26, 2010; 13 previews, 47 performances. Setting: Act 1: A sheltered spot on the outskirts of an Irish town, Kilbeggan, early summer; Act 2: The office of the Silver Wings Motor Services, early summer, seven years later; Act 3: The same, a few months later. U.S. premiere of a 1947 play presented in three acts with two intermissions.

Shawn Fagan and Rosie Benton in Wife to James Whelan
(photo by Carol Rosegg)

What the Public Wants by Arnold Bennett; Director, Matthew Arbour; Set, Roger Hanna; Costumes, Erin Murphy; Lighting, Marcus Doshi; Sound, Daniel Kluger; Props, Deb Gaouette; Hair/Wigs, Gerard Kelly; PSM, Kathy Snyder; ASM, Lauren McArthur; Production Manager, Sherri Kotimsky; Illustration, Stefano Imbert; Graphics, Jude Dvorak; Assistant Production Manager, Wayne Yeager; Wardrobe, Karle J. Meyers; Assistant Set, Zhanna Gurvich; Assistant Costumes, Hunter Kaczarowski; Assistant Lighting/Programmer, Sara Gosses; Technical Director, Carlo Adinolfi; **Cast:** Rob Breckenridge (Sir Charles Worgan), Marc Vietor (Francis Worgan), Douglas Rees (Saul Kendrick/John Worgen), Jeremy Lawrence (Simon MacQuoid/Holt St. John/James Brindley), Ellen Adair (Emily Vernon), Birgit Huppuch (Henrietta Blackwood/Annie Worgan), Laurie Kennedy (Mrs. Worgan), Mary Baird (Mrs. Downes)

Mint Theatre; First Preview: January 14, 2011; Opening Night: January 27, 2011; Closed March 13, 2011; 26 previews, 42 performances. Setting: Act 1: Private office of Sir Charles Worgan, a November afternoon; Act 2: The same, four months later; Act 3: Library of John Worgan at Bursley, in Five Towns, a Sunday evening in July; Act 4: Private office of Sir Charles, a few days later. Revival of a 1909 play presented in four acts with two intermissions after Acts 1 and 2. First produced 1909 by the Stage Society in London, the first New York production was produced by The Theatre Guild in 1922.

A Little Journey by Rachel Crothers; Director, Jackson Gay; Set, Roger Hanna; Costumes, Martha Hally; Lighting, Paul Whitaker; Sound, Jane Shaw; Props, Joshua Yocum; Dramaturg, Heather J. Violanti; PSM, Samone B. Weissman; ASM, Andrea Jo Martin; Production Manager, Sherri Kotimsky; Illustration, Stefano Imbert; Graphics, Hey-Jude Graphics; Assistant Production Manager/Technical Director, Wayne Yeager; Wardrobe, Karle J. Meyers; Assistant Set, Zhanna Gurvich; Assistant Costumes, Amanda Jenks; Programmer/Assistant Lighting, Nelson Emig; **Cast:** Rosemary Prinz (Mrs. Bay), Chet Siegel (Lily), Laurie Birmingham (Mrs. Welch), Anthony L. Gaskins (Porter), McCaleb Burnett (Jim West), Jennifer Blood (Annie), Victoria Mack (Kittie Van Dyck), Joey Parsons (Ethel Halstead), Samantha Soule (Julie Ruterford), John Wernke (AAlfred Bemis), Craig Wroe (Leo Stern), Ben Hollandsworth (Frank), Ben Roberts (Charles), Douglas Rees (Mr. Smith/Conductor)

Mint Theatre; First Preview: May 12, 2011; Opening Night: June 6, 2011; Closed July 17, 2011; 24 previews, 43 performances. Setting: Spring, 1914; the inside of a Pullman sleeping car bound for the Pacific Coast. Revival of a play presented in two acts. Originally presented in New York at the Little Theatre (Helen Hayes Theatre) and later the Vanderbilt Theatre December 26, 1918–August, 1919, playing 252 performances.

Samantha Soule and McCaleb Burnett in A Little Journey
(photo by Richard Termine)

The New Group

Fifteenth Season

Artistic Director, Scott Elliott; Executive Director, Geoffrey Rich; Managing Director, Oliver Dow; Director of Development, Jamie Lehrer; Associate Artistic Director, Ian Morgan; General Manager, Elisabeth Bayer; Artistic Associate, James Gittins; Director of Special Events/Individual Giving, Cristina Galeano; Marketing Associate, Laura Padilla; Production Supervisor, Peter R. Feuchtwanger/PRF Productions; Casting, Judy Henderson; Press, Bridget Klapinski, Seven17 PR

Blood From a Stone by Tommy Nohilly; Director, Scott Elliott; Set, Derek McLane; Costumes, Theresa Squire; Lighting, Jason Lyons; Sound, Bart Fasbender; Special Effects, Jeremy Chernick; Dialect Coach, Doug Paulson; PSM, Valerie A. Peterson; Assistant Director, Marie Masters; ASM, Stephanie Cali; Props, Matt Hodges; Assistant Design, Jason Sherwood (set), Amanda Jenks (costumes), Grant Wilcoxen (lighting), William Neal (sound), Sarah Bird (special effects); **Cast:** Gordon Clapp (Bill), Thomas Guiry (Matt), Natasha Lyonne (Sarah), Ann Dowd (Margaret), Ethan Hawke (Travis), Daphne Rubin-Vega (Yvette)

Acorn Theatre on Theatre Row; First Preview: December 13, 2010; Opening Night: January 12, 2011; Closed February 19, 2011; 23 previews, 46 performances. Setting: A small town in Connecticut; a Wednesday through Friday in December in the recent past. World premiere of a new play presented in three acts with one intermission between Acts 2 and 3.

Ann Dowd and Ethan Hawke in Blood From a Stone *(photo by Monique Carboni)*

Marie and Bruce by Wallace Shawn; Director, Scott Elliott; Set, Derek McLane; Costumes, Jeff Marshie; Lighting, Jason Lyons; Sound, Shane Rettig; PSM, Valerie A. Peterson; Assistant Director, Marie Masters; ASM, Stephanie Cali; Props, Lily Fairbanks; Assistant Design: Jason Sherwood (set), Kyle Lacolla (costumes), Grant Wilcoxen (lighting), Justin Smiley (sound); Light Board Programmer, Greg Solomon; **Cast:** Cindy Katz (Ann/Waitress), Alison Wright (Gloria), Marisa Tomei (Marie), Frank Whaley (Bruce), Devin Ratray (Herb), Russell G. Jones (Nils/Bert), Adam Trese (Frank), Tina Benko (Janet), Alok Tewari (Ralph/Ed)

Acorn Theatre on Theatre Row; First Preview: March 14, 2011; Opening Night: April 5, 2011; Closed May 7, 2011; 21 previews, 34 performances. Revival of a play presented without intermission. Originally presented at the Theatre Upstairs at the Royal Court in London in 1979; New York premiere at the Public Theater February 3–March 15, 1980 (see *Theatre World* Vol. 36, page 149).

Marisa Tomei and Frank Whaley in Marie and Bruce *(photo by Monique Carboni)*

One Arm by Tennessee Williams; Adapted for the stage and directed by Moisés Kaufman; Co-presented by the Tectonic Theater Project (Moisés Kaufman, Artistic Director; Greg Reiner, Executive Director; Tiffany Redmon, Administrative Coordinator); Set, Derek McLane; Costumes, Clint Ramos; Lighting, David Lander; Original Music & Sound, Shane Rettig; Associate Director & Dramaturg, Jimmy Maize; Dialect Coach, Doug Paulson; Fight Director, David Anzuelo; Dramaturg, David G. Schultz; PSM, Valerie A. Peterson; Props, Lily Fairbanks; Associate Set, Shoko Kambara; Assistant Design: Jason Sherwood (set), Tristan Raines (costumes), Phil Kong (lighting), Janie Bullard and Justin Smiley (sound); Light Board Programmer, Ken Elliott; Wigs, Charles LaPointe; **Cast:** Noah Bean (Narrator, Sean, ensemble), Steven Hauck (Lester Chaplain, ensemble), Claybourne Elder (Ollie Olsen), Christopher McCann (Prison Guard, Yachtsman, ensemble), Todd Lawson (Divinity Student, Sailor, Middle-Aged Homosexual, ensemble), Greg Pierotti (Cherry, an in the Park, Middle-Aged Homosexual, ensemble), KC Comeax (Willy, Sailor, ensemble), Larisa Polonsky (Lila, Girl in the French Quarter, Nurse, ensemble)

Acorn Theatre on Theatre Row; First Preview: May 19, 2011; Opening Night: June 9, 2011; Closed July 2, 2011; 21 previews, 25 performances. Setting: 1967; Los Angeles, New Orleans, New York, and several other cities in the U.S. New York premiere of a play based on a short story and unproduced screenplay presented without intermission. World premiere produced by the Steppenwolf Theatre Company, About Face Theatre, and Techtonic Theater in Chicago at the Steppenwolf Downstairs Theatre December 2-19, 2004.

Claybourne Elder and Todd Lawson in One Arm *(photo by Monique Carboni)*

New Victory Theater

Fifteenth Season

President, Cora Cahan; Executive VP, Lisa Lawer Post; VP of Operations, Jarret M. Haynes; Curatorial/Progamming, Mary Rose Lloyd; Development SVP, Cheryl Kohn; Education Director, Edie Demas; Finance VP, Kim Dobbie Neuer; NVT Director of Theater Operations, Melinda Berk; Director of Production, David Jensen; NVT Technical Director, Robert Leach, NVT Production Coordinator, Colleen Davis; Public Relations Director, Laura Kaplow-Goldman; Marketing Director, Lauren P. Fitzgerald; IT Director, Michael Reisman; Facilities Manager, , Benno van Noort; Ticket Services, Robin Leeds; New 42nd Street Studios/The Duke on 42nd Street Director of Operations, Alma Malabanan- McGrath

Puss in Boots (*El Gato con botas*) by Xavier Montsalvatge; Presented by Tectonic Theater Project and Gotham Chamber Opera in association with Blind Summit Theatre (London); Director, Moisés Kaufman; Conductor, Neal Goren; Puppet Director, Mark Down; Set, Andromache Chalfant; Costumes, Clint Ramos; Lighting, David Lander; Choreography, Seán Curran; **Cast:** Ginger Costa-Jackson/Karin Mushegain/Leah Wool (Cat), Valerie Ogbonnaya/Nadine Sierra (Princess), Stephen LaBrie/Craig Verm (Miller), Peter Castaldi/Kyle Pfortmiller (King), Kevin Burdette/David Salsbery Fry (Ogre); Puppeteers: Stefano Brancato, Joe Gallina, Jonothan Lyons, Marta Mozelle Macrostie, James Ortiz, Aaron Schroeder, Jessica Scott, Teddy Yudain

New Victory Theatre; October 2-10, 2010; 10 performances. U.S. premiere of an opera for young audiences presented in Spanish and English without intermission.

A scene from in Puss in Boots *(photo by Eric P. Mull)*

ZooZoo Created by Carol Triffle and Jerry Mouawad; Presented by Imago Theatre (Portland, Oregon); Original Music, Katie Griesar; Lighting, Jeff Forbes; Creature Fabrication, Carol Triffle, Jerry Mouawad, Mark Forrest, Cati Thomas; PSM, Chris Balo; Company Stage Manager, Kayla Scrivner; **Cast:** CarlosAlexis Cruz, Jonathan Godsey, Alexander L. Hill, Joseph Lymous, Fiely Matias

New Victory Theatre; October 15-24, 2011; 10 performances. New York premiere of a visual theatre production presented without intermission.

Nevermore: The Imaginary Life and Mysterious Death of Edgar Allan Poe Conceived by Jonathan Christenson and Bretta Gerecke; Written, directed, and composed by Jonathan Christenson; Presented by Catalyst Theatre (Edmonton, Canada); Design, Bretta Gerecke; Choreography, Laura Krewski; Music/Sound, Wade Staples; Production Manager, James Robert Boudreau; Stage Manager, John Raymond; ASM, Candice Charney or Wayne Paquette; Props, Amy Kucharuk; Design Associate, Daniela Masellis; Voice and Text Coach, Betty Moulton; Sound Operator, Kevin Green; Costume Associate, Sheena Haug; **Cast:** Shannon Blanchet (Chorus, Nancy Valentin, Emira Royster, Mrs. Samuel Osgood,

Ms. Duval), Adam Cope (Chorus, Henry Poe, Bill Burton, Raven), Beth Graham (Chorus, Dresser, Rosalie Poe, Fanny Allen, Virginia Clem, Ann Carter Lee, Society Lady), Matthew Hulshof (Edgar, Ensemble), Carson Nattrass (Chorus, Pallearer, Metzengerstein's Horse, The Imp, Corpse, Alexander Shelton, Rufus Griswold), Garrett Ross (Chorus, David Poe, Jock Allan, Corpse, Raven, Mr. Bliss), Vanessa Sabourin (Chorus, Eliza Poe, Miss Duval, Muddy Clem, Society Lady)

New Victory Theatre; October 29-November 7, 2010; 8 performances. U.S. premiere of a new musical presented in two acts.

Egg and Spoon by Marcello Chiarenza and Patrick Lynch; Presented by Lyngo Theatre Company (London/Venice); Director, Marcello Chiarenza; Costumes/Lighting, Elana Marini; Chreographer/Assistant Director, Patrick Lynch; Set, Marcelllo Chiarenza; Sound, Carlo Capelli; Stage Manager/Technician; Keta Newborn; **Cast:** Patrick Lynch (Percy), Airlie Scott (April)

Studio 3A/B New 42nd Street Studios; November 2-21, 2010; 42 performances. A multi-sensory interactive theatrical production presented without intermission.

Squirm Burpee Circus: A Vaudevillian Melodrama Presented by the Handsome Little Devils (Denver); Artistic Director, Mike Huling; Director, Armitage Shanks; Choreograpy, Dan Newsome and Matthew Schneider; Artistic Manager, Cole Schneider; Set, Michael and Dan Huling; Costumes, Sarah Campbell; Lighting, Joey Wartnerchaney; **Cast:** Mike Huling (Mike the Handsome), Dave Clay (Dashing Dave), Cole Schneider (The Lovely Little Lolo), Jason Knauf (The Baron Vegan von Hamburger)

New Victory Theatre; November 13-28, 2010; 17 performances. New York premiere of a circus/variety show presented without intermission.

Momentum Created and presented by Myumana (Tel Aviv); Artistic Director/Creators/Directors/Music and Lyrics, Eylon Nuphar and Boaz Berman; Co-Founder/Producer, Roy Ofer; Artistic Advisor/Musical Editor/Effects Advisor, Ido Kagan; Artistic Advisors, David Ottone, Giuliano Peparini; Lighting, Roy Milo and Eylon Nuphar; Sound, Amir Schorr; Costumes/Sets/Props, Michael Kramenko and Yaron Zino; **Cast:** Ruth Aharoni, Talia Bik, Sergio Braams, Vicky Burrel, Michael Fcigenbaum, Silvia Garcias de Ves, "Kikeh" Enrique Jacinto, Alexandra Jezouin, Spike Levy, Roberto "Beto" Mendez, Natalie Pik, Aka Jean Claude Thiemele, Tim Vranken, Hila Yaffe

New Victory Theatre; December 4, 2010-January 2, 2011; 29 performances. U.S. premiere of a physical theatre piece presented without intermission.

A scene from in Momentum *(photo by Mayumana)*

Nearly Lear Adapted by Susanna Hamnet and Edith Tankus from Shakespeare; Presented by Susanna Hamnett; Initial Resarch in Association with Emma Rice and Mike Shepherd (Kneehigh Theatre); Director, Edith Tankus; Set, Lindsay Anne Black; Lighting, Michelle Ramsay; Sound, Gavin Fearon; Film, David Parker; **Cast:** Susanna Hamnet (The Fool)

Duke on 42ⁿᵈ Street; January 7-16, 2011; 8 performances. U.S. premiere of a solo performance play presented without intermission.

Susanna Hamnet in Nearly Lear *(photo by Doug Forster)*

Circus INcognitus Created, directed, presented by Jamie Adkins; Costumes, Katrin Leblond; Lighting, Nicholas Descoteaux; Music Composition and Arrangements, Lucie Cauchon; **Cast:** Jamie Adkins

New Victory Theatre; February 11-27, 2011; 17 performances. New York premiere of a solo performance circus/variety piece presented without intermission.

Skellig by David Almond; Presented by the Birmingham Stage Company (U.K.); Director, Phil Clark; Design, Jackie Trousdale; Music, Jak Poore; Lighting, Jason Taylor; Sound, Lewis Fowler; Production Manager, Adrian Littlejohns; **Cast**: Ellen Callender (Mrs. McKee), Colin R. Campbell (Dad), Christopher Chamberlain (Rasputin), Neal Foster (Skellig), Victoria Hamnett (Ensemble), Matthew Harrison (Ensemble), Dean Logan (Michael), Charlotte Palmer (Mum), Jak Poore (Coot), Charlie Sanderson (Mina)

New Victory Theatre; March 4-April 13, 2011; 8 performances. U.S. premiere of a play presented in two acts.

Mischief Created by Sue Buckmaster, Arthur Pita, and Sophia Clist; Presented by Theatre-Rites (London) and Arthur Pita; Director, Sue Buckmaster; Choreography, Arthur Pita; Visual Artist, Sophia Clist; Music, Charlie Winston; Lighting, Guy Hoare; Costume Supervisor, Alice Wilson; Puppet Maker, Tony Mason; Production Manager, Simon Sturgess; **Cast:** Claire Cunningham, Rachel Donovan, Gavin Eden, Valentina Golfieri, Phil King, Mohsen Nouri, Alexander Varona, Frank Wilson

New Victory Theatre; March 18-27, 2011; 8 performances. U.S. premiere of a physical theater and dance piece presented without intermission.

Boom Town Written by Steven Ragatz; Presented by Cirque Mechanics (Las Vegas, Nevada); Director, Chris Lashua; Co-Director/Choreography, Aloysia Gavre; Lighting, Deanna Fitzgerald; Set/Rigging Design, Sean Riley; Acrobat Act

Creator, Michael "Tex" Redinger; Composer, Michael Picton; Costumes, Belinda Lee Long; **Cast:** Steven Ragatz, Clint Bobzien, Elena Day, Hannah Bobzien, Timber Brown, Michael Hills, Charlotte Greenblatt, Wes Hatfield, Kerren McKeeman, Lindsay Orton, Michael "Tex" Redinger

New Victory Theatre; April 8-24, 2011; 17 performances. Off-Broadway premiere of a theatrical circus presented without intermission.

Potato Needs a Bath Created by Shona Reppe and Andy Manley; Presented by Shona Reppe Puppets (Fife, Scotland); Director, Andy Manley; Technical Manager/Company Stage Manager, Tamlin Wiltshire; Set, Shona Reppe; Composer, David Trouton; Costumes, Alison Brown; Management, Catherine Wheels Theatre Company; **Cast:** Shona Reppe (Performer)

Studio 3A/B New 42nd Street Studios; April 8-24, 2011; 26 performances. U.S. premiere of a solo performance and puppet theatre piece presented without intermission.

The Tragical Life of Cheeseboy by Finegan Kruckemeyer, conceived by Andy Packer; Presented by Sligsby Theatre Company (Adelaide, Australia); Director, Andy Packer; Set/Costumes/Props, Wendy Todd; Design Consultant/Lighting, Geoff Cobham; Sound, Nick O'Connor; Music, Quincy Grant; Production Manager, Roland Partis; Illustrator, Andy Ellis; New Media Artist, Simone Mazengarb; New Media Consultant, Sophie Hyde; **Cast:** Stephen Sheehan, Samuel McMahon, Rory Walker

Duke on 42ⁿᵈ Street; April 29-May 8, 2011; 10 performances. U.S. premiere of a play for young audiences presented without intermission.

Peter and Wendy Based on the novel by J.M. Barrie, adaptation by Liza Lorwin; Created and presented by Mabou Mines; Director, Lee Breuer; Composer, Johnny Cunningham; Puppets/Set/Lighting, Julie Archer; Associate Lighting, Steven L. Shelley; Fight Director, B.H. Barry; Costumes, Sally Thomas; Sound, Edward Cosla; PSM, Judith Schoenfeld; **Cast:** Karen Kandel (Narrator); Puppeteers: Lute Breuer, Basil Twist, Lindsay Abromaitis-Smith, Sam Hack, Jenny Subjack Piezas, Sarah Provost, Jessica Chandlee Smith, Jessica Scott, Amanda Villalobos

New Victory Theatre; May 6-21, 2011; 14 performances. Revival of a play with puppetry presented in two acts. Originally presented by Mabou Mines at the New Victory February 1, 1996 with most of this company (see *Theatre World* Vol. 53, page 148).

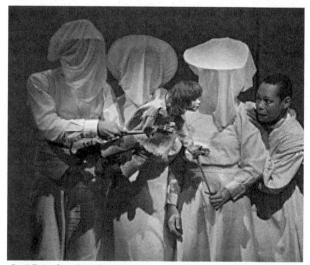

Basil Twist, Sam Hack, Sarah Provost, and Karen Kandel in Peter and Wendy *(photo by Richard Termine)*

New York Gilbert & Sullivan Players

Thirty-sixth Season

Artistic Director & General Manager/Director/Music Director/Set Design/Conductor, Albert Bergeret; Managing Director, David Wannen; Music by Sir Arthur Sullivan and Librettos by Sir William S. Gilbert; Costumes, Gail Wofford; Lighting, Brian Presti; Technical Director/PSM, David Sigafoose; ASM, Annette Dieli; Head of Wardrobe, Corey Groom; Administratve Intern, Joseph Rubin; Assistant Music Director, Andrea Stryker-Rodda; Orchestra Manager, Larry Tietze; Press, Peter Cromarty

Utopia, Limited or, The Flowers of Progress Co-Director, David Auxier; **Cast:** David Wannen (King Paramount), Stephne Quint (Scaphio), Stephen O'Brien (Calynx), Michael Galante (Lord Dramaleigh), Cameron Smith (Captain Fitzbattleaxe), Quinto Ott (Captain Sir Edward Corcoran), Richard Alan Holmes (Mr. Goldbury), Michael Connolly (Sir Bailey Barre), David Macaluso (Mr. Blushington), Laurelyn Watson Chase (The Princess Zara), Sarah Caldwell Smith (The Princess Nekaya), Amy Helfer (The Princess Kalyba), Erika Person (The Lady Sophy), Katie Hall (Salata), Jenny Millsap (Melente), Brooke Collins (Phylla), Ensemble: Ted Bouton, Susan Case, Elisabeth Cernadas, Carol Davis, Tom Donelan, Louis Dall'Ava, Victoria Devany, Alan Hill, James La Rosa, Daniel Lockwood, Rebecca O'Sullivan, Chris-Ian Sanchez, Angela Smith, Andrea Stryker-Rodda, Andrew Taines, Matthew Wages, Lauren Wenegrat, Eric Werner, Emily Wright

Symphony Space; November 21, 2010; 1 performance. Setting: A Utopian Palm Grove and the Throne Room in King Paramount's Palace. Revival of an operetta presented in two acts.

Stephen Quint, Laurelyn Watson, and David Wannen in Utopia, Limited (photo by William Reynolds)

The Yeomen of the Guard or, The Merryman and His Maid Choreography, Janis Ansley-Ungar and David Auxier; Set, Richard Manfredi and Albere; Costumes, Jan Holland, Gail J. Wofford; **Cast:** Keith Jurosko (Sir Richard Cholmondeley), Daniel Greenwood (Colonel Fairfax), Richard Alan Holmes (Sergeant Meryll), Paul Betz (Leonard Meryll), Stephen Quint (Jack Point), David Wannen (Wiltred Shadbull), Lucian Russell (The Headsman), Daniel Lockwood (First Yeoman), Ted Bouton (Second Yeoman), Lance Olds (First Citizen), William Whitefield (Second Citizen), Laurelyn Watson Chase (Elsie Maynard), Erika Person (Phoebe Meryll), Angela

Smith (Dame Carruthers), Sarah Hutchison (Kate); Ensemble: Louis Dall'Ava, Thomas Donelan, Michael Galante, Alan Hill, Quinto Ott   Citizens of the Tower Susan Case, Michael Connolly, Victoria Devany, Katie Hall, Amy Maude Helfer, David Macaluso, James Mills   Jenny Millsap, Rebecca O'Sullivan, Monique Pelletier, Lauren Wenegrat

Symphony Space; December 5, 2010; 1 performance. Setting: Tower Green; 16th Century. Revival of an operetta presented in two acts.

The Mikado or, The Town of Titipu Co-Stage Direction, David Auxier; Co-Costume Design, Kayko Nakamura; **Cast:** David Wannen (The Mikado of Japan), Cameron Smith or Daniel Greenwood (Nanki-Poo), David Macaluso or Stephen Quint (Ko-Ko), Louis Dall'Ava (Pooh-Bah), David Auxier (Pish-Tush), Sarah Smith (Yum-Yum), Rebecca Sullivan (Pitti-Sing), Amy Maude Helfer (Peep-Bo), Caitlin Burke or Angela Smith (Katisha); Ensemble: Michael Connolly, Lauren Frankovich, Michael Galante, Katie Hall, Alan Hill, Sarah Hutchison, James Mills, Lance Olds, Quinto Ott, Monique Pelletier, Jennifer Piacenti, Natalie Ross, Chris-Ian Sanchez, Matthew Wages

Symphony Space; December 29, 2010–January 2, 2011; 5 performances. Setting: A Japanese Garden. Revival of an operetta presented in two acts.

Trial by Jury and **G&S a la Carte** Trial by Jury: Choreography, David Auxier; **Cast:** Stephen Quint (The Learned Judge), Richard Alan Holmes (Counsel for the Plaintiff), Cameron Smith (The Defendant), Ted Bouton (Foreman of the Jury), David Wannen (Usher), Kimilee Bryant (The Plaintiff Angelina); Ensemble: Caitlín Burke, Michael Connolly, Louis Dall'Ava, Michael Galante, Daniel Greenwood, Katie Hall, Alan Hill, James Mills, Jenny Millsap, Stephen O'Brien, Lance Olds, Rebecca O'Sullivan, Monique Pelletier, Jennifer Piacenti, Chris-Ian Sanchez, Angela Christine Smith, Sarah Caldwell Smith, Matt Wages, Lauren Wenegrat, William Whitefield, Emily Wright; **G&S a la Carte:** Book and direction by David Auxier; **Cast:** Richard Alan Holmes (Richard D'Oyly Carte), Caitlín Burke (Helen Lenoir), Stephen Quint (Arthur Sullivan), Stephen O'Brien (W.S. Gilbert), Kimilee Bryant (Miss Nelly Bromley), David Auxier (Walter, a G&S Fan)

Symphony Space; March 20, 2011; 1 performance. Revival of a one-act operetta and revival of an original musical soireé presented with intermission.

Laurelyn Watson Chase and Stephen Quint in Trial by Jury (photo by Carol Rosegg)

New York Theatre Workshop

Twenty-eighth Season

Artistic Director, James C. Nicola; Managing Director, William Russo; Associate Artistic Director, Linda S. Chapman; General Manager, C. Barrack Evans; Development, Alisa Schierman; Education, Bryn Thorsson; Finance and Administration, Rachel McBeth; Production/Facilities Manager, Julie M. Mason; Casting, Jack Doulin; Literary Associate, Geoffrey Scott; Artistic Associates, Michael Greif, Michael Friedman, Ruben Polendo, Alex Lewin; Marketing Associate, Rebekah Paine; Technical Director, Brian Garber; Press, Richard Kornberg, Don Summa

The Little Foxes by Lilian Hellman; Director, Ivo van Hove; Design, Jan Versweyveld; Costumes, Kevin Guyer; Sound/Video, Thibaud Delpeut; Video, Tal Yarden; PSM, Winnie Y. Lok; ASM, Rachel Motz; Assistant Directors, Rafael Gallegos, Kirk Jackson; Assistant Lighting/Electrician, John Anselmo Jr.; Sound/Video Supervisor, Jamie McElhinney; Costume Shop Manager, Jeffrey Wallach; Props, Matt Hodges; Production Assistant, Edward Herman; Assistant Set, Tim Brown; Assistant Lighting, Justin Partier; Assistant Sound, Jason Sebastian; Assistant Video, Taili Wu; Wardrobe, Arianna E. Funk; Light Board Programmer, Alex Fabozzi; **Cast:** Tina Benko (Birdie Hubbard), Marton Csokas (Ben Hubbard), Sanjit De Silva (William Marshall), Lynda Gravatt (Addie), Elizabeth Marvel (Regina Giddens), Cristin Milioti (Alexandra Giddens), Thomas Jay Ryan (Oscar Hubbard), Greig Sargeant (Cal), Christopher Evan Welch (Horace Giddens), Nick Westrate (Leo Hubbard)

East 4th Street Theatre; First Preview: September 10, 2010; Opening Night: September 21, 2010; Closed October 31, 2010; 58 performances. A new version of a revival of a play presented without intermission. Originally presented at New York's National Theatre February 15, 1939 starring Tallulah Bankhead, playing 410 performances. The play has had three major Broadway revivals in 1967 (starring Anne Bancroft and George C. Scott), 1981 (starring Elizabeth Taylor), and 1997 (starring Stockard Channing).

Tina Benko and Elizabeth Marvel in The Little Foxes *(photo by Jan Versweyveld)*

Three Pianos Written and arranged by the cast; Music ("Winterreise") by Franz Schubert, text by Wilhelm Muller; Director, Rachel Chavkin; Set/Illustration, Andreea Mincic; Lighting, Austin R. Smith; Sound, Matt Hubbs and Dave Malloy; Costumes, Jessica Pabst; Video, Dave Malloy; PSM, Jessie Vacchiano; Stage Manager, Rebecca S. Fleming; Assistant Director, Christopher Bowser; Production Assistant, Patrick Clayton; Assistant Set, Jonathan Cottle, Ryan Trupp; Assistant Lighting, Nick Houfek; Movement Coach, Dan Safer; Master Electrician, John Anselmo Jr.; Sound/Video Supervisor, Ryan Holsopple; Props, Matt Hodges; Costume Shop Manager, Jeffrey Wallach; **Cast:** Rick Burkhardt, Alec Duffy, James Malloy

East 4th Street Theatre; First Preview: November 7, 2010; Opening Night: December 19, 2010; Closed January 9, 2011; 48 performances. Off-Broadway premiere of a theatrical song cycle presented in two parts without intermission. Originally presented in association with the Onotological-Hysterical Incubator at Theater at St. Mark's Church February 2010.

Dave Malloy, Alec Duffy, and Rick Brukhardt in Three Pianos
(photo by Joan Marcus)

Peter and the Starcatcher Text by Rick Elice, based on the novel by Dave Barry and Ridley Pearson; Directors, Rogers Rees and Alex Timbers; Music, Wayne Barker; Movement, Steven Hoggett; Music Director, Marco Paguia; Set, Donyale Werle; Costumes, Paloma Young; Lighting, Jeff Croiter; Sound, Darron L West; Fight Director, Jacob Grigolia-Rosenbaum; Dramaturgy, Ken Cerniglia; PSM, Clifford Schwartz; ASM, Katherine Wallace; Casting, Jack Doulin, Tara Rubin; Assistant Director, Lillian King; Associate Design: Grady Barker, Meghan Buchanan (set), Grant Yeager (lighting); Assistant Design: Justin Couchara (set), David Mendizabal (costumes), Cory Pattak (lighting), Charles Coes (sound); Sound Supervisor, Toby Algya; Props, Meghan Buchanan, Matt Hodges; Script Assistant, Alisa Zeljeznjak; Assistant Technical Director, Jon Rodriguez; Electrician, John Anselmo Jr.; Costume Shop Manager, Jeffrey Wallach; **Cast:** Teddy Bergman (Fighting Prawn), Arnie Burton (Mrs. Bumbrake), Adam Chanler-Berat (Boy), Matt D'Amico (Slank), Kevin Del Aguila (Smee), Brandon Dirden (Captain Scott), Carson Elrod (Prentiss), Greg Hildreth (Alf), Celia Keenan-Bolger (Molly), Karl Kenzler (Lord Aster), Eric William Love (Sailor/Pirate), Steve Rosen (Black Stache), David Rossmer (Ted); Musicians: Marco Paguia or Dan Green (Piano), Deanne Prouty (Percussion)

East 4th Street Theatre; First Preview: February 18, 2011; Opening Night: March 9, 2011; Closed April 24, 2011; 66 performances. World premiere of a new play with music presented in two acts. Originally presented in a "Page to Stage" workshop production at La Jolla Playhouse in 2009.

The Shaggs: Philosophy of the World Book, story, and lyrics by Joy Gregory; Story, music, and lyrics by Gunnar Madsen; Story and direction by John Langs; A co-production with Playwrights Horizons (please see production listing on page 220 in this volume).

Pan Asian Repertory Theatre

Thirty-fourth Season

Artistic Producing Director, Tisa Chang; Communications Director, Abigail Felder; Artistic Associate, Ron Nakahara; Workshop Instructor, Ernest Abuba; Fight Choreographer, Michael G. Chin; Outreach Associate/House Manager, Danny Gomez; Webmaster, Auric Abuba; Production Manager, Jay Janicki; Box Office Manager, Monet Hurst-Mendoza; Bookkeeper, Rosemary Kahn; Graphics, Ramon Gil & Chris Loh; Advertising, Miller Advertising; Photo Archivist, Corky Lee; Press, Keith Sherman and Associates

Vietnam Project II: Past and Present

We Are Written and directed by Nguyen Thi Minh Ngoc; Translations, Ian Bui; Set, Kim Tran; Costumes, Bao Tron Chi; Lighting, Ji-youn Chang; Music, Trinh Cong Son; Singer, Kim Minh; Guitarist, Duc Tri; **Cast:** Lê Khanh, Thái Hòa Lê, Ngoc Dang, Leon Le, Nguyen thi Minh Ngoc, Chantal Thuy, Tienne Vu

West End Theatre at St. Paul's; Opening Night: March 18, 2011; Closed March 26, 2011. World premiere of a theatrical piece with storytelling, music, and traditional Vietnamese theatrical techniques presented in Vietnamese and English without intermission.

Ngoc Dang in We Are

Thai-Hoa Le and Chantal Thuy in We Are *(photos by Corky Lee)*

Monster by Derek Nguyen; Director, Kaipo Schwab; Set, Gian Marco Lo Forte; Costumes, Carol Pelletier; Lighting, Jiyoun Chang; Video Coordinator, Rocco D'Santi; Stage Manager, Wendy Ouellette; ASM, A.J. Dobbs; **Cast:** Daniel Lê (Detective Tang Tran), Deanna Gibson (Katie Van Dorph/Molly), Justin R. G. Holcomb (Wray Ballard/Priest), Tonia Jackson (Shawna Washington/Rosa Martinez), Brad Lewandowski (Eric Henderson), Patricia Randell, (Flora Bonnard), Claro de los Reyes (Khoi Nguyen), Tran T. Thuc Hanh (Woman/Mai Vi Pham)

West End Theatre at St. Paul's; First Preview: March 30, 2011; Opening Night: April 5, 2011; Closed April 17, 2011. Setting: The California desert suburb of Sun Valley. New York premiere of a play presented in two acts. World premiere presented by East West Players April 17, 2002.

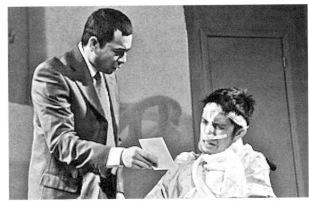

Daniel Lê and Claro de los Reyes in Monster

Daniel Lê and Deanna Gibson in Monster

Readings and Workshops

Acting/Writing Lab Presentation Bruce Mitchell Room; January 6, 2011; scenes and shorts from Pan Asian's performance and writing workshops; Included: *This Korean Story* by Susan Kim; *Dance* by Jillian Hassett; *Infinitude* by Sung Rno, performed by Johnson Chong; *Intentions of a Father* by Dorim Lee; Two untitled pieces by Julia Amsterdam; Timothy Liu in a monologue from *Hamlet*; *a good sc(rub)* by Kira Neel; *All This Intimacy* by Rajiv Joseph, with Rachel Lin (Jen), Johnson Chong (Ty); *Party* by Jillian Hassett; Johnson Chong in a monologue from *Measure for Measure*; *Once Upon a Time in China* by John Quincy Lee

Newworks 2011 Chen Dance Center; May 18-21, 2011; a series of readings of new plays and solo performance pieces; Plays Included. *Recess* by Una Aya Osato; *American Mixed Tape* by Allen Hope Sermonia; *The Women of Tu-Na House* by Nancy Eng; Solo performance shorts included: *Party* by Jillian Hasset; a *aood sc(rub)* by Kira Neel; *Unfelt Wonder* by Angela Santillo

Pearl Theatre Company

Twenty-seventh Season

Artistic Director, J.R. Sullivan; Managing Director, Shira Beckerman; Production Manager/Technical Director, Gary Levinson; Dramaturg, Kate Farrington; Marketing & Press, Aaron Schwartzbord; Development Manager, Angi Taylor; Audience Services Manager, Courtney Breslin; Artistic Adminstrator, Sarah Wozniak; Management Associate, Michael Levinton; Costume Shop Manager, Niki Hernandez-Adams; Education, Carol Schultz

The Sneeze by Michael Frayn, adapted from plays and stories by Anton Chekhov; Director, J.R. Sullivan; Set, Jo Winiarski; Costumes, Barbara A. Bell; Lighting, Ann G. Wrightson; Sound, Jane Shaw; Movement Coach/Assistant Director, Kali Quinn; Fight Director, Rod Kinter; PSM, Lisa Ledwich; Production Assistant, Samantha Gass; Props/Assistant Set, Buist Bickley; Costume Design Assistant, Caitlin Cisek; **Cast:** Rachel Botchan (Murashkina/Brizzhalov's Wife/ Natalya Stepanovna), Bradford Cover (Kamyshev/Brizzhalov/Smirnov/A Traveler), Dominic Cuskern (Champugne/Cart Driver/ Chubukov), Robert Hock (Luka/ Svetlovidov), Chris Mixon (Parvel/Chervyakov/Nyukhin), Edward Seamon (Misha/Nikita Ivanich), Lee Stark (Chervyakov's Wife/Popova)

City Center Stage II; First Preview: September 17, 2010; Opening Night: September 26, 2010; Closed October 31, 2010; 9 previews, 37 performances. Setting: A small theatre in a Russian Province. New York premiere of a 1983 play with eight scenes in two acts.

The Company in The Sneeze *(photo by Gregory Costanzo)*

Rosmersholm by Henrik Ibsen, adapted by Mike Poulton; Director, Elinor Renfield; Set, Harry Feiner; Costumes, Niki Hernandez-Adams; Lighting, Stephen Petrilli; Sound, Toby Jaguar Algya; Additional Casting, Stephanie Klapper; PSM, Dale Smallwood; Assistant to the Director, Michelle Foster; Casting Assistants, Lauren O'Connell, Tyler Albright; Prop Master, Buist Bickley; Assistant Costumes, Anna Gerdes; Wigs, Amanda Miller; **Cast:** Bradford Cover (Johannes Rosmer), Margot White (Rebecca West), Austin Pendleton (Doctor Kroll), Dan Daily (Ulrik Brendel), Dominic Cuskern (Peder Mortensgaard), Robin Leslie Brown (Mrs. Helseth); Understudy: Jason Aspery (Rosmer/Kroll)

City Center Stage II; First Preview: November 12, 2010; Opening Night: November 21, 2010; Closed December 19, 2010; 9 previews, 29 performances. Setting: The parlor and study in Rosmersholm (the house of Rosmer), over two days in late summer. American premiere of a new version of a classic play presented in two acts.

The Misanthrope by Molière, translated by Richard Wilbur; Director, Joseph Hanreddy; Set, Harry Feiner; Costumes, Sam Fleming; Lighting, Stephen Petrilli; Sound, M.L. Dogg; PSM, Dale Smallwood; Rehearsal ASM, Michal V. Mendelson; Production Assistant, Katherine Schroeder; Props, Buist Bikckley; Wigs, Gerald Kelly; **Cast:** Sean McNall (Alceste), Shawn Fagan (Philinte), Kern McFadden (Oronte/Guard), Janie Brookshire (Célimène), Dominic Cuskern (Basque/Dubois), Robin LeMon (Eliante), Matthew Amendt (Acaste), Patrick Halley (Clitandre/u.s. Alceste), Joey Parsons (Arsinoé); Acting Apprentices: Michael Frishman, Paul Kite, Blair Lewin, Lauren Nordvig, Chris Richards

City Center Stage II; First Preview: January 14, 2011; Opening Night: January 23, 2011; Closed February 20, 2011; 9 previews, 30 performances. Setting: Célimène's house in Paris. Revival of a classic play presented in two acts.

Janie Brookshire and Kern McFadden in The Misanthrope *(photo by Jacob J. Goldberg)*

Wittenberg by David Davalos; Director, J.R. Sullivan; Set, Jo Winiarski; Costumes, Liz Covey; Lighting, Stephen Petrilli; Sound, Barry G. Funderburg; PSM, Erin Albrecht; Production Assistant, Emily Rolston; Assistant to the Director, Katherine Schroeder; Props, Buist Bickly; Assistant Props, Joshua Yocum; Wardrobe, Mary Margaret Powers; Draper, Anna Gerdes; Board Operator, Emily Ewing; **Cast:** Scott Greer (John Faustus, *a doctor*), Sean McNall (Hamlet, *a senior, major undecied*), Chris Mixon (Rev. Fr. Martin Luther, *professor and a confessor*), Joey Parsons (The Eternal Feminine)

City Center Stage II; First Preview: March 11, 2011; Opening Night: March 20, 2011; Closed April 17, 2011; 9 previews, 30 performances. Setting: The last week of October, 1517; Wittenberg, Germany – the town and its university. New York premiere of a new play presented in two acts. Originally produced by the Arden Theatre Company.

Scott Greer, Sean McNall, and Chris Mixon in Wittenberg *(photo by Sam Hough)*

Playwrights Horizons

Fortieth Season

Artistic Director, Tim Sanford; Managing Director, Leslie Marcus; General Manager, Carol Fishman; Director of New Play Development, Adam Greenfield; Director of Musical Theatre/Literary Associate, Kent Nicholson; Casting, Alaine Alldaffer, Laura Stanczyk; Production Manager, Christopher Boll; Development, Jill Garland; Controller, Jack Feher; Marketing, Eric Winick; Director of Ticket Central, Ross Peabody; School Director, Helen R. Cook; Company Manager, Caroline Aquino; Technical Director, Brian Coleman; Advertising, Eliran Murphy Group; Press, The Publicity Office, Marc Thibodeau, Michael S. Borowski

Me, Myself & I by Edward Albee; Produced in arrangement with Elizabeth Ireland McCann; Director, Emily Mann; Set, Thomas Lynch; Costumes, Jennifer von Mayrhauser; Lighting, Kenneth Posner; Sound, Darron L West; PSM, Alison Cote; ASM, Marisa Levy; Stage Management Resident, Allison Cottrell; Directing Resident, Lisa Szolovits; Associate Set, Charlie Corcoran; Assistant Design: Grant Yeager (lighting), Suzanee Chesney (costumes), Matt Hubbs (sound); Prop Supervisor, Desireé Maurer; Costume Supervisor, Tiia E. Torchia; Wardrobe Supervisor, Carrie Buettner; Lighting Supervisor, Douglas Filomena; Audio Supervisor, Dylan Carrow; Graphic Design, Patrick Flood; Scenic Artist, Hannah Davis; **Cast:** Zachary Booth (OTTO), Preston Sadleier (otto), Elizabeth Ashley (Mother), Brian Murray (Dr.), Natalia Payne (Maureen), Stephen Payne (The Man)

Mainstage Theatre; First Preview: August 24, 2010; Opening Night: September 12, 2010; Closed: October 31, 2010; 24 previews, 51 performances. New York premiere of a new play presented in two acts. World premiere produced at the McCarter Theatre Center (Princeton, New Jesery) January 18, 2008.

Elizabeth Ashley, Brian Murray, Zachary Booth, Preston Sadler, and Natalia Payne in Me, Myself & I *(photo by Joan Marcus)*

After the Revolution by Amy Herzog; Director, Carolyn Cantor; Set, Clint Ramos; Costumes, Kaye Voyce; Lighting, Ben Stanton; Original Music and Sound, Fitz Patton; PSM, Hannah Cohen; Stage Management Resident, Ryan Gohsman; Directing Resident, Knud Adams; Assistant Design: Craig Napoliello (set), Sarah Gosnell (costumes), Carl Faber (lighting), Mark Van Hare (sound); Scenic Artist, Samantha Yaeger; Props Supervisor, Desireé Maurer; Costume Supervisor, Tiia E. Torchia; Wardrobe Supervisor, Jessie June Shipley; Lighting Supervisor, Douglas Filomena; Audio Supervisor, Dylan Carrow; **Cast:** Peter Friedman (Ben), Mare Winningham (Mel), Mark Blum (Leo), Lois Smith (Vera), Katharine Powell (Emma), Elliot Villar (Miguel), David Margulies (Morty), Meredith Holzman (Jess)

Peter Jay Sharp Theater; First Preview: October 21, 2010; Opening Night: November 10, 2010; Closed December 12, 2010; 24 previews, 37 performances. Setting: New York and Boston in May and June of 1999. New York premiere of a new play presented in two acts. World premiere presented at Williamstown Theatre Festival June 22, 2010 with most of this cast.

Lois Smith and Katharine Powell in After the Revolution *(photo by Joan Marcus)*

A Small Fire by Adam Bock; Director, Trip Cullman; Set, Loy Arcenas; Costumes, Ilona Somogyi; Lighting, David Weiner; Original Music and Sound, Robert Kaplowitz; PSM, Lori Ann Zepp; Stage Management Resident, Allison Cottrell; Directing Resident, Lisa Szolovits; Assistant to Mr. Bock, James Ryan Caldwell; Assistant Design: Dexter Hernandez, Joey Mendoza, Dax Valdes (set), Jessica Wagener (costumes), Sarah Jakubasz (lighting); Associate Sound, Jessica Paz; Scenic Artist, Samantha Yaeger; Automation, Ry Pepper; Deck Carpenter, John Underwood; Props Supervisor, Desireé Maurer; Assistant Props, Eric Berninghausen, Sarah Engelke; Costume Supervisor, Tiia E. Torchia; Costumes Assistant, Sarah Reever; Lighting, Supervisor, Douglas Filomena; Wardrobe, Carrie Buettner; Audio Supervisor, Dylan Carrow; **Cast:** Michele Pawk (Emily Bridges), Victor Williams (Billy Fontaine), Reed Birney (John Bridges), Celia Keenan-Bolger (Jenny Bridges)

Mainstage Theatre; First Preview: December 16, 2010; Opening Night: January 6, 2011; Closed: January 30, 2011; 23 previews, 27 performances. World premiere of a new play presented without intermission.

Michele Pawk, Celia Keenan-Bolger, and Reed Birney in A Small Fire *(photo by Joan Marcus)*

Kin by Bathsheba Doran; Director, Sam Gold; Set, Paul Steinberg; Costumes, David Zinn; Lighting, Jane Cox; Sound, Matt Tierney; Dialects, Stephen Gabis; PSM, Alaina Taylor; ASM, Katrina Herrmann; Stage Management Resident, Ryan Gohsman; Directing Resident, Knud Adams; Assistant Design: Michael V. Moore (set), Jacob Climer (costumes), Bradley King (lighting), Janie Bullard, Alex Neumann (sound); Scenic Artist, Hannah Davis; Automation, Philip Tokarsky; Carpenters, Stephen Burt, Will Duty, David Nelson; Props Supervisor, Desireé Maurer; Costume Supervisor, Tiia E. Torchia; Wardrobe Supervisor, Jill Frese; Lighting Supervisor, Douglas Filomena; Audio Supervisor, Dylan Carrow; Props Assistants, Eric Berninghausen, Sarah Engelke; Costume Assistant, Sarah Reever; Light Board, Lisa Hufnagel; Audio Board, Sarah Gates; **Cast:** Suzanne Bertish (Linda), Bill Buell (Max), Kristen Bush (Anna), Patch Darragh (Sean), Laura Heisler (Helena), Matthew Rauch (Simon/Gideon), Cotter Smith (Adam), Concetta Tomei (Kay), Molly Ward (Rachel)

Mainstage Theatre; First Preview: February 25, 2011; Opening Night: March 21, 2011; Closed: April 17, 2011; 29 previews, 30 performances. World premiere of a new play presented without intermission.

Go Back to Where You Are by David Greenspan; Director, Leigh Silverman; Set, Rachel Hauck; Costumes, Theresa Squire; Lighting, Matt Frey; PSM, Kyle Gates; Stage Management Resident, Allison Cottrell; Directing Resident, Lisa Szolovits; Assistant Design: Lauren Rockman (set), Amanda Jenks (costumes), Oliver Wason (lighting); Scenic Artists, Samantha Yaeger, Carolyn Bonanni; Properties Supervisor, Desireé Maurer; Costume Supervisor, Tiia E. Torchia; Wardrobe Supervisor, Janet Anderson; Lighting Supervisor, Douglas Filomena; Audio Supervisor, Dylan Carrow; Graphic Design, Bradford Louryk; Production Artwork, Aaron Epstein; **Cast:** Brian Hutchison (Bernard), David Greenspan (Passalus), Tim Hopper (God/Malcolm), Lisa Banes (Claire), Mariann Mayberry (Charlotte), Stephen Bogardus (Tom), Michael Izquierdo (Wally)

Peter Jay Sharp Theater; First Preview: March 24, 2011; Opening Night: April 12, 2011; Closed May 1, 2011; 21 previews, 22 performances. Setting: The east end of Long Island, summer. World premiere of a new play presented without intermission.

The Shaggs: Philosophy of the World Book and lyrics by Joy Gregory, music and lyrics by Gunnar Madsen; Based on the true story of The Shaggs; Co-Produced with New York Theatre Workshop (James C. Nicola, Artistic Director; William Russo, Managing Director); Director, John Langs; Choreography, Ken Roht; Set, Mimi Lien; Costumes, Emily Rebholz; Lighting, Geoff Korf; Sound, Darron L West; Music Director, Aaron Gandy; Orchestrations/Vocal Arrangements, Gunnar Madsen; Music Coordinator, John Miller; Dialect Coach, Stephen Gabis; Additional Press, Richard Kornberg and Associates; PSM, Lori Lundquist; ASM, Katrina Herrmann; Dance Captain, Jamey Hood; Assistant to the Director, Augustus Heagerty; Assistant Choreographer, William Popp; Wigs, Leah Loukas; Assistant Design: Brett Banakis, Laura Jellinek (set), Katie Hartsoe (costumes), Yuriy Nayer (lighting), Matt Hubbs (sound); Co-Technical Director, David Nelson; Supervisors: Desireé Maurer (props), Tiia E. Torcia (costumes) Douglas Filomena (lighting), Dylan Carrow (sound); Automation, Nick DeFrange; Deck Carpenter, Adam Walck; **Cast:** Peter Friedman (Austin Wiggin), Jamey Hood (Dot Wiggin), Sarah Sokolovic (Betty Wiggin), Emily Walton (Helen Wiggin), Annie Golden (Annie Wiggin), Kevin Cahoon (Charley/Bobby), Cory Michael Smith (Kyle), Steve Routman (Mr. Wilson/Exeter Talent Show Host/Russ/Hank); Band: Aaron Gandy (Conductor/Keyboard), LeRoy Bach (Guitar/Keyboard), Mark Vanderpoel (Bass), David Jerome Hilliard (Drums)

Musical Numbers: Verses in the Body, Verses in the Body (reprise), Career Day, Impossible You, Annie's Lessons, Don't Say Nothing Bad About My Dad, Show Me the Magic, Words Into Wonder, Things I Wonder, Destiny, Philosophy of the World–Practice, Austin's Howl, Flyin, The Night Before, Studio Montage, Ordinary Day, This Is Real, Poster Girls, My Head Is an Empty Birdcage, Driving Home (The Rage), Never Fade, Philosophy of the World (final reprise)

Mainstage Theatre; First Preview: May 12, 2011; Opening Night: June 7, 2011; Closed July 3, 2011; 14 previews, 27 performances. Setting: Fremont, New Hampshire; 1969 and 1989. New York premiere of a new musical presented in two acts. Midwest Premiere by the Lookingglass Theatre Company (Chicago). Developed in workshop by Geva Theatre Center (Rochester, New York). An earlier version was presented by The Powerhouse Theatre (Los Angeles), and at the 2005 New York Musical Theatre Festival.

Lisa Banes and David Greenspan in Go Back to Where You Are *(photo by Joan Marcus)*

Peter Friedman, Annie Golden, Sarah Sokolovic, Emily Walton, and Jamey Hood in The Shaggs: Philosophy of the World *(photo by Joan Marcus)*

Primary Stages

Twenty-fifth Season

Founder and Executive Producer, Casey Childs; Artistic Director, Andrew Leynse; Managing Director, Elliot Fox; Associate Artistic Director, Michelle Bossy; Literary Manager, Tessa LaNeve; Development, Jessica Sadowski Comas; Marketing, Shanta Mali; General Manager, Reuben Saunders; Production Supervisor, Peter R. Feuchtwanger; Casting, Stephanie Klapper; Press, O+M Company, Rick Miramontez, Philip Carrubba

Secrets of the Trade by Jonathan Tolins; Presented in association with Ted Snowdon; Director, Matt Shakman; Set, Mark Wellington; Costumes, Alejo Vietti; Lighting, Mike Durst; Original Music and Sound, John Gromada; PSM, Sarah Cadell; ASM, Kelly Ice; Assistant Design: Larry Brown (set), China Lee (costumes), Amanda Clegg Lyon (lighting), Matthew Walsh (sound); Props, Alexandra Morton; Assistant Directors, Josh Breslow, Benjamin Kern; Carpenters, John Martinez, Tom Goehring; Electricians, Tom Dyer, Robert Murray; Audio, David Arnold, Erin Ballentine; Wardrobe, Laura Bowman; Light Board Programmer, Jonathan Dunkle; Light/Sound Board, Jessica Ferguson; Production Assistants, Veronica Falborn, Steve Fareri; **Cast:** Mark Nelson (Peter Lipman), Noah Robbins (Andrew Lipman), Amy Aquino (Joanne Lipman), Bill Brochtrup (Bradley), John Glover (Martin Kerner)

59E59 Theater A; First Preview: July 27, 2010; Opening Night: August 10, 2010; Closed September 4, 2010; 14 previews, 27 performances. Setting: 1980-1990; New York, California, and Massachusettes. New York premiere of a new play presented in two acts. Originally produced by the Black Dahlia Theatre (Los Angeles, California).

Noah Robbins and John Glover in Secrets of the Trade *(photo by James Leynse)*

In Transit Book, music, and lyrics by Kristen Anderson-Lopez, James-Allen Ford, Russ Kaplan, Sara Wordsworth; Based on a concept created with Gregory T. Christopher and Karla Lant; Produced in association with Baruch/Viertel/Routh/Frankel Group, Jane Bergere, Jodi Glucksman, Ken Greiner, Chip Meyrelles, Christina Papagjika, Janet Rosen; Director/Musical Staging, Joe Calarco; Music Director, Mary-Mitchell Campbell; Set, Anna Louizos; Costumes, Jennifer Caprio; Lighting, Jeff Croiter; Sound, Jon Weston; PSM, Andrew Neal; ASM, Kelly Hess; Assistant Director, Kenneth Ferrone; Associate Music Director, Adam Wachter; Associate Design: Aimee Dombo (set), Paul Carey (costumes), Jason Strangfeld (sound); Assistant Design: Sydney Maresca (costumes), Zach Blane (lighting);

Props, Samuel Froeschle; **Cast:** Steve French (Chris/Steven/Dave/Coffee Guy), Celisse Henderson (Momma/Booth Lady/Ms. Williams), Hannah Laird (Ali/Nanny), Chesney Snow (Boxman), Graham Stevens (Nate/Cab Driver), Denise Summerford (Jane/Kathy), Tommar Wilson (Trent/Hunter/Train Conductor)

Musical Numbes: Not There Yet, No Dental, Four Days Home, Maxed Out, Saturday Night Obsession, Wingman, But Ya Know, Keep It Goin, A Little Friendly Advice, The Moving Song, Choosing Not to Know, Getting There, Finale

59E59 Theater A; First Preview: September 21, 2010; Opening Night: October 5, 2010; Closed October 30, 2010; 14 previews, 27 performances. Setting: NYC, now. World premiere of a new musical presented without intermission.

Denise Summerford, Hanna Laird, Steve French, Tommar Wilson, Graham Stevens, Cellisse Henderson, and (back) Chesney Snow in In Transit *(photo by James Leynse)*

Black Tie by A.R. Gurney; Presented in association with Jamie deRoy, Barry Feirstein, Daniel Frishwasser, Ted Snowdon; Director, Mark Lamos; Set, John Arnone; Costumes, Jess Goldstein; Lighting, Stephen Strawbridge; Original Music and Sound, John Gromada; Props, Faye Armon; PSM, Matthew Melchiorre; ASM, Amanda Spooner; Assistant Design: Adam Karavatakis (set), Nick Kolin (lighting), Janie Bullard (sound); Associate Costumes, China Lee; Prop Assistant, Marina Guzman; Carpenters, John A. Martinez, J. Michael Zally; Electricians, Tom Dyer, Yuriy Nayer; Audio, David A. Arnold, Erin Ballentine; Light/Sound Board, Jesscia Ferguson; Wardrobe Supervisor, Laura Bowman; Production Assistant, Erin Teachman; **Cast:** Gregg Edelman (Curtis), Daniel Davis (Curtis' Father), Carolyn McCormick (Mimi), Elvy Yost (Elsie), Ari Brand (Teddy)

59E59 Theater A; First Preview: January 25, 2011; Opening Night: February 8, 2011; Closed March 27, 2011 2010; 14 previews, 49 performances. Setting: Early evening on a Friday in mid-August, in a hotel near the southern tip of Lake George and the Adirondacks. World premiere of a new play presented without intermission.

Carolyn McCormick, Daniel Davis, Ari Brand, and Gregg Edelman in Black Tie *(photo by James Leynse)*

The Public Theater

Fifty-fifth Season

Artistic Director, Oskar Eustis; Executive Director, Andrew Hamingson; General Manager, Andrea Nellis; Associate Artistic Director, Mandy Hackett; Associate Producer, Jenny Gersten; Development, Casey Reitz; Marketing, Nella Vera; Communications, Candi Adams; Casting, Jordan Thaler, Heidi Griffiths; Capital Projects, Adrienne Dobsovits; Finance, Daniel C. Smith; Director of Joe's Pub, Shanta Thake; Director of Musical Theatre Initiative, Ted Sperling; Director of Shakespeare Initiative, Barry Edelstein; Under the Radar, Mark Russell; Special Projects, Maria Goyanes; Master Writer Chair, Suzan-Lori Parks; Director of Production, Ruth E. Sternberg; Information Technology, Robert Cohn; Ticket Services, Jimmy Goodsey; Press, Sam Neuman

The Mercant of Venice by William Shakespeare; Director, ; Set, Mark Wendland; Costumes, Jess Godstein; Lighting, Ken Posner; Composer, Dan Moses Schreier; Sound, Acme Sound Partners; Fight Director, Thomas Schall; PSM, Stephen M. Kaus; Stage Manager, Buzz Cohen; Vocal Coach, Kate Wilson; Assistant Director, Laura Savia; Associate Lighting, Aaron Spivey; Props Master, Faye Armon; Assistant Design: Jonathan Collins, Rachel Nemec (set), Alex Fogel (lighting), Jason Crystal (sound); Dramaturg, Barry Edelstein; **Cast:** Byron Jennings (Antonio), Francois Battiste (Salerio), Matthew Rauch (Solanio), Hamish Linklater (Bassanio), Bill Heck (Lorenzo), Jesse L. Martin (Gratiano), Lily Rabe (Portia), Marianne Jean-Baptiste (Nerissa), Al Pacino (Shylock), Nyambi Nayambi (Prince of Monaco), Jesse Tyler Ferguson (Launcelot Gobbo), Heather Lind (Jessica), Max Wright (Prince of Arragon), Richard Topol (Tubal), Gerry Bamman (Duke of Venice); Ensemble: Happy Anderson, Liza J. Bennett, Tyler Caffall, Cary Donaldson, Luke Forbes, Bryce Gill, Shalita Grant, Jade Hawk, Tia James, Kelsey Kurz, Brian MacDonald, Dorien Makhloghi, Joe Short

Delacorte Theater; First Preview: June 12, 2010; Opening Night: June 30, 2010; Closed August 1, 2010; 9 previews, 15 performances. Revival of a classic play presented in two acts. This production transferred to Broadway later this season (see page 46 in this volume).

Lily Rabe, Byron Jennings, and Al Pacino in The Merchant of Venice *(photo by Joan Marcus)*

The Winter's Tale by William Shakespeare; Director, Michael Greif; Set, Mark Wendland; Costumes, Clint Ramos; Lighting, Ken Posner; Original Music, Tom Kitt; Sound, Acme Sound Partners; Puppetry, Lake Simons; Music Director, Keith Cotton; Choreographer, Dontee Kiehn; PSM, Michael McGoff; Stage Manager, Winnie Y. Lok; Fight Director, Thomas Schall; Vocal Coach, Deborah Hecht; Music Coordinator, Michael Keller; Assistant Director, Patricia McGregory; Associate Design: Aaron Spivey (lighting), Jessica Pabst (costumes); Prop Master, Faye Armon; Dramaturg, Barry Edelstein; **Cast:** Ruben Santiago-Hudson (Lontes), Jesse L. Martin (Polixenes), Linda Emond (Hermione), Alexander Maier

(Mamillius), Byron Jennings (Camillo), Gerry Bamman (Antigonus), Marianne Jean-Baptiste (Paulina), Shalita Grant (Emilia/Mopsa), Bethany Heinrich (Serving Woman to the Queen/Dorcas), Liza J. Bennett and Tia James (Serving Women to the Queen), Nyambi Nyambi (Cleomenes), Matthew Rauch (Dion), Bill Heck, Richard Topol (Sicilian Lords), Francois Battiste (Sicilian Lord/Florizel), Happy Anderson (Sicilian Lord/Soldier/A Mariner), Tyler Caffall, Cary Donaldson and Luke Forbes (Sicilian Lords/Soldiers), Max Wright (Shepherd), Jesse Tyler Ferguson (Clown), Hamish Linklater (Autolycus), Heather Lind (Perdita); Musicians: Keith Cotton (Conductor/Synthesizer/Guitar), Grant Braddock (Drums/Percussion), Peter Sachon (Cello), Antoine Silverman (Violin)

Delacorte Theater; First Preview: June 9, 2010; Opening Night: July 1, 2010; Closed July 31, 2010; 9 previews, 15 performances. Revival of a classic play with new original music presented in two acts.

Linda Emond, Ruben Santiago-Hudson, and Jesse L. Martin in The Winter's Tale *(photo by Joan Marcus)*

Gatz Text from *The Great Gatsby* by F. Scott Fitzgerald; Created by Elevator Repair Service (John Collins, Artistic Director; Ariana Smart Truman, Producer); Director, John Collins; Associate Director, Steve Bodow; Set, Louisa Thompson; Costumes, Coleen Werthmann; Lighting, Mark Barton; Sound, Ben Williams; PSM, Sarah Hughes; Stage Manager, Ruth E. Sternberg; Assistant Costume Master, Sydney Ledger; Assistant Design: Campbell Ringel (costumes), Oliver Wason (set); ERS Production Manager, B.D. White; Production Assistant, Catherine Barricklow; Lead Props, Claire Karoff; Production Audio, Ann-Marie Dalenberg; Wardrobe Supervisor, T. Michael Hall; Production Electrician, Zach Murphy; **Cast:** Scott Shepherd (Nick), Jim Fletcher (Jim), Kate Scelsa (Lucille), Susie Sokol (Jordan), Victoria Vazquez (Daisy), Gary Wilmes (Tom), Aaron Landsman (George), Laurena Allan (Myrtle), Annie McNamara (Catherine), Vin Knight (Chester), Ben Williams (Michaelis), Mike Iveson (Ewing), Ross Fletcher (Henry C. Gatz)

Martinson Hall; First Preview: September 26, 2010; Opening Night: October 3, 2010; Closed November 28, 2010; 5 previews, 69 performances. New York premiere of a play presented in 4 acts with two intermissions and one dinner break. ERS premiered the nearly eight-hour theatrical event in May 2006 at the Kunsten Festival des Arts in Brussels. The U.S. premiere played the Walker Arts Center in Minneapolis in September 2006.

In the Wake by Lisa Kron; Director, Leigh Silverman; Set, David Korins; Costumes, Susan Hilferty; Lighting and Projections, Alexander V. Nichols; Sound, Darron L. West; PSM, Matha Donaldson; Stage Manager, Katrina Herrmann; Assistant Director, Johnson Henshaw; Assistant Costume Manager, Sydney Ledger; Associate Set, Amanda Stephens; Associate Costumes, Marina Reti; Assistant Lighting, Heather Graff; Associate Sound, M. Florian Staab; Production Assistant, Samantha Flint; Production Audio, Elizabeth Rhodes; Wardrobe Supervisor, Amy Hensberry; Production Electrician, Zach Murphy; Lead Props Artisan, Eric Hart; **Cast:** Jenny Bacon (Amy), Michael Chernus (Danny), Miriam

Gary Wilmes, Laurena Allan, Scott Shepherd, Annie McNamara, Vin Knight, and Kate Scelsa in Gatz *(photo by Joan Marcus)*

F. Glover (Tessa), Marin Ireland (Ellen), Deirdre O'Connell (Judy), Susan Pourfar (Kayla), Danielle Skraastad (Laurie)

Newman Theater; First Preview: October 19, 2010; Opening Night: November 1, 2010; Closed November 21, 2010; 16 previews, 23 performances. New York premiere of a new play presented in two acts. Originally presented by Center Theatre Group and Berkeley Repertory Theatre at the Kirk Douglas Tehatre in Los Angeles March 21, 2010 (see *Theatre World* Vol. 66, page 356).

Danielle Skraastad, Susan Pourfar, Marin Ireland, Miriam F. Glover, and Michael Chernus in In the Wake *(photo by Joan Marcus)*

Compulsion by Rinne Groffe; Co-presented by Berkeley Repertory Theatre and Yale Repertory Theatre; Director, Oskar Eustis; Set, Eugene Lee; Costumes, Susan Hilferty; Lighting, Michael Chybowski; Sound, Darron L West; Video and Projections, Jeff Sugg; Puppet Design and Supervision, Matt Acheson; PSM, Buzz Cohen; Stage Manager, Sean M. Thorne; Assistant Director, Johanna Gruehut; Associate Sound, M. Florian Staab; Associate Video and Projections, Shawn Duan; Assistant Design: Tristan Jeffers, Patrick Lynch (set), Kara Harmon (costumes), Kate Ashton (lighting), Eric Novak (puppets); Production Assistants, Maggie Swing, Brandon Voight; Production Audio, Asa Wember; Production Video, Josh Higgason; Wardrobe Supervisor, T. Michael Hall; Wig Supervisor, Rachel Brown; Production Electrician, Zach Murphy; Light Board Programmer, Tim Kaufman; Props Crew Head, Amelia Freeman-Lynde; **Cast:** Hannah Cabell (Miss Mermin, Mrs. Silver), Matte Osian (Mr. Thomas, Mr. Harris, Mr. Ferris, Mr. Matzliach), Mandy Patinkin (Mr. Silver); Puppeteers: Emily Decola, Daniel Fay, Eric Wright

Martinson Hall; First Preview: February 1, 2011; Opening Night: February 17, 2011; Closed March 13, 2011; 14 previews, 22 performances. World premiere of a new play presented in two acts. This co-production was first presented at Yale Repertory January 29, 2010 and at Berkeley Repertory September 16, 2010.

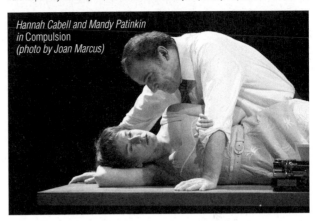

Hannah Cabell and Mandy Patinkin in Compulsion *(photo by Joan Marcus)*

The Intelligent Homosexual's Guide to Capitalism and Socialism with a Key to the Scriptures by Tony Kushner; Co-presented with Signature Theatre Company in association with the Guthrie Theater; Director, Michael Greif; Set, Mark Wendland; Costumes, Clint Ramos; Lighting, Kevin Adams; Sound, Ken Travis; Composer, Michael Friedman; Fight Director, Rick Sordelet; PSM, Martha Donaldson; Stage Manager, Alison DeSantis; Dramaturg, Antonia Grilikhes-Lasky; Assitant Director, Erik Pearson; Props, Faye Armon; Script Supervisor, Johnson Henshaw; **Cast:** Michael Cristofer (Gus Marcantonio), Stephen Spinella (Pill), Linda Emond (Empty), Steven Pasquale (V), Brenda Wehle (Clio), K. Todd Freeman (Paul), Danielle Skraastad (Maeve), Matt Servitto (Adam), Hettienne Park (Sooze), Michael Esper (Eli), Molly Price (Shelle)

Newman Theater; First Preveiew: March 23, 2011; Opening Night: May 5, 2011; Closed June 12, 2011; 50 previews, 44 performances. Setting: A brownstone on Clinton Street, Carroll Gardens, Brooklyn, and a couple of side trips to Manhattan; Friday June 15 through Sunday June 17, 2007. New York premiere of a new play presented in three acts with two intermissions. World premiere at the Guthrie Theatre May 15, 2009 (see *Theatre World* Vol. 65, page 326).

Michael Cristofer, K. Todd Freeman, Linda Emond, Stephen Spinella, Hettienne Park, Brenda Wehle, and Steven Pasquale in The Intelligent Homosexual's Guide to Capitalism and Socialism with a Key to the Scriptures *(photo by Joan Marcus)*

Co-Productions at Other Venues

The Human Scale by Lawrence Wright; Co-presented by 3-Legged Dog (Kevin Cunningham, Executive Artistic Director; Aaron Louis, Producing Director); Director, Oskar Eustis; Associate Director/Hebrew Translation, Johanna Gruenhut; Lighting, Deb Sullivan; Video, Aaron Harrow; Sound, Matt Hubbs; Scenic Consultant, David Korins; Composer, Michael Friedman; PSM, Lori Lindquist; Vocal Coach, Robert Perillo; Video Image Coordinator, Sheryl Mendez; Production Manager, Leighann Snyder; Assistant Video, Oriol Muñoz; Technical Directors, Anthony Cerrato, Eric Dyer; Violin, Rob Moose; 3LD Staff: Media Director, Aaron Harrow; Media Design/Promotions, Piama Habibullah; Company Manager/Associate Producer, Karin Martins; **Cast:** Lawrence Wright (Performer)

3LD Art & Technology Center; First Preview: October 2, 2010; Opening Night: October 7, 2010; Closed October 31, 2010; 6 previews, 26 performances. World premiere of a new solo performance play with multimedia presented without intermission.

Lawrence Wright in The Human Scale *(photo by Joan Marcus)*

The Great Game: Afghanistan A series of short plays: (Part 1 –1842-1830: Invasions & Independence): *Monologue* by Siba Shakib, *Bugles at the Gates of Jalalabad* by Stephen Jeffreys, *Duologue* by Siba Shakib, *Durand's Line* by Ron Hutchinson, *Verbatim* edited by Richard Norton-Taylor, *Campaign* by Amit Gupta, *Now Is the Time* by Joy Wilkinson; (Part 2–1979-1996: Communism, The Mujahideen & The Taliban): *Black Tulips* by David Edgar, *Monologue* by Siba Shakib, *Wood for the Fire* by Lee Blessing, *Miniskirts of Kabul* by David Greig, *Duologue* by Siba Shakib, *The Lion of Kabul* by Colin Teevan; (Part 3–1996-2010: Enduring Freedom): *Honey* by Ben Ockrent, *The Night Is Darkest Before the Dawn* by Abi Morgan, *Verbatim* edited by Richard Norton-Taylor, *On the Side of the Angels* by Richard Bean, *Verbatim Part 2* edited by Richard Norton-Taylor, *Canopy of Stars* by Simon Stephens; Presented by The Tricycle Theatre (Nicolas King, Artistic Director; Mary Lauder, General Manager) in association with NYU Skirball Center; Directors, Nicolas Kent and Indhu Rubasingham; Project Designer, Pamela Howard; Designers, Miriam Nabarro, Carl B. Taylor; Lighting, David I. Taylor; Original Lighting, James Farncombe; Sound, Tom Lishman; Associate Design, Miriam Nabarro; Assistant Director, Rachel Grunwald; Dialect Coach, Majella Hurley; Fight Director, Bret Yount; Production Manager, Shaz McGee; Technical Director/Stage Manager, Bartolo Cannizzaro, Assistant Stage Managers, Sarah Alford Smith, Karen Habens, Ed Borgnis; **Cast:** Daniel Betts, Sheena Bhattessa, Michael Cochrane, Karl Davies, Vincent Ebrahim, Nabil Elouahabi, Shereen Martineau, Tom McKay, Daniel Rabin, Danny Rahim, Raad Rawi, Jemma Redgrave, Cloudia Swann, Rick Warden

Skirball Center at NYU; First Preview: December 1, 2010; Opening Night: December 7, 2010; Closed December 19, 2010; 27 performances (9 of each part). U.S. premiere of three evenings of short plays presented in repertory, each part presented with intermission.

Shereen Martineau and Sheena Bhattessa in Night Is Darkest Before Dawn, *one of the plays in Part 3 of The Great Game: Afghanistan (photo by John Haynes)*

Belarus Free Theatre Three plays in repertory by Belarus Free Theatre, presented in association LaMaMa ETC: *Being Harold Pinter* adapted and directed by Vladimir Shcherban; *Zone of Silence* Created by Natalia Loliada, Nikolai Khalezin, Vladimir Shcherban, and Konstantin Steshik; *Discover Love* written and directed Nikolai Khalezin with the participation of Natalia Koliada, choreographed by Olga Skvortsova, intro by MC Coppa, musical fusion by Laur Biazhanin; BFT General Producers, Natalia Koliada and Nikolai Khalezin; PSM, David Bonnia; Production Manager, Andrew Kircher; Stage Managers, Laur Biarzhanin, Artsem Zhaliazniak, Irina Yaroshevich, Aliaksei Shyrnevich; Technical Director, Mark Tambella; **Casts:** *Being Harold Pinter:* Nikolai Khalezin, Pavel Gorodnitski, Yana Rusakevich, Oleg Sidorchyk, Irina Yaroshevich, Denis Tarasenko, Marina Yurevich; *Zone of Silence:* Pavel Gorodnitski, Yana Rusakevich, Oleg Sidorchik, Denis Tarasenko, Marina Yurevich; *Discover Love:* Oleg Sidorchyk, Marina Yurevich, Pavel Gorodnitski

LaMaMa ETC; Opening Night: March 13, 2011; Closed May 15, 2011; 39 performances. U.S. premieres of three plays and theatrical pieces presented in Russian and Belarus with titles, in repertory.

A scene from in Being Harold Pinter, *part of Belarus Free Theatre (photo by Joan Marcus)*

Public Lab (Fifth Season)

That Hopey Changey Thing Written and directed by Richard Nelson; Set/Costumes, Susan Hilferty; Lighting, Jennifer Tipton; Sound, Scott Lehrer; PSM, Pam Salling; Stage Manager, Amber Wedin; Assistant Director, David F. Champman; Production Manager, Elizabeth Moreau; Assistant Costume Master, Sydney Ledger; Props, Susan Barras; **Cast:** Jay O. Sanders (Richard Apple), Maryann Plunkett (Barbara Apple), Laila Robins (Marian Apple Platt), J. Smith-Cameron (Jane Apple Halls), Jon DeVries (Benjamin Apple), Shuler Hensley (Tim Andrews)

Anspacher Theater; First Preview: October 26, 2010; Opening Night: November 2, 2010; Closed November 14, 2010; 8 previews, 14 performances. Setting: New York: The dining room in Barbara Apple's house on Center Street between approximately 7pm and 9pm on Tuesday November 2, 2010. World premiere of a new play presented without intermission.

Maryann Plunkett, Jay O. Sanders, Jon DeVries, J. Smith-Cameron, nd Shuler Hensleay in That Hopey Changey Thing *(photo by Joan Marcus)*

Timon of Athens by Wiliam Shakespeare; Director, Barry Edelstein; Set, Neil Patel; Costumes, Katherine Roth; Lighting, Russell H. Champa; Sound, Leon Rothenberg; Video, Andrew C. Kircher; Wigs, Paul Huntley; Fight Director, Thomas Schall; Voice and Text Coach, Shane Ann Younts; Music, Curtis Moore; PSM, James Latus; Stage Manager, Tom Taylor; Guitar, Simon Kafka; Production Manager, Elizabeth Moreau; **Cast:** Richard Thomas (Timon), Max Casella (Apemantus), Reg E. Cathey (Alcibiades), Mark Nelson (Flavius), David Manis (Lucius/Senator of Athens), Chris McKinney (Lucullus), Triney Sandoval (Sempronius/Senator of Athens), Che Ayende (Servilius), Cary Donaldson (Lucilius), Tom Bloom (Senator of Athens/An Old Athenian/A Stranger), Chris McKinney (Senator of Athens), Brian Keane (A Merchant/An Officer of the Senate), Anthony Manna (A Jeweler/Caphis), Greg McFadden (A Poet), Orville Mendoza (A Painter), Joe Paulik (Cupid/Philotus)

Anspacher Theater; First Preview: February 15, 2011; Opening Night: March 1, 2011; Closed March 6, 2011; 17 previews, 7 performances. Revival of a play presented in two acts. This production introduced Shakespearean plays into the Public Lab process.

Omid Abtahi and Tala Ashe in Urge for Going *(photo by Carol Rosegg)*

Urge for Going by Mona Mansour; Director, Hal Brooks; Set, Jason Simms; Costumes, Jenny Mannis; Lighting, Tyler Micoleau; Music and Sound, Ryan Rumery and Christian Frederickson; Fight Director, Lisa Kopitsky; Dialect Coach, Charlotte Fleck; PSM, Michael Domue; Stage Manager, Erin Kraus; Assistant Director, Colette Robert; Dramaturgy Associate, Dana Tanner Kennedy; Arabic Consultant, Hend Ayoub; Production Manager, Elizabeth Moreau; **Cast:** Omid Abtahi (Jul), Jacqueline Antaramian (Abir), Tala Ashe (Jamila), Demosthenes Chrysan (Hamzi), Ramsey Faragallah (Adham), Ted Sod (Ghassan)

Anspacher Theater; First Preview: March 25, 2011; Opening Night: April 10, 2011; Closed April 17, 2011; 19 previews, 8 performances. Setting: A refugee camp in South Lebanon, 2003. World premiere of a new play presented without intermission.

Knickerbocker by Jonathan Marc Sherman; Director, Pippin Parker; Set, Peter Ksander; Costumes, Gabirel Berry; Lighting, Jeff Croiter; Sound, Walter Trarbach; Projections, Shawn Duan; Original Music, Marc Parenti; Pamela Salling; Stage Manager, Maggie Swing; Assistant Director, Elizabeth Carlson; Company Manager, Daniel Hoyos; Production Manager, Elizabeth Moreau; Playwright Assistant, Adam Shulman; Prop Master, Amelia Freeman-Lynde; Assistant Production Manager, Catherine Barricklow; **Cast:** Mia Barron (Pauline), Alexander Chaplin (Jerry), Bob Dishy (Raymond), Christina Kirk (Tara), Drew Madland (Steve), Zak Orth (Chester), Ben Shenkman (Melvin)

Anspacher Theater; First Preview: May 6, 2011; Opening Night: May 19, 2011; Closed May 29, 2011; 14 previews, 13 performances. Setting: The Knickerbocker Bar and Grill at 9th and University Place, New York City; April to October, 2008. World premiere of a new play presented without intermission.

Alexander Chaplin and Zak Orth in Knickerbocker *(photo by Carol Rosegg)*

Richard Thomas and the Cast in Timon of Athens *(photo by Joan Marcus)*

Rattlestick Playwrights Theater

Sixteenth Season

Co-Founder/Artistic Director, David Van Asselt; Managing Director, Brian Long; Production Manager, Eugenia Furneaux-Arends; Literary Managers, Denis Butkus, Julie Kline, Daniel Talbott; Literary Associates, Brian Miskell, Mary Laws; Box Office Manager/Marketing Associate, Dana Edwards; Marketing & Development Interns, Mary Laws, Sara Rappaport; Press, O+M Company, Richard Hillman

Little Doc by Dan Klores; Director, John Gould Rubin; Set, David Rockwell; Costumes, Clint Ramos; Lighting, Nicole Pearce; Sound, Jill BC DuBoff; Creative Consultant, Linda Larkin; Fight Director, David Anzuelo; Voiceover, Eric Cook; PSM, Meredith Dixon; ASM, Melissa Mae Gregus; Casting, Calleri Casting; Props/Scenic Artist, Eugenia Furneaux-Arends; Assistant Props/Scenic Artist, Ashley Pridemore; Technical Director, Brian Smallwood; Assistant Technical Director, Katie Tackacs; Assistant Director, Sherri Kronfeld; Associate Set, Gaetane Bertol; Assistant Design: Anita La Scala (set), Kate R. Mincer (costumes), Ien Denio (sound); Lighting Programmer, Chris Thielking; **Cast:** Adam Driver (Rick), Salvatore Inzerillo (Angelo), Stephen Marcus (Weasel/Seymore), Tobias Segal (Billy), Bill Tangradi (Lenny), Dave Tawil (Manny), Joanne Tucker (Peggy)

Rattlestick Theater 224 Waverly; First Preview: June 1, 2010; Opening Night: June 17, 2010; Closed July 17, 2010; 7 previews, 25 performances. Setting: Brooklyn, 1975; the living room of a one-bedroom apartment under the "el" and above a neighborhood bar. World premiere of a new play presented without intermission.

Adam Driver, Dave Tawil, Steven Marcus, Billy Tngradi, Joanne Tucker, and Tobias Segal in Little Doc *(photo by Sandra Coudert)*

underneathmybed by Florencia Lozano; Presented in association with Piece By Piece Productions; Director, Pedro Pascal; Set, Raul Abrego; Costumes, Olivera Gajic; Lighting, Nicole Pearce; Video, S. Katy Tucker; Fight Director, David Anzuelo; PSM, Melissa Mae Gregus; ASM, Michael John Carroll; Casting, Judy Bowman; Assistant Director, Lyssa Mandel; Props/Scenic Artist, Eugenia Furneaux-Arends; Assistant Props/Scenic Artist, Katie Takacs; Assistant Technical Director, Ian Heitzman; Assistant Lighting, Chris Thielking; Associate Projections, luckydave; Carpenters, Nina Alexander, Jermiah Fox, Nick Monroy; Lighting Team, The Lighting Syndicate; **Cast:** Vanessa Aspillaga (Daisy), Maria Cellario (Tia Toti), Matthew Dellapina (Kaspar), Audrey Esparza (Josefina), Vivia Font (Paola), Charles Goforth (Doctor M.), Yetta Gottesman (Jean), Paula Pizzi (Lizbel), Marina Pulido (S), Ed Trucco (Esteben)

Rattlestick Theater 224 Waverly; First Preview: September 1, 2010; Opening Night: September 9, 2010; Closed October 26, 2010; 7 previews, 31 performances. World premiere of a new play presented in two acts.

Paula Pizzi, Audrey Esparza, Vivia Font, Vanessa Aspillaga, Maria Cellario, and Ed Trucco in underneathmybed *(photo by Sandra Coudert)*

There Are No More Big Secrets by Heidi Schreck; Director, Kip Fagan; Set, John McDermott; Costumes, Jessica Pabst; Lighting, Matt Frey; Sound, Daniel Kluger; Projections, luckydave; PSM, Melissa Mae Gregus; ASM, Michael Denis; Casting, Calleri Casting; Props/Scenic Artist, Eugenia Furneaux-Arends; Assistant Props/Scenic Artist, Ashley Pridemore; Assistant Director, Stella Powell-Jones; Assistant to Ms. Schreck, Diana Stahl; Technical Director, Katie Takacs; Assistant Technical Director, Kate Stack; Carpenters, Ian Heitzman, Nick Monroy, John McDermott; Lighting, The Lighting Syndicate; Lighting Programmer, Holly Burnell; Program Design, Catherine Duennebier, Kathryn Hathaway; **Cast:** Nadia Alexander (Lana), Dagmara Dominczyk (Nina), Gibson Frazier (Charles), Christina Kirk (Maxine), Adam Rothenberg (Gabe)

Rattlestick Theater 224 Waverly; First Preview: November 5, 2010; Opening Night: November 14, 2010; Closed December 18, 2010; 7 previews, 29 performances. World premiere of a new play presented in two acts.

Christina Kirk, Gibson Frazier, Dagmara Domincyz, and Adam Rothenberg in There Are No More Big Secrets *(photo by Sandra Coudert)*

The Hallway Trilogy Three plays: *Rose, Parrffin,* and *Nursing* by Adam Rapp; Directors, Adam Rapp (Part 1: *Rose*), Daniel Aukin (Part 2: *Paraffin*), Trip Cullman (Part 3: *Nursing*); Sets, Beowulf Boritt; Costumes, Jessica Pabst; Lighting, Tyler Micoleau; Music/Sound, Eric Shimelonis; PSMs, Melissa Mae Gregus, Meredith Dixon; ASMs, Michael Denis, Rebecca Spinac; Casting, Calleri Casting; Fight Director, Thomas Schall; Special Effects, Jeremy Chernick; Production Manager, Hilary Krishnan; Props/Scenic Artists, John McDermott, Eugenia Furneaux-Arends; Hair/Makeup, Erin Kennedy Lunsford; Wardrobe Supervisor, Jennifer Jefferson; Assistant Props, Ashley Pridemore; Assistant Sound, Phil Carluzzo; Assistant Directors, Dana Jané, Jordana Kritzer, Mary Laws; Technical Director, Katie Takacs; Language Specialist, Dana Jané; Playwright Assistant, Michael Swift; Production Assistants, Katie Fergerson, Judy Merrick, Katrina Herrmann; Lighting, The Lighting Syndicate; Program, Jennifer Nesbitt; Graphics, Achilles Lavidis; **Cast:** William Apps (Orest/Denny), Robert Beitzel (Ido/Joe), Guy Boyd (O'Neill/Marty), Louis Cancelmi (Jerry/Andy), Maria Dizzia (Rahel/Joan), Logan Marshall-Green (Richard B/Lloyd), Sue Jean Kim (Dena/Tour Guide), Nick Lawson (Marbles/Leshik), Sarah Lemp (Megan/Erin), Danny Mastrogiorgio (Louie Zap/Kevin), Julianne Nicholson (Mary/Margo), Jeremy Strong (Lucas/Journalist), Katherine Waterston (Rose), Stephen Tyrone Williams (Cory/Guard)

Rattlestick Theater 224 Waverly; First Preview: February 6, 2011; Opening Night: February 20, 2011; Closed March 27, 2011; 9 previews (3 of each part), 51 performances (18 of Part 1; 18 of Part 2; 15 of Part 3). Setting: A lower east side hallway, 1953, 2003, and 2053. Three plays presented in rotating repertory (with Sunday marathons of all three plays), each play presented without intermission.

Casron McCullers Talks About Love by Suzanne Vega; Director, Kay Matschullat; Music, Suzanne Vega and Duncan Shiek; Additional Music, Michael Jefrey Stevens; Music Director, Gerry Leonard; Set, Louisa Thompson; Costumes, Jessica Pabst; Lighting, Lenore Doxsee; Sound, Nick Kourtides; PSM, Melissa Mae Gregus; Hair and Makeup, Leah Loukas; Assistant Director, Mahayana Landowne; Technical Director, Katie Takacs; Assistant Technical Director, Stephen McKenney; Props/Scenic Artist, Eugenia Furneaux-Arends; Production Assistants, Katrina Herrmann, Sam Horwith; Lighting, The Lighting Syndicate; Casting, Calleri Casting; Graphics, Achilles Lavidis; Program, Jennifer Nesbitt; **Cast:** Suzanne Vega (Carson), Joe Iconis (Pianist), Andy Stack (Guitarist)

Rattlestick Theater 224 Waverly; First Preview: April 20, 2011; Opening Night: May 5, 2011; Closed June 5, 2011; 7 previews, 34 performances. World premiere of a new play with live music presented without intermission.

Suzanne Vega in Carson McCullers Talks About Love *(photo by Sandra Coudert)*

Sue Jean Kim, Louis Cancelmi, Logan Marshall-Green, and Maria Dizzia in Nursing, the third installment in The Hallway Trilogy *(photo by Sandra Coudert)*

Roundabout Theatre Company

Forty-fifth Season

Artistic Director, Todd Haimes; Managing Director, Harold Wolpert; Executive Director, Julia C. Levy; Associate Artistic Director, Scott Ellis; Founding Director, Gene Feist; Artistic Development/Casting, Jim Carnahan; Development, Lynne Gugenheim Gregory; Marketing/Sales Promotion, David B. Steffen; Education, Greg McCaslin; General Manager, Sydney Beers; General Manager of the Steinberg Center, Rachel E. Ayers; Finance, Susan Neiman; IT Director, Antonia Palumbo; Database Operations, Wendy Hutton; Production Manager, Aurora Productions; Associate Production Manager, Michael Wade; Company Manager at the Steinberg, Nicholas Caccavo; Press, Boneau/Bryan-Brown, Jessica Johnson, Matt Polk, Amy Kass, Emily Meagher

The Language Archive by Julia Cho; Director, Mark Brokaw; Set, Neil Patel; Costumes, Micael Krass; Lighting, Mark McCullough; Original Music and Sound, David Van Tieghem; PSM, William H. Lang; Dialect Coach, Ben Furey; Casting, Carrie Gardner; Assistant Director, Alec Strum; Associate Costumes, Tracy Christensen; Assistant Design: Caleb Levengood (set), Robert Denton (lighting), Brandon Wolcott (sound); Assistant to Costume Designer, Annie Tippe; Costumer, Virginia Johnson; Master Technician, Nicholas Wolff Lyndon; Wardrobe Supervisor, Amy Kitzhaber; Props Supervisor, Peter Sarafin; Sound Supervisor, Elizabeth Coleman; Automation Programmer, Adam Lang; Production Carpenter, Rebecca O'Neill; Production Electrician, Tom Dyer; **Cast:** Matt Letscher (George), Heidi Schreck (Mary), Betty Gilpin (Emma), Jayne Houdyshell (Alta & others), John Horton (Resten & others)

Laura Pels Theatre; First Preview: September 24, 2010; Opening Night: October 17, 2010; Closed December 19, 2010; 28 previews, 72 performances. New York premiere of a new play presented in two acts. World premiere at South Coast Repertory March 26, 2010.

John Horton, Matt Letscher, Betty Gilpin, and Jayne Houdyshell in The Language Archive *(photo by Joan Marcus)*

The Milk Train Doesn't Stop Here Anymore by Tennessee Williams; Director, Michael Wilson; Set, Jeff Cowie; Costumes, David C. Woolard; Lighting, Rui Rita; Original Music and Sound, John Gromada; PSM, Susie Cordon; Hair and Makeup, Mark Adam Rampmeyer; Dialect Coach, Gillian Lane-Plescia; Movement Director, Peter Pucci; ASM, Allison Sommers; Assistant Director, Christopher Schilder; Associate Lighting, Carl Faber; Assistant Design: Thomas Charles LeGalley (costumes), Alex Neumann, Janie Bullard (sound); Assistant to Mr. Rita, Austin Bransgrove; Master Technician, Nicholas Wolff Lyndon; Wardrobe Supervisor, Amy Kitzhaber; Hair/Makeup Supervisor, Renee Kelly; Props Supervisor, Matt Hodges; Fight Consultant, Mark Olsen; Production Carpenter, Rebecca O'Neill; Production Electrician, Tom Dyer; Sound Supervisor, Elizabeth Coleman; Automation Programmer, Martin Perrin; Dramaturg, Christopher Baker; Assistant to Mr. Wilson, Amy Ashton; **Cast:** Olympia Dukakis (Flora Goforth), Maggie Lacey (Frances Black "Blackie"), Curtis Billings (Giulio), Elisa Bocanergra (Simonetta), Darren Pettie (Christopher Flanders), Edward Hibbert (Witch of Capri); Understudies: Curtis Billings (Christopher), Kevin Fugaro (Giulio), Gordana Rashovich (Flora, Witch), Amanda Todor (Blackie, Simonetta)

Laura Pels Theatre; First Preview: January 7, 2011; Opening Night: January 30, 2011; Closed April 4, 2011; 27 previews, 79 performances. Setting: Flora Goforth's mountaintop villa on Italy's Divina Costiera. A day in August, 1962, and the next day. Revival of a play presented in two acts. Originally presented in Spoleto, Italy in 1962, the first New York production opened at the Morosco Theatre in January 16–March 16, 1963 playing 69 performances (see *Theatre World* Vol. 19, page 55). This production was inspired by a revival at Hartford Stage in May 2008.

Maggie Lacey, Darren Pettie, and Olympia Dukakis in The Milk Train Doesn't Stop Here Anymore *(photo by Joan Marcus)*

Death Takes a Holiday Book by Thomas Meehan and Peter Stone, music and lyrics by Maury Yeston; Based on the play by Alberto Casella and rewritten for the American stage by Walter Ferris; Director, Doug Hughes; Choreography, Peter Pucci; Music Supervision and Direction, Kevin Stites; Sets, Derek McLane; Costumes, Catherine Zuber; Lighting, Kenneth Posner; Sound, Jon Weston; Hair and Wigs, Tom Watson; Orchestrations, Larry Hochman; Music Coordinator, John Miller; PSM, James FitzSimmons; ASM, Katherine Wallace; Dance Captain, Mara Davi; Associate Director, David Hilder; Assistant Choreographers, Mike Kirsch, Zach Villa; Associate Design: Shoko Kambara (set), Nikki Moody (costumes), Jason Strangfeld (sound); Assistant Design: Ryan Park (costumes), Nick Solyom, Anshuman Bhatia (lighting), Sean Foote (sound); Master Technician, Nicholas Wolff Lyndon; Props, Kathy Fabian, Carrie Mossman, Tim Ferro; Wardrobe Supervisor, Amy Kitzhaber; Hair and Wig Supervisor, Tom Augustine; Additional Orchestrations, Danny Troob, Bruce Coughlin; Keyboard Programmer, Randy Cohen; Music Copying, Emily Grishman, Katharine Edmonds; **Cast:** Jill Paice (Grazia Lamberti), Michael Siberry (Duke Vittorio Lamberti), Rebecca Luker (Duchess Stepanie Lamberti), Max von Essen (Corrado Montelli), Mara Davi (Alice Lamberti), Alexandra Socha (Daisy Fenton), Jay Jaski (Lorenzo), Linda Balgord (Contessa Evangelina Di San Danielli), Simon Jones (Dr. Dario Albione), Don Stephenson (Fidele), Patricia Noonan (Sophia), Joy Hermalyn (Cora), Kevin Earley* (Death/Prince Nikolai Sirki), Matt Cavenaugh (Major Eric Fenton); Understudies/Standbys: Glory Crampton (Stephanie, Contessa Di San Danielli, Cora), Jay Jaski (Corrado Montelli, Major Eric Fenton), Patricia Noonan (Grazia Vittorio Lamberti), Jessica Vosk (Alice, Daisy Fenton, Sophia), Jim Walton (Vittorio Lamberti, Dr. Albione, Fidele); Orchestra: Kevin Stites (Conductor/

Keyboard), Greg Jarrett (Associate Conductor/Keyboard), Steve Lynon and John Winder (Woodwinds), Rheagan Osteen (French Horn), Timothy Schadt (Trumpet), Bill Ellison (Bass), Eric Poland (Percussion), Martin Agee (Violin/Concertmaster), Laura Bontrager (Cello)

Musical Numbers: In the Middle of Your Life (Prologue), Nothing Happened, How Will I Know, Centuries, Why Do All Men, Shiki's Arrival, Death is in the House, Alive, Life's a Joy, Who is this Man, Life's a Joy (reprise), Shimmy Like They Do in Paree; Roberto's Eyes, Alone Here with You, Something's Happened, Losing Roberto, What Do You Do, More and More, Finally to Know, I Though That I Could Live, December Time, Pavane, More and More (reprise), In the Middle of Your Life (reprise)

Laura Pels Theatre; First Preview: June 10, 2011; Opening Night: July 12, 2011; Closed September 4, 2011; 45 previews, 50 performances. Setting: The Villa Felicita, on the lakeside in Northen Italy in the summer of 1921. World premiere of a new musical presented in twenty-three scenes in two acts.

*Julien Ovenden was originally cast as "Death/Prince Nikolai Sirki" but had to bow out on August 3rd. Mr. Earley, his understudy, had performed the role from July 19 and on opening night, and permanently stepped officially through the rest of the run.

Jill Paice and Kevin Earley in Death Takes a Holiday *(photo by Joan Marcus)*

Roundabout Underground

Tigers Be Still by Kim Rosenstock; Director, Sam Gold; Set and Costumes, Dane Laffrey; Lighting, Japhy Weideman; Sound, Fitz Patton; PSM, Kyle Gates; ASM, Jamie Lynne Sullivan; Associate Producers, Jill Rafson, Josh Fiedler; Roundabout Underground Curator, Robyn Goodman; Production Manager, Michael Wade; Assistant Production Manager, Joel Krause; Assistant Director, Portia Krieger; Assistant Design: Scott Tedman-Jones (set), Mark Van Hare (sound); Carpenter, Casey Krueger; Electrician, Danielle Clifford; Sound Supervisor, Erin Ballantine; Wardrobe Supervisor, Ashley Rose Horton; **Cast:** Halley Feiffer (Sherry), Reed Birney (Joseph), John Magaro (Zack), Natasha Lyonne (Grace)

Blackbox Theatre; First Preview: September 10, 2011; Opening Night: October 6, 2010; Closed November 28, 2010; 28 previews, 60 performances. Setting: Present day in a suburban town. World premiere of a new play presented without intermission.

The Dream of the Burning Boy by David West Read; Director, Evan Cabnet; Set, Lee Savage; Costumes, Jessica Wegener Shay; Lighting, Ben Stanton; Sound, Jill BC DuBoff; PSM, Charles M. Turner III; ASM, Courtney James; Casting, Carrie Garnder; Production Manager, Michael Wade; Roundabout Underground Curator, Robyn Goodman; Associate Producers, Jill Rafson, Josh Fiedler; Technical Director, Christopher M. Soley; Prop Supervisor, Meghan Buchanan; Assistant Director, Joseph Hendel; Assistant Costumes, Kristina Makoloski; Assistant to Sound Designer, Ien DeNio; Board Operator, Seth Morgan; Wardrobe Supervisor, Ashley Rose Horton; Scenic Charge, Danielle Clifford; Sound Supervisor, Erin Ballentine; **Cast:** Reed Birney (Larry), Josh Caras (Dane), Matt Dellapina (Steve), Jessica Rothenberg (Chelsea), Jake O'Connor (Kyle), Alexandra Socha (Rachel), Kristie Dale Sanders (Andrea)

Black Box Theatre; First Preview: February 25, 2011; Opening Night: March 23, 2011; Closed May 15, 2011; 30 previews, 63 performances. Setting: The present; a small high school in Suburban America. World premiere of a new play presented without intermission.

Halley Feiffer, Natasha Lyonne, and John Magaro in Tigers Be Still *(photo by Joan Marcus)*

Jessica Rothenberg, Jake O'Connor, Reed Birney, and Alexandra Socha in The Dream of the Burning Boy *(photo by Joan Marcus)*

Second Stage Theatre

Thirty-second Season

Artistic Director, Carole Rothman; Executive Director, Casey Reitz; Associate Artistic Director, Christopher Burney; General Manager, Don-Scott Cooper/Dean A. Carpenter; Finance, Janice B. Cwill; Development, Sarah Bordy; Marketing, Larua DiLorenzo; Sales, Noel Hattem; Marketing Associates, Nathan Leslie; Ticket Services Manager, Greg Turner; Production Manager, Jeff Wild; Casting, MelCap Casting; Technical Director, Robert G. Mahon III; Press, The Hartman Group, Tom D'Ambrosio, Michelle Bergmann

Wings by Arthur Kopit; Director, John Doyle; Sets, Scott Pask; Costumes, Ann Hould-Ward; Lighting, Jane Cox; Sound, Bray Poor; Projections, Peter Nigrini; PSM, Roy Harris; Stage Manager, Rosie Goldman; Associate Design: Christine Peters (set), Christopher Vergara (costumes), Bradley King (lighting), C. Andrew Bauer (projections); Assistant Design: Charles Coes (sound), Daniel Vatsky (projections); Production Electrician, John Tees III; Audio Master, Mark Huang; Props Master, Susan Barras; Wardrobe Supervisor, Ashley Farra; Carpenters, Rob Boyle, Bryan McGuckin; Board Operators, Sarah Bullock, John Kemp; Production Assistant, Ashley Nelson; **Cast:** Jan Maxwell (Emily Stilson), January LaVoy (Amy), Michael Weller (Doctor One), Adam Heller (Doctor Two/Mr. Brownstein), Anne L. Nathan (Nurse One), Beth Dixon (Nurse Two/Mrs. Timmins), Teagle F. Bougere (Billy/Attendant)

Second Stage; First Preview: October 5, 2010; Opening Night: October 24, 2010; Closed November 21, 2010; 23 previews, 32 performances. Revival of a play presented without intermission. World premiere at Yale Repertory Theatre March 3, 1978. Originally produced on Broadway by the Kennedy Center at the Lyceum Theatre January 28–May 5, 1979 playing 113 performances.

Jan Maxwell in Wings *(photo by Joan Marcus)*

Gruesome Playground Injuries by Rajiv Joseph; Director, Scott Ellis; Set, Neil Patel; Costumes, Jeff Mahshie; Lighting, Donald Holder; Sound, Ryan Rumery; Original Music, Gwendolyn Sanford and Brandon Jay; PSM, Barclay Stiff; Stage Manager, Davin De Santis; Assistant Director, Kate Pines; Production Assistant, Brittany Kramer; Associate Design: Stephen K. Dobay (set), Kyle LaColla (costumes), Carolyn Wong (lighting); Assistant Design: Ryan Bona (lighting), M. Florian Staab (sound); Makeup, Arielle Toelke; Props Master, Susan Barras; Wardrobe Supervisor, Ashley Farra; Carptenter, Bryan McGuckin; Board Operators, Sarah Bullock, John Kemp; **Cast:** Jennifer Carpenter (Kayleen), Pablo Schreiber (Doug)

Second Stage; First Preview: January 5, 2011; Opening Night: January 31, 2011; Closed February 19, 2011; 31, previews, 23 performances. New York premiere of a new play presented without intermission. World premiere at the Alley Theatre October 21, 2009.

Pablo Schreiber and Jennifer Carpenter in Gruesome Playground Injuries *(photo by Joan Marcus)*

By the Way, Meet Vera Stark by Lynn Nottage; Director, Jo Bonney; Set, Neil Patel; Costumes, Emilio Sosa; Lighting, Jeff Croiter; Sound, John Gromada; Film, Tony Gerber; Dialect Coach, Stephen Gabis; Projections, Shawn Sagady; PSM, Lori Ann Zepp; Stage Manager, Eileen Ryan Kelly; Hair and Makeup, J. Jared Janas, Rob Greene; Production Assistant, Kendall Booher; Assistant Director, David Mendizábal; Period Coach, Darryl Quinton; Associate Design: Stephen K. Dobay (set), Ashley Farra (costumes); Assistant Design: Robert Denton (lighting), Janie Bullard (sound); Production Electrician, John Tees; Audio Master, Jana Hoglund; Props Master, Susan Barras; Wardrobe Supervisor, Ashley Farra; Light Board Programmer, Anup Aurora; **Cast:** Sanaa Lathan (Vera Stark), Stephanie J. Block (Stephanie J. Block), Kimberly Hébert Gregory (Lottie/Carmen Levy-Green), Karen Olivo (Annie Mae/Afua Assata Ejobo), Daniel Breaker (Leroy Barksdale/Herb Forrester), David Garrison (Fredrick Slasvick/Brad Donovan), Kevin Isola (Maximillian Von Oster/Peter Rys-Davies)

Second Stage; First Preview: April 6, 2011; Opening Night: May 9, 2011; Closed June 12, 2011; 39 previews, 39 performances. Setting: Hollywood, 1933, 1973, 2003. World premiere of a new play presented in two acts.

Stephanie J. Block and Sanaa Lathan in By the Way, Meet Vera Stark *(photo by Joan Marcus)*

All New People by Zach Braff; Director, Peter DuBois; Set, Alexander Dodge; Costumes, Bobby Frederick Tilley II; Lighting, Japhy Weideman; Sound, M.L. Dogg; Projections, Aaron Ryhne; PSM, Lori Ann Zepp; Stage Manager, Ahsley J. Nelson; Production Assistant, Lizz Gatzunis; Assistant Director, Reginald Douglas; Hanging Effect, Aaron Verdery; Dialect Coach, Stephen Gabis; Film Segment Producer, Igor Srubshchik; Associate Design: Kevin Judge (set), Ashley Farra (costumes), Justin Partier (lighting), Ned Stresen-Reuter (projections); Assistant Design: Akiko Kosaka (set), Gary Slootskiy (lighting), Chris Barlow (sound); Production Electrician, John Tees; Audio Master, M.L. Dogg; Projections Programmer, Daniel Brodie; Props Master, Susan Barras; Wardrobe Supervisor, Ashley Farra; Carpenters, Jonathan Maloney, Bryan McGuckin; Light Board Programmer, Anup Aurora; Board Operators, Sarah Bullock, Jorge Cortes; Film UPM, Bill Sell; Film Cinematography, Tom Houghton; Orignal Song "Rally" written by Allie Moss; **Cast:** Justin Bartha (Charlie), Krysten Ritter (Emma), David Wilson Barnes (Myron), Anna Camp (Kim); Special Film Appearances: Kevin Conway, Tony Goldwyn, S. Epatha Merkerson

Second Stage; First Preview: June 28, 2011; Opening Night: July 25, 2011; Closed August 14, 2011; 31 previews, 24 performances. World premiere of a new play presented without intermission.

Justin Bartha, Krysten Ritter, Ana Camp, and David Wilson in All New People (photo by Joan Marcus)

Second Stage Uptown Series

Sex Lives of Our Parents by Anna Kerrigan; Director, Carolyn Cantor; Set, Andromache Chalfant; Costumes, Jessica Ford; Lighting, Tyler Micoleau; Sound, Jill BC DuBoff; PSM, Winnie Y. Lok; Stage Manager, McKenzie Murphy; Assistant Director, Zach Chotzen-Freund; Production Assistant, Kristen Torgrimson; Assistant Design: Kim Newton (costumes), Marika Kent (lighting), Janie Bullard (sound); Prop Master, Susan Barras; Production Electrician, John Tees III; Production Carpenter, Steve Rosenberg; Production Sound, Mark Huang; Wardrobe Supervisor, Cornelia Wall; **Cast:** Teddy Bergman (Elliot/Nurse), Lisa Emery (Charlotte), Daniel Jenkins (Christopher), Virginia Kull (Virginia), Ben Rappaport (Jeff/Rodney), Mark Zeisler (Henry/Lucas)

McGinn/Cazale Theatre; First Preview: June 7, 2011; Opening Night: June 22, 2011; Closed July 3, 2011; 17 previews, 13 performances. World premiere of a new play presented without intermission.

Ben Rappaport, Virginia Kull, and Lisa Emery in Sex Lives of Our Parents (photo by Carol Rosegg)

The Talls by Anna Kerrigan; Director, Carolyn Cantor; Set, Dane Laffrey; Costumes, Jenny Mannis; Lighting, Japhy Weideman; Sound, M.L. Dogg; PSM, Winnie Y. Lok; Stage Manager, McKenzie Murphy; Assistant Director, Roxann Mtjoy; Production Assistant, Amy Groeschel; Assoicate Lighting, Justin Partier; Assistant Design: Alexis Distler (set), Kristin Fiebig (costumes), John Kemp (sound); Props Master, Susan Barras; Production Electrician, John Tees III; Production Sound, Hark Huang; Production Carpenter, Steve Rosenberg; Wardrobe Supervisor, Cornelia Wall; **Cast:** Gerard Canonico (Russell James), Timothée Chalamet (Nicholas Clarke), Shannon Esper (Isabelle Clarke), Lauren Holmes (Catherine Clarke), Michael Oberholtzer (Christian Clarke), Peter Rini (Mr. John Clarke), Christa Scott-Reed (Mrs. Anne Clarke)

McGinn/Cazale Theatre; First Preview: August 1, 2011; Opening Night August 15, 2011; Closed August 26, 2011; 15 previews, 14 performances. Setting: Oakland, California; May 1970. World premiere of a new play presented without intermission.

Christa Scott-Reed and Peter Rini in The Talls (photo by Joan Marcus)

Signature Theatre Company

Twentieth Season

Founding Artistic Director, James Houghton; Executive Director, Erika Mallin; Associate Artistic Director, Beth Whitaker; General Manager, Adam Bernstein; Development, Katherine Jaeger-Thomas; Marketing, David Hatkoff; Production Manager, Paul Ziemer; IT Manager, Jeffrey Goodman; Box Office Manager, Stephanie Farhood; Casting, Telsey + Company; Press, Boneau/Bryan-Brown, Juliana Hannett, Matt Ross, Jim Byk, Emily Meagher; Legacy Playwright, Tony Kushner

Angels in America: A Gay Fantasia on National Themes *Part 1: Millennium Approaches; Part 2: Perestroika* by Tony Kushner; Director, Michael Grief; Sets, Mark Wendland; Costumes, Clint Ramos; Lighting, Ben Stanton; Sound, Ken Travis; Projections, Wendall K. Harrington; Music, Michael Friedman and Chris Miller; Hair and Wigs, Charles G. LaPointe; Dialect Coach, Deborah Hecht; Fight Director, Rick Sordelet; Aerial Design, Paul Rubin; Makeup, Cookie Jordan; Additional Costumes, Jeff Mahshie; PSM, Monica A Cuoco; Stage Manager, Joshua Pilote; Assistant Director, Adam Shulman; SDC Sir John Gielgud Directing Fellow, Saheem Ali; Assistant to the Director, Matt McCollum; Special Effects Coordinator, Jeremy Chernick; Production Dramaturg, Kirsten Bowen; Dramaturg, Antonia Grilikhes-Lasky; Assistant Set, Jon Collins; Assistant Costumes, Jacob Climer, Kyle LaColla, Jessica Pabst; Assistant Lighting, Ben Krall; Assistant Sound, Jessica Paz; Projections Assistant, Caite Hevner; Projection Animation, David Beidny, David Berry, Bo Eriksson; Projection Research, Anya Klepikov; Properties Master, Sarah Bird; Associate Properties Master, Dana Lewman; Production Carpenter, Steve Lorick; Production Electrician, The Lighting Syndicate; Production Sound and Video Supervisor, Graham Johnson; Wings, Martin Izquierdo; Puppetry, Lake Simons; Master Carpenters, Peter MacBeth, Rory Mulholland; Projections Programmer, Paul Vershbow; Light Board Programmer/Operator, Bridget Chervenka; Wardrobe Supervisor, Vanessa Watters; Wig Supervisor, Colleen P. Herman; Deck Carpenters, Kara Aghabekian, Michael Demyan; Production Assistants, Michael Block, Stephen Ehrlich, Dee Dee Katchen, Jenn McNeill, Stephen Ravet; Production Artwork, Milton Glaser; Assistant to Mr. Kushner, Kyle Warren; Casting Associates, Jade King Carroll, Joseph Ward, Nicole Watson; **Cast:** Robin Bartlett (Hannah Pitt), Christian Borle (Prior Walter), Bill Heck (Joe Pitt), Zoe Kazan (Harper Pitt), Billy Porter (Belize), Zachary Quinto (Louis Ironson), Robin Weigert (The Angel), Frank Wood (Roy Cohn); Cast Replacements: *February 2, 2011:* Lynne McCullough (Hannah Pitt), Michael Urie (Prior Walter), Adam Driver (Louis Ironson), Keira Keeley (Harper Pitt), Sofia Jean Gomez (The Angel); *March 29, 2011:* Jonathan Hadary (Roy Cohn)

Peter Norton Space; First Preview: September 14, 2010; Opening Night: October 28, 2010; Closed April 24, 2011; 256 performances. Setting: Late Fall and early winter in New York City; 1985-1986; Epilogue takes place in 1990. Revival of two plays performed in repertory (with some one-day marathons); each part presented with two intermissions. The world premiere of *Millenium Approaches* opened at the Walter Kerr Theatre May 4, 1993. *Perestroika* opened at the Walter Kerr November 23, 1993 and and performed in repertory with *Millenium Approaches*. Both productions closed December 4, 1994 after playing 367 performances and 216 performances respectively (see *Theatre World* Vol. 49, page 49; Vol. 50, pages 35 and 71). This production was extended four times from its original closing date of December 19, 2010. Zachary Quinto received a 2011 Theatre World Award for his performance in this production.

Zachary Quinto and Christian Borle in Angels in America, Part 1: Millenium Approaches *(photo by Joan Marcus)*

Robin Bartlett and Christian Borle in Angels in America, Part 2: Perestroika *(photo by Richard Termine)*

Frank Wood, Billy Porter, Robin Bartlett, Zoe Kazan, Bill Heck, Robin Weigert, Zachary Quinto, and Christian Borle in Angels in America, Part 2: Peristroika *(photo by Richard Termine)*

Sofia Jean Gomez and Michael Urie in Angels in America, Part 2: Peristroika *(photo by Joan Marcus)*

Billy Porter and Michael Urie in Angels in America, Part 2: Peristroika *(photo by Joan Marcus)*

The Intelligent Homosexual's Guide to Capitalism and Socialism with a Key to the Scriptures by Tony Kushner; Presented in association with the Public Theater (please see production details on page 223 in this volume).

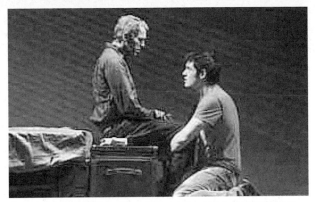

Stephen Spinella and Michael Esper in The Intelligent Homosexual's Guide to Capitalism and Socialism with a Key to the Scriptures *(photo by Joan Marcus)*

The Illusion by Tony Kushner, adapted from Pierre Corneille's *L'Illusion Comique*; Director, Michael Mayer; Set, Christine Jones; Costumes, Susan Hilferty; Lighting, Kevin Adams; Sound, Bray Poor; Music, Nico Muhly; Fight Director, Rick Sordelet; Hair and Wigs, Tom Watson; PSM, Paul J. Smith; ASM, Michael Rico Cohen; Assistant Director, Kareem Fahmy; Production Dramaturg, Kristen Bowen; Assistant Set, Jonathan Collins; Assistant Costumes, Kara Harmon; Assistant Lighting, Robert Denton; Assistant Sound, Nicholas Pope; Assistant to the Composer, Trevor Gureckis; Properties Master, Sarah Bird; Assistant Properies Master, Michelle Davis; Technical Director, Kurt Gardner; Master Carpenter, Rory Mulholland; Production Electrician, The Lighting Syndicate; Production Sound Supervisor, Graham Johnson; Light Board Programmer/Operator, Bridget Chervenka; Wardrobe Supervisor, Vanessa Watters; Wardrobe Crew, Mary Rutherford; Deck Carpenters, Kara Aghabekian, Kurtis Rutherford; Production Assistant, Lauren Klein; **Cast:** David Margulies (Pridamant of Avignon), Henry Stram (The Amanuensis/Gerontc), Lois Smith (Alcandre), Finn Wittrock (Calisto/Clindor/Theogenes), Amanda Quaid (Melibea/Isabelle/Hippolyta), Merritt Wever (Elicia/Lyse/Clarina), Sean Dugan (Pleribo/Adraste/Prince Florilame), Peter Bartlett (Matamore)

Peter Norton Space; First Preview: May 17, 2011; Opening Night: June 5, 2011; Closed July 17, 2011; 56 perrformances. Setting: The seventeenth century, in the cave of the magician Alcandre, near Remulac, a small town in the south of France. Revival of a play presented in two acts. Originally presented by the Perry Street Theatre in 1988.

Peter Bartlett and Finn Wittrock in The Illusion *(photo by Joan Marcus)*

Soho Rep

Thirty-fifth Season

Artistic Director, Sarah Benson; Executive Director, Tania Carmargo; Producer, Rob Marcato; Literary & Humanities Manager, Raphael Martin; Production & Facilities Manager, Robbie Saenz de Viteri; Development Associate, Leslie Caiola; Management Assistant, Julie Griffith; Writer/Director Lab Co-Chairs, Daniel Manley & Rob Marcato; Box Office, William Burke; Development Consultant, Jennie Greer; Founding Artistic Directors, Marlene Swarz and Jerry Engelbach; Graphic Design, An Art Service; Press, Sam Rudy Media Relations, Dale Heller

Orange, Hat & Grace by Gregory S. Moss; Director, Sarah Benson; Set, Rachel Hauck; Lighting, Matt Frey; Costumes, David Hyman; Sound, Matt Tierney; Hair & Makeup, Jon Carter; Fight Director, J. David Brimmer; Props, Michelle Davis; PSM, Terri K. Kohler; Production Manager, Robbie Saenz de Viteri; Technical Director, Dave Nelson; ASM, Annette Adamska; Assistant Design: Oliver Wason (lighting), Joshua P. Burns (costumes), Jason Sebastian (sound); Assistant Director, Knud Adams; Wardrobe Supervisor, Mia Bednowtiz; Hair Supervisor, Chelsea Roth; Sound Board, Bobby McElver; Electricians, The Syndicate; Set Construction, Sightlines Fabrication, Hartford Stage; Production Assistants, Rachel Karp, Walter Ryon, Kelley Van Dilla; **Cast:** Stephanie Roth Haberle (Orange), Matthew Maher (Hat), Reyna de Courcy (Grace)

Soho Rep (Walkerspace); First Preview: September 15, 2010; Opening Night: September 22, 2010; Closed October 10, 2010. World premiere of a new experimental play presented without intermission.

Matthew Maher and Stephanie Roth Haberle in Orange, Hat & Grace
photo by Carol Rosegg)

Jomama Jones: Radiate Written and composed by Jomama Jones (Daniel Alexander Jones) and Bobby Halvoson with Sharon Bridgforth, Grisha Coleman, and Amy Hunt; Developed with New Dramatists Full Stage NYC Program; Director, Kym Moore; Music Director, Bobby Halvorson; Set, Arnulfo Maldonado; Lighting, Lucrecia Briceno and David Bengali; Costumes, Oana Botez Ban; Gowns, Oana Botez-Ban, Ron Cesario; Sound, Nick Kourtides; Press for Jomoma Jones, Heidi Riegler; Assistant Director, Oona Curley; Associate Lighting, Barbara Samuels; Wardrobe Supervisor, Mia Bednowitz; Production Assistants, Rachel Karp, Walter Ryon; **Cast:** Jomama Jones, Helga Davis and Sonya Perryman (*The Sweet Peaches*), Jing Xu; Musicians: Bobby Halvorson (Guitar), Michael O'Brien (Bass), Sean Dixon (Drums), Ted Cruz (Trumpet/French Horn), John Raymond (Trumpet sub)

Soho Rep (Walkerspace); First Preview: December 29, 2010; Opening Night: January 4, 2011; Closed January 15, 2011. World premiere of a musical performance event presented without intermission.

Sonya Perryman, Jomama Jones, and Helga Davis in Jomama Jones: Radiate *(photo by Nisha Sondhe)*

born bad by Debbie Tucker Green; Director, Leah C. Gardiner; Set, Mimi Lien; Lighting, Michael Chybowski; Costumes, Paul Tazewell; Sound and Original Music, Matt Sherwin; PSM, Beth Stegman; ASM, Lily Perlmutter; Dramaturg, Raphael Martin; Casting, Rob Marcato; Dialect Coaches, Jaime Lincoln Smith and Charlotte Fleck; Technical Director, Nate Lemoine; Assistant Director, Liz Thaler; Assistant Costumes, Kara Harmon; Assistant Lighting, Justin Partier; Wardrobe Supervisor, Mia Bednowitz; Associate Producer, Jason Bruffy; **Cast:** Quincy Tyler Bernstine (Sister #1), Crystal A. Dickinson (Sister #2), Elain Graham (Mum), LeRoy James McClain (Brother), Michael Rogers (Dad), Heather Alicia Simms (Dawta)

Soho Rep (Walkerspace); First Preview: March 31, 2011; Opening Night: April 7, 2011; Closed May 7, 2011. U.S. premiere of a new play presented without intermission.

Elaine R. Graham, Michael Rogers, Heather Alicia Simms, and Crystal A. Dickinson in born bad *(photo by Carol Rosegg)*

Readings

Writer/Director Lab Reading Series Downtown's premiere program for new plays; Included: *Fort Lee* by Lloyd Suh, directed by Sarah Rasmussen (March 28, 2011); *Loop Tape* by Andy Bragen, directed by Mike Donahue (April 4, 2011); *Takar-Azuka!* by Susan Soon He Stanton, directed by Alice Reagan (April 11, 2011); *The Dead, Inc.* by Michael Yates Crowley, directed by Rachel Chavkin (April 25, 2011); *When I Had Three Sisters* by Jason Pizzarello, directed by Lila Neugebauer (May 9, 2011)

Theatre for a New Audience

Thirty-second Season

Artistic Director, Jeffrey Horowitz; Chairman, Theodore Rogers; Managing Director, Dorothy Ryan; General Manager, Theresa von Klug; Development, James L. Lynes; Education, Katie Miller; Finance, Elizabeth Lees; Capital Campaign Director, Rachel Lovett; Associate Artistic Director, Arin Arbus; Associate General Manager/Company Manager, Lee Helms; Press, Bruce Cohen

Notes from Underground by Fyodor Dostoevsky, adapted by Bill Camp and Robert Woodruff; Based on the translation by Richard Peavear and Larissa Volokhonsky; Presented by Yale Repertory Theatre in association with the Baryshnikov Arts Center; Director, Robert Woodruff; Set, David Zinn; Costumes, Moria Sine Clinton; Lighting, Mark Barton; Composer/Sound, Michaël Attias; Projections, Peter Nigrini; Associate Projections, Daniel Vatsky; Production Dramaturgy, Amy Boratko; Vocal Coaches, Andrew Wade and Walton Wilson; Casting, Tara Rubin; Fight Director, Rick Sordelet; PSM, Kris Longley-Postema; Production Manager, B.D. White; Technical Director, Megan Caplan; Associate Sound, Philip Owen; Associate Video, Daniel Vatsky; **Cast:** Bill Camp (Man), Merritt Janson (Liza/Musician), Michaël Attias (Apollon/Musician)

Baryshnikov Arts Center; First Preview: November 7, 2010; Opening Night: November 11, 2010; Closed November 20, 2010. New York premiere of a new play based on a classic novel presented without intermission. Originally presented at Yale Repertory Theatre March 20, 2009.

Bill Camp in Notes from Underground *(photo by Joan Marcus)*

Cymbeline by William Shakespeare; Presented by Fiasco Theater; Directors, Noah Brody and Ben Steinfeld; Set, Jean-Guy Lecat; Costumes, Whitney Locher; Lighting, Tim Cryan; Fabulous Trunk, Jacques Roy; Vocal & Text Consultants, Cicely Berry, Robert Neff Williams; Fight Director, Noah Brody; Music Director, Ben Steinfeld; PSM,, Anne Michelson; Production Manager, B.D. White; Fight Consultant, J. Allen Suddeth; Assistant Director, Gillian Williams; Assistant Design: Pierre Lebon (set), Haley Lieberman (costumes), Ariel Pierce (lighting); **Cast:** Jessie Austrian (Imogen), Noah Brody (Posthumus/Roman Captain), Paul L. Coffey (Pisanio/Philario/Caius Lucius/Guiderius), Andy Grotelueschen (Cymbeline/Cloten/Cornelius), Ben Steinfeld (Iachimo/Arviragus), Emily Young (Queen/Frenchman/Belaria)

New Victory Theater; First Preview: January 13, 2011; Opening Night: January 16, 2011; Closed January 31, 2011. U.S. premiere of a new version of a classic play presented in two acts.

Andy Grotelueschen, Ben Steinfeld, Jessie Austrian, Noah Brody, Paul L. Coffey, and Emily Young in Cymbeline *(photo by Gerry Goodstein)*

The Merchant of Venice by William Shakespeare; Director, Darko Tresnjak; Set, John Lee Beatty; Costumes, Linda Cho; Lighting, David Weiner; Sound/Composer, Jane Shaw; Hair & Wigs, Charles LaPointe; Vocal Coach, Claudia Hill-Sparks; Video Artist, Matthew Myhrum; Casting, Deborah Brown; PSM, Renee Lutz; Production Manager, Bridget Welty; ASM, Marjorie Ann Wood; Tour Management, Paul M. Rambacher; Tour Producer, Thomas O. Kriegsmann; Company Manager, Tyler Soltis; **Cast:** F. Murray Abraham (Shylock), Andrew Dahl (Balthasar), Grant Goodman (Solanio), Lucas Hall (Bassanio), Kate MacCluggage (Portia), Christen Simon Marabate (Nerissa), Melissa Miller (Jessica), Jacob Ming-Trent (Launcelot Gobbo), Vince Nappo (Lorenzo), Tom Nelis (Antonio), Christopher Randolph (The Prince of Arragon/Tubal), Matthew Schneck (Salerio), Ted Schneider (Gratiano), Raphael Nash Thompson (The Prince of Morocco); Understudies: Jonathan Epstein, Catherine Gowl

Michael Schimmel Center at Pace University; Opening Night: February 27, 2011; Closed March 13, 2011. Setting: Venice and Belmont, the near future. Revival of a classic play presented in two acts. This production was previously presented by Theatre for a New Audience at the Duke on 42nd Street January 7–March 11, 2007.

Macbeth by William Shakespeare; Director, Arin Arbus; Set/Masks, Julian Crouch; Costumes, Anita Yavich; Lighting, Marcus Dohsi; Composer/Sound, Sarah Pickett; Vocal Coach, Andrew Wade; Dramaturg, Jonathan Kalb; Fight Director, B.H. Barry; Casting, Deborah Brown; PSM, Joanne E. McInerney; Production Manager, B.D. White; ASM, Katrina Lynn Olson; Hair/Wigs, Tom Watson; Technical Director, Adam Shive; Associate Sound, Jana Hogland; **Cast:** Justin Blanchard (Malcolm), Annika Boras (Lady Macbeth), Denis Butkus (Lennox), Peter Jay Fernandez (Duncan/Old Man/Doctor), Ian Holcomb (Donalbain/Messenger), Albert Jones (Macduff), John Christopher Jones (Porter/Servant), Robert Langdon Lloyd (Ross), Saxon Palmer (Witch/Seyton), Marquis Rodriguez (Fleance/Young Macduff/Young Siward), Roslyn Ruff (Lady Macduff/Gentlewoman), Christian Rummel (Sergeant/Englis Doctor/Menteith), Tommy Schrider (Witch/Murderer), John Douglas Thompson (Macbeth), Graham Winton (Banquo/Siward), Andrew Zimmerman (Witch/Murderer)

Duke on 42nd Street; First Preview: March 12, 2011; Opening Night: March 20, 2011; Closed April 22, 2011. Setting: Scotland and the English court. Revival of a classic play presented in two acts.

Vineyard Theatre

Thirtieth Season

Artistic Director, Douglas Aibel; Executive Director, Jennifer Garvey-Blackwell; General Manager, Reed Ridgley; Associate Artistic Director, Sarah Stern; Development, Scott Pyne; Marketing, Jonathan Waller; Education, Gad Guterman; Production Manager, Ben Morris; Assistant General Manager, Dennis Hruska; Marketing and Development Associate, Eric Emch; Box Office Manager, Literary Fellow, Louise Gough; Development Fellow/Executive Assistant, Erica Mann; Education Instructor, Dax Valdez; Casting, Henry Russell Bergstein; Press, Sam Rudy, Bob Lasko, Dale Heller

Middletown by Will Eno; Director, Ken Rus Schmoll; Sets/Costumes, David Zinn; Lighting, Tyler Micholeau; Sound, Jill BC DuBoff; PSM, Charles Turner III; ASM, Courtney James; Assistant Director, Will Wiseheart; Assistant Design: Tim McMath (set), Jacob Climer (costumes), Marika Kent (lighting), Patrick Metzger (sound); **Cast:** Heather Burns (Mrs. Swanson), Cindy Cheung (Female Tourist/Woman on Date/Attendant 2), Johanna Day (Aunt/Female Doctor/Intercom), Georgia Engel (Librarian), David Garrison (Public Speaker/Greg/Male Doctor), Ed Jewett (Male Tourist/Freelancer/Radio Host), McKenna Kerrigan (Tour Guide/Atendant/Music Host), James McMenamin (Mechanic), Michael Park (Cop), Linus Roache (John Jodge), Olivia Scott (Sweetheart), Pete Simpson (Landscaper/Ground Control/Man on Date/Janitor)

Gertrude and Irving Dimson Theatre; First Preview: October 13, 2010; Opening Night: November 3, 2010; Closed December 5, 2010; 21 previews, 34 performances. World premiere of a new play in two acts.

Linus Roache and Heather Burns in Middletown *(photo by Carol Rosegg)*

Interviewing the Audience by Zach Helm; Originally created by Spalding Gray; Directing Consultant, Sarah Stern; Set and Lighting Consultant, Kevin Adams; Sound Consultant, Brett Jarvis; PSM, Megan Smith; **Cast:** Zach Helm (Interviewer)

Gertrude and Irving Dimson Theatre; First Preview: February 3, 2011; Opening Night: February 10, 2011; Closed February 27, 2011; 7 previews, 19 performances. An interactive theatre experience with audience participation presented without intermission.

Zach Helm in Interviewing the Audience *(photo by Carol Rosegg)*

Picked by Christopher Shinn; Director, Michael Wilson; Set, Rachel Hauck; Costumes, Mattie Ullrich; Lighting, Russell H. Champa; Sound, Jill BC DuBoff; PSM, Cole Bonenberger; ASM, Shane Schnetzler; Assistant Director, Christopher Schilder; Assistant Design: Heather Lockard (costumes), Dani Clifford (lighting), Patrick Metzger (sound); Prop Master, Lily Fairbanks; Master Carpenter/Deck Supervisor, Eric Brooks; Deck Carpenter, Will Duty; Wardrobe Supervisor, Jessica Moy; Sound Board Operator, Stephanie Riddle; Production Assistant, Amy Lynch; **Cast:** Mark Blum (John), Tom Lipinski (Nick), Michael Stahl-David (Kevin), Liz Stauber (Jen), Donna Hanover (Casting Director/TV Personality)

Gertrude and Irving Dimson Theatre; First Preview: April 6, 2011; Opening Night: April 20, 2011; Closed May 22, 2011. World premiere of a new play presented in two acts.

Liz Stauber and Michael Stahl-David in Picked *(photo by Carol Rosegg)*

Developmental Lab

Now. Here. This. Book by Hunter Bell and Susan Blackwell, music and lyrics by Jeff Bowen; Based on a collaboration by the Company; Director, Michael Berresse; Music Director, Larry Pressgrove; **Cast:** Hunter Bell, Susan Blackwell, Jeff Bowen, Heidi Blickenstaff

Gertrude and Irving Dimson Theatre; June 4-19, 2010. Developmental production of a new musical presented without intermission.

Women's Project

Thirty-third Season

Producing Artistic Director, Julie Crosby, PhD.; Associate Artistic Director, Megan E. Carter; Associate Producer, Elizabeth R. English; Marketing, Deane Brosnan; General Manager, Karron Karr; Grants Manager, Elz Cuya; Theater Manager/Social Media Coordinator, Monet Hurst-Mendoza; Production Manager, Aduro Productions (Carolyn Kelson & Jason Janicki); Education Director, Johnmichael Rossi; Casting, Alaine Alldaffer & Lisa Donadio; Financial Services, Patricia Taylor; Press, Bruce Cohen

Apple Cove by Lynn Rosen; Director, Giovanna Sardelli; Set, Scott Bradley; Costumes, Amy Clark; Lighting, Japhy Weideman; Sound, Bart Fasbender; PSM, Jack Gianino; Stage Manager, Kelly "Kiki" Hess; Assistant Director, Nicole A. Watson; Assistant Costumes, Anne E. Grosz; Assistant Lighting, Dani Clifford; Assistant Sound, Dylan Carrow; Properties Master, Zach Roland; Wardrobe Supervisor, Amanda Jenks; Production Assistant, James Lanius; Casting Assistant, Darragh Garvey; Sound Board Operator, Ryan Gravett; Master Electrician, Adrian Kozlow; Master Carpenter, Daniel Thomas, **Cast:** Paul Carlin (Gary Hall), Erin Gann (Alan King), Allison Mack (Edie King); Dion Mucciacito (Duke), Kathy Searle (Mary Hall)

Julia Miles Theatre; First Preview: January 29, 2011; Opening Night: February 6, 2011; Closed March 6, 2011; 8 previews, 24 performances. Setting: A gated suburban community in a part of the country where it is always warm; the present – summer through spring. New York premiere of a new play presented without intermission. First produced by Todd Mountain Theater Project at the Roxbury Arts Group in Roxbury, New York in August 2005. Developed at the Lark Play Development Center, New York.

Kathy Searle, Paul Carlin, Allison Mack, Dion Mucciacito, and Erin Gann n Apple Cove (photo by Carol Rosegg)

Room Based on the writings of Virginia Woolf, adapted by Jocelyn Clarke; Co-presented with SITI Company (Anne Bogart, Artistic Director; Megan Wanlass Szalla, Executive Director); Director, Anne Bogart; Set, Neil Patel; Costumes, James Schuette; Original Lighting, Christopher Akerlind; Associate Lighting, Brian H. Scott; Soundscape, Darron L West; Movement Dramaturg, Barney O'Hanlon; PSM, Kris Longley-Postema; Sound Board Operator, Asa Wember; Light Board Operator, Kate Conover; Production Electrician, Adrian Kozlow; Production Carpenter, Danny Thomas; Spot, James Lanius; **Cast:** Ellen Lauren (Performer)

Julia Miles Theatre; First Preview: March 12, 2011; Opening Night: March 14, 2011; Closed March 27, 2011; 2 previews, 16 performances. Revival of a solo performance play presented without intermission. Originally presented in 2000 at the Wexner Center for the Arts in Columbus, Ohio. The New York premiere was presented at Classic Stage Company in May 2002.

Dion Mucciacito and Allison Mack in Apple Cove (photo by Carol Rosegg)

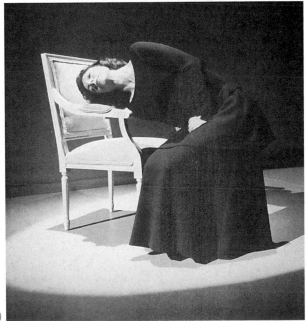

Ellen Lauren in Room (photo by AJ Zanyk/Wexner Center)

York Theatre Company

Forty-second Season

Artistic Director, James Morgan; Associate Artistic Director, Brian Blythe; Managing Director, Elisa Spencer Kaplan; Development and Communications, Kerry Watterson; Marketing Manager, Phil Haas; Audience Services Manager, Devin Guinn/Cristin Whitley; Company Manager, Carolyn Kuether; Development Associate, Shahna Sherwood; Graphics Associate, Jeb Knight; Reading Series Coordinator, Jeff Landsman; Founding Director, F. Janet Hayes Walker; Chairman of the Board, W. David McCoy; Casting, Geoff Josselson; Press, O+M Company

Falling for Eve Book by Joe DiePietro, music by Bret Simmons, lyrics by David Howard; Based on *Adam Alone* by David Howard; Co-presented by 1113 Productions (Steven Ulman, Executive Producer), Director, Larry Raben; Musical Staging, Lee Martino; Music Director/Arrangements, Kim Douglas Steiner; Set, Beowulf Boritt; Costumes, Bobby Pearce; Lighting, Herrick Goldman; PSM, Megan Schneid; ASM, Paul O'Toole; Props, Buist Bickley; Casting, Michael Cassara; Marketing Consultant, HHC Marketing; Production Manager, Scott DelaCruz; Assistants to the Director, Jessica Gordon, Toph McRae; Musical Staging Assistant, Charlie Williams; Assistant Set, Jo Winiarski; Associate Lighting, Susan Nicholson; Production Electrician, Joe Ben Deal; Wardrobe Supervisor, Zoe Zoephel; **Cast:** Jennifer Blood (Sarah), Nehal Joshi (Michael), Adam Kantor (God He), Jose Llana (Adam), Sasha Sloan (God She), Krystal Joy Brown (Eve); Musicians: Kim Douglas Steiner (Conductor/Keyboards), David Purcell (Drums/Percussion), Rob Jacoby (Woodwinds), Daniel Levy (Guitars/Bass)

Jose Llana, Sasha Sloan, and Krystal Joy Brown in Falling For Eve
(photo by Carol Rosegg)

Musical Numbers: The Creation Prelude; God, It's Good To Be Me; Another Day In Paradise; I Like You; Only Human; Apple, Apple, Apple, Apple; I've Got Plans For You; Where Will I Sleep Tonight?; Now What?; There's A Space Next To Me; Good Things Are A Comin'; Just Beyond Where The World Ends; Eve; Once A Life Ago; Something Just Happened To Me; Paradise Is You

Theatre at St. Peter's Church; First Preview: July 6, 2010; Opening Night: July 15, 2010; Closed: August 8, 2010. World premiere of a new musical presented without intermission.

The Road to Qatar! Book and lyrics by Stephen Cole, music by David Krane; Director, Philip George; Choreography, Bob Richard; Music Arrangements/Orchestrations, David Krane; Music Director, David Caldwell; Sets/Costumes/Puppet Design, Michael Bottari and Ronald Case; Lighting, Martin Vreeland; Projections, Chris Kateff; Marketing Consultant, HHC Marketing; General Manager for Coltrane LLC, Brierpatch Productions; PSM, Sarah Hall; ASM, Sarah Butke or Kelly Ice; Production Manager, Tyler Wise; Technical Director, Wyatt Kuether; Production Supervisor, Deirdre Brennan; Props, Dani Hurley; Shadow Puppets, Dani Hurley; Wardrobe Supervisor, Chadd McMillan; **Cast:** James Beaman (Michael), Bruce Warren (Farid), Bill Nolte (Mansour), Keith Gerchak (Jeffrey), Sarah Stiles (Nazirah); Orchestra: David Caldwell (Conductor/Piano), Mike Kuennen (Accoustic and Electric Bass), Perry Cavari (Drums/Percussion), Steve Greenfield (Reed One), Rick Walburn (Reed Two)

Musical Numbers: Opening, Oil!, The Road to Qatar!, Everything is Bigger, Farid's Song, Must Be, Safari, Good Things Come in Threes, Dancing as Fast as We Can, Doesn't Matter, Nazirah's in London, Give 'em What They Want, Aspire, Aspire (reprise), The Other Side of the World, Oh What a Show!, Finale

Theatre at St. Peter's Church; First Preview: January 25, 2011; Opening Night: February 3, 2011; Closed February 27, 2011. Setting: February-November 2005; New York City, Dubai, Bratislava, London, and Qatar. New York premiere of a new musical presented without intermission. World premiere at Lyric Stage (Dallas) October 9-24, 2009 (see *Theatre World* Vol. 66, page 376).

Sarah Stiles, Bill Nolte, James Beaman, Keith Gerchak, and Bruce Warren in The Road to Qatar! *(photo by Carol Rosegg)*

Tomorrow Morning Book, music, and lyrics by Laurence Mark Wythe; Co-presented by Hilary A. Williams; Director, Tom Mullen; Choreography, Lorin Lotarro; Music Director, John Bell; Orchestrations/Vocal Arrangements, Laurence Mark Wythe; Guirtar Arrangements, Dougal Irvine; Additional Orchestrations, Matt Brind and Brett Rowe; Set, Dan P. Conley; Costumes, Bill Morey; Lighting, Kirk Bookman; Projections and Sound, Mike Tutaj; Marketing Consultant, HHC Marketing; PSM, Sarah Butke; ASM, Sarah Hall or Paul O'Toole; Production Manager, Tyler Wise; Technical Director, Wyatt Kuether; Properties, Aaron Quintana; Wardrobe Supervisor, Chadd McMillan; Master Electrician, Zach Simon-Curry; Master Carpenter, Chris Robinson; **Cast:** D.B. Bonds (Jack), Autumn Hurlbert (Kat), Matthew Hydzik (John), Mary Mossberg (Catherine); Orchestra: John Bell (Conductor/Piano), Micah Burgess (Guitar), Alan Stevens Hewitt (Bass), Jeremy Yaddaw (Drums)

Musical Numbers: Everything Changes, What It Takes, The Reasons, I Remember, The Secret Tango, Catherine's Moment, Every Day, Invetory/POVs, The Girl in the Mirror, The Game Show, Look What We Made, Self Portrait, All About Today

Theatre at St. Peter's Church; First Preview: March 21, 2011; Opening Night: March 30, 2011; Closed April 23, 2011. Setting: In and around a house in Los Angeles, now and ten years ago. World premiere of a new musical presented without intermission.

Musicals In Mufti– Musical Theatre Gems in Staged Concert Performances – Twenty-fifth Series

Coco Book and lyrics by Alan Jay Lerner, music by André Previn, suggested from the life of Coco Chanel; Director, Mark D. Kaufmann; Music Director/Pianist, Michael Horsley; Lighting, Joe Ben Deal; PSM, Emily James Durning; ASM, Paul O'Toole; **Cast:** Andrea Marcovicci (Coco), Charles Kimbrough (Louis Greff), Susan Blommaert (Pignol), Brian Hissong (Alex, Bernstone, Albert), Tom Galantich (Dr. Pettijean, Charles, Ginsbourne), Robert Lenzi (Julian, Rosenberry, Armand), Heather Parcells (Solange), Adriana McPhee (Jeanine, Docaton), Julie Kotarides (Colette), David Turner (Sebastian), Peter Lockyer (Georges), Michelle Lookadoo (Simone), Jessica Grové (Noelle), Lewis Cleale (Papa, Berkwit)

Theatre at St. Peter's Church; September 10-12, 2010; 5 performances. Setting: Paris 1953-54; The House of Chanel, the Salon/Workroom and Coco's Apartment. Staged concert version of a revival of a musical presented in two acts. The original production opened at the Mark Hellinger Theatre December 18, 1969 starring Katherine Hepburn, and played 329 performances.

The Roar of the Greasepaint, The Smell of the Crowd Book, music, and lyrics by Leslie Bricusse and Anthony Newley; Director, Marcia Milgrom Dodge; Music Director, Ethyl Will; Lighting, Chris Robinson; PSM, Emily James Durning; ASM, Paul O'Toole; **Cast:** Veronica Kuehn (Kid/Violet Urchin), Ruthie Ann Miles (Bully/Red Urchin), Eliza Hayes Maher (Orange Urchin), Elly Noble (Yellow Urchin), Brandi Burkhardt (Girl/Green Urchin), Kay Trinidad (Blue Urchin), Zonya Love (Indigo Urchin), Jim Brochu (Sir), Josh Grisetti (Cocky), Quentin Earl Darrington (Q.E.D.)

Theatre at St. Peter's Church; October 1-3, 2010; 5 performances. Setting: A rocky place; Dawn. Staged concert version of a revival of a musical presented in two acts. The original production opened at the Shubert Theatre May 16, 1965 playing 231 performances.

I Remember Mama Music by Richard Rodgers, lyrics by Martin Charnin, book by Thomas Meehan; Additional Lyrics, Raymond Jessel; Based on the play by John Van Druten; Director, Michael Montel; Music Director, Mark Hartman; Lighting, Lois Catanzo; PSM, Emily James Durning; ASM, Paul O'Toole; **Cast:** Erin Mackey (Katin), Juliette Allen Angelo (Christine), Tanner Tompkins (Dagmar), Marissa O'Donnell (Johanna), Zach Landes (Nils), Howard McGillin (Papa), Jacquelyn Piro Donovan (Mama), Price Waldman (McGuire, Sailro, Doctor, Admirer), Maureen Silliman (Aunt Trina, Dame Sybill Fitzgibbons), Becky Barta (Aunt Sigrid, Nurse, Admirer), Michael J. Farina (Peter Thorkelson, Sailor, Admierer), George S. Irving (Uncle Chris)

Theatre at St. Peter's Church; October 8-10, 2010; 5 performances. Setting: San Francisco, 1910-1911. Staged concert version of a revival of a musical presented in two acts. The original production opened at the Majestic Theatre May 31, 1979 playing 108 performances.

I Love My Wife Book and lyrics by Michael Stewart, music by Cy Coleman; Director, Carl Andress; Music Director, Matt Castle; Lighting, Kirk Bookman; Lighting Supervisor, Steve O'Shea; Assistant Director, Marc Tumminelli; PSM, Emily James Durning; ASM, Paul O'Toole: **Cast:** Jenni Barber (Cleo), Heidi Blickenstaff (Monica), Matt Castle (Stanley [piano]), Josh Grisetti (Alvin), Jesse Means (Quenton [drums]), Adam Monley (Wally), Louis Tucci (Harvey [bass]), Scott Wakefield (Norman [guitar/banjo])

Theatre at St. Peter's Church; October 22-24, 2010; 5 performances. Setting: Trenton, New Jersey; 1977. Staged concert version of a revival of a musical presented in two acts. The original production opened at the Ethel Barrymore Theatre April 17, 1977 playing 857 performances.

Mary Mossberg, D.B. Bonds, Matthew Hydzik, and Autumn Hurlbert in Tomorrow Morning *(photo by Carol Rosegg)*

Annika Boras and John Douglas Thompson in Macbeth
(photo by Gerry Goodstein)

Rebecca Luker and Michael Siberry in Death Takes a Holiday
(photo by Joan Marcus)

Laurelyn Watson Chase in The Mikado (photo by Michael A. Nemeth)

Robin Leslie Brown and Margot White in Rosmersholm
(photo by Gregory Costanzo)

Karl Kenzler, Celia Keenan-Bolger, and the Company in Peter
and the Starcatcher (photo by Joan Marcus)

OFF-OFF-BROADWAY
June 1, 2010–May 31, 2011

Top: Seth Blum and Elizabeth McMonagle in Hush The Musical, presented by Charles "Rooc" Mandracchia in association with Frizzi & Lazzi Theatre Company

Center: Chris Bannow and Ian McWethy in Electra in a One-Piece, presented at the Wild Project by Good Company (photo by Sam Hough)

Bottom: Jennifer Harder, Nikole Beckwith, and Andy Phelan in MilkMilkLemonade at Astoria Performing Arts (photo by Rhys Harper)

Off-Off-Broadway: A Year of Transition

By Shay Gines, Founder, New York Innovative Theatre Foundation

The 2010-2011 season was one of transition for the Off-Off-Broadway (OOB) community. A number of prominent OOB pioneers passed away, the community witnessed some of their most beloved and long-established performance venues shutter, and many companies and artists found themselves at a crossroads: choosing to either relocate to more economically and artistically enticing cities or remain in the Big Apple and face an environment that is pushing independent theatre artists further and further from the heart of the Theatre District.

With the passing of Ellen Stewart, Lanford Wilson, and Doric Wilson, OOB lost some of the most renowned artists who helped build the vibrant and kinetic Off-Off-Broadway community.

Ellen Stewart, the infamously outspoken and opinionated founder and artistic director of La MaMa, passed away on January 13, 2011. Her memorial service at St. Patrick's Cathedral was filled with friends, family, and many of the artists whose lives she had touched. "There is a full house here today," said La MaMa Board President, Frank Carucci, "which would have made Ellen very happy." During her forty-nine years as artistic director, La MaMa grew from a tiny basement cabaret to a two-building arts complex on East 4th Street—from a modest company presenting the work of friends and relatives to an iconic, groundbreaking institution that is known around the world. Stewart was a cornerstone of the OOB community and became known as OOB's "Mama." Her passing was acutely felt.

In March of 2011, OOB lost Lanford Wilson. One of the most prolific playwrights to come from the OOB community, Wilson began his career at the Caffé Cino. He also worked at La MaMa and many other independent theatre houses. It is at the Cino that Wilson met and began work with his lifelong collaborator, director Marshall Mason. Together they forged a forty-year partnership that resulted in some of the most heartfelt and celebrated plays of their generation. In 1969, Wilson, along with many other playwrights and directors from the OOB scene, founded the Circle Repertory Company. While he had many successes—including receiving the Pulitzer Prize for Drama in 1980—he remained an adamant supporter of independent artists, regularly stating that, "We all share a common experience, a common identity."

Only two months later, in May 2011, gay rights activist and playwright Doric Wilson passed away. Wilson is believed to be the first resident playwright of the Caffé Cino. According to playwright Robert Patrick, Wilson's work helped "establish the Cino as a venue for new plays, and materially contributed to the then-emerging concept of Off-Off-Broadway." Many of Wilson's plays documented the underground Village scene of the '50s and '60s, including the Stonewall Riots that ignited the Gay Liberation movement in New York City in 1969. Wilson later went on to found TOSOS (The Other Side Of Silence), an OOB company dedicated to illuminating the gay and lesbian experience. It is not surprising that Wilson's plays about the origins of the Gay Rights movement found their legs in OOB. Shared characteristics like the fact that both sectors work outside mainstream America and have struggled for legitimacy made OOB the perfect conduit for these plays that sought to challenge the status quo.

Each of these extraordinary artists and leaders imprinted their unique characteristics on to the DNA of the OOB community. They infused it with their own enthusiastic integrity and tenacious Do It Yourself spirit that are hallmarks of the community today. Their influence, guidance, and support will be dearly missed. And while no one will ever take the place of Ellen Stewart or Doric Wilson, the younger generation of OOB artists is already grooming outspoken advocates and community leaders to address current challenges and discover new artistic avenues.

One of the most immediate challenges facing the OOB community is a lack of performance space. Over the last decade, OOB has lost more than 25% of their performance venues across the city. These spaces have either been demolished to make way for new developments (housing or commercial developments) or repurposed into non-performance venues. This distressing trend sets OOB companies and artists on a chronic cycle of displacement that successively pushes them further and further from the heart of the Theatre District, and often out of reach of audiences.

It has long been believed that this is a natural part of urban renewal. Artists find cheap space in depressed areas of town, create a theatre, and invest in the space. Audiences come to performances, generating evening foot traffic, which decreases crime and vandalism in that area. The audience members also spend money in the neighborhood, which increases the income of the local businesses, which in turn invest more in their stores and the neighborhood, which helps bring in more customers and audience members. More businesses open shops, property values increase, rents go up, and soon the artists can no longer afford to keep their space in a neighborhood that they helped revitalize. It is a pattern that is too familiar to the OOB community, and the classic gentrification story, but it has a detrimental effect on long-term sustainability of culture development in New York City.

On August 31, 2010, the Ohio Theatre on Wooster Street ended its twenty-nine year run and closed its doors forever. In 2008, the owners of the building, who had always been supporters of the theatre, found themselves no longer able to keep up with the financial demands of the maintenance and preservation of the building and decided to sell. The new owners had no desire to rent to an independent theatre on a shoestring budget. And with that, one of the most fertile and beloved Off-Off-Broadway venues was gone. The Ohio was home to many theatre companies and some of the most influential OOB artists of our time and it will be sadly missed.

Center Stage's issues began in 2008 when rent for their space dramatically increased. It was particularly difficult timing for the fifteen-year-old company, which was feeling the adverse effects of the recession. Sponsors, corporate funding, and donations started to dry up and fewer OOB companies were able to pay sublet rental deposits up front. Budget cuts and layoffs did not make up the financial gap and after a hard-fought year of just trying to retain the space long enough to honor their remaining sublet agreements, Center Stage closed up shop in the spring of 2011.

Founded in 1955, Theater Ten Ten was New York City's longest continuously operated Off-Off Broadway theatre. For fifty-five years this company presented shows in the theatre of the Park Avenue Christian Church. However, in the winter of 2010, the church ministry began reevaluating its mission and use of its facility. As part of that effort, Theater Ten Ten was dissolved in the summer of 2010 and the venue is no longer available for use by the theatre community.

These are only a few examples of some of OOB's most established and much-loved spaces that are now clothing boutiques or offices. While these losses are hard to bear, the OOB community is persevering. The company that ran Center Stage Developing Artists Theater Company is currently seeking new space. Theater Ten Ten reemerged as Theater 2020 with performances at various locations in Brooklyn. And in the fall of 2011, the manager of the Ohio Theatre took over the former Wings Theatre space in the Archive Building, and the New Ohio Theatre was born.

While these individual companies continue to seek opportunities, the community as a whole has recognized sustainable real estate as a persistent problem and is looking for innovative ways to address it. The OOB community is working hand-in-hand with community boards throughout the city to support a proposal that would offer tax relief to landlords who rent space at below market value to nonprofit performing arts organizations. The idea has promise and has garnered support from all twelve of Manhattan's community boards and several elected officials. Further work is yet to be done on the issue, and support from the outer boroughs is still required. However, if passed, this tax abatement could have long-term benefits for OOB with respect to its ability to retain facilities and provide a more stable environment for artists.

Not only does OOB endeavor to create a more favorable rental environment, it is also seeks opportunities to purchase facilities outright. OOB companies like Horse Trade Theater Group are looking to purchase spaces that can then become permanent fixtures of the community and not dependent on sympathetic landlords. Horse Trade manages several spaces in the East Village, including Under St. Marks. Horse Trade's non-exclusive rental agreements provide very inexpensive performance space to many OOB productions. So when the owners of 94 St. Marks Place announced that they were putting the building on the market, the community rushed to endorse the purchase of the small black box theatre in the basement. The demonstration of support "from the community helped us garner a great deal of press, and hardened our landlord's resolve to not just sell at whatever price he could get," said Managing Director Erez Ziv. While Horse Trade cannot afford to purchase the entire building, the outpouring of support helped them to broker a deal with the owner for an extended lease until 2019 as well as an agreement to consider turning the building into a condominium which would allow Horse Trade the opportunity to purchase the theatre space it now occupies. These discussions are still preliminary and anything can happen in the next seven years, but this was a decisive step for the troupe in acquiring a permanent space.

The loss of performance space is not the only challenge facing artists in New York City. In an article for *Crain's Business* entitled "Artists Fleeing the City," journalist Miriam Kreinin Souccar reported that "Artists have long struggled in New York, moving into rough areas, gentrifying them and then getting forced out. But as the city has gotten increasingly expensive, there are few such neighborhoods left to move to, forcing a growing number of artists to abandon the city."

OOB artists are no strangers to hard times. While it is not easy being the proverbial "starving artist," they understand the struggles of pursuing an artistic dream while trying to make ends meet. Living and working in one of the most culturally rich and artistically fertile cities in the world is worth the effort. However, over the last few years that struggle has become increasingly arduous. Housing costs continue to rise, day jobs are harder to come by, costs of living have increased, and the city is offering fewer incentives for artists. Meanwhile, other cities such as Detroit, Cleveland, and Philadelphia are actively luring artists with competitive arts-friendly initiatives.

Part of the allure of New York City is the artistic community. 40,000 artists strong, OOB is one of the largest arts communities in the world. These artists pay taxes, support local businesses, are involved in civic activities, and perhaps most importantly, contribute to the identity of the city. Can city officials and corporate entities stop the flight of artists before the creative talent pool is thoroughly depleted? Are current cultural development initiatives enough to keep artists in the city? It is difficult to imagine the Big Apple without an independent theatre scene pushing the boundaries of American theatre. However, it would not be such a bad alternative to see those same artists taking their Do It Yourself, OOB brand of theatre and spreading it across the nation. Perhaps that is the next big transition for this community.

This year the OOB community was met with change and loss. However, OOB is constantly growing, evolving and adapting. Transition is a part of the communal identity and there is no doubt that the result of that transition will be worth purchasing a ticket to see.

Resources for this section: OffOffOnline, NYTheatre.com, Innovative Theatre Foundation, TheatreMania.com

Andrew Colteaux and Kat Yew in the Yara Arts Group presentation of Raven *(photo by Lee Wexler)*

Abigail Rose Solomon and Shara Ashley Zeiger (front) Kendall Rileigh and Maxwell Zener (rear) in Savage in Limbo, *presented by Rosalind Productions and The Platform Group (photo by Suzi Sadler)*

3Graces Theater Co.

www.ThreeGracesTheater.org

As It Is In Heaven Director, Ludovica Villar-Hauser; Stage Manager, Gary Adamsen; Lighting, Joshua Scherr; Costumes, Shelly Norton, Veneda Truesdale; Cast: Margot Avery, Kathleen Bishop, Rachel Cantor, Carla Cantrelle, Kelli Lynn Harrison, Kate Kearney-Patch, Annie McGovern, Megan Tusing, DeWanda Wise; Cherry Lane Theatre; May 20–June 11, 2011

9Thirty Theatre Company

www.9TTC.org

The Birds Director, Aaron Gonzalez; Original Music, James Stewart; Stage Manager, Mikey Beyrouti; Lighting, Mikey Beyrouti; Set, Aaron Gonzalez; Costumes, Dana Dobreva; Puppets, Lillian Clements; Cast: Freddie Bennett, Patrick Bonck, Matthew Jellison, Nicole Hodges, Kim Ramirez, Eric Sutton; Greek Cultural Center; August 10–21, 2010

AAI Productions

7sinsin60.com

7 Sins in 60 Minutes by Paula Clzmar, Cheryl L. Davis, Olga de la Fuente, Chisa Hutchinson, Natalia Naman, Anne Phelan, Melisa Tien; Director, Melanie Sutherland; Lighting, Joyce Liao; Cast: Duane Cooper, Cortnie Loren Miller, Michael Rosete, Karen Sours; Producer, Lanie Zipoy; Graphics, Stephanie Bart-Horvath; HERE Arts Center; July 11–15, 2010

Abbie, the play L.L.C.

President and Artistic Director, Bern Cohen; Production Manager, Wendy Czerwinski; Co-Producer, Jason Scheff

Abbie Written and performed by Bern Cohen; Director, Thomas Caruso; Stage Manager and AV Designer, Morgan Paul Freeman; Lighting, Zachary Spitzer; Production Manager, Wendy Czerwinski, Technical Director, Sean Ryan; Production Coordinator, Brittany Gischner; Production Assistant, Patrick Scheid; Assistant Producer, Penny Bittone, Lighting Board Operator, Tim Guccione; Publicists, Sam Morris PR; West End Theater; January 6–29, 2011

Abingdon Theater

Woman Before A Glass by Lanie Robertson; Abingdon Theater Stage II; May 17–29, 2011

The Nanjing Race by Reggie Cheong-Leen; Director, Brian Tom O'Connor; Stage Manager, Genevieve Ortiz; Lighting and Set, Andrew Lu; Costumes, Pam Prior; Sound, David Margolin Lawson; Fight Choreographer, Rick Sordelet; Production Manager, John Trevellini; Casting Director, William Schill; Press, Shirley Herz Associates/Bob Lasko; Assistant Stage Manager, Christine Kwon; Photographer, Kim T. Sharp; Cast: James Chen, Marcus Ho, Ian Wen; Dorothy Strelsin Theatre; October 29–November 21, 2010

How I Fell In Love by Joel Fields; Director, Jules Ochoa; Stage Manager, Genevieve Ortiz; Lighting, Travis McHale; Set, Wilson Chin, David Arsenault; Costumes, Kimberly Matela; Sound, Ian Wehrle; Production Manager, John Trevellini; Casting Director, William Schill; Press, Shirley Herz Associates/Bob Lasko; Assistant Director, Benji Shaw; Assistant Stage Manager, Sarah Livant Photographer, Kim T. Sharp; Cast: Mark Doherty, Polly Lee, Tommy Schrider, Roya Shanks; Dorothy Strelsin Theatre; January 21–February 13, 2011

Summer In Sanctuary by Al Letson; Director, Rob Urbinati; Stage Manager,

Mark Hoffner; Lighting, Andrew Lu; Costumes, Karen Anselm; Sound, David Margolin Lawson; Production Designer, Jared Mezzocchi; Production Manager, John Trevellini; Cast: Al Letson, Willie Evans Jr.; Dorothy Strelsin Theatre; March 25–April 27, 2011

AC Productions

How I Killed My Roommate... and Got Away With It by John Pallotta; Director, Anita Clay; Cast: Robert McKeon, Heather Bunch, Matt Sternberg, Katherine Eliott, Anita Clay, Marie Accardi, Diane Accardi, Emma Peele, Ryan Masterson, Jen Finger; Producers Club–The Grand Theatre; August 25, 2010

Access Theater

www.accesstheater.com

READINGS AND WORKSHOPS

Open Access: Plays in Progress: *An Evening of Works in Progress* by members of the Stevedore Confederacy/Access Theater Writer's; *The Zebra Shirt of Lonely Children* Written and performed by Mattew Trumbull; *Fold The Close* by Tabetha Xavier; *The House of Mr. Orange* Director, Susan Bowen; Co-Produced by Blue Coyote Theater Group; Access Theatre; March 30–April 3, 2011

Active Theater

www.theactivetheater.com

Venus Flytrap by Anthony Dodge; Director, Marcia Milgrom Dodge; Stage Manager, Peter Lawrence, Angela Kiessel; Lighting, Paul Miller; Set, Michael Schweikardt; Costumes, Bobby Pearce; Sound, Acme Sound Partners; Co-Producer, Craig Haffner, Karl E. Held; Wigs and Hair, Edward J. Wilson; Assistant Stage Manager, Pamela Remler; Cast: Xanthe Elbrick, Raissa Dorff, Jason Emmanuel, Grace Gealey, Matt Loney, Jose Luaces, Richard B. Watson; The Workshop Theater; November 4–14, 2010

Bridgeboy by Matthew Keuter; Director, Nathaniel Shaw; Stage Manager, Kerry J. Lynch; Lighting, Yuiry Nayer; Set, Craig Napoliello; Costumes, Matthew Kessler; Sound, Jacob Subotnik; Cast: Lisa Altomare, Catherine Curtin, Michael Andrew Daly, Anthony Inneo, James Judy, Rhyn McLemore, Mary Jo Mecca, David Ojala; The Workshop Theater; February 24–March 6, 2011

READINGS AND WORKSHOPS

Body Language by Jennie Contuzzi; Director, Nathaniel Shaw; Samantha Buck, Michael McGlone, Catherine Curtin, Lou Carbonneau, Rob Sheridan; Pearl Studios; March 24, 2011

Adaptive Arts Theater Company

www.adaptiveartstheater.org

Artistic Director, Marielle Duke; Co-Founder, Christian Toth; Associate Artistic Director, Gabby Sherba; Artistic Associate, Michael Mraz; Artistic Associate, Eric Bland; Educational Associate, Collin McConnell; Educational Associate, Melanie McCauley

Alice Sit by the Fire by J.M. Barrie; Director, Marielle Duke; Musical Director, Patrick Metzger; Stage Manager, Devan Hibbard; Set, Olivia Harris; Sound, Patrick Metzger; Composer, Patrick Metzger; Producer, Carlyann Oquendo; Cast: Gabby Sherba, Shelley Little, Catherine McNelis, Christian Toth, Leigh Poulos, Mark Souza, Alex Engquist, Jillian Homlish, Emily Perkins; IRT; March 13–20, 2011

FESTIVALS

Adaptive Arts' 60 Second Play Festival; Director, Marielle Duke and John Hurley; IRT; March 20, 2011

Burritos by Tim Errickson, Cast: Bob D'Haene, Ryan Andes and Justin Holcomb; *Interview, 1949* by Beth Danesco, Cast: Justin Holcomb; *Have You Seen My…* by Arthur M. Jolly, Cast: Ryan Andes and Emily King Brown; *Under my Coat is the Truth* by Greg Romero, Cast: Ilana Meredith, Emily King Brown and Sabrina Farhi; *Cold* by Stacey Lane, Cast: Sabrina Farhi and Spencer Robinson; *Philometry* by Nelson Diaz-Marcano, Cast: Ilana Meredith, Bob D'Haene, and Spencer Robinson; *100% Unbreakable for Infinity* by Beth Danesco, Cast: Alex Engquist, Spencer Robinson and Alexandra Giacona; *Alaska* by Alexis Roblan, Cast: Ali Giacona and Jess DiCarlo; *About Facebook* by Eric Bland, Cast: Jess DiCarlo and Joseph Ryan; *Candy Heart* by Marek Muller, Cast: Jonah LeDoux and Jess DiCarlo; *Dirty Laundry* by Michael Bradley, Cast: Jonah LeDoux and Renee Hermiz; *Oh Cynthia!!!* by C.L. Weatherstone; Cast: Jeff Roth; *Tempting Fate* by Wyatt Williams, Cast: Joseph Ryan and Jeff Roth; *One Minute Relationship* by Mike Poblete; Cast: Alex Engquist and Gabby Sherba; *Endless Song of Happiness* by August Schulenberg, Cast: Ryan Andes and Gabby Sherba; *Outer Space Beats Hollywood Every Time* by Corey Pajka, Cast: Jonah, LeDoux, Justin Holcomb, and Emily King Brown; *Pirate Pete* by Evan Baker, Cast: Cameron and Ryan Andes; *Teleprompter* by Asher Wyndham, Cast: Isaiah Tanenbaun; *War is in the Air* by Jae Kramisen, Cast: Isaiah Tanenbaum and Patrick Poole; *Let it Burn* by Jae Kramisen, Cast: Patrick Poole and Alley Scott; *One, Two, Three* by Ilana Meredith, Cast: Alley Scott and Kristen Vaughn; *Exercise in Futility* by Adam Hundley, Cast: Kristen Vaughn and Johnna Adams; *Hat Trick* by Isaac Rathbone, Cast: Ben VanderBoom and Roger Nasser; *10 Going on 40* by Hollie Rosenberg, Cast: Roger Nasser and Heather Cunningham; *Not Expecting That* by Arthur M. Jolly, Cast: Roger Nasser and Ben VanderBoom; *Pancake Philosophy* by Beth Danesco, Cast: Ben VanderBoom and Stephanie Cox-Williams; *Yes I Am* by Eric Bland, Cast: Ben VanderBoom and Becky Byers; *Shoe Box* by Stacey Lane, Cast: Ben VanderBoom, Stephanie Cox-Williams , Becky Byers ,Lex, Friedman, Shelly Ray, Michael Moss, and Rebecca Davis; *Best Day Ever* by Crystal Skillman, Cast: Becky Byers, Rebecca Davis, Stephanie Cox-Williams, Lex Friedman, Shelly Ray, Michael Moss; *Ex Ghosts* by Arthur M. Jolly, Cast: Michael Moss, Shelly Ray, and Lex Friedman; *Contradictions* by Suzanne Lamberg, Cast: Michael Moss, Rebecca Davis

Autism Initiative; Shetler Studios; October 24, 2010

X-ray Vision at the Motel 9 by Ian August, Director, Marielle Duke, Cast: Eric Bland and Alex Engquist; *Rain* by Garry Williams, Director, August Schulenburg, Cast: Ken Glickfeld, Alisha Spielmann, Jane Taylor, Isaiah Tanenbaum; *Prodigal Father* by Isaac Rathbone, Director, Dev Bondarin, Cast: John Greenleaf and John Gardner; *Walk into the Sea* by Elaine Romero, Director, Jerry Ruiz, Cast: Sandra Delgado, J.J. Perez, Teddy Canez

READINGS AND WORKSHOPS

Deus Ex Machina by Jessica Loria; Director, Christopher Thomasson; Cast: Heather Cunningham, Alex Engquist, Erin Gorski; IRT; March 14, 2011

Welcome Back, Llyod by Isaac Rathbone; Matthew Groff; Cast: Alley Scott, Patrick Avella, Joe Beaudin; IRT; March 19, 2011

The Hand that Moves by August Schulenburg; Cast: Kari Swenson Riely, Alisha Spielmann, Paula Roman, Godfrey Simmons, Mariam Habib; IRT; March 19, 2011

Akiz Productions

Hanako Junction Written and directed by Roderic Wachovsky; Choreographer, Giovanni Villari; Stage Manager, Michael Palmer; Lighting, Joyce Liao; Set, Mark Symczak; Costumes, Carolyn Hoffman; Sound, Peter Sylvester; Cast: Jonathan Cantor, Bill Dante, Nadia Gan, Elena McGhee; Gene Frankel Theatre; April 11–20, 2011

Algonquin Production and The Present Company

Protected by Timothy Scott Harris; Director, Timothy Scott Harris; Cast: Dee Dee Friedman, Cam Kornman, Jeff Paul, Bill Tatum, Matt Walker; Connelly Theater; August 13–27, 2010

AliveWire Theatrics

www.AliveWireTheatrics.com

Besharet by Chana Porter; Director, Scott Rodrigue; Stage Manager, Erica Holtz; Lighting, Jason Miller; Set, Eric Berninghausen; Costumes, Emily Peterson; Sound, Dan Snazelle; Cast: MacLeod Andrews, Tia Stivala, William Green, Olivia Rorick; P.S. 122; March 7–27, 2011

American Bard Theater Company

www.americanbard.org

Measure for Measure by William Shakespeare; Director, Natalie Doyle Holmes; Musical Director, Mary Riley; Stage Manager, Jeanne E. Travis; Composer, William TN Hall; Lighting, Daniel Winters; Set, Natalie Doyle Holmes, Erin Gilbreth, Pamela Leverenz; Costumes, Christine Kahler; Sound, Jeanne E. Travis, Mary Riley; Photographer, Carrie Crow; Graphics, Herbert Lascina; Web Designer, Robbie Holmes; House Manager, Fred Gilbreth; Box Office Manager, Tiffany Kintigh; Casting Director, Damon Kinard; Cast: Bryan L. Cohen, Bill Galarno, Erin Gilbreth, Timothy C. Goodwin, Jack Herholdt, Ross Hewitt, Sam Laakso, Stephen Medvidick, Andrew Oppenheim, Mary Riley, Lily Warpinski, Cheri Wicks; Payan Theater; November 4– 13, 2010

Much Ado About Nothing by William Shakespeare; Director, John Basil; Original Music, Scott O'Brien; Choreographer, Alisa Claire; Stage Manager, Michelle Foster; Lighting, Mark Hankla; Costumes, Robin McGee; Sound, Scott O'Brien; Cast: A.J. Cote', Alicia Giangrisostomi, Chris Kateff, Liz Keefe, Taylor Miller, Rainard Rachele, Ryan Rinkel, Basil Rodericks, Chris Seiler, Brian Silliman, Joseph Small, Graham Stevens, Jay Stratton, Erica Swindell, Robert Lee Taylor, Zac Walker, Nate Washbur; American Globe Theater; February 25–March 26, 2011

Four by Tenn: *Small Craft Warnings, A Perfect Analysis Given by a Parrot, Summer at the Lake* and *The Case of the Crushed Petunias* by Tennessee Williams; Director, Seth Duerr; Stage Manager, Elizabeth Luchs; Lighting, Daniel Winters; Set, Elyse Handelman; Costumes, Sean Sullivan; Sound, Artem Kulakov; AV Design, Ben Lundberg; Production Manager, Jim Armstrong; Dramaturg, Natalie Doyle Holmes; Casting Assistant, Sarah Overturf; House Manager, Fred Gilbreth; Box Office Manager, Ross Hewitt; Marketing Assistant, Lily Warpinsk; Cast: Graham Anderson, Spencer Aste, Bryan L. Cohen, Joe Dawson, Erin Gilbreth, Keith Merrill, Mary Riley, Gwenevere Sisco, Jane Strauss, Timothy Warmen, Lucas A. Wells, Cheri Wicks, Renee Williams; Shetler Studio 54; April 9–23, 2011

READINGS AND WORKSHOPS

Sommer Sonnets by William Shakespeare; Director, Natalie Doyle Holmes, Andrew Eisenman; Jack Herholdt, Ross Hewitt, Marley Riley, Cheri Wicks; Weist Barron Studios; August 5, 2010

American Centaur

www.Americanglobe.org

K5 Adapted from Shakespeare; Director, The Company; Producer, Ali Skye Bennet and Luis Christian Dilorenzi; Cast: Cory Antiel, Alex Borinsky, Devin Bokaer, Michael Bradley Cohen, Rowan Magee, Justin Perkins; TheaterLab; November 2–3, 2010; also performed at IRT Theater in May 2011

When Richard Ordered the Sun to Set Adapted from Shakespeare; Director, The Company; Puppet Carver, Jon O'Brien; Cast: Cory Antiel, Devin Bokaer, Michael Bradley Cohen, Rowan Magee, Justin Perkins; IRT Theater; May 13–15, 2011

READINGS AND WORKSHOPS

Merhant of Venice by Adapted from Shakespeare; Director, The Company; Montgomery St. Gardens; June 26, 2010

Lord, What These Weathers are Cold! Adapted from Anonymous; Cast: Cory Antiel, Clare Barron, Arla Berman, Devin Bokaer, Alex Borinsky, Michael Bradley Cohen, Rowan Magee, Emma Marks, Justin Perkins; Montgomery St. Gardens; December 16, 2010

The American Theatre of Actors

The Prince of Hell's Kitchen by Steve Silver; Director, Laurie Rae Waugh; Cast: Meghan Sara Karre, Thomas J. Kane, Steve Silver, Steven F. DeFonte and Amy Losi; American Theatre of Actors; November 17–21, 2010

American Thymele Theatre

Alcestis by Euripides; Director, Lorca Peress; Original Music, Kostas Kouris; Cast: Paul Mischeshin, Frederick Mayer, Goran Ivanovski, Vasile Flutur, Michael Honda, Perri Yaniv, Julian M. Sapala, Steven Unger, Jessica Levesque, Christopher Ryan,Densie Fiore, Emilly Medina, Harry Oram, Zenon Zeleniuch, Luke Vedder and Anthony Michael Stok; Various parks in NYC; July 6–10, 2010

anna&meredith

www.annaandmeredith.com

Gormanzee & Other Stories by Anna Moench; Director, Meredith Steinberg; Original Music, David Moench; Choreographer, Meredith Steinberg; Puppet Design, Erin Smith; Cast: Edward Bauer, Jean Ann Douglass, Dave Edson, Sarah Elmaleh, Molly Gaebe,Claire Gresham, Elisa Matula, Nathan Richard Wagner; Flea Theatre; July 7–25, 2010

Apple Core Theater Company

www.applecoretheatercompany.org

Producing Artistic Director, Allison Taylor; Associate Artistic Director, Walter J. Hoffman

As Is by William M. Hoffman; Director, Walter J. Hoffman; Original Music, Joemca; Lighting, Walter J. Hoffman; Set, Nikki Egana Stadler; Costumes, David Zwiers; Sound, Joemca; Cast: Jeff Auer, Emily King Brown, Jason Griffith, Brian Hopson, Jessica Luck, Todd Michael, Ryan Stadler, David Zwiers; Studio Theater at Theatre Row; October 14–31, 2010

Artistic New Directions

www.artisticnewdirections.org

Artistic Co-Directors, Kristine Niven, Janice L. Goldberg

Running by Arlene Hutton; Director, Lori Walter and Beth Lincks; Stage Manager, Kate Erin Gibson and Jacob Callie Moore; Lighting, Rob Strohmeir; Set, Eric Nightengale; Costumes, Marguerita Delgado; Production Assistant, Becca Worthington; Cast: Seth Barrish, Lee Brock; Players Theatre; September 9–20, 2010

Psychomachia by Jennifer Lane; Director, Robin A. Paterson; Stage Manager, Becky Lynn Dawson; Lighting, Robin A. Paterson; Set, Robin A. Paterson; Costumes, Nicole Montemarono; Sound, Trystan Tazon; Co-Producers, Janice L. Goldberg, Kristine Niven; Cast: Ashlie Atkinson, Kyle Groff, Frank Deal, Arthur French, John Calvin Kelly, Cynthia Mace, Jennifer Laine Williams; Theatre 54; December 1–19, 2010

The Rubber Room by Gary Garrison and Roland Tec; Director, Janice L. Goldberg, Kathleen Brant, Dan Dinero, Mathew Shepard, Michael Rock; Stage Manager, Seymour, Amy VonVett, Leta Tremblay, Clay Martin, Lori Lundquist; Lighting, Marie Yokoyama; Set, Yoon Choi; Costumes, Nicole Montemarno; Producers, Janice L. Goldberg, Kristine Niven; Cast: Cooper Shaw, Allison Goldberg, Richard Hoehler, Jacob Callie Moore, Kristine Niven, Jill Melanie Wirth, Kari Swenson Riely, Ben Sumrall, Mary Ruth Baggott, Dan Patrick Brady, Sheila Stasack, Cecily Benjamin, John Calvin Kelly, John Brady, Amanda Ladd; Produced in association with the Workshop Theatre Company, Emerging Artists, Midtown Direct Rep; Theatre 54; February 9–20, 2011

Eclectic Evening of Shorts IV, Boxers & Briefs by Raphael Badagliacca ,William Fowkes, Drew Larimore, Joseph Gallo, Wayne Paul Mattingly, David Martin, Josh McIlvain, Patrick Nash, Randy Noojin, Charles Niven, Donald Steele, Bara Swain, Jeffrey Sweet, Jill Melanie Wirth, David Wirth; Director, Patricia Birch, Joseph Gallo, Heather Cohn, Scotty Watson, Megan Cooper, Clay Martin, Kelly Haran, Kristine Niven, Kathryn Long, Wendy Peace, Randy Noojin, Catherine Siracusa, Nick Stimler, David Wirth; Stage Manager, Leta Tremblay; Lighting, Marie Yokoyama; Producers, Janice L. Goldberg, Kristine Niven; Artistic Intern, Frank-Thomas Grogan; Cast: Douglas Manes, Wende O'Reilly, Wendy Joy Mercer, Quinn Warren, David Crommett, Josh Adler, Amanda Ladd, Frank Hankey, Margo Hammond, Zach Kleinsmith, Thomas McGinn, Kristine Niven, Bruce Colbert, Kati Brazda, Bill Tatum, Jason Hart, Ashley Rebecca King; Theatre 54; March 25–April 3, 2011

FESTIVALS

Go Solo! III; Huron Club at Soho Playhouse; November 29–December 1, 2010

A Mike and a Mirror Written and performed by Jane Marx, Director, Michael Morrow; *Stones* Written and performed by Margo Hammond, Director, Frank Hankey; *Getting Back Shantel* by Drew Larimore; *Rap* by Soce, Director, Ethan Matthews, Cast: Jeff Randal Rose; *Overheard* Written and performed by Larry Rosen; *In This Economy* Written and performed by Mark Levine, Director, Jo Bellamo; *A Shaman in My House* Written and performed by Karen Shasha, Director, David Schecter; *No Childhood Left Behind* Written and performed by Robin Goldfin, Original Music, Oren Neiman, Director, David L. Carson; *Friends* Written and performed by Mike Toro; *Famous* Written and performed by Sandi Carroll, Director, Jane Nichols; *When I Grow Up* by Donald Steele, Director, Michael Boonstra, Cast: Luke Hubbard; *American Addict* by Ricky Butler, Director, Ron Barba, Cast: Ricky Butler; *Jewish Female Geriatric Rap* Written and performed by Dev Rogers, Music by Don Slovin

READINGS AND WORKSHOPS

The New Me by Margo Hammond; Director, Kathryn Long; Shetler Studios; October 17, 2010

Impromtu-tu Written and performed by Scotty Watson; Bridge Theatre; November 17, 2010

After Anne Frank Written and performed by Carol Lempert; Director, Janice L. Goldberg; Bridge Theatre; April 17, 2011

Artists Empire

www.artistsempirepictures.com

Keep Your Baggage With You (at all times) by Jonathan Blitstein; Director, Daniel Talbott; Choreographer, David Anzuelo; Lighting, Benjamin Tevelow; Set, Eugenia Furneaux-Arends; Costumes, Tristan B. Raines; Sound, Janie Bullard;

Cast: Daniel Abeles, Jessica Dickey, Nate Miller, Laura Ramadei, Danielle Devito, Sanford Wilson, Sam Horwith; Theater for the New City; September 16–28, 2010

Astoria Performing Arts Center

www.apacny.org

Executive Director, Taryn Sacramone; Artistic Director, Tom Wojtunik; Production Manager, Annie Jacobs; Marketing Director, Dave Charest; Press, Katie Rosin; Casting Director, Wojcik|Seay; Resident Seter, Michael P. Kramer

MilkMilkLemonade by Joshua Conkel; Director, José Zayas; Stage Manager, Alex Mark; Lighting, Bruce Steinberg; Set, Jason Simms; Costumes, Sydney Maresca; Sound, David Margolin Lawson; Choreographer, Nicole Beerman; Cast: Jess Barbagallo, Nikole Beckwith, Michael Cyril Creighton, Jennifer Harder, Andy Phelan; Good Shepherd United Methodist Church; October 28–November 13, 2010

The Human Comedy Music by Galt MacDermot, Libretto by William Dumaresq, From the Story by William Saroyan; Director, Tom Wojtunik; Music Director, Jeffrey Campos; Stage Manager, Olivia O'Brien; Choreographer and Associate Director, Christine O'Grady; Lighting, Dan Jobbins; Set, Michael P. Kramer; Costumes, Hunter Kaczorowski; Sound, David A. Thomas; Props Designer, Ashlee Springer; Cast: Amie Bermowitz, Nathan Brisby, Victoria Bundonis, Chris Causer, Philip Deyesso, Jonathan Gregg, Tauren Hagans, Deidre Haren, Marcie Henderson, Rayna Hickman, D. William Hughes, Michael Jones, Andrew Leggieri, Aaron J. Libby, Jean Liuzzi, Douglas Lyons, Anthony Pierini, Richard Vernon, Rachel Rhodes-Devey; Good Shepherd United Methodist Church; May 5–May 28, 2011

FESTIVAL

The 4th Annual New York One-Minute Play Festival; Good Shepherd United Methodist Church; September 25–26, 2010

Playwrights: David Simpatico, Daniel McCoy, Michael Golmaco, Meghan Sass, Webb Wilcoxen, Pat Lin, Joshua Conkel, Matt Gunn Park, Corina Copp, Laurel Haines, Erica Saleh, Bekah Brunstetter, Janine Nabers, Alexis Clements, Eric Bland, Peter Gil-Sheraton, Jen Silverman, Mallery Avidon, Anna Moench, Eric Winick, Maya Macdonald, Paul Thureen & Hannah Bos, James Carter, Tanya Saracho, Micah Bucey, Tom X. Chao, Rose Martula, Andrea Ciannavei, Enrique Urueta, Ben Cikanek, Liz Duffy Adams, Michael Bradford, Robert Saietta, Tommy Smith, Alejandro Morales, Avi Glickstein, Matthew Paul Olmos, Michael John Garces, Adam Szymkowicz, Callie Kimball, Sibyl Kempson, Caridad Svich, Clay McLeod Chapman, Anton Dudley, Qui Nguyen, & Saviana Stanescu; Directors: Robert Ross Parker, Scott Ebersold, Jordana Williams, Dominic D'Andrea, Morgan Gould, Melanie Williams, Tom Wojtunik; Cast: Ronan Babbitt, Scott Rad Brown, Richard D. Busser, Becky Comtois, James Comtois, Rachel Craw, Brian Ferrari, Keely Flaherty, Jenny Gom, Tommy Hettrick, Christine Holt, Katie Iacona, Hana Kalinksi, Matthew Kinney, Anna La Madrid, Preston Martin, Chris Masullo , Sophie Mears, Colin Murphy, Tom Pecinka, Ian Quinlan, Jen Ring, Emily Riordan, Seth Shelden, Marc Sinoway, Andrea Marie Smith, Jennifer Gordon Thomas, Megan Tusing, Temar Underwood, Amir Wachterman, Jacob Wilhelmi, Sean Williams, TJ Witham, Catherine Yeager

READINGS AND WORKSHOPS

Doctoring by Nastaran Ahmadi; Director, Jessi D. Hill; Stage Manager, Amanda Johnson; Cast: Corena Chase, Jon Levenson, Brian McManamon, Jenny Seastone Stern; Good Shepherd United Methodist Church; September 16, 2010

The Groaning Board by Wendy MacLeod; Director, Moritz von Stuelpnagel; Stage Manager: Alex Mark; Cast: Brielle Silvestri, Matt D'Amico, Richmond Hoxie, Chris Kipniak, Susie Pourfar, Patricia Randell, Matthew Wilkas, Gameela Wright; Good Shepherd United Methodist Church; December 9, 2010

It Is Done by Alex Goldberg; Director, Tom Wojtunik; Cast: Amanda Johnson, Matt Kalman, Catia Ojeda, Ean Sheehy; Good Shepherd United Methodist Church; February 10, 2011

Afterglow (A Comedie of Bad Manners) by Sarah Overman; Director, Jessi D. Hill; Cast: Amanda Johnson, Dan Amboyer, Erin Buckley, Susan Ferrara, Emily Hagburg, Ryan Hilliard, Jared McGuire, Catia Ojeda; Good Sheperd United Methodist Church; March 28, 2011

Hand to God by Robert Askins; Director, Dylan McCullough; Cast: Jonathan Gregg, Steven Boyer, Geneva Carr, Frank Deal, Kevin O'Donnell, Amelia Pedlow; Good Shepherd United Methodist Church; May 23, 2011

Ateh Theater Group

Weekend at an English Country Estate by Sara Montgomery; Director, Paul Urcioli; Stage Manager, Darryllee VanOudenhove; Lighting, Carlton Ward; Set, Sara C. Walsh; Costumes, Katja Andreiev; Cast: Mick Lauer, Alyssa Lott, Madeleine Maby, Sara Montgomery, Julia Moss, Elizabeth Neptune, Jacques Roy, Joe Stipek, Charlie Wilson; Access Theater; October 14–31, 2010

Athena Theatre

www.AthenaTheatre.com

Artistic Director: Veronique Ory

Beirut by Alan Bowne; Director, Zoppa Brothers; Stage Manager, Cassie Dorland; Lighting, Ross Graham; Set, Joseph C. Heitman; Costumes, Hadas Tzur; Sound, Colin J. Whitely; Technical Director, Chimmy Anne Gunn; Assistant Stage Managers, Ruth Gersh and James W. Guido; Scenic Artist and Props Master, Jon Knust; Fight Choreographer, Robert Tuftee; Producer, Athena Theatre Company, Exhibit Z, Stephen P. Palmese; Cast: Meital Dohan, Sammi Rotibi, Tony Ray Rossi, Veronique Ory, Paul Bomba, Russell Jordan; Theatre Row; January 5–January 22, 2011

READINGS AND WORKSHOPS

Waking Up by Augusto Federico Amador; Director, Erma Duricko; Cast: Bobby Brower, Brionne Davis, Veronique Ory, Aldo Pisano, Ryan Castro; Primary Stages; November 8, 2011

The Australian-America Production Company

www.productioncompany.org

Goodbye New York, Goodbye Heart by Lally Katz; Director, Oliver Butler; Stage Manager, Jeff Meyers; Lighting, Carolyn Wong; Set, Valerie Bart; Costumes, Carolyn Hoffmann; Sound, Asa Wember; Cast: Nicolle Bradford, Brian Robert Burns, Erin Maya Darke, Andrew Dawson, Ryan King, Polly Lee, Samantha Sherman, Danielle Slavick, Lucy Walters, Rae C. Wright; HERE Arts Center; December 1–21, 2010

Bandwagon Productions

www.baltimoreinblackandwhite.com

Baltimore in Black and White by Jason Odell Williams; Director, Charlotte Cohn; Choreographer, Tocarra Cash; Lighting, Lauren Parrish; Set, David L. Arsenault; Costumes, Carolyn Hoffmann-Schneider; Sound, Asa Wember; Cast: Christopher Burris, Judy Jerome, Paul Perroni, Chris Burke, Anthony Vaughn Merchant, Charleigh E. Parker, Catia Ojeda, Sdrina Renee; the cell; May 11–21, 2011

Julie Yarwood, John Philip, Linda Elizabeth Freund, Andrew Loren Resto, Philip Stoehr, Brandon Ruckdashel, Barbara Mundy and Courtney Jean Allen in the Manhattan Theatre Source production of Two Steps Forward (photo by Bruce-Michael Gelbert)

Madelyn Schwartz, Emelise Aleandri, Seth Blum, and Tommy J. Dose in Hush The Musical, presented by Charles "Rooc" Mandracchia in association with Frizzi & Lazzi Theatre Company

Bill Connington in Razors Edge Productions' Princes of Darkness (photo by Beau Allulli)

Denny Lawrence, Christa Kimlicko Jones, Nick Cianfrogna, William Franke, Helen Merino, and Heather Hill in Theatre East's production of The Soldier Dreams (photo by Sherri Jackson)

Jarret Kerr, Tommy Nelms, Sarah Wharton, and Angelica Reeve in Percival's Big Night presented by Organs of State (photo by the Kathleen Ching)

Vit Horejs in a scene from Kacha and the Devil, *presented by the Czechoslovak-American Marionette Theatre (photo by Lee Wexler)*

Emily Hartford in Rabbit Hole Ensemble's The Tragic Story of Doctor Frankenstein *(photo by Edward Elefterion)*

Nora Martinez DeBenedetto, Paige O'Malley, Brian Morgan, Tom Tyburski, Florence Pape, and David Plotka in Little Red *presented by Phoenix Theatre Ensemble (photo by John Crittenden)*

(Clockwise from top): Keith Chandler, Anna Foss Wilson, Evelyn Sullivan, and Tim Donovan in Transatlantica *at the Operating Theater (photo by Peter Hoerburger)*

Brian Dykstra, Susan Ferrara, and Lori Prince in First Prize, *presented by kef theatrical productions (photo by Ry Pepper)*

Barefoot Theatre Company

www.barefoottheatrecompany.org

Producing Artistic Director, Francisco Solorzano; Co-Artistic Director, Nicole Haran; Managing Director, Victoria Malvagno; Producing Director, Christopher Whalen; Literary Manager, Therese Plaehn

Emergency Used Candles by Ciara Montlto; Director, Victoria Malvagno; Stage Manager, John Beverly; Lighting, Josh Iacovelli; Set, Tom Lenz; Costumes, Victoria Malvagno; Sound, Francisco Solorzano; Understudy/Assistant Stage Manager, Samantha Fontana; Dramaturg, Nicole Haran.; Cast: Samantha Fontana; The Cherry Lane Theatre (Studio Theatre); November 4–20, 2010

Teeth Of The Sons by Joseph Sousa; Director, Nicole Haran; Stage Manager, Charles Casano; Lighting, Niluka Hotaling; Set, Josh Iacovelli; Costumes, Victoria Malvagno; Sound, Francisco Solorzano; Producing Director, Christopher Whalen; Associate Producing Director, Cristina Fernandez; Assistant Stage Manager, Michael Pierre Louis; Cast: Will Allen, Casander M.J. Lollar, Shayna Padovano, Joseph Sousa, Donald P. Flories; The Cherry Lane Theatre (Studio Theatre); April 11–May 14, 2011

READINGS AND WORKSHOPS

2nd Annual bareNaked Reading Series by Jose Rivera, Kristoffer Diaz, Lucy Boyle, Mike Reiss, Jason Furlani, Kyle Bradstreet; Director, Nicole Haran, Debra Kempermier, Pamela Seiderman, Heidi Hendlesman, John Hurley; Cast: Francisco Solorzano, Therese Plaehn, Gabe Fazio, John Ventigmilia, Caitlin Fitzgerald, Sally Wingert, John Gazzale, Jeremy Brena, Charles Everett, Socorro Santiago, Patrizia Hernandez, T. Ryder Smith, Roderick Nash, Lisa Anderson, Anna Chlumsky; The Cherry Lane Theatre (Studio Theatre); November 15–30, 2010

bareNaked Reading Series LA by Israel Horovitz, Mike Reiss, Francisco Solorzano, Joseph Sousa, Daniel Graff, Lila Rose Kaplan, Courtney Sieberling, Tim Plaehn, Lina Patel; Director, Francisco Solorzano, Christopher Whalen, Therese Plaehn, Nicole Haran; Cast: Patricia Ricardson, Frank Collison, Christopher Whalen, Samantha Fontana, Francisco Solorzano, Therese Plaehn, Mike Rossi, Tyler Fascett, Will Allen, Alona Dadiani, Jerry O'Donnell, Joseph Sousa, Anika Solveig and live music by The Public Trust, Gina Pens; Art Of Acting Studio, Los Angeles, California; February 21–26, 2011

Sins Of The Mother Written and directed by Israel Horovitz; Cast: Chris Cooper, Ethan Hawke, Francisco Solorzano, Michael Stuhlbarg; Cherry Lane Theatre Mainstage; May 2, 2011

Basement Workshop Series Cast: Village Iliad Written and performed by Samantha Fontana; Director, Victoria Malvagno; Cherry Lane Theatre Studio Theatre; May 2–9, 2011

Barrow Street Theatre

Capsule 33 by Thaddeus Phillips and Tatiana Mallarino; Directed and performed by Thaddeus Phillips; September 17–October 16, 2010

The BE Company

www.thebecompany.org

Sex on Sunday by Chisa Hutchinson; Director, Jade King Carroll; Original Music, Fritz Myers; Stage Manager, Kelly Vieau; Lighting, Ian DelDuca; Set, Jay Rohloff; Costumes, Ashley Farra; Sound, Fritz Myers; Cast: Amber Gray, Jeremy Rishe, Nedra McClyde, Nyahale Allie, Lolita Foster, Benton Greene; Urban Stages; March 19–April 3, 2011

The Beautiful Soup Theater Collective

www.beautifulsoupweebly.com

Hamlet by William Shakespeare; Director, Steven Carl McCasland; Choreographer, Ellyn Stein; Stage Manager, Griffin Parker; Lighting, Gabriella DeGaetano; Sound, Steven Carl McCasland; Cast: Rory Allan Meditz, John Johmann, John Caldara, Jackie Jacobi, Tracy Jennissen, Kristen Vaphides, Kathleen Moran; Horse Trade Theatre–Red Room; November 5–14, 2010

The Berserker Residents

The Annihilation Point by Tim Sawicki; Director, Dan Rothenberg; Stage Manager, Jonathan Welsh; Lighting, James Jackson; Set, Lisi Stoessel; Costumes, Alisa Sickora Kleckner; Sound, Mark Valenzuela; Technical Director, Rajiv Shah; Cast: Justin Jain, David Johnson, Bradley K Wrenn; Abrons Arts Center; January 9–16, 2011

Billie Holiday Theatre

www.thebillieholiday.org

Brothers from the Bottom Written and directed by Jackie Alexander; Stage Manager and Lighting, Avan; Set, Felix E. Cochren; Costumes, Helen L. Simmon-Collen; Assistant Stage Manager, Jaime Durant; Cast: Nicoye Banks, Thaddeus Daniels, Warner Miller, Neko Parham, Anja Lee, Joy Hooper; October 15–19, 2010

The Legend of Buster Neal Written and directed by Jackie Alexander; Stage Manager and Lighting, Avan; Set, Felix E. Cochren; Costumes, Helen L. Simmons-Collen; Cast: Charles Anthony Burks, Sidiki Fofana, Stephen Hill, Dennis Johnson, Patrick Mitchell, Nathan Purdee; February 18–March 27, 2011

The Right Reverend Dupree in Exile Written and directed by Jackie Alexander; Stage Manager and Lighting, Avan; Set, Felix E. Cochren; Costumes, Helen L. Simmons-Collen; Cast: Ralph McCain, Marcelle Gover, Brandon Jones, Eboni Witcher, Rege C. Lewis; April 29–June 26, 2011

Bindlestiff Family Cirkus

www.bindlestiff.org

Executive Director, Keith Nelson; Artistic Director, Stephanie Monseu; Youth Program Director, Viveca Gardiner; Volunteer Coordinator, Ellia Bisker

Buckaroo Bindlestiff's Wild West Jamboree Written, Directed and performed by Keith Nelson and Stephanie Monseu; Set and Costumes, Stephanie Monseu; AV Designer, Keith Nelson; Rocking Horse Ranch, Highland NY; February 20–April 23, 2010

Buccaneer Bindlestiff's Swashbucking Cirkus Written, Directed and performed by Keith Nelson and Stephanie Monseu; Costumes, Stephanie Monseu; Sound, Keith Nelson; Pier 1, Riverside Park, NYC; July 22, 2010

Bindlestiff Family Cirkus Cabaret Written, Directed and performed by Keith Nelson and Stephanie Monseu; Musical Director, Francisco Monroy; Stage Manager, Ellia Bisker; Dixon Place, New York, NY; March 14–April 25, 2010

Bindlestiff Open Stage Variety Show Written, Directed and Stage Managed by Keith Nelson; Lighting, Sound and AV Design, Kris Anton; Galapagos Art Space; January 3–May 5, 2011

Bindlestiff Cavalcade of Youth; Director, Viveca Gardiner; Coney Island USA; November 7, 2010

Bindlestiff Family Cirkus Written, Directed and performed by Keith Nelson and Stephanie Monseu; Musical Director, Sabrina Chap; Spiegeltent, Bard College; June 2010

FESTIVALS

NYC Unicycle Festival Governors Island, Grant's Tomb, and a group ride from Brooklyn Bridge to Coney Island; September 3–5, 2010

Ghostwalk Hudson; Multiple venues in Hudson, NY; November 5, 2010

PRESENTED PRODUCTIONS

Shoebox Tour Produced by Shoebox–www.shoeboxtour.com; Pratt Institute; March 30, 2010

Hey Ya Brothers Produced by Hey Ya Brothers–www.heyyabrothers.com; The Point, Bronx, NY; June 19, 2010

The Bitter Poet

www.thebitterpoet.com

The Bitter Poet: Looking For Love In All The Wrong Black Box Performance Spaces; Under St Marks; February 25–March 6, 2011

Black Henna Productions

blackhennaproductions.com

The Unlikely Adventure of Race McCloud, Private Eye Director, Tom Hoefner; Original Music, Andrew Barkan; Choreographer, Eugene Solfanelli; Lighting, Ian McDonald; Costumes, Pavie Mirzaali; Art Design, Kevin Gillespie; Cast: Tom Brown, Cas Marino, Fiona Kearns; American Theatre of Actors; September 9 -19, 2010

Blessed Unrest

www.blessedunrest.org

Machinal by Sophie Treadwell; Director, Damen Scranton; Stage Manager, Jaimie Van Dyke; Lighting, Benjamin C. Tevelow; Set, Rachel Gilmore & Benjamin C. Tevelow; Costumes, Rachel Gilmore; Sound, Damen Scranton; Cast: Zenzelé Cooper, Eunjee Lee, Nurit Monacelli, Sophie Nimmanit, Celli Pitt, Darrell Stokes, Laura Wickens, Jason Winfield; Interart Annex; February 19–March 14, 2011

ArtCamp SexyTime FootBall by Teddy Jefferson, Matt Opatrny, Damen Scranton and the Ensemble; Director, Jessica Burr; Choreographer, Jessica Burr; Stage Manager, Jaimie Van Dyke; Lighting, Benjamin C. Gevelow; Set, Rachel & Benjamin C. Gevelow; Costumes, Rachel Gevelow; Sound, Damen Scranton; Cast: Dave Edson, Nick Micozzi, Catherine Gowl, Jason Griffin, Vaishnavi Sharma, Ian Wen, Laura Wickens; Interart Annex; May 5–23, 2011

READINGS AND WORKSHOPS

ArtCamp SexyTime FootBall WorkShop With text by Teddy Jefferson and Matt Opatrny; Director, Jessica Burr; Stage Manager, Jaimie Van Dyke; Lighting, Rachel Gevelow; Cast: Dave Edson, Catherinc Gowl, Jason Griffin, Nick Micozzi, Sophie Nimmannit, Damen Scranton, Laura Wickens; Interart Theatre; December 3, 2010

The Storm by Aleksandr Ostrovsky, translated and adapted by Laura Wickens; Director, Jessica Burr; Stage Manager, Jaimie Van Dyke; Lighting, Michael McGee; Cast: Dave Edson, Catherine Gowl, Jason Griffin, Eunjee Lee, Sophie Nimmannit, Darrell Stokes, April Sweeney, David Townsend, Ian Wen; Interart Theatre; December 18, 2010

PRESENTED PRODUCTIONS

Music Mélange Stage Manager, Jaimie Van Dyke; Cast: Amir Vahab, Paul Brill, Threeds, Sean Statser, Nuno Antunes, Adrien Morejen, Boris Shpitalnik, Matt Muszynski, Ed Gonzales, Hannah Wilson & Vaishnavi Sharma; Interart Theatre; March 25–26, 2011

How Do You Do? A Cabaret. Produced and Performed by Celli Pitt; Musical Director Gerard Barnes; Interart Theatre; June 18, 2011

Blue Roses Productions

Tom's Children by Kara Lee Corthron, Gary Giovannetti, Tom Matthew Wolfe, John Yearley, Richard Cottrell, Dawson Moore and Craig Pospisil; Director, Erma Duricko; Stage Manager, Megan Smith; Lighting, Joanna Emmott; Sound, Tim Brown; Producer, Karen Eterovich; Cast: Dominic Comperatore, Marissa Danielle Duricko, Heather Lee Harper, Jim Ireland, Blair Sams, George Sheffey; Abingdon Theater Mainstage; January 28–30, 2011

BOO-Arts Productions

www.boo-arts.com

Founder and Artistic Director: Kathleen O'Neill, Founder and Producing Director Dana Monagan; Social Media Director, London Griffith

READINGS AND WORKSHOPS

A Daughter of Israel by David Stallings; Director, Kathleen O'Neill; Stage Manager, London Griffith; Cast: Melanie Brook, Daniella Chai, Melissa Dugherty, Shira Kobren and Adi Kurtchik; Looking Glass Theatre; November 11–21, 2010

The Addicts by Ed Malin; Director, Kathleen O'Neill; Manhattan Theatre Source; April 9, 2010

Boomerang Theatre Company

www.boomerangtheatre.org

The Tempest by William Shakespeare; Director, Sara Thigpen; Stage Manager, Laura Gomez; Costumes, Annie Simon; Assistant Director, Beth Ann Leone; Assistant Stage Manager, Michelle Foster; Cast: Spencer Aste, Kent Burnham, David Carlyon, Bob D'Haene, Jonathan Dewberry, Jason Loughlin, Catherine McNelis, Vinnie Penna, Shannon Thomason, Christian Toth, Amanda Tudor, Luis Vega, Schylar Westbrook; Central Park, NYC; June 19–July 18, 2010

Venus Observed by Christopher Fry; Director, Cailin Heffernan; Stage Manager, Kate Erin Gibson; Lighting, Kia Rogers; Set, Nikki Black; Costumes, Cheryl McCarron; Sound, Jacob Subotnick; Special Effects, Joseph Mathers; Cast: Spencer Aste, Saluda Camp, John Greenleaf, Samantha Ives, Ryan Lee, Jason Loughlin, Thea McCartan, Paul Nugent, Buzz Roddy, Kristen Vaughan; The Connelly Theater; September 9–October 3, 2010

Uncle Vanya by Anton Chekhov; Director, Philip Emeott; Stage Manager, Stephanie Brookover; Lighting, Kia Rogers; Set, Nikki Black; Costumes, Cheryl McCarron; Sound, Jacob Subotnick; Fight Director, Carrie Brewer; Prop Designer, Stephanie Cox-Williams; Cast: Richard Brundage, Lauren Kelston, James Leach, Joseph Mathers, Dolores McDougal, Ann Parker, Ed Schultz, Eve Udesky, Bill Weeden; The Connelly Theater; September 11–October 10, 2010

Endless Summer Nights by Tim Errickson; Director, Christopher Thomasson; Stage Manager, Michelle Foster; Lighting, Kia Rogers; Set, Nikki Black; Costumes, Cheryl McCarron; Sound, Jacob Subotnick; Props Designer, Stephanie Cox-Williams; Assistant Stage Manager, Samantha Steiger; Cast: Becky Byers, Bret Hoskins, Synge Maher, Michael Criscuolo, Joe Mathers, Nora Hummel; The Connelly Theater; September 17–October 9, 2010

Brave New World Repertory Theatre

www.bravenewworldrep.org

Producer/Artistic Director, Claire Beckman; Managing Director, David Frutkoff; Associate Artistic Director, John Morgan, Cynthia Babak; Creative Consultant, Amy Ilias; Education Director, Stacey Cervellino

As You Like It by William Shakespeare; Director, Claire Beckman; Cast: Cynthia Babak, William Brenner, Nixon Cesar, Karl Greenberg, Dave Hall, Kevin Hogan, Catherine Mancuso, John Edmond Morgan, Eleanor Ruth, Joe Salgo, Stephen Sheffer, Franny Silverman, Christine Siracusa, Scott Voloshin, Kimber-Lee Alston, Dilya Kurbonova, Christina Offley; The Oriental Pavilion in Prospect Park; July 22–August 12, 2010

The American Clock, a vaudeville based in part on Studs Terkel's Hard Times by Arthur Miller; Director, Cynthia Babak; Music Director, Amanda Gookin; Stage Manager, Nataliya Vasilyeva; Lighting, Simon Cleveland; Set, John Morgan; Costumes, Lisa Renee Jordan; Sound, Benjamin Furiga; AV Design, Cynthia Babak; Producer, Claire Beckman; Assistant Director, Kellie Mecleary; Assisstant Stage Manager Patrick Mahaney; Austin Bransgrove, Assistant Lighting; Choreographer, Caroline Ryburn; Pianist, Andy Arena; Musicians, Chris Cornwall, Mark August, Amanda Gook; Cast: Andy Arena, Mark August, Alice Barrett-Mitchell, Doug Barron, Tara Bast, Claire Beckman, Nixon Cesar, Chris Cornwall, Gary Cowling, Isidore Elias, Jeff Golde, Alvin Hippolyte, Kevin Hogan, Cathy Mancuso, John Morgan, Caroline Ryburn, Joe Salgo, Stuart Zagnit, Kevin Hogan, Joe Salgo, John Edmond Morgan, Scott Voloshin, Evan Thompson, Claire Beckman, Sandra Mills Scott, Franny Silverman, Alice Barrett-Mitchell, Tara Bast; Brooklyn Lyceum; March 3–13, 2011

Brick Theater

www.bricktheater.com

Theater of the Arcade: Five Classic Video Games Adapted for the Stage by Jeff Lewonczyk; Director, Gyda Arber; Original Music, Frank Padellaro and Chris Chappell; Lighting, Ian W. Hill; Cast: Fred Backus, Hope Cartelli, Stephen Heskett, Kent Meister, Josh Mertz, Robert Pinnock, Shelley Ray; The Brick Theater; July 13, 2010–July 25, 2010

The Tremendous Tremendous by Marc Bovino, Joe Curnutte and Stephanie Wright Thompson; Director, Jeff Withers; Musical Director, Michael Dalto; Stage Manager, Karina Martins; Lighting, Mike Inwood; Set, The Mad Ones; Costumes, Sydney Gallas; Sound, Stowe Nelson; Makeup Design, Michale Anthony; Cast: Marc Bovino, Joe Curnutte, Michael Dalto, Stephanie Wright Thompson, Henry Vick; Co-Produced with The Mad Ones The Brick; March 31–April 16, 2011

The Little Chaos Director, Stiven Luka; Lighting and Set, William Moody; Costumes, Enver Chakartash; Cast: Brock Harris, Ronald Peet, Raimonda Skeryte; The Brick; April 21–30, 2011

Time: A Complete Explanation in Three Parts Cast: Alejandro Acierto, Gelsey Bell, Brian McCorkle, Esther Neff, Paul Pinto, Matthew Stephen Smith, Jeffrey Young; Co-produced with Panoply Performance Laboratory (PPL) and thingNY; The Brick; May 4–14, 2011

Guide and Infinite Progress Cast: Cara Sheffler and Luke Cissell; Co-produced with New Madrid Productions;The Brick; May 19 – 20, 2011

FESTIVALS

Too Soon Festival; Brick Theater; June 6–24, 2010; Included: *Happily After Tonight* Written and directed by Mateo Moreno; *Death is a Scream* Written and performed by Esther Crow, Director, Rabeah Ghaffari; *Chemistry* Written and performed by Danny Bowes and Jillian Tully, Director, Danny Bowes; *Jeannine's Abortion: A Play in One Trimester* by Eric Bland, Director, Hope Cartelli; *That Old Soft Shoe* by Matt Freeman, Director, Kyle Ancowitz, Produced by Blue Coyote Theater Group; *Redbeard and Domicella* by Kasia Nikhamina, Director,

Michael Rau, Produced by Hearth Gods; *Hack! an I.T. Spaghetti Western* by Crystal Skillman, Director, John Hurley, Produced by Impetuous Theater Group; *Dandilion and the Bicycle Powered Cloud Plane* by Heather Coffey and Andy Hadaway, Director, Heather Coffey, Produced by The Tiny Black Hearts; *RIP JD: A Celebration of Death* by Erin Austin and Ross Evans, Director, Ross Evans, Produced by Plastic Flamingo

New York Clown Theatre Festival; Brick Theater; September 3–26, 2010; Included: *Manchego: The Birth of Cheese* Written and directed by Ambrose Martos; *How to Give Up on Your Dreams: Without Really Trying* Written and directed by Bony Lil; *Send In the Angels* Produced by CDCC Productions; *Perhaps, Perhaps Quizás* Produced by Clown Me In; *Clowns in Gowns* Written and directed by Adrianna Chavez and Heidi Rider; *Coney Island Chris* Written and directed by Chris Allison; *The Kapinski Private Eye Academy* Produced by F.O. Fire; *A-Dressing History* Produced by Fool's Academy; *The Wow Show* Produced by Have Vaude-Ville Travel Productions; *Channel One* Produced by James and JF; *Neon Lights* Written and performed by Jeff Seal and Chris Manley, Director, Danny Manley; *Hula Hell is Miss Saturn* Produced by Miss Saturn; *The Last Show You'll Ever See* Produced by Nomadic Theatre; *Ms. Pretty Smart, Secret Agent* Written, directed and performed by Olivia Lehrman; *Legs and All* Written, directed and performed by Summer Shapiro and Peter Musante; *Carmen the Mopera* Director, Avner Eisenberg, Produced by The Eccentric Company; *Cirkus Luna!* Produced by Theatre Group Dzieci; *Ferdinand the Magnificent!* Produced by Third Base!; *Morro and Jasp Do Puberty* Produced by Unit Productions

Broken Glass Theatre

www.brokenglasstheatre.org

Inferno by Kate Moran; Director, Kat Moran; Lighting, Taylor Tobin; Set, Ali Goldaper; Costumes, Erin Frumet; Sound, Anthony Jones; Adapted from Dante; Executive Producer, Nathan Zebedeo; Producer, Katie Chambers; Props Design, Ali Goldaper; Graphic Design, Miranda Leiggi; Cast: Robbie Baum, Danielle Devine, Sarah Knittel, Whit Leyenberger, Kamelle Mills, Clint Okayama, Nicole Roberts, Christina Stone, Terence Stone and Marchelle Thurman; Under St Marks; April 21–24, 2011

The Bushwick Starr

www.thebushwickstarr.org

In The Pony Palace/Football Written and directed by Tina Satter; Musical Arrangement, Chris Giarmo, Bobby McElver; Lighting, Zack Tinkleman; Set, Andrea Minic; Costumes, Michael DeAngelis; Cast: Moe Angelos, Jess Barbagallo, Eliza Bent, Nikki Calonge, Emily Davis, Erin Markey, Glennis McMurray, Kourtney Rutherford, Julia Sirna-Frest; Produced in association with Half Straddle; The Bushwick Starr; February 10-26, 2011

Here at Home by Eric Bland; Director, Shannon Sindelar; Lighting, Jon Luton; Set, Andreea Mincic; AV Design, Ryan Holsopple; Cast: D.J. Mendel, Hollis Witherspoon, Ryan Holsopple and Eric Blan; The Bushwick Starr; May 12–28, 2011

C.A.G.E. Theatre Company

The Tempest by William Shakespeare; Directors, Monica Alia and Michael Hagins; Cast: Michael Hagins, Molly Gilman, Rebecca Overholt, Enrique Huili, Thomas Cox, Sharon Cacciabaudo, Whitney Stone, Danny Sauls, Kenneth Scott Thompson, Ambar Aranaga, Daniel Largo; Looking Glass Theatre; September 16–19, 2010

Cake Productions

www.cakeproductions.org

Speaking in Tongues Director, Louis Wells; Stage Manager, Courtney Ferrell; Lighting, Jessica Burgess; Set, Lea Anello; Costumes, Mark Caswell; Sound, Louis Wells; Cast: Brooke Berry, Joachim Boyle, Sarah Brill, Francesca Day, Christopher Halladay, Christopher McLinden, Bryan Kaplan, Marta Kuersten, David Douglas; NYTW's 4th Street Theatre; November 4–20, 2010

Canal Park Playhouse

www.canalparkplayhouse.com

Properties of Play Director, Shea Elmore; Production Coordinator, Serena Pomerantz; Cast: Amanda Miller, Carolyn McCandlish, Julio Peña, Sarah-Doe Osborne; Canal Park Playhouse; November 29–January 1, 2011

Cantwell/Newsom Productions

Avenue of the Americas by Martin Blank; Director, Katherine M. Carter; Cast: Virginia Bartholomew, Timothy J. Cox, Chris Davis, Leo Goodman, Laura Yost; 45th Street Theatre; January 21–February 6, 2011

Castillo Theatre

www.castillo.org

Artistic Director, Dan Friedman; Managing Director, Diane Stiles; Theatre Sales and Marketing Director, Gail Peck; Resident Scenic and Video Designer, Joseph Spirito; Technical Director, Kenneth Horgan; Youth Onstage! Program Manager, Craig Pattison

The Proverbial Loons in Musical Improv Comedy at Castillo Director, David Nackman; Musical Director, Frank Spitznagel; Stage Manager, Juanda Hall, Fulton Hodges; Set, Joseph Spirito; Costumes, Emilie Charlotte; Producer, Kate Henselmans; Coach, Tara Copeland; Cast: David Nackman, J.B. Opdycke, Andy Parker, Marian Rich, Cathy Rose Salit, Frank Spitznagel; Castillo Theatre; October 2010–June 2011

Playing with Heiner Muller by Heiner Muller; Translated by Carl Weber, Helen Fehervary, Sue-Ellen Case and Marc D. Silberman; Music and Lyrics by Fred Newman; Director, Gabrielle L. Kurlander; Music Director, David Belmont; Stage Manager, Sean McCain; Lighting, Rachelle Beckerman; Set, Joseph Spirito; Costumes, EmilieCharlotte; Sound, David Belmont; AV Design, Paula Miranda, Joseph Spirito; Producer, Jim Horton; Choreographer, Lonne Moretton; Music Producer, Michael Walsh; Assistant Director, Antoine RL Joyce; Additional texts by Fred Newman and Nichelle Brown; Cast: Keldrick Crowder, Fulton C. Hodges, Ava Jenkins, Sylenia Lewis, John Rankin III; Castillo Theatre; November 5–December 12, 2010

Mr. Hirsch Died Yesterday by Fred Newman; Director, Woodie King Jr.; Stage Manager, Fulton C. Hodges; Lighting, John Eckert; Set, Joseph Spirito; Costumes, Carolyn Adams, EmilieCharlotte; Sound, David Belmont; AV Design, Paula Miranda, Joseph Spirito; Producer, Jessica Massad; Dramaturg, Dan Friedman; Cast: Lindsay Arber, Dana Berger, Debbie Buchsbaum, Lenora B. Fulani, Zoe Geltman, Joseph Mallon, Reynaldo Piniella, Ben Prayz, Katya Pucci, Moshe Yassur; Castillo Theatre; January 21–February 20, 2011

Young Playwrights from Castillo (Part One): *Nine Falls from Grace: The Political Guide to Navigating Heaven* by Darnelle Cadet, *I Am What I Am Not* by William H.E.J. Santos, *Bruised* by Sita Sarkar; Director, Ruby Lawrence, Ben Vershbow, Brittney Jensen; Lighting, Mike Megliola; Set, Damon Avent; Costumes, EmilieCharlotte, May Chan, Carla Rey Rowe; Festival Director, Craig Pattison; Festival Producer, L. Thecla Farrell; Cast: Michael Alcide, Jessica

Garcia, Kristal Geraldino, George Hawkins, Randy Higgins, Aliyaa Lambert, Shalisha McIntosh, Shaakirah Medford, Luz Monica Montanez, Jeanell Reynoso, Renea Speed; Castillo Theatre; March 4–6, 2001

License to Dream by Fred Newman; Director, David Nackman; Musical Director, David Belmont, Michael Walsh; Stage Manager, Lauren Williams; Lighting, John Eckert; Set, Joseph Spirito; Costumes, EmilieCharlotte; AV Design, Paula Miranda, Joseph Spirito; Producer, John Rankin III; Production Supervisor, Jim Horton; Assistant Director, David Blasher; Music, David Truskinoff; Lyrics, Fred Newman; Choreographer, Javier Dzul; Dance Captain, Robin Taylor; Cast: Ivanova Aguilar, Kyla Ernst Alper, Cornelius Brown, Kimarra Cannonier, Christian Colon, Melissa Rose Corning, Lauren Curet, Ty Evans, Rosemarie Madera, Matthew Sparks, Robin Taylor; Castillo Theatre; April 29–June 5, 2011

Che by Mario Fratti; Director, Madelyn Chapman; Stage Manager, Sharon R. Brown; Lighting, Rachelle Beckerman; Set, Joseph Spirito; Costumes, EmilieCharlotte; Sound, Sean O'Halloran; AV Design, Joseph Spirito; Assistant Director, Peter Cook; Dramaturg, Dan Friedman; Producer, Jim Horton; Cast: Purba Atandrila, Randy Higgins, Leticia King, Joneise McCrae, Samantha Randolph, Esteban Rodriguez-Alverio, Rejinal Simon, Faith Vann; Castillo Theatre; May 7–June 6, 2010

Risky Revolutionary by Fred Newman; Director, David Nackman; Stage Manager, Ellen Korner; Lighting, Rachelle Beckerman; Set, Joseph Spirito; Costumes, EmilieCharlotte; Sound, Sean O'Halloran; AV Design, Joseph Spirito; Dramaturg, Dan Friedman; Producer, Diane Stiles; Cast: Arturo Castro, Luca Rodrigues, Chris Triana; Castillo Theatre; May 7–June 6, 2010

FESTIVALS

Mario Fratti-Fred Newman Political Play Series 2010; Castillo Theatre; August 2, 2010–August 23, 2010; Included: *The Third Crossing* by Debora Threedy, Director, Peter James Cook; *Put Your Trust* in God and Keep Your Powder Dry by Michael Vukadinovich, Director, Valentina Fratti; *Tangled* by Nicole Anderson-Cobb, Director, Woodie King Jr.; *Another Kind of Hunger* by Judith Marie Wallace, Director, Eric Vitale

Great Black Plays and Playwrights Series; Castillo Theatre; June 11, 2010–June 26, 2010; Included: *Meetings* by Mustapha Matura, Director, Seret Scott; *The Sty of the Blind Pig* by Phillip Hayes Dean, Director, Patricia White; *A Recent Killing* by Amiri Baraka, Director, Hampton V. Clanton; *What the Winesellers Buy* by Ron Milner, Director, Justin Lord; *Long Time Since Yesterday* by P.J. Gibson, Director, Bette Howard; *TopDog/UnderDog* by Suzan-Lori Parks, Director, Jamie Richards; *Wedding Band* by Alice Childress, Director, Chuck Smith; *Crumbs From the Table of Joy* by Lynn Nottage, Director, Marjorie Moon; *Flyin' West* by Pearle Cleage, Director, Lydia Fort

READINGS AND WORKSHOPS

Macbeth–a Youth Onstage! workshop by William Shakespeare; Director, Craig Pattison; Castillo Theatre; July 29–31, 2010

NON-REDISDENT PRODUCTIONS

Shirley Chisholm: Catalyst for Change by Ajene Washington; Adapted from speeches and writings by Shirley Chisholm; Director, Imani; Produced by Woodie King Jr.'s National Black Touring Circuit; Castillo Theatre; February 18–20, 2011

CELEBRITY AUTOBIGRAPHY

Gay Pride Edition Director, Eugene Pack & Dayle Reyfel; Cast: Rachel Dratch, Cheyenne Jackson, Kristen Johnston, John Cameron Mitchell, Eugene Pack, Dayle Reyfel, Bruce Vilanch, B.D. Wong; The Gramercy Theater; June 26, 2010

The Cell

www.thecelltheatre.org

Founding Artistic Director, Mancy Manocherian;Artistic Director, Kira Simring; Managing Director, Pat Jones; Director of Development & Marketing Garlia Cornelia Jones; Technical Director, Lee Terry; Web Director, Chris Gabriel

...And Then You Go On, An Anthology of the Works of Samuel Beckett Written and performed by Bob Jaffe; Director, Peter Wallace; Lighting, Lee Terry; Set, Jill Klinow Jaffe; Costumes, Marilyn Salvatore; The Cell; March 23–April 10, 2011

Centripetus Theatre Company

Spring Awakening: A Sin of Omission Adapted by Toby Bercovici and Emily Denison, based on the original by Frank Wedekind; Director, Toby Bercovici; Stage Manager, Alexandra Chilton; Lighting, Jonathan Hicks; Choreographer, Madelyne Camera; Assistant Stage Manager/Assistant Lighting, Imani Denson-Pittman; Cast: Duncan Grossman, Michael Greehan, Christian Hoots, Samuel Perry, Gregory Boover, Annelise Nielsen, Brittany Costa, Emma Cohen, Linda Tardif; Looking Glass Theatre; July 7–17, 2010

Charles "Rooc" Mandracchia in Association wit Frizzi& Lazzi Theatre Company

www.hushthemusical.com

Producer, Charles Mandracchia, Emelise Aleandri

Hush The Musical Libretto by Emelise Aleandri from a play by Etta Cascini; Director, Charles Mandracchia; Musical Director, Mitch Marcus; Cast: Seth Blum, Emelise Aleandri, Madelyn Schwartz, Tommy J. Dose, Elizabeth McMonagle; Triad Theatre NYC; May 19–26, 2011

Cheryl King Productions

www.stageleftstudio.net

Play Dead by William LoCasto; Director, Theresa Gambacorta; Cast: Jay Alvarez, Raissa Dorff, John Gazzale, Kathleen Locklar; Stage Left Studio; November 17–21, 2010

Fearless Moral Inventory by Frank Blocker; Director, Helena Gleissner; Lighting, Mary Catherine Moore; Set, Edward Morris; Costumes, Murray Scott Changar; Sound, Kenneth Allen; Choreographer, Kathy Kelly Christos; Stage Left Studio; February 15–June 28, 2010

Chicago City Limits

www.chicagocitylimits.com

Executive Producer, Paul Zuckerman; Linda Gelman, Producer; Julia Young, Associate Producer; Joe DeGise II, Resident Company Director; Rob Schiffmann, Touring Company Director

Chicago City Limits On Ice Director, Joe DeGise II; Musical Director, Andrew Resnick; Stage Managers and Lighting, Emilie Hanson, Sarah Mills; Cast: Joe DeGise II, Annie Schiffmann, Rob Schiffmann, Stefan Schick; Broadway Comedy Club; December 1, 2010

The Civilians

In the Footprint by Steven Cosson, Jocelyn Clarke; Original Music and Lyrics by Michael Friedman; Director, Steve Cosson; Cast: Matthew Dellapina, Greg McFadden, Colleen Werthmann, Billy Eugene Jones, Donnetta Lavinia Grays and Simone Moore; The Irondale Center; November 22–December 11, 2010

Clout in the Mug Productions

Dolores and North of Providence Director, Alberto Bonilla; Stage Manager, Jasmin Sanchez; Set, Rachel Kenner; Cast: John Golaszewski , Rebecca Nyahay, Sat Charn Fox , Rachel Cornish; Teatro La Tea; January 27–February 12, 2011

Clubbed Thumb

Roadkill Confidential by Sheila Callaghan; Director, Kip Fagan; Stage Manager, Sunneva Stapleton; Lighting, Jeanette Oi-Suk Yew; Set, Peter Ksander; Costumes, Jessica Pabst; Sound, Bart Fasbender; AV Design, Shaun Irons and Lauren Petty; Cast: Alex Anfanger, Rebecca Henderson, Polly Lee, Matthew Maguire and Danny Mastrogiorgio; 3LD Art and Technology Center; September 10–28, 2010

The Collective NY

www.thecollective-ny.org

Artistic Director: Victoria Dicce, Kevin Kane; Managing Director: Lisa Kicielinski, Robert Z. Grant

Someone Who'll Watch Over Me by Frank McGuinness; Director, Robert Z Grant; Stage Manager, Krista Amigone; Lighting, Alex Fabozzi; Set, Robert Z. Grant; Costumes, Krista Amigone; Sound, Mark Parenti; Executive Producers: Victoria Dicce, Nina Mehta, Jeff Berg; Cast: Kevin Kane, Brian Leider, Mike Houston; New York Theatre Workshop, and Teatro Circulo; June 17–August 8, 2011

The Common Tongue

www.tctnyc.org

Artistic Director: Lila Dupree, Danny Mitarotondo; Development Director, Shawn Kathryn Kane

Connect Five: Four Plays. *One Audience.* Included: *The Make-Out Queen, Last Night, Young, The Room and A Richard* by Bronwen Prosser, Wendy MacLeod, Danny Mitarotondo, Lucy Thurber; Directors, Kathryn Walsh, Karen Kohlhaas, Shannon Fillion, Mo Zhou; Stage Manager, Ellen Mezzera; Lighting, Colin Scott; Set, Sarah Muxlow; Producers, Danny Mitarotondo and Lila Dupree; Photographer, Suzi Sadler; Press, Emily Owens; Graphics, Houston Kraft; Cast: Lila Dupree, Sarah Kauffman, Kathleen Littlefield, Blaze Mancillas, Heather Oakley, Michael Pantozzi, Bronwen Prosser; The Ars Nova Building; January 5–16, 2011

READINGS AND WORKSHOPS

Color the Sky by Patrick Henry Flynn; Director, Danny Mitarotondo; Producer, Lila Dupree and Danny Mitarotondo; Cast: David Blais, Lila Dupree, Judith Jones, John Shea, Angelica Torn, Shai Trichter, Beth Woodard; The Geraldine Page Salon for the Arts; May 20, 2010

Company XIV

www.companyxiv.com

Nutcracker Rouge by Jeff Takacs; Directed and Choreographed by Austin McCormick; Lighting, Gina Scherr; Set, Props and Costumes, Zane Pihlstrom; Sound, Austin McCormick; Cast: Jeff Takacs,Michael Hodge, Sean Gannon, Mina Lawton, Marisol Cabrera,Yeva Glover, Davd Martinez, Marla Phelan, Delphina Parenti, Laura Careless; 303 Bond St Theater; December 10, 2010–January 9, 2011

Lover. Muse. Mockingbird. Whore. by Charles Bukowski; Director, Austin McCormick; Lighting, Gina Scherr; Set and Costumes, Zane Pihlstrom; 303 Bond Street; April 17–May 8, 2011

Le Cirque Feerique by Austin McCormick and Jeff Takacs; Director, Austin McCormick; Lighting, Gina Scherr; Set and Costumes, Zane Pihlstrom; Chorepgrapher, Austin McCormick; Cast: Marisol Cabrera, Laura Careless, Yeva Glover, Gioia Marchese, Austin McCormick, Davon Rainey and Jeff Takacs, Brooke Bryant, Brett Umlauf and Amber Youell; 303 Bond Street; May 9–June 6, 2010

Coyote REP Theatre Company

www.coyoterep.org

Questions My Mother Can't Answer Written and performed by Andrea Caban; Director, Rachel Eckerling; Stage Manager, Danielle Buccino; Lighting, Jason Byron Teague; Sound, Marcelo Añez; NYTW's 4th Street Theatre; August 15–27, 2010

The New Normal by Donnetta Lavinia Grays; Director, Isaac Byrne; Original Music, Mitch Greenhill; Stage Manager, Katie Chai; Lighting, Jason Byron Teague; Set, Patrick Gegen; Costumes, Emily Lippolis; Sound, Mitchell Greenhill; Co-Producer, Jack Sharkey; Fight Direction, Jacob Grigolia-Rosenbaum; Featured Art, Sandi Davis; Cast: Michael Mason, Nell Mooney, Andrea Caban, Emily Rossell; Wings Theatre; October 13–23, 2010

READINGS AND WORKSHOPS

The Dogwatcher by Emily Bohannan; Cast: Sameerah Luqmaan-Harris; Ripely-Grier Studios; May 2, 2011

Sick by Greg Ayers; Director, Paul Dobie; Cast: Chris Bert, Alex Brightman, Andrea Caban, Jessica Disalvo, Ben Hollandsworth, Brian Munn, Josh Odsess-Rubin, Tom Patterson, Anita Sabherwal; Ripley-Grier Studios; May 9, 2011

They Were Ours by Larry Manogue and William Walter White; Director, Elizabeth Gardiner; Cast: Rob Bradford, Le-Anne Garland, Jason Alan Griffin, Jeanne LaSala, Joel Leffert, Tim McKiernan, Teresa Meza, Josh Odsess-Rubin, Tom Patterson, chandra thomas; Ripley- Grier Studios; May 16, 2011

The Review by Donnetta Lavinia Grays; Director, Iaasc Byrne; Cast: Jeanne LaSala, Lea Robinson, Elizabeth Whitney, Ellen David; Ripley-Grier Studios; May 23, 2011

Creation Production Company

A World Apart by Susan Mosakowski; Director, Jean Radich; Lighting, Mark Barton; Set, Lee Savage; Costumes, Jennifer Moeller; Sound, Robert Murphy; Cast: Antoinette LaVecchia, Andy Paris, Amelia Workman; Flea Theater Mainstage; February 6–26, 2011

Crimson Kitty Productions

www.crimsonkitty.com

Guyz and Dollz Cast: Hosted by Harmonica Sunbeam & Tyra Allure Ross; Cast: Vouge Evolution, Rose Wood, Tyra Allure Ross, Harmonica Sunbeam, Switch N' Play, Bambi Galore, Go Go Harder Faster Stronger, Charlie Demos, Tiah Carrera, Carmen Carrera, Jerymiah Versali; China 1 Antique Lounge and Stage; June 13, 2010

Auralfixia: An Erotic Cabaret Cast: Juliet Jeske, Busty Kitten, Lydia Love, Charlie Demos, Audacia Ray; Bowery Poetry Club; August 5, 2010–December 2, 2010

Magick! A Sextacular Holiday Feast! Cast: Dame Cuchifrita,Brandon B., Rachel Cleary, Charlie Demos; Bowery Poetry Club; December 2, 2010–December 2, 2010

Cross-Eyed Bear Productions

www.duncanpflaster.com

Producer/Playwright, Duncan Pflaster

The Thyme of the Season Written and directed by Duncan Pflaster; Original Music, Matthew Applebaum; Costumes, Mark Richard Caswell; Original Music, Matthew Applebaum; Cast: Eric C. Bailey, Clara Barton Green, Rebecca Hirota, Tania Jeudy, Shawn McLaughlin, Ryan G. Metzger, Kelly Nichols, Michelle Ramoni, Luke Strandquist, Michelle O'Connor, Matthew Applebaum; Gene Frankel Theatre; June 5–28, 2010

Cuchipinoy Productions

cuchipinoy.com

Co-Founding Artistic Director, Rodney E. Reyes; Co-Founding Artistic Director, Mario Corrales; Production Manager, Anna Payumo

PRESENTED PRODUCTIONS

In the Indian Night Sky by Reshma Sapre; Produced by Hathi Chiti Books for Kids–hathichiti.com; Director, Rodney E. Re; Performed by Cuchipinoy Productions; Asia Society; October 30, 2011

Czechoslovak-American Marionette Theatre

czechmarionettes.org

Artistic Director, Vit Horejs; Executive Director, Bonnie Sue Stein; Associate Artistic Director, Theresa Linnihan; Costumes, Michelle Beshaw

Johannes Dokchtor Faust, a Petrifying Puppet Comedye by Anonymous; Director, Vit Horejs; Musical Director, Jonathan Cross; Stage Manager, Alan Barnes Netherton; Cast: Deborah Beshaw, Michelle Beshaw, Jonathan Cross, Vit Horejs, Theresa Linnihan; DUMBO Arts Festival; September 25–26, 2010; also peformed at Bohemian National Hall, June 5, 2011

Mr. M. Written and directed by Vit Horejs; Music Director, Adrienne Cooper; Stage Manager, Michael Collins; Lighting, Federico Restrepo; Set and Costumes, Michelle Beshaw; Cast: Ronny Wasserstrom, Hannah Temple, Steven Ryan, Theresa Linnihan, Vit Horejs, Adrienne Cooper, Michelle Beshaw, Deborah Beshaw; Theater for the New City; April 4–May 8, 2011; also performed at The JCC in Manhattan

Kacha and the Devil Written and directed by Vit Horejs; Set, Vit Horejs, Costumes, Marika Blossfeldt; Cast: Vit Horejs; New York Public Libraries in 4 borroughs; July 15, 2010–June 25, 2011

Dare To Speak Productions

I Plead Guilty Written and directed by Natalia Pelevine; Stage Manager, Catriona Rubenis-Stevens; Lighting, Jeff Nash; Sound, Daniel Dungan; Props Designer, Jane Stein; Cast: Dana Pelevine, Evgenyia Radilova; Gene Frankel Theatre; May 18–29, 2011

Dark Luna

Us vs. Them by Wesley Broulik; Director, Michelle Seaton; Original Music, Hal Logan; Stage Manager, Courtney Ferrell; Lighting and Set, Ed Hill; Costumes, Caitlin Doukas; Cast: Wesley Broulik, Dannie Flanagan, Eric Michael Gillett, Brooke Page, Maria Itzel Siegrist, Michelle Seaton, and Siouxsie Suarez; Roy Aria Off Broadway Theatre; March 4,–26, 2011

Pas-sage by Wesley Broulik; Director, Michelle Seaton; Lighting and Set, Edward Hill; Costumes, Caitlin Doukas; Cast: Wesley Broulik, Mindi L. Logan; Roy Arias Off Broadway Theatre; March 12–23, 2011

Del Valle Productions, Inc.

www.delvalleproductions.com

Brownsville Bred Written and performed by Elaine Del Valle; Director, Paul J. Michael; Stage Manager, Patrick Woodall; Lighting, Joie Bauer; Nuyorican Poets Cafe; June 9–August 25, 2010

DeterminedMe Productions

www.michellefelicehartley.com

Life Encounters Written and performed by Michelle F. Hartley; Lighting and Sound, Tina Lee Jones; Payan Theater; May 24–29, 2011

Diversity Players of Harlem

www.diversityplayersofharlem.com

Die Laughing the Stage Play by Marq Overton; Director, Dwight Ali Williams; Stage Manager, Bekah Hernandez; Lighting, Bekah Hernandez; Costumes, Tara Devincenzo; Cast: Dennis LA White; Roy Arias Off Broadway Theatre; October 5–17, 2010

Dixon Place

www.dixonplace.org

Founder & Executive Director, Ellie Covan; Finance Director, Benjamin Soencksen; Director of Programming, Mimi McGurl; Development Director, Catherine Porter; Marketing Director, Tim Ranney; Technical Director, Rob Lariviere

Washboard Jungle benefit July 1, 2010

VERTititGo Written, Performed, Director, Jibz Cameron; Sound, Mateah Baim; Creative Consulting, Kate Volk; Produced by Dynasty Handbag; July 2–31, 2010

After Collapsing by Laura Berlin; July 2, 2010

Gay 101: A Primer by Frank GeCaro; July 6, 2010

Blatant by Jack Shamblin; July 6, 2010

Adam Tendler July 7, 2010; August 13, 2010; October 4, 2010; January 24, 2011; February 14, 2011

Atmosphere of the Moon Produced by Olson/Appleton; July 8, 2010

U.V.A. Produced by Ultraviolet Astronomy ; July 8, 2010

Realness Produced by Gender Fabulous! ; July 9, 2010

The Fury of the Gods by Susana Cook; July 10, 2010

Babyfat or Skinnybaby July 12, 2010

Jeep Ries Partnering] July 12, 2010

Sinking Hearts by Joshua Conkel; July 12, 2010

The Vanishing City: 1975 July 13, 2010

That Man: Peter Berlin July 13, 2010

The Gay Ivy July 14, 2010

Living on the Real by Michael Lynch and Steve Kaufman; July 14, 2010; October 29, 2010

Queer and Curious: Bauman, Stronger, Morrison and Satter ; July 15, 2010

Brooklyn Book of Shadows July 15, 2010

Fabulous Artistic Guys Get Overtly Tramatized Sometimes: The Musical! July 16, 2010

Straight Talk by Jeff McMahon; July 19, 2010

Live Feed Produced by Black Took Collective; July 19, 2010

Drag Show Produced by Video Verite; July 20, 2010

Under Exposed July 21–August 8, 2010

The Material World by DanFishback; July 22, 2010

One Man Show July 23, 2010

Butch Burlesque July 24, 2010

Take the Mic Hosted by Marti Gould Cummings; July 26, 2010; September 27, 2010; October 25, 2010; December 27, 2010; January 31, 2011; February 28, 2011; March 28, 2011; April 25, 2011; May 30, 2011

Blazek/Patek July 27, 2010

Gerrification July 27, 2010

The Law Project by Heather Gold; July 28, 2010

Syrup in Our Shorts July 28, 2010

Smithsoniansmith Created by Scott Heron and Hijack Dance; Arwen Wilder, Kristin van Loon, Scott Heron; July 29–August 7, 2010

Wet. Hot. Mess July 29, 2010

Annie Lanzillotto July 30, 2010

Penetrating the Space by Kim Katzberg July 31, 2010; October 8–16, 2010

Loving & Daring Projection Design, Nancy Brooks Brody; Produced by LAVA; June 3–20, 2010

Little Theatre June 7, 2010; August 13, 2010; November 8, 2010; December 13, 2010; January 24, 2011; February 14, 2011; March 14, 2011; April 4, 2011; May 9, 2011

Money Talks with Citizen Reno June 7- 21, 2010; October 11, 2010; November 3, 2010; November 23, 2010; December 21, 2010; January 11, 2011; February 7, 2011

The Bulldyke Chronicles June 12, 2010; August 11, 2010; November 13, 2010; December 18, 2010; January 22, 2011; February 19, 2011; April 16, 2011; May 21, 2011

27 Tips for Banishing the Rule June 22–23, 2010

Byrne/Larimer/Finwall June 24–25, 2010

Tweed–Fractured Classicks Pic-Up June 29–30, 2010

Draw the Circle August 2, 2010

Exilkabarett by Ariel Federow August 2, 2010; October 26, 2010

The Dog and Pony Show August 3–4, 2010

The Ones August 3, 2010

D'FunQT: A Big D'Lo Show August 5, 2010

I Light Up My Life August 6, 2010; October 7–14, 2010

Kankana Banerjee September 3, 2010

Crossing Boundaries September 7, 2010; November 17, 2010; May 31, 2011

John Dyer September 7, 2010; October 5, 2010; November 2, 2010; December 7, 2010

Circuit Bending September 8, 2010; October 13, 2010; November 10, 2010; December 8, 2010

Confined by Emily Berry; Composer, Daniel Bernard Roumain; Script Contributions, Todd Craig; Video Design, Gail Scott White; Sara Roer, Nicole McClam, Yuko Mitsuishi, Milvia Pacheco, Emily Berry, Shonnese C.L. Coleman; Produced by Mondo Can Commission; September 10–25, 2010

The Hichristina Shows by Fritz Donnelly and Christina Ewald; September 10, 2010; November 12, 2010

Experiments and Disorders September 14, 2010; November 2, 2010; March 23, 2011; May 3, 2011

Carousel September 15, 2010; January 19, 2011; February 16, 2011

Autobahn de fe September 15, 2010

Another Life by Karen Malpede September 21, 2010

Brink by Jessica Morgan, Kriota Willberg September 22–23, 2010; January 26–27, 2011

Fear Mongers: Fireside Chats About Horror Films September 22, 2010; October 26, 2010; November 23, 2010; December 21, 2010; January 31, 2011

Trav S.D's Last Chance Saloon September 24, 2010

Hollow September 25, 2010; January 22, 2011

Moving Men ; September 28, 2010; October 19, 2010

Puppet Blok gets PUNCHED! September 29–30, 2010; April 21, 2001

Lady HaHa by Kate Clinton; October 1, 2010

Radio Purgatory Produced by Theater THE; October 7–30, 2010

Belladonna:Benefit Performance October 12, 2010

Running Into Me October 13, 2010

The Hey-Ya Brothers Comedy Hour October 16, 2010; November 13, 2010; December 18, 2010; January 19, 2011; March 19, 2011

The Downtown Clown Revue October 18, 2010; November 15, 2010; December 20, 2010; January 17, 2010; February 21, 2011; March 21, 2011

Fireside Puppet Chats October 27, 2010; December 15, 2010; April 22, 2011; May 18, 2011

Puppet Blok: The Rainbow Connection October 27, 2010

Little Tainted Blood October 28, 2010

Five 'TIL by Edwin Lee Gibson; November 4–20, 2010

Blatant November 4, 2010

A Quiet Sip of Coffee November 5, 2010

QT November 9, 2010; January 18, 2010; February 22, 2011; May 25, 2011

Canned Ham November 14, 2010; March 3–26, 2011

The Wilde Road by Lyn Hejinian, Carla Harryman; Produced by Belladonna; November 16, 2010; December 14, 2010

348 ; November 18, 2010

The Maestrosities November 19, 2010

Crones, Ducks & Babes November 20, 2010

Page to Stage: Futana November 22, 2010

A Very Mary Holiday November 29, 2010

Bowery History: A Celebration Hosted by Kent Barwick; Poor Baby Bree; Dixon Place; November 30, 2010

Heist Dixon Place; December 1, 2010

Let Them Eat Cake by Holly Jughes, Maureen Angelos and Megan Carney; December 2–18, 2010

Moisty The Snowman Saves Christmas December 3–11, 2010

Talks with Citizens Reno December 6, 2010

The Astral Kinetic Urban Project December 7, 2010

Puppet Blok: Hudson to China December 15, 2010

Lost Lounge January 8–16, 2011

Panda NYC Live: An Evening of Performance January 12, 2011; February 24, 2011; May 13, 2011

Random Acts of Blindness by Geoffrey Pomeroy; January 19, 2011

Terry Dame & Electric Junkyard Gamelan January 20, 2011

Phantom Band January 21, 2011

Trav S.D.'s Bohemian Theme Park January 21, 2011

Red Bastard January 25, 2011

Pete Sturman January 26, 2011

Page to Stage: Glow January 27, 2011

Ruby Streak Trapeze Studio January 28, 2011

Adam Sank Hosts Inside the Comic's Studio January 29, 2011

Jeffrey Marsh February 1, 2011

These Robes, Those Robes February 2, 2011; May 6–7, 2011

Clear February 3–19, 2011

Puppet Blok by Spica Wobbe and Kate Brehm; February 23, 2011

The Tragedy of Maria Macabre by Rachel Klein; March 2, 2011

Page to the Stage by Lisa Clair and Gred Zuccolo; March 7, 2011

TiVo the Resistance! Produced by Logic LTD; March 10, 2011

Tweed–ButtHairFlies "R" Free March 11–12, 2011

Chinaberry Sidewalks by Rodney Crowell; March 16, 2011

I Wanted it to Have a How and I Wanted it to Have a Verb March 18, 2011

Jon Keith Brunelle/Valerie Work March 22, 2011

Resisdance March 30, 2011

Lane Gifford/Valerie Green March 31, 2011

Bindlestiff Family Cirkus Winter Cabaret April 1–2, 2011

The History of Kisses Written and performed by David Cale; April 5, 2011

Projection April 6, 2011

Nuevo Laredo April 8–23, 2011

Page to the Stage by Adam Burnett & Matt Reeck; April 11, 2011

ThingNY & PPL by Alison Ward; April 15, 2011

Secret City April 17, 2011; May 22, 2011

Gasland April 18, 2011

Life and Death in the Temple of Solitude April 23, 2011

Page to Stage: Understand by Alexandra Collier; May 4, 2011

Language as Action Produced by Kathy Engel; May 5, 2011

Cinco de Maestro May 5, 2011

Under Exposed May 10, 2011

Two Angry Comedies About Love by Sister Sylvester May 12, 2011

Big and Salty by Chris Wells, Jeremy Bass and Emma Griffin May 14, 2011

Work It Out with Anne and Scott May 14, 2011

Page to the Stage: The Mother Gene by Rachel Schroeder May 16, 2011

Belladonna: Prose Event May 17, 2011

Puppet Blok!: The Kid Inside by Alissa Hunnicut May 18, 2011

The Proof May 19, 2011

The Egg Progect May 20 -28, 2011

Page to the Stage by Maxwell and Milo Tramer, Ryan Tracy; May 23, 2011

Girl Adventure: Parts 1–4 by Nina Morrison; May 24, 2011

The Famous Accourdion Orchestra by Bob Goldberg; May 25, 2011

Only, Only, Me, Just... Director, Paola Irun; May 26, 2011

Anti-Diva May 27, 2011

FeMUSEum by Lois Weaver, Carmelita Tropicana, Amy Lame and Bird la Bird; May 29, 2011

Dog Run Rep

The Man Who Ate Michael Rockefeller by Jeff Cohen; Director, Alfred Preisser; Lighting, Jay Scott; Set, Heather Wolensky; Costumes, Kimberly Glennon; Cast: David Brown Jr., Shannon A. L. Dorsey, Tracy Jack, David King, Sean Lum, Daniel Morgan Shelley, Aaron Strand, Rawle Williams; West End Theatre; September 12 –October 3, 2010

Dramatic Question Theatre and Puerto Rican Traveling Theatre

FESTIVALS

Insight Series 2010 Included: *Firehouse* by Pedro Antonio Garcia; Director, Mark Bloom; *Coda for Freddy Blue* by Fred Crecca; Director, Rick Mowat; *The Albatross* by Delilah R. Sanchez; Director, Sally Burtenshaw; 47th Street Playhouse; June 3–20, 2010

Dream Up Festival

A Taste of Altruistic; Wardrobe of the Living Dead and Choose Your Grown Adventure by Maximilian Avery Clark and Jennifer Fedor; Director, Brock H. Hill; Theater for the New City; August 20–September 5, 2010

The Drilling Company

www.drillingcompany.org

Love's Labours Lost by William Shakespeare; Director, Kathy Curtis; Set, Brittany Vosca; Costumes, Lisa Renee Jordan; Sound, Chris Rummel; Cast: Jordan Feltner, Jasper Stolfter, Anwen Darcy, Amanda Dillard, Anna Parratore, Mckey Carpenter, Dave Marantz, Jack Hevholds, Matt Burns, Stephen Drabicki, Nicola Murphy, Michael Gnat, Paul Guskin, Abe Koogler, Gabriella Mazza, Tim Realbuto, Jasmine Mone; Municipal Parking Lot; July 8–July 24, 2010

Julius Caesar by William Shakespeare; Director, Hamilton Clancy; Costumes, Rebecca Lord; Cast: Selene Beretta, Ivory Aquino, Mark Jeter, Brandon Riley, Bill Green, Bobby Plasencia, Brian D. Hills, Leila Okafor, Marianna Caldwell, Joann Sacco, Bill Green, Amanda C. Fuller, Jarad Benn; Municipal Parking Lot; July 29–August 14, 2010

HO! Written and performed by Brian Dykstra; Director, Margarett Perry; Lighting, Chad Lefebvre; Set, David Arsenault; Drilling Company Theatre Lab; November 27–December 19, 2010

Reservoir by Eric Henry Sanders; Director, Hamilton Clancy; Lighting, M. Crowe and CahdLefebvre; Set, Jennifer Varbalow; Costumes, Lisa Renee Jordan; Sound, Sue Ann Holton; Cast: Alessandro Colla, McKey Carpenter, NAthan Ramos, Karla Hendrick, Amanda Dillard; Drilling Company Theatre Lab; January 6–16, 2011

Bird Brain by Vern Thiessen; Director, Hamilton Clancy; Stage Manager, Mary Jane Newman; Lighting, Miriam Crowe; Set, Jennifer Varbalow; Sound, Chris Rummel; Assistant Director, Karla Hendrick; Graphic Design, Phillip De Vita; Cast: Hamilton Clancy, Anwen Darcy, Aimee Whelan; The Drilling Company; January 16 –February 7, 2011

Home of the Great Pecan by Stephen Bittrich; Director, Hamilton Clancy; Original Music, Candy Land and the Goolaks; Lighting, Miriam Crowe; Set, Jennifer Varbalow; Cast: Jessi Gormezano, Brandon Riley, Roberto DeFelice, Dave Marantz , dan Teachout, Veronica Crus, Bill Green , Steve Schmmit, Amanda Dillard, Scott Baker, Amanda Fuller, Victoria Campbell, Jarad Benn; Drilling Company Theatre Lab; January 20–February 6, 2011

Happiness by Stephen bittrich, Brian Dykstra, Paul Hufker, Israela margalit, Laura Marks, Andrea Moon, Deborah Savage, C.Denby Swanson; Director, Hamilton Clancy, Sarah Biesinger, Katie McHugh, Eric Nightengale, Randy Noojin; Stage Manager, Sarah Biesinger; Lighting, Miriam Crowe; Set, Jennifer Varablow; Costumes, Lisa Renee Jordan; Sound, Ashley Marie Scoles; Production Assistant, Company Manager, Stephanie Pezolano; Graphics, Phillip DeVita; Publicity, Jonathan Slaff; Cast: Josh Adler, Kevin Best, Stephen Bittrich, Nina Burns, Rebecca Darke, Ryan Fyke, Dennis Gagamiros, Jessi Blue Gormenzano, Miguel Govea, Bill Green, Eric Jennings, Darren Lipari, Dave Marantz, Lisa Pettersson, Jed Peterson, Kendall Rileigh, Sara Schabach; The Drilling Company; May 12–29, 2011

The Frog Singer by Laura Strausfeld; Director, Eric Nightengale; Sound, Eric Nightengale; Projection and Puppet Designer Laura Strausfeld; Cast: John Heath, Joann Sacco and Claudia Orenstein; The Drilling Company Theatre; May 15–June 6, 2010

Duel Theatre

www.dueltheatre.org

Tape Director, Jim Wise; Stage Manager, Rachel Harpham; Set, Eric Broadwater; Cast: Brandon McMillen, James Savage, Jessiee Datino; Center Stage, NY; November 13–27, 2010

Dysfunctional Theatre Company

www.dysfunctionaltheatre.org

Artistic Director, Amy Overman; Director of Development, Justin Plowman; Director of Development, Dysfunctional Classics Series, Peter Schuyler; President, Paul Wells, Vice President, Rick Vorndran, Treasurer, Jennifer Gill; Secretary, Rob Brown

A Cavalcade of Curiosities by F. Scott Fitzgerald, J.O.S. Hartung, Daniel Keleher, Danna Call, Hrosvitha, Trav S.D.; Director, Justin Plowman, Nicole Lee Aiossa, Eric Chase, Amy Overman, Peter Schuyler; Lighting, Eric Chase; Sound, Justin Plowman; Cast: Nicole Lee Aiossa, Ann Breitbach, Rob Brown, Danaher Dempsey, Adam Files, Christopher Gilkey, Josh Hartung, Cedric Jones, Marissa Levien, Vivian Meisner, Cara Moretto, Tom O'Connor, Vince Phillip, Peter Schuyler, Amy Beth Sherman, Stephanie Willing; The Red Room; March 14–23, 2011

READINGS AND WORKSHOPS

Brew of the Dead II: Oktoberflesh by Patrick Storck; Director, Justin Plowman; Cast: Nicole Lee Aiossa, Eric Chase, Tom O'Connor, Amy Overman, Peter Schuyler; Under St. Marks; October 31, 2010

East River Commedia

eastriver.org

A Couple of Poor Polish Speaking Romanian by Dorota Maslowska; Director, Paul Bargetto; Original Music and Sound, Lukasz Szalankiewicz; Set and Costumes, Doris Mirescu; Video, Patrick Flynn; Cast: Troy Lavallee, Robin Singer, Robert Saietta, Herbie Go, Nora Woolley, Amanda Broomell, Steven Conroy, Stephanie Shipp; February 10 – 26, 2011

FESTIVALS

UndergroundZero Festival (4th Annual) (see Festival listings in this section) PS 122; July 6 – 25, 2010

EBE Ensemble

www.ebeensemble.com

Romeo & Juliet by William Shakespeare; Director, Dev Bondarin; Stage Manager, Jessica Polanco; Costumes, Amanda Jenks; Original Music, Frederick Alden Terry; Fight Choreographer, Turner Smith; Live Foley Design, Joshua B. Jenks and Nancy Valladares; Cast: Eric Alba, Judy Alvarez, Ugo Chukwu , Joshua Luria, Camille Mazurek, Nicholas Reinhardt, Len Rella, Elizabeth Spano, Montgomery Sutton, Steve Viola; Prospect Park; July 24–August 7, 2010

The Girl from Nashville by Steven Michael Walters; Director, Kristine Ayers; Choreographer, Turner Smith; Stage Manager, Andrea Herbert; Lighting, Tsubasa Kamei; Set, David Ogle; Costumes, Amanda Jenks; Sound, Joshua B Jenks; Cast: Brad Makarowski, Jessica Renee Russell, Dan Sharkey, Montgomery Sutton, Erin Wilhelm; Abingdon Theatre;

December 3–18, 2010

Elephants on Parade 2011: *The Day the Devil Passed Through Harper County* by Daniel Welser Carrol; *The Sandbox* by Matthew Hanf, *Waiting for Godot* by Alexander Motyl, *The Fairy Tale of America* by Michael Niederman, *1-800-HELP-U-WRITE* by Chris Purnell, *The Right Reasons* by Tom Sime; Director, Tracy Cameron Francis, Elyzabeth Gorman, Barbara Harrison, Rebecca Lewis-Whitson, Bobbi Masters, Adrian Wattenmaker; Choreographer, Turner Smith; Stage Manager, Bekah Hernandez; Lighting, Lauren Bremen; Set, Cory Rodriguez; Costumes, Amanda Jenks & Genevieve Hudson Price; Sound, Joshua B. Jenks;

Props, Lauren Genutis; Cast: Eric Alba, Rin Allen, Penny Bittone, Alex Celeste Muniz, Joe Mullen, Mary Notari, Nick Reinhardt, Elizabeth Spano, Ryan Willard; 4th Street Theater; April 5–16, 2011

El Gato Teatro

www.elgatoteatro.com

Gabriella Barnstone; Artistic Director

Nuevo Laredo Directed and Choreographed by Gabriella Barnstone; Stage Manager, Anna Kroup; Lighting, Garin Marschall; Set, Paul Douglas Olmer; Costumes, Oana Botez-Ban; Sound, Nicholas Colvin; Cast: David Hale, Audrey Ellis, Carlton Ward; April 8–23, 2011

Emerging Artists Theatre

www.emergingartiststheatre.org

Spring EATFest 2011 Series A: *Staying Put* by Kathleen Warnock; *The Takeover* by Barbara Lindsay, *Clean* by Audrey Cefaly; Lighting, Tamora Wilson; Set, Tim McMath; Costumes, Nicole Wee; Cast: Desmond Dutcher, Matt Stapleton, Richard Cottrell, Laura Fois, Glory Gallo, Blanche Cholet, Caitlin Johnston; TADA! Theater; March 7–19, 2011; Series B: *Sweat* by Jon Spano; *Reservations Cancelled* by John Zygmunt; *Assisted Living* by Jeffrey Newman; *Matchpoint* by Chris Widney; Lighting, Tamora Wilson; Set, Tim McMath; Costumes, Nicole Wee; Cast: Tommy Day Carey, Bernard Burlew, Paul Herbig, Matt Boethin, Augustine Hargrove, Brook Zelcer, Erin Hadley, Valerie David, Deb Armelino, Elizabeth Bell, Irene Longshore; TADA! Theater; March 8–20, 2011; Series C: *The Chiselers* by Mark Finley; Director, Melissa Attebery; Lighting, Tamora Wilson; Set, Tim McMath; Costumes, Nicole Wee; Cast: Eric Chase , Chuck Saculla, Marie Wallace, Karen Stanion, Andrea Alton; TADA! Theater; March 9–20, 2011

READINGS AND WORKSHOPS

EAT New Works Series TADA! Theater; April 25 – May 15, 2011

Endtimes Productions

www.endtimesproductions.org

Naked Holidays: NYC 2010: *Naked Holidays Opening* by George Larkin; *Splooge* by Steve Lewis; *The Real Toy Story* by Leah Dashe; *Jack and Jill in Christmastown* by David Dannenfelser; *Who is Kris Kringle?* by Eric R. Pfeffinger; *No One Enjoys Christmas More Than Hitler* by Leal Vona and Adam Tullis, *The Naked People Play* by Stacey Lane, *Naked Holidays Follies* by Steve Strangio; Director, Russell Dobular; Choreographer, Tiffany Herriott; Stage Manager, Mike Beyrouti; Cast: Ann Breitbach, Eli Bridges, Danielle Cautela, Victoria Clare, Alessandro Colla, Alex Dunbar, Alinca Hamilton, Heather Lee Harper, Christopher Johnston, Serena Miller, Levi Morger, Christina Roman, Sarah Schoofs, Fernando Sousa, Alley Scott, Jonathan Steinberg, Ruthie Ste; Ace of Clubs; December 10–30, 2010

Manson: The Musical! Director, Russell Dobular; Musical Director, Serena Miller; Lighting, Jeremy Pape; Set, Chris Cornwell; Assistant Director, Leah Dashe; Assistant Musical Director, Marek Sapieyevski; Choreographer, Tiffany Herriobett; Dance Captain, Heather Lee Harper; Cast: Dylan Weinberger, Alex Dunbar, Kevin Paul Smith, Danielle Cautela, Emily Woo Zeller, Molly McAdoo, Briana Packen, Lena Hudson, Sarah Marek, Chris Cornwell, Anthony Mead, Alessandro Colla, Marek Sapieyevski, Victoria Clare, Cheri Paige Fogelman; Ace of Clubs; October 24–December 19, 2010

Extant Arts

www.extantarts.org

Ghosts Director, Sophie Hunter; Choreographer, Sarah Outhwaite; Stage Manager, Julia Singer; Lighting, Melissa Mizell; Set, Fiammetta Horvat; Costumes, Hunter Kaczorowki; Sound, Asa Wember; Cast: Anthony Holds, Paulo Quiros, LeeAnne Hutchison, Justine Salata; Access Theater Black Box; November 5–21, 2010

F*It Club

www.f-itclub.tumblr.com

The Spring Fling Included *If* by Anna Ziegler, *Drunk* by Bekah Brunstetter, *Minotaur Scavenger Hunt* by Caroline V. McGraw, *The Short, Sad Biography of the Magician's Assistant* by Ashlin Halfnight, *Come Here* by Isaac Oliver, *French Toast and Parsley* by Brooke Berman, *We Have The Music* by Mark Schultz, *Our Trip To Ohio* by Greg Keller; Director, Josh Hecht, May Adrales, Lila Neugebauer, Laura Savia, Heidi Handelsman, Victor Maog; Stage Manager, Veronica Graveline; Lighting, Daniel Winters; Set, Sarah Martin; Costumes, Jennifer Jacob; Sound, Tim Boyce; Cast: Ali Ahn, Clayton Apgar, Jeanine Bartel, Marty Brown, Sara Buffamanti, Kevin Dwyer, Julie Fitzpatrick, Ben Graney, Stephen Graybill, Jessica Howell, Mara Kassin, Ryan King, Roger Lirtsman, Joseph Midyett, Allyson Morgan, Morgan Reis, David Ross, Amanda Say, Danielle Slavick; IRT Theater; April 27–May 8, 2011

Fallen Swallow/Laughing Pigeon

Alice by Teresa Ann Virginia Bayer; Director, Brian Hashimoto; Assistant Director, Jay Spriggs; Cast: Caroline Calkins, Rivka Borek, Jessica Carlsen, Savvy Clement, John DeSilvestri, Matt Roth, Nick Roesler, Franz Quitt, Lauren Weinberg, and Ali Rivera; Archip Gallery Theater; June 23–26, 2010

Fifty 7 Productions

www.fifty7productions.org

Fallen by Kyle Spidle; Director, Corinne Lee; Lighting, Shane Terenzi; Costumes, Joshua McKinley Cook; Executive Producer, Peter Wells; Photographer, Cortney Jenee Brown; Cherry Lane Studio; September 9–19, 2010

F.I.G. Theater Group

Director/Producer Cilque Brown

Black Metropolis Written and directed by Cilque Brown; Stage Manager, Michele Marinace; Lighting and Sound, Arno Austin; Associate Director, Ben Black and Paula Flynn; Associate Stage Manager, Patricia Diggs; Cast: Duane Granston, Charles Williams, Robert Tyler, Ben Black, Donnell Jenkins, Merson Narcisse, Eric Harris, Johnny Faulkner, Kelly Anne Wadler, Mustafa Gatollari, Holly Rhea, Angela Rostick, Jennifer Akabue, Paula Flynn, Deidre King, Michele Marinace, Tyies; Producers Club; October 9–November 20, 2010

Under the Same Moon Written and directed by Cilque Brown; Stage Manager, Kojo Koama; Lighting and Sound, Arno Austin; Associate Director, Ben Black, Paula Flynn; Associate Stage Manager, Deirdre King; Cast: Ben Black, Kojo Boama, Denise Collins, Bettina Colley, Ron Denson, Omar Clyburn, Paula Flynn, Kyle Brown, Bonnie Jones, Deirdre King, Holly Rhea, Angela Rostick, Jake Taylor, Charles Williams; Producers Club; February 19–May 16, 2011

Firebone Theatre

www.firebonetheatre.com

A Mysterious Way by Barrett Hileman; Director, Steven Walters; Cast: Gene Defrancis; Red Room; September 9–18, 2010

The Flea Theater

theflea.org

Artistic Director, Jim Simpson; Producing Director, Carol Ostrow; Managing Director, Beth Dembrow; Technical Director, Liz Blessing; Marketing and Membership Manager, Dane Joseph; Assistant to the Producing Director, Sarah Wansley

Office Hours by A.R. Gurney; Director, Jim Simpson; Set, Kate Sinclair Foster; Lighting, Jeanette Yew; Costumes, Jessica Pabst; Sound, Jill BC DuBoff; Projection Design, David Prittie; Cast: Holly Chou, Louiza Collins, Tommy Crawford, Bjorn DuPaty, Katherine Folk-Sullivan, Andy Gershenzon, Raúl Sigmund Julia, Betsy Lippitt, Maren Langdon, Turna Mete, John Russo, Wilton Yeung; September 18–November 7, 2010

Looking At Christmas by Steven Banks; Director, Jim Simpson; Set, Kate Sinclair Foster; Lighting, Jeanette Oi-Suk Yew; Costumes, Gabriel Berry; Sound, Jill BC DuBoff; Cast: Brett Aresco, Crystal Arnette, Allison Buck, Holly Chou, Jack Corcoran, Christian Adam Jacobs, Raúl Sigmund Julia, Betsy Lippitt, Turna Mete, Michael Micalizzi, Briana Pozner, John Russo; November 20–December 30, 2010

American Sexy by Trista Baldwin; Director, Mia Walker; Set, Kate Sinclair Foster; Lighting, Joe Chapman; Costumes, Katie Hartsoe; Sound, Colin Whitley; Cast: Atomi Blair, Veracity Butcher, Seth Moore, Scott Morse, Briana Pozner, Ian Quinlan, Nicky Schmidlein, and Ron Washington; January 15–March 6, 2011

Dance Conversations 2011 Panalists: Laurence Yadi, Nicolas Cantillon, Maira Duarte, Jason Sosnowski, Patrice M. Regnier, Rachel Korenstein, Daniel Charon, Valerie Green, Sarah Levitt, Benjamin Wegman, Amos Pinhasi, Barkin, Amber Sloan, Jessica DiMauro, Lenora Lee, Eunhee Lee, Barbie Diewald, Lucy York Struever, Rebecca Stronger, Maré Hieronimus, Daniela Hoff, Roxanne Steinberg, Shannon Gillen, Michael Freeman, David Appel, Stefanie Nelson, Preeti Vasudevan, Claire Porter; Moderators: Jessica Ray, Gus Solomons Jr, Gina Gibney, Reggie Wilson, Melinda Ring, Pele Bauch; February 28–March 13, 2011

Music with a View 2011 Hosts: Annie Gosfield, Roger Kleier, Preston Stahly, Robert Rowe, Randall Woolf, James Moore, Alan Pierson, Atau Tanaka, David T. Little, Ian Moss, Peter Catapano, Daniel Felsenfeld, Robert Beaser; Cast: Marco Cappelli, Sam Crawford, Molly Thompson, Anney Bonney, Dither, Emily Manzo, Kevin Bourisquot, Aled Roberts, Martha Mooke, Agatha Kasprzyk, Vision Fugitive, Noé Cuellar, Joseph Kramer, Dafna Naphtali, LEMUR Bots, Ted Hearne, Philip White, Jonathan Chen, Armando Bayolo, Cornelius Dufallo, Atau 4 hands iPhone, Phyllis Chen, Rob Dietz, Peri Mauer, Lukas Ligeti, Marimba Lumina, Lisa Coons, Maria Tegzes, Lorenda Ramou, Jiri Kaderabek, Sidney Samberg, Jonathan Elliott; March 22–April 3, 2011

Future Anxiety by Laurel Haines; Director, Jim Simpson; Set, Kyle Chepulis; Lighting, Brian Aldous; Costumes, Sydney Gallas; Sound, Patrick Metzger; Graphics, David Prittie; Props, Kate Sinclair Foster; Stage Manager, Michelle Kelleher; Cast: Brett Aresco, Allison Buck, Holly Chou, Ugo Chukwu, Katherine Folk-Sullivan, Grant Harrison, Alex Herrald, Josephine Huang, Amanda Idoko, Raúl Sigmund Julia, Yvette King, Vin Kridakorn, Maren Langdon, Betsy Lippitt, Seth Moore, Joy Notoma, Reynaldo Piniella, Donaldo Prescod, Joann Sacco, Anita Sabherwal, Keola Simpson, Hansel Tan, Monica Wyche; April 15–May 26, 2011

Just Cause Written and directed by Zack Russell; Stage Manager, Daniella Caggiano; Set, Kate Sinclair Foster; Lighting, Brian Tovar; Costumes, Katie Hartsoe; Sound, Janie Bullard; Cast: Brett Aresco, Crystal Arnette, Allison Buck, Tommy Crawford, Greg Engbrecht, Katherine Folk-Sullivan, Eric Folks, Alex Herrald, Raúl Sigmund Julia, Georgia X Lifsher, Betsy Lippitt, Sean McIntyre, Kate Michaud, Briana Pozner, Ian Quinlan, Cynthia Whalen, Wilton Yeung; May 6–June 6, 2011

FESTIVALS

#serials@theflea: cycles 1 & 2 January 21–March 28, 2011; Included: *Too Little Too Late* by Lucy Alibar; *HBO's Generation Kill* by Josh Barrett; *Follow Me Down* by Patrick Barrett; *Spidermusical* by Randy Blair and Tim Drucker; *Michael & Edie* by Rachel Bonds; *The Bird Girl* by E.J.C. Calvert; *The Recommendation* by Jonathan Caren; *Sexy JayJay* by Charlotte Miller, *The Only One* by Nikole Beckwith, *The Fall of the House of Sunshine* by Jonathan Goldberg, *The Escape* by Isaac Kruger, *Oliver Eats Cake* by Christopher Oscar Peña, *Bea Arthur and the Knights of the Round Table* by Joe Tracz, *It's Happening* by Jon Bass, *Unfuck Yourself Rhys Bauer!* by Josh Barrett, *Legal Tender* by Lucas Kavner; Directors, Nicole Greene, Mia Walker, Mary Birnbaum, Jeremy Bloom, Jess Chayes, Tamara Fisch, Kel Haney, Luke Harlan, Kate Pines, Brian Smith, Allison Troup-Jensen, Sarah Elizabeth Wansley, Mark Duncan; Cast: Tiffany Abercrombie, Brett Aresco, Crystal Arnette, Musa Bacon, Satomi Blair, Allison Buck, Veracity Butcher, Ugo Chukwu, Thomas Crawford, Brent Dixon, Greg Engbrecht, Bobby Foley, Katherine Folk-Sullivan, Grant Harrison, Halima Henderson, Alex Herrald, Harrison Hill, Josephine Huang, Amanda Idoko, Eric Folks, Michael Goldlist, Morgan Harris

NON-RESIDENT PRODUCTIONS

Metamorphoses Adapted and diected by Peter Bramley; Original Music, Lucy Egger; Produced by Pants on Fire; January 5–30, 2011

Flux Theatre Ensemble

www.fluxtheatre.org

Artistic Director, August Schulenburg; Managing Director, Heather Cohn; Marketing Director, Kelly O'Donnell; Company Members, Tiffany Clementi, Isaiah Tanenbaum, Matthew Archambault

Dog Act by Liz Duffy Adams; Director, Kelly O'Donnell; Musical Director, Gerad Keenan; Stage Manager, Cat Adler-Josem; Lighting, Kia Rogers; Set, Jason Paradine; Costumes, Lara de Bruijn; Sound, Elizabeth Rhodes; Assistant Director, Tiffany Clementi; Cast: Becky Byers, Liz Douglas, Lori E. Parquet, Zack Robidas, Julian Stetkevych, Chris Wight; Clemente Soto Vélez Cultural Center; February 4–20, 2011

READINGS AND WORKSHOPS

Miss Lilly Gets Boned Or: The Loss of All Elephant Elders by Bekah Brunstetter; Director, Heather Cohn; Judson Memorial Church; December 15, 2010

Hearts Like Fists by Adam Szymkowicz; Keith Powell; Judson Memorial Church; September 15, 2010

Folding Chair Classical Theatre

www.foldingchairtheatre.org

A MidSummer Night's Dream by William Shakespeare; Director, Marcus Geduld; Access Theater; May 5–June 4, 2011

The Foolish Theatre

www.foolishtheatre.org

Skin Deep by Rich Orloff; Director, Jeffrey C. Wolf; Stage Manager, Susan Sunday; Lighting, David A. Sexton; Set, Craig M. Napoliello; Costumes, Jonathan Knipscher; Sound, Jeffrey C. Wolf; Cast: William Green, Dee Dee Friedman, Mary Theresa Archbold, Robby Sharpe, Timothy Scott Harris; Theatre 54; October 16–November 6, 2010

Fordham Alumni Theatre Company

What May Fall by Peter Gil Sheridan; Director, Morgan Gould; Stage Manager, Stephenie Suski; Lighting, Ryan Seelig; Set, Chad McCarver; Costumes, Dana Covarrubias; Sound, Tim Chaffee and Chris Barlow; Cast: Tom Deckman, Annie Purcell, Amelia Workman, Chris Bester, Kate Morgan Chadwick, Maria McConville, Marco Formosa, Jessica Howell, Ian McWethy; Pope Auditorium at Fordham University; July 21–31, 2010

The Forge

www.theforgenow.com

Immortal: The Gilgamesh Variations Group adaptation by Charles Borkhuis, Erin Browne, Jane Ann Crum, Jeffrey James Keyes, Barbara Lanciers, Leonard Madrid, Gretchen Michelfeld, Kay Mitchell, Juanita Rockwell, Barry Rowell, Gabriel Shanks ; Director, Gabriel Shanks; Original Music, Christian B. Carey; Choreographers: KT Peterson, Gabriel Shanks, Barbara Lanciers; Stage Manager, Jeni Shanks; Lighting, Erik Bruce; Set, Allen Cutler; Costumes, Anne Liberman; Puppet and Props Designer, Allen Cutler; Cast: Oscar Castillo, Nathaniel P. Claridad, Cherrye J. Davis, Kamelle Mills, Nolan Muna, KT Peterson, Eugene the Poogene, Catherine Porter, Terence Stone, Benjamin Thys; The Bushwick Starr; January 20–30, 2011

The Frog & Peach Theatre Co., Inc.

www.frogandpeachtheatre.org

Artistic Director, Lynnea Benson

Cymbeline by William Shakespeare; Director, Lynnea Benson; Stage Manager, Blair Hotchner; Lighting, Joseph Kehoe; Set, Marc D. Malamud; Costumes, Jessa-Raye Court; Sound, Lynnea Benson; Movement Consultant, Tom Knutson; Combat Designer, Marcus Watson; Original Music, Ted Zurkowski; Original Score, Bobby Lawlor; Technical Director, Kevin J. Davies; Associate Producer, Alexandra H. Rubin; Cast: Karen Lynn Gorney, Ross Beshear, Vivien Landau, Jonathan Marballi, Erick Gonzalez, Michael Broadhurst, Steve Mazzacone, Jonathan Reed Wexler, Stephen Siano, Kevin G. Shinnick, David Arthur Bachrach, Rosa Valenze Gilmore, Patrick Roberts, Kathleen Choe; The West End Theatre; October 7–31, 2010

Twelfth Night by William Shakespeare; Director, Lynnea Benson; Music Director, Ted Zurkowski; Stage Manager, Balir Hotchner; Lighting, Leo Malkin; Set, Peter Adams; Costumes, Jessa-Raye Court; Sound, Lynnea Benson; Composer, Ted Zurkowski; Movement & Gesture Coach, Tom Knutson; Combat Designer, Marcus Watson; Technical Director, Kevin J. Davies; Aisistant Stage Manager, Ryan Dreyer, Irene Hernandez, Associate Producer, Alexandra H. Rubin; Cast: Lenny Ciotti, Amy Quint, Eric DySart, Jonathan Marballi, Michael Broadhurst, Steve Mazzoccone, Jane Cortney, Erick Gonzalez, Leah Reddy, Brando Boniver, Kyla D'Souza, Collin Blackard, Mark Sage Hamilton, Peter Forde, Monty Nummi, and Matthew Bayer; The West End Theatre; April 21–May 15, 2011

Brent McBeth, Joel Jeske, Danny Gardner in Parallel Exit's Room 17B (photo by Jim Moore)

Bob Brader in Spitting In The Face Of The Devil, presented by the John Montgomery Theatre Company (photo by Tracy Olsen)

Cara Moretto and Adam Swiderski in Spacemen from Space, presented by Gemini CollisionWorks (photo by Ian W. Hill)

Christopher Borg and Joey Rizzolo in Locker #4173b at the New York Neo-Futurists (photo by Anton Nickel)

Marc Bovino, Joe Curnutte, Michael Dalto, Stephanie Wright Thompson and Henry Vick in The Tremendous Tremendous, presented The Mad Ones & The Brick (photo by Andrew Smrz)

Laura Wickens, Nick Micozzi, Ian Wen, Jason Griffin, Vaishnavi Sharma, Catherine Gowl, and Dave Edson in Blessed Unrest's production of ArtCamp SexyTime FootBall (photo by David Anthony)

Darrell James in St Nicholas at Theatre of the Expendable (photo by Dorian Nisinson)

Hunter Gilmore and Sheila Joon in Two Gentlemen of Verona at Judith Shakespeare Company NYC (photo by Deb Failla)

A scene from Eclectic Evening of Shorts IV: Boxers & Briefs presented by Artistic New Directions (photo by Konrad Brattke)

Helena Serdyuk, Benjamin Rishworth, Carol Jacobanis,and Laura Dragomir in the ShakespeareNYC production of A Midsummer Night's Dream (photo by Al Foote III)

The Gallery Players

www.galleryplayers.com

Candide or Optimism by TJ Edwards; Director, Neal J. Freeman; Lighting, Scott Andrew Cally; Costumes, Dara Fargotstein; Sound, Jack Kennedy; Cast: Patrick Toon, Kyle Minshew, Andrew Davies, Kyle Metzger, Amanda McCallum, Minna Taylor; June 3, 2010–June 20, 2010

What the Butler Saw by Joe Orton; Director, Zac Hoogendyk; Lighting, Austin R. Smith; Set, Starlet Jacobs; Costumes, Erica Evans; Sound, Ann Warren; Cast: David Sedgwick, Tom Cleary, , Kane Prestenback, Nicole Fitzpatrick, Emily Taplin Boyd, September 11–26, 2010

Reefer Madnes Music by Dan Studney, lyrics by Kevin Murphy; Director, Dev Bondarin; Choreographer, Joe Barros; Stage Manager, Jodi Witherell; Lighting, Dan Jobbins; Set, Lilia Trenkova; Costumes, Soule Golden; Sound, Kim Fuhr; Props Design, Jennifer Stimple; Cast: Natalia Barzilai, Laura Elizabeth Brandel, Robert Conte, Joshua M. Feder, Katharine Pettit, Travis Slavin; October 23–November 14, 2010

Dancing at Lughnasa by Brian Friel; Director, Heather Siobhan Curran; Lighting, Richard T Chamblin; Set, Jared Rutherford; Costumes, Travis Chinick; Sound, Julianne Merrill; Cast: Susan Ferrara, Kelsey Formost, Zac Hoogendyk, Amanda McCallum, Therese Plaehn, Jasper Soffer, Richard Vernon, Leigh Williams; December 4–19, 2010

The Drowsy Chaperone Book by Bob Martin and Don McKellar: Music and Lyrics by Lisa Lambert and Greg Morrison; Director, Hans Friedrichs; Choreographer, Christine O'Grady; Stage Manager, Nicholas Rainey; Lighting, Brad Peterson; Set, Jared Rutherford; Costumes, Ryan J. Moller; Sound, Kimberly Fuhr-Carbone; Cast: Whitney Branan, Jennifer DiDonato, Tauren Hagans, Robert Anthony Jones, Edward Juvier, Lorinne Lampert, Aaron J. Libby, Jake Mendes, Trey Mitchell, Jan-Peter Pedross, Colin Pritchard, Megan Rosenblatt, Chloe Sabin, Dawn Trautman, Craig Treubert, Tyler Wallach, Eric Weaver; January 29–February 20, 2011

Jitney by August Wilson; Director, Gregory Simmons; Stage Manager, Tamesis Eve Batiste; Lighting, Porsche McGovern; Set, Brian Ireland; Costumes, Sara Baldocchi-Byrne; Sound, Ted Pallas; Cast: Gil Charleston, Kwaku Driskell, Lawrence James, Barry L Johnson, Franck Juste, Ivan Moore, Iman Richardson, Terrence Charles Rodgers, Lawrence Winslow; March 19–April 3, 2011

Oliver! by Lionel Bart; Director, Neal J. Freeman; Choreographer, Josie Bray; Stage Manager, Matt Remington; Lighting, Tracy Lynn Wertheimer; Set, Cory Rodriguez; Costumes, Megan Q. Dudley; Sound, Ann Warren; Cast: Stephanie Holser, Judy Molner, Tony Lance, Jesse Turtz, Eric Stephenson, Bill Krakauer, Audrey Heffernan Meyer, Michael Mizwicki, Hayley Richelson, Melissa Gonzalez, Zenovia Gonzalez, Nicholas Gonzalez, Zev Lane, David Morales, Asher Muldoon, Caroline Ros, River Alexander, Dominic Cuskern, Zac Morechai, Yakov Klugman, Stacie Bono, Leah Jennings, Debra Thais Evans; April 20–May 22, 2011

Gemini CollisionWorks

collisionwork.livejournal.com

The Wedding of Berit Johnson & Ian W. Hill: A Theatre Study by Ian W. Hill & Berit Johnson Written and directed by Ian W. Hill; Stage Manager, Berit Johnson; Lighting, Sound and Set, Ian W. Hill; Costumes, Karen Flood; AV Design, Ian W. Hill & Berit Johnson; Produced in association with The Brick Theater, Inc.; Cast: Ian W. Hill, Berit Johnson, Gita Borovsky, Maggie Cino, Edward Einhorn, Sarah Engelke, Matt Gray, Daniel McKleinfeld, Sally McKleinfeld, Timothy McCown Reynolds, Sean Rockoff, Dina Rose, Frank Cwiklik, Bryan Enk, Luana Josvold, Christiaan Koop; The Brick; June 19–26, 2010

Spacemen from Space! An Exciting New Serial for the Stage in 6 Thrill-Packed Episodes! Written and directed by Ian W. Hill; Music Director, Adam Swiderski & Berit Johnson; Stage Manager, Berit Johnson; Lighting, Set and Sound, Ian W. Hill; Costumes, Karen Flood; AV Design, Ian W. Hill & Berit Johnson; Original Music, Ian W. Hill & Berit Johnson; Produced in association with The Brick Theater, Inc.; Cast: Alex Amery, Ethan Angelica, Aaron Baker, Eric C. Bailey, David Berent, Ali Skye Bennet, George Bronos, Josh Hartung, Stephen Heskett, Ian W. Hill, Justin RG Holcomb, James Isaac, Douglas MacKrell, Roger Nasser, Cara Moretto, Amy Overman, Yvonne Roen, Trav S.D., Adam Swiderski, William Webber, Stephanie Willing; The Brick; August 12–22, 2010

Devils by John Whiting; Director, Ian W. Hill; Stage Manager, Berit Johnson; Lighting, Set and Sound, Ian W. Hill; Produced in association with The Brick Theater, Inc.; Cast: David Arthur Bachrach, Olivia Baseman, Lynn Berg, George Bronos, Lindsey Beth Carter, Sarah Malinda Engelke, Saara Falk, Ian W. Hill, Mike Hill, Justin RG Holcomb, Michael Jablonski, Norah Elise Johnson, Candace Rachel Lawrence, Michael Marion, Justin Maruri, Samuel Muniz, Eric Oleson, Christian Toth, Shelley Ray, Timothy McCown Reynolds, Noah Schultz, Anna Stromberg, David Watson, Morgan Anne Zipf; The Brick; August 14–29, 2010

Gingold Theatrical Group

www.projectshaw.com

Artistic Director, David Staller; General Manager, Cori Gardner; Office Manager, Meredith Dixon

Village Wooing & **Interlude at the Playhouse** by George Bernard Shaw; Director, David Staller; Cast: Brian Murray, Veanne Cox; The Players Club; June 21, 2010

Man and Superman by George Bernard Shaw; Director, David Staller; The Players; July 19, 2010

Candida by George Bernard Shaw; Director, David Staller; The Players Club; September 27, 2010

Captain Brassbound's Conversion by George Bernard Shaw; Director, David Staller; The Players; October 25, 2010

How He Lied To Her Husband & **The Fascinating Foundling** by George Bernard Shaw; David Staller; The Players; November 22, 2010

Heartbreak House by George Bernard Shaw; Director, David Staller; Cast: Elie Dunn; The Players; December 20, 2010

Androcles and the Lion by George Bernard Shaw; Director, David Staller; The Players; January 24, 2011

GTG'S Valentine's Day Surprise Songs, Poems, Letters and Shaw's Wicked One-Act *Overruled* by George Bernard Shaw; Music by Noel Coward, Irving Berlin, and Frank Loesser; Director, David Staller; The Players; February 14, 2011

Great Catherine and **Annjanska** by George Bernard Shaw; David Staller; The Players; March 28, 2011

Shaw & Shakespeare by George Bernard Shaw; Director, David Staller; The Players; April 25, 2011

You Never Can Tell by George Bernard Shaw; David Staller; The Players; May 23, 2011

Getting Married by George Bernard Shaw; Director, David Staller; The Players; June 20, 2011

Glass Beads Theatre Ensemble

www.glassbeadstheatre.org

Artistic Director, Mari Gorman

Lily of the Conservative Ladies by Michael Locascio; Director, Mari Gorman; Stage Manager, Chimmy Gunn; Lighting, Travid McHale; Cast: Danna Call, Christopher Estrada, Ondina Frate, Roy Havrilack, Stuti Kejriwal, Suzi Lindner, Devon Talbott; June Havoc Theatre; February 3–27, 2011

Godlight Theatre

www.godlighttheatrecompany.org

Clifford Chase's Winkie by Matt Pelfrey; Director, Joe Tantalo; Cast: Nick Paglino, Greg Konow, Adam Kee, Elliot Hill, Sean Phillips, Chris Cipriano, Michael Shimkin, Erin Wheelock and Geraldine Johns; 59E59 Theaters; March 5–April 10, 2011

An Impending Rupture of the Belly by Matt Pelfrey; Director, Joe Tantalo; Lighting and Set, Maruti Evans; Sound, Andrew Recinos; Cast: Nick Paglino, Lawrence Jansen, Deanna McGovern, Gregory Konow, Ryan O'Callaghan; The Lion at Theatre Row; November 17–December 4, 2010

Good Company

www.goodcompanynyc.org

Artistic Director, David Ruttura; Artistic Associate, Isaac Oliver; General Manager, Melanie Hopkins

Electra in a One-Piece by Isaac Oliver; Director, David Ruttura; Original Music, Ryan Scott Oliver; Lighting, Paul Toben and Jeremy Cunningham; Set, Kenneth Grady Barker; Costumes, Moria Sine Clinton; Sound, Jason Crystal; Dustin O'Neill for Projection Design; Cast: Chris Bannow, Ian McWethy, Michael Brusasco, Matt Park, Erika Rolfsrud, Amanda Scot Ellis, Melanie Hopkins, Austin Mitchell, Matthew Park; Wild Project; October 28–November 14, 2010

Greek Cultural Center

www.greekculturalcenter.org

Executive Board President, Elias Neofotistos; Treusurer, Anita Toumaras; Secretery, Elefteria Tourtoulis; Vise President: Kalliopi Giannatos; Members of the Executive Board: Dora Gotsis, Thanasis Tsouvelis

The Mystery of Irma Vep by Charles Ludlam; Director, Evangelos Alexiou-Christos Alexiou; Manager, Socratis Gerokostas-Apostolos Spiropoulos; Lighting, Drew Florida; Set, Christos Alexandridis and Evangelos Alexiou; Costumes, Evangelos Alexiou-Christos Alexandridis; Sound, Thanasis Tzouvelis; AV Design, Myrto Ioanna Kassis; Light Operator, Andronikos Diomis; Sound Operator, Kimon Diomis; Press Translator, Alex Malaos; Set Construction, Demetres Beryeles; Cast: Evangelos Alexiou, Christos Alexandridis; Greek Cultural Center; October 29–December 12, 2010

Babies Are Brought By the Stork by Thanasis Papathanasiou-Michalis Reppas; Director, Ioanna Katsarou; Stage Manager, Sofia Tsekoura and Alkis Sarantinos; Lighting, Drew Florida; Set, Christos Alexandridis-Ioanna Katsarou; Costumes, Ioanna Katsarou; Sound, Thanasis Tsouvelis; AV Design, Myrto Ioanna Kassis; Costume Assistant, Fay Tamiolaki; Light Operator, Billy Koumoutjeas; Sound Operator, Makis Papamichael; Englsh translator, Loukas Skipitaris; Hair-Wig Stylist, Christophe Bouchet, Press Translator, Alex Malaos, Technical Director, Maria Gouveris; Cast: Christos Alexandridis, Yiannis Amouris, Dimitris Bozinis, Theodora Loukas, Kristina Siapkara, Phyto Stratis, Sophia Tsekoura; Greek Cultural Center; March 11–April 17, 2011

The p-ROJECT based on The Persians by Aeschylus; Director, Ioanna Katsarou and Dimitris Bozinis; Musical Director, Dimitris Dimitrakopoulos; Stage Manager, Sofia Tsekoura; Lighting, Drew Florida; Set, Marina Gkoumla; Costumes, Dimitris Bozinis-Ioanna Katsarou; Sound, Dimitris Dimitrakopoulos; AV Design, Myrto Ioanna Kassis; Assistant Director, Sofia Tsekoura; Special Set Construction, Christos Alexandridis; Vocal Coaching, Peter Ludwig; English Translation, Chryssanthi Katsarou Ventouratos; Light operator, Sofia Tsekoura; Sound operator, Theodora Loukas; Cast: Ioanna Katsarou and Dimitris Bozinis; Produced in association with Eclipses Group Theater; Greek Cultural Center-Eclipses Group Theater; May 6–22, 2011

The Greenpoint Division

www.greenpointdivision.com

Michael & Edie by Rachel Bonds; Director, Robert Saenz de Viteri; Lighting, Natalie Robin; Sound, John Dupre; Art Installation by Hugh Morris; Cast: Matthew Micucci, Stephanie Wright Thompson, Jocelyn Kuritsky, Jacob Wilhelmi, and Gabel Eiben; Access Theater Black Box; December 3–19, 2010

The Group Theatre Too

The Things We Do For Love by Noel Katz; Director, Justin Boccitto; Musical Director, Christine de Frece; Producer, Steven Bidwell; Cast: Steven Bidwell, Stephen Mitchell Brown, Christine de Frece, Vanessa Dunleavy, Rebecca Kubaska, Brad Siebeking and Noel Katz; The Duplex; May 2–3, 2011

Choreographer's Canvas 2011 Director, Justin Boccitto; Stage Manager, Joseph Benesh; Lighting, Tim Ruppen; Sound, Eric Baron; Associate Producer, Mary Ann Penzero; Production Assistant, Jamie Marcus; Company Manager, Cristina Marie; Cast: James Atkinson, Michelle Barber, Michael Blevins, Justin Boccitto, Bob Boross, Emily Bufferd, Crystal Chapman, Jim Cooney, Bobby Hedglin-Taylor, Marian Hyun, Jason Marquette, Christohper Noffke, Kelly Peters, Jonathan Riedel, Sue Samuels, Amit Shah, Nick; Manhattan Movement & Arts Center; May 11, 2011

Ground Up Productions

www.GroundUpProductions.org

Letter From Algeria by Michael I. Walker; Director, Adam Fitzgerald; Stage Manager, Devan Hibbard; Lighting and Set, Travis McHale; Costumes, Amanda Jenks; Cast: Patrick Murney, JD Taylor, Rufus Collins, Amanda Jane Cooper; Abingdon Theatre Complex; October 29–November 20, 2010

Grounded Aerial

www.groundedaerial.com

Insectinside Written and directed by Karen A. Fuhrman; Original Music, John Medeski; Brooklyn Lyceum; April 26–29, 2011

The Guerrilla Shakespeare Project

www.GuerrillaShakespeare.com

The Taming of the Shrew by William Shakespeare; Director, Kim Martin-Cotton; Sound, Melissa Mizell; Cast: Geordie Broadwater, Kimiye Corwin, Ginger Eckert, Jordan Kaplan, Paul Klementowicz, Michael Larson, Madeleine Maby, Jordan Reeves, Jacques Roy, Tom Schwans; The Medicine Show Theatre; March 17–April 3, 2011

Hamm & Clov Stage Company

www.hammandclov.org

Holly Villaire, Producing Artistic Director

Ardnaglass on the Air by Jimmy Kerr; Director, Geraldine Hughes; Stage Manager, Alexis Qualls; Lighting, Joe Novak; Set, Pierre Kraitsowits; Cast: Jimmy Kerr, Jo Kinsella, Jonathan Judge-Russo and Maureen Brehoney Brady; Performed as a part of the 2010 1st Irish Festival; Manhattan Theatre Source; September 13–25, 2010

Handcart Ensemble

Kings: The Siege of Troy by Christopher Logue; Director, Jim Milton; Cast: Dana Watkins and J. Eric Cook; Workshop Theater; March 11–April 3, 2011

Harlem Creations

www.ilostmyheartinhaiti.com

I Lost My Heart in Haitl by Michelle Anglin; Directed and Original Music by Anngeannette Pinkston; Stage Manager, Michael Calise; Lighting, James Carter; Set, Michelle Anglin; Cast: Sandra Miller, Ava Jenkins, Ben Guralnik, Adrienne Witt, Nina Kompanek, Sabrina DeLee, James Williams, Anna Nellnois, Kamal Bashir, Kyara Kelley, Jeanica Toussaint, Nicholas Jenkins; Producer's Club Grand Theatre; August 10–21, 2010

HERE Arts Center

here.org

Artistic Director, Kristin Marting; Producing Director, Kim Whitener; Director Dream Music Puppetry Program, Basil Twist; Producer Dream Music Puppetry Program, Barbara Busackino; General Manager, Amanda Cooper; Development Director, Paul Menard; Marketi

Candy Tastes Nice Written and performed by Miranda Huba; Director, Shannon Sindelar; Sound, Bobby McElver; Lighting, Jeanette Oi-Suk Yew; Dorothy B. Williams Theatre; July 7–10, 2010

Sweet Motherhood by Jeremy Kareken in collaboration with Lee M. Silver; Director, Michael Bigelow Dixon; Costumes Design, Kari Love; Sound, Bruce Ellman; Set, Ray Neufeld; Video Design, Zoe Woodworth; Lighting, Christopher Brown; Production Stage Manager, Press Rep, Jim Baldassare; Photographer Carol Rosegg; Produced by Matthew Kreiner, Rachel Ford, Sara Bisman; Cast: Caroline Clooney and Michael De Nola; HERE Mainstage Theatre; July 8–31, 2010

Read My Mind by Damon Heath Sager; Director, Ryan Hugh McWilliams; Sound, Roger Mulligan; Video Designer, Ryan Hugh McWilliams; Lighting, Ilana Guttin; Casting and Consultation, Keith Justin Foster; Cast: Katie Hyde Lewars, Darren marc, Maia Karo, Jesse R. Tendler, Mike Quirk, Danielle Devine; Produced by The Gossip Factory; Dorothy B. Williams Theatre; July 20–24, 2010

Poste Restante Cast: Bonnie Duncan and Tim Gallagher; Produced by They Gotta Be Secret Agents; Dorothy B. Williams Theatre; July 16–18, 2010

For a Girl to Disappear July 20–28, 2010

Fog by Eugene O'Neill; Director, Katalina Mustatea; Costumes, Alicia Papanek; Lighting, Matthew Taylor; Choreographer, Yoshito Sakuraba; Original Music, Fredo Viola; Photographer, Melissa Lynn; Poster and Video Designer, Aaron Needham; Stage Manager, Glen Kinnaird; Cast: Kristina Skovby, Doug Rossi, Shaun Yates, Will de Meo; Produced by InOktober Productions; Dorothy B. Williams Theatre; July 28–August 1, 2010

Alberts I–V Sound, Broken Chord Collective; Film, Jayce Bartok and Andres Karu; Design Consultors, Thomas Dunn and Anya Klepikov; Live Electronics, Paula Matthusen; Cast: Aaron Meicht, Scott Blumenthal, Paula Matthusen, Wil Smith, and Daniel Baker; Produced by OZET; Dorothy B. Williams Theatre; August 5–8, 2010

USER 927 by Katharine Clark Gray; Director, David Hilder; Cast: Kelly McAndrew, Erika Rolfsrud, Alvin Keith, Gerry Lehane, Jake Paque, Anna Kull, Arielle Lever & David Julian Melendez; Produced by Fatboy, Self Defense, Rearviewmirror, Widows; HERE Mainstage Theatre; August 5–8, 2010

Struck by Robert Saietta and Rebecca Hart; Director, Joan Jubett; Original Music, Rebecca Hart; Cast: Rebecca Hart, Robert Saietta, Stephen Bradbury, Martina Potratz, David Bennett and Tommy McGinn; Dorothy B. Williams Theatre; August 31–September 2, 2010

Oedipus After Colonus by Robert Kelly; Director, Crichton Atkinson; Sound, Brenda Hutchinson; Video Designer, Andrew Lush and Richard Gartrell; Producer, Joel T. Clark; Cast: Carey Harrison; Produced by Dangerous Ground Productions; Dorothy B. Williams Theatre; September 8–12, 2010

Border Towns Director, Nick Brooke, Jenny Rohn; Sound, Jeremy Wilson; Set, Sue Rees; Lighting, Michael Giannitti; Costumes, Simone Duff; Composer, Nick Brooke; Music Director, Mary Montgomery Koppel; Stage Manager, Enrico Wey; Cast: Laura Bohn, Michael Chinworth, Chris Giarmo, Laryssa Husiak, Kamala Sankaram, Laura Stinger, Dax Valdes; Produced by The Cabinet; HERE Mainstage Theatre; September 10–18, 2010

Haratio Created by Ely Key, Antonguilio Panizzi, and Samuel Smith-Stevens; Dorothy B. Williams Theatre; September 15–18, 2010

Polanski Polanski by Saviana Stanescu; Director, Tamilla Woodard; Video Designer, Jake Witlen; Sound, Hillary Charnas; Lighting, Joyce Liao; Costumes, Amelia Dombrowski; Graphics, Allen Spector; Assistant Director and Photographer, Nancy Keegan; Stage Manager, Naomi Anhorn; Cast: Grant Neale; Produced by Nomad Theatreical; Dorothy B. Williams Theatre; September 22–25, 2010

Sleeping Beauty Written, Directed and performed by Colette Garrigan; Lighting, Laurent Filo; Consultants, Robin Frédéric and Pascaline Herveet; Original Music, Pascaline Herveet; Dorothy B. Williams Theatre; September 28–October 2, 2010

Microcrisis by Michael Lew; Director, Ralph B. Peña; Set, Clint Ramos; Costumes, Theresa Squire; Lighting, Japhy Weideman; Sound, Shane Rettig; Choreographer, Dax Valdes; Cast: Jackie Chung, David Gelles, William Jackson Harper, Lauren Hines, Alfredo Narciso, Socorro Santiago; Produced by Ma-Yi Theatre Company; September 28–October 23, 2010

Panic! Euphoria! Blackout by Ellen Maddow; Director, Katie Pearl; Lighting and Set, Lenore Doxsee; Costumes, Kiki Smith; Choreographer, Faye Driscoll; Cast: Randolph Curtis Rand, Mary Schultz, and Paul Zimet; Produced by The Talking Band; October 7–23, 2010

The Fortune Teller Created and Director, Erik Sanko and Jessica Grindstaff; Lighting, Andrew Hill; Marionette Designer, Erik Sanko; Sound, Andy Green; Architectural Designer, Selin Maner; Interior Design Team: Deana, Matt Acheson, Fatimah Durkee, Chloe Foglia, Jessica Grindstaff, Michelle Harper, Alex Haring, Robert Jami; Original Music, Danny Elfman and Erik Sanko; Art Director and Project Manager Jessica Grindstaff; Cast: Gavin Friday; Produced by Phantom Limb; Dorothy B. Williams Theatre; November 4–December 4, 2010

Soul Leaves Her Body Director, Peter Flaherty and Jennie MaryTai Liu; Designers: Scott Hirsch, Peter Ksander, Lucky Dragons, Austin Switser, Brandon Wolcott, Wendy Yang Bailey, Pablo Colapinto, and Jeanette Yew; Choreographer, Jennie MaryTai Liu; Cast: Leslie Cuyjet, Sean Donovan, Jennie MaryTai Liu, and Wai Ching Ho, Jackie Au, Makoto Hirosoko, Wai Ching Ho, Leslie Ho, Howah Hung, Rachel Lin, Jennie Mary Tai Liu, Eric Ng, Suetmann Wong; HERE Mainstage Theatre; November 5–23, 2010

Goodbye New York, Goodbye Heart Produced by The Production Company; December 1–21, 2010

Phobophilia Cast: Stephen Lawson and Aaron Pollard; Produced by 2BOYS.TV; Dorothy B. Williams Theatre; January 5–10, 2011

Mosheh by Yoav Gal; January 26–February 5, 2011

Next by Stephen Gracia; Produced by Abraxas Stage Company; February 2–19, 2011

Dead Fish by Rachael Holder; Director, Tarik Davis; Designer, Brett Banakis; Producer, Laura K. Nicoll; Cast: Arjun Gupta, Wade Allain-Marcus, Melle Powers, Halima Henderson, and Vella Lovell; February 9–12, 2011

Sleep of Reason Written and directed by Rachel Frank; Lighting, Greg Goff; Costume and Set and Construction, Rachel Frank; Cast: Angelica Pinna-Perez, Ruthie Scarpino, Dan Theisen, and Melanie Torres; February 18–19, 2011

Project Brand New Produced by Project Arts Centre; February 22, 2011

Shéhérazade! Written, Directed and performed by Maria Beloso Hall in collaboration with Frederic Ruiz and Philippe Risler; Costume and Set, Nefertiti La Foraine; Music Director and Percussion, Joël Grare; February 23, 2011

Instant Vaudeville Produced by Second Generation (2G); February 25–26, 2011

The Last Story Written & Director, Ka a elan; Cast: Tajna Tanovi , Scott Wallace; Graphics, Mirko Ili Corp; Produced by Theater TAS; March 2–12, 2011

Feeder: A Love Story by James Carter; Director, Jose Zayas; Set, Peter Ksander; Video Designer, Alex Koch; Costumes, Suzanne Chesney; Lighting, Bruce Steinberg; Sound, David Margolin Lawson; Producer, Ying Le, Arwen Lowbridge; Press Rep, Emily Owens, PR; Cast: Jennifer Conley Darling, Pierre-Marc Diennet; Produced by terraNOVA Collective; March 6–26, 2011

Ligeia by Edgar Allan Poe; Director, Selma Trevino; Conceived & Performed by William Trevino; Produced by Corporeal Arts Incorporated; March 18–20, 2011

Unheard Written and directed by Charles B. Murray; Nathan Lucrezio; Produced by Euphonixs, Inc.; March 24–26, 2011

Atta Boy Written and Produced by Brian Bauman; Director, Brian Bauman and Ricardo Bracho; Set, Christo Allegra; Sound, Seth Abrames; Lighting, John Eckert; Assistant Lighting, Adam Green; Cast: Heidi Carlsen, Robb Martinez, Jason Zeren; Produced by Perfect Disgrace Theatre; Dorothy B. Williams Theatre; March 29–April 1, 2011

2 out of 3: Breaking Statistics by Dana Edell; Produced by viBe; April 2–3, 2011

Tomorrow's Shore: A Reimagining of Beckett's Endgame by Marissa Mickelberg; Production Designer, Andrew Wingert; Lighting, Oliver Wason; Sound, Nicole Carroll; Stage Manager, Carrie Jean Fox; Cast: Andrew MacLarty, Amy P. Miller, Timothy Isaac Mellema and Jamie Soltis; April 7–9, 2011

Epona's Labyrinth by Ivana Catanese and Kameron Steele; Director, Kameron Steele; Lighting, Ayumu Saegusa; Costumes Designer, Mitsushi Yanaihara; Video Designer, Keisuke Takahashi; Sets Designer, Shige Moriya; Sound and Original Music, SKANK; Choreographer, Mikuni Yanaihara; Stage Manager, Catherine Coffey; Dramaturg, Pete McCabe; Managing Producer, Ivana Catanese; Produced by The South Wing in collaboration with Nibroll art collective; HERE Mainstage Theatre; April 7–23, 2011

Time Capsules To Space Created by Zarah Cabañas; Produced by FireflyLab; April 15–17, 2011

Another Place Written and directed by Melissa F. Moschitto; Lighting, Ryan Metzler; Assistant Lighting, Shaun Suchan; Set, Justin Couchara; Assistant Set, Kristina Herne; Costumes, Christina Kim; Assistant Sound, Justin Stasiw; Conceived by The Anthropologists; Dramaturg, Louise Gough; Producer, Anna Hayman; Associate Producer, Jason Najjoum; Stage Manager, Christine Boutin, Production Assistant, Lisa Haedrich; Cast: Raniah Day, Joseph Diomede, Jean Goto, Jonathan Maccia and Karly Maurer; Produced by The Anthropologists; Dorothy B. Williams Theatre; April 27–29, 2011

Puppet Parlor Cast: Hanne Tierney, Malgosia Szkandera, Joey Arias, Basil Twist, Chris DeVille; Dorothy B. Williams Theatre; April 30–May 1, 2011

18 Paintings Created and Director, Dylan Stephen Levers; Set, Liz Jenetopulos; Lighting, Charlie Winter; Costumes, Savana Leveille; Sound, Kevin Brouder; Puppetry Designer and Additional Sound, Ien DeNio; Stage Manager, Chaele Davis; Producer, Eve Rybnick; Cast: Laurel Atwell, Kirstan Clifford, Megan Hanley, Daniel Joseph LeBlanc, Carolyn McCandlish, Olivia Mora, Peter Rothbard; Dorothy B. Williams Theatre; May 4–7, 2011

The Tempest by William Shakespeare; Director, David Herskovits; Lighting, Lenore Doxsee; Assistant Lighting, Natalie Robin; Set, David Birn; Costumes, Carol Bailey; Sound, Kate Marvin, David Herskovits; Original Music, Thomas Cabaniss, Julia Greenberg and Robin Goldwasser, Robert Johnson, Kate Marvin, Mel Marvin, John Morton, and David Rosenmeyer; Stage Manager, Joseph Fletcher; Assistant Stage Manager, Kathleen Purcell; Assistant Director, Maia Karo; Cast: Clare Barron, Purva Bedi, James Ferguson, Yehuda Hyman, Mia Katigbak, Meg MacCary, Nana Mensah, Mary Neufeld, Hubert Point-Du Jour, Steven Rattazzi, J.H. Smith III; May 4–28, 2011

Move It! Produced by Parallel Exit; May 9, 2011

Pieces of Papter Project–Aspirations of 9/11 Written and directed by Michael Simon Hall; Lighting, Justin Partier; Video Design, Shawn Boyle; Sound Engineer, Billy Bagget; Cast: Patrick Avella, Clodagh Bowyer, Susanna Buckley, Aaron Chartrand, Tino Christopher, Lars Drew, Marco Greco, Marlene Hamerling, Bob Hart, Stacey Haughton, Elizabeth Flynn-Jones, Sergio Martinez, Karen Mester, Maureen Mueller, Mary Murphy, Preya Patel; Dorothy B. Williams Theatre; May 12–14, 2011

Between Two Worlds Written and directed by Eileen Connolly; Video Designer, Edgar Santiago; Choreographed by Sean Roschman and Eileen Connolly; Cast: Andhy Mendez, Annalisa Chamberlin, Joseph Goodrich, Connie Rotunda, Kyle Quiring, Dannie Flanagan, Maryann Peterson, Sean Roschman; Produced by Wallis Knot Theatre & Roschman Dance Collaboration; May 15–18, 2011

The Money Show Created by Lauren Murphy and Megan Maczko; Produced by Cheddar Gorillas Productions; May 20–22, 2011

READINGS AND WORKSHOPS

Lush Valley Think Tank #3: Freedom July 7, 2010

Petrohead! by Rochelle Bright; Produced by Toi Trade Theatre Co; Dorothy B. Williams Theatre; August 16, 2010

Lush Valley Think Tank #4: Equality August 18, 2010

HARP Work-in-Progress September 13, 2010

FESTIVALS

CultureMart Festival; HERE Arts Center; January 7–23, 2011; Included: *Wooden* by Laura Peterson; *Floating Point Waves* Created by Ximena Garnica and Shige Moriya, Produced by LEIMAY, CAVE and The New York Butoh Festival, in collaboration with Roland Toledo and Jeremy Slater; *Botch* Cast: Christina Campanella and John Rose; *Lush Valley* Conception Mahayana Landowne, Kristin Marting and Tal Yarden, Original and adapted text by Robert Lyons, Cast: Marc Bovino, Oana Botez, Matthew Lewis, Irene Longshore, Rudy Mungaray, Mariana Newhard, Clint Ramos, Abigail Ramsay, Jane Shaw, Suzi Takahashi and Dax Valdes; *A Marriage: 1* by Nick Vaughan and Jake Margolin; *The Strangest* by Betty Shamieh, Director, Jose Zayas; *Chimera* by Deborah Stein and Suli Holum; *Miranda* by Kamala Sankaram; *Epyllion* by Lindsay Abromaitis-Smith; *Panel Discussions* Panalists: Jesse Zaritt, Karen Shimakawa, Donna Uchizono, Ximena Garnica, Kristin Marting, Tal Yarden, Yana Landowne, Jake Margolin, Nick Vaughan, Joe Diebes, Pete McCabe, Kamala Sankaram, Joe Diebes, Christina Campanella, Yoav Gal, Nick Brooke; January 11–21, 2011; *City Council Meeting* by Aaron Landsman; Directed and Dramaturged by Mallory Catlett; January 12–13, 2011

The Hive Theatre

Artistic Director, Matthew A.J. Gregory

Panama by Mike Folie; Director, Diana Glazer; The Cell Theatre; November 9, 2010

Horse Trade

www.horseTRADE.info

The Pumpkin Pie Show: Amber Alert by *Diminishing Returns*; *Gladiatorum*; *Sixteen Again*; *Diary Debris*; Parent/Teacher by Clay McLeod Chapman; Sound, RadioTheatre; Cast: Clay McLeod Chapman, Hannah Timmons, Hannah Cheek; The Kraine Theater; October 14–30, 2010

Donnie and the Monsters by Robert J. Gibbs; Director, Heidi G. Grumelot; Stage Manager, Ashley Zednick; Set, Ariel Schecter; Sound, Hanna Weddle; Puppet & Prop Design, Elaine Jones; Assistand Director, Nicole Gehring; Cast: Richard Altmanschofer, Paul Herbig, Yury Lomakin, JB Rot , and Matt Wise; Under St. Marks; September 2–18, 2010

Mimi and Gustav in Love and Pirates! by Denis Woychuk; Director, Steve Brennan; Musical Director, Caitlin Rodgers; Cast:; Kraine Theater; November 6–December 19, 2010

Thank You For Being A Friend Book by Nick Brennan; Music by Jeff Thomson; Lyrics by Luke Jones and Cisco Cardenas; Director, Nick Brennan; Musical Director, Adam Gubman; Choreographer, Amy Corcoran; Production Designer, Luke Jones; Cast: Mimi Imfurst, Jake Lemmenes, Susan Campanaro, Jason B. Schmidt, Belinda Hodler; Kraine Theatrer; June 13–August 1, 2010

FESTIVALS

The Fire This Time Festival; Red Room; January 17–30, 2011; Included: *The Flower Thief* by Pia Wilson; *Casket Sharp* by Radha Blank; *The Scorpion and the Fox* by Jesse Cameron Alick; *The Big Crunch or...(the eternal return)* by Christine Jean Chambers; *Exodus* by Camille Darby; *The Bitter Seraph of Sugar Hill* by Marcus Gardley; *Breakfast* by Yusef Miller; *Third Grade* by Dominique Morisseau; *The Anointed* by Germono Toussaint; *Gypsy Moth* by Kelley Nicole Girod; *On Troubled Waters* by Derek Lee McPhatter; Director, Kelly Nicole Girod, Derek Lee McPhatter, Germono Toussaint

The Drafts Fest: Accidental Discharge Impossible Red Room; May 5–14, 2011; Included: *Hard to Kill* by Aliza Einhorn, Director, Danny Sharron; *Senile Agitation* by Quinn D. Eli, Director, Shay Gines; *Paper Rose of Sarajevo* by Eric Kingrea, Director, Nicole Watson; *A Better Destiny for Bethany* by Derek McPhatter, Director, Nicole Gerhing; *The Bling and the Bang Of It* by Megan Hill, Director, Axel Avin Jr.; *Pigeons, Sharks, and Vixens* by Matthew-Lee Erlbach, Director, Randi Rivera; Cast: Penny Pollack, Gary Warchola, Amanda Von Nostrand, Quinn Warren, JB Rote, Evan Taylor Walker, Yesenia Tromp, Matthew Wise, Penny Pollack and Matthew Wise

The Corporate Personhood Play Festival; Kraine Theater; December 7–15, 2010; Included: *Dammit, Office Girl!* by James Comtois, Director, Danny Sharron; *Brooklyn Skank* by Fernanda Coppel, Director, Donya K. Washington; *The Foundation* by Jerome Parker, Director, Axel Avin Jr.; *Target Monologue* by Leegrid Stevens, Director, Rachel Wohlander; *Oh, Donna* Written & Director, Lucile Baker Scott

NON-RESIDENT PRODUCTIONS

Based on a True Story: The Sex Edition Produced by Wreckio Ensemble; Director, Christopher Bamonte with Randi Berry, Dechelle Damien and Karly Maurer; Under St. Marks

Buckle Up: The Jorney of a Ride Home Produced by Sanity Island; Director, JP Shuffman; Light Design, Brian Douglas, Costumes, Jen Perney; Set JP Schuffman; Under St. Marks

Cut Produced by The Management; Director, Meg Sturiano; Cast: Nicole Beerman, Megan Hill, and Joseph Varca; Under St. Marks

Dirty Little Machine by Miranda Huba; Director, Nathan Schwartz; Cast: Nic Grelli, Joanne Wilson; Produced by AnimalParts Theatre; Red Room; May 19–June 4, 2011

Right Cross Rhapsody by Todd Michael; Director, Walter Hoffmann; Set and Costumes, David Zwiers; Lighting and Sound Desigers, Walter Hoffman, Chandler Wild & Joemca; Original Music, Lisa Ferber, Joemca; Cast: Jeff Auer, Courtney Cook, Matt Garner, Jason Griffith, Brian Hopson, Jessica Luck, Todd Michael, and Ryan Stadler; Produced by Grayce Productions; Red Room; June 10–26, 2010

Hobo Grunt Cycle Written and directed by Kevin Augustine; Props and Set, Gloria Sun; Lighting, Ayuma Saegusa; Video Designer, Raine Vivian; Sound, Aldo Perez and Miguel Weissman; Costumes, Ana Marie Salamat, Mandy Tam and Candida Nichols; Cast: Kevin Augustine, Adam Ende, Ora Fruchter, and Joshua Holden; Produced by Lone Wolf Tribe; Kraine Theater; April 7–24, 2011

Jewqueen Created and Performed by Julia Arazi, Sarah Bishop-Stone, Das Elkin, Diana Konopka, Michael Levinton, Rodney Pallanck, Laura von Holt; Produced by Little Lord (a theater company); Under St. Marks; March 17–18, 2011

The Kentucky Goblin Siege by Jeff Sproul; Director, Lindsey Moore; Sound, Jeremy Mather; Fight Chorographer, Kenneth Nicholas; Costumes Caroline O'Hare; Puppet Designer, Anna Paniccia and Puppet Heap; Set, Jak Prince; Stage Manager, Sarania Hertilus; Cast: Jeremy Banks, Alicia Barnatchez, Jesse Bernath, Sabrina Farhi, Jeremy Mather, Michele McNally, Mike Quirk, Alexis Robbins, Jeff Sproul, Christine Sullivan, D. Robert Wolcheck,Elizabeth Dapo, Ryan-Michele Healey, Lisa Nussbaum; Produced by No Tea Productions; Kraine Theater; October 20–November 24, 2010

Legs and All Written, Directed and performed by Summer Shapiro & Peter Musante; Produced by Summer Shapiro & Peter Musante; Kraine Theater; October 2–16, 2010

Lonsome Winter by Joshua Conkel and Megan Hill; Director, Meg Sturiano; Stage Manager, Chiara DiLello; Costumes, Joshua Conkel; Set, Jason Sims; Sound, Meg Sturiano; Lighting, Grant Wilcoxen; Cast: Megan Hill, Nicole Beerman, Kristen Hopkins, Nick Lewis, Joshua Conkel; Produced by The Management; Under St. Marks; December 2–19, 2010

Under Consideration by Chris Cragin, Pia Wilson, Bridget Kelso, Sevan Greene, Sukari Jones, Aaron Levy, Anna Moench, Jerome Parker, and Stella Fawn Ragsdale; Produced by The Ghostlights; Kraine Theatre; April 14–16, 2011

Work: A Play by Jeremy Mather, Lindsey Moore, & Jeff Sproul; Produced by No Tea Production ; Director, Lindsey Moore; Set and Costumes, Lindsey Moore; Cast: Jeremy Banks, Alicia Barnatchez, Jesse Bernath, Sabrina Farhi, Jeremy Mather, Michele McNally, Alexis Robbins, Jeff Sproul, and D. Robert Wolcheck; Under St. Marks

The House of Yes

www.houseofyes.org

Circus of Circus by Kae Burke; Director, Rachel Klein; Choreographer, Rachel Klein and Angela Harriel; Stage Manager, Marina Steinberg; Lighting, Julia Lavault; Set, Emma Chammah, Pak Kei Mak, and Ethan O'Hara; Costumes, Kae Burke; Sound, Marshall Moran; Aerial and Circus Rigging Design, Kae Burke; Cast: Benjamin Cerf, Ashley Monroe, Kae Burke, Shannon Turner, Ryan Murray Shinji, Evgenia Radilova, Natasha Ortiz, Eric Schmalenberger, David Slone, Valton Jackson, Angela Harriel and the Love Show Dancers; October 1 –16, 2010

Hudson Warehouse

hudsonwarehouse.net

Trojan Women Written and directed by Nicholas Martin Smith; Stage Manager, Peter Howard; Costumess, Drew Rosene and Emily Rose Parman; Producer, Susane Lee; Cast: Ruth Nightengale, Lindsay Kitt Wiebe, Chel Shipley, Molly Garber, Amanda Renee Baker, Julia E.C. Jones, Sydney Stanton, Kate Tenetko, Margaret Woodard, Chris Behan, Nick DeVita, Augustine Hargrave, Peter Howard, Kelly King, Darla Delane, Drew Rosene; Soldiers and Sailors Monument; June 3 – 27, 2010

Cyrano by Edmond Rostand; Director, Nicholas Martin Smith; Choreographer, Jared Kirby; Cast: David Palmer Brown, Matt Fraley, Amanda Jones, Joseph Hamel, Emily Rose Parman, Vince Phillip, Valerie O'Hara, Chel Shipley, Ryan Patrick Lingle, Roger Dale Stude, Coulby Jenkins; Soldiers and Sailors Monument; July 8 – August 1, 2010

Romeo and Juliet by William Shakespeare; Director, Nicholas Martin Smith; Costumes, Drew Rosene; Cast: Tyler D. Hall, Gustavo Obregon, Drew Rosene, Jesse Michael Mothershed, Vince Philip, Nike DeVita, J.T. Maloy, Valerie O'Hara, David Palmer Brown, Amanda Renee Baker, Amanda Ochoa, George K. Wells, Jerry Mouse Nwosuocha, J.T. Maclay; Soldiers and Sailors Monument; August 5 – 29, 2010

Hyper Aware Theater Company

www.hyperawaretheater.blogspot.com

Wild Blue by Gary Ferrar and Louis Aquiler; Director, Gary Ferrar; Original Music, Patrick Gaughan; Cast: Chad Miller, George Walsh, Jeremy Weber, Erin Ronder, Ariana Murphy; The Access Theater; March 29–April 10, 2011

IATI Theater

www.iatiTheater.org

The Smell of Popcorn Director, Jorge B. Merced; Choreographer, Mike Yahn; Stage Manager, Karina Fernandez; Lighting and Set, Jason Sturm; Cast: Javier E. Gomez, Luciana Faulhaber; Teatro IATI; September 8–19, 2010

Haunting The Reynosos by Henry Guzmán; Director, Roberto Cambeiro; Lighting, Miguel Angel Valderrama; Set, Ji-youn Chang; Costumes, Christina Giannini; Sound, William González; Cast: Winston Estevez, Fabián González, Betsy Pujols, Laura Spalding, Teresa Yenque; December 1–12, 2010

Incubator Arts Project

www.incubatorarts.org

Producing Director, Samara Naeymi; Fiscal Management & Administration, Mimi Johnson; Development Director, Arwen Lowbridge; Curator, Technical Director, Brendan Regimbal; Curator, Shannon Sindelar; Curator/Director of the MUSIC program, Travis Just

Buddy Cop Produced by The Debate Society; June 3–12, 2010

Short Form 2010 June 23–25, 2010

the Little Death: Vol. 1 by Matt Mark; July 8–17, 2010

Red Over Red by Shannon Sindelar and Ryan Holsopple; Director, Shannon Sindelar; Sound, Ryan Holsopple; Live Projections Desing, Ryan Holsopple and Mirit Tal; Scenic Design, Andreea Mincic; Lighting, Jon Luton; Costumes, Ramsey Scott; Jet Crash Sound by Tim Cramer; DJ Mendel, Caitlin McDonough-Thayer, Shauna Kelly and Ryan Holsopple; Produced by 31Down–31down.org; July 22–August 2, 2010

The Internet Produced by Everywhere Theatre Group; August 12–28, 2010

AW Keats! Keats MotherF***er Produced by Reconnoiter; September 2–4, 2010

Brandywide Distillery Fire by Michael Gardner and Matt Freeman; September 8–18, 2010

Field 309 Produced by Title: Point Productions; September 23–October 2, 2010

The Void Produced by Hybrid Stage Projects; October 7–16, 2010

(oh my god I am so) THIRST (y) Produced by Little Lord a Theatre Company; October 21–30, 2010

Montgomery Park or Opulence by Karinne Keithley; November 4–13, 2010

Timberbrit Produced by Firestarter Productions; November 18–20, 2010

Emancipatory Politics: A Romantic Tragedy Produced by Old Ken Road; December 2–11, 2010

Boat Produced by Magnus, Miller and Truman; December 16–18, 2010

Tom Ryan Thinks He's James Mason by Daniel Fish; Directed; January 6–22, 2011

Dance Marathon Produced by Bluemouth Inc.; January 6–8, 2011

Innova Produced by Object Collection; January 6–11, 2011

Saturn Nights Produced by The Longest Lunch; January 27–February 5, 2011

Medea /and Medea /For Medea Produced by Red Handle; February 17–26, 2011

Are They Edible Produced by Yew's Jeanette Oi-Suk; March 3–5, 2011

Carla & Lewis Produced by The Ecocide Projects; March 10–19, 2011

The Inexplicable Redemption of Agent G Produced by Vampire Cowboy's; March 24–April 16, 2011

Opal Produced by The Nerve Tank; April 28–May 7, 2011

Clap for the Wolfman Produced by Shannon Gillen and Guests; May 12–14, 2011

May Days May 20–28, 2011

InProximity Theatre Company

www.InProximityTheatre.org

Sight Unseen by Donald Margulies; Director, Dorothy Lyman; Stage Manager, Jasmin Sanchez; Lighting, Lisa Soverino; Set, James J. Fenton; Costumes, Court Watson; Sound, Jeremy Lee; Propmaster, Michael Mattie; Assistant Stage Manager, Eva Owens; Producer, Jolie Curtsinger; Associate Producer, Michael Poignand; Cast: Laurie Schaefer, Bryn Boice, Jonathan Todd Ross, Brent Vimtrup; Theatre 54 @Shetler Studios; September 23–October 10, 2010

Navy Pier by John Corwin; Director, Bryn Boice; Stage Manager, Jasmin Sanchez; Lighting, Lisa Soverino; Set, James J. Fenton; Sound, Amy Altadonna; Producer, Jolie Curtsinger, Laurie Schaefer; Associate Producer, Jenna Gottlieb; Cast: Josh Clayton, Jolie Curtsinger, Michael Poignand, Laurie Schaefer; Theatre Row–Studio Theatre; May 5–22, 2011

InViolet Repertory Theater in association with New York Theatre Workshop

invioletrep.com

40 Weeks by Michael Henry Harris; Director, Danton Stone; Stage Manager, Megan Griffith; Lighting, Melissa Mzell; Set, Lauren Helpern; Costumes, Lisa Loen; Sound, Josh Liebert; Cast: Ronan Babbitt, Jorge Cordova. Michelle David, Megan Hart and Deanna Sido; Fourth Street Theatre; February 22–26, 2011

Iron Jaw Company

www.ironjawcompany.com

Founders, Erica Linderman, Kitty Lindsay, Teresa Reynolds

Women of Manhattan by John Patrick Shanley; Director, Will Warren; Dorothy Strelsin Theatre; September 30 – October 3, 2010

Narrator 1 by Erin Browne; Director, Kitty Lindsay; Stage Manager, Eileen Arnold; Lighting, Jake Degroot; Set, Stephanie Barkley; Sound, Phillip Rudy; Cast: Rachael Hip-Flores, Marco Formosa, Jennifer Harder, Kyle Kirkpatrick, Matthew Murumba, Aiden O'Shea and Cotton Wright; Lion Theatre; May 11–28, 2011

IRT Theater

www.irttheater.org

Artistic/Executive Director, Kori Rushton; Associate Artistic Director, Ben Vershbow; Managing Director, Veronica Graveline; Technical Director, Matt Vieira

Carnival Round the Central Figure by Diana Amsterdam; Director, Karen Kohlhaas; Musical Director, David James Boyd; Stage Manager, Veronica Graveline; Lighting, Eric Southern; Set, Walt Spangler with Melissa Shakun and Jisun Kim; Costumes, Katja Andreiev; Producer, Kori Rushton/IRT Productions; Managing Producer, Jaki Silver; Assistant Managing Producer, Danielle Connor; Assistant Director, Rick Cekovsky; Assistant Director, Arden Walentowski; Public Relations, Springer Assosciates PR; Graphic Design, Kave; Cast: Carla Briscoe, Ted Caine, Janna Emig, Brandon Kyle Goodman, Stephanie Hsu, Raymond Hill, David Michael Kirby, Shane LeCocq, Christine Rowan, Kori Rushton, Rebecca Schoffer, Livia Scott, Cynthia Silver, Danni Simon, Ed Stelz; IRT Theater; January 13–30, 2011

John Montgomery Theatre Company

www.jmtcinc.com

Artistic Director, Suzanne Bachner; Executive Director, Bob Brader; Founder, Patrick Hillan; Artistic Associate, Francis O'Flynn; Resident Graphics, Michael Koch; Resident Photographer, Scott Wynn; Resident Video Producer, Shar Adrias

Spitting In The Face Of The Devil Written and performed by Bob Brader; Director, Suzanne Bachner; Lighting, Cory Pattak; Graphics, Michael Koch; Video Production, Shar Adrias; Photographer, Scott Wynn; Theatre Row Studio Theatre; June 11, 2010; also performed at The London Fringe, June 2010; The Omega Institute, July 2010 and The Atlantic Fringe, September 2010

Spitting In The Face Of The Devil–60 minute version Written and performed by Bob Brader; Director, Suzanne Bachner; Lighting, Cory Pattak; Developer, Suzanne Bachner; Graphics, Michael Koch; Video Production, Shar Adrias; Photographer, Scott Wynn; Theatre Row Studio Theatre; November 12, 2010

READINGS AND WORKSHOPS

Follow Me Written and directed by Suzanne Bachner; Cast: Bob Brader, Becky Byers, Nathan Faudree, Einar Gunn, Judy Krause & Mateo Moreno; West Chelsea

Arts Building; January 27, 2010

Josiah Theatre Works

Tribute (forget me not) Written and directed by Nickolas Long, III; Original Music, Nickolas Long, III, K.Will, Sophia Loren Coffee, Andrea Womack, TJ-Breezy; Stage Manager, Andrea Womack; Cast: Gerard Dure, James Roach, Andrea Womack, Cumali, Bryant Mccallister, Chanton Mcelwain; Paul Michael's The Network; February 18, 2011

Judith Shakespeare Company NYC

www.judithshakespeare.org

Artistic Director and Producer, Joanne Zipay; Associate Artistic Director, Jane Titus; Associate Producer, Ginny Hack

Two Gentlemen of Verona by William Shakespeare; Director, Joanne Zipay; Original Music, Austin Moorhead; Stage Manager, Sandra M. Bloom; Lighting, Lois Catanzaro; Set, Joshua David Bishop; Costumes, Ashley Betton; Cast: Alvin Chan, Alexandra Devin, Amy Driesler, Marie Bridget Dundon, Bill Galarno, Hunter Gilmore, Suzanne Hayes, Rachael Hip-Flores, Sheila Joon, Peggy Suzuki, Natasha Yannacanedo, Candide; TBG Theatre; August 4 –22, 2010

KADM Productions

The Inventor, The Escort, The Photographer, Her Boyfriend and His Girlfriend Written and directed by Matt Morillo; Choreographer, Gillian Brooke Todd; Lighting, Amith A. Chandrashaker; Set, Mark Marcante; Cast: David R. Doumeng, Tom Pilutik, Jessica Durdock Moreno, Emily Campion, Maria Rowene; Theater for the New City; January 6–March 5, 2011

kef theatrical productions

www.kefproductions.com

Artistic Director, Adam Fitzgerald; Producing Director, Lori Prince; Director of Education and Outreach, Kimberly Strafford; Marketing Manager, Matthew Menter; Associate Producer, Adam J. Rosen

First Prize by Israela Margalit; Director, Margarett Perry; Stage Manager, Jessa Nicole Pollack; Lighting, Travis McHale; Set, David L. Arsenault; Costumes, Nicole Wee; Sound, Colin Whitely; Cast: Brian Dykstra, Susan Ferrara, Christopher Hirsh and Lori Prince; ArcLight Theatre; April 28–May 21, 2011

READINGS AND WORKSHOPS

Cradle & All by Jay Russell; Director, Adam Fitzgerald; Cast: Harry Bouvy, Finnerty Steeves, Steven Strafford and Amy Warren; The Arc Light Theatre; May 11, 2011

Inappropriate: The Concert Director, Adam Fitzgerald; Cast: Lisa Brescia, Kristy Cates, Ali Ewoldt, Brad Giovanine, Danielle Grabianowski, David Gurland, Katie Lee Hill, Brianne Mai, Rob Maitner, Jeremy Ritz, Steven Strafford, Christopher Totten, Adena Walker, Cassie Wooley and Lee Zarrett; Lucky Strike; September 13, 2010

Old Fashioned Piano Party Director, Adam Fitzgerald; Cast: Pilita Danes, Colin Israel, Zachary Prince, Marcos Sanchez, Christopher Sloan and Katie Zaffrann. With accompaniment by Michael Harren; Laurie Beechman Theatre; November 7, 2011

Methtacular! by Steven Strafford; Director, Adam Fitzgerald; Music Director, Michael Harren; Producer, Justin Brill; Theatre Row Studios; January 31, 2011

Kids with Guns

kidswithguns.com

Co-Artistic Director, Ben Cikanek; Co-Artistic Director, Mike Klar

Wolves by Delaney Britt Brewer; Director, Mike Klar; Stage Manager, Meredith Brown; Lighting, Maruti Evans; Set, Maruti Evans; Costumes, Heather Klar; Sound, John Colaruotolo; Producer, Ben Cikanek; Producer, Mike Klar; Choreography Consulting, Jessica Jolly; Technical Director, Vadim Malinskiy; Cast: Josh Tyson, Elizabeth A. Davis, Richard Saudek, Sarah Baskin, Megan Hart, Doug Roland, Julie Fitzpatrick, Vikki Vasiliki Eugenis, Isaac Jin Solstein; 59E59 Theaters; August 4–21, 2010

La Criatura Theater

www.lacriatura.org

The Orphans by Karina Casiano; Directed and Choreographed by Karina Casiano and Daniel Irizarry; Original Music, Andrés Rotmistrovsky; Stage Manager, Edna Lee Figueroa; Lighting, María Cristina Fusté; Set, Jorge Dieppa; Costumes, Awymarie Riollano; Sound, Karina Casiano; Cast: Daniel Irizarry, Karina Casiano; Produced in association with La MaMa Experimental Theatre; December 2–12, 2010

LABA

www.14streety.org/laba

A Wonderfully Flat Thing by Valerie Work, Manju Shandler and Basmat Hazan; Director, David Winitsky; Original Music, Tamar Muskal; Choreographer, Jesse Zaritt; Stage Manager, Sarah Koehler; Lighting, David Tirosh; Set, Manju Shandler; Puppet Design, Manju Shandler; Cast: Jake Goodman, Emily Hartford, Shawn Shafner, Sarah Painter, Sarae Garcia; 14th Street Theatre; December 18, 2010–January 16, 2011

LaMaMa Experimental Theatre Club

www.lamama.org

Artistic Director, Mia Yoo; Managing Director, Mary Fulham; Associate Director, Beverly Petty; Programming Director for The Club; La MaMa Moves! Curator, Nicky Paraiso; Puppet Series Curator, Denise Greber; Experiments Curator, George Ferencz; Poetry Electric Curator, William Electric Black; Coffeehouse Chronicles Curator, Chris Kapp; Associate Director of Development, Kaori Fujiyabu: Special Projects Manager & International Relations, Denise Greber; Resident Artistic Associate, Kiku Sakai; Bookkeeper, Melissa Slattery; Director of Archive, Ozzie Rodriguez; Archive Staff: Kaori Fujiyabu, Michal Gamily, Shigeko Suga; Marketing, Discovering Oz Communications; IT Support, Eugene the Poogene; Production Manager, Mark Tambella; Technical Supervisor, Juan Merchan; Resident Sound, Tim Schellenbaum; Technical Staff: Jack Reynolds, Carla Bosnjak, Sarah Murphy, David Bonilla, Miguel Valderama, Michael Greber; Ulrich Fladl; Box Office/House Staff: Alexa Criscitiello, Shannon Foy, Michael Greber, Peter Jubinsky; Great Jones Staff: Michael Arian, Merry Geng, Pearse Redmond, Doug Major, Valois Mickens, Cathy Shaw; La Galleria: Matt Nasser, Louis Laurita, Adriana Farmiga, Sara Galassini

A prayer for Japan A benefit for Japan; with A Shinto Ritual, Kinding Sindaw, Matou, Emi Toko, The Silver Cloud Dancers & Singers and Pua Ali'i 'Ilima and Vicky Holt Takamine; April 25, 2011

A Tribute to Jim Neu Memorial Tribute; November 20, 2010

Against Progress Spotlight Catalonia at Prelude 2010 Festival by Esteve Soler; Curated by Mallory Catlett; Director, Dan Safer; Translator, Hillary J. Gardner; October 5, 2010

Beautiful Fire by Joseph Webb; February 18–20, 2011

Being Harold Pinter by Harold Pinter; Adapted by Vladimir Shcherban, and letters of Belarusian political prisoners; Director, Vladimir Shcherban; Stage Manager, Aliaksei Shyrnevich, Laur Biarzhanin, Artsem Zhaliazniak; Cast: Nikolai Khalezin, Pavel Gorodnitski, Yana Rusakevich, Oleg Sidorchik, Irina Yaroshevich, Denis Tarasenka, Marina Yurevich; produced by Belarus Free Theatre; La MaMa Experimental Theatre; April 21–May 15, 2011

Belarus Free Theatre in Repertory by Belarus Free Theatre; co-presented with Public Theatre; [Being Harold Pinter], [Zone of Silence] Director, Vladimir Shcherban; [Discover Love] Directed and written by Nikolai Khalezin; April 13–May 15, 2011

Broken Nails–A Marlene Dietrich Dialogue Written and performed by Anna Skubik; La MaMa Experimental Theatre; November 11–21, 2010

Buried up to my neck while thinking outside the box by George Emilio Sanchez; March 25–27, 2011

Cabaret Central: Political Snorts by NYU Performance Composition; Director, Liz Swados; December 7, 2010

Cancer's a Bitch Annual Fundraiser by The National LGBT Cancer Network; Cast: Bitch and Eddie Sarfaty; October 19, 2010

Christmas in Nickyland 2010 by Nicky Paraiso; Performances by The Alien Comic aka Tom Murrin, Mike Albo, Jim Andralis, Larry Krone, Betsy Bates, Ellen Fisher, Ching Gonzalez, Joseph Keckler, Jon Kinzel, Vicky Shick, Patricia Hoffbauer, George Emilio Sanchez, Ishmael Houston-Jones, Yvonne Meier, Matt Nasser, Edgar Oliver, Chris Tanner Cruce, Lance Cruce; December 18–19, 2010

CoffeeHouse Chronicles '11 Director, Chris Kapp; Ongoing

Experiments '11; Experimental play reading series; Curated by George Ferencz; Ongoing

Folktales from Asia and Africa by Jane Catherine Shaw; Director, Jane Catherine Shaw; Set, Jane Catherine Shaw; Puppet Designer, Jane Catherine Shaw ; Cast: Jane Catherine Shaw; La MaMa Experimental Theatre; October 16–November 7, 2010

Gingerbread Story A benefit for La MaMa and Broadway Cares/ Equity Fights AIDS; by Laura Benanti, Kim Ima and Gail

Lerner; June 6, 2011

Girl/Group: A daughter's tale by Susan Murphy; Director, Mario Giacalone; June 17–26, 2011

Hamyul/Hamlet by William Shakespeare; Director, Byungkoo Ahn; June 23–July 10, 2011

I Am Going To Run Away October 1–10, 2010

I Am Going to Run Away Written, Directed and performed by Bree Benton; Original Music, Franklin Bruno; La MaMa Experimental Theatre; October 1–10, 2010

International Migration Art Festival A closing event of IMAFestival; a concert by Georgia Cee; May 3, 2011

I Fioretti In Musica Written and directed by Gian Marco Lo Forte; Original Music, Sasha Zamler-Carhart & Ryan Carter; Choreographer, Philip Montana; Stage Manager, Karen Oughtred; Lighting, Ji-youn Chang; Set, Gian Marco Lo Forte; Costumes, Angela Wendt & Gabriel Berry; Sound, Ryan Carter; Puppet and Mask Designer, Jane Catherine Shaw & Abby Felder; Cast: singers Megan Schubert, Patrick Fennig, Charles Matthew Hill, Mathew Knickman and Raymond Bailey; puppeteers and dancers Laura Arend, Courtney Dana Baron, Spencer Bazzano, Kimberly Diamond, Silvia Giampaola, Dorothy James Loechel, Dana Marcolina, Kayla Ma; La MaMa Experimental Theatre; October 1–17, 2010

Jonathan Hart Makwaia in Concert by Jonathan Hart; Cast: Ian Magilton, Inki Storleer, Jonathan Hart Makwaia;February 25- 27, 2011

La MaMa Fall Gala Honoring Cheryl Henson Cast: Basil Twist, Roman Paska, Federico Restrepo, Tom Lee, Erik Sanko, Jessica Grindstaff, Lake Simons, John Dyer; Dan Hurlin, Mark Russell, Theodora Skipitares, Leslie Carrara Rudolf, Lolly, Caroll Spinney, Oscar the Grouch; October 25, 2010

La MaMa-Loped with Jesse Cameron Alick, Lucile Scott, Scout Durwood; February 14, 2011

La MaMa Teen Dance Festival: A New Generation Director, Martha Tornay; with East Village Dance Project (EVDP); November 26–28, 2010

My Life, My Diary, My Dance by Chloe Arnold; Director, Ted Louis Levy; Original Music, Choclatt Jared, Harold O'Neil, Kenny Alston; February 11–13, 2011

Nicholas Gorham: One Drop Passing Written and Conceived by Nicholas Gorham; Director, Matt Nasser; Choreographer, Joshua Weidenmiller; Original Music, Andrew Sotomayor; February 4 – 5, 2011

Pass The Blutwurst, Bitte Director, John Kelly; Choreographer, John Kelly; Stage Manager, Mike Taylor; Lighting, Stan Pressner; Set, Huck Snyder; Costumes, James Reilly; Projection Designer, Anthony Chase; Cast: John Kelly, Eric Jackson Bradley, Tymberly Canale, Mackenhan Meehan, Luke Murphy; La MaMa Experimental Theatre; December 2–19, 2010

Peter Sciscioli(New York)/Ana Sofrenovic(Belgrade) Created and Performed by Peter Sciscioli and Ana Sofrenovic; Moderated by Marya Wethers; April 10, 2011

Poetry Electric 11' Director, William Electric Black; Ongoing

Project: Lohan by D'Arcy Drollinger; Director, Ben Rimalower; Choreographer, John Paolillo; Stage Manager, Darrin Maurer; Lighting, Wilburn Bonnell; Set, Chris Minard; Costumes, Ryan J. Moller; Sound, Andrew Puccio; AV Design, ; Projection Designer, Jason Courson; Cast: D'Arcy Drollinger, Cindy Goldfield, Emily McGowan, Brandon Olson, Brian Reiss, Clayton Dean Smith; La MaMa Experimental Theatre; April 29–May 15, 2011

Purge (Puhdistus) by Sofi Oksanen; Translated by Eva Buchwald; Director, Zishan Ugurlu; Stage Manager, Jes Levine; Lighting, Tsubasa Kamei; Set, Zishan Ugurlu; Costumes, Oana Botez Ban; Sound, Fernando Arruda; Cast: Maren Bush, Peter Franzen, Jillian Lindig, Tony Naumovski, Grant Neale, Larisa Polonsky, Alexander Ristov; La MaMa Experimental Theatre; February 11–20, 2011

Shadow '11 a festival of concert playreadings celebrating Black History Month; February 24–27, 2011

Stationary Excess and Karen Davis does La MaMa Written and Created by Tim Cowbury; Cast: Jessica Latowicki, Karen Davis, Jess Barbagallo, Emily Davis, Julia Sirna-Frest; Produced by by Made in China; April 15–24, 2011

The American Human BeatBox Festival Curated by Kid Lucky; Cast: Doug E Fresh, Rabbi D, Butterscotch, Shockwave; May 15–18, 2011

The GIMF Project: IF by Heidi Latsky; June 16–18, 2011

Trav S.D.'s Tent Show Tetragrammaton by Trav S.D.; March 17–April 3, 2011

Waiting For The Dream Director, Irina Brook; Sound and Lighting, Thibault Ducros; Cast: Augustin Ruhabura, Christian Pelissier, Emmanuel Guillaume, Gerald Papasian, Hovnatan Avedikian, Jerry Di Giacomo; November 3–7, 2010

FESTIVALS

La MaMa Moves Dance Festival; LaMaMa; May 27–June 19, 2011; Included: *Barrish* by Sarah A.O. Rosner, A.O. Movement Collective; *Contemporary Israeli Dance Week* Curated by Michal Gamily; *Dancing Divas* Cast: Yvonne Rainer, Peggy Choy, Patricia Hoffbauer, Leslie Satin & David Botana, Mary Seidman; *Dancing for Joan* Performed by Chen and Dancers, Yoshiko Chuma and Robert Black, Nicholas Leichter and Will Rawls, David Dorfman Dance, Archie Burnett, Javier Ninja, Doug Elkins, Heidi Latsky, Doug Varone and Dancers, Martha Graham All-City Panorama; *Denouement* by Austin McCormick/ Company XIV; La

MaMa Experimental Theatre; *East Village Dance Project* Choreographer, Martha Tornay, Dawson, Leiber; *Etudes for an Astronaut* by Lance Gries; *Hula Moves* by Pua Ali'i 'Ilima and Vicky Takamine; *Mandorla* by Jenny Rocha Dance; *NY International* La MaMa Moves Dance Festival; *NYU Collaboration Project* Cast: Casey Boyle, Brighid Greene, Claudia Anata Hubiak, Igor Konyukhov, Michael Laskaris, Russell Stuart Lilie, Allie Pfeffer, Phoebe Sandford; *Solos, Duets, Trios and… Intricate Intimacies*

Perforations Festival New York Curated and Produced by Zvonimir Dobrovic; Cast: Ivo Dimchev (Bulgaria)**;** BADco. (Croatia)**;** Sanja Mitrovic (Serbia)**;** Igor Josifov (Macedonia)**;** Petra Kovaic (Croatia)**;** Željko Zorica (Croatia)**;** Slovenian Youth Theater (Slovenia)**;** Via Negativa (Slovenia)**;** and Ivica Buljan/Mini Teater (Croatia/ Slovenia); March 11 – 20, 2011

Under The Radar Festival (see Festivals below); LaMaMa; January 5–16, 2011

Being Harold Pinter Director, Vladimir Shcherban; Produced by Belarus Free Theatre; *Dutch A/V* Written and Presented by Reggie Watts and Tommy Smith; Director, Tommy Smith; *Gob Squad's Kitchen (You've Never Had It So Good)* by Gob Squad; *Living In Exile* by Jon Lipsky; Director, Christopher McElroen; *Show Your Face!* Director, Matjaz Pograjc; Presented by Betontanc and Umka.lv

NON-RESIDENT PRODUCTIONS

American Hurrah Revisited & The Mother's Return by Jean Claude Van Itallie; Director, Josh Adler; Cast: Autumn Horn, Cam Kornman, Diana De Luna, Helen Nesteruk, Lou Boretto, Matthew Tischler, Noelle Neglia, Randy Noojin; Produced by Theatre Research Ensemble (TReE); October 15–24, 2010

Bong Bong Bong against the Walls, Ting Ting Ting in our Heads Written and directed by Dario D'Ambrosi; Stage Manager, Alessandro Corazzi; Set, Aurora Buzzetti; Puppet Designer, Aurora Buzzetti; Cast: Ashley C. Williams, George Drance, Theresa Linnihan; Produced by Pathological Theatre-Italy; La MaMa Experimental Theatre; October 14 –31, 2010

Camp Wanatachi by Natalie Elizabeth Weiss & Bekah Brunstetter; Director, Matt Cowart; Original Music, Natalie Elizabeth Weiss; Electronic Music by Machinedrum aka Travis Stewart; Choreographer, Vanessa Walters; Stage Manager, Andrea Wales; Lighting and Set, Marc Janowitz; Costumes, Ren LaDassor; Sound, Matt Koenig & Ellis Traver; Cast: Krystina Alabado, Liz Byrne, Hannah DelMonte, Alyse Alan Louis, Thom Miller, Marissa O'Donnell, Natalie Elizabeth Weiss, Keaton Whittaker; Produced by Ian Pai; La MaMa Experimental Theatre; January 21–February 6, 2011

Chopin–An Impression La MaMa Puppet Series; Written and Conceived by Leslaw Piecka & Wojciech Szelachowski; Director, Leslaw Piecka; Choreographer, Jolanta Kruszewska; Original Music, Fryderyk Chopin; Produced by Bialystock Puppet Theatre-Poland; October 21–November 7, 2010

Fab! Festival and block party Cast: Valery Oisteanu, Paul Mills aka Poez, Ilka Scobie, Gian Marco Lo Forte, Velez Moore, Kid Lucky and Federico Restrepo & LOCO 7; East 4th Street (Between Bowery and 2nd Avenue); Produced by Fourth Arts Block; September 25, 2010

Fall and Recover Conceived and Choreographed by John Scott; Original Music, Rossa O'Snodaigh; Lighting, Eamon Fox; Sound, Tim Schellenbaum; Cast: Francis Acilu, Julie Chi, Philip Connaughton, Aisling Doyle, Faranak Mehdi Golhini, Solomon Ijigade, Sebastiao Mpembele Kamalandua, Kiribu, Patience Namehe, Nina, Elizabeth Suh, Haile Tkabo, Mufutau Kehinde Yusuf; Produced by Irish Modern Dace Theatre;La MaMa Experimental Theatre; March 26–April 9, 2011

Heaven On Earth by Chuck Mee; Directed and Choreographed by Dan Safer; Lighting, Jay Ryan; Set, Jay Ryan; Costumes, Deb O; Sound, Ryan Maeker; Video Designer, Kaz Phillips; Cast: Abigail Browde, Heather Christian, Sean Donovan, Mike Mikos, Sophie Cattani, Antoine Oppenheim, Francois Sabourin, Scott Shepherd; Produced by Witness Relocation; La MaMa Experimental Theatre; February 17, 2011

Hope Speaks Director, Jonathan McCrory; Lighting, Marika E Kent; Cast: Chanel Carroll, Cherrye J. Davis, Eric Lockley, Jonathan McCrory, Kimberly Young, Kisa Willis; Produced by The Movement Theatre Company; April 1 – 9, 2011

How and Why I Robbed My First Cheese Store by Mike Gorman; Director, Dave Bennettd; Stage Manager, Ashley Rossetti; Lighting, John Eckert; Set, Donald Eastman; Costumes, Gabriel Berry; Sound, Tim Schellenbaum; Cast: Melody Bates, Mary Notari, Joe Mullen, Alan B. Netherton, Thomas Piper, Travis York; Produced by Forty Hour Club; La MaMa Experimental Theatre; May 19–June 5, 2011

ImageNation Cast: Guillermo Gómez-Peña; Produced by Hemispheric Institute; June 13, 2011

In Retrospect Directed and Choreographed by Federico Restrepo; Original Music, Elizabeth Swados; Stage Manager, Beatrice Davies; Lighting and Set, Federico Restrepo; Costumes, Denise Greber; Sound, Sebastian Quiroga; Puppet Designer, Federico Restrepo; Cast: LOCO7 Dance Puppet Theatre Company–Federico Restrepo, Denise Greber, Allison Hiroto, Sara Galassini, Katherine Correa; Produced by Loco 7 Dance puppet Theatre Company; La MaMa Experimental Theatre; November 12–28, 2010

Lysistrata Directed and Conceived by Theodora Skipitares; Choreographer, Angela Harriell; Music and Lyrics, Skip Shirley; Lighting, Jesse Belsky; Costumes, Lara de Bruijn; Video Design, Aaron Long, Kay Hines; Produced by Skysaver Productions; February 3 – 13, 2011

Mapping Moebius Conceived and Director, Ildiko Nemeth; Choreographer, Julie Atlas Muz; Lighting, Federico Restrepo; Visual and Project Designed, Laia Cabrera; Illustration and Animation, Isabelle Duverger; Cast: Chris Tanner, Markus Hirnigel Schmitz; Produced by New Stage Theatre Company; December 2 – 19, 2010

Raven Director, Virlana Tkacz; Original Music, Alla Zagaykevych, Aurelia Shrenker, Eva Salina Primack; Choreographer, Shigeko Suga; Stage Manager, Natia Tatchin; Lighting, David Bonilla; Costumes, Keiko Obremski; Sound, Tim Schellenbaum; Projection Designer, Volodymyr Klyuzko & Mikhail Shraga; Cast: Andrew Colteaux, Maren Bush, Sean Eden, Kat Yew; Produced by Yara Arts Group; La MaMa Experimental Theatre; April 8–24, 2011

Ritter, Dene, Voss by Thomas Bernhard; Translated by Kenneth Northcott and Peter Jansen; Director, Adam Seelig; Cast: Shannon Perreault, Maev Beaty, Jordan Pettle; Produced by One Little Goat Theatre from Toronto; La MaMa Experimental Theatre; September 23–October 10, 2010

The Elder Project by Gloria Miguel, Lisa Mayo and Steve Elm; Director, Muriel Miguel & Steve Elm; Produced by Spiderwoman Theater; March 5 – 6, 2011

The Golden Racket Cast: Jennifer Miller, Becca Blackwell, Erin Markey, Jenny Romaine and Carlton Ward; Produced by Circus Amok; June 10 – 12, 2011

The Law of Remains by Reza Abdoh; Directed and Designed by Zishan Ugurlu; Performed by members of the 25th graduating class of Theater program at Eugene Lang College, The New School for Liberal Arts; May 10 – 11, 2011

The Orphans by Karina Casiano; Directed and performed by Daniel Irizarry & Karina Casiano; Produced by La Criatura Theatre; December 2 – 12, 2010

The Painted Bird: Bastard Director, Pavel Zustiak; Original Music, Christian Frederickson; Choreographer, Pavel Zustiak; Lighting, Joe Levasseur; Set, Nick Vaughan; Sound, Tim Schellenbaum; Projection Designer, Manny Palad; Cast: Jaroslav Vinarsky; Created in collaboration with Jaro Vinarsky; Produced by Palissimo Company; La MaMa Experimental Theatre; November 11–21, 2010

The Walk Across America For Mother Earth by Taylor Mac; Director, Paul Zimet; Original Music, Ellen Maddow; Choreographer, Nikki Zialcita; Stage Manager, Robert Signom III; Lighting, Lenore Doxsee; Set, Anna Kiraly; Costumes, Machine Dazzle; Make-Up Designer, Darrell Thorne; Cast: Will Badgett, Viva DeConcini, James Tigger! Ferguson, Daphne Gaines, Taylor Mac, Ellen Maddow, Frank Paiva, Steven Rattazzi, Tina Shepard, Jack Wetherall, Alex Franz Zehetbauer, Nikki Zialcita; Produced by Talking Band; La MaMa Experimental Theatre; January 19–30, 2011

Three from Tennessee by Tennessee Williams; Director, Cosmin Chivu, Grant Kretchik and Ruis Woertendyke; Produced by Pace University Drama; March 4 – 6, 2011

Transience 2 Choreographer, Kumi Kuwahata; Cast: Gisele Assi, Kimie Nishizawa, Kumi Kuwahata, Xianix Barrera; Produced by White Art Dance Group; December 14-15, 2010

Wake Up, You're Dead Director, Aaron Haskell; Original Music, Julia Joseph & Nicholas Walsorf; Choreographer, Aaron Haskell; Set, Paul Smithyman; Costumes, Candice Thompson; Cast: Robert Anthony, Aaron Haskell, Chris Lee, Maggie Macdonald, Hattie Mae Williams and Korey Phillip; Produced by Brooklyn Art Department (B.A.D.); La MaMa Experimental Theatre; October 29–November 7, 2010

We couldn't call it what we wanted to call it, so we called it HOLY CRAP!! by Iñigo Ramírez de Haro; Translated by Ronald Rand & Inigo Ramirez de Haro; Director, Erica Gould; Original Music, and Sound, Scott O'Brien; Lighting, Driscoll Otto; Set, Stephen Dobay; Costumes, Kevin Thacker; Cast: Stephen Mo Hanan; Produced by Ronald Rand Production; La MaMa Experimental Theatre; April 28–May 15, 2011

Winter Sun: A Celebration of Traditional Music from the Carpathians Directed and Created by Virlana Tkacz; Cast: Aurelia Shrenker, Eva Salina Primack, Julian Kytasty, Kat Yew, Deanna Klapishchack, Yuliyan Yordanov, Valeriy Zhmud, Shigeko Suga, Paul Brantley, Alexander Katreczko, Ron Lawrence, Kiku Sakai; Produced by Yara Arts Group; December 26, 2010

Lauren Rayner Productions

www.laurenrayner.com

Executive Producer, Lauren Rayner

Mendacity Written and directed by Lauren Rayner; Stage Manager, Lauren Heirigs; Lighting, Tony Lepore; Set, Jim Rayner; Sound, Jonathan Hull; AV Design, Jay Kilachand; Producer, Benjamin Mack; Producer / Creative Collaborator, Rachel Kerry; Choreographer, Shiloh Goodin; Creative Collaborators: Joseph Samuel Wright, Ryan Scoble, Sarah Newswange; Cast: Ali Kresch; Presented as part of the FRIGID Festival; Kraine Theater; February 24–March 11, 2011

Lesser America

www.lesseramerica.com

Squealer by Jonathan Blitstein; Director, Daniel Talbott; Stage Manager, Michael Denis; Lighting, Brad Peterson; Set, Eugenia Furneaux-Arends; Costumes, Tristan Raines; Sound, Janie Bullard; Cast: Daniel Abeles, Jamie Law, Nick Lawson, Sarah Lemp, Nate Miller, Laura Ramadei; Theater for the New City; May 5 –21, 2011

Lighthouse Theatre

www.thelighthousetheatre.com

Lunatic: A Love Story Written and performed by Rachel Adler; Center Stage, NY; May 27–June 12, 2010

Literally Alive

www.literallyalive.com

A Christmas Carol by Brenda Bell; Director, Carlo Rivieccio; Original Music, Michael Sgouros; Choreographer, Stefanie Smith; Stage Manager, Kerianne Murphy; Lighting, Josh Iacovelli; Cast: DJ Canaday, Timothy Ryan Bartlett, Eric Fletcher, Kalen J. Hall, Brianna Hurley, Jessica Bay Blyweiss, Kayleigh E. Shuler, Richelle Blauvelt; Players Theatre & Players Loft; November 27–December 30, 2010

Little Lord (a theater company)

www.littlelord.org

(oh my god I am so) THIRST(y) Adopted from Eugene O'Neill; Director, Michael Levinton; Stage Manager, Anna Kroup; Lighting, Simon Cleveland; Set, Jason Simms; Costumes, Sydney Maresca; Sound, Kate Marvin; Cast: Tonya Canada, Megan Hill, Polly Lee, Michael Levinton, Hugh Sinclair, Laura von Holt, Donya K. Washington, Stephanie Weeks & Merlin Whitehawk; Ontological Hysterical Theatre; October 21–30, 2010

Jewqueen Created and Performed by Julia Arazi, Sarah Bishop-Stone, Das Elkin, Diana Konopka, Michael Levinton, Rodney Pallanck, Laura von Holt; Under St. Marks; March 18–19, 2011

The Living Theatre

livingtheatre.org

Korach Written and directed by Judith Malina; Original Music, Sheila Dabney, Carlo Altomare, Steve Taylor; Choreographer, Carlo Altomare; Cast: Albert Lamont, Andrew Greer, Anna Agostino, Ben Cerf, Brent Barker, Casimira Altomare, Cecilie Greve, Charles Fairbanks, Chelsey Clime, Gia Krahne, Homa Hynes, Jay Dobkin, Jerry Goralnick, Kennedy Yanko, Kyle Ryan, Maria Guzman, Martin Munoz, Monica Hunken, Sarah Bella Ald, Tom Walker, Sheila Dabney; The Living Theatre; February 2–26, 2011

Looking Glass Theatre

www.lookingglasstheatrenyc.com

Betsy is Bored, Bored, Bored, Bored, Bored! by Judy Sheehan; Director, Amanda Thompson; Lighting, Ryan Metzler; Cast: Toccara Castleman, Suzee Dunn, Ryan McCurdy, Jacquelyn Schultz and Mary Beth Walsh; Looking Glass Theatre; October 16–November 21, 2010

Three By the Sea by Donna Latham; Director, Julia Martin; Musical Stage Manager, Julia Frieri; Lighting, Ryan Metzler; Set, Clifton Chadick; Costumes, Kristina Sneshkoff; Sound, Eric C. Dente; Puppet Designer, Honey Goodenough & Ryan Dillon; Cast: Elise Bernlohr, Laura Borgwardt, Maggie Delgadillo, Rob Esris, Jacob Mondry, Ali Schmidt and Zach Tait; Looking Glass Theatre; March 5–April 10, 2011

Just A Reading by Ryan Glass; Director, Chanda Calentine; Choreographer, Helen McTernan; Lighting, Ryan Metzler; Cast: Jenn Boehm, Michael Sean Cirelli, Brandon Ferraro, Cas Marino, Alexandra Mingione, Stephen Reich; Looking Glass Theatre; April 28–May 15, 2011

Mad Dog Theatre Company

www.maddogbarks.com

All the Way From China by Barry Levey; Director, Joel Waage; Stage Manager, Sarah Gleissner; Lighting, Richard Chamblin; Cast: Ghafir Akbar, Heather Kelley, Kevin O'Callaghan; Gene Frankel Theatre; November 10–21, 2010

The Mad Ones

madone.wordpress.com

The Tremendous Tremendous by Marc Bovino, Joe Curnutte, Stephanie Wright Thompson; Director, Jeffrey Withers; Lighting, Mike Innwood; Set, The Mad Ones and Gabel Eiben; Costumes, Sydney Gallas; Sound, Stowe Nelson; Cast: Marc Bovino, Joe Curnutte, Michael Dalto, Stephanie Wright Thompson, Henry Vick; Brick Theater; March 31–April 16, 2011

Maieutic Theatre Works (MTWorks)

www.mtworks.org

A Home Across The Ocean by Cody Daigle; Director, Dev Bondarin; Stage Manager, Carolynn Richer; Lighting, Dan Gallagher; Set, Blair Mielnik; Costumes, Rachel Dozier-Ezell; Sound, Kimberly Fuhr-Carbone; Cast: Alex Bond, Mark Emerson, Lavita Shaurice Burr, David Stallings, Dathan B. Williams; The Studio Theater @ Theatre Row; September 16–October 2, 2010

The Family Shakespeare by David Stallings; Director, Antonio Miniño; Original Music, Jessie Montgomery; Stage Manager, Carolynn Richer; Lighting, Dan Gallagher; Set, Blair Mielnik; Costumes, Rachel Dozier-Ezell; Sound, Jessie Montgomery; Cast: Eric C. Bailey, Sarah Chaney, Alexandra Cohen-Spiegler, Jason Emanuel, Diánna Martin, Frankie Seratch, Peter B. Schmitz, Corey Tazmania and Cotton Wright; June Havoc Theatre; April 14–April 30, 2011

Manhattan Theatre Source

theatresource.org

The Little Mermaid by Brenda Bell; Director, Stefanie Smith; Original Music, Michael Sgouros; Choreographer, Stefanie Smith; Stage Manager, Kerianne Murphy; Lighting, Amanda Sheets; Set, Christian Amato; Costumes, Mia Bienovich; Cast: Eric Fletcher, Jovanni Guzman, Brianna Hurley, Jenna Lipe, Danielle Beckmann, Yuka Ibi, Kayleigh Shuler, Jillian Severin, Yuka Ibi; Players Theatre & Players Loft; March 12–May 22,2011

Things At The Doorstep: An Evening of Horror Based on the Works of H.P. Lovecraft: *The Hound* by Greg Oliver Bodine; *I Am Providence* by Nat Cassidy; Director, DeLisa M. White; Stage Manager, Laura Schlachtmeyer; Lighting, Kia Rogers; Sound, Jay Spriggs; Cast: Nat Cassidy, Greg Oliver Bodine; Produced in association with Greg Oliver Bodine, and Nat Cassidy; ManhattanTheatreSource; January 6–29, 2011

Two Steps Forward by John Philip and Andrew Loren Resto; Director, Michael Portantiere; Cast: Courtney Allen, Linda Elizabeth, Barbara Mundy, John Philip, Andrew Loren Resto, Brandon Ruckdashel, and Julia Yarwood; Produced by 3A Productions; Manhattantheatresource; May 5 –21, 2011

FESTIVALS

Ingenius Short Play Festival: *What is This* by Jen Thatcher; *Lips Upon Cheeks* by Alaina Hammond; *Impossible to Leave* by Laura Schlachtmeyer; *Destination* by Vivian Neuwirth; *Misary, Apathy and Despair* by John McKinney; *Deuteranomal* by Jessica Fleitman; *I, Carpenter* by Greg Oliver Bodine, *My Baby* by Vincent Marano; Lighting, Kia Rodgers; Sound, Jay Spriggs; Cast: James Edward Bection, Bennett Harrell, Jessica Lynn Jennings, Ken Caughlin, Mark

Levy, Robin Kurtz, Charles Hinshaw, Julie Allen, Ross Pivec, Vivian Neuwirth, Steven Schnetzer, Rebecca Davis, Annalisa Loefler, Harry Peerce, Quinn Warren, Elizabeth Fonta; ManhattanTheatreSource; January 12–22, 2011

Marion Attal Theater

marionattaltheater.org

Portrayed : The Unbearable Burden Of Deciding What To Do Before Dying by James Holland; Director, Michael Petranek; Original Music, Julien Jardin; Stage Manager, Anais Zapirain; Lighting, Amy Wowak; Set, Katie-Jo Glover; Costumes, Lea Betremieux; Cast: Lindsey Ashlen, Marion Attal, Monroe Robertson; The Invisible Dog; September 16–October 10, 2010

Mergatroyd Productions

www.mergatroyd.org

President, Nancy McClernan

Julia & Buddy Written and directed by N. G. McClernan; Musical Director and Stage Manager, N. G. McClernan; Presented as part of the Midtown International Theatre Festival Short Subjects; Cast: Daniel Genalo, Kat Chua; Jewel Box Theatre; July 13–18, 2010

Even Odds Written and directed by N. G. McClernan; Presented as part of the John Chatterton Short Play Lab; Cast: Krista Hasinger, Mike Durell; Roy Arias Studios; September 18–19, 2010

The Slash Written and directed by N. G. McClernan; Stage Manager, Katie Kavett; Presented as part of the MidWinter Madness Festival Cast: Carolyn Paine, Amanda Thickpenny, Mike Durrel, Abe Lebovic; Roy Arias Studios; February 16–20, 2011

READINGS AND WORKSHOPS

Friday Night Footlights reading by N. G. McClernan; Cast: Daniel Genalo, Claire Warden, Bruce Barton; Dramatists Guild; January 14, 2011

Metropolitan Playhouse

www.metropolitanplayhouse.org

The Drunkard Director, Francis X. Kuhn; Choreographer; Original Music, Bix Bettwy; Stage Manager, Eileen Arnold; Lighting, Christopher Weston; Set, Matthew Allar; Costumes, Sidney Fortner; Cast: Michael Hardart, Ben Gougeon, Howard Thoresen, Cyrus Newitt, Bix Bettwy, Eli Green, William J. Allgood, Leigh Shannan, Charlotte Hampden, Kendall Rileigh, Rosina Fernhoff, Jessica Doherty, Jennifer Angela Bishop; Metropolitan Playhouse; September 18–October 17, 2010

Uncle Tom's Cabin by George L. Aiken; Director, Alex Roe; Original Music, Bix Betty; Choreographer, Scott Barrow; Stage Manager, Heather Olmstead; Lighting, Christopher Weston; Set, Alex Roe; Costumes, Sidney Fortner; Cast: George Lee Miles, Rick Delaney, Richard Waits, Marcie Hendersen, Alex Marshall-Brown, Lisa Riegel, J. M. McDonough, Dan Snow, Peter Tedeschi, Helen Highfield; Metropolitan Playhouse; November 13–December 12, 2010

The White Person's Guide to the Harlem Renaissance Written and directed by David Lally; Cast: Trent Carson, Eli Green, Steven Lally, Alex Marshall-Brown, Shaundra Noll; Metropolitan Playhouse; January 20–29, 2011

The Great Divide by William Vaughn Moody; Director, Michael Hardart; Lighting, Christopher Weston; Set, Emily Inglis; Costumes, Sidney Fortner; Cast: Tomothy Weinert, Tony Zazella, Michael I. Walker, Arthur Harold, Ray Crisara, Joe Gioco, Lauren Sowa, Elizabeth Inghram, Wendy Merritt; Metropolitan Playhouse; March 5–April 3, 2011

One-Third of a Nation by Arthur Arent; Director, Alex Roe; Stage Manager, Katy Moore; Lighting, Christopher Weston; Set, Alex Roe; Costumes, Lena Sands; Cast: Paul Bomba, Brian Harlan Brooks, Peter S. Feliz, Sidney Fortner, Brad Fraizer, Ben Gougeon, Meghan Hoffman, Teresa Kelsey, Me'Lisa Sellers, Howard Thoreson, Leo G. Gitelman; Metropolitan Playhouse; April 23–May 22, 2011

A Play Date with Ivan Ulz Written and directed by Ivan Ulz; Cast: Ian Ulz, Leah Wells; The Metropolitan Playhouse; May 7–22, 2011

Adventure Theater by Kenn Adam; Director, Laura Livingston; Cast: Michael Durnin, Shaundra Noll, Laura Livingston; Metropolitan Playhouse

Michael Chekhov Theatre Company

www.chekhovtheatre.com

An Ideal Husband by Oscar Wilde; Director, Peter Giser; Set, Arash Mokhtar; Costumes, Liz DeBetta; Cast: Arash Mokhtar, Tony Martinelli, Steve Abbruscato, Elias Buehler, Liz DeBetta, Lauren Cavicchioli, Katie Hilliard, Judy Guyll, D'Arcy Fellona, Chelsea Mauger; 45th Street Theatre – Upstairs; July 15–20, 2010

The Late Henry Moss by Sam Shepard; Director, Christine Ann Sullivan; Original Music, Brian Sullivan; Stage Manager, Emilie Zifkin; Lighting, Joan Racho-Jansen; Set, Terri Tomola; Cast: Tom Pavey, Paul Newport, John Torres, Raymond Hill, Sonia Torres, Thomas Francis Murphy; 45th Street Theatre – Upstairs; July 25–August 17, 2010

The Beauty Queen of Leenane by Martin McDonagh; Director, Ann Bowen; Stage Manager, Russ Marisak; Lighting, Joan Racho-Jansen; Set, Joan Racho-Jansen; Cast: Goran Ivanovski, Evangeline Johns, Thomas Francis Murphy, Duvall O'Steen; 45th Street Theatre; August 30–September 28, 2010

The Servant of Two Masters by Carlo Goldoni; Director, Peter Giser; Choreographer, Peter Giser; Costumes, Peter Giser; Sound; Cast: Arash Mokhtar, Peter Giser, David Elyha, John Rice, Luigi DiGangi, Marken Greenwood, Krysten Kimmett, Katie Hilliard, Emily Dahlke, Annarosa Mudd; 45th Street Theatre – Upstairs; November 1 –22, 2010

Milk Can Theatre Company

www.milkcantheatre.org

Malfi, Inc. by Bethany Larsen; Director, Julie Fei-Fan Balzer; Choreographer, Ian Roettger; Stage Manager, Katie Kavett; Lighting, Wilburn Bonnell; Set, Kacie Hultgren; Costumes, Sarah Gosnell; Sound, Chris Larsen; Cast: Sofia Barclay, Michael Cicetti, Anthony Gaskins, Peter Gray, Olivia Gillatt, Miranda Jonte, Jed Peterson, Hannah Tamminen; Theatre 54; November 10–21, 2010

Mind The Art Entertainment

www.MindTheArtEntertainment.com

Holiday in Hell by Charles O'Hara; Director, Jackie Bartone & Christian De Gré; Set, Joseph Reese Anderson; Sound, Michael Berberich; Cast: Ashley C. Williams, Charles O'Hara, McKey Carpenter, Skyler Adams, Rose Zisa, Gabor Szetey, Sandy Bauleo, RJ Lewis; Center Stage, NY; March 29–April 20, 2011

The Timing of a Day by Owen Panettieri; Director, Joey Brenneman; Cast: Justin Anselmi, R. Elizabeth Woodard, Nik Kourtis, Miguel Govea; Center Stage, NY; March 31–April 17, 2011

Josh Tyson, Vikki Vasiliki Eugenis,and Julie Fitzpatrick in the Kids With Guns production of Wolves (photo by Ben Cikanek)

Vandit Bhatt and Poonam Basu in Theater2020's Romeo & Juliet
(photo by David Fuller)

Laurie Schaefer, Brent Vimtrup, Jonathan Todd Ross in Sight Unseen, presented by InProximity Theatre Company (photo by Lisa Soverino)

Philomena Bindlestiff and Mr. Pennygaff in the Bindlestiff Family Cirkus New Vaudeville Revue (photo by Ed Flores)

The cast of Rising Sun Performance Company's Last Supper
(photo by David Anthony)

Kevin Hogan and Alvin Hippolyte in The Halloween Plays *at Brave New World Repertory Theatre (photo by Steve Bartel)*

Becky Byers in Nosedive Productions' Little One *(photo by Aaron Epstein)*

Bern Cohen in Abbie, *presented at the West End Theatre (photo by Sam Morris)*

Andrew Cooksey, Denise Collins, Leon Adrian, Jarred Solomon, Ben Black and Paula Flynn in F.I.G. Theater Group production of Under the Same Moon *(photo by Raymond D. Carnegie)*

Jaime Espinal and Susan Rybin in the Thalia Spanish Theatre production of No Problemo Amigo *(photo by Michael Palma)*

Mind The Gap Theatre

www.mindthegaptheatre.com

BritBits 7 short play series by Paula D'Alessandris, Bronwen Denton-Davis, Sam Peter Jackson, Richard Manton-Hollis, Camilla Maxwell, Brian Pracht, Laura Stevens, Chris Thorpe; Director, Paula D'Alessandris, Camilla Maxwell, Stephanie Staes; Stage Manager, Lauren Arneson; Lighting, Isaac Winston; Cast: Peter Cormican, Daniel Damiano, Martin Ewens, Anna Frankl-Duval, Lain Gray, Emma Gordon, Adriana Llabres, Sarah Manton, Camilla Maxwell, Cailin McDonald, Mia Moreland, Simon Pearl, Adam Jonas Segaller, Hannah Scott, Ruthie Stephens, Frances Uku; Manhattan Theatre Source; June 9–18, 2010

Under The Blue Sky by David Eldridge; Director, Paula D'Alessandris; Stage Manager, Kate Erin Gibson; Lighting, Kate Erin Gibson; Set, Kristin Costa; Cast: Stuart Williams, Sarah Manton, Jonathan Tindle, Elizabeth Jasicki, Richard Hollis, Christine Rendel; Kraine Theater; May 19–June 5, 2011

READINGS AND WORKSHOPS

Mr. Nobody by Philip Ralph; Director, Paula D'Alessandris; Cast: Andy de la Tour, Susan Wooldridge, Katie Fabel; Atlantic Theater Studios; November 21, 2010

adrenalin…heart by Georgia Fitch; Paula D'Alessandris; Cast: Lain Gray, Mia Moreland; Atlantic Theater Studios; November 14, 2010

Theatre Uncut by Dennis Kelly, Lucy Kirkwood, Laura Lomas, Anders Lustgarten, Mark Ravenhill, Jack Thorne and Clara Brennan; Workshop Theater; March 19, 2011

The Modern Stage

Miracle Day Written and directed by Tom Sime; Cast: Adam Smith, Kristina Olson, Damian Maffei, Marcella Goheen; Bleecker Street Theatre; May 10–June 15, 2010

Monica Hunken and Co.

www.monicahunken.com

Blondie of Arabia Written and performed by Monica Hunken; Lighting, Jessica Lynn Hinkle and Evan True; Living Theatre; September 22–October 9, 2010

Moose Hall Theater Company

www.moosehallisf.org

The Comedy of Errors by William Shakespeare; Director, Ted Minos; Lighting, Catherine Bruce; Set, Ted Minos; Costumes, Catherine Bruce; Sound, Luke St. Francis; Cast: Seth Austin, Alvin Chan, Rick Delaney, Marie Bridget Dundon, Nikki Ferry, Leo Gianopoulos, John Graham, Emily Vigoda, Kacie Leblong, Stephen Medvidick, Sean MacBride Murray, Jodie Pfau, Matt Reeves, Mary Riley, Kevin G. Shinnick, Dan Vidor; Inwood Hill Park Peninsula; June 2–19, 2010

Tombstone: Saga of the Americans Story by Ted Minos and Aaron Simms, Written by Ted Minos; Director, Aaron Simms; Choreographer, Ray Rodriguez; Lighting, Cathy Bruce; Set, Aaron Simms; Costumes, Cathy Bruce and Aaron Simms; Sound, Ted Minos; Fight Choreographer, Ray A. Rodriguez; Cast: Kevin Shinnick, Ross Pivac, Leo Giannopoulos, Rick Delaney, Lauren Schroeder, Tara Gadomski, Alexandra Dixon, Alicia Fitzgerald, Samantha Bruce, David Mead, Kyle Kensrue, Eli Bridges, Ash Edwards, Gregory Kostal, Yoko Hyun, Sam Bailer, Michael Hagins, Carla Birkhofer, Marisa Dalpiaz, Amanda Griemsmann, Gustavo Heredia; The View Theater; July 14–31, 2010

Mortal Folly Theatre Company

mortalfollytheatre.org

A Midsummer Night's Dream by William Shakespeare; Director, Katherine Harte-DeCoux; Assistant Director, Stacee Mandeville; Original Music, Amanda Gookin; Choreographer, Nathan DeCoux; Stage Manager, Stevie Mock; Lighting, Rafael Cubela; Set, Chris Cornwell; Costumes, Alexis Balaoing; Sound, Amanda Gookin; Cast: Mark August, Rob Bellsey, Alyssa Borg, Seton Brown, Laura King, Katherine McDowell, Matthew Rini, Liz Sklar, Hannah Sloat, Jenelle Sosa, David Stroh, Melanie Stroh, Jeffrey Sutton; Richmond Shepard Theatre; June 2–20, 2010

Merely Players by William Shakespeare & Others; Original Music by Amanda Gookin; 5C Cultural Center Café; August 22, 2010

Macbeth by William Shakespeare; Director, Katherine Harte-DeCoux; Assistant Director, Stacee Mandeville; Original Music, Amanda Gookin; Choreographer, Nathan DeCoux; Stage Manager, Bekah Hernandez; Lighting, Bekah Hernandez; Set, John Short; Costumes, Alexis Balaoing; Sound, Amanda Gookin; Cast: Mark August, Alyssa Borg, Erik Cheski, Sam Eggers, David A Ellis, Josey Nicole Housley, Bryant Martin, Matthew Rini, John Short, Liz Sklar, Hannah Sloat, Brandon Smith, Melanie Stroh, Robert Lee Taylor; Gene Frankel Theatre; December 1 –19, 2010

Mountebanks

travsd.wordpress.com

Trav S.D.'s Tent Show Tetragrammaton: *Universal Rundle, The Strange Case of Grippo the Ape Man* Written and Directed by Trav S.D.; Original Music, Trav S.D.; Choreographer, Becky Byyers; Stage Manager, Aaron Heflich Shapiro; Lighting, Jeff Nash; Set and Costumes, Julez Kroboth; Sound, Tom Bibla; Cast: Trav S.D., Bob Laine, Tom Bibla, Stephen Heskett, Catherine Porter, Timothy McCown Reynolds, Hope Cartelli, Jeff Lewonczyk, Art Wallace, Josh Hartung, Sarah Malinda Engelke, Sara Malinda Engelke; La MaMa Experimental Theatre; March 17–April 3, 2011

The Movement Theatre Company

www.themovementtheatrecompany.org

Bintou by Chantal Bilodeau; Director, David Mendizábal; Original Music, Yusuke Namiki; Choreographer, Willie Teacher; Stage Manager and Set, Jamal Jordan; Lighting, T. Rick Hayashi; Costumes, Jesca Prudencio; Cast: Audrey Hailes, Cherrye Davis, Joy Caldwell; Harlem School of the Arts; June 24–July 10, 2010

MultiStages

www.eljallartsannex.com/multistages.htm

Lorca Peress, Artistic Director

READINGS AND WORKSHOPS

Temple of the Souls, A Musical Drama by Anita Velez-Mitchell; Director, Lorca Peress; Composer, Dean Landon and Anika Paris; Music Director, Bruce Baumer; Pearl Studios; April 17, 2011

Murder Mystery Manhattan

mysterymanhattan.com

Vesuvio and Philomena's Wedding to Die For Written and directed by Keith Dougherty; Cast: Keith Dougherty, Natalie Wilder, Patrick Shea and Maureen Van Trease; July 15, 2010

Neighborhood Productions

thewifebytommysmith.wordpress.com

The Wife by Tommy Smith; Director, May Adrales; Stage Manager, Tara Nachtigall; Lighting, Gina Scherr; Set, Ji-Youn Chang; Costumes, Becky Bodurtha; Sound, Hillary Charnas; Cast: Noel Joseph Allain, Travis Allen, Jakob Knoll, Mary Jane Gibson, Caitlin McDonough-Thayer, Ayesha Ngaujah; Access Gallery; December 2 –19, 2010

Nero Fiddled

nerofiddled.net

Artistic Director, Noah Diamond; Artistic Director, Amanda Sisk

Groucho on the Air by Noah Diamond; Director, Amanda Sisk; Musical Director, DJ Thacker; AV Design, Noah Diamond; Cast: Noah Diamond, Amanda Sisk; Bushwick Project for the Arts; January 29, 2011

The New Acting Company

www.childrensaidsociety.org/pcc/nac

Snow White by Kathy Keane; Director, Stephen Michael Rondel; Choreographer, Daniella Rabbani; Stage Manager, Sarah Perlin; Lighting, Ben Tevelow; Set, Carl Tallent; Costumes, Mark Salinas; Sound, Stephen Michael Rondel; Cast: Josie Pelham, Tanya O'Debra, Alexandra Dickson, Synge Maher, Moe Rosen, Fergus Scully, Michael Titone, Olivia Berke, Elizabeth Ely, Zoe Ilic & Sophie Shuster; The New acting Company; April 22 –May 15, 2011

New Lion's Productions

Comedie of Errors by William Shakespeare; Director, Lauren Keating; Stage Manager, Emily Tabachuk; Set, Daniel Zimmerman; Costumes, Tristan Raines; Sound Cast: Tina Diaz, Claire Morrison, Nadia Hulett, Joyce Miller, Matt Lents as Luciano, Anna Marquardt, Meghan Powe; Central Park; July 30–August 15, 2010

New Paradise Laboratories and The Riot Group

www.freedomclubtheshow.com

Freedom Club by Adriano Shaplin; Director, Whit MacLaughlin; Stage Manager, Emily Rea; Lighting, Maria Shaplin; Set, Matt Saunders; Costumes, Rosemarie E. McKelvey; Sound, Whit MacLaughlin and Adriano Shaplin; AudioVisual, Jorge Cousineau; Cast: Drew Friedman, McKenna Kerrigan, Jeb Kreager, Mary McCool, Paul Schnabel, Adriano Shaplin and Stephanie Viola; Connelly Theater; January 6–15, 2011

New Perspectives Theatre Company

www.newperspectivestheatre.org

Artistic Director, Melody Brooks; General Manager, Catharine Guiher; Associate Artistic Director, C. Amanda Maud; Program Manager, Celia Braxton; Managing Associate and Marketing Coordinator, Jenny Greeman; Artistic Associate/Asst. Director Apprentice Program, Kerry Watterson; Resident Production Designer, Meganne George

Mother of God! by Michele A. Miller; Director, Melody Brooks; Cast: Charles E. Gerber, Karin De La Penha, Erwin Falcon, Ray Rodriguez, Marisa Petsakos, Keith Walker, Kkeona Welch; Richmond Shepard Theatre; March 11–26, 2011

Travelin' Shoes Written and performed by Denise Lock; Director, Jeffery V. Thompson; New Perspectives Theatre Company; May 11–22, 2011

FESTIVAL

In the Papers! September 20–26, 2010; Production Designer, Meganne George; Lighting, Joyce Liao; Included: *Mary and East* by Stacy Osei-Kuffour, Director, Pat Golden; *Vanishing Print* by Calla Videt, Director, Jenny Greeman; *Dead People's Things* by Ione Lloyd, Director, Jenny Greeman; *Quimera in the Storm* by Rosebud Ben-Oni, Director, Melody Brooks

The New Stage Theatre Comapny

www.newstagetheatre.org

Mapping Möbius by Colm O'Shea, Marie Glancy O'Shea and Ildiko Nemeth; Director, Ildiko Nemeth; Stage Manager, Fabiyan Pemble-Belkin; Lighting, Federico Restrepo; Set and Sound, Ildiko Nemeth; Costumes, Ildiko Nemeth, Javier Bone Carbone and Lisa Kathryn Hokans; AV Design, Laia Cabrera and Ildiko Nemeth; Choreograper, Julie Atlas Muz; Cast: Dana Boll, Kaylin Lee Clinton, Catherine Correa, Maria Cuartero, Markus Hirnigel, Sunrise Marks, Florencia Minniti, BJ Rubin, Peter B. Schmitz, Jeanne Lauren Smith, Chris Tanner; Presented in association with La MaMa E.T.C.; La MaMa E.T.C.; November 2–December 19, 2010

New Worlds Theatre Project

www.newworldsproject.org

Producing Artistic Director, Ellen Perecman; Managing Director, Scott Matthews

Displaced Wedding by H. Leivick; Adaptation by Ellen Perecman; Director, David Winitsky; Original Music, Live Footage; Lighting, Colin D. Young; Set, Bill Clarke; Costumes, Michelle Bohn; Cast: Maisha Azadi, Chris Bannow, Gian-Murray Gianino, Michael Goldlist, Alvin Keith, Ema Lakovlc, Trish Mc Call, Tyler Merna, Emily Schoen, Yelena Shmulenson, Franny Silverman; West End Theater; December 11–January 2, 2011

New York Classical Theatre

newyorkclassical.org

The Rover by Aphra Behn; Director, Karin Coonrod; Production Designer, Oona Ban; Cast: M. Scott McClean, April Sweeney, Kersti Bryan, Cooper D'Ambrose; World Financial Center; March 2–20, 2011

New York Neo-Futurists

www.nyneofuturists.org

Too Much Pride Makes the Baby Go Gay: 30 Gay Plays in 60 Straight Minutes Written and performed by the New York Neo-Futurists; Kraine Theatre; June 25–26, 2010

30 Half-Nekkid Plays in 60 Half-Nekkid Minutes Written, Director, the New York Neo-Futurists Ensemble; Cast: Christopher Borg, Cara Francis, Ryan Good, Nicole Hill, Rob Neill, Joey Rizzolo and Lauren Sharpe; Kraine Theater; August 20–21, 2010

(un)afraid Written and performed by Jill Beckman, Cara Francis, Ricardo Gamboa, Daniel McCoy; Director, Rob Neill; Choreographer, Lauren Sharpe; Stage Manager, Laura Schlachtmeyer; Lighting, Lauren Parrish; Set, Liz Jenetopulos; Costumes, Hunter Kaczorowski; Sound, Christopher Loar; Video Designer, Adam

Smith; Production Manager, Jennie Miller; Assistant Stage Manager, Shane Reader; Living Theatre; October 14–November 6, 2010

Too Much Light Makes the Baby Go Blind Written and performed by Jill Beckman, Christopher Borg, Roberto Colindrez, Jeffery Cranor, Cara Francis, Ryan Good, Alicia Chaisson, Eevin Hartsough, Nicole Hill, Jacquelyn Landgraf, Erica Livingston, Christopher Loar, Daniel McCoy, Rob Neill, Joey Rizzolo, Lauren Sharpe, Lauren Sharpe, Adam Smith; Kraine Theater; November 19, 2010–June 4, 2011

Locker #4173b by Joey Rizzolo and Christopher Borg; Director, Justin Tolley; Stage Manager, Ashley Nelson; Lighting, Lauren Parrish; Costumes, Ashley Rose Horton; Sound, John Emmett O'Brien; Video Designer, Sydney Buchan; Production Manager, Meg Bashwiner; Assistant Stage Manager, Aliee Chan; Cast: Christopher Borg, Joey Rizzolo, Yolanda Kay Wilkinson, Nicole Hill; The Monkey; April 28–May 21, 2011

Nicu's Spoon

www.spoontheater.org

Beautiful Thing by Jonathan Harvey; Director, Michelle Kuchuk; Choreographer and Costumes, Stephanie Barton-Farcas; Stage Manager, Phillip Chavira; Lighting, Steven Wolf; Set, John Trevellini; Sound, Michelle Kuchuk; Cast: Julie Campbell, Micheal Abourizk, Trip Langley, Rebecca Lee Lerman, Tim Romero; Spoon Theatre; July 7–25, 2010

Kimberly Akimbo by David Lindsay-Abaire; Director, Oliver Conant; Stage Manager, Juni Li; Lighting, Steven Wolf; Set, Alvaro Sena; Costumes, S. Barton-Farcas; Cast: Wynne Anders, David Tully, Elizabeth Bell, William Reid and Phrannie Lyons; Spoon Theatre; October 6–24, 2010

Cinderelle Written and directed by Nick Linnehan; Musical Director, Ian Wherle; Stage Manager, Phillip Chavira; Lighting, Costumes and Set, Alvaro Sena; Cast: Elizabeth Carey, Stephen Drabicki, Scott Andrews, Phillip Lewis, Haley Selmon, Emanuel Pinkhasov; Spoon Theatre; January 5–30, 2011

Bad Seed by Maxwell Anderson; Director, S. Barton-Farcas; Original Music, Damon Law; Stage Manager, Juni Ii; Lighting, Steven Wolf; Set and Sound, S. Barton-Farcas; Costumes, Rien Schlecht; Cast: Lee Eden, Sharon Hunter, Mark Armstrong, Tim Romero, Wynne Anders, Morgan Sills, Milton Elliott, Matt De Rogatis, Katie Labahn, Michael Abourizk, Diane Shilling; Nicu's Spoon Theatre; April 6–24, 2011

Nosedive Productions

www.nosediveproductions.com

The Little One by James Comtois; Director, Pete Boisvert; Choreographer, Qui Nguyen; Stage Manager, Guinevere Pressley; Lighting, Daniel Winters; Set, Tim McMath; Costumes, Betsy Strong; Sound, Patrick Shearer; Special Effects Designer, Stephanie Cox-Williams; Cast: Patrick Shearer, Christopher Yustin, Ryan Andes, Jeremy Goren, Becky Byers, Rebecca Comtois, Stephanie Cox-Williams, Melissa Roth, Kraine Theater; June 17–July 10, 2010

Nylon Fusion Collective

nylonfusion.org

Fuente Ovejuna by Lope De Vega; Director, Andy Goldberg; Original Music, Sandra Rubio; Choreographer, Josie Bray; Stage Manager, Beth Stegman; Lighting, Aaron Speavy; Set, Shoko Kambara; Costumes, AMelia Drombrowski; Cast: Katherine Barron, Marisa Dargahi, Andres de Vengoechea, Ivette Dumeng, Alex Dunbar, David Henry Gerson, Jorge Hoyos, Seth James, Elliot Joseph, Justin Maruri, David Powers, Michael R. Rosete, Ina Marie Smith, Galit Sperling, Jacob

Troy, Nick Walkonis; Clemente Soto Velez Cultural Center; June 23–July 3, 2010

Wisdom Of Obscurity by Elliot Joseph; Director, Mahayana Landowne; Choreographer, Bryce Bermingham; Stage Manager, Hannah Folger; Lighting, Lee Terry; Set, Brian Saxon; Costumes, Lorna Martin-Latner; Sound, Karen Derby; Cast: Alfred Gingold, Jonathan Blakeley, Elliot Joseph, Mac Brydon, Kaia Foss, Nnamudi Amobi, Lauren Swann; Manhattantheatresource; April 14–30, 2011

Paper Dragon by Alisha Silver; Director, Lori Kee; Stage Manager, Hannah Folger; Lighting, Lee Terry; Set, Brian T Saxton; Sound, Karen Derby; Cast: Caroline Bloom, Jennifer Betit Yen, Ivette Dumeng, Justin Maruri, Kevin Melendez, Joseph Schommer, Meghan Jones, Jacob Troy; Manhattan Theatre Source; April 17–30, 2011

READINGS AND WORKSHOPS

The Writers Collective Reading Series Included: *In the Center of the Fire* by Alisha Silver; *Uh Fairy Tale* by Joseph Wright; *Sleeping with Strangers* by Jack Karp; *Cake Light* by Courtney Brooke Lauria; *E = (mc)^3* by Calla Videt; *The First Settlers* by Kelly Davis; *Smudge* by Walker Sampson; *The Tutor* by Ka; Clemente Soto Velez; June 17–29, 2010

Oberon Theatre Ensemble

www.OberonTheatre.org

Othello by William Shakespeare; Director, Cara Reichel; Stage Manager, Dee Dee Katchen; Lighting, Isabella Byrd; Set, Ann Bartek; Cast: Daniel Morgan Shelley, Stewart Walker, Simon Feil, Randy Howk, Jennifer Blood, Jessica Angleskahn, Jane Cortney, Chris Seiler, David Matthew Douglas, Nate Faust, Lowell Byers, Matt W. Cody, Whitney Kam Lee, Rene Reyes; The Kirk @ Theatre Row Studios; June 3–24, 2010

Order by Christopher Stetson Boal; Director, Austin Pendleton; Stage Manager, Jenna Lazar; Lighting, Isabella Byrd; Set, Ann Bartek; Costumes, Mark Richard Caswell; Sound, Andrew Sherman; Cast: James Edward Becton, Gabe Bettio, Mac Brydon, Brad Fryman, William Laney, Amanda Plant, Ryan Tramont, James Washington; The Kirk @ Theatre Row Studios; June 6–26, 2010

Odyssey Productions

www.odyssey-productions.org

The Country Wife by William Wycherley; Director, Bradford Cover; Original Music, George MacDonald; Stage Manager, Jamie Lynne Sullivan; Lighting, Shelly Rodriguez; Costumes, Hwi-won Lee; Cast: Victor Barranca, Brent Bateman, Ron Bopst, Katie Bruestle, Stanley Brode, Matthew Cohn, Olivia Gilliatt, Allison Hirschlag, Allison Layman, Meg MacCary, Caitlin McMahon, Kyle Minshew, Adam Patterson; American Theatre of Actors; July 9–18, 2010

On the Square Productions

www.onthesquareproductions.com

Monroe, Illinois: Over Here/Townie by Aaron Wigdor Levy; Director, Deborah Wolfson; Stage Manager, Shannon Ancrum; Set, Greg Westby; Costumes, Mikey Goodmark; Sound, Greg Westby; Cast: Cyrilla Baer, Becca Hackett, Rachel McPhee, Doug Roland; Flea Theatre; December 8, 2010–December 21, 2010

In Your Image by Rob Benson; Director, Deborah Wolfson; Lighting, Dan Gallagher; Set, Kacie Hultgren; Costumes, Noel Falene Anderson; Cast: Rob Benson, Roger Clark, John Michalski; 59 E 59 Theaters; February 10–27, 2011

One Year Lease

www.oneyearlease.org

The Killing Room by Daniel Keene; Director, Nick Flint; Original Music, Nathan Leigh; Stage Manager, Rosy Garner; Lighting, Mike Riggs; Set, James Hunting; Costumes, Kay Lee; Sound, Nathan Leigh; Cast: Christopher Baker, Danny Bernardy, Sarah-Jane Casey, David Deblinger, Babis Gousias, Sameerah Luqmaan-Harris, Danielle Heaton, Richard Saudek; Teatro Círculo; March 10–April 2, 2011

Opening Doors Theatre Company

www.odtconline.org

Artistic & Managing Director, Suzanne Adams

Drat! The Cat! Music by Milton Schafer, book & lyrics by Ira Levin; Director, Jeremy Gold Kronenberg; Musical Director, Ted Kociolek; Choregoraphy, Christine Schwallenberg; Producer, Billie Di Stefano; Stage Manager, Esi Stogah; Cast: Richard Rice Alan, Danny Blaylock, Mark Emerson, Debra Thais Evans, Gladiss Gressley, Bridget Harvey, Emily Jenda, Edward Juvier, Jillian Prefach, Nick Reynolds; Duplex Cabaret Theatre; November 8–12, 2010

Operating Theater

www.operatingtheater.org

Artistic Director, Jason Schuler; Producing Director, Dori Ann Scagnelli

Transatlantica by Kenny Finkle; Director, Jason Schuler; Stage Manager, Helene Montagna; Lighting, Peter Hoerburger; Set, Gian Marco Lo Forte; Costumes, Jennifer Paar; Sound, Kim Carter; Producer, Dori Ann Scagnelli and Jason Schuler; Associate Producer, Tim Donovan Jr.; Scenic Artisit, Carolyn Bonanni; Original Music, Keith Caputo and Ryan Oldcastle; Additional Music, Rebecca Kupersmith; Puppet Engineer, Mathieu Lorain Dignard; Puppets, Jason Schuler; Cast: Tim Donovan Jr., Evelyn Sullivan, Anna Foss Wilson, Keith Chandler, Pierre-Marc Diennet, Eben Moore; 4th Street Theatre; October 1–23, 2010

OptiMystics

Billy Carver and the Children in Mind Written and directed by Montserrat Mendez; Lighting, Kia Rogers; Set, Montserrat Mendez; Costumes, Jenny Green; Sound, Patrick Metzger; Cast: Jenny D. Green, Armistead Johnson, Monroe Robertson, Lauren Roth, Aimee Whelan, Stuart Williams, Nathan Willis; Manhattan Theatre Source; July 7–24, 2010

Organs of State

www.organsofstate.org

Artistic Director, Guy Yedwab; Managing Director, Ben Lundberg; Production Manager, Marika Kent

The End by Guy Yedwab; Director, Ben Lundberg; Stage Manager, Susie Duecker; Set, Ben Lundberg; Costumes, Guy Yedwab; Spotlight Operator, Euthymios Logothetis; Produced in association with Pipeline Theatre Company; Cast: Guy Yedwab, Will Notini; The Wings; September 21–28, 2010

The Story of the Chisel Boy by J.C. Torres; Director, Ben Lundberg; Lighting, Marika Kent; Set, Andy Yanni; Sound, Ben Lundberg; Cast: Lisa Long, Adriana Spencer, Paul Ashey, Timothy Long; Paradise Factory; December 15–19, 2010

Percival's Big Night by Jarret Kerr; Director, Will Sullivan; Stage Manager, Amanda Hillsberg; AV Design, Ben Lundberg; Cast: Tommy Nelms, Sarah Wharton, Jarret Kerr, Angelica Reeve; The Monkey; January 25–February 6, 2011

The First Ladies Project Director, Annie Tippe; Stage Manager, Kaela GarvinLighting, Marika Kent; Set, Rachel Schneider; Costumes, Eleot Reich; Sound, Eric Biel; AV Design, Ben Lundberg; Conceived by Claire Downs; Associate Set, Walter Ryon; Master Carpentry, Joel Fullerton; Mad Beats, James Monaco; Poster Design, Robyn Ng; Events, Will Notini; Marketing, Ben Lundberg, Euthymios Logothetis; Cast: Claire Downs, Annie Tippe, Dana Clinkman, Ryann Weir, Kim Blanck; 4th Street Theater; April 21–May 1, 2011

Other Side Productions

www.othersideproductions.org

Eurydice by Sara Ruh; Director, Thom Fogarty; Original Music, Jim Campilongo; Choreographer, Thom Fogarty; Production Designer, Thom Fogarty; Cast: Quincy Ellis, Lulu Fogarty, Caitlin Rose McMahon, Aidan O'Shea, Patrick Ellison Shea, Adam Patterson and Joe Tannenbaum; The Bridge Theater; January 27–February 6, 2011

Overcoat Theater

An Evening with Ryan Paulson & H.R. Britton Written and directed by H.R. Britton & Ryan Paulson; Director, Ryan Paulson, Raj Varma; Cornelia Street Café; July 22, 2010

Packawallop Productions

www.packawallop.org

Artistic Director, Scott Ebersold; Producing Director, Jay Aubrey

Paper Cranes by Kari Bentley-Quinn; Director, Scott Ebersold; Stage Manager, Amy Francis Schott; Lighting, Scott Bolman; Set, Jared Rutherford; Costumes, Jennifer Paar; Sound, Ryan Maeker; Assistant Sound, Chantel Pascente; Cast: Melissa Hammans, Sarah Lord, Eric T. Miller, Susan Louise O'Connor, Cynthia Silver; Access Theater; April 15–May 8, 2011

READINGS AND WORKSHOPS

The Lounge Series: Turning the Glass Around by Pia Wilson; Director, Shelley Butler; New Georges; November 16, 2011

The Lounge Series: How Soon Is Now?; TheaterLab; January 31, 2011

The Lounge Series: Loteria by Carmen Pelaez; Director, Carl Andress; Access Theater; May 2, 2011

Paisley in Blue Productions

Vanya adapted from Anton Chekhov; Director, Onur Karaoglu; Original Music, Erato A. Kremmyda; Lighting, Marie Yokoyama; Set, Marie Yokoyama; Cast: Christopher John Domig, Meera Kumbhani, Elizabeth Lee Malone, Jason Martin; 2 Great Jones; April 14–30, 2011

The Panoply Performance Laboratory

www.panoplylab.org

The Last Dreams of Helene Weigel or How to Get Rid of The Feminism Once and For All by Esther Neff and Brian McCorkle; Director, Esther Neff; Choreographer, Esther Neff; Set, Liz Jenatopolus; Costumes, Lena Sands; Sound, Brian McCorkle; AudioVisual and Puppet Design, Panoply Design; Cast: Andrea Suarez, Tom Swirly, Katie Johnston, Matthew Stephen Smith, Kate Garfield, Loren

Barnese, Matthew Gonzalez, Jessica Bathurst; Surreal Estate; July 25, 2009–August 1, 2010

Parallel Exit

www.parallelexit.net

Mark Lonergan, Artistic Director; Monika Jouvert, General Manager

Room 17B by Mike Dobson and Joel Jeske; Director, Mark Lonergan; Musical Director, Mike Dobson; Stage Manager, Olivia O'Brien; Lighting, Maruti Evans; Set, Maruti Evans; Composer, Mike Dobson; Choreographers, Danny Gardner and Brent McBeth; Cast: Mike Dobson, Danny Gardner, Joel Jeske, Brent McBeth; 59E59 Theaters; January 13–February 6, 2011

Parenthesis

parenthesistheater.com

The Lady's Not for Burning by Christopher Fry; Director, Bryan Close; Stage Managers, Michelle Foster and Brooke Elsinghorst; Lighting, Lucrecia Briceno and Tim Cryan; Set, Michael V. Moore; Costumes, Kirche Zeile; Sound, Asa Wember; Cast: Matthew Baldiga, Gwen Ellis, Nick Fesette, Danny Makali'i Mittermeyer, Anna Olivia Moore, Jefferson Slinkard, Rob Skolits, Jean Tafler, Jared Thompson, Isaac Woofter; Walkerspace; May 21–June 11, 2011

Partial Comfort Productions

partialcomfort.org

Artistic Directors: Chad Beckim, Molly Pearson; Company Manager, Jessika Doyel; Marketing Director, Lindsey Austen; Casting, Judy Bowman; Press, Ron Lasko, Spin Cycle

A Bright New Boise by Samuel D. Hunter; Director, Davis McCallum; Original Music, Ryan Rumery; Stage Manager, Tara Nachtigall; Lighting, Raquel Davis; Set, Jason Simms; Costumes, Whitney Locher; AV Design, Rocco D'Santi; Cast: Andrew Garman, Sarah Nina Haydon, Danielle Slavick, John Patrick Doherty, Matt Farabee; The Wild Project; September 15–October 2, 2010

Passajj Productions

Wuthering Heights, a Romantic Musical by Paul Dick; Director, Mat Gutchick; Musical Director, Michael Sheetz; Stage Manager, Michael Palmer; Lighting, Scott Needham; Set, Tim McMath; Costumes, Nicole Pezzola; Cast: Erin Wegner Brooks, Jonathan Grunert, Dawn Timm, Scott Ramsey, John Weigand, Bill Newhall, Weston Wells Olson, Eric Van Tielen, Mollie Vogt-Welch, Deena Eddy; Mint Theater; June 11–27, 2010

Peculiar Works Project

www.peculiarworks.org

Co-Founders and Co-Producers: Ralph Lewis, Catherine Porter, Barry Rowell

Can You Hear Their Voices? by Hallie Flanagan and Margaret Ellen Clifford; Director, Ralph Lewis and Barry Rowell; Musical Director, Seth Bedford; Stage Manager, Susan D. Lange; Lighting, David Castaneda; Set, Nikolay Levin; Costumes, Deb O; AV Design, Matt Tennie; Producing Associate: Cathy Carlton Production dramaturg; Gwen Orel; Press, Jim Baldassare; Cast: Tonya Canada, Patricia Drozda, Sarah Elizondo, Ken Glickfeld, Mick Hilgers, Christopher Hurt, Derek Jamison, Ben Kopit, Carrie McCrossen, Catherine Porter, Rebecca Servon; 2 Great Jones Street, NYC; June 3–27, 2010

PegLeg Productions/
Culture Project's Women Center Stage 2011

www.womencenterstage.org

Hold Music by Calla Videt and B. Walker Sampson; Director, Calla Videt; Choreographer, Rick and Jeffrey Kuperman; Stage Manager, Kara Kaufman; Lighting, Mary E. Stebbins; Set, Ji-youn Chang; Costumes, Ginia Sweeney; Video Design for Trevor Martin; Cast: Merrie Jane Brackin, Arlo Hill, Josh Odsess-Rubin, Avery Pearson, Mickey Sumner and Aya Tucker; Living Theatre; March 12–28, 2011

Perfromance Space 122

Artistic Director, Vallejo Gantner; Managing Director, Winnie Fung; Director of Production, Derek Lloyd; Communications & Branding Manager, Laura Nicoll; Creative Technology Developer, Alex Reeves; Individual Giving and Special Events Manager, Lori Vroegi

Strange Action Created by Isabel Lewis; Dramaturge, Josep Maynou; Isabel Lewis, Josep Maynou; June 3–6, 2010

The Octoroon Written and directed by Branden Jacobs-Jenkins in collaboration with Johnson Henshaw and Allison Lyman; Director, Costumes, Abigail Hahn; Sound, Jesse Rudoy; Make-Up, John Carter; Light Design, Kevin Hardy; Producer, Johnson Henshaw; Dramaturg, Allison Lyman; Assistant Director, Lacy Warner; Cast: Travis York, Chris Manley, Gabe Levey, Jake Hart, Margaret Flanagan, Amber Gray, Mary Wiseman, LaToya Lewis, Kim Gainer, Sasheer Zamata; ; June 26–July 3, 2010

The Pied Piper of the Lower East Side Produced by The Amoralists; July 29–August 3, 2010

Happy in the Poorhouse Produced by The Amoralists; July 29–August 3, 2010

Mundo Overloadus by Michael Lederer; Produced by C de B Productions & The Dubrovnik Shakespeare Festival; September 7–12, 2010

Hetero by Lachaud; Director, Arthur Nauzyciel; September 11–14, 2010

The Map of Lost Things by Darragh Martin; Puppets, Katey Parker; Original Music Donovan Seidle; Katey Parker; Produced by The Invisible Company; September 16–26, 2010

Graham & Frost by Belinda McKeon; Director, Thomas G. Waites; Lighting and Set, Tsubasa Kemei and Jennifer Stimple; Sound, Jeremy Joyce; Costumes, Brian Einersen; Cast: Steven Randazzo, Enrico Ciotti and Dan Shaked; Produced by The Sullivan Project in association with Alycia Aumuller, Maedhbh McCullagh, Todd Miller and Williston Productions; September 17–October 3, 2010

The Sea Museum by Darrieussecq; Director, Daniel Pettrow; Produced by French Institute Alliance Francaise–www.fiaf.org; September 18–19, 2010

Hotel Savoy Concept and Staging by Dominic Huber; Sound, Knut Jensen; Additional Script Contribution, Lara Koerte; Dramaturgy: Anne Hoelck; Assistant Director & Prop Design, Fabian Offert and Paula Reissig; Co-Producer, Dominic Huber and Philipp Leist; Cast: Wickham Boyle, Howard des Chenes, Tom Gallucio, Léna Greenberg, Chandler Gregoire, Timothy Hospodar, Michael Simmons, Richard Stein, Issac Taylor, Heather Warner, Phillip Gulley; Produced by Dominic Huber; September 30–October 31, 2010

Our Hit Parade Hosts, Bridget Everett and Kenny Mellman; Cast: Erin Markey, Jenn Harris, Julie Atlas Muz, The Kitty Litter, Corn Mo, Hank & Cupcake, Bookmark and Share, Reggie Watts, Erin Markey, Amber Martin, Adrienne Truscott, The Kitty Litter, plus Marga Gomez and Dan Fishback; Produced by Avant-Garde-Arama!; October 1–2, 2010

I Am Saying Goodnight Audio/Visual Design, Joanna Seitz; Lighting, Jonathan Belcher; Conceived and Director, Amanda Loulaki; Created by Rebecca Brooks, Carolyn Hall, Becky Serrell, Pedro Osorio and Amanda Loulaki; Original Music,

Georgios Kontos, Giannis Aggelakas and Nikos Veliotis; Cast: Carolyn Hall, Becky Serrell, Pedro Osorio and Amanda Loulaki; Produced by Amanda Loulaki and Short Mean Lady; October 13–October 16, 2010

Them Created by Ishmael Houston-Jones, Dennis Cooper and Chris Cochrane; Lighting, Joe Levasseur; Cast: Joey Cannizzaro, Felix Cruz, Jeremy Pheiffer, Niall Noel, Jacob Slominski, Arturo Vidich, Enrico D. Wey; ; October 21–30, 2010

Supergabriela Director, Cosmin Manolescu; Choreographer, Cosmin Manolescu; Cast: Camille Mutel, Litsa Kiousi, Cosmin Manolescu; Produced by Cosmin Manolescu & Serial Paradise Company; November 4–5, 2010

Now and Nowhere Else Created by Diane Madden, Joey Truman, Peter Warren, Pål Asle Pettersen and Jim Dawson; Produced by Iver Findlay & Marit Sansmark; November 10–14, 2010

Lay of the Land Created by Tim Miller; December 1–11, 2010

Rumble Ghost Written and Choreographed by Jack Ferver; Dramaturge, Josh Lubin-Levy; Costumes Design, Reid Bartelme; Original Music, Calder Singer; Cast: Benjamin Asriel, Reid Bartelme, Christian Coulson, Carlye Eckert, Jack Ferver, Michelle Mola, Breanna O'Mara; December 8–12, 2010

Brothers and Sisters and Motherfuckers Written, Directed and performed by Jibz Cameron; Animation, Amy Von Harrington; Video and Set, Lauren Brown; Costumes, Hayden Dunham; Hair and Makeup, Holli Smith; Sound, A.V. Linton and Jibz Cameron; Producer, Jibz Cameron and Amy Von Harrington; Produced by Dynasty Handbag; December 15–19, 2010

Every House Has a Door Director, Lin Hixon; Created by Lin Hixson and Matthew Goulish; January 25–26, 2011

Storm Still Cast: Rick Burkhardt, Andy Gricevich, Ryan Higgins; Produced by The Nonsense Company; February 19–March 6, 2011

East 10th Street: Self Partait with Empty House Written & Performed by Edgar Oliver; Director, Randy Sharp; Lighting, David Zeffren; Sound, Steve Fontaine; March 18–April 2, 2011

Swan!!! by Jack Ferver; Cast: Jenn Harris, Randy Harrison, Christian Coulson, Matthew Wilkas; Produced by QWAN Company; ; March 10–12, 2011

Supernormal Written and performed by Tom Shillue; March 16–April 2, 2011

The Escape Artist Script and Visual Concept, John Kelly; Original Music, John Kelly, Carol Lipnik, Claudio Monteverdi, John Barry; Dramaturge, Dudley Saunders; Video Design, Jeff Morey; Cast: John Kelly; Musicians: John BiPinto, Nioka Workman, Justin Smith; April 15–30, 2011

Radio Play by Reggie Watts and Tommy Smith; Director, Kip Fagan; Cast: Reggie Watts, H.I. Bonner, Beth Hoyt, Mary Jane Gibson, Marshall York, Jen Rondeau; May 6–22, 2011

FESTIVALS

soloNOVA Arts Festival 2010 (see Festivals below); Produced by terraNOVA Collective; ; May 26–June 6, 2010

4th Annual Underground Zero Festival (see Festivals below); Produced by East River Commedia; ; July 6–25, 2010

COIL Festival 2011 (see Festivals below); January 5–15, 2011

Festival of Ideas for A New City ; May 4–8, 2011

Phoenix Theatre Ensemble

www.phoenixtheatreensemble.org

Co-Artistic Director, Craig Smith; Co Artistic Director, Elise Stone; Co-Artistic Director, Amy Wagner; Co-Artistic Director, Brian Costello; Co-Artistic Director, Kelli Holsopple; Co-Artistic Director, Kathy Menino; Co-Artistic Director, Joe Menino

Hapgood by Tom Stoppard; Director, John Giampetro; Stage Manager, Miriam Hyfler; Lighting, Jay Ryan; Set, Jay Ryan; Costumes, Colleen Kesterton; Sound, Elizabeth Rhodes; Dialect Coach, Kohli Calhoun; Graphics, Monty Stilson; Technical Director, Vadim Malinskiiy; Cast: Brian A. Costello, Keith Hamilton-Cobb, Joseph J. Menino, Jason O'Connell, David Regelmann, Craig Smith, Elise Stone, Jack Tartaglia, Josh Tyson; The Wild Project; December 2–12, 2010

Little Red Book, Kathy Menino; Music & Lyrics, Ellen Mandell; Director, Jeremy Williams; Music Director, Ellen Mandell; Stage Manager, Donna Gearhardt Healey; Lighting, Jay Ryan; Set, Jeff Duer; Choreographer, Jeremy Williams; Scenic Artist, Erin Duer; Image Design Lantzy; Photography, John Crittenden; Graphic Design, Monty Stilson; Cast: Nora Martinez DeBenedetto, Paige O'Malley, Brian Morgan, Tom Tyburski, Florence Pape, David Plotka; The Wild Project; December 4–11, 2010

The Emperor's New Clothes by Kathy Menino; Director, Jeremy Williams; Musical Director, Ellen Mandell; Stage Manager, Donna Gearhardt Healey; Lighting, Jay Ryan; Set, Erin Duer; Costumes, Erin Duer; Adaptor, Kathy Menino; Original Music and Song, Ellen Mandel; Choreographer, Jeremy Williams; Image Design, Meghan Lantzy; Graphic Design, Monty Stilson; Photographer, John Crittenden; Cast: Laura DiCerto, Florence Pape, Paige O'Malley, Brian Morgan, Kyra Bowman, Douglas Santiago; The Wild Project; February 21–12, 2011

Iphegenia at Aulis by Euripedes; Director, Amy Wagner; Stage Manager, Miriam Hyfler; Lighting and Set, Maruti Evans; Costumes, Suzanne Chesney; Sound, Elizabeth Rhodes; Graphics, Monty Stilson; Technical Director, Vadim Malinskiiy; Cast: Cheryl Cochran, Brian A. Costello, Amy Fitts, Kelli Holsopple, John Lenartz, Lawrence Merritt, Joseph J. Menino, Laura Piquado, Elise Stone, & Josh Tyson; The Wild Project; March 3–13, 2011

READINGS AND WORKSHOPS

A Man's A Man by Bertolt Brech & Eric Bentley; Director, Amy Wagner; Music, Arnold Black; Musical Director, Ellen Mandel; Cast: Brian A. Costello, Amy Fitts, Ariel Estrada, Kelli Holsopple, Joseph J. Menino, Grant Neale, Laura Piquado, Elise Stone, Josh Tyson, Anthony Willis Jr.; The Wild Project; November 16–21, 2010

Silent Partners by Charles Marowitz; Director, Scott Shattuck; Based on The Brecht Memoir by Eric Bentley; Cast: Michael Surabian, Brian Costello, John Lenartz, Laura Piquado, LeeAnne Hutchison, Josh Tyson, David Rigelmann; Lighting, Jay Ryan; Stage Manager, Amanda Karmas; The Wild Project; February 22–27, 2011

Mother Courage and Her Children by Bertolt Brecht & Eric Bentley; Director, Robert Hupp; Composer, Darius Milhaud; Music Arrangement, Ellen Mandel; Cast: Brian A. Costello, Ariel Estrada, Amy Fitts, Kelli Holsopple, Rudy Lawless, John Lenartz, Dan Matisa, Joseph J. Menino, Laura Piquado, Craig Smith, Elise Stone, & Josh Tyson; The Wild Project; May 10–15, 2011

Ping Chong & Company

www.pingchong.org

Artistic Director, Ping Chong; Managing Director, Bruce Allardice; Associate Director, Sara Zatz; General Manager, Jane Jung; Production Associate/Education Coordinator, Jesca Prudencio

Throne of Blood Written and directed by Ping Chong; Stage Manager, Amy Miranda Warner; Lighting, Darren McCroom; Set, Christopher Acebo; Costumes, Stefani Mar; Sound, Todd Barton; AV Design, Maya Ciarrocchi; Assistant Stage Manager, Mandy Younger; Movement and Fight Director, John Sipes; Associate Fight Director, U. Jonathan Toppo; Voice Director, Sara Becker; Movement Consultant, Darrell Bluhm; Noh choreography and Cultural Advisor, Ako; Cast: Kevin Kenerly, Ako, Danforth Comins, Jonathan Haugen, JaMario Stills, Richard Howard, Michael Winters, Cristofer Jean, Gregory Linington, Peter Macon, James Newcomb, U. Jonathan Toppo, Elijah Alexander, Kacy-Earl David, Emily Sophia

Knapp, Eddie Lopez; Angus Bowmer Theatre, Oregon Shakespeare Festival; Howard Gilman Opera House, Brooklyn Academy of Music; July 21–November 13, 2010

Secret Survivors Written and directed by Sara Zatz; Stage Manager, Courtney Golden; Lighting, Brant Thomas Murray; Project Coordinator, Amita Swadhin; Technical Director, Rachael Harris; Cast: Amita Swadhin, Gabriella Callender, Lucia Leandro Gimeno, RJ Maccani, Diana Sands; Produced in association with El Museo del Barrio; El Teatro, El Museo del Barrio; March 12, 2011

Inside/Out...voices from the disability community Written and directed by Ping Chong and Sara Zatz; Stage Manager, Courtney Golden; Lighting, Brant Thomas Murray; Produced in association with VSA Cast: Josh Hecht, Monique Holt, Christopher Imrosciano, Vivian Cary Jenkins, Matthew S. Joffe, Zazel-Chavah O'Garra, Blair Wing, Mind Pfeffer; Flynn Center, Burlington VT; Round House Theatre, Bethesda MD; Amaryllis Theatre, Philadelphia PA; May 15–June 23, 2011

READINGS AND WORKSHOPS

Cry for Peace: Voices from the Congo by Ping Chong and Kyle Bass with Sara Zatz; Director, Ping Chong; Produced in association with Syracuse Stage and Ping Chong & Company; Beckett Theatre; April 5, 2011

Pioneers Go East Company

www.pioneersgoeast.org

Artistic Director, Gian Marco Lo Forte; Marketing, Abby Felder; Resident Artists: Mark Tambella, Gabriel Berry, Angela Wendt, Ji-Youn Chang, Rocco D'Santi

I Fioretti in Musica–opera in danza by Gian Marco Lo Forte; Director, Gian Marco Lo Forte; Musical Director, Sasha Zamler-Carhart; Stage Manager, Karen Oughtred; Lighting, Jiji Chang; Set, Gian Marco and Mark Tambella; Costumes, Gabriel Berry & Angela Wendt; AV Design, Jiji Chang & Rocco D'Santi; Puppet Designer, Cathy Shaw and Abby Felder; Drawing and paintings projection Mark Tambella; Choreographer, Philip Montana; Composer, Sasha Zamler-Carhart and Ryan Carter; Cast: Courtney Dana Baron; Kayla Mason; Laura Arend; Miriam Rosenberg; Emanuele Nigro, Dana Marcolina, Spencer Bazzano, Bradley Williams, Jason Zeren, Dorothy James Loechel, Kim Diamond, Silvia Gianmpaola; Megan Schubert; Patrick Fennig; Matt Knickman; Co-production La Mama ETC and Pioneers Go East Company; La MaMa ETC; September 30–October 15, 2010

Pipeline Theatre Company

Fat Kids On Fire by Bekah Brunstetter; Director, Peter Frechette; Stage Manager, Fernando Contreras; Lighting, Rick Hayashi; Set, Ian Crawford; Costumes, Meagan Kensil & Brian Maxsween; Sound, Liam Nelligan; Cast: John Early, Shane Zeigler, Sydney Matthews, Susan Blair Ross, Andrea Ciannavei, Megan Linde, Andi Potamkin; Wings Theatre; September 17–October 2, 2010

The Caucasian Chalk Circle by Bertolt Brecht; Director, Anya Saffir; Original Music, Cormac Bluestone; Choreographer, Alison Beatty; Stage Manager, Jessika Doyel; Lighting and Set, Eric Southern; Costumes, Katja Andreiev; Props Designer, Zealan Salemi; Cast: Sam Dash, John Early, Matthew Hanson, Glenn Hergenhahn, Maura Hooper, Daniel Johnsen, Jacquelyn Landgraf, Charley Layton, Vladimir Margolin, Sydney Matthews, Brian Maxsween, Joyce Miller, Alex Mills, Ronald Peet, Michael R. Piazza, Marek Sapieyevski, Chloe Wepper; Theater for the New City; March 5–19, 2011

The Platform Group

Artistic Director: Shara Ashley Zeiger

Savage in Limbo by John Patrick Shanley; Director, Brian Tom O'Connor; Stage Manager, Marcie Friedman; Lighting, Isabella Byrd; Set, Andrew Lu; Sound, Anthony Trentinella; Assistant Director and Assistant Stage Manager, Julia Frieri; Producer, Abigail Rose Solomon; Cast: Shara Ashley Zeiger, Abigail Rose Solomon, Maxwell Zener, Fabio Taliercio, Kendall Rileigh; Co-produced with Rosalind Productions; The Drilling Company Theatre; February 11–March 27, 2011

Playhouse Creatures Theatre Co.

playhousecreatures.org

The Libertine Director, Eric Tucker; Stage Manager, Gina Costaglioa; Lighting, Les Dickert; Set, Layra Taber Bacon; Costumes, Angela Huff; Cast: Joseph W. Rodriguez, Eric Doss, Harry Oram, Ross bennett Hurwitz, Patricia Duran, Claire Warden, Libby Arnold, Sara Koestner; Kirk Theatre; November 5–20, 2010

PLG Arts

www.plgarts.org

Daydream adapted from William Shakespeare; Director, Rohana Elias-Reyes; Stage Manager, Gloria Yetter; Cast: Adrian Cervantes Mejia, Kubbi, T. Scott Lilly, Laura Frenzer, Tomike' Lee Ogugua, Lynda Kennedy, Albert Elias; Prospect Park›s Imagination Playground; June 5–27, 2010

Point of You Productions

www.pointofyou.org

Executive Director, Johnny Blaze Leavitt; Artistic Director, Jeff Love; Administrative Director, Melanie Kunchinksi Rodriguez; Director or Operations, Sean Rodriguez; Technical Director, Gerard J. Savoy; Production Director, Marc Adam Smith

Summers in the City by Ellis Cahill, Kathleen Rose Fletcher, Nicholas Walker Herbert, Johnny Blaze Leavitt, Peggy Lee, Jeff Love, Leslie Marseglia, Olivia Worden, Ceren Zorlu; Director, Jeff Love, Monica Blaze Leavitt, Alyssa Mann, Marc Adam Smith, Paul Weissman, Ceren Zorlu; Cast: Brandon Beilis, Ellis Cahill, Jessie Fahay, Kathleen Rose Fletcher, Marlise Garde, Annalee Hardison, Cedric Jones, Karron Karr, Johnny Blaze Leavitt, Monica Blaze Leavitt, Jeff Love, Meghan Love, Alyssa Mann, Leslie Marseglia, Rita MenWeep, Gerard J. Savo; Gotham City Improv; August 3–5, 2010

A Midwinter's Tale by Johnny Blaze Leavitt based on a screenplay by Kenneth Branagh; Director, Jeff Love; Stage Manager, Olivia Schlueter Corey; Lighting, Keri Thibodeau; Set, Gerard J. Savoy; Sound, Jeff Love; Lighting Assistance, Christine Boutin; Fight Coordinator, Gerard J. Savoy; Dialect Coach, Monica Blaze Leavitt; Graphic Design, Melanie Kuchinski Rodriguez, Stislow Design & Illustration; Photographer, Sean Rodriguez; Cast: Kathleen Rose Fletcher, Nick Herbert, Chris Keating, Johnny Blaze Leavitt, Meghan Love, Leslie Marseglia, Gerard J. Savoy, Tina Trimble Savoy, Olivia Schlueter-Corey, Christopher Shelton, Felicia Eugenia Velasco, Paul Weissman, Morgan White; American Theatre of Actors; March 3–13, 2011

Potomac Theatre Project

www.potomactheatreproject.org

A Question of Mercy by Dave Rabe; Director, Jim Petosa; Stage Manager, Lisa McGinn; Lighting, Hallie Zieselman; Set, Christina Galvez; Costumes, Emma Ermotti; Sound, Andrew Duncan Will; AV Design, Ross Bell; Furniture Design, Eleanor Kahn; Cast: Alex Cranmer, Paula Langton, Mat Nakitare, Martha Newman and Tim Spears; Atlantic Stage 2; July 6–August 1, 2010

The Thief and Plevna: Meditations on Hatred by Howard Barker; Director, Richard Romagnoli; Stage Manager, Alex Mark, Lisa McGinn; Lighting, Hallie Zieselman; Set, Christina Galvez; AudioVisual, Ross Bell; Cast:; Atlantic Stage 2; July 12–31, 2010

Lovesong of the Electric Bear by Snoo Wilson; Director, Cheryl Faraone; Stage Manager, Alex Mark, Lisa McGinn; Lighting, Hallie Zieselman; Set, Christina Galvez; Costumes, Danielle Nieves; Sound, Jimmy Wong; AV Design, Ross Bell; Atlantic Stage 2; July 13–August 1, 2010

Project: Theater

www.projecttheater.org

My Custom Van by Based on the book of essays by Michael Ian Black; Adapted by Project: Theater; Director, Joe Jung; Stage Manager, Jacob Seelbach; Lighting, Chad Lefebvre; Set, J.J. Bernard & Francois Portier; Costumes, Jessi Blue Gormezano; Sound, Joe Jung; AV Design, Joe Jung & Chad Lefebvre; Cast: Amanda Byron, Laura Dillman, Ruark Downey, Brian Frank, Joe Jung, Andrew McLeod, Brian Sell, Joshua Tussin; The Drilling Company Theatre; July 1-10, 2011

Mark My Words Written and performed by Jessi Blue Gormezano; Director, Joe Jung and Hannah Wilson; Stage Manager, Carmen Torres; Lighting, Amanda Byrd; Set, J.J. Bernard & Francois Portier; Costumes, Jessi Blue Gormezano; Sound, Joe Jung; The Drilling Company Theatre; April 21–April 24, 2011

William and the Tradesmen Written and directed by Eli James; Director, Craig Wroe; Stage Manager, Carmen Torres; Lighting, Alex Goldberg; Set, J.J. Bernard & Francois Portier; Costumes, Eli James; Sound and AV Design, Joe Jung; Cast: Eli James; The Drilling Company Theatre; April 28–May 1, 2011

READINGS AND WORKSHOPS

Our Bar by Project: Theater; Director, Jessi Blue Gormezano and Hannah Wilson; Cast: Joe Jung, Andrew McLeod, Ken Ferrigni, Jennifer Logue, Sarah Schabach, Brian Sell, Amy Hattemer, Jenny Schutzman, Shira Kobren, Ruthie Scarpino, Greg Engbrecht, Laura Dillman, Brian Frank and numerous others.; Failte Irish Whiskey Bar; On-going

Project Y Theatre Company

www.projectytheatre.org

The Revival by Samuel Brett Williams; Director, Michole Biancosino; Stage Manager, Patrick Clayton; Lighting, Ben Hagen; Set, Kevin Judge; Costumes, Emily Pepper; Sound, Amit Prakash; Cast: Trent Dawson, Raymond Mcanally, Aidan Sullivan; Lion Theatre; September 9–25, 2010

Pulse Ensemble Theatre

www.pulseensembletheatre.org

Chaos Theory by Anuvab Pal; Director, Alexa Kelly; Stage Manager, Brian Richardson; Lighting, Steve O'Shea; Set, Zhanna Gurvich; Sound, Louis Lopardi; Cast: Rita Wolf; The Barrow Group Theatre; May 26–June 19, 2010

MacBeth by William Shakespeare; Director, Alexa Kelly; Cast: Jeff Burchfield, Paul Pontrelli, Akeem Folkes, Brian Richardson, Renee Flemings, Aam Jonas Segaller, Danny Makali'i Mittermeyer, Shawn Williams, Mathew J, Harris, Mia Anderson, Wendy Snow, Erica Chambers, Regina Gibson, Gregory Wool, Kara Addington and Le; Riverbank State Park; August 12–28, 2010

Purple Rep

www.purplerep.com

Co-Artistic Director, Larry Kunofsky; Co-Artistic Director, Mariah MacCarthy; Co-Producer and Company Manager, Katharine Sullivan; Co-Producer and Production/General Manager, Tzipora Kaplan

The All-American Genderf*ck Cabaret by Mariah MacCarthy; Director, Heidi Handelsman; Choreographer, Brandon Whited; Stage Manager, Liz Richards; Lighting, Lois Catanzaro; Set, Tim McMath; Costumes, Polina Roytman; Sound, Jay Spriggs; Cast: Esteban Benito, Kim Gainer, Yeauxlanda Kay, Jamhl Garrison-Lowe, Lauren Hennessy, Catherine Lefrere, Lindsay Naas, Jordan Tierney, and Wes Urish; Paradise Factory Theatre; April 8–30, 2011

The Un-Marrying Project by Larry Kunofsky; Director, Rachel Eckerling; Original Music, Jay Spriggs; Choreographer, Brandon Whited; Stage Manager, Michael Denis; Lighting, Lois Catanzaro; Set, Tim McMath; Costumes, Polina Roytman; Sound, Jay Spriggs; Video Designer, Daniel Heffernan; Cast: Jolly Abraham, Abraham Amkpa, Katie Atcheson, Nic Grelli, Brian Miskell, Diana Oh, and Bill Weeden; Paradise Factory Theatre; April 9–30, 2011

Queens Players

www.thequeensplayers.com

The Persecution And Assassination Of Jean Paul Marat As Performed By The Inmates Of The Asylum At Charenton Under The Direction Of The Marquis De Sade by Peter Weiss; Director, Kelly Johnston; Cast: Annabelle Beaver, Charlotte Dunn, Chelsea D'Aprile, Danielle Devine, Gina Trebiani, Howah Hung, Lena Cigleris, Meytal Navarro, Stephanie LaVardera, Tonya M. Edwards; Secret Theatre; October 14–30, 2010

Saint Joan by George Bernard Shaw; Director, Ken Neil Hailey; Original Music, Cory Hibbs; Costumes, Tom Kleinert; Cast: Eric Stephenson, Greer Samuels, David Douglas, Graciany Miranda, Alex Panich, Janice Acevedo, Eric William Whitehead, Robert Eigen, Tim Moore, Bruce Barton, Dave Fink, Jonathan Zipper, Cory Hibbs, Kurt Roediger, Jaike Foley-Schultz and Peter Judd; Secret Theatre; October 28–November 13, 2010

Three Sisters by Anton Chekhov; Director, Alberto Bonilla; Stage Manager, Jasmin Sanchez; Cast: Daniel Smith, Peter Guaracci, Sarah Bonner; The Secret Theatre; March 9–26, 2011

Queens Shakespeare Inc

www.secrettheatre.com

The Merchant of Venice by William Shakespeare; Director, Nanette Asher; Stage Manager, Tara Schmidt; Sound, Justin Asher; Production Manager, Lighting and Set, Jonathan Emerson and Joe Sebring; Cast: Kelly Addyman, Nikki Bohm, Jonathan Emerson, Liam Ferguson, Adam Gallinat, Matt Harris, Bradley LeBoeuf, Leila Okafor, Michael Pichardo, Dave Reck, Camilla Skoglie, Anwar Uddin, Celeste Van Vroenhoven; Bowne Street Community Church; June 3–27, 2010

A MidSummer Night's Dream by William Shakespeare; Director, Jonathan Emerson; Stage Manager, Tara Schmitt; Lighting, Joe sebring; Set, Jonathan Emerson; Costumes, Helyn Messenger; AV Design, Joe Sebring and William Johnson; Cast: Melissa Damas, Anna Wallace Deering, Jonathan Emerson,

Kathleen Fletcher, Kyrian Friedenberg, Adam Gallinat, Bradley LeBoeuf, Steven Martin, Helyn Messenger, Patrick Mahoney, Jessica Mchugh, Natasha Murray, Sarah Penchef, Sajeev Pillai, Ross Pivec; The Secret Theatre; May 18–26, 2011

Queens Theatre

Julius Caesar by William Shakespeare; Director, Richard Mazda; Cast: Alex Cape, Anthony Martinez, Amelia Gonzalez, Ashley Denise Robinson, Bethanne Haft, Camilla Skoglie, David Fink, Elizabeth Bernhardt, Gil Ron, Greer Samuels, Jake Cullens, Jeffrey Coyne, Joe Mullen, Jonathan Emerson, Juan Castano, Kaitlyn Huczko, Kara Addington, Lena Gora, Michelle Pucci, Rachel Pfennigwerth, Sarah Bonner, Suzanne Lenz, Tyrus Holden; The Secret Theatre; September 16 –October 2, 2010

Theatre Du Grand-Guignol: Tales of Horror and Fear: *The Final Kiss* by Maurice Level; *Tics, or Doing the Deed* by Rene Berton; Director, Ariel Francoeur; Cast: Jeni Ahlfeld, Kirsten Anderson, Sean Demers, Catherine Ellsberg, Beth Heidere, Dave Herigstad, Tim Lalumia, Jenny Levine, Amy Lytle, Teddy Lytle, Greg Petroff, Jack Rondeau; The Secret Theatre; October 14–31, 2010

The Knight of the Burning Pestle by Sir Francis Beaumont; Director, Richard Mazada; Stage Manager, Rachel Pfenningwerth; Costumes, Helyn Messenger; Photographer, Sean MacBride Murray; Videographer, Perry Katz; Cast: Alex Cape, Alex Stine, Ariel Rosen-Brown, Avery Manuel, Brian Walters, Helyn Messenger, Jonathan Emerson, Joshua Warr, Kate Siepert, Philip J. Rossi, Randy Warshaw, Ross Pivec, Shannon Pritchard, Thom Brown; The Secret Theatre; February 17– March 5, 2011

Rabbit Hole Ensemble

www.rabbitholeensemble.com

Before Your Very Eyes by Edward Elefterion; Director, Edward Elefterion; Stage Manager, Brooke Leigh-Barefoot Bell; Lighting, Sam Gordon; Set, Patrick Mills; Costumes, Michael Tester; Sound, David Liao; Assistant Stage Manager, Christina Bracco; Press, Emily Hartford; Special Event Planning, Jessica Quimby; Cast: Bobby Abido, Diana Delacruz, Sanam Erfani, Elyse Knight, Damon Pooser; Clemete Soto Velez Center, Flamboyan Theatre; May 19–June 13, 2010

The Tragic Story of Doctor Frankenstein by Stanton Wood; Directed and Choreographed by Edward Elefterion; Lighting and Sound, Edward Elefterion; Costumes, Pei-Chi Su; Graphics, David Liao; Press, James Gerontzos; Special Events, Jessica Quimby; Cast: Arthur Aulisi, Emily Hartford, Elyse Knight, Jocelyn O'Neil, Lauren Cook, Nikki Dillon; BAX/Brooklyn Arts Exchange; October 28– November 13, 2010

Doctor Frankenstein's Magical Creature by Stanton Wood; Directed and Choreographed by Edward Elefterion; Lighting, Sound and Set, Edward Elefterion; Costumes, Pei-Chi Su; Graphics, David Liao; Press, Nikki Dillon; Special Events, Jessica Quimby; Cast: Arthur Aulisi, Nikki Dillon, Emily Hartford, Elyse Knight, Jocelyn O'Neil, Rachel Pearl; Old First Reformed Church; March 17–April 2, 2011

READINGS AND WORKSHOPS

The Legend of Ichabod Crane by Dan Kitrosser; Director, Edward Elefterion; Theatre for Communities Project Administrator, Emily Hartford; Accompanist, Ilan Isakov; Various locations throughout Brooklyn; September 2010

RadioTheatre

www.radiotheatrenyc.com

The Time Machine by Dan Bianchi; Adapted from H.G. Wells; Directed and Original Music by Dan Bianchi; Set, Dan Bianchi; Sound, Dan Bianchi, Wes Shippee; Cast: Frank Zilinyi, Kate Siepert; Red Room; December 12, 2010– January 10, 2011

The H.P.Lovecraft Festival : *Dagon* I, *The Dunwich Horror*, *Pickman's Model*, *From Beyond*, *The Beast In The Cave*, *The Music of Erich Zann* by Dan Bianchi; Directed and Original Music by Dan Bianchi; Lighting, Set and Sound, Dan Bianchi; Cast: Natalie Martin, Alfred Gingold, Peter Reznikoff; Kraine Theater; March 17–April 3, 2011

The Haunting of 85 East 4th Street Written and directed by Dan Bianchi; Produced in association with Horse Trade Theater Group; Kraine Theater; April 10–October 31, 2010

Random Accomplice

The Promise by Douglas Maxwell; Director, Johnny McKnight; Lighting, Dave Shea; Sound, Karen MacIver; AudioVisual, Tim Reid; Set and Costumes, Lisa Sang; 59E59 Theaters; April 3–17, 2011

Razors Edge Productions

www.zombietheplay.com

President, Bill Connington

Princes of Darkness Written and performed by Bill Connington; Directed and Choreographed by Rachel Klein; Stage Manager, Naomi Anhorn; Lighting, Kia Rogers; Costumes, Rachel Klein; Sound, Sean Gill; Assistant Stage Manager, Caitlin Lyons; Sound Recording, Danny Bonner; Theater for the New City; August 8–14, 2010

I Stand Before You Naked by Joyce Carol Oates; Director, Bill Connington; Stage Manager, Naomi Anhorn; Lighting, Yuriy Nayer; Casting; Robin Carus; Assistant Stage Manager; Caitlin Lyons: Cast: Elizabeth Pojanowski, Karin de la Penha, Bree Williamson, Jennifer McCabe, Melissa Miller, Abby Royle, Janet Carroll, Nikka Lanzarone, Barbara Walsh, Mary Stout, Stephanie D'Abruzzo, Annmarie Benedict, Randy Redd; Gerald W. Lynch Theater; November 28, 2011

READINGS AND WORKSHOPS

A Cheever Evening by A.R. Gurney; Director, Dan Cordle; Stage Manager, Caitlin Lyons; Cast: Bill Connington, Stephanie D'Abruzzo, Michael Laurence, Nick Sullivan, Juliette Bennett, Annmarie Benedict; New York Society Library; October 21, 2010

Love Letters by A.R. Gurney; Director, Dan Cordle; Stage Manager, Caitlin Lyons; Cast: Bill Connington, Annmarie Benedict; New York Society Library; October 28, 2010

Red Fern Theatre Company

www.redferntheatre.org

Good Egg by Dorothy Fortenberry; Director, Kel Haney; Original Music, Colin Wambsgans; Choreographer, Karl Maier; Stage Manager, Michal V. Mendelson; Lighting, Chuan-Chi Chan; Set, Scott Dougan; Costumes, Katherine Akiko Day; Sound, Katherine A. Buechner; Assistant Director and Marketer, Megan Eileen Kosmoski; Rehearsal Stage Manager and Puppet Designer, Kate Pressman; Press Representation, Katie Rosin/KampfirePR; Cast: Andrea Day, Dan McCabe; 14th Street Y, The; October 21–November 7, 2010

Gentrifusion: *First of the Month* by Carla Ching, *Robert Mapplethorpe Doesn't Live Here Anymore* by Joshua Conkel, *Inhabited* by Michael John Garcés, *Ours is the Future. Ours is the Past.* by Jon Kern, *(2) 11* by Janine Nabers, *Crawl* by Crystal Skillman; Director, John Giampietro, Colette Robert, and Moritz von Stuelpnagel; Stage Manager, Michal V. Mendelson; Lighting, Marie Yokoyama; Set and Costumes, Katherine Akiko Day; Sound, Colin J. Whitely; Photographer, Dennis W. Ho; AV Design, Dennis W. Ho; Artistic Producer, Andrea Day, Kel Haney; Props Designer and Marketer, Megan Eileen Kosmoski; Production Manager,

Laura Anderson; Rehearsal Stage Manager and Assistant Director, Michelle Foster; Cast: Sheldon Best, Rajesh Bose, Tim Cain, Molly Carden, Wayne T. Carr, Gilbert Cruz, Andrea Day, Frank Harts, Nathan Hinton, Devin Norik, Eugene Oh, Casey Robinson, Michael Schantz, André St. Clair Thompson, Federico Trigo, Megan Tusing, Tai Verley, Tiffany Villarin; 14th Street Y, The; January 27–February 13, 2011

A Shot Away: Personal Accounts of US Military Sexual Trauma by Donna Fiumano-Farley; Director, Melanie Moyer Williams; Stage Manager, Michael Aaron Jones; Lighting, Marie Yokoyama; Set, Katherine Akiko Day; Costumes, Elizabeth Barrett Groth; Sound, Colin J. Whitely; Properties Designer and Marketer, Megan Eileen Kosmoski; Assistant Director, Christine J. Schmidt; Assistant Director, Barbara Harrison; Press Representation, Katie Rosin & Kampfire PR; Artistic Associate, Kel Haney; Cast: Laura Anderson, Dana Berger, Grant Chang, Elizabeth Flax, Jessica Myhr, Jeff Pierce, Tara Ricasa, Jackie Sanders, Rafe Terrizzi, and Ian Way; 14th Street Y, The; March 31–April 17, 2011

READINGS AND WORKSHOPS

A Shot Away: Personal Accounts of Military Sexual Trauma by Donna Fiumano-Farley; Director, Melanie Moyer Williams; Cast: Laura Anderson, Dana Berger, Elizabeth Flax, Anna Kull, Amelia Mathews, Emily Riordan, and Cheri Wicks; The Theater at the 14th Street Y; October 24, 2010

We in Silence Hear a Whisper by Jon Kern; Director, Melanie Moyer Williams; Cast: Brian Coats, James Chen, Rory Lipede, Kendall Rileigh and Devere Rogers; The Theater at the 14th Street Y; November 2, 2010

We in Silence Hear a Whisper by Jon Kern; Director, Melanie Moyer Williams; Cast: Sheldon Best, James Chen, Laura Heidinger, Rory Lipede and Devere Rogers; The Theater at the 14th Street Y; February 8, 2011

Red Shark Productions

www.macbeth2011.com

Macbeth by William Shakespeare; Director, Kelly Johnston; Stage Manager, Katy Moore; Lighting, Crystal M. Lee; Costumes, Kerry Gibbons; Sound, Howard Fredrics; Cast: Matthew Barbot, Victor Barranca, Samantha Dena, Tim Dowd, Andy English, Tony von Halle, Hailey Heisick, Tania Jeudy, Sheila Joon, Anthony Martinez, Connor McCabe, Paul J Miller, Emily Mitchell, Nick Palladino, AJ Patton, Michael Raver, Annie Rubino, Christine Seisle; Wings Theatre; March 10–27, 2011

Redd Tale Theatre Company

www.reddtale.org

The Triumph of Love Written and directed by Will Le Vasseur; Original Music, Robert Roxby; Choreographer, James Dorfer & Will Le Vasseur; Stage Manager, Brittany Ray; Lighting, Set, Costume and Sound, Will Le Vasseur; Cast: Virginia Bartholomew, Tom Cleary, Rainbow Dickerson, Robert Dyckman, Cameran Hebb, Lynn Kenny, Brad Lewandowski, and James Stewart; Nicu's Spoon Theatre; August 5–29, 2010

Macbeth by William Shakespeare; Director, Will Le Vasseur; Original Music, Robert Roxby; Fight Choreographer, Mike Yahn; Movement Choreographer, Rebecca Millstein & Will Le Vasseur; Stage Manager, Brittany Ray; Lighting, Set, Costume and Sound, Will Le Vasseur; Cast: Morgan Auld, Virginia Bartholomew, Elyse Beyer, MJ Brackin, Michael Komala, Sam Laakso, Brad Lewandowski, Jodi Mara, Collin McConnell, Jack Nicolaus, Maria Silverman, Melissa Smith, and James Stewart; Nicu's Spoon Theatre; August 6–28, 2010

REPAlliance

The Giver Director, Tyrus Holden; Cast: Logan Riley Bruner, Ken Neil Hailey, Katie Braden; Secret Theatre; March 29–April 20, 2011

Repertorio Español

www.repertorio.org

La Gringa by Carmen Rivera; Director, René Buch; Lighting, Set and Costumes, Robert Weber Federico; Sound, Carlos Bernales, Rafael Moscoso; September 10, 2010–May 15, 2011

El insólito caso de mis' Piña Colada (The Preposterous Case of Miss Piña Colada) by Carlos Ferrari; Director, René Buch; Stage Manager, Fernando Then; Lighting, Set and Costumes, Robert Weber Federico; Sound, Alfonso Rey; September 11, 2010–August 31, 2011

La casa de Bernarda Alba (The House of Bernarda Alba) by Federico García Lorco; Director, René Buch; Lighting, Set and Costumes, Robert Weber Federico; Sound, Marshall Coid; September 25, 2010–June 1, 2011

La vida en los Esclavos Unidos(Life in the United Slaves) by Saulo Garcia; Director, Juan Carlos Talero; September 18, 2010–August 31, 2011

El Insomnio Americano (American Insomniac) by Saulo Garcia; Director, Leandro Fernández; September 19, 2010–March 8, 2011

Way to Heaven by Juan Mayorga; Director, René Buch; Lighting Derek Wright; Costume and Sound, Patrick Johnson; September 28, 2010–May 31, 2011

Crónica de una muerte anunciada (Chronicle of a Death Foretold) by Fabio Rubiano; Director, Jorge Ali Triana; Musical Director, Ricardo Jaramillo; Set, Luis Alfonso Triana; Costumes, Rosario Lozano; Sound, Marcela Molina; October 1, 2010–August 31, 2011

La fiesta del chivo (The Feast of the Goat) by Jorge Ali Triana and Veronica Triana; Director, Jorge Ali Triana; Lighting, María Cristina Fusté; Set and Costumess, Regina García, Julian Hoyos; Sound, Jimmy Ianaka; October 1, 2010–August 31, 2011

La casa de los Espiritus(The House of the Spirits) by Caridad Svich; Director, José Zayas; Lighting Robert Weber Federico; Set, Robert Weber Federico, Alex Koch; Costumes, Robert Weber Federico; Sound, David Margolin Lawson; October 1, 2010–August 31, 2011

Vagón (Boxcar) by Silvia González; Director, René Buch; Lighting, Set and Costumes, Robert Weber Federico; Sound, Alfonso Rey; October 1, 2010–August 31, 2011

Doña Flor y sus dos maridos (Doña Flor and Her Two Husbands) by Jorge Alí Triana, Verónica Triana; Director, Jorge Alí Triana; Lighting, Set and Costumes, Robert Weber Federico; Sound, Jimmy Tanaka; October 1, 2010–August 31, 2011

Pantaleón y las visitadoras (Pantaleon and the Visitors) by Jorge Alí Triana, Verónica Triana; Director, Jorge Alí Triana; Musical Director, Andrés Cabas; Set, Robert Weber Federico, Alex Koch; Sound, Alfonso Rey, October 1, 2010–August 31, 2011

El Quijote by Santiago García; Director, Jorge Ali Triana; Lighting, María Cristina Fusté; Set, Robert Weber Federico; Costumes, Paula Juliana Pérez; Sound, Jimmy Tanaka; October 1, 2010–August 31, 2011

La vida es sueño (Life is a Dream) by Pedro Calderón de La Barca; Director, René Buch; Lighting, Set and Costumes, Robert Weber Federico; Sound, Jimmy Tanaka; October 1, 2010–August 31, 2011

Ana en el Trópico (Anna in the Tropics) by Nilo Cruz; Director, René Buch; Lighting, Robert Weber Federico; Set, Robert Weber Federico; Costumes, Robert Weber Federico; Sound, Hector Martignon; Cast: Francisco Gattorno, Denise Quiñones, Ricardo Barber; October 15, 2010–August 31, 2011

Asi que pasen cinco años (Once Five Years Pass) by Federico García Lorca; Director, René Buch; January 13–August 31, 2011

En el tiempo de las mariposas(In the Ttime of the Butterflies) by Caridad Svich; Director, José Zayas; February 15–August 31, 2011

No hay mejor amigo, ni peor enemigo(No Better Friend, No Worse Enemy) by Carlos J. Serrano; Director, José Zayas; Stage Manager, Fernando Then; Lighting, Set and Costumes, Robert Weber Federico; Sound, Jane Shaw; AV Design, Jon Bremmer, Alex Koch; Cast: Anthony Alvarez, Ricardo Hinoa, Raúl Durán, Iliana Guibert, Indio Meléndez, Alfonso Rey, Edgar Caraballo; May 11–September 31, 2011

Resonance Ensemble

www.resonanceensemble.org

Artistic Director, Eric Parness; Managing Director, Rachel Reiner; Literary Manager, Haley A. Ward; Benefit Coordinator, Elizabeth Kandel

Shakespeare's Slave by Steven Fechter; Director, Eric Parness; Original Music, Nick Moore; Stage Manager, Sean McCain; Lighting, Joe Doran; Set, Sarah B. Brown; Costumes, Mark Richard Caswell; Sound, Nick Moore; Cast: Chris Ceraso, Zack Calhoon, Lucille Duncan, Nancy Nagrant, Romy Nordlinger, Steven Pounders, David L. Townsend, Stewart Walker, Shaun Bennet Wilson; Clurman Theatre; May 24–June 18, 2011

H4 based on William Shakespear; Director, Allegra Libonati; Original Music, David Hancock Turner; Stage Manager, Jessie Vacchiano; Lighting, Joe Doran; Set, Sarah B. Brown; Costumes, Brenda Abbandandolo; Sound, David Hancock Turner; Media Designer, Johnathan Carr; Cast: Dorothy Abrahams, Alice Bahlke, Joie Bauer, Michael Chmiel, Brian D. Coats, Joe Jung, Michael Nathanson, Jensen Olaya, Steven Pounders, Timothy McCown Reynolds, Brian Silliman; Clurman Theatre; May 27–June 18, 2011

Retro Productions

www.retroproductions.org

Benefactors by Michael Frayn; Director, Peter Zinn; Stage Manager, Ricardo Rust; Lighting, Justin Sturges; Set, Jack and Rebecca Cunningham; Costumes, Ben Philipp; Sound, Jeanne Travis; Cast: Heather E. Cunningham, David Ian Lee, Matthew Semler and Kristen Vaughan; Spoon Theatre; November 3–20, 2010

Women and War by Jack Hilton Cunningham; Director, Peter Zinn; Stage Manager, Jenny Kennedy; Lighting, Justin Sturges; Set, Jack Cunningham and Rebecca Cunningham; Costumes, Rebecca Cunningham and Casandera MJ Lollar; Sound, Jeanne Travis; Board Operators: Ricardo Rust, Jeanne Travis; Cast: Lowell Byers, Heather E. Cunningham, Lauren Kelston, Casandera M. J. Lollar, Elise Rovinsky; The Spoon Theatre; November 9–March 9, 2011; also performed at The Archlight Theater; January 11-12, 2011 as a co-production with The Bleecker Company

Dear Ruth by Norman Krasna; Director, Richard Roland; Stage Manager, Ricardo Rust; Lighting, Jacqueline Reid; Set, Jeff Stander; Costumes, Viviane Galloway and Jeannette Aultz; Sound, Jeanne Travis; Property Designer, Heather Cunningham and Cassie Dorland; Cast: Becky Byers, Heather E. Cunningham, Douglas B. Giorgis, Joe Mathers, David Sedgewick, Alisha Spielmann, Matilda Szydagis, and Matthew Trumbull, Shay GInes; Spoon Theatre; May 4–21, 2011

Riant Theatre

www.therianttheatre.com

Founder and Artistic Director, Van Dirk Fisher

FESTIVALS

Strawberry One Act Festival: Summer 2011; (See Festivals below); St. Clement's; August 12–22, 2010

Strawberry One-Act Festival: Winter 2011; (See Festivals below); The Dudson Guild Theatre; February 7–12, 2011

READINGS AND WORKSHOPS

Hearts Gamble by Kee Seymore; Director, Sean Gallagher; Cast: Kee Seymore, Sean Gallagher, Mike Gregorek, Damian Santucc, Melinda Stewar, Kyla Garcia; Stage Manager, Bhret Boone

Rising Phoenix Repertory

www.risingphoenixrep.org

Ceremony by Mark Schultz; Director, Brian Roff; Cast: Evan Crommett, Alex Flores, and Meg Gibson; Seventh Street Small Stage; September 16–29, 2010

Rising Sun Performance Company

www.risingsunnyc.com

The Last Supper by Dan Rosen; Director, Akia; Stage Manager, Alexandra Deurr; Lighting, Dan Jobbins; Set, Jak Prince; Costumes, Tiffini Minatel; Sound, Ryan Kilcourse; AV Design, Matthew Kreiner; Original Musical Score, Christopher Bowen; Lighting, Dan Jobbins; Sound, Ryan Kilcourse; Media Design, Matthew Kreiner; Costumes, Tiffini Minatel; Set, Jak Prince; Fight Direction, Turner Smith; Cast: David Anthony, Joe Beaudin, Lindsay Beecher, April E. Bennett, Michael Bernardi, Susan Burns, Patrick J. Egan, Christopher Enright, Ben Friesen, Marianna Guillen , Erik Gullberg, Larry Guttman; Produced in association with Horse TRADE Theater Group Red Room Theater; April 28–August 5, 2010

Encounters in a non-lucid state. Rising Sun's 4th Annual One Act Series: *Cookies* by John Patrick Bray; *Binge Honeymoon* by Rebecca Stokes; Residue by Stacey L; Director, Leal Vona, Kelly Hawkins; Stage Manager, Jak Prince; Costumes, Leigh Ann Ryklin; AV Design, Tim Butterfield; Cast: Becky Sterling, Michael Jones, Allison Whittinghill, Anthony Mead, Erica Lutz; Produced in association with Horse TRADE Theater Group; Red Room Theater; August 5–21, 2010

Goodnight Lovin' Trail by John Patrick Bray; Director, Akia; Stage Manager, Lindsay Beecher; Lighting, Set, Costume and Sound, Akia; Cast: Olivia Rorick, Nic Mevoli, Lindsay Beecher, Joe Beaudin; Presented as part of FRIGID NY Festival; The Red Room; February 23–March 5, 2011

Mash Up! Director, Akia, Maura Kelly, Lindsay Beecher & Ted Gorodetzky; Stage Manager, Nzinga Williams; Costumes, Barbara Erin Delo; AV Design, Derek Shore; Production Manager, Lindsay Beecher; Literary Management, Michael Ross Albert and John Patrick; Cast: Akia, Amanda Berry, David Anthony, EJ Assi, Elizabeth Burke, Jason Vinoles, Joe Beaudin, Kate Foster ,Kate Grimes, Kitty Lindsey, Larry Gutman, Lela Bryant, Lindsay Beecher , Lindsey Smith, Michael Bernardi, Michael Burns, Mimi Jefferson; Kraine Theater; June 22, 2011

READINGS AND WORKSHOPS

The Mermaid off of Staten Island by Kate Foster; Presented at FRIGID NY; Red Room; March 5, 2011

Robroy Mountjoy Productions

www.robroymountjoyproductions.com

Bubblemakers Written and directed by Robroy Mountjoy; Original Music, Greg Indelicato, Robroy Mountjoy; Stage Manager, Orlando Iriarte; Lighting, Greg Indelicato; Costumes, Shatisha Bryant; Sound, Greg Indelicato; Cast: Orlando Iriarte, Benjamin Torres, Shatisha Bryant, Marguerite Simpkins, Vincent Lopez, Jessica Dicembri, Walter Tabelisma, Kyemma Vivian Campbell, Ann Van Gieson, Magnolia Nunez; Producer's Club Grand Theatre; February 3–6, 2011

Rosalind Productions Inc.
& The Platform Group in association with The Drilling Company

rosalindproductions.com

Savage in Limbo by John Patrick Shanley; Director, Brian Tom O'Connor; Stage Manager, Marcie A. Friedman; Lighting, Isabella F. Byrd; Set, Andrew Lu; Sound, Anthony Trentinella; Cast: Abigail Rose Solomon, Shara Ashley Zeiger, Fabio Taliercio, Maxwell Zener, Kendall Rileigh; Drilling Company Theatre Lab; February 11–March 5, 2011

Rose Upon the Rood

Gibraltar by Patrick Fitzgerald; Director, Terry Kinney and Patrick Fitzgerald; Choreographer, Patrick Fitzgerald; Lighting, Mark Wickham; Set, Tara Kennedy and Mark Wickham; Costumes, Tara Kennedy; Sound, Mark Wickham; Cast: Patrick Fitzgerald, Cara Seymour; Bowery Electric; October 11–November 29, 2010

Scandinavian American Theater Company

www.satcnyc.org

Miss Julie Adapted by Craig Lucas from August Strindberg's drama, based on a literal translation by Anders Cato; Director, Henning Hegland; Lighting, Joe Novak; Set, Henning Hegland and Julia Przedmojska; Costumes, Julia Przedmojska; Sound, Amy Altadonna; AV Design, Sebastian Nyman Agdur; Production Manager, Elin Eggertsdottir; Choreographer, Vigdis Hentze Olsen; Cast: Lisa Pettersson, Albert Bendix, Anette Norgaard; Victor Borge Hall Scandinavia House; June 10–19, 2010

Seeing Place Theater

www.seeingplacetheater.com

Waiting for Lefty by Clifford Odets; Director, Brandon Walker and Reesa Graham; Cast: David Arthur Bachrach, Thomas Beaudoin, Steven Beckingham, Christoper Bischoff, Jon Dalin, John Gazzale, John Greenleaf, Joshua Everett Johnson, Norah Elise Johnson, Ned Lynch, Tyler Moss, Dothan Negrin, Adam Reich, Anna Marie Sell, Bonnie Singer, Nick Velkov, Brandon Walker, Jamie Watson, Joseph Mancuso; American Theatre of Actors, Sargent Theatre; June 9–26, 2010

Look Back in Anger by John Osborne; Director, Reesa Graham; Lighting, Christopher Michael Ham; Set, Sound and Costumes, Lillian Wright; Cast: Keenan Caldwell, Rick Delaney, Adam Reich, Anna Marie Sell, and Brandon Walker; American Theatre of Actors, Sargent Theatre; October 13–30, 2010

Twelfth Night by William Shakespeare; Director, Brandon Walker; Lighting, Joshua Rose; Cast: David Arthur Bachrach, Michael Clay, Erin Cronican, Jorge Hoyos, Michael Jefferson, Ben Leasure, Ned Lynch, Nathan Ramos, David Sedgwick, Anna Marie Sell, Lindsay Teed, and Brandon Walker; American Theatre of Actors, Sargent Theatre; March 30 –April 16, 2011

ShakespeareNYC

King Lear by Wiliam Shakespeare; Director, Beverly Bullock; Stage Manager, Lily Ardalan; Lighting, James Bedell; Set and Costumes, Beverly Bullock; Sound, John D. Ivy; Fight Director, Al Foote III; Directory of Photographer, Mike Stodden; Cast: King Lear, Bill Fairbairn; Goneril, Carol Jacobanis; Albany, Michael Bartoli; Regan, Patricia McNamara; Cormwall, Marc Greece; Cordelia, Katherine Kelly Lidz; King of France, Justin Gallo; Burgundy, Thane Floreth; Kent, Peter Herrick; Gloucester, Ron Drey; The Lion Theatre, Theatre Row; February 10–11, 2011

A Midsummer Night's Dream by William Shakespeare; Director, Beverly Bullock; Stage Manager, Lily Ardalan; Lighting, James Bedell; Set and Costumes, Beverly Bullock; Sound, John D. Ivy; Fight Director, Al Foote III: Director of Photograpy, Mike Stodden; Cast: Hermia, Katherine Kelly Lidz, Brian Morvant, Valerie Redd, Joseph Mitchell Parks, Peter Herrick, Patricia McNamara, John Montague, Joseph Small, Benjamin Rishworth; The Lion Theatre, Theatre Row; February 4–5, 2011

Shelby Company

www.shelbycompany.org

The Land Whale Murders by Jonathan A. Goldberg; Director, Tom Ridgely; Stage Manager, Marianne Broome; Lighting, Greg Goff; Set, Chris Simms; Costumes, Deanna Frieman; Sound, M. L. Dogg; Fight Choreographer, Rod Kinter; Cast: Nathaniel Kent, Carl Howell, Amy Landon, Jennifer Joan Thompson, Richard Holliman, Robert Michael McClure; Theater 3; December 2–18, 2010

The Shelter

www.thesheIternyc.org

F***ing Christmas by Jonathan Ashley, Kitty Lindsay, Michael Kingsbaker, Dave Lankford, Beth Jastroch, Meghan Jones, Melinda Smart; Director, Jonathan Ashley, Kitty Lindsay, Beth Jastroch, Dave Lankford, Michael Kingsbaker, Meghan Jones; Lighting, Chris Noke; Set, Jonathan Ashley; Costumes, Colleen Schmitz; Light Board Operator, James Rich; Cast: Jonathan Ashley, Meghan Jones, Michael Kingsbaker, Dave Lankford, Michael Bernstein, Paco Lozano, Eugene Turonis, T. D. White, Maggie Alexander, Loren Dunn, Andy Hassell, Meghan Jones, Natalya Krimgold, Emily Turonis, Leslie Kendall Dye, Cynthia Shaw; The WorkShop Theatre Company's Main Stage; December 9 –12, 2010

Night Windows:*Perfume and Maple* by Melinda Smart, *Freak Closet* by Beth Jastroch, *Night of the Living* by Dave Lankford; Director, Beth Jastroch, Meghan Jones, Olivia Killingsworth; Stage Manager, Michael Denis; Lighting, Jake Fine; Set, Brandon Hardy; Sound, Andy Cohen; Producer, Meghan Jones; Producer, Kitty Lindsay; Technical Director, Jonathan Ashley; Music, Alec Head; Cast: Emily Robin Fink, Paco Lozano, Ginger Kearns, Michael Kingsbaker, Belle Caplis, Dave Lankford; The WorkShop Theater Main Stage; May 5 -15, 2011

READINGS AND WORKSHOPS

The Reading Series, Part Two by Beth Jastroch, Wendy Mae Shelton, Maiken Wiese, Meghan Jones, Kitty Lindsay; Gene Frankel Theatre; March 14, 2011

SickLittle Productions

Outer Puppets Series II—The Horror! Written and directed by Richard Hinojosa & Jason Griffith; Original Music Tristan McKay; Cast: Jonathan Harford, Lindsay MacNaughton, Ann Gillespie, Richard Hinojosa and Jason Griffith; Under St Marks; June 9–24, 2010

Sister Sylvester

sistersylvester.org

Play America (Life is Short, Wear Your Party Pants) by Matthew Wilson; Director, Kathryn Hamilton; Choreographer, Kathryn Hamilton; Stage Manager, Arienne Pelletier; Set, Damon Pelletier; Costumes, Alison Ward; AV Design, Peter Clough; Cast: Brandt Adams, Jennifer La Fleur, Devin Burnam, Terence Mintern, Monica Santana, Marcus Dillon, Akua Doku, Nick Lehane, Face Yu, Lauren Glover, Damon Pelletier, Ingrid Gillming, Melissa Mensah, Lilian Velasquez, Mary Wiseman and Cyrus Moshrefi; Convent of St. Cecilia; August 20–30, 2010

Skysaver Productions

theodoraskipitares.com

Lysistrata by Aristophanes; Adapted, Designed and Director, Theodora Skipitares; Cast: Daniel Irizarry, Antonevia Ocho-Coultes, Minna Taylor, Raquel Cion, La MaMa Experimental Theatre; February 3–12, 2011

Slant Theatre Project

Binge by Thomas Ward; Director, Adam Knight; Lighting, Isabella Byrd; Set, Jonathan Wentz; Costumes, Kristina Makowski; Assistant Director, Shelby Hibbs; Cast: Brent Bateman, John G. Preston, Therese Barbato, David Lee Nelson; 78th Street Theatre Lab; July 29–August 8, 2010

Smith Street Stage

www.smithstreetstage.com

Romeo & Juliet by William Shakespeare; Director, Robbie Sublet; Original Music, Ruark & Blaise Downey; Choreographer, Jessica Weiss; Stage Manager, Cynthia Vazquez; Costumes, Laura Waringer; Cast: Jonathan Hopkins, Joby Earle, Sam Rosenberg, Sean Dillon, Beth Ann Leone; Carroll Park; August 16–28, 2010

Jesus Christ Superstar Music by Andrew Lloyd Webber, Lyrics by Tim Rice; Director, Jonathan Hopkins; Musical Director, Ruark Downey; Cast: J.D. Desharnais, Blaise Downey, Ruark Downey, Beth Ann Leone, Elliot Roth, and Joshua Tussin; Carroll Park; April 23, 2011

Spider Webb Productions

www.spiderwebbproductions.com

The Contract by James Webb; Director, Karl Williams; Stage Manager, Kaitlin Hernandez; Lighting, Isaac Winston; Set, Leigh-Ann Ryklin; Costume and Sound, Leigh-Ann Ryklin; Cast: Joy Jones, Albert Christmas, James Webb; Kraine Theater; October 5–19, 2010

St. Bart's Players

www.stbartsplayers.org

Closer Than Ever Lyrics by Richard Maltby Jr.; Music by David Shire; Director, Hector Coris; Originally Conceived by Steven Scott Smith; Cast: Laura Apruzzese, Harley Diamond, Hope Landry, Chad Miller, Dominic Paolillo, Angela Shultz, Merrill Vaughn and Jonathan Whitton; Park Avenue Christian Church Theater; November 12–21, 2010

The Stolen Chair Theatre Company

www.stolenchair.org

Stage Kiss by Kiran Rikhye; Director, Jon Stancato; Lighting, Daniel Winters; Set, David Bengali; Costumes, Sarah Riffle; Cast: Liz Eckert, Liza Wade Green, Andy Phelan, Noah Schultz; Andy Phelan, Noah Schultz, Liz Eckert, Liza Wade Green; Wings Theatre; January 27–March 5, 2011

Kinderspiel by Kiran Rikhye; Director, Jon Stancato; Lighting, Daniel Winters; Set, David Bengali; Costumes, Julie B. Schworm; Cast: David Berent, Liz Eckert, Liza Wade Green, Laura Heidinger,

David Skeist; Wings Theatre; February 3–March 5, 2011

The Storm Theatre

www.stormtheatre.com

Arrah na Pogue by Dion Boucicault; Director, Peter Dobbins; Stage Manager, Robyn Lee; Lighting, Michael Abrams; Set, Ken Larson; Costumes, Laura Taber Bacon; Sound, Adam Salberg; Cast: Spencer Aste, Joie Bauer, Jonathan Blakeley, Christine Bullen, Griffin DuBois, Michelle Kafel, Laura King, Jessica Levesque, Sawyer Mastandrea, Jennie McGuinness, Ted McGuinness, Phil Mills, Nicola Murphy, Paul Nugent, Patrick Rosendale, Anthony Russo; Theatre of the Church of Notre Dame; March 11–April 2, 2011

Noon Divide by Paul Claudel; Director, Peter Dobbins and Stephen Logan Day; Cast: Brian J. Carter, Kate Chamuris, Peter Dobbins, Chris Kipiniak; Produced in association with Blackfriars Repertory Theatre; Theatre of the Church of Notre Dame; October 29–November 20, 2010

The Straddler

Trousers by Don Monaco; Director, Dan Monaco; Cast: Marty Brown, Todd Pate; Interborough Repertory Theatre; March 24–April 9, 2011

Swedish Cottage Marionette Theatre

The Secret History of the Swedish Cottage Written and directed by Matt Acheson and Tom Lee; Lighting, Miranda Hardy; Set, Matt Acheson and Tom Lee; Sound, Matt Swed and Matt Acheson; Puppet Designer, Matt Acheson and Tom Lee; Cast: Cory Antiel, Kate Brehm, Candice Burridge, Daniel Fay, Retta Leaphart, Jonothon Lyons, James Mack, GV Maldonado, Kervin Peralta, Kevin White, Darnell Wickham; Swedish Cottage Marionette Theatre; January 18–May 31, 2011

Sweeter Theater Productions

www.sweetertheater.com

Fracturing by Deanna Neil; Director, Maura Farver; Stage Manager, Colin Miller & Amy Francis Schott; Lighting, Andy Fritsch; Set, Josh Zangen & Sean Ryan

Jennings; Costumes, Summer Lee Jack; Sound, Palmer Hefferan; Cast: Timur Kocak, Andrew Langton, Tamara Flannagan, Allie Dunbar, Robyn Frank, Charlotte Patton, Colleen Smith Wallnau; Flamboyan Theatre–CSV Cultural Center; July 8–18, 2010

T. Schreiber Studio

www.tschreiber.org

Balm in Gilead by Lanford Wilson; Director, Peter Jensen; Musical Director, Stephanie Seward; Original Music, Mickey Theis; Choreographer, Jessica Osborne; Stage Manager, Liz Richards; Lighting, Eric Cope; Set, Matt Brogan; Costumes, Anne Wingate; Sound, Andy Cohen; Producing Director, Barb Kielhofer; Technical Director, Mike Dazé; Ian Bell; Assistant Director, Julia Kelly; Asst. Stage Manager, Victoria Loye; Publicist, Lanie Zipoy; Props Designer, Diamando Stratakos; Composer, Mickey Theis; Cast: Seth Allen, Ian Bell, Esteban Benito, Jill Bianchini, Dennis Brito, Tommy Buck, Lowell Byers, Ian Campbell Dunn, Belle Caplis, Amanda Catrini, Lawrence Crimlis, Lily DePaula, Warren Douglas, Jordan Feltner, Stephanie Iscovitz, Brad Martocello, Mariel Matero, Jevon McFerrin, Erica Lauren McLaughlin, Alona Metcalf, Sebastian Montoya, Michael Murray, Jason Pumarada, Orlando J. Rivera, Olivia Roric, Stephanie Seward, Lisa Sobin, Eric Spear, Christine Vega, Stewart Villilo, Jonathan Wilde, Richard Zekaria; Gloria Maddox Theatre; October 14–December 18, 2010

The Changing Room by David Storey; Director, Terry Schreiber; Stage Manager, Liz Richards; Lighting, Dennis Parichy; Set, Hal Tiné; Costumes, Anne Wingate; Sound, Andy Cohen; Producing Director, Barb Kielhofer; Dialect Coach, Page Clements; Technical Director, Mike Dazé; Makeup Designer, Amanda Donelan; Assistant Stage Manager, Victoria Loye; Publicist, Lanie Zipoy; Props Designer and Associate Set, Chris Minard, Olivia Killingsworth; Cast: Eric Percival, Matthew Ballinger, Marcin Paluch, Mike Dazé, Luke Guldan, David Donahoe, Lowell Byers, Brian Podnos, Sean Gallagher, Peter Judd, Justin Noble, Nick Fesette, Sean Patterson, Josh Sienkiewicz, Randy Miles, Rick Forstmann, Edward Campbell; Gloria Maddox Theatre; February 25–April 3, 2011

You Never Can Tell by George Bernard Shaw; Director, Robert Verlaque; Choreographer, Jessica Osborne; Stage Manager, Victoria Loye; Lighting, Eric Cope; Set, Chris Minard; Costumes, Steven Daniels; Sound, Andy Cohen; Producing Director, Barb Kielhofer; Dialect Coach, Page Clements; Choreographer, Jessica Osborne; Technical Director, Josh Sienkiewicz; Publicist, Lanie Zipoy; Assistant Director, Michael W. Murray; Assistant Costumer, Phoebe Kamijo; Cast: Helen Abell, Townsend Ambrecht, Lucy Avery Brooke, Lowell Byers, Laurence Cantor, Seth James, Peter Judd, Randy Miles, Marilyn Mineo, Jessica Osborne, Edwin Sean Patterson, Kyle Storey, Noelle P. Wilson; T. Schreiber Studio; May 12–June 19, 2011

READINGS AND WORKSHOPS

Big Country by Chris Barlow; Director, Morgan Gould; T. Schreiber Studio; July 21–30, 2011

Take Wing And Soar Productions, Inc

www.takewingandsoar.org

Producing Artistic Director, Debra Ann Byrd; Associate Artistic Director, Timothy D. Stickney; Press, Penny Landau; Marketing & Promotions, Natalie Clarke; Director of Volunteer Services, LaZette McCants; Assistant to the Chief Executive, Mercedes

Anthony and Cleopatra by William Shakespeare; Director, Petronia Paley; Stage Manager, Annette Nelson-Wright; Lighting, James Carter; Set, Heather Wolensky; Costumes, David Withrow; Sound, David D. Wright; Producer, Debra Ann Byrd, Sheila Speller; Dramaturg, Dr. Mark Ringer; Press, Penny Landau/MAYA PR; Marketing & Promotions, Natalie Clarke; House Manager, LaZette McCants;

Sound Tech, Joshua Glenn.; Cast: Michael Early, Debra Ann Byrd, Althea Alexis, Andi Bohs, Nehassaiu deGannes, Andre Dell, Lawrence Floyd, Terrell M. Green, David Heron, Aixa Kendrick, Mark Lang, Gerrad Lobo, Tom Martin, Alejandro Santoni, Norman Anthony Small, Amar Srivastava; The Poet's Den Theater; March 17–27, 2011

READINGS AND WORKSHOPS

Massinissa, The Man Who Betrayed Hannibal To Rome by Lorey Hayes; Director, Alfred Preisser; Cast: Anthony Alessandro, Robert Arcaro, Leon Addison Brown, Michael J. Burg, Debra Ann Byrd, Michael Chenevert, Marie Eusebe, Edward Furs, Hazell Goodman, Omatara Labinja, Leopold Lowe, Tomike Ogugua, Roscoe Orman, April Dae Rochon, Timothy D. S; American Negro Theatre; October 20, 2010

Measure For Measure by William Shakespeare; Director, Dathan B. Williams; Cast: Richarda Abrams, Leigh Ellen Caudill, Zenzelé Cooper, Leone Harman, David Harrell, Natalie Hegg, Franz Jones, Alvin Keith, Evelyn Lorena, Tom Martin, Christopher Michael McLamb, Guthrie Nutter, Leila Okafor, Beverley Prentice, Shaina Simmon; The Poet's Den Theater; November 11, 2010

An Ideal Husband by Oscar Wilde; Director, Kevin Connell; Cast: James Edward Becton, Wendi Joy Franklin, Jasmine Mahboob, Peter Martin, Kevyn Morrow, Petronia Paley, Christopher Stokes, Charles E. Wallace, Stacy Yokoyama; Stage Manager, Cati Pishal, Producer/Artistic Director, Debra Ann Byrd; The Poet's Den Theater; December 17, 2010

The Talking Band

New Island Archipelago Written and directed by Paul Zimet; Choreographer, Hilary Easton; Original Music, Ellen Maddow; Stage Manager, Julia Funk; Lighting, Nan Zhang; Set, Nic Ularu; Costumes, Olivera Gajic; AudioVisual, Simon Tarr; Cast: Todd D'Amour, James Himmelsbach, Kristine Lee, Bianca Leigh, Ellen Maddow, Steven Rattazzi, Tina Shepard, Harry Mann, Beth Meyers; 3LD Art and Technology Center; May 24–June 6, 2010

The Teacup Company

The Umbrella Plays by Stephanie Janssen; Director, Daniel Talbott; Stage Manager, Hannah Woodward; Lighting, Brad Peterson; Set, Eugenia Furneaux-Arends; Costumes, Tristan Raines; Cast: Macleod Andrews, Matt Dixon, Natalie Gold, Jan Leslie Harding, Stephanie Janssen, Christ Stack, Samantha Soule; March 31–April 10, 2011

TeaCup Productions LLC

www.teacupproductions.com

The Alexis & Destiny Chronicles: Love Sick & Sick of Love Producer's Club; May 20–June 11, 2011

The Tempest Ladies, LLC

www.tempestladies.com

Founding Ensemble Members: Stella Berg, Laura Borgwardt, Holly Hart, Jana Stambaugh; Ensemble Members: Julia Giolzetti, Laura Bess Jernigan

The Tempest by William Shakespeare; Director, The Tempest Ladies Ensemble; Cast: Stella Berg, Laura Borgwardt, Dana Clinkman, Holly Hart, Sarah Olbrantz, Jana Stambaugh; Roy Arias Theatre; September 23–27, 2010

Kevin Kane in Someone Who'll Watch Over Me, presented by *The Collective NY* (photo by Alex Fabozzi)

Xanthe Elbrick and Jose Luaces in *The Active Theater production of* Venus Flytrap (photo by Jason Watson)

Becky Byers, David Sedgewick, Heather E. Cunningham and Alisha Spielmann in Retro Productions' Dear Ruth (photo by Kristen Vaughan)

Andre St. Clair Thompson and Devin Norik in Gentrifusion, *presented by the Red Fern Theatre Company (photo by Jordan Popalis)*

Leanne Linsky, Robert Gonzales Jr., and Shana Wiersum in Dead White Males, presented by *Tongue in Cheek Theater (photo by Justin Boykin)*

Kaia Foss and Jonathan Blakeley in the Nylon Fusion Collective production of *Wisdom Of Obscurity* (photo by Nikolitsa Boutieros)

Uma Incrocci and Alex Emanuel in Untitled Theater Company #61's Do Androids Dream of Electric Sheep? *(photo by Arthur Cornelius)*

Christos Alexandridis and Evangelos Alexiou in The Mystery of Irma Vep *at the Greek Cultural Center (photo by Drew Florida)*

Jason Griffith and Ryan Stadler in the Apple Core Theater Company's As Is *(photo by Katherine Miles Jones)*

terraNOVA Collective

www.terranovacollective.org

Artistic Director, Jennifer Conley Darling; Associate Artistic Director, James Carter; Managing Director, Diane Alianiello; Groundbreakers Program Director, Jessi D. Hill

Feeder: A Love Story by James Carter; Director, José Zayas; Stage Manager, Michal V. Mendelson; Lighting, Bruce Steinberg; Set, Peter Ksander; Costumes, Suzanne Chesney; Sound, David Margolin Lawson; AV Design, Alex Koch; Producer, Arwen Lowbridge; Cast: Jennifer Conley Darling, Pierre-Marc Diennet; HERE; March 6–27, 2011

FESTIVALS

soloNOVA Arts Festival; 9th Space at Performance Space 122; May 11–May 28, 2011

Santa Claus is Coming Out Written and performed by Jeffrey Solomon, Director, Joe Brancato; *Woman of Leisure and Panic* Written, Choreographed and Performed by Charlotte Bydwell; *...and stockings for the ladies* by Attila Clemann; Director, Zach Fraser, Cast: Brendan McMurtry-Howlett; *Polanski, Polanski* by Saviana Stanescu, Director, Tamilla Woodard, Lighting, Joyce Liao, Costumes, Amelia Dombrowski, Sound, Hillary Charnas; Video Designer, Jake Witlen, Cast: Grant Neale; *Questions My Mother Can't Answer* Written and performed by Andrea Caban, Director, Rachel Eckerling; *Jobz* Written and performed by Joseph Keckler, Director, Josh Hecht; *Tar Baby* by Desiree Burch and Dan Kitrosser, Performed by Desiree Burch and Director, Isaac Byrne

Thalia Spanish Theatre

www.thaliatheatre.org

Executive and Artistic Director, Mr. Angel Gil Orrios; Administrative Director, Kathryn Giaimo; Managing Director, Soledad Lopez; Technical Director, Fabricio Saquicela

Colombia: Passion & Soul/Alma y Pasion Director, Armando Moreno and Wilson Fernando Mesa; Musical Director, Harold Gutierrez; Stage Manager, Fernando Mesa; Lighting and Set, Angel Gil Orrios; Costumes, Armando Moreno and Fernando Mesa; Sound, Jaime Castillo; AV Design, Fabricio Saquicela; Thalia Spanish Theatre; October 1–November 7, 2010

From Fuente Ovejuna to Ciudad Juarez by Lope de Vega; adapted by Sergio Adillo; Director, Lucia Rodriguez Miranda; Music Director, Mireya Ramos; Stage Manager, Armando Moreno; Lighting, Fabricio Saquicela; Set, Lucia Rodriguez Miranda; Costumes, Lucia Cuba; Sound, Deborah Gros; AV Design, Fabricio Saquicela; Cast: Maria-Itzel Siegrist, Sergio Adillo, Anthony Cotto, Melinna Bobadilla, Andres Martinez, Maria Parra Peyramaure, Laura Santos, Alvarez, Victoria Tapias Guzman, Franco Galecio, Mariachi Flor de Toloache; Produced in association with The Cross Border Project Thalia Spanish Theatre; December 3–11, 2010

you TANGO? Director, Angel Gil Orrios; Musical Director, Raul Jaurena; Stage Manager, Armando Moreno; Lighting, Fabricio Saquicela; Set, Angel Gil Orrios; Costumes, Soledad Lopez; Sound, Jaime Castillo; AV Design, Angel Gil Orrios; ; Cast: Marga Mitchell, Pablo Pereya, Ivan Terrazas, Sara Grdan, Diego Ocampo, Mariana Fresno, Raul Jaurena, Pablo Aslan, Maurizio Najt, Sergio Reyes, Beledo.; Thalia Spanish Theatre; January 28–March 20, 2011

No Problemo Amigo by Jaime Espinal; Director, Angel Gil Orrios; Musical Director, Los 3 Certidos; Stage Manager, Martha Osorio; Lighting, Angel Gil Orrios; Set, Angel Gil Orrios; Costumes, Soledad Lopez and Armando Moreno; Sound, Jaime Castillo; AV Design, Fabricio Saquicela; Supertitles, Andres Martinez-Tutek; Makeup Designer, Rena Most; Cast: Jaime Espinal, Susan Rybin, Jesus Martinez, Francisco Fuertes, Alicia Kaplan, Alexandra Gutierrez, Yolanda Castillo, Premier Solis, Juan Fernando Gaviria, Juanfer Ossa, Andres Martinez-

Tutek, Diego Arango, Federico Giraldo, Pablo Naval, Jesus Acosta, Juan; Thalia Spanish Theatre; May 6–June 19, 2011

Theater for The New City

www.theaterforthenewcity.net

Executive Director, Crystal Field; Development Director, Courtney Harge; Administrator, Jon Weber; Production Manager, Mark Marcante; Lighting Director, Alexander Bartenieff; Technical Director, Sarah Harris; Literary Manager, Michael Scott-Price

My Boyfriend is a Zombie by William Electric Black and Gary Schreiner; Director, William Electric Black; Lighting, Federico Restrepo; Costumes, Tilly Grimes; Choreographer, Jeremy Lardieri; Mak-up Designer, Kate Tsang; Cast: Nicole Patullo, Cara S.Liander, Allison Troesch and Macah Coates, Jamaal Kendall, Jeremy Lardieri, Lenin Alevante and Matthew Hooper, Erin Salm, Verna Hampton, Gary Schreiner, Saadi Zain,and James Mussen; Theater for the New City; June 3–27, 2010

Gone Fission, or Alternative Power Written and directed by Crystal Field; Original Music, Joseph Vernon Banks; Various parks in NYC; July 31–September 12, 2010

The Dybbuk Written and directed by Julia Pascal; Choreographed and Designed by Thomas Kampe; Theater for the New City; August 10–25, 2010

Around the Night Park by Maria Micheles; Director, Richard Vetere; Cast: ; Theatrer for the New City; August 23–September 2, 2010

Auto Graphic Novel Written, Directed and performed by Johnny Klein; Theater for the New City; August 29–September 4, 2010

The Foolish Disciple by Juan Rulfo, adaptation by German Jaramillo; Director, German Jaramillo; Musical Director, Pablo Mayor; Lighting, Miguel Angel Valderrama; Set, Luis Roldan; Costumes, Felix Ciprian; Cast: Ramiro Sandoval, Pedro Espinosa, Anita Guzman, Jimena Ladino, Juanita Lara, Wilmar Saldarriaga, Juan Esteban Velez, Jorge Luis Vera; Community Space Theater; October 7–24, 2010

Trio by Mario Fratti; Director, Stephan Morrow; Lighting Alex Bartonieff; Set, Mark Marcante; Cast: Billy Marshall Jr., Brandon McDonough, Chris Kerson, Jennifer Loryn, Joe Ambrose, Patrick McCarthy, Rachael McOwen, Rose Gregorio, Sean Phillips; Cino Theater; October 7–24, 2010

Dawoud Kringle Cast: Sohrab Saadat, Ravish Momin; Community Space Theater; October 13, 2010

Only Love Will Do by Walt Stepp; Director, Lissa Moira; Lighting, William Giraldo; Set, David Zen Mansley; Cast: Danny Ashkenasi, Louisa Bradshaw, Jason Colllins, Robert Homeyer, Richard O'Brien; Cabaret Theater; November 10–28, 2010

Angry Young Women by Matt Morillo; Director, Bobbi Masters; Lighting and Set, Eric Cope; Cast: Kitty Lindsay, Laurie Berich, Shara Ashley Zeiger, Paul Eddy, Ivan Perez, David Jenkins, Angelica Rose Sirabella, Darlene Rae Heller, Mia van de Water, Julia Giolzetti; Cabaret Theater; December 2–12, 2010

Nonviolent Executions Written and performed by Steve Ben Israel; Community Space Theater; December 3–4, 2010

A Christmas Carol Written and directed by David Zen Mansley; Community Theater; December 16–19, 2010

Dollface by David Foreman and B.J. Sebring; Director, David Foreman and B.J. Sebring; Stage Manager, Katy Moore; Lighting Alex Bartenieff; Set, Mark Marcante; Costumes, Natalie Lunn; Cast: Linda Shell, Davis Tass Rodriguez, Collin Carr, David Forman, Kathryn Kates, Karen Gale, Ben Prayz, Polly McKie, Mike Backes, C.J. Williams, Harry Forman, Harmony Stempel, Diana Forman, Veronica Forman; Johnson Theater; December 23, 2010–January 9, 2011

A Process of Elimination by Gene Ruffini; Director, Celine Havard; Stage Manager, Carol A Sullivan; Lighting, Alexander Bartenieff; Set, David Zen Mansley; Costumes, Guiomar Giraldo; Sound, Zephan Ellenbogen; Cast: Dan Burkarth, Mitchell Conway, Colleen Cosgrove, Michael Gnat, Stephen Hansen, Joseph Lyons, Gabriella Mazza, Lisa Tracy; Cino Theater; December 30, 2010–January 16, 2011

The Inventor Written and directed by Matt Morillo; Lighting, Amith A Chandrashaker; Set, Mark Marcante; Cast: David R Doumeng, Jessica Durdock Moreno, Tom Pilutik, Emily Campion, Maria Rowene; Community Theater; January 6–29, 2011

Age Out by Tom Diriwachter; Director, Jonathan Weber; Lighting and Set, Mark Marcante; Cast: Bob Homeyer, Peter Welch, Nicholas John Mazza, Oliver Thrun, Patrick Pizzolorusoo, Alexander Simmons, Michael Wetherbee; Cabaret Theater; January 13–30, 2011

Starry Messenger by Ira Hauptman; Director, Susan Einhorn; Lighting, Jeff Greenberg; Set and Costumes, Meghan E Healey; Sound, Nel Paese; Cast: Brian Gagne, Jorge Luna, Elisa Matula, Jeremy Rishe, Marnye Young, Lou Vuolo, David Little; Cino Theater; January 27–February 13, 2011

The Fishcatcher Experiment by Eugenia Macer-Story; Director, Eugenia Macer-Story; Lighting, Mark Marcante; Set, Eugenia Macer-Story; Cast: Michael Lois Bernardi, Cait Bliss, Caiti Maloney, Geovanni Gopradi, Nick Pacifico, Jessica Cermak, Von Jacobs, Primy Rivera, Matthew Dean Wood, Neal Kodinsky, Melene Sosi, Pateina Murray; Cabaret Theater; February 3–20, 2011

Help me Jump Over the Show Written and directed by Bina Sharif; Lighting Alex Bartenieff; Set, Lytza Colon; Community Space Theater; February 3–27, 2011

The Inventor, The Escort, The Photographer, Her Boyfirend and His Girlfriend Written and directed by Matt Morillo; Lighting, Amith A Chandrashaker; Set, Mark Marcante; Costumes, Cast: David R Doumeng, Jessica Durdock Moreno, Tom Pilutik, Emily Campion, Maria Rowene; Cabaret Theater; February 24–March 5, 2011

Infallibility by Matt Barbot; Director, David Zen Mansley; Lighting, William Giraldo; Costumes, Zen, Jess Hart, Caren Johanns, Caiti Maloney; Sound, Joy Lindsheid, William Girakdo; Cast: David Zen Mansley, Justin Williams, Zachary Fineblum, Nicholas Troilo, George Isaacs, Kevin Peralta; Community Theater; March 3–13, 2011

Before God Was Invented Written and directed by Lissa Moira; Musical Director, Chris Wade; Lighting and Sound, William Giraldo; Set and Costumes, David Zen Masley; Cast: Chelsey Clime, Tjasa Ferme, Ashley Ford, Andrew Greer, Nora Munde Gustuson, George Isaacs, David Zen Mansley, Leanna Mercadante, Vicki Oceguera, Brik Olson, Daniel Vidor, Erica Hochstedler; Community Theater; March 17–April 3, 2011

Birds on Fire Written and directed by Barbara Kahn; Stage Manager, Bill Bradford; Lighting and Set, Mark Marcante; Costumes, Alice J Garland; Sound, Joy Linsheid; Cast: Robert Gonzales Jr., Benjamin Pike, Tommy Kearney, Amanda Yachechak, Gusta Johnson, Anna Podolak, Zoe Annastassiou, Sarah Shankman, Brian F Waite, Benjamin Pike, Noelle Tate; Cino Theater; March 17–April 10, 2011

Stars and Stripes by Walter Corwin; Director, David Aronson, David Weinstein, Walter Corwin; Lighting, Alex Bartenieff; Cast: Lei Zhou, Natalia Korablina, Lucy Cottrell, Indigo Pavlov, Dan Kelly, David Weinstein, Arthur Abrams; Cabaret Theater; March 24, 2011–April 10, 2011

Awake In A World That Encourages Sleep Written and directed by Raymond J Barry; Lighting, Sarah Harris; Set, Markus Maurette; Cast: Tacey Adams, Raymond J Barry, Joseph Culp; Johnson Theater; March 31–April 24, 2011

Keira and Isabella Written and directed by Anthony Laura; Set, Micaela Carolan; Cast: Danielle Carroll, Lisa DiFiore, Jordan Gosnell, Amy Losi, Patricia Nicastro, David Reck, Lisa Rosado, Michelle Silvani, Ashley Spivak; Community Theater; April 6–10, 2011

Only Love Will Do by Walt Stepp; Director, Lissa Moira; Stage Manager, Lighting, William Giraldo; Set, David 'Zen' Mansley; Cast: Danny Ashkenasi, Louisa Bradshaw, Jason Collins, Robert Homeyer, Richard O'Brien; Cabaret Theater; April 15–May 1, 2011

Catch Her In The Lie Written and directed by Philip Suraci; Musical Director, Joseph Albano Feiger; Lighting, Alex Bartenieff; Set, Mark Marcante; Costumes, Kat Martin; Cast: Matthew Richard Antezzo, Briana Bartenieff, Monica Bell, Mercer Borris, Josh Feiger, Ava Kuslansky, Delfin Gokhan Meekan, Tiffany Otero, Franny Rae, Ayumi Patterson, Antoine Saunders, Asha Simon, Brandon Smith, Malcom Zelaya; Cino Theater; May 5–22, 2011

The Death of Don Juan by Elodie Lauten; Director, Robert Lawson; Music Director, Elodie Lauten; Stage Manager, Robert Mendoza; Lighting, Alexander Bartenieff; Costumes, Anna Thomford; AV Design, Ron Benjamin; Cast: Arianna Armon, Alisha Desai, Mary Hurlbut, Courtenay Symonds, Douglas McDonnell, Jonathan Hirshman, Elodie Lauten; Johnson Theater; May 5–22, 2011

Squealer by Jonathan Blitstein; Director, Daniel Talbott; Musical Director, Allison Tartalia; Lighting, Brad Peterson; Set, Eugenia Furneaux-Arends; Costumes, Tristan Scott Barton Raines; Sound, Janie Bullard; Cast: Daniel Abeles, Jamie Law, Nick Lawson, Sarah Lamp, Nate Miller, Laura Ramadei; Cabaret Theater; May 5–21, 2011

Winter Wedding by Hanoch Levin; Director, David Wilinger; Lighting Chris Brown; Set, Mark Marcante; Costumes, Caridel Cruz; Translated by Lauren Hessing and David Wilinger; Original Music, Arthur Abrams; Cast: Debra Zane, Tony Greenleaf, Primy Rivera, Nikki Ilioupolis, Charles Dinstuhl, Joe Barna, Beth Bailis, Rachel Wolf, Gus Weinstein, Brandon Judell, Rob Weinzimer, Al Patrick Jo and Songdance; Theater for the New City; May 5–22, 2011

FESTIVALS

Dream Up Festival August 8–5, 2010; Included: *Chutes & Latters* and *Other Dangerous Games* by Christopher Massimine; *Bright Images* by Ken Gaertner, Director, Mark Bloom; *Bitch* by Sean Pomposello, Director, Matt M. Morrow; *Gloves for Guns* by David Lawson, Director, Michael Padden; *It Ain't No Sin* by Michael Patrick Flanagan Smith, Director, Meghan Finn; *My Artichoke Heart* by Naima Kristel Philips, Directed Simon Adinia Hanukai; *One Drop* by Andrea Fulton, Director, Ward Nixon; *Realpolitik* by elyse Cogan and Ivy Livingston; *Second Empire* by TL; DR Collective; *Seymour or the Last Fallen Angel* by Ashley Christopher Leach, Director, J. Andew McNeal; *Shakespeare is Dead* by Alex Mills, Direccted by Tom Costello; *Stand Clear of the Closing Doors: A Subway Musical and Romance* Written, Director, Richard S. Rose; *The Dudleys!* by Leegrid Stevens, Director, Matt Torney; *The New York Monologues* by Mike Poblete, Director, Ruth McGowan; *The Sky is Melting* by Elizabeth Woodbury, Director, Amy Brewczynski; *Trapped, An Evening of Two One-Act Dramas* by Darlene Troiano and Dawn Sofia, Directed Michael Beckett; *Wabi Sabi Not Wasabi* by Ming Peiffer, Director, Kat Yen; *What the Sparrow Said* by Danny Mitarotando, Director, Shannon Fillion

NON-RESIDENT PRODUCTIONS

Dansor/Dansouth; Johnson Theater; November 16–17, 2010

Bread & Puppet Produced by Bread and Puppet Theater; Johnson Theater; December 2–19, 2011

Times Square Angel by Charles Busch; Johnson Theater; December 13, 2010

Modigliani Produced by The Malisa Theatre Company; By Dennis McIntyre; Director: Michael Luggio; Community Space Theater; December 28, 2010–January 1, 2011

Thunderbirds Pow-Wow Produced by Thunderbird American Indian Dancers; Johnson Theater; January 28–February 6, 2011

Mr M. by Vit Horejs; Produced by The Czechslovak-American Marionette Theatre Supported by GOH Productions; Community Theater; April 14–May 1, 2011

Theater Nyx

www.theaternyx.com

Artistic Director, Alex Mallory; Executive Director, Jenni Marks

Ravel by Samantha Collier; Director, Alex Mallory; Stage Manager, Jill Wurzburg; Lighting, Ryan Metzler; Set, Geoffrey Waltz; Costumes, Mikey Goodmark; Sound, Dave Horowitz; Mask Designer, Steph Cathro; Cast: Samantha Cooper, Kelsey Moore, Elizabeth Claire Taylor; Looking Glass Theatre; August 5–15, 2010

Theater Reconstruction Ensemble

www.reconstructionensemble.org

A Doll's House by Henrik Ibsen; Director, John Kurzynowski; Lighting and Set, Natalie Robin; Sound, Kate Marvin; Producers: John Kurzynowski and Sydney Matthews; Cast: Jaclyn Backhaus, Pete Forester, Stacy Jordan, Anastasia Olowin & Jon Riddleberger; Access Theater; April 14–17, 2011

Theater THE

www.theaterthe.com

Radio Purgatory created by Theater THE; Director, Barry Goldman; Original Music, Aldo Perez; Stage Manager, Alison Graeffe; Lighting, David Tirosh; Set, Karl Allen; Costumes, Ramona Ponce; Sound, Aldo Perez; AV Design, Tatsushi Tahara; Cast: Aldo Perez, Jenny Lee Mitchell, Matthew Talmage. Jonathon Roberts, Richard Ginocchio, Matt Muszynski; October 7–30, 2010

TheaterPeace

theaterpeace.org

Catch Her in the Lie Written and directed by Philip Suraci; Original Music, Joseph Albano Feiger; Choreographer, Steffanie White; Stage Manager, Jacqueline Donnaruma; Lighting, Alex Bartenieff; Set, Mark Marcante; Costumes, Kat Martin; Sound, Joseph Albano Feiger; Masks Designer, Spica Wobbe; Cast: Monica Bell, Mercer Borris, Josh Feiger, Ava Kuslansky, Matthew Antezzo, Brandon Smith, Malcom Zelaya, Brianna Bartenieff, Antoine Saunders, Asha Simon, Jacob Berck-Sasofsky, Tiffany Otero, Frances Raybaud, Delfin Meehan, Ayumi Patterson, Ty Cotton, Kimbe; Theater for the New City; May 5–22, 2011

Theatre 167

www.theatre167.org

You Are Now the Owner of this Suitcase by Mando Alvarado, Jenny Lyn Bader, Barbara Cassidy, Les, Hunter, Joy Tomasko, Gary Winter, Stefanie Zadravec; Director, Ari Laura Kreith; Lighting, Nicole Pearce; Set, Michael Wilson Morgan; Cast: Patricia Becker, Rajesh Bose, Kim Carlson, Arlene Chico-Lugo, Kathleen Choe, Bernardo Cubria, Ross DeGraw, Oscar Fabela, Samuel T. Gaines, John P. Keller, Stephanie LaVardera, Waldo Mayo, Emma Ramos; PS 69; March 12–27, 2011

Theatre 4 the People

theatre4thepeople.com

A Grimm Reality by Bekah Brunstetter, Cassandra Hume, Chisa Hutchinson, Zack Freidman, Dan Kitrosser; Director, Isaac Byrne; Musical Director, Evan Greene; Stage Manager, Catherine DeCioccio; Set, David Ogle; Costumes, Cherie A. Roberts; Cast: Amber Bloom, Isaac Byrne, Alexander Farrell, Emily Hartford,

Cassandra Hume, Chris Cromwell, Dan Kitrosser, Edward Chin-Lyn, Elizabeth Kensek, Evan Greene, Giuditta Lattanzi, Kara Ayn Napolitano, Kyle Welling, Lalo Esquivel, Paul Fears, Roberta Colindrez; Bryant Park; July 24–August 14, 2010

Theatre Askew

theatreaskew.com

A Night at the Tombs written and performed by Bianca Leigh; Director, Tim Cusack; Music by Jeff Whitty, Taylor Mac, Jeff Domoto, Barb Morrison, Matty Pritchard, and Isam Rum; Bowery Poetry Club; June 24–August 5, 2010

Theatre C

www.theatreC.org

Producing Artistic Director, Carlos Armesto; Associate Producer, Lauren Rayner

disOriented by Kyoung H. Park; Director, Carlos Armesto; Stage Manager, Chapel Folger; Lighting, Jake DeGroot; Set, Adam Koch; Costumes, Carla Bellisio; Sound, David M. Lawson; Line Producer, Evan O'Brient; Producing Associate, Lauren Rayner; Choreographer, Elisabetta Spuria; Production Manager and Technical Director, Ashley Crocket; Props Coordinator, Jamie Bressler; Cast: Ariel Estrada, Daniel K. Isaac, Talym Jinn Kim, Julian Leong , Bert Matias, Amy Kim Washke, Virginia Wing; Peter Jay Sharp Theater; February 16–March 7, 2011

Binding Written and performed by Jesse Zaritt; Director, Basmat Hazan; Stage Manager, John Murdock; Lighting, David Tirosh; Set, Daniel Zimmerman; Costumes, Manju Shandler; Sound, Sharath Patel, Hillary Charnas; AV Design, David Tirosh; Lead Producer, Carlos Armesto; Line Producer, Cat Tate Starmer; Producing Associate, Lauren Rayner; Production Consultant, Heather Klein; PS 122; May 5–29, 2011

READINGS AND WORKSHOPS

The Ugly Swan by Sammy Buck; Director, Carlos Armesto; Music Director and Composer, Dan Acquisto; Producing Associate, Lauren Rayner; Pearl Studios; December 13, 2010

Shoot the Piano Player by Charles Smith; Director, Carlos Armesto; Producer, Margot Harley; Lyrics, Lois Walden; Music, David Sherman; Music Director, Sean Driscoll; Casting, Michael Cassara; New 42nd Street Studios; November 16, 2010

Theatre East

www.theatreeast.org

Artistic Director, Judson Jones; Managing Director, Todd Eric Hawkins; Associate Artistic Director, Christa Kimlicko Jones; Associate Director, Joseph Parks;Director of Development, William Franke; Company Manager, Daryl Wendy Strauss; Marketing Director, Shorey Walker

The Soldier Dreams by Daniel MacIvor; Director, Judson Jones; Stage Manager, Megan O'Brien; Lighting, Jessica M. Burgess; Set, Lea Anello; Sound, Scott O'Brien; Voice and Dialect Coach, Kohli Calhoun; Production Manager, Eric Kasprisin; Cast: Nick Cianfrogna, William Franke, Heather Hill, Bryan Jarrett, Christa Kimlicko Jones, Denny Lawrence, Helen Merino, Joseph Mitchell Parks; The Lion, Theatre Row; March 25–April 9, 2011

READINGS AND WORKSHOPS

Pretty Chin Up by Andrea Ciannavei; Director, Michele Chivu; Cast: Shawtane Bowen, Andrea Ciannavei, Bronwen Coleman, Trevor Long, Sid Williams, Helen Merino; Stella Adler Studios; July 20, 2010

The Soldier Dreams by Daniel MacIvor; Director, Judson Jones; Cast: William Franke, Christa Kimlicko Jones, Denny Lawrence, Helen Merino, Heather Hill, Tom Pacio, Joseph Mitchell Parks, Matt Savins; June Havoc, Abingdon Theatre; September 9, 2010

Theatre of the Expendable

www.theatreoftheexpendable.org

Artistic Director, Jesse Edward Rosbrow; Staff Producer, Arienne Pelletier; Director of Communications, Justin Howard; Associate Director of Development, Geoffrey Barrows

St. Nicholas by Conor McPherson; Director, Jesse Edward Rosbrow; Stage Manager, Melissa A. Nathan; Lighting, Ryan Metzler; Costume and Properties Consultant, Jennifer Raskopf; Graphics, Duncan Pflaster; Audience Development, Michael Roderick; Press, Emily Owens PR; Producer, Alexander Koo; Producer, Arienne Pelletier; Producer, Jesse Edward Rosbrow; Cast: Darrell James; The WorkShop Theater; June 17–July 3, 2010

Three Legged Dog (3LD)

3leggeddog.org

Artistic Director, Kevin Cunningham; Producing Director, Aaron Louis, Media Director, Aaron Harrow; Promotions Manager, Piama Habibullah; Company Manager, Karina Martins; Development and Artistic Associate, Joellen Dolan; Program Associate Maxim Tumenev

Men Go Down Written and directed by John Jahnke; Stage Manager, Karen Oughtred; Lighting, Bruce Steinberg; Set, Peter Ksander; Costumes, Romona Ponce; Sound, Kristin Worrall; Video Designer, Taili Wu, Andrew Schneider, and Rebecca Adomo; Cast: Melody Bates, Alexander Borinsky, Tim Eliot, Michael Ingle, Mikeah Jennings, Liz Santoro, Hillary Spector, Tanisha Thompson; Produced in association with Hotel Savant; 3LD; January 6 – 23, 2011

Spy Garbo by Sheila Schwartz; Director, Kevin Cunningham; Original Music, Aldo Perez; Production Stage Manager, Danielle Teague-Daniels; Lighting, Laura Mroczkowski; Set, Neal Wilkinson; Costumes, Clint Ramos; Sound Desiger, Marcelo Anez; Video Designer, Aaron Harrow, Jeff Morey and Peter Norrman; Dramaturg, Sarah Cameron Sunde; Produced in association with Affinity Company Theater; 3LD; March 6 – April 10, 2011

Tiffany Hayden-Williamson Productions, LLC

www.thwstories.com

The Atmosphere Written and directed by Tiffany Hayden-Williamson; Cast: David Brandyn, Leigh Chan, TJ Collins Jr., Elann Danziger, Judith Kenny, Nina Maxwell, Zefralyn Osborn, Robyn Young; Brooklyn Music School Playhouse; May 19 –May 20, 2011

Tin Lily Productions

www.tinlily.org

Fefu and her Friends by Maria Irene Fornes; Director, Jillian Johnson; Stage Manager, Jessica Mason; Lighting, Allison Carney; Set, Joshua David Bishop; Costumes, Izzy Fields; Cast: Tai Verley, Cait Bliss, Katie Stults, Annie Branson, Nora Jane Williams, Kyle June Williams, Sasha Kaye, Katie Middleton; Center for Performance Research; November 12–December 5, 2010

Tongue in Cheek Theater Productions

www.tictheater.com

Jake Lipman, Producing Artistic Director

Dead White Males: A Year in the Trenches of Teaching by William Missouri Downs; Director, Brock H. Hill; Stage Manager, Katy Moore; Lighting, Brock H. Hill; Set, Virginia Monte; Costumes, Michael Piatkowski; Sound, Philip Rothman; Cast: Brady Adair, Robert Gonzalez Jr., Jake Lipman, Graciany Miranda, Shana Wiersum, Leanne Linsky and Brynne Kraynak; The Bridge Theater; October 6, 2010–October 16, 2010

The Drunken City Written and directed by Brock H. Hill; Choreographer, Merete Muenter; Stage Manager, Allison Lemel; Lighting, Set and Costumes, Meagan E. Miller-McKeever; Sound, Philip Rothman; Cast: Michael Gene Conti, Reiss Gaspard, A.J. Heekin, Jake Lipman, Shelley Little and Shana Wiersum; Shetler Studio 54; April 27–May 7, 2011

Toy Box Theatre Company

www.toyboxtheatre.org

Woyzeck Adapted and Directed Jonathan Barsness; Original Music, Colonna Sonora; Choreographer, Elisabeth Motley; Stage Manager, Sara Troficanto; Lighting, Alex Moore; Set, Kacie Hultgren; Costumes, Kate Mincer; Sound, James Sparber; Cast: Juan Luis Acevedo, Amy Bloomberg, Ron Bopst, Ryan Colwell, Sarah Hankins, David Michael Holmes, Ryan Reilly, Clare Schmidt; Teatro IATI; October 22–November 12, 2010

FESTIVALS

Plus One Solo Show Festival–October 2010; Stage Manager, Allison Lemel; The Bridge Theatre @ Shetler Studios; October 10–11, 2010; Included: *JACKed Up* Written and performed by Mark Gessner, Director, James Angiola; *I'm Fired!* Written and performed by Margie Suvalle, Director, Matt Hoverman; *Can't the Revolution Wait?* Written and performed by Jamila Webb, Director, Dawn-Elin Fraser

Plus One Solo Show Festival–May 2011; Stage Manager, Allison Lemel;The Bridge Theatre @ Shetler Studios; May 1–2, 2011; Included: *The Glory of Love* Written and performed by Sarah Aili, Director, Matt Hoverman; *Pipelayer's Union* Written and performed by Glynn Borders, Director, Heather Guthrie; *Swamp Girl Written and performed* by Debra Castellano, Director, Matt Hoverman

True Light Productions

www.oncampustheplay.com

On Campus by Steve Sherman; Director, Marc Santa Maria; Stage Manager, Estie Sarvasy; Lighting, Chad Lefebvre; Set, Daniel Zimmerman; Costumes, Jake Millgard; Sound, Brandon Wolcott; Props Design, Jake Millgard; Cast: Caitlin Gold, Jake Millgard, Osvaldo Plasencia, Sarah Saunders, Steve Sherman, Ed Stelz, Chloe Tuttle; 14th Street Y, The; March 10–26, 2011

Turtle Shell Producitons

turtleshellproductions.com

Summer by Martin M. Zuckerman; Director, John Cooper; Lighting, Christian DeAngelis; Set, Kyle Dixon; Costumes, A. Christina Giannini; Sound, Josh Millican; AV Design, Jason Craigs; Cast: John P. Keller, Mark Mikulski, Daren Kelly, Christiane Seidel, Brooke Novak, Pauline Walsh; Turtle's Shell Theater; April 29–May 30, 2011

Two Beard Productions

Smoking Section by Brian Pollock; Director, Robert Mark; Set, Brian Pollock; Cast: Brian Pollock, Robert Mark, Nick Maccarone, Jeane Marie, Emma Peele, Chris Bucci, Meaghan B Fluitt, Ronnie Charles, William Downes, Emily Hanson; Producer's Club Grand Theatre; November 4–7, 2010

Two Turns Theater Company

www.twoturns.com

The Turn of the Screw by Jeffrey Hatcher; Director, Ken Cerniglia; Cast: Vince Gatton, Christina LaFortune; Merchant's House Museum; November 11–21, 2010

Untitled Theater Company #61

www.untitledtheater.com

Artistic Director, Edward Einhorn; Associate Artistic Director, Henry Akona

Do Androids dream of Electric Sheep? Written and directed by Edward Einhorn; Musical Director, Henry Akona; Stage Manager, Berit Johnson; Lighting, Jeff Nash; Set, Neal Wilkinson; Costumes, Carla Gant; Sound, Henry Akona; AV Design, Jared Mezzochi; Puppet Designer, Barry Weil; Props Designer, Berit Johnson; Fight Choreographer, Dan Zisson; Assisant Directors, Tom Berger and Patrice Miller; Cast: Timothy Babcock, Alex Emanuel, Ian W. Hill, Uma Incrocci, Christian Pedersen, Yvonne Roen, Trav SD, Alyssa Simon, Ken Simon, Moira Stone; 3LD Art & Technology Center; November 18–December 10, 2010

Urban Research Theater

www.urbanresearchtheater.com

Play/War by Ben Spatz; Director, Maximilian Balduzzi and Ben Spatz; Original Music, Ben Spatz; Choreographer, Maximilian Balduzzi; Cast: Ben Spatz, Maximilian Balduzzi; Medicine Show Theatre; July 16–August 14, 2010

Valhalla Productions

Class A by Cameron Moir; Director, Alyse M. Frosch; Cast: David Arkema, Parker Hurley, Andrew J. Langton, Andrew Lerner, Olga Malykhin, Hailey McCarty, Cameron Moir, Seth Norris, Susan Young and Peter Zerneck; Gene Frankel Theatre; February 24–27, 2011

Vampire Cowboys

www.vampirecowboys.com

Artistic Directors, Qui Nguyen and Robert Ross Parker; Managing Director, Abby Marcus; Producing Director, Nick Francone; Associate Producer, Daniel Rech; General Manager, Dan Rogers

The Inexplicable Redemption of Agent G by Qui Nguyen; Director, Robert Ross Parker; Stage Manager, Danielle Buccino; Lighting, Nick Francone; Set, Nick Francone; Costumes, Jessica Wegener Shay; Sound, Shane Rettig; AV Design, Matthew Tennie; Puppet Designer, David Valentine; Choreographer, Jamie Dunn; Fight Directors, Adam Scott Mazer and Qui Nguyen; Assistant Director, Dan Rogers; Assistant Stage Managers Emily Edwards and Amy VonVett; Sound Operator, Jeanne Travis; Produced in association with Incubator Arts Project; Cast: William Jackson Harper, Jon Hoche, Bonnie Sherman, Paco Tolson, Amy Kim Waschke; Incubator Arts Project; March 24–April 16, 2011

Variations Theatre Group

www.variationstheatregroup.com

Fool For Love by Sam Shepard; Director, Rich Ferraioli; Lighting, Christopher Weston; Set, R. Allen Babcock; Sound, John Albano; Cast: Kirk Gostkowski, Collin Meath, Christina Elise Perry; Access Theater Black Box; February 23–March 5, 2011

Vital Theatre Company

Angelina Ballerina The Musical Book and Lyrics by Susan DiLallo; Original Music, Ben Morss; Director, Sam Viverito; Musical Director, Michael Borth; Stage Manager, Shani Colleen Murfin; Lighting, Michael Gottlieb; Set, Kyle Dixon; Costumes, Elisabeth Vastola; Choreographer, Sam Viverito; Assistant to the Director, Lynn Sterling; Based on the characters by Katherine Holabird and Helen Craig; Cast: Whitney Autumn Meyer, Amy White, Kevin Michael Wade, Cassie Okenka, Amber Coartney, Eric Restivo, Jake Weinstein, Sarah Elaine Hoffman, Alexis Field, Amanda Yachechak, Kara Jones, Jessica Freitas, Ronn Burton, Maggie Gomez-Madonia, TIffany Weisend, Harmon; McGinn/Cazale Theatre; October 2, 2010–March 13, 2011

Velma Gratch & the Way Cool Butterfly Book and Lyrics by Michelle Marie Elliott; Original Music, Danny Larsen; Director, Linda Ames Key; Music Director, Mark Evans; Stage Manager, Kristina Vnook; Lighting, Lois Catanzaro; Set, Tim McMath; Costumes, Sarah Riffle; Choreographer, Bethany M. White; Based on the book by Alan Madison; Cast: Alex Viola, Maggie Wetzel, Breanna Bartley, Alex Krasser, Ashley Klanac, Peter Burke, Alexandra Paddock, Lauren Nestor; McGinn/Cazale Theatre; January 9–February 27, 2011

Awesome Allie, First Kid Astronaut Book by Scott Elmegreen, Music and Lyrics by Drew Fornarola; Director, Jeremy Dobrish; Musical Director, Michael Pettry; Stage Manager, Kristina Vnook; Lighting, Josh Bradford; Set, Jon Collins; Costumes, Bobby Pearce; Choreographer, Christine O'Grady; Cast: Dara Hartman, Erica Wilpon, Joshua David Bishop, Chris Kind, Ashley Laverty, Michael Walker; McGinn/Cazale Theatre; March 12–April 26, 2011

Pinkalicious, The Musical Book and Lyrics by Elizabeth Kann and Victoria Kann; Original Music, John Gregor; Director, Teresa K. Pond; Musical Director, Jad Bernardo; Stage Manager, Katie Gorum and Nataliya Vasilyeva; Set, Adam Koch; Costumes, Cherie Cunningham; Sound Engineer, Anna Hardisty; Choreographer, Dax Valdes; On-going

Vortex Theater Company

www.vortextheater.com

Haunted House Created by Vortex Theater Company; October 12–31, 2010

Wide Eyed Productions

www.wideeyedproductions.com

A Girl Wrote It: *Clementine* by Lynda Green, *Selection* by Kris Montgomery, *The Return of Toodles Von Flooz* by Lisa Ferber, *Plight of the Apothecary* by Elizabeth Birkenmeier; Director, Justin Ness; Stage Manager, Lesley Stone; Lighting, Joe Novak; Sound, Colin Whitely; AV Design, Brian Bernhardt; Cast: Colin McFadden, William Reid, Michael Komala, Andrew Harriss, Tom Carman, Eric Whitten, Kirsta Peterson, Lucy McRae, Becky Sterling Rygg, Lisa Mamazza, Brianne Mai, Melissa Johnson, Allison Moody; Red Room; February 3, 2010–February 20, 2011

Henry VI part III by William Shakespeare; Director, Adam Marple; Stage Manager, Pisa Waikwamdee; Lighting, Joe Novak; Set, Ji-youn Chang; Sound, Colin Whitely; Cast: Al Foote III, Sky Seals, Nat Cassidy, Ben Newman, Jake Paque, Jerrod Bogard, Andrew Harriss, Justin Ness, Amy Lee Pearsall, Bari

Robinson, Anthony Doqaj, Candace Thompson, Justin R.G. Holcomb, Kelly McCrann, Kym Smith, Lucy McRae, Moses Villarama, R Paul, Trevor Dallier; East 13th Street Theatre; July 1–24, 2010

The Prairie Plays: High Plains & My Daughter Keeps Our Hammer by Brian Watkins; Director, Kristin Skye Hoffmann and Anthony Reimer; Lighting, Joe Novak; Sound, Trevor Dallier and Brian Watkins; Cast: Brian Watkins, Amy Lee Pearsall, Katie Schorr; Under St Marks; November 4–21, 2010

Wilson Exclusive Talent Productions

www.wetprods.com

Producer/Director/Writer, Stephanie Lynn Wilson

A Wound In Time Written and directed by Stephanie Lynn Wilson; Musical Director, Wil Milton and Rodney Carter; Lighting, Sam Chico; Set and Sound, Stephanie Lynn Wilson; Makeup Designer, Ryss; Cast: Bisa Dawes, Alan Cordoba, Darryl Reillly, Soleidy Mendez, Ryss, Irma Cadiz, Hoji Fortuna, Alan Liddell, Steve DeVito; Nuyorican Poets Cafe; October 22–November 1, 2010

READINGS AND WORKSHOPS

Blood Makes The Red River Flow Written and directed by Stephanie Lynn Wilson; Cast: Malika Iman, Christiana Blain, Ron Rivera, Candace Purcell, Richard York, Harold Mathieu; Space On White

Wings Theatre

wingstheatre.com

A House Full of Dust by Bella Poynton; Director, Amanda Thompson; Cast: Oakley Boycott, Lars Drew, Alejandra Escalante, Renee Petrofes, George Saulnier, Jordan Tierney, and Jim Staudt; Wings Theatre; August 10–29, 2010

Repo Returns by Terrance Zdunich and Darren Smith; Director, Jordana Dlugacz and James Prego; Wings Theatre; July 10, 2010

Woman Seeking... a theatre company

wstheater.webs.com

The Torch-Bearers by George Kelly; Director, Christine Mosere; Assistant Director, Sonia Perez; Stage Manager, Chris Scofield; Set, Kim Rosin; Lighting, Judy Wolcott; Costumes, Vivica Sanai; Set Building, Eric Helland; Assistant Stage Manager, Amanda Montoya; Photographer, Colin McKenna; Cast: Eleanor Moseley, Kate Szyperski, Laurie Bialik, Larry Albert, Susan Connors, Richard Nguyen Sloniker, Kayti Barnett, Rachel Jackson, Brandon Felker, Rebecca Olson, Eric Helland, Laura Hanson; Richard Hugo House; December 3– 19, 2010

Woodie King Jr's New Federal Theater

Knock Me A Kiss Written and directed by Charles Smith; Cast: Erin Cherry, André De Shields, Gillian Glasco, Morocco Omari, Sean Phillips, and Marie Thomas; Abrons Arts Center; November 21–December 5, 2010

Working Theater

www.theworkingtheater.org

Honey Brown Eyes by Stefanie Zadravec; Director,Erica Schmidt; Cast: Edoardo Ballerini, Sue Cremin, Gene Gillette, Beatrice Miller, Daniel Serafini-Sauli & Kate Skinner; The Clurman Theatre at Theatre Row; January 9 – February 6, 2011

WorkShop Theater Company

www.workshoptheater.org

Verbatim Verboten by Michael Martin; Director, Jonathan Pereira; Cast: Jonathan Pereira, Dan Patrick Brady, Cecily Benjamin, Kelly Anne Burns, Loren Dunn, Anne Fizzard, Richard Kent Green, Mike Smith Rivera, Amanda Sayle, Tracy Shar; Produced in association with Alvin Out Productions; WorkShop Theater Mainstage; Apirl 16–September 17, 2010

The Navigator by Eddie Antar; Director, Leslie Kincaid Burby; Lighting and Set, Duane Pagano; Sound, Quentin Chiapetta; Cast: Joe Franchini, Michael Gnat, Kelly Anne Burns, Nicole Taylor; The Workshop Theater, The Jewel Box; September 16–October 2, 2010

Interchange by Ken Jaworowski; Director, Thomas Coté; Lighting, Yuriy Nayer; Set, Craig Napoliello; Costumes, Catherine Siracusa; Sound, David Schulder; Cast: Liz Amberly, Cecily Benjamin, Shaun Bennet Wilson, Daniel Damiano, Gerry Goodstein, Riley Jones-Cohen, Wende O'Reilly, Jeff Paul, David M. Pincus, Sean Singer; Workshop Theater; October 7–October 30, 2010

A Christmas Carol Adapted and Performed by Greg Oliver Bodine; Director, Shana Solomon; WorkShop Theater, Jewel Box Theater; December 19 – 21, 2010

Tartuffe by Moliere; Director, Charles E. Gerber; Translated by Paul Weidner; Cast: Kelly Anne Burns, Daniel Damiano, Ellen Dolan, DeeDee Friedman, Charles E. Gerber, Noah Keen, David M. Mead, Gerrianne Raphael, Mike Smith Rivera, Natalie Smith, Bill Tatum, Jonathan Weber; WorkShop Theatre; January 15 – 19, 2011

Kings: The Siege of Troy by Christopher Logue; Adapted by Jim Milton; Work-Shop Theatre; March 10 – April 2, 2011

Lizzie Borden at Eight O'Clock by Mitch Giannunzio; Director, Kenneth Tigar; Stage Manager, Alma Negro; Cast: Ellen Barry; The Workshop Theater, Produced in association with Alvin Out Productions; The Jewel Box; March 24–April 3, 2011

FESTIVALS

Cold Snaps 2010 The Workshop Theater/ The Jewel Box; December 2–18, 2010; Included: *Fly Season* by John McKinney, *Fourteen Million* by Liz Amberly, *Green Star, Gold Star* by David M. Mead, *Layover* by Loren Dunn, *Lionel* by Joanne Joseph, *One is the Road* by Mark Loewenstern, *Sunday Afternoon* by Frank Hertle, *A Weekend in Filey* by Jennifer Fell Hayes; Director, Adriana Baer, Thomas Coté, Gerrianne Raphael, Ryan Lee, Jessica Creane, Leslie Kincaid Burby, David M. Mead, Kathy Gail MacGowan; Stage Manager, Michael Palmer, Joshua Quinn; Lighting and Set, Richard Kent Green; Sound, John McKinney; AV Design, Howard Better; Cast: C.K. Allen, Mary Ruth Baggot, Dan Patrick Brady, David Palmer Brown, Ethan Cadoff, Daniel Damiano, Letty Ferrer, Anne Fizzard, Ken Glickfeld, Charlotte Hampden, Bob Manus, Amanda Sayle, Stephania Schramm, Laurie Schroeder, Joanie Schumacher, Georgia Southern, Jonathan We, Dan Patrick Brady

They That Have Borne The Battle: One-Act Festival Workshop Theater; May 5–28, 2011; Included: *Air Force 525* by Marylee Martin, *Bethesda* by Bob Stewart, *Breakfast With Charlie* by Bob Manus, *The Fatwa of Corpman Johnny Jones* by Greg Oliver Bodine, *On the Advice of an Old Friend* by David M. Mead, *Vowed and Wowed* by Rich Orloff; Director, Katie Braden, Jessica Creane, Ryan Lee, Passion, David M. Pincus; Stage Manager, Joshua Quinn; Lighting and Set, Richard Kent Green; Costumes, Alexa Devin; Sound, John McKinney; Cast: Chance Andersen, Greg Oliver Bodine, Ellen Dolan, Burt Edwards, Anne Fizzard, Ken Glickfeld, Sam Gooley, Leslie Gwyn, Mark Hofmaier, Howah Hung, Elena Hurst, Maya Katherine Jasinska, Whitney Kirk, Whitney Kam Lee, Bob Manus, David C. Marshall, Clare Patterson, Bill Tatum

READINGS AND WORKSHOPS

The Garden by Loren Dunn; Director, Eric Dente; Stage Manager, Joshua Quill; Coordinating Producer, Anne Fizzard; Cast: Ellen Barry, Dan Patrick Brady, Ken

Glickfeld, Susan Izatt, Laura E. Johnston, Brenna Palughi, Ben Sumrall, Bjorn Thorstad, Matthew Wise; WorkShop Theater, Jewel Box Theater; October 21–30, 2010

Somewhere Waiting for You by Kathryn Paulsen; Director, Katrin Hilbe; Co-ordinating Producer, Katie Yamulla; Cast: Anthony Bowden, Liz Forst, Michael Gnat, Lucy McMichael, Bill Tatum, Amanda Tudor, Richard Vernon, Katie Yamulla; WorkShop Theater; October 26, 2010

Mama's Gonna Buy You... by Chisa Hutchinson; Cast: James Edward Becton, Cecily Benjamin, Daniel Carlton, Tammi Clayton, Richard Kent Green, Laura E. Johnston, Christina Romanello Boyle, Tiffany Rothman, Diana Sheivprasad; WorkShop Theater, Jewel Box Theater; November 4–6, 2010

The Waiting Room by Robert Karmon; Director, Robert Kalfin; Michael Gnat, David Pincus, Richard B. Watson, Natalie Mosco, Sean Singer, Ben Sumrall, Jack Tartaglia, Matthew Wechsler, Richard Kent Green; WorkShop Theater, Jewel Box Theater; November 21, 2010

Save Me: The Amazing Adventures of Patchgirl by Ben Alexander, Director, Richard Kent Green; *Location* by Leslie Gwyn, Director, Jessica Creane; *Synagoguery* by Michael Lazan, Director, Eddie Antar; WorkShop Theater, Jewel Box Theater; February 17–19, 2011

The Silver Fox by Donna DeMatteo; Director, David M. Mead; Cast: Christina Romanello Boyle, Letty Ferrer, Natalie Smith, David Palmer Brown; WorkShop Theater, Jewel Box Theater; March 3–5, 2011

Beat Chick by Prudence Wright Holmes and Joanne Joseph; Director, Prudence Wright Holmes; Stage Manager and Board Operator, Dan Patrick Brady; Production Manager, Jeff Paul; Cast: David Palmer Brown, Brad Coolidge, Anne Fizzard, Richard Kent Green, Andy Lindberg, Tom Pennachini, Leigh Shannon; WorkShop Theater, Jewel Box Theater; March 17–19, 2011

Someone's Knocking by Rich Orloff; Director, Leslie Kincaid Burby; Sound, Quentin Chiapetta and MediaNoise; Production Manager, Georgia Southern; Cast: Kelly Anne Burns, Dee Dee Friedman, Richard Kent Green, Timothy Scott Harris, Rita Rehn, Mike Smith Rivera WorkShop Theater, Jewel Box Theater; April 21–23, 2011

The Writer's Forum

www.theatresource.org

Better Lucky Than Smart by Jonathan Kravetz; Director, Joseph Beuerlein; Cast: Jay Leibowitz, Joe Masi, Brandon Potter, Valerie Hager, Sarah Doudna, Natasha William; ManhattanTheatreSource; August 18–Septemer 4, 2010

WTE Theatre

www.wtetheatre.org

Stinky Flowers and the Bad Banana by Croft Vaughn; Director, David A. Miller; Original Music, Alana McNair; Stage Manager, Barbara Dente; Lighting, Kate Ashton and Sam Gordon; Set, Jennifer Varbalow; Costumes, Bradley Erickson; Multi-Media Designer, Matt Burnett, Jeff Heyman, Double Blind; Cast: Michael J. Donnolly, Lauren Sowa, Robert James Grimm III, Dorothy Abrahams , Chuck Blasius; Under St Marks; October 7–24, 2010

Xoregos Performing Company

www.xoregos.com

Harlem on My Mind by Ade Ademola, Grace Cavalieri, Dave DeChristopher, Kimberly Shelby-Szyszko; Director, Shela Xoregos; Musical Director, Eugene

Abrams; Cast: Paule Aboite, Andrew R. Cooksey, Keldrick Crowder, Z.Louis Finney, Sydney Allyson Francis, Emani Spence; Metropolitan Playhouse; January 18–29, 2011

Yara Arts Group

Winter Sun Created by Yara Arts Group; Director, Virlana Tkacz; Musical Director, Julian Kytasty; Stage Manager, Sue Jane Stoker; Lighting, David Bonilla; Set, Watoku Ueno; AV Design, Mikhail Shraga and Peyton Skyler Harrison; Translator, Virlana Tkacz and Wanda Phipps; Choreographer, Shigeko Suga; Cast: Ivan Zelenchuk, Mykola Zelenchuk, Mykola Ilyuk, Vasyl Tymchuk, Ostap Kostyuk, Aurelia Shrenker, Eva Salina Primack, Kat Yew, Deanna Klapishchak, Shigeko Suga, Yuliyan Yordanov, Musicians: Julian Kytasty, Paul Brantley, Alexander Katreczko, and Valeriy Zh; La MaMa Ellen Stewart Theatre; December 26, 2011

Raven Inspired by the poetry of Oleh Lysheha; Director, Virlana Tkacz; Music Director, Alla Zagaykevych, Aurelia Shrenker and Eva Salina Primack; Stage Manager, Nadia Tatchin; Lighting, David Bonilla and Evhen Kopyov; Set, Watoku Ueno; Costumes, Keiko Obremski; Sound, Tim Schellenbaum; AV Design, Volodymyr Klyuzko & Mikhail Shraga; Additional Music, Julian Kytasty; Cast: Andrew Colteaux, Marena Bush, Sean Eden, Kat Yew; La MaMa ETC; April 8–24, 2011

The York Shakespeare Company

www.yorkshakespeare.org

Artistic Director, Seth Duerr

The Punishing Blow by Randy Cohen; Director, Seth Duerr; Kirk Theater; August 13, 2010–August 28, 2010

Long Day's Journey Into Night by Eugene O'Neill; Director, Seth Duerr; Stage Manager, Angie McCormack; Lighting, Driscoll Otto; Set, Stephen K. Dobay; Costumes, Sean Sullivan; Sound, John D. Ivy; Graphics, Ehren Ziegler; Cast: Bill Fairbairn, Rebecca Street, Seth Duerr, Alexander Harvey; Theatre Row Theatre; May 29–June 12, 2010

Macbeth by William Shakespeare; Director, Seth Duerr; Stage Manager, Stanley L. Ralph; Set, Elyse Handelman; Lighting, Bradley King; Costumes, Kevin Thacker; Sound, John D. Ivy; Cast: Seth Duerr, Bob Armstrong, Sarah Bowles, Andrew Broussard, Cristina Carrión, MaConnia Chesser, Clifton Dunn, Patrick Goss, Gabe Green, Davis Hall, Joseph Hamel, Jared Kirby, Everett O'Neil, Christian Rizzuti, Jenn Remke, Mickey Ryan, Jerilyn Sackler, Fred Stuart, Jeffrey Evan Thomas, Jeff Topf, Renee Williams and Roger Yeh; Clurman @ Theatre Row; October 30–November 13, 2010

Richard II by William Shakespeare; Director, Seth Duerr; Stage Manager, Stanley L. Ralph; Set, Elyse Handelman; Lighting, Bradley King; Costumes, Kevin Thacker; Sound, John D. Ivy; Cast: Seth Duerr, Bob Armstrong, Sarah Bowles, Andrew Broussard, Cristina Carrión, MaConnia Chesser, Clifton Dunn, Patrick Goss, Gabe Green, Davis Hall, Joseph Hamel, Jared Kirby, Everett O'Neil, Christian Rizzuti, Jenn Remke, Mickey Ryan, Jerilyn Sackler, Fred Stuart, Jeffrey Evan Thomas, Jeff Topf, Renee Williams and Roger Yeh;Clurman @ Theatre Row; October 30–November 13, 2010

Yurikoff Productions

Gods at the End of the World by Oliver Thrun; Director, Matthew Kreiner; Lighting, Alexander Bartenieff; Set, Mark Marcante; Sound, Jeremy Pape; Cast: Klemen Novak, Trevor Kluckman, Kevin Paul Smith, Alex Escher, Megan Lee, Meghan Sinclair, Elizabeth Dilley, Stephanie Haring; Theater for the New City; June 17–July 3, 2010

Zimmertyne Productions

zimmertyne.wordpress.com

The Exquisite Corpse Festival: *Exquisite Corpse* by Jason Tyne-Zimmerman, *Unsaddest Factory* by Matthew Grzybowski, *Exquisite Corpse* by Stacy Davidowitz, Eric Samuelsen, and Ben Lewis, *Exquisite Corpse* by John Patrick Bray, Anton Dudley, and Jonathan Lynch; Director, Rick Joyce, Matthew Kriener, Adam Dworkin, Dan Balkin, Akia, Willow Norton, Josh Penzell; Original Music, Douglas Gillin, Miss FD, Scott Porter, Tin Pan, Haircut 1234, Loli Lux; Stage Manager, Jason Tyne-Zimmerman; Space on White; December 10, 2010–January 9, 2011

FESTIVALS

The 9.13 Project

Brecht Forum; June 9–20, 2010

Produced by One Armed Man, Inc.; Currated by Adam Klasfeld

Citizen Paine by Bill Hollenbach

Marx in Soho by Howard Zinn

The Report of My Death by Adam Klasfeld

Finks by Joe Gilford

FreEpLaY: Antigone Remix by the Strike Anywhere Performance Ensemble

Works-In-Progress Administration by Julie Halpern and Crystal Skillman

Military Act(ion)s by Layna Fisher, john michaelrossi, Tony Pennino and Drew Hildebrand

Captain Ferguson's School for Balloon Warfare by Isaac Rathbone

In My Name by Steven Hevey

EVENTS

Roundtable: McCarthyism Then and Now with Joe Gilford and Julie Halpern; Moderated by Adam Klasfeld

Scratch That–Chalkboard Improv and Poetry with The Strike Anywhere Performance Ensemble and The New **World Waking!–A Song Cycle for Peace** Concept, Music & Lyrics by Steve Schalchlin

An Evening with Vinie Burrows

The Bococa Arts Festival

bococaartsfestival.com

Various Locations; June 18–26, 2010

Interrogation Room by Dru Johnston; Director,, Ray Chao; Cast: Andy Schnecflock, Nikki Gold, Joe Cummings, Griffin DuBois; Produced by Sou Chanhthirath

Orestes 2.0 by Charles Mee; Director,, Marc Stuart Weitz; Cast: Kevin Dedes, Caitlin Talbot, Natalie Hegg, Tovah Suttle, Quinn Mander, Brian Stevens, and Drew Hirshfield; Produced by The Children's Theatre Company–thechildrenstheatrecompany.weebly.com

Podcast Plays by Wendy Burbank, Katie McKenna, Sam Schreiber, Friedrich Durrenmatt; Director,, Sergei Burbank; Cast: Produced by Conflict of Interest Theater Company–conflicttheater.podomatic.com

Stephen King High School: The Musical! Conceived and Composed by Jamie King and Sam Rosenberg with Book and Lyrics by Jamie King; Director,, Jonathan Hopkins; Cast: Sam Rosenberg, Sarah Jane Marek, Kendra Treichler,

Alessandro Colla, Bob Barth, Brianna Tyson, Leal Vona, Jamie King and Chris Montgomery; Produced by The Bococa Arts Festival–www.skhsm.com

The Beard by Michael McClure; Director, Kristyn R. Smith; Cast: Eric Whitten, Kate Russell; Produced by Silent Bugler Productions

COIL Festival

www.ps122.org

P.S. 122; January 5 – 15, 2011

Kim Nobel Will Die by Kim Nobel; UpStairs @ PS 122; January 11–15, 2011

Hello Hi There by Annie Dorsen; UpStairs @ PS 122; January 6–14, 2011

Symptom Produced by The BodyCartography Project; DownStairs @ PS 122; January 7–10, 2011

Rabbi Rabino Produced by Vivi Tellas; DownStairs @ PS 122; January 5–15, 2011

Holiday Produced by Ranters Theatre; DownStairs @ PS 122; January 6–15, 2011

Ouveture Alcina Produced by Teatro Delle Albe; UpStairs @ PS 122; January 5–10, 2011

Stories Left to Tell Conceived and Director, Kathleen Russo and Lucy Sexton; Created from unpublished works of Spalding Gray; Cast: Ain Gordon, Kathleen Chalfant, Hazelle Goodman, Bob Holman, Rich Kind, David Straithairn, Jonathan Ames, Whoopi Goldberg; DownStairs @ PS 122; January 5–11, 2011

A Disaster Begins by Ain Gordon; DownStairs @ PS 122; January 10, 2011

Rumble Ghost by Jack Ferver; UpStairs @ PS 122; January 7–9, 2011

I am Saying Goodnight Produced by Amanda Loulaki & Short Mean Lady; UpStairs @ PS 122; January 7–11, 2011

The FRIGID Festival

frigidnewyork.info

Horse Trade Theatre Group Venues; February 23 – March 13, 2011

Co-Founder and Managing Director, Erez Ziv; Artistic Director, Heidi Grumelot; Bookkeeper, Shula Kaplan and Nicole Gerhing; Publicity, Emily Owens; Webmistress Emleigh Worlf

Fucking Girls by Ben Thompson; Kraine Theatre; February 23–March 6, 2011

Hi, How Can I Help You? by Scout Durwood; Kraine Theatre; February 24–March 5, 2011

JapJAP Produced by Keep It Movin' Productions; Kraine Theatre; February 25–March 6, 2011

Joe: The Perfect Man Produced by Crowning Monkey; Kraine Theatre; February 25–March 6, 2011

Mendacity Produced by Lauren Rayner Productions; Kraine Theatre; March 11, 2011

My Pal Izzy–The Early Life and Music of Irving Berlin Produced by Sisterscene Productions; Kraine Theatre; February 24–March 5, 2011

The Mysterious Mystery of Mystery Street Produced by Blame Your Fate Productions; Kraine Theatre; February 24–March 6, 2011

The Oregon Trail: Quest for the West! Produced by No. 11 Productions; Kraine Theatre; March 12, 2011

Scarlet Woman Produced by SunsetGun Productions; Kraine Theatre; February 23–March 5, 2011

YIPPIE! Produced by The Beggars Group; Kraine Theatre; February 23–March 5, 2011

The Bitter Poet: Looking for Love in All the Wrong Blackbox Performance Spaces Under St. Marks; February 25–March 6, 2011

Funny a trunk show Under St. Marks; February 24–March 6, 2011

I Love You (We're F*#ked) by Kevin Thornton; Under St. Marks; February 24–March 6, 2011

Inside Straight by George Ridgeway; Under St. Marks; February 25–March 6, 2011

A Kind Kind Man Produced by Stasz/Pruitt Productions; Under St. Marks; February 24–March 5, 2011

Oneymoon (A Honeymoon for One) Produced by Dutch Girl Productions; Under St. Marks; February 23–March 3, 2011

Paradise Lost Produced by ACM Productions; Under St. Marks; 40609

Pretty-N-Papi Produced by Awkward at Best; Under St. Marks; February 24–March 5, 2011

Saving Tania's Privates Produced by AJ Epstein Productions; Under St. Marks; 40610

Boatload Produced by Stars and Hearts; Red Room; February 25–March 6, 2011

Fate, Fury and Musical Theatre: A Kind of Cabaret Produced by The Furies Theatre Company; Red Room; March 10, 2011

Goodnight Lovin' Trail Produced by Rising Sun Performance Company; Red Room; March 13, 2011

The Hyperbolist by Joe Mazza; Red Room; February 24–March 6, 2011

The Shorebound Swim With a One Click Kick: A Tragedy of Reason Produced by The Lucky Artist Theater Company; Red Room; February 23–March 6, 2011

There is No Good News by David Mogolov; Red Room; February 24–March 6, 2011

We Might Be Experimenting on You Produced by Collision Productions; Red Room; March 7–8, 2011

Wonder Woman: A How To Guide for Little Jewish Girls by Cyndi Freeman; Red Room; March 10, 2011

Year of the Slut Produced by JJ Rockstar Productions; Red Room; February 24–March 5, 2011

Midtown International Theatre Festival

www.midtownfestival.org

Various Locations; July 12 – August 1, 2010

Executive Director, John Chatterton; Managing Producer, Emileena Pedigo; Senior Artistic Director, Lisa Dozier; Artistic Director for Musicals, Jamibeth Margolis; MITF Co-Artistic Director, Gerald vanHeerden;Artistic Director for Germanic Productions, Dan

A Sweet Word of Advice by Sophia Romma; Director, Sophia Romma; Naomi McDougall Jones as Svetlana Moiseyevna; Tosh Marks as Lieutenant James Perso Arrivederci; Cast: Carolyn Seiff, Allan Mirchin

Alice and Elizabeth's One Woman Show by Alice Barden; The Dorothy Strelsin Theatre; July 16–27, 2010

All Folked Up Written and directed by Joshua R. Pangborn; Artist, Nicholas Keller; Cast: Ron Barba, Anthony Castellano, Danielle Connor, Genevieve Frey, Michele MacShane, Jill Maybruch, Leslie C. Nemet, Mickey O'Sullivan, Stephen Suarez

An Ode to the Washermen by Andre Richardson Hogan II

Asian Belle by Michelle Glick; The Dorothy Strelsin Theatre; July 15–August 1, 2010

Blow by Blow by Jen Forcino; Director, Sally Burtenshaw

Can I Really Date a Guy That Wears a Yamulke? by Amy Holson-Schwartz; Produced by Marc L. Bailin & Holson Productions; The Beckett Theatre; July 17–30, 2010

Civil War Voices Book, James R. Harris; Original Musical Arrangements, Mark Hayes; Produced by Alma Villegas and Bob Ost/Wildly Productive Productions in association with Rough and Ready LLC, Jaye Maynard and Sheila Geltzer; June Havoc Theatre; July 24–August 1, 2010

Closure by Meri Wallace; Director, Arthur French, Duncan Pflaster, Debra Savage, Andrew Rothkin and Karen Raphaeli; Produced by Meri Wallace and Karen Raphaeli; The Main Stage Theaer

Colored People's Time by Leslie Lee; Produced by Negro Ensemble Company; The Beckett Theatre

Conspiracy: A Love Story Book and Lyrics, Victor Lesniewski; Original Music, Ronnie Reshef; Director, Elizabeth Carlson; Cast: Mark Cajigao, Elaine Moran, Eddie Schnecker, Danielle Treuberg; Produced by TrackTwelve Productions; June Havoc Theatre; July 14–21, 2010

Etty by Susan Stein; Director, Austin Pendleton; www.ettyplay.org; The Dorothy Strelsin Theatre; July 17–31, 2010

Fête Written and performedy by Raquel Cion; Director, Cynthia Cahill

Gray Matters by Jacques Lamarre; Director, Joshua Lee Ramos; Cast: Stephen Sherman, April Woodall, Jen Anaya, Kathryn Kates; Produced by Emerson Theater Collaborative–www.emersontheatercollaborative.org; The Main Stage Theater; July 17–31, 2010

Hey Mary! by Bella Poynton

Hot Mama Mahatma by Karen Fitzgerald; Director, Matt Hoverman

How I Became an Astronaut by Fara Greenbaum

How Many Goodbyes Must I Say by Raymond Jones

In Our Own Image by Christopher Heath; Produced by Agony Productions; The Main Stage Theater; July 18–31, 2010

Inside Voices at the Girl Aquarium by Gina Inzunza; Director, Marcus Yi; Cast: Angela Collard, Katya Collazo, Danielle Geeslin, Lotus Huynh, Betty Kaplan, Ingrid Running

Julia and Buddy Written and directed by N. G. McClernan; www.mergatroyd.org

Layla and Harley Together Again by Jonathan Wallace; Director, Jonathan Wallace and Ed Matthews; Cast: Elisa Abatsis, Orion Delwaterman, Tatiana Gomberg, Aaron Kapner, Cinda Lawrence, Ed Matthews, Dave Powers, Ian Roettger; Produced by Howling Moon Cab Company; The Dorothy Strelsin Theatre; July 14–31, 2010

Literary Disruption by James V. O'Connor; Director, Paula Riley; June Havoc Theatre; July 19–August 1, 2010

Love Humiliation Karaoke by Enzo Lombard; Produced by DQDI Productions; The Dorothy Strelsin Theatre; July 29–August 1, 2010

Love Me Tinder by Martin Dove; Produced by Mike Reardon and Write Paths Studio; The Main Stage Theater; July 21–August 1, 2010

Love Stinks by Kate Rader; Director, Gary Cavello

Lovers Book, Music and Lyrics by Christopher Massimine; Director, Christopher M. Czyz; Will Taylor, Courtney Hammond; Produced by Massimine, Roytman & Presentations; The Beckett Theatre; July 15–August 1, 2010

Magdalena's Crossing by Carolyn Nur Wistrand; Director, Elena Araoz; Choreographer, Carlos A. Cruz Velázquez; Cast: Flor Bromley, Jennica Carmona, Gabriel Gutiérrez, Cary Hite, Adriana Llabrés, Clem McIntosh, Melinda Peinado, Alejandra Piñeiro, Aamira Welthy, Natalie Woolams-Torres

Merrily Merrily Merrily by Becca Schlossberg; Director, Madeleine Rose Parsigian; Produced by Robert Intile Jr. and Alina Gutierrez; June Havoc Theatre

Most Likely To: The Senior Superlative Musical Book, Music and Lyrics by Michael Tester; Director, Abbe Gail Cross; Cast: Andrew J. Beck, Gina Marie Bilardi, Amanda Castanos, Alexander Greif, Christopher Hlinka, Katherine Hoffmann, Steven Liberto, Lyle Colby Mackston, Melissa Rapelje, Lauren Renner, Sarah Sixt, Matthew Walsh, Jesse Zeidman; Produced by Broadway Clubhouse–www.broadwayclubhouse.com; The Beckett Theatre; July 16–31, 2010

Never Norman Rockwell by Kyle Baxter; Director, Anthony Gargano; Cast: Elizabeth Allerton, Sarah Barry, Paul Bellantoni, Dan Belmont, DR Mann Hanson, Austin Mitchell, Michael Selkirk; Produced by The Collective Objective; The Beckett Theatre

Once Upon a Mama

Peking Roulette by Ben Thompson; Director, Anna Grace; Composer, Michelangelo Sosnowitz; Production Stage Manager, Kelly Vieau; Assistant Stage Manager, Chad Helmer; Cast: Kim Williams, Kristen Hung; The Dorothy Strelsin Theatre; July 15–31, 2010

Prevailing Wins by Robin Bond; Director, Michele Pace; Produced by Divine Productions, in association with Strings Attached Theater Company; June Havoc Theatre; July 14–27, 2010

ResurGENTS: The Reappearance of Hope by Damion Sanders and Lawrence Floyd; Produced by Obsidian Media Group; June Havoc Theatre; July 12–August 1, 2010

Screenplay by Scott Brooks; Director, Jenny Greeman; Jonathan Sale, Diana De La Cruz, Heather Dilly, Scott Brooks; Produced by Badlands Theatre Co.; The Main Stage Theater; July 17–31, 2010

Searching for Soula by Marisa Petsakos; Director, Don Bill

Stonewall by Jase Egan; Director, Brett Miro

Tallish Tales by Amy Kitzhaber; Adapted for the Stage by Amy Kitzhaber, based on the book "Slovenly Betsy" by Dr. Heinrich Hoffman; The Dorothy Strelsin Theatre

Ten Reasons I Won't Go Home With You Book, Kelly Nichols; Lyrics, Bobby Cronin, Jason Purdy, Andrew Byrne, and Blake Hackler; Music, Alan Bukowiecki, Bobby Cronin, Jason Purdy, Andrew Byrne, Steven Silverstein, and Phillip Chernyak; Produced by Burning Nickels Productions, Phil Newsom Productions & Michael Roderick–; June Havoc Theatre; July 17–29, 2010

The Burning by Lori Fischer; Director, Melissa Maxwell; Cast: Bonnie Barrios, Christina Ghubril, Miguel Govea, and America Soli Pabon

The Gospel According to Josh Written and performed by Joshua Rivedal; Director, Joshua Gaboian; Produced by –www.thegospelaccordingtojosh.com; The Dorothy Strelsin Theatre; July 16–August 1, 2010

The Hyenas Got It Down by Daniel Damiano; Director, Aaron Gonzalez; Daniel Damiano

The King of Bohemia: The Life and Times of Franz Kafka by Jeffrey Boles; Produced by Jeffrey Boles and ReniGraef Productions; The Main Stage Theater; July 17–August 1, 2010

The Reunion Plays by J. Boyett

The Starship Astrov by Duncan Pflaster; Produced by Oberon Theatre Ensemble; The Beckett Theatre; July 17–31, 2010

The Tragedie of Cardenio by Ben Bartolone; Produced by Brain Trust Productions; June Havoc Theatre; July 22–28, 2010

Three American Women by Lori Marra; Directed; June Havoc Theatre

Til Death Do Us Part? by Daniel Jean; Director, Fulton C. Hodges

Until We Find Each Other by Brooke Berman; Director, David Winitsky; Produced by MSK Productions; The Main Stage Theater; July 20–August 1, 2010

Visionaries: A Night of Two Shorts by Vivian Vertes; Director, Dina Epshteyn; Cast: Amelia Anderson, Janet Dunson, and Larry Greenbush

What Makes You Think I Want To Talk To You? by Martin Joseph; Director, Carl Ford; The Dorothy Strelsin Theatre

READINGS AND WORKSHOPS

Becoming Kinky by Ted Swindley; Director, Jamibeth Margolis; Produced by Ted Swindley Productions Inc.

Blacks and Whites Written and directed by Phillip W. Weiss; Produced by Phil's Literary Works LLC

For the Duration by Ross Berger; Produced by Amy Fogelman

Hadleyburg Lyrics, Mae Richard; Music, John Cliffon; Book, Bob Griffiths; Director, Gerald vanHeerden; Produced by VMHF Theatricals

Miss Pell is Missing by Leonard Gershe; Director, Daniel Haley; Produced by Wildcat Theatricals

Rising by Carolyn Nur Wistrand; Director, Marie McKinney; Produced by Negro Ensemble Company

Safari's Song Written and directed by Catherine Owens-Herrmann; Produced by Owens-Herrmann Entertainment LLC

Soleda Red and Yellow by Raymond Jones; Director, Charles Weldon; Produced by Negro Ensemble Company

New York International Fringe Festival

fringenyc.org

Various Locations; August 13 – 29, 2010

Producing Artistic Director, Elena K. Holy; President, Board of Directors, Shelley Burch; Festival Administrator, Britt Lafield; Festival Technical Director, Gregg Bellon; Venue Production Coordinator, Scott D. Mancha and Maggie Sinak; Operations Manager, John Trevellini

(UN)Natural by Conceived by Richard Hess; Director, Richard Hess; Produced by The Lost Theatre–www.un-naturaldisaster.com; ; August 14–27, 2010

12 Incompetent Men (And Women!) by Ian McWethy; Director, Jeff Glaser; Produced by –www.12incompetentmen.us; SoHo Playhouse; August 18–29, 2010

23 Feet in 12 Minutes: The Death and Rebirth of New Orleans by Mari Brown; Director, David Travis; Produced by Word on the Street Productions–www.wordonthestreetplays.org; Players Loft; August 23–29, 2010

3boys by Becca Schlossberg; Director, Madeleine Rose Parsigian; Produced by Merrily3 Productions–www.3boysnyc.com; 4th Street Theatre; August 22–28, 2010

Abraham's Daughters by Elissa Lerner; Produced by Danish Duck Productions–www.abrahamsdaughterstheplay.com; SoHo Playhouse; August 15–28, 2010

Ah Kua Show by Leona Lo; Director, Richard Chua; Produced by Talk Sense Pte. Ltd.–www.ahkuashow.wordpress.com; The Club @ LaMaMa; August 21–26, 2010

AK-47 Sing-Along by Samara Weiss; Director, Lucy Cashion; Produced by ERA–www.ak47singalong.com; HERE Mainstage Theater; August 13–21, 2010

All Day Suckers by Susan Dworkin; Director, Jessica Bauman; Produced by New Feet Productions and Adam Blanshay; The Robert Moss Theatre; August 19–28, 2010

Alligator Summer by Dylan Lamb; Director, Robert Ribar; Produced by Limelight Productions–www.alligatorsummer.blogspot.com; The Robert Moss Theatre; August 14–23, 2010

Alternative Methods by Patricia Davis; Director, Josh Liveright; Produced by Patricia Davis Productions–www.alternativemethodstheplay.com; First Floor Theatre @ LaMama; August 15–28, 2010

The Altoona Dada Society Presents The Velvet Gentleman by Jon Steinhagen; Director, Kevin P. Hale; Produced by Playlab NYC–www.playlabnyc.org; Studio at Cherry Lane Theater; August 13–26, 2010

American Gypsy by Ben Whiting; Director, Alexander Marshall; Produced by MagicMouth Theatre Company–www.magicmouth.org; The Kraine Theatre; August 22–29, 2010

Amsterdam Abortion Survivor by Micha Wertheim; www.michawertheim.nl; SoHo Playhouse; August 13–27, 2010

And a Wake-up by Megan Condit; Director, Bruce Faulk; Produced by S&G Productions–www.andawakeup.com; The New School for Drama Theatre; August 15–23, 2010

Art of Attack by Asa Merritt; Director, Joshua Brody; Produced by The Cadre–www.artofattackplay.com; First Floor Theatre at LaMaMa; August 18–27, 2010

As I Am Fully Known by Emily Rieder; Director, Andrew Oswald; Produced by The 8'oClocks–www.the8oclocks.com; First Floor Theatre at LaMaMa; August 14–29, 2010

As You Like It by William Shakespeare; Director, Greg Thornton; Produced by BAMA Theatre Company–www.bamatheatrecompany.org; Connelly Theater; August 17–28, 2010

Bagabones by Jonathan Nosan; www.bagabonestheshow.org; First Floor Theatre at LaMaMa; August 13–26, 2010

Banshee of Bainbridge by Jim Tierney; Director, Diánna Martin; www.bansheeofbainbridge.com; The Robert Moss Theatre; August 13–27, 2010

Baristas by Evan Twohy; www.baristasplay.com; The Kraine Theatre; August 15–28, 2010

The Battle of Spanktown by Jeffrey Pfeiffer; Director, Heidi Handelsman; Produced by The Potluck–www.thebattleofspanktown.tumblr.com; August 14–27, 2010

The Beatitudes by Justin Allen; Choreographer: Melanie Cortier; Produced by Eidolon Ballet–www.thebeatitudes.weebly.com; August 14–20, 2010

The Boogyman Thumbs A-1-A by Carl Holder, Carter Hudson and Eddie Prunoske; Director, Eddie Prunoske; Produced by Glass Bandits–www.gbtheater.com; The New School for Drama; August 14–22, 2010

Tiny Geniuses by Emily Feldman; Director, Jay Briggs; Produced by Bourbon Barrel Ensemble–www.tinygeniuses.tumblr.com; HERE Mainstage Theater; August 13–24, 2010

Bunked!: A New Musical by Alaina Kunin and Bradford Proctor; Director, Seth Sikes; Original Music: Bradford Proctor; Produced by Kunin Productions–www.bunkedthemusical.com; Lucille Lortel Theatre; August 17–25, 2010

Burning In China by Gary Moore; Director, Caleb Deschanel; Produced by Dark Light Theater–www.burninginchina.com; 4th Street Theatre; August 17–28, 2010

Butterfly, Butterfly, Kill Kill Kill! by Patrick Harrison; Director, Patrick Harrison; Original Music, Dave Harrington; Choreographer Adam Scott Mazer and Ian Picco; Produced by Depth Charge–www.depthcharge.us; First Floor Theatre at LaMaMa; August 13–19, 2010

By Hands Unknown by Kym Gomes; Director, Harvey Huddleston and Kym Gomes; Produced by BravaCompany/Chelsea Rep LAB–www.byhandsunknown.com; The New School for Drama Theatre; August 13–19, 2010

Cats Don't Grin Written and directed by Francois Carre; www.francoiscarre.com; Studio at Cherry Lane Theater; August 13–28, 2010

Classically Trained, Practically Broke Franca Vercelloni in collaboration with Myrna E. Duarte and John David West; Director, Myrna E. Duarte and John David West; Produced by Monkey With A Knife Productions–www.classicallytrainedpracticallybroke.com; The Club @ LaMaMa; August 14–28, 2010

The Conveniences of Modern Living Conceived, Developed and Created by Daniel John Kelley and Emily Plumb; Director, Emily Plumb; Produced by Jilted Pigeon Productions–www.conveniencesofmodernliving.weebly.com; Players Theatre; August 17–28, 2010

Cookie by Chad Beckim; Director, Janet Bobcean; Produced by 61 Academy in Association with Partial Comfort Productions–www.cookietheplay; The Robert Moss Theatre; August 19–27, 2010

Daddy Day Produced by Bert Hana–www.berthana.nl; First Floor Theatre @ LaMama; August 13–18, 2010

Dear Harvey by Patricia Loughrey; Original Music, Thomas Hodges; Produced by Diversionary Theatre–www.diversionary.org; SoHo Playhouse; August 20–28, 2010

Did You Do Your Homework? Written and performed by Aaron Braxton; www.aaronbraxton.com; Players Loft; August 14–26, 2010

Dream of the Marionettes / Le Rêve des Marionettes by Johanna Divine and Christy Leichty; Director, Steven Cooper and Christy Leichty; Original Music: Johanna Divine and Daniel Coolik, Choreographer: John Vincent; Produced by Les Marionettes Productions–www.dreamofthemarionettes.com; The Ellen Stewart Theatre @ LaMaMa; August 26, 29, 2010

Driving the Saudis by Jayne Amelia Larson; Director, Charlie Stratton; www.drivingthesaudis.info; SoHo Playhouse; August 15–27, 2010

Energy Man by Ramon Sanchez; Director, Heather McAllister; Produced by Hope Theatre, Inc.–www.myspace.com/hopetheatre; The Cherry Pit; August 16–28, 2010

Eternity in an Hour by Tim Bruce (after the works of William Blake); Director, Eric Loren and Monia Giovannangeli; Original Music Victor Vertunni, Choreographer: Monia Giovannangeli and Marja Merisalo; Produced by Theatre of Eternal Values–www.eternityinanhour.info; The New School for Drama theatre; August 13–22, 2010

Evan O'Television in Double Negatives by Evan O'Sullivan; Produced by O'Television Productions–www.evanotv.com; HERE Dorothy B. Williams Theatre; August 19–28, 2010

Faster Than the Speed of White by Pushkar Sharma and Sathya Sridharan; Original Music Chuck Kim;

Produced by Brownstar–www.brownstarrevolution.com; 4th Street Theatre; August 20–26, 2010

Faye Lane's Beauty Shop Stories by Faye Lane; Director, Jay Rogers; www.BeautyShopStories.com; The Club @ LaMaMa; August 14–23, 2010

Feed the Monster by Stephanie Ehrlich; Director, Michael Roderick; www.feedthemonstershow.com; The Club @ LaMaMa; August 14–26, 2010

Flesh-Light Stories by Rod Nash; Director, Michel Chahade; Produced by Open Source Theater–www.OSTHEATER.com; The New School for Drama Theatre; August 18–26, 2010

For the Kingdom of Fatherland by Shabana Rehman; Director, Stephen Rosenfeld; Produced by Shabana Rehman in Association with American Comedy Institute–www.shabana.no; The New School for Drama Theatre; August 13–24, 2010

For the Birds by Siobhan Donnellan; Produced by Blue Wren Collective—www.bluewrencollective.com; Studio at Cherry Lane Theatre; August 21–28, 2010

The Fourth Estate by Glenda Frank; Director, Rebecca Hengstenberg; www.glendafrank.com; The Cherry Pit; August 17–25, 2010

Friends Like These by Gregory Crafts; Director, Sean Fitzgerald and Vance Roi Reyes; Produced by Theatre Unleashed—www.friendsliketheseplay.com; The Cherry Pit; August 24–28, 2010

Friends of Dorothy: An Oz Cabaret by Rita MenWeep and Scot Marshall; Director, Megan Doss; Produced by Conatus Productions—www.conatusproductions.com; The Ellen Stewart Theatre @ LaMaMa; August 16–22, 2010

Garage by Dive Theatre; Director, Michael Hogwood; Produced by Dive Theatre—www.divetheatre.com; 4th Street Theatre; August 14–29, 2010

Gate B23 Written and directed by Debbie Slevin; Produced by Greymatters Productions; Tom Noonan's Paradise Factory; August 14–21, 2010

Get Rich Cheating by Jeff Kreisler; Director, Anne Teutschel; Produced by Up Top Productions—www.GetRichCheating.com; SoHo Playhouse; August 15–27, 2010

Getting Even with Shakespeare by Matt Saldarelli; Director, Laura Konsin; Produced by Self Fulfilling Productions—www.gettingevenwithshakespeare.com; Players Theatre; August 14–27, 2010

The Order of Blattaria, A Kid's Guide to Survival Written and directed by Michael Wulffhart and David Herbelin; Original Music: Karl Jaecke, Choreographer: David Herbelin; Produced by Arimaw Productions—www.TheOrderOfBlattaria.com; ;

Ghost of Dracula by Kenneth Molloy, based on characters created by Bram Stoker; Director, Daniel Johnsen; Produced by Colby Day Productions; Connelly Theater; August 13–29, 2010

A Gilgl Fun a Nigun (The Metamorphasis of a Melody) by I. L. Peretz; Director, Pascal Holtzer; Produced by Le Theatre en l'Air/Der LuftTeater—www.lufteater.com; 4th Street Theatre; August 14–24, 2010

The Girl in the Park by Matt Owen; Produced by Dalliance Theater—www.DallianceTheater.com; Players Theatre; August 18–28, 2010

GirlPower: Survival of the Fittest Director, Ashley Marinaccio, Elizabeth Koke and Jessica Greer Morris; Produced by Project Girl Performance Collective and Co-Op Theatre East—www.projectgirlperformancecollective.org; The Robert Moss Theatre; August 15–26, 2010

Good Good Trouble On Bad Bad Island by Joshua Mikel; Director, Chad Larabee; Produced by Endstation Theatre Company—www.endstationtheatre.org; The Robert Moss Theatre; August 16–28, 2010

The Great Galvani Written and directed by Shawn Reddy; Produced by The Magpies—www.themagpiesproject.com; Players Loft; August 18–29, 2010

Ground To Cloud Written and directed by Christine Marie; Produced by Christine Marie and Ensemble—www.CimiMarie.com; The New School for Drama Theatre; August 19–26, 2010

Group by Daniel McCoy; Director, Heidi Handelsman; Produced by Crosstown Playwrights; The Kraine Theatre; August 13, 27, 2010

The Guardian's Author Written and directed by Thomas D. Praino; www.theguardiansprojectauthor.blogspot.com; 4th Street Theatre; August 14–29, 2010

Hamlet Shut Up Story by William Shakespeare, Adapted by Jonas Oppenheim and the Ensemble ; Director, Jonas Oppenheim; Original Music: Josh Senick; Produced by Sacred Fools Theater Company—www.hamletshutup.com; First Floor Theatre @ LaMama; August 14–21, 2010

Hamlettes by Patrick Shaw; Director, Lillian Meredith; Produced by FullStop Collective—www.fullstopcollective.org; The Cherry Pit; August 14–28, 2010

Happy Birthday, Mom Written and directed by Meghan Gambling; Produced by Teaspoon Productions—www.happybdaymom.biz; The Cherry Pit; August 13–19, 2010

Have a Nice Life Music and Lyrics, Conor Mitchell; Book, Matthew Hurt; Director, Bill Felty; Musical Director, Tom Brady; Choreographer, Nancy Berman Kantra; Produced by Nice People Theatre Company—www.nicepeopletheatre.org; Lucille Lortel Theatre; August 20–22, 2010

Headscarf and the Angry Bitch by Zehra Fazal; www.zehrafazal.com; Studio at Cherry Lane theatre; August 13–20, 2010

Hearts Full of Blood by James Asmus; Director, Andrew Hobgood; Produced by The New Colony—www.thenewcolony.org; HERE Mainstage Theater; August 24–29, 2010

The Height of the Eiffel Tower by Morgana O'Reilly; Director, and Co-Creator Abigail Greenwood; Produced by Rambunctious Productions—www.rambunctious.co.nz; 4th Street Theatre; August 13–18, 2010

Hello, I Must Be Going by Albi Gorn; Director, Alan Fox; Produced by M&M Productions Acting Company, Inc. ; Tom Noonan's Paradise Factory; August 14–19, 2010

Heron & Crane by Kirk German; Director, Kirk German & Heather Huggins; Original Music: Travis Cooper; Choreographer Lisa del Rosario; Produced by DA! Theatre Collective—www.datheatrecollective.org; Studio at Cherry Lane; August 18–21, 2010

Heterosexuals by Lee Papa; Director, Mark Creter; Produced by Up Top Productions in Association with the Rude Pundit—www.heterosexualstheplay.blogspot.com; The Cherry Pit; August 17–25, 2010

high five by Angela Hanks; www.highfiveplay.webs.com; The Cherry Pit; August 13–27, 2010

Hip Hop High-The Musical by Z-Man and Cindy Topps; Director, Jana Mattioli and Z-Man; Music and Lyrics: Z-Man; Choreographer: Jonah Biddle and Shani Alston; Produced by Z-Man Films and Records—www.hiphophighthemusical.com, The Ellen Stewart Theatre @ LaMaMa; August 13–28, 2010

How Alfo Learned to Love Women by Vincent Amelio; Director, Kathleen Bishop; Produced by Broken Bat Productions—www.howalfolearnedtolovewomen.blogspot.com; Connelly Theater; August 14–26, 2010

How My Mother Died of Cancer, and Other Bedtime Stories by Chris Kelly; Director, Laura Moss; Produced by Robert Intile Jr. and Alina Gutierrez in association with The Dreamscape Theatre—www.cancerplay.com; Robert Moss Theatre; August 13–22, 2010

The Hurricane Katrina Comedy Festival by Rob Florence; Director, Dann Fink; Produced by Batture Productions—www.KatrinaComedy.net; SoHo Playhouse; August 13–29, 2010

The Hyperbolist by Joe Mazza; Director, Dan Kerr-Hobert, Joe Mazza and Susan Ask; Produced by bang-bang-fou!—www.joemazza.org; HERE Dorothy B. Williams Theatre; August 14–27, 2010

I am what I am not Choreographer: Gessica Paperini and Marjolayne Auger; Produced by The New Young Choreographers—www.imwhatimnot.blogspot.com; August 14–25, 2010

In Loco Parentis by Michael DeVito; Director, Jonathan Warman; www.inlocoparentisplay.com; 4th Street Theatre; August 14–28, 2010

In the Schoolyard by Paulanne Simmons; Original Music: Rachel Kaufman; Lyrics: Paulanne Simmons; Director, James Martinelli; www.intheschoolyard.com; The Ellen Stewart Theatre @ LaMaMa; August 19–29, 2010

I Don <3 U Ne Mor by Daren Taylor; Director, John Hurley; Original Music: Frank Grullon and Cathy Thomas; Produced by The Awakening Project—www.idonheartUthemusical.com; Lucille Lortel Theatre; August 22–28, 2010

Insurmountable Simplicities by Roberto Casati and Achille Varzi; Adapted by Natalie Glick; Director, Natalie Glick; www.insimplicitiesplay.com; ; August 16–29, 2010

An Idiot by Jeff Tabnick; Adapted fro Doestoevsky's The Idiot; Director, Eric Nightengale; Produced by Propinquity Productions–www.propinquityproductions. com; The Kraine Theatre; August 14–28, 2010

Interfaith by Martin D. Hill, with Jen Ryan, RikSansone, Mike MacEachern; Produced by Understanding with The Rev. Bill & Betty; Really Christian Broadcasting Network–www.revbillandbetty.com; The Robert Moss Theatre; August 19–29, 2010

Invader? I Hardly Know Her by Jason Powell; www.invaderihardlyknowher. com; SoHo Playhouse; August 14–28, 2010

Jen and Liz in Love by Jesse Weaver; Director, Lory Henning; Produced by BrunetteRedhead Productions–www.bbrproductions.org; The Kraine Theatre; August 18–28, 2010

Jew Wish Written and performed by Rachel Eckerling–www.jewwishtheshow. com; Players Theatre; August 14–20, 2010

Julius Caesar: The Death of a Dictator Based on text by William Shakespeare; Adapted by Orson Welles; Director, Leon Shanglebee; Original Music:Metallica; Choreographer: Nicole Langevin; Produced by The Gangbusters Theatre Company–www.gangbusterstheatre.com; HERE Mainstage Theater; August 14–22, 2010

Jurassic Parq: The Broadway Musical by Emma Barash, Marshall Pailet, Bryce Norbitz and Steve Wargo; Director, Marshall Pailet; Choreographer: Hayley Podschun; www.JurassicParq.blogspot.com; The Ellen Stewart Theatre @ LaMaMa; August 20–27, 2010

Just in Time–Judy Holliday Story by Bob Sloan; Director, Bob Sloan; www. thejudyhollidaystory.com; SoHo Playhouse; August 15–28, 2010

Lemonade: A Play of World Domination by Jais Brohinsky; Director, David Denson; www.lemonadetheplay.com; Tom Noonan's Paradise Factory; August 13–21, 2010

Lenny's Dead by Alex Giacin; Director, John Long; Produced by Goshen Players–www.goshenplayers.org; The Kraine Theatre; August 15–26, 2010

Letters to Clio-Part II, Margarita by Jennifer S. Jones; Director, Jessica Lefkow; Produced by LTC Productions–www.letterstoclio.com; Studio at Cherry Lane Theatre; August 14–27, 2010

Living on the Edge Written, Directed and Choreographed by Nadia Lesy; Produced by Bullettrun–www.bullettrun.com; The Ellen Stewart Theatre @ LaMaMa; August 13–22, 2010

Lost and Found by John Pollono; Director, Andrew Block; Produced by Rogue Machine Theatre–www.lostandfoundplay.com; The Cherry Pit; August 16–27, 2010

Love in the Time of Swine Flu: A comedyabout sex, dating andeverything else terrifying by Derek Dupuy, CJ Hunt, Mike Spara, Grace Blakeman and Alison Phillips; Produced by Stupid Time Machine–www. stupidtimemachine.com; ; August 13–21, 2010

MacChin: The Lamentable Tragedie of Jay Leno Written and directed by Zachary Stewart; Produced by The Hamburger Theatre Company–www.macchin. tumblr.com; Players Theatre; August 14–27, 2010

The Mad 7 -A Mystical Comedy with Ecstatic Dance by Yehuda Hyman; Director, Mara Isaacs; Choreographer: Yehuda Hyman; Produced by The Mad 7 Team–www.themad7.com; 4th Street Theatre; August 13–29, 2010

Made in Taiwan by Michelle Krusiec; Director, Andy Belser; www. michellekrusiec.com/mit.html; The New School for Drama Theatre; August 14–24, 2010

Magical Exploding Boy by Dean Evans; Produced by Chicago Physical Theater–www.magicalexplodingboy.com; 4th Street Theatre; August 13–27, 2010

The Maid of Orleans by Friedrich Schiller; Director, Pamela Wilkinson; Translated and Adapted by Pamela Wilkinson; Produced by Demimonde Theatre & Opera Co.–www.themaidoforleans.com; Connelly Theater; August 14–27, 2010

Manon/Sandra by Michel Tremblay; Director, Pia Furtado; Produced by The Theory of Everything–www.thetheoryofeverything.co.uk; The New School for Drama Theatre; August 14–20, 2010

Marilyn Monroe: wouldn't it be fascinating Written and directed by Erik Zambrano; Produced by Zambrano Tomorrow–www.erikzambrano.com; The New School for Drama Theatre; August 14–26, 2010

Masks Written and directed by Terryl Daluz and Mann Alfonso; Produced by Masks Productions–www.masksproductions.com; The Kraine Theatre; August 21–29, 2010

A Matter of Choice by Chad Beckim; Director, Alicia Dempster and T.C. Burtt; Produced by Freed Purple Monkey Theatrics–www.freedpurplemonkeytheatrics. com; SoHo Playhouse; August 13–21, 2010

The Means by Kirk White; Director, Jim Wren; Produced by Plaid Wall–www. letuskillyou.com; SoHo Playhouse; August 14–28, 2010

Menny and Mila Book, Music and Lyrics by Paul Schultz; Director, Sofia L. Geier; Choreographer: Kate Scott ; Produced by Rosetree Productions; Lucille Lortel Theatre; August 17–28, 2010

Miss Kim by Gina Kim and Ryan Tofil; Director, Matthew Corozine–www. misskimtheplay.com; Players Theatre; August 13–27, 2010

Miss Magnolia Beaumont Goes to Provincetown by Joe Hutcheson; Director, Cheryl King; Produced by Cheryl King Productions–www. MissMagnoliaBeaumont.com; Studio at Cherry Lane Theatre; August 14–26, 2010

The Mission by Jules Tasca; Director, KenTerrell; Produced by Curan Repertory Company–www.curan.org; The Kraine Theatre; August 17–24, 2010

Missionary Position Written and performed by Steven Fales; Produced by gEveryman Productions–www.mormonboy.com; SoHo Playhouse; August 14–27, 2010

Mobius by Michael Lopez-Saenz; Produced by Emmett Productions–www. mobiustheplay.com; HERE Mainstage Theater; August 14–25, 2010

The Momentum by Boo Killebrew, Geoffrey Decas O'Donnell, Jordan Seavey and TJ Witham; Produced by CollaborationTown–www.collaborationtown.org; The Robert Moss Theatre; August 14–28, 2010

Monetizing Emma by Felipe Ossa; Director, Leah Bonvissuto; Produced by Thackeray Walsh LLC–www.monetizingemma.com; HERE Mainstage Theater; August 14–25, 2010

The Morning After/The Night Before Book, Music, and Lyrics by Jeff Bienstock; Director, Diana Glazer; Produced by Cracked Windshield Productions–www.tmatnb.com; Lucille Lortel Theatre; August 18–28, 2010

My Broken Brain by Michael Hirstreet; Developed and Director, Leah Benavides; Produced by DreamStem Productions–www.michaelhirstreet.blogspot.com; Players Loft; August 14–28, 2010

My Three Moms Written and performed by Virginia Bryan; Director, Leslie Collins; Produced by –www.mythreemomstheshow.com; Players Loft; August 15–28, 2010

My Dad's Crazier Than Your Dad: A Scientific Inquiry by Katharine Heller; Director, Nell Balaban; Produced by Dragonchase Inc.–www.mydadscrazier.com; August 13–27, 2010

My Name is Ruth Written and directed by Claire Porter; Produced by The 34 West Theater Company–www.34west.org; Connelly Theater; August 15–22, 2010

Namely, Muscles Produced by –www.cportables.com; 4th Street Theatre; August 14–20, 2010

The Nightmare Story by Alex Falberg, Arya Shahi, Ben Ferguson, Curtis Gillen, Daniel Weschler, Matt Nuernberger, Ryan Melia; Produced by PigPen Theatre Co.–www.PigPenTheatre.com; The club @ LaMaMa; August 13–21, 2010

No One Finer Than Frank Shiner by Sinead Daly; Director, Danielle Kourtesis; Produced by The Ladies of Caos–www.ladiesofcaos.wordpress.com; Studioat Cherry Lane Theatre; August 16–28, 2010

Omarys Concepcion Lopez Perez Goes to Israel (to speak to God at the Wailing Wall) by Leila Arias; Produced by –www.leilaarias.com; Players Loft; August 13–29, 2010

One Thumb Out by Tom MacLachlan; Director, Zoe Carides; Produced by Kitta Cunningham Productions–www.onethumbout.com; The Robert Moss Theatre; August 25–29, 2010

Open Heart Written and directed by Joe Salvatore; Produced by Joes & Co.–www.openhearttheplay.com; The First Floor Theatre @ LaMaMa; August 19–29, 2010

The Order of Blattaria, A Kid's Guide to Survival Written and directed by Michael Wulffhart and David Herbelin; Original Music Karl Jaecke ; Produced by Arimaw Productions–www.TheOrderOfBlattaria.com; August 25–29, 2010

Our Condolences by Lauren Olson; Director, Rachel Hamilton; Produced by –www.ourcondolencestheshow.com; Studio at Cherry Lane Theatre; Agust 14–28, 2010

Over and Over Written and directed by Tim Aumiller; Produced by No Hope Productions–www.nohopeproductions.com; Studio at Cherry Lane Theatre; August 18–28, 2010

Over There by PJ Walsh; Director, Dion Flynn; Produced by 60 Miles North Productions–www.overtheresoloshow.com; Players Theatre; August 13–25, 2010

P.O. by Scott Klavan; Director, Ian Streicher; Produced by Buddy-Pal Productions–www.pofringeplay.com; The Kraine Theatre; August 13–28, 2010

Passchendaele by John Rafter Lee; Director, Jonathan Winn and Jessica McVea; Produced by Thesia Arts–www.passchendaele.org; The Robert Moss Theatre; August 14–28, 2010

A Personal Warstories of a Mumbai Terror Attacks Written and directed by Divya Palat; Produced by Balancing Act Productions–www.divyapalat.net; August 15–22, 2010

Perspectives Choreographer: Stephanie Dixon, Mary Beth Leigh, Tamora Petitt and Karen Voyles; Produced by Deliquescent Designs–www.deliquescentdesigns.com; ; August 13–21, 2010

Picking Palin Written and directed by Stephen Padilla; Produced by A Family Affair Films–www.pickingpalin.com; Connelly Theater; August 13–28, 2010

Picture Incomplete, A New Musical! Book and Lyrics: Trent Armand Kendall; Music and Lyrics Michael Polese; Director, Greg Ganakas; Music Director and Arrangements: Adam Klipple; Choreographer Greg Ganakas and Trent Armand Kendall ; Produced by Onemoe Music, LLC–www.pictureincomplete.com; The club @ LaMaMa; August 13–27, 2010

The Pig, The Farmer, and The Artist by David Chesky; Director, A. Scott Parry; Conductor: Anthony Aibel; Produced by –www.davidchesky.com; The Ellen Stewart Theatre @ LaMaMa; August 18–28, 2010

Pigeons, Knishes and Rockettes by Diana Rissetto; Director, Ilana Becker; Produced by –www.pigeonsknishesandrockettes.com; The Cherry Pit; August 14–24, 2010

Platinum Book and Lyrics by Will Holt & Bruce Vilanch; Director, Ben West; Original Music: Gary William Friedman; Choreographer: Rommy Sandhu; Produced by UnsungMusicalsCo. Inc.–www.PlatinumTheMusical.com; Lucille Lortel Theatre; August 17–21,2010

Playing By Air Director, Jacob Weiss; Produced by –www.playingbyair.com; ; August 20–28, 2010

Pope! An Epic Musical Written and Lyrics by Justin Moran; Director, Greg Moran; Original Music: Christopher Pappas; Music Director: Adam Podd; Produced by Louder, Faster, Better!–www.popethemusical.com; Lucille Lortel Theatre; August 21–28, 2010

Prey by Scott Decker; Director, Geoffrey Cantor; Produced by Red Rope Productions–www.preytheplay.com; The Kraine Theatre; August 14–24, 2010

The Princes of Persuasion by Ithai Benjamin & Rebeca Raney; Director, Ithai Benjamin; Produced by Recipes For Romance–www.princesofpersuasion.com; HERE Dorothy B. Williams Theater; August 14–26, 2010

Protected Written and directed by Timothy Scott Harris; Produced by Algonquin Productions–www.protectedtheplay.com; Connelly Theater; August 13–27, 2010

Questions My Mother Can't Answer by Andrea Caban; Director, Rachel Eckerling; Produced by Coyote REP Theatre Company–www.questionsmymothercantanswer.com; 4th Street Theatre; August 15–27, 2010

A Raisin in the Salad: Black Plays for White People by Kevin R. Free; Director, Christopher Burris; Produced by Bryan E. Glover in association with P4:13, Inc.–www.blackplaysforwhitepeople.com; Players Theatre; August 13–23,2010

Rash by Jenni Wolfson; Director, Jen Nails; Produced by Jennikins Productions–www.rashsolo.blogspot.com; HERE Dorothy B. Williams Theater; August 13–28, 2010

Return to the Onion Cellar Written and directed by Samantha Boyd–www.ReturnToTheOnionCellar.com; The Ellen Stewart Theatre @ LaMaMa; August 14–27, 2010

Richard 3 by William Shakespeare; Adapted and Director, James Presson; Produced by Less Than Rent Productions–www.LessThanRentProductions.com; The Ellen Stewart Theatre @ LaMaMa; August 14–20, 2010

Rites of Privacy by David Rhodes; Director, Charles Loffredo; Produced by Moving Parts Theater–www.ritesofprivacy.com; HERE Dorothy B. Williams Theater; August 14–28, 2010

The River Valeo by Trey Tatum; Director, Bridget Leak; ; Cast: ; Produced by DOG P!SS Theatre Company–www.therivervaleo.com; The Kraine Theatre; August 15–29, 2010

Ruby Wilder by Brooke Allen; Director, Eric Hoff; Produced by Not Waiting Productions–www.notwaiting.intuitwebsites.com; The Robert Moss Theatre; August 13–18, 2010

Running by Arlene Hutton; Director, Beth Lincks and Lori Wolter; Produced by The Journey Company–www.arlenehutton.com; The Cherry Pit; August 13–20, 2010

Saving Throw Versus Love by Larry Brenner; Director, Dann Fink; Produced by Rhetorical Question Players–www.savingthrowvslove.viviti.com; Players Theatre; August 15–24, 2010

Scared Skinny: a one (hundred pound lighter) woman show by Mary Dimino; Director, Lisa Milinazzo; Produced by Small Pond Entertainment–www.scared-skinny.com; Tom Noonan's Paradise Factory; August 13–21, 2010

The Scavenger's Daughter by Colm Magner; Produced by Ar Dair Dog and Drama Co.–www.thescavengersdaughter.org; 4th Street Theatre; August 19–28, 2010

The Secretaries by Maureen Angelos, Babs Davy, Dominique Dibbell, Peg Healey and Lisa Kron; Director, Mark Finley; Produced by TOSOS–www.thesecretariestosos.com; Lucille Lortel Theatre; August 20–29, 2010

A Separate Peace by John Knowles; Director, Jason McConnell Buzas; Adapted by Brian Foyster; Produced by Running Horse Productions–www.aseparatepeace.info; Connelly Theater; August 15–28, 2010

Shaheed: The Dream and Death of Benazir Bhutto by Anna Khaja; Director, Heather De Michele; Produced by Off-Chance Productions—www.ShaheedThePlay.com; ; August 13–28, 2010

Shh! by Theo Goodell, A. Nora Long and Dawn M. Simmons; Director, A. Nora Long; Produced by New Exhibition Room—www.newexhibitionroom.org; The Cherry Pit; August 26–28, 2010

Shine: A Burlesque Musical by Cass King, John Woods, Sam Dulmage; Director, Roger Benington; Produced by The Wet Spots—www.shinemusical.com; The Ellen Stewart Theatre @ LaMaMa; August 14–28, 2010

South Beach Rapture by David Caudle; Director, Michelle Bossy; Produced by The Plum—www.southbeachrapture.com; ; August 15–25, 2010

South Pathetic by Jim David; Director, Peter Smith; Produced by New Conservatory Theatre Center Of San Francisco/Trash de Blanc—www.jimdavid.com; Tom Noonan's Paradise Factory; August 14–21, 2010

Spellbound-A Musical Adventure Written, Music, Lyrics and Orchestrated by Paul Deakin & Christian De Gré; Produced by Mind The Art Entertainment & Robert R. Blume—www.SpellboundTheMusical.com; The Ellen Stewart Theatre @ LaMaMa; August 15–27, 2010

Squeeze the Dollar, Change Your Life by Sigal Shoham; Director, David Ford; Studio at Charry Lane Theatre; August 14–23, 2010

Stand Fast by Ron Brawer & Tom Wirtshafter; Director, Michael Page; Produced by Barrow Street Productions; HERE Mainstage; August 13–26, 2010

Standing Up: Bathroom Talk & Other Stuff We Learn From Dad by Tracey Conyer Lee; Director, Kevin R. Free; Produced by Only40Entertainment—www.tleestandingup.blogspot.com; Players Theatre; August 17–28, 2010

Strange Love in Outer Space by Janyia Antrum; Director, Christopher Mirto; Original Music, Nick Morgan; Produced by The Contasia Players—www.strangeloveinouterspace.com; The Cherry Pit; August 14–23, 2010

Stripes: The Mystery Circus by Sarah Hayward, in collaboration with Marguerite Witvoet; Director, Johanna Mercer; Music Director, Marguerite Witvoet; Choreographer, Tara Cheyenne Friedenberg; Produced by Wayward Productions—www.sarahhayward.ca; Studio at Cherry Lane Theatre; August 20–28, 2010

The Swearing Jar by Kate Hewlett; Director, Rosemary Andress; Music and Lyrics, Kate Hewlett; Arrangement, Christopher Stanton; Produced by The Bridge Theatre Company in Association with 6AM Tango Productions—www.thebridgetheatrecompany.com; Connelly Theater; August 14–29, 2010

Swaha: Rituals of Union Choreographer, Guru Durga Charan Ranbir, Guru Kelucharan Mohapatra, Taiis Pascal-Charles; Director, Taiis Pascal-Charles and Leena Mohanty; Produced by Trinayan Dance Theater—www.trinayan.org/swaha; ; August 15–22, 2010

T-O-T-A-L-L-Y! Written and Choreographed by Kimleigh Smith; Director, Paula Killen; Produced by T-O-T-A-L-L-Y! KimLeigh Productions—www.totallykimleigh.com; ; August 18–28, 2010

Tangled Yarn by Anais Tekerian, Kevork Mourad; Director, Kevork Mourad; Produced by Tangled Lines Productions—www.tangledyarn.net; 4th Street Theatre; August 15–26, 2010

Terms of Dismemberment: A Musical with Heart…and Other Body Parts Book & Lyrics, Dorothy Marcic ; Director, Hinton Battle; Original Music, Frank Sanchez, Lyrics and Music, Mehr Mansuri; Assistant Director, Kenneth Ferrone; Produced by Dr. Dorothy Productions—www.termsofdismemberment.com; Lucille Lortel Theatre; August 18–28, 2010

Terror SuperHighway by Kevin McHatten; Director, James Phillip Gates; Produced by Roust Theatre Company—www.RoustTC.com; Studio at Cherry Lane Theatre; August 14–27, 2010

the tim&micah project: Selection Written, Directed and Choreographed by tim&micah; Produced by the tim&micah project—www.timandmicahproject.com;

The Robert Moss Theatre; August 20–29, 2010

The Timing Of A Day by Owen Panettieri; Director, Joey Brenneman; Produced by Mind The Art Entertainment—www.mindtheartentertainment.com; 4th Street Theatre; August 18–28, 2010

Together This Time Book, Zac Kline; Original Music, Andrew Heyman; Lyrics, Andrew Heyman and Zac Kline; Produced by —www.togetherthistime.com; Lucille Lortel Theatre; August 18–26, 2010

Trick Boxing Written, Directed and Choreographed by Megan McClellan and Brian Sostek; Produced by Sossy Mechanics—www.SossyMechanics.com; Connelly Theater; August 15–26, 2010

Tristan & Isolde by Josie Peterson; Director, Josie Peterson and Lio Sigerson; Produced by The Shore Theater—www.theshoretheater.com; Connelly Theater; August 17–28, 2010

The Twentieth-Century Way by Tom Jacobson; Director, Michael Michetti; Produced by The Theatre @ Boston Court—www.tinyurl.com/Twentieth-Century; Players Theatre; August 14–24, 2010

Two Girls Written and performed by Gabrielle Maisels; Director, Joey Brenneman; Produced by —www.gabriellemaisels.blogspot.com; Connelly Theater; August 19–25, 2010

Two Sizes Too Small by Jessica Kane; Produced by YMMSBILYA Productions—www.twosizestoosmall.com; The club @ LaMaMa; August 13–25, 2010

UBA Bounce Directed and Choreographed by Eva Dean; Produced by Eva Dean Dance—www.evadeandance.org; ; August 15–28, 2010

Venus and Mona by Leslie Bramm; Director, Melissa Attebery; Fight Choreographer, Carrie Brewer; Produced by Three Crows Theatre—www.venusandmona.com; The Kraine Theatre; August 15–27, 2010

Veritas by Stan Richardson; Director, Ryan J. Davis; Produced by Ryan J. Davis, Stan Richardson, and Nathan Vernon—www.VeritasThePlay.com; HERE Mainstage Theater; August 20–28, 2010

Violators Will Be Violated by Casey Smith; Director, Jennifer A. Skinner; Produced by Circle X Theatre Co.—www.violatorswillbeviolated.com; Players Loft; August 15–28, 2010

Viva La Evolucion! by Diana Yanez; Director, Marjorie Duffiled; Developed by Diana Yanez, Marjorie Duffield; Cast: Diana Yanez; Produced by AtomicTuna Productions & Travel Large—www.vivalaevoluciontheshow.com; SoHo Playhouse; August 19–29, 2010

Vinnie Vidivici Written and directed by Vince Santoro; Produced by Panther Canyon Productions—www.vincesantoro.com; The club @ LaMaMa; August 23–28, 2010

Viva Los Bastarditos! by Jake Oliver; Produced by Jake Oliver (Productions)—www.bastarditos.com; The Ellen Stewart Theatre @ LaMaMa; August 14–24, 2010

Wanton Displays of Affection by Zach Smilovitz; Director, Yael Kiken, Zach Smilovitz & Liam White; Produced by University of Michigan's Basement Arts—www.wantondisplays.com; The Cherry Pit; August 13–25, 2010

War Zones Written and directed by Laura Brienza; Produced by—www.warzonestheplay.com; HERE Dorothy B. Williams Theater; August 13–24, 2010

West Lethargy Written and directed by Stephen Kaliski; Produced by Page 121 Productions—www.page121productions.org; The Kraine Theatre; August 18–26, 2010

When Last We Flew by Harrison David Rivers; Director, Colette Robert; Produced by DRD Theatricals & Eric Louie—www.WhenLastWeFlew.com; Lucille Lortel Theatre; August 19–29, 2010

When Lilacs Last Written and directed by Tony Devaney Morinelli; Produced by —www.whenlilacslast.com; Connelly Theater; August 22–29, 2010

William and the Tradesmen by Eli James; Director, Francesco Campari; Produced by —www.williamandthetradesmen.com; The club @ LaMaMa; August 14–25, 2010

A Woman of no Distinction Written and directed by Claire Fleury–www.clairefleury.com; Studio at Cherry Lane Theatre; August 16–23, 2010

New York Musical Theatre Festival

www.nymf.org

September 27–October 17, 2010

Executive Director & Producer, Isaac Robert Hurwitz; Director of Programming, Mike Cohen; Director of Development, Scott Pyne; Director of Operations, Lynn Spector; General Manager, Jeremy Youett; Associate General Manager, Kim Shaw

Above Hell's Kitchen Book, Music, and Lyrics by Jonathan Spottiswoode

Bloodties Book, Music, and Lyrics by Ned Massey

Fellowship! Book by Kelly Holden-Bashar and Joel McCrary; Music by Allen Simpson; Lyrics and Additional Material by Brian D. Bradley, Lisa Fredrickson, Kelly Holden-Bashar, Joel McCrary, Edi Patterson, Steve Purnick, Cory Rouse, Allen Simpson, Ryan Smith, Peter Allen Vogt, and Matthew Stephen Young

Fingers and Toes Book, Music, and Lyrics by Logan Medland

Frog Kiss Book and Lyrics by Charles Leipart; Music by Eric Schorr; Based on the Stephen Mitchell novella The Frog Prince

The Great Unknown Book by William Hauptman; Music and Lyrics by Jim Wann

The History of War Book by Chip Zien; Music by Deborah Abramson; Lyrics by Amanda Yesnowitz

I Got Fired: A Semi-Autobiographical Sort-of-True Revenge Musical Book, Music, and Lyrics by Keith Varney

Jay Alan Zimmerman's Incredibly Deaf Musical Book, Music, and Lyrics by Jay Alan Zimmerman

The Most Ridiculous Thing You Ever Hoid Book by Andy Seiler, Jim Beckerman, and Fred Wemyss; Lyrics by Jim Beckerman and Andy Seiler; Music by Jim Beckerman

My Mother's Lesbian Jewish Wiccan Wedding Book, Music, and Lyrics by David Hein and Irene Carl Sankoff

Nighttime Traffic Book, Music, and Lyrics by Alex Wyse

Pandora's Box Book by Maria S. Schlatter; Music and Lyrics by Glen Roven; Based on the film Gazon Maudit

Petrouchka Concept by Matthew Neff; Music by Michelangelo Sosnowitz; Directed and Choreographed by Matthew Neff

POPart: The Musical Book and Lyrics by Daryl Lisa Fazio; Music by Aaron McAllister

Shine! The Horatio Alger Musical Book by Richard Seff; Music by Roger Dean Anderson; Lyrics by Lee Goldsmith

Show Choir! – The Musical Book, Music, and Lyrics by Donald Garverick and Mark McDaniels

Special Letter Book and Lyrics by In Seon Park; Music by Chang Wook Ma

The Tenth Floor Book by Sara Cooper; Music and Lyrics by J. Sebastian Fabal

Tess, a new rock opera Book, Music and Lyrics by Annie Pasqua; Additional Book, Music, and Lyrics by Jenna Pasqua; Based on Tess of the d'Urbervilles by Thomas Hardy

Therapy Rocks Book by Kaethe Fine, Nat Bennett and Karen Bishko; Music and Lyrics by Karen Bishko

Things As They Are Book and Lyrics by John Dietrich; Music by Jonathan Comisar

Trails Book by Christy Hall, Music by Jeff Thomson; Lyrics by Jordan Mann

Trav'lin Book by Allan Shapiro and Gary Holmes; Music and Lyrics by J.C. Johnson and friends

V-Day Book, Music, and Lyrics by David Rossmer and Steve Rosen

Vote for Me: A Musical Debate Book, Music, and Lyrics by Scott Elmegreen and Drew Fornarola

Without You by Anthony Rapp, featuring Music and Lyrics by Jonathan Larson

READINGS AND WORKSHOPS

8Minute Musicals

Beautyfull Book by Jill Jaysen; Music and Lyrics by Mark Shepard; Conceived by Jill Jaysen and Jena Wider

If It Only Even Runs a Minute Conceived by Kevin Michael Murphy and Jennifer Ashley Tepper

My Life: Today Book by Zakiyyah Alexander, Lisa Danser, Sara Patterson and Jeff Statile; Music by Steven Jamail; Lyrics by Steven Jamail and Sara Patterson

Oklahomo: The Adventures of Dave and Gary Book, Music, and Lyrics by Jesse Gage

Our Country Book by Dan Collins, Music and Lyrics by Tony Asaro; Based on an original concept by Tony Asaro

Water and Power Book and lyrics by Jeff Lantos; Music by Bill Augustine

Food on the Aisle Book and Lyrics by Donna Kaz, Music by Gerald Stockstill

Most Likely to Die Book and Lyrics by Christopher Barnes; Music by Ryan Mercy

Roofless Book, Music and Lyrics by Tim Long and Jerome Johnson

Planet Connections Theatre Festivity

planetconnections.org

Various Locations; June 3–27, 2010

Executive Director/Artistic Curator, Glory Kadigan; Assistant Associate Director, Andi Cohen; Assistant Managers: Allison Brzezinski, Amber Gallery, Chaz Graytok, Jesse Edward Rosbrow, Lisa Kopitsky, Bonnie Gleicher, Ross Baum, Box Office Staff, Shawn Ban

11 Seconds of Esctasy Written and directed by Rol Escudero; Produced by ETdC Projects' Lab Production; The Robert Moss Theater; June 8–22, 2010

4 1/2 Hours: Across the Stones of Fire by Jeff Biggers; Director, Stephanie Pistello; Produced by Coal Free Future Project; The Gene Frankel Theatre; June 4–13, 2010

A Brown Monkey Goes to McDonald's Written and performed by Sahil Farooqi; Director, Regie Cabico; The Gene Frankel Theatre; June 11–23, 2010

A Dream About Sunflowers by Jonathan Wallace; Director, Amber Gallery; Produced by Howling Moon Cab Company; The Gene Frankel Theatre; June 10–26, 2010

Are You There Zeuz? It's Me, Electra Written and directed by Aliza Shane; Bleecker Street Theatre; June 2010

BJ: A Musical Romp Book & Lyrics by Peter Dagger, Original Music, Eric Leboe; Director, Matt Britten; Produced by Peter and Matt's Production Company; The Gene Frankel Theatre; June 15–25, 2010

Cake by Felipe Ossa; Director, Leah Bonvissuto; Green Room Theatre; June 2010

Clandestine by Glory Boewn, Ann Gillespie, Alex Goldberg, Duncan Pflaster, Nandita Shenoy and Jonathan Wallace; Director, Luke Harlan, Cindy N. Kawasaki, Rachel Klein, Michael Schwartz; Cast: Teisha Bader, Rosebud Baker, Luciana Faulhaber and Mariel Matero; Produced by NewGround Theatre Company; The Gene Frankel Theatre; June 3–20, 2010

Danny Written and directed by Andrew Rothkin; Produced by White Rabbit Theatre & Kim M. Jones; Green Room Theatre; June 3–27, 2010

Decadent Acts Written and directed by Ashley Marinaccio; Produced by Co-op Theatre East; The Robert Moss Theater; June 15–24, 2010

Dig & Be Dug: The Gospel of Lord Buckley Written and performed by Ryan Knowles; Director, David Kraft; Produced by Interprod Theatre; The Gene Frankel Theatre; June 3–15, 2010

Down the Rabbit Hole Written and performed by Erin Jividen; Director, Angela Astle; Produced by EJ Rocks/Erin Jividen; The Robert Moss Theater; June 3–14, 2010

Fox Tales by Gabrielle Fox; Director, Tony Howarth; The Gene Frankel Theatre; June 3–20, 2010

Give Till It Hurts Book, Music & Lyrics by Dorothy Marcic; Director, Hinton Battle; Produced by Dr. Dorothy Productions; The Robert Moss Theater; June 4–26, 2010

Good Lonely People by Carol Carpenter; Director, Dianna Martin; Produced by MTWorks; The Robert Moss Theater; June 4–26, 2010

Green! Produced by The Mistake and The Icky House Club; The Gene Frankel Theatre; June 8–26, 2010

His Beauty by Ashley Jacobson; Director, Nadine Friedman; The Gene Frankel Theatre; June 5–26, 2010

Hourglass by Richard L. Gaw; Director, Rose Ginsberg; The Gene Frankel Theatre; June 4–17, 2010

One Hand Clapping Written and directed by Adam Samtur; The Gene Frankel Theatre; June 4–17, 2010

I Don't Want to Hurt Your Feelings Written and directed by Emma Koenig; The Robert Moss Theater; June 5–13, 2010

Liner Notes by John Patrick Bray; Director, Erin Smiley; Produced by (re:) Directions Theatre Company; The Robert Moss Theater; June 3–25, 2010

Love Me by Jason Grossman; Director, Daryl Boling; Produced by Funny…. Sheesh Productions; The Robert Moss Theater; June 10–25, 2010

Made for Each Other by Monica Bauer; Director, John Fitzgibbon; The Robert Moss Theater; June 13–26, 2010

Manhattan Project by Ricardo Garcia; Translated by Adolfo Perz Alvarez, Directed and Designed by Oscar A. Mendoza, Musical Director, Xavier Paez Haubold; Produced by Mush-room Theatre Design; The Robert Moss Theater; June 6–23, 2010

Recovery by Mark J. Williams; The Gene Frankel Theatre; June 17–26, 2010

Scherzo by David Alex Andrejko; Director, Ellen Orenstein; Produced by Blueprint Theatre Project ; The Robert Moss Theater; June 3–26, 2010

Small Bites: A Smorgasbord of One-Act Comedies Written and Direced by J.C. Svec; Produced by Tribe Productions; The Gene Frankel Theatre; June 16–26, 2010

Sunrise, Sunset or Breakfast with Julia Written and performed by Julia Sandra Rand; Director, Nicole Potter; Produced by Diva Duo; The Gene Frankel Theatre; June 12–21, 2010

Tess, A New Rock Opera Music and Lyrics by Annie Pasqua and Jenna Pasqua; Produced by Big Lady Productions; The Robert Moss Theater; June 9–22, 2010

The Green Knight by Brian Rady; Director, Jeremy Bloom; Green Room Theatre; June 2010

The Picture of Dorian Gray by Oscar Wilde; Adapted for the Stage and Director, Glory Bowen; Produced by G-Money Productions; The Robert Moss Theater; June 5–21, 2010

The Riverside Symphony Produced by Ignited States Production Company; The Robert Moss Theater; June 5–26, 2010

The Six Month Cure by Lenny Schwartz; Director, Norah Turnham; Produced by Daydream Theatre Company; The Gene Frankel Theatre; June 18–20, 2010

The Thyme of the Season Written and directed by Duncan Pflaster; Produced by Cross-Eyed Bear Productions; The Gene Frankel Theatre; June 5–23, 2010

The Untitled Project Conceived by Calla Videt; The Gene Frankel Theatre; June 4–13, 2010

Uncle Shelby's Wunderpantry of Possibilities Produced by Shelby Company; The Gene Frankel Theatre; June 6–26, 2010

War Crimes by Sergei Burbank; Director, Sara Wolkowitz; Produced by Conflict of Interest Theatre Company; The Robert Moss Theater; June 10–20, 2010

Women on Love Written and Musical Direction by Katya Stanislavskaya; Director, Marlo Hunter; The Gene Frankel Theatre; June 7, 2010

American Cow Girl Written and performed by Lauren Marie Albert; The Gene Frankel Theatre; June 8, 2010

Another Place Written and directed by Melissa F. Moschitto; Produced by The Anthropologists; The Robert Moss Theater; June 24, 2010

Cat Gets Credit Card! by William Butler; Director, Richard Butler; The Robert Moss Theater; June 21, 2010

In The Wilderness by John Kearns; Produced by Boann Books & Media, LLC; The Robert Moss Theater; June 15, 2010

Laurie Deacon and The Night Caller Written and directed by Sean Gill; Produced by Junta Juliel Productions; The Robert Moss Theater; June 17, 2010

Married Plus One by Dorothy Marcic; Director, Michelle BestThe Robert Moss Theater; June 22, 2010

Prostate Dreams by Sal Phoenix Atlantis; The Robert Moss Theater; June 16, 2010

Revolution Book and Lyrics by Anne Berlin; Original Music, Andy Cohen; Director, Valentina Fratti; Produced by Krazy Kat; The Robert Moss Theater; June 10, 2010

Samuel French Inc. Off-Off-Broadway Short Play Festival

oob.samuelfrench.com; Lion Theater; July 13–18, 2010; Included: *#4* by Harley Adams; *A Map of Our Country* by Andrew Kramer; *The Tragic Death of Emily Brown* by Mohammad Yousuf; *Antipasto* by Bryan Harnetiaux; *The Bear (A Tragedy)* by E.J.C. Calvert; *Black Meat* by Trey Tatum; *Caution* by Lauren Yee; *Christians Having Sex in Silence* by Paul David Young; *Climb the Smallest Mountain* by Michael Gordon Shapiro; *The Complicated* by Jessica Lafrance and Andrew L. Smith; *The Concrete Wall* by J.C. Svec; *Dance Lessons* by Josh Koenigsberg; *Delphinium Mansion* by Libby Leonard; *A Different Kind of Animal* by Thomas Higgins; *Europeans Kiss on Three Cheeks* by Tom Grady; *Facing the Window* by Tom Matthew Wolfe; *Fan-Boy* by Megan Sass; *Flood* by Kirby Fields; *For the Winter* by Michael Ross Albert; *Gun Metal Blue Bar* by K. Frithjof Peterson; *A*

History of Kites by Josh Beerman; The Incident Report by EM Lewis; Knuckleheads by James McLindon; Laid Plans by Josh Sohn; The Magician and the Memory by Michael Vukadinovich; Mind Control by Debbie Lamedman; The More-Than One by Rebecca Lynne Fullan; The Mud is Thicker in Mississippi by Dennis A. Allen II; The Peacekeeper by Edward Pomerantz; The Pen is Mightier by Joshua Cole; Perfect Weather by Eric Fallen; Pigskin by Gabriel Dean; Schwartz! (Hansel und Gretel) by J. Julian Christopher; Skin Deep by Mary Lynn Dobson; Smart Phone by Nick Jones; Ugly Couples in Los Angeles by Cameron Michael Porsandeh; What Dies Inside Us While We Live by Jessica Hinds; White Embers by Saviana Stanescu; Wipe Away by Mark Snyder; Ya Heard Me by Daniella Shoshan

Shortented Attention Span's 2010 Horror Festival

Players Theatre; October 7–24, 2010; Produced by Shortened Attention Span–www.shortenedattentionspan.com; Included: Lizzy Bugs Boogie by John DiBenedetto; Greyhound by Will Snider; Visitation Rites by Jerome Schwartz; Love Stinks by J. Boyett; A Cougars Tale by Adriana Spencer and Erin E. McGruff; Bye, George by Charles Messina; See Saw Kill by Michael Bradley Block; Lonesome Devil by Ben Lewis; TMZ: Too Many Zombies by Jamie King; Devil and the Cleaner by Robert LoManto; Lady and The Vamp by Stacy Davidowitz; Curiosity by Mim Granahan; Wolf Manhood by David Williams; [death]match.com by Erin Moughon; Prom Night of The Living Dead by Anna Grace and Kris Chung

Strawberry One Act Festival

Produced by Riant Theatre–www.therianttheatre.com

Summer 2010 Theatre at St. Clement's; August 12–22, 2010; Included: Fireman Written and directed by Stephen Brown; The Handback Click-Clack Girls Written and directed by Anthony Fusco ; Why They Came by Jessica Hinds; Director, Lucia Peters; Beyond Open Lines by Emmanuel Fleischmann; Director, Mark Bloom; Blind Sided by Cynthia Talia Ferri; Director, Jonathan Libman; The Meteor Season Written and directed by Keaton Weiss; Mirror,Mirror Written and directed by Norman Weinstein; Dream Wedding! by Ellen Orchid; Director, Whitney Aronson; Curveball by Brendan Burke; Director, Sarah V. Michelson; The Session by Chris Ferretti; Director, Julie Wallach; Hiroshi – Me, Me, Me by Natalie Menna; Day Dreams by Paul Trupia; Director, Becky Copley; Soul of a Poet by Isaac Shapiro; Directed Heather Arnson; Toast with Champale by Veronica Newton; Director, Ali Ayala; Close to Home Written and directed by Jonathan Cook; The Assessment by J.M. Eisenman, Justin Shapiro; The Benevolents Written and directed by Devin Doyle; Summer Breezes in the City of the Dead by Lucas T. Syed; Adult Books by Jonathan Ashley; Gay Haiku by Samuel Perwin; Director, Mary Birnbaum; Heroes Written and directed by Joseph Lizardi; Playing the Game by Holly Hunt; Director, Susan Tromans; Simply Me A musical with Mitchell Robert; Musical Director, Albee Barr; The Audition by Leroy Antonio Edwards; Director, Carol Kostendiech; Relationship Court by Sergio Solorzano; Director, Sergio Solorzano and Adam Brome; The Losing Game by Kristen Seavey Cards; Home Sweet Home Written and directed by Eljon Wardally; Something Like Penquins by Levi Wilson; Director, Mario Corry; Taste of Bad Medicine by John Vitkovich; Heart Slam by David Risk; Gentleman and Scholar by John Martin; Director, Nat Habib

Winter 2011 The Hudson Guild Theatre; February 7–12, 2011; Included: Create Me Pegasus by Amy E. Witting; Cast: Billy Weimer, Elanna White; Waiting for Obama: A Night At the Hall of Presidents by Caitlin Tegart; Director, Neil W. Casey; Cast: Timothy Dunn, Winton Noel, Ben Rameaka, Michael Hartney, Matt Fisher, John Murray, Will Hines; The House of Fallen Snow by Merridith Allen; Cast: Marie Anello, Kristina Erikson, Robert L. Haber, Andrew Pigott, Aristotle Stamat; Punching Glass by Amanda Idoko; Cast: Lavita Burr, Amanda Idoko, Madalyn McKay, Rosemary Thomas; The Weekend by Josie Parrelli; Obituary Blues by Von H. Washington Sr.; My Mom is a Sex Therapist Written and performed by Cara Maltz and Stephan Varnier; Thank you Ten by Mara Wilson; Clown Love by

Carla Ching; Cast: Michael Swartz, Ricardo Perez Gonzalez, Amanda Boekelheide; Home Movies by Lee Eypper; Director, Sarah Henkins; Mismatched Socks by Melissa Kuch; Three Smart Fellows by Arthur S. Brown; Nighthawks by Daniel Alexander Tobin; Status: A music drama for the digital age by Brian Myers; The House of Fallen Snow by Merridith Allen; The Rookie by Bob Zaslow; Pieces of No Traveler by Penny Pollak; Salamander Stew by Michael Fixel; Director, Juliet Fixel; A Matter of Choice by Paul Trupia; Winter Flowers by Lily Rusek; Director, Heather Arnson; Always Faithful by Joseph Lizardi; Waiting Written and directed by Yael Gidron; The River view by Stephen G. Martin; The Third Pulpit by Ed Stever; Bryan and Kim by Adam Delia; Conkers by Holly Hamilton; When the Bed Bugs Bite by Terry M. Sandler; Standing on Ceremony by Laurence C. Schwartz; The Bridge by Rick Charles Mueller; Cast: Kaelin Birkenhead, Rick Koch,Rick Charles Mueller, Seth Rosenfeld; Broken by Greg Redlawsk; Sarah's Blood by Rebekah L. Pierce; WerQ! The Dragsical by Ashton Pina

UndergroundZero Festival (4th Annual)

PS 122; July 6 – 25, 2010

Produced by East River Commedia–eastriver.org

LA Party by David Barlow; Conceived and Director, Phil Soltanoff

The Ring Cycle: Part 1 Director, Dave Dalton; Produced by Performance Lab 115

Father of Lies Directed and Adapted by Jose Zayas

The Adventures of Alvin Sputnik: Deep Sea Explorer Created and Performed by Tim Watts; Produced in association with terraNOVA Collective

The National Diet of Japan Director, Cole Wimpee; Produced by Aztec Economy

The Last Burlesque Show in the World Presented by Pinchbottom Burlesque; Produced by Collective: Unconscious

Half Awake and Falling Through the Sky by Mercedes Murphy and Heather Benton; Conceived and Director, Mercedes Murphy

Marriage of Convenience Written and directed by Ian Rowlands; Performed by Christian Conn

Quiet To Departure Choreographed and Performed by Leigh Evans

Aspettando Nil (Waiting for Nil) Conceived and Director, Faviana Iacozilli; Produced by Lafabbrica Compagnia

Are We Here Yet? Director, Anna Brenner

The Concretes (after Vladimir Sorokin) Director, Alexandru Mihaescu; Produced by Green Hours Theater

Creating Illusion Written and performed by Jeff Grow; Director, Jessi D. Hill; Produced in association with terraNOVA Collective

The Human Voice (La Voix Humaine) by Francis Poulenc; Director, Shoshona Currier; Performed by Kristina Wilson

Polanski by Saviana Stanescu, Director, Tamilla Woodard; Preformed by Grant Neale

Blue Dress Reduction by Eliza Bent, Jasmin Hoo and Elizabeth Stevenson; Director, Meghan Finn

The Parting Glass by Dermot Bolger; Produced by Axis Ballymun in association with terraNOVA Collective

From Dawn till Night (The Earth is Uninhabitable Like the Moon) Director, Doris Mirescu; Produced by Dangerous Ground Productions

Forever Art Director, Johanna Zielinski; Produced by Theater Bielefeld

Tales of the Body Director, Tomeu Gomila; Produced by Au Ments Theater Company; Original Music, Kiko Barrenengoa and Mariano Torres

AutoMotive (American Trilogy part 1) Director, Paul Bargetto; Produced by East River Commedia

Broke Wide Open Written and performed by Rock Wilk, Director, Tamilla Woodard

Under the Radar Festival

www.undertheradarfestival.com

Various Locations; January 5 – 16, 2011

Artistic Director & Producer, Mark Russell; Associate Artistic Producer, Meiyin Wang

Ameriville Written, Created and Performed by UNIVERSES; Developed and Director, Chay Yew; Cast: Steven Sapp, Mildred Ruiz, Gamal Chasten, William Ruiz; The Public Theatre; January 5–16, 2011

Being Harold Pinter Adapted and Director, Vladimir Shcherban; Producer, Nikolai Khalezin and Natalia Koliada; Produced by Under The Radar and LaMaMa–www.lamama.org; LaMaMa; January 5–16, 2011

Bonanza Produced by STUK, Vooruit, KVS; Robert Moss Theatre; January 6–16, 2011

Correspondances Created by Kettly Noël and Nelisiwe Xaba; The Public Theatre; January 7–16, 2011

Dutch A/V by Reggie Watts; LaMaMa; January 5–16, 2011

Gob Squad's Kitchen (You've Never Had It So Good) Creaded by the Gob Squad; Produced by Under The Radar, LaMaMa, Gob Squad, Volksbuehne am Rosa-Luxemburg-Platz Berlin–www.lamama.org; LaMaMa; January 6–8, 2011

Jump by David Greenspan; Director, JoAnne Akalaitis; Performed and Composed by Nora York; The Public Theatre; January 11–15, 2011

Living In Exile by Jon Lipsky; Director, Christopher McElroen; Cast: T Ryder Smith; Presented in Assocation with LaMaMa–www.lamama.org; LaMaMa; January 6–16, 2011

Phobophilia Cast: Stephen Lawson and Aaron Pollard; Produced by HERE; HERE Arts Space; January 5–10, 2011

Show Your Face Produced by Under The Radar and LaMaMa, Betontanc and Umka LV–www.lamama.org; LaMaMa; January 10–11, 2011

The Interminable Suicide of Gregory Church by Daniel Kitson; Produced by St. Ann's Warehouse–www.stannswarehouse.org; St. Ann's Warehouse; January 6–16, 2011

The Walk Across America for Mother Earth by Taylor Mac; Director, Paul Zimet; Produced by La MaMa and The Talking Band–www.lamama.org; LaMaMa; January 15–16, 2011

Too Late! Antigone (contest #2) Devised and Director, Enrico Casagrande and Daniela Nicolò; Silvia Calderoni and Vladimir Aleksic; www.publictheater.org; The Public Theatre; January 6–15, 2011

Vice Versa Based on Cock and Bull by Will Self; Producer, Les Subsistances; Sophie Cattani, Antoine Oppenheim, François Sabourin; January 6–15, 2011

Vision Disturbance by Christina Masciotti; Director, Richard Maxwell; Cast: Linda Mancini and Jay Smith; Produced by New York City Players; Abrons Arts Center Henry Street Settlement; January 12–14, 2011

Watch Me Work Conceived and Performed by Suzan-Lori Parks; The Public Theatre; January 5–16, 2011

Watt by Samuel Beckett Director, Tom Creed; Texts from the novel selected by Barry McGovern; Cast: Barry McGovern; The Public Theatre; January 6–16, 2011

Your Brother. Remember? Conceived, directed, edited, performed by Zachary Oberzan; January 5–16, 2011

ADDITIONAL INDEPENDENT PRODUCTIONS

Balls! The Testosterone Plays by Monica Bauer; Director, John D. FitzGibbon; Cast: Aaron Gonzalez, Nick Ruggeri, John Fico; Workshop Theater; November 20–December 5, 2010

Be a Good Little Widow by Bekah Brunstetter; Director, Stephen Brackett; Cast: Jill Eikenberry, Chad Hoeppner, Jonny Orsini, Wrenn Schmidt; Ars Nova; May 2–14, 2011

A Creed for Those Who Have Suffered by Camilla Maxwell; Director, Stephanie Staes; Cast: Ralph Aiken, Anna Frankl-Duval, Danai Epithymiadi, Meredith Hackett, Eric Johnston, Adriana Llabres and Jonathan Schlieman; Manhattan Repertory Theatre; July 11–15, 2010

Etiquette Unraveled by Lake Simons and Chad Lynch; Director, Chad Lynch; Lighting, Ayumu Saegusa; Cast: Lake Simons; Red-Space; February 5 – 13, 2011

The Hail Mary Plays: Singing Adonis & Fade to Black by Chuck Orsland; Director, Lawrence Frank & Gary Filsinger; Cast: Flint Beverage, Margaret Champagne, Jessica Alexandra Green, Jeff Greene, Monica Jones, Tony White, Elizabeth Allerton,Collin Biddle, Mike Durell, Molly Evensky, Matthew Salmela; Studios 353; March 4–25, 2011

Night Moves by Joseph Coyne; Director, Joe Paradise; Producer, Robert Bryson; Michael Chekov Theatre; March 3 –8, 2011

Now Repeat in Steinese by Gertrude Stein; Director, Ryan Bronz, Kurt Braunohler, Heidi Carlsen, Andrew Frank, Mark Grenier, Drew Pisarra, Laura Sheedy; Producer, Drew Pisarra; Under St Marks; June 1–29, 2010

Odysseus DOA Written and directed by Stephen Svoboda; Production Stage Manager, Mark Mocahbee; Lighting, John Czajkowski; Set, Michiko Kitayama; Costumes, Kristi McKay; Sound and Visual Effects Designer, Stephen Svoboda; Cast: Laura Austin, John Bixler, Binaifer Dabu, Brett Davenport, Maha McCain, Kate Metroka, Adam Perabo, Darian Sundberg, Temar Underwood, Nathan Young; Lion Theatre; March 16 – 21, 2011

Stretch Marks by Angela Kariotis; Director, Florinda Bryant; Cast: Angela Kariotis; www.angelakariotis.com; Stage Left Studio; May 12–June 9, 2011

You Shouldn't Be Here Written and performed by Kelly Dwyer; Under St Marks; February 23–March 6, 2011

PROFESSIONAL REGIONAL COMPANIES

Top: The Company of Much Ado About Nothing *at the Alabama Shakespeare Festival (photo by Phil Scarsbrook)*

Center: Elizabeth Bunch and Todd Waite in the Alley Theatre's Pygmalion *(photo by T. Charles Erickson)*

Bottom: Luke Robertson, Jimi Kocina, Veronika Duerr, and Lakisha Michelle May in Spoon Lake Blues *at Alliance Theatre (photo by Greg Mooney)*

In Living Color

By Rob Weinert-Kendt, Associate Editor, *American Theatre* magazine

It would be presumptuous and premature to pronounce the 2010-11 regional theatre season as the one that at last reflected a post-racial America, but there is a good case to be made that American theatres are at last starting to look more like the country they serve, both backstage and at the front of the house. Indeed, the diversity evident in the American theatre this past season—not only ethnic but aesthetic—represents a distinct step forward from 1990s-style multiculturalism, in which the tendency was to attempt to give each under-represented group its own compartment and fiefdom. This was the model employed, for instance, by Los Angeles' influential Center Theatre Group, which had separate developmental labs for Asian, black, and Latino artists.

One of those departments was run in its heyday by Singapore-born playwright/director Chay Yew (*Porcelain*, *A Language of Their Own*), who spent the better of last season as a freelance director, helming a Hurricane Katrina-themed piece called *Ameriville* by the hip-hop theatre ensemble Universes at Bethesda, at Maryland's Round House Theatre, as well as directing various productions in his home base of New York City. But at season's end, he was named artistic director of Chicago's Victory Gardens Theater—a troupe begun in 1974 with a multicultural mission, though run by a white artistic director, Dennis Zacek.

A similar thing had happened in Chicago in October, when Timothy Douglas, an African-American director and performer, was named to succeed James Bohnen as the head of Chicago's Remy Bumppo Theatre Company, which last season staged a diet of Wilde, Albee, and Stoppard. And in February, Baltimore's CENTERSTAGE announced longtime Artistic Director Irene Lewis' replacement: London-born Ghanaian playwright Kwame Kwei-Armah. Lewis' last directing gig there was a production of Harold Pinter's *The Homecoming*.

None of these three theatre companies occupies a specific ethnic niche (or "ghetto," to use a starker word), either in their programming or in the audiences they serve. The fact that they now happen to be run by non-white artistic directors is a measure of meritocratic progress since the days when a given region's black artists, for example, would all vie to do the "black play" in the theatre season's "black slot" (often in February), and audiences of color would attend accordingly. Over the years, even as that rigidly circumscribed programming has slowly given way to more diversity on the stages of America's regional theatres, the makeup of their administrative offices has lagged somewhat behind the curve. Now that that imbalance is also at last changing, the fare on American stages is certain to change, as well—not just cosmetically but integrally.

This past season, of course, did not yet reflect the programming taste of any of these brand-new artistic leaders, but encouraging signs of change were everywhere. At the Oregon Shakespeare Festival in Ashland, two of the season's biggest events were the premiere of *American Night*, an edgily hilarious take on our nation's immigration history and hysteria, by the Los Angeles-based Chicano comedy trio Culture Clash, and a staging by New York-based avant gardist Ping Chong of Akira Kurosawa's 1957 film, itself an adaptation of *Macbeth*. Meanwhile, at Alabama Shakespeare Festival, the season kicked off with African-American writer Pearl Cleage's *The Nacirema Society Requests the Honor of Your Presence at a Celebration of Their First One Hundred Years*, a romantic comedy about black debutantes in Montgomery, in a coproduction with Atlanta's Alliance Theatre. The Alliance was also behind a unique adaptation, coproduced by Pasadena Playhouse: Director/choreographer Debbie Allen's "urban" retake on Dickens' *Oliver Twist*, in a new musical called simply *Twist*.

Indeed, coproductions and partnerships were another way theatres embraced promising voices this past season. In the San Francisco Bay Area, three companies of varying size each presented a piece of an ambitious African-influenced trilogy by Tarell Alvin McCraney: The Magic Theatre took on *The Brothers Size*, Marin Theatre Company mounted *In the Red and Brown Water*, and American Conservatory Theater presented *Marcus, or the Secret of Sweet*. Across

the country, the Boston area featured a similar intra-theatre repertory of works by the laconic slacker-chic playwright Annie Baker, with *Circle Mirror Transformation* at Huntington Theatre Company, *Body Awareness* at SpeakEasy Stage Company, and *The Aliens* at Company One.

Another trilogy, Regina Taylor's autobiographical *Trinity River Plays* (which include *Jar Fly*, *Rain*, and *Ghoststory*), was presented in its entirety by two major theatres: the Dallas Theatre Center and Chicago's Goodman Theatre. Indeed, as the Windy City's largest theatrical institution, the Goodman has been a leader in forward-thinking collaborations, forming a bond with its city's Latino-focused Teatro Vista and commissioning and producing *El Nogalar*, an adaptation of Chekhov's *Cherry Orchard* from local talent Tanya Saracho.

People of color are not the only under-represented voices on American stages. White writers from small-town, red-state America—or at least, those who take life in the American heartland as their subject matter—are also a kind of minority at the nation's major theatres. Idaho-bred Samuel D. Hunter, who has had success Off-Broadway with plays like *A Bright New Boise*, finally had his first professional production back in his home state when Boise Contemporary Theater premiered his suicide-themed drama *Norway*, in a coproduction with Indianapolis' Phoenix Theatre.

And speaking of coproductions, one of the nation's most ambitious new-works programs, the National New Play Network's Continued Life of New Plays Fund, makes matching theatres with new plays its mission. The result is what they diplomatically term "rolling world premieres," so that each theatre can conceivably claim to have been part of a play's first production. This season, with the fund's help, Aditi Brennan Kapil's kaleidoscopic immigrant tale *Agnes Under the Big Top* made the rounds of Connecticut's Long Wharf Theatre and Minneapolis' Mixed Blood Theatre, while Steve Yockey's magic-realist drama *afterlife: a ghost story* bowed at New Orleans' Southern Rep and Watertown, Massachusetts' New Repertory Theatre. Each of these will go on to at least one more future production in future seasons; other plays that began the first leg of their journey under the program this season were Theresa Rebeck's *What We're Up Against*, about workplace sexism, produced at the Magic Theatre; Stephen Sach's art-history comedy *Bakersfield Mist*, debuted at Los Angeles' Fountain Theatre; and A. Rey Pamatmat's teen-bonding play *Edith Can Shoot Things and Hit Them*, which premiered at the Actors Theatre of Louisville's Humana Festival of New American Plays.

Humana is just one of many play festivals at which the nation's regional theatres (not to mention agents and commercial producers) shop for fresh material and writers. Others include Portland's Time-Based Arts Festival, which admittedly favors devised performance pieces over plays per se, but at which one of the season's most auspicious properties made its bow: monologuist Mike Daisey's *The Agony and the Ecstasy of Steve Jobs*, a sharp bite into the cult of Apple which went on to play at Berkeley Repertory Theatre, Washington, D.C.'s Woolly Mammoth Theatre, and Seattle Repertory Theatre. (Its New York run would go on to open, fortuitously, a week after Jobs' death in the fall of 2011.)

At another of the nation's most influential gatherings, Philadelphia's Live Arts Festival, another work began a season-long trajectory. New York-based Elevator Repair Service's newest literary adaptation, *The Select (The Sun Also Rises)*, treated Hemingway's macho classic with plenty of gusto, if in a less comprehensive way than ERS' previous opus *Gatz* (a seven-hour, word-for-word rendition of *The Great Gatsby*). En route to a New York run, *The Select* showed up at ArtsEmerson, a brand new presenting/producing space in Boston's theatre district.

You might think that new theatre openings would be scarce in a recession, but ArtsEmerson was not the only new player on the scene this past season. In Washington, D.C., Arena Stage opened the sparkling, multi-stage Mead Center for American Theater with a multicultural new production of *Oklahoma!* helmed by Artistic Director Molly Smith. And Arena's ambitions are not merely architectural. Also bowing this year were the theatre's Visiting Companies Initiative, which copresents work by smaller companies from D.C. and elsewhere, and the American Voices New Play Institute. Though started the previous summer, the Institute kicked it up a notch this year with an auspicious convening of playwrights and theatre leaders, and with the hiring of Polly Carl, a dramaturg and new-works leader who had worked previously at Minneapolis' Playwrights Center and Chicago's Steppenwolf Theatre, as the institute's director.

As we are still in a faltering economy, the news was not all good this past season. For every theatre that beat the odds and came back from the brink (as was the case with the Pasadena Playhouse, which rallied after a Chapter 11 bankruptcy the previous summer, and with Atlanta's Actor's Express, rescued by an emergency fundraising plea in the spring), there were sad tales of closure or restructuring. Florida Stage's closure at season's end left Palm Beach theatre supporters confused and heartbroken; though its financial troubles had begun with the 2008 recession, they were compounded by a a recent move to a new facility and a consequent shedding of subscribers. Florida Stage is especially missed for its role as a home for new work; its last season included *Cane*, the first in a planned trilogy about local history by the company's resident playwright, Andrew Rosendorf.

In Seattle, the news out of the beloved Intiman Theatre was no less upsetting, if perhaps less surprising. Drama had swirled for months around the mid-season departure of managing director Brian Colburn, and repeated emergency fundraising pleas were not reassuring. The Intiman finally announced that its season would end prematurely at the end of its spring production of *All My Sons*, and that new Artistic Director Kate Whoriskey would be let go along with a number of staff members. (A tentative plan to revive the forty-year-old theatre during the summer of 2012 has since surfaced.)

Revival of the Fittest

When theatres retrench in hard times, they often reduce their commitment to risk-taking new works, relying instead on tried-and-true classics. While thankfully that was not really the case this past season, there were plenty of signs that theatres, in addition to keeping their fingers on the pulse of young writing, were also attending to the canon, both with revivals of classics and of familiar twentieth-century works. Christopher Sergel's adaptation of *To Kill a Mockingbird* and August Wilson's *Ma Rainey's Black Bottom* were two of the season's most-produced plays *not* by Shakespeare.

One way theatres keep the classics as interesting as new works is to reimagine them in ways both radical and timeless. In *An Iliad*, which bowed in the fall at Princeton, New Jersey's McCarter Theatre Center and at Portland Center Stage (with New York and Chicago runs still to come), actor Denis O'Hare and director Lisa Peterson turned the Homeric epic into a visceral, intimate evening of solo storytelling. Another twist on Homer came at Georgia Shakespeare in Atlanta, where director/adaptor Richard Garner's *The Odyssey: a Journey Home* framed the action in a contemporary VA hospital, with a nurse reading the story to a wounded soldier, who then recalled the picaresque tale in flashback.

At American Conservatory Theater, consummate clown Bill Irwin returned with his and Mark O'Donnell's freewheeling adaptation of Molière's shape-shifting farce *Scapin*. Watertown, Massachusetts' New Repertory Theatre presented Theresa Rebeck's *Dollhouse*, a contemporized take on Ibsen's classic, and Lookingglass Theatre Company, which specializes in wildly creative adaptations, gave Chicago Amanda Dehnert's dark, athletic *Peter Pan (a Play)*.

Chicago witnessed another auspicious "revisal" of a beloved show: At American Theater Company, director P.J. Paparelli teamed with Jim Jacobs, a surviving co-creator of the rock 'n' roll musical *Grease*, and restored much of the show's original Northside local color, along with plenty of adolescent raunch, that had been cut before the show's New York productions and film version. *The Original Grease*, which came with an "R" rating, opened in the spring and ran through the summer nights. Meanwhile, at San Diego Repertory Theatre, a less well-known musical, Ed Bullins and Mildred Kayden's salty New Orleans backstager *Storyville*, got a lavish rethinking by director Ken Page.

Revivals that did not take as many liberties but which were nonetheless auspicious included the premiere of Tony Kushner's *Angels in America* in Mormon country,

in a production by Salt Lake Acting Company (Part One, *Millennium Approaches* was fully staged, while Part Two, *Perestroika*, got just a staged reading). North Carolina, meanwhile, was visited by not one but two incarnations of *Angels*: *Millennium* was staged at North Carolina Stage in Asheville, and both plays were mounted at Playmakers in Chapel Hill. These were not even the only notable Kushner revivals: Denver's Curious Theatre Company also produced his *Homebody/Kabul*, written before 9/11 but still unfortunately as timely as ever.

As the year marked what would have been Tennessee Williams' centennial, more than the usual flurry of revivals graced regional stages, from *A Streetcar Named Desire* at Williamstown Theatre Festival in Massachusetts to *Camino Real* at Anchorage, Alaska's Cyrano's Theatre Company. Another late American master, Horton Foote, had a unique revival at Cleveland Play House: an all-black staging of his masterpiece *A Trip to Bountiful*. And though when Steppenwolf planned its revival of Lanford Wilson's bittersweet 1973 classic *The Hot l Baltimore*, Wilson was still alive—and in fact consulted with director Tina Landau about the production—his untimely death during the show's previews made it a lovely posthumous tribute to an American original.

Other notable revivals included the triumphant return of Richard Greenberg's best-known work, *Three Days of Rain*, to the theatre that premiered it, Costa Mesa, California's South Coast Repertory; the Kennedy Center's splashy, acclaimed revival of Stephen Sondheim and James Goldman's showbiz valentine *Follies*; and director Mary Zimmerman's sprightly retake on Leonard Bernstein's *Candide*, both at the Goodman and at Washington, D.C.'s Shakespeare Theatre Company.

That *Follies* would eventually make it to Broadway, and at presstime there was still hope that Zimmerman's *Candide* might, too. A number of other musical productions in regional theatres—where Broadway now regularly does its out-of-town tryouts—vied for the affections not only of local audiences but of visiting New York muckety-mucks. They included Alan Menken and Glenn Slater's gospel-tinged romantic comedy *Leap of Faith* at Center Theatre Group's Ahmanson Theatre; a rendition of the Oscar-winning *Little Miss Sunshine* by William Finn and James Lapine at the La Jolla Playhouse; an adaptation of the cheerleader comedy *Bring It On* at the Alliance Theatre, with direction and choreography by Andy Blankenbuehler and a star-studded creative team (songs by *In the Heights*' Lin-Manuel Miranda and *Next to Normal*'s Tom Kitt, book by *Avenue Q*'s Jeff Whitty); a musical of Armistead Maupin's iconic *Tales of the City*, also with a book by the busy Whitty and a score by the Scissor Sisters' Jake Shears, staged (where else?) at American Conservatory Theater in San Francisco; *Prometheus Bound*, American Repertory Theater's hard-rocking take on the Greek myth with music by System of a Down and a book by *Spring Awakening*'s Steven Sater; and a musical based on Shirley Jackson's *We Have Always Lived in the Castle* at New Haven's Yale Repertory Theatre, with a book by Adam Bock and songs by Todd Almond.

Musicals were not the only works inspired by non-theatrical sources this past season. Popular books turned into plays with Matthew Spangler's stage version of Khaled Hosseini's *The Kite Runner* at Cleveland Play House and Actors Theatre of Louisville; Rupert Holmes' stage adaptation of John Grisham's *A Time To Kill* at Arena Stage; actor Bill Camp and director Robert Woodruff's stark, raving take on Dostoevsky's *Notes From Underground* at La Jolla Playhouse; Caridad Svich's multilingual stage version of Isabel Allende's *The House of the Spirits* at both Denver Center Theatre and Mixed Blood; and Lemony Snicket's own co-adaptation, with director Tony Taccone, actor Geoff Hoyle, and puppeteers from Phantom Limb, of his meta-musical romp *The Composer Is Dead*, at Berkeley Rep.

In With the New

While there is no shame in adapting and reviving, the live arts are, by definition, most alive when they are living. So even as the Arena Stage, for instance, honored an American master with its Edward Albee Festival in the spring—with Steppenwolf's revelatory revival of *Who's Afraid of Virginia Woolf?* as its centerpiece—it brought us something new from the still-kicking playwright with *Homelife*, a prequel to his seminal one-act *The Zoo Story*, now conjoined as a two-act with the title *At Home at the Zoo*. Similarly, another living legend, Athol

Fugard, did not rest on his laurels but debuted a searing new moral drama, *The Train Driver*, on either coast: at the Fountain and at Long Wharf.

This year's most-produced plays (as tallied at the beginning of each season by Theatre Communications Group) included several listed above, as well as hits from previous seasons: Lynn Nottage's *Ruined*, Sarah Ruhl's *In the Next Room, or the vibrator play*, both Tracy Letts' *Superior Donuts* and *August: Osage County*, Yasmina Reza's *God of Carnage*. Of these, only Ruhl also brought forth a brand new play, *Stage Kiss* at the Goodman, which, given her productivity and track record, certainly will not be the last we hear of it.

What other auspicious new plays are we likely to see proliferating on stages in the coming seasons? A few playwrights increased their odds of being produced by, well, producing a lot of new writing: The busy Rajiv Joseph (whose *Bengal Tiger in the Baghdad Zoo* and *Gruesome Playground Injuries* both wended their way through the regions to New York acclaim in recent years) debuted the taut high school drama *The North Pool* at Palo Alto, Caliornia's TheatreWorks as well as the art-themed mystery *The Monster at the Door* at the Alley Theatre in Houston. Another oft-produced scribe, Jeffrey Hatcher, premiered two plays about major twentieth-century theatrical figures, depicting a key historical moment between acting legends Alfred Lunt and Lynne Fontanne in *Ten Chimneys* at Arizona Theatre Company and imagining a zany case of writer's block on the part of dramatist George S. Kaufman with *Louder Faster* (co-written with Jeffrey Simonson) at Pittsburgh's City Theatre.

Up-to-the-minute contemporary concerns dominated or at least haunted many of the year's most auspicious new plays. Lisa D'Amour's bewitching four-hander *Detroit* at Steppenwolf showcased recession-era jitters, while Bill Cain's harrowing *9 Circles* put a recently returned Iraq War vet through a Dantean virtual hell. K.J. Sanchez and Emily Ackerman's *ReEntry*, created from interviews with veterans of wars in Iraq and Afghanistan, took a more circumspect but no less probing look at the challenges of returning military, in a production at Baltimore's CENTERSTAGE. In Tucson, Arizona, the fearless Borderlands Theatre mounted Kara Hartzler's immigration-themed *No Roosters in the Desert*. Anna Deavere Smith brought her rumination on aging, the body, and health care, *Let Me Down Easy*, to Arena Stage, La Jolla Playhouse, and San Diego Rep. And David Henry Hwang riffed on Chinese and American competition and misunderstanding in the comedy *Chinglish* at the Goodman.

The concerns of Rinne Groff's *Compulsion* at Berkeley Rep may have been rooted in the post-Holocaust era, as a Meyer Levin-like author crusaded for the exclusive rights to Anne Frank's diary, but in the lead role, Mandy Patinkin made his passion immediate. Playwright Charles Smith mined a similarly dark chapter of history for *The Gospel According to James*, a commission from Indiana Repertory Theatre inspired by the history of a real-life lynching in the state in 1930, with Tony-winning actor Andre De Shields as a present-day survivor of the crime. In a powerfully personal excavation, Jonathan Moscone, artistic director of California Shakespeare Theater in Berkeley, teamed with Berkeley Rep Artistic Director Tony Taccone to co-write *Ghost Light*, a look back at the assassination of Moscone's father, San Francisco Mayor George Moscone, who was killed alongside gay

martyr Harvey Milk in 1978; it premiered in the summer at Oregon Shakespeare Festival. And another past/present juxtaposition fired Karen Zacarias' *Legacy of Light*, in which women scientists 260 years apart struggle with pregnancy and their place in the world, in production at Philadelphia's People's Light & Theatre Company, Richmond, Virginia's Barksdale Theatre, and Boston's Lyric Stage Company.

Science was also the theme of *Darwinii* at Cleveland Public Theatre. This raucuous comedy about unnatural selection was penned by Brett Keyser and Glen Berger—who, before he became a co-writer on Broadway's *Spider-man* musical, wrote such smart, mind-bending comedies as *Great Men of Science, Nos. 21 & 22*, and *Underneath the Lintel*. Another up-and-coming young playwright, Jordan Harrison, cast a skeptical eye on technology in *Futura*, an Orwellian cautionary fable about a world without printed type, at Portland Center Stage and Pasadena, California's Theatre @ Boston Court. And at Steppenwolf, Laura Eason's edgy two-hander, *Sex With Strangers*, used the brave new world of blogs and web publishing as the backdrop for a cat-and-mouse romantic power play.

Older-school media were the subject of *The Method Gun*, a piece from Austin, Texas' Rude Mechanicals that satirized the cult of acting gurus and played at ArtsEmerson, Columbus, Ohio's Wexner Center for the Arts, and the Center Theatre Group's Kirk Douglas Theatre; and of *Tales From Hollywood*, Christopher Hampton's fictionalized take on the shared Tinseltown exile of German WWII expat writers Bertolt Brecht and the Mann brothers, Heinrich and Thomas, at West L.A.'s Odyssey Theatre.

If American stages represented under-served audiences and subject matter this season—and continue to do so in the future—it will be thanks finally not to the people who run the theatres, or even those who attend them, but the daring, diverse artists who create the work. And in casting one last glance at the season, we are encouraged to see that the American theatre is in good hands. Kirsten Greenidge, for instance, contributed a nuanced look at confused social striving in 1970s and '80s-era black New England in *Bossa Nova* at Yale Repertory Theatre. Pulitzer winner Nilo Cruz returned to his roots with the Cuban Revolution-era romance *The Color of Desire* at Actors Playhouse in Coral Gables, Florida.

John Cariani, whose day job is as a loose-limbed Broadway triple threat but who also wrote the enormously popular regional hit *Almost, Maine*, contributed another play set in his home state, *Last Gas*, at Maine's Portland Stage. Stephen Karam, another regional favorite for *Speech and Debate*, wrote the affecting dark comedy *Sons of the Prophet*, which premiered at Huntington Theatre Company (in a coproduction with New York's Roundabout Theatre, where it went on to extravagant acclaim in the fall of 2011).

And two productions you're likely to see around the country include *The Complete World of Sports (abridged)*, the latest franchise from the Reduced Shakespeare Company, which kicked off at Boston's Merrimack Repertory Theatre and later Pittsburgh Public Theater, and *Traces*, an unclassifiable show from Cirque du Soleil-trained acrobats that is like an artier *Stomp*, which made its U.S. bow at Denver Performing Arts Center. If theatre has taught us anything, it is that it comes in all colors, shapes, and sizes. For every kind of theatre, there is a season.

ACT–A Contemporary Theatre

Seattle, Washington

Forty-sixth Season

Artistic Director, Kurt Beattie; Executive Director, Gian-Carlo Scandiuzzi; Artistic Associate and Casting Director, Margaret Layne; Literary Manager, Anita Montgomery; Artistic Manager, Nicole Boyer Cochran; Producing Director, Joan Toggenburger; PSM, Jeffrey K. Hanson; Costume Director, Carolyn Keim; Technical Director, Steve Coulter

The Trip to Bountiful by Horton Foote; Director, Victor Pappas; Sets, Matthew Smucker; Costumes, Frances Kenny; Lighting, Rick Paulsen; Sound, Christopher Walker; Dialect, Alyssa Keene; SM, Erin B. Zatloka; Cast: Ian Bell (Houston Ticket Agent); Mary Kae Irvin (Jessie Mae Watts); Charles Leggett (Sherriff); Jessica martin (Thelma); Marianne Owen (Carrie Watts); Wesley Rice (Roy/2nd Houston Ticket Agent); Paul Morgan Stetler (Ludie Watts); May 7–June 6, 2010

The Female of the Species by Joanna Murray-Smith; Director, Allison Narver; Sets, Robert A. Dahlstrom; Costumes, Deb Trout; Lighting, Geoff Korf; Sound, Brendan Patrick Hogan; Dialect, Alyssa Keene; SM, JR Welden; Cast: Mark Chamberlin (Theo Reynolds); Renata Friedman (Molly Rivers); Suzy Hunt (Margot Mason); Tim Hyland (Frank); Morgan Rowe (Tess Thorton); Paul Morgan Stetler (Bryan Thorton); June 18–July 18, 2010

Yankee Tavern by Steven Dietz; Director, Steven Dietz; Sets, Matthew Smucker; Costumes, Marcia Dixcy Jory; Lighting, Rick Paulsen; Sound, Brendan Patrick Hogan; SM, Jeffry K. Hanson; Cast: Charles Leggett (Ray); Jennifer Lee Taylor (Janet); Shawn Telford (Adam); R. Hamilton Wright (Palmer); July 30–August 29, 2010

The Lady With All the Answers by David Rambo; Director, Valerie Curtis-Newton; Sets, Martin Christoffel; Costumes, Melanie Taylor Burgess; Lighting, Robert Aguilar; Sound, Brendan Patrick Hogan; SM, JR Welden; Dialect, Judith Shahn; Cast: Julie Briskman (Eppie Lederer "Ann Landers"); September 10–October 31, 2010

The Lieutenant of Inishmore by Martin Mcdonagh; Director, Kurt Beattie; Sets, Thomas Lynch; Costumes, Catherine Hunt; Lighting, Mary Louise Geiger; Sound, Brendan Patrick Hogan; SM, Jeffry K. Hanson; Fight Director, Robert Macdougall; Dialect, Alyssa Keene; Acrobatics Coach, Ryan Daudistel; Cast: Jeffrey Fracé (Padraic); Seán G. Griffin (Donny); Elise Hunt (Mairead); Tim Hyland (Christy); David Roby (James/Joey); MJ Sieber (Davey); Brian D. Simmons (Braden); October 15–November 14, 2010

A Christmas Carol by Charles Dickens; Adapted by Gregory A. Falls; Director, Allison Narver; Sets, Shelly Henze Schermer; Costumes, Deb Trout; Lighting, Michael Wellborn; Sound/Music, Brendan Patrick Hogan; Original Sound, Steven M. Klein; Choreographer, Wade Madsen; SM, JR Welden, Jeffrey K. Hanson; Dialect, Alyssa Keene; Cast: Ian Bell (Mr. Fezziwig/Topper, Poor Man/Gent #1/Business Man #1/Narrator); Daniel Brockley (Middle Scrooge/Beggar/Ali Baba/Spirit #3); Mark Chamberlin (Ebenezer Scrooge); Burton Curtis (Marley/Old Joe/Bread Lady/Guest); Sylvie Davidson (Belle/Niece/Mrs. Dilber/Narrator); Alban Dennis (Bob Cratchit/Jonathan/Robinson Crusoe); Brandon Engman (Turkey Boy/Singing Thief/Undertaker's Assistant/Master Fezziwig); Sean G. Griffin (Ebenezer Scrooge); Andrew Haggerty (Peter Cratchit); Sarah Harlett (Mrs. Fezziwig/Sister/Sugarplum Seller/Charwoman); Frank Lawler (Fred/Dick/Grocer/Businessman #2); David Anthony Lewis (Spirit #2/Ragpicker/Gent #2/Narrator); Eli Lotz (Charles Cratchit/Young Scrooge); Jessica Martin (Spirit #1/Guest #2); Kasey Percich (Martha Cratchit/Miss Fezziwig); Patience Probst (Elizabeth Cratchit/Want); Morgan Roberts (Belinda Cratchit/Fan, Lil Fezziwig); Sarah Roberts (Tiny Tim/Ignorance); Morgan Rowe (Mrs. Cratchit/Fezziwig Dancer); Diana Huey (Ladies u/s); John Ulman (Gentlemen's u/s); November 28–December 20, 2010

Actors Theatre of Louisville

Louisville, Kentucky

Forty-seventh season

Artistic Director, Marc Masterson; Managing Director, Jennifer Bielstein

The Kite Runner by Khaled Hesseini; Adapted by Matthew Spangler; Director, Marc Masterson; Sets, Michael B Raiford; Costumes, Lorraine Venberg; Lighting, Brian J Lilienthal; Sound, Matt Callahan; Props, Mark Walston; Wigs, Heather Fleming; Musical Supervisor, Salar Nader; SM, Kathy Preher; Dramaturg, Carrie Hughes; Fight Director, k. Jenny Jones; Dialect, Rocco Dal Vera; Cast: Aadya Bedi (Soraya/Ensemble), Apollo Dukakis (Rahim Khan/ Ensemble), Nasser Faris (Baba/Ensemble), Jose Peru Flores (Young Amir/Ensemble), Ariya Ghahramani (Kamal/Ensemble), Omar Koury (Farid/Ensemble), Salar Nader (Tabla Player), Matt Pascua (Hassan/Sohrab/Ensemble), Kario Pereira-Bailey (Wali/Ensemble), Annie Pesch (Mrs. Nguyen/Ensemble), James Saba (Ali/Zaman/Omar Faisal/Ensemble), Zarif Kabier Sadiqi (Assef/Ensemble), Remi Sandri (General Taheri/Ensemble), Jos Viramontes (Amir); August 21–September 25, 2010

Dracula by Bram Stoker; Originally dramatized by John L Balderston and Hamilton Deane; Adapted and directed by William McNulty; Sets, Paul Owen; Costumes, Lorraine Venberg; Lighting, Tony Penna; Original Music/Sound, Benjamin Marcum; Props, Joe Cunningham; Media Designer, Philip Allgeier; Wigs/Makeup, Heather Fleming; SM, Kimberly J First; Dramaturg, Adrien-Alice Hansel; Fight Director, k. Jenny Jones; Cast: Marc Bovino (Renfield), James Whalen (Count Dracula), Havalah Grace (Ms. Sullivan), William McNulty (Van Helsing), Simon Kendall (Dr. Seward), Ryan Westwood (Mr. Briggs), Gisela Chipe (Lucy), Joseph Midyett (Jonathan Harker), Dinah Berkeley (Undead Ensemble), Alex Hernandez (Undead Ensemble), Emily Kunkel (Undead Ensemble), Eleanor McKenna (Undead Ensemble), Emily Steinbach (Undead Ensemble); September 17–31, 2010

The Mystery of Irma Vep by Charles Ludlam; Director, Sean Daniels; Sets, Michael B Raiford; Costumes, Lorraine Venberg; Lighting, Brian J Lilienthal; Sound, Matt Callahan; Props, Mark Walston; Wigs, Heather Fleming; SM, Paul Mills Holmes; ASM, Kathy Preher; Dramaturg, Amy Wegener; Cast: Larry Bull (Jane Twisden/Lord Edgar Hillcrest/Intruder), Blake DeLong (Nicodemus Underwood/Lady Enid Hillcrest/Alcazar/Pev Amri); Apprentices: Jordan Brodess (Egyptian), Daniel Desmarais (Egyptian), Devin Olson (Egyptian), Brandon Peters (Egyptian), Zach Virden (Egyptian); October 5–October 30, 2010

A Christmas Story by Philip Grecian; Based on the motion picture *A Christmas Story* distributed by Warner Bros.), written by Jean Shepherd, Leigh Brown and Rob Clark, and on the book In God We Trust, All Others Pay Cash by Jean Shepherd; Director, Sean Daniels; Sets, Scott Bradley; Costumes, Lorraine Venberg; Lighting, Brian J Lilienthal; Sound, Matt Callahan; Props, Mark Walston; Properties Master, Joe Cunningham; Wigs, Heather Fleming; Media, Philip Allgeier; Choreographer, Delilah Smith; SM, Kathy Preher; ASM, Paul Mills Holmes; Dramaturg, Amy Wegener; Cast: Katie Weible Blackerby (Miss Shields), Jahne Kobi Brown (Helen Weathers), Carter Caldwell (Scut Farkas), Liam Craig (Ralph Parker), Justin R.G. Holcomb (The Old Man), Will DeVary (Flick), Jack Lindsey (Schwartz), Arabella Paulovich (Ester Jane), Gabe Weible (Randy), Jessica Wortham (Mother), Henry Miller (Ralphie Parker); Apprentices: Jordan Brodess (Elf), Alex Stage (Elf), Rebecca Haden (Elf), Elizabeth Schwarzrock (Elf), William O. Steele IV (Elf), Devin Olson (Elf), Kerri J. Alexander (Elf), Sean Michael Palmer (Elf); November 9–November 29, 2010

Barefoot in the Park by Neil Simon; Director, Marc Masterson; Sets, Tom Tutino; Costumes, Lorraine Venberg; Lighting, Brian J Lilienthal; Sound, Matt Callahan; Props, Mark Walston; Wigs, Heather Fleming; SM, Stephen Horton; Dramaturg, Sarah Lunnie; Cast: Clyde Tyrone Harper (The Delivery Man), V Craig Heidenreich (Victor Velasco), Aaron Munoz (The Telephone Man), Jane Pfitsch (Corie Bratter), Lee Aaron Rosen (Paul Bratter), Peggy J Scott (Mrs. Banks); November 16–December 18, 2010

A Christmas Carol by Charles Dickens; Adapted by Barbara Field; Director, Sean Daniels; Sets, Paul Owen; Costumes, Lorraine Venberg; Lighting, Deb Sullivan; Sound, Matt Callahan; Props, Mark Walston; Properties Master, Joe Cunningham; Media, Phillip Allgeier; Wigs, Heather Fleming; Music Supervisor, David Keeton; Movement Supervisor, Delilah Smyth; SM, Paul Mills Holmes; ASM, Kimberly J First; Dramaturg, Sarah Lunnie; Cast: Ciaran Davis Brown (Boy Scrooge/Simon/Tom Cratchit), Alexis Broncovic (Belle/Mrs. Fred), Alexandria Chand (Marjoram/Caroler/Fezzi Guest), Elise Coughlan (Caroler/Fezzi Guest), John Gregorio (Fred/Mr. Fezziwig), Gylf Forsberg (Peter/Townsperson), Brad Heberlee (Bob Cratchit), Ann Hodapp (Mrs. Grigsby/Cook), David Keeton (Grasper/Townsperson), Clare Rose Kresse (Belinda/Fezzi Guest), Helen Lister (Tiny Tim/Ensemble), Fred Major (Old Joe/Schoolmaster) , Bill McNulty (Scrooge), David Ryan Smith (Ghost of Christmas Present/Forrest), Douglas Scott Sorenson (Marley), Celina Stachow (Mrs. Cratchit), Navida Stein (Mrs. Fezziwig), Lindsey Noel Whiting (Ghost of Christmas Past/Mrs. Blakely); Apprentices: Kerri Alexander (Townsperson/Party Guest), Martina Bonolis (Dorthea/Marigold), Jordan Brodess (Puss in Boots/Townsperson/Party Guest), Daniel Desmarais (Dick Wilkins/Topper), Rebecca Haden (Sophia/Petunia), Ellen Haun (Fan/Fezzi Guest), Devin Olson (Edwards/Townsperson/ Undertaker/Party Guest), Sean Michael Palmer (Ghost of Christmas Future/Ali Baba/ Townsperson/Party Guest), Elizabeth Schwarzrock (Martha Cratchit/Party Guest), Alex Stage (Robinson Crusoe/Townsperson/Party Guest), Ryan Westwood (Young Ebenezer/Pall Bearer); December 7–December 23, 2010

The Second City: It Takes a 'Ville! Created by The Second City; Additional materials created by Tim Baltz and Ed Furman; Director, Mick Napier; Sets, Ryan Wineinger; Lighting, Brian J Lilienthal; Props, Joe Cunningham; SM, Kimberly Miller; Dramaturg, Mik Mroczynski; Musical Director, Matt Cohen; Cast: Lauren Dowden, Jennifer Estlin, Mitchell Fain, John Hartman, Anthony Irons, Steve Waltien; January 4–February 6, 2011

Ma Rainey's Black Bottom by August Wilson; Director, Ron OJ Parson; Sets, Michael Ganio; Costumes, Lorraine Vengberg; Lighting, Brian J Lilienthal; Sound, Matt Callahan; Props, Mark Walston; Wigs, Heather Fleming; SM, Paul Mills Holmes; ASM, Kimberly J First; Dramaturg, Jessica Reese; Cast: Jonathan Butler-Duplessis (Sylvester), Jonathan Gillard Daly (Irvin), Anthony Fleming III (Levee), Joshua Loren (Policeman), Erynn Mackenzie (Dussie Mae), William McNulty (Sturdyvant), Greta Oglesby (Ma Rainey), Ernest Perry, Jr. (Cutler), A.C. Smith (Slow Drag), Alfred H. Wilson (Toledo); January 18–February 13, 2011

Humana Festival

BOB by Peter Sinn Nachtrieb; Director, Sean Daniels; Sets, Michael B. Raiford; Costumes, Lorraine Venberg; Lighting, Brian J Lilienthal; Sound, Matt Callahan; Props, Joe Cunningham; Media, Philip Allgeier; Wigs, Heather Fleming; SM, Paul Mills Holmes; Dramaturg, Sarah Lunnie; Cast: Jeffrey Binder (Bob), Aysan Celik (Chorus 1), Polly Lee (Chorus 2), Danny Scheie (Chorus 3), Lou Sumrall (Chorus 4); March 24–April 17, 2011

A Devil at Noon by Anne Washburn; Director, Steve Cosson; Sets, Brian Sidney Bembridge; Costumes, Lorraine Venberg; Lighting, Jeff Nellis; Sound, Matt Hubbs; Props, Joe Cunningham; Media, Philip Allgeier; Mime Consultant, Emmanuelle Delpech-Ramey; SM, Stephen Horton; Dramaturg, Janice Paran; Cast: Joseph Adams (Chet Ellis), Ross Bickell (Bob Seward/Moon Man), Rebecca Hart (Lois L), Brandon T Miller (Tom/Don Larkin), David Ross (Dennis/Philip Hutchens), Matthew Stadelmann (Colin McAdams/Phone guy); February 27–April 3, 2011

Edith Can Shoot Things and Hit Them by A. Rey Pamatmat; Director, May Adrales; Sets, Brian Sidney Bembridge; Costumes, Connie Furr-Soloman; Lighting, Jeff Nellis; Sound, Benajmin Marcum; Props, Joe Cunningham; Media, Philip Allgeier; Fight Director, Drew Fracher; SM, Kimberly J. First; Dramaturg, Michael Bigelow Dixon; Cast: Teresa Avia Lim (Edith) John Norman Schneider (Kenny), Cory Michael Smith (Benji); March 11–April 2, 2011

The Edge of Our Bodies Written and directed by Adam Rapp; Sets, Tom Tutino; Costumes, Kristopher Castle; Lighting, Keith Parham; Original Music, Christian Frederickson and Ryan Rumery; Props, Mark Walston; SM, CJ LaRoche; Assistant Director/Dramaturg, Lila Neigebauer; Cast: Catherine Combs (Bernadette); March 22–April 3, 2011

Elemeno Pea by Molly Smith Metzler; Director: Davis McCallum; Sets, Michael B Raiford; Costumes, Lorraine Venberg; Lighting, Brian J Lilienthal; Sound, Matt Callahan; Props, Mark Walston; Wigs, Heather Fleming; SM, Kathy Preher; Dramaturg, Amy Wegener; Cast: Cassie Beck (Devon), Kimberly Parker Green (Simone), Daniel Pearce (Ethan), Gerardo Rodriquez (Jos-B), Sara Surrey (Michaela); March 8–April 3, 2011

Maple and Vine by Jordan Harrison; Director, Anne Kauffman; Sets, Brian Sidney Bembridge; Costumes, Connie Furr Soloman; Lighting, Jeff Nellis; Sound, Benjamin Marcum; Props, Alice Baldwin; Media, Philip Allgeier; Wigs, Heather Fleming; SM, Melissa Rae Miller; Dramaturg, Amy Wegener; Cast: Kate Turnbull (Katha), Peter Kim (Ryu), Paul Niebanck (Dean), Jeanine Serralles (Ellen/Jenna), Jesse Pennington (Roger/Omar); March 4–April 3, 2011

The following short plays were presented under the title *The End*, and were performed March18–April 3, 2011:

The End (The Apprentice Showcase) by Dan Dietz, Jennifer Haley, Allison Moore, A. Rey Pamatmat, and Marco Ramirez; Directors, Amy Attaway, Michael Legg; Co-conceived and developed with Sarah Lunnie; Sets, Ryan Wineinger; Costumes, Lindsay Chamberlin; Lighting, Brian J Lilienthal; Sound, Matt Callahan; Props, Alice Baldwin; Wigs, Heather Fleming; SM, Jessica Potter; Fight Director, Joe Isenberg; Dramaturg, Sarah Lunnie

This is How it Ends by A. Rey Pamatmat; Cast: Sean Michael Palmer (Jake), Emily Kunkel (Annie), Daniel Desmarais (Pestilence), Victoria Alvarez-Chacon (Death), Devin Olson (War), Martina Bonolis (Famine)

The One about the Astroid by Marco Ramirez; Cast: Peter Vergari

La Reina de los Ángeles by Jennifer Haley; Cast: Zach Virden (Trent), Brandon Peters (Ryan), Lizzie Schwarzrock (Lila), Rebecca Haden (Jillian), Monica Bergstrand (Mindi), Will Steele (Jake), Kerri Alexander (Director)

The One That Ends Itself by Marco Ramirez; Cast: Alex Stage

Apocalypse Apartments by Allison Moore; Cast: Ryan Westwood (Mick), Lizzie Schwarzrock (Zoe), Peter Vergari (Tyler), Rebecca Haden (Stace), Dinah Berkeley (Piper), Zach Virden (Eric)

La Muerte by Marco Ramirez; Cast: Alex Hernandez (Slick), Jordan Brodess (Mouse), Kerri Alexander (La Muerte)

4B by Marco Ramirez; Cast: Alex Stage (Pete), Ryan Westwood (Mikey)

The One They Call the Bloop by Marco Ramirez; Cast: Kerri Alexander

Promageddon by Dan Dietz; Cast: Scott Swezey (Gil), Jordan Brodess (Theo), Havalah Grace (Dot), Ellen Haun (Alexis), Dinah Berkeley (Kimmy)

Ten-Minute Plays

April 2–April 3, 2011

Hygiene by Gregory Hischak; Director, Kent Nicholson; Sets, Ryan Wineinger; Costumes, Lisa Weber; Lighting, Nick Dent; Sound, Paul Doyle; Props, Jay Tollefsen, Mark Walston; Wigs, Heather Fleming; Media, Philip Allgeier; SM, Kathy Preher; Dramaturg, Rachel Lerner-Ley; Cast: Teresa Avia Lim (Wendy), Daniel Pearce (Howard), Sara Surrey (Rita)

Chicago, Sudan Written and performed by Marc Bamuthi Joseph; Director, Michael John Garcés; Sets, Ryan Wineinger; Costumes, Lindsay Chamberlin; Lighting, Nick Dent; Sound, Paul Doyle; Props, Jay Tollefsen, Mark Walston; Wigs, Heather Fleming; Media, Philip Allgeier; SM, Kathy Preher; Dramaturg, Rachel Lerner-Ley

Mr. Smitten by Laura Eason; Director, Kent Nicholson; Sets, Ryan Wineinger; Costumes, Lindsay Chamberlin; Lighting, Nick Dent; Sound, Paul Doyle; Props, Jay Tollefsen, Mark Walston; Wigs, Heather Fleming; Media, Philip Allgeier; SM, Kathy Preher; Dramaturg, Rachel Lerner-Ley; Cast: Cassie Beck (Anna), Gerardo Rodriquez (Dr. Loomis)

Alabama Shakespeare Festival

Montgomery, Alabama

Thirty-seventh Season

Producing Artistic Director, Geoffrey Sherman

Festival Stage

Cowgirls Conceived by Mary Murfitt; Book by Betsy Howie; Music and lyrics by Mary Murfitt; Original Story Development, Kevin Murphy; Director, Karen Azenberg; Musical Director, Mary Ehlinger; Sets, Peter Hicks; Costumes, Katrina Cahalan-Wilhite; Lighting, Paul Wonsek; Sound, Richelle Thompson; SM, Tanya J. Searle; PA, Melissa Van Swol; SDC Observer, Shari Johnson; Cast: Angela C. Howell (Jo Carlson), Pearl Rhein (Rita), Tamra Hayden (Lee), Jessica Tyler Wright (Mary Lou), Chelsea Costa (Mo), Carrie Cimma (Mickey); June 13–July 11, 2010

The Nacirema Society Requests the Honor of Your Presence at a Celebration of Their First One Hundred Years by Pearl Cleage; Director, Susan Booth; Assistant to the Director, Bari Newport; Sets, Peter Hicks; Costumes, Susan Mickey; Lighting, Phil Monat; Sound, Richelle Thompson; Dramaturg, Celise Kalke; SM, Tanya J. Searle; PA, Cheryl Hanson; Cast: Trezana Beverly (Grace Dubose Dunbar), Naima Carter Russell (Gracie Dunbar), Chinai J. Hardy (Marie Dunbar), Andrea Frye (Catherine Adams Green), Kevin Alan Daniels (Bobby Green), Tonia Jackson (Alpha Campbell Jackson), Karan Kendrick (Lillie Campbell Jackson), Jasmine Guy (Janet Logan), Neda Spears (Jessie Roberts); September 26–October 10-2010

Peter Pan by Jerome Robbins; Adapted from Sir James M. Barrie; Music, Moose Charlap; Lyrics, Carolyn Leigh; Additional Music, Jule Styne; Additional Lyrics, Betty Comden, Adolph Green; Director, Geoffrey Sherman; Choreographer, Karen Azenberg; Musical Director, Tom Griffin; Fight Director, John Manfredi; Sets, John Iacovelli; Costumes, Patrick Holt; Lighting, Paul Wonsek; Sound, Richelle Thompson; Assistant Choreographer/Dance Captain, Lenny Daniel; Assistant Musical Director, Joel Jones; Dramaturg, Susan Willis; SM, Tanya J. Searle; ASM, Melissa Von Swol; PA, Cheryl Hanson, Bronwen Hernandez; Casting, Elissa Myers Casting, Paul Fouquet, CSA; Cast: Sarah Litzsinger (Peter Pan), Rodney Clark (Mr. Darling/Captain Hook), Lynna Schmidt (Mrs. Darling), Emily Kinney (Wendy), Greyson Hammock and Tyler Lewin (John), Joseph Sims and Crispin South (Michael), Caitlin McGee (Liza/Mermaid/Older Wendy/Wendy u/s), Billy Sharpe (Smee), Eleni Kanalos (Tiger Lily), Kevin Curtis (Slightly), Maria Totten (Tootles/Peter Pan u/s), Roy San Filipo (Curly/Nana u/s), Eric Shorey (Nibs), Anthony Napoletano (Twin #1), Nathaniel Braga (Twin #2), Tyler Jakes (Nana/Crocodile), Roger Preston Smith (Mullins/Indian/Mr. Darling/Capt Hook u/s), Richard Gatta (Starkey/Indian), Lenny Daniel (Cecco/Indian), Kent Zimmerman (Noodler/Indian), Adam Pellegrine (Jukes/Indian), Rachel McIsaac (Indian/Mermaid/Twin #1/Twin #2/ Tiger Lilly u/s), Tara Herweg (Older Wendy/Mrs. Darling/Liza u/s), Breanna Newton, Savannah Rigby (Jane), Erik Gullberg (Indian), Seth Rabinowitz (Indian/Pirate), Corey Triplett (Indian/Pirate), Brett Warnke (Indian), Kevin Callaghan (Pirate/Starkey/Mullins/Smee u/s); November 21–December 31-2010

Bear Country by Michael Vigilant; Director, Tim Rhoze; Sets, Katherine Ross; Costumes, Elizabeth Novak; Lighting, Tom Rodman; Sound, Brett Rominger; SM, Melissa Van Swol; PA, Whitney Keeter; Cast: Rodney Clark (Coach Bryant), William Peden (Young Bryant/ Young Coach Bryant), Christopher Burns (Uncle/ Coach Cowan/Coach Hank/Football Player/Reporter/Television Announcer/ Technician/Attorney/Racist), James Bowen (Radio Announcer/Friend/Floor Manager/Grandpa/Student Protestor); January 16–January 23, 2011

Julius Caeser by William Shakespeare; Director, Geoffrey Sherman; Composer, James Conely; Fight Director, Marcus Lane; Sets, Peter Hicks; Costumes, Elizabeth Novak; Lighting, Paul Wonsek; Sound, Brett Rominger; Dramaturg, Susan Wills; SM, Tanya J. Searle; ASM, Melissa Von Swol; PA, Cheryl Hanson; Cast: Rodney Clark (Julius Caeser/Ghost of Caeser), Corey Triplett (Octavius Caeser/Trebonius), Peter Simon Hilton (Marcus Antonius), Erik Gullberg (M. Emilius Lepidus/Popilius Lena/Marullus/Plebian/Servant to Antony/Soldier), Eric Hoffman (Cicero/Artemidorus/Cobbler/Soldier), Tyler Jakes (Publius/Strato/ Plebian/Soldier/ Messenger), Stephen Paul Johnson (Marcus Brutus), Thom Rivera (Cassius), Phillip Christian (Casca/Lucilius), James Bowen (Ligarius/ Messala), Brik Berkes (Decius Brutus/Cinna/Titinius), Seth Rabinowitz (Metellus Cimber/Flavius/Soldier), Kevin Callaghan (Cinna/Pindarus), Greta Lambert (Soothsayer), Nandita Shenoy (Lucius), Caitlin McGee (Plebian/Servant to Caesar), Tata Herweg (Servant to Octavius/Calphurnia), Jenny Mercein (Portia); February 4–May 21, 2011

Much Ado About Nothing by William Shakespeare; Director, Diana Von Fossen; Composer, James Conely; Movement Specialist, Parul Kapoor; Fight Director, Marcus Lane; Sets, Peter Hicks; Costumes, Brenda Van der Weil; Lighting, Paul Wonsek; Sound, Richelle Thompson; Dramaturg, Bruce Mann; SM, Melissa Van Swol; ASM, Tanya J. Searle; PA, Cheryl Hanson; Cast: Thom Rivera (Don Pedro), Peter Simon Hilton (Benedick), Erik Gullberg (Claudio), Corey Triplett (Balthasar), Phillip Christian (Don John), Brik Berkes (Brachio), Seth Rabinowitz (Conrad), Stephen Johnson (Leonato), Caitlin McGee (Hero), Jenny Mercein (Beatrice), Rodney Clark (Antonio), Tara Herweg (Margaret/a Sexton), Nandita Shenoy (Ursula), James Bowen (Friar), Eric Hoffman (Dogberry), Kevin Callahan (Verges), Brett Warnke (First Watchman), Tyler Jakes (Second Watchman/Boy/Messenger); March 11–May 21, 2011

Moonlight and Magnolias by Ron Hutchinson; Director, Geoffrey Sherman; Sets, Peter Hicks; Costumes, Elizabeth Novak; Lighting, Paul Wonsek; Sound, Richelle Thompson; Dramaturg, Susan Willis; Fight Director, Marcus Lane; SM, Tanya J. Searle; ASM, Melissa Van Swol; PA, Cheryl Hanson; Cast: Brik Berkes (Ben Hecht), Thom Rivera (Victor Fleming), Eric Hoffman (David O. Selznick), Miss Poppenghul (Nandita Shenoy); April 20–May 29, 2011

Menopause: The Musical Book and lyrics by Jeannie Linders; Supervising Director, Seth Greenleaf; Choreography Supervisor, Daria Melendez; Sets, Bud Clark; Costumes, Sue Hill; Lighting/National Production Manager, Ryan Patrigde; Company Manager/ASM, Neal Gardner; SM, Marc Carmen; Production Supervisor, Thomas Madden; Choreography, Patty Bender; Original Direction, Kathryn Conte; Cast: Emily David (Professional Woman), Patti Gardner (Soap Star), Pammie O'Bannon (Earth Mother), Sandy DeWoddy (Iowa Housewife), P.J. Jenkins (u/s); July 10–July 24, 2011

Octagon Stage

The House on Pooh Corner by A.A. Milne; Adapted by Bettye Knapp; Director, Nancy Rominger; Costumes, Aaron Turner; Lighting, Tom Rodman; Sound, Layne Weldon; Dramaturg, Susan Willis; Voice/Dialect Coach, Greta Lambert; SM, Bronwen Hernandez; PM, Chris Haugh; Cast: Tyler Jakes (Christopher Robin/ Owl), Corey Triplett (Winnie-the-Pooh), Caitlin McGee (Piglet), Seth Rabinowitz (Eeyore), Erik Gullberg (Tigger/Early/Late), Tara Herweg (Kanga), Kevin Callaghan (Roo), Brett Warnke (Rabbit), VOICE (Diana Von Fossen); September 24–October 22, 2010

The Flagmaker of Market Street by Elyzabeth Gregory Wilder; Director, Leah C. Gardiner; Sets, Peter Hicks; Costumes, Pamela Scofield; Lighting, Tom Rodman; Sound, Richelle Thompson; Dramaturg, Susan Willis; SM, Jen Nelson Lane; PA, Bronwen Hernandez; Dialect Coach, Dr. Daniel Black; Cast: Jack Koenig (George Cowles), Nikki E. Walker (Mae), Brian Wallace (William Bibb), Adria Vitlar (Lydia Frost); February 6–May 21, 2011

Blood Divided by Jeffrey L. Chastang; Director, Nancy Rominger; Sets, Peter Hicks; Costumes, Pamela Scofield; Lighting, Tom Rodman; Sound, Brett Rominger; Dramaturg, Marlon Bailey; SM, Jen Nelson Lane; PA, Bronwen Hernandez; Cast: Jack Koenig (Dr. William "Owen" Baldwin), Brian Wallace (William "Lowndes" Yancey), Sloan Grenz (Willie "Buddy Willie" Baldwin), Billy Eugene Jones (Jim Hale); February 20–March 20, 2011

Alley Theatre

Houston, Texas

Sixty-fourth Season

Artistic Director, Gregory Boyd; Managing Director, Dean R. Gladden

Hubbard Stage

The Mousetrap by Agatha Christie; Director, Gregory Boyd; Sets, Linda Buchanan; Costumes, Tricia Barsamian; Lighting, Michael Lincoln; Sound, Pierre Dupree; SM, Elizabeth M. Berther; ASM, Rebecca R.D. Hamlin Cast: Jeffrey Bean (Detective Sergeant trotter), James Belcher (Major Metcalf), Elizabeth Bunch (Mollie Ralston), Josie de Guzman (Miss Casewell), Chris Hutchison (Giles Ralston), Anne Quackenbush (Mrs. Boyle), John Tyson (Mr. Paravicini), Todd Waite (Christopher Wren); July 8–August 8, 2010

Peter Pan, or The Boy Who Would Not Grow Up by J.M. Barrie in a new version by John Caird, Trevor Nunn; Director, Gregory Boyd; Sets, Hugh Landwehr; Costumes, Constance Hoffman; Lighting, Beverly Emmons; Music Composition/Sound, Rob Milburn, Michael Bodeen; Dramaturgs, Mark Bly, Lauren Halvorsen; Fight Director, Brian Byrnes; Flying Effects ZFX, Inc.; SM, Elizabeth M. Berther, Terry Cranshaw; Cast: Leraldo Anzaldua (Skylights), Jeffrey Bean (Smee), James Belcher (Cecco), James Black (Mr. Darling/Captain James Hook), Thomas Brazzle (Alsatian Fogerty), Brian Byrnes (George Scourie/Robt. Mullins), Elizabeth Bunch (Wendy), Patrick Damien Earl (Nana/Chay Turley/Bill Jukes), Luis Gonzalez (Nibs/The Crocodile), Dylan Godwin (Tootles), Chris Hutchison (Alf Mason), Julia Krohn (Liza/Curly), Katrina Lenk (Mrs. Darling/Slightly), Kalob Martinez (Canary Robb), Emily Neves (Michael/Jane), David Rainey (Noodler/Cookson), Jay Sullivan

A Christmas Carol–A Ghost Story of Christmas by Charles Dickens; Adapted and originally directed by Michael Wilson; Director, James Black; Sets, Tony Straiges; Costumes, Alejo Vietti; Lighting, Rui Rita; Original Music, John Gromada; SM, Terry Cranshaw; Cast: Jeffrey Bean (Ebenezer Scrooge), James Belcher (Bert/Spirit of Christmas Present), Elizabeth Bunch (Mrs. Fezziwig/Mrs. Cratchit), Dylan Godwin (Mr. Marvel), Paul Hope (Second Solicitor/Mr. Fezziwig), Chris Hutchison (Bob Cratchit), Charles Krohn (Undertaker/Old Joe), Julia Krohn (Mary Pidgeon/Spirit of Christmas Past), Emily Neves (Belle/Fred's Wife), Melissa Pritchett (Ghostly Apparition/Fred's Sister-in-Law), David Rainey (Mrs. Dilber/Jacob Marley), John Tyson (First Solicitor/Fiddler); November 19–December 27, 2010

God of Carnage by Yasmina Reza; Translated by Christopher Hampton; Director, Wilson Milam; Sets, Eugene Lee; Costumes, Deb Trout; Lighting, Geoff Korf; Sound, Matt Starritt; Set Assistant, Patrick Lynch; SM, Jessica C. Bomball; Assistant Director, Holly R. Coombs; Cast: Hans Altwies (Michael Novak), Denis Arndt (Alan Raleigh), Bhama Roget (Annette Raleigh), Amy Thone (Veronica Novak); In Association with Seattle Repertory Theatre; January 7–January 30, 2011

August: Osage County by Tracy Letts; Director, Jackson Gay; Sets/Lighting, Kevin Rigdon; Costumes, Alejo Vietti; Sound, Pierre Dupree; Fight Direction, Brian Byrnes; Dramaturg, Lauren Halvorsen; SM, Terry Cranshaw; ASM, Rebecca R.D. Hamlin; Cast: Jeffrey Bean (Bill Fordham), James Belcher (Charlie Aiken), James Black (Steve Heidebrecht), Elizabeth Bunch (Karen Weston), Louisa Flaningam (Mattie Fae Aiken), Sarah Gay (Johnna Monevata), Josie de Guzman (Barbara Fordham), Jennifer Harmon (Violet Weston), Chris Hutchison (Little Charles Aiken), Charles Krohn (Beverly Weston), Emily Neves (Jean Fordham), Todd Waite (Sheriff Deon Gilbeau); February 18–March 13, 2011

Amadeus by Peter Shaffer; Director, Jonathan Moscone; Sets, Daniel Ostling; Costumes, Katherine Roth; Lighting, Christopher Akerlind; Sound, Rob Milburn, Michael Bodeen; Assistant Director, Elizabeth Bunch; Dramaturg, Robert Shimko; New York Casting, Alaine Alldaffer; SM, Julie Haber; Cast: Stanley Bahorek (Wolfgang Amadeus Mozart), Jeffrey Bean (Antonio Salieri), James Belcher (Baron Van Swieten), James Black (Count Orsini-Rosenberg), Patrick Damien Earl (Priest/Citizen of Vienna), Dylan Godwin and Adam Van Wagoner (The Venticelli),

Chris Hutchison (Joseph II), Steve Irish (Major Domo/Citizen of Vienna), Amanda Kingston (Katherina Cavalieri/Citizen of Vienna), Charles Krohn (Johann Kilian Von Strack), Kalob Martinez (Salieri's Cook/Citizen of Vienna), Emily Neves (Citizen of Vienna), Melissa Pritchett (Constanze Weber), Anne Quackenbush (Teresa Salieri/Citizen of Vienna), David Rainey (Giuseppe Bonno/Citizen of Vienna), Santry Rush (Salieri's Valet/Citizen of Vienna); April 1–May 1, 2011

Pygmalion by George Bernard Shaw; Director, Anders Cato; Sets, Neil Patel; Costumes, Alejo Vietti; Lighting, Rui Rita; Original Music/Sound, Josh Schmidt; Dialect/Voice/Text Coach, Sara Becker; Dramaturg, Lauren Halvorsen; SM, Elizabeth M. Berther; ASM, Rebecca R.D. Hamlin; Cast: Jeffrey Bean (Bystander), James Belcher (Bystander), James Black (Colonel Pickering), Elizabeth Bunch (Eliza Doolittle), Patrick Damien Earl (Bystander), SuEllen Estey (Mrs. Eynsford-Hill), Chris Hutchison (Freddy Eynsford-Hill), Melissa Pritchett (Clara Eynsford-Hill), Elizabeth Shepherd (Mrs. Higgins), Lyndsay Sweeney (Bystander), John Tyson (Alfred Doolittle), Kay Walbye (Mrs. Pearce), Todd Waite (Henry Higgins); May 20–June 12, 2011

Neuhaus Stage

St. Nicholas by Conor McPherson; Director, James Black; Sets/Costume/Lighting, Kevin Rigdon; SM, Terry Cranshaw; Cast: James Black (A Man); July 15–August 8, 2010

A Behanding in Spokane by Martin McDonagh; Director, James Black; Sets, Kevin Rigdon; Costumes, Kelly James-Penot; Lighting, Clint Allen; Sound, Pierre Dupree; Dramaturg, Lauren Halvorsen; New York Casting, Laura Stanczyk, CSA; SM, Rebecca R.D. Hamlin; Cast: Sean-Michael Bowles (Toby), Chris Hutchison (Mervyn), Emily Neves (Marilyn), Andrew Weems (Carmichael); August 27–September 26, 2010

The Santaland Diaries by David Sedaris; Adapted for the stage by Joe Mantello; Director, David Cromer; Sets, Karin Rabe; Lighting, Kevin Rigdon; Costumes, Blair Gulledge; Sound, Pierre Dupree; SM, Elizabeth M. Berther; Cast: Todd Waite (Crumpet); November 21–December 31, 2010

A Weekend with Pablo Picasso by Herbert Siguenza; Director, Todd Salovey; Sets/Costumes, Giulio Cesare Perrone; Lighting, Clint Allen; Original Music/Sound, Bruno Louchouarn; Projection, Victoria Petrovich; Dramaturg, Mark Bly; SM, Elizabeth M. Berther; Cast: Herbert Siguenza (Pablo Picasso); World Premiere; January 22–February 27, 2011

The Monster at the Door by Rajiv Joseph; Director, Daniella Topol; Sets, Kevin Rigdon; Costumes, Amy Clark; Lighting, Tyler Micoleau; Sound, BC DuBoff; Dramaturg, Mark Bly; Fight Direction, Brian Byrnes; SM, Terry Cranshaw; Cast: Rebecca Brooksher (Tonise), Adam Green (Jesse), Portia (Maya), Brian Reddy (Vince), James A. Stephens (Fergueson); World Premiere; April 29–May 29, 2011

Alliance Theatre

Atlanta, Georgia

Forty-third Season

Artistic Director, Susan V. Booth; General Manager, Max Leventhal

Alliance Stage

Twist by William F. Brown; Director/Choreographer, Debbie Allen; Sets, Todd Rosenthal; Costumes, Emilio Sosa; Lighting, Rick Belzerr; Composer/Musician, Tena Clark, Gary Prim; Sound, Peter Fitzgerald; SM, David Blackwell; PSM, Pat A. Flora; Cast: Paul Aguirre (Potlatch/Ensemble), E. Wade Benson (Mr. Prudhomme), Alaman Diadhiou (Twist), Duane Asanté Ervin (Pistol), Kyle Garvin (Skillet/Ensemble), Jared Grimes (Roosevelt/Ensemble), Shawna M. Hamic (Miss Cotton/Ensemble), Matthew Johnson (Boston), Olivia-Diane Joseph (Della), Tracy Kennedy (Crazah Chesterfield), Aijia Lise (Angela/Ensemble), Pat McRoberts (Lucius Thatcher), Melissa Lola Youngblood (Naomi/Ensemble), John Fisher (Ensemble), Chantel Heath (Ensemble), Jamie Katz (Ensemble), Rikki McKinney

(Ensemble), Chondra La-Tease Profit (Ensemble), Malaiyka Reid (Ensemble), Brett Sturgis (Ensemble), Dougie Styles (Ensemble), Zaire Adams (Children's Ensemble), Trey Best (Children's Ensemble), Sabrina Cmelak (Children's Ensemble), Nickolas Eibler (Children's Ensemble), Michael George (Children's Ensemble), Beau Harmon (Children's Ensemble), Chandler Kinney (Children's Ensemble), Chase Maxwell (Children's Ensemble), Madison Minniti (Children's Ensemble); September 1–October 3, 2010

The Nacirema Society Requests the Honor of Your Presence at a Celebration of Their First One Hundred Years by Pearl Cleage; Director, Susan V. Booth; Sets, Peter Hicks; Costumes, Susan E. Mickey; Lighting, Phil Monat; Sound, Richelle Thompson; PSM, lark hackshaw; Dramaturg, Celise Kalke; Cast: Trezana Beverley (Grace Dunbar), Kevin Alan Daniels (Bobby Green), Andrea Frye (Catherine Adams Green), Jasmine Guy (Janet Logan), Chinai J. Hardy (Marie Dunbar), Tonia Jackson (Alpha Campbell Jackson), Karan Kendrick (Lillie Campbell Jackson), Naima Carter Russell (Gracie Dunbar), Neda Spears (Jessie Roberts); World Premiere; October 20–November, 2010

Middle School the Musical by The Cast of *Middle School the Musical*; Director, Rosemary Newcott; PSM, Liz Campbell; Cast: Keith A. Hale (Dr. K), Bernard D. Jones (Junebug), Diany Rodriguez (Cesario), Sharisa Whatley (July), Jacob York (Tubbs); World Premiere; October 23–October 30, 2010

A Christmas Carol by Charles Dickens; Director, Rosemary Newcott; Sets, D. Martyn Bookwalter; Costumes, Mariann Verheyen; Lighting, Diane Ferry Williams; Sound, Clay Bennine; PSM, Pat A. Flora; Cast: Christy Baggett (Ensemble), Elizabeth Wells Berkes (Belle/Ensemble), Kylie Brown (Fan/Martha/Ensemble), Ritchie Crownfield (Ensemble), Christopher DesRoches (Young Scrooge/Ensemble), JeNie Fleming (Mrs. Cratchit/Ensemble), Neal A. Ghant (Bob Cratchit), Bart Hansard (Fezzwig/Christmas Present/Ensemble), Bernard D. Jones (Peter/Ensemble), Chris Kayser (Ebenezer Scrooge), Joe Knezevich (Fred/Ensemble), Royce Mann (Tiny Tim/Ensemble), Tendal Mann (Daniel/Ignorance/Ensemble), Daniel Thomas May (Marley/Ensemble), Bernardine Mitchell (Mrs. Fezziwig/Mrs. Dibler/Ensemble), Sinatra Osm (Dick/Ensemble), Tessa Lene Palisoc (Belinda/Ensemble), Courtney Patterson (Christmas Past/Peg/Ensemble), Drad Raymond (Topper/Ensemble), Ivy Catherine Rogers (Josephine/Ensemble), Jordan Shoulberg (Melinda/Want/Ensemble), James Washburn III (Wyatt/Ensemble), Laurie Williamson (Bess/Ensemble); November 26–December 24, 2010

Bring It On: The Musical by Jeff Whitty; Director/Choreographer, Andy Blankenbuehler; Sets, David Korins; Costumes, Andrea Lauer; Lighting, Jason Lyons; Composer/Musician, Tom Kitt, Lin-Manuel Mirand, Amanda Green; Sound, Brian Ronan; Video, Jeff Sugg; PSM, Lisa Dawn Cave; Cast: Antwan Bethea (Ensemble), Nick Blaemire (Randall/God-like Voice), Courtney Corbeille (Ensemble), Ariana DeBose (Nautica), Brandon Espinoza (Steven/ Announcer/Ensemble), Kelly Felthous (Eva), Shawn Alynda Fisher (Swing), Brooklyn A. Freitag (Ensemble), Gregory Haney (La Cienega), Rod Harrelson (Swing), Dominique Johnson (Cameron/Ensemble), Stephanie C. Klemons (Alexis/Ensemble), Janet Krupin (Kylar/ Announcer), Amanda Lea LaVergne (Campbell), Melody Mills (Ensemble), Michael Mindlin (Cheer Camp Leader/Ensemble), Griffin Myers (Swing), Michael Naone-Carter (Ensemble), David Ranck (Ensemble), Ryann Redmond (Bridget), Elena Ricardo (Ensemble), Kate Rockwell (Skylar/Judge Voice), Billie Sue Roe (Swing), Jon Rua (Twig/Announcer/Ensemble), LaQuet Sharnell ("Legendary" Singer/Ensemble/Soloist), Ephraim M. Sykes (Ensemble), Sheldon Tucker (Ensemble), Adrienne Warren (Danielle), Lauren Whitt (Ensemble); World Premiere; January 15–February 20, 2011

Honk! Music by George Stiles; Book and lyrics by Anthony Drewe; Director, Rosemary Newcott; Sets, Kat Conley; Lighting, Pete Shinn; Costumes, Sydney Roberts; Sound, Clay Benning; PSM, Liz Cambell; Cast: Christy Baggett (Ida/Pink Foot/Froglet), Cynthia D. Barker (Grace/Dot/Froglet/Mother Swan), Leslie W. Bellair (Maureen/Penny/Snowy/Froglet), J.C. Long (Turkey/Ducklings/Barnacles/Main Bullfrog/Father Swan/ASM), Brandon O'Dell (Drake/Jay Bird/Greylag/Froglet), Eugune H. Russell IV (Cat), Justin Tanner (Ugly/Dance Captain); March 5–March 20, 2011

August: Osage County by Tracy Letts; Director, Susan V. Booth; Sets, Leslie Taylor; Costumes, Mariann Verheyen; Lighting, Ken Yunker; Sound, Clay Benning; PSM, Pat A. Flora; Dramaturgs, Patrick McColery, Bari Newport; Cast: Andrew Benator (Little Charles), Brenda Bynum (Violet Weston), Jill Jane Clements (Mattie Fae Aiken), Carolyn Cook (Ivy Weston), Richard Garner (Charlie Aiken), Del Hamilton (Beverly Weston), Bart Hansard (Sheriff Deon Gilbeau), Chris Kayser (Bill Fordham), Tess Malis Kincaid (Barbara Fordham), Joe Knezevich (Steve Heidebrecht), Bethany Anne Lind (Jean Fordham), Courtney Patterson (Karen Weston), Diany Rodriguez (Johnna Monevata); April 1–April 24, 2011

Hertz Stage

Sammy & Me by Wendy Dann and Eric Jordan Young; Director, Wendy Dann; Sets, Brian Sidney Bembridge; Lighting, Marcus Doshi; Costumes, Toni-Leslie James; Sound, Joanna L. Staub; PSM, R. Lamar Williams; Dramaturg, Celise Kalke; Cast: Eric Jordan Young (Me); October 1–October 24, 2010

The Second City Miracle on 1280 Peachtree Street by T.J. Shanoff and Seth Weitberg; Director, Billy Bungeroth; PSM, R. Lamar Williams; Cast: Randy Havens (Ensemble), Tara Ochs (Ensemble), Amy Roeder (Ensemble), Micah Sherman (Ensemble), Ric Walker (Ensemble), Claudia Michelle Wallace (Ensemble); World Premiere; November 5–December 12, 2010

Carapace by David Mitchell Robinson; Director, Judith Ivey; Sets/Costumes, Lex Liang; Lighting, John Ambrosone; Sound, Clay Benning; PSM, R. Lamar Williams; Cast: David de Vries (Jeff), Paul Hester (Kyle), Mark Kincaid (Ted), Joe Knezevich (Peter), Tony Larkin (Brian), Bethany Anne Lind (Margo); World Premiere; February 11–March 16, 2011

Spoon Lake Blues by Josh Tobiessen; Director, Davis McCallum; Sets, Marion Williams; Costumes, Sydney Roberts; Lighting, Jane Cox; Sound, Clay Benning; PSM, Lark Hackshaw; Dramaturg, Celise Kalke; Cast: Veronika Duerr (Abigail), Jimi Kocina (Brady), Lakisha Michelle May (Caitlin), Luke Robertson (Denis); World Premiere; April 1–April 24, 2011

American Conservatory Theater

San Francisco, California

Fourty-fourth Season

Artistic Director, Carey Perloff; Executive Director, Ellen Richard

Scapin by Molière; Adapted by Bill Irwin and Mark O'Donnell; Director, Bill Irwin; Sets, Erik Flatmo; Costumes, Beaver Bauer; Lighting, Nancy Schertler; Composers/Musicians, Randall Craig, Keith Terry; Sound, Jake Rodriguez; Dramaturg, Michael Paller; PM, Jeff Rowlings; SM, Danielle Callaghan; Cast: René Augesen (Zerbinette), Randall Craig (George), Geoff Hoyle (Geronte), Bill Irwin (Scapin), Omozé Idehenre (Nerine), Steven Anthony Jones (Argante), Patrick Lane (Leander), Keith Pinto (Gendarme/Porter 2), Keith Terry (Fred), Gregory Wallace (Octave), Ashley Wickett (Hyacinth), Jud Williford (Sylvestre); September 16–October 23, 2010

Marcus; or The Secret of Sweet by Tarell Alvin McCraney; Director, Mark Rucker; Sets, Loy Arcenas; Lighting, James F. Ingalls; Costumes, Lydia Tanji; Sound, Andre Pluess; SM, Elisa Guthertz; PM, Jeff Rowlings; Cast: Shinelle Azoroh (Osha), Omozé Idehenre (Shaunta Iyun), Margo Hall (Oba/Shun/Elegua), Jared McNeill (Terrell), Richard Prioleau (Marcus Eshu), Gregory Wallace (Ogun Size), Tobie L. Windham (Oshoosi Size/Shua); West Coast Premiere; October 29–November 21, 2010

A Christmas Carol by Charles Dickens; Adapted by Carey Perloff and Paul Walsh; Music by Karl Lundeberg; Choreography by Val Caniparoli; Director, Domenique Lozano; Based on the original direction by Carey Perloff; Sets, John Arnone; Costumes, Beaver Bauer; Lighting, Nancy Schertler; Sound, Jake Rodriguez; SM, Karen Szpaller; Dramaturg, Michael Paller; PM, Jeff Rowlings; Cast: Matthew Avery (Davey/Alfred), Shinelle Azoroh (Belle), Ashley Baker (French Plum/Martha Cratchit), Samuel Joseph Berston (Rory Wilkins/Ned Cratchit), James Carpenter

(Ebenezer Scrooge), Bonnie Castleman (Turkish Fig), Dan Clegg (Clerk/Young Scrooge/ Businessman), Stephanie DeMott (Dorothy/Beth), Penelope Devlin (Sarah Wilkins), Emma Rose Draisin (Little Fan), Marisa Duchowny (The Ghost of Christmas Past), Ella Francis (Want), Alan Frenkel-Andrade (Boy Dick/ Ignorance), Anthony Fusco (Ebenezer Scrooge, Dec. 5 and 20), Cindy Goldfield (Charitable/Ruth/Produce Seller), Eva Huzella (French Plum), Brian Jansen (Alan/ Topper), Jenna Johnson (Ermengarde/Mary/Mrs. Filcher), Richardson Jones (Giles the Fiddler/Thomas/Gang Member), Steven Anthony Jones (The Ghost of Christmas Present), Patrick Lane (Fred/Jim/Gang Member), Alexandra Lee (Precious Wilkins/Gang Member), Sharon Lockwood (Mrs. Dilber/Mrs. Fezziwig), Shelby Lyon (Turkish Fig), Delia MacDougall (Anne Cratchit), Samatha Martin (Sally Cratchit), Jarion Monroe (Mr. Fezziwig/Businessman), Nicholas Pelczar (Bob Cratchit), Caroline Pernick (Spanish Onion), Richard Prioleau (Produce Seller/Businessman), Tobiah Richkind (Peter Cratchit), Joshua Roberts (Burt/ Businessman), Max Rosenak (Dick Wilkins/Businessman), Julian Carlo Santos (Edward/Gang Member), Sadie Eve Scott (Tiny Tim Cratchit), Rachel Share-Sapolsky (Belinda Cratchit), Tony Sinclair (Boy Scrooge/Boy in Sunday Clothes), Willian David Southall (Clerk/Spanish Onion), Howard Swain (Charitable), Ashley Wickett (Felicity/Annabelle), Jack Willis (Marley); December 2–24, 2010

Clybourne Park by Bruce Norris; Director, Jonathan Moscone; Sets, Ralph Funicello; Costumes, Katherine Roth; Lighting, Alexander V. Nichols; Sound, Jeff Mockus; Dramaturg, Michael Paller; PM, Jeff Rowlings; SM, Elisa Guthertz; Cast: René Augesen (Bev/Kathy), Manoel Felciano (Jim/Tom/Kenneth), Anthony Fusco (Russ/Dan), Omozé Idehenre (Francine/Lena), Emily Kitchens (Betsy/ Lindsey), Richard Thieriot (Karl/Steve), Gregory Wallace (Albert/Kevin); West Coast Premiere; January 20–February 20, 2011

The Homecoming by Harold Pinter; Director, Carey Perloff; Sets, Daniel Ostling; Costumes, Alex Jaeger; Lighting, Alexander V. Nichols; Sound, Cliff Caruthers; Dramaturg, Michael Paller; PM, Jeff Rowlings; SM, Kimberly Mark Webb; Cast: René Augesen (Ruth), Adam O'Byrne (Joey), Anthony Fusco (Teddy), Andrew Polk (Lenny), Kenneth Welsh (Sam), Jack Willis (Max); March 3–27, 2011

No Exit by Jean-Paul Sartre; The Virtual Stage and Electric Company Theatre production; Adapted from French by Paul Bowles; Conceived and directed by Kim Collier; Sets, Jay Gower Taylor; Costumes, Kristen McGhie; Lighting, John Webber; Sound, Brian Linds; Video, Andy Thompson; PM, Jeff Rowlings; SM, Jan Hodgson; Cast: Lucia Frangione (Estelle), Laara Sadiq (Inez), Andy Thompson (Cradeau), Jonathon Young (The Valet); April 7–May 1, 2011

Armistead Maupin's Tales of the City: A New Musical Libretto by Jeff Whitty, Music and lyrics by Jake Shears, John Garden; Based on Armistead Maupin's *Tales of the City* and *More Tales of the City*; Choreography by Larry Keigwin; Director, Jason Moore; Sets, Douglas W. Schmidt; Costumes, Beaver Bauer; Lighting, Robert Wierzel; Sound, John Shivers; Associate Sound Designer, David Patridge; Orchestrator, Bruce Coughlin; Arrangements, Stephen Oremus and Carmel Dean; Music Supervisor, Carmel Dean; Music Director/Conductor, Cian McCarthy; Dramaturg, Michael Paller; Casting, Melcap Casting, David Caparelliotis; PM, Jeff Rowlings; SM, Karen Szpaller; Cast: Judy Kaye (Anna Madrigal), Mary Birdsong (Mona Ramsey), Josh Breckenridge (Jon Fielding, etc.), Manoel Felciano (Normal Neal Williams), Diane J. Findlay (Mother Mucca, etc.), Patrick Lane (Brian Hawkins), Kathleen Elizabeth Monteleone (DeDe Halcyon-Day, etc.), Richard Poe (Edgar Halcyon), Julie Reiber (Connie Bradshaw, etc.), Andrew Samonsky (Beauchamp Day, etc.), Wesley Taylor (Michael "Mouse" Tolliver), Betsy Wolfe (Mary Ann Singleton), Keith A. Bearden (Ensemble), Jessica Coker (Ensemble), Kristoffer Cusick (Ensemble) Jason Hoover (Ensemble), Alex Hsu (Ensemble), Kimberly Jensen (Ensemble), Stuart Marland (Ensemble), Jeff McLean (Ensemble), Pamela Myers (Ensemble), Alexis Papedo (Ensemble), Josh Walden (Ensemble); World Premiere; May 18–July 31, 2011

The American Repertory Theater

Cambridge, Massachusetts

Thirty-first Season

Artistic Director, Diane Paulus; Producer/Acting Managing Director, Diane Borger

Cabaret Book by Joe Masteroff; Based on the play by John Van Druten; Stories by Chistopher Isherwood; Music by John Kander; Lyrics by Fred Ebb; Director, Steven Bogart; Sets/Costumes, David Israel Reynoso; Lighting, Nicholas D. Vargelis; Sound, Clive Goodwin; SM, Katherine Shea; Movement Director, Steven Mitchell Wright; Casting, Ariane Barbanell; Production Associate, Taylor Adamik; Assistant Director, Jillian Singer; Voice Coach, Karen Kopryanski; Dramaturg, Jessica Green; Cast: Amanda Palmer (Emcee), Aly Trasher (Sally Bowles), Matt Wood (Cliff Bradshaw), Thomas Derrah (Fraulein Schneider), Remo Airaldi (Herr Schultz), David Costa (Ernst Ludwig), Claire Elizabeth Davies (Fraulein Kost), Jeremy Geidt (Max), Lucille Duncan (Rosie), Gaetano Pugliese (Louie), Eric Johnson (Frenchie), Tamara Hickey (Texas), Renee-Marie-Brewster (Fritzie), Jordy Lievers (Helga), Christopher I. Thomas (Bobby), Ed Walsh (Victor), Annika Franklin (Hansel); August 31–October 29, 2010

Alice vs. Wonderland Adapted by Brendan Shea; Based on Lewis Carroll's *Alice's Adventures in Wonderland* and *Through the Looking Glass*; Director, János Szász; Sets, Riccardo Hernandez; Costumes, David Israel Reynoso; Lighting, Maruti Evans; Sound, Clive Goodwin; Choreographer, Cheryl Turski; SM, Kevin Schlagle; Dramaturg, Sara Bookin-Weiner; Cast: Annika Franklin (Mary Ann/ Black Dahlia), Vincent Selhorst-Jones (White Rabbit/Spade #2), Angela Gulner (Alice 1), Nick Crandall/Derek Lettman (Door 1/Cheshire Cat), Ed Walsh (Door 2/ Lory/White Knight), Jared Eaton (Door 3/Duck/March Hare), Erikka Walsh (Alice 2), Sarah Jadin (Dodo/Tweedledum/Alice 4/Black Dahlia), Megan Brotherton (Tweedledee/Alice 4/Space #5), Steven Good (Mouse/Spade #7), Christian Grunnah (Pat/Caterpillar/Knave), Faith Imafidon (Alice 3), Christopher Staley (Caterpillar/Mad Hatter), Jennifer Soo (Alice 5), M. Zach Bubolo (Dormouse/King of Hearts), Renee-Marie Brewster (Alice 6/Black Dahlia), Jordy Lievers (Queen of Hearts/Black Dahlia); September 18–October 9, 2011

The Blue Flower by Jim and Ruth Bauer; Director, Will Pomerantz; Movement Director, Tom Nelis; Special Arrangement, Stephen Schwartz, Andrew Levine, Steve Tate; Sets, Marsha Ginsberg; Costumes, Carol Bailey; Lighting, Justin Townsend; Sound, Clive Goodwin; Cast: Daniel Jenikins (Max), Meghan McGeary (Hannah), Tom Nelis (Fairytale), Lucas Kavner (Franz), Teal Wicks (Maria), Conner Christiansen (Typewriter Man), Paul Shafer (Sewing Machine Man); December 1, 2010–January 8, 2011

R. Buckminster Fuller: The History (and Mystery) of The Universe by D.W. Jacobs; Director, D.W. Jacobs; SM, Adele Nadine Trauh; Dramaturg, Annie DiMario; ASM, Chris de Camillis; Production Associate, Sarah Gasser; Cast: Thomas Derrah (R. Buckminster Fuller); January 14, 2011–Limited Engagement

Ajax by Sophocles; In a new translation by Carles Connaghan; Director, Sarah Benson; Sets/Costume, David Zinn; Lighting, Justin Townsend; Sound, Matt Tierney; Video, Greg Emetax; Casting, Stephen Kopel; Fight Consultant, Felix Ivanov; SM, Katie Ailinger; Voice/Speech, Nancy Houfek; Assistant Director, Kathryn Kozlark; Dramaturg, Laura Henry; ASM, Ryan A. Anderson; Assistant Dramaturg, Christina Farris; Cast: Kaaron Briscoe (Athena), Ron Cephas Jones (Odysseus), Brent Harris (Ajax), Remo Airaldi (Chorus Leader), Linda Powell (Tecmessa), Mesafint Goldfeld (Eurysaces), Nick Crandall (Messenger), Nathan Darrow (Teucer), James Joseph O'Nel (Menelaus), Thomas Derrah (Agamemnon); February 12–March 13, 2011

Death and the Powers by Robert Pinsky and Randy Weiner; Music by Tod Machover; Libretto by Robert Pinski; Director, Diane Paulus; Conductor, Gil Rose; Production Design, Alex McDowell; Choreography, Karole Armitage; Costumes, David C. Woolard; Lighting, Donald Holder; Sound, Chris Full; Visual/Software Design, Peter Torpey; Media Design, Matt Checkowski; Sound Technology, Ben Bloomberg; Associate Director, Andrew Eggert; Manager, Sisie Siu Cohen; Robot Mechanical Design, Bob Hsiung; Robotic Control Systems, Michael

Miller; Interaction Design, Elena Jessop; Assistant Director, Allegra Libonati; Assistant Lighting Designer, Rebecca Makus; PSM, Nancy Harrington; SM, Julie Baldauff, Carolyn Boyd, Dana Stremming; Technology Development, Opera of the Future Group, MIT Media Lab; Cast: James Maddalena (Simon Powers), Emily Albrink (Evvy), Sara Heaton (Miranda), Hal Cazalet (Nicholas), Douglas Dodson (The United Way), David Kravitz (The United Nations), Tom McNichols (The Administration); March 18– March 25, 2011

Prometheus Bound by Steven Sater; Adapted from the play by Aeschylus; Music by Serj Tankian; Director, Diane Paulus; Choreography, Stephen Petronio; Sets, Riccardo Hernandez; Costumes, Emily Rebholz; Lighting, Kevin Adams; Sound, Clive Goodwin; Orchestrations, Serj Tankian; Vocal Design, AnnMarie Milazzo; Music Supervisors, Debra Barsha, Lance Horne; Band Leader, Vincent Pedulla; Casting, Melcap Casting; SM, Katherine Shea; Associate Director, Allegra Libonati; Dramaturg, Ryan McKittrick, Sara Bookin-Weiner, Tyler Monroe; Cast: Gavin Creel (Prometheus), Lea DeLaria (Force), Michael Cunio (Oceanos), Gabriel Ebert (Hepaistos/Hermes), Jo Lampert (Daughter of the Aether), Celina Carvaijal (Daughter of the Aether), Ashley Flanagan (Daughter of the Aether), Uzo Aduba (Io), Emmanuel Avellanet (Groupie), Kevin Lin (Groupie, Bart Mather (Groupie); February 25–April 2, 2011

Arden Theatre Company

Philadelphia, Pennsylvania

Twenty-third Season

Producing Artistic Director, Terrence J. Nolen; Managing Director, Amy L. Murphy

Arcadia Stage

Ghost Writer by Michael Hollinger; Director, James J. Christy; Sets, David P. Gordon; Costumes, Charlotte Cloe Fox Wind; Lighting, Jerold R. Forsyth; Sound, Jorge Cousineay; SM, Alec E. Ferrell; Cast: Megan Bellwoar (Myra Babbage), Patricia Hodges (Vivian Woolsey), Douglas Rees (Franklin Woolsey); World Premiere; September 9–November 7, 2010

A Moon for the Misbegotten by Eugene O'Neill; Director, Matt Pfeiffer; Sets, Matt Saunders; Costumes, Alison Roberts; Lighting, Thom Weaver; Sound, James Sugg; SM, Alec E. Ferrell; Cast: Grace Gonglewski (Josie Hogan), Eric Hissom (James Tyrone, Jr), Sean Lally (Mike Hogan), Allen Radway (T. Stedman Harder), H. Michael Walls (Phil Hogan); January 6–February 27, 2011

Wanamaker's Pursuit by Rogelio Martinez; Director, Terrence J. Nolen; Sets, James Kronzer; Costumes, Richard St. Clair; Lighting, F. Mitchell Dana; Sound, Jorge Cousineau; Dramaturg, Edward Sobel; SM, Stephanie Cook; Cast: David Bardeen (Leo Stein), Shawn Fagan (Picasso/LaRue/Guard/Franz Reichelt/ Fencing Instructor), Wilbur Edwin Henry (Paul Poiret), Jürgen Hooper (Nathan Wanamaker), Geneviève Perrier (Denise Poiret), Catharine K. Slusar (Gertrude Stein); World Premiere; March 31–May 22, 2011

F. Otto Haas Stage

The Threepenny Opera Play with music after John Gay's *The Beggar's Opera*, in Three Acts; Music by Kurt Weill; German translation, Elisabeth Hauptmann; Adaptation/Lyrics, Bertolt Brecht; English translation of dialogue, Robert MacDonald; English translation of lyrics, Jeremy Sams; Used by arrangement with European American Music Corporation, agent for The Kurt Weill Foundation for Music, Inc., agent for the Brecht Estate; Director, Terrence J. Nolen; Sets, Tom Gleeson; Costumes, Rosemarie E. McKelvey; Lighting, Thom Weaver; Sound/Video, Jorge Cousineau; Musical Director, Eric Ebbenga; Fight Director, John Bellomo; Dramaturg, Sarah Ollove; SM, John Flack; Cast: Terence Archie (MacHeath), Liz Filios (Lucy Brown), Victoria Frings (Polly Peachum), Scott Greer (Peachum), Doug Hara (Filch/Jimmy/Old Whore), Jamal Lee Harris (Chain-Saw Bob/Constable), Darren Michael Hengst (Matt of the Mint/Beggar), Brianna Horne (Vixen), Sean Lally (Crook-Fingered Jake), Anthony Lawton (Tiger Brown), Mary Martello (Mrs. Peachum), Sebastian Naskaris (Ned), Bi Jean Ngo (Walt/

Nelly), Clare O'Malley (Dolly), Ken Robinson (Smith/Reverend Kimball), Amanda Schoonover (Betty/Beggar), Rachel Wallace (Jenny); September 30–November 7, 2010

The Borrowers by Mary Norton; Adapted by Charles Way; Director, Whit MacLaughlin; Sets, Lewis Folden; Costumes, Rosemarie E. McKelvey; Lighting, Drew Billiau; Sound/Original Music, Nathan Roberts; Puppets, Aaron Cromie; SM, Stephanie Cook; Cast: Scott Boulware (Pod), Delanté G. Keys (Boy), Bi Jean Ngo (Arrietty), Steve Pacek (Crampfurl, Spiller, Gypsy Boy, Eggletina), Catharine K. Slusar (Homily), Jo Twiss (Mrs. Driver/Aunt Lupy); December 1, 2010–January 30, 2011

Superior Donuts by Tracy Letts; Director, Edward Sobel; Sets, Kevin Depinet; Costumes, Alison Roberts; Lighting, Michelle Habeck; Sound, Rob Kaplowitz; SM, Katharine M. Hanley; Fight Director, John V. Bellomo; Cast: Jennifer Barnhart (Officer Randy Osteen), Ian Bedford (Kiril Ivakin), Jake Blouch (Kevin Magee), Nancy Boykin (Lady Boyle), James William Ijames (Franco Wicks), David Mackay (Max Tarasov), Pete Pryor (Luther Flynn), Craig Spidle (Arthur Przybyszewski), Brian Anthony Wilson (Officer James Bailey); March 3–April 3, 2011

The Flea and the Professor Based on the story by Hans Christian Andersen, by Jordan Harrison; Music, Richard Gray; Lyrics, Jordan Harrison, Richard Gray, Director, Anne Kauffman; Sets, Louisa Thompson, Costumes, Olivera Gajic; Lighting, Thom Weaver; Sound, Rob Kaplowitz; Music Director, Dan Kazemi; Choreographer, Jenn Rose; SM, Alec E. Ferrell; Cast: Aaron Cromie (The Sea Captain/The Loyal Subject), Scott Greer (The Flea), Alex Keiper (The Cannibal Princess), Mary Martello (The Cannibal Queen), Robert McClure (The Professor), Annie McNamara (The Storyteller), Kim Sullivan (The Cannibal King/ Hans Christian Andersen); World Premiere; May 4–June 12, 2011

Arena Stage at the Mead Center for American Theater

Washington, D.C.

Sixty-first Season

Artistic Director, Molly Smith; Managing Director, Edgar Dobie

Oklahoma! Music by Richard Rodgers; Book and lyrics by Oscar Hammerstein II; Director, Molly Smith; Choreographer, Parker Esse; Music Director, George Fulginiti-Shakar; Sets, Eugene Lee; Costumes, Martin Pakledinaz; Lighting, Michael Gilliam; Sound, Timothy M. Thompson; Fight Choreographer, David Leong; Dramaturg, Janine Sobeck; NY Casting Director, Paul Hardt; Arena Casting Director, Daniel Pruksarnukul; SM, Susan R. White; Cast: Philip Michael Baskerville (Cord Elam), Kurt Boehm (Male Swing), E. Faye Butler (Aunt Eller), Cyana Cook (Ellen), Emilee Dupré (Vivian), Lucas Fedele (Ike Skidmore), Eleasha Gamble (Laurey), Semhar Ghedremichael (Aggie), Jessica Hartman (Female Swing), Andrew Hodge (Slim), Nehal Joshi (Ali Hakim), Anton Harrison LaMon (Jess), Cara Massey (Gertie), Hugh Nees (Andrew Carnes), Annie Petersmeyer (Virginia), Aaron Ramey (Jud Fry), Shane Rhoades (Fred/Dance Captain), Nicholas Rodriguez (Curly), Vincent Rodriguez III (Sam), June Schreiner (Ado Annie Carnes), Kyle Vaughn (Mike/Dream Curly), Cody Williams (Will Parker), Hollie E. Wright (Sylvie/Dream Laurie), Jessica Wu (Kate); October 22–December 30, 2010

every tongue confess by Marcus Gardley; Director, Kenny Leon; Sets, Tom Lynch; Costumes, Ilona Somogyi; Lighting, Allen Lee Hughes; Composer, Dwight Andrews; Sound, Timothy M. Thompson; Dramaturg, Nakissa Etemad; NY Casting Director, Alaine Alldaffer; Fight Director, Joe Isenberg; Arena Casting Director, Daniel Pruksarnukul; SM, Kurt Hall; Cast: Jason Dirden (Shadrack), Crystal Fox (Missionary/Tender Meeks), Autumn Hurlbert (Benny Pride), Jim Ireland (Stoker Pride), Leslie Kritzer (Bernadette), Eugene Lee (Elder/Jeremiah), F. Roger Mitchell (Brother/Bobby), Jonathan Peck (Blacksmith), Phylicia Rashad (Mother Sister); November 9, 2010–January 2, 2011

Jonathon Young and Andy Thompson in American Conservatory Theatre's production of No Exit (photo by Michael Julian Berz)

Remo Airaldi and Linda Powell in Ajax at the American Repertory Theatre (photo by Michael Lutch)

Hal Cazalet and James Maddalena in American Repertory Theatre's Death and the Powers (photo by Jonathan Williams)

Bill Irwin and Geoff Hoyle in Scapin at American Conservatory Theatre (photo by Kevin Berne)

Doug Hara and Brianna Horne in Arden Theatre Company's production of The Threepenny Opera (photo by Mark Garvin)

Kim Sullivan, Aaron Cromie, Scott Greer, Mary Martello, and Alex Keiper in the Arden Children's Theatre production of The Flea and the Professor (photo by Mark Garvin)

Mongezi Ntaka, David Foreman, Waldo Robertson, Rachael Holmes, and Daniel Ssuuna in Arena Stage at the Mead Center for American Theater's production of Ruined (photo by Joan Marcus)

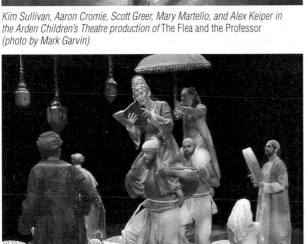

The Company of The Arabian Nights at Arena Stage at the Mead Center for American Theater (photo by Stan Barouh)

Bob Sorenson and Oliver Wadsworth in The Mystery of Irma Vep at the Arizona Theatre Company (photo by Tim Fuller)

Georgette Timoney, Bill Timoney, and Jason Harper in A Christmas Story at Arkansas Repertory Theatre (photos by Ben Krain)

Naomi Jacobson and Steve Hendrickson in Arizona Theatre Company's World Premiere of Ten Chimneys (photo by Tim Fuller)

Let Me Down Easy by Anna Deavere Smith; Director, Leonard Foglia; Music/Lyrics, Joshua Redman; Sets, Riccardo Hernandez; Costumes, Ann Hould-Ward; Lighting, Dan Ozminkowski; Movement Coach, Elizabeth Roxas-Dobrish; Vocal Coach, Amy Stoller; based on the original by Jules Fisher and Peggy Eisenhauer; Sound, Ryan Rumery; Projections, Zachary Borovay; Dramaturg, Alisa Solomon; SM, Joe Smelser; Cast: Anna Deavere Smith; December 31, 2010–February 13, 2011

The Arabian Nights by Mary Zimmerman; Adapted from *The Book of the Thousand Nights and One Night*, in association with Berkeley Repertory Theatre, Kansas City Repertory Theatre and Lookingglass Theatre Company; Director, Mary Zimmerman; Sets, Daniel Ostling; Costumes, Mara Blumenfeld; Lighting, T.J. Gerckens; Sound/Original Music, André Pluess; SM, Cynthia Cahill; Cast: Barzin Akhavan (Harun al-Rashid), Usman Ally (Madman), Terence Archie (Greengrocer/Robber), David DeSantos (King Shahryar), Minita Gandhi (Slave Girl), Allen Gilmore (Scheherezade's Father/Ishak of Mosul), Susaan Jamshidi (Butcher/Sympathy the Learned), Ronnie Malley (Poor Man/Musician), Luis Moreno (Clarinetist/Sage), Maureen Sebastian (Dunyazade/Azizah), Nicole Shalhoub (Perfect Love/The Other Woman), Louis Tucci (Jafar/Sheik al-Fadl), Stacey Yen (Scheherezade), Evan Zes (Sheik al-Islam/Abu al-Hasan); January 14–February 20, 2011

Who's Afraid of Virginia Woolf? by Edward Albee; Steppenwolf Theatre Company; Director, Pam MacKinnon; Sets, Todd Rosenthal; Costumes, Nan Cibula-Jenkins; Lighting, Allen Lee Hughes; Sound, Rob Milburn, Michael Bodeen; Fight Choreographer, Nick Sandys; Steppenwolf Casting Director, Erica Daniels; Arena Casting Director, Daniel Pruksarnukul; SM, Malcolm Ewen; Cast: Carrie Coon (Honey), Madison Dirks (Nick), Amy Morton (Martha), Tracy Letts (George); February 25–April 10, 2011

At Home at the Zoo by Edward Albee; Director, Mary B. Robinson; Sets, James Noone; Costumes, T. Tyler Stumpf; Lighting, Nancy Schertler; Sound, Timothy M. Thompson; Fight Director, Joe Isenberg; Dramaturg, Aaron Malkin; NY Casting Director, MelCap Casting/David Caparelliotis, CSA; Arena Casting Director, Daniel Pruksarnukul; SM, Martha Knight; Cast: Jeff Allin (Peter), Colleen Delany (Ann), James McMenamin (Jerry); February 25–April 24, 2011

Ruined by Lynn Nottage; Director, Charles Randolph-Wright; Sets, Alexander V. Nichols; Costumes, ESosa; Lighting, Michael Gilliam; Sound/Original Music, Lindsay Jones; Music Coordinator, Mongezi Chris Ntaka; Fight Director, Robb Hunter; Dialect, Kim James Bey; Movement Consultant, Keith Lamelle Thomas; Dramaturg, Amrita Ramanan; NY Casting Director, Tara Rubin Casting; Arena Casting Director, Daniel Pruksarnukul; SM, Kurt Hall; Cast: Segun Akande (Soldier), Jeremiah W. Birkett (Christian), Clifton Duncan (Jerome Kisembe), JaBen A. Early (Simon), David Foreman (Percussionist), Donnetta Lavinia Grays (Salima), Rachael Holmes (Sophie), James Johnson (Soldier/Aid Worker), Jenny Jules (Mama Nadi), Jamairais Malone (Josephine), Mongezi Chris Ntaka (Guitarist), Babs Olusanmokum (Cmdr. Osembenga), Lawrence Redmond (Mr. Hariri), Waldo Robertson (Guitarist), Daniel Ssuuna (Traditional African Instrumentalist/Laurent), Jude Tibeau (Soldier), Psalmayene 24 (Fortune); Ensemble: Jamar Brown, Ellentinya I. Dodd, Thony Mena, Jason Phillips, David Samuel, Anastasia Stewart, Hectorlyne P. Wuor; April 22–June 5, 2011

A Time to Kill by Rupert Holmes; Director, Ethan McSweeney; Sets, James Noone; Costumes, Karen Perry; Lighting, York Kennedy; Sound/Original Music, Lindsay Jones; Video Design, Jeff Sugg; Fight Choreographer, David Leong; Script Wrangler, Aaron Malkin; Dialect, Lynn Watson; NY Casting Director, Tara Rubin Casting; Arena Casting Director, Daniel Pruksarnukul; SM, Susan R. White; Cast: Sebastian Arcelus (Jake Brigance), Jeffrey M. Bender (Billy Ray Cobb/Terrell Grist/Dr. Rodeheaver), Rosie Benton (Ellen Roark), Brennan Brown (Rufus Buckley), Erin Davie (Carl Jane Brigance), Trena Bolden Fields (Norma), Jonathan Lincoln Fried (Wizard for Mississippi/Dr. W.T. Bass), Dion Graham (Carl Lee Hailey), JC Hayward (Felicia Albright), Deborah Hazlett (Drew Tyndale/Cora Cobb), Joe Isenberg (Pete Willard/D.R. Musgrove), Chiké Johnson (Ozzie Walls), Michael Marcan (Cameraman), Hugh Nees (Vernon Pate), Nisa Shelton (Tonya Hailey), Evan Thompson (Judge Omar Noose), John C. Vennema (Lucien Willbanks); May 6–June 19, 2011

Arizona Theatre Company

Phoenix and Tucson, Arizona

Forty-fourth Season

Artistic Director, David Ira Goldstein; Interim Managing Director, Jessica Andrews

Backwards in High Heels Conceived and developed by Lynnette Barkley, Christopher McGovern; Book/Musical Arrangements/Original Songs, Christopher McGovern; Music by George Gershwin, Irving Berlin, Jerome Kern; Director, Scott Schwartz; Co-creator, Lynnette Barkley; Musical Director/Conductor, Christopher McGovern; Choreographer, Patti Colombo; Sets, Walt Spangler; Costumes, Alejo Vietti; Lighting, Jeff Croiter; Sound, Abe Jacob; Associate Director, Laura Josepher; PSM, Glenn Bruner; Co-producers, Asolo Repertory Theatre, The Cleveland Playhouse, SanJose Repertory Theatre; Cast: Matthew LaBanca (MarcusDirector/Fred Astaire/Others), Heather Lee (Lela), James Patterson (Frank), Benjie Randall (Joe/Bill McMath/George Schaffer/Lew Ayres/Others), Christianne Tisdale (Martha May/Louise/Ethel Merman/ Others), Anna Aimee White (Ginger Rogers), Cameron Herderson (Associate Choreographer/u/s), Temple of Music and Art, September 10–October 2, 2010; Herberger Theater Center, October 7–24, 2010

Ma Rainey's Black Bottom by August Wilson; Director, Lou Bellamy; Sets, Vicki Smith; Costumes, Mathew J. LeFebvre; Lighting, Don Darnutzer; Sound, Brian Jerome Peterson; Music Consultant, Sanford Moore; Fight Director, Brent Gibbs; SM, Bruno Ingram; ASM, Glenn Bruner, Alena Fast; Co-producer, Penumbra Theatre Company; Cast: James T. Alfred (Levee), Lerea Carter (Dussie Mae), James Craven (Cutler), Abdul Salaam El Razzac (Toledo), William John Hall, Jr. (Slow Drag), Phil Kilbourne (Irvin), Brendan Guy Murphy (Policeman), Jevetta Steele (Ma Rainey), Michael Tezla (Sturdyvant), Ahanti Young (Sylvester), Temple of Music and Art, October 16– November 6, 2010; Herberger Theater Center, November 11–28, 2010

Woody Guthrie's American Song Songs and writings by Woody Guthrie, Conceived and adapted by Peter Glazer, Orchestrations/Vocal Arrangements, Jeff Waxman, Director, Randal Myler; Music Director, Dan Wheetman; Sets, Vicki Smith; Costume, Kish Finnegan; Lighting, Michael Gilliam; Sound, Abe Jacob; Projections Designer, Jeffrey Cady; PSM, Glenn Bruner; ASM, Bruno Ingram, Tim Toothman, Ashley Simon; Cast: Jason Edwards (Ensemble), Sally Mayes (Ensemble), Kenita R. Miller (Ensemble), Ryan Nearhoff (Ensemble), Jim Newman (Ensemble), Mark Baczynski (Musician), David P. Jackson (Musician), David Miles Keenan (Assistant Musical Director/Musician); Temple of Music and Art, November 27–December 22, 2010; Herberger Theater Center, December 30, 2010–January 16, 2011

Ten Chimmneys by Jeffrey Hatcher; Director, David Ira Goldstein; Sets, John Ezell; Costumes, Marcia Dixcy Jory; Lighting, Dennis Parichy; Sound/Composer, Josh Schmidt; PSM, Glenn Bruner; ASM, Alena Fast; Cast: Suzanne Bouchard (Lynn Fontanne), Anna Bullard (Uta Hagen), Steve Hendrickson (Alfred Lunt), Naomi Jacobson (Louise Greene), Linda Stephens (Hattie Sederholm), Marcus Truschinski (Carl Sederholm), Michael Winters (Sydney Greenstreet); World Premiere; Temple of Music and Art, December 28, 2010–February 12, 2011; Herberger Theater Center, February 15– March 6, 2011

Lost in Yonkers by Neil Simon; Director, Samantha K. Wyer; Set, Michael Schweikardt; Costumes, David K. Mickelsen; Lighting, David Lee Cuthbert; Resident Sound Designer, Brian Jerome Peterson; Dialect Coach, Dianne Winslow; SM, Timothy Toothman; ASM, Ashley Simon; Cast: Maxx Carlisle–King (Arty), Ryan DeLuca (Jay), Kate Goehring (Bella), Judy Kaye (Grandma), Preston Maybank (Louie), Kerry McCue (Gert), Spencer Rowe (Eddie), James Conway (Eddie u/s), Megan Davis (Gert u/s), Anna Lauren Farrell (Bella, u/s), Joe Hubbard (Louie, u/s), Connor Kesslering (Jay u/s), Preston Maguire (Arty u/s), Leannè Whitewolf-Charlton (Grandma u/s); Temple of Music and Art, February 2–March 19, 2011; Herberger Theater Center; March 22–April 10, 2011

The Mystery of Irma Vep by Charles Ludlam; Director, David Ira Goldstein; Set, Drew Boughton; Costume, David Kay Mickelsen; Lighting, Michael Gilliam; Sound, Brian Jerome Peterson; Composer, Roberta Carlson; PSM, Glenn Bruner;

ASM, Timothy Toothman; Cast: Bob Sorenson (Jane Twisden/Lord Edgar Hillcrest/an Intruder), Oliver Wadsworth (Nicodemus Underwood/Lady Enid Hillcrest/Alcazar/Pev Amri), Karl Hussey (Mr. Sorenson u/s), Mike Reasor (Mr. Wadsworth u/s); Temple of Music and Art, March 21–April 30, 2011; Herberger Theater Center, May 4–May 29, 2011

Arkansas Repertory Theatre

Little Rock, Arkansas

Thirty-fifth Season

Artistic Director, Bob Hupp; Managing Director, Michael McCurdy

Evita by Tim Rice; Director, Cliff Fannin Baker; Choreographer, Lynne Kurdziel-Formato; Musical Director, Helen Gregory; Sets, Don Yanick; Costumes, Marianne Custer, Lighting, Mike Eddy; Sound, M. Jason Pruzin; Video, Matt Rozzell; Props, Lynda J. Kwallek; PSM, Patrick Lanczki, Assistant PSM, Libby Mickle; PM, Rafael Colon Castanera; Casting, Maria Eberline; Cast: Alan Bennett (Ensemble/Magaldi u/s), Matthew Buffalo (Ensemble), Al Bundonis (Peron), Joi Chen (Ensemble), Peter Davenport (Ensemble/Peron u/s), Maria Eberline (Eva Peron), Katie Emerson (Mistress/Ensemble), Liz Griffith (Ensemble/Eva u/s), Adam Ioele (Ensemble), Antonio Jimenez (Ensemble/Che u/s), Laura Medford (Ensemble/Mistress u/s), Javar La'trail Parker (Ensemble), Rick Qualls (Ensemble/Agustin Magaldi), Freddy Ramirez (Tango Specialty/Ensemble), Molly Rosenthal (Ensemble), Rachal Small (Ensemble), Allision Stodola Wilson (Ensemble/Dance Captian), David Tankersley (Ensemble), David Villella (Che); September 10–October 3, 2010

Hamlet by William Shakespeare; Director, Robert Hupp; Fight Director, D.C. Wright; Sets, Mike Nichols; Costumes, Margaret McKowen; Lighting, Matthew Webb; Sound, M. Jason Pruzin; Props, Lynda J. Kwallek; Composer, Ellen Mandel; PSM, Tara Kelley; PM, Rafael Colon Castanera; Vocal Coach, Karen Q. Clark; Cast: Tom Bateman (Cornelius/Lucianus/ Gentleman), Harris Berlinsky (Polonius), J. Center (Franciso/Player King/Grave Digger/ Norwegian soldier), Avery Clark (Hamlet), Nikki Coble (Ophelia), Ben Gibson (Claudius' Soldier), Angie Gilbert (Gertrude's Assistant/Player Queen/Gertrude u/s), Peter Leake (Lord/ Player/Fortinbras/Fight Captain), Kenneth Lee (Horatio), Michael Markham (Barnardo/ Rosencrantz/Lord). Barbara McCulloh (Gertrude), Colin McPhillamy (Ghost/Claudius), Matt Morley (Claudius' Soldier), Joel Rainwater (Guildenstern/Osric), Joseph Reese (Marcellus/ Player/Captain/Priest), Shannon Michael Wamser (Laertes); October 29–November 14, 2010

A Christmas Story by Philip Grecian; Director, Nicole Capri; Sets, Mike Nichols; Costumes, Shelly Hall; Lighting, Andrew Meyers; Sound, M. Jason Prusin; Lynda J. Wallek; PSM, Patrick Lanczki; PM, Rafael Colon Castanera; Cast: Matthew Carey (Scut Farkus), John Logan Darr (Randy), Spencer Davis (Flick), Cole Ewing (Ralphie), C.J. Fowler (Grover Dill/ Schwartz/ Ralphie/Scut u/s), Will Frueaff (Grover Dill/Flick/Ralphie/Randy u/s), Jason Harper (Ralph), Julia Landfair (Emily Jane, Esther Jane u/s), Damon McKinnis (Schwartz), Laura Medford (Miss Shields), Marina Redlich (Ester Jane), Abby Shourd (Emily Jane), Bill Timoney (Old Man), Georgette Reilly Timoney (Mother); December 3–December 26, 2010

A Raisin In The Sun by Lorraine Hansberry; Director, Rajendra Ramoon Maharaj; Sets, Mike Nichols; Costumes, Trish Clark; Lighting, Matthew Webb; Sound, M. Jason Pruzin; Props, Lynda J. Kwallek; PSM, Patrick Lanczki; PM, Rafael Colon Castanera; Cast: Segun Akande (Joseph Asagai), Tyrese Treyvon Bluford (Travis Younger), Lynnette R. Freeman (Ruth Younger), Jon Froehich (Karl Lindner, Fight Captain), Michael Chenevert (George Murchison), Laurence A. Stepney (Bobo), Phyllis Yvonne Stickney (Lena Younger), Christopher B. Straw (Moving Man), Hisham Tawfiq (Walter Lee Younger), Myxolydia Tyler (Beneatha Younger), Anthony Dewayne Williams Jr. (Travis Younger), S. Juain Young; January 21–February 6, 2011

Hairspray by Mark O'Donnell, Thomas Meehan; Music, Marc Shaiman; Lyrics, Scott Wittman, Marc Shaiman; Orchestrations, Harold Wheeler; Arrangements by Marc Shaiman; Director/Choreographer, Robert Kovach; Costumes, Michael Bottari, Ronald Case; Lighting, Michael J. Eddy; Sound, M. Jason Pruzin; Wigs, Gerard Kelly; PSM, Patrick Lanczki; Costume Coordinator/PM, Rafael Colon Castanera; ASM, Mary Stazewski; Musical Director, Corinne Aquilina; Cast: Kelsie Adkisson (Ensemble/Dynamite), Tommaso Antico (Link Larkin), Morgan Brown (Little Inez) Iris Burruss (Ensemble/Dynamite), Lillian Castillo (Tracy Turnblad), Brendan Chambers (Ensemble), P. Jay Clark (Harriman F. Spritzer/Mr. Pinky/ Principal/Edna u/s), Kevin Crumpler (IQ/Ensemble), Katye Dunn (Ensemble), Katie Emerson (Penny Pingleton), David Errigo, Jr. (Ensemble/Link Larkin u/s), Lavon Fisher-Wilson (Motormouth Maybelle), Gregory J, Hanks (Dance Captain/ Ensemble), Stacy Hawking (Ensemble), Antyon Le Monte (Seaweed J. Stubbs), Michael Lowe (Ensemble), Kimberly Marable (Ensemble/ Dynamite), Laura Medford (Amber Von Tussle), Matt Morley (Ensemble), Kenny Morris (William Turnblad), Rick Qualls (Corny Collins), Sandy Rosenberg (Female Authority Figure), Molly Rosenthal (Ensemble), Mary Katelin Ward (Dance Captain/ Ensemble/Penny u/s), Cory Washington (Ensemble, Seaweed u/s), Andi Watson (Velma Von Tussle), D. Scott Withers (Edna Turnblad); April 8–May 8, 2011

The 39 Steps Adapted by Patrick Barlow; Novel by John Buchan; Director, Robert Hupp; Sets, Mike Nichols; Costumes, Rafael Colon Castanera; Lighting, Matthew Webb; Sound, M. Jason Pruzin; PSM, Erin Albrecht; Wig, Poua Yang; Cast: Avery Clark (Richard Hannay), Nikki Coble (Anabella Schmidt/Pamela/Margaret), Jason Collins (Clown #2), Jason Guy (Clown #1), June 10–June 26, 2011

Barrington Stage Company

Pittsfield, Massachusetts

Sixteenth Season

Artistic Director, Julianne Boyd; Richard M. Parison Jr., Managing Director

The Whipping Man by Matthew Lopez; Director, Christopher Innvar; Sets, Sandra Goldmark; Costumes, Kristina Lucka; Lighting, Scott Pinkney; Sound, Brad Berridge; PM, Tristan Wilson; Casting, Pat McCorkle CSA; SM, Kate J. Cudworth; Cast: LeRoy McClain (John), Clarke Peters (Simon), Nick Westrate (Caleb); May 26–June 13, 2010

Sweeney Todd: The Demon Barber of Fleet Street by Stephen Sondheim and Hugh Wheeler; Director, Julianne Boyd; Choreographer, Shonn Wiley; Music Director, Darren R. Cohen; Sets, Wilson Chin; Costumes, Jen Moeller; Lighting, Philip S. Rosenberg; Sound, Ed Chapman; Production Director, Tristan Wilson; Fight Choreographer, Michael Burnet; Dialect Coach, Stephen Gabis; Casting, Pat McCorkle CSA; SM, Renee Lutz; Cast: Shonn Wiley (Anthony), Jeff McCarthy (Sweeney Todd), Christianne Tisdale (Beggar Woman), Harriet Harris (Mrs. Lovett), Ed Dixon (Judge Turpin), Timothy Shew (Beadle Bamford), Sarah Stevens (Johanna), Zachary Clause (Tobias), Branch Woodman (Pirelli/Ensemble), Allan Snyder (Jonas Fogg/Ensemble), Traci Bair (Ensemble), Paul Betz (Ensemble), Analisa Leaming (Ensemble), Ailsa May (Ensemble), John Rapson (Ensemble), Jamie Rosenstein (Ensemble), Amanda Salvatore (Ensemble), Billy Shaw (Ensemble); June 17– July 17, 2010

Freud's Last Session by Mark St. Germain; Suggested by "The Question of God" by Dr. Armand M. Nicholi, Jr.; Director, Tyler Marchant; Sets, Brian Prather; Costumes, Mark Mariani; Lighting, Clifton Taylor; Sound, Beth Lake; Casting, Pat McCorkle CSA; SM, Kate J. Cudworth; Cast: Mark H. Dold (C.S. Lewis), Martin Rayner (Sigmund Freud); June 22–July 3, 2010

Pool Boy Music and lyrics by Nikos Tsakalakos; Book and lyrics by Janet Allard; Director, Daniella Topol; Choreographer, Shonn Wiley; Music Director, Matt Castle; Sets, Brian Prather; Costumes, Holly Cain; Lighting, Nicole Pearce; Sound, Brad Berridge; Vocal Arrangements, Nikos Tsakalakos. Angelique Mouyis; Casting, Pat McCorkle CSA; SM, Michael Andrew Rodgers; Musical Theatre Lab Artistic Producer, William Finn; Cast: Jay Armstrong Johnson (Nick), Cortney Wolfson (April), Cliff Bemis (Mr. Lopes), Jon Benjamin Schneider (Jack), John Hickok (Mr. Rodney Duval), Sara Gettelfinger (Ms. Donna Duval); Sorab Wadia (The Sultan of Nubai); July 13–August 8, 2010

Art by Yasmina Reza; Translation by Christopher Hampton; Director, Henry Wishcamper; Sets, Robin Vest; Costumes, Jenny Mannis; Lighting, Matthew Richards; Original Music/Sound, Bart Fasbender; Production Director, Tristan Wilson; Fight Choreographer, Michael Burnet; Casting, Pat McCorkle CSA; SM, Wesley Apfel; Cast: Brian Avers (Yvan), Michael Countryman (Marc), David Garrison (Serge); July 22–August 7, 2010

Absurd Person Singular by Alan Ayckbourn; Director, Jesse Berger; Sets, Jo Winiarski; Costumes, Sara Jean Tosetti; Lighting, Peter West; Sound, Brad Berridge; Production Director, Tristan Wilson; Dialect, Stephen Gabis; Fight Choreographer, Michael Burnet; Casting, Pat McCorkle CSA; SM, Renee Lutz; Cast: Julia Coffey (Jane), Robert Petkoff (Sidney), Graeme Malcolm (Ronald), Henny Russell (Marion), Finnerty Steeves (Eva), Christopher Innvar (Geoff); August 12–29, 2010

The Memory Show Book and lyrics by Sara Cooper; Music, Zach Redler; Director, Joe Calarco; Music Director, Vadim Feichtner; Sets, Brian Prather; Costumes, Kristina Sneshkoff; Lighting (Joel Shier); Sound (Adair Mallory); Casting, Pat McCorkle, CSA; SM, Michael Andrew Rodgers; Musical Theatre Lab Artistic Producer, William Finn; Cast: Catherine Cox (Mother), Leslie Kritzer (Daughter); August 18–29, 2010

The Crucible by Arthur Miller; Director, Julianne Boyd; Sets, David Barber; Costumes, Kristina Sneshkoff; Lighting, Scott Pinkney; Sound, Brad Berridge; Production Director, Tristan Wilson; Casting, Pat McCorkle CSA; SM, Renee Lutz; Cast: Christopher Innvar (John Proctor), Kim Stauffer (Elizabeth Proctor), Jessica Griffin (Abigail Williams), Robert Zukerman (Deputy Governor Danforth), Fletcher McTaggart (Reverend John Hale), Peter Samuel (Reverend Parris), Edward Cating (Judge Hathorne), Gordon Stanley (Giles Corey), Rosalind Cramer (Rebecca Nurse/Sarah Good), Jeffrey Kent (Thomas Putnam), Glen Barrett (Francis Nurse), Matt Neely (Ezekiel Cheever), Betsy Hogg (Mary Warren), Starla Benford (Tituba), Peggy Pharr Wilson (Mrs. Ann Putnam), Maggie Donnelly (Mercy Lewis), Caroline Mack (Betty Parris), Gabrielle Smachetti (Susanna Walcott); October 6–24, 2010

Zero Hour Written and performed by Jim Brochu; Lighting, Zach Blane; Production Director, Jeff Roudabush; Casting, Pat McCorkle, CSA; SM, Michael Andrew Rodgers; Associate Producer, Natasha Sinha; May 18–June 10, 2011

Barter Theatre

Abingdon, Virginia

Seventy-eighth Season

Producing Artistic Director, Richard Rose; Associate Artistic Director-Production, Camille Davis; Associate Director, Nicholas Piper, Katy Brown; Director of Advancement, Jayne Duehring; Managing Director, Jeremy Wright; Director of Patron Sales and Services, Lori Hester

The Full Monty Music and lyrics, David Yazbek; Book, Terrence McNally; Based on the Motion Picture Released by Fox Searchlight Pictures; Written by Simon Beaufoy; Director, Richard Rose; Choreographer, Amanda Aldridge; Music Director, Steve Sensenig; Dance Captain, Sean Campos; Sets, Dale F. Jordan; Costumes, Kelly Jenkins; Lighting, Dale F. Jordan; Sound, Bobby Beck; SM, Holley Housewright; ASM, Jayme Tinti; Cast: Kristen Gehling (Georgie Bukatinsky), Sean Campos (Buddy "Keno" Walsh), David McCall (Reg Willoughby), Dan Folino (Jerry Lukowski), Ezra Colón (Dave Bukatinsky), Ben Mackel (Malcolm MacGregor), J. Casey Barrett (Ethan Girard), Logan Fritz, Matthew Torbett (Nathan Lukowski), Ashlie Roberson (Susan Hershey), Roslyn Seale (Joanie Lish), Kelli Winn (Estelle Genovese), Ashley Campos (Pam Lukowski), Nicholas Piper (Teddy Slaughter), Mary Lucy Bivins (Molly MacGregor), Rick McVey (Harold Nichols), Jill Anderson (Vicki Nichols), Mary Lucy Bivins (Jeanette A. Burmeister), Jasper McGruder (Noah "Horse" T. Simmons), Nathan Whitmer (Minister/Tony Giordano), David McCall (Police Sergeant), Bryan Pridgen (Ensemble); Barter Theatre; September 17–November 13, 2010

The Woman in Black by Stephen Mallatratt; Based on the novel by Susan Hill; Director, Tricia Matthews; Sets, Samina Vieth; Costumes, Adrienne Webber; Lighting, Heather Brooke Eisenhart; Sound, Bobby Beck; SM, Cindi A. Raebel; Cast: Eugene Wolf (Actor), Michael Poisson (Kipps); Barter Stage II; Septemer 3–November 13, 2010

Sherlock Holmes and the Case of the Jersey Lily by Katie Forgette; Director, Katy Brown; Sets, Ian Zywica; Fight Choreographers, Ezra Colón, Sean Campos; Fight Captain, Sean Campos; Costumes, Amanda Aldridge; Lighting, Dale F. Jordan; Sound, Bobby Beck: SM, Cindi A. Raebel; ASM, Jayme Tinti; Cast: Jill Anderson (Mrs. Lillie Langtry), Sean Campos (John Smythe/Abdul Karim), Nicholas Piper (Sherlock Holmes/Mrs. Padgett), Rick McVey (Dr. Watson), Mary Lucy Bivins (Mrs, McGlynn/Mrs. Irma Tory), David McCall (Oscar Wilde), Eugene Wolf (Professor Moriarty); World Premiere; Barter Theatre; October 1–November 13, 2010

Where Trouble Sleeps by Catherine Bush, Adapted from the novel by Clyde Edgerton; Director, Jasper McGruder; Sets, Dale F. Jordan; Costumes, Liz Whittemore; Lighting, Heather Brooke Eisenhart; Sound, Bobby Beck; Fight Choreographer/Captain, Ezra Colón; Original Music, Ben Mackel; SM, Holley Housewright; Cast: Nathan Whitmer (Sergeant Floyd), Ashley Campos (Alease Toomey), Matthew Torbett (Stephen Toomey), Logan Fritz (Terry Daniels), Ezra Colón (Train Redding), Ben Mackel (Blake Redding), Kristen Gehling (Dorothea Clark), Michael Poisson (Preacher Crenshaw), Kelli Winn (Cheryl Daniels), Nathan Whitmer (Harvey Toomey), Evalyn Baron (Bea Blaine), Dan Folino (Jack Umstead); World Premiere; Barter Stage II; October 9–November 13, 2010

It's a Wonderful Life Adapted by Richard Rose from the Frank Capra film; Director, Katy Brown; Music Director, Steve Sensenig; Assistant Music Director, Ben Mackel; Fight Choreographer/Captain, Ezra Colón; Dance Choreographer, Amanda Aldridge; Sets, Dale F. Jordan; Costumes, Amanda Aldridge; Lighting, Dale F. Jordan; Sound, Bobby Beck; SM, Jayme Tinti; Cast: Rick McVey (George Bailey), J. Casey Barret (Mr. Gower), Eugene Wolf (Mr. Martini/Mr. Potter), Rebecca McGraw (Ma Bailey), Nathan Whitmer (Bert, et al), Ben Mackel (Ernie), Jill Anderson (Mary Hatch Bailey), Kevin O'Bryan (Michael Bailey/Young George Bailey), Clara Gambrel/Abby Graham (Janie Bailey), Peter Morison/Daniel Osborne (Pete Bailey), Annie Osborne/Chloe Smith (Beth Anne Bailey/Young Harry Bailey/Young Violet Bick) Virginia Rachel Pillion/Caroline Rose Wilson (Zuzu), Ezra Colón (Clarence Odbody), Peter Morison/Daniel Osborne (Young Sam Wainwright), Clara Gambrel/Abby Graham (Young Mary Hatch), Michael Poisson (Uncle Billy), Rebecca McGraw (Cousin Tilly/Others), Dan Folino (Mr. Tom Bailey), J. Casey Barret (Potter's man/Others, Ashley Campos (Violet Bick/Others), David McCall (Harry Bailey/Others), Dan Folino (Sam Wainwright); Barter Theatre; November 19–December 26, 2010

A Tuna Christmas by Jaston Williams, Joe Sears, Ed Howard; Director, Mary Lucy Bivins; Sets, Samina Vieth; Costumes, Adrienne Webber; Wig/Makeup, Ryan Fischer; Lighting, Samina Vieth; Sound, Bobby Beck; Cindi A. Raebel; Cast, Nicholas Piper (Thurston Whellis/Bertha Bumiller/Others), Sean Campos (Arles Struvie/Vera Carp/Others); Barter Stage II; November 23–December 26, 2010

XANADU Book by Douglas Carter Beane; Music and lyrics by Jeff Lynne and John Farrar, Originally produced by Robert Ahrens, Dan Vickery, Tara Smith, B. Swibel, Sara Murchson, Dale Smith, Cari Smulyan; Based on the Universal Pictures film; Screenplay by Richard Danus and Marc Rubel; Director, Richard Rose; Choreographer, Amanda Aldridge; Music Director, Steve Sensenig; Sets, Scott Aronow; Costumes, Amanda Aldridge; Wigs/Makeup, Ryan Fischer; Lighting, Dale F. Jordan; Sound, Bobby Beck; Dance Captain, Sean Campos; SM, Cindi A. Raebel; ASM, Jayme Tinti; Cast: Ben Mackel (Sonny Malone), Ashley Campos (Kira), Lacretta Nicole (Erato), J. Casey Barrett (Euterpe), Ezra Colón (Melpomene) Mary Lucy Bivins (Thalia), Sean Campos (Terpsicore), Hannah Ingram (Calliope), Michael Poisson (Danny Maguire/Zeus); Musicians: Urania, Muse of Keyboards, Steve Sensenig; Polyhymnia, Muse of Synthesizer, Brandon Sturiale; Drummer, Jerry Greene; Barter Theatre; February 4–April 16, 2011

Civil War Voices by James R. Harris; With music of the period and original arrangements by Mark Hayes; Director, Susanne Boulle; Assistant Director, Katy Brown: Music Director, W. Brent Sawyer; Sets, Dale F. Jordan: Costumes, Michele Macadaeg; Wigs/Makeup, Ryan Fischer; Lighting, Andrew Morehouse; Sound, Bobby Beck; SM, Karen N. Rowe; Cast: Eugene Wolf (Narrator), Tricia Matthews (Grandmother), Wendy Piper (Mother), Rick McVey (Father), Adam J. MacDonald (Theophilus Perry), Holly Williams (Harriet Perry), Chavez Ravine (Elizabeth Keckley), Dan Folino (Joshua Lawrence Chamberlain), Arthur W. Marks (Cook), Nathan Whitmer (Slave Master), Scott Gendel (pianist), Claire Morison (violin player); Barter Stage II; February 11–April 16, 2011

Treasure Island by Robert Louis Stevenson; Adapted by Richard Rose; Director, Richard Rose; Assistant Director, Katie Becker; Musical Composer, Peter Yonka; Fight Choreographer, Michael G. Chin; Fight Captains, Sean Campos, Ezra Colón; Sets, Dale F. Jordan; Costumes, Ryan Fischer; Lighting, Dale F. Jordan; Sound, Bobby Beck; SM, Karen N. Rowe, ASM, Jayne Tinti; The Cast: Eugene Wolf (William "Billy" Bones), J. Casey Barrett (Adult Jim Hawkins), Kevin O'Bryan (Young Jim Hawkins), Nicholas Piper (Dr. David Livesay) Ben Mackel (Tom Redruth), Dan Folino (Richard Joyce), Ezra Colón (Black Dog), J. Casey Barrett (Mrs. Hawkins), Adam J. MacDonald (Blind Pew), Sean Campos (Job Anderson), Arthur W. Marks (Kidd Johnson), Michael Poisson (Squire John Trelawny), Will Stutts (Long John Silver), Dan Folino (Israel Hands), Ben Mackel (Tom Morgan), Eugene Wolf (Mr. Arrow), Adam J. MacDonald (Captain Alexander Smollett), Ezra Colón (Abraham Gray), Ben Mackel (Taylor), Dan Folion (Allan), Ezra Colón (O'Brien), Dan Folino (no name), Eugene Wolf (Ben Gunn); Barter Theatre; February 18–April 16, 2011

Age of Arousal by Linda Griffiths, Wildly inspired by George Gissing's The Odd Woman; Director, Karen Sabo; Sets, Samantha Vieth; Costumes, Amanda Aldridge; Wigs/Makeup, Ryan Fischer; Lighting, Andrew Morehouse; Sound, Bobby Beck; Props, Chase Molden; SM, Cindi A. Raebel; Cast: Mary Lucy Bivins (Mary Barfoot), Hannah Ingram (Rhoda Nunn), Wendy Piper (Virginia Madden), Tricia Matthews (Alice Madden), Holly Williams (Monica Madden), Nathan Whitmer (Everard Barfoot); Barter Stage II; February 26–April 16, 2011

Circumference of a Squirrel by John Walch; Director, Katy Brown; Sets, Derek Smith; Costumes, Liz Whittemore; Lighting, Andrew Morehouse; Sound, Bobby Beck; SM, Seymour; Cast: Nicholas Piper (Chester); Barter Stage II; April 30–August 13, 2011

Elvis Has Left the Building by Duke Ernsberger and V. Cate; Director, Nicholas Piper; Sets, Dale F. Jordan; Costumes, Kelly Jenkins; Lighting, Andrew Morehouse; Sound, Bobby Beck; Wigs/Makeup, Ryan Fischer; SM, Seymour; Cast: Eugene Wolf (The Colonel), Mary Lucy Bivins (Trudy), Bryan Pridgen (Roscoe), Dan Folino (Candy), Hannah Ingram (Jill Tanner); World Premiere; Barter Stage II; May 13–August 13, 2011

Disney's Beauty and the Beast Music by Alan Menken, Lyrics by Howard Ashman and Tim Rice, Book by Linda Woolverton; Director, Richard Rose; Choreographer, Amanda Aldridge; Music Director, Steve Sensenig; Sets, Daniel Ettinger; Costumes, Amanda Aldridge; Lighting, Michael Barnett; Sound, Bobby Beck; Props, Ricky Hesson; Wigs/Makeup, Ryan Fischer; Assistant Choreography/Dance Captain, Ashley Campos; Dance Assistant, Cay Harkins; Fight Captain, Sean Campos; SM, Cindi A. Raebel; ASM, Jayme Tinti; Cast: Tricia Mattthews (Mrs. Potts), Cooper Woodard, Abigail Conde (Chip), Sean Campos (Beast), Holly Williams (Belle), Ben Mackel (Lefou), Nathan Whitmer (Gaston), Michael Poisson (Maurice), Rick McVey (Cogsworth), Jamal Crowell (Lumiere), Ashley Campos (Babette), Marnee Hollis (Madam de la Grand Bouche), David Alford (Ensemble), J. Casey Barrett (Ensemble), Sarah Bumgarner (Ensemble), Abbey Elliott (Ensemble), Samuel Floyd (Esemble), Jesse Jones (Ensemble), Justin Tylr Lewis (Ensemble), Christian Mansfield (Ensemble), Joshua O'Bryan (Ensemble), Erin Parker (Ensemble), Ashlie Roberson (Ensemble), Libby Tatum (Ensemble), Mandy Williams (Ensemble), Kelli Winn (Ensemble), Aria Brinkley (Ensemble), Kinser Crutchfield (Ensemble), Aleander Eleas (Ensemble); Steve Sensenig (Conductor); Barter Theatre; May 28–August 13, 2011

Saving Old Smokey by Ron Osborne; Director, Mary Lucy Bivins; Music Director, Steve Sensenig; Music Assistant, Eugene Wolf; Sets, Cheri Prough DeVol; Costumes, Liz Whittemore; Lighting, Michael Barnett; Sound, Bobby Beck; Props, Ricky Hesson; Wigs/Makeup, Ryan Fischer; SM, Seymour; Cast, Marnee Hollis (Emma), Tricia Matthews (Jinks), Erin Parker (Olive), Ashley Campos (Tammy), Rick McVey (Howard), Ashlie Roberson (Cordelia); World Premiere; Barter Theatre; June 9–August 13, 2011

Alfred Hitchcock's The 39 Steps Adapted by Patrick Barlow from the novel by John Buchnan, from the movie by Alfred Hitchcock; Director, Katy Brown; Sets, Derek Smith; Costumes, Karen Brewster; Lighting, Andrew Morehouse; Sound, Bobby Beck; Props, Ricky Hesson; Wigs/Makeup, Ryan Fischer; SM, Cindi A. Raebel; ASM, Jayme Tinti; Cast, Nathan Whitmer (Richard Hannay), Hannah Ingram (Annabella Schmidt/Pamela/Margaret), Ben Mackel (Clown #1), Sean Campos (Clown # 2); Barter Stage II; June 17–August 13, 2011

2010 National Tours

Forever Plaid (National Tour) Writer/Original Director/Choreographer, Stuart Ross; Musical Continuity Supervisor/Arranger, James Raitt; Original Producer, Gene Wolsk; Director/Choreographer, Robert Randle; Music Director (Barter Theatre), Steve Sensenig; Musical Director (tour) Lee Harris; Sets, Dale F. Jordan; Costumes, Kelly Jenkins; Lighting, Michael Barnett; Sound, Bobby Beck; Dance Captain, Scott Guthrie; Casting, Paul Russell; SM, Daniel LeMein; Cast: Kevin Greene (Francis), Chris Vaughn (Smudge), Steven Douglas Stewart (Sparky), Byron DeMent (Jinx), Scott Guthrie (u/s); Pianist, Lee Harris; Bass Player, Garrett Jones. Crew: Fall 2010 Company Manager, Derek Spack; Spring 2011 Company Manager, Ed Whitehead; Tech Dirctor/Prod. Carpenter Crew (Stephen Vess); Wardrobe/Props Running Crew, Johnathan Menius; Master Electrician, Rahme Rayes; Sound, Kim Hines. September 24–November 8

The Diary of Anne Frank (National Tour) by Frances Goodrich, Albert Hackett; Edited by Otto Frank; Based upon the book Anne Frank: The Diary of a Young Girl; Director, Richard Rose; Sets, Dale F. Jordan; Costumes, Amanda Aldridge; Lighting, Cheri Prough DeVol; Sound, Bobby Beck; Music Composer, Peter Yonka; SM, Christopher C. Dunlop. Cast: Danny Vaccaro (Mr. Otto Frank), Rebecca Reinhardt (Miep Gies), Hannah Ingram (Mrs. Van Daan), Robin Bloodworth (Mr. Van Daan), Greg Pragel (Peter Van Daan), Tricia Matthews (Mrs. Edith Frank), Julie Scholl (Margot Frank), Kelly Klein (Anne Frank), Gregory Mach (Mr. Kraler), Gannon McHale (Mr. Dussel). Crew: Company Manager, Ed Whitehead; Tour TD, Charles "Bo" Howard; Carpenter/Props, Mollie Slattery; Wardrobe, Rachel Marie Brown; Master Electrician, Richard Spomer; Sound, Robert Peterson. September 30, 2010–February 10, 2011

Berkeley Repertory Theatre

Forty-second Season

Artistic Director, Tony Taccone; Managing Director, Susan Medak; Associate Artistic Director, Les Waters; General Manager, Karen Racanelli

Compulsion A co-production with The Public Theater and Yale Repertory Theatre; Written by Rinne Groff; Director, Oskar Eustis; Sets, Eugene Lee; Costumes, Susan Hilferty; Lighting, Michael Chybowski; Sound, Darron L West; Video/Projection, Jeff Sugg; Puppet Design/Supervision, Matt Acheson; PSM, Michael Suenkel; ASM, Karen Szpaller; Cast: Mandy Patinkin (Mr. Silver), Hannah Cabell (Miss Mermin/Mrs. Silver), Matte Osian (Mr. Thomas/Mr. Harris/Mr. Ferris/Mr. Matzliach), Emily DeCola (Puppeteer), Daniel Patrick Fay (Puppeteer) Eric Wright (Puppeteer); World Premiere; Thrust Stage; September 13–October 31, 2010

Lemony Snicket's The Composer Is Dead Conceived for the stage by Lemony Snickct, Phantom Limb (Jessica Grindstaff and Erik Sanko, Artistic Director), Tony Taccone, Geoff Hoyle; The Magic of Living, Breathing Theater; Written by Lemony Snicket; Film Produced by Lisa Cook; Director of Photography, Martin Rosenberg; Underscoring, Matthew Compton, Asa Taccone; Puppeteers; Erik

Sanko, Oliver Dazell; The Composer is Dead, Written by Lemony Snicket; Music by Nathaniel Stookey; Recorded music originally commissioned and performed by The San Francisco Symphony; Conducted by Edwin Outwater; Director, Tony Taccone; Sets/Costume/Puppetry, Jessica Grindstaff and Erik Sanko; Lighting/Projection, Alexander Nichols; Sound, James LeBrecht; SM, Michael Suenkel; ASM, Kimberly Mark Webb; Cast: Geoff Hoyle; Puppeteers; Jenny Campbell, Frankie Cordero, Marta Mozelle MacRostie, Edouard Sanko, Ronny Wasserstrom; Additional Voices: Bettina Devin, Roger L. Jackson, Jarion Monroe, Asher Terra, Erin-Kate Whitcomb; World Premiere; Roda Theatre; November 26, 2010–January 16, 2011

The Last Cargo Cult Created and performed by Mike Daisey; Directed by Jean-Michele Gregory; Sets/Lighting, Seth Reiser; Thrust Stage; January 11–February 20, 2011

The Agony and the Ecstasy of Steve Jobs Created and performed by Mike Daisey; Director, Jean-Michele Gregory; Sets/Lighting, Seth Reiser; Thrust Stage; January 20–February 27, 2011

Ruined Co-production with the Huntington Theatre and La Jolla Playhouse; Written by Lynn Nottage; Director, Liesl Tommy; Choreographer, Randy Duncan; Sets, Clint Ramos; Costumes, Kathleen Geldardl; Lighting, Lap Chi Chu; Sound/Original Music, Broken Chord; Dramaturg, Shirley Fishman; Fight Director, Steve Rankin; SM, Anjee Nero; Casting, Alaine Alldaffer; West Coast Casting, Amy Potozkin; Cast: Oberon K.A. Adjepong (Christian), Pascale Armand (Salima), Jason Bowen (Fortune), Carla Duren (Sophie), Wendell B. Franklin (Jerome Kisembe), Zainab Jah (Josephine), Joseph Kamal (Mr. Harari), Adesoji Odukogbe (Musician 2), Kola Ogundiran (Laurent), Okieriete Onaodowan, (Simon), Tonye Patano (Mama Nadi), Adrian Roberts (Commander Osembenga), Alvin Terry (Musician 1); Roda Theatre; February 25–April 10, 2011

Three Sisters by Anton Chekhov; A new version by Sarah Ruhl; Based on a literal translation by Elise Thoron with Natalya Paramonova and Kristin Johnsen-Neshati; In association with Yale Repertory Theatre; Director, Les Waters; Sets, Annie Smart; Costumes, Ilona Somogyi; Lighting, Alexander V. Nichols; Sound, David Budries; Musical Director, Julie Wolf; Dramaturg, Rachel Steinberg; SM, Michael Suenkel; ASM, Cynthia Cahill; Casting, Amy Potozkin, Janet Foster; Cast: Wendy Rich Stetson (Olga), Heather Wood (Irina), James Carpenter (Chebutykin), Thomas Jay Ryan (Tuzenbach), Sam Breslin Wright (Solyony), Natalia Payne (Masha), Barbara Oliver (Anfisa), Richard Farrell (Ferapont), Bruce McKenzie (Vershinin), Alex Moggridge (Andrei), Keith Reddin (Kulygin), Emily Kitchens (Natasha), David Abrams (Fedotik), Cobe Gordon (Rode); Thrust Stage; April 8–May 22, 2011

Limited Season

The Great Game: Afghanistan Tricycle Theatre's production; Written by Richard Bean, Lee Blessing, David Edgar, David Greig, Amit Gupta, Ron Hutchinson, Stephen Jeffreys, Abi Morgan, Richard Norton-Taylor, Ben Ockrent, Simon Stephens, Colin Teevan, Joy Wilkinson; Director, Nicolas Kent and Indhu Rubasingham; Project Designer, Pamela Howard; Lighting, David I. Taylor (based on original lighting by James Farncombe); Sound, Tom Lishman; Associate Designer, Miriam Nabarro; Assistant Director, Rachel Grunwald; Cast: Daniel Betts, Sheena Bhattessa, Michael Cochrane, Karl Davies, Vincent Ebrahim, Nabil Elouahabi, Shereen Martineau, Tom McKay, Daniel Rabin, Danny Rahim, Raad Rawi, Jemma Redgrave, Cloudia Swann, Rick Warden; West Coast Premiere; Roda Theatre; October 22–November 7, 2010

Let Me Down Easy Conceived, written and performed by Anna Deavere Smith; In association with Arena Stage, presenting the Second Stage's production; Director, Leonard Foglia; Sets, Riccardo Hernandez; Costumes, Ann Hould-Ward; Lighting, Dan Ozminkowski (based on design by Peggy Eisenhower and Jules Fisher); Sound, Ryan Rumery; Original Music Elements, Joshua Redman; Projection Design, Zachary Borovay; Dialect, Amy Stoller; Movement, Elizabeth Roxas-Dobrish; Hair, Anthony Dickey; Makeup, Maria Verel; Dramaturg, Alisa Solomon; Artistic Associate, Kimber Riddle; Assistant Director, Keturah Stickann; Associate Movement Coach, Michael Thomas; SM, Joseph Smelser (May 28–

July 10), Cynthia Cahill (August 10–September 4); ASM, Ronee Penoi (May 28–July 10), Karen Szpaller (August 10–September 4); Roda Theatre, May 28–July 10, 2011; Encore run: Thrust Stage, August 10–September 4, 2011

Special Presentations

An Evening with Robin Williams

Going on the Road Down Under

Recharging the Batteries.....Again

Roda Theatre, October 10–13, 2011

The Arabian Nights Adapted from *The Book of the Thousand Nights and One Night* translated by Powys Mathers; Remounted in Berkeley by Heidi Stillman and Mary Zimmerman In association with Arena Stage, Kansas City Repertory Theatre, and Lookingglass Theatre Company; Written and directed by Mary Zimmerman; Sets, Daniel Ostling; Costumes, Mara Blumenfeld; Original Composition/Sound, Andre Pluess and The Lookingglass Ensemble; Lighting, T.J. Gerckens; SM, Cynthia Cahill; Casting, Stephanie Klapper, Amy Potozkin; Cast: Barzin Akhavan (Harun Al-Rashid/Others), Terence Archie (Greengrocer/Robber/Others), David DeSantos (King Shahryar), Minita Gandhi (Slave Girl/Others), Allen Gilmore (Scheherezade's Father/Ishak of Mosul/Others), Susaan Jamshidi (Butcher/Sympathy the Learned/Others), Ronnie Malley (Poor Man/Musician/Others), Luis Moreno (Clarinetist/Sage/Others), Jonathan Raviv (Madman/Others), Maureen Sebastian (Dunyazade/Azizah/Others), Nicole Shalhoub (Perfect Love/The Other Woman/Others), Louis Tucci (Jafar/Sheik Al-Fadl/Others), Stacey Yen (Scheherezade), Evan Zes (Sheik Al-Islam/Abu Al-Hasan/Others), Thrust Stage, December 11–30, 2010

Berkshire Theatre Group: Berkshire Theatre Festival

Stockbridge and Pittsfield, Massachusettes

Eighty-third Festival Season

First Season as a merged organization with The Colonial Theatre

Artistic Director/CEO, Kate Maguire

Moonchildren by Michael Weller; Director, Karen Allen; Sets, John Traub; Costumes, George Veale; Lighting, Shawn E. Boyle; Sound, J Hagenbuckle; SM, Laura Wilson; Cast: Hale Appleman (Bob), Kale Browne (Mr. Willis/Cootie's Dad), Aaron Costa Ganis (Dick), Carter Gill (Norman), Matt Harrington (Cootie), Jesse Hinson (Ralph/Effing), Andrew Joffe (Bream/The Milkman), Jeff Kent (Lucky), Norma Kuhling (Kathy), Joe Paulik (Mike), Samantha Richert (Shelly), Miriam Silverman (Ruth), David Wade Smith (Uncle Murray); The Unicorn Theatre; July 2–July 16, 2011

The Who's Tommy Music and lyrics by Pete Townsend; Book by Pete Townsend and Des McAnuff; Director, Eric Hill; Musical Director, Randy Redd; Choreographer, Gerry McIntyre; Sets, Gary English; Costumes, David Murin; Lighting, Matthew Adelson; Sound, J Hagenbuckle; Projections, Shawn E. Boyle; SM, Stephen Horton; Cast: Jordan Barbour (The Specialist/Chorus), James Barry (Captain Walker), Rory Donovan (Minister/Mr. Simpson/Chorus), Randy Harrison (Rommy/Narrator), Christopher Gurr (Uncle Ernie), Jaclyn Miller (Dance Captain), Jenny Powers (Mrs. Walker), Angela Robinson (Acid Queen), Ben Rosenblatt (Cousin Kevin/Chorus), Hannah Shankman (Sally Simpson/Nurse/Chorus) Zi Alikhan (Pinball Lad/Chorus), Aaron Barcelo (Hawker/Chorus), Chris Chianesi (Lover/Pinball Lad/Chorus), Brett Dameron (Pinball Lad/Chorus), Rebecca Leigh (Ensemble), Connor McNinch (Tommy Age 10), Paige Scott (Tommy Age 4), Chris Vecchia (Ensemble); The Colonial Theatre; July 9–July 16, 2011

Sylvia by A. R. Gurney; Director, Anders Cato; Sets, R. Michael Miller; Costumes, Olivera Gajic; Lighting, Tyler Micoleau; Sound, Scott Killian; SM, Carola LaCoste; Cast: David Adkins (Greg), Rachel Bay Jones (Sylvia), Walter Hudson (Tom, Phyllis, Leslie), Jurian Hughes (Kate); The Fitzpatrick Main Stage; July 16–July 30, 2011

Dutch Masters by Greg Keller; Director, Brian Roff; Sets, Jason Simms; Costumes, Laurie Churba Kohn; Lighting, Japhy Weideman; Sound, Bray Poor; PSM, Peter Durgin; SM, Betsy Selman; Cast: Amari Cheatom (Eric), Christian Coulson (Steve); The Unicorn Theatre; July 23–August 6, 2011

In the Mood by Kathleen Clark; Director, Marc Bruni; Sets, Lee Savage; Costumes, Laurie Churba Kohn; Lighting, David Lander; Sound, Scott Killian; SM, Stephen Horton; Cast: Stephen Buntrock (Nick Elliot), Arnie Burton (Edward Horton), Jennifer Cody (Carolyn Shore), Johanna Day (Sally Elliot), Erin Dilly (Perri Rubin), Damian Young (Derek Rubin); The Fitzpatrick Main Stage; August 6–August 13, 2011

Finian's Rainbow Music by Burton Lane; Book by E.Y. Harburg and Fred Saidy; Lyrics by E.Y. Harburg; Director, Kyle Fabel; Musical Director, Aaron Jodoin; Sets, Randall Parsons; Costumes, Lara De Bruijn; Lighting, Paul Hackenmueller; Sound, Gillian Moon; Movement, Isadora Wolfe; SM, Dana Gal; Cast: Aaron Barcelo (Woody Mahoney), Ryan Chittaphong (Sheriff), Rory Donovan (Finian McLonergan), Ashley Everage (The Maid), Ricardo Gayle (Howard), Joshua Marx (Buzz Collins), Julius Reese (Henry), Aubrey Sinn (Sharon McLonergan), Margaret Wild (Susan Mahoney), Robbie Williams (Senator Rawkins), Aaron Carlton Wright (Og), Julia Anrather (Ensemble), Rachael Balcanoff (Ensemble), Madeline Calandrillo (Ensemble), Natasha Edwards (Ensemble), Erica Frighetto (Ensemble), Amy Secunda (Ensemble), Zach Sorrow (Ensemble); The Unicorn Theatre; August 13–August 27, 2011

Period of Adjustment by Tennessee Williams; Director, David Auburn; Sets, R. Michael Miller; Costumes, Wade Laboissonniere; Lighting, Mary Louise Geiger; Sound, Scott Killian; SM, Laura Wilson; Cast: Rebecca Brookshcr (Isabel Haverstick), Mark Corkins (Mr. McGillicudy), Mia Dillon (Mrs. McGillicudy), Paul Fitzgerald (Ralph Bates), Anny Giobbe (Dorothea Bates), C.J. Wilson (George Haverstick); The Fitzpatrick Main Stage; August 20-September 3 , 2011

Birthday Boy by Chris Newbound; Director, Wes Grantom; Sets, Kenneth Grady Barker; Costumes, Charles Schoonmaker; Lighting, Derek Wright; Sound, Phil Pickens; SM, Kyle S. Urquhart; Cast: Nick Dillenburg (Julian), Tara Franklin (Melora), Keira Naughton (Arianne), James Ludwig (Matt); The Unicorn Theatre; August 31-September 3 and September 29-October 16, 2011

California Shakespeare Theater

Orinda, California

Thirty-eighth Season

Artistic Director, Jonathan Moscone; Managing Director, Susie Falk

Titus Andronicus by William Shakespeare; Director, Joel Sass; Sets, Emily Greene; Costumes, Paloma H. Young; Lighting, Russell H. Champa; Sound, Andre Pluess; Dramaturg, Philippa Kelly; Fight Director, Dave Maier; Choreographer, Marybeth Cavanaugh; Text/ Language Coach, Lynne Soffer; PSM, Laxmi Kumaran; Casting Director, Jessica Richards; Cast: James Carpenter (Titus Andronicus), Anna Bullard (Lavinia), Rob Campbell (Saturninus), Chad Deverman (Demetrius), Shawn Hamilton (Aaron), Dan Hiatt (Marcus), Delia MacDougall (Quintus/ Nurse/Goth), David Mendelsohn (Chiron), Nicholas Pelczar (Lucius/Clown), Stacy Ross (Tamora), Liam Vincent (Bassianus/Publius/Goth), Caleb Alexander (Young Lucius), Galen Murphy-Hoffman (Martius/Aemilius), Jody Christian (Ensemble), Willem Long (Ensemble), Geoffrey Nolan (Ensemble), Paris Hunter Paul (Ensemble), Valerie Wagenfeld (Ensemble); Bruns Memorial Amphitheater; June 1–26, 2011

The Verona Project by Amanda Dehnert; Director Amanda Dehnert; Sets, Daniel Ostling; Costumes, Melissa Torchia; Lighting, David Lee Cuthbert; Music Producer/Sound, Joshua Horvath; Dramaturg, Joy Meads; Additional lyrics, Megan Trinrud; Vocal/Text Coach, Domenlque Lozano; Fight Director, Dave Maier; PSM, Megan Q. Sada; Cast: Arwen Anderson (Julia); Dan Clegg (Proteus); Marisa Duchowny (Pro's Mom/Sylvio's Mom); Philip Mills (Sylvio); Harold Pierce (Speed); Nate Trinrud (Valentine); Elena Wright (Thuria/Val's Mom); Adam Yazbeck (The Duke); Bruns Memorial Amphitheater; July 6–31, 2011

Candida by George Bernard Shaw; Director, Jonathan Moscone; Sets, Annie Smart; Costumes, Anna Oliver; Lighting, York Kennedy; Sound, Will McCandless; Dialect, Lynne Soffer; PSM, Laxni Kumaran; Cast: Julie Eccles (Candida); Anthony Fusco (Reverend James Morell); Nick Gabriel (Eugene Marchbanks); Alexandra Henrikson (Miss Proserpine Garnett); Jarion Monroe (Mr. Burgess); Liam Vincent (Reverend Lexy Mill); Bruns Memorial Amphitheater; August 10–September 4, 2011

The Taming of the Shrew by William Shakespeare; Director, Shana Cooper; Sets, Scott Dougan; Costumes, Katherine O'Neill; Lighting, York Kennedy; Sound, Jake Rodriguez; Movement, Erika Chong Shuch; Fight Director, Dave Maier; Dramaturg, Philippa Kelly; Vocal/Text Coach, Nancy Carlin; PSM, Corrie Bennett; Cast: Dan Clegg (Tranio); Rod Gnapp (Baptista); Alexandra Henrikson (Bianca); Dan Hiatt (Grumio/Vincentio); Slate Holmgren (Petruchio); Joan Mankin (Curtis/ Pedant/Widow); Nicholas Pelczar (Lucentio); Danny Scheie (Gremio/Tailor); Erica Sullivan (Katherine); Liam Vincent (Hortensio); Theo Black (Biondello); Bruns Memorial Amphitheater; September 21–October 16, 2011

Casa Mañana Theatre

Fort Worth, Texas

Fifty-third Season

President and Executive Producer, Wally Jones

The Sound of Music Music by Richard Rodgers; Lyrics by Oscar Hammerstein II; Book by Howard Lindsay, Russel Crouse; Director/Choreographer, Alan Coats; Music Director, Edward G. Robinson; Sets, Mark Halpin; Costumes, Tammy Spencer; Lighting, John Bartenstein; Hair/Wig/Makeup, Patricia Delsordo; Sound, Jonathan Parke; PM, Dave McManus; SM, Leigh'Ann Andrews; Cast: Jacquelyn Piro Donovan (Maria Rainer), Steve Blanchard (Captain von Trapp), Patty Goble (Mother Abbess), Mary McElree (Liesl von Trapp), Cooper Rodgers (Friedrich von Trapp), Caitlin Hale Daniels (Louisa von Trapp), Bobby Rochelle (Kurt von Trapp), Brooke Verbois (Brigitta von Trapp), Lauren Magee (Marta von Trapp), Cosette Cook (Gretl von Trapp), Dennis Yslas (Max Detweiler), Diana Sheehan (Elsa Schraeder), Tyce Green (Rolf), Brian Mathis (Herr Zeller), Deborah Brown (Frau Schmidt), Doug LoPachin (Franz), Becky Turner (Sister Berthe), Sarah Comley (Sister Margaretta), Theresa Thompson (Sister Sophia), Christopher J. Deaton (Admiral von Schreiber/Priest); September 11-19, 2010

The Best Little Whorehouse in Texas Book by Larry L. King, Peter Masterson; Music and lyrics by Carol Hall; Director, Michael Susko; Choreographer, Josh Rhodes; Music Director, Lisa LeMay; Sets, Mark Halpin; Lighting, John Bartenstein; Costumes, Tammy Spencer; Hair/Wig/Makeup, Patricia Delsordo; Sound, Jonathan Parke; SM, Leigh'Ann Andrews; PM, Dave McManus; Cast: Ruta Lee (Miss Mona Stangley), Ed Dixon (Sheriff Ed Earl Dodd), David Coffee (C.J. Scruggs/Governor), Joe Sturgeon (Melvin P. Thorpe), Greg Dulcie (Edsel Mackey/Bandleader), Neil Rogers (Senator Wingwoah/Mayor Rufus Poindexter), Liz Mikel (Jewel), Paige Wheat (Angel), Melissa Farmer (Shy), Amber Nicole Guest (Doatsey Mae/Eloise); October 23–31, 2010

Evita Music by Andrew Lloyd Webber; Lyrics by Tim Rice; Director/Choreographer, Richard Stafford; Associate Director/Choreographer, Jonathan Stahl; Music Director, Craig Barna; Sets, Mark Halpin; Costumes, Tammy Spencer; Hair/ Wig/ Makeup Design, Patricia Delsordo; Lighting, Samuel Rushen; Sound, Jonathan Parke; SM, Leigh'Ann Andrews; PM, Dave McManus; Cast: Lauren Kennedy (Eva Perón), Kevin Gray (Che), Greg Dulcie (Perón), Jonathan Bragg (Magaldi), Ashley Arnold (Mistress); February 5–13, 2011

Hairspray Book by Mark O'Donnell, Thomas Meehan; Music and lyrics by Marc Shaiman; Lyrics by Scott Wittman; Director, Casey Hushion; Choreographer, Josh Rhodes; Music Director, Aimee Hurst Bozarth; Costumes, Tammy Spencer; Hair/ Wig/ Makeup, Patricia Delsordo; Lighting, Samuel Rushen; Sound, Shannon Slaton; PM, Dave McManus; SM, Leigh'Ann Andrews; Cast: Jennifer Foster (Tracy Turnblad), David Coffee (Edna Turnblad), John Arthur Greene (Link Larkin), Laura

Nikki Coble and Avery Clark in Arkansas Repertory Theatre's production of The 39 Steps *(photos by Stephen Thorton)*

John Hickok, Jay Armstrong Johnson, and Sara Gettelfinger in Barrington Stage Company's Pool Boy *(photo by Kevin Sprague)*

Martin Rayner and Mark H. Dold in Freud's Last Session at Barrington Stage Company *(photos by Kevin Sprague)*

Sean Campos and Nicholas Piper in A Tuna Christmas *at Barter Theatre* *((photo by Kevin Sprague)*

Jill Anderson in Barter Theatre's Sherlock Holmes and the Case of the Jersey Lily *(photo by Leah Prater)*

Mike Daisey in The Agony and the Ecstasy of Steve Jobs *at Berkeley Repertory Theatre (photo by Kevin Berne)*

Mandy Patinkin in the world premiere production of Compulsion *at Berkeley Repertory Theatre (photo by Kevin Berne)*

Slate Holmgren and Erica Sullivan in The Taming of the Shrew *at California Shakespeare Theater (photo by Kevin Berne)*

The Company of California Shakespeare Theater's world-premiere production of The Verona Project *(photo by Kevin Berne)*

Wetsel (Penny Pingleton), Donell James Foreman (Seaweed J. Stubbs), Sainty Reid (Amber von Tussle), Cara Statham Serber (Velma Von Tussle), Jarret Mallon (Corny Collins), Sheran Goodspeed Keyton (Motormouth Maybelle), Sydney Porter (Little Inez), Doug LoPachin (Wilbur Turnblad), Christopher J. Deaton (Harriman F. Spitzer/Mr. Pinky/Principal/ Guard), Sarah Gay (Prudy Pingleton/ Gym Teacher/Matron), Tesia Kwarteng (Dynamite), Adrianna Hicks (Dynamite), Jo-Rhea Dalcour (Dynamite); August 13–21, 2011

CENTERSTAGE

Baltimore, Maryland

Forty-eighth Season

Artistic Director, Irene Lewis

The Pearlstone Theater

The Wiz Book by William F. Brown; Music and lyrics by Charlie Smalls, Based on the story *The Wonderful Wizard of Oz* by L. Frank Baum; Director, Irene Lewis; Music Director/ Orchestrator, Eric Svejcar; Choreographer, Willie Rosario; Sets, Christopher Barreca; Costumes, Candice Donnelly; Lighting, Rui Rita; Sound, David Budries; PSM, Bret Torbeck, Julianne Franz; ASM, Christopher Michael Borg; Dramaturg, James Magruder, Otis Ramsey-Zöe; Fight Choreographer, J. Allen Suddeth; Assistant Choreographer, Brian Barry; Associate Music Director, Victor Simonson; Hair/Wigs, Jon Carter; Cast: Eric B. Anthony (Scarecrow), Jonathan Burke (Ensemble), Tym Byerz (Ensemble), Kristen N. Dowtin (Dorothy), Manoly Farrell (Ensemble/Dance Captain), LaTrisa A. Harper (Ensemble), Daisy Hobbs (Ensemble), Mel Johnson, Jr. (Tin Man), Kingsley Leggs (Uncle Henry/ The Wiz), Alison Mixon (Ensemble), MaShawn Morton (Ensemble/Fight Captain), Alfie Parker, Jr. (Ensemble), Wayne W. Pretlow (Lion), Angela Robinson (Auntie Em/Glinda), Gwen Stewart (Addaperle/Evillene); September 29–November 7, 2010

The Homecoming by Harold Pinter; Director, Irene Lewis; Sets, Riccardo Hernández; Costumes, Catherine Zuber; Lighting, Mark McCullough; Sound, David Budries; PSM, Lloyd Davis, Jr.; ASM, Raine Bode, Kathryn Ambrose; Fight Choreography, J. Allen Suddeth; Dialect Coach, Gillian Lane-Plescia; Dramaturg, Whitney Eggers; Cast: Jarlath Conroy (Max), Trent Dawson (Lenny), Steven Epp (Teddy), Felicity Jones (Ruth), Sebastian Naskaris (Joey), Laurence O'Dwyer (Sam); January 26–February 20, 2011

Snow Falling on Cedars Adapted by Kevin McKeon from the novel by David Guterson; Director, David Schweizer; Sets, Allen Moyer; Costumes, David Burdick; Lighting, Christopher Akerlind; Sound/Music, Ryan Rumery; Dramaturg, Gavin Witt; Fight Choreographer, Lewis Shaw; Cast: Laura Kai Chen (Hatsue Miyamoto), Danny Gavigan (Carl Heine, Jr.), Kristin Griffith (Etta Heine/Mrs. Chambers), Anjanette Hall (Susan Marie Heine), Neal Hemphill (Art Moran), Glenn Kubota (Hisao Imada/Mr. Nitta/Zenhichi Miyamoto), Kenneth Lee (Kabuo Miyamoto), Michael McKenzie (Nels Gudmundsson/Carl Heine, Sr.), Owen Scott (Abel Martinson); Timothy Sekk (Ishmael Chambers), Bernard Burak Sheredy (Alvin Hooks); Ching Valdes-Aran (Fujiko Imada/Mrs. Nitta); March 9–April 3, 2011

The Head Theater

ReEntry by Emily Ackerman and KJ Sanchez; Director, KJ Sanchez; Sets/ Costumes, Marion Williams; Lighting, Russell H. Champa; Sound, Zachary Williamson; Projections, Alex Koch; Military Consultant, Joe Harrell; PSM, Denise Cardarelli; Dramaturg, Whitney Eggers, Gavin Witt; Cast: Joe Harrell (CO/Others), Sameerah Luqmaan-Harris (Mom/Maria/Others), Bobby Moreno (Charlie/Tommy), PJ Sokso (John/Pete/Others), Sheila Tapia (Liz/Marine Wife/ Others); November 10–December 19, 2010

The Second City Does Baltimore Created for CENTERSTAGE by The Second City; Additional material created by Megan Grano and T.J. Shanoff; Director, Matt Hovde; Music Director, Joe Drennan; Sets, Jennifer Stearns; Lighting, Lesley Boeckman; Sound, Amy C. Wedel; PSM, Josh Miller; Dramaturg, Gavin

Witt; Cast: Warren Phynix Johnson (Ensemble), Brett Lyons (Ensemble), Dana Quercioli (Ensemble), Tim Sniffen (Ensemble), Niccole Thurman (Ensemble), Megan Wilkins (Ensemble); December 30, 2010–February 20, 2011

Crime & Punishment Adapted by Curt Columbus and Marilyn Campbell from the novel by Fyodor Dostoevsky; Director Jason Loewith; Sets, Walt Spangler; Costumes, Janice Pytel; Lighting, Colin K. Bills; Sound, Joshua Horvath; PSM, Captain Kate Murphy; Dramaturg, Whitney Eggers; Fight Director, Lewis Shaw; Cast: Lauren Culpepper (Sonia), Eric Feldman (Raskolnikov), John Leonard Thompson (Porfiry); Apr 13–May 15, 2011

Center Theatre Group

Los Angeles, California

Forty-fourth Season

Artistic Director, Michael Ritchie; Managing Directors, Charles Dillingham

Ahmanson Theatre

Leap of Faith Based on the Motion Picture *Leap of Faith* (produced by Paramount Pictures Corporation and written by Janus Cercone); Music by Alan Menken; Book by Janus Cercone, Glenn Slater; Lyrics by Glenn Slater; Director/ Choreographer, Rob Ashford; Sets, Robin Wagner; Costumes, William Ivey Long; Lighting, Donald Holder; Sound, John Shivers; Wigs/Hair, Paul Huntley; Casting, Telsey + Company; Orchestrations, Michael Starobin, Joseph Joubert; Vocal and Incidental Arrangements/Music Supervisor, Michael Kosarin; Dance Arrangements, David Chase; Music Direction, Brent-Alan Huffman; PSM, Steven Zweigbaum; SM, Susie Walsh, Michelle Blair; Associate Choreographer, Chris Bailey; Associate Director, Stephen Sposito; Associate Producer, Neel Keller; Cast: Brad Anderson (Tom), Nicholas Barasch (Boyd McGowan), Krystal Joy Brown (Ornella), Michelle Duffy (Emma Schlarp), Jarrod Emick (Sheriff Will Braverman), Raúl Esparza (Jonas Nightingale), Harvey Evans (Mugs), Jennie Ford (Dance Captain/Swing), Bob Gaynor (Fred), Kendra Kassebaum (Sam), Shannon Lewis (Susie Raylove), Kecia Lewis-Evans (Ida Mae Sturdevant), Michael X. Martin (Jake), Leslie Odom, Jr. (Ricky Sturdevant), Darcie Roberts (Rita), Bryce Ryness (Dude), Brooke Shields (Marva McGowan), C.E. Smith (Titus), Alex Michael Stoll (Robert Raylove), Dennis Stowe (Caesar), Brandon Wardell (Amos), Karl Warden (Swing), Charlie Williams (Deputy Wayne Storm, Assistant Dance Captain); Ensemble: Bradley Benjamin, Tom Berklund, Christopher Bones, Ta'Rea Campbell, Eric L. Christian, Ashley Blair Fitzgerald, Angela Grovey, Maurice Murphy, Anise E. Ritchie, Ariel Shepley, Katherine Tokarz, Natalie Willes; World Premiere; September 11–October 24, 2010

Next to Normal Music by Tom Kitt; Book and lyrics by Brian Yorkey; Director, Michael Greif; Sets, Mark Wendland; Costumes, Jeff Mahshie; Lighting, Kevin Adams; Sound, Brian Ronan; Casting, Telsey + Company; Production Supervisor, Judith Schoenfeld; PSM, Michael McGoff; SM, Rachel Zack; ASM, Timothy Eaker; Technical Supervisor, Larry Morley; General Management, 321 Theatrical Management; Orchestrations, Michael Starobin, Tom Kitt; Music Supervisor, Charlie Alterman; Music Director, Bryan Perri; Vocal Arrangements, Annmarie Milazzo; Musical Staging, Sergio Trujillo; Cast: Curt Hansen (Gabe), Emma Hunton (Natalie), Jeremy Kushnier (Dr. Madden/Dr. Fine), Alice Ripley (Diana), Preston Sadleir (Henry), Asa Somers (Dan); Understudies: Caitlin Kinnunen, Perry Sherman, Pearl Sun, Jason Watson; West Coast Premiere; November 23, 2010–January 2, 2011

33 Variations Written and directed by Moisés Kaufman; Tectonic Theater Project Production; Music, Ludwig van Beethoven; Sets, Derek McLane; Costumes, Janice Pytel; Lighting, David Lander; Sound, André J. Pluess; Projection, Jeff Sugg; Additional Costumes, David C. Woolard; Hair/ Wigs, Charles LaPointe; Choreographer, Daniel Pelzig; Casting, James Calleri; Associate Producer, Neel Keller; PSM, Linda Marvel, David Lober; SM, Melissa M. Spengler, Susie Walsh; Cast: Don Amendolia (Anton Diabelli), Jane Fonda (Dr. Katherine Brandt), Zach Grenier (Ludwig van Beethoven), Greg Keller (Mike Clark), Susan Kellermann

(Dr. Gertrude Ladenburger), Samantha Mathis (Clara Brandt), Grant James Varjas (Anton Schindler), Diane Walsh (Pianist/Musical Director); Ensemble/Understudies: Scott Barrow, Caitlin O'Connell, Yvonne Woods Slaten; January 30–March 6, 2011

God of Carnage by Yasmina Reza; Translation, Christopher Hampton; Director, Matthew Warchus; Sets/Costumes, Mark Thompson; Lighting, Hugh Vanstone; Sound, Simon Baker, Christopher Cronin; Music, Gary Yershon; Casting, Daniel Swee; PSM, David S. Franklin; Associate Set, Nancy Thun; Associate Lighting, Ted Mather; Associate Costumes; Daryl A. Stone; Production Management, Aurora Productions; General Management, STP/David Turner & Chris Morey; Associate Director, Beatrice Terry; Cast: Jeff Daniels (Alan), Hope Davis (Annette), James Gandolfini (Michael), Marcia Gay Harden (Veronica); Standbys: Hugo Armstrong, Orlagh Cassidy; West Coast Premiere; April 5–May 29, 2011

Les Misérables Cameron Mackintosh 25th Anniversary Production; Based on the novel by Victor Hugo; Music by Claude-Michel Schönberg; Lyrics by Herbert Kretzmer; Original French text, Alain Boublil, Jean-Marc Natel; Additional material, James Fenton; Original Adaptation/Direction, Trevor Nunn, John Caird; Directors, Laurence Connor, James Powell; Original Orchestrations, John Cameron; New Orchestrations, Chris Jahnke; Additional Orchestrations, Stephen Metcalfe, Stephen Brooker; Music Supervisor, Dan Bowling; Music Director, Robert Billig; Musical Staging, Michael Ashcroft; Sets, Matt Kinley; Costumes, Andreane Neofitou; Lighting, Paule Constable; Sound, Mick Potter; Projections, Fifty-Nine Productions; Additional Costumes, Christine Rowland; PSM, Trinity Wheeler; SM/Assistant Fight Captain, Heather Chockley; ASM, Mitchell B. Hodges; Cast: Richard Todd Adams (Factory Foreman/Lesgles), Cathryn Basile (Crazy Whore), Julie Benko (Innkeeper's Wife), Justin Scott Brown (Marius), Cole Burden (Courfeyrac), Josh Caggiano (Gavroche), Colin DePaula (Gavroche), Jason Forbach (Feuilly), Katherine Forrester (Little Cosette/Young Éponine), Lucia Giannetta (Factory Girl), Ian Patrick Gibb (Constable/Jean Prouvaire), Cooper Grodin (Combeferre/Fauchelevent), Shawna M. Hamic (Madame Thénardier), Chasten Harmon (Éponine), Jeremy Hays (Enjolras), Ethan Paul Khusidman (Gavroche), Beth Kirkpatrick (Old Woman), Anastasia Korbal (Little Cosette/Young Éponine), Michael Kostroff (Thénardier), Jenny Latimer (Cosette), Cornelia Luna (Wigmaker), Benjamin Magnuson (The Bishop of Digne/Babet), J. Mark McVey (Jean Valjean), Betsy Morgan (Fantine), Max Quinlan (Laborer/Montparnasse), John Rapson (Farmer/Bamatabois/Claquesous), Sarah Shahinian (Young Whore), Alan Shaw (Constable/Joly), Joseph Spieldenner (Innkeeper/Grantaire/Major Domo), Joe Tokarz (Champmathieu/Brujon/Loud Hailer), Andrew Varela (Javert); Swings: Richard Barth, Ben Gunderson, Jason Ostrowski (Dance Captain), Rachel Rincione, Natalie Weiss; Ensemble/Understudies: Briana Carlson-Goodman, Casey Erin Clark, Aliya Victoriya; 25th Anniversary Production; June 14–July 31, 2011

Kirk Douglas Theatre

Stoop Stories Written and performed by Dael Orlandersmith; Consulting Director, Jo Bonney; Original Music/Sound, Eric Shimelonis; Costumes, Dian Camarillo; Lighting, Richard Peterson; AP, Neel Keller; PSM, Barclay Stiff; West Coast Premiere; July 7–11, 2010

Bones by Dael Orlandersmith; Director, Gordon Edelstein; Sets, Takeshi Kata; Costumes, Ellen McCartney; Lighting, Lap-Chi Chu; Sound, Adam Phalen; AP, Neel Keller; Dramaturg, Pier Carlo Talenti; Casting, Bonnie Grisan; PSM, Barclay Stiff; Cast: Khandi Alexander (Claire), Tessa Auberjonois (Leah), Tory Kittles (Steven), Doug Webb (Saxophones), Nedra Wheeler (Bass); World Premiere; July 30–August 8, 2010

Venice Book and direction by Eric Rosen; Music by Matt Sax; Lyrics by Matt Sax, Eric Rosen; A co-production with Kansas City Repertory Theatre; Additional Music, Curtis Moore; Sets/Costumes, Meghan Raham; Lighting, David Weiner; Sound/Music Production/Incidental Music, Joshua Horvath; Projection, Jason H. Thompson; Casting, Bonnie Grisan, Stephanie Klapper; Dramaturg, Mike Sablone; Fight Direction, Steve Rankin; Associate Producer, Kelley Kirkpatrick; PSM, Anjee Nero, David Lober; SM, Cate Cundiff; Music Direction/Arrangements/Orchestrations, Curtis Moore; Choreography, John Carrafa, Tanisha Scott; Associate Music Direction/Keyboard, David Manning; Drums/Percussion, Brandon Draper; Dance Captain, Aleander Selma; Cast: Uzo Aduba (Anna Monroe), Erich Bergen (Michael Victor), Rodrick Covington (Markos Monroe), J.D. Goldblatt (Theodore Westbrook), Andrea Goss (Willow Turner), Preston Mui (Ensemble/Drew Andrews/Dance Captain), Javier Muñoz (Venice Monroe), Victoria Platt (Emilia Monroe), Angela Wildflower Polk (Hailey Daisy), Matt Sax (Clown MC), Donald Webber, Jr. (Ensemble/Andy Andrews/Fight Captain), Morgan Weed (Ensemble/Reporter); World Premiere Production; October 7–November 14, 2010

Jamie Adkins' Circus INcognitus Created and performed by Artistic Director, Jamie Adkins; Production Direction/Photography/Web Design, Amanda Russell; Lighting, Nicolas Descoteaux; Costumes, Katrin Leblond; Music Composition/Arrangement, Lucie Cauchon; Sound Track Musician, Anne-Marie Levasseur; Touring Technical Director, Lionel Dechamps; PSM, Elle Aghabala; January 15–23, 2011

The Author by Tim Crouch; Directors, Karl James, a smith; Lighting, Christopher Kuhl; Original Lighting, Matt Drury; Sound, Ben Ringham, Max Ringham; Associate Producer, Kelley Kirkpatrick; PSM, Elle Aghabala; Cast: Tim Crouch, Chris Goode, Vic Llewellyn, Esther Smith; North American Premiere; February 15–27, 2011

The Cripple of Inishmaan by Martin McDonagh; Druid and Atlantic Theater Company production; Director, Garry Hynes; Sets/Costumes, Francis O'Connor; Lighting, Davy Cunningham; Sound, John Leonard; Composer, Colin Towns; United States Casting, Laura Stanczyk; Irish Casting, Maureen Hughes; Fight Director, J. David Brimmer; Company Stage Director/ASM, Sarah Lynch; PSM, David H. Lurie; Production Manager, Eamonn Fox; Cast: Liam Carney (BabbyBobby), Nancy E. Carroll (Mammy O'Dougal), Ingrid Craigie (Kate), Dermot Crowley (JohnnyPateenMike), Clare Dunne (Slippy Helen), Laurence Kinlan (Bartley), Dearbhla Molloy (Eileen), Tadhg Murphy (Billy Claven), Paul Vincent O'Connor (Doctor McSharry); April 5–May 1, 2011

Juan and John Created and performed by Roger Guenveur Smith; Associate Director, Patricia McGregor; Costumes, Candice Cain; Lighting, Justin Townsend; Sound/Video, Marc Anthony Thompson; Associate Producer, Kelley Kirkpatrick; PSM, Elle Aghabala; May 17–May 29, 2011

The Method Gun by Kirk Lynn; Director, Shawn Sides; Created and performed by Rude Mechs; Production Manager/Technical Director, Madge Darlington; Sets, Leilah Stewart; Costumes, Katey Gilligan; Lighting, Brian H Scott; Sound/Composer, Graham Reynolds; PSM/Projection, Lowell Bartholomee; Projection, Michael Mergen; Dramaturg, Adrien-Alice Hansel; Cast: Thomas Graves (Carl Reyholt as Pablo/Paper Boy/Tamale Vendor/Doctor), Hannah Kenah (Connie Torrey as Colored Woman/Mexican Woman), Lana Lesley (Koko Bond as Negro Woman/Nurse), E. Jason Liebrecht (Robert "Hops" Gilbert as Steve), Shawn Sides (Elizabeth Johns as Eunice); June 14–26, 2011

This by Melissa James Gibson; Playwrights Horizons production; Director, Daniel Aukin; Sets, Louisa Thompson; Costumes, Jessica Pabst; Lighting, Matt Frey; Original Sound, Matt Tierney; Original Music, Peter Eldridge; Original Casting, Alaine Alldaffer; Casting, Erika Sellin; Associate Artistic Director, Kelley Kirkpatrick; PSM, Elle Aghabala; SM, Cate Cundiff; Cast: Saffron Burrows (Jane), Eisa Davis (Marrell), Glenn Fitzgerald (Alan), Gilles Marini (Jean-Pierre), Darren Pettie (Tom); July 30–August 28, 2011

Mark Taper Forum

The Lieutenant of Inishmore by Martin McDonagh; Director, Wilson Milam; Sets, Laura Fine Hawkes; Costumes, Stephanie Kerley Schwartz; Lighting, Brian Gale; Sound, Cricket S. Myers; Fight Director, Steve Rankin; Special Prosthetic Effects, Matthew W Mungle; Special Effects, Waldo Warshaw; Original Music, Matt McKenzie; Dialect, Carla Meyer; Casting, Erika Sellin; AP, Neel Keller; PSM, David S. Franklin; SM, Michelle Blair; Cast: Ian Alda (Joey), Andrew Connolly (Christy), Coby Getzug (Davey), Sean G. Griffin (Donny), Kevin Kearns (Brendan), Zoe Perry (Mairead), Chris Pine (Padraic), Brett Ryback (James); Understudies:

PJ Brown, Greg Bryan, Annie Burgstede, Jonathan Lipnicki; June 30–August 8, 2010

The Glass Menagerie by Tennessee Williams; The Long Wharf Theatre production; Director, Gordon Edelstein; Sets, Michael Yeargan; Costumes, Martin Pakledinaz; Lighting, Jennifer Tipton; Sound, David Budries; Casting, James Calleri; Additional Casting, Erika Sellin, Carrie Gardner; Associate Producer, Neel Keller; PSM, Robyn Henry; SM, Christopher J. Paul; Cast: Patch Darragh (Tom Wingfield), Judith Ivey (Amanda Wingfield), Keira Keeley (Laura Wingfield), Ben McKenzie (Jim O'Connor); Understudies: Colleen Foy, Betsy Randle, Arron Shiver; September 1–October 17, 2010

Harps and Angels Music and lyrics by Randy Newman; Conceived by Jack Viertel; Director, Jerry Zaks; Musical Staging, Warren Carlyle; Sets, Stephan Olson; Costumes, Stephanie Kerley Schwartz; Lighting, Brian Gale; Sound, Philip G. Allen; Projection, Marc I. Rosenthal; Music Direction/Arrangements, Michael Roth; Orchestrations, David O, Michael Roth; Music Consultant/Additional Arrangements, Nadia DiGiallonardo; Casting, Laura Stanczyk; Associate Producer, Neel Keller; PSM, David S. Franklin; SM, Nate Genung; Dance Captain, Christa Jackson; Cast: Ryder Bach, Storm Large, Adriane Lenox, Michael McKean, Katey Sagal, Matthew Saldivar; Understudies: Graham Fenton, Christa Jackson, Andy Taylor, Nell Teare; World Premiere; November 10–December 22, 2010

John Lithgow's Stories by Heart Conceived, written and performed by John Lithgow; Lighting, Eric Cornwell; Producer/Manager, Staci Levine; January 4–February 13, 2011

Burn This by Lanford Wilson; Director, Nicholas Martin; Sets, Ralph Funicello; Costumes, Gabriel Berry; Lighting, Ben Stanton; Sound, Cricket S. Myers; Original Music, Peter Golub; Fight Director, Steve Rankin; Casting, Erika Sellin; Associate Producer, Kelley Kirkpatrick; PSM, David Lober; SM, Michelle Blair; Cast: Brooks Ashmanskas (Larry), Ken Barnett (Burton), Zabryna Guevara (Anna), Adam Rothenberg (Pale); Understudies: Emily Sandack, Matthew J. Williamson (Fight Captain); March 23–May 1, 2011

Poor Behavior by Theresa Rebeck; Director, Doug Hughes; Sets, John Lee Beatty; Costumes, Catherine Zuber; Lighting, Ben Stanton; Original Music/Sound, David Van Tieghem; Casting, MelCap Casting; Associate Artistic Director, Neel Keller; by Special Arrangement with Jeffrey Finn; PSM, Barclay Stiff; SM, Michelle Blair, John Randolph Ferry; Cast: Johanna Day (Ella), Sharon Lawrence (Maureen), Reg Rogers (Ian), Christopher Evan Welch (Peter); Understudies: Leslie Stevens, Nick Toren; World Premiere; September 7–October 16, 2011

Cincinnati Playhouse in the Park

Cincinnati, Ohio

Fifty-first Season

Producing Artistic Director, Edward Stern; Executive Director, Buzz Ward

Robert S. Marx Theatre

High by Matthew Lombardo; Director, Rob Ruggiero; Sets, David Gallo; Costumes, Jess Goldstein; Lighting, John Lasiter; Sound/Composer, Vincent Olivieri; PSM, Jenifer Morrow; ASM, Joseph Millett; Cast: Kathleen Turner (Sister Jamison Connelly), Evan Jonigkeit (Cody Randall), Michael Berresse (Father Michael Delpapp); World Premiere; September 4–October 2, 2010

You Can't Take It With You by Moss Hart and George S. Kaufman; Director, Steven Woolf; Sets, John Ezell; Costumes, Elizabeth Covey; Lighting, Peter E. Sargent; Sound, Rusty Wandall; PSM, Jenifer Morrow; Second Stage Manager, Andrea L. Shell; ASM, Joseph Millett; Cast: Carol Schultz (Penelope Sycamore), Stephanie Cozart (Essie), Rachel Leslie (Rheba), Tony Campisi (Paul Sycamore), Scott Schafer (Mr. DePinna), Jamie LaVerdiere (Ed), Scott Whitehurst (Donald), Joneal Joplin (Martin Vanderhof), Amelia McClain (Alice), Todd Lawson (Henderson/The Man), Benjamin Eakeley (Tony Kirby), Anderson Matthews (Boris Kolenkhov), Amy Warner (Gay Wellington), Jeffrey Hayenga (Mr. Kirby), Barbara

Kingsley (Mrs. Kirby/Grand Duchess Olga Katrina), Colin Gold (Jim), Matthew David Gellin (Mac); October 16–November 13, 2010

A Christmas Carol by Charles Dickens; Adapted by Howard Dallin; Director, Michael Evan Haney; Assistant Director, Stephen Skiles; Sets, James Leonard Joy; Costumes, David Murin; Lighting, Kirk Bookman; Sound/Composer, David B. Smith; Lighting Contractor, Susan Terrano; Music Director, Rebecca N. Childs; Choreographer, Dee Anne Bryll; SM, Andrea L. Shell; Second Stage Manager, Jenifer Morrow; Cast: Bruce Cromer (Ebenezer Scrooge), Nick Rose (Mr. Cupp/Percy/Rich Man at Fezziwig's), Lelund Durond (Mr. Sosser/Topper/Man with Shoe Shine/Guest at Fezziwig's), Andy Prosky (Bob Cratchit/Schoolmaster Oxlip), Keith Merrill (Fred), Gregory Procaccino (Jacob Marley/Old Joe), Dale Hodges (Ghost of Christmas Past/Mrs. Peake), Noah Lentini (Boy Scrooge/Guest at Fezziwig's/Bootblack/Streets), Isabella Siska (Fan/Rich Daughter at Fezziwig's/Streets), Keith Jochim (Mr. Fezziwig/Ghost of Christmas Present), Amy Warner (Mrs. Fezziwig/Patience/Streets), Mark St. Cyr (Dick Wilkins/Poor Caroler/Streets), Mariana Fernández (Scrubwoman (Mary) at Fezziwig's/Streets), Todd Lawson (Young and Mature Scrooge/Ghost of Christmas Future), Sabrina Veroczi (Belle/Catherine Margaret), Matthew David Gellin (Constable at Fezziwig's/Poulterer/Rich Caroler/Streets), Regina Pugh (Mrs. Cratchit/Laundress at Fezziwig's/Streets), Christopher Marc Wells (Peter Cratchit/Gregory/Apprentice at Fezziwig's/Streets), Allison Edwards (Belinda Cratchit/Guest at Fezziwig's/Streets), Julianne Fox (Martha Cratchit/Guest at Fezziwig's/Streets), Owen Gunderman (Tiny Tim), Anne Marie Damman (Rose/Rich Caroler/Guest at Fezziwig's/Streets), Riley Nattermann (Ignorance/Matthew/Rich Son at Fezziwig's/Streets), N'doumbe Ngom (Want/Guest at Fezziwig's/Streets), Colin Gold (Man with Pipe/Guest at Fezziwig's/Streets), Marie Pope (Mrs. Dilber/Guest at Fezziwig's/Streets); Kevin-Michael Chu (Undertaker/Guest at Fezziwig's/Streets), Javier Gresham (George/Charles/Apprentice at Fezziwig's/Streets), Rae Dohar (Poor Caroler/Rich Mother at Fezziwig's/Streets); December 2–30, 2010

Over the Tavern by Tom Dudzick; Director, Michael Evan Haney; Sets, Paul Shortt; Costumes, Dorothy Marshall Englis; Lighting, Dennis Parichy; Sound, Rusty Wandall; SM, Andrea L. Shell, Second Stage Manager, Jenifer Morrow; Cast: Spencer Davis Milford (Rudy), Darrie Lawrence (Sister Clarissa), Celeste Ciulla (Ellen Pazinski), Braden Phillips (Georgie), Eric Nelsen (Eddie), Katie McClellan (Annie), Kevin Cutts (Chet Pazinski), Anne Marie Damman (Nurse), Mark St. Cyr (Orderly); January 22–February 19, 2011

Gee's Bend by Elyzabeth Gregory Wilder; Director, Derrick Sanders; Sets, Jack Magaw; Costumes, Reggie Ray; Lighting, Thom Weaver; Sound/Composer, Justin Wellington; Music Director, Timothy W. Carpenter; PSM, Jenifer Morrow; Second Stage Manager, Andrea L. Shell; ASM, Wendy Dorn; Cast: Bakesta King (Sadie), Nikkole Salter (Nella), Cherene Snow (Alice/Asia), Quentin Earl Darrington (Macon); March 12–April 9, 2011

Beehive Created by Larry Gallagher; Director/Choreographer, Pamela Hunt; Musical Director, Michael Sebastian; Sets, James Morgan; Lighting, Mary Jo Dondlinger; Sound, David B. Smith; SM, Joseph Millett; Second Stage Manager, Jenifer Morrow; Ensemble: Lauren Dragon, Lisa Estridge, Jennie Harney, Kristin Maloney, Debra Walton, Jessica Waxman; April 23–May 22, 2011

Thompson Shelterhouse Theatre

The Understudy by Theresa Rebeck; Director, Michael Evan Haney; Sets/Lighting, Kevin Rigdon; Costumes, Gordon DeVinney; Sound, Chuck Hatcher; SM, Andrea L. Shell; ASM, Joseph Millett; Cast: David Christopher Wells (Harry), R. Ward Duffy (Jake), Kelly Hutchinson (Roxanne); September 18–October 17, 2010

The Second City Does Cincinnati: Pride and Porkopolis by Matt Hovde and Seth Weitberg; Director, Mick Napier; Musical Director, Jonathan Wagner; Lighting, Andrew J. Hungerford; SM, Donald E. Claxon; Ensemble: Ryan Archibald, Katie Caussin, Joe Dempsey, Sayjal Joshi, Anthony LeBlanc, Andel Sudik, Micah Sherman, Edgar Blackmon; World Premiere; November 6, 2010–January 16, 2011

The Piano Teacher by Julia Cho; Director, Edward Stern; Sets, Joseph P. Tilford; Costumes, Gordon DeVinney; Lighting, Thomas C. Hase; Sound, Fitz Patton; SM, Joseph Millett; Cast: Dale Hodges (Mrs. K), Joy C. Hooper (Mary Fields/Student 1/Parent A/Student C), Johnson Chong (Michael/Student 2/Parent B/Student D); February 12–March 13, 2011

Behind the Eye by Carson Kreitzer; Director, Mark Wing-Davey; Sets, Peter Ksander and Douglas Stein; Costumes, Emily Rebholz; Lighting, Blake Burba; Sound/Composer, Ryan Rumery; Projections/Video, Peter Flaherty; SM, Andrea L. Shell; Cast: Sarah Agnew (Lee Miller), Dee Pelletier (Woman: Tanja/Nusch/Audrey/Colette), Alan Cox (Man One: Man Ray/Roland Penrose), Alex Podulke (Man Two: Antony/Registry Clerk/Paul Eluard/Dave Scherman), James Saba (Man Three: Guide/Aziz/Picasso/Colette's Husband/Doctor); World Premiere; April 2–May 1, 2011

The Pavilion by Craig Wright; Director, D. Lynn Meyers; Sets, Bill Clarke; Costumes, Gordon DeVinney; Lighting, Phil Monat; Sound, Matthew Callahan; PSM, Jenifer Morrow; Cast: Jeffrey Kuhn (Narrator), Jay Stratton (Peter), Anney Giobbe (Kari); May 14–June 12, 2011

Cleveland Play House

Cleveland, Ohio

Ninety-fifth Season

Artistic Director, Michael Bloom; Managing Director, Kevin Moore

Drury Theatre

The 39 Steps by Patrick Barlow; Director, Peter Amster; Sets, Linda Buchanan; Lighting, Michael Lincoln; Sound/Composer, Victoria Toy Delorio; Costumes, Tracy Dorman; PSM, Stuart Plymesser; Assistant Director, Deborah Magid; Dialect, Jerrold Scott; Cast: Nick Sandys (Richard Hannay), Rob Johansen (Clown 1), Joe Foust (Clown 2), Sarah Nealis (Annabella Schmidt /Margaret/Pamela); September 17–October 10, 2010

This Wonderful Life by Steve Murray; Director, Peter Amster; Sets, Jeffrey W. Dean; Lighting, Aaron Muhl; Sound, Kevin Kennedy; SM, Jennifer Matheson Collins; Cast: James Leaming (Narrator/All Characters); November 26–December 19, 2010

The Trip to Bountiful by Horton Foote; Director, Timothy Douglas; Sets, Tony Cisek; Lighting, Christopher Studley; Sound, James C. Swonger; SM, Jennifer Matheson Collins; Costumes, Toni-Leslie James; Assistant Director, Bridget Leak; Cast: Lizan Mitchell (Carrie Watts), Doug Brown (Roy/Ensemble), Howard W. Overshown (Ludie Watts), Chinai J./Hardy (Jessie Mae Watts), Jessica Frances Dukes (Thelma), Lawrence Redmond (Sheriff/Ensemble); February 4–27, 2011

Legacy of Light by Karen Zacarias; Director, Bart DeLorenzo; Sets, Takeshi Kata; Lighting, Matthew Richards; Sound, James C. Swonger; SM, Lisa J. Snodgrass; Costumes, David Kay Mickelsen; Music Arranger/Composer, Tiffany Goff; Fight Choreographer, Ron Wilson; Cast: Cerris Morgan-Moyer (Emilie du Chatelet), Clancy O'Connor (Saint-Lambert/Lewis), Lenny Von Dohlen (Voltaire), Paul Michael Valley (Peter/Monsieur du Chatelet), Michelle Duffy (Olivia/Wet Nurse), Amelia Pedlow (Millie/Pauline); April 8–May 1, 2011

Bolton Theatre

The Kite Runner by Matthew Spangler; Director, Marc Masterson; Sets, Michael B. Raiford; Lighting, Brian J. Lilienthal; Sound, Matt Callahan; SM, Shannon Habenicht; Costumes, Lorraine Venberg; Wigs, Heather Fleming; Musical Supervisor, Salar Nader; Dialect, Rocco Dal Vera; Fight Director, K. Jenny Jones; Cast: Aadya Bedi (Soraya/Ensemble), Apollo Dukakis (Rahim Khan/Ensemble), Nasser Faris (Baba/Ensemble), Jose Peru Flores (Young Amir/Ensemble), Ariya Ghahramani (Kamal/Ensemble), Omar Koury (Farid/Ensemble), Salar Nader (Tabla Player), Matt Pascua (Hassan/Sohrab, Ensemble), Kario Pereira-Bailey (Wali/Ensemble), Annie Pesch (Mrs. Nguyen/Ensemble), James Saba (Ali/Zaman/Omar Faisal/Ensemble), Zarif Kabier Sadiqi (Assef/Ensemble), Remi Sandri (General Taheri/Ensemble), Jos Viramontes (Amir); October 15–November 7, 2010

Backwards in High Heels by Lynnette Barkley and Christopher McGovern; Director, Scott Schwartz; Sets, Walt Spangler; Lighting, Jeff Croiter, Grant Yeager; Sound, Brian Jerome Peterson; SM, Shannon Habenicht; Costumes, Alejo Vietti; Musical Director, Tim Robertson; Choreography, Patti Colombo, Cameron Henderson; Associate Director, Laura Josepher; Cast: Anna Aimee White (Ginger), Heather Lee (Lela), Christianne Tisdale (Martha May/Louise/Ethel Merman/Others), Matthew LaBanca (Marcus/Director/Fred Astaire/Others), Benjie Randall (Joe/Bill McMath/George Schaffer/Lew Ayres/Others), James Patterson (Jack Culpeeper/Hermes Pan/Jimmy Stewart/Others); January 7–30, 2011

Baxter Stage

My Name is Asher Lev by Aaron Posner; Director, Laura Kepley; Sets, Antje Ellermann; Lighting, Michael Lincoln; Original Music/Sound, Lindsay Jones; SM, Shannon Habenicht; Costumes, Jeffrey Van Curtis; Dialect, Charles Kartali; Cast: Noel Joseph Allain (Asher Lev), Elizabeth Raetz (Rivkeh Lev/Anna Schaeffer/Rachel), Tom Alan Robbins (Aryeh Lev/Uncle Yitzchok/Rebbe/Jacob Kahn); March 4–April 3, 2011

Dallas Theater Center

Dallas, Texas

Fifty-third Season

Artistic Director, Kevin Moriarty; Managing Director, Mark Hadley (through December 2010), Heather Kitchen (March 2011–present)

Henry IV by William Shakespeare; Director, Kevin Moriarty; Sets, John Coyne; Costumes, Jennifer Ables; Lighting, Jeff Croiter; Sound, Broken Chord Collective; Voice /Speech Coach, Thom Jones; Fight Director, Christopher DuVal; PM, Jeff Gifford; PSM, Melissa Daroff; Assistant Director, John Aldous; Casting, Lee Trull; Cast: Kurt Rhoads (King Henry IV), Randy Moore (Sir John Falstaff), Regan Adair (Vernon), Graham Dudley (Peto), Hassan El-Amin (Northumberland), Ricco Fajardo (Lancaster), Alexander Ferguson (Clarence), Chamblee Ferguson (Westmoreland), Micah Figueroa (Gloucester), Matthew Gray (Worcester), Dexter Hostetter (Pistol), Cliff Miller (Poins), Cedric Neal (Warwick), Sean O'Connor (Hastings), Beethovan Oden (Blunt), John Taylor Phillips (Glendower), Bryan Pitts (Douglas), Abbey Siegworth, Lady Percy, Doll Tearsheet), Teddy Spencer (Bardolph), Paul Stuart (Hotspur), Christina Vela (Mistress Quickly), Steven Walters (Prince Hal); September10–October 10, 2010

The Trinity River Plays by Regina Taylor; Director, Ethan McSweeny; Sets, Todd Rosenthal; Lighting, Tyler Micoleau; Costumes, Karen Perry; Sound, Steven Cahill; Additional Composition, Daryl Waters; Dialect, Sally Nystuen Vahle; Fight Director, Matthew E. Ellis; Wigs/Hair, Valerie Gladstone; Dramaturg, Janice Paran; PM, Jeff Gifford; SM, T. Paul Lynch; Assistant Directors, Bryan Hunt, Patrick Walsh; Cast: Karen Aldridge (Iris), Christiana Clark (Jasmine), Samuel Ray Gates (Jack), Penny Johnson Jerald (Rose), Jefferson A. Russell (Ray Earl/Frank), Jacqueline Williams (Daisy); November 5–December 5, 2010

A Christmas Carol by Charles Dickens; Adapted by Richard Hellesen; Music by David de Berry; Director, Matthew Gray; Music Director/Choreographer, Lindy Heath Cabe; Sets, Bob Lavalle; Costumes, Wade Laboissonniere; Lighting, Matthew Richards; Dialect, Emily Gray; PM, Jeff Gifford; SM, Melissa Daroff; ASM, Chris Wathen; Casting, Lee Trull; Cast: Chamblee Ferguson (Ebenezer Scrooge), Liz Mikel (The Ghost of Jacob Marley), Regan Adair (Bob Cratchit/Ensemble), J. Brent Alford (The Ghost of Christmas Present/Fezziwig/Charitable Gentleman/Ensemble), Christian St. John Chiles (Edward Cratchit/Ensemble), Caitlin Hale Daniels (Belinda Cratchit/Ensemble), Mark Fisher (Tiny Tim/Boy Scrooge/Ensemble), David Gorena (Dick Wilkins/Lower Class Husband/Ensemble), Emily Gray (Mrs. Cratchit/Ensemble), Jake Gray (Peter Cratchit/Ensemble), Tiffany Hobbs (Laundress/Ensemble), Aidan Langford (Edward Cratchit, Ensemble), Marlhy Murphy (Tiny Tim/Boy Scrooge/Ensemble), Alex Organ (Topper/Charitable Gentleman/Ensemble), Cedric Neal (The Ghost of Christmas Past/Ensemble), Paoloma Renteria (Belinda Cratchit/Ensemble), Cara Statham Serber

(Fred's Wife/Ensemble), Abbey Siegworth (Belle/Ensemble), Halle Tomlinson (Beggar Child/Ensemble), Lee Trull (Fred/Young Scrooge/Old Joe/Ensemble), Christina Vela (Mrs. Fezziwig/ Charworman/ Ensemble), Ben Villasenor (Peter Cratchit/Ensemble), Rachel Werline (Martha Cratchit/Fan/ Ensemble); November 26–December 24, 2010

Arsenic and Old Lace by Joseph Kesselring; Director, Scott Schwartz; Sets, Anna Louizos; Costumes, William Ivey Long; Lighting, Jeff Croiter; Sound, Curtis Craig; Composer/Lyricist, Michael Holland; Wigs, Paul Huntley; PM, Jeff Gifford; PSM, Melissa Draoff: ASM, Korey Kent; Casting Tara Rubin casting; Cast: Betty Buckley (Martha Brewster), Tovah Feldshuh (Abigail Brewster), J. Brent Alford (Teddy Brewster), James Crawford (Officer O'Harra), Jason Douglas (Jonathan Brewster), Nehal Joshi (Dr. Einstein), Chris McCreary (Officer Brophy), Sean O'Connor (Officer Klein), Steve Powell (Mr. Gibbs/Mr. Witherspoon), Diana Sheehan (Understudy for Ms. Buckley and Ms. Feldshuh), Abbey Siegworth (Elaine Harper), Paul Taylor (Lt. Rooney/Reverend Doctor Harper), Lee Trull (Mortimer Brewster); February 4–March 13, 2011

Dividing the Estate by Horton Foote; Director, Joel Ferrell; Sets, John Arnone; Costumes, Claudia Stephens; Lighting, Matthew Richards; Sound, Bruce Richardson; Wig Design, Dave Bova; PM, Jeff Gifford; SM, Kathryn Davies; Casting, Lee Trull; Cast: June Squibb (Stella Gordon), Kurt Rhoads (Lewis Gordon), Nance Williamson (Mary Jo), Akin Babatunde (Doug), Lynn Blackburn (Paulene), Katherine Bourne (Irene Ratliff), Kieran Connolly (Bob), Gail Cronauer (Lucille), Kristin Frantz (Sissie), Matthew Gray (Son), Emily Habeck (Emily), Tiffany Mann (Cathleen), Liz Mikel (Mildred); March 11–April 9, 2011

Cabaret Music by John Kander, Lyrics by Fred Ebb, Book by Joe Masteroff; Director/ Choreographer, Joel Ferrell; Sets, Bob Lavallee; Costumes, Clint Ramos; Lighting, Lap Chi Chu; Sound, Ray Nardelli; Music Director/Conductor, Elaine Davidson; Associate Choreographer, Kent Zimmerman; Wigs, Dave Bova; PM, Jeff Gifford; SM, Melissa Daroff; Casting Lee Trull; ASM, Korey Kent; Cast: Wade McCollum (Emcee), Kate Wetherhead (Sally Bowles), David Coffee (Herr Schultz), Walter Lee Cunningham, Jr. (Frenchie/Ensemble), Jeremy Dumont (Herman/Ensemble), Chamblee Ferguson (Ernst Ludwig), Katharine Gentsch (Rosie/Ensemble), Tiffany Hobbs (Fritzie/Ensemble), Julie Johnson (Fraulein Scheider), Elise Lavallee (Helga/ Ensemble), Traci Lee (Texas/Ensemble), Jason Moody (Hans/Ensemble), Alex Ross (Victor/ Ensemble), Teddy Spencer (Max/Ensemble), Lee Trull (Clifford Bradshaw), Sally Nystuen Vahle (Fraulein Kost), Merrill West (Lulu/Ensemble), Ken Zimmerman (Bobby/Ensemble); April 22–May 22, 2011

The Wiz Book by William F. Brown; Music and lyrics by Charlie Smalls; Director, Kevin Moriarty; Choreographer, Christopher Lance Huggins; Music Director, Lindy Heath Cabe; Sets, Jo Winiarski; Costumes, Wade Laboissonniere; Lighting, Jaymi Lee Smith; Sound, Charles R. Parsely II; Conductor, Elaine Davidson; Wigs, Cookie Jordan; PM, Jeff Gifford; SM, Eric Tysinger; ASM, Chris Wathen; Casting, Tara Rubin; Local Casting, Lee Trull; Cast: Trisha Jeffrey (Dorothy), Hassan El-Amin (Henry/The Wiz), Sydney James Harcourt (the Tinman), James Tyrone lane (the Scarecrow), Denise Lee (Auntie Em/Glenda), Liz Mikel (Adaperle/ Evillene), David Ryan Smith (the Cowardly Lion), Claude Alexander III (Dallas Black Dance Theatre), Katricia Eaglin (Dallas Black Dance Theatre), Richard A. Freeman, Jr. (Dallas Black Dance Theatre), Candace Hamblett-Holford (Dallas Black Dance Theatre), Michelle Hebert (Dallas Black Dance Theatre), Diana Hererra (Dallas Black Dance Theatre), Rachel McSween (Dallas Black Dance Theatre), Amber J. Merrick (Dallas Black Dance Theatre), Derrick Smith (Dallas Black Dance Theatre), Sean Smith (Dallas Black Dance Theatre), Jamie Thompson (Dallas Black Dance Theatre), Tyrone C. Walker (Dallas Black Dance Theatre), Major Attaway (Vocalist), Feleceia Benton (Vocalist), Stephanie Hall (Vocalist), Calvin Roberts (Vocalist); July 8–August 7, 2011

Delaware Theatre Company

Wilmington, Delaware

Thirty-Second Season

Executive Director, Mary Ann Ehlshlager

Sylvia by Ar.R.Gurney; Director, David Stradley; Sets, Adam Riggar Costumes, Janus Stefanowicz; Lighting, Shelley Hicklin; Sound, John Stovicek; PSM, Danielle B. Rose; ASM, Bayla Rubin; Cast: Maggie Lakis (Sylvia), Hollis McCarthy (Kate), Kurt Zischke (Greg), Dave Jadico (Tom/Phyllis/Leslie); October 19–November 7, 2010

Around the World in 80 Days Adapted by Mark Brown from the novel by Jules Verne; Director, Aaron Posner; Assistant Director, Megan Nicole O'Brien; Sets, Brian Sidney; Costumes, Rachel Healy; Lighting, Thom Weaver; Sound, Andre Pluess; PSM, Danielle B. Rose; ASM, Debbie Lau; Cast: Farah Bala (Aouda/ Newspaperman/Priest), Dan Hodge (Detective Fix/ Andrew Stuart/Conductor/ Elephant Owner/Young Parsi/Oysterpuff/Rev. Wilson's Servant), James Ijames (Passepartout/James Sullivan), Benjamin Lloyd (James Forester/Gauthier Ralph/ British Consul/Director of Police/Sir Francis/Judge Obadih/Chinese Broker/Ship Clerk/Bunsby/ Proctor/Engineer/Mudge/Clerk/Captain Speedy/Ship Engineer/ Train Clerk), Greg Wood (Phileas Fogg); December 1–19, 2010

Lucy by Damien Atkins; Director, David Stradley; Sets, Alexis Distler; Costumes, Rosemarie McKelvey; Lighting, Joshua Shulman; Sound, Fabian Obispo; PSM, Danielle B Rose; ASM, Bayla Rubin; Cast: Kate Eastwood Norris (Vivian), Andrea Green (Lucy), Charlie DelMarcelle (Gavin); Karen Peakes (Julia); Ross Beschler (Morris); January 19–February 6, 2011

Blithe Spirit by Nöel Coward; Director, Domenick Scudera; Sets, John Raley; Costumes, Brian Strachan; Lighting, Shelley Hicklin; Sound, John Stovicek; PSM, Danielle B Rose; ASM, Debby Lau; Cast: Sarah Doherty (Edith), Christie Parker (Ruth), James Michael Reilly (Charles), Peter DeLaurier (Mr. Bradman), Ceal Phelan (Mrs. Bradman), Meghan Colleen Moroney (Madame Arcati), Beth Hylton (Elvira); March 2–20, 2011

Chasin' Dem Blues by Kevin Ramsey; Director, Kevin Ramsey; Co-music Directors, Nate Buccieri, Eric Noden; Sets, Matthew Myhrum; Costumes, Janus Stefanowicz; Lighting, Joshua Shulman; Sound, John Stovicek; PSM, Danielle B Rose; ASM, Bayla Rubin; Cast: Doug Eskew (Blue), Jannie Jones (Queen), Eric Noden (Harp), Nate Buccieri (Professor), Mike De Castro (Traps), April 13–May 1, 2011

The Denver Center Theatre Company

Denver, Colorado

Thirty-first Season

Artistic Director, Kent Thompson

The Ricketson Theatre

The 39 Steps Adapted by Patrick Barlow; Director, Art Manke; Sets, Michael C. Smith; Costumes, David Kay Mickelsen; Lighting, Charles R. MacLeod; Sound, William Burns; Composer, Steven Cahill; Dramaturg, Douglas Langworthy; PM, Edward Lapine; SM, A. Phoebe Sacks; Cast: Sam Gregory (Richard Hannay), Larry Paulsen (Clown 1), Rob Nagle (Clown 2), Victoria Mack (Pamela/Annabella/Margaret); September 10–November 14, 2010

Map of Heaven by Michele Lowe; Director, Evan Cabnet; Sets, David M. Barber; Costumes, Clint Ramos; Lighting, Charles M. MacLeod; Sound, Williams Burns; Dramaturg, Douglas Langworthy; PM, Edward Lapin; SM, A. Phoebe Sacks; Cast: Stephanie Janssen (Lena Gates), Angela Reed (Rebecca Marks), Jessica Love (Jen Gates), Quentin Maré (Ian Gates), Vivia Font (Gail Kleizer), Genesis Oliver (Delivery Boy); January 14–February 26, 2011

Ruined by Lynn Nottage; Director, Seret Scott; Sets, Michael Ganio; Costumes, David Kay Mickelsen; Lighting, Jane Spencer; Sound, William Burns; Composer, Keith E. Johnston; Dramaturg, Douglas Langworthy; PM, Edward Lapine; SM, A. Phoebe Sacks; Cast: Kim Staunton (Mama Nadi), Joy Jones (Josephine), Tallia Brinson (Sophie), Daphne Gaines (Salima), Harvey Blanks (Christian), Sam Gregory (Mr. Harari), Wallian Oliver Watkins (Jerome Kisembe), Sheldon Woodley (Fortune), Keith Hamilton Cobb (Commander Osembenga), Maurice Jones (Soldier/Ensemble), Biko Eisen-Martin (Soldier/Ensemble), Ron McBee (Musician/Ensemble), Keith E. Johnston (Musician/Ensemble); March 18–April 30, 2011

The Space Theatre

House of the Spirits Based on the novel by Isabel Allende with songs by Caridad Svich; Director, José Zayas; Sets, Robert Mark Morgan; Costumes, Deborah M. Dryden; Lighting, Jane Spencer; Sound, Jason Ducat; Composer, Jane Shaw; PM, Edward Lapine; SM, Rachel Ducat; Cast: Drew Cortese (Esteban Garcia), Meghan Wolf (Alba), Franca Sofia Barchiesi (Clara), Dion Mucciacito (Pedro Tercero/Guard/Barabbas), Allison Pistorius (Rosa The Beautiful/ Blanca/Woman 4), John Hutton (Esteban Trueba), Jeanne Paulsen (Nivea/Woman 2), Lawrence Hecht (Severo/Pedro Garcia/Fr. Antonio/Man 1), Dena Martinez (Pancha/Woman 1), Jeanine Serralles (Ferula/Count Satigny/Woman 3), Lanna Joffrey (Transito Soto); September 17–October 23, 2010

Reckless by Craig Lucas; Director, Scott Schwartz; Sets, Kevin Rigdon; Costumes, Clare Henkle; Lighting, Charles R. MacLeod; Sound, Jason Ducat; PM, Edward Lapine; SM, Mark D. Leslie; Cast: Drew Cortese (Tom), Julia Motyka (Rachel), Jeffrey M. Bender (Lloyd), Leslie O'Carroll (Pooty), Tyrone Mitchell Henderson (Roy/Tim Timko), Kathleen M. Brady (Trish/Sue), Gabra Zackman (Doctors); November 12–December 18, 2010

The Catch by Ken Weitzman; Director, Lou Jacob; Sets, James Kronzer; Costumes, Ilona Somogyi; Lighting, Jane Spencer; Sound and Composition, Jane Shaw; PM, Edward Lapine; SM, Rachel Ducat; Cast: Nicoye Banks (Darryl Love), Mike Hartman (Sid Zipnik), Ian Merrill Peakes (Gary Zipnik), Makela Spielman (Beth Zipnik), Pun Bandhu (Michael Nomura), Wai-Ching Ho (Ruth Nomura); January 21–February 26, 2011

Superior Donuts by Tracy Letts; Director, Bruce K. Sevy; Sets, Lisa M. Orzolek; Costumes, Meghan Anderson Doyle; Lighting, Charles R. MacLeod; Sound, Jason Ducat; Dramaturg, Chad Henry; PM, Edward Lapine; SM, Chris C. Ewing, Kurt Van Raden; Cast: Kathleen M. Brady (Lady Boyle), Jeanne Paulsen (Officer Randy Osteen), Robert Sicular (Max Tarasov), Earl Baker Jr. (Officer James Bailey), Mike Hartman (Arthur Przybyszewski), Sheldon Best (Franco Wicks), John Hutton (Luther Flynn), Scott Thomas (Kevin Magee), Jeffrey Evan Thomas (Kiril Ivakin); April 1–May 7, 2011

The Stage Theatre

Dracula Adapted by Charles Morey; Director, Gavin Cameron-Webb; Sets, Vicki Smith; Costumes, Kevin Copenhaver; Lighting, Don Darnutzer; Sound, Craig Breitenbach; Original Music Composer, Gary Grundei; PM, Edward Lapine; SM, Christopher C. Ewing; Cast: Harry Carnahan (Jonathan Harker), Kathleen M. Brady (Peasant Woman/Mrs.Westenra), Jeffrey Roark (Peasant Man/Maxwell/Reporter/Workman), Tamara Hoffman (Peasant/Bride/Maid), Mandi Madsen (Peasant/Bride), Lincoln Thompson (Peasant Man/Reporter/Attendant), Caitlin Wise (Peasant/Bride/Cockney Tart), Philip Pleasants (Abraham Van Helsing), Margaret Loesser Robinson (Mina Murray Harker), Sofia Jean Gomez (Lucy Westenra), M. Scott McLean (Arthur Holmwood), Jeremiah Wiggins (Dr. John Seward), Michael McKenzie (R. M. Renfield), Mike Hartman (Coachman/Capt. Swales/Reporter/Workman), Anthony Marble (Count Dracula); October 1–October 31, 2010

A Christmas Carol by Charles Dickens; Adapted by Richard Hellesen; Director, Bruce K. Sevy; Sets, Vicki Smith; Costumes, Kevin Copenhaver; Lighting, Don Darnutzer; Sound, Craig Breitenbach; Music, David de Berry; Cast: Philip Pleasants (Ebenezer Scrooge), James Michael Reilly (Bob Cratchit), Jordan Coughtry (Fred), Mike Hartman (Ghost of Jacob Marley), Kate Hurster (Ghost of Christmas Past/Fred's Wife), Jeffrey Roark (Schoolmaster/Belle's Husband), Jacob Pearce (Ebenezer the Child), Kate Lubotsky (Fan), M. Scott McLean (Ebenezer the Young Man), Michael Fitzpatrick (Fezziwig), Renée Brna (Belle/Martha), Larry Bull (Ghost of Christmas Present), Linda Mugleston (Mrs. Fezziwig/Mrs. Cratchit), Augustus Lane Filholm (Peter), Zoe Miller (Belinda), Jack Lilley (Edward), Charlie Korman (Tiny Tim), Andy Jobe (Ghost of Christmas Yet to Come), Lexi Lubotsky (Want), Gabe Simmons (Ignorance), Bryce Baldwin (Boy in the Street); November 26–December 24, 2010

A Midsummer Night's Dream by William Shakespeare; Director, Kent Thompson; Sets, John Iacovelli; Costumes, Bill Black; Lighting, Don Darnutzer; Sound, Craig Breitenbach; Composer, Gregg Coffin; PM, Edward Lapine; Cast: Keith Hamilton Cobb (Theseus), Philip Pleasants (Egeus), Leigh Nichols Miller (Lysander), Drew Cortese (Demitrius), Paul Hebron (Philostrate), John Hutton (Oberon), Michael Wartella (Puck), Sam Gregory (Quince), Stephen Weitz (Snug), Lawrence Hecht (Bottom), Chad Callaghan (Flute), Tom Coiner (Snout). Randy Moore (Starveling), Tamara Hoffman (Hippolyta), Caitlin Wise (Hermia), Allison Pistorius (Helena), Kathleen McCall (Titania), Mandi Madsen (First Fairy), Kate Lubotsky (Cobweb), Keely Kritz (Peaseblossom), Zoe Miller (Moth), Lexi Lubotsky (Mustardseed), Gabe Simmons (Indian Boy); January 28–February 26, 2011

Traces a Les 7 Doigts de la Main Production; Director/Choreographer, Shana Carroll, Gypsy Snider; General Management, 321 Theatrical Management; Artists: Mason Ames, Valérie Benoît-Charbonneau, Mathieu Cloutier, Bradley Henderson, Phillippe Nomand-Jenny, Xia Zhengqi, Florian Zumkehr, Héloïse Bourgeois, Sen Lin, William Underwood; March, 11–May18, 2011

The 5th Avenue Theatre

Seattle, Washington

Twenty-second Season

Executive Producer and Artistic Director, David Armstrong; Managing Director, Bernadine C. Griffin; Producing Director, Bill Berry

In The Heights Music, lyrics, and original concept by Lin-Manuel Miranda; Book by Quiara Alegría Hudes; Director, Thomas Kail; Choreographer, Andy Blankenbuehler; Music Supervisor/Arranger/Orchestrator, Alex Lacamoire; Musical Director, Justin Mendoza; Sets, Anna Louizos; Costumes, Paul Tazewell; Lighting, Howell Binkley; Sound, Acme Sound Partners; Arranger/Orchestrator, Bill Sherman; Music Coordinator, Michael Keller; Casting, Telsey + Company; Tour Marketing/Publicity, Allied Live; GM, John S. Corker; Technical Supervisor/PM, Brian Lynch/Theatretech, Inc.; PSM, Marian Dewitt; SM, Joel Rosen, Katrina Stevens; ASM, Jennifer Leigh Wheeler; Wigs, Charles LaPointe; Fight Director, Ron Piretti; Associate Director, Casey Hushion; Producers, Kevin McCollum, Jeffrey Seller, Jill Furman Willis, Sander Jacobs, Robyn Goodman/Walter Grossman, Peter Fine, Sonny Everett/Michael Skipper; Associate Producers, Ruth Hendel, Harold Newman; Cast: Jose-Luis Lopez (Graffiti Pete), Joseph Morales (Usnavi), David Baida (Piragua Guy/Ensemble), Elise Santora (Abuela Claudia), Genny Lis Padilla (Carla), Isabel Santiago (Daniela), Daniel Bolero (Kevin), Natalie Toro (Camila), Chris Chatman (Sonny), Rogelio Douglas Jr. (Benny), Lexi Lawson (Vanessa), Arielle Jacobs (Nina), Sandy Alvarez (Ensemble), Christina Black (Ensemble), Natalie Caruncho (Ensemble), Oscar Cheda (Ensemble), Dewitt Cooper III (Ensemble), Wilkie Ferguson (Ensemble), Rayanne Gonzales (Ensemble), Rebecca Kritzer (Ensemble), April Ortiz (Ensemble), Joel Perez (Ensemble), Carlos Salazar (Ensemble), Brandon Contreras (Swings), Karlee Ferreira (Swings), Kristina Fernandez (Swings), Michael Fielder (Dance Captain/Swings), Morgan Matayoshi (Dance Captain/Swings), Antuan Raimone (Swings); September 28–October 17, 2010

A Christmas Story: The Musical! Based upon the motion picture *A Christmas Story*; Originating author, Jean Shepherd; Book by Joseph Robinette; Music and lyrics by Benj Pasek, Justin Paul; Director, Eric Rosen; Choreographer, Kelly Devine; Music Direction/Supervision, Ian Eisendrath; Orchestrations, Larry Blank; Sets, Walt Spangler; Costumes, Elizabeth Hope Clancy; Lighting, Howell Binkley; Sound, Ken Travis; Associate Choreographer, Richard J. Hinds; Dance

Matt Harrington, Joe Paulik, Samantha Richert, and Carter Gill in Moonchildren at Berkshire Theatre Group: Berkshire Theatre Festival (photo by Christy Wright)

Lauren Kennedy and Company in Casa Mañana Theatre's production of Evita (photo by Curtis Brown)

Michael McKenzie, Laura Chen, Glen Kubota, Ching Valdes-Aran, and Kenneth Lee in CENTERSTAGE's production of Snow Falling on Cedars (photo by Richard Anderson)

Eric Feldman, John Leonard Thompson, and Laura Culpepper in Crime and Punishment at CENTERSTAGE (photo by Richard Anderson)

Raúl Esparza in the world premiere of Leap of Faith at Centre Theatre Group (photo by Craig Schwartz)

Matt Sax and the Company of Venice in the world premiere production at Center Theatre Group (photo by Craig Schwartz)

Kathleen Turner and Evan Jonigkeit in the world premiere of Cincinnati Playhouse in the Park's production of High (photo by Sandy Anderwood)

Bakesta King and Cherene Snow in the Cincinnati Playhouse in the Park's production of Gee's Bend (photo by Sandy Anderwood)

Lizan Mitchell and Howard W. Overshown in The Trip to Bountiful at Cleveland Play House (photo by Roger Mastroianni)

Greg Wood, James Ijames, Benjamin Lloyd, and Dan Hodge in Around the World in 80 Days at Delaware Theatre Company (photo by Matt Urban)

Kurt Zischke and Maggie Lakis in Sylvia at Delaware Theatre Company (photo by Matt Urban)

Jeffrey M. Bender and Julia Motyka in the Denver Center Theatre Company's production of Reckless (photo by Terry Shaprio)

Arrangements, August Eriksmoen; Associate Music Director, Faith Seetoo; New York Casting, Stephanie Klapper; PSM, Amy Gornet; ASM, Jessica C. Bomball, Bret Torbeck; Cast: Frank Corrado (Jean Shepherd), John Bolton (The Old Man), Anne Allgood (Mother), Clarke Hallum (Ralphie Parker), Matthew Lewis (Randy Parker), Dexter Johnson (Flick), River Aguirre (Schwartz), Ashton Herrild (Scut Farkus), Keenan Barr (Grover Dill), Drea Gordon (Esther Jane), Olivia Mora (Mary Beth), Shaye Hodgins (Classmate), Erich Schleck (Classmate), Cameron Washington (Classmate), Mira Wellington (Classmate), Carol Swarbrick (Miss Shields/Others), Jadd Davis (Radio Quartet/Others), Candice Donehoo (Radio Quartet/Others), Brandon O'Neill (Radio Quartet/Others), Billie Wildrick (Radio Quartet/Others), Eric Polani Jensen (Pierre Andre/Others), Ty Willis (Tree Salesman/Others), Frances Leah King (Mrs. Dill/Others), Matt Wolfe (Santa/Others), Orville Mendoza (Elf/Waiter/Others), Jenny Shotwell (Elf/Others), Krystle Armstrong (Elf/Others/Dance Captain), Wilder Cufley (u/s), Larson Eernissee (u/s), Walker Caplan (u/s), Jared Michael Brown (Swings), Sarah Davis (Swings); November 26–December 30, 2010

Vanities Produced in partnership with ACT–A Contemporary Theatre; Based on the original play by Playwright, Jack Heifner; Director/Musical Staging, David Armstrong; Composer/Lyrics, David Kirshenbaum; Music Direction/Supervision, Ian Eisendrath; Sets, Matthew Smucker; Costumes, Catherine Hunt; Lighting, Tom Sturge; Sound, Ken Travis; Assistant Sound Design, Brendan Hogan; ASM, Jeffrey K. Hanson, JR Welden; Assistant Director, Eric Jensen; Assistant Lighting Design, Susannah Scott; Associate Music Director, Faith Seetoo; Dialect, Alyssa Keene; Cast: Cayman Ilika (Kathy), Jennifer Sue Johnson (Joanne), Billie Wildrick (Mary), Abby Duke Pollard (u/s); ACT–A Contemporary Theatre; February 4–May 1, 2011

Next to Normal Composer/Co-orchestrator, Tom Kitt; Librettist/Lyricist, Brian Yorkey; Director, Michael Greif; Choreographer, Sergio Trujillo; Sets, Mark Wendland; Costumes, Jeff Mahshie; Lighting, Kevin Adams; Sound, Brian Ronan; Co-orchestrator, Michael Starobin; Music Supervisor, Charlie Alterman; Music Director, Bryan Perri; Vocal Arrangements, Annmarie Milazzo; Casting, Telsey + Company; PSM, Michael McGoff; SM, Rachel Zack; ASM, Timothy Eaker; Technical Supervisor, Larry Morley; Production Supervisor, Judith Schoenfeld; General Management, 321 Theatrical Management; Assistant Director, Laura Pietropinto; Associate Choreographer, Dontee Kiehn; Producers, David Stone, James L. Nederlander, Barbara Whitman, Patrick Catullo, Second Stage Theatre; Cast: Curt Hansen (Gabe), Emma Hunton (Natalie), Jeremy Kushnier (Dr. Madden/Dr. Fine), Alice Ripley (Diana), Preston Sadleir (Henry), Asa Somers (Dan), Pearl Sun (Standby), Jason Watson (Standby/u/s), Caitlin Kinnunen (u/s), Perry Sherman (u/s); February 22–March 13, 2011

9 to 5 The Musical Based on the 20th Century Fox Picture originally produced on Broadway by Robert Greenblatt; Composer/Lyricist, Dolly Parton; Book by Patricia Resnick; Director/ Choreographer, Jeff Calhoun; Associate Director, Richard J. Hinds; Co-Choreographer, Lisa Stevens; Sets, Kenneth Foy; Costumes, William Ivey Long; Lighting, Ken Billington; Sound, Steve Canyon Kennedy; Projection Designer, Benjamin Pearcy; Music Director/Additional Orchestrations/Vocal and Incidental Music Arrangements, Stephen Oremus; Orchestrator, Bruce Coughlin; Dance Arranger/Co-orchestrator, Alex Lacamoire; Musical Director/Conductor, Martyn Axe; Assistant Conductor/Keyboard II, Christopher D. Littlefield; Music Coordinator, Michael Keller; Casting, Telsey + Company; Hair/Wigs, Paul Huntley, Edward J. Wilson; Aerial Effects Designer, Paul Rubin; Production Supervisor, John R. Edkins; PSM, Timothy R. Semon; SM, CCME. Cameron Holsinger; ASM, Karyn Meek; Company Manager, Chris Danner; Associate Company Manager, Miguel Ortiz; General Management, Nina Lannan Associates; Producers, Blumenthal Performing Arts Center, Fox Theatricals, Theatre Under The Stars (TUTS, Robert G. Bartner, ATG, Independent Presenters Network, James L. Nederlander, Music Theatre International; Cast: Dee Hoty (Violet Newstead), Diana DeGarmo (Doralee Rhodes), Mamie Parris (Judy Bernly), Joseph Mahowald (Franklin Hart Jr.), Kristine Zbornik (Roz Keith), Gregg Goodbrod (Joe/Ensemble), Micah Shepard (Dwayne/ Ensemble), Jesse JP Johnson (Josh/Ensemble), Wayne Schroder (Dick/Detective/Tinsworthy/ Ensemble), Jane Blass (Margaret/Ensemble), April Nixon (Kathy/Ensemble), Michelle Marmolejo (Maria/Ensemble), Natalie

Charlé Ellis (Missy/Ensemble), Paul Castree (Bob Enright/Ensemble), Autumn Guzzardi (Candy Striper/Ensemble), Randy Aaron (Ensemble), Janet Dickinson (Ensemble), Ryah Nixon (Ensemble), Rick Pessagno (Assistant Dance Captain/Ensemble), Mark Raumaker (Ensemble), Brian Beach (Swings), Sarah Dacey Charles (Swings), Marjorie Failoni (Dance Captain/Swings), K.J. Hippensteel (Swings), Travis Waldschmidt (Swings); April 5–April 24, 2011

Guys and Dolls Based on a story and characters by Damon Runyon; Composer/Lyricist, Frank Loesser; Book by Jo Swerling and Abe Burrows; Director, Peter Rothstein; Choreographer, Noah Racey; Music Director, Joel Fram; Sets, Kate Sutton-Johnson; Costumes, Gregory A. Poplyk; Lighting, Tom Sturge; Sound, Ken Travis; Hair/Makeup, Mary Pyanowski; New Orchestrations, Bruce Monroe; Dance Music Arrangements, Mark Hummel; Dialect, Alyssa Keene; Associate Sound Designer, Zach Williamson; Associate Music Director, Dwight Beckmeyer; Assistant to the Director, Benjamin Shaw; PSM, Amy Gornet; ASM, E. Sara Barnes, Stina Lotti; Cast: Todd Buonopáne (Nicely-Nicely Johnson), Greg McCormick Allen (Benny Southstreet), Allen Galli (Rusty Charlie), Katherine Strohmaier (Sarah Brown), Clayton Corzatte (Arvide Abernathy), Ann McCormick Allen (Agatha), Bradford Farwell (Harry the Horse), Jim Gall (Lt. Brannigan/Fight Captain), Daniel C. Levine (Nathan Detroit), Billie Wildrick (Miss Adelaide), Brandon O'Neill (Sky Masterson), Matt Farnsworth (Sky Masterson), Joshua Carter (Joey Biltmore/Guys), Bob De Dea (Charlie/Guys), Brittany Jamieson (Mimi/Dolls), Laura Kenny (General Cartwright), David Drummond (Big Jule), David Alewine (Dance Captain/Guys), Gabriel Corey (Guys), Ross Cornell (Guys), Bojohn Diciple (Guys), Christian Duhamel (Guys), Eric Esteb (Guys), Jonathan Paul Lee (Guys), Daniel Oakden (Guys), Dane Stokinger (Guys), Trina Mills (Dolls), Kasey Nusbickel (Dolls), Katie Rooney (Dolls), Jessica Skerritt (Dolls), Mara Solar (Dolls); May 12–June 5, 2011

Disney's Aladdin the New Stage Musical Based on the Disney film written by Ron Clements, John Musker, Ted Elliott and Terry Rossio; Directed and produced by Ron Clements and John Musker; Music, Alan Menken; Co-lyricist, Howard Ashman, Tim Rice; Book/ Additional Lyrics, Chad Beguelin; Director/Choreographer, Casey Nicholaw; Music Director/ Music Supervisor/ Vocal and Incidental Music Arranger, Michael Kosarin; Orchestrator, Danny Troob; Sets, Anna Louizos; Costumes, Gregg Barnes; Lighting, Natasha Katz; Sound, Ken Travis; Hair, Josh Marquette; Illusion Designer, Joe Eddie Fairchild; Fight Choreographer, Geoffrey Alm; Dance Arranger, Glen Kelly; Associate Director, Scott Taylor; Associate Choreographer, John Macinnis; Associate Music Director/Associate Conductor, Ian Eisendrath; Associate Set Designer, Michael Carnahan; Associate Costume Designer, Sky Switser; Associate Lighting Designer, Peter Hoerburger; Casting, Tara Rubin Casting; Technical Supervision, Troika Entertainment; PSM, Clifford Schwartz; ASM, Jessica C. Bomball, Holly R. Coombs; Disney Theatrical Productions; Cast: Brian Gonzales (Babkak), Andrew Keenan-Bolger (Omar), Brandon O'Neill (Kassim/Spooky Voice/Tiger God), Nikki Long (Dance Captain/Ensemble), Daisy Hobbs (Ensemble/Woman), Tia Altinay (Ensemble/Attendant/Belly Dancer/ Vendor), Kristin Culp (Ensemble/Belly Dancer), Nick DeSantis (Ensemble/Razoul), Ronald Duncan (Ensemble), C.J. Eldred (Intern/Guard), David Janett (Ensemble/Servant), Kenway Hon Wai K. Kua (Ensemble/Vendor/Guard), Stanley Martin (Ensemble/Henchman), Creighton J. Oliver (Intern/Servant), Shanna Marie Palmer (Ensemble/Attendant/Belly Dancer/Fight Captain), Bobby Pestka (Ensemble/Prince Hassim/Guard), Connor Russell (Intern/Royal Page), Manuel Santos (Ensemble/Prince Abdullah/Servant), Allysa Shorte (Ensemble/Attendant/Belly Dancer), Daniel J. Watts (Ensemble/Guard/Prince Salim), Matt Wolfe (Ensemble/Henchman/Apple Vendor/Guard), Adam Jacobs (Aladdin), Jonathan Freeman (Jafar), Don Darryl Rivera (Iago), Seán G. Griffin (Sultan), Courtney Reed (Jasmine), James Monroe Iglehart (Genie); July 8–July 31, 2011

Geffen Playhouse

Los Angeles, California

Sixteenth Season

Producing Director, Gil Cates; Artistic Director, Randall Arney; Managing Director, Ken Novice

Ruined by Lynn Nottage; Director, Kate Whoriskey; Sets, Derek McClane; Costumes, Paul Tazewell; Lighting, Peter Kaczorowski; Sound, Michael Bodeen; SM, Mary K. Klinger; PM, Daniel Ionazzi; Cast: Quincy Tyler Bernstine (Salima), Cherise Boothe (Josephine), Tongayi Chirisa (Kisembe/Soldier/Miner), Carl Cofield (Fortune/ Soldier/Miner), Russell G. Jones (Christian), Simon Shabantu Kashama (Guitarist), Tom Mardirosian (Mr. Harari), Ron McBee (Pascal/Soldier), Portia (Mama Nadi), Condola Rashad (Sophie), David St. Louis (Osembenga/ Soldier/Miner, Stephen Tyrone Williams (Simon/Laurent/Soldier/Miner/Aid Worker); Gil Cates Theater; September 7–October 17, 2010

Hershey Felder in Maestro: The Art of Leonard Bernstein by Hershey Felder; Director, Joel Zwick; Sets, Francois Pierre Couture; Lighting, Michael Gilliam; Music, Leonard Bernstein, Sound, Erik Carstensen; SM, GiGi Garcia; PM, Dan Ionazzi; Cast: Hershey Felder (Leonard Bernstein); Gil Cates Theater; November 2–December 12, 2010

The Break of Noon by Neil LaBute; Director, Jo Bonney; Sets, Neil Patel; Lighting, David Weiner; Costumes, Emilio Sosa; Sound, Darron L. West; SM, Christina Lowe; PM, Daniel Ionazzi; Cast: Tracee Chimo (Host/Gigi), John Earl Jelks (Lawyer/ Detective), Kevin Anderson (John Smith), Catherine Dent (Ginger/ Jesse); Gil Cates Theater; January 25–March 6, 2011

In Mother Words by Joan Stein and Susan Rose; Director, Lisa Peterson; Sets, Rachel Hauck; Costumes, David Woolard; Lighting, Christopher Kuhl; Sound, Jill DuBoff; SM, Young Ji; PM, Daniel Ionazzi; Ensemble: James Lecesne, Saidah Arrika Ekulona, Jane Kaczmarek, Amy Pietz; Audrey Skirball Kenis Theater; February 15–May 1, 2011

The Escort: An Explicit Play for Discriminating People by Jane Anderson; Director, Lisa Petersen; Sets, Richard Hoover; Costumes, Laura Bauer; Lighting, Rand Ryan; Sound, Paul James Prendergast; SM, Jimmie McDermott; PM, Daniel Ionazzi; Cast: Polly Draper (Rhona), James Eckhouse (John/Howard/Waiter), Maggie Siff (Charlotte), Gabriel Sunday (Lewis/Mathew); Gil Cates Theater; March 29–May 8, 2011

Superior Donuts by Tracy Letts; Director, Randall Arney; Sets, John Arnone; Costumes, Laura Bauer; Lighting, Daniel Ionazzi; Sound, Richard Woodbury; SM, Michele Miner; PM, Daniel Ionazzi; Cast: Gary Cole (Arthur), Brian Abraham (Kiril Ivakin), Damon Gupton (Officer James Bailey), Edi Gathegi (Franco Wicks), Mary Beth Fisher (Randy), Paul Dillon (Luther Flynn), Matt McTighe (Kevin), Kathryn Joosten (Lady Boyle), Ron Bottitta (Max); Gil Cates Theater; May 31–July 10, 2011

Extraordinary Chambers by David Wiener; Director, Pam McKinnon; Sets, Myung Ili Cho; Costumes, Alex Jaeger; Lighting, Lap Chi Chu; Sound, Vincent Olivieri; SM, Young Ji; PM, Daniel Ionazzi; Cast: Marin Kinkle (Mara), Francois Chau (Dr. Heng), Greg Watanabe (Sopoan), Mather Zickel (Carter), Kimiko Gelman (Rom Chang); Audrey Skirball Kenis Theater; May 24–July 3, 2011

Georgia Shakespeare

Atlanta, Georgia

Twenty-fifth Season

Richard Garner, Producing Artistic Director

Shrew: the Musical Conceived, adapted and directed by John R. Briggs; Music and lyrics by John R. Briggs, Dennis West; Original Arrangements, Dennis West; Sets, Rochelle Barker; Costumes, Douglas J. Koertge; Lighting, Liz Lee; Sound, Clay Benning; SM,Margo Kuhne; Vocal Director, Ann-Carol Pence; Choreographer, Jen MacQueen; Musical Orchestrations, Eric Alexander; Accompanist, Clay Causey; Cast: Joe Knezevich (Petruchio), Park Krausen (Kate), Chris Kayser (Grumio), Ann Marie Gideon (Bianca), Neal A. Ghant (Lucentio), Brian Kurlander (Hortensio), Daniel Thomas May (Tranio), Allen O'Reilly (Baptista), Tim McDonough (Gremio), Allan Edwards (Vincentio/Georgio), Casey Hoekstra (Biondello), Courtney Patterson (Widow), Brad Sherrill (Banker), Brian Harrison (Harrison), Caitlin McWethy (Phillis), Megan Pickrell (Griselle), Tucker Weinmann (Nathaniel); June 9–August 8, 2010

Love's Labour's Lost by William Shakespeare; Director, Janice Akers; Sets, Kat Conley; Costumes, Sydney Roberts; Lighting, Mike Post; Composer, Kendall Simpson; SM, Robert Schultz; Cast: Brian Kurlander (King Ferdinand of Navarre), Brad Sherrill (Biron), Neal A. Ghant (Longaville), Daniel Thomas May (Dumain), Chris Kayser (Boyet), Tim McDonough (Don Armado/King of France), Allan Edwards (Holofernes/Marcade), Brian Harrison (Nathaniel), Joe Knezevich (Costard), Tucker Weinmann (Moth), Carolyn Cook (Princess of France), Park Krausen (Rosaline), Courtney Patterson (Maria), Casey Hoekstra (Dull/ Forester/ Marcade's Gentleman), Caitlin McWethy (Katharine), Ann Marie Gideon (Jaquenetta), Megan Pickrell (Lady Caterer/Nurse) ; June 9–August 8, 2010

King Lear by William Shakespeare; Director, Sabin Epstein; Sets, Angela Balogh Calin; Costumes, Christine Turbitt; Lighting, Mike Post; Composer, Laura Carpman; Sound, Clay Benning; Fight Directors, Scot Mann, Kelly Martin; SM, Margo Kuhne; Cast: Tim McDonough (King Lear), Brian Kurlander (Duke of Cornwall), Brad Sherrill (Duke of Albany), Allen O'Reilly (Earl of Kent), Allan Edwards (Earl of Gloucester), Joe Knezevich (Edgar), Daniel Thomas May (Edmund), Neal A. Ghant (Oswald), Chris Kayser (Fool), Carolyn Cook (Goneril) Courtney Patterson (Regan), Park Krausen (Cordelia), Ensemble: Ann Marie Gideon, Brian Harrison, Casey Hoekstra, Caitlin McWethy, Megan Pickrell, Tucker Weinmann; June 9–August 8, 2010

The Legend of The Sword in the Stone Based on the work of T.H. White; Adapted and directed by Tim Conley and Allen O'Reilly; Composer, Kendall Simpson; Sets, Tim Conley; Costumes, Katy Munroe; Lighting, Katie McCreary; Sound, Brian Smith; SM, Katie Pfohl; Cast: Brian Harrison (Merlin), Casey Hoekstra (Kay/Others), Caitlin McWethy (Wart); Ann Marie Gideon (Sir Ector/ Morganna/Archimedes/Others); July 20–August 7, 2010

The Odyssey: A Journey Home Based on the work of Homer; Adapted by Richard Garner and the GS Company; Director, Richard Garner; Sets, Kat Conley; Costumes, Sydney Roberts; Lighting, Mike Post; Composer, Kendall Simpson; Sound, Clay Benning; Dramaturg, Jane Barnette; SM, Margo Kuhne; Vocal Coach, Elisa Carlson; Cast: Joe Knezevich(Odysseus), Tess Malis Kincaid (Penelope/ Others), Carolyn Cook (Athena/Others), Chris Kayser (Zeus/Others), Neal A. Ghant (Eurylochus/Others), Bruce Evers (Cyclops/Others), Zechariah Pierce (Antinous/ Others), Eliana Marianes (Nausicaa/Others), Craig Thompson (Telemachus/ Others), Enoch King (Amphinomous/Others); October 6–October 31, 2010

A Christmas Story Based on the motion picture *A Christmas* Story, written by Jean Shepherd, Leigh Brown and Rob Clark; and on the book *In God We Trust, All Others Pay Cash* by Jean Shepherd; Written by Philip Grecian; Director, Drew Fracher; Sets, Kat Conley; Costumes, Sydney Roberts; Assistant Costume Design, Marianne Martin; Lighting, Mike Post; Sound, Benjamin Marcum; SM, Margo Kuhne; Cast: Cooper Driskell (Ralphie), Allan Edwards (Ralph/Narrator), Mark Kincaid (The Old Man), Sherman Fracher (Mother), Ian L'Abate (Randy), Eric Broner (Flick), Whit Weinmann (Scut), Giovanni Tortorici (Schwartz) LaLa Cochran (Miss Shields), Alice Garriga (Helen), Shea Jones (Esther Jane); December 7–December 24 , 2010 3

Geva Theatre Center

Rochester, New York

Thirty-eighth Season

Artistic Director, Mark Cuddy; Executive Director, Tom Parrish

Amadeus by Peter Shaffer; Director, Paul Mason Barnes; Sets, Bill Clarke; Costumes, Dorothy Marshall Englis; Lighting, Kendall Smith; Sound, Rusty Wandall; Assistant Director, Kathryn Moroney; Dramaturg, Marge Betley; SM, Kirsten Brannen; ASM, Skip Greer; Cast: Royce Bleier (Ensemble), Vincent Carbone (Ensemble), Kate Dylan (Ensemble), Tim Ellison (Ensemble), Michael Fitzpatrick (Count Johann Kilian van Strack), Laura Griffith (Constanze Weber), Brent Harris (Antonio Salieri), Brad Heberlee (Joseph II), Richmond Hoxie (Count Franz Orsini-Rosenberg), David Graham Jones (Venticelli), Darrell Lance (Ensemble), Patricia Lewis (Ensemble), Stephanie McKee (Ensemble), Ned Noyes (Venticelli), Jim Poulos (Wolfgang Amadeus Mozart), Robert Rutland (Baron Gottfried van Swieten), Ricky Thomas (Ensemble), Rachael Yoder (Ensemble); September 7–October 3, 2010

Carry It On by Philip Himberg and Maureen McGovern. Director, Philip Himberg; Musical Director, Jeffrey Harris; Sets, Neil Patel; Costumes, Gayle Baizer; Lighting Design, David Lander; Projection Design, Maya Ciarrocchi; Sound, Ian Hildreth; Dramaturg, Marge Betley; PSM, Robert V. Thurber; ASM, Kirsten Brannen. Cast: Maureen McGovern; October 12–November 14, 2010

A Christmas Carol by Charles Dickens; Adapted for the stage by Mark Cuddy, Music and lyrics by Gregg Coffin; Director, Mark Cuddy; Sets, Adam Koch; Costumes, Devon Painter; Lighting, Paul Hackenmueller; Musical Director, Gregg Coffin; Sound, Lindsay Jones; Projections Design, Dan Scully; Choreographer, Meggins Kelley; Assistant Sound Designer, Will Pickens; Projections Programmer, Ben Keightley; Dramaturg, Jean Gordon Ryon; SM, Kirsten Brannen; ASM, Veronica Aglow. Cast: Melissa Rain Anderson (Mrs. Cratchit, Mrs. Fezziwig, Mrs. Dilber), Ethan Beckwith-Cohen (The Child Ebenezer, Boy Cratchit, Ignorance), Tali Beckwith-Cohen (Tiny Tim), Royce Bleier (Londoner), Lucas Brown (The Child Ebenezer, Boy Cratchit, Ignorance), Vincent Carbone (Londoner),Kasey Dickinson (Girl Cratchit, Want, Turkey Girl), Emelia Duserick (Fan, Miss Fezziwig), Kate Dylan (Londoner), Tim Ellison (Londoner), Gavin Flood (The Young Ebenezer, Peter Cratchit), Mina Konuksever (Miss Fezziwig, Belinda Cratchit),Kevin Ligon (Businessman, Fezziwig, The Ghost of Christmas Present), Kara Lindsay (Belle, Fred's Wife, Martha Cratchit, Young Wife), Stephanie McKee (Londoner), Erin McManus (The Ghost of Christmas Past, Turkey Girl), Sage Melcher (Miss Fezziwig, Servant Girl), Kara Minute (Londoner), Michael Motkowski (The Young Ebenezer, Peter Cratchit), Megan Mueller (Tiny Tim), Ned Noyes (Fred, Apprentice Ebenezer, Young Husband), Guy Paul (Ebenezer Scrooge), Jim Poulos (Bob Cratchit, Dick Wilkins, Sailor, Undertaker's Man), Julie Sandler (Girl Cratchit, Want, Turkey Girl), Remi Sandri (The Ghost of Jacob Marley, Schoolmaster, Miner, Topper, Businessman), Carina Scalice (Miss Fezziwig, Servant Girl), Michael Sheehan (Londoner), Ricky Thomas (Londoner), Taylor Tydings (Fan, Miss Fezziwig), Mark Weeg (Fiddler), Alizabeth York (The Ghost of Christmas Past, Turkey Girl), Annaleigh York (Miss Fezziwig, Belinda Cratchit), Rachael Yoder (Londoner); November 26–December 26, 2010.

I'll Be Geneseeing You: The Second City Does Rochester. Material created by the cast of The Second City; Additional material created by Jean Villepique and Ed Furman; Director, Jimmy Carlson; Musical Director, Lisa McQueen; Lighting, Derek Madonia; Sound, Ian Hildreth; SM, J. Jackson Smith. Cast: Hilary Bauman, Shad Kunkle, Michael Lehrer, Tawny Newsome, Ric Walker, Beth Winslow; January 4–January 20, 2010

Over the Tavern by Tom Dudzick; Director, Skip Greer; Sets, John Iacovelli; Costumes, B. Modern; Lighting, John Wylie; Sound, Dan Roach; Assistant Director, Susan Ware; Dramaturg, Eric Evans; SM, Kirsten Brannen; ASM, Veronica Aglow. Cast: Jesse Allis (Eddie), Forrest Gertin (Rudy), Lara Hillier (Annie), Celia Howard (Sister Clarissa), Arnie Mazer (Chet), Nick Magnanti (Rudy and Georgie u/s), Brigitt Markusfeld (Ellen), Andrew Rondeau (Georgie); February 15–March 13, 2011

Radio Golf by August Wilson; Director, Timothy Bond; Sets, William Bloodgood; Costumes, Susan E. Mickey; Lighting, Thomas C. Hase; Sound, Jon Herter; Associate Lighting Designer, Troy Martin O'Shia; Associate Sound Designer, Ian Hildreth; Dramaturg, Kyle Bass; SM, Christine Lomaka; ASM, Kirsten Brannen; Cast: Richard Brooks (Harmond Wilks), Thomas Jefferson Byrd (Elder Joseph Barlow), Crystal Fox (Mame Wilks), LeLand Gantt (Sterling Johnson), G. Valmont Thomas (Roosevelt Hicks); March 22–April 17, 2011

The Music Man Book, music and lyrics by Meredith Willson; Story by Meredith Willson and Franklin Lacey; Director, Mark Cuddy; Choreographer, Peggy Hickey; Musical Direction, Don Kot; Sets, G.W. Mercier; Costumes, Pamela Scofield; Lighting, Thomas Munn; Sound, Will Pickens; Video Animation, Dan Roach; Assistant Lighting Designer, Joel Atella; Dramaturg, Jean Gordon Ryon; SM, Frank Cavallo; ASM, Veronica Aglow. Cast: Jessica Azenberg (Ensemble), John Bolton (Harold Hill), Lucas Brown (Ensemble), Larry Bull (Charlie Cowell), Henry Clapp (Ensemble), Jon Clunies (Olin Britt/Salesman), Max Coller (Winthrop Paroo), Sawyer Duserick (Ensemble), Gavin Flood (Ensemble), Gerard Floriano (Ensemble/Olin Britt u/s), Sophia Louise Fusilli (Ensemble), Andre Garner (Marcellus), Rayanne Gonzales (Alma Hix), Skip Greer (Mayor Shinn), Kelley Hamilton (Ensemble), Susan J. Jacks (Maud Dunlop/Eulalie Shinn u/s), Sean Jernigan(Oliver Hix), Brandon La (Ensemble), Analisa Leaming (Marion Paroo), Roy Lightner (Ensemble/Dance Captain), Sarah Kay Marchetti (Ensemble), Robin Masella (Ensemble/Zaneeta u/s), Jordan McNees (Ensemble), Kristen Mengelkoch (Ethel Toffelmier/Marion u/s), Cass Morgan (Mrs. Paroo), Kyle Mueller (Winthrop Paroo), Megan Mueller (Ensemble), Brittany Murchie (Ensemble), Chloe Phelps (Ensemble), Kilty Reidy (Constable Locke/Marcellus/Harold Hill u/s), Jerrod F. Royster (Ensemble), Jeff Salisbury (Ensemble), Adriana Scalice (Amaryllis), Daniel Vito Siefring (Ensemble/Constable Locke u/s), Jennifer Smith (Eulalie Shinn), Rachel Solomon (Mrs. Squires/Mrs. Paroo u/s), Melissa Steadman (Zaneeta Shinn), Johnny Stellard (Ensemble/Tommy Djilas u/s), Trevor Strader (Ewart Dunlop), Emma Sykes (Gracie Shinn), Justin Urso (Tommy Djilas), Allie Waxman (Ensemble), Stephen Wilde (Jacey Squires), Patrick Willaert (Ensemble/Oliver Hix/Jacey Squires/Ewart Dunlop u/s), Alizabeth York (Amaryllis), Annaleigh York (Gracie Shinn); April 27–June 5, 2011

Goodman Theatre

Chicago, Illinois

Eighty-sixth Season

Artistic Director, Robert Falls; Executive Director, Roche Schulfer

Albert Theatre

Candide Newly adapted from the Voltaire by Mary Zimmerman; Book adapted from the Voltaire by Hugh Wheeler; Music by Leonard Bernstein; Lyric by Richard Wilbur; Additional Lyrics, Stephen Sondheim, John Latouche, Lillian Hellman, Dorothy Parker, Leonard Bernstein; Director, Mary Zimmerman; Choreographer, Danny Pelzig; Music Director, Doug Peek; Costumes, Mara Blumenfeld; Lighting, T.J. Gerckens; Sound, Richard Woodbury; Sets, Dan Ostling; Casting, Adam Belcuore, Alan Paul; New York Casting, Telsey & Company; Additional Arrangements and Orchestrations, Doug Peek; PSM, Joseph Drummond; SM, T. Paul Lynch; A co-production with Shakespeare Theatre Company; Cast: Larry Yando (Pangloss/Others), Geoff Packard (Candide), Lauren Molina (Cunegonde), Erik Lochtefeld (Maximilian/Others), Margo Seibert (Paquette/Others), Rebecca Finnegan (Baroness/Vanderdendur/Others), Govind Kumar (Servant/Others), Tom Aulino (Baron/Martin/Others), Emma Rosenthal (Bird/Others), Jesse J. Perez (Soldier/Cacambo/Others), Jonathan Weir (Soldier/Governor/Others), Joey Stone (Soldier/Señor/Others), Rob Lindley (Anabaptist/Captain/Others), Thomas Adrian Simpson (Innkeeper/Schoolteacher/Others), Joe Tokarz (Orator/Grand Inquisitor/Others), Tracy Lynn Olivera (Orator's Wife/Others), Spencer Curnutt (Sailor/Others), Tempe Thomas (Queen of El Dorado/Others), Hollis Resnik (Old Lady); September 17–October 31, 2010

A Christmas Carol by Charles Dickens; Adapted by Tom Creamer; Director, William Brown; Sets, Todd Rosenthal, Costumes, Heidi Sue McMath; Lighting, Robert Christen; Sound, Cecil Averett; Music, Andrew Hansen; Casting, Adam Belcuore; PSM, Alden Vasquez; SM, Jamie Wolfe; Musical Director, Andrew Hansen; Vocal Director, Malcolm Ruhl, Choreographer, Susan Hart; Dance Captain, Katie Jeep; Young Performer Supervisor, Meg Grgurich; Assistant to the Choreographer, Robyn Robbins; Cast: John Judd (Ebenezer Scrooge), Ron Rains (Bob Cratchit), Michael Perez (Mr. Ortle), Lisa Tejero (Miss Crumb), Andy Truschinski (Fred), Tim Gittings (Poulterer/Schoolmaster/Topper/Old Joe), Emma Gordon (Child in Doorway/Pratt/Emily Cratchit/Ignorance), Naren Chaudhry (William/Want), Susan Felder (Charwoman/Mrs. Fezziwig), Anish Jethmalani (Ghost of Jacob Marley), Susan Shunk (Ghost of Christmas Past/Philomena/Young Woman), Grant Mitchell (Scrooge as Boy), Megan Delaney (Fan/Belinda Cratchit), Eric Parks (Scrooge as Young Man/Tree seller/Ghost of Christmas Future), Nate Burger (Dick Wilkins/Young Man), John Lister (Mr. Fezziwig/Chestnut seller), Tiffany Scott (Belle/Catherine), Penelope Walker (Ghost of Christmas Present), Christine Sherrill (Mrs. Cratchit), Grant Mitchell (Peter Cratchit), Peyton Young (Martha Cratchit), Cameron Joseph Conforti (Tiny Tim Cratchit), Katie Jeep (Abby/Mrs. Dilber), Aaron Holland (Percy/ Undertaker), Justin Amolschd (French horn/Mr. French), Gregory Hirte (Violin/Mr. Sawyer), Malcolm Ruhl (Accordion/Mr. Keys); November 19–December 31, 2010

The Trinity River Plays by Regina Taylor; Director, Ethan McSweeny; Sets, Todd Rosenthal; Costumes, Karen Perry; Lighting, Tyler Micoleau; Sound, Steve Cahill; Additional Composition, Daryl Waters; Dramaturgs, Tanya Palmer, Janice Paran; Casting, Logan Vaughn; PSM, T. Paul Lynch; SM, Joseph Drummond; Fight Director, Matthew E. Ellis; Wigs/Hair, Valerie Gladstone; A co-production with Dallas Theatre Center; Cast: Penny Johnson Jerald (Rose/She Who Looks Like Rose), Karen Aldridge (Iris), Jacqueline Williams (Daisy), Christiana Clark (Jasmine), Samuel Ray Gates (Jack), Jefferson A. Russell (Ray Earl/Frank); World Premiere; January 15–February 20, 2011

God of Carnage by Yasmina Reza; Translated by Christopher Hampton; Director, Rick Snyder; Sets, Takeshi Kata; Costumes, Birgit Rattenborg Wise; Lighting, Robert Christen; Sounds, Richard Woodbury; Casting, Adam Belcuore; Dramaturg, Neena Arndt; PSM, Alden Vasquez; SM, Jamie Wolfe; Cast: Mary Beth Fisher (Veronica), Keith Kupferer (Michael), Beth Lacke (Annette), David Pasquesi (Alan); Albert Theatre; March 5–April 17, 2011

Stage Kiss by Sarah Ruhl; Director, Jessica Thebus; Sets, Todd Rosenthal; Costumes, Linda Roethke; Lighting, James F. Ingalls; Sound, Andre J. Pluess; Dramaturg, Neena Arndt; Casting, Adam Belcuore; PSM, Joseph Drummond; SM, T. Paul Lynch, Jamie Wolfe; Fight Choreographer, Nick Sandys; Fight Captain, Mark L. Montgomery; Cast: Jenny Bacon (She), Mark L. Montgomery (He); Jeffrey Carlson (Kevin/Butler/Doctor/Pimp), Erica Elam (Millicent/Laurie), Scott Jaeck (Husband/Harrison), Ross Lehman (Director), Sarah Tolan-Mee (Millie/Maid/Angela); World Premiere; April 30–June 5, 2011

Chinglish by David Henry Hwang; Director, Leigh Silverman; Sets, David Korins; Costumes, Anita Yavich; Lighting, Brian MacDevitt; Sound, Darron West; Projections, Jeff Sugg; Casting, Adam Belcuore; New York Casting, Telsey & Company; Translator, Candace Chong; Cultural Advisors, Joanna L. Lee, Ken Smith; Dramaturg, Tanya Palmer; PSM, Alden Vasquez; SM, Jamie Wolfe; Associate Set Designer, Rod Lemmond; Assistant Lighting Designer, Ariel Benjamin, Sarah Tundermann; Associate Projection Designer, Shawn Duan; Australian Dialect Coach, Christine Adaire; Assistant Director, Johnson Henshaw; Cast: Jennifer Lim (Xu Yan), Angela Lin (Miss Qian/Prosecutor Li), Christine Lin (Zhao), Stephen Pucci (Peter Timms), James Waterston (Daniel Cavanaugh), Johnny Wu (Bing/Xu Geming), Larry Zhang (Minister Cai Guoliang); World Premiere; June 18–July 31, 2011

Chicago Shakespeare Theater

Being Harold Pinter Adapted and directed by Vladimir Scherban; General Producers, Natalia Kaliada, Nikolai Khalezin; SM, Aliaksei Shyrnevich, Laur Biarzhanin, Artsem Zhaliazniak. In association with Northwestern University, The League of Chicago Theatres and Chicago Shakespeare Theater; Cast: Nikolai Khalezin, Pavel Haradnitski, Yana Rusakevich, Aleh Sidorchyk, Irene Iarochevitch, Dzianis Tarasenka, Maryna Yurevich; Owen Theatre, January 27–29, 2011; Northwestern University, February 4–13, 2011; February 18–20, 2011

Owen Theatre

The Seagull by Anton Chekhov; Adapted and directed by Robert Falls; Translator, George Calderon; Sets, Todd Rosenthal; Costumes, Ana Kuzmanic; Lighting, Keith Parham; Sound, Richard Woodbury; Casting, Adam Belcuore; Dramaturg, Neena Arndt; PSM, Kimberly Osgood; SM, Jamie Wolfe; Cast: Mary Beth Fisher (Arkadina), Stephen Louis Grush (Konstantin), Francis Guinan (Sorin), Heather Wood (Nina), Steve Pickering (Shamrayev), Janet Ulrich Brooks (Polina), Kelly O'Sullivan (Masha), Cliff Chamberlain (Trigorin), Scott Jaeck (Dorn), Demetrios Troy (Medvedenko), Dieterich Gray (Yakov), Will Allan (Servant), Laura T. Fisher (Cook), Rebecca Buller (Maid); October 16–November 21, 2010

Mary by Thomas Bradshaw; Director, May Adrales; Sets, Kevin Depinet; Costumes, Ana Kuzmanic; Lighting, Keith Parham; Sound, Andrew Hansen; Casting, Adam Belcuore; New York Casting, David Caparelliotis; Dramaturg, Tanya Palmer; PSM, Kimberly Osgood; Dialect, Christine Adaire; Violin Coach, Inger Carle; Cast: Alex Weisman (David), Eddie Bennett (Jonathan), Scott Jaeck (James), Barbara Garrick (Dolores), Myra Lucretia Taylor (Mary), Cedric Young (Elroy), Steve Pickering (Priest); World Premiere; February 5–March 6, 2011

El Nogalar by Tanya Saracho; Director, Cecilie D. Keenan; Sets, Brian Sidney Bembridge; Costumes, Christine Pascual; Lighting, Jesse Klug; Music/Sound, Joe Cerqua; Dramaturg, Kristin Leahey; PSM, Rita Vreeland; SM, Kimberly Osgood; Cast: Charín Alvarez (Maité), Sandra Delgado (Valeria), Carlo Lorenzo Garcia (López), Bert Matias (Fulgencio), Christina Nieves (Anita), Yunuen Pardo (Dunia); World Premiere; March 26–April 24, 2011

Goodspeed Musicals

East Haddam, Connecticut

Forty-seventh Season

Executive Director, Michael P. Price; Associate Producer, Bob Alwine; Line Producer, Donna Lynn Cooper Hilton

Goodspeed Opera House

Annie Get Your Gun Music and lyrics by Irving Berlin; Original Book, Herbert and Dorothy Fields; Revisions, Peter Stone; Director, Rob Ruggiero; Choreographer, Noah Racey; Musical Director, Michael O'Flaherty; Assistant Musical Director, William J. Thomas; Orchestrations, Dan DeLange; Sets, Michael Schweikardt; Costumes, Alejo Vietti; Lighting, John Lasiter; Hair, Charles LaPointe; Sound, Jay Hilton; PM, R. Glen Grusmark; PSM, Bradley G. Spachman; ASM, Derek Michael DiGregorio; Dialect, Gillian Lane-Plescia; Dance Captain, Amos Wolff; Cast: David McDonald (Buffalo Bill Cody), Kevin Earley (Frank Butler), Rebecca Watson (Dolly Tate), Andrew Cao (Tommy Keeler), Chelsea Morgan Stock (Winnie Tate), James Beaman (Charlie Davenport), Bill Nabel (Foster Wilson/Ensemble), Michael Nichols (Chief Sitting Bull), Jenn Gambatese (Annie Oakley), Joy Rachel Del Valle (Jessie), Marissa Smoker (Nellie), Griffin Birney (Little Jake), Orville Mendoza (Running Deer/Waiter/ Bandleader/ Ensemble), Con O'Shea-Creal (Eagle Feather/Ensemble), Amos Wolff (Porter/Ensemble), Bill Nabel (Pawnee Bill/Ensemble), Brandon Andrus (Messenger/Ensemble), Dorothy Stanley (Mrs. Sylvia Potter-Porter/Ensemble), Ensemble: Sean Coughlin, Pilar Millhollen, Natalie Ryder, Molly Tynes, Aaron Young, Noah Aberlin, Hartleigh Buwick, Jake Poulios; April 16–June 27, 2010

Carnival! Music and lyrics by Bob Merrill; Book by Michael Stewart; Director, Darko Tresnjak; Choreographer, Peggy Hickey; Musical Director, Michael O'Flaherty; Sets, David P. Gordon; Costumes, Fabio Toblini; Lighting, John Lasiter; Sound, Jay Hilton; Hair, David H. Lawrence; Puppet Design, Robert Smythe; Aerial Choreographer, Joshua Dean; Magic Consultant, Mark Kalin; PM, R. Glen Grusmark; PSM, Bradley G. Spachman; ASM, Derek Michael DiGregorio; Assistant Musical Director, F. Wade Russo; Dance Captain, Robin Masella; Cast: Price Waldman (Grobert), Laurent Giroux (Schlegel), Mike McGowan (Marco), Michelle Blakely (Rosalie), Lauren Worsham (Lili), Nathan Klau (Jacquot), Adam Monley (Paul), Ensemble: Joshua Dean, Ben Franklin, Timothy Hughes, Kara Kimmer, Robin Masella, Clifton Samuels, Amy Shure, Justin Urso, Price Waldman, Dana Winkle, Miquel Edson, Melissa Steadman; July 9–September 18, 2010

How to Succeed in Business Without Really Trying Music and lyrics by Frank Loesser; Book by Abe Burrows, Jack Weinstock, Willie Gilbert; Director, Greg Ganakas; Choreographer, Kelli Barclay; Musical Director, Michael O'Flaherty; Orchestrations, Dan DeLange; Sets, Adrian W. Jones, Costumes, Gregory Gale; Lighting, Paul Miller; Sound, Jay Hilton; Hair, Ashley Ryan; PM, R. Glen Grusmark; PSM, Bradley G. Spachman; ASM, Derek Michael DiGregorio; Assistant Musical Director, William J. Thomas; Dance Captain, Matthew Kilgore; Cast: Senator Christopher J. Dodd (Voice of Narrator), Brian Sears (J. Pierrepont Finch), James Beaman (Milt Gatch), Brian Ogilvie (Jenkins), Matthew Kilgore (Tackaberry), Drew Taylor (Peterson), Ronn Carroll (J.B. Biggley), Natalie Bradshaw (Rosemary Pilkington), Aaron Serotsky (Bert Bratt), Erin Maguire (Smitty), Tom Deckman (Bud Frump), Jennifer Smith (Miss Jones), Richard Vida (Mr. Twimble), Nicolette Hart (Hedy LaRue), Lianne Marie Dobbs (Miss Krumholtz), John Scacchetti (Toynbee), Jerry Christakos (Benjamin Ovington), Richard Vida (Wally Womper), Ensemble: James Beaman, Jerry Christakos, Lianne Marie Dobbs, Sara Marie Hicks, Matthew Kilgore, Natalie Newman, Brian Ogilvie, Kristin Piro, John Scacchetti, Drew Taylor, Micki Weiner, Peter Mills, Kellyn Uhl; September 24–November 28, 2010

The Norma Terris Theatre

Band Geeks Music by Mark Allen, Gaby Alter, Tommy Newman; Lyrics by Gaby Alter, Tommy Newman; Book by Tommy Newman, Gordon Greenberg; Concept, Tommy Newman; Director, Gordon Greenberg; Choreographer, Denis Jones; Musical Director, David Loud; Orchestrations, Lynne Shankel; Sets, Anna Louizos; Costumes, Gregg Barnes; Lighting, Jeff Croiter; Sound, Jay Hilton; Technical Director, Adam Goodrum; PSM, Chris Zaccardi; Dance Captain, Patti Murin; Cast: Jared Gertner (Elliot), Katie Klaus (Laura), Michael Winther (Mr. Hornsby), F. Michael Haynie (Spitz), Patti Murin (Nicole), Ruthie Ann Miles (Molly), Michael Millan (Kyle), Nkrumah Gatling (Alvin), Jacey Powers (Natalia), Jill Abramovitz (Principal Dixon), Matt Braver (Stewart), Tommar Wilson (Jake); May 13–June 6, 2010

Radio Girl Book by Daniel Goldfarb; Music by Henry Krieger; Lyrics by Susan Birkenhead; Director/Choreographer, Christopher Gattelli; Musical Director, Andy Einhorn; Musical Arranger, Sam Davis; Sets, Anna Louizos; Costumes, Gregg Barnes; Lighting, Jeff Croiter; Sound, Jay Hilton; PSM, Thomas J. Gates; Technical Director, Adam Goodrum; ASM, Chris Zaccardi; Dance Captain, Pam Remler; Cast: Stephen Bienskie (Radio Announcer), Michele Ragusa (Lola), Andy Einhorn (Lucius), John Bolton (Orville Smithers), Gabriella Malek (Rebecca Winstead), Joey Sorge (Uncle Harry), Anthony Holds (Tony Kent), Lee Meriwether (Aunt Miranda), Meredith Patterson (Gwen), Orson Bean (Homer Busby), Liz Larsen (Melva), Ensemble: Andrew Boetcher, Ariel Reid, Pam Remler, Allie Schauer, David Spangenthal, Richard Riaz Yoder; July 29–August 22, 2010

Roald Dahl's James and the Giant Peach Music and lyrics by Benj Pasek, Justin Paul; Book by Timothy Allen McDonald; Director, Graciela Daniele; Choreographer, Michael Tracy, Pilobolus; Musical Director, Chris Fenwick; Orchestrations, August Eriksmoen; Dance Arranger, Sam Davis; Vocal Arranger, Justin Paul; Sets, Christopher H. Barreca, Lighting, Stephen Strawbridge; Sound, Jay Hilton; PSM, Bernita Robinson; ASM, Meg Friedman; Technical Director, Adam Goodrum; Assistant Director, Maddie Kelly; Dance Captain, Nick Gaswirth;

Cast: Chelsea Krombach (Mrs. Trotter/Ladybug/Ensemble), Jim Stanek (Mr. Trotter/Green Grasshopper/Ensemble), Justin Lawrence Hall (James), Steve Rosen (Marvo the Magician), Ruth Gottschall (Spiker), Danny Dillon (Sponge), Kate Wetherhead (Spider/Ensemble), Nick Gaswirth (Centipede/Ensemble), Destan Owens (Earthworm), Ensemble: Otis Cook (Pilobolus), Heather Jeane Favretto (Pilobolus), Jessica Hershberg, , Edwin Olvera (Pilobolus), Roberto Olvera (Pilobolus), Destan Owens, Marissa Palley, Nicholas Park, Annika Sheaff (Pilobolus), Derek Stratton (Pilobolus), Minami Yusui; October 21–November 21, 2010

Great Lakes Theater

Cleveland, Ohio

Forty-ninth Season

Producing Artistic Director, Charles Fee; Executive Director, Robert Taylor

Othello by William Shakespeare; Director, Risa Brainin; Sets, Russell Metheny; Lighting, Michael Klaers; Costumes, Kim Krumm Sorenson; Composer, Michael Keck; Fight Choreographer, Ken Merckx; SM, Corrie E. Purdum; Cast: David Alan Anderson (Othello), David Anthony Smith (Iago), Kevin Crouch (Cassio), Eduardo Placer (Roderigo), Aled Davies (Brabantio), Chris Richards (Duke of Venice/Soldier), Richard Klautsch (Lodovico), M.A. Taylor (Gratiano), Sara M. Bruner (Desdemona), Laura Perrotta (Emilia), Jodi Dominick (Bianca), Dakotah Brown (Montano), Kyle Downing (Soldier), Eric Perusek (Soldier), Robert M. Smith (Soldier), James Weaver (Soldier); Hanna Theater; September 24–October 31, 2010

An Ideal Husband by Oscar Wilde; Director, Sari Ketter; Sets, Nayna Ramey; Lighting, Marcus Dilliard; Costumes, Jason Lee Resler; Composer, Michael Keck; Choreographer, Helene Peterson; SM, Tim Kinzel; Cast: Richard Klautsch (Sir Robert Chiltern, Bart), Aled Davies (The Earl of Caversham, KG), Eduardo Placer (Vicomte De Nanjac), Kevin Crouch (Mr. Montford), Chris Richards (Mason), M. A. Taylor (Phipps), Jodi Dominick (Lady Gertrude Chiltern), Sara M. Bruner (Miss Mabel Chiltern), Maryann Nagel (Lady Markby), Laura Perotta (Mrs. Laura Chevely), Liz Conway (The Countess of Basildon, (Olivia), Layla Schwartz (Mrs. Marchmont (Margaret)), Dakotah Brown, Kyle Downing, Andee Leach, Andrew Morton, Eric Perusek, Kaci Scott (Guests at the Chiltern's Reception/Servants/Footmen); Hanna Theater; October 1–31, 2010

A Christmas Carol by Charles Dickens; Adapted and directed by Gerald Freedman; Staged by Victoria Bussert; Assistant Director, Sara M. Bruner; Sets, John Ezell and Gene Emerson Friedman; Lighting, Mary Jo Dondlinger, Cynthia Stillings; Costumes, James Scott; Sound, Tom Mardikes, Stan Kozak; Music Adapter/Arranger, Robert Waldman; Music, Stuart Raleigh, Choreographer, David Shimotakahara; Dance Staging, Pandora Robertson; SM, Corrie E. Prudum; ASM, Kim Kinzel; Cast: Donald Carrier (Father/Bob Cratchit), Laura Perrotta (Mother/Fred's Wife/Fezziwig Guest/Dance Captain), Rachel M. Jones (Miss Elizabeth/ Fan/Fezziwig Guest/Martha Cratchit), Rod Lawrence (Master Richard/Dick Wilkins/Peter Cratchit), Natalie Welch (Miss Abagail/Fezziwig Guest/Belinda Cratchit), Jackson Daugherty (Master Robert/Adolescent Scrooge/Fezziwig Guest/James Cratchit), Isabela Moner (Miss Polly/Sara Cratchit/Want), Cameron Danielle Nelson (Master William/Tiny Tim), Matthew Taylor (Master William/Tiny Tim), Aled Davies (Samuels/Ebenezer Scrooge), David Anthony Smith (Muggeridge/Christmas Present/Fezziwig Guest/Debtor), Jodi Dominick (Jane/Mrs. Cratchit/Fezziwig Guest/Charwoman), Kevin Crouch (Nephew Fred/Young Scrooge/Fezziwig Guest), M. A. Taylor (First Charity Man/Fezziwig Guest/Joe the Keeper), Darryl Lewis (Second Charity Man/Mr Fezziwig/Helmsman/Rich Man), Eduardo Placer (Streetsinger/Christmas Past/Christmas Future), Cassidy Josephine Nelson (Sled Boy/Boy Scrooge/Ignorance), Mackenzie Dale Durken (Skate Girl), Lynn Robert Berg (Marley/ Lighthouse Keeper/Rich Man/Undertaker), Laura Welsh Berg (Belle/Fezziwig Guest/Debtor's Wife), Maryann Nagel (Mrs. Fezziwig/Cynthia/Laundress), Dudley Swetland (Miner/ Topper/Rich Man), Kalie Malish (Soloist/Street Child), Cameron Andrew Howell (Delivery Boy), Eva Christina Holtkamp (Street Child); Ohio Theater; December 3–23, 2010

The Complete Works of William Shakespeare (Abridged) by Adam Long, Daniel Singer, Jess Winfield; Director, Charles Fee; Assistant Director, Sara M. Bruner; Sets, Gage Williams; Lighting, Rick Martin; Costumes, Charlotte Yetman; Sound, Peter John Still; Choreographer, Helene Peterson; Fight Choreographer, Ken Merckx; SM, Corrie E. Purdum, Tim Kinzel; Cast: Paul Hurley, Jason O'Connell, M. A. Taylor; Hanna Theater; March 11–27, 2011

The Two Gentlemen of Verona by William Shakespeare; Director, Charles Fee; Sets, Russell Metheny; Lighting, Michael Chybowski; Costumes, Star Moxley; Sound, Peter John Still; Music, Matthew Webb; Percussion, Andrew Pongracz; SM, Corrie E. Purdum; Cast: Neil Brookshire (Valentine), Paul Hurley (Proteus), M. A. Taylor (Speed), Lee Stark (Julia), Jodi Dominick (Lucetta/Outlaw), Dudley Swetland (Antonio), Robert Williams (Panthino/Outlaw), Nika Ericson (Silvia), David Anthony Smith (Launce), Mojo/Rallo (Crab), Eduardo Placer (Thurio), Aled Davies (Duke), Sara M. Bruner (Outlaw/Host), Eric Perusek (Eglamour); Hanna Theater; April 8–23, 2011

Guthrie Theater

Minneapolis, Minnesota

Forty-eighth Season

Artistic Director, Joe Dowling

Wurtele Thrust Stage

The Master Butchers Singing Club by Marsha Norman (based upon the novel by Louise Erdrich); Director and developer, Francesca Zambello; Sets, David Korins; Costumes, Jess Goldstein; Lighting, Mark McCullough; Sound, Rob Milburn, Michael Bodeen; Musical Supervisor/Incidental Music, Kevin Stites; Dramaturg, Jo Holcomb; Voice/Dialect Coach, Lucinda Holshue; Movement, Marcela Lorca; Fight Director, Peter Moore; PSM, Russell W. Johnson; ASM, Jason Clusman, Michele Harms; Associate Director, Jason Snow; Cast: Sheila Tousey (Step and a Half), Lee Mark Nelson (Fidelis Waldvogel), Emily Gunyou Halaas (Delphine Watzka), Katie Guentzel (Eva Waldvogel), Charlie Brady (Cyprian Lazarre), M. Cochise Anderson (Ancestor), Ryan McCartan (Franz Waldvogel), Peter Thomson (Doctor Heech), Terry Hempleman (Roy Watzka), Tracey Maloney (Clarisse Stubbs), Bill McCallum (Sheriff Hock), Jennifer Blagen (Tante), Maeve Moynihan (Mazarine), Jake Ingbar (Karl), Sean Cackosi, Rebecca Hurd, Logan Pedersen (Young People of Argus); September 11–October 30, 2010

A Christmas Carol by Charles Dickens; Adaptation, Crispin Whittell; Director, Joe Dowling; Sets, Walt Spangler; Costumes, Mathew J. LeFebvre; Lighting, Christopher Akerlind; Composer, Keith Thomas; Sound, Scott W. Edwards; Dramaturg, Michael Lupu; Voice/Dialect Coach, Gillian Lane-Plescia; Movement, Joe Chvala; PSM, Russell W. Johnson; ASM, Jason Clusman, Chris A. Code; Associate Director, Benjamin McGovern; Cast: Sam Bardwell (Topper/Dick Wilkins), Virginia S. Burke (Robinson Crusoe's Parrot/Mrs. Cratchit), Ali Rose Dachis (Deidre Fezziwig/Sally), Bob Davis (Old Joe/ Mr. Fezziwig), Kate Eifrig (Ghost of Christmas Past), Nic Few (Ghost of Christmas Present/Bull), Nathaniel Fuller (George/Mr. Sykes/Bear), Ebenezer Scrooge (Daniel Gerroll), Summer Hagen (Daisy Fezziwig), Hugh Kennedy (Mr. Wimple/David/Belle's Husband/Ghost of Christmas Future), Kathryn Lawrey (Dora Fezziwig/Jane), James Leighton (Young Scrooge/Tim's Priest), Kris L. Nelson (Bob Cratchit, Donald), Lee Mark Nelson (Jacob Marley/Mr. Bones/Scrooge's Priest), Isabell Monk O'Connor (Mrs. Dilber/Bumble), Noah Putterman (Fred/Daniel), Angela Timberman (Merriweather), Suzanne Warmanen (Bunty/Mrs. Fezziwig), Christine Weber (Wimple's Wife/Belle/Kitty); November 19–December 30, 2010

The Winter's Tale by William Shakespeare; Director, Jonathan Munby; Sets, Alexander Dodge; Costumes, Linda Cho; Lighting, Oliver Fenwick and Philip S. Rosenberg; Composer, Adam Wernick; Sound, Scott W. Edwards; Choreographer, Daniel Pelzig; Voice/Language, Andrew Wade; Dramaturg, Carla Steen; SM, Chris A. Code; ASM, Michele Harms, Justin Hossle; Assistant Director, Andy Ottoson; Cast: Ansa Akyea (Archidamus/Lord), Christina Baldwin (Emilia), Raye Birk

(Doctor/Shepherd), John Catron (Jailer/Young Shepherd), Bob Davis (Camillo), Sean Michael Dooley (Cleomenes/Mariner), Tyson Forbes (Dion/Bear/ Shepherd's Servant), Emily Gunyou Halaas (Lady/Mopsa), Michael Hayden (Leontes), Michael Thomas Holmes (Autolycus), Juan Rivera Lebron (Lord/Florizel), Bill McCallum (Polixenes), Michelle O'Neill (Hermione), Suzanne Warmanen (Lady/Oracle/Dorcas), Christine Weber (Guard/ Perdita), Stephen Yoakam (Antigonus/Time), Noah Coon (Mamillius), Devon Solwold (Mamillius); January 29–March 27, 2011

Arsenic and Old Lace by Joseph Kesselring; Director, Joe Dowling; Sets, John Lee Beatty; Costumes, Christine A. Richardson; Lighting, Tom Mays; Sound, Scott W. Edwards; Dramaturg, Michael Lupu; Voice/Dialect Coach, Christine Adaire; Movement, Marcela Lorca; PSM, Russell W. Johnson; ASM, Jason Clusman; Assistant Director, Anthony Nelson; Cast: Michael Booth (Officer Klein), Bob Davis (Teddy Brewster), Tyson Forbes (Jonathan Brewster), Nathanial Fuller (Rev. Dr. Harper/Mr. Witherspoon), Jonas Goslow (Mortimer Brewster), Terry Hempleman (Officer O'Hara), Hugh Kennedy (Officer Brophy), Kathryn Lawrey (Elaine Harper), Kris L. Nelson (Dr. Einstein), Kristine Nielson (Abby Brewster), Peter Thomson (Mr. Gibbs/Lt. Rooney), Sally Wingert (Martha Brewster); April 9–June 5, 2011

H.M.S. Pinafore by Gilbert and Sullivan; Director, Joe Dowling; Music Director/Arrangement, Andrew Cooke; Choreography/Musical Staging, David Bolger; Sets, Frank Hallinan Flood; Costumes, Fabio Toblini; Lighting, Malcolm Rippeth; Sound, Scott W. Edwards; Dramaturg, Jo Holcomb; Voice/Dialect Consultant, Lucinda Holshue; SM, Chris A. Code; ASM, Martha Kulig, Timothy Markus; Assistant Director, James McNamara; Cast: Christina Baldwin (Buttercup), Robert O. Berdahl (Captain Corcoran), Barbara Bryne (Queen Victoria), Aleks Knezevich (Ralph Rackstraw), Seri Johnson (Cousin Hebe), Heather Lindell (Josephine), Robb McKindles (Bill Bobstay), Jason Simon (Dick Deadeye), Peter Thomson (Sir Joseph Porter), J. Tyler Whitmer (Bob Becket), Joseph Bigelow, Nathan Bird, Nathaniel Braga, Alfie Parker Jr., Adrian Pena, Adam Sarette, Brian Skellenger, Brian Sostek (Sailors), Lauren Asheim, Timotha Lanae, Molly Sue McDonald, Tinia Moulder, Simone Perrin, Kersten Rodau (Sisters/ Cousins/ Aunts), Adam Lendermon, Nicholas McGough, Laura Rudolph (Swings); June 18–August 28, 2011

McGuire Proscenium Stage

The Great Game: Afghanistan by Richard Bean, Lee Blessing, David Edgar, David Greig, Amit Gupta, Ron Hutchinson, Stephen Jeffreys, Abi Morgan, Ben Ockrent, Simon Stephens, Colin Teevan and Joy Wilkinson; Directors, Nicholas Kent, Indhu Rubasingham; Cast: Daniel Betts, Sheena Bhattessa, Michael Cochrane, Karl Davies, Vincent Ebrahim, Nabil Elouahabi, Shereen Martineau, Tom McKay, Daniel Rabin, Danny Rahim, Raad Rawi, Jemma Redgrave, Cloudia Swann, Rick Warden; September 29–October 17, 2010

The 39 Steps Adapted by Patrick Barlow from the novel by John Buchan from the movie of Alfred Hitchcock; Director, Joel Sass; Sets, Richard Hoover; Costumes, Amelia Cheever; Lighting, Barry Browning; Sound, Reid Rejsa; Shadow Puppets, Michael Sommers; Dramaturg, Carla Steen; Voice/Dialect Coach, Lucinda Holshue; Movement, Marcela Lorca; SM, Martha Kulig; ASM, Justin Hossle; Assistant Director, Julie Kurtz; Cast: Robert O. Berdahl (Richard Hannay), Sara Agnew (Annabella Schmidt/Margaret/ Pamela), Jim Lichtscheidl (Clown), Luverne Seifert (Clown); October 30–December 26, 2010

Romeo and Juliet and The Comedy of Errors by William Shakespeare; Director (Romeo and Juliet), Penny Metropulos; Director (The Comedy of Errors), Ian Belknap; Cast: Kaliswa Brewster, Ray Chapman, Elizabeth Grullon, Whitney Hudson, Jonathan C. Kaplan, Jason McDowell-Green, Stephen Pilkington, Alejandro Rodriguez, Benjamin Rosenbaum, John Skelley, Jamie Smithson, Sid Solomon, Elizabeth Stahlmann; January 8–January 30, 2011

Arms and the Man by George Bernard Shaw; Director, Ethan McSweeny; Sets, Walt Spangler; Costumes, Murell Horton; Lighting, Robert Wierzel; Sound, Richard Woodbury; Dramaturg, Carla Steen; Speech/Dialect Coach, Wendy Waterman, Erika Bailey; Movement, Marcela Lorca; SM, Martha Kulig; ASM, Timothy Markus; Assistant Director, Patrick Walsh; Cast: J.C. Cutler (Nicola), Peter Michael Goetz

(Major Paul Petkoff), Kate Eifrig (Catherine Petkoff), Jim Lichtscheidl (Bluntschli), Summer Hagen (Louka), Mariko Nakasone (Raina Petkoff), Jason Rojas (Russian Officer), Major Sergius Saranoff (Michael Schantz); March 19–May 8, 2011

God of Carnage by Yasmina Reza; Director, John Miller-Stephany; Sets, Todd Rosenthal; Costumes, Mathew J. LeFebvre; Lighting, Marcus Dilliard; Sound, Scott W. Edwards; Dramaturg, Jo Holcomb; Voice/Speech Coach, Lucinda Holshue; Movement, Marcela Lorca; SM, Michele Harms; ASM, Justin Hossle; Assistant Director, Jon Ferguson; Cast: Tracey Maloney (Annette Raleigh), Bill McCallum (Alan Raleigh), Jennifer Blagen (Veronica Novak), Chris Carlson (Michael Novak); May 28–August 7, 2011

The Huntington Theatre Company

Boston, Massachusetts

Twenty-ninth Season

Artistic Director, Peter DuBois; Managing Director, Michael Maso

Bus Stop by William Inge; Director, Nicholas Martin; Sets, James Noone, Costumes, Miranda Hoffman; Lighting, Philip Rosenberg; Sound, Alex Neumann; PSM, Leslie Sears; SM, Kevin Robert Fitzpatrick; Cast: Noah Bean (Bo), Adam LeFevre (Will Masters), Will LeBow (Carl), Stephen Lee Anderson (Virgil Blessing), Ronete Levenson (Elma), Karen MacDonald (Grace), Nicole Rodenburg (Cherie), Henry (Dr. Gerald Lyman); September 17–October 17, 2010

Circle Mirror Transformation by Annie Baker; Director, Melia Bensussen; Sets, Cristina Todesco, Costumes, Bobby Frederick Tilley II; Lighting, Dan Kotlowitz; Sound, David Remedios; PSM, Kathryn Most; SM, Josieanne M. Lemieux; Cast: Betsy Aidem (Marty), Nadia Bowers (Theresa), Michael Hammond (James), Jeremiah Kissel (Schultz), Marie Polizzano (Lauren); October 15–November 14, 2010

Vengeance is the Lord's by Bob Glaudini's; Director, Peter DuBois; Sets, Eugene Lee; Costumes, Mimi O'Donnell; Lighting, Japhy Weideman; Sound, Ben Emerson; Composer, David Van Tieghem; PSM, Carola Morone; SM, Leslie Sears; Cast: Larry Pine (Mathew Horvath), Roberta Wallach (Margaret Horvath), Lee Tergesen (Woodrow Horvath), Katie Kreisler (Roanne Horvath), Karl Baker Olson (Donald Horvath), Johnny Lee Davenport (Parcel Manning), Trevor Long (Milo); November 12–December 12, 2010

Ruined by Lynn Nottage, Director, Liesl Tommy; Choreography, Randy Duncan; Sets, Clint Ramos; Costumes, Kathleen Geldard; Lighting, Lap Chi Chu; Original Music/Sound/Music Direction, Brochen Chord; PSM, Anjee Nero; SM, Leslie Sears; Cast: Tonye Patano (Mama Nadi), Oberon K.A. Adjepong (Christian), Pascale Armand (Salima), Jason Bowen (Fortune), Carla Duran (Sophie), Wendell B. Franklin (Jerome), Zainab Jah (Josephine), Joseph Kamal (Mr. Harari), Adesoji Odukogbe (Musician 2), Kola Ogundiran (Laurent), Okieriete Onaodowan (Simon), Adrian Roberts (Commander Osembenga), Alvin Terry (Musician 1); January 7–February 6, 2011

Educating Rita by Willy Russell; Director, Maria Aitken; Sets, Allen Moyer; Costumes, Nancy Brennan; Lighting, Joel E. Silver; Original Music/Sound, Seaghan McKay; PSM, Carola Morrone LaCoste; SM, Amy Weissenstein; Andrew Long (Frank), Jane Pfitsch (Rita); March 11–April 10, 2011

Sons of the Prophet by Stephen Karam; Director, Peter DuBois, Sets, Anita Louizos; Costumes, Bobby Frederick Tilley II; Lighting, Japhy Weideman; Sound, M.L. Dogg; Cast: Kelsey Kurz (Joseph), Gloria (Joanna Gleason), Dan McCabe (Charles), Yusef Bulos (Bill), Dee Nelson (Dr. Manor/Ensemble), Charles Socarides (Timothy), Lizbeth Mackay (Mrs. McAndrew/Ensemble), Vin (Jonathan Louis Dent); April 1–May 1, 2011

Richard III/The Comedy of Errors by William Shakespeare; Propeller Theatre Company; Director, Edward Hall; Sets/Costume, Michael Pavelka, Lighting, Ben Ormerod; Music, Propeller; Additional Arrangements/Original Music, Jon Trenchard; Adaptation, Edward Hall, Roger Warren; Tony Bell (Queen Margaret/

Pinch), Kelsey Brookfield (Lord Rivers/Duchess of York/Courtesan), Dugald Bruce-Lockhart (Sir Richard Ratcliffe/Antipholus of Syracuse), Wayne Cater (Bishop of Ely/Balthasar), Richard Clothier (The Duke of Ephesus/Richard Duke of Gloucester), John Dougall (George Duke of Clarence/Lord Stanley/Ageon), Richard Frame (Richard Duke of York/Murderer/Dromio of Syracuse), Robert Hands (King Edward IV/Earl of Richmond/Adriana), Chris Myles (Duke of Buckingham/Aemilia), David Newman (Sir William Catesby/Luciana),Thomas Padden (Lord Hastings/Duke of Norfolk/Angelo), Sam Swainsbury (Edward Prince of Wales/Murderer/Antipholus of Ephesus), Dominic Tighe (Queen Elizabeth/Officer), Jon Trenchard (Dromio of Ephesus/Lady Anne); May 18–June 19, 2011

Illinois Theatre Center

Park Forest, Illinois

Thirty-fifth Season

Producing Artistic Director, Etel Billig; Associate Director, Jonathan R. Billig

Anna Christie by Eugene O'Neill; Director, Etel Billig; Sets/Lighting, Jonathan R. Billig; Costumes, Pat Decker; Cast: Tori Buckey (Anna), Scott Lynch-Giddings (Chris), Ernest W. Ray (Mat), Jean Roberts (Marthy), David Boettcher (Johnny/Sailor), Don Tieri (Larry/Sailor); September 24–October 10, 2010

The Real Thing by Tom Stoppard; Director, David Perkovich; Sets/Lighting, Jonathan R. Billig; Costumes, Pat Decker; Cast: Michael Joseph Mitchell (Henry), Melissa Carlson (Annie), Regina Leslie (Charlotte), Eric Leonard (Max), Luke Daigle (Billy), Latherine Banks (Debbie), Jude Willis (Brodie); October 29–November 14, 2010

The Apple Tree Music by Jerry Bock; Lyrics by Sheldon Harnick; Book by Bock, Harnick and Jerome Coopersmith; Director, Etel Billig; Choreogrpaher, Frank Roberts; Sets/Lighting, Roy G. Biv; Costumes, Pat Decker; Cast: Katrina Kuntz (Eve/Barbara/Ella), Glenn Stanton (Adam/ Sanjar/Flip), Frank Roberts (Snake/Balladeer/Narrator), Ernest W. Ray (Voice of God/King Arik/Producer); Ensemble: Jameson Wentworth App, Morgan Glynn Briggs, Tom McGunn, Danielle Scampini; December 3–December 19, 2010

Intimate Apparel by Lynn Nottage; Director, Etel Billig; Sets/Lighting, Jonathan R. Billig; Costumes, Pat Decker; Cast: Kona N. Burks (Esther), Kevin McKillip (Mr. Marks), Sandra Adell (Mrs. Dickson), Thurston Hill (George), Candace C. Edwards (Mayme), Calliope Porter (Mrs. Van Buren); January 28–February 13, 2011

Boeing, Boeing by Marc Camoletti; Director, David Boettcher; Sets/Lighting, Jonathan R. Billig; Costumes, Pat Decker; Cast: Martin Yurek (Bernard), Joe Lehman (Robert), Jean Roberts (Bertha), Mary K. Nigohosian (Janet), Katherine Dell Cikanek (Jacqueline), Angela Beyer (Judith); March 4–March 20, 2011

The Glorious Ones Book and lyics by Lynn Ahrens, Music by Stephen Flaherty; Director/ Choreographer, Frank Roberts; Sets/Lighting, Roy G. Biv; Costumes, Pat Decker; Cast: Jason Speling (Flaminio), Caron Buinis (Colombina), Jeny Wasilewski (Armanda), Jameson Wentworth App (Francesco), David Lipschutz (Pantalone), Jill Sesso (Isabella), Tom McGunn (Dottore); April 15–May 1, 2011

Indiana Repertory Theatre

Indianapolis, Indiana

Thirty-ninth Season

Artistic Director, Janet Allen; Managing Director, Steven Stolen

OneAmerica Stage

Holes by Louis Sachar; Director, David Bradley; Sets, Robert M. Koharchik; Lighting, Lap Chi Chu; Costumes, Wendy Meaden; Sound, Todd Mack Reischman; SM, Nathan Garrison; ASM, Joel Markus; Composer, Fabian Obispo; Dramaturg,

Richard J Roberts; Dialect Coach, Nancy Lipschultz; Fight Choreographer, Drew Vidal; Cast: Nick Abeel (Stanley Yelnats), David Anderson (X-Ray), Ryan Artzberger (Judge/Mr. Sir), Wayne T. Carr (Police Officer/Sam/ Attorney General), Jaron Cook (Magnet), Mark Goetzinger (Myra's Father/Sheriff/Jesse), Jennifer Johansen (Stanley's Mother/Sarah/Kate Barlow), Matthew Joseph Lindblom (Zigzag), Constance Macy (Myra/Warden/Mrs. Collingwood/ Linda Walker), Brandon Merriweather (Armpit), Robert Neal (Police Officer/Igor Barkov/Trout Walker), Mauricio Suarez (Zero), Ben Tebbe (Stanley's Father/Mr. Pendanski/Elya/ Toughest Kid in Camp), Milicent Wright (Madame Zeroni/Ms. Morengo/Zero's Mother); September 25–November 6, 2010

A Christmas Carol by Charles Dickens; Adapted by Tom Haas; Director, Richard J Roberts; Sets, Russell Metheny; Lighting, Michael Lincoln; Costumes, Murell Horton; Composer, Andrew Hopson; Choreographer, David Hochoy; Musical Director, Christopher Ludwa; SM, Nathan Garrison; ASM, Joel Markus; Cast: David Alan Anderson (Fezziweg/Ghost of Christmas Present/Old Joe), Ryan Artzberger (Ebenezer Scrooge), Matthew Brumlow (Fred/Young Scrooge/Broker), Mark Goetzinger (Portly Gentleman/Schoolmaster/Topper), Jennifer Johansen (Sister of Mercy/Roses Sister/Charwoman), Constance Macy (Mrs. Cratchit/ Mrs. Fezziweg/ Plump Sister), Robert Neal (Marley's Ghost/Lamplighter/Ghost of Christmas Future/Poulterer's Man), Jerry Richardson (Bob Cratchit/Postboy/ Broker), Ben Tebbe (Waiter/Young Marley/ Nutley/Undertaker), Cora Vander Broek (Felicity/Ghost of Christmas Past/Laundress), Leah Walsh (Fan/Belle/ Martha), Noah Bush, Noah Huber (Waif/Henry Cratchit/Ignorance/Turkey Boy), Tessa Buzzetti, Alexandra Young (Belinda Cratchit/Young Fan), Taylor Kleyn, Grant Gourley (Peter Cratchit/Adolescent Scrooge/Dick Wilkins), Ethan Holder, Kalea Spurlock (Tiny Tim/Boy Scrooge), Delaney Jackson, Sally Root (Betsy Cratchit/ Want); November 21–December 26, 2010

The Diary of Anne Frank by Frances Goodrich and Albert Hackett; Adapted by Wendy Kesselman; Director, Janet Allen; Sets, Bill Clarke; Lighting, Ann G. Wrightson; Costumes, Linda Pisano; Wigs, Amanda Bailey; Composer/Sound, Andrew Hopson; Dramaturg, Richard J Roberts; SM, Nathan Garrison, Danny Kuenzel; AD, Mark Kamie; Casting, Rich Cole, Claire Simon; Cast: Rebecca Buller (Anne Frank), Craig Wroe (Otto Frank), Denise Cormier (Edith Frank), Erin Neufer (Margot Frank), Kathleen Wise (Miep Gies), Jacob Liberman (Peter van Daan), Terence Goodman (Mr. Kraler), Constance Macy (Mrs. van Daan), Paul Kiernan (Mr. van Daan), Rob Johansen (Mr. Dussel), Brian Noffke (First Man), John Goodson (Second Man), Sam Fain (Third Man); January 18–February 24, 2011

The Gospel According to James by Charles Smith; Director, Chuck Smith; Sets, Linda Buchanan; Lighting, Kathy A. Perkins; Costumes, Rachel Anne Healy; Composer/Sound, Ray Nardelli; Dramaturgs, Janet Allen, Richard J Roberts; SM, Nathan Garrison, Joel Grynheim; Casting, Claire Simon; Cast: André De Shields (James), Linda Kimbrough (Marie), Marcus Davis Hendricks (Tommy Shipp), Tyler Jacob Rollinson (Abe Smith), Anthony Peeples (Apples), Keith D. Gallagher (Claude), Kelsey Brennan (Mary), Christopher Jon Martin (Hoot Ball), Diane Kondrat (Bea Ball); March 22–April 10, 2011

The 39 Steps by Alfred Hitchcock; Adapted by Patrick Barlow; Director, Peter Amster; Sets, Linda Buchanan; Lighting, Michael Lincoln; Costumes, Tracy Dorman; Composer/Sound, Victoria Delorio; Dramaturg, Richard J Roberts; SM, Nathan Garrison; Cast: Matthew Brumlow (Richard Hannay), Sarah Nealis (Annabella Schmidt/ Margaret/Pamela/others), Rob Johansen (Clown 1), Tom Aulino (Clown 2); April 20–May 14, 2011

Upperstage

Mary's Wedding by Stephen Massicotte; Director, James Still; Sets, Gordon R. Strain; Lighting, Betsy Cooprider-Bernstein; Costumes, Guy Clark; Sound, Ryan Peavey; Composer, Brian Grimm; Dramaturg, Richard J Roberts; SM, Amy Denkmann; Casting, Claire Simon; Cast: Zach Kenney (Charlie), Gwendolyn Whiteside (Mary), Brian Grimm (Cello Player); November 3–December 4, 2010

Neat by Charlayne Woodard; Director, Richard J Roberts; Sets, Robert M. Koharchik; Lighting, Ryan Koharchik; Costumes, Wendy Meaden; Sound, Ryan Peavey; SM, Amy K. Denkmann; Cast: Milicent Wright (Charlayne); February 10–March 6, 2011

Fire in the Garden by Ken Weitzman; Director, Larissa Kokernot; Sets, Robert M. Koharchik; Lighting, Ryan Koharchik; Costumes, Guy Clark; Sound, Todd Mack Reischman; Dramaturg, Richard J Roberts; Stage Manager, Delia Neylon; Cast: Ryan Artzberger; February 12–27, 2011

In Acting Shakespeare by James DeVita; Sets, Robert M. Koharchik; Lighting, Ryan Koharchik; Sound, Fitz Patton; SM, Amy K. Denkmann; Cast: James DeVita; February 17–March 6, 2011

Kansas City Repertory Theatre

Kansas City, Missouri

Forty-sixth Season

Artistic Director, Eric Rosen; Managing Director, Cynthia Rider; Producing Director, Jerry Genochio

Saved Music and lyrics by Michael Friedman; Book and lyrics by John Dempsey and Rinne Groff; Director Gary Griffin; Assistant Director, Kyle Hatley; Music Director/Conductor, Jasper Grant; Sets, Walt Spangler; Costumes, Megan Turek; Lighting, Jason Lyons; Sound, Joshua Horvath; PSM, Brooke Redler; Cast: Justis Bolding (Hilary Faye); Laura Huizenga (Mary); Doogin Brown (Jesus/ Nurse/Mitch); Graham Rowat (Pastor Mike); David Hull (Dean); Patrick Andrews (Roland); Izzie Baldwin (Tia); Gillian Goldberg (Cassandra); Felicia Finley (Lillian); Nick Spangler (Patrick); September 10–October 3, 2010

Harriet Jacobs by Lydia R. Diamond; Director, Jessica Thebus; Sets, Collette Pollard; Costumes, Jeremy W. Floyd; Lighting, J.R. Lederle; Projections, Jeffrey Cady; Composer/Sound, Andre Pluess; Movement Director, Tyrone Aiken; Assistant Director, Rebecca Stevens; PSM, Mary R. Honour; Cast: Nambi Kelley (Harriet Jacobs), Cheryl Lynn Bruce (Grandma), Phillip James Brannon (Tom), David Fonteno (Master Norcom), Shamika Cotton (Mary), Ronica Riddick (Mistress Norcom), Gilbert Glenn Brown (Samuel Treadwell Sawyer), Damon Russel Armstrong (Daniel); October 22–November 21, 2010

A Christmas Carol by Charles Dickens; Adapted for the stage by Barbara Field; Director, Kyle Hatley; Sets, John Ezell; Costumes, Lacy L. Hansen; Projections/ Lighting, Jeffrey Cady; Music Director/Accompanist, Mark Ferrell; Additional Music, Eryn Preston; Sound, John Story; Movement Coach, Jennifer Martin; Assistant Director, Eric Graves; PSM, Brooke Redler; Cast: Zachary Andrews (Fred), Allan L. Boardman (Old Joe), Greg Brostrom (Albert Hall), Rufus Burns (Dick Wilkins), TJ Chasteen (Young Ebenezer), Noel Collins (Topper), Walter Coppage (Bob Cratchit), Corey Eaton (Ignorance), Kat Endsley (Laundress), Peggy Friesen (Mrs. Fezziwig/Harp Accompanist), Jim Gall (Ghost of Christmas Present), Marcus Garlington (Peter), Kelly Gibson (Giggly Sister), Nick Grant (Peter), Jennie Greenberry (Poulterer's Wife), Katie Hall (Belinda), Whittaker Hoar (Tiny Tim), Gary Neal Johnson (Ebenezer Scrooge), Katie Kalahurka (Ghost of Christmas Past), Jack Kincaid (Tiny Tim), Sarah LaBarr (Aunt Fezziwig), Addison Landes (Want), Paolo Laskero (Simon), Emily Peterson (Fan), Matthew Rapport (Ghost of Christmas Future), Mark Robbins (Jacob Marley), Stephanie Roberts (Mrs. Cratchit), Vanessa Severo (Belle), Anna Stastny (Belinda), Mia Vaught (Ignorance), Margaret Veglahn (Want), Kathleen Warfel (Grandma), Cheryl Weaver (Charwoman), Austin Zollars (Simon); Additional ensemble: Mattie Bell, Jane Carr, Francis Cooper, Regan Grant, Jane Kincaid, Megan Secrest; November 19–December 26, 2010

Another American: Asking and Telling Written and performed by Marc Wolf; Lighting, Jason Lyons; Music/Soundscape, David Van Tieghem; PSM, Samantha Greene; Original direction by Joe Mantello; All roles by Marc Wolf; January 14–February 6, 2011

Circle Mirror Transformation by Annie Baker; Director, Kyle Hatley; Sets, Meghan Raham; Costumes, Megan Turek; Lighting/Projections, Jeffrey Cady; Sound, Michael Griggs; Assistant Director, Jess Akin; PSM, Mary R. Honour; Cast: Tom Aulino (Schultz), Izzie Baldwin (Lauren), Mark Robbins (James), Lee Roy Rogers (Marty), Kim Stauffer (Theresa); February 18–March 20, 2011

Kimiko Gelman and Greg Watanabe in Extraordinary Chambers *at Geffen Playhouse (photo by Michael Lamont)*

James Eckhouse and Maggie Siff in Geffen Playhouse's production of The Escort: An Explicit Play for Discriminating People *(photo by Michael Lamont)*

Joe Knezevich and Park Krausen in Shrew: the Musical *at Georgia Shakespeare (photo by Jen Hofstetter)*

The Company of at Goodspeed Musicals' production of Carnival! *(photo by Diane Sobolewski)*

The Company of Annie Get Your Gun *at Goodspeed Musicals (photo by Diane Sobolewski)*

David Anthony Smith and David Alan Anderson in the Great Lakes Theater production of Shakespeare's Othello *(photo by Roger Mastroianni)*

John Bolton and the Company of Geva Theatre's The Music Man *(photo by Ken Huth)*

Kona N. Burks and Kevin McKillip in
Intimate Apparel *at Illinois Theatre Center*
(photo by Warren Skalski)

Georgia Cohen, Mary Bacon, and Molly Camp in Crimes of the Heart
at McCarter Theatre Center (photo by T. Charles Erickson)

The Company of My Fair Lady *at Lyric Stage*
(photo by James Jamison)

Cabaret Book by Joe Masteroff; Based on the play by John Van Druten and stories by Christopher Isherwood; Music by John Kander; Lyrics by Fred Ebb; Broadway production directed and produced by Harold Prince; Music Director/Conductor/Pianist, Anthony T. Edwards; Orchestrator, Doug Peck; Choreographer, Richard J. Hinds; Sets, Jack Magaw; Costumes, Sarah Beers; Lighting, David Weiner; Sound, Zachary Williamson; PSM, Brooke Redler; Cast: Brian Sills (Master of Ceremonies), Charles Fugate (Ernst Ludwig), Claybourne Elder (Clifford Bradshaw), Hollis Resnik (Fraulein Schneider), Vanessa Severo (Fraulein Kost), Gary Neal Johnson (Herr Schultz), Kara Lindsay (Sally Bowles), Kit Kat Klub Boys: KC Comeaux (Bobby), Bryan LaFave (Victor), Jerry Jay Cranford (Max), Kit Kat Klub Girls: Kym Chambers Otto, Jenny Florkowski, Colleen Grate, Mandy Morris, Emily Shackelford; March 18–April 10, 2011

Peer Gynt by Henrik Ibsen; Adapted and directed by David Schweizer; Sets, David Zinn; Costumes, Christina Wright; Lighting/Projections, Darrel Maloney; Sound/Composition, Ryan Rumery; Assistant Director, Arika Larson; PSM, Mary R. Honour; Cast: Danny Gavigan (Peer Gynt/Buttonmoulder/Others), Birgit Huppuch (Ase/Solveig/Others), Luis Moreno (Peer Gynt/Troll King/Others), Kate Cullen Roberts (Ingrid/Anitra/Others), Evan Zes (Peer Gynt/Mads Moen/Others); April 22–May 22, 2011

La Jolla Playhouse

La Jolla, California

Forty-first Season

Artistic Director, Christopher Ashley; Managing Director, Michael S. Rosenberg

Subscription Shows

Surf Report by Annie Weisman; Director, Lisa Peterson; Sets, Rachel Hauck; Costumes, David Zinn; Lighting, Ben Stanton; Original Music/Sound, John Gromada; Dramaturg, Shirley Fishman; SM, Jennifer Leigh Wheeler; Cast: Matthew Arkin (Hal), Zoë Chao (Bethany), Linda Gehringer (Judith), Gregory Harrison (Bruce) and Liv Rooth (Jena); World Premiere; Mandell Weiss Forum; June 15–July 11, 2010

A Midsummer Night's Dream by William Shakespeare; Director, Christopher Ashley; Sets, Neil Patel; Costumes, David C. Woolard; Lighting, Howell Binkley; Composers, Mark Bennett and Felix Mendelssohn; Choreography, Andrew Pacho; Orchestrations, Wayne Barker; Musical Direction, Eric Stern; Puppetry, Basil Twist; Dramaturg, Shirley Fishman; SM, Anjee Nero; Cast: Kyle Anderson (Fairy), Ken Berkeley (Fairy-Acrobat), Amelia Campbell (Hermia), Cate Campbell (Fairy), Maggie Carney (Peter Quince), Maritxell Carrero (Fairy), Matthew Cusick (Fairy-Acrobat), Matthew Patrick Davis (Tom Snout/Wall), Sara Garcia (Fairy), Zachary Harrison (Starveling/Moonshine), Tim Hopper (Lysander), Seán Mahon (Demetrius), Jonathan McMurtry (Egeus), Hugo Medina (Snug/Lion), Martin Moran (Puck), Amanda Naughton (First Fairy), Daniel Oreskes (Theseus/Oberon), Tatyana Petruk (Fairy Acrobat), Christopher Douglas Reed (Flute/Thisbe), Lucas Caleb Rooney (Nick Bottom), J. Smith-Cameron (Helena), Anne Stella (Fairy), Charlayne Woodard (Hippolyta/ Titania), Bowman Wright (Fairy); Sheila and Hughes Potiker Theater;July 20–August 22, 2010

Limelight: The Story of Charlie Chaplin by Christopher Curtis and Thomas Meehan; Music and Lyrics by Christopher Curtis; Directors, Warren Carlyle and Michael Unger; Sets, Alexander Dodgel; Costumes, Linda Cho; Lighting, Paul Gallo; Sound, Jon Weston; Projection Design, Zachary Borovay; Choreography, Warren Carlyle; Orchestrations, Douglas Besterman; Musical Direction, Bryan Perri; Dramaturg, Gabriel Greene; SM, Frank Hartenstein; Cast: Aaron Acosta (Ensemble), LJ Benet (Young Sydney), Ashley Brown (Oona/Hannah), Jenn Colella (Hedda Hopper), Courtney Corey (Old Hannah/Ensemble), Matthew Patrick Davis (Ensemble), Justin Michael Duval (Ensemble), Sara Edwards (Ensemble), Eddie

Korbich (Karno), Ben Liebert (Ensemble), Alyssa Marie (Ensemble), Rob McClure (Charlie Chaplin), Brooke Sunny Moriber (Mildred), Jennifer Noble (Ensemble), Kürt Norby (Ensemble), Carly Nykanen (Ensemble), Ron Orbach (Sennett/McGranery), Jessica Reiner-Harris (Ensemble), Roland Rusinek (Alf), Jake Evan Schwenke (Young Charlie/Jackie), Kirsten Scott (Ensemble), Matthew Scott (Sydney); World Premiere; Mandell Weiss Theatre;September 7–October 17, 2010

Dostoevsky's Notes from Underground; A Yale Repertory Theatre Production; Adapted by Bill Camp and Robert Woodruff; Translation, Richard Pevear, Larissa Volokhonsky; Director, Robert Woodruff; Sets, David Zinn; Costumes, Moria Siné Clinton; Lighting, Mark Barton; Sound/Original Music, Michaël Attias; Projection Design, Peter Nigrini; SM, Kris Longely-Postema; Cast: Michaël Attias (Apollon/Musician), Bill Camp (Man), Merritt Janson (Liza/Musician); Sheila and Hughes Potiker Theatre; September 17–October 17, 2010

Ruined by Lynn Nottage; Co-production with Huntington Theatre Company and Berkeley Repertory Theatre; Director, Liesl Tommy; Sets, Clint Ramos; Costumes, Kathleen Geldard; Lighting, Lap Chi Chiu; Sound/Original Music, Broken Chord; Choreography, Randy Duncan; Dramaturg, Shirley Fishman; SM, Anjee Nero; Cast: Oberon K.A. Adjepong (Christian), Pascale Armand (Salima), Jason Bowen (Fortune), Carla Duren (Sophie), Wendell B. Franklin (Jerome), Zainab Jah (Josephine), Joseph Kamal (Mr. Harari), Adesoji Odukogbe (Musician 2), Kola Ogundiran (Laurent), Okieriete Onaodowan (Simon), Tonye Patano (Mama Nadi), Adrian Roberts (Commander Osembenga), Alvin Terry (Musician 1); Mandell Weiss Theatre; November 16–December 19, 2010

Little Miss Sunshine by James Lapine; Music and Lyrics by William Finn; Director, James Lapine; Sets, David Korins; Costumes, Jennifer Caprio; Lighting, Ken Billington; Sound, Dan Moses Schreier; Musical Direction, by Vadim Feichtner; Choreography, Christopher Gattelli; Orchestrations, Michael Starobin; Hair/Makeup, Dave Bova; Music Arrangements, Will Aronson; PSM, J. Philip Bassett; Cast: Felicity Bryant (Pageant Girl), Bradley Dean (Ensemble), Sophia DeLange (Pageant Girl), Madi Rae DiPietro (Pageant Girl), Carmen Ruby Floyd (Ensemble), Hunter Foster (Richard Hoover), Malcolm Gets (Frank Ginsberg), Sue Goodman (Ensemble), Kishka Grantz (Pageant Girl), Georgi James (Oliver Hoover), Dick Latessa (Grandpa), Alyssa Marie (Ensemble), David Meyers (Ensemble), Eliseo Roman (Ensemble), Andrew Samonsky (Ensemble), Jennifer Laura Thompson (Sheryl Hoover), Taylor Trensch (Dwayne Hoover), Ryan Wagner (Ensemble), Sally Wilfert (Ensemble), Zakiya Young (Ensemble); World Premiere; Mandell Weiss Theatre; February 15–March 27, 2011

Page to Stage Productions

John Leguizamo: Diary of a Madman by John Leguizamo; Director, Fisher Stevens; Sets, Happy Massee; Production Management/Lighting, Rus Snelling; Stage Management/Projection Design, Aaron Gonzalez; Starring John Leguizamo; Mandell Weiss Theatre, March 4– 14, 2010; Shank Theatre, May 18–29, 2010; Subsequently opened on Broadway as *Ghetto Klown,* March 2011

Cankerblossom Conceived and created by Pig Iron Theatre Company; Text, Tim Sawicki & Pig Iron Theatre Company; Music, Rosie Langabeer; Director, Dan Rothenberg; Sets/Animation, Mimi Lien; Costumes, Leslie Ann Rogers; Lighting, James Clotfelter; Sound, Nick Kourtides; Projection Design, Josh Higgason; Cardboard Creations, Beth Nixon; SM Hannah Wichmann; Cast: Hinako Arao, Beth Nixon, David Sweeny, Alex Torra; Mandell Weiss Forum; August 12–15, 2010

Educational Touring Production:

Frida Libre by Karen Zacarías; POP Tour Production, Commissioned by La Jolla Playhouse; Music, Deborah Wicks La Puma; Director, Rosemary Newcott; Sets, Ian Wallace; Costumes, Thomas Charles LeGalley; Sound, Deborah Wicks La Puma; Dramaturg, Shirley Fishman; Movement Consultant, Anjanette Maraya Ramey; SM, Hannah Ryan; Cast: Camden Gonzales (Frida), Rae Henderson (Ensemble), Steve Limones (Alex), Steven Lone (Maestro/Ensemble); World Premiere

Long Wharf Theatre

Forty-sixth Season

Artistic Director, Gordon Edelstein; Managing Director, Ray Cullom

Mainstage

Ella: The Musical by Jeffrey Hatcher; Conceived by Rob Ruggiero and Dyke Garrison; Director, Rob Ruggiero; Music Director, George Caldwell; Music Supervision/ Arrangements, Danny Holgate; Sets, Michael Schweikart; Costumes, Alejo Vietti; Wigs, Charles LaPointe; Lighting, John Lasiter; Sound, Michael Miceli; SM, Richard Costabile; Cast: Tina Fabrique (Ella), George Caldwell (pianist), Harold Dixon (Norman), Rodney Harper (drums), Joilet Harris (Ella cover), Ron Haynes (trumpet), Cliff Kellam (bass); September 22–October 17, 2010

The Train Driver by Athol Fugard; Director, Gordon Edelstein; Sets, Eugene Lee, Lighting, Chris Akerlind; Costume, Susan Hilferty; Sound, John Gromada; SM, Cole Bonenberger; Cast: Roelf Visagie (Harry Groener), Simon Hanabe (Anthony Chisholm); October 27–November 21, 2010

The Old Masters by Simon Gray; Director, Michael Rudman; Sets, Alexander Dodge; Costumes, Toni-Leslie; Lighting, James Peter Kaczorowski; Sound/ Original Music, John Gromada; Casting, Jack Doulin; SM, Bonnie Brady; Cast: Sam Waterston (Bernard Berenson), Rufus Collins (Edward Fowles), Brian Murray (Joseph Duveen), Shirley Knight (Mary Berenson), Heidi Schreck (Nicky Mariano). Produced by John Martello and Elliot Martin; January 19–February 13, 2011

Italian American Reconciliation by John Patrick Shanley; Director, Eric Ting; Sets, Scott Bradley, Costumes, Linda Cho; Lighting, Russell Champa; Sound, Sarah Pickett; Casting, James Calleri, CSA; SM, Megan Schwarz Dickert; Cast: Lisa Birnbaum (Janice), Mike Crane (Huey), Stephanie DiMaggio (Teresa), John Procaccino (Aldo), Socorro Santiago (Aunt May); April 27–May 22, 2011

Stage II

Shirley Valentine by Willy Russell; Director, Gordon Edelstein; Sets, Frank Alberino; Costumes, Martin Pakledinaz; Lighting, Rui Rita; Sound, Ryan Rumery; SM, Jason Hindelang; Cast: Judith Ivey (Shirley Valentine); December 2, 2010– January 2, 2011

Agnes Under the Big Top by Aditi Brennan Kapil; Director, Eric Ting: Sets, Frank Alberino; Costumes, Jessica Wegener Shay; Lighting, Tyler Micoleau; Sound/Composition, Katie Down; Composition, Sam Ghosh; Dialects, Amy Stoller; Dramaturg, Liz Engelman; Casting, James Calleri CSA; SM, Megan Schwarz Dickert; Cast: Eshan Bay (Happy), Francesca Choy-Kee (Agnes), Michael Cullen (Shipkov), Laura Esterman (Ella), Sam Ghosh (Busker), Gergana Mellin (Roza); March 2–April 3, 2011

Lyric Stage

Dallas County, Texas

Eighteenth Season

Founding Producer, Steven Jones; Managing Director, Valerie Galloway Chapa

Bye Bye Birdie by Michael Stewart; Music by Charles Strouse; Lyrics by Lee Adams; Director, Cheryl Denson; Choreographer, Ann Nieman, Music Director, Jay Dias, Sets, Christopher Potter, Mamie Trotter, Woody Mahaone; Costumes, Drenda Lewis; Lighting, Julie N. Moroney; Sound, Bill Eickenloff; Props, Jane Quetin; SM, Margaret J. Soch; Cast: Steve Barcus (Albert Peterson), Catherine

Carpenter Cox (Rose Alvarez), Daniel R. Johnson (Conrad Birdie), Mary McElree (Kim MacAfee), Mike Gallagher (Mr. MacAfee), Wendy Welch (Mrs. MacAfee), Chet Monday (Randolph MacAfee), Charlotte Franklin (Mae Peterson), Mackenzie Orr (Hugo Peabody), Emily Jackson (Ursula Merkle), Lee Jamison (Gloria Rasputin), Katharine Gentsch (Sad Girl/Ensemble), Graham Galloway (Sad Girl/ Ensemble), Caitlin Galloway (One Boy Girl/Ensemble), Lindsay Sawyer (One Boy Girl/Ensemble), James Williams (Mayor/ Ensemble), Vicki Dean (Mayor's Wife/Ensemble), Kristi Rowan (Mrs. Merkle/Ensemble), Raleigh Tyler (Harvey Johnson/Ensemble), Ben Giddings (Charles Maude/Men's Quartet), Martin Antonio Guerra (Men's Quartet/Ensemble), Eric Domuret (Men's Quartet), Babakayode Ipaye (Men's Quartet/Ensemble), Alex Aultshuler (Ensemble), Eric Daniel Aultman (Ensemble), Meredith Cole (Ensemble), Ryan Cowles (Ensemble), Cameron Leighton Kirkpatrick (Ensemble), Ty Taylor (Ensemble), Feleceia Benton (Ensemble), Dayton Spencer Dobbs (Ensemble), John Venable (Ensemble); June 18–27, 2010

My Fair Lady by Alan Jay Lerner and Frederick Loewe; Director/Choreographer, Len Pfluger; Music Director, Jay Dias; Sets, Kenneth Foy; Costumes, Cathleen Edwards, Drenda Lewis; Lighting, Julie N. Moroney; Sound, Scott A. Eckert; Orchestrations, Robert Russell Bennett, Phillip J. Lang; Props, Jane Quetin; SM, Margaret J. Soch; Cast: Kimberly Whalen (Eliza Doolittle), J. Brent Alford (Henry Higgins), Gary Taggart (Colonel Pickering), Sonny Franks (Alfred Doolittle), Noelle Stanley (Mrs. Pierce), Dayton Spencer Dobbs (Jamie), Keith Warren (Harry), Daniel R. Johnson (Freddy Eynsford-Hill), Juli Erickson (Mrs. Higgins), Jay Taylor (Bartender), Vicki Dean (Mrs. Hopkins/Lady Boxington), James Williams (Butler/Lord Boxington), Graham Galloway (Flower Girl), Lucia A. Welch (Mrs. Eynsford-Hill); Ensemble: Eric Daniel Aultman, Feleceia Benton, Mallory Michaellann Brophy, Courtney Dahl, Vicki Dean, Caitlin Galloway, Graham Galloway, Katharine Gentsch, Martin Antonio Guerra, Amber Nicole Guest, Sarah Harder, Joseph Holt, Will Huse, Babakayode Ipaye, Augustine Jalomo, Kali Katzmann, Thomas Christopher Renner, Michael Anthony Sylvester, Dana Taylor, Jay Taylor, Lucia A. Welch, James Williams; September 10–19, 2010

The Night of the Hunter by Claibe Richardson and Stephen Cole; Based on the novel by Davis Grubb; Director, Cheryl Denson; Music Director, Scott A. Eckert; Sets, Scott Osborne; Lighting, Julie S. Moroney; Costumes, Drenda Lewis; Sound, J.D. Sones; Props, Jane Quetin; SM, Margaret J. Soch; Orchestrations, Donald Johnston; Additional Orchestrations, Scott A. Eckert; Cast: Lois Sonnier Hart (Rachel Cooper), Jack Vangorden (John), Marlhy Murphy (Pearl), Sonny Franks (Ben), Julie Johnson (Willa); Davis Gaines (Preacher), Susan Metzger (Miz Cunningham), Doug Jackson (Uncle Birdie), Deborah Brown (Icey Spoon), Steven D. Morris (Walt Spoon), Stephanie Spalding (Nellie Boyd), Vicki Dean (Mamie Ernest), Shelbie Mac (Ruby), Lily Monday (Mary), Dani Altshuler (Clary), Eric Daniel Aultman (Drugstore Cowboy), Dayton Spencer Dobbs (Prison Guard/ Police), Daniel R. Johnson (Drugstore Cowboy), Keith J. Warren (Minister/Police/ Drugstore Cowboy), James Williams (Warden); October 29–November 7, 2010

Flora The Red Menace by David Thompson; Music by John Kander; Lyrics by Freb Ebb; Director/Choreographer, Ann Nieman; Music Director, Scott A. Eckert; Sets, Jane Quetin; Costumes, David Blades; Lighting, Julie N. Moroney; Sound, Bill Eickenloff; Stage Manager, Margaret J. Soch; Cast: Kristin Dausch (Flora), Keith J. Warren (Harry), Danielle Estes (Charlotte), Calvin Roberts (Willy/Others), Jeff McGee (Mr. Weiss/ Others), Jacklyn Staff (Maggie/Others), Thomas Christopher Renner (Kenny/Others), K. Doug Miller (Mr. Stanley/Others); February 11–26, 2011

McCarter Theatre Center

Princeton, New Jersey

Thirty-eighth Season

Artistic Director, Emily Mann; Managing Director, Tim Shields

Berlind Theatre

Aurélia's Oratorio Created and directed by Victoria Thierrée Chaplin; Technical Direction, SM, Gerd Walter; Lighting, Laura de Bernadis, Philippe Lacombe; Sound, Victoria Thierrée Chaplin; Sets, Victoria Thierrée Chaplin; Costumes, Victoria Thierrée Chaplin, Jacques Peridiguez, Veronique Grand, Monika Schwarzl; Cast: Aurélia Thierrée, Jaime Martinez; September 10–October 17, 2010

The How and the Why by Sarah Treem; Director, Emily Mann; Sets, Daniel Ostling; Costumes, Jennifer Moeller; Lighting, Stephen Strawbridge; Sound, Robert Kaplowitz; Casting, Laura Stanczyk, CSA; Dramaturg, Carrie Hughes; PSM, Alison Cote; Cast: Mercedes Ruehl (Zelda Kahn), Bess Rous (Rachel Hardeman); World Premiere; January 7–February 13, 2011

Sleeping Beauty Wakes Book by Rachel Sheinkin; Music by Brendan Milburn; Lyrics by Valerie Vigoda; Director, Rebecca Taichman; Music Direction, James Sampliner; Choreography, Doug Varone; Sets, Riccardo Hernandez; Costumes, Miranda Hoffman; Lighting, Christopher Akerlind; Sound, Leon Rothenberg; Projection, Peter Nigrini; Supervising Orchestrator, James Sampliner; Arrangements, Brendan Milburn; Casting, Laura Stanczyk, CSA; PSM, Cheryl Mintz; Cast: Steve Judkins (Murray), Adinah Alexander (Hadara), Jimmy Ray Bennett (Leon), Donna Vivino (Cheryl), Bryce Ryness (Orderly), Kecia Lewis-Evans (Doctor), Bob Stillman (King), Aspen Vincent (Beauty); April 29–June 5, 2011

Matthews Theatre

An Iliad Adapted from Homer by Lisa Peterson and Denis O'Hare; Translation, Robert Fagles; Director, Lisa Peterson; Sets, Rachel Hauck; Costumes, Marina Draghici; Lighting, Scott Zielinski; Music/Sound, Mark Bennett; PSM, Cheryl Mintz; Cast: Stephen Spinella (Poet); October 19–November 7, 2010

A Christmas Carol by Charles Dickens; Adaptation, David Thompson; Director, Michael Unger; Music/Lyrics, Michael Starobin; Choreography, Rob Ashford; Sets, Ming Cho Lee; Costumes, Jess Goldstein; Lighting, Stephen Strawbridge; Sound, Brian Ronan; Musical Director, Charles Sundquist; Choreography Supervisor, Jennifer Paulson Lee; Dialect, Gillian Lane-Plescia; Casting, Laura Stanczyk, CSA; Supervising SM, Cheryl Mintz; Cast: Justin Blanchard (Jacob Marley/Mr. Stocks), Cherise Boothe (Christmas Present), Bill Buell (Mr. Fezziwig/Old Joe), Jonathan Crombie (Bob Cratchit), Christ Dunlop (Young Scrooge/Mr. Bonds), Piper Goodeve (Fan/Mrs. Bonds/Dance Captain), James Ludwig (Fred/Schoolmaster/ Undertaker), Graeme Malcolm (Ebenezer Scrooge), Janet Metz (Mrs. Cratchit), Pippa Perthree (Mrs. Dilber), Michele Tauber (Mrs. Fezziwig/Mrs. Stocks/Laundress), Stephanie Umoh (Lily/Belle) Ensemble: Rachel Baker, Neville Braithwaite, Mary Leigh Christine, Kara Dombrowski, Justin Flexen, Timothy Grady, Brody Hessin, K.C. Leiber, Mike Miller, Emma Ritchie, Nicholas Yenson; Children: Danny Hallowell, Mariel Edokwe, Jake Urban, Kate Fahey, Ileena Irin Irving, Elisa Rodriguez, Tom Rodriguez, Noah Hinsdale, Hope Springer, Cara Barkenbush, Camryn McAuliffe, Matthew Kuenne, Annika Goldman, Adam LeCompte; December 5–26, 2010

Crimes of the Heart by Beth Henley; Director, Liesl Tommy; Sets, Andromache Chalfant; Costumes, Marion Williams; Lighting, Ann G. Wrightson; Sound, Karin Graybash; Dialect, Thom Jones; Casting, Laura Stanczyk, CSA; PSM, Cheryl Mintz; Cast: Mary Bacon (Lenny MaGrath), Brenda Withers (Chick Boyle), Lucas Van Engen (Doc Porter), Georgia Cohen (Meg MaGrath), Molly Camp (Babe Botrelle), Dustin Ingram (Barnette Lloyd); March 8–27, 2011

Merrimack Repertory Theatre

Lowell, Massachusetts

Thirty-third Season

Artistic Director, Charles Towers; Executive Director, Steven Leon

The Reduced Shakespeare Company The Complete World of Sports by Reed Martin and Austin Tichenor; Director, Reed Martin, Austin Tichenor; Costumes, Julia Kwitchoff; Wardrobe, Lee Viliesis; Sound, Zach Moore, Joe Winkler; Props, Elizabeth Bazzano, Alli Bostedt; Backdrop Design, Dottie Marshall Englis; Backdrop Painting/ Construction, Scott Loebl; GM, Jane Martin; Office Manager, Alli Bostedt; SM, Emily F. McMullen; Fight Song Arranger, Jon Webber; Poster/Logo, Scott Brushnell; Legal Counsel, Sharon Colchamiro, Esq.; Creative Cash Control, Joanne Nagel; Company Founder, Daniel Singer; Cast: Reed Martin (Reed), Austin Tichenor (Austin), Matt Rippy (Matt); September 9–October 30, 2010

Four Places by Joel Drake Johnson; Director, Charles Towers; Sets, Bill Clarke; Lighting, Jeff Adelberg; Costumes, Deb Newhall; Cast: Carole Monferdini (Peggy); Kate Udall (Ellen), John Wojda (Warren), Laura Latreille (Barb); East Coast Premiere; October 14–November 7, 2010

Beasley's Christmas Party by C.W. Munger; Director, Carl Forsman; Sets, Beowulf Boritt; Costumes, Theresa Squire; Lighting, Josh Bradford; Sound, Will Pickens; Cast: Joey Collins (Man 2), Crystal Finn (Woman 1), Tony Ward (Man 1); New England Premiere; November 26–December 19, 2010

Tryst by Karoline Leach; Director, Joe Brancato; Sets, Michael Schweikardt; Costumes, Alejo Vietti; Lighting, Martin Vreeland; Sound, Johnna Doty; Cast: Mark Shanahan (George Love), Andrea Maulella (Adelaide Pinchin); January 6–30, 2011

The Exceptionals by Bob Clyman; Director, Charles Towers; Sets, Judy Gailen; Costumes, Deb Newhall; Lighting, Brian Lilienthal; Cast: Carolyn Baeumler (Gwen), Judith Lightfoot Clarke (Claire), Catherine Eaton (Allie), Joseph Tisa (Tom); World Premiere; February 10–March 6, 2011

Two Jews Walk Into A War... by Seth Rozin; Director, Melia Bensussen; Sets, Richard Chambers; Costumes, Judy Gailen; Lighting, Dan Kotlowitz; Sound, David Remedios; Cast: Jeremiah Kissel (Zeblyan), Will Lebow (Ishaq); March 17–April 10, 2011

A Picasso by Jeffrey Hatcher; Director, Charles Towers; Sets/Costumes, Campbell Baird; Lighting, Brian Lilienthal; Cast: Mark Zeisler (Picasso), Kate Udall (Miss Fischer); April 21–May 15, 2011

Music Theatre of Wichita

Wichita, Kansas

Thirty-ninth Season

Producing Artistic Director, Wayne Bryan

Gypsy Book by Arthur Laurents; Music by Jule Styne; Lyrics by Stephen Sondheim; Director, Wayne Bryan; Choreographer, Amy Baker; Musical Director, Thomas W. Douglas; Sets, Michael Anania, Charles O'Connor, XuZheng He; Costumes, Thomas G. Marquez, Sarah Reever; Lighting, David Neville; Sound, David Muehl; Hair/Wigs, Raymond J. Torres; Props, Ray Wetmore; PM, David Neville; PSM, Emily F. McMullen; SM, Tiffany K. Orr; Company Manager/Associate Producer, Nancy Reeves; Cast: Karen L. Robu (Rose), Lisa Rohinsky (Louise), Timothy W. Robu (Herbie), Eloise Kropp (June), Johnny Stellard (Tulsa), Addison Baker (Baby June), Gina Austin (Tessie Tura), Patty Reeder (Miss Cratchitt/Mazeppa), Cynthia Atchison (Electra), Faith Northcutt (Young Louise), John Boldenow (Pop / Mr. Goldstone), Richard Campbell (Uncle Jocko / Cigar), Michael J. Parker (Weber / Kringelein/Phil), Skyler Adams (Yonkers), Chistopher Wood (L.A./Bougeron-Cochon), Josh Smith (Kansas/Tulsa u/s), Daxton Bloomquist (Flagstaff), Baltimore

(James Tolbert), Jacob Gutierrez (George/Cow Dancer/Pastey), Natasha Scearse (Agnes/Showgirl), Sasha Hutchings (Marjorie May/Showgirl), Erin Clemons (Showgirl), Kaleigh Cronin (Waitress/Showgirl), Kimberly Fauré (Showgirl/Dance Captain), Emily Mechler (Showgirl/Renee), Keaton Fish (Newsboy), Marak Gann (Newsboy), Justin Kim (Clarence/Newsboy), Gavin Myers (Newsboy), Brennan O'Rourke (Newsboy), Morgan Purdy (Balloon Girl/Baby June u/s), Lauren Voigt (Contestant/Young Louise u/s); June 9–13, 2010

Smokey Joe's Café: The Songs of Leiber and Stoller Words and music by Jerry Leiber and Mike Stoller; Director/Choreographer, Darren Lee; Associate Director/Choreographer, Melanie Lockyer; Musical Director, Thomas W. Douglas; Sets, Tara A.Houston; Costumes, Tiia E. Torchia; Lighting, David Neville; Sound, David Muehl; Hair/Wigs, Raymond J. Torres; Props, Ray Wetmore; PM, David Neville; PSM, Emily F. McMullen; SM, Tiffany K. Orr; Company Manager/Associate Producer, Cast: Lawrence Cummings, Kimberly Fauré, Kolby Kindle, Grasan Kingsbury, Kevyn Morrow, Betti O., Darcie Roberts, Josh Sassanella, Debra M.. Walton, Skyler Adams, Erin Clemons, Kaleigh Cronin, Jacob Gutierrez, Sasha Hutchings, Hannah Meredith Killebrew, Eloise Kropp, Sam Lips, Emily Mechler, Kevin Munhall, Natasha Scearse, Josh Smith, Johnny Stellard, James Tolbert, Jenny Wine, Christopher Wood; Onstage band: Thomas W. Douglas (conductor/piano), Jesse Warkentin (associate conductor/synthesizer), Rod Martens (guitar), Eric Crawford (bass), Dave Dobbins (saxophones), Steve Hatfield (drums), Ginger Zyskowski (percussion); June 23–27, 2010

Crazy for You: The New Gershwin Musical Music and lyrics by George Gershwin and Ira Gershwin; Book by Ken Ludwig; Director, James Brennan; Choreographer, Alan Coats; Original Broadway Choreography by Susan Stroman; Musical Director, Thomas W. Douglas; Sets, Michael E. Downs, J.B. Wilson; Costumes, Thomas G. Marquez; Lighting, David Neville; Sound, David Muehl; Hair/Wigs, Raymond J. Torres; Props, Ray Wetmore; PM, David Neville; PSM, Emily F. McMullen; SM, Tiffany K. Orr; Company Manager/Associate Producer, Nancy Reeves; Cast: David Elder (Bobby Child), Darcie Roberts (Polly Baker), Matthew Shepard (Bela Zangler), Kimberly Fauré (Irene Roth), Andreas de Rond (Lank Hawkins), Mary Lou Phipps-Winfrey (Mother), John Boldenow (Everett Baker), Timothy W. Robu (Eugene), Karen L. Robu (Patricia), Kaleigh Cronin (Tess/Dance Captain), Natasha Scearse (Patsy), Skyler Adams (Production Tenor/Pete), Erin Clemons (Vera), Jacob Gutierrez (Wyatt), Tanner Lee Hanley (Jimmy), Shannon Hucker (Mitzi), Sasha Hutchings (Elaine), Hannah Meredith Killebrew (Louise), Eloise Kropp (Susie), Sam Lips (Junior), Emily Mechler (Betsie/Polly u/s), Sophie Menas (Margie), Peter Mills (Ike), Kevin Munhall (Moose), Josh Smith (Billy), Johnny Stellard (Custus/Lank u/s), Jenny Wine (Sheila), Christopher Wood (Harry); July 7–11, 2010

Annie Book by Thomas Meehan; Music by Charles Strouse; Lyrics by Martin Charnin; Director/ Choreographer, Roger Castellano; Musical Director, Thomas W. Douglas; Sets, Ming Cho Lee; Costumes, Cathleen Edwards; Lighting, David Neville; Sound, David Muehl; Hair/Wigs, Raymond J. Torres; Props, Ray Wetmore; PM, David Neville; PSM, Tiffany K. Orr; SM, Emily F. McMullen; Company Manager/Associate Producer, Nancy Reeves; Cast: Alyssa Danley (Annie), Michael DeVries (Oliver Warbucks), Jennifer Perry (Miss Hannigan), Denis Lambert (Rooster), Emily Mechler (Grace Farrell), Kaleigh Cronin (Lily St. Regis), Charles Parker (FDR), Timothy W. Robu (Drake), Johnny Stellard (Bert Healy/Eddie/Ensemble), Laura Smith (Molly), Gabbe Meloccaro (Pepper), Rebecca Jensen (Duffy), Sally Olmstead (July), Caroline Boesen (Tessie), Lucy Anderson (Kate), Skyler Adams (Fred/Ickes/Ensemble/Rooster u/s). Erin Clemons (Ensemble), Andreas de Rond (Policeman/ Ensemble), Ryan Ehresman (Jimmy Johnson/Ensemble), Kimberly Fauré (Company Dance Captain/ Mrs. Greer/Boylan Sister/Ensemble), Jacob Gutierrez (Fred McCracken/Ensemble), Tanner Lee Hanley (Dog Catcher #1/Sound Effects Man/Ensemble), Shannon Hucker (Peggy/Ensemble), Sasha Hutchings (Cecille/Ensemble), Hannah Meredith Killebrew (Boylan Sister/Ensemble), Kolby Kindle (Bundles/ Ensemble), Eloise Kropp (Jane/Ensemble), Sam Lips (Ira/Judge Brandeis/Ensemble), Sophie Menas (Annette/Boylan Sister/Ensemble). Peter Mills (Louis Howe/Ensemble), Kevin Munhall (Appleseller/Ensemble), Michael J. Parker (Lt. Ward/Morganthau/Ensemble), Sarah Quinn (Young People's Dance Captain/Ensemble), Natasha Scearse (Sophie/Ensemble/

Lily u/s), Josh Smith (Dog Catcher #2/Artie/ Ensemble), Jenny Wine (Star-to-Be/Perkins/Ensemble/Grace u/s), Christopher Wood (Hull/ Ensemble), Dani Young (Mrs. Pugh/Ensemble/Miss Hannigan u/s), Dudley (Sandy), Kirby (Caught Dog), and Talia Bauchmoyer, Hannah Brock, Kathryn Bunting, Maria Collins, Sydney Dahlgren, Michaela Chang Edwards, Hannah Gonzalez, Abby Grier, Emma Gunderson, Gracie Johnston, Abigail Ottaway, Morgan Purdy, Emily Smith, Lacey Wellemeyer (Young New Yorkers); July 21–25, 2010

Curtains Book by Rupert Homes; Music by John Kander; Lyrics by Fred Ebb; Original book and concept by Peter Stone; Additional Lyrics by John Kander and Rupert Holmes; Director, Mark Madama; Choreographer, Peggy Hickey; Musical Director, Thomas W. Douglas; Sets, J Branson; Costumes, Debbie Roberts; Lighting, David Neville; Sound, David Muehl; Hair/Wigs, Raymond J. Torres; Props, Ray Wetmore; PM, David Neville; PSM, Emily F. McMullen; SM, Tiffany K. Orr; Company Manager/Associate Producer, Nancy Reeves; Cast: Larry Raben (Lt. Frank Cioffi); Darcie Roberts (Georgia Hendricks); Paula Leggett Chase (Carmen Bernstein); Claybourne Elder (Aaron Fox); Jody Cook (Christopher Belling); Timothy W. Robu (Oscar Shapiro); Emily Mechler (Niki Harris); Kimberly Fauré (Bambi Bernét); Johnny Stellard (Bobby Pepper), Andreas de Rond (Daryl Grady), Michael J. Parker (Sidney Bernstein), Kevin Munhall (Randy Dexter), Christopher Wood (Harv Fremont), Karen L. Robu (Jessica Cranshaw/Carmen u/s), Kolby Kindle (Johnny Harmon), Jacob Gutierrez (Detective O'Farrell/Ensemble), Thomas W. Douglas (Sasha Iljinsky), Skyler Adams (Ensemble/Aaron u/s), Kaleigh Cronin (Ensemble), Tanner Lee Hanley (Ensemble), Shannon Hucker (Ensemble), Hannah Meredith Killebrew (Ensemble), Eloise Kropp (Ensemble/Dance Captain/Bambi u/s), Sam Lips (Ensemble), Sophie Menas (Ensemble), Peter Mills (Ensemble), Sarah Quinn (Ensemble), Josh Smith (Ensemble), Natasha Scearse (Ensemble); August 4–8, 2010

North Carolina Theatre

Raleigh, North Carolina

Twenty-seventh and Twenty-eighth Season

President and CEO, Lisa Grele Barrie; Artistic Director, Casey Hushion; Producer, Carolee Baxter

Annie by Thomas Meehan; Music by Charles Strouse; Lyrics by Martin Charnin; Director, Casey Hushion; SM, William Alan Coats; Hair/Makeup, Patricia DelSordo; Costumes, Ann M. Bruskiewitz; Lighting, Craig Stelzenmuller; Sound, Shannon Slaton; Choreographer, Vince Pesce; Music Director, Edward G. Robinson; Animal Trainer, William Berloni; Orchestra Contractor, Nancy Whelan; Associate Director, Heather Patterson King; First Production Assistant, Eric Tysinger; Props, Laurie Johnson; Master Carpenter, Tommy Reed; Wardrobe, Meredith Scott; Sound Assistant, Eric Feuerstein; Assistant to Director, Andrew Madsen; Assistant to the Producer, Katie Lynch; Company Management Assistant, Tricia Young; English Bernhardt (Annie), Mikey (Sandy), Katherine Anderson (Chorus), Kate Blain (Chorus), Joey Calveri (Rooster), Tim Caudle (Chorus/Lt. Ward/Morgenthau), Andrew Chappelle (Chorus/Dog Catcher), Allison Chochrane (Orphan), Molly Deans (Chorus), Gracie Deloache (Orphan), Mary Kate Englehardt (Molly), Jennifer Frankel (Chorus/Ronnie Boylan/ Dance Captain/ Hannigan u/s), Katherine "KK" Fristch (July/Annie u/s), Terri Gervais (Chorus/Mrs. Pugh), Elgin Giles (Chorus), Eric Michal Gillett (FDR), Laurel Harris (Chorus/Connie Boylan/A Star To Be), Dana Zihlman Harshaw (Lily St. Regis), Kelsey Healey (Tessie), Avery Hoerdemann (Orphan), Brian Michael Hoffman (Chorus/Bundles/Ickes/SFX Man), Hannah Hoskins (Orphan), Mary Callan Kelso (Orphan), Heather Patterson King (Chorus/Sophie/Perkins), Hayley Lundberg (Orphan), Eric Mann (Chorus/Fred McCracken), Jeremy Mills (Chorus), Christy Morton (Grace Farrell), Brian Norris (Chorus/Bert Healy), Adrienne C. Perry (Chorus), Payton Prince (Duffy), Alexa Robertson (Kate), Jennifer Swiderski (Chorus/Bonnie Boylan), Tom Treadwell (Chorus/Drake), Alexis Van Venrooy (Orphan), Cady Van Venrooy (Orphan), Kelsey Walston (Pepper), Matthew-Jason Willis (Chorus/Howe); July 24–August 1, 2010

Little Shop Of Horrors by Howard Ashman; Music by Alan Menken; Director/Choreographer, Casey Hushion; Music Director/Conductor, Julie Bradley; SM, Candace E. Hoffman; ASM, Eric Tysinger; Lighting, John Bartenstein; Sound, Shannon Slaton; Costumes, Ann M. Bruskiewitz; Hair/Make-Up, Patricia DelSordo; Props, Laurie Johnson; Master Carpenter, Tommy Reed; Assistant Director/Choreographer, Todd Michel Smith; Assistant Programming/Lighting Designer, Kevin Cook; Master Electrician/Lighting Board Op, Lucas Johnson; Wardrobe Supervisor, Meredith Scott; A1 Sound Engineer, Eric Carney; A2/RF Technician, Brian L. Hunt; 2nd ASM, Helen A. Barnes; Rehearsal Pianists, Nancy Whelan & Coty Cockrell; Sound Assistant, Eric Feuerstein; Carpentry Assistant/Stagehand, Edward Kirby; Stitchers, Emma Bevacqua, Elaine Brown, & Robert Odom; Dressers, Kay Hedrick & Brittnye Batchelor; Assistant to the Director, Stacie Alston; TUTS Technical Director, Ivy Whisnant; Production Photographer, Curtis Brown Photography. Noah Putterman (Seymour), Gina Milo (Audrey), Stephen Berger (Mushnik), Evan Casey (Orin and Everybody Else), Rebecca Covington (Street Urchin/Ronnette), Parker Fitzgerald (Audrey II Manipulator), Michael James Leslie (Voice of Audrey II), Natalie Renee (Street Urchin/Crystal), Danielle K Thomas (Street Urchin/Chiffon); September 18–September 26, 2010

The Producers by Mel Brooks; Director/Choreographer, Bill Burns; Music Director/Conductor, Edward G. Robinson; SM, William Alan Coats; Assistant Director/Choreographer, Shari Jordan; ASM, Eric Tysinger; Lighting, John Bartenstein; Sound/A1 Sound Engineer, Brian L. Hunt; Costumer, Ann M. Bruskiewitz; Hair/Make-Up, Patricia DelSordo; Associate Music Director/Contractor, Nancy Whelan; Properties Mistress, Laurie Johnson; Master Carpenter, Tommy Reed; Assistant Programming/Lighting Designer, Kevin Cook; Master Electrician/Lighting Board Op, Craig Mowery; Wardrobe Supervisor, Meredith Scott; Wardrobe Assistant, Casey Watkins; Hair/Make-Up Assistants, Elisa Acevedo, Joyce Hawkins; Rehearsal Pianists, Nancy Whelan and Jesse Kapsha; Dance Captain, Shari Jordan; Director/Choreographer's Assistant, Kelsey Walston; Assistant SM, Andrieu Doyle; Production Photographer, Curtis Brown Photography. Michael McCormick (Max Bialystock), Stacey Todd Holt (Leo Bloom), Stuart Marland (Roger DeBris), Steven Ted Beckler (Franz Liebkind), Lara Seibert (Ulla), Christopher Sloan (Carmen Ghia), Alexander Aguilar (Chorus), Nicole Batalias (chorus), Bree Branker (Chorus), Sarah Burns (Chorus), Thay Floyd (Chorus), Tyler Foy (Chorus), Ian Gleason (Chorus/Lead Tenor), Erica Hamilton (Chorus), Kinsie Howell (Chorus), Lisa Jolley (Chorus), Shari Jordan (Chorus/Usherette/Dance Captain), Meredith Jones (Chorus), Judy Long (Chorus/Shirley), Jeremy Mills (Chorus), Ryan Naimy (Chorus), A.J. Sullivan (Chorus/Mr. Marks), Mackenzie Warren (Chorus) and Matthew-Jason Willis (Chorus); February 12–February 20, 2011

Hello, Dolly! by Michael Stewart; Music and lyrics by Jerry Herman; Director, Casey Hushion; Choreographer, Vince Pesce; Music Director/Conductor, Edward G. Robinson; SM, William Alan Coats; ASM, Eric Tysinger; Lighting, Craig Stelzenmuller; Sound, Brian L. Hunt; Costumes, Ann M. Bruskiewitz; Hair/Make-Up, Patricia DelSordo; Associate Music Director/Contractor, Nancy Whelan; Properties Mistress, Aline Johnson; Master Carpenter, Tommy Reed; Associate Sound Designer, Eric Collins; Rehearsal Pianists, Nancy Whelan & Jesse Kapsha; Directors Assistant, Katherine Finan; Stage Management Assistant, Anna Rains; Prodcuction Photographer, Curtis Brown Photography. Jacquelyn Piro Donovan (Dolly), Stephen Godwin (Horace Vandergelder), Matt Loehr (Cornelius), Gail Bennett (Irene Malloy), Michael Baxter (Chorus), Josie Bodle (Chorus), Lindsey Bracco (Chorus), Garrett Broadwell (Chorus), Bailey Buntain (Ermengarde), Pauline Cobrda (Ernestina/Chorus/Dolly u/s), Joseph Cullinane (Chorus), Meredith Davis (Chorus), Andrieu Doyle (Chorus), Jason Mark Durst (Chorus), Hazel Edmond (Chorus), Matt Gibson (Chorus), Elgin Giles (Chorus), Kelsey Healey (Kid's Chorus), Meredith Jones (Chorus), Steve Konopelski (Choruse/Dance Captain), Julie Kotarides (Chorus), Nicholas Kraft (Kid's Chorus), Becca Lee (Chorus), Hayley Lundberg (Kid's Chorus), Halle Morse (Minnie Fay), Jeremy Morse (Barnaby), Drew Nellessen (Chorus), Danny Norris (Rudolph/Chorus), Kristin Sears (Chorus), Jason Sparks (Ambrose), Jared Titus (Chorus), Mackenzie Warren (Chorus), and Matthew-Jason Willis (Chorus); May 7–14, 2011

The Old Globe

San Diego, California

Seventy-sixth Season

Executive Producer, Louis G. Spisto

Lowell Davies Festival Theatre

King Lear by William Shakespeare; Director, Adrian Noble; Sets, Ralph Funicello; Costumes, Deirdre Clancy; Lighting, Alan Burrett; Sound/Original Music, Christopher R. Walker; Original Music, Shaun Davey; Fight Director, Steve Rankin; Vocal/Dialect Coach, Claudia Hill-Sparks; SM, James Latus; Cast: Michael Stewart Allen (Duke of Cornwall), Donald Carrier (Duke of Albany), Andrew Dahl (Oswald), Ben Diskant (King of France), Craig Dudley (Doctor), Christian Durso (Duke of Burgundy), Robert Foxworth (King Lear), Catherine Gowl (Cordelia), Charles Janasz (Earl of Gloucester), Joseph Marcell (Earl of Kent), Steven Marzolf (Curan/ Herald), Jonno Roberts (Edmund), Aubrey Saverino (Regan), Adrian Sparks (Old Man), Emily Swallow (Goneril), Bruce Turk (Fool), Jay Whittaker (Edgar); Ensemble: Shirine Babb, Grayson DeJesus, Kevin Hoffmann, Andrew Hutcheson, Jordan McArthur, Brooke Novak, Ryman Sneed, Bree Welch; June 12–September 23, 2010

The Taming of the Shrew by William Shakespeare; Director, Ron Daniels; Sets, Ralph Funicello; Costumes, Deirdre Clancy; Lighting, Alan Burrett; Sound/Original Music, Christopher R. Walker; Original Music, Shaun Davey; Fight Director, Steve Rankin; Vocal/Dialect Coach, Claudia Hill-Sparks; SM, James Latus; Cast: Michael Stewart Allen (Tranio), Shirine Babb (Widow), Donald Carrier (Hortensio), Craig Dudley (Tailor/Vincentio), Charles Janasz (Pedant/Curtis), Joseph Marcell (Gremio), Jordan McArthur (Biondello), Jonno Roberts (Petruchio), Adrian Sparks (Baptista Minola), Emily Swallow (Katherine), Bruce Turk (Grumio), Bree Welch (Bianca), Jay Whittaker (Lucentio); Ensemble: Andrew Dahl, Grayson DeJesus, Ben Diskant, Christian Durso, Kevin Hoffmann, Andrew Hutcheson, Steven Marzolf; June 16–September 26, 2010

The Madness of George III by Alan Bennett; Director, Adrian Noble; Sets, Ralph Funicello; Costumes, Deirdre Clancy; Lighting, Alan Burrett; Sound/Original Music, Christopher R. Walker; Original Music, Shaun Davey; Fight Director, Steve Rankin; Vocal/Dialect Coach, Claudia Hill-Sparks; SM, James Latus; Cast: Michael Stewart Allen (Fox), Miles Anderson (George III), Shirine Babb (Lady Pembroke), Donald Carrier (Sheridan), Andrew Dahl (Prince of Wales), Grayson DeJesus (Ramsden), Ben Diskant (Greville), Craig Dudley (Dundas), Christian Durso (Braun), Robert Foxworth (Dr. Willis), Kevin Hoffmann (Duke of York), Andrew Hutcheson (Fortnum), Charles Janasz (Thurlow), Joseph Marcell (Sir George Baker), Steven Marzolf (Captain Fitzroy), Jordan McArthur (Papandiek), Brooke Novak (Margaret Nicholson), Ryman Sneed (Maid), Adrian Sparks (Sir Lucas Pepys/Sir Boothby Skrymshir), Emily Swallow (Queen Charlotte), Bruce Turk (Dr. Richard Warren), Jay Whittaker (William Pitt); Ensemble: Catherine Gowl, Aubrey Saverino, Bree Welch; June 19–September 24, 2010

Old Globe Theatre

Robin and the 7 Hoods–A New Musical Book by Rupert Holmes; Lyrics by Sammy Cahn; Music by Jimmy Van Heusen; Based on the original screenplay by David R. Schwartz; Produced with the permission of Warner Brothers Theatrical Ventures; Music Supervisor/Vocal and Incidental Music Arrangements, John McDaniel; Director/Choreographer, Casey Nicholaw; Sets, Robert Brill; Costumes, Gregg Barnes; Lighting, Kenneth Posner; Sound, John Shivers; Sound, David Patridge; Hair/Wigs, Josh Marquette; Orchestrator, Bill Elliott; Music Director, Mark Hummel; Dance Music Arranger, David Chase; SM, Peter Wolf; Cast: Will Chase (Little John Dante), Adam Heller (Lieutenant Nottingham), Rick Holmes (P.J. Sullivan), Jeffrey Schecter (Willie Scarlatti), Eric Schneider (Robbo Ortona), Amy Spanger (Alana O'Dell), Kelly Sullivan (Marian Archer); Ensemble: Timothy J. Alex, Clyde Alves, Graham Bowen, Andrew Cao, Cara Cooper, Paige Faure, Lisa Gajda, Stephanie Gibson, Carissa Lopez, Vasthy Mompoint, Beth Johnson Nicely, Aleks Pevec, Sam Prince, Tally Sessions, Brian Shepard, Anthony Wayne; World Premiere; July 14–August 29, 2010

Brighton Beach Memoirs by Neil Simon; Director, Scott Schwartz; Sets, Ralph Funicello; Costumes, Alejo Vietti; Lighting, Matthew McCarthy; Sound, Paul Peterson; Original Music, Michael Holland; Dialect, Jan Gist; SM, Diana Moser; Cast: David Bishins (Jack Jerome), Bonnie Black (Blanche Morton), Sloan Grenz (Stanley Jerome), Austyn Myers (Eugene Jerome), Joseph Parks (Stan Jerome), Allie Trimm (Nora Morton), Brandon Uranowitz (Eugene Jerome), Julia Vanderwiel (Laurie Morton), Karen Ziemba (Kate Jerome); September 14–November 7, 2010

Broadway Bound by Neil Simon; Director, Scott Schwartz; Sets, Ralph Funicello; Costumes, Alejo Vietti; Lighting, Matthew McCarthy; Sound, Paul Peterson; Original Music, Michael Holland; Dialect, Jan Gist; SM, Diana Moser; Cast: David Bishins (Jack Jerome), Bonnie Black (Blanche Morton), Howard Green (Ben Epstein), Joseph Parks (Stan Jerome), Brandon Uranowitz (Eugene Jerome), Karen Ziemba (Kate Jerome); September 17–November 7, 2010

Dr. Seuss' How the Grinch Stole Christmas! Book and lyrics by Timothy Mason; Music by Mel Marvin; Original production conceived and directed by Jack O'Brien; Director/Choreography restaged by James Vasquez; Original Choreography, John DeLuca; Musical Direction, Ron Colvard; Additional Choreography, Bob Richard; Sets, John Lee Beatty; Costumes, Robert Morgan; Lighting, Pat Collins; Sound, Paul Peterson; Orchestrations, Anita Ruth; Vocal Arrangements/Incidental Music, Joshua Rosenblum; Dance Music Arranger, David Krane; Leila Knox, SM; Cast: Jeff Skowron (The Grinch), Logan Lipton (Young Max), Martin Van Treuren (Old Max), Remy Margaret Corbin, Shea Starrs Siben (Cindy-Lou Who), Melinda Gilb (Mama Who), Steve Gunderson (Papa Who), Eileen Bowman (Grandma Who), Phil Johnson (Grandpa Who), Emma Ford, Skylar Starrs Siben (Annie Who), Samantha Wang , Julia Way (Betty-Lou Who), Leif Erik Isaacson, Dylan Nalbandian (Boo Who), Trevor Juliano Lerma, Lane Palhegyi (Danny Who); Ensemble: Aaron Acosta, Liam James Brandt, Felicity Bryant, Dominique Castillo, Courtney Corey, Randall Dodge, Madeline Edwards, Anna George, Kyle J. Jackson, Samantha Littleford, Allison Ma, Kürt Norby, Karyn Overstreet, Lou Francine Rasse, Emma Rasse, Anise Ritchie; November 20–December 26, 2010

Jane Austen's Emma–A Musical Romantic Comedy Book, music and lyrics by Paul Gordon; Direction, Jeff Calhoun; Sets, Tobin Ost; Costumes, Denitsa Bliznakova; Lighting, Michael Gilliam; Sound, John H. Shivers; Sound, David Patridge; Music Supervisor, Brad Haak; Music Direction, Laura Bergquist; SM, Thomas J. Gates; Cast: Adam Daveline (Robert Martin), Richert Easley (Mr. Woodhouse), Suzanne Grodner (Miss Bates), Kelly Hutchinson (Mrs. Bates/Mrs. Elton), Brian Herndon (Mr. Elton), Dani Marcus (Harriet Smith), Adam Monley (Mr. Knightley), Patti Murin (Emma Woodhouse), Amanda Naughton (Mrs. Weston), Don Noble (Mr. Weston), Allison Spratt Pearce (Jane Fairfax), Will Reynolds (Frank Churchill); January 15–March 6, 2011

Rafta, Rafta... by Ayub Khan-Din; Based on *All in Good Time* by Bill Naughton; Director, Jonathan Silverstein; Sets, Alexander Dodge; Costumes, Christal Weatherly; Lighting, Lap Chi Chu; Sound, Paul Peterson; Dialect, Gillian Lane-Plescia; Movement Consultant, Reetu Patel; Music Consulant, Mark Danisovszky; SM, Diana Moser; Cast: Shalin Agarwal (Etash Tailor), Geeta Citygirl Chopra (Lopa Dutt), Amir Darvish (Jivaj Bhatt), Nasser Faris (Laxman Patel), Ariya Ghahramani (Jai Dutt), Mahira Kakkar (Vina Patel), Caralyn Kozlowski (Molly Bhatt), Kamal Marayati (Eeshwar Dutt), Gita Reddy (Lata Patel), Rachid Sabitri (Atul Dutt); March 22–April 24, 2011

August: Osage County by Tracy Letts; Director, Sam Gold; Sets, David Zinn; Costumes, Clint Ramos; Lighting, Japhy Weideman; Sound, Fitz Patton; Dialect, Jan Gist; SM, Diana Moser; Cast: Joseph Adams (Bill Fordham), Guy Boyd (Charlie Aiken), Todd Cerveris (Sheriff Deon Gilbeau), Robert Foxworth (Beverly Weston), Kimberly Guerrero (Johnna Monevata), Carla Harting (Ivy Weston), Ronete Levenson (Jean Fordham), Robert Maffia (Steve Heidebrecht), Lois Markle (Violet Weston), Kelly McAndrew (Karen Weston), Angela Reed (Barbara Fordham), Robin Pearson Rose (Mattie Fae Aiken), Haynes Thigpen (Little Charles Aiken); May 7–June 12, 2011

Sheryl and Harvey White Theatre

The Last Romance by Joe DiPietro; Director, Richard Seer; Sets, Alexander Dodge; Costumes, Charlotte Devaux; Lighting, Chris Rynne; Sound, Paul Peterson; SM, Lavinia Henley; Cast: Patricia Conolly (Rose Tagliatelle), Joshua Jeremiah (The Young Man), Paul Michael (Ralph Bellini), Marion Ross (Carol Reynolds); July 30–September 12, 2010

Welcome to Arroyo's by Kristoffer Diaz; Director, Jaime Castañeda; Sets, Takeshi Kata; Costumes, Charlotte Devaux; Lighting, Matthew Richards; Sound, Paul Peterson; Musical Direction, Shammy Dee; Projections, Aaron Rhyne; Stage Manager, Elizabeth Lohr; Cast: Wade Allain-Marcus (Trip Goldstein), Tala Ashe (Lelly Santiago), Byron Bronson (Officer Derek), Andres Munar (Alejandro Arroyo), GQ (Nelson Cardenal), Amirah Vann (Amalia Arroyo); September 25–October 31, 2010

The Winter's Tale by William Shakespeare; Director, Ray Chambers; Sets, Sean Fanning; Costumes, Michelle Hunt Souza; Lighting, Chris Rynne; Sound, Kevin J. Anthenill; Voice/Speech, Jan Gist; SM, Natashja Kelly; Cast: Shirine Babb (Paulina), Ethan Stone (Antigonus/Servant/Lord from Bohemia), Adam Daveline (Shepherd/ Cleomenes/Prison Keeper), Grayson DeJesus (Clown/1st Lord/2nd Guard), Ben Diskant (Autolycus/2nd Lord), Christian Durso (Leontes), Andrew Hutcheson (Polixenes/ Officer), Jesse Jensen (Florizel/1st Guard/1st Attendant), Rachael Jenison (Perdita), Allison Spratt Pearce (Time/2nd Lady), Deborah Radloff (Archidamus/Mopsa/1st Gentlewoman), Ryman Sneed (Hermione), Jonathan Spivey (Camillo/2nd Attendant/Mariner), Bree Welch (Emilia/Dorcas), Robby Young (Mamillius); November 7–November 14, 2010

Plaid Tidings–A Special Holiday Edition of Forever Plaid Book, direction, and choreography by Stuart Ross; Sets, Sean Fanning; Costumes, Charlotte Devaux; Lighting, Chris Rynne; Sound, Paul Peterson; Music Direction, Don LeMaster, Associate Music Director, Steven Withers; SM, Elizabeth Stephens; Cast: David Brannen (Sparky), Leo Daignault (Jinx), Jason Heil (Smudge), Michael Winther (Frankie); November 27–December 26, 2010

Death of a Salesman by Arthur Miller; Director, Pam MacKinnon; Sets, Marion Williams; Costumes, Mathew J. LeFebvre; Lighting, Rui Rita; Sound, Jeremy J Lee; SM, Lavinia Henley; Cast: Jordan Baker (The Woman), Jeffrey DeMunn (Willy Loman), Ben Diskant (Bernard), Jesse Jensen (Stanley), Robin Moseley (Linda), Tyler Pierce (Happy), John Procaccino (Charley), Deborah Radloff (Jenny/Letta), Lucas Caleb Rooney (Biff), Ryman Sneed (Miss Forsythe), Adrian Sparks (Uncle Ben), Jonathan Spivey (Howard Wagner/2nd Waiter); January 22–February 27, 2011

Groundswell by Ian Bruce; Director, Kyle Donnelly; Sets, Kate Edmunds; Costumes, Denitsa Bliznakova; Lighting, Russell H. Champa; Sound, Lindsay Jones; Dialect, Gillian Lane-Plescia; Casting, Samantha Barrie, CSA; SM, Annette Yé; Cast: Antony Hagopian (Johan), Owiso Odera (Thami), Ned Schmidtke (Smith); March 12–April 17, 2011

Life of Riley by Alan Ayckbourn; Director, Richard Seer; Sets/Costumes, Robert Morgan; Lighting, Chris Rynne; Sound, Paul Peterson; Dialect, Jan Gist; SM, Elizabeth Stevens; Cast: David Bishins (Simeon), Ray Chambers (Jack), Rebecca Gold (Tilly), Dana Green (Tamsin), Colin McPhillamy (Colin), Henny Russell (Kathryn), Nisi Sturgis (Monica); American Premiere; April 30–June 5, 2011

Olney Theatre Center

Olney, Maryland

Seventy-second Season

Artistic Director, Jim Petosa; Managing Director, Amy Marshall

Trumpery by Peter Parnell; Director, Jim Petosa; Producing Director, Brad Watkins; Technical Director, Eric Knauss; Company Manager, Sean Cox; Costume Shop Manager, Jeanne Bland; Sets, Jeremy W. Foil, James Kronzer; Costumes, Nicole V. Moody; Lighting, Daniel MacLean Wagner; SM, Tim Burt; Sound,

Elisheba Ittoop; Associate Lighting, Brian Engel; Cast: Ian LeValley (Darwin), James Chatham/Ari Goldbloom-Helzner (George), Christine Hamel (Emma), Shelley Bolman (Hooker), Hannah Lane Farrell (Annie/Girl), James Slaughter (Owen/Williams/ Vicar/Protester), Nick DePinto (Huxley), Jeffries Thaiss (Wallace); April 14–May 9, 2010

Forever Plaid Written, originally directed and choreographed by Stuart Ros; Music continuity, supervision and arrangements by James Raitt; Director/ Choreographer, Bobby Smith; Musical Director, Aaron Broderick; Producing Director, Brad Watkins; Technical Director, Eric Knauss; Company Manager, Bobby Maglaughlin; Costume Shop Manager, Jeanne Bland; Sets, HannaH J Crowell; Costume Coordinator, Jeanne Bland; Lighting, Brian Engel; SM, Diane Teng; Sound, GW Rodriguez; Cast: Ben Martin (Jinx), Ben Lurye (Sparky), Patrick Cragin (Frankie), Dan Van Why (Smudge), John Dellaporta (Swing); July 7–August 1, 2010

The Savannah Disputation by Evan Smith; Director, John Going; Producing Director, Brad Watkins; Technical Director, Eric Knauss; Company Manager, Bobby Maglaughlin; Costume Shop Manager, Jeanne Bland; Sets, James Wolk; Costumes, Liz Covey; Lighting, Dennis Parichy; SM, Renee E. Yancey; Wigs, Anne Nesmith; Dialect, Steve Satta; Sound, Christopher Baine; Cast: Brigid Cleary (Mary), Beth Hylton (Melissa), Michele Tauber (Margaret), Jeff Allin (Father Murphy); July 28–August 22, 2010

Dinner with Friends by Donald Margulies; Director, Jim Petosa; Producing Director, Brad Watkins; Technical Director, Eric Knauss; Company Manager, Bobby Maglaughlin; Costume Shop Manager, Jeanne Bland; Sets, James Kronzer; Costumes, Howard Vincent Kurtz; Lighting, Daniel MacLean Wagner; SM, Josiane M. Lemieux; Sound, Christopher Baine; Cast: Paul Morella (Gabe), Julie-Ann Elliott (Karen), Peggy Yates (Beth), Jeffries Thaiss (Tom); August 25–September 26, 2010

Misalliance by George Bernard Shaw; Director, John Going; Producing Director, Brad Watkins; Technical Director, Eric Knauss; Company Manager, Bobby Maglaughlin; Costume Shop Manager, Jeanne Bland; Sets, James Wolk; Costumes, Liz Covey; Lighting, Dennis Parichy; SM, Renee E. Yancey; Wigs, Anne Nesmith; Dialect, Nancy Krebs; Sound, GW Rodriguez; Cast: Joel Reuben Ganz (John Tarleton, Jr), Matthew McGloin (Bentley Summerhays), Patricia Hurley (Hypatia Tarleton), Anne Stone (Mrs. Tarleton), Dudley Knight (Lord Summerhays), Joe Vincent (John Tarleton), Alex Podulke (Joseph Percival), Andrea Cirie (Lina Szczepanowska), Drew Kopas (Julius Baker "Gunner"); September 29–October 24, 2010

Annie Book by Thomas Meehan, Music by Charles Strouse, Lyrics by Martin Charnin; Director, Mark Waldrop; Musical Director, Christopher Youstra; Choreographer, Tara Jeanne Vallee; Producing Director, Brad Watkins; Technical Director, Eric Knauss; Company Manager, Bobby Maglaughlin; Costume Shop Manager, Jeanne Bland; Sets, Ming Cho Lee; Sound, Christopher Baine; SM, Renee E. Yancey; Costumes, Theoni Aldredge; Wig, Anne Nesmith; Lighting, Charlie Morrison; Cast: Heidi Kaplan, Sadie Rose Herman (Molly), Adalia Jimenez/Nia Smith (Pepper), Kylie Sage Cooley, Lily Discepolo (Duffy), Rachel Olivia Condliffe, Jacqueline Kempa (July), Sydney Maloney, Colette Youstra (Tessie), Caitlin Deerin (Annie), Madeline Heyman, Carolyn Youstra (Kate), Channez McQuay (Miss Hannigan), Alan Hoffman (Bundles), Andrew Sonntag (Dog Catcher), Jason Lott (Officer Ward), Janet Aldrich (Sophie the Kettle), James Konicek (Apple Seller), Carrie A.Johnson (Grace Farrell), James Konicek (Drake), Janet Aldrich (Mrs. Greer), Jamie Ogden (Mrs. Pugh), George Dvorsky (Daddy Warbucks), Autumn Seavey (Star to Be), Jenna Sokolowski (Roxy Usherette), Bobby Smith (Rooster Hannigan), Jenna Sokolowski (Lily St. Regis), Andrew Sonntag (Bert Healy), Bobby Smith (Sound Effects Man), Alan Hoffman (Fred McCracken), Jason Lott (Jimmy Johnson), Janet Aldrich (Bonnie Boylan), Jamie Ogden (Connie Boylan), Allie Parris (Ronnie Boylan), Jason Lott (Kaltenborn's Voice), Andrew Sonntag (Ickes), Janet Aldrich (Frances Perkins), Alan Hoffman (Hull), Jason Lott (Morganthau), Rob McQuay (FDR), Leo Christopher Sheridan (Howe), Alan Hoffman (Justice Brandeis); Ensemble: Janet Aldrich, John Dellaporta, Alan Hoffman, James Konicek, Jason Lott, Rob McQuay, Jamie Ogden,

Allie Parris, Autumn Seavey, Leo Christopher Sheridan, Bobby Smith, Jenna Sokolowski, Andrew Sonntag; November 17, 2010–January 16, 2011

A Christmas Carol, A Ghost Story of Christmas Adapted by Paul Morella from the original novella by Charles Dickens; Artistic Coordinator, Jim Petosa; Costumes, Jeanne Bland, Pei Lee; Lighting, Sonya Dowhaluk; Sound, Edward Moser, GW Rodriguez; Props, Alisha Rider; SM, Corey Williams; ASM, Kyle Blair; Cast: Paul Morella; December 16, 2010–January 2, 2011

Joseph and the Amazing Technicolor Dreamcoat Lyrics by Tim Rice; Music by Andrew Lloyd Webber; Director, David Hilder; Musical Director, Christopher Youstra, Choreographer, Wendy Seyb; Producing Director, Brad Watkins; Technical Director, Eric Knauss; Company Manager, Bobby Maglaughlin; Costume Shop Manager, Jeanne Bland; Sets, Eugenia Furneaux-Arends; Costumes, Ivania Stack; Lighting, Dan Covey; SM, Renee E. Yancey; Sound, GW Rodriguez; Cast: Eleasha Gamble (Narrator), TJ Langston/Sean Silvia (Boy), R. Scott Williams (Jacob/Potiphar), Alan Wiggins (Joseph), Stephawn Stephens (Reuben), Ben Lurye (Simeon/Butler), Nick Lehan (Levi), Jeramiah Miller (Naphtali), Kurt Boehm (Issachar/Sphinx), Vincent Kempski (Asher), Parker Drown (Dan), LC Harden Jr. (Zebulon/Baker), Russell Sunday (Gad/Pharaoh), Andrew Sonntag (Benjamin), Mardee Bennett (Judah), Heather Marie Beck (Mrs. Potiphar/Wife); MaryLee Adams (Wife/Camel), Erin Driscoll (Wife/Ishmaelite), Jamie Eaker (Wife/ Ishmaelite), Ashleigh King (Wife/Camel), Briana Marcantoni (Wife); Ensemble: MaryLee Adams, Heather Marie Beck, Mardee Bennett, Kurt Boehm, Erin Driscoll, Parker Drown, Jamie Eaker, LC Harden Jr., Vincent Kempski, Ashleigh King, Nick Lehan, Ben Lurye, Briana Marcantoni, Jeramiah Miller, Andrew Sonntag, Stephawn Stephens, Russell Sunday; February 23–April 3, 2011

Farragut North by Beau Willimon; Director, Clay Hopper; Producing Director, Brad Watkins; Technical Director, Eric Knauss; Company Manager, Bobby Maglaughlin; Costume Shop Manager, Jeanne Bland; Sets, Cristina Todesco; Costumes, Ivania Stack; Lighting, Nicholas Houfek; SM, Renee E. Yancey; Sound, GW Rodriguez; Cast: Danny Yoerges (Stephen Bellamy), Susan Lynskey (Ida Horowicz), Bruce Nelson (Paul Zara), Kevin Haser (Ben), Elisabeth Ness (Molly), Alan Wade (Tom Duffy), Timothy Andres Pabon (Frank/Waiter); April 27–June 5, 2011

Oregon Shakespeare Festival

Ashland, Oregon

Seventy-sixth Season

Artistic Director, Bill Rauch; Executive Director, Paul Nicholson

Angus Bowmer Theatre

Measure for Measure by William Shakespeare; Director, Bill Rauch; Sets, Clint Ramos; Costumes, ESosa; Lighting, David Weiner; Video/Projections, Shawn Sagady; Composer/ Arrangements, Susie García; Music Supervisor, Michael Keck; Choreographer, Alonzo Lee Moore IV; Phil Killian Directing Fellow, Jerry Ruiz; Dramaturg, Barry Kraft; Voice/Text, Rebecca Clark Carey; Fights, U. Jonathan Toppo; SM, D. Christian Bolender; PA: Karen Hill; Cast: Anthony Heald (Vincentio), Isabell Monk O'Connor (Escalus), René Millán (Angelo), Kenajuan Bentley (Lucio), Jim L. Garcia (Veteran/Barnardine/Ensemble), Cristofer Jean (Mistress Overdone/Abhorson/ Ensemble), Ramiz Monsef (Pompey), Mandie Jenson (Kate Keepdown/Ensemble), Tony DeBruno (Provost), Frankie J. Alvarez (Claudio), Alejandra Escalante (Juliet/Ensemble), Jonathan Dyrud (Froth/Peter/ Ensemble), David Dials (Thomas/Ensemble), Stephanie Beatriz (Isabela), K.T. Vogt (Francisca/Secretary), Tyrone Wilson (Elbow/Ensemble), Kalindi Garcia (Stenographer/Ensemble), Brooke Parks (Mariana/Ensemble), Mary Alfaro (Musician/Ensemble), Vaneza M. Calderón (Musician/ Ensemble), Susie García (Musican/Ensemble); February 18–November 6, 2011

To Kill a Mockingbird by Harper Lee; Adapted for the stage by Christopher Sergel; Director, Marion McClinton; Sets/Projections, David Gallo; Costumes, Deborah M. Dryden; Lighting, Dawn Chiang; Composer/Sound, Michael Bodeen,

Rob Milburn; Shadow Projections, Lynn Jeffries; Associate Director, Patricia McGregor Dramaturg, Martine Kei Green; Voice/Text, Evamarii Johnson; Fights, U. Jonathan Toppo; SM, Jeremy Eisen; ASM, Mara Filler. Cast: Dee Maaske (Jean Louise Finch), Braden Day (Jem), Kaya Van Dyke (Scout), James Edmondson (Walter Cunningham/Ensemble), Mark Murphey (Atticus Finch), Isabell Monk O'Connor (Calpurnia), Judith Delgado (Mrs. Dubose/Ensemble), Leo Pierotti (Dill), Russell Lloyd (Mr. Radley/Ensemble), Michael J. Hume (Judge Taylor/Ensemble), Peter Frechette (Heck Tate), Howie Seago (Bob Ewell/Ensemble), Tyrone Wilson (Rev. Sykes/Ensemble), Brad Whitmore (Mr. Gilmer/Ensemble), Susannah Flood (Mayella Ewell), Peter Macon (Tom Robinson), David Salsa (Boo Radley/Ensemble); February 19–July 3, 2011

The Imaginary Invalid by Molière; Adapted by Oded Gross and Tracy Young; Director, Tracy Young; Sets/Costumes, Christopher Acebo; Lighting, Lap Chi Chu; Composer/Sound, Paul James Prendergast; Choreographer, Ken Roht; Projections, Michael K. Maag: Dramaturg, Lydia G. Garcia; Voice/Text, David Carey; Fights, U. Jonathan Toppo; SM, Jill Rendall; PA, Karl Alphonso; Cast: David Kelly (Argan), K.T. Vogt (Toinette/Ensemble), Rodney Gardiner (Guy/Ensemble), Kimbre Lancaster (Angelique/Ensemble), Nell Geisslinger (Louison/ Ensemble), Terri McMahon (Beline/Ensemble), Christopher Livingston (Cleante/Ensemble), U. Jonathan Toppo (Monsieur De Bonnefoi/Ensemble), Daisuke Tsuji (Thomas Diafoirus/ Ensemble), Robert Vincent Frank (Monsieur Diafoirus/Ensemble), Jeffrey King (Beralde/ Ensemble), Chris Carwithen (Fleurant/Ensemble), Daniel T. Parker (Doctor Purgon/Ensemble); February 20–November 6, 2011

August: Osage County by Tracy Letts; Director, Christopher Liam Moore; Sets, Neil Patel; Costumes, Alex Jaeger; Lighting, James F. Ingalls; Composer/Sound, Andre J. Pluess; Phil Killian Directing Fellow, Jerry Ruiz; Dramaturg, Lydia G. Garcia; Voice/Text, Rebecca Clark Carey; Fights, U. Jonathan Toppo; SM, Amy Miranda Warner; ASM, Mandy Younger; Cast: Richard Elmore (Beverly Weston), Judith-Marie Bergan (Violet Weston), DeLanna Studi (Johnna Monevata), Terri McMahon (Ivy Weston), Catherine E. Coulson (Mattie Fae Aiken), Tony DeBruno (Charlie Aiken), Bill Geisslinger (Bill Fordham), Robynn Rodriguez (Barbara Fordham), Savannah Edson (Jean Fordham), Armando Durán (Sheriff Deon Gilbeau), Kate Mulligan (Karen Weston), Jeffrey King (Steve Heidebrecht), Brent Hinkley (Little Charles Aiken); April 20–November 5, 2011

The African Company Presents Richard III by Carlyle Brown; Director, Seret Scott; Sets, Richard L. Hay; Costumes, Shigeru Yaji; Lighting, Dawn Chiang; Composer/Sound, Todd Barton; Dramaturg, Martine Kei Green; Voice/Text, Rebecca Clark Carey; Fights, U. Jonathan Toppo; SM, Jill Rendall; PA, D Westerholm; Cast: Charles Robinson (Papa Shakespeare), Kevin Kenerly (James Hewlett), Peter Macon (William Henry Brown), Tiffany Rachelle Stewart (Ann Johnson), Gina Daniels (Sarah), Michael Elich (Stephen Price), Mark Murphey (Constable-man); July 20–November 5, 2011

New Theatre

The Language Archive by Lisa Cho; Director, Laurie Woolery; Sets, Christopher Acebo; Costumes, Christal Weatherly; Lighting, Geoff Korf; Composer/Sound, Todd Barton; Dramaturg, Lue Morgan Douthit; Voice/Text, David Carey; Fights, U. Jonathan Toppo; SM, Gwen Turos; ASM, Mandy Younger; Cast: Rex Young (George), Kate Mulligan (Mary), Susannah Flood (Emma), Judith Delgado (Alta/Ensemble), Richard Elmore (Resten/Ensemble); February 24–June 17, 2011

Julius Caesar by William Shakespeare; Director, Amanda Dehnert; Sets, Richard L. Hay; Costumes, Linda Roethke; Lighting, Robert Peterson; Composer/Sound, Fabian Obispo; Dramaturg, Lue Morgan Douthit; Voice/Text, Scott Kaiser; Fights, U. Jonathan Toppo; Stage Manager, Gwen Turos; PA, D Westerholm; Cast: Vilma Silva (Julius Caesar), Jonathan Haugen (Brutus), Gregory Linington (Cassius), Danforth Comins (Mark Anthony), Anthony Heald (Cobbler/Cicero/Publius/ Cinna/Pindarus), Kenajuan Bentley (Flavius/Trebonius/Octavius Caesar), Kevin Kenerly (Casca/Lepidus/Messala), Ako (Soothsayer/Caius Ligarius/Volumnius), Brooke Parks (Marullus/Decius Brutus/Titinius), Gina Daniels (Cinna/Portia/ Cato), Frankie J. Alvarez (Lucius/Metellus Cimber/Caesar's Servant/Octavius' Servant); New Theatre; March 23–November 6, 2011

Ghost Light by Tony Taccone; Conceived and Developed by Jonathan Moscone and Tony Taccone; Director, Jonathan Moscone; Sets, Todd Rosenthal; Costumes, Meg Neville; Lighting, Christopher Akerlind; Composer/Sound, Andre J. Pluess; Projections/Video Design, Maya Ciarrocchi; Dramaturg, Alison Carey; Voice/ Text, David Carey; SM, Health Belden; ASM, Mandy Younger; Cast: Christopher Liam Moore (Jon), Robynn Rodriguez (Louise/Ensemble), Bill Geisslinger (Prison Guard/Ensemble), Derrick Lee Weeden (Mister/Ensemble), Ted Deasy (Basil/Ensemble), Peter Frechette (Film Director/Ensemble), Danforth Comins (Loverboy/ Ensemble), Tyler James Myers (Boy), Danielle Chaves (Ensemble), Isaac Kosydar (Ensemble); World Premiere; June 28–November 5, 2011

Elizabethan Stage

Henry IV, Part Two by William Shakespeare; Director, Lisa Peterson; Sets, Rachel Hauck; Costumes, David C. Woolard; Lighting, Jane Cox; Composer/ Sound, Paul James Prendergast; Dramaturg, Alan Armstrong; Voice/Text, David Carey; Fights, U. Jonathan Toppo; SM, Amy Miranda Warner; ASM, Mara Filler; Cast: Rodney Gardiner (Rumour/Pistol/Gower/ Harcourt/Messengers), Al Espinosa (Lord Bardolph/Earl of Warwick), Jeffrey King (Earl of Northumberland/ Earl of Westmoreland), Eddie Lopez (Travers/Fang/Wart/ Thomas), Mark Bedard (Lord Hastings/ William/Feeble/Beedle/ Constable), Michael J. Hume (Archbishop of York/Justice Silence), Chris White (Lord Mowbray/Peto/ Bullcalf), Michael Winters (Falstaff), Braden Day (Falstaff's Page), Jack Willis (Lord Chief Justice), Kimberly Scott (Mistress Quickly), Brian Demar Jones (Snare/Mouldy/ Humphrey), Brent Hinkley (Bardolph), John Tufts (Prince Hal), Howie Seago (Ned Poins), Vilma Silva (Lady Northumberland/Davy), Christine Albright (Lady Percy), Daisuke Tsuji (Francis/Shadow/Prince John), Nell Geisslinger (Doll Tearsheet), Richard Howard (King Henry IV), David Demuth (Earl of Surrey/Ensemble), Juan C. Parada (Sir John Colevile/Ensemble), Winston Bischof (Ensemble), Zach Myers (Ensemble); May 31–October 7, 2011

The Pirates of Penzance, or the Slave of Duty Music by Arthur Sullivan; Libretto by W.S. Gilbert; Director, Bill Rauch; Music Director/Conductor, Daniel Gary Busby; Choreography, Randy Duncan; Sets, Michael Ganio; Costumes, Deborah M. Dryden; Lighting, Jane Cox; Sound, Kai Harada, Joanna Lynne Staub; Associate Music Director/Additional Vocal/Orchestra Arrangements, Darcy Danielson; Additional Lyrics, Robin Goodrin Nordli; Dramaturg, Judith Rosen; Voice/Text, David Carey; Associate Director, Miriam A. Laube; Associate Choreographer, Jacklyn Miller; Fights, U. Jonathan Toppo; SM, Heath Belden; ASM, Karl Alphonso; Cast: Michael Elich (The Pirate King), Robert Vincent Frank (Samuel), Eddie Lopez (Frederic), Robin Goodrin Nordli (Ruth), David Kelly (Major-General Stanley), Khori Dastoor (Mabel), Kate Hurster (Edith), Amber A. Harris (Kate), Mandie Jenson (Isabel), Emily Sophia Knapp (Celia), Kimbre Lancaster (Daphne), Cristofer Jean (Sergeant of Police/Pirate), Chris Carwithen (Pirate/Police), Ted Deasy (Pirate/Police), Al Espinosa (Pirate/Police), Rodney Gardiner (Pirate/Police), Christopher Livingston (Pirate/Police), René Millán (Pirate/Police), Daniel T. Parker (Pirate/Police), Kimberly Scott (Pirate/Police), Daisuke Tsuji (Pirate/Police), Chris White (Pirate/Police), Emily S. Caldwell (Puppeteer), Miles Fletcher (Puppeteer), Lauryn Hochberg (Puppeteer), Tim Homsley (Puppeteer), Blaine Johnston (Puppeteer), Juan C. Parada (Puppeteer); Orchestra: Patricia M. Berlet, Lori Calhoun, Scott Cole, Arlene Tayloe, Darcy Danielson, Alison Dresser, Bruce Dresser, Mark Jacobs, Kristin Kessler, Jim Malachi, Jacob Phelps-Ransom, Katheryn Jean McElrath, Bruce McKern, Michal Palzewicz; June 1–October 8, 2011

Love's Labor's Lost by William Shakespeare; Director, Shana Cooper; Sets, Christopher Acebo; Costumes, Christal Weatherly; Lighting, Marcus Doshi; Composer/Sound, Paul James Prendergast; Choreographer, Jessica Wallenfels; Dramaturg, Lue Morgan Douthit; Voice/Text, Rebecca Clark Carey; SM, D. Christian Bolender; PA, Karen Hill; Cast: Mark Bedard (Ferdinand), Gregory Linington (Berowne), Ramiz Monsef (Longaville), John Tufts (Dumaine), Kate Hurster (The Princess of France), Stephanie Beatriz (Rosaline), Tiffany Rachelle Stewart (Maria), Christine Albright (Katherine), Robin Goodrin Nordli (Boyet), Jack Willis (Don Adriano de Armado), Emily Sophia Knapp (Moth), Gina Daniels (Jaquenetta), Charles Robinson (Sir Nathaniel), Michael Winters (Holofernes),

Carolyn Baeumler, Judith Lightfoot Clarke, Catherine Eaton, and Joseph Tisa in The Exceptionals *at Merrimack Repertory Theatre (photo by Meghan Moore)*

Mark Zeisler and Kate Udall in Merrimack Repertory Theatre's A Picasso *(photo by Meghan Moore)*

Karen L. Robu in Gypsy *at Music Theatre of Wichita (photo by Jerry Fritchman)*

Lawrence Cummings, Josh Sassanella, Kevyn Morrow, Grasan Kingsbury, and Kolby Kindle in Smokey Joe's Café: The Songs of Leiber and Stoller *at Music Theatre of Wichita (photo by Christopher Clark)*

Jacquelyn Piro Donovan in North Carolina Theatre's Hello, Dolly! *(photo by Curtis Brown)*

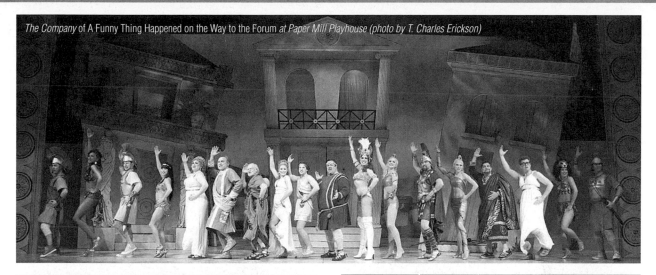

The Company of A Funny Thing Happened on the Way to the Forum at Paper Mill Playhouse (photo by T. Charles Erickson)

Hayden Tee and Kimberly Burns in Pittsburgh Public Theater's production of Camelot (photo by Pittsburgh Public Theater)

Matthew Carlson and Kathryn Hunter-Williams in PlayMakers Repertory Company's production of Angels in America (photo by Jon Gardiner)

The Company in As You Like It at PlayMakers Repertory Company (photo by Jon Gardiner)

Joseph Graves in An Iliad at Portland Center Stage (photo by Owen Carey)

Brad Whitmore (Dull), Ako (Madame Marcade), Jonathan Haugen (Costard), Brian Demar Jones (Forester/Attendant), Josh Bowen (Attendant); June 2–October 9, 2011

Paper Mill Playhouse

Millburn, New Jersey

Thirty-seventh Season

Mark S. Hoebee, Producing Artistic Director; Todd Schmidt, Managing Director

Hairspray by Mark O'Donnell, Thomas Meehan; Music by Mark Shaiman; Lyrics by Scott Wittman; Based on the New Line Cinema Film written and directed by John Waters; Orchestrations, Harold Wheeler; Arrangements, Marc Shaiman; Direction re-created by Matt Lenz; Choreography re-created by Michele Lynch; Sets, Michael Allen Costumes, Brian Hemesath; Lighting, Paul Miller; Sound, Randy Hansen; Hair/Wigs, Mark Adam Rampmeyer; Casting, SM, Telsey + Company; Press Representative, Shayne A. Miller, Thomas J. Gates; Music Supervisor, Tom Helm; Music Director, Joe Elefante; ASM, Andrea Cibelli; Cast: Chistine Danelson (Tracy Turnblad), Kasey Marino (Corny Collins), Kathleen Elizabeth Monteleone (Amber Von Tussle), Jake Wilson (Brad), Deidre Haren (Tammy), Alex Rolecek (Fender), Laurie Veldhee (Brenda), Callan Bergmann (Sketch), Beth Cheryl Tarnow (Shelley), Christopher Messina (IQ), Dani Spieler (Lou Ann), Constantine Rousouli (Link Larkin), Susan Mosher (Prudy Pingleton), Christopher Sieber (Edna Turnblad), Alex Ellis (Penny Pingleton), Donna English (Velma Von Tussle), Kevin Meaney (Harriman F. Spritzer), Lee Roy Reams (Wilbur Turnblad), Kevin Meaney (Principal), Caliaf St. Aubyn (Seaweed J. Stubbs), Christopher Brasfield (Duane), Tyrick Wiltez Jones (Gilbert), Shelese Franklin (Lorraine), Kyshawn K. Lane (Thad)Iris Burruss, Nicole Powell, Rashidra Scott (The Dynamites), Kevin Meaney (Mr. Pinky), Susan Mosher (Gym Teacher), Arielle Campbell (Little Inez), Iris Burruss (Pearl), Nicole Powell (Cindy), Rashidra Scott (Peaches), Natasha Yvette Williams (Motormouth Maybelle), Kevin Meaney, Susan Mosher (Police Officers), Susan Mosher (Matron), Kevin Meaney (Guard), Callan Bergmann, Christopher Brasfield, Iris Burruss, Shelese Franklin, Dedire Haren, Tyrick Wiltez Jones, Kyshawn K. Lane, Christopher Messina, Nicole Powell, Alex Rolecek, Rashidra Scott, Dani Spieler, Beth Cheryl Tarnow, Laurie Veldheer, Jake Wilson (Denizens of Baltimore); September 22–October 17, 2010

Les Misérables by Cameron Mackintosh; A musical based on the novel by Victor Hugo; The New 25th Anniversary Production; Music by Claude-Michel Schönberg; Lyrics by Herbert Kretzmer; Original French Text by Alain Boublil and Jean-Marc Natel; Additional material by James Fenton; Original production adapted and directed by Trevor Nunn and John Caird; Original orchestrations by John Cameron; Directed by Laurence Connor and James Powell; New orchestrations, Chris Jahnke; Additional orchestrations, Stephen Metcalfe, Stephen Brooker; Musical Supervisor, Daniel Bowling; Musical Director, Peter White; Musical Staging, Michael Ashcroft; Sound, Mick Potter; Lighting, Paule Constable; Costumes, Andreane Neofitou; Sets, Matt Kinley (inspired by the paintings of Victor Hugo); Additional costumes, Christine Rowland; Dance Captain, Jason Ostrowski; Cast: Lawrence Clayton (Jean Valjean), Andrew Varela (Javert), Benjamin Magnuson (The Bishop of Digne), Richard Todd Adams (Factory Foreman), Betsy Morgan (Fantine), Lucia Giannetta (Factory Girl), Cathryn Basile, Julie Benko, Casey Erin Clark, Briana Carlson-Goodman, Sarah Shahinian (Whores), Heather Jane Rolff (Old Crone), Cornelia Luna (Crone), John Rapson (Bamatabois), Katherine Forrester, Anastasia Korbal (Little Cosette), Shawna M. Hamic (Madame Thénardier), Katherine Forrester, Anastasia Korbal (Young Éponine), Michael Kostroff (Thénardier), Josh Caggiano, Lewis Grosso (Gavroche), Chasten Harmon (Éponine), Jenny Latimer (Cosette), Jon Fletcher (Montparnasse), Benjamin Magnuson (Babet), Richard Todd Adams (Brujon), John Rapson (Claquesous), Jeremy Hays (Enjolras), Justin Scott Brown (Marius), Cooper Grodin (Combeferre), Jason Forbach (Feuilly), Cole Burden (Courfeyrac), Alan Shaw (Joly), Joseph Spieldenner (Grantaire), Joe Tokarz (Lesgles), Ian Patrick Gibb (Jean Prouvaire), Richard Barth, Ben Gunderson, Jason Ostrowski,

Rachel Rincione, Natalie Weiss (Swings)Cathryn Basile, Julie Benko, Casey Erin Clark, Briana Carlson-Goodman, Lucia Giannetta, Cornelia Luna, Heather Jane Rolff, Sarah Shahinian, Aliya Victoriya (Ensemble); November 19–December 26, 2010

The 25th Annual Putnam County Spelling Bee! Music and lyrics by William Finn; Book by Rachel Sheinkin; Based upon C-R-E-P-U-S-C-U-L-E, an original improvisational play created by Rebecca Feldman; Additional material by Jay Reiss; Director, Marc Bruni; Choreographer, Wendy Seyb; Sets, Anna Louizos; Costumes, Alejo Vietti; Lighting, David Lander; Wigs, Leah J. Loukas; Music Director, Andy Einhorn; ASM, Katrina Lynn Olson; Associate Scenic Design, Hilary Noxon; Assistant Costume Design, Thomas Charles LeGalley; Assistant Lighting Design Ben Pilat; Moving Light Programmer, Victor Seastone; PA, Ruth Zang; Guest Speller Coordinator, David PershickaElectronic Music Design and Programming, Bruce Samuels; Cast: Ephie Aardema (Logainne Schwartzandgrubenierre), Will Blum (William Barfée), Lyle Colby Mackston (Leaf Coneybear), Marla Mindelle (Rona Lisa Peretti), Olivia Oguma (Marcy Park), Jerold E. Solomon (Mitch Mahoney), Ali Stroker (Olive Ostrovsky), David Volin (Vice Principal Douglas Panch), Brandon Yanez (Chip Tolentino); January 19–February 13, 2011

A Funny Thing Happened On The Way To The Forum Book by Burt Shevelove and Larry Gelbart; Music and lyrics by Stephen Sondheim; Originally produced on Broadway by Harold S. Prince; Director, Mark Waldrop; Choreographer, Vince Pesce; Sets, Ray Klausen; Costumes, Matthew Hemesath; Lighting, F. Mitchell Dana; Sound, Randy Hansen; Hair/Wigs, Mark Adam Rampmeyer; Casting, Telsey + Company; Press Representative, Shayne A. Miller; PSM, Lois L. Griffing; Music Supervisor, Tom Helm; Music Director, Ed Goldschneider; ASM, Thomas Recktenwald, Ruth Zang; Assistant Director, Kyle Brand; Assistant Choreographer, Jennifer Jenkins; Associate Scenic Design, Randall Parsons; Assistant Costume Design, Travis Chinick; Assistant Lighting Design, Brenda Veltre; Moving Light Programmer, Matt Hudson; Assistant Sound Design, Julie Pittman; PA, Stephanie Halbedel; Electronic Music Design and Programming, Synthlink LLC, Jim Harp; Cast: Paul C. Vogt (Prologus), Ryan Dietz, Michael Timothy Howell, Bret Shuford (The Proteans), Justin Bowen (Hero), Chelsea Krombach (Philia), Greg Vinkler (Senex), Beth Mcvey (Domina), John Scherer (Hysterium), Stephen Berger (Marcus Lycus), Paul C. Vogt (Pseudolus), Kristine Bendul (Tintinabula), Chondra L. Profit (Panacea), Anne Otto, Lara Seibert (The Geminae), Kristine Covillo (Vibrata), Liz Mckendry (Gymnasia), Chet Carlin (Erronius), Stephen R. Buntrock (Miles Gloriosus); March 16–April 10, 2011

Curtains Book by Rupert Holmes; Music by John Kander; Lyrics by Fred Ebb; Original Book and Concept by Peter Stone; Additional lyrics by John Kander and Rupert Holmes; Director, Mark S. Hoebee; Choreographer, Joann M. Hunter; Music Director/Conductor, Tom Helm; Sets, Robert Andrew Kovach; Costumes, Tracy Christensen; Lighting, Charlie Morrison; Sound, Randy Hansen; Hair/Wigs, Rob Greene, J. Jared Janas; Casting, Telsey + Company; PSM, Shayne A. Miller, Thomas J. Gates; ASM, Rebecca S. Fleming, Patrick David Egan; Assistant Director, Adam Dworkin; Assistant Choreographer, Scott Taylor; Associate Scenic Design, Steve Barnes; Assistant Costume Design, Kathleen McAllister; Assistant Lighting Design, John Burkland; Moving Light Programmer, Tim Rogers; Music Preparation, Richard Rockage; Electronic Music Design and Programming, Synthlink LLC, Jim Harp; Special Effects, Waldo Warshaw; Cast: Robert Newman (Lieutenant Frank Cioffi), Kim Zimmer (Carmen Bernstein), Amanda Rose (Niki Harris), Helen Anker (Georgia Hendricks), Kevin Kern (Aaron Fox), Ed Dixon (Christopher Belling), Aaron Galligan-Stierle (Daryl Grady), Rye Mullis (Johnny Harmon), Dick Decareau (Oscar Shapiro), David Elder (Bobby Pepper), Anne Horak (Bambi Bernét), Daniel Marcus (Sidney Bernstein), Tom Helm (Sasha Iljinsky), Happy Mcpartlin (Jessica Cranshaw), Ian Liberto (Randy Dexter), Joshua James Campbell (Harv Fremont), Colin Bradbury (Detective O'farrell), Ashley Arcement (Female Swing), Patrick O'neill (Male Swing/Dance Captain); Ensemble: Monique Alhaddad, Colin Bradbury, Joshua James Campbell, Lauren Decierdo, Mathew Deguzman, Taurean Everett, Becca Kloha, Mary Ann Lamb, Ian Liberto, Happy Mcpartlin, Molly Tynes, Kyle Vaughn, Dana Winkle; April 27–May 22, 2011

Philadelphia Theatre Company

Philadelphia, Pennsylvania

Thirty-fifth Season

Producing Artistic Director, Sara Garonzik; Managing Director, Shira Beckerman

The 25th Annual Putnam County Spelling Bee Music and lyrics by William Finn, book by Rachel Sheinkin; Conceived by Rebecca Feldman; Director, Marc Bruni; Music Director, Andy Einhorn; Choreography, Wendy Seyb; Set, Anna Louizos; Costumes, Alejo Vietti; Lighting, David Lander; Sound, Nick Kourtides; Cast: Ephie Aardema (Logainne), Will Blum (Barfée), Lyle Colby Mackston (Leaf Coneybear), Marla Mindelle (Rona Lisa Peretti), Olivia Oguma (Marcy Park), Jerold E. Solomon (Mitch Mahoney), Ali Stroker (Olive Ostrovsky), David Volin (Douglas Panch), Brandon Yanez (Chip Tolentino); November 12–December 12, 2010

Race by David Mamet; Director, Scott Zigler; Set/Lighting, Kevin Rigdon; Costumes, Teresa Squires; Cast: Jordan Lage (Jack), Nicole Lewis (Susan), John Preston (Charles), Ray Anthony Thomas (Henry); January 12–February 20, 2011

Let Me Down Easy Written and performed by Anna Deavere Smith; Director, Leonard Foglia; Sets, Riccardo Hernandez; Costumes, Ann Hould-Ward; Lighting, Don Ozminkowski; Sound, Ryan Rummery; Projections, Zachary Borovay; Original Music, Joshua Redman; March 18–April 10, 2011

Ruined by Lynn Nottage; Director, Maria Mileaf; Set, Antje Ellermann; Lighting, Russell H. Champa; Costumes, Janus Stefanowicz; Sound, Bart Fasbender; Cast: Oberon K.A. Adjepong (Christian), Sean-Michael Bowles (Simon), Khris Davis (Rebel Soldier), James Ijames (Fortune), Kes Khemnu (Kisembe), Jamil A.C. Mangan (Osembenga), Paul Meshejian (Mr. Harari), Erika Rose (Salima), Heather Alicia Simms (Mama), Chandra Thomas (Josephine), Keona Welsh (Sophie); May 20–June 12, 2011

Pittsburgh Public Theater

Pittsburgh, Pennsylvania

Thirty-sixth Season

Producing Artistic Director, Ted Pappas

The Royal Family by George S. Kaufman and Edna Ferber; Director, Ted Pappas; Sets, James Noone; Costumes, Susan Tsu; Lighting, Kirk Bookman ; Sound, Zach Moore; SM, Ruth E. Kramer; Cast: Zeva Barzell (Della), James Fitzgerald (Jo), Tony Bingham (McDermott/Gunga), Ross Bickell (Herbert Dead), Jennifer Regan (Kitty Dean), Lindsey Kyler (Gwen Cavendish), Evan Alex Cole (Perry Stewart), Jenny Sterlin (Fanny Cavendish), Larry John Meyers (Oscar Wolfe), Helena Ruoti (Julie Cavendish), David Whalen (Anthony Cavendish), Daryll Heysham (Gilbert Marshall), Karen Merritt (Miss Peake), Matt Lang (Hallboy), Charlie Wein (Hallboy); September 30–October 31, 2010

Talley's Folly by Lanford Wilson; Director, Pamela Berlin; Sets, Michael Schweikardt; Costumes, Candice Donnelly; Lighting, Chris Dallos; Sound, Zach Moore; SM, Fred Noel; Cast: Andrew Polk (Matt Friedman), Julie Fitzpatrick (Sally Talley); November 11–December 12, 2010

The Complete World of Sports (abridged) by The Reduced Shakespeare Company; SM, Elaine M. Randolph; Cast: Reed Martin, Matt Rippy, Austin Tichenor; January 4–9, 2011

Camelot by Alan Jay Lerner and Frederick Loewe; Director, Ted Pappas; Music Director, F. Wade Russo; Sets, James Noone; Costumes, Alejo Vietti; Lighting, Kirk Bookman; Sound, Zach Moore; SM, Ruth E. Kramer; Cast: Hayden Tee (Arthur), Dieter Bierbrauer (Sir Dinadan), Alex Coleman (Merlyn), Greggory Brandt (Sir Sagramore), Mark Campbell (Sir Lionel), Kimberly Burns (Guenevere), Daisy Hobbs (Nimue), Keith Hines (Lancelot), Ted Watts, Jr. (Squire Dap), Noble Shropshire (Pellinore), Don DiGiulio (Mordred), Joshua Brelsford and Dustin

Butoryak (Tom), Zanna Fredland, Amanda Frennier, Christina McCann, Sarah Ziegler (Ladies), Joe Jackson, Joe Paparella, Matthew Charles Thompson (Knights), Jonathan Pendergrass and Ben Thorpe (Pages); January 20–February 20, 2011

Circle Mirror Transformation by Annie Baker; Director, Jesse Berger; Sets/Costumes, David M. Barber; Lighting, Don Darnutzer; Sound, Zach Moore; SM, Fred Noel; Cast: Lauren Blumenfeld (Lauren), Bridget Connors (Marty), Daina Michelle Griffith (Theresa), Daniel Krell (Schultz), John Shepard (James); March 3–April 3, 2011

Superior Donuts by Tracy Letts; Director, Ted Pappas; Set, Michael Schweikardt; Costumes, Amy Clark; Lighting, Phil Monat; Sound, Zach Moore; SM, Fredric H. Orner; Cast: Donald Corren (Max Tarasov), Antoinette LaVecchia (Officer Randy Osteen), Wali Jamal (Officer James Bailey), Sharon Brady (Lady Boyle), Anderson Matthews (Arthur Przybyzewski), Brandon Gill (Franco Wicks), Daryll Heysham (Luther Flynn), Joe Jackson (Kevin Mcgee), David Agranov (Kiril Ivakin); April 14–May 15, 2011

God of Carnage by Yasmina Reza; Director, Ted Pappas; Translator, Christopher Hampton, Sets, Anne Mundell; Costumes, Ted Pappas; Lighting, Phil Monat; Sound, Zach Moore; SM, Fred Noel; Cast: Susan Angelo (Annette Raleigh), Ted Koch (Michael Novak), Deirdre Madigan (Veronica Novak), David Whalen (Alan Raleigh); May 26–June 26, 2011

PlayMakers Repertory Company

Chapel Hill, North Carolina

Thirty-fifth Season

Producing Artistic Director, Joseph Haj; Managing Director, Hannah Grannemann

Mainstage

As You Like It by William Shakespeare; Director, Joseph Haj; Sets, Peter Ksander; Costumes, Anne Kennedy; Lighting, Charlie Morrison; Sound, Ryan J. Gastelum; Composer, Michael Yionoilis; Choreographer, Erin Dangler; SM, Sarah Smiley, Charles K. Bayang; Cast: David Adamson (Corin/Martext/Adam), Dee Dee Batteast (Follower to Duke Senior), Brett Bolton (Charles/Second Lord/Follower to Duke Senior/Follower to Duke Frederick/Duke Frederick and Duke Senior's Second Lord), James E. Brinkley (William), John Brummer (Silvius), Jeffrey Blair Cornell (Duke Senior/Duke Frederick), Kelsey Didion (Phebe), John Dreher (Jaques de Boys/Duke Frederick and Duke Senior's First Lord/Follower to Duke Senior/Follower to Duke Frederick), KG Garcia (Oliver), Matt Garner (Le Beau/Follower to Duke Senior), Katja Hill (Audrey), Jimmy Kieffer (Touchstone), Lauren Klingman (Follower to Duke Senior), Derrick Ledbetter (Orlando), Marianne Miller (Rosalind), Katie Paxton (Amiens/Follower to Duke Senior), Scott Ripley (Jaques), Josh Tobin (Dennis/Follower to Duke Senior), Alice Whitley (Celia); September 22–October 10, 2010

Fences by August Wilson; Director, Seret Scott; Sets, Jan Chambers; Costumes, Helen Q. Huang; Lighting, Peter West; Sound, Ryan J. Gastelum; SM, Charles K. Bayang, Sarah Smiley; Cast: Erik LaRay Harvey (Lyons), Kathryn Hunter-Williams (Rose), Thomasi McDonald (Jim Bono), Charlie Robinson (Troy), Iania Smith (Raynell), Ray Anthony Thomas (Gabriel), Yaegel Welch (Cory); October 27–November 14, 2010

Shipwrecked! An Entertainment by Donald Margulies; Director, Tom Quaintance; Sets, Robin Vest; Costumes, Rachel E. Pollock; Lighting, Tyler Micoleau; Sound, Ryan J. Gastelum; SM, Sarah Smiley; Cast: Dee Dee Batteast (Player), Kelsey Didion (Ensemble), Jimmy Kieffer (Player), Lauren Klingman (Ensemble), Derrick Ledbetter (Player), Scott Ripley (Louis de Rougemont), Josh Tobin (Ensemble); December 1–19, 2010

Angels in America, Part 1: Millennium Approaches and Part 2: Perestroika (in rotating repertory) by Tony Kushner; Director, Brendon Fox; Sets, Narelle Sissons; Costumes, Jan Chambers; Lighting, Pat Collins; Sound,

Ryan J. Gastelum; SM, Charles K. Bayang, Sarah Smiley; Cast: Matthew Carlson (Prior Walter), Christian Conn (Joe Pitt), Jeffrey Blair Cornell (Roy Cohn), Julie Fishell (Hannah Pitt), Avery Glymph (Belize), Kathryn Hunter-Williams (The Angel), Jeffrey Meanza (Louis Ironson), Marianne Miller (Harper Pitt); January 29–March 6, 2011

Big River: The Adventures of Huckleberry Finn; Music and lyrics by Roger Miller; Book by William Hauptman; Adapted from the novel by Mark Twain; Director, Joseph Haj; Choreographer, Casey Sams; Music Director, Jack Herrick; Sets, McKay Coble; Costumes, Bill Black; Lighting, Charlie Morrison; Sound, Ryan J. Gastelum; SM, Charles K. Bayang, Sarah Smiley; Cast: David Adamson (Second Man/Counselor Robinson/Ensemble); LeDawna Akins (Alice/Ensemble); Brett Bolton (First Man/Sheriff Bell/Ensemble); Bryan Burton (Ben/Hank/ Young Fool/Ensemble); Jason Edward Cook (Huck); Jeffrey Blair Cornell (King/Ensemble/ Dance Captain); DeDe Corvinus (Widow Douglas/Sally Phelps/Ensemble); Toshia Cunningham (Alice's Daughter/Ensemble); David Aron Damane (Jim); Kelsey Didion (Miss Watson/Strange Woman/Ensemble); Ray Dooley (Judge Thatcher/Harvey Wilkes/Silas Phelps/Ensemble); John Dreher (Tom Sawyer/Ensemble); Matt Garner (Simon/Lafe/Ensemble); Meredith Jones (Mary Jane Wilkes/Ensemble); Jimmy Kieffer (Pap/Doctor/Ensemble); Katie Paxton (Dick/Andy/ Susan/Ensemble/Asst. Dance Captain); Scott Ripley (Duke/Ensemble); Jessica Sorgi (Joanna Wilkes/Ensemble); Josh Tobin (Jo Harper/Ensemble); April 6–24, 2011

PRC² Second Stage

Happy Days by Samuel Beckett; Director, Rob Melrose; Sets, Michael Locher; Costumes, McKay Coble; Lighting, Chuck Catotti; Original Sound, Cliff Caruthers; Sm, Charles K. Bayang; Cast: Ray Dooley (Willie), Julie Fishell (Winnie); September 8–12, 2010

Exit Cuckoo (nanny in motherland) by Lisa Ramirez; Director, Colman Domingo; Cast: Lisa Ramirez; January 12–16, 2011

The Year of Magical Thinking by Joan Didion; Director, Mark DeChiazza; Sets, Peter Ksander; Costumes, Rachel E. Pollock; Lighting, Jesse Belsky; Sound, Ryan J. Gastelum; SM, Sarah Smiley; Cast: Ellen McLaughlin; April 27–May 1, 2011

Portland Center Stage

Portland, Oregon

Twenty-third Season

Artistic Director, Chris Coleman; Associate Artistic Director, Rose Riordan

Mainstage

Sunset Boulevard Book and lyrics by Don Black and Christopher Hampton; Music by Andrew Lloyd Webber; Director, Chris Coleman; Musical Director/Conductor, Rick Lewis; Choreographer, Joel Ferrell; Sets, G.W. Mercier; Costumes, Jeff Cone; Original Costume Design, Anthony Powell; Lighting, Robert Wierzel; Sound, Casi Pacilio; Video Designer, Patrick Weishampel; Dialect, Mary McDonald-Lewis; Fight Director, John Armour; SM, Mark Tynan; ASM, Jamie Hill; PA, Joey Edwards; New York Casting, Harriet Bass; Cast: Linda Mugleston (Norma Desmond), Larry Daggett (Max von Meyerling), Kevin Reed (Joe Gillis), Sarah Stevens (Betty Shaefer), Michael Brian Dunn (Sheldrake/Pet Undertaker/John/Salesman #2/Richard/ Jones/Reporter), Jessica Lisa Elovsson (Dawn/Lisa/Technician/1st Beautician/ Ensemble), Tony Falcon (Cop/Myron/Glen/Salesman #4/Indian Brave/Myron/Cop/Ensemble), Courtney Freed (Secretary/Dawn/Larissa/Stagehand/Jean/ Technician/Doctor/ Reporter/ Ensemble), Lisa Karlin (Joanna/Stagehand/Delilah/1st Masseuse/Newsreel Crew/Ensemble), Robert Andrew Koutras (Stagehand/Sammy/Salesman #1/Samson/Newsreel Crew/Ensemble), Emily Leonard (Mary/ Stagehand/Astrologer /Reporter/Ensemble), Paul Louis Lessard (Cop/Younger Man/Cliff/ Salesman #5/Director of Photography/ Stagehand/Ensemble), Lindsay Luppino (Anita/Sandy/ Larissa/

Stagehand/2nd Beautician/Ensemble), Leif Norby(Cop/Morino/ Joe/Stagehand/Jane/Manfred/ Hogeye/Ensemble), Jeffrey Pew (Artie Green/Salesman #6/Reporter/Ensemble), Kurt Raimer (Cop/Finance Man #1/Stagehand/Actor/Salesman #7/Adam/ Guard/Newsreel Crew/Ensemble), Robert Stoeckle (Cop/Finance Man# 2/Barman/Salesman #3/Actor #4/ DeMille/Ensemble), Tracy J. Wholf (Dancing Girl/Liz/Waitress/ Danielle/ Stagehand/Heather/ Analyst/Reporter/Ensemble); September 14–October 17, 2010

A Christmas Story by Phil Grecian; Co-author, Jean Shepherd, Bob Clark, Leigh Brown; Director, Rose Riordan; Sets, Tony Cisek; Costumes, Jeff Cone; Lighting, Nancy Shertler; Sound, Casi Pacilio; Fight Director, Ted deChatelet; SM, Jamie Hill; ASM, Liam Kaas-Lentz; ASM, Mark Tynan; PA, Joseph Edwards; Cast: Aliemah Bradley (Ensemble, Girl u/s), Michael Cline (Ralphie), Dylan Earhart (Flick), Harrison Goyette (Randy), Aimee Martin (Helen), Henry Martin (Ensemble, Boy u/s), Ethan McKay (Schwartz), Darius Pierce (Adult Ralph), Laura Faye Smith (Miss Shields), Ebbe Roe Smith (The Old Man), Valerie Stevens (Mother), Calvin Whitney (Scut Farkus), Hannah Wilson (Esther Jane); November 21–December 26, 2010

The Imaginary Invalid by Molière; Adaptor, Constance Congdon; Director, Chris Coleman; Sets, William Bloodgood; Costumes, Jeff Cone; Lighting, Peter Maradudin; Sound, Casi Pacilio; Composer, Randall Tico; Musical Supervisor, Rick Lewis; SM, Liam Kaas-Lentz; ASM, Jamie Hill; PA, Lydia Comer; Cast: Christine Calfas (Beline), Barry Del Sherman (Dr. Purgeon), Hollye Gilbert (Angelique), Sharonlee Mclean (Toinette), David Margulies (Argan), John Wernke (Cleante/Fleurant), Danny Wolohan (De Bennefoi/Claude); January 11–February 6, 2011

One Flew Over the Cuckoo's Nest by Dale Wasserman, from the Ken Kesey novel; Director, Rose Riordan; Sets, Tony Cisek; Costumes, Jeff Cone; Lighting, Diane Ferry Williams; Sound, Sam Kusnetz; Fight Director, Ted deChatelet; SM, Mark Tynan; PA, Joseph Edwards; Cast: Bobby Bermea (Aide Willaims), Craig Bockhorn (Cheswick), Stephen Caffrey (Dale Harding), Rich Cashin (Ruckley), Gretchen Corbett (Nurse Ratched), R. Ward Duffy (Randle McMurphy), Michael Fisher-Welsh (Dr. Spivey), Val Landrum (Sandra), Amy Newman (Nurse Flinn), Tim Sampson (Chief Bromden), Wally Schmidt (Patient Ensemble), Nick Schultz (Patient Ensemble), Vin Shambry (Aide Warren), John Shuman (Patient Ensemble), Ebbe Roe Smith (Scanlon), Robert M. Thomas (Patient Ensemble), Ryan Tresser (Billy Bibbit), Tracy S. Turner (Aide Turkel), Sara Catherine Wheatley (Candy Starr); February 22–March 27, 2011

Opus by Michael Hollinger; Director, Brendon Fox; Sets, James Kronzer; Costumes, Holly Poe Durbin; Lighting, Patricia Collins; Sound, Casi Pacilio; SM, Liam Kaas-Lentz; PA, Lydia Comer; Cast: Matthew Boston (Dorian), Chris Coleman (Elliot), Chris Hietikko (Carl), Greg Jackson (Alan), Sarah Stevens (Grace); April 12–May 8, 2011

One Night with Janis Joplin by Randy Johnson; Writer/Director, Randy Johnson; Musical Director/Arranger, Len Rhodes; in association with the Estate of Janis Joplin and Jeffrey Jampol for JAM, Inc.; Sets/Lighting, Justin Townsend; Costumes, Jeff Cone; Sound, Casi Pacilio; Projections Designer, Darrel Maloney; SM, Mark Tynan; ASM, Jamie Hill; ASM, Stephanie Mulligan; PA, Joseph Edwards; Casting, Randy Dupre, JRD Los Angeles; Cast: Cat Stephani (Janis Joplin), Sabrina Elayne Carten (The Blues Singer), Moriah Angeline (Background Vocalist/Janis u/s), Marisha Wallace (Background Vocalist/Blues Singer u/s); Band: Tyler Evans (Keyboard), Patrick Harry (Bass), Mitch Wilson (Drums), Gavriel de Tarr (Trumpet), Anton Van Oosbree (Trumpet), David Milne (Saxophone), Stephen Flakus (Guitar), Ross Seligman (Guitar); May 24–July 3, 2011

Ellyn Bye Studio

An Iliad Co-adaptor, Denis O'Hare, Lisa Peterson; Director, Penny Metropulos; Sets, William Bloodgood; Costumes, Jeff Cone; Lighting, Diane Ferry Williams; Sound, Sterling Tinsley; SM, Liam Kaas-Lentz; PA, Aubree Lynn, Lydia Comer; Cast: Joseph Graves (Storyteller); September 28–November 21, 2010

The Santaland Diaries by David Sedaris; Adaptor, Joe Mantello; Director, Wendy Knox; Sets/Costumes, Jessica Ford; Lighting, Don Crossley; Sound, Sarah Pickett; SM, Mark Tynan; PA, Aubree Lynn; Cast: Wade McCollum (Crumpet the Elf); November 30, 2010–January 2, 2011

futura by Jordan Harrison; Director, Kip Fagan; Sets, Mimi Lien; Costumes, Jeff Cone; Lighting, Matt Frey; Sound, Casi Pacilio; Projection Designer, Luke Norby; Fight Director, Ted deChatelet; Composer, Jana Losey; SM, Jamie Hill; PA, Aubree Lynn; Casting, Rose Riordan; Cast: Phillip Clark (Edward), Lori Larsen (The Professor), Chris Murray (Gash), Kerry Ryan (Grace); February 1–March 27, 2011

BUST by Lauren Weedman; Director, Allison Narver; Sets/Lighting, Allen Hahn; Sound, Mark Nichols; SM, Jamie Hill, Stephanie Mulligan; PA, Aubree Lynn; Cast: Lauren Weedman (as herself); April 23–June 19, 2011

The Repertory Theatre of St. Louis

St. Louis, Missouri

Forty-fourth Season

Artistic Director, Steven Woolf; Managing Director, Mark Bernstein

Virginia Jackson Browning Mainstage

You Can't Take It With You by Moss Hart and George S. Kaufman; Director, Steven Woolf; Sets, John Ezell; Costumes, Elizabeth Covey; Lighting, Peter E. Sargent; Sound, Rusty Wandall; Casting, Rich Cole; PSM, Glenn Dunn; ASM, Shannon B. Sturgis, PM, Edward M. Coffield; Cast: Stephanie Cozart (Essie Carmichael), Carol Schultz (Penny Sycamore), Rachel Leslie (Rheba), Tony Campisi (Paul Sycamore), Scott Schafer (Mr. De Pinna), Jamie LaVerdiere (Ed Carmichael), Scott Whitehurst (Donald), Joneal Joplin (Grandpa Vanderhof), Amelia McClain (Alice Sycamore), Todd Lawson (Henderson/The Man), Benjamin Eakeley (Tony Kirby), Anderson Matthews (Boris Kolenkhov), Susie Wall (Gay Wellington), Jeffrey Hayenga (Mr. Kirby), Barbara Kingsley (Mrs. Kirby/ Grand Duchess Olga Katrina); September 8–October 3, 2010

High by Matthew Lombardo; Director, Rob Ruggiero; Sets, David Gallo; Costumes, Jess Goldstein; Lighting, John Lasiter; Sound/Composer, Vincent Olivieri; Casting, Pat McCorkle, C.S.A.; Assistant Director, Nick Eilerman; PSM, Champe Leary; ASM, Tony Dearing; PM, Edward M. Coffield; Cast: Kathleen Turner (Sister Jamison Connelly), Michael Berresse (Father Michael Delpapp), Evan Jonigkeit (Cody Randall); World Premiere; October 13–November 7, 2010

Over the Tavern by Tom Dudzick; Director, Michael Evan Haney; Sets, Paul Shortt; Costumes, Dorothy Marshall Englis; Lighting, Dennis Parichy; Sound, Rusty Wandall; Casting, Rich Cole; Child Casting, Carrie Houk C.S.A.; PSM, Glenn Dunn; ASM, Shannon B. Sturgis; PM, Edward M. Coffield; Cast: Spencer Davis Milford (Rudy), Darrie Lawrence (Sister Clarissa), Celeste Ciulla (Ellen), Braden Phillips (Georgie), Eric Nelsen (Eddie), Katie McClellan (Annie), Kevin Cutts (Chet); December 1–26, 2010

The Fall of Heaven by Walter Mosley (Based on his novel *The Tempest Tales*); Director, Seth Gordon; Sets, Robert Mark Morgan; Costumes, Myrna Colley-Lee; Lighting, Michael Lincoln; Sound, Rusty Wandall; Casting, Rich Cole; PSM, Champe Leary; ASM, Tony Dearing; PM, Edward M. Coffield; Cast: Bryan Terrell Clark (Tempest), Corey Allen (Joshua Angel), Rachel Leslie (Alfreda/Darlene/ Ensemble), Kenya Brome (Branwyn), Jeffrey C. Hawkins (Basil Bob/Voices of Saint Peter, Mr. Chin and Mr. Akbar), Jerome Lowe (Ensemble), Borris York (Ensemble); January 5–30, 2011

Macbeth by William Shakespeare; Director, Paul Mason Barnes; Sets, Michael Ganio; Costumes, Dorothy Marshall Englis; Lighting, Kenton Yeager; Sound, Rusty Wandall; Fight Directors, Brian A. Peters and Shaun Sheley; Casting, Rich Cole; Child Casting, Carrie Houk C.S.A.; PSM, Glenn Dunn; ASM, Shannon B. Sturgis; PM, Edward M. Coffield; Cast: Timothy D. Stickney (Macbeth), Caris Vujcec (Lady Macbeth), Jerry Vogel (Duncan/Menteith), Ben Nordstrom (Malcolm), Greg Fink (Donalbain), Jason Cannon (Banquo/Caithness), Kyle

Acheson (Fleance), Christopher Hickey (Ross), Chris Bolan (Lennox), Michael James Reed (Macduff), Nancy Bell (Lady Macduff/Angus), Nathaniel McIntyre (Captain/Siward), Michael Curtin (Young Siward/Soldier), Michael Keyloun (Witch/Murderer/Servant/Doctor), Shanara Gabrielle (Witch/Murderer/ Servant/ Gentlewoman), David Graham Jones (Witch/Porter/Seyton), Alex Donovan, Maria Knasel, Drew Redington, Julia Schweizer, Elizabeth Teeter (Macduff Children), Ensemble: Hillary Brainerd, Jake Golliher, Scott Joy, Scears Lee IV, McKenna Liesman, Colton Pometta; February 9–March 6, 2011

Beehive The 60's Musical Created by Larry Gallagher; Director/Choreographer, Pamela Hunt; Musical Director, Michael Sebastian; Sets, James Morgan; Costumes, John Carver Sullivan; Lighting, Mary Jo Dondlinger; Sound, Rusty Wandall; Casting, Rich Cole; PSM, Glenn Dunn; ASM, Tony Dearing; PM, Edward M. Coffield; Cast: The Players: Lauren Dragon, Lisa Estridge, Jennie Harney, Kristin Maloney, Debra Walton, Jessica Waxman; The Band: Michael Sebastian (Piano), John Brophy (Drums), Mike Buerk (Saxophone), Jay Hungerford (Bass), Steve Schenkel (Guitar), Andy Tichenor (Trumpet); March 16–April 10, 2011

Emerson Studio Theatre

The Year of Magical Thinking by Joan Didion; Director, Priscilla Lindsay; Sets, Rob Koharchik; Costumes, Wendy Meaden; Lighting, Ryan Koharchik; Sound, Justin Been; PSM, Emilee Buchheit; PM, Edward M. Coffield; Cast: Fontaine Syer (Joan); January 12–30, 2011

In the Next Room or the vibrator play by Sarah Ruhl; Director, Stuart Carden; Sets, Gianni Downs; Costumes, Dorothy Marshall Englis; Lighting, Mark Wilson; Sound/Composer, Mikhail Fiksel; Casting, Rich Cole; PSM, Champe Leary; PM, Edward M. Coffield; Cast: Annie Purcell (Catherine Givings), Ron Bohmer (Dr. Givings), Amy Landon (Annie), Michael James Reed (Mr. Daldry), Emily Dorsch (Sabrina Daldry), Krystel Lucas (Elizabeth), David Christopher Wells (Leo Irving); March 9–27, 2011

The Grandel Theatre (Studio Theatre Series)

Next Fall by Geoffrey Nauffts; Director, Seth Gordon; Sets, Brian Sidney Bembridge; Costumes, Lou Bird; Lighting, John Wylie; Sound, Rusty Wandall; Casting, Rich Cole; PSM, Shannon B. Sturgis; PM, Edward M. Coffield; Cast: Marnye Young (Holly), Ben Nordstrom (Brandon), Susan Greenhill (Arlene), Keith Jochim (Butch), Jeffrey Kuhn (Adam), Colin Hanlon (Luke); October 27–November 14, 2010

Imaginary Theatre Company

Chanticleer! Book, music and lyrics by Brian Hohlfeld; Director, Kat Singleton; Musical Director, Neal Richardson; Sets, Scott Loebl; Costumes, Dorothy Marshall Englis; PSM, Danny Maly; Director of Education, Marsha Coplon; Cast: Ann Ashby (Henrietta/Fern), Lakeetha Blakeney (Chanticleer), Jordan Reinwald (Fox/Pig), Christian Vieira (Scooter/Phil); Touring October 18, 2010–April 2, 2011

The Nutcracker by Sarah Brandt; Based on the story by E.T.A. Hoffmann; Music and lyrics/Musical Director, Neal Richardson; Director, Bruce Longworth; Choreographer, Ellen Isom; Sets, Scott Loebl; Costumes, Dorothy Marshall Englis; PSM, Danny Maly; Director of Education, Marsha Coplon; Cast: Ann Ashby (Maria), Lakeetha Blakeney (Mother/Mouse/Fairy/Townsperson), Jordan Reinwald (Godfather/Mouse King/Fairy/Mayor), Christian Vieira (Father/ Nutcracker/Fritz); World Premiere; Touring November 8, 2010–December 31, 2010

Trail of Tears by Kathryn Schultz Miller; Director, Jason Cannon; Musical Director, Neal Richardson; Sets, Scott Loebl; Costumes, Garth Dunbar; PSM, Danny Maly; Director of Education, Marsha Coplon; Cast: Ann Ashby (Snow Owl/ Others), Lakeetha Blakeney (President Andrew Jackson/Others), Jordan Reinwald (Walking Bear/Others), Christian Vieira (Chosen One); Touring January 18–April 2, 2011

San Jose Repertory Theatre

San Jose, California

Thirtieth Season

Artistic Director, Rick Lombardo; Managing Director, Nick Nichols

Black Pearl Sings! by Frank Higgins; Director, Rick Lombardo; Sets, John Iacovelli; Costumes, Frances Nelson McSherry; Lighting, Daniel Meeker; Sound, Rick Lombardo; Vocal Coach, Kate McCormick; Casting Director, Bruce Elsperger; Dramaturg, Karen Altree Piemme; PM, Christopher Morris; PSM, Laxmi Kumaran; ASM, Peter Royston; Cast: Jannie Jones (Alberta "Pearl" Johnson), Jessica Wortham (Susannah Mullally); West Coast Premiere; September 2–26, 2010

Secret Order by Bob Clyman; Director, Chris Smith; Sets/Media, David Lee Cuthbert; Costumes, B. Modern; Lighting, Pamila Gray; Sound, Steve Schoenbeck; Casting Director, Bruce Elsperger; Dramaturg, Karen Altree Piemme; PSM, Joshua M. Rose; ASM, Jaimie L. Johnson; PM, Christopher Morris; Cast: Robert Krakovski (Robert Brock), Julian López-Morillas (Saul Roth), Kathryn Tkel (Alice Curiton), James Wagner (William Shumway); Understudies: Anaseini Katoa (Alice Curiton); Regional Premiere; October 14–November 7, 2010

Backwards in High Heels: The Ginger Musical Conceived and developed by Lynette Barkley and Christopher McGovern; Book/Musical Arrangements/ Original Songs, Christopher McGovern; Director, Scott Schwartz; Choreographer, Patti Colombo; Musical Director/Conductor, Tim Robertson; Sets, Walt Spangler; Costumes, Alejo Vietti; Lighting, Grant Yeager; Associate Director, Laura Josepher; Associate Choreographer, Cameron Henderson; Casting Director, Alison Franck; PSM, Laxmi Kumaran; ASM, Peter Royston, PM, Christopher Morris; Cast: Anna Aimee White (Ginger Rogers), Heather Lee (Lela), Christianne Tisdale (Martha May/Louise/Ethel Merman/Others) Matthew LaBanca (Marcus/Director/Fred Astaire/Others), Benjie Randall (Joe/Bill McMath/George Schaffer/Lew Ayres/ Others), James Patterson (Jack Culpepper/Hermes Pan/Jimmy Stewart/Others); Band: Tim Robertson (Keyboards), Russ Gold (Percussion), Michael Corner (Reeds), Andrew Currier (Upright Bass), Robin Snyder (Cello); Understudies: Cameron Henderson (Male Roles), Benjie Randall (Fred Astaire); Regional Premiere; November 24–December 19, 2010

The Dresser by Ronald Harwood, Director, Rick Lombardo; Sets, Kent Dorsey; Costumes, Cathleen Edwards; Lighting, David Lee Cuthbert; Sound, Steve Schoenbeck; Dialect, Kimberly Mohne Hill; Casting Director, Bruce Elsperger; Dramaturg, Karen Altree Piemme; PSM, Laxmi Kumaran; ASM, Gina Marie Hayes; Cast: Ken Ruta (Sir), Rachel Harker (Her Ladyship), Lynne Soffer (Madge), Blake Ellis (Oxenby), Julian López-Morillas (Geoffrey Thornton), Blythe Foster (Irene), Drew Benjamin Jones (Knight/Albany), Jason Kapoor (Gloucester), Shane Rhoades (Knight/Gentleman), Adam Sessa (Kent); Understudies: Black Ellis (Norman), Julian López-Morillas (Sir), Drew Benjamin Jones (Oxenby); January 27–February 20, 2011

Legacy of Light by Karen Zacarías, Director, Kirsten Brandt; Sets, William Bloodgood; Costumes, Brandin Barón; Lighting/Media, David Lee Cuthbert; Sound, Jeff Mockus; Fight Director, Dave Maier; Casting Director, Bruce Elsperger; Dramaturg, Karen Altree Piemme; PSM, Laxmi Kumaran; ASM, Deirdre Rose Holland; Cast: Rachel Harker (Émilie du Châtelet), Carrie Paff (Olivia/Wet Nurse), Mike Ryan (Peter/Monsieur du Châtelet, Kathryn Tkel (Millie/Pauline), Miles Gaston Villanueva (Saint-Lambert/Lewis), Robert Yacko (Voltaire); Understudies: Sara Luna (Millie/Pauline), Kevin Wulf (Saint-Lambert/Lewis); West Coast Premiere; March 24–April 17, 2011

Love in American Times by Philip Kan Gotanda, Director, Rick Lombardo; Sets, Robin Sanford Roberts; Costumes, Cathleen Edwards; Lighting/Media, David Lee Cuthbert; Original Composition/Sound, Tamara Roberts; Fight Choreographer, Dave Maier; Casting Director, Bruce Elsperger; Dramaturg, Karen Altree Piemme; PSM, Stephanie Schliemann; ASM, Kathleen J. Parsons; Cast: J. Michael Flynn (Jack Heller), Linda Park (Scarlett Mori-Yang), Rosina Reynolds (Desiree/Mrs. Green/Abby), Craig Marker (Calvin/Edward), Arwen Anderson (Evelyn/Sophie), Gabriel Marin (Bartender/Cheese Master/Mr. Stein/Hector), Zarah Mahler (Jazz Singer/Mrs. Stein/Lyonee); Understudies: Gabriel Marin (Edward), Vanessa Alvarez (Sophie/Female Ensemble), Jason Kapoor (Male Ensemble); World Premiere; May 12–June 5, 2011

Seattle Repertory Theatre

Seattle, Washington

Forty-eighth Season

Artistic Director, Jerry Manning; Managing Director, Benjamin Moore

Bagley Wright Theatre

God of Carnage by Yasmina Reza; Director, Wilson Milam; Sets, Eugene Lee; Costumes, Deb Trout; Lighting, Geoff Korf; Sound, Matt Starritt; Assistant Scenic Designer, Patrick Lynch; Fight Choreographer, Geoffrey Alm; SM, Jessica C. Bomball; ASM, Holly R. Coombs; Cast: Hans Altwies (Michael Novak), Amy Thone (Veronica Novak), Denis Arndt (Alan Raleigh), Bhama Roget (Annette Raleigh); October 1–October 24, 2010

Dancing at Lughnasa by Brian Friel; Director/Movement, Sheila Daniels; Sets, Etta Lilienthal; Costumes, Constanza Romero; Lighting, L.B. Morse; Sound/ Composer, Paul James Prendergast; Movement, Jessica Wallenfels; Dialect, Gin Hammond; SM, Amy Poisson; ASM, Miranda C. Pratt; Cast: Cheyenne Casebier (Rose), Troy Fischnaller (Gerry), Benjamin Harris (Michael), Gretchen Krich (Maggie), Todd Jefferson Moore (Father Jack), Linda K Morris (Agnes), Mari Nelson (Kate), Elizabeth Raetz (Chris); November 12–December 5, 2010

The Brothers Size by Tarell Alvin McCraney; Director, Juliette Carrillo; Sets, Mikiko Suzuki MacAdams; Costumes, Constanza Romero; Lighting, Geoff Korf; Sound, Matt Starritt; Composer, Kathryn Bostic; Movement Consultant, Sonia Dawkins; Vocal Consultant, Judith Shahn; Consultant for Yoruba Mythology, Nina Angela Mercer; SM, Bret Torbeck; ASM, Micahel B. Paul; Cast: Warner Miller (Oshoosi), Yaegel T. Welch (Ogun), Eddie R. Brown III (Elegba); February 4–February 27, 2011

Of Mice and Men by John Steinbeck; Director, Jerry Manning; Sets, Jennifer Zeyl; Costumes, Deb Trout; Lighting, Robert J. Aguilar; Original Music/Sound, Robertson Witmer; Fight Choreographer, Robert Macdougall; Dialect, Judith Shahn; SM, Stina Lotti; ASM, Jessica C. Bomball; Cast: Eric Ray Anderson (The Boss), Teagle F. Bougere (Crooks), Troy Fischnaller (George), Jim Gall (Slim), Seán G. Griffin (Candy), Elise Karolina Hunt (Curley's Wife), Charles Leggett (Lennie), Ray Tagavilla (Carlson), Seanjohn Walsh (Curley), William A. Williams (Whit); March 18–April 10, 2011

The Agony and the Ecstasy of Steve Jobs by Mike Daisey; Director, Jean-Michele Gregory; Cast: Mike Daisey; Sets/Lighting, Seth Reiser; SM, Anne Kearson; April 22–May 22, 2011

Leo Kreielsheimer Theatre

Three Tall Women by Edward Albee; Director, Allison Narver; Sets, Matthew Smucker; Costumes, Melanie Taylor Burgess; Lighting, Allen Hahn; Sound/ Composer, Paul James Prendergast; SM, Lori Amondson; Cast: Megan Cole (A), Suzanne Bouchard (B), Alexandra Tavares (C), Nick Garrison (Boy); October 22–November 28, 2010

The K of D, an urban legend by Laura Schellhardt; Director/Co-scenic Designer, Braden Abraham; Co-scenic Designer, L.B. Morse; Costumes, Denise Damico; Lighting, Robert J. Aguilar; Sound, Matt Starritt; Stage Manager, Amy Poisson; Cast: Renata Friedman (The Girl); January 14–February 20, 2011

This by Melissa James Gibson; Director, Braden Abraham; Sets/Lighting, L.B. Morse; Costumes, Christine Meyers; Sound, Gino Scarpino; Composer, Peter Eldridge; Music Consultant, Tim Symons; French Dialect Consultant, Brianne Helmick; SM, Cristine Anne Reynolds; Cast: Hans Altwies (Tom), Cheyenne Casebier (Jane), Nick Garrison (Alan), Ryan Shams (Jean-Pierre), April Yvette Thompson (Marrell); April 8–May 15, 2011

Shakespeare Theatre Company

Washington, D.C.

Twenty-fifth Season

Artistic Director, Michael Kahn; Managing Director, Chris Jennings

All's Well That Ends Well by William Shakespeare; Director, Michael Kahn; Sets, Court Watson; Costumes, Robert Perdziola; Lighting, Charlie Morrison; Composer, Adam Wernick; Sound, Martin Desjardins; Choreographer, Karma Camp; Wigs, Anne Nesmith; Voice/Text Coach, Ellen O'Brien; Assistant Director, Jenny Lord; Literary Associate, Akiva Fox; SM, Joseph Smelser; ASM, Benjamin Royer; Cast: Bev Appleton (First Elder Lord), Michael Bakkensen (Parolles), Nick DePinto (Dumaine the Elder), Conrad Feininger (Second Elder Lord/ Duke of Florence), Daniel Flint (Interpreter/ Ensemble), Adam Green (Lavatch), Kevin Hasser (Ensemble), Russell Jonas (Ensemble), Marsha Mason (Countess of Rossillion), Natalie Mitchell (Diana), Caitlin O'Connell (Widow Capilet), Barbara Pinolini (Mariana/Reynalda), Charity Pomeroy (Ensemble), Tony Roach (Bertram), John William Schiffbauer (Ensemble), Miriam Silverman (Helena), Ted van Griethuysen (King of France), Kristen Varvaris (Ensemble), Paxton Whitehead (Lafew), Scott Woltz (Ensemble), Kevin Woods (Ensemble), Danny Yoerges (Dumaine the Younger); Lansburgh Theatre; September 7–October 30, 2010

Candide by Leonard Bernstein; Directed and newly adapted from the Voltaire by Mary Zimmerman; Presented by HRH Foundation; Choreographer, Daniel Pelzig; Music Director/Additional Arrangements/Orchestrations, Doug Peck; Sets, Daniel Ostling; Costumes, Mara Blumenfeld; Lighting, T.J. Gerckens; Sound, Richard Woodbury; New York Casting, Adam Belcuore, David Muse, Alan Paul Casting, Telsey + Company; Assistant Director, Jenny Lord; Literary Associate, Akiva Fox; SM, Beth Ellen Spencer; ASM, Benjamin Royer; Cast:Tom Aulino (Baron/Martin/Others), Spencer Curnutt (Sailor/Others), Rebecca Finnegan (Baroness/Vanderdendur/Others), Govind Kumar (Servant/Others), Rob Lindley (Anabaptist/ Captain/Others), Erik Lochtefeld (Maximilian/Others), Lauren Molina (Cunegonde), Tracy Lynn Olivera (Orator's Wife/Others), Geoff Packard (Candide), Jesse J. Perez (Soldier/Cacambo/ Others), Hollis Resnik (Old Lady), Emma Rosenthal (Bird/Others), Margo Seibert (Paquette/ Others), Thomas Adrian Simpson (Innkeeper/Schoolteacher/Others), Chris Sizemore (Orator/ Grand Inquisitor/Others), Joey Stone (Soldier/Señor/Others), Tempe Thomas (Queen of El Dorado/Others), Jonathan Weir (Soldier/Governor/Others), Larry Yando (Pangloss/Others); Sidney Harman Hall; November 26, 2010–January 9, 2011

Cymbeline by William Shakespeare; Director, Rebecca Bayla Taichman; Sets, Riccardo Hernandez; Costumes, Miranda Hoffman; Lighting, Christopher Akerlind; Composer/Sound, Andre Pluess; Choreographer, Zoe Scofield; Fight Director, Rick Sordelet; Voice/Text Coach, Ellen O'Brien;Specialty Object Designer (Book), Janie Geiser; Casting, Telsey + Company; Resident Casting Director, Daniel Rehbehn; Assistant Director, Jenny Lord; Literary Associate, Akiva Fox; SM, Jennifer Rae Moore; ASM, Elizabeth Clewley; Cast: Katie Atkinson (Ensemble), Justin Badger (Polydore [Guiderius]), Mark Bedard (Posthumus Leonatus), Zoe Wynn Briscoe (Girl), Brian Clowdus (Ensemble), Franchelle Stewart Dorn (Queen), Adam Ewer (Ensemble), Gretchen Hall (Imogen), Benjamin Horen (Ensemble), Adrian LaTourelle (Iachimo), Andrew Long (Caius Lucius), Leo Marks (Cloten), Alex Morf (Cadwal [Arviragus]), Dee Pelletier (Storyteller), Michael Rudko (Morgan [Belarius]), Todd Scofield (Philario), Kevin Stevens (Ensemble), Tom Story (Cloten's Lord/Ensemble), Ted van Griethuysen (Cymbeline), Jenn Walker (Helen), James Whalen (Ensemble), Hannah Wolfe (Ensemble), William Youmans (Pisanio); Lansburgh Theatre; January 18–March 6, 2011

An Ideal Husband by Oscar Wilde; Director, Keith Baxter; Sets, Simon Higlett; Costumes, Robert Perdziola; Lighting, Peter West; Sound, Martin Desjardins; Casting, Stuart Howard, Amy Schecter, Paul Hardt, Additional Casting, Joyce Nettles Casting; Resident Casting Director, Daniel Rehbehn; Voice/Dialect Coach, Ellen O'Brien; Wigs, Anne Nesmith; Assistant Director, Jenny Lord; Literary Associate, Akiva Fox; SM, Brandon Prendergast; ASM, Benjamin Royer; Cast: Kevin Bergen (Mr. Montford), Travis Blumer (Ensemble), Claire Brownell

(Mabel Chiltern), Lise Bruneau (Mrs. Marchmont), Louis Cupp (Ensemble), Logan DalBello (Prinz Friedrich/Ensemble), Nick Dillenburg (Vicomte de Nanjac), Caitlin Diana Doyle (Ensemble), Cameron Folmar (Lord Goring), Greg Gallagher (Ensemble), Emily Joshi-Powell (Ensemble), Martha Karl (Ensemble), Warren Katz (Mason), Floyd King (Phipps), Tessa Klein (The Countess of Basildon), Rachel Pickup (Lady Chiltern), Emily Raymond (Mrs. Cheveley), Nancy Robinette (Lady Markby), David Sabin (The Earl of Caversham/K.G.), John William Schiffbauer (Ensemble), Anne Stone (Duchess of Maryborough), Paul Stuart (Ensemble), Gregory Wooddell (Sir Robert Chiltern); Sidney Harman Hall; March 8–April 16, 2011

Old Times by Harold Pinter; Director, Michael Kahn; Set, Walt Spangler; Costumes, Jane Greenwood; Lighting, Scott Zielinski; Sound, Martin Desjardins; CSA Casting, Laura Stanczyk; Resident Casting Director, Daniel Rehbehn; Voice/ Dialect Coach, Ellen O'Brien; SM, Beth Ellen Spencer; ASM, Elizabeth Clewley; Cast: Steven Culp (Deeley), Tracy Lynn Middendorf (Kate), Holly Twyford (Anna); May 17–July 3, 2011

The Merchant of Venice by William Shakespeare; Director, Ethan McSweeny; Sets, Andrew Lieberman; Costumes, Jennifer Moeller; Lighting, Marcus Doshi; Composer/Sound, Steven Cahill; Choreographer, Karma Camp; Wigs, Dave Bova; Casting Director, McCorkle Casting, Ltd.; Resident Casting Director, Daniel Rehbehn; Voice/Dialect Coach, Deena Burke; Assistant Director, Jenny Lord; SM, Bonnie Brady; ASM, Benjamin Royer; Cast: Gordon Adams (Ensemble), Travis Blumer (Ensemble), Matthew Carlson (Lorenzo), Julia Coffey (Portia), Carl Cofield (Prince of Morocco), Drew Cortese (Bassanio), Aubrey Deeker (Gratiano), Vaneik Echeverria (Prince of Arragon), Drew Eshelman (Duke), Adam Ewer (Ensemble), Tim Getman (Solanio), Emily Joshi-Powell (Ensemble), Kai Moeller (Ensemble), Andy Murray (Salerio), Mark Nelson (Shylock), Daniel Pearce (Launcelot Gobbo), Amelia Pedlow (Jessica), Benjamin Pelteson (Tubal), Khalil Reddick (Ensemble), Derek Smith (Antonio), Kevin Stevens (Ensemble), Paul Stuart (Ensemble), Liz Wisan (Nerissa), Hannah Wolfe (Ensemble), June 21–July 24,2011

South Coast Repertory

Costa Mesa, California

Forty-seventh season

Artistic Directors, David Emmes, Martin Benson, Marc Masterson; Managing Director, Paula Tomei

Segerstrom Stage

Misalliance by George Bernard Shaw; Director, Martin Benson; Sets, Ralph Funicello; Lighting, Tom Ruzika; Original Music, Michael Roth; Costumes, Maggie Morgan; Dramaturg, Kelly Miller; PM, Joshua Marchesi; SM, Jamie A. Tucker; Cast: Daniel Bess (John Tartleton Jr.), JD Cullum (Julius Baker), Richard Doyle (Lord Summerhays), Waytt Fenner (Bentley Summerhays), Peter Katona (Joseph Percial), Melanie Lora (Hypatia Tarleton), Dakin Matthews (John Tarleton), Kirsten Potter (Lina Szcepanowska), Amelia White, (Mrs. Tarleton); September 10– October 10, 2010

Becky Shaw by Gina Gionfriddo; Director, Pam MacKinnon; Sets, Daniel Ostling; Costumes, Sara Ryung Clement; Lighting, Lap Chi Chu; Sound/Original Music, Michael K. Hooker; Dramaturg, Kelly L. Miller; PM, Joshua Marchesi; SM, Chrissy Church; Cast: Tessa Auberjonois (Suzanna Slater), Brian Avers (Max Garrett), Angela Goethals (Becky Shaw), Graham Michael Hamilton (Andrew Porter), Barbara Tarbuck (Susan Slater); October 22–November 21, 2010

A Christmas Carol by Charles Dickens; Adapted by Jerry Patch; Director, John-David Keller; Assistant Director, Hisa Takakuwa; Sets, Thomas Buderwitz; Costumes, Dwight Richard Odle; Lighting, Donna and Tom Ruzika; Musical arrangement/Composer, Dennis McCarthy; Sound, Drew Dalzell; Vocal Director, Dennis Castellano; Choreography, Sylvia C. Turner; SM, Jamie A. Tucker; Cast: Christian Barillas Undertaker/Young Ebenezer), Daniel Blinkoff (Bob Cratchit), Jennifer Chu (Toy Lady/Sally/Scavenger), Gregg Daniel (Marley/Spirit of

The Company of One Flew Over the Cuckoo's Nest *at Portland Center Stage (photo by Owen Carey)*

Shanara Gabrielle, Michael Keyloun, David Graham Jones, and Timothy D. Stickney in Macbeth *at The Repertory Theatre of St. Louis (photo by Eric Woolsey)*

Yaegel T. Welch, Eddie R. Brown III, and Warner Miller in The Brothers Size *at Seattle Repertory Theatre (photo by Chris Bennion)*

Megan Cole and Suzanne Bouchard in Seattle Repertory Theatre's production of Three Tall Women *(photo by Chris Bennion)*

Dylan DoVale, Ryan Jones, Jaycob Hunter, Jordan Bellow, Rudy Martinez, Emmett Lee Stang, Susannah Schulman, Jennifer Stang, and Patrick Kerr in A Midsummer Night's Dream *at South Coast Repertory (photo by Henry DiRocco)*

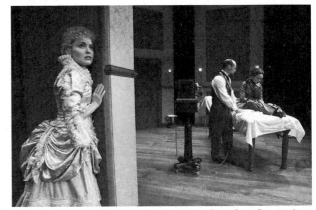

Kathleen Early, Andrew Borba, and Rebecca Mozo in South Coast Repertory's production of In the Next Room or the vibrator play *(photo by Henry DiRocco)*

The Company of Stages St. Louis' production of Big River: The Adventures of Huckleberry Finn *(photo by Whitney Curtis)*

Tracy Letts and Brenda Barrie in Steppenwolf Theatre Company's production of Middletown *(photo by Michael Brosilow)*

Anna O'Donoghue and Jacqueline Baum in The Miracle Worker *at Syracuse* Stage *(photo by Michael Davis)*

Jamie Farmer, Samuel Whited, and David Compton in Tennessee Repertory's production of A Christmas Story *(photo by Harry Butler)*

Peter Vann, Patrick Waller, and Nate Eppler in The 39 Steps *at Tennessee* Repertory *(photo by Harry Butler)*

Stephen Berenson and the Company in the world premiere of The Completely Fictional – Utterly True–Final Strange Tale of Edgar Allan Poe *(photo by Mark Turek)*

Christmas Yet-to-Come), Richard Doyle (Solicitor/Spirit of Christmas Past/ Gentleman), Karen Hensel (Mrs. Fezziwig/Solicitor), John-David Keller (Mr. Fezziwig/Gentleman), Art Koustik (Joe/Ensemble), Timothy Landfield (Spirit of Christmas Present), William Francis McGuire (Fred/Gentleman), Hal Landon Jr. (Ebenezer Scrooge), Puja Mohindra, (Laundress/Belle/Ensemble), Jennifer Parsons (Mrs. Cratchit), Ensemble: Jordan Bellow, Cory Nestor, Kalie Quiñones, Emmett Lee Stang; Children: Allison Baayoun, Kelsey Bray, Lauren Cocroft, Nikki Daurio, Kailyn Leilani Dunkelman, Henry Ficcadenti, Kelsey Kato, Megan Larnerd, Guy McEleney, Emma Smith, Harvey J. Sutton, Tessa Taylor, Erika Tran, Blaze H.K. Whiting, Ethan Williams-Dalgart, Katherine Zofrea; November 27–December 26, 2010

A Midsummer Night's Dream by William Shakespeare; Directed by Mark Rucker; Sets, Cameron Anderson; Costumes, Nephelie Adndonyadis; Lighting, Lap Chi Chu; Original Music, John Ballinger, Ken Roht; Choreography, Ken Roht; Music Director, John Ballinger; Sound, Kimberly Egan; Dramaturg, John Glore; PM, Joshua Marchesi; SM, Jamie A. Tucker; Cast: Elijah Alexander (Oberon/ Theseus), Rob Campbell (Puck/Philostrate), Richard Doyle (Robin Starveling), Kathleen Early (Hermia), Nick Gabriel (Lysander), Dana Green (Helena), John-David Keller (Snug), Patrick Kerr (Nick Bottom), Hal Landon Jr. (Peter Quince), Michael Manuel (Francis Flue), William Francis McGuire (Egeus/Snout), Susannah Schulman (Hippolyta/Titania), Tobie Windham (Demetrius), Fairies: Jordan Bellow, Dylan DoVale, Jaycob Hunter, Ryan Jones, Rudy Martinez, Emmett Lee Stang, Jennifer Stang; January 21–Febaury 20, 2011

Silent Sky by Lauren Gunderson; Director, Anne Justine D'Zmura; Sets, John Iacovelli; Costumes, David Kay Mickelson; Lighting, York Kennedy; Original Music, Lewis Flinn; Projection Design, John Crawford; Dramaturg, John Glore; PM, Joshua Marchesi; SM, Chrissy Church; Cast: Erin Cottrell (Margaret Leavitt), Colette Kilroy (Annie Cannon), Monette Magrath (Henrietta Leavitt), Nick Toren (Peter Shaw), Amelia White (Williamina Fleming); World Premiere; April 1–May 1, 2011

Three Days of Rain by Richard Greenberg; Director, David Emmes; Sets, Tom Buderwitz; Costumes, Holly Poe Durbin; Lighting, Lonnie Rafael Alcaraz; Sound, Cricket Myers; Dramaturg, Kimberly Colburn; PM, Joshua Marchesi; SM, Jamie A. Tucker; Cast: Brendan Hines (Pip/Theo), Kevin Rahm (Walker/Ned), Susannah Schulman (Nan/Lina); May 13–June 12, 2011

Julianne Argyros Stage

In the Next Room or the vibrator play by Sarah Ruhl; Director, Casey Stangl; Sets, John Arnone; Costumes, David Kay Mickelson; Lighting, Daniel Ionazzi; Original Music/Sound, Jim Ragland; Dialect, Philip D. Thompson; Dramaturg, Kimberly Colburn; PM, Jackie S. Hill; SM, Kathryn Davies; Cast: Andrew Borba (Dr. Givings), Kathleen Early (Catherine Givings), Tracey A. Leigh (Elizabeth), Ron Menzel (Leo Irving), Rebecca Mozo (Sabrina Daldry), Tom Shelton (Mr. Daldry), Libby West (Annie); September 26–October 17, 2010

Sideways Stories from Wayside School by Louis Sachar; Adapted for the stage by John Olive; Director, Anne Justine D'Zmura; Sets, Sibyl Wickersheimer; Costumes, Nephelie Andonyadis; Lighting, Thomas Ontiveros; Sound, Kimberly Egan; Dramaturg, Kimberly Colburn; PM, Jackie S. Hill; SM, Kathryn Davies; Cast: Josh Nathan (Myron), Jennifer Chu (Bebe), Greg Watanabe (Dameon), Erika Whalen (Leslie), Amy Tolsky (Rondi), David Vegh (Louis), Larry Bates (Mrs. Gorf/Mr. Pickle/Miss Valooosh/Mr. Gorf/Voices), Jennifer Parsons (Mrs. Jewls); November 5–21, 2011

Circle Mirror Transformation by Annie Baker; Director, Sam Gold; Sets, David Zinn; Costumes, Angela Balough Calin; Lighting, Mark Barton; Sound, Leah Gelpe; Asst. Sound, David Roy; Dramaturg, Kelly Miller; PM, Jackie S. Hill; SM, Jennifer Ellen Butler; Cast: Linda Gehringer (Marty), Arye Gross (Schultz), Marin Hinkle (Theresa), Lily Holleman (Lauren), Brian Kerwin (James); January 9–31, 2011

Lucky Duck by Bill Russell and Jeffrey Hatcher; Music by Henry Krieger; Lyrics by Bill Russell; Director, Art Manke; Sets, Fred Kinney; Costumes, Angela Balogh Calin; Lighting, Jaymi Lee Smith; Sound, Cricket S. Myers; Dramaturg, Kimberly

Colburn; PM, Jackie S. Hill; SM, Jennifer Ellen Butler; Cast: Renee Brna (Mildred Mallard, Wren, Priggy), Gloria Garayua (Millicent Mallard, Verblinka, Chicken Little), Jamey Hood (Serena), Brian Ibsen (Wolf), Nicholas Mongiardo-Cooper (Clem Coyote, Free-Range Chicken) Tom Shelton (King, Cop, Armand Dillo), Jeffrey Christopher Todd (Drake, Carl), Amy Tolsky (Mrs. Mallard, Gossetella, Queen); February 11–27, 2011

The Weir by Conor McPherson; Director, Warner Shook; Sets, Thomas Buderwitz; Costumes, Angela Balogh Cain; Lighting, Peter Maradudin; Sound, Jim Ragland; Dialect, Philip D. Thompson; Dramaturg, Kimberly Colburn; PM, Joshua Marchesi; SM, Jennifer Sherman; Cast: Richard Doyle (Jack), James Lancaster (Finbar), Kirsten Potter (Valerie), Daniel Reichert (Jim), Tony Ward (Brendan); March 13–April 3, 2011

Completeness by Itamar Moses; Director, Pam MacKinnon; Sets, Christopher Barreca; Costumes, Sara Ryung Clement; Lighting, Russell H. Champa; Sound/ Original Music, Bray Poor; Dramaturg, Kelly Miller; PM, Jackie S. Hill; SM, Jennifer Ellen Butler; Cast: Brooke Bloom (Lauren/Katie/Nell), Johnathan McClain (Don/Clark/Franklin), Karl Miller (Elliot), Mandy Siegfried (Mandy); World Premiere; April 17–May 8, 2011

The Emperor's New Clothes by Lynn Ahrens and Stephen Flahery; Director, Nick DeGruccio; Sets, Fred Kinney; Costume, Soojin Lee; Lighting, Tom Ruzika; Sound, Drew Dalzell; Dramaturg, Kelly Miller; PM, Jackie S. Hill; SM, Jennifer Ellen Butler; Cast: Todd Nielson (William), Diana Burbano (Deena), Alex Miller (Marcus), Chad Borden (Swindler), Jeffrey Christopher Todd (Arno); May 20– June 5, 2011

STAGES ST. LOUIS

St. Louis, Missouri

Twenty-Fourth Season

Artistic Director, Michael Hamilton; Executive Producer, Jack Lane; Managing Director, Ron Gibbs

Big River: The Adventures of Huckleberry Music and lyrics by Roger Miller; Book by William Hauptman; Adapted from the novel by Mark Twain; Direction and musical staging by Michael Hamilton; Choreographer, Dana Lewis; Musical Direction, Lisa Campbell Albert; Sets, James Wolk; Costumes, Lou Bird; Lighting, Matthew McCarthy; Orchestral Design, Stuart M. Elmore; PSM, Stacy A. Blackburn; PM, Joseph M. Novak; New York Casting by Gayle Seay and Scott Wojcik, Wojcik/Seay Casting; Cast: Leah Berry (Mary Jane Wilkes/TP), Darrel Blackburn (The King), Justin Bowen (Tom Sawyer), John Flack (Judge/Harvey Wilkes/Silas Phelps/Skiff2) , Kyle P. Gunby (Jo Harper/Ruffian 3/Mover), Lynn Humphrey (Widow Douglas/TP2/Harmonium Player), Kelsie Johnson Betsy, Alice's Daughter), Alexis Kinney (Joanna Wilkes/Becky Thatcher), John Kinney (Dick/Ruffian 2/Mourner/Mover), Andrew Kruep (Simon/Ruffian 1/Mourner/ Mover), Larry Mabrey (Mark Twain/TP/Covict/Doctor), Ben Nordstrom (Ben Rogers/Andy/Young Fool/Mover/Convict), Richard Pruitt (Pap Finn/Hank/Sheriff Bell/Convict), Lisa M. Ramey (Alice), Ken Robinson (Jim), David Schmittou (Duke), Shaun Sheley (Schoolmaster/Bricktown Overseer/Counselor Robinson/ Convict/ Overseer), Adam Shonkwiler (Huckleberry Finn), Katy Tibbets (Susan Wilkes/TP), Zoe Vonder Haar (Miss Watson/Sally Phelps), Darrin Wood (Overseer/Skiff 1/Lafe/Mourner/Grave Digger/Convict), Boris York (Bill/Convict); May 28–June 27, 2010

Promises, Promises Book by Neil Simon, based on the film *The Apartment* by Billy Wilder and I.A.L. Diamond; Music by Burt Bacharach; Lyrics by Hal David; Produced for the Broadway Stage by David Merrick; Direction and musical staging by Michael Hamilton; Choreographer, Dana Lewis; Musical Direction, Lisa Campbell Albert; Sets, Mark Halpin; Costumes, John Inchiostro; Lighting, Matthew McCarthy; Orchestral Design, Stuart M. Elmore; PSM, Stacy A. Blackburn; PM, Joseph M. Novak; New York Casting by Gayle Seay and Scott Wojcik, Wojcik/Seay Casting; Cast: Darrel Blackburn (Jesse Vanderhof), Abbey

Elliott (Miss Kreplinski/Miss Polanski), Kari Ely (Peggy Olson/1st Receptionist), John Flack (Mr. Eichelberger), Michael Halling (J.D. Sheldrake), Ellen Isom (Ginger/2nd Receptionist), Edward Juvier (Dobitch), Tari Kelly (Fran Kubelik), Andrew Laudel (New Young Executive), Patrick Martin (Bartender Eddie/Knicks Fan/ Karl Kubelik), Ben Nordstrom (Chuck Baxter), Richard Pruitt (Dr. Dreyfuss), Lisa M. Ramey (Vivien Della Hoya), Mark Roland (Bartender Eugene/Knicks Fan), David Schmittou (Kirkeby), Sarah Staker (Ms. Ross), April Strelinger (Sylvia Gilhooley/Lum Ding Hostess), Katy Tibbets (Standby for Fran), Maria Tholl (Company Nurse/Helen Sheldrake), Nic Thompson (Waiter), Brandi Wooten (Marge Macdougall), Borris York (Company Doctor); July 16–August 15, 2010

The Aristocats Music and lyrics by Richard M. Sherman and Robert B. Sherman, Al Rinker and Floyd Huddleston, Terry Giklyson; Music adapted, arranged and additional music by Bryan Louiselle; Book adapted and additional lyrics by Michael Bernard; Based on the 1970 Disney film *The Aristocats*; Direction and choreography by Stephen Bourneuf; Musical Direction, Al Fischer; Sets, Mark Halpin; Costumes, John Inchiostro; Lighting, Matthew McCarthy; Orchestral Design, Stuart M. Elmore; PSM, Stacy A. Blackburn; PM, Joseph M. Novak; New York Casting by Gayle Seay and Scott Wojcik, Wojcik/Seay Casting; Cast: Kari Ely (Madame/Abigail), Lisa Christine Fahey (Marie, an Aristocat), Kyle P. Gunby (Toulouse, an Aristocat), Edward Juvier (Roquefort), John Kinney (Berlioz), Ben, Nordstrom (Wacky Cat /LaFayette), Taylor Pietz (Amelia), Pamela Reckamp (Duchess), David Schmittou (Thomas O'Malley), Shaun Sheley (Edgar), Nic Thompson (Hep Cat/Vichy), Borris York (Scat Cat/Napoleon); August 4–August 15, 2010

State Fair Music by Richard Rodgers; Lyrics by Oscar Hammerstein II; Book by Tom Briggs and Louis Mattioli; Based on the screenplay by Oscar Hammerstein II and the novel by Phil Strong; Direction and musical staging by Michael Hamilton; Choreography by Dana Lewis; Musical Direction, Lisa Campbell Albert; Sets, James Wolk; Costumes, Lou Bird; Lighting, Matthew McCarthy; Orchestral Design, Stuart M. Elmore; PSM, Stacy A. Blackburn; PM, Joseph M. Novak; New York Casting by Gayle Seay and Scott Wojcik, Wojcik/Seay Casting; Cast: Stephanie Brown (Barker/Vendor), Lani Corson (Eleanor, Wayne's girlfriend/ Barker/Vendor), Mike Dowdy (Hank Munson/ Judge/Fairgoer), Zak Edwards (Charlie/Uncle Sam/Fairtone), Preston Ellis (Wayne Frake), Kari Ely (Melissa Frake), Laura Ernst (Judge/Fairgoer), Lisa Christine Fahey (Fairgoer), John Flack (Lem/Fairgoer), Julie Hanson (Margy Frake), Hollie Howard (Emily Arden), Abigail Isom (Violet), Colin Israel (Harry), Andrew Laudel (Faritone/ Judge), Jim Newman (Pat Gilbert), Taylor Pietz (Vivian/Midway Dancer/Judge), Lisa M. Ramey (Jeanne/Midway Dancer), Whit Reichert (Dave Miller/Judge Heppenstahl), Mark Roland (Fairtone/Gus/Routabout), Shaun Sheley (The Astounding Stralenko/The Chief of Police), Nic Thompson (Fairtone/Roustabout), Joseph Torello (Clay/Fair Announcer), Christopher Vettel (Abel Frake), Zoe Vonder Haar (Mrs. Edwin Metcalf), Matthew Winnegge (Fairtone/Fairgoer), Darin Wood (The Hoop-la Barker); September 3–October 3, 2010

Steppenwolf Theatre Company

Chicago, Illinois

Thirty-third Season

Artistic Director, Martha Lavey; Executive Director, David Hawkanson

Main Stage

Detroit by Lisa D'Amour; Director/Ensemble, Austin Pendleton; Sets, Kevin Depinet; Costumes, Rachel Healy; Lighting, Kevin Rigdon; Sound, Josh Schmidt; Dramaturg, Polly Carl; Fight Choreography, Matt Hawkins; SM, Michelle Medvin; ASM, Rose Marie Packer; Cast: Kevin Anderson (Kenny), Kate Arrington (Sharon), Ian Barford (Ben), Robert Breuler (Frank), Laurie Metcalf (Mary); Downstairs Theatre; September 9–November 7, 2010

Edward Albee's Who's Afraid of Virginia Woolf? by Edward Albee; Director, Pam MacKinnon; Sets, Todd Rosenthal; Costumes, Nan Cibula-Jenkins;

Lighting, Allen Lee Hughes; Sound, Rob Milburn, Michael Bodeen; SM, Malcolm Ewen; ASM, Deb Styer; Cast: Tracy Letts (George), Amy Morton (Martha), Carrie Coon (Honey), Madison Dirks(Nick); Downstairs Theatre; December 2, 2010–February 13, 2011

Sex with Strangers by Laura Eason; Director/Associate Artist, Jessica Thebus; Sets, Todd Rosenthal; Costumes, Ana Kuzmanic; Lighting, J.R. Lederle; Sound/ Original Music, Andre Pluess, Kevin O'Donnell; Dramaturg, Polly Carl; SM, Christine D. Freeburg; ASM, Kathleen E. Petroziello; Cast: Sally Murphy (Olivia), Stephen Louis Grush (Ethan); Upstairs Theatre; January 20–May 15, 2011

The Hot L Baltimore by Lanford Wilson; Director/Ensemble, Tina Landau; Sets, James Schuette; Costumes, Ana Kuzmanic; Lighting, Scott Zielinski; Sound, Rob Milburn, Michael Bodeen; SM, Deb Styer; ASM, Rosie Marie Packer; Cast: Alana Arenas (Jackie), Kate Arrington (Suzy), Jon Michael Hill (Bill Lewis), James Vincent Meredith (Mr. Katz), Yasen Peyankov (Mr. Morse), Molly Reagan (Millie), de'Adre Aziza (April), Jeremy Glickstein (John/Taxi Driver/ Delivery Boy), Sean Allan Krill (The Man), TaRon Patton (Mrs. Oxenham), Namir Smallwood (Jamie), Samuel Taylor (Paul Granger III), Allison Torem (The Girl) and Jacqueline Williams (Mrs. Bellotti); Downstairs Theatre; March 24– May 29, 2011

Middletown by Will Eno; Director, Les Waters; Sets, Antje Ellermann; Costumes, Janice Pytel; Lighting, Matt Frey; Sound, Richard Woodbury; SM, Laura D. Glenn; ASM, Michelle Medvin; Cast: Alana Arenas (Tour Guide/Sweetheart/Attendant #2/Intercom), Tim Hopper (Public Speaker/Male Tourist/Greg/ Freelancer/Male Doctor/Radio Science Show Host), Ora Jones (Aunt/ Female Doctor/ Classical Music Show Host), Martha Lavey (Librarian), Tracy Letts (John Dodge), Brenda Barrie (Mary Swanson), Molly Glynn (Female Tourist/Woman on Date/Attendant), Keith Kupferer (Man on Date/Landscaper/Janitor/ Ground Control), Danny McCarthy (The Cop) and Michael Patrick Thornton (Mechanic); Downstairs Theatre; June 16–August 14, 2011

Steppenwolf for Young Adults

To Kill a Mockingbird by Harper Lee; Dramatized by Christopher Sergel; Director, Hallie Gordon; Sets, Collette Pollard; Costumes, Myron Elliott; Lighting, J.R. Lederle; Sound, Victoria Delorio; Fight Choreography, Jeffrey Baumgartner; SM, Laura D. Glenn; ASM, Cassie Wolgamott; Cast: Alan Wilder (Mr. Cunningham/ Judge Taylor), Abu Ansari (Tom Robinson), Carolyn Defrin (Jean Louise Finch), James D. Farruggio (Heck Tate), Caroline Heffernan (Scout Finch), Franette Liebow (Miss Maude Atkinson), Zachary Keller (Dill/Walter Jr.), Larry Neumann, Jr. (Bob Ewell), Elaine Roth (Mrs. Dubose), Gary Simmers (Arthur 'Boo' Radley/ Mr. Gilmer), Philip R. Smith (Atticus Finch), Sandra Watson (Calpurnia), Bubba Weiler (Jem), Claire Wellin (Mayella Ewell) and Dexter Zollicoffer (Reverend Sykes); Upstairs Theatre; October 12–November 14, 2010

Samuel J. and K. by Mat Smart; Director, Ron OJ Parson; Sets, Jack Magaw; Costumes, Melissa Torchia; Lighting, J.R. Lederle; Sound, Kevin O'Donnell; Dramaturg, Polly Carl; Fight Choreography, David Chrzanowski; SM, Beth Ellen Spencer; Cast: Cliff Chamberlain (Samuel J.), Samuel G. Roberson, Jr. (Samuel K.); Upstairs Theatre; February 22– March 13, 2011

First Look Repertory of New Work

The Etiquette of Vigilance by Robert O'Hara; Director, Timothy Douglas; Sets, Scott Neale; Costumes, Elizabeth Flauto; Lighting, Marcus Doshi; Sound, Rick Sims; Dramaturg, Rebecca Rugg; SM, Angela M. Adams; Festival Producer, Polly Carl; Program Assistant, Whitney Dibo; Cast: Alana Arenas (Lorraine) with Alfred H. Wilson (Travis); Garage Theatre; October 27–November 14, 2010

The Old Masters by Sam Marks; Director, Daniel Aukin; Sets, Scott Neale; Costumes, Elizabeth Flauto; Lighting, Marcus Doshi; Sound, Rick Sims; Dramaturg, Sarah Slight; SM, Adam Ganderson; Festival Producer, Polly Carl; Program Assistant, Whitney Dibo; Cast: Anne Adams (Lara Yount), Natasha Lowe (Olive Redding) and Jay Whittaker (Ben Schmitt); Garage Theatre; October 28–November 14, 2010

The North Plan by Jason Wells; Director, Kimberly Senior; Sets, Scott Neale; Costumes, Elizabeth Flauto; Lighting, Marcus Doshi; Sound, Rick Sims;

Dramaturg, Joy Meads; SM, Jonathan Nook; Festival Producer, Polly Carl; Program Assistant, Whitney Dibo; Cast, Jennifer Engstrom (Tanya Shepke), Tom Hickey (Dale Pittman), Timothy Edward Kane (Carlton Berg), Brian King (Bob Lee), Tamberla Perry (Shonda Cox) and Will Zahrn (Chief Swenson); Garage Theatre; October 29–November 14, 2010

Syracuse Stage

Syracuse, New York

Thirty-eighth Season

Producing Artistic Director, Timothy Bond; Managing Director, Jeffrey Woodward

No Child... by Nilaja Sun; Directed, Timothy Bond; Lighting, Dave Bowman; Sound, Jonathan R. Herter; Projection Designer, Brenna Merritt; SM, Laura Jane Collins; Cast: Reenah L. Golden; September 21–October 10, 2010

The 39 Steps Adapted by Patrick Barlow, from the novel by John Buchan, from the movie of Alfred Hitchcock; Director, Peter Amster; Sets, Linda Buchanan; Costumes, Tracy Dorman; Lighting, Michael Lincoln; Music/Sound, Victoria Delorio; PSM, Stuart Plymesser; Cast: Joe Foust (Clown 2), Rob Johansen (Clown 1), Sarah Nealis (Annabella Schmidt/Margaret/Pamela), Nick Sandys (Richard Hannay); October 20–November 7, 2010

A Christmas Story Based on the motion picture by Jean Shepherd, Leigh Brown and Bob Clark; Adapted by Philip Grecian; Director, Seth Gordon; Sets, Michael Ganio; Costumes, David Kay Mickelsen; Lighting, Richard Winkler; Sound, Jonathan R. Herter; Cast: Timothy Davis-Reed (Ralph), Nicholas Deapo (Ralphie), Sara Goodwin (Esther Jane), Madison Gregory (Helen), Charles Kartali (Old Man), Hunter Metnick (Randy), Danny Mulvihill (Farkus), Pat Nesbit (Mrs. Shields), Ted Potter (Flick, Ralphie u/s), Tristan Tierney (Shwartz), Elizabeth Ann Townsend (Mother); November 30–December 30, 2010

Rent Music, lyrics and book by Jonathan Larson; Director/Choreographer, Anthony Salatino; Musical Direction, Sarah Pickett; Sets, Troy Hourie; Costumes, Jessica Ford; Lighting, Dawn Chiang; Sound, Jonathan R. Herter; Videography, Daniel Aguilera; PSM, Stuart Plymesser; Cast: Stanley Bahorek (Mark), Jordan Barbour (Tom Collins), Ross Baum (Ensemble), LilyAnn Carlson (Ensemble), Ken Clark (Roger), John Duff (Ensemble), Aisling Halpin (Ensemble), Jené Hernandez (Mimi), Antwayn Hopper (Benny, Ensemble), Mary Claire King (Ensemble), Katie LaMark (Ensemble), Sammy Lopez (Ensemble), Mia Michelle McClain (Ensemble), Matthew Hazen McGuire (Ensemble), Eric Meyers (Ensemble), Marcelo Pereira (Ensemble), Rashidra Scott (Joanne), Jose Sepulveda (Angel), Hannah Shankman (Maureen/Ensemble); January 18–February 13, 2011

Radio Golf by August Wilson; Director, Timothy Bond; Sets, William Bloodgood; Lighting, Thomas C. Hase; Costumes, Susan E. Mickey; Sound, Jonathan R. Herter; PSM, Christine Lomaka; Cast: Richard Brooks (Harmond Wilks), Thomas Jefferson Byrd (Elder Joseph Barlow), Crystal Fox (Mame), LeLand Gantt (Sterling), G. Valmont Thomas (Roosevelt Hicks); February 23–March 13, 2011

The Miracle Worker by William Gibson; Director, Paul Barnes; Sets, Michael Vaughn Sims; Costumes, Tracy Dorman; Lighting, Lonnie Rafael Alcaraz; Sound, Jonathan R. Herter; PSM, Stuart Plymesser; SM, Kerri J. Lynch; Cast: Maxwel Anderson (Servant), Jacqueline Baum (Helen), Brenna Carolan Carlin (Young Woman of the Asylum), Christof Deboni (Jimmie), Lucy DiGenova (Blind Girl), Eric Gilde (James Keller), Malcolm Ingram (Doctor), Anya Johnson (Young Woman of the Asylum), Emma Mae Karp (Blind Girl), Aliyah A. Kilpatrick (Martha), Hadiya Asha Lee (Blind Girl), Lanya Liebler-Bendix (Blind Girl), Nia Lloyd (Blind Girl), Madison Lynch (Blind Girl/Helen u/s), Craig MacDonald (Anagnos), Celia Madeoy (Aunt Ev), Jenaha McLearn (Blind Girl/ Young Woman of the Asylum), Shauna Miles (Viney), Anna O'Donoghue (Annie Sullivan), Tess Polachek (Young Woman of the Asylum), James Lloyd Reynolds (Keller), Regan Thompson (Kate Keller), Hannah Travis (Blind Girl), Jamaal Wade (Percy); Canine: Sonar Findling (Belle); February 23–March 13, 2011

The Clean House by Sarah Ruhl; Director, Michael Barakiva; Sets, John Iacovelli; Costumes, Oana Botez-Ban; Lighting, Thomas C. Hase; Music/Sound, Ryan Rumery; Projections, Kate Freer and David Tennent; PSM, Stuart Plymesser; Cast: David Adkins (Charles), Gisela Chipe (Matilde), Alma Cuervo (Ana), Carol Halstead (Lane), Linda Marie Larson (Virginia); May 4–22, 2011

Tennessee Repertory Theatre

Nashville Tennessee

Twenty-sixth Season

Producing Artistic Director, René D. Copeland

To Kill a Mockingbird Adapted by Christopher Sergel from the novel by Harper Lee; Director, René D. Copeland; Sets, Gary C. Hoff; Costumes, Trish Clark; Lighting, Phillip Franck; Sound/Composition, Paul Carrol Binkley, Technical Director, Tyler Axt, SM, David Wilkerson; Cast: Chip Arnold (Atticus Finch), Matthew Carlton (Nathan Radley/Judge Taylor),David Compton (Bob Ewell), Christopher Dean (Jem Finch), Isaiah Frank (Dill), Margaux Granath (Scout Finch), Denice Hicks (Miss Maudie/Mrs. Dubose/Miss Stephanie), Bakari King (Tom Robinson), Mary McCallum (Helen Robinson), Marin Miller (Mayella Ewell), Shelean Newman (Jean Louise Finch), Rodrikus Springfield (Reverend Sykes), Jennifer Whitcomb-Oliva (Calpurnia), Samuel Whited (Heck Tate/Walter Cunningham), Bobby Wyckoff (Boo/Mr. Gilmer); October 2–30, 2010

A Christmas Story Adapted by Phillip Grecian based on the motion picture by Jean Shepherd, Leigh Brown and Bob Clark; Director, Lauren Shouse; Sets, Gary C. Hoff; Costumes, Trish Clark; Lighting, Michael Barnett; SM, Cecelia Lighthall; Cast: Shane Bridges (Scut Farkas/Ensemble), David Compton (The Old Man/Ensemble), Jamie Farmer (Mother/Ensemble), Andrew Kanies (Randy/Ensemble), Eric D. Pasto-Crosby (Schwartz/Ensemble), Samuel Whited (Ralph/Ralphie), David Wilkerson (Flick/Ensemble); November 20–December 18, 2010

Yankee Tavern by Steven Dietz; Director, René D. Copeland; Sets, Gary C. Hoff; Costumes, Trish Clark; Lighting, Michael Barnett; Sound, Paul Carrol Binkley; Technical Director, Tyler Axt, SM, David Wilkerson; Cast: Henry Haggard (Ray), Cori Laemmel (Janet), Maurice Ralston (Palmer), Patrick Waller (Adam); February 5–19, 2011

The 39 Steps Adapted by Patrick Barlow from the film of Alfred Hitchcock based on the novel by John Buchan, René D. Copeland; Sets, Gary C. Hoff; Costumes, Trish Clark; Lighting, Michael Barnett; Sound, Paul Carrol Binkley; Technical Director, Tyler Axt; SM, David Wilkerson; Cast: Nate Eppler (Richard Hannay), Peter Vann (Clown 1), Patrick Waller (Clown 2), Martha Wilkinson (Annabella Schmidt/Pamela/Margaret); March 19–April 2, 2011

Pump Boys and Dinettes Created by John Foley, Mark Hardwick, Debra Monk, Cass Morgan, John Schimmel, Jim Wann; Co-directors, René D. Copeland, Pam Atha; Sets, Gary C. Hoff; Costumes, Trish Clark; Lighting, Phillip Franck; Musical Direction, Paul Carrol Binkley; Choreography, Pam Atha; Technical Director, Tyler Axt; SM, David Wilkerson; Cast: Brad Albin (Eddie), Jeff Boyet (Jim), Brooke Bryant (Prudie), Taylor Jones (Jackson), Martha Wilkinson (Rhetta), Jeffrey Williams (L.M.); April 23–May 14, 2011

Trinity Repertory Company

Providence, Rhode Island

Forty-seventh Season

Artistic Director, Curt Columbus; Executive Director, Michael Gennaro; Production Director, Laura E. Smith; Associate Production Director, Mark Turek; General Manager, Pamela Adams; Director of Marketing and Public Relations, Marilyn Busch

The Chace Theater

Camelot Book and lyrics by Alan Jay Lerner; Music by Frederick Lowe; Director, Curt Columbus; Musical Direction/Additional Arrangements, Michael Rice; Choreographer, Sharon Jenkins; Sets, Eugene Lee; Lighting, Michael Gottlieb; Costumes, William Lane; Sound, Peter Sasha Hurowitz; Props, S. Michael Getz; PSM, Melissa Rae Miller; Cast: Janice Duclose (Morgan Le Frey/Ensemble), Mauro Hantman (Merlyn/Ensemble), Barbara Meek (Pellinore), Stephen Thorne (Arthur), Joe Wilson Jr. (Lancelot), Rebecca Gibel (Guenevere), Christopher Berry (Sir Dinadan/ Ensemble), Jaelyn Blanchard (Nimue/ Ensemble), Vichet Chum (Sir Lionel/ Ensemble), Charlotte Graham (Lady Anne/ Ensemble), Jamey Grisham (Mordred); September 10–October 10, 2011

A Christmas Carol by Charles Dickens; Adapted by Adrian Hall and Richard Cumming; Director, Michael Perlman; Musical Director, Michael Rice; Sets, Michael McGarty; Lighting, Dan Scully; Costumes, William Lane; Sound, Peter Sasha Hurowitz; Choreographer, Jude Sandy; Props, S. Michael Getz; PSM, Robin Grady; Cast: Mauro Hantman (Ebenezer Scrooge), Janice Duclos (Mrs. Partlet /Mrs. Fezziwig), Rachael Warren (Ghost of Christmas Past), Joe Wilson Jr. (Ghost of Christmas Present 2), Matt Clevy (Marley), Richard Donnelly (Fezziwig/ Topper/Old Joe), Rebecca Gibel (Lucy), Jude Sandy (Ghost of Christmas Present 1), Monica Willey (Fan), Richard Williams (Cratchit), Brandon Drea (Fred), Madeleine Lambert (Belle), Zarina Shea (Mrs. Cratchit), Liam Clancy (Turkey Boy/Young Scrooge), Emeline Herreid (Belinda/Young Belle), Jonah King (Tiny Tim), Julianna McGuirl (Belinda/Young Belle), Peter Medici (Tiny Tim), Kateryne Nelson-Guerrero (Martha/Young Fan), Elliott Peters (Turkey Boy/Young Scrooge), Nigel Richards (Young Marley/Peter), Brian Roque (Young Marley/Peter), Abby Spare (Martha/Young Fan); November 19–December 31, 2010

The Crucible by Arthur Miller; Director, Brian McEleney; Set/Lighting, Eugene Lee; Costumes, William Lane; Sound, Peter Sasha Hurowitz; PSM, Robin Grady; Cast: Angela Brazil (Susannah Walcott/ Elizabeth Proctor), Mauro Hantman (Reverend John Hale), Barbara Meek (Tituba/ Rebecca Nurse/ Judge Hathorne), Anne Scurria (Ann Putnam/Francis Nurse/ Martha Corey), Fred Sullivan Jr. (Thomas Putnam/ Deputy Governor Danforth), Stephen Thorne (John Proctor), Rachel Warren (Mary Warren), Bob Berky (Reverend Samuel Paris), Olivia D'Ambrosio (Abigal Williams/ John Herrick), Terrell Donnell Sledge (Mercy Lewis/ Giles Corey), John Tracey (Betty Parris/ Ezekiel Cheever); February 4–March 13, 2011

Steel Magnolias by Robert Harling; Director, Brian Mertes; Sets, Michael McGarty; Lighting, Dan Scully; Costumes, William Lane; Sound, Broken Chord; PSM, Lisa McGinn; Cast: Janice Duclos (M'Lynn), Barbara Meek (Clairee), Anne Scurria (Ousier), Rachel Warren (Truvy), Alexandra Lawrence (Annelle), Madeleine Lambert (Shelby); April 15–May 15, 2011

The Dowling Theater

Absurd Person Singular by Alan Aykborn; Director, Brian McEleney; Sets, Michael McGarty; Lighting, John Ambrosone; Costumes, William Lane; Sound, Peter Sasha Hurowitz; PSM, Buzz Cohen; Cast: Angela Brazil (Jane), Stephen Berenson (Sidney), Timothy Crowe (Ronald), Anne Scurria (Marion), Phyllis Kay (Eva), Fred Sullivan Jr. (Geoffrey); October 5–November 21, 2010

It's A Wonderful Life: A Live Radio Play by Joe Landry; Co-directors, Curt Columbus, Tyler Dobrowsky; Sets; Michael McGarty; Lighting, John Amrosone; Costumes, Alison Walker Carrier; Sound, Peter Sasha Hurowitz; PSM, Kristin Gibbs; Cast: Stephen Berenson (Clarence the Angel/Others), Angela Brazil (Mary Hatch/Others), Timothy Crowe (Old Man Potter/Others), Anne Scurria (Violet Bick/Others), Fred Sullivan Jr. (George Baily/Others); December 2, 2010–January 2, 2011

Yellowman by Dael Orlandersmith; Director, Laurie Carlos; Sets, Seitu Jones; Lighting, Michael Wangen; Costumes, William Lane; Sound, Peter Sasha Hurowitz; PSM, Elizabeth Moloney; Cast:), Joe Wilson Jr. (Eugene), Rachel Christopher (Alma); February 25–April 3, 2010

The Completely Fictional- Utterly True- Final Strange Tale of Edgar Allen Poe by Stephen Thorne; Director, Curt Columbus; Sets, Susan Zeeman Rogers; Lighting, Keith Parham; Costumes, William Lane; Sound, Peter Sasha Hurowitz; Props, S. Michael Getz; PSM, Melissa Rae Miller; Cast: Brian McEleney (Poe), Stephen Berenson (The Kindly Doctor), Angela Brazil (Nurse Roget/Mlle. Valdemar/Others), Mauro Hantman (Doctor John Moran/ Frazzled Doctor/ Others), Phyllis Kay (Nurse Price/Osgood/Widow/VanKirk/Eliza/Others), Fred Sullivan Jr. (Charles Dickens), Joe Wilson Jr. (Griswold/Religious Doctor/John Allan/Others), Lauren Lubow (Nurse Pym/Lynch/Virginia/Others), Charlie Thurston (Edgar/VanKirk/Others); May 6–June 10, 2011

Virginia Stage Company

Norfolk, Virginia

Thirty-second Season

Artistic Director, Chris Hanna; Managing Director, Keith Stava

The Diary of Anne Frank by Frances Goodrich and Albert Hackett; Adapted by Wendy Kesselman; Director, Chris Hanna; Sets, Dick Block; Costumes, Jeni Schaefer; Lighting, A. Nelson Ruger IV; Sound, Kim Fuhr; Casting Director, Harriet Bass; PSM, Matthew G. Marholin; Cast: Amelia Pedlow (Anne Frank), Robert Dorfman (Otto Frank), Lori Wilner (Edith Frank), Zoe Winters (Margot Frank), Amber Wood (Miep Gies), Patrick Martlette (Peter van Daan), Ron Newman (Mr. Kraler), Anne-Marie Cussoon (Mrs. Van Daan), Kenny Morris (Mr. Van Daan), John Seidman (Mr. Dussel); September 21–October 10, 2010

The New Pink by Chris Hanna; Director, Chris Hanna; Sets, Samuel W. Flint; Costumes, Jeni Schaefer; Lighting, Traci Klainer; Casting Director, Harriet Bass; PSM, Matthew G. Marholin; Cast: Tandy Cronyn (Gail), Jack Davidson (Roy), Rob Wilson (Gary); October 26–November 14, 2010

A Christmas Carol by Charles Dickens; Adapted by Virginia Stage Company; Director, Patrick Mullins; Sets/Lighting, A. Nelson Ruger IV; Costumes, Jeni Shacfer; Sound, Sharath Patel; Musical Director, Barton Kuebler; PSM, Matthew G. Marholin; Cast: Matthew Cabbil (Fred), Kevin R. Free (Ghost of Christmas Past), Shelby Mason (Ensemble), Peter Moore (Scrooge), Andy Paterson (Bob Cratchit), Jay Reese (Young Scrooge, Peter Cratchit), Valerie Sanchez (Modern Child), Tina Stafford (Mrs. Cratchit), Chris Van Cleave (Jacob Marley), Cayley Waldo (Belle), Evette Marie White (Ghost of Christmas Past), Jack Whitelaw (Tiny Tim), Alba Woolard (Ensemble); December 3– December 24, 2010

SCKBSTD–A New Musical from Bruce Hornsby Music and lyrics by Bruce Hornsby; Lyrics by Chip deMatteo; Book by Clay McLeod Chapman; Director, John Rando; Sets, Narelle Sissons; Costumes, Jennifer Caprio; Lighting, Robert Wierzel; Sound, Jessica Paz; Projection Designer, Darrel Maloney; Music Director, Jodie Moore; PSM, Matthew G. Marholin; Casting, Jim Carnahan, CSA, Kate Boka; Music Supervisor, Kimberly Grigsbby; Choreographer, Scott Wise; Cast: Charles Franklin (Timothy Reynolds), Robert Cuccioli (Norman Rhodes), Kevin Mambo (Sheriff Delbert Rogers), William Parry (William), Riley Costello (Chip/ The Paperboy), Jayne Paterson (Sally Rogers), Rosa Curry (Jenny), Garrett Long (Wendy/Susan), Jill Paice (Afton Reynolds), Marcus Lovett (Jim Reynolds), Kenneth Cavett (Postman), Karl Warden (UPS Man), Eugene Barry-Hill (FedEx Man), Brynn Williams (Jill Rogers); January 18–February 6, 2011

The Last Five Years Written and composed by Jason Robert Brown; Director, Patrick Mullins; Sets, Terry Summers Flint; Costumes, Kelly Kasper; Lighting, Traci Klainer Polimeni; Sound, Danny Erdberg; Musical Director, Barton Kuebler; Casting, Harriet Bass; PSM, Matthew G. Marholin; Cast: Summer Broyhill (Cathy Hiatt); Colin Isreal (Jame Wllerstein); Band: Barton Kuebler (Conductor/ Keyboards), Allegra Havens (Violin), Leslie Fritelli, Dionne Wright (Cello), Eldon Sully (Guitar), Wes Smith (Bass); February 22–March 13, 2011

Radio Golf by August Wilson; Director, Derrick Sanders; Sets, Tony Cisek; Costumes, Jeni Schaefer; Lighting, Thom Weaver; Sound, Elisheba Ittoop; PSM, Matthew G. Marholin; Cast: Morocca Omari (Harmond Wilks), Tracey N. Bonner

(Mame Wilks), E. Roger Mitchell (Roosevelt Hicks), Cedric Young (Sterling Johnson), Ellis Foster (Elder Joseph Barlow); March 29–April 17, 2011

Westport Country Playhouse

Westport, Connecticut

Eightieth Season

Artistic Director, Mark Lamos; Managing Director, Michael Ross

Dinner with Friends by Donald Margulies; Director, David Kennedy; Sets, Lee Savage; Costumes, Emily Rebholz; Lighting, Matthew Richards; Sound, Fitz Patton; Fight Director, Mark Silence; PSM, Bonnie Brady; Cast: Mary Bacon (Beth), David Aaron Baker (Tom), Steven Skybell (Gabe), Jenna Stern (Karen); June 1–19, 2010

Happy Days by Samuel Beckett; Director, Mark Lamos; Sets/Costumes, John Arnone; Lighting, Stephen Strawbridge; Sound, Stephen Strawbridge; Dialect, Stephen Gabis; PSM, Matthew Melchiorre; Cast: Dana Ivey (Winnie), Jack Wetherall (Willie); July 6– 24, 2010

I Do! I Do! Book and lyrics by Tom Jones, Music by Harvey Schmidt; Director, Susan H. Schulman; Choreographer, Michael Lichtefeld; Musical Director, Joel Fram; Sets, Wilson Chin; Costumes, Devon Painter; Lighting, Philip Rosenberg; Sound, Domonic Sack; PSM, Melanie T. Morgan; Cast: Kate Baldwin (Agnes), Lewis Cleale (Michael); August 10–28, 2010

The Diary of Anne Frank by Frances Goodrich and Albert Hackett; Adapted by Wendy Kesselman; Director, Gerald Freedman; Sets, John Ezell; Costumes, Willa Kim; Lighting, Travis McHale; Sound, Rusty Wandall; PSM, Matthew Melchiorre; Cast: Ari Brand (Peter Van Daan), Lauren Culpepper (Margot Frank), Molly Ephraim (Anne Frank), Mitch Greenberg (Otto Frank), Felicity Jones (Edith Frank), Lou Liberatore (Mr. Dussel), Mimi Lieber (Mrs. Van Daan), Allen McCullough (Mr. Kraler), Steve Vinovich (Mr. Van Daan), Monica West (Miep), Philip M. Gardiner, Jack Kesy, Nicholas Wilder (Men); September 28–October 30, 2010

Beyond Therapy by Christopher Durang; Director, David Kennedy; Sets, Lee Savage; Costumes, Jennifer Caprio; Lighting, Jeff Croiter; Sound, John Gromada; PSM, Matthew Melchiorre; Cast: Trent Dawson (Stuart), Nick Gehlfuss (Andrew), Jeremy Peter Johnson (Bruce), Nicole Lowrance (Prudence), Kathleen McNenny (Charlotte), Stephen Wallem (Bob); April 26–May 14, 2011

Woolly Mammoth Theatre Company

Washington, DC

Thirtieth Season

Artistic Director Howard Shalwitz, Managing Director Jeffrey Herrmann

One Man Lord of the Rings Written and performed by Charles Ross; Director, TJ Dawe; PSM Christine Fisichella; July 5–August 1, 2010

Gruesome Playground Injuries by Rajiv Joseph; Director, John Vreeke; Sets, Misha Kachman; Costumes, Franklin Labovitz; Lighting, Colin K. Bills; Sound, Christopher Baine; Dramaturg, Miriam Weisfeld; Cast: Gabriela Fernandez-Coffey (Kayleen), Tim Getman (Doug); May 17–June 19, 2010

Thirty-first Season

In the Next Room or the vibrator play by Sarah Ruhl; Director, Aaron Posner; Sets, Daniel Conway; Lighting, Colin K. Bills; Costumes, Helen Huang; Composer, James Sugg; PSM, Taryn Friend; Dramaturg, Kristin Leahey; Cast: Katie deBuys (Mrs. Givings), Jessica Frances Dukes (Elizabeth), Kimberly Gilbert (Mrs. Daldry), Eric Hissom (Dr. Givings), James Konicek (Mr. Daldry), Sarah Marshall (Annie), Cody Nickell (Leo Irving); August 23–October 3, 2010

House of Gold by Gregory S. Moss; Director, Sarah Benson; Sets/Costumes, David Zin; Lighting, Colin K. Bills; Sound, Matt Tierney; Projection, Aaron Fisher; Cast: Randy Blair (Jasper), Kaaron Briscoe (The Girl), James Flanagan (Joseph M Lonely Jr), William Hayes (Apollonian Boy 2), Mitchell Hébert (Detective), Ben Kingsland (Apollonian Boy 3), Andrew M. Lincoln (Apollonian Boy 1), Michael Russotto (Man); November 1–28, 2010

A Girl's Guide to Washington Politics Written and Performed by Chicago's The Second City; Director, Bill Bungeroth; PSM, Shawn Pace; Musical Director, Diana Lawrence; Lighting, Andrew F. Griffin; Sets, Klyph Stanford; Ensemble: Joey Bland, Brooke Breit, Lili-Anne Brown, Lori Mcclain, Rebecca Sohn; December 8, 2010 – January 9, 2011

Oedipus el Rey by Luis Alfaro; Director, Michael John Garcés; Sets, Misha Kachman; Lighting, Colin K. Bills; Music/Sound, Ryan Rumery; PSM, Lindsay Pryor; Fight Choreographer, Lorraine Ressegger; Dramaturg, John M. Baker; Cast: Mando Alvarado (Coro), David Anzuelo (Laius), Jaime Robert Carrillo (Coro), Romi Dias (Jocasta), Gerard Ender (Tiresias), Andres Munar (Oedipus), Jose Joaquin Perez (Creon); February 7–March 6, 2011

The Agony and the Ecstasy of Steve Jobs Created and performed by Mike Daisey; Director, Jean-Michele Gregory; Sets/Lighting, Seth Reiser; PSM, Jason R. Caballero; Dramaturg, Miriam Weisfeld; March 21–April 17, 2011

Too Much Light Makes the Baby Go Blind Created by Greg Allen; Written, directed and performed by The Neo-Futurists; Ensemble: Greg Allen, Bilal Dardai, Megan Mercier, John Pierson, Caitlin Stainken; April 20–May 1, 2011

Bootycandy by Robert O'Hara; Director, Robert O'Hara; Sets, Tom Kamm; Lighting, Colin K. Bills; Costumes, Kate Turner-Walker; Sound, Lindsay Jones; PSM, William E. Cruttenden III; Dramaturg, Miriam Weisfeld; Ensemble: Phillip James Brannon, Jessica Frances Dukes, Sean Meehan, Laiona Michelle, Lance Coadie Williams; May 30–July 3, 2011

Yale Repertory Theatre

New Haven, Connecticut

Forty-Fifth Season

Artistic Director, James Bundy; Managing Director, Victoria Nolan; Associate Artistic Director, Jennifer Kiger

We Have Always Lived in the Castle Book and lyrics by Adam Bock; Music and lyrics by Todd Almond; Based on the novel by Shirley Jackson; Director, Anne Kauffman; Music Director, Dan Lipton; Musical Staging, Seán Curran; Sets, David Zinn; Costumes, Ilona Somogyi; Lighting, Stephen Strawbridge; Sound, Tony Smolenski IV; Orchestrations, Todd Almond, Dan Lipton; Dramaturg, Amy Boratko; Casting Directors; Tara Rubin, Laura Schutzel; SM, James Mountcastle; Cast: Alexandra Socha (Mary Katherine [Merricat] Blackwood), Jenn Gambatese (Constance Blackwood), Bill Buell (Julian Blackwood), Sean Palmer (Charles Blackwood), Heather Ayers (Maggie Donell), Joy Franz (Mrs. Prudhomme, Lucille Wright, Ellen Blackwood), William Parry (Mr. Elbert, John Blackwood), Carly Hughes (Stella Suggs), Richard Todd Adams (Jim Donell), Matt Pearson (Joe Durham), Beth McVey (Mrs. Taggert, Helen Clarke, Dorothy Blackwood), Ryan Murphy (Joe Jr., Thomas Blackwood); University Theatre; World Premiere; September 17–October 9, 2010

A Delicate Balance by Edward Albee; Director, James Bundy; Sets, Chien-Yu Peng; Costumes, Aaron P. Mastin; Lighting, Alan C. Edwards; Sound/Composer, Sarah Pickett; Dramaturg, Catharine M. Kollros; Casting Directors, Tara Rubin, Laura Schutzel; SM, Lindsey Turteltaub; Cast: Kathleen Chalfant (Agnes), Edward Herrmann (Tobias), Ellen McLaughlin (Claire), Kathleen Butler (Edna), John Carter (Harry), Keira Naughton (Julia); Yale Repertory Theatre; October 22–November 13, 2010

Bossa Nova by Kirsten Greenidge; Director, Evan Yionoulis; Sets, Ana M. Milosevic; Costumes, Summer Lee Jack; Lighting, Laura J. Eckelman; Sound, Michael Vincent Skinner; Dialect, Jane Guyer; Casting Directors, Tara Rubin, Laura Schutzel; SM, Lee Micklin; Cast: Ella Joyce (Lady Paradis), Francesca Choy-Kee (Dee Paradis), Libby Woodbridge (Grace Mahoney), Tommy Schrider (Micheal Cabot); Malenky Welsh (Jane Paradis), Emily Dorsch (Joan Cabot); World Premiere; Yale Repertory Theatre; November 26–December 18, 2010

The Piano Lesson by August Wilson; Director, Liesl Tommy; Sets, Dede M. Ayite; Costumes, Jennifer Salim; Lighting, Alan C. Edwards; Sound, Junghoon Pi; Dramaturg, Cheng-Han Wu; Vocal/Dialect Coach, Beth McGuire; Casting Directors, Tara Rubin, Laura Schutzel; Music Director, Eisa Davis; Fight Director, Rick Sordelet; SM, Allison Hall Johnson; Cast: LeRoy McClain (Boy Willie), Keith Randolph Smith (Doaker), Charles Hudson, III (Lymon), Eisa Davis (Berniece), Malenky Welsh (Maretha), Tyrone Mitchell Henderson (Avery), Charles Weldon (Wining Boy), Joniece Abbott-Pratt (Grace); Yale Repertory Theatre; January 28–February 19, 2011

Romeo and Juliet by William Shakespeare; Director, Shana Cooper; Composer, Gina Leishman; Choreographer, Seán Curran; Sets, Po-Lin Li; Costumes, Leon Dobkowski; Laura J. Eckelman; Sound, Jennifer Lynn Jackson; Dramaturg, Kee-Yoon Nahm; Fight Director, Rick Sordelet; Vocal Coach, Grace Zandarski; Casting Directors, Tara Rubin, Laura Schutzel; SM, Kirsten Parker; Cast: Brian Robert Burns (Gregory/Ensemble), Catherine Castellanos (Lady Montague/Ensemble), William DeMeritt (David/Friar John), John Patrick Doherty (Mercutio), Marcus Henderson (Tybalt), Chris Henry (Benvolio), Irene Sofia Lucio (Juliet), Cynthia Mace (Nurse), Graeme Malcolm (Prince), Christopher McHale (Montague), Seamus Mulcahy (Peter), Andy Murray (Capulet), Fisher Neal (Abram, Ensemble), Joseph Parks (Romeo), Christina Rouner (Lady Capulet), Blake Segal (Balthasar/Ensemble), Alice Shih (Ensemble), Gabriel Sloyer (Sampson/Ensemble), Sarah Sokolovic (Rosaline/Ensemble), Henry Stram (Frian Laurence), Kathryn Zukaitis (Ensemble); University Theatre; March 11–April 2, 2011

Autumn Sonata by Ingmar Bergman; Director, Robert Woodruff; Literal Translation, Wendy Weckwerth; Music Director, Michaël Attias; Sets, Riccardo Hernandez; Costumes, Candice Donnelly; Lighting, Jennifer Tipton; Sound, Chad Raines; Dramaturg, Amy Boratko, Hannah Rae Montgomery; Vocal Coach, Walton Wilson; Casting Directors, Tara Rubin, Laura Schutzel; SM, Lindsey Turteltaub. Cast: Olek Krupa (Viktor), Rebecca Henderson (Eva), Candy Buckley (Charlotte), Merritt Janson (Helena), Paul Brantley (Leonardo); Yale Repertory Theatre; U.S. Premiere; April 15–May 7, 2011

Special Events

Noboundaries A Series of Global Performances Presented by World Performance Project at Yale and Yale Repertory Theatre

The Case of the Spectator Created and Performed by María Jerez; Iseman Theater; American Premiere; September 23–25, 2010

The Method Gun Created by Rude Mechs; Written by Kirk Lynn; Director, Shawn Sides; Yale Repertory Theatre; February 23–26, 2011

Nameless forest Conceived and directed by Dean Moss in collaboration with Sungmyung Chun; Co-produced by Gametophyte, Inc. and MAPP International Productions; Special Preview Engagment; Iseman Theater; March 31–April 2, 2011

Charles Franklin and Robert Cuccioli in SCKBSTD–A New Musical from Bruce Hornsby *at Virginia Stage Company (photo by David Polston)*

Kate Baldwin and Lewis Cleale in I Do! I Do! *at Westport Country Playhouse (photo by T. Charles Erickson)*

Lori McClain, Joey Bland, Brooke Breit, Lili-Anne Brown, and Rebecca Sohn in A Girl's Guide to Washington Politics *at Woolly Mammoth Theatre Company (photo by Stan Barouh)*

The Company of The Piano Lesson *at Yale Repertory Theatre (photo by Joan Marcus)*

Alexandra Socha in We Have Always Lived in the Castle *at Yale Repertory Theatre (photo by Joan Marcus)*

THEATRICAL AWARDS

2010–2011

Top: John Lloyd Young performs the opening number at the Theatre World Awards (photo by Michael and Laura Viade)

Center: Patina Miller and Jonathan Groff at the Theatre World Awards (photo by Michael Ileeney)

Bottom: Zoe Caldwell (front) with the cast of The Motherf**ker with the Hat: Bobby Cannavale, Annabella Sciorra Elizabeth Rodriguez, Chris Rock, and Yul Vázquez (photo by Bruce Glikas)

Ellen Barkin of The Normal Heart

Desmin Borges of The Elaborate Entrance of Chad Deity

Halley Feiffer of The House of Blue Leaves

Grace Gummer of Arcadia

Rose Hemingway of How to Succeed in Business Without Really Trying

John Larroquette of How to Succeed in Business Without Really Trying

Heather Lind of The Merchant of Venice

Patina Miller of Sister Act

Arian Moayed of Bengal Tiger at the Baghdad Zoo

Jim Parsons of The Normal Heart

Zachary Quinto of Angels in America: A Gay Fantasia on National Themes

Tony Sheldon of Priscilla Queen of the Desert

Dorothy Loudon Award

Seth Numrich of War Horse

Lunt-Fontanne Award for Ensemble Excellence

The Cast of The Motherf**ker with the Hat

Bobby Cannavale

Chris Rock

Elizabeth Rodriguez

Annabella Sciorra

Yul Vázquez

67th Annual Theatre World Awards

Tuesday, June 7, 2011 at the August Wilson Theatre

Originally dubbed *Promising Personalities* in 1944 by co-founders Daniel Blum, Norman MacDonald, and John Willis to coincide with the first release of *Theatre World*, the definitive pictorial and statistical record of the American theatre, the Theatre World Awards, as they are now known, are the oldest awards given for debut performances in New York City, as well as one of the oldest honors bestowed on New York actors.

Administered by the Theatre World Awards Board of Directors, a committee of current New York drama critics chooses six actors and six actresses for the Theatre World Award who have distinguished themselves in Broadway and Off-Broadway productions during the past theatre season. Occasionally, Special Theatre World Awards are also bestowed on performers, casts, or others who have made a particularly lasting impression on the New York theatre scene.

The Dorothy Loudon Foundation in conjunction Theatre World Awards presented the third annual Dorothy Loudon Award (formerly known as the *Starbaby Award*) at the ceremony. Dorothy Loudon, a former Theatre World Award winner and repeated presenter at past ceremonies, was an ardent supporter of the Theatre World Awards and a dear friend to John Willis. The Dorothy Loudon Award for Excellence in the Theatre is presented to a performer who made an auspicious Broadway or Off-Broadway performance in the season.

This year the Lunt-Fontanne Award for Ensemble Excellence was introduced and will be presented as deemed worthy by the Theatre World Awards to an outstanding Broadway or Off-Broadway ensemble. This award is sponsored by Aaron Frankel in devoted honor of Alfred Lunt and Lynn Fontanne.

The Awards ceremony also included a loving video memorial and tribute to John Willis, the "father" of the Theatre World Awards and longtime editor of this publication, who passed away June 25, 2010.

The Theatre World Award is designed by Wade F. Dansby 3 in the spirit of the previous Theatre World Janus statuette, created by internationally recognized artist Harry Marinsky, keeping the Janus tradition with an etching of the original sculpture adapted from the Roman myth of Janus. Janus was the God of Entrances, Exits and All Beginnings - with one face appraising the past and the other anticipating the future.

The Theatre World Award winners are selected by a committee of New York drama critics: David Cote (*Time Out New York* and NY1's *On Stage*), Joe Dziemianowicz (*New York Daily News*), Peter Filichia (*Star-Ledger* and *TheaterMania.com*), Harry Haun (*Playbill*), Matthew Murray (*TalkinBroadway.com*), Frank Scheck (*New York Post* and *The Hollywood Reporter*), and Linda Winer (*Newsday*). The Theatre World Awards Board of Directors is: Barry Keating (President), Erin Oestreich (Vice President), Cara Lustik (Secretary), Jon Lonoff (Treasurer), Mary K. Botosan, Vern T. Calhoun, Dorothy W. Kopelman, Tom Lynch, Kati Meister, Sal Scarmardo, Jane Stuart. Board Emeritus: Thom Christopher, Marianne Tatum, Jamie deRoy, Ben Hodges, Walter Willison, Doug Holmes, Patricia Elliott, Leigh Giroux, Scott Denny; Advisors: Jason Cicci, Christopher Cohen, Randall J. Hemming, Gordon Kelly, Michael Messina, Barry Monush, Matthew Murray, Flora Stamatiades.

THE CEREMONY Writer and Host, Peter Filichia; Producers, Mary K. Botosan & Erin Oestreich; Executive Producer, Kati Meister; Director, Barry Keating; Music Director/Accompanist, Henry Aronson; Associate Director, Jeremy Quinn; Production Stage Manager, Kimothy Cruse; Stage Manager, Alden Fulcomer; Stephen Wilde; Press Agent, Jim Baldassare; General Manager, Jon Lonoff; Lighting Consultant, Wendy Luedtke; Photographers, Bruce Glikas, Konrad Brattke, Michael Viade, Michael Heeney; Video Photographer, Bradshaw Smith; Presented on the set of the *Jersey Boys*, scenic design by Klara Zieglerova, lighting design by Howell Binkley, sound design by Steve Canyon Kennedy

THEATRE WORLD AWARDS STAFF AND CREW Assistant Stage Managers, Stephen Ferri, Christina Lowe, Michael Mele; Assistant Director, Steve Edlund; Graphic Artist/Program Design, Dorothy W. Kopelman; Cover Art/Poster, Justin

"Squigs" Robertson; Guest Coordinator, Lon Lonoff; Volunteer Coordinators, Jane Stuart, Stephen Wilde; Alumni Liaison, Brenda Smiley; Video Editor, Jon Simon; Hair/Makeup, Brian Mann Nance

JUJAMCYN THEATRES Jordan Roth (President), Paul Libin (Executive Vice President), Jack Viertel (Senior Vice President), Meredith Villatore (Chief Financial Officer), Jennifer Hershey (Vice President, Building Operations), Michah Hollingsworth (Vice President, Company Operations), Hal Goldberg (Theatre Operations)

AUGUST WILSON THEATRE STAFF Willa Burke (Manager), Nick Russo (Treasurer), Dan Dour (Carpenter), Scott Mulrain (Propertyman), Robert Fehrbach (Electrician), Ralph Santos (Engineer)

JERSEY BOYS PRODUCTION STAFF Sandy Carlson (Company Manager), Michelle Bosch (Production Stage Manager), Richard Hester, (Production Supervisor), Peter Fulbright (Technical Supervisor), Jeff Parvin (Production Manager)

JERSEY BOYS CREW FOR THE THEATRE WORLD AWARDS Carpentry, Michael Kelly; Electrician, Brian Amam; Properties, Emiliano Pares; Sound Board, Julie Randolph; Fly Automation, Ron Fucarino; Flyman, Peter Wright; Light/Video Operator, Gary Marlin; Projection Programmer, Paul Vershbow

WINNERS Ellen Barkin (*The Normal Heart*), Desmin Borges (*The Elaborate Entrance of Chad Deity*), Halley Feiffer (*The House of Blue Leaves*), Grace Gummer (*Arcadia*), Rose Hemingway (*How to Succeed in Business Without Really Trying*), John Larroquette (*How to Succeed in Business Without Really Trying*), Heather Lind (*The Merchant of Venice*), Patina Miller (*Sister Act*), Arian Moayed (*Bengel Tiger at the Baghdad Zoo*), Jim Parsons (*The Normal Heart*), Zachary Quinto (*Angels in America: A Gay Fantasia on National Themes*), Tony Sheldon (*Priscilla Queen of the Desert*); **Dorothy Loudon Award:** Seth Numrich (*War Horse*): **Lunt-Fontanne Award for Ensemble Excellence:** The Cast of *The Moherf**ker with the Hat*. Bobby Cannavale, Chris Rock, Elizabeth Rodriguez, Annabella Sciorra, Yul Vázquez

PRESENTERS Tammy Blanchard – *Gypsy* (2003); Gabriel Byrne – *The Moon for the Misbegotten* (2000); Zoe Caldwell – *Slapstick Tragedy* (1966); Billy Crudup – *Arcadia* (1995); Jonathan Cake – *Medea* (2003); Jason Danieley – *Candide* (1997); Blythe Danner – *The Miser* (1969); Edie Falco – *Side Man* (1999); Tovah Feldshuh – *Yentl* (1976); Jonathan Groff – *Spring Awakening* (2007); Carla Gugino – *After the Fall* (2005); John Leguizamo – *Spic-O-Rama* (Special Award 1993); Andrea McArdle – Annie (1977)

PERFORMERS John Lloyd Young – *Jersey Boys* (2006): Opening Number "Since I Don't Have You"; Karen Akers – *Nine* (1982): "I'll Be Seeing You" for the John Willis Tribute; Ernestine Jackson – *Raisin* (1974): Closing Number "If I Were a Bell"

SPECIAL GUESTS Rosemary Harris – *The Climate of Eden* (1953); Lionel Larner, Executive Director of the Dorothy Loudon Foundation; Aaron Frankel, The Lunt-Fontanne Award for Excellence

2011 THEATRE WORLD AWARD WRANGLER Carly Rose Sonenclar from the cast of *Wonderland*

VOLUNTEERS Kevin Albanese, Tom Bernagozzi, Geoff Botosan, Sarah Chalfy, Kelly Childress, Christine Cirker, Anthony Competello, Peter Dagger, Oleg Deyle, Christiana Farruggia, Robby Farruggia, Carly Glenn, Jeremiah Hernandez, Angela Ho, Sharon Hunter, Andrea Kempfer, Maria Kohut, Kristin Kotalo, Kelsey Maples, Andrea Marano, Lea McKenna-Garcia, Shawn Nabors, Kali Una Norris, Jillian Sayegh, Joshua Strone, James Sheridan, Emily Turner, Michael Twaine

SPONSORSHIP The Dorothy Loudon Foundation, Aaron Frankel, Alan & Arlene Alda, Sonia Alden Foundation Inc, Paul Craffey, Laurence Fishburne, Mario Frangoulis, Laurence Guittard, Estelle Parsons, Dodger Properties, Ron Jordan Roberts, Rev. Joshua Ellis, Joan Hovis Eubanks, Patrice Wymore Flynn, David Fritz, Fritz Travel, Nancy Giles, Doris Blum Gorelick, Christopher Goutman, Rosalind Harris, Linda Hart, Cecilia Hart Jones, James Earl Jones, Spiro Malas,

Brian Stokes Mitchell, The Shubert Organization, Joseph S. Tocci, Michael Viade, Leilani Jones Wilmore, John Lloyd Young, Jane Alexander, Karen Allen, Thomas Amorosi, Maureen Anderman, Lou Antonio, Orson Bean, Warren Berlinger, Thomas Bernagozzi, Sylvia Brown-Sanders, Brent Carver, Maxwell Caulfield, Thom Christopher, Jason Cicci, Esther Cohen, Barbara Cook, O. David Deitz, Bambi Dejesus, Edward Evanko, Harvey Evans, Kenneth Fakler, Brian Farrell, Wendy Federman, Tovah Feldshuh, Michael Filerman Trust, Barbara Flood (Feldman), Miriam Fond, Bette-Lee Fox, Gavin Lee, Gail Gerber, Daniel Gerroll, Anita Gillette, Marlene Gould, Harry Groener, Conrad Janis, Ernestine Jackson, Mark Jacoby, Julie Kagan, Margery Klain, Jack F. Lee, Kelsey Maples, Daisy Maryles, John McMartin, Scott Mauro Entertainment, Anthony Meisel, James Miller, Marianne Mills, Charles M. Mirotznik, Athena and Patrick Monahan, Ann Morrison, Karen Plesher, Susan L. Raanan, Kay Radtke, Peter & Helen Carey Raudenbush, M. Reedy, Marcia Roberts, Cliff Robertson, Greg Roosi, Emily Saines, L. Ables Sayre, Leslie Shreve, Sheila Smith, Linda Soo Hoo, Elisa Loti Stein, Philip Suraci / Christina Biddle, Marianne Tatum, Aubrey Lee Thacker Jr., Linda Thorson, Jane Trese, Blake Walton, Andrea Zuckerman

SPECIAL THANKS Actors' Equity Association, Rob Adler, Alyssa Arminio, The Araca Group, Attitude Car Service, Joseph Baker, Molly Barnett, Michelle Bergmann, Doris Blum, Boneau/Bryan-Brown, Kayla Borg, Geoff Botosan, Brasserie Cognac, Konrad Brattke, Broadway Beat, Broadway.com, Broadway Stars, roadwayWorld.com, Nicole Capatasto, Sandy Carlson, John Cerullo, Paul Craffey, Christine Cirker, Custom Glass Etching, Tom D'Ambrosio, Julie Danni, Michael David, Scott Denny, Dodger Properties, Wade F. Dansby 3, Amanda Dekker, Patricia Elliott, Brian Ferdman, Paul Foley, Aaron Frankel, Leigh Giroux, Bruce Glikas, Goodpenny, Jackie Green, Josh Grisetti, Kelly Guiod, The Hartman Group, Michael Heeney, Randy J. Hemming, HIT Entertainment, Ben Hodges, Micah Hollingworth, Home Work People Real Estate, Florian Hugo, International Poster Centre, Ernestine Jackson, Jujamcyn Theaters, Jeremy Katz, Kevin Kilner, Albert Kim, King Displays, Lionel Larner, Jackie LaVanway, Angelina Lippert, Susan Loyd, Kelsey Maples, Rosanne Martino, Beverly D. Mac Keen, Emily Meagher, Aaron Meier, Lindsay Meck, Michael Messina, Dona Miller, Barry Monush, Annick Muller, Matthew Murray, The National Arts Club, O&M, Kristine Penny, Joe Perrotta, Playbill, Prestone Printing, Richard Ridge, Ron Roberts, Cliff Robertson, Justin 'Squigs' Robertson, Rosco Lighting, Jeff Rose, Rosenberg, Neuwirth & Kuchner, CPAs, Matt Ross, Jordan Roth, Sam Rudy, Anne Runolfsson, Wayne Sapper, Jerry Shafninsky, Mark Schlegel, Heath Schwartz, Marisa Sechrest, Jon Simon & Goodpenny, Stephanie Shaw, Brenda Smiley, Bradshaw Smith, Andy Synder, Michael Strassheim, Marianne Tatum, TheaterMania, Richard Terrano, Susanne Tighe, Abbie Van Nostrand, Charles Vargas, Michael Viade, Jack Vrtar, S. Walter Art Department, Wayne Wolfe, Michael Wright, Sarah Ziering

SUPPORT Theatre World Awards After-Party generously sponsored by **Brasserie Cognac**; Additional sound equipment provided by **Michael Andrews Audio Visual Systems**; Gift bag and promotional items supplied by: The Araca Group, Daryl Roth Productions, Decca Records/Universal Music, Drama Book Shop, E1Entertainment, Hal Leonard, Performing Arts Publishing Group, HIT Entertainment, HomeWorkPeople,

Real Estate and Staffing, Jon Lonoff, Caroline Newhouse, Prestone Printing, Randall J. Hemming, Rosco Lighting, Samuel French Publishing, Sony Music, Ten Chimneys, Theatermania, Type A Marketing

The Theatre World Awards, Inc. is a 501 (c)(3) nonprofit organization, and our annual presentation is made possible by the generous contributions of previous winners and friends. For more information please visit thewebsite at www.theatreworldawards.org.

Tax-deductible contributions can be sent via PayPay to info@theatreworldawards.org, or checks and money orders sent to:

Theatre World Awards, Inc.

Box 246 Radio City Station

New York, NY 10101-0246

Presenters Jonathan Cake and Billy Crudup (BG)

Heather Lind (MLV)

Tovah Feldshuh displays the Theatre World Awards poster created by Justin "Squigs" Robertson (BG)

Arian Moayed (MLV)

Lionel Larner, Seth Numrich, and Blythe Danner (BG)

Presenters John Leguizamo, Carla Gugino, Edie Falco, and Gabriel Byrne (BG)

Tony Sheldon and Tovah Feldshuh (BG)

1953 Winner Rosemary Harris introduces the John Willis tribute video (MLV)

Rose Hemingway and Andrea McArdle (BG)

Ellen Barkin and Gabriel Byrne (BG)

Grace Gummer (MLV)

Aaron Frankel introduces the new Lunt-Fontanne Award for Ensemble Excellence that will be presented as part of the Theatre World Awards (MLV)

1966 Winner Zoe Caldwell presents the Lunt-Fontanne Award (MLV)

Chris Rock accepts the Lunt-Fontanne Award on behalf of the cast of The Motherf**ker with the Hat: Elizabeth Rodriguez, Yul Vázquez, Annabella Sciorra, and Bobby Cannavale (MLV)

Desmin Borges and John Lequizamo (JB)

Jason Danieley and Arian Moayad (JB)

Halley Feiffer and Edie Falco (KB)

Karen Akers presents a loving tribute song to John Willis (MLV)

Carla Gugino and Zachary Quinto (BG)

Halley Feiffer (MLV)

John Larroquette and Tammy Blanchard (BG)

Tony Sheldon (MH)

Zoe Caldwell and Rosemary Harris (BG)

Patina Miller (MLV)

Theatre World Awards Host Peter Filicia (MLV)

2005 Winner Mamie Gummer with her sister 2011 winner Grace Gummer (BG)

Ernestine Jackson (1974 Winner from Raisin) closes out the ceremony with a dazzling performance of "If I Were a Bell" from Guys and Dolls (MLV)

A photo tribute to John Willis (MLV)

Theatre World Award producer Kati Meister, 1957 Winner Cliff Robertson at the after-party at Brasserie Congac (MLV)

Zachary Quinto (center) with Theatre World Awards producers Erin Oestreich and Mary Botosan (BG)

Musical Director Henry Aronson (MLV)

Seth Numrich and Heather Lind, cast mates from this year's production of The Merchant of Venice (MLV)

Tovah Feldshuh, John Lloyd Young, and 1983 Winner Linda Thorson (KB)

Ellen Barkin accepts the award for Jim Parsons who was not able to attend the ceremony (MLV)

Presenters Jonathan Cake, Blythe Danner, and Jonathan Groff (MLV)

Photos by Bruce Glikas (BG), Michael Heeney (MH), onrad Brattke (KB), and Michael & Laura Viade (MLV)

Rose Hemingway (MLV)

Previous Theatre World Award Recipients

1944-45: Betty Comden (*On the Town*), Richard Davis (*Kiss Them For Me*), Richard Hart (*Dark of the Moon*), Judy Holliday (*Kiss Them for Me*), Charles Lang (*Down to Miami* and *The Overtons*), Bambi Linn (*Carousel*), John Lund (*The Hasty Heart*), Donald Murphy (*Signature* and *Common Ground*), Nancy Noland (*Common Ground*), Margaret Phillips (*The Late George Apley*), John Raitt (*Carousel*)

1945-46: Barbara Bel Geddes (*Deep Are the Roots*), Marlon Brando (*Truckline Café* and *Candida*), Bill Callahan (*Call Me Mister*), Wendell Corey (*The Wind is Ninety*), Paul Douglas (*Born Yesterday*), Mary James (*Apple of His Eye*), Burt Lancaster (*A Sound of Hunting*), Patricia Marshall (*The Day Before Spring*), Beatrice Pearson (*The Mermaids Singing*)

1946-47: Keith Andes (*The Chocolate Soldier*), Marion Bell (*Brigadoon*), Peter Cookson (*Message for Margaret*), Ann Crowley (*Carousel*), Ellen Hanley (*Barefoot Boy With Cheek*), John Jordan (*The Wanhope Building*), George Keane (*Brigadoon*), Dorothea MacFarland (*Oklahoma!*), James Mitchell (*Brigadoon*), Patricia Neal (*Another Part of the Forest*), David Wayne (*Finian's Rainbow*)

1947-48: Valerie Bettis (*Inside U.S.A.*), Edward Bryce (*The Cradle Will Rock*), Whitfield Connor (*Macbeth*), Mark Dawson (*High Button Shoes*), June Lockhart (*For Love or Money*), Estelle Loring (*Inside U.S.A.*), Peggy Maley (*Joy to the World*), Ralph Meeker (*Miser Roberts*), Meg Mundy (*The Happy Journey to Trenton and Camden* and *The Respectful Prostitute*), Douglass Watson (*Antony and Cleopatra*), James Whitmore (*Command Decision*), Patrice Wymore (*Hold It!*)

1948-49: Tod Andrews (*Summer and Smoke*), Doe Avedon (*The Young and Fair*), Jean Carson (*Bravo!*), Carol Channing (*Lend an Ear*), Richard Derr (*The Traitor*), Julie Harris (*Sundown Beach*), Mary McCarty (*Sleepy Hollow*), Allyn Ann McLerie (*Where's Charley?*), Cameron Mitchell (*Death of a Salesman*), Gene Nelson (*Lend an Ear*), Byron Palmer (*Where's Charley?*), Bob Scheerer (*Lend an Ear*)

1949-50: Nancy Andrews (*Touch and Go*), Phil Arthur (*With a Silk Thread*), Barbara Brady (*The Velvet Glove*), Lydia Clarke (*Detective Story*), Priscilla Gillette (*Regina*), Don Hanmer (*The Man*), Marcia Henderson (*Peter Pan*), Charlton Heston (*Design for a Stained Glass Window*), Rick Jason (*Now I Lay Me Down to Sleep*), Grace Kelly (*The Father*), Charles Nolte (*Design for a Stained Glass Window*), Roger Price (*Tickets, Please!*)

1950-51: Barbara Ashley (*Out of This World*), Isabel Bigley (*Guys and Dolls*), Martin Brooks (*Burning Bright*), Richard Burton (*The Lady's Not For Burning*), Pat Crowley (*Southern Exposure*), James Daly (*Major Barbara* and *Mary Rose*), Cloris Leachman (*A Story for a Sunday Evening*), Russell Nype (*Call Me Madam*), Jack Palance (*Darkness at Noon*), William Smithers (*Romeo and Juliet*), Maureen Stapleton (*The Rose Tattoo*), Marcia Van Dyke (*Marcia Van Dyke*), Eli Wallach (*The Rose Tattoo*)

1951-52: Tony Bavaar (*Paint Your Wagon*), Patricia Benoit (*Glad Tidings*), Peter Conlow (*Courtin' Time*), Virginia de Luce (*New Faces of 1952*), Ronny Graham (*New Faces of 1952*), Audrey Hepburn (*Gigi*), Diana Herbert (*The Number*), Conrad Janis (*The Brass Ring*), Dick Kallman (*Seventeen*), Charles Proctor (*Twilight Walk*), Eric Sinclair (*Much Ado About Nothing*), Kim Stanley (*The Chase*), Marian Winters (*I Am a Camera*), Helen Wood (*Seventeen*)

1952-53: Edie Adams (*Wonderful Town*), Rosemary Harris (*The Climate of Eden*), Eileen Heckart (*Picnic*), Peter Kelley (*Two's Company*), John Kerr (*Bernardine*), Richard Kiley (*Misalliance*), Gloria Marlowe (*In Any Language*), Penelope Munday (*The Climate of Eden*), Paul Newman (*Picnic*), Sheree North (*Hazel Flagg*), Geraldine Page (*Mid-Summer*), John Stewart (*Bernardine*), Ray Stricklyn (*The Climate of Eden*), Gwen Verdon (*Can-Can*)

1953-54: Orson Bean (*John Murray Anderson's Almanac*), Harry Belafonte (*John Murray Anderson's Almanac*), James Dean (*The Immoralist*), Joan Diener (*Kismet*), Ben Gazzara (*End as a Man*), Carol Haney (*The Pajama Game*), Jonathan Lucas (*The Golden Apple*), Kay Medford (*Lullaby*), Scott Merrill (*The Threepenny Opera*), Elizabeth Montgomery (*Late Love*), Leo Penn (*The Girl on the Via*

Flaminia), Eva Marie Saint (*The Trip to Bountiful*)

1954-55: Julie Andrews (*The Boy Friend*), Jacqueline Brookes (*The Cretan Woman*), Shirl Conway (*Plain and Fancy*), Barbara Cook (*Plain and Fancy*), David Daniels (*Plain and Fancy*), Mary Fickett (*Tea and Sympathy*), Page Johnson (*In April Once*), Loretta Leversee (*Home is the Hero*), Jack Lord (*The Traveling Lady*), Dennis Patrick (*The Wayward Saint*), Anthony Perkins (*Tea and Sympathy*), Christopher Plummer (*The Dark is Light Enough*)

1955-56: Diane Cilento (*Tiger at the Gates*), Dick Davalos (*A View from the Bridge*), Anthony Franciosa (*A Hatful of Rain*), Andy Griffith (*No Time for Sergeants*), Laurence Harvey (*Island of Goats*), David Hedison (*A Month in the Country*), Earle Hyman (*Mister Johnson*), Susan Johnson (*The Most Happy Fella*), John Michael King (*My Fair Lady*), Jayne Mansfield (*Will Success Spoil Rock Hunter?*), Sarah Marshall (*The Ponder Heart*), Gaby Rodgers (*Mister Johnson*), Susan Strasberg (*The Diary of Anne Frank*), Fritz Weaver (*The Chalk Garden*)

1956-57: Peggy Cass (*Auntie Mame*), Sydney Chaplin (*Bells Are Ringing*), Sylvia Daneel (*The Tunnel of Love*), Bradford Dillman (*Long Day's Journey Into Night*), Peter Donat (*The First Gentleman*), George Grizzard (*The Happiest Millionaire*), Carol Lynley (*The Potting Shed*), Peter Palmer (*Li'l Abner*), Jason Robards (*Long Day's Journey Into Night*), Cliff Robertson (*Orpheus Descending*), Pippa Scott (*Child of Fortune*), Inga Swenson (*The First Gentleman*)

1957-58: Anne Bancroft (*Two for the Seesaw*), Warren Berlinger (*Blue Denim*), Colleen Dewhurst (*Children of Darkness*), Richard Easton (*The Country Wife*), Tim Everett (*The Dark at the Top of the Stairs*), Eddie Hodges (*The Music Man*), Joan Hovis (*Love Me Little*), Carol Lawrence (*West Side Story*), Jacqueline McKeever (*Oh, Captain!*), Wynne Miller (*Li'l Abner*), Robert Morse (*Say, Darling*), George C. Scott (*Richard III*)

1958-59: Lou Antonio (*The Buffalo Skinner*), Ina Balin (*A Majority of One*), Richard Cross (*Maria Golovin*), Tammy Grimes (*Look After Lulu*), Larry Hagman (*God and Kate Murphy*), Dolores Hart (*The Pleasure of His Company*), Roger Mollien (French Theatre National Populaire), France Nuyen (*The World of Suzie Wong*), Susan Oliver (*Patate*), Ben Piazza (*Kataki*), Paul Roebling (*A Desert Incident*), William Shatner (*The World of Suzie Wong*), Pat Suzuki (*Flower Drum Song*), Rip Torn (*Sweet Bird of Youth*)

1959-60: Warren Beatty (*A Loss of Roses*), Eileen Brennan (*Little Mary Sunshine*), Carol Burnett (*Once Upon a Mattress*), Patty Duke (*The Miracle Worker*), Jane Fonda (*There Was a Little Girl*), Anita Gillette (*Russell Patterson's Sketchbook*), Elisa Loti (*Come Share My House*), Donald Madden (*Julius Caesar*), George Maharis (*The Zoo Story*), John McMartin (*Little Mary Sunshine*), Lauri Peters (*The Sound of Music*), Dick Van Dyke (*The Boys Against the Girls*)

1960-61: Joyce Bulifant (*Whisper to Me*), Dennis Cooney (*Every Other Evil*), Sandy Dennis (*Face of a Hero*), Nancy Dussault (*Do Re Mi*), Robert Goulet (*Camelot*), Joan Hackett (*Call Me By My Rightful Name*), June Harding (*Cry of the Raindrop*), Ron Husmann (*Tenderloin*), James MacArthur (*Invitation to a March*), Bruce Yarnell (*The Happiest Girl in the World*)

1961-62: Elizabeth Ashley (*Take Her, She's Mine*), Keith Baxter (*A Man for All Seasons*), Peter Fonda (*Blood, Sweat and Stanley Poole*), Don Galloway (*Bring Me a Warm Body*), Sean Garrison (*Half-Past Wednesday*), Barbara Harris (*Oh, Dad, Poor Dad, Mamma's Hung You in the Closet and I'm Feeling So Sad*), James Earl Jones (*Moon on a Rainbow Shawl*), Janet Margolin (*Daughter of Silence*), Karen Morrow (*Sing, Muse!*), Robert Redford (*Sunday in New York*), John Stride (*Romeo and Juliet*), Brenda Vaccaro (*Everybody Loves Opal*)

1962-63: Alan Arkin (*Enter Laughing*), Stuart Damon (*The Boys from Syracuse*), Melinda Dillon (*Who's Afraid of Virginia Woolf?*), Robert Drivas (*Mrs. Dally Has a Lover*), Bob Gentry (*Angels of Anadarko*), Dorothy Loudon (*Nowhere to Go But Up*), Brandon Maggart (*Put It in Writing*), Julienne Marie (*The Boys from Syracuse*), Liza Minnelli (*Best Foot Forward*), Estelle Parsons (*Mrs. Dally Has a Lover*), Diana Sands (*Tiger Tiger Burning Bright*), Swen Swenson (*Little Me*)

1963-64: Alan Alda (*Fair Game for Lovers*), Gloria Bleezarde (*Never Live Over a Pretzel Factory*), Imelda De Martin (*The Amorous Flea*), Claude Giraud (*Phèdre*),

Ketty Lester (*Cabin in the Sky*), Barbara Loden (*After the Fall*), Lawrence Pressman (*Never Live Over a Pretzel Factory*), Gilbert Price (*Jerico-Jim Crow*), Philip Proctor (*The Amorous Flea*), John Tracy (*Telemachus Clay*), Jennifer West (*Dutchman*)

1964-65: Carolyn Coates (*The Trojan Women*), Joyce Jillson (*The Roar of the Greasepaint – The Smell of the Crowd*), Linda Lavin (*Wet Paint*), Luba Lisa (*I Had a Ball*), Michael O'Sullivan (*Tartuffe*), Joanna Pettet (*Poor Richard*), Beah Richards (*The Amen Corner*), Jaime Sanchez (*Conerico Was Here to Stay* and *The Toilet*), Victor Spinetti (*Oh, What a Lovely War*), Nicolas Surovy (*Helen*), Robert Walker (*I Knock at the Door* and *Pictures in the Hallway*), Clarence Williams III (*Slow Dancing on the Killing Ground*)

1965-66: Zoe Caldwell (*Slapstick Tragedy*), David Carradine (*The Royal Hunt of the Sun*), John Cullum (*On a Clear Day You Can See Forever*), John Davidson (*Oklahoma!*), Faye Dunaway (*Hogan's Ghost*), Gloria Foster (*Medea*), Robert Hooks (*Where's Daddy?* and *Day of Absence*), Jerry Lanning (*Mame*), Richard Mulligan (*Mating Dance* and *Hogan's Ghost*), April Shawhan (*3 Bags Full*), Sandra Smith (*Any Wednesday*), Leslie Ann Warren (*Drat! The Cat!*)

1966-67: Bonnie Bedelia (*My Sweet Charlie*), Richard Benjamin (*The Star-Spangled Girl*), Dustin Hoffman (*Eh?*), Terry Kiser (*Fortune and Men's Eyes*), Reva Rose (*You're A Good Man, Charlie Brown*), Robert Salvio (*Hamp*), Sheila Smith (*Mame*), Connie Stevens (*The Star-Spangled Girl*), Pamela Tiffin (*Dinner at Eight*), Leslie Uggams (*Hallelujah, Baby*), Jon Voight (*That Summer – That Fall*), Christopher Walken (*The Rose Tattoo*)

1967-68: David Birney (*Summertree*), Pamela Burrell (*Arms and the Man*), Jordan Christopher (*Black Comedy*), Jack Crowder – a.k.a. Thalmus Rasulala (*Hello, Dolly!*), Sandy Duncan (*Ceremony of Innocence*), Julie Gregg (*The Happy Time*), Stephen Joyce (*Stephen D.*), Bernadette Peters (*George M*), Alice Playten (*Henry, Sweet Henry*), Michael Rupert (*The Happy Time*), Brenda Smiley (*Scuba Duba*), Russ Thacker (*Your Own Thing*)

1968-69: Jane Alexander (*The Great White Hope*), David Cryer (*Come Summer*), Blythe Danner (*The Miser*), Ed Evanko (*Canterbury Tales*), Ken Howard (*1776*), Lauren Jones (*Does a Tiger Wear a Necktie?*), Ron Leibman (*We Bombed in New Haven*), Marian Mercer (*Promises, Promises*), Jill O'Hara (*Promises, Promises*), Ron O'Neal (*No Place to Be Somebody*), Al Pacino (*Does a Tiger Wear a Necktie?*), Marlene Warfield (*The Great White Hope*)

1969-70: Susan Browning (*Company*), Donny Burks (*Billy Noname*), Catherine Burns (*Dear Janet Rosenberg, Dear Mr. Kooning*), Len Cariou (*Henry V* and *Applause*), Bonnie Franklin (*Applause*), David Holliday (*Coco*), Katharine Houghton (*A Scent of Flowers*), Melba Moore (*Purlie*), David Rounds (*Child's Play*), Lewis J. Stadlen (*Minnie's Boys*), Kristoffer Tabori (*How Much, How Much*), Fredricka Weber (*The Last Sweet Days of Isaac*)

1970-71: Clifton Davis (*Do It Again*), Michael Douglas (*Pinkville*), Julie Garfield (*Uncle Vanya*), Martha Henry (*The Playboy of the Western World, Scenes From American Life*, and *Antigone*), James Naughton (*Long Days Journey Into Night*), Tricia O'Neil (*Two by Two*), Kipp Osborne (*Butterflies Are Free*), Roger Rathburn (*No, No, Nanette*), Ayn Ruymen (*The Gingerbread Lady*), Jennifer Salt (*Father's Day*), Joan Van Ark (*School for Wives*), Walter Willison (*Two by Two*)

1971-72: Jonelle Allen (*Two Gentlemen of Verona*), Maureen Anderman (*Moonchildren*), William Atherton (*Suggs*), Richard Backus (*Promenade, All!*), Adrienne Barbeau (*Grease*), Cara Duff-MacCormick (*Moonchildren*), Robert Foxworth (*The Crucible*), Elaine Joyce (*Sugar*), Jess Richards (*On The Town*), Ben Vereen (*Jesus Christ Superstar*), Beatrice Winde (*Ain't Supposed to Die a Natural Death*), James Woods (*Moonchildren*)

1972-73: D'Jamin Bartlett (*A Little Night Music*), Patricia Elliott (*A Little Night Music*), James Farentino (*A Streetcar Named Desire*), Brian Farrell (*The Last of Mrs. Lincoln*), Victor Garber (*Ghosts*), Kelly Garrett (*Mother Earth*), Mari Gorman (*The Hot l Baltimore*), Laurence Guittard (*A Little Night Music*), Trish Hawkins (*The Hot l Baltimore*), Monte Markham (*Irene*), John Rubinstein (*Pippin*), Jennifer Warren (*6 Rms Riv Vu*), Alexander H. Cohen (Special Award)

1973-74: Mark Baker (*Candide*), Maureen Brennan (*Candide*), Ralph Carter (*Raisin*), Thom Christopher (*Noel Coward in Two Keys*), John Driver (*Over Here*), Conchata Ferrell (*The Sea Horse*), Ernestine Jackson (*Raisin*), Michael Moriarty (*Find Your Way Home*), Joe Morton (*Raisin*), Ann Reinking (*Over Here*), Janie Sell (*Over Here*), Mary Woronov (*Boom Boom Room*), Sammy Cahn (Special Award)

1974-75: Peter Burnell (*In Praise of Love*), Zan Charisse (*Gypsy*), Lola Falana (*Dr. Jazz*), Peter Firth (*Equus*), Dorian Harewood (*Don't Call Back*), Joel Higgins (*Shenandoah*), Marcia McClain (*Where's Charley?*), Linda Miller (*Black Picture Show*), Marti Rolph (*Good News*), John Sheridan (*Gypsy*), Scott Stevensen (*Good News*), Donna Theodore (*Shenandoah*), Equity Library Theatre (Special Award)

1975-76: Danny Aiello (*Lamppost Reunion*), Christine Andreas (*My Fair Lady*), Dixie Carter (*Jesse and the Bandit Queen*), Tovah Feldshuh (*Yentl*), Chip Garnett (*Bubbling Brown Sugar*), Richard Kelton (*Who's Afraid of Virginia Woolf?*), Vivian Reed (*Bubbling Brown Sugar*), Charles Repole (*Very Good Eddie*), Virginia Seidel (*Very Good Eddie*), Daniel Seltzer (*Knock Knock*), John V. Shea (*Yentl*), Meryl Streep (*27 Wagons Full of Cotton*), The Cast of *A Chorus Line* (Special Award)

1976-77: Trazana Beverley (*for colored girls...*), Michael Cristofer (*The Cherry Orchard*), Joe Fields (*The Basic Training of Pavlo Hummel*), Joanna Gleason (*I Love My Wife*), Cecilia Hart (*Dirty Linen*), John Heard (*G.R. Point*), Gloria Hodes (*The Club*), Juliette Koka (*Piaf...A Remembrance*), Andrea McArdle (*Annie*), Ken Page (*Guys and Dolls*), Jonathan Pryce (*Comedians*), Chick Vennera (*Jockeys*), Eva LeGallienne (Special Award)

1977-78: Vasili Bogazianos (*P.S. Your Cat Is Dead*), Nell Carter (*Ain't Misbehavin'*), Carlin Glynn (*The Best Little Whorehouse in Texas*), Christopher Goutman (*The Promise*), William Hurt (*Ulysses in Traction, Lulu*, and *The Fifth of July*), Judy Kaye (*On the 20th Century*), Florence Lacy (*Hello, Dolly!*), Armelia McQueen (*Ain't Misbehavin'*), Gordana Rashovich (*Fefu and Her Friends*), Bo Rucker (*Native Son*), Richard Seer (*Da*), Colin Stinton (*The Water Engine*), Joseph Papp (Special Award)

1978-79: Philip Anglim (*The Elephant Man*), Lucie Arnaz (*They're Playing Our Song*), Gregory Hines (*Eubie!*), Ken Jennings (*Sweeney Todd*), Michael Jeter (*G.R. Point*), Laurie Kennedy (*Man and Superman*), Susan Kingsley (*Getting Out*), Christine Lahti (*The Woods*), Edward James Olmos (*Zoot Suit*), Kathleen Quinlan (*Taken in Marriage*), Sarah Rice (*Sweeney Todd*), Max Wright (*Once in a Lifetime*), Marshall W. Mason (Special Award)

1979-80: Maxwell Caulfield (*Class Enemy*), Leslie Denniston (*Happy New Year*),Boyd Gaines (*A Month in the Country*), Richard Gere (*Bent*), Harry Groener (*Oklahoma!*), Stephen James (*The 1940's Radio Hour*), Susan Kellermann (*Last Licks*), Dinah Manoff (*I Ought to Be in Pictures*), Lonny Price (*Class Enemy*), Marianne Tatum (*Barnum*), Anne Twomey (*Nuts*), Dianne Wiest (*The Art of Dining*), Mickey Rooney (*Sugar Babies* – Special Award)

1980-81: Brian Backer (*The Floating Light Bulb*), Lisa Banes (*Look Back in Anger*), Meg Bussert (*The Music Man*), Michael Allen Davis (*Broadway Follies*), Giancarlo Esposito (*Zooman and the Sign*), Daniel Gerroll (*Slab Boys*), Phyllis Hyman (*Sophisticated Ladies*), Cynthia Nixon (*The Philadelphia Story*), Amanda Plummer (*A Taste of Honey*), Adam Redfield (*A Life*), Wanda Richert (*42nd Street*), Rex Smith (*The Pirates of Penzance*), Elizabeth Taylor (*The Little Foxes* – Special Award)

1981-82: Karen Akers (*Nine*), Laurie Beechman (*Joseph and the Amazing Technicolor Dreamcoat*), Danny Glover (*Master Harold...and the Boys*), David Alan Grier (*The First*), Jennifer Holliday (*Dreamgirls*), Anthony Heald (*Misalliance*), Lizbeth Mackay (*Crimes of the Heart*), Peter MacNicol (*Crimes of the Heart*), Elizabeth McGovern (*My Sister in This House*), Ann Morrison (*Merrily We Roll Along*), Michael O'Keefe (*Mass Appeal*), James Widdoes (*Is There Life After High School?*), Manhattan Theatre Club (Special Award)

1982-83: Karen Allen (*Monday After the Miracle*), Suzanne Bertish (*Skirmishes*), Matthew Broderick (*Brighton Beach Memoirs*), Kate Burton (*Winners*), Joanne Camp (*Geniuses*), Harvey Fierstein (*Torch Song Trilogy*), Peter Gallagher (*A Doll's Life*), John Malkovich (*True West*), Anne Pitoniak (*'Night Mother*), James Russo

(*Extremities*), Brian Tarantina (*Angels Fall*), Linda Thorson (*Streaming*), Natalia Makarova (*On Your Toes* – Special Award)

1983-84: Martine Allard (*The Tap Dance Kid*), Joan Allen (*And a Nightingale Sang*), Kathy Whitton Baker (*Fool For Love*), Mark Capri (*On Approval*), Laura Dean (*Doonesbury*), Stephen Geoffreys (*The Human Comedy*), Todd Graff (*Baby*), Glenne Headly (*The Philanthropist*), J.J. Johnston (*American Buffalo*), Bonnie Koloc (*The Human Comedy*), Calvin Levels (*Open Admissions*), Robert Westenberg (*Zorba*), Ron Moody (*Oliver* – Special Award)

1984-85: Kevin Anderson (*Orphans*), Richard Chaves (*Tracers*), Patti Cohenour (*La Boheme* and *Big River*), Charles S. Dutton (*Ma Rainey's Black Bottom*), Nancy Giles (*Mayor*), Whoopi Goldberg (*Whoopi Goldberg*), Leilani Jones (*Grind*), John Mahoney (*Orphans*), Laurie Metcalf (*Balm in Gilead*), Barry Miller (*Biloxi Blues*), John Turturro (*Danny and the Deep Blue Sea*), Amelia White (*The Accrington Pals*), Lucille Lortel (Special Award)

1985-86: Suzy Amis (*Fresh Horses*), Alec Baldwin (*Loot*), Aled Davies (*Orchards*), Faye Grant (*Singin' in the Rain*), Julie Hagerty (*The House of Blue Leaves*), Ed Harris (*Precious Sons*), Mark Jacoby (*Sweet Charity*), Donna Kane (*Dames at Sea*), Cleo Laine (*The Mystery of Edwin Drood*), Howard McGillin (*The Mystery of Edwin Drood*), Marisa Tomei (*Daughters*), Joe Urla (*Principia Scriptoriae*), Ensemble Studio Theatre (Special Award)

1986-87: Annette Bening (*Coastal Disturbances*), Timothy Daly (*Coastal Disturbances*), Lindsay Duncan (*Les Liaisons Dangereuses*), Frank Ferrante (*Groucho: A Life in Revue*), Robert Lindsay (*Me and My Girl*), Amy Madigan (*The Lucky Spot*), Michael Maguire (*Les Misérables*), Demi Moore (*The Early Girl*), Molly Ringwald (*Lily Dale*), Frances Ruffelle (*Les Misérables*), Courtney B. Vance (*Fences*), Colm Wilkinson (*Les Misérables*), Robert DeNiro (Special Award)

1987-88: Yvonne Bryceland (*The Road to Mecca*), Philip Casnoff (*Chess*), Danielle Ferland (*Into the Woods*), Melissa Gilbert (*A Shayna Maidel*), Linda Hart (*Anything Goes*), Linzi Hateley (*Carrie*), Brian Kerwin (*Emily*), Brian Mitchell (*Mail*), Mary Murfitt (*Oil City Symphony*), Aidan Quinn *A Streetcar Named Desire*), Eric Roberts (*Burn This*), B.D. Wong (*M. Butterfly*), Tisa Chang and Martin E. Segal (Special Awards)

1988-89: Dylan Baker (*Eastern Standard*), Joan Cusack (*Road* and *Brilliant Traces*), Loren Dean (*Amulets Against the Dragon Forces*), Peter Frechette (*Eastern Standard*), Sally Mayes (*Welcome to the Club*), Sharon McNight (*Starmites*), Jennie Moreau (*Eleemosynary*), Paul Provenza (*Only Kidding*), Kyra Sedgwick (*Ah, Wilderness!*), Howard Spiegel (*Only Kidding*), Eric Stoltz (*Our Town*), Joanne Whalley-Kilmer (*What the Butler Saw*); Pauline Collins of *Shirley Valentine* (Special Award), Mikhail Baryshnikov (Special Award)

1989-90: Denise Burse (*Ground People*), Erma Campbell (*Ground People*), Rocky Carroll (*The Piano Lesson*), Megan Gallagher (*A Few Good Men*), Tommy Hollis (*The Piano Lesson*), Robert Lambert (*Gypsy*), Kathleen Rowe McAllen (*Aspects of Love*), Michael McKean (*Accomplice*), Crista Moore (*Gypsy*), Mary-Louise Parker (*Prelude to a Kiss*), Daniel von Bargen (*Mastergate*), Jason Workman (*Jason Workman*), Stewart Granger (*The Circle* – Special Award), Kathleen Turner (*Cat on a Hot Tin Roof* – Special Award)

1990-91: Jane Adams (*I Hate Hamlet*), Gillian Anderson (*Absent Friends*), Adam Arkin (*I Hate Hamlet*), Brenda Blethyn (*Absent Friends*), Marcus Chong (*Stand-up Tragedy*), Paul Hipp (*Buddy*), LaChanze (*Once on This Island*), Kenny Neal (*Mule Bone*), Kevin Ramsey (*Oh, Kay!*), Francis Ruivivar (*Shogun*), Lea Salonga (*Miss Saigon*), Chandra Wilson (*The Good Times Are Killing Me*); Tracey Ullman (*The Big Love* and *Taming of the Shrew*), Ellen Stewart (Special Award)

1991-92: Talia Balsam (*Jake's Women*), Lindsay Crouse (*The Homecoming*), Griffin Dunne (*Search and Destroy*), Laurence Fishburne (*Two Trains Running*), Mel Harris (*Empty Hearts*), Jonathan Kaplan (*Falsettos* and *Rags*), Jessica Lange (*A Streetcar Named Desire*), Laura Linney (*Sight Unseen*), Spiro Malas (*The Most Happy Fella*), Mark Rosenthal (*Marvin's Room*), Helen Shaver (*Jake's Women*), Al White (*Two Trains Running*), The Cast of *Dancing at Lughnasa* (Special Award), Plays for Living (Special Award)

1992-93: Brent Carver (*Kiss of the Spider Woman*), Michael Cerveris (*The Who's Tommy*), Marcia Gay Harden (*Angels in America: Millennium Approaches*), Stephanie Lawrence (*Blood Brothers*), Andrea Martin (*My Favorite Year*), Liam Neeson (*Anna Christie*), Stephen Rea (*Someone Who'll Watch Over Me*), Natasha Richardson (*Anna Christie*), Martin Short (*The Goodbye Girl*), Dina Spybey (*Five Women Wearing the Same Dress*), Stephen Spinella (*Angels in America: Millennium Approaches*), Jennifer Tilly (*One Shoe Off*), John Leguizamo and Rosetta LeNoire (Special Awards)

1993-94: Marcus D'Amico (*An Inspector Calls*), Jarrod Emick (*Damn Yankees*), Arabella Field (*Snowing at Delphi* and *4 Dogs and a Bone*), Aden Gillett (*An Inspector Calls*), Sherry Glaser (*Family Secrets*), Michael Hayden (*Carousel*), Margaret Illman (*The Red Shoes*), Audra McDonald (*Carousel*), Burke Moses (*Beauty and the Beast*), Anna Deavere Smith (*Twilight: Los Angeles, 1992*), Jere Shea (*Passion*), Harriet Walter (*3Birds Alighting on a Field*)

1994-95: Gretha Boston (*Show Boat*), Billy Crudup (*Arcadia*), RalphFiennes (*Hamlet*), Beverly D'Angelo (*Simpatico*), Calista Flockhart (*The Glass Menagerie*), Kevin Kilner (*The Glass Menagerie*), Anthony LaPaglia (*The Rose Tattoo*), Julie Johnson (*Das Barbecü*), Helen Mirren (*A Month in the Country*), Jude Law (*Indiscretions*), Rufus Sewell (*Translations*), Vanessa Williams (*Kiss of the Spider Woman*), Brooke Shields (Special Award)

1995-96: Jordan Baker (*Suddenly Last Summer*), Joohee Choi (*The King and I*), Karen Kay Cody (*Master Class*), Viola Davis (*Seven Guitars*), Kate Forbes (*The School for Scandal*), Michael McGrath (*Swinging on a Star*), Alfred Molina (*Molly Sweeney*), Timothy Olyphant (*The Monogamist*), Adam Pascal (*Rent*), Lou Diamond Phillips (*The King and I*), Daphne Rubin-Vega (*Rent*), Brett Tabisel (*Big*), The Cast of *An Ideal Husband* (Special Award)

1996-97: Terry Beaver (*The Last Night of Ballyhoo*), Helen Carey (*LondonAssurance*), Kristin Chenoweth (*Steel Pier*), Jason Danieley (*Candide*), Linda Eder (*Jekyll & Hyde*), Allison Janney (*Present Laughter*), Daniel McDonald (*Steel Pier*), Janet McTeer (*A Doll's House*), Mark Ruffalo (*This Is Our Youth*), Fiona Shaw (*The Waste Land*), Antony Sher (*Stanley*), Alan Tudyk (*Bunny Bunny*), The Cast of *Skylight* (Special Award)

1997-98: Max Casella (*The Lion King*), Margaret Colin (*Jackie*), Ruaidhri Conroy (*The Cripple of Inishmaan*), Alan Cumming (*Cabaret*), Lea Delaria (*On the Town*), Edie Falco (*Side Man*), Enid Graham (*Honour*), Anna Kendrick (*High Society*), Ednita Nazario (*The Capeman*), Douglas Sills (*The Scarlet Pimpernel*), Steven Sutcliffe (*Ragtime*), Sam Trammel (*Ah, Wilderness!*), Eddie Izzard (Special Award), The Cast of *The Beauty Queen of Leenane* (Special Award)

1998-99: Jillian Armenante (*The Cider House Rules*), James Black (*Not About Nightingales*), Brendan Coyle (*The Weir*), Anna Friel (*Closer*), Rupert Graves (*Closer*), Lynda Gravátt (*The Old Settler*), Nicole Kidman (*The Blue Room*), Ciáran Hinds (*Closer*), Ute Lemper (*Chicago*), Clarke Peters (*The Iceman Cometh*), Toby Stephens (*Ring Round the Moon*), Sandra Oh (*Stop Kiss*), Jerry Herman (Special Award)

1999-2000: Craig Bierko (*The Music Man*), Everett Bradley (*Swing!*), Gabriel Byrne (*A Moon for the Misbegotten*), Ann Hampton Callaway (*Swing!*), Toni Collette (*The Wild Party*), Henry Czerny (*Arms and the Man*), Stephen Dillane (*The Real Thing*), Jennifer Ehle (*The Real Thing*), Philip Seymour Hoffman (*True West*), Hayley Mills (*Suite in Two Keys*), Cigdem Onat (*The Time of the Cuckoo*), Claudia Shear (*Dirty Blonde*), Barry Humphries (*Dame Edna: The Royal Tour* – Special Award)

2000-2001: Juliette Binoche (*Betrayal*), Macaulay Culkin (*Madame Melville*), Janie Dee (*Comic Potential*), Raúl Esparza (*The Rocky Horror Show*), Kathleen Freeman (*The Full Monty*), Deven May (*Bat Boy*), Reba McEntire (*Annie Get Your Gun*), Chris Noth (*The Best Man*), Joshua Park (*The Adventures of Tom Sawyer*), Rosie Perez (*References to Salvador Dali Make Me Hot*), Joely Richardson (*Madame Melville*), John Ritter (*The Dinner Party*), The Cast of *Stones in His Pocket* – Seán Campion & Conleth Hill (Special Awards)

2001-2002: Justin Bohon (*Oklahoma!*), Simon Callow (*The Mystery of Charles Dickens*), Mos Def (*Topdog/Underdog*), Emma Fielding (*Private Lives*), Adam Godley (*Private Lives*), Martin Jarvis (*By Jeeves*), Spencer Kayden (*Urinetown*), Gretchen Mol (*The Shape of Things*), Anna Paquin (*The Glory of Living*), Louise Pitre (*Mamma Mia!*), David Warner (*Major Barbara*), Rachel Weisz (*The Shape of Things*)

2002-2003: Antonio Banderas (*Nine*), Tammy Blanchard (*Gypsy*), Thomas Jefferson Byrd (*Ma Rainey's Black Bottom*), Jonathan Cake (*Medea*), Victoria Hamilton (*A Day in the Death of Joe Egg*), Clare Higgins (*Vincent in Brixton*), Jackie Hoffman (*Hairspray*), Mary Stuart Masterson (*Nine*), John Selya (*Movin' Out*), Daniel Sunjata (*Take Me Out*), Jochum ten Haaf (*Vincent in Brixton*), Marissa Jaret Winokur (*Hairspray*), Peter Filichia and Ben Hodges (Special Awards)

2003-2004: Shannon Cochran (*Bug*), Stephanie D'Abruzzo (*Avenue Q*), Mitchel David Federan (*The Boy From Oz*), Alexander Gemignani (*Assassins*), Hugh Jackman (*The Boy From Oz*), Isabel Keating (*The Boy From Oz*), Sanaa Lathan (*A Raisin in the Sun*), Jefferson Mays (*I Am My Own Wife*), Euan Morton (*Taboo*), Anika Noni Rose (*Caroline, or Change*), John Tartaglia (*Avenue Q*), Jennifer Westfeldt (*Wonderful Town*), Sarah Jones (*Bridge and Tunnel* – Special Award)

2004-2005: Christina Applegate (*Sweet Charity*), Ashlie Atkinson (*Fat Pig*), Hank Azaria (*Spamalot*), Gordon Clapp (*Glengarry Glen Ross*), Conor Donovan (*Privilege*), Dan Fogler (*The 25th Annual Putnam County Spelling Bee*), Heather Goldenhersh (*Doubt*), Carla Gugino (*After the Fall*), Jenn Harris (*Modern Orthodox*), Cheyenne Jackson (*All Shook Up*), Celia Keenan-Bolger (*The 25th Annual Putnam County Spelling Bee*), Tyler Maynard (*Altar Boyz*)

2005-2006: Harry Connick Jr. (*The Pajama Game*), Felicia P. Fields (*The Color Purple*), Maria Friedman (*The Woman in White*), Richard Griffiths (*The History Boys*), Mamie Gummer (*Mr. Marmalade*), Jayne Houdyshell (*Well*), Bob Martin (*The Drowsy Chaperone*), Ian McDiarmid (*Faith Healer*), Nellie McKay (*The

Threepenny Opera), David Wilmot (*The Lieutenant of Inishmore*), Elisabeth Withers-Mendes (*The Color Purple*), John Lloyd Young (*Jersey Boys*)

2006–2007: Eve Best (*A Moon for the Misbegotten*), Mary Birdsong (*Martin Short: Fame Becomes Me*), Erin Davie (*Grey Gardens*), Xanthe Elbrick (*Coram Boy*), Fantasia (*The Color Purple*), Johnny Galecki (*The Little Dog Laughed*), Jonathan Groff (*Spring Awakening*), Gavin Lee (*Mary Poppins*), Lin-Manuel Miranda (*In the Heights*), Bill Nighy (*The Vertical Hour*), Stark Sands (*Journey's End*), Nilaja Sun (*No Child…*), The Actors Fund (Special Award)

2007–2008: de'Adre Aziza (*Passing Strange*), Cassie Beck (*The Drunken City*), Daniel Breaker (*Passing Strange*), Ben Daniels (*Les Liaisons Dangereuses*), Deanna Dunagan (*August: Osage County*), Hoon Lee (*Yellow Face*), Alli Mauzey (*Cry-Baby*), Jenna Russell (*Sunday in the Park with George*), Mark Rylance (*Boeing-Boeing*), Loretta Ables Sayre (*South Pacific*), Jimmi Simpson (*The Farnsworth Invention*), Paulo Szot (*South Pacific*)

2008–2009: David Alvarez (*Billy Elliot The Musical*), Chad C. Coleman (*Joe Turner's Come and Gone*), Jennifer Grace (*Our Town*), Josh Grisetti (*Enter Laughing The Musical*), Haydn Gwynne *Billy Elliot The Musical*), Colin Hanks (*33 Variations*), Marin Ireland (*reasons to be pretty*), Trent Kowalik (*Billy Elliot The Musical*), Kiril Kulish (*Billy Elliot The Musical*), Susan Louise O'Connor (*Blithe Spirit*), Condola Rashad (*Ruined*), Geoffrey Rush (*Exit the King*), Josefina Scaglione (*West Side Story*), Wesley Taylor (*Rock of Ages*); The Cast of *The Norman Conquests* (Special Award)

2009–2010: Nina Arianda (*Venus in Fur*), Chris Chalk (*Fences*), Bill Heck (*The Orphans' Home Cycle*), Jon Michael Hill (*Superior Donuts*), Scarlett Johansson (*A View from the Bridge*), Keira Keeley (*The Glass Menagerie*), Sahr Ngaujah (*Fela!*), Eddie Redmayne (*Red*), Andrea Riseborough (*The Pride*), Heidi Schreck (*Circle Mirror Transformation*), Stephanie Umoh (*Ragtime*), Michael Urie (*The Temperamentals*); Dorothy Loudon Award: Bobby Steggert (*Yank!* & *Ragtime*)

Andrea McArdle and Dorothy Loudon at the 1977 Theatre World Awards

John Leguizamo at the 1993 Theatre World Awards

MAJOR NEW YORK THEATRICAL AWARDS

American Theatre Wing's Antoinette Perry "Tony" Awards

Sunday, June 12, 2011 at the Beacon Theatre; 65th annual; Host: Neil Patrick Harris. Presented for distinguished achievement in the Broadway theatre by The American Theatre Wing (Theodore S. Chapin, Chairman; Howard Sherman, Executive Director) and The Broadway League (Paul Libin, Chairman; Charlotte St. Martin, Executive Director); Tony Awards Production General Managers, Alan Wasser and Allen Williams; Executive Producers, Ricky Kirshner and Glenn Weiss/ White Cherry Entertainment; Production Director, Glen Weiss; 2010–2011 Tony Awards Nominating Committee (appointed by the Tony Awards Administration Committee): Victoria Bailey (Executive Director, Theatre Development Fund), David Caddick (Music Supervisor), Ben Cameron (Program Director for the Arts - Doris Duke Charitable Foundation), Kathleen Chalfant (Actor), Hope Clarke (Stage Director/Choreographer/Actor), Thomas Cott (Producer/Management Consultant), André De Shields (Actor), Edgar Dobie (Producer/General Manager/ Managing Director, Arena Stage Washington, DC), Gordon Edelstein (Director/ Artistic Director of Long Wharf Theatre), Beverly Emmons (Lighting Designer), Michael Greif (Director), Paulette Haupt (Director of the Music Theatre Conference at The O'Neill Center), Mark Hollmann (Composer/Lyricist), Elena K. Holy (Founder - The International Fringe Festival), Robert Kamlot (Retired General Manager), Moisés Kaufman (Director/Playwright/Artistic Director, Tectonic Theater), Robert Kimball (Author), Pia Lindström (Former Reporter/Theatre Critic), Todd London (Artistic Director, New Dramatists), Donna McKechnie (Actor/Choreographer), Jon Nakagawa (Producer of Contemporary Programming - Lincoln Center), Alice Playten (Actor), Theresa Rebeck (Playwright), Susan H. Schulman (Director), Rosemarie Tichler (Theatre Executive, Educator/Casting Director), Tamara Tunie (Actor/Producer), William Tynan (Actor/Reporter), Kevin Wade (Playwright/Screenwriter), Doug Wright (Playwright/Screenwriter), Andrew Zerman (Retired Casting Director).

Best Play: *War Horse* by Nick Stafford, Produced by Lincoln Center Theater, André Bishop, Bernard Gersten, National Theatre of Great Britain, Nicholas Hytner, Nick Starr, Bob Boyett, War Horse LP

Nominees: *Good People* by David Lindsay-Abaire, Produced by Manhattan Theatre Club, Lynne Meadow, Barry Grove; *Jerusalem* by Jez Butterworth, Produced by Sonia Friedman Productions, Stuart Thompson, Scott Rudin, Roger Berlind, Royal Court Theatre Productions, Beverly Bartner/Alice Tulchin, Dede Harris/Rupert Gavin, Broadway Across America, Jon B. Platt, 1001 Nights/ Stephanie P. McClelland, Carole L. Haber/Richard Willis, Jacki Barlia Florin/Adam Blanshay; *The Motherf**ker with the Hat* by Stephen Adly Guirgis, Produced by Scott Rudin, Stuart Thompson, Public Theater Productions, Oskar Eustis, Joey Parnes, Labyrinth Theater Company, Stephen Adly Guirgis, Mimi O'Donnell, Yul Vázquez, Danny Feldman, Fabula Media Partners LLC, Jean Doumanian, Ruth Hendel, Carl Moellenberg, Jon B. Platt, Tulchin Bartner/Jamie deRoy

Best Musical: *The Book of Mormon* Produced by Anne Garefino, Scott Rudin, Roger Berlind, Scott M. Delman, Jean Doumanian, Roy Furman, Important Musicals LLC, Stephanie P. McClelland, Kevin Morris, Jon B. Platt, Sonia Friedman Productions, Stuart Thompson

Nominees: *Catch Me If You Can* Produced by Margo Lion, Hal Luftig, Stacey Mindich, Yasuhiro Kawana, Scott & Brian Zeilinger, The Rialto Group, The Araca Group, Michael Watt, Barbara & Buddy Freitag, Jay & Cindy Gutterman/Pittsburgh CLO, Elizabeth Williams, Johnny Roscoe Productions/Van Dean, Fakston Productions/Solshay Productions, Patty Baker/Richard Winkler, Nederlander Presentations, Inc., Warren Trepp, Remmel T. Dickinson, Paula Herold/Kate Lear, Stephanie P. McClelland, Jamie deRoy, Barry Feirstein, Rainerio J. Reyes, Rodney Rigby, Loraine Boyle, Amuse Inc., Joseph & Matthew Deitch/Cathy Chernoff, Joan Stein/Jon Murray, The 5th Avenue Theatre; *The Scottsboro Boys* Produced by Barry and Fran Weissler, Jacki Barlia Florin, Janet Pailet/Sharon A. Carr/Patricia R.

Klausner, Nederlander Presentations, Inc./The Shubert Organization, Beechwood Entertainment, Broadway Across America, Mark Zimmerman, Adam Blanshay/ R2D2 Productions, Rick Danzansky/Barry Tatelman, Bruce Robert Harris/Jack W. Batman, Allen Spivak/Jerry Frankel, Bard Theatricals/Probo Productions/Randy Donaldson, Catherine Schreiber/Michael Palitz/Patti Laskawy, Vineyard Theatre; *Sister Act* Produced by Whoopi Goldberg & Stage Entertainment, The Shubert Organization and Disney Theatrical Productions

Best Book of a Musical: *The Book of Mormon* by Trey Parker, Robert Lopez, and Matt Stone

Nominees: *Bloody Bloody Andrew Jackson* by Alex Timbers; *The Scottsboro Boys* by David Thompson; *Sister Act* by Cheri Steinellner, Bill Steinkellner, and Douglas Carter Beane

Best Original Score (music and/or lyrics) Written for the Theatre: *The Book of Mormon* Music & Lyrics by Trey Parker, Robert Lopez, and Matt Stone

Nominees: *The Scottsboro Boys* Music & Lyrics by John Kander and Fred Ebb; *Sister Act* Music by Alan Menken, Lyrics by Glenn Slater ; *Women on the Verge of a Nervous Breakdown* Music & Lyrics by David Yazbek

Best Revival of a Play: *The Normal Heart* by Larry Kramer; Produced by Daryl Roth, Paul Boskind, Martian Entertainment, Gregory Rae, Jayne Baron Sherman/ Alexander Fraser

Nominees: *Arcadia* by Tom Stoppard, Produced by Sonia Friedman Productions, Roger Berlind, Stephanie P. McClelland, Scott M. Delman, Nicholas Quinn Rosenkranz, Disney Theatrical Group, Robert G. Bartner, Olympus Theatricals, Douglas Smith, Janine Safer Whitney; *The Importance of Being Earnest* by Oscar Wilde, Produced by Roundabout Theatre Company, Todd Haimes, Harold Wolpert, Julia C. Levy; *The Merchant of Venice* by William Shakespeare, Produced by The Public Theater, Oskar Eustis, Andrew D. Hamingson, Jeffrey Richards, Jerry Frankel, Debbie Bisno & Eva Price, Amy Nederlander, Jonathan First, Stewart F. Lane & Bonnie Comley, Universal Pictures Stage Productions, Merritt Forrest Baer, The Araca Group, Broadway Across America, Joseph & Matthew Deitch, JK Productions, Terry Allen Kramer, Cathy Chernoff/Jay & Cindy Gutterman, Mallory Factor/Cheryl Lachowicz, Joey Parnes, The Shubert Organization

Best Revival of a Musical: *Anything Goes* Produced by Roundabout Theatre Company, Todd Haimes, Harold Wolpert, Julia C. Levy

Nominees: *How to Succeed in Business Without Really Trying* Produced by Broadway Across America, Craig Zadan, Neil Meron, Joseph Smith, Michael McCabe, Candy Spelling, Takonkiet Viravan/Scenario Thailand, Hilary A. Williams, Jen Namoff/Fakston Productions, Two Left Feet Productions/Power Arts, Hop Theatricals, LLC/Paul Chau/Daniel Frishwasser/Michael Jackowitz, Michael Speyer-Bernie Abrams/Jacki Barlia Florin-Adam Blanshay/Arlene Scanlan/TBS Service

Best Performance by a Leading Actor in a Play: Mark Rylance, *Jerusalem*

Nominees: Brian Bedford, *The Importance of Being Earnest*; Bobby Cannavale, *The Motherf**ker with the Hat*; Joe Mantello, *The Normal Heart*; Al Pacino, *The Merchant of Venice*

Best Performance by a Leading Actress in a Play: Frances McDormand, *Good People*

Nominees: Brian Bedford, *The Importance of Being Earnest*; Bobby Cannavale, *The Motherf**ker with the Hat*; Joe Mantello, *The Normal Heart*; Al Pacino, *The Merchant of Venice*

Best Performance by a Leading Actor in a Musical: Norbert Leo Butz, *Catch Me If You Can*

Nominees: Josh Gad, *The Book of Mormon*; Joshua Henry, *The Scottsboro Boys*; Andrew Rannells, *The Book of Mormon*; Tony Sheldon, *Priscilla Queen of the Desert*

Best Performance by a Leading Actress in a Musical: Sutton Foster, *Anything Goes*

Nominees: Beth Leavel, *Baby It's You!*; Patina Miller, *Sister Act*; Donna Murphy, *The People in the Picture*

Best Performance by a Featured Actor in a Play: John Benjamin Hickey, *The Normal Heart*

Nominees: Mackenzie Crook, *Jerusalem*; Billy Crudup, *Arcadia*; Arian Moayed, *Bengal Tiger at the Baghdad Zoo*; Yul Vázquez, *The Motherf**ker with the Hat*

Best Performance by a Featured Actress in a Play: Ellen Barkin, *The Normal Heart*

Nominees: Edie Falco, *The House of Blue Leaves*; Judith Light, *Lombardi*; Joanna Lumley, *La Bête*; Elizabeth Rodriguez, *The Motherf**ker with the Hat*

Best Performance by a Featured Actor in a Musical: John Larroquette, *How to Succeed in Business Without Really Trying*

Nominees: Colman Domingo, *The Scottsboro Boys*; Adam Godley, *Anything Goes*; Forrest McClendon, *The Scottsboro Boys*; Rory O'Malley, *The Book of Mormon*

Best Performance by a Featured Actress in a Musical: Nikki M. James, *The Book of Mormon*

Nominees: Laura Benanti, *Women on the Verge of a Nervous Breakdown*; Tammy Blanchard, *How to Succeed in Business Without Really Trying*; Victoria Clark, *Sister Act*; Patti LuPone, *Women on the Verge of a Nervous Breakdown*

Best Scenic Design of a Play: Rae Smith, *War Horse*

Nominees: Todd Rosenthal, *The Motherf**ker with the Hat*; Ultz, *Jerusalem*; Mark Wendland, *The Merchant of Venice*

Best Scenic Design of a Musical: Scott Pask, *The Book of Mormon*

Nominees: Beowulf Boritt, *The Scottsboro Boys*; Derek McLane, *Anything Goes*; Donyale Werle, *Bloody Bloody Andrew Jackson*

Best Costume Design of a Play: Desmond Heeley, *The Importance of Being Earnest*

Nominees: Jess Goldstein, *The Merchant of Venice*; Mark Thompson, *La Bête*; Catherine Zuber, *Born Yesterday*

Best Costume Design of a Musical: Tim Chappel & Lizzy Gardiner, *Priscilla Queen of the Desert*

Nominees: Martin Pakledinaz, *Anything Goes*; Ann Roth, *The Book of Mormon*; Catherine Zuber, *How to Succeed in Business Without Really Trying*

Best Lighting Design of a Play: Paule Constable, *War Horse*

Nominees: David Lander, *Bengal Tiger at the Baghdad Zoo*; Kenneth Posner, *The Merchant of Venice*; Mimi Jordan Sherin, *Jerusalem*

Best Lighting Design of a Musical: Brian MacDevitt, *The Book of Mormon*

Nominees: Ken Billington, *The Scottsboro Boys*; Howell Binkley, *How to Succeed in Business Without Really Trying*; Peter Kaczorowski, *Anything Goes*

Best Sound Design of a Play: Christopher Shutt, *War Horse*

Nominees: Acme Sound Partners and Cricket S. Myers, *Bengal Tiger at the Baghdad Zoo*; Simon Baker, *Brief Encounter*; Ian Dickinson for Autograph, *Jerusalem*

Best Sound Design of a Musical: Brian Ronan, *The Book of Mormon*

Nominees: Peter Hylenski, *The Scottsboro Boys*; Steve Canyon Kennedy, *Catch Me If You Can*; Brian Ronan, *Anything Goes*

Best Direction of a Play: Marianne Elliott and Tom Morris, *War Horse*

Nominees: Joel Grey and George C. Wolfe, *The Normal Heart*; Anna D. Shapiro, *The Motherf**ker with the Hat*; Daniel Sullivan, *The Merchant of Venice*

Best Direction of a Musical: Casey Nicholaw and Trey Parker, *The Book of Mormon*

Nominees: Rob Ashford, *How to Succeed in Business Without Really Trying*; Kathleen Marshall, *Anything Goes*; Susan Stroman, *The Scottsboro Boys*

Best Choreography: Kathleen Marshall, *Anything Goes*

Nominees: Rob Ashford, *How to Succeed in Business Without Really Trying*; Casey Nicholaw, *The Book of Mormon*; Susan Stroman, *The Scottsboro Boys*

Best Orchestrations: Larry Hochman & Stephen Oremus, *The Book of Mormon*

Nominees: Doug Besterman, *How to Succeed in Business Without Really Trying*; Larry Hochman, *The Scottsboro Boys*; Marc Shaiman & Larry Blank, *Catch Me If You Can*

Special Tony Award for Lifetime Achievement in the Theatre: Athol Fugard; Philip J. Smith

Regional Theatre Tony Award: Lookingglass Theatre Company (Chicago, Illinois)

Isabelle Stevenson Award for Service: Eve Ensler

Special Tony Award: Handspring Puppet Company

Tony Honor for Excellence in the Theatre: William Berloni; The Drama Book Shop; Sharon Jensen and Alliance for Inclusion in the Arts

PAST TONY AWARD-WINNING PRODUCTIONS Awards listed are Best Play followed by Best Musical, and, as awards for Best Revival and the subcategories of Best Revival of a Play and Best Revival of a Musical were instituted, they are listed respectively.

1947: No award given for musical or play **1948:** *Mister Roberts* (play) **1949:** *Death of a Salesman*; *Kiss Me, Kate* (musical) **1950:** *The Cocktail Party*; *South Pacific* **1951:** *The Rose Tattoo*; *Guys and Dolls* **1952:** *The Fourposter*; *The King and I* **1953:** *The Crucible*; *Wonderful Town* **1954:** *The Teahouse of the August Moon*; *Kismet* **1955:** *The Desperate Hours*; *The Pajama Game* **1956:** *The Diary of Anne Frank*; *Damn Yankees* **1957:** *Long Day's Journey into Night*; *My Fair Lady* **1958:** *Sunrise at Campobello*; *The Music Man* **1959:** *J.B.*; *Redhead* **1960:** *The Miracle Worker*; *Fiorello!* & *The Sound of Music* (tie) **1961:** *Becket*; *Bye Bye Birdie* **1962:** *A Man for All Seasons*; *How to Succeed in Business Without Really Trying* **1963:** *Who's Afraid of Virginia Woolf?*; *A Funny Thing Happened on the Way to the Forum* **1964:** *Luther*; *Hello, Dolly!* **1965:** *The Subject Was Roses*; *Fiddler on the Roof* **1966:** *The Persecution and Assassination of Marat as Performed by the Inmates of the Asylum of Charenton Under the Direction of the Marquis de Sade*; *Man of La Mancha* **1967:** *The Homecoming*; *Cabaret* **1968:** *Rosencrantz and Guildenstern Are Dead*; *Hallelujah Baby!* **1969:** *The Great White Hope*; *1776* **1970:** *Borstal Boy*; *Applause* **1971:** *Sleuth*; *Company* **1972:** *Sticks and Bones*; *Two Gentlemen of Verona* **1973:** *That Championship Season*; *A Little Night Music* **1974:** *The River Niger*; *Raisin* **1975:** *Equus*; *The Wiz* **1976:** *Travesties*; *A Chorus Line* **1977:** *The Shadow Box*; *Annie* **1978:** *Da*; *Ain't Misbehavin'*; *Dracula* (innovative musical revival) **1979:** *The Elephant Man*; *Sweeney Todd* **1980:** *Children of a Lesser God*; *Evita*; *Morning's at Seven* (best revival) **1981:** *Amadeus*; *42nd Street*; *The Pirates of Penzance* **1982:** *The Life and Adventures of Nicholas Nickelby*; *Nine*; *Othello* **1983:** *Torch Song Trilogy*; *Cats*; *On Your Toes* **1984:** *The Real Thing*; *La Cage aux Folles*; *Death of a Salesman* **1985:** *Biloxi Blues*; *Big River*; *A Day in the Death of Joe Egg* **1986:** *I'm Not Rappaport*; *The Mystery of Edwin Drood*; *Sweet Charity* **1987:** *Fences*; *Les Misérables*; *All My Sons* **1988:** *M. Butterfly*; *The Phantom of the Opera*; *Anything Goes* **1989:** *The Heidi Chronicles*; *Jerome Robbins' Broadway*; *Our Town* **1990:** *The Grapes of Wrath*; *City of Angels*; *Gypsy* **1991:** *Lost in Yonkers*; *The Will Rogers' Follies*; *Fiddler on the Roof* **1992:** *Dancing at Lughnasa*; *Crazy for You*; *Guys and Dolls* **1993:** *Angels in America: Millenium Approaches*; *Kiss of the Spider Woman*; *Anna Christie* **1994:** *Angels in America: Perestroika*; *Passion*; *An Inspector Calls* (play revival); *Carousel* (musical revival) **1995:** *Love! Valour! Compassion!*; *Sunset Boulevard*; *The Heiress*; *Show Boat* **1996:** *Master Class*; *Rent*; *A Delicate Balance*; *King and I* **1997:** *Last Night of Ballyhoo*; *Titanic*; *A Doll's House*; *Chicago* **1998:** *Art*; *The Lion King*; *View from the Bridge*; *Cabaret* **1999:**

Side Man; Fosse; Death of a Salesman; Annie Get Your Gun **2000:** *Copenhagen; Contact; The Real Thing; Kiss Me, Kate* **2001:** *Proof; The Producers; One Flew Over the Cuckoo's Nest; 42nd Street* **2002:** Edward Albee's *The Goat, or Who Is Sylvia?; Thoroughly Modern Millie; Private Lives; Into the Woods* **2003:** *Take Me Out; Hairspray; Long Day's Journey Into Night; Nine* **2004:** *I Am My Own Wife; Avenue Q; Henry IV; Assassins* **2005:** *Doubt; Monty Python's Spamalot; Glengarry Glen Ross; La Cage aux Folles* **2006:** *The History Boys; Jersey Boys; Awake and Sing!; The Pajama Game* **2007:** *The Coast of Utopia; Spring Awakening; Journey's End; Company* **2008:** *August: Osage County; In the Heights; Boeing-Boeing; South Pacific* **2009:** *God of Carnage; Billy Elliot The Musical; The Norman Conquests; Hair* **2010:** *Red; Memphis; Fences; La Cage aux Folles*

Drama Desk Awards

Monday, May 23, 2011 at Hammerstein Ballroom; 56th annual; Host: Harvey Fierstein. Originally known as the Vernon Rice Awards until 1964 (named after the former *New York Post* theatre critic); Presented for outstanding achievement in the 2010–2011 season for Broadway, Off-Broadway, and Off-Off Broadway productions, voted on by an association of New York drama reporters, editors and critics; Executive Producer, Robert R. Blume; Consulting Producer, Lauren Class Schneider; Director of Ceremony, Jeff Kalpak; Line Producer, Rich Bittner; Gala Producer Christopher Raphael; Special Events Director, Randie Levine-Miller; Director of Publicity, Les Schecter and Springer Associates; Associate Producer, Red Carpet Media, Renee McCurry; Frank Fiorucci; Blume Media Group Ltd.; Production Associate Producers, Joseph Callari, Les Schecter; Media Sponsors, *TheaterMania.com* and The Broadway Channel; Board of Directors: Isa Goldberg (President), Leslie Hoban Blake (Vice President), Charles Wright (Treasurer and 2nd Vice President), Richard Ridge (Secretary), Arlene Epstein, Elysa Gardner, Randy Gener, John Istel, David Kaufman, Sam Norkin, William Wolf; Nominating Committee: Barbara Siegel – Chairperson (*TheaterMania.com* and *TalkinBroadway.com*), Jason Clark (*Slant Magazine*), Anita Gates (*Freelance, The New York Times, theatergossip.com*), Lawrence Harbison (Senior Editor and Columnists for *Smith & Kraus, Inc.*), Gerard Raymond (*Back Stage*), Richard Ridge (*Broadway Beat TV*), Douglas Strassler (*Show Business Magazine*)

Outstanding Play: *War Horse* by Nick Stafford

Nominees: Jon Robin Baitz, *Other Desert Cities*; Adam Bock, *A Small Fire*; Stephen Adly Guirgis, *The Motherf**ker With the Hat*; Samuel D. Hunter, *A Bright New Boise*; Rajiv Joseph, *Bengal Tiger at the Baghdad Zoo*; David Lindsay-Abaire, *Good People*

Outstanding Musical: *The Book of Mormon*

Nominees: *In Transit; Priscilla Queen of the Desert; See Rock City & Other Destinations; Sister Act; The Kid*

Outstanding Revival of a Play: *The Normal Heart*

Nominees: *Born Yesterday; The House of Blue Leaves; The Importance of Being Earnest; The Merchant of Venice; Three Sisters*

Outstanding Revival of a Musical: *Anything Goes*

Nominees: *Hello Again; How to Succeed in Business Without Really Trying*

Outstanding Actor in a Play: Bobby Cannavale, *The Motherf**ker With the Hat*

Nominees: Charles Busch, *The Divine Sister*; Al Pacino, *The Merchant of Venice*; Geoffrey Rush, *The Diary of a Madman*; Mark Rylance, *Jerusalem*; Michael Shannon, *Mistakes Were Made*; Paul Sparks, *Dusk Rings a Bell*

Outstanding Actress in a Play: Frances McDormand, *Good People*

Nominees: Nina Arianda, *Born Yesterday*; Stockard Channing, *Other Desert Cities*; Laurie Metcalf, *The Other Place*; Michele Pawk, *A Small Fire*; Lily Rabe, *The Merchant of Venice*

Outstanding Actor in a Musical: Norbert Leo Butz, *Catch Me If You Can*

Nominees: Colin Donnell, *Anything Goes*; Daniel Radcliffe, *How to Succeed in Business Without Really Trying*; Andrew Rannells, *The Book of Mormon*; Tony Sheldon, *Priscilla Queen of the Desert: The Musical*; Christopher Sieber, *The Kid*

Outstanding Actress in a Musical: Sutton Foster, *Anything Goes*

Nominees: Beth Leavel, *Baby It's You!*; Patina Miller, *Sister Act*; Donna Murphy, *The People in the Picture*; Sherie Rene Scott, *Women on the Verge of a Nervous Breakdown*

Outstanding Featured Actor in a Play: Brian Bedford, *The Importance of Being Earnest*

Nominees: Christian Borle, *Peter and the Starcatcher*; Boyd Gaines, *The Grand Manner*; Logan Marshall-Green, *The Hallway Trilogy*; Zachary Quinto, *Angels in America*; Tom Riley, *Arcadia*; Yul Vázquez, *The Motherf**ker With the Hat*

Outstanding Featured Actress in a Play: Edie Falco, *The House of Blue Leaves*

Nominees: Lisa Emery, *The Collection & A Kind of Alaska*; Julie Halston, *The Divine Sister*; Sarah Nina Hayon, *A Bright New Boise*; Celia Keenan-Bolger, *Peter and the Starcatcher*; Linda Lavin, *Other Desert Cities*; Judith Light, *Lombardi*

Outstanding Featured Actor in a Musical: John Larroquette, *How to Succeed in Business Without Really Trying*

Nominees: Adam Godley, *Anything Goes*; Brian Stokes Mitchell, *Women on the Verge of a Nervous Breakdown*; Rory O'Malley, *The Book of Mormon*; Bob Stillman, *Hello Again*; Tom Wopat, *Catch Me if You Can*

Outstanding Featured Actress in a Musical: Laura Benanti, *Women on the Verge of a Nervous Breakdown*

Nominees: Kerry Butler, *Catch Me if You Can*; Victoria Clark, *Sister Act*; Jill Eikenberry, *The Kid*; Nikki M. James, *The Book of Mormon*; Patti LuPone, *Women on the Verge of a Nervous Breakdown*; Laura Osnes, *Anything Goes*

Outstanding Director of a Play: Joel Grey and George C. Wolfe, *The Normal Heart*

Nominees: Trip Cullman, *A Small Fire*; Moisés Kaufman, *Bengal Tiger at the Baghdad Zoo*; Davis McCallum, *A Bright New Boise*; Daniel Sullivan, *The Merchant of Venice*; Kirjan Waage and Gwendolyn Warnock, *Baby Universe*

Outstanding Director of a Musical: Casey Nicholaw and Trey Parker, *The Book of Mormon*

Nominees: Rob Ashford, *How to Succeed in Business Without Really Trying*; Joe Calarco, *In Transit*; Jack Cummings III, *Hello Again*; Jack Cummings III, *See Rock City & Other Destinations*; Kathleen Marshall, *Anything Goes*

Outstanding Choreography: Kathleen Marshall, *Anything Goes*

Nominees: Rob Ashford, *How to Succeed in Business Without Really Trying*; Scott Graham and Steven Hoggett, *Beautiful Burnout*; Steven Hoggett, *Peter and the Starcatcher*; Casey Nicholaw, *The Book of Mormon*; Siudy, *Between Worlds*

Outstanding Music: Trey Parker, Robert Lopez & Matt Stone, *The Book of Mormon*

Nominees: Brad Alexander, *See Rock City & Other Destinations*; Alan Menken, *Sister Act*; Marc Shaiman, *Catch Me if You Can*; Mike Stoller and Artie Butler, *The People in the Picture*; David Yazbek, *Women on the Verge of a Nervous Breakdown*

Outstanding Lyrics: Trey Parker, Robert Lopez & Matt Stone, *The Book of Mormon*

Nominees: Rick Crom, *Newsical The Musical — Full Spin Ahead*; Jack Lechner, *The Kid*; Adam Mathias, *See Rock City & Other Destinations*; Glenn Slater, *Sister Act*; Scott Wittman and Marc Shaiman, *Catch Me if You Can*

Outstanding Book of a Musical: Adam Mathias, *See Rock City & Other Destinations*

Nominees: Kristen Anderson-Lopez, James-Allen Ford, Russ Kaplan and Sara Wordsworth, *In Transit*; Iris Rainer Dart, *The People in the Picture*; Stephan Elliott and Allan Scott, *Priscilla Queen of the Desert: The Musical*; Trey Parker, Robert Lopez and Matt Stone, *The Book of Mormon*; Michael Zam, *The Kid*

Outstanding Orchestrations: Larry Hochman & Stephen Oremus, *The Book of Mormon*

Nominees: Mary-Mitchell Campbell, *Hello Again*; Bruce Coughlin, *The Burnt Part Boys*; Simon Hale, Jim Abbott and David Yazbek, *Women on the Verge of a Nervous Breakdown*; Marc Shaiman and Larry Blank, *Catch Me if You Can*; Lynne Shankel, *The Extraordinary Ordinary*

Outstanding Music in a Play: Wayne Barker, *Peter and the Starcatcher*

Nominees: Kathryn Bostic, *Bengal Tiger at the Baghdad Zoo*; Lars Petter Hagen, *Baby Universe*; Alan John, *The Diary of a Madman*; Tom Kitt, *The Winter's Tale*; Dan Moses Schreier, *The Merchant of Venice*

Outstanding Revue: *Rain: A Tribute to the Beatles on Broadway*

Nominations: *Fyvush Finkel Live!*; *Newsical The Musical — Full Spin Ahead*

Outstanding Set Design: Derek McLane, *Anything Goes*

Nominees: Rachel Hauck, *Orange, Hat & Grace*; David Korins and Zachary Borovay, projection design), *Lombardi*; Derek McLane, *Bengal Tiger at the Baghdad Zoo*; Tony Straiges, *Treasure Island*; Mark Wendland, *The Merchant of Venice*

Outstanding Costume Design: Tim Chappel & Lizzy Gardiner, *Priscilla Queen of the Desert*

Nominees: Desmond Heeley, *The Importance of Being Earnest*; Ann Hould-Ward, *A Free Man of Color*; Martin Pakledinaz, *Anything Goes*; Ann Roth, *The Book of Mormon*; Paloma Young, *Peter and the Starcatcher*

Outstanding Lighting Design: David Lander, *Bengal Tiger at the Baghdad Zoo*

Nominees: Jean Kalman, *John Gabriel Borkman*; R. Lee Kennedy, *See Rock City & Other Destinations*; Laura Mroczkowski, *Spy Garbo*; Ben Stanton, *The Whipping Man*; David Weiner, *A Small Fire*

Outstanding Sound Design in a Musical: Brian Ronan, *Anything Goes*

Nominees: Lindsay Jones, *The Burnt Part Boys*; Michael Rasbury, *Hello Again*; Brian Ronan, *The Book of Mormon*; Jon Weston, *In Transit*

Outstanding Sound Design in a Play: Acme Sound Partners and Cricket S. Myers, *Bengal Tiger at*

the Baghdad Zoo

Nominees: Acme Sound Partners, *The Merchant of Venice*; Ian Dickinson, *John Gabriel Borkman*; Brett Jarvis, *Baby Universe*; Bray Poor, *Wings*; Eric Shimelonis, *The Hallway Trilogy*

Outstanding Solo Performance: John Leguizamo, *Ghetto Klown*

Nominees: Daniel Beaty, *Through the Night*; Mike Birbiglia, *Mike Birbiglia's My Girlfriend's Boyfriend*; Juliette Jeffers, *Batman and Robin in the Boogie Down*; Colin Quinn, *Colin Quinn Long Story Short*; Joanna Tope, *The Promise*

Unique Theatrical Experience: *Sleep No More*

Nominees: *Being Harold Pinter*, *Circus Incognitus*; *Gatz*, *Play Dead*; *Room 17B*;

Outstanding Ensemble Performances: *In Transit*; *The Normal Heart*

Special Awards: A.R. Gurney (Playwright); Reed Birney (Actor); Scott Elliott (Artistic Director, The New Group); Pearl Theatre Company; Creative team of *War Horse*: Paule Constable, Marianne Elliott, 59 Productions, Adrian Kohler with Basil Jones for Handspring Puppet Company, Tom Morris, Rae Smith, Christopher Shutt, Toby Sedgwick, Adrian Sutton and John Tams

PAST DRAMA DESK AWARD-WINNING PRODUCTIONS From 1954–1974, non-competitive awards were presented to various artists: performers, playwrights, choreographers, composers, designers, directors, theatre companies and occasionally to specific productions. In 1975 the awards became competitive, and citations for Outstanding New Play (P) – or in some instances Outstanding New American Play (AP) and Outstanding New Foreign Play (FP), Outstanding Musical (M), Musical Revue (MR), Outstanding Revival, (R) –and later, Outstanding Play Revival (RP) and Outstanding Musical Revival (RM)– were instituted and presented as the season demanded. If year or a specific category within a year is missing, no production awards were presented in that year or specific category.

1955: *The Way of the World*; *A Thieve's Carnival*; *Twelfth Night*; *The Merchant of Venice* **1956:** *The Iceman Cometh* **1963:** *The Coach with Six Insides*; *The Boys from Syracuse* **1964:** *In White America*; *The Streets of New York* **1970:** *Borstal Boy* (P); *The Effect of Gamma Rays on Man-in-the-Moon Marigolds* (AP); *Company* (M) **1975:** *Same Time, Next Year* (AP), *Equus* (FP); **1976:** *Streamers* (P); *The Royal Family* (R) **1977:** *A Texas Trilogy* (AP); *The Comedians* (FP); *Annie* (M) **1978:** *Da* (P); *Ain't Misbehavin'* (M) **1979:** *The Elephant Man* (P); *Sweeney Todd*, *The Demon Barber of Fleet Street* (M) **1980:** *Children of a Lesser God* (P); *Evita* (M) **1981:** *Amadeus* (P); *Lena Horne: The Lady and Her Music* (M) **1982:** *"Master Harold"…and the boys* (P); *Nine* (M); *Entertaining Mr. Sloan* (R) **1983:** *Torch Song Trilogy* (P); *Little Shop of Horrors* (M); *On Your Toes* (R) **1984:** *The Real Thing* (P); *Sunday in the Park with George* (M); *Death of a Salesman* (R) **1985:** *As Is* (P); *A Day in the Death of Joe Egg* (R) **1986:** *A Lie of the Mind* (P); *The Mystery of Edwin Drood* (M); *Lemon Sky* (R) **1987:** *Fences* (P); *Les Misérables* (M) **1988:** *M. Butterfly* (P); *Into the Woods* (M); *Anything Goes* (R) **1989:** *The Heidi Chronicles* (P); *Jerome Robbins' Broadway* (M); *Our Town* (R) **1990:** *The Piano Lesson* (P); *City of Angels* (M); *Gypsy* (R) **1991:** *Lost in Yonkers* (P); *The Secret Garden* (M); *And the World Goes Round* (MR); *A Little Night Music* (R) **1992:** *Lips Together, Teeth Apart* (P); *Crazy for You* (M); *Guys and Dolls* (R) **1993:** *Jeffrey* (P); *Kiss of the Spider Woman* (M); *Anna Christie* (R) **1994:** *Angels in America: Perestroika* (P); *Passion* (M); *Howard Crabtree's Whoop-Dee-Doo* (MR); *An Inspector Calls* (RP); *She Loves Me* (RM) **1995:** *Love! Valour! Compassion!* (P); *Showboat* (M); *The Heiress* (R) **1996:** *Master Class* (P); *Rent* (M); *A Delicate Balance* (RP); *The King and I* (RM) **1997:** *How I Learned to Drive* (P); *The Life* (M); *Howard Crabtree's When Pigs Fly* (MR); *A Doll's House* (RP); *Chicago* (RM) **1998:** *The Beauty Queen of Leenane* (P); *Ragtime* (M); *A View from the Bridge* (RP); *1776* (RM) **1999:** *Wit* (P); *Parade* (M); *Fosse* (MR); (tie) *Death of a Salesman* and *The Iceman Cometh* (RP); *You're a Good Man, Charlie Brown* (RM) **2000:** *Copenhagen* (P); *Contact* (M); *The Real Thing* (RP); *Kiss Me, Kate* (RM) **2001:** *Proof* (P); *The Producers* (M); *Forbidden Broadway 2001: A Spoof Odyssey* (MR); *The Best Man* (RP); *42nd Street* (RM) **2002:** (tie) *The Goat, or Who Is Sylvia?* and *Metamorphoses* (P); *Private Lives* (RP); *Into the Woods* (RM) **2003:** *Take Me Out* (P); *Hairspray* (M); *Long Day's Journey Into Night* (RP); *Nine* (RM) **2004:** *I Am My Own Wife* (P); *Wicked* (M); *Henry IV* (RP); *Assassins* (RM) **2005:** *Doubt* (P); *Monty Python's Spamalot* (M); *Forbidden Broadway: Special Victims Unit* (MR); *Twelve Angry Men* (RP); *La Cage aux Folles* (RM) **2006:** *The History Boys* (P); *The Drowsy Chaperone* (M); *Awake and Sing!* (RP); *Sweeney Todd, The Demon Barber of Fleet Street* (RM) **2007:** *The Coast of Utopia* (P); *Spring Awakening* (M); *Journey's End* (RP); *Company* (RM) **2008:** *August: Osage County* (P); *Passing Strange* (M); *Forbidden Broadway: Rude Awakening* (MR); *Boeing-Boeing* (RP); *South Pacific* (RM) **2009:** *Ruined* (P); *Billy Elliot The Musical* (M); *The Norman Conquests* (RP); *Hair* (RM) **2010:** *Red* (P); *Memphis* (M); Tie: *A View from the Bridge* and *Fences* (RP); *La Cage aux Folles* (RM)

Village Voice Obie Awards

Monday, May 16, 2011 at Webster Hall; 56th annual; Hosts: S. Epatha Merkerson and David Hyde Pierce. Presented for outstanding achievement in Off- and Off-Off-Broadway theater in the 2010–2011 season; Founded in 1955 by Village Voice cultural editor Jerry Tallmer; Judges: Michael Feingold (Committee Chair and *Village Voice* chief theatre critic), Alexis Soloski (*Village Voice* theatre critic), Hilton Als (*The New Yorker*), David Henry Hwang (Playwright); Evan Yionoulis (Director), Andy Propst (*TheatreMania/AmericanTheaterWebccom*); Produced by Eileen Phelan; Publicity by Gail Parenteau; Presenters: Alec Baldwin, Andrew Rannells, Arian Moayad, Frank Wood, Jim Parsons, John Larroquette, Liev Schreiber, Lin-Manuel Miranda, Mamie Gummer, Margaret Colin, Nina Arianda, Patina Miller, Rose Hemingway; Performance by Anthony Rapp and his band.

Best New American Play: ($1,000): *The Elaborate Entrance of Chad Deity* by Kristoffer Diaz (Second Stage)

Performance: Andre Braugher, *The Whipping Man* (Manhattan Theatre Club); Michael Chernus, *In the Wake* (The Public Theater); Ethan Hawke, *Blood From a Stone* (The New Group); Hamish Linklater, *The School for Lies* (Classic Stage); Laurie Metcalf, *The Other Place* (MCC Theater); Thomas Sadoski, *Other Desert Cities* (Lincoln Center Theater); Scott Shepherd, *Gatz* (The Public Theater); Brenda Wehle, *The Intelligent Homosexual's Guide to Capitalism and Socialism With a Key to the Scriptures* (The Public Theater); Charlayne Woodard, *The Witch of Edmonton* (Red Bull Theater); F. Murray Abraham, sustained excellence of performance

Playwrighting: Samuel D. Hunter, *A Bright New Boise* (The Wild Project); Jonas Hassen Khemiri, *Invasion!* (Soho Rep)

Direction: Austin Pendleton, *Three Sisters*; Roger Rees and Alex Timbers, *Peter and the Starcatcher* (New York Theatre Workshop); Leigh Silverman, *In the Wake* (The Public Theater) and *Go Back to Where You Are* (Playwrights Horizons)

Design: Jill BC DuBoff (sustained excellence of sound design); Donyale Werle (sustained excellence of set design)

Special Citations: *Sleep No More*, Design and direction by Felix Barrett; Co-Design by Livi Vaughan and Beatrice Minns ; Choreography by Maxine Doyle; Sound by Stephen Dobbie; Lighting by Euan Maybank; Costumes by David Israel Reynoso

Young Jean Lee, *We're Gonna Die*

Debbie Tucker Green (playwright) and Leah C. Gardiner (director), *Born Bad*

Ross Wetzsteon Memorial Award ($1,000): Belarus Free Theatre

Obie Theater Grants ($10,000 divided among winners): Metropolitan Playhouse and Wakka Wakka

PAST OBIE AWARD-WINNING BEST NEW PLAYS If year is missing, no award was given that season; multiple plays were awarded in some seasons.

1956: *Absalom, Absalom* **1957:** *A House Remembered* **1959:** *The Quare Fellow* **1961:** *The Blacks* **1962:** *Who'll Save the Plowboy?* **1964:** *Play* **1965:** *The Old Glory* **1966:** *The Journey of the Fifth Horse* **1970:** *The Effect of Gamma Rays on Man-in-the-Moon Marigolds* **1971:** *The House of Blue Leaves* **1973:** *The Hot L Baltimore* **1974:** *Short Eyes* **1975:** *The First Breeze of Summer* **1976:** *American Buffalo, Sexual Perversity in Chicago* **1977:** *Curse of the Starving Class* **1978:** *Shaggy Dog Animation* **1979:** *Josephine* **1981:** *FOB* **1982:** *Metamorphosis* in Miniature; *Mr. Dead and Mrs. Free* **1983:** *Painting Churches*; *Andrea Rescued*; *Edmond* **1984:** *Fool for Love* **1985:** *The Conduct of Life* **1987:** *The Cure*; *Film Is Evil, Radio Is Good* **1988:** *Abingdon Square* **1990:** *Prelude to a Kiss*; *Imperceptible Mutabilities in the Third Kingdom*; *Bad Benny*; *Crowbar*; *Terminal Hip* **1991:** *The Fever* **1992:** *Sight Unseen*; *Sally's Rape*; *The Baltimore Waltz* **1994:** *Twilight: Los Angeles, 1992* **1995:** *Cryptogram* **1996:** *Adrienne Kennedy* **1997:** *One Flea Spare* **1998:** *Pearls for Pigs and Benita Canova* **2001:** *The Syringa Tree* **2004:** *Small Tragedy* **2009:** *Ruined* **2010:** *Circle Mirror Transformation*

Outer Critics Circle Awards

Thursday, May 26, 2011 at Sardi's Restaurant; 61st annual. Presented for outstanding achievement for Broadway and Off-Broadway productions during the 2010–2011 season. Winners are voted on by theatre critics of out-of-town periodicals and media. Executive Committee: Simon Saltzman (President), Mario Fratti (Vice-President), Patrick Hoffman (Corresponding Secretary), Stanley L. Cohen (Treasurer), Glenn Loney (Historian & Member-at-Large), Rosalind Friedman (Recording Secretary), Aubrey Reuben, Thomás Gentile, Harry Haun (Members-at-Large); Presenters: Charles Busch, Julie Halston, Brian d'Arcy James, Swoosie Kurtz.

Outstanding New Broadway Play: *War Horse*

Nominees: *Bengal Tiger at the Baghdad Zoo*; *Good People*; *The Motherf**ker With the Hat*

Outstanding New Broadway Musical: *The Book of Mormon*

Nominees: *Priscilla Queen of the Desert*; *Sister Act*; *Women on the Verge of a Nervous Breakdown*

Outstanding New Off-Broadway Play: *Other Desert Cities*

Nominees: *Blood From a Stone*; *Kin*; *The Other Place*

Outstanding New Off-Broadway Musical: *The Kid*

Nominees: *Freckleface Strawberry*; *In Transit*; *Tomorrow Morning*

Outstanding New Score (Broadway or Off-Broadway): *The Book of Mormon*

Nominees: *Catch Me If You Can*; *Sister Act*; *Women on the Verge of a Nervous Breakdown*

Outstanding Revival of a Play: *The Normal Heart*

Nominees: *Born Yesterday*; *The Importance of Being Earnest*; *The Merchant of Venice*

Outstanding Revival of a Musical: *Anything Goes*

Nominees: *How to Succeed in Business Without Really Trying*; *Hello Again*; *A Tree Grows in Brooklyn*

Outstanding Director of a Play: Marianne Elliott and Tom Morris, *War Horse*

Nominees: Emma Rice, *Brief Encounter*; Anna D . Shapiro, *The Motherf**cker With the Hat*; Daniel Sullivan, *Good People*

Outstanding Director of a Musical: Casey Nicholaw and Trey Parker, *The Book of Mormon*

Nominees: Rob Ashford, *How to Succeed in Business Without Really Trying*; Kathleen Marshall, *Anything Goes*; Jerry Zaks, *Sister Act*

Outstanding Choreography: Kathleen Marshall, *Anything Goes*

Nominees: Rob Ashford, *How to Succeed in Business Without Really Trying*; Ross Coleman, *Priscilla Queen of the Desert*; Casey Nicholaw, *The Book of Mormon*

Outstanding Actor in a Play: Mark Rylance, *Jerusalem*

Nominees: Reed Birney, *The Dream of the Burning Boy*; Bobby Cannavale, *The Motherf**ker With the Hat*; Joe Mantello, *The Normal Heart*; Al Pacino, *The Merchant of Venice*

Outstanding Actress in a Play: (tie) Nina Arianda, *Born Yesterday* & Frances McDormand, *Good People*

Nominees: Edie Falco, *The House of Blue Leaves*; Judith Light, *Lombardi*; Laurie Metcalf, *The Other Place*

Outstanding Actor in a Musical: Josh Gad, *The Book of Mormon*

Nominees: Norbert Leo Butz, *Catch Me If You Can*; Daniel Radcliffe, *How to Succeed in Business Without Really Trying*; Tony Sheldon, *Priscilla Queen of the Desert*; Aaron Tveit, *Catch Me If You Can*

Outstanding Actress in a Musical: Sutton Foster, *Anything Goes*

Nominees: Victoria Clark, *Sister Act*; Beth Leavel, *Baby It's You*; Patina Miller, *Sister Act*; Donna Murphy, *The People in the Picture*

Outstanding Featured Actor in a Play: Brian Bedford, *The Importance of Being Earnest*

Nominees: Evan Jonigkeit, *High*; Stacy Keach, *Other Desert Cities*; Seth Numrich, *War Horse*; Yul Vázquez, *The Motherf**cker With the Hat*

Outstanding Featured Actress in a Play: Elizabeth Rodriguez, *The Motherf**ker With the Hat*

Nominees: Renée Elise Goldsberry, *Good People*; Linda Lavin, *Other Desert Cities*; Estelle Parsons, *Good People*; Alison Pill, *The House of Blue Leaves*

Outstanding Featured Actor in a Musical: Adam Godley, *Anything Goes*

Nominees: Colin Donnell, *Anything Goes*; Chester Gregory, *Sister Act*; John Larroquette, *How to Succeed in Business Without Really Trying*; John McMartin, *Anything Goes*

Outstanding Featured Actress in a Musical: Laura Benanti, *Women on the Verge of a Nervous Breakdown*

Nominees: Nikki M. James, *The Book of Mormon*; Patti LuPone, *Women on the Verge of a Nervous Breakdown*; Marla Mindelle, *Sister Act*; Laura Osnes, *Anything Goes*

Outstanding Scenic Design (Play or Musical): Neil Murray, *Brief Encounter*

Nominees: Desmond Heeley, *The Importance of Being Earnest*; Derek McLane, *Bengal Tiger at the Baghdad Zoo*; Todd Rosenthal, *The Motherf**ker With the Hat*

Outstanding Costume Design (Play or Musical): Tim Chappel and Lizzy Gardiner, *Priscilla Queen of the Desert*

Nominees: Lez Brotherston, *Sister Act*; Desmond Heeley, *The Importance of Being Earnest*; Lizz Wolf, *Baby It's You!*

Outstanding Lighting Design (Play or Musical): Paule Constable, *War Horse*
Nominees: Natasha Katz, *Sister Act*; David Lander, *Bengal Tiger at the Baghdad Zoo*; Malcolm Rippeth, *Brief Encoutner*

Outstanding Solo Performance: John Leguizamo, *Ghetto Klown*

Nominees: Daniel Beaty, *Through the Night*; Mike Birbiglia, *My Girlfriend's Boyfriend*; Michael Shannon, *Mistakes Were Made*

John Gassner Playwriting Award: Matthew Lopez, *The Whipping Man*

Nominees: Amy Herzog, *After the Revolution*; David West Read, *The Dream of the Burning Boy*; Kim Rosenstock, *Tigers Be Still-at-Large*

Special Citations: Ellen Barkin for her outstanding Broadway debut in *The Normal Heart*; Adrian Kohler with Basil Jones for Handspring Puppet Company for design, fabrication and direction for *War Horse*

PAST OUTER CRITICS CIRCLE AWARD-WINNING PRODUCTIONS

Awards listed are for Best Play and Best Musical; as other categories were cited, they are indicated as such: (R) Best Revival; (RP) Best Play Revival; (RM) Best Musical Revival; (BP) Best Productions; (OP) Best Off-Broadway Play; (OM) Best Off-Broadway Musical. Beginning with 1990, shows listed are: Best (New) Play, Best (New) Musical, Best Play Revival, Best Musical Revival, Best Off-Broadway Play, Best New Off-Broadway Musical. In 1999, the awards were qualified as "Outstanding" instead of "Best"; if year is missing, no production awards were presented.

1950: *The Cocktail Party*; *The Consul* **1951:** *Billy Budd*; *Guys and Dolls* **1952:** *Point of No Return*; no musical award **1953:** no play award; *Wonderful Town* **1954:** *The Caine Mutiny Court-Martial*; *Kismet* **1955:** *Inherit the Wind*; *Three for Tonight* **1956:** *The Diary of Anne Frank*; *My Fair Lady* **1957:** *Long Day's Journey Into Night*; *My Fair Lady* **1958:** *Look Homeward, Angel*; *The Music Man* **1959:** *The Visit*; no musical award **1960:** *The Miracle Worker*; *Bye Bye Birdie* **1962:** *Anything Goes* (R) **1964:** *The Trojan Women* (R-classic); *The Lower Depths* (R-modern) **1965:** (BP) – *Oh What a Lovely War*; *Tartuffe* **1966:** (BP) – *Wait a Minim!*; *Mame* **1967:** (BP) – *America Hurrah*; *Cabaret*; *You Know I Can't Hear You When the Water's Running*; *You're A Good Man, Charlie Brown* **1968:** (BP) – *Rosencrantz and Guildenstern are Dead*; *The Price*; *George M!*; *Your Own Thing* **1969:** *Dames at Sea* (OM) **1970:** *Child's Play*; *Company*; *The White House Murder Case* (OP); *The Last Sweet Days of Isaac* (OM) **1971:** (BP) – *A Midsummer Night's Dream*; *Follies*; *No, No, Nanette* **1972:** *Sticks and Bones* and *That Championship Season*; no musical award **1974:** *A Moon for the Misbegotten* and *Noel Coward in Two Keys*; *Candide* **1975:** *Equus*; no musical award **1977:** *for colored girls…*; *Annie* **1978:** *Da*; no musical award **1979:** *The Elephant Man*; *Sweeney Todd, the Demon Barber of Fleet Street* **1980:** *Children of a Lesser God*; *Barnum* **1981:** *Amadeus*; *The Pirates of Penzance* (R); *March of the Falsettos* (OM) **1982:** *"Master Harold"…and the Boys*; *Nine*; *A Soldier's Play* (OP) **1983:** *Brighton Beach Memoirs*; *Cats*; *You Can't Take It With You* (RP); *On Your Toes* (RM); *Extremities* (OP); *Little Shop of Horrors* (OM) **1984:** *The Real Thing*; *La Cage aux Folles*; *Death of a Salesman* (R); *Painting Churches* (OP); *A… My Name is Alice* (Revue) **1985:** *Biloxi Blues*; *Sunday in the Park With George*; *Joe Egg* (R); *The Foreigner* (OP); *Kuni-Leml* (OM) **1986:** *I'm Not Rappaport*; *The Mystery of Edwin Drood*; *Loot* (R); *A Lie of the Mind* (OP); *Nunsense* (OM) **1987:** *Fences*; *Les Les Misérables*; *All My Sons* (R); *The Common Pursuit* (OP); *Stardust* (OM) **1988:** *M. Butterfly*; *The Phantom of the Opera*; *Anything Goes* (R); *Driving Miss Daisy* (OP); *Oil City Symphony* and *Romance, Romance* (OM) **1989:** *The Heidi Chronicles*; *Jerome Robbins' Broadway* **1990:** *The Grapes of Wrath*; *City of Angels*; *Cat on a Hot Tin Roof*; *Gypsy*; *Prelude to a Kiss*; *Closer Than Ever* **1991:** *Lost in Yonkers*; *Miss Saigon*; *Fiddler on the Roof* (R); *The Sum of Us*; *Falsettoland*; *And the World Goes Round* (Revue) **1992:** *Dancing at Lughnasa*; *Crazy for You*; *The Visit*; *Guys and Dolls*; *Marvin's Room*; *Song of Singapore* **1993:** *The Sisters Rosensweig*; *The Who's Tommy*; *Anna Christie*; *Carnival*; *Jeffrey*; *Ruthless!* **1994:** *Angels in America*; *Kiss of the Spider Woman*; *An Inspector Calls*; *She Loves Me*; *Three Tall Women*; *Annie Warbucks* **1995:** *Love! Valour! Compassion!*; *Sunset Boulevard*; *The Heiress*; *Show Boat*; *Camping with Henry and Tom*; *Jelly Roll* **1996:** *Master Class*; *Victor/Victoria*; *Inherit the Wind*; *The King and I*; *Molly Sweeney* and *Picasso at the Lapin Agile*; *Rent* **1997:** *The Last Night at Ballyhoo*; *The Life*; *A Doll's House*; *Chicago*; *How I Learned to Drive*; *Howard Crabtree's When Pigs Fly* **1998:** *The Beauty Queen of Leenane*; *Ragtime*; *A View from the Bridge*; *Cabaret*; *Never the Sinner* and *Gross Indecency: The Three Trials of Oscar Wilde*; *Hedwig and the Angry Inch* **1999:** *Not About Nightingales*; *Fosse*; *The Iceman Cometh*; *Annie Get Your Gun* and *Peter Pan* and *You're A Good Man, Charlie Brown*; *Wit*; *A New Brain* **2000:** *Copenhagen*; *Contact*; *A Moon for the Misbegotten*; *Kiss Me, Kate*; *Dinner With Friends*; *The Wild Party* **2001:** *Proof*; *The Producers*; *The Best Man* and *One Flew Over the Cuckoo's Nest*; *42ⁿᵈ Street*; *Jitney*; *Bat Boy: The Musical* **2002:** *The Goat, or Who Is Sylvia?*; *Urinetown the Musical* and *The Dazzle*; *Morning's at Seven*; *Oklahoma!*; *tick, tick…BOOM!* **2003:** *Take Me Out*; *Hairspray*; *A Day in the Death of Joe Egg*; *Nine*; *The Exonerated*; *A Man of No Importance* **2004:** *I Am My Own Wife*; *Wicked*; *Henry IV*; *Wonderful Town*; *Intimate Apparel*; *Johnny Guitar* and *The Thing About Men* **2005:** *Doubt*; *Monty Python's Spamalot*; *Twelve Angry Men*; *La Cage aux Folles*; *Fat Pig* and *Going to St. Ives*; *Altar Boyz* **2006:** *The History Boys*; *Jersey Boys*; *Awake and Sing!*; *Sweeney Todd, the Demon Barber of Fleet Street*; *Stuff Happens*; *Grey Gardens* **2007:** *The Coast of Utopia*; *Spring Awakening*; *Journey's End*; *Company*; *Indian Blood*; *In the Heights* **2008:** *August: Osage County*; *Xanadu* and *Young Frankenstein*; *The Homecoming*; *South Pacific*; *Dividing the Estate*; *Adding Machine* **2009:** *God of Carnage*; *Billy Elliot The Musical*; *The Norman Conquests*; *Hair*; *Ruined*; *The Toxic Avenger* **2010:** *Red*; *Memphis*; *Fences*; *La Cage aux Folles*; *The Orphans' Home Cycle*; *The Scottsboro Boys* and *Bloody Bloody Andrew Jackson*

Lucille Lortel Awards

Sunday, May 1, 2011 at NYU Skirball Center; 26th annual; Hosts: Samantha Bee and Zach Braff. Presented by the League of Off-Broadway Theatres and Producers for outstanding achievement Off-Broadway. The 2010–2011 awards voting committee consisted of Randy Anderson (SDC), Arnold Aronson (Columbia University School of the Arts), Terry Berliner (SDC), Tiffany Little Canfield (Telsey + Company), Julie Crosby (Women's Project), Amy Danis (MARS Theatricals), Peter Filichia (*The Star-Ledger*), George Forbes (Off-Broadway League), Susan Gallin (Susan Gallin Productions), Eleanor Goldhar (Guggenheim Foundation), Melanie Herman (MH Productions), Linda Herring (Tribeca Performing Arts Center), Walt Kiskaddon (AEA), Russell Lehrer (AEA), Richard Price (TDF), Mark Rossier (New York Foundation for the Arts), Philip Taylor (NYU Steinhardt Program in Educational Theatre), Rosemarie Tichler, Barbara Toy (American Theatre Wing), Elisabeth Vincentelli (*New York Post*).

Outstanding Play: *The Elaborate Entrance of Chad Deity* by Kristoffer Diaz (Second Stage)

Nominees: *In the Wake* by Lisa Kron (The Public Theater); *Other Desert Cities* by Jon Robin Baitz (Lincoln Center Theater); *Peter and the Starcatcher* by Rick Elice, based on the novel by Dave Barry and Ridley Pearson (New York Theatre Workshop); *The Coward* by Nick Jones (Lincoln Center Theater/LCT3)

Outstanding Musical: *Bloody Bloody Andrew Jackson* Music and Lyrics by Michael Friedman, Book by Alex Timbers (The Public Theater/Center Theatre Group/Les Freres Corbusier)

Nominees: *In Transit* Music, Lyrics and Book by Kristen Anderson-Lopez, James-Allen Ford, Russ Kaplan, Sara Wordsworth (Primary Stages with the Baruch/Viertel/Routh/Frankel Group, Jane Bergere, Jodi Glucksman, Ken Greiner, Chip Meyrelles, Christina Papagjika, and Janet Rosen); *The Burnt Part Boys* Music by Chris Miller, Lyrics by Nathan Tysen, Book by Mariana Elder (Playwrights Horizons/Vineyard Theatre); *The Kid* Music by Andy Monroe, Lyrics by Jack Lechner, Book by Michael Zam (The New Group); *We the People: America Rocks!* Book by Joe Iconis, Songs by Brad Alexander and Kevin Del Aguila, Eli Bolin and Sam Forman, Joe Iconis, Tommy Newman, Ryan Scott Oliver, Adam Overett, Mark Weiner and Erik Weiner and Jordan Allen-Dutton (Theatreworks USA)

Outstanding Revival: *Angels in America: A Gay Fantasia on National Themes/Part 1: Millennium Approaches, Part 2: Perestroika* by Tony Kushner (Signature Theatre Company)

Nominees: *The Collection* & *A Kind of Alaska* by Harold Pinter (Atlantic Theater Company); *The Little Foxes* by Lillian Hellman (New York Theatre Workshop); *The Misanthrope* by Moliere, translated by Richard Wilbur (Pear Theatre Company); *Three Sisters* by Anton Chekhov, translated by Paul Schmidt (Classic Stage Company)

Outstanding Solo Show: *My Girlfriend's Boyfriend* Written and performed by Mike Birbiglia

Nominees: *Through the Night* Written and performed by Daniel Beaty

Outstanding Director: John Collins, *Gatz*

Nominees: Anne Kauffman, *This Wide Night*; Joe Mantello, *Other Desert Cities*; Joe Mantello, *The Other Place*; Leigh Silverman, *In the Wake*

Outstanding Choreography: Steven Hoggett, *Peter and the Starcatcher*

Nominees: Tracy Bersley, *The Witch of Edmonton*; Danny Mefford, *Bloody Bloody Andrew Jackson*; Annie-B Parson, *Orlando*; Gail Pennington Crutchfield, *Freckleface Strawberry*

Outstanding Lead Actor: Christian Borle, *Peter and the Starcatcher*

Nominees: Desmin Borges, *The Elaborate Entrance of Chad Deity*; André Braugher, *The Whipping Man*; Michael Shannon, *Mistakes Were Made*; Jeremy Strong, *The Coward*

Outstanding Lead Actress: Laurie Metcalf, *The Other Place*

Nominees: Tracee Chimo, *Bachelorette*; Edie Falco, *This Wide Night*; Elizabeth Marvel, *The Little Foxes;* Michele Pawk, *A Small Fire*

Outstanding Featured Actor: Thomas Sadoski, *Other Desert Cities*

Nominees: Michael Chernus, *In the Wake*; Noah Galvin, *The Burnt Part Boys*; David Patrick Kelly, *When I Come to Die*; David Margulies, *After the Revolution*

Outstanding Featured Actress: Kristen Schaal, *The Coward*

Nominees: Laura Heisler, *Kin*; Linda Lavin, *Other Desert Cities*; Deirdre O'Connell, *In the Wake*; Lois Smith, *After the Revolution*

Outstanding Scenic Design: Donyale Werle, *Bloody Bloody Andrew Jackson*

Nominees: Rachel Hauck, *This Wide Night*; Anna Louizos, *In Transit*; Jan Versweyveld, *The Little Foxes*; Donyale Werle, *Peter and the Starcatcher*

Outstanding Costume Design: Gabriel Berry, *The Coward*

Nominees: Jennifer Caprio, *In Transit*; Cait O'Connor, *The Witch of Edmonton*; Emily Rebholz, *This Wide Night*; David Zinn, *Other Desert Cities*

Outstanding Lighting Design: Ben Stanton, *The Whipping Man*

Nominees: Betsy Adams, *When I Come to Die*; Mark Barton, *Gatz*; Matt Frey, *This Wide Night*; Jesse Klug, *The Elaborate Entrance of Chad Deity*

Outstanding Sound Design: Mikhail Fiksel, *The Elaborate Entrance of Chad Deity*

Nominees: Fitz Patton, *The Other Place*; Mic Pool, *The 39 Steps*; Jon Weston, *In Transit*; Ben Williams, *Gatz*

Outstanding Alternative Theatrical Experience: *Gatz* Produced by Elevator Repair Service (The Public Theater)

Lifetime Achievement Award: Lynne Meadow, Manhattan Theatre Club

Service to Off-Broadway Award: Gary Glaser, Partner at Seyfarth Shaw LLP

PAST LUCILLE LORTEL-AWARD WINNING PRODUCTIONS Awards listed are Outstanding Play and Outstanding Musical, respectively, since inception.

1986: *Woza Africa!*; no musical award **1987:** *The Common Pursuit*; no musical award **1988:** no play or musical award **1989:** *The Cocktail Hour*; no musical award **1990:** no play or musical award **1991:** *Aristocrats*; *Falsettoland* **1992:** *Lips Together, Teeth Apart*; *And the World Goes 'Round* **1993:** *The Destiny of Me*; *Forbidden Broadway* **1994:** *Three Tall Women*; *Wings* **1995:** *Camping with Henry & Tom*; *Jelly Roll!* **1996:** *Molly Sweeney*; *Floyd Collins* **1997:** *How I Learned to Drive*; *Violet* **1998:** (tie) *Gross Indecency* and *The Beauty Queen of Leenane*; no musical award **1999:** *Wit*; no musical award **2000:** *Dinner With Friends*; *James Joyce's The Dead* **2001:** *Proof*; *Bat Boy: The Musical* **2002:** *Metamorphoses*; *Urinetown* **2003:** *Take Me Out*; *Avenue Q* **2004:** *Bug*; *Caroline or Change* **2005:** *Doubt*; *The 25th Annual Putnam County Spelling Bee* **2006:** *The Lieutenant of Inishmore*; *The Seven* **2007:** *Stuff Happens*; (tie) *In the Heights* and *Spring Awakening* **2008:** *Betrayed*; *Adding Machine* **2009:** *Ruined*; *Fela! A New Musical* **2010:** *The Orphans' Home Cycle*; *The Scottsboro Boys*

New York Drama Critics' Circle Award

Monday, May 9, 2011; 76th annual. Presented by members of the press in the New York area. New York Drama Critics' Circle Committee: Adam Feldman – President (*Time Out New York*), – Vice President (*New York Post*), Joe Dziemianowicz – Treasurer (*The Daily News*), Eric Grode – Recording Secretary (non-voting), Hilton Als (*The New Yorker*), Melissa Rose Bernardo (*Entertainment Weekly*), Scott Brown (*New York*), David Cote (*Time Out New York*), Michael Feingold (*The Village Voice*), Robert Feldberg (*The Bergen Record*), David Finkle (*TheatreMania.com*), Elysa Gardner (*USA Today*), Eric Haagensen (*Back Stage*), Mark Kennedy (*Associated Press*), Jesse Oxford (*New York Observer*), David Rooney (*Variety*), Frank Scheck (*New York Post*), David Sheward (*Back Stage*), John Simon

(*Bloomberg News*), Alexis Soloski (*The Village Voice*), Marilyn Stasio (*Variety*), Steven Suskin (*Variety*), Terry Teachout (*Wall Street Journal*), Linda Winer (*Newsday*), Richard Zoglin (*Time*); Emeritus: Howard Kissel (*New York Daily News*), Michael Sommers (*Newhouse*)

Best Play: *Good People* by David Lindsay-Abaire

Best Foreign Play: *Jerusalem* by Jez Butterworth

Best Musical: *The Book of Mormon* by Trey Parker, Matt Stone, and Robert Lopez

Special Citations: The Broadway revival of *The Normal Heart*; Mark Rylance for *La Bete* and *Jerusalem*; Direction, design, and puppetry of *War Horse*

PAST DRAMA CRITICS' CIRLCE AWARD-WINNING PRODUCTIONS AND CITATIONS From 1936 to 1962, the New York Drama Critics' Circle presented awards for Best American Play, Best Foreign Play, and Best Musical, although some years no awards were given in specific categories. For entries below during those years, the first entry (unless otherwise indicated) is for Best American Play, (F) for Best Foreign Play, and (M) for Best Musical. For listings from 1962 to the present, the first listing (unless otherwise indicated) is for Best Play, and proceeding listings are as follow (depending on which awards were cited): (A) Best American Play; (F) Best Foreign Play; (M) Best Musical. Special Citations, periodically presented, are indicated as (SC).

1936: *Winterset* **1937:** *High Tor* **1938:** *Of Mice and Men, Shadow and Substance* (F) **1939:** *The White Steed* (F) **1940:** *The Time of Your Life* **1941:** *Watch on the Rhine, The Corn Is Green* (F) **1942:** *Blithe Spirit* (F) **1943:** *The Patriots* **1944:** *Jacobowsky and the Colonel* (F) **1945:** *The Glass Menagerie* **1946:** *Carousel* (M) **1947:** *All My Sons, No Exit* (F), *Brigadoon* (M) **1948:** *A Streetcar Named Desire, The Winslow Boy* (F) **1949:** *Death of a Salesman, The Madwoman of Chaillot* (F), *South Pacific* (M) **1950:** *The Member of the Wedding, The Cocktail Party* (F), *The Consul* (M) **1951:** *Darkness at Noon, The Lady's Not for Burning* (F), *Guys and Dolls* (M) **1952:** *I Am a Camera, Venus Observed* (F), *Pal Joey* (M), *Don Juan in Hell* (SC) **1953:** *Picnic, The Love of Four Colonels* (F), *Wonderful Town* (M) **1954:** *Teahouse of the August Moon, Ondine* (F), *The Golden Apple* (M) **1955:** *Cat on a Hot Tin Roof, Witness for the Prosecution* (F), *The Saint of Bleecker Street* (M) **1956:** *The Diary of Anne Frank, Tiger at the Gates* (F), *My Fair Lady* (M) **1957:** *Long Day's Journey into Night, The Waltz of the Toreadors* (F), *The Most Happy Fella* (M) **1958:** *Look Homeward Angel, Look Back in Anger* (F), *The Music Man* (M) **1959:** *A Raisin in the Sun, The Visit* (F), *La Plume de Ma Tante* (M) **1960:** *Toys in the Attic, Five Finger Exercise* (F), *Fiorello!* (M) **1961:** *All the Way Home, A Taste of Honey* (F), *Carnival* (M) **1962:** *Night of the Iguana, A Man for All Seasons* (F), *How to Succeed in Business Without Really Trying* (M) **1963:** *Who's Afraid of Virginia Woolf?, Beyond the Fringe* (SC) **1964:** *Luther, Hello Dolly!* (M), *The Trojan Women* (SC) **1965:** *The Subject Was Roses, Fiddler on the Roof* (M) **1966:** *Marat/Sade, Man of La Mancha* (M), *Mark Twain Tonight* - Hal Holbrook (SC) **1967:** *The Homecoming, Cabaret* (M) **1968:** *Rosencrantz and Guildenstern Are Dead, Your Own Thing* (M) **1969:** *The Great White Hope, 1776* (M) **1970:** *Borstal Boy, The Effect of Gamma Rays on Man-in-the-Moon Marigolds* (A), *Company* (M) **1971:** *Home, The House of Blue Leaves* (A), *Follies* (M), **1972:** *That Championship Season, The Screens* (F), *Two Gentlemen of Verona* (M), *Sticks and Bones* (SC), *Old Times* (SC) **1973:** *The Changing Room, The Hot L Baltimore* (A), *A Little Night Music* (M) **1974:** *The Contractor, Short Eyes* (A), *Candide* (M) **1975:** *Equus, The Taking of Miss Janie* (A), *A Chorus Line* (M) **1976:** *Travesties, Streamers* (A), *Pacific Overtures* (M) **1977:** *Otherwise Engaged, American Buffalo* (A), *Annie* (M) **1978:** *Da, Ain't Misbehavin'* (M) **1979:** *The Elephant Man, Sweeney Todd* (M) **1980:** *Talley's Folly, Betrayal* (F), *Evita* (M), Peter Brook's *Le Centre International de Créations Théâtricales* at La MaMa ETC (SC) **1981:** *A Lesson from Aloes, Crimes of the Heart* (A), *Lena Horne: The Lady and Her Music* (SC), *The Pirate of Penzance* at New York Shakespeare Festival (SC) **1982:** *The Life and Adventures of Nicholas Nickleby, A Soldier's Play* (A) **1983:** *Brighton Beach Memoirs, Plenty* (A), *Little Shop of Horrors* (M), *Young Playwrights Festival* (SC) **1984:** *The Real Thing, Glengarry Glen Ross* (F), *Sunday in the Park with George* (M), Samuel Beckett

(SC) **1985:** *Ma Rainey's Black Bottom* **1986:** *A Lie of the Mind, Benefactors* (A), *The Search for Signs of Intelligent Life in the Universe* (SC) **1987:** *Fences, Les Liaisons Dangereuses* (F), *Les Misérables* (M) **1988:** *Joe Turner's Come and Gone, The Road to Mecca* (F), *Into the Woods* (M) **1989:** *The Heidi Chronicles, Aristocrats* (F), *Bill Irwin: Largely New York* (SC) **1990:** *The Piano Lesson, Privates on Parade* (F), *City of Angels* (M), **1991:** *Six Degrees of Separation, Our Country's Good* (F), *The Will Rogers Follies* (M) Eileen Atkins - *A Room of One's Own* (SC) **1992:** *Dancing at Lughnasa, Two Trains Running* (A) **1993:** *Angels in America: Millenium Approaches, Someone Who'll Watch Over Me* (F), *Kiss of the Spider Woman* (M) **1994:** *Three Tall Women, Twilight: Los Angeles, 1992* - Anna Deavere Smith (SC) **1995:** *Arcadia, Love! Valour! Compassion!* (A), Signature Theatre Company's Horton Foote Season (SC) **1996:** *Seven Guitars, Molly Sweeny* (F), *Rent* (M), New York City Center's *Encores!* (SC) **1997:** *How I Learned to Drive, Skylight* (F), *Violet* (M), *Chicago* - Broadway revival (SC) **1998:** *Art, Pride's Crossing* (A), *Lion King* (M), *Cabaret* – Broadway revival (SC) **1999:** *Wit, Closer* (F), *Parade* (M), David Hare (SC) **2000:** *Jitney, James Joyce's The Dead* (M), *Copenhagen* (F) **2001:** *The Invention of Love, The Producers* (M), *Proof* (A) **2002:** *Edward Albee's The Goat, or Who is Sylvia?, Elaine Stritch: At Liberty* (SC) **2003:** *Take Me Out, Talking Heads* (F), *Hairspray* (M) **2004:** *Intimate Apparel*, Barbara Cook (SC) **2005:** *Doubt, The Pillowman* (F) **2006:** *The History Boys, The Drowsy Chaperone* (M), John Doyle, Sarah Travis and the Cast of *Sweeney Todd* (SC), Christine Ebersole (SC) **2007:** *The Coast of Utopia, Radio Golf* (A), *Spring Awakening* (M), *Journey's End* (SC) **2008:** *August: Osage County, Passing Strange* (M) **2009:** *Ruined, Black Watch* (F); *Billy Elliot The Musical* (M); Angela Lansbury (SC); Gerard Alessandrini for *Forbidden Broadway* (SC); Matthew Warchus and the Cast of *The Norman Conquests* (SC) **2010:** *The Orphans Home Cycle*; Lincoln Center Festival (SC); Viola Davis (SC); Annie Baker for *Circle Mirror Transformation* and *The Aliens* (SC)

Drama League Awards

Friday, May 20, 2011; Broadway Ballroom at The Marriott Marquis; 77th annual. Host: Kathleen Turner; Presented for distinguished achievement in the New York theater; winners are selected by members of the League; Drama League President, Jano Herbosch; Executive Director, Gabriel Shanks; Honorary Co-Chairs: Edie Falco, Billy Crudup, Tom Wopat, Judith Light, Sanaa Lathan, Sutton Foster, John Leguizamo, Estelle Parsons, Cherry Jones; Presenters: Daniel Radcliffe, Josh Gad, Andrew Rannells, Patina Miller, James Earl Jones, Douglas Aibel, Robin Williams, John Kander.

Play: *War Horse*

Musical: *The Book of Mormon*

Revival of a Play: *The Normal Heart*

Revival of a Musical: *Anything Goes*

Performance: Mark Rylance, *Jerusalem* and *La Bête*

Julia Hansen Award for Excellence in Directing: Susan Stroman

Achievement in Musical Theatre: Liza Minnelli

Unique Contribution to Theater: Whoopi Goldberg

Pulitzer Prize Award Winners for Drama

Established in 1917; Administered by the Pulitzer Prize Board, Columbia University; Lee C. Bollinger, President. Winner is chosen by a jury, composed of three to four critics, one academic and one playwright, however the board has final authority over choice. Presented for an outstanding drama or musical presented in New York or regional theater. The award goes to the playwright but production of the play as well as the script, is taken into account.

2010 Winner: *Clybourne Park* by Bruce Norris

PAST PULITZER PRIZE WINNERS If year is missing, no award was presented that year.

1918: *Why Marry?* by Jesse Lynch Williams **1920:** *Beyond the Horizon* by Eugene O'Neill **1921:** *Miss Lulu Bett* by Zona Gale **1922:** *Anna Christie* by Eugene O'Neill **1923:** *Icebound* by Owen Davis **1924:** *Hell-Bent for Heaven* by Hatcher Hughes **1925:** *They Knew What They Wanted* by Sidney Howard **1926:** *Craig's Wife* by George Kelly **1927:** *In Abraham's Bosom* by Paul Green **1928:** *Strange Interlude* by Eugene O'Neill **1929:** *Street Scene* by Elmer Rice **1930:** *The Green Pastures* by Marc Connelly **1931:** *Alison's House* by Susan Glaspell **1932:** *Of Thee I Sing* by George S. Kaufman, Morrie Ryskind, Ira and George Gershwin **1933:** *Both Your Houses* by Maxwell Anderson **1934:** *Men in White* by Sidney Kingsley **1935:** *The Old Maid* by Zoe Atkins **1936:** *Idiot's Delight* by Robert E. Sherwood **1937:** *You Can't Take It with You* by Moss Hart and George S. Kaufman **1938:** *Our Town* by Thornton Wilder **1939:** *Abe Lincoln in Illinois* by Robert E. Sherwood **1940:** *The Time of Your Life* by William Saroyan **1941:** *There Shall Be No Night* by Robert E. Sherwood **1943:** *The Skin of Our Teeth* by Thornton Wilder **1945:** *Harvey* by Mary Chase **1946:** *State of the Union* by Howard Lindsay and Russel Crouse **1948:** *A Streetcar Named Desire* by Tennessee Williams **1949:** *Death of a Salesman* by Arthur Miller **1950:** *South Pacific* by Richard Rodgers, Oscar Hammerstein II, and Joshua Logan **1952:** *The Shrike* by Joseph Kramm **1953:** *Picnic* by William Inge **1954:** *The Teahouse of the August Moon* by John Patrick **1955:** *Cat on a Hot Tin Roof* by Tennessee Williams **1956:** *The Diary of Anne Frank* by Frances Goodrich and Albert Hackett **1957:** *Long Day's Journey Into Night* by Eugene O'Neill **1958:** *Look Homeward, Angel* by Ketti Frings **1959:** *J.B.* by Archibald MacLeish **1960:** *Fiorello!* by Jerome Weidman, George Abbott, Sheldon Harnick, and Jerry Bock **1961:** *All the Way Home* by Tad Mosel **1962:** *How to Succeed in Business Without Really Trying* by Abe Burrows, Willie Gilbert, Jack Weinstock, and Frank Loesser **1965:** *The Subject Was Roses* by Frank D. Gilroy **1967:** *A Delicate Balance* by Edward Albee **1969:** *The Great White Hope* by Howard Sackler **1970:** *No Place to Be Somebody* by Charles Gordone **1971:** *The Effect of Gamma Rays on Man-in-the-Moon Marigolds* by Paul Zindel **1973:** *That Championship Season* by Jason Miller **1975:** *Seascape* by Edward Albee **1976:** *A Chorus Line* by Michael Bennett, James Kirkwood, Nicholas Dante, Marvin Hamlisch, and Edward Kleban **1977:** *The Shadow Box* by Michael Cristofer **1978:** *The Gin Game* by D.L. Coburn **1979:** *Buried Child* by Sam Shepard **1980:** *Talley's Folly* by Lanford Wilson **1981:** *Crimes of the Heart* by Beth Henley **1982:** *A Soldier's Play* by Charles Fuller **1983:** *'night, Mother* by Marsha Norman **1984:** *Glengarry Glen Ross* by David Mamet **1985:** *Sunday in the Park with George* by James Lapine and Stephen Sondheim **1987:** *Fences* by August Wilson **1988:** *Driving Miss Daisy* by Alfred Uhry **1989:** *The Heidi Chronicles* by Wendy Wasserstein **1990:** *The Piano Lesson* by August Wilson **1991:** *Lost in Yonkers* by Neil Simon **1992:** *The Kentucky Cycle* by Robert Schenkkan **1993:** *Angels in America: Millenium Approaches* by Tony Kushner **1994:** *Three Tall Women* by Edward Albee **1995:** *Young Man from Atlanta* by Horton Foote **1996:** *Rent* by Jonathan Larson **1998:** *How I Learned to Drive* by Paula Vogel **1999:** *Wit* by Margaret Edson **2000:** *Dinner with Friends* by Donald Margulies **2001:** *Proof* by David Auburn **2002:** *Topdog/Underdog* by Suzan Lori-Parks **2003:** *Anna in the Tropics* by Nilo Cruz **2004:** *I Am My Own Wife* by Doug Wright **2005:** *Doubt* by John Patrick Shanley **2007:** *Rabbit Hole* by David Lindsay-Abaire **2008:** *August: Osage County* by Tracy Letts **2009:** *Ruined* by Lynn Nottage **2010:** *Next to Normal* by Tom Kitt and Brian Yorkey

REGIONAL AND OTHER THEATRICAL AWARDS

American Theatre Critics Association Awards

Steinberg New Play Award and Citations

April 2, 2011; Ceremony at the Humana Festival at Actors Theatre Louisville; founded in 1977. The Harold and Mimi Steinberg/ATCA Awards honor new plays that had their world premieres in the previous year in professional productions outside New York City. From 1977–1984 ACTA gave only one play a citation. After 1985, three citations were awarded. Currently the new play award comes with a $25,000 prize and the two other citations are awarded a $7,500 prize.

2011 New Play Award: *Nine Circles* by Bill Cain (premiered at Marin Theatre Company); **Citations:** *The Good Counselor* by Kathryn Grant (premiered at Premiere Stages at Kean University); *The History of Invulnerability* by David Bar Katz (premiered at Cincinnati Playhouse in the Park)

Past Recipients (after 1986, first entry is the principal citation): **1977:** *And the Soul Shall Dance* by Wakako Yamauchi **1978:** *Getting Out* by Marsha Norman **1979:** *Loose Ends* by Michael Weller **1980:** *Custer* by Robert E. Ingham **1981:** *Chekhov in Yalta* by John Driver and Jeffrey Haddow **1982:** *Talking With* by Jane Martin **1983:** *Closely Related* by Bruce MacDonald **1984:** *Wasted* by Fred Gamel **1985:** (no principal citation) *Scheherazade* by Marisha Chamberlain, *The Shaper* by John Steppling, *A Shayna Maidel* by Barbara Lebow **1986:** *Fences* by August Wilson; *Fugue* by Lenora Thuna; *Hunting Cockroaches* by Januscz Glowacki **1987:** *A Walk in the Woods* by Lee Blessing; *The Film Society* by John Robin Baitz; *Back to the World* by Stephen Mack Jones **1988:** *Heathen Valley* by Romulus Linney; *The Voice of the Prairie* by John Olive; *The Deal* by Matthew Witten **1989:** *The Piano Lesson* by August Wilson; *Generations* by Dennis Clontz; *The Downside* by Richard Dresser **1990:** *2* by Romulus Linney; *Pick Up Ax* by Anthony Clarvoe; *Marvin's Room* by Scott McPherson **1991:** *Two Trains Running* by August Wilson; *Sincerity Forever* by Mac Wellman; *The Ohio State Murders* by Adrienne Kennedy **1992:** *Could I Have This Dance* by Doug Haverty; *American Enterprise* by Jeffrey Sweet; *Miss Evers' Boys* by David Feldshuh **1993:** *Children of Paradise: Shooting a Dream* by Steven Epp, Felicity Jones, Dominique Serrand, and Paul Walsh; *Black Elk Speaks* by Christopher Sergel; *Hurricane* by Anne Galjour **1994:** *Keely and Du* by Jane Martin **1995:** *The Nanjing Race* by Reggie Cheong-Leen; *Rush Limbaugh in Night School* by Charlie Varon; *The Waiting Room* by Lisa Loomer **1996:** *Amazing Grace* by Michael Cristofer; *Jungle Rot* by Seth Greenland; *Seven Guitars* by August Wilson **1997:** *Jack and Jill* by Jane Martin; *The Last Night of Ballyhoo* by Alfred Uhry; *The Ride Down Mount Morgan* by Arthur Miller **1998:** *The Cider House Rules, Part II* by Peter Parnell; *Jitney* by August Wilson; *The Old Settler* by John Henry Redwood **1999:** *Book of Days* by Lanford Wilson; *Dinner With Friends* by Donald Margulies; *Expecting Isabel* by Lisa Loomer **2000:** *Oo-Bla-Dee* by Regina Taylor; *Compleat Female Stage Beauty* by Jeffrey Hatcher; *Syncopation* by Allan Knee **2001:** *Anton in Show Business* by Jane Martin; *Big Love* by Charles L. Mee; *King Hedley II* by August Wilson **2002:** *The Carpetbagger's Children* by Horton Foote; *The Action Against Sol Schumann* by Jeffrey Sweet; *Joe and Betty* by Murray Mednick **2003:** *Anna in the Tropics* by Nilo Cruz; *Recent Tragic Events* by Craig Wright; *Resurrection Blues* by Arthur Miller **2004:** *Intimate Apparel* by Lynn Nottage; *Gem of the Ocean* by August Wilson; *The Love Song of J. Robert Oppenheimer* by Carson Kreitzer **2005:** *The Singing Forest* by Craig Lucas; *After Ashley* by Gina Gionfriddo; *The Clean House* by Sarah Ruhl; *Madagascar* by J.T. Rogers **2006:** *A Body of Water* by Lee Blessing; *Red Light Winter* by Adam Rapp; *Radio Golf* by August Wilson **2007:** *Hunter Gatherers* by Peter Sinn Nachtrieb; *Opus* by Michael Hollinger; *Guest Artist* by Jeff Daniels **2008:** *33 Variations* by Moises Kaufman; *End Days* by Deborah Zoe Laufer; *Dead Man's Cell Phone* by Sarah Ruhl **2009:** *Song of Extinction* by E.M. (Ellen) Lewis; *Great Falls* by Lee Blessing; *Superior Donuts* by Tracy Letts **2010:** *Equivocation* by Bill Cain; *Time Stands Still* by Donald Margulies; *Legacy of Light* by Karen Zacarias

M. Elizabeth Osborn Award

April 2, 2011; Ceremony at the Humana Festival at Actors Theatre Louisville; established in 1993. Presented by the American Theatre Critics Association in memory of Theatre Communications Group and American Theatre play editor M. Elizabeth Osborn to an emerging playwright who has not received other major national awards, has not had a significant New York production, and whose work has not been staged widely in regional theatres; $1,000 prize and recognition in the *Best Plays Theater Yearbook* edited by Jeffrey Eric Jenkins.

2011 Winner: Cori Thomas for *When January Fells Like Summer* (premiered at City Theatre, Pittsburgh, Pennsylvania)

Past Recipients: 1994: *Hurricane* by Anne Galjour **1995:** *Rush Limbaugh in Night School* by Charlie Varon **1996:** *Beast on the Moon* by Richard Kalinoski **1997:** *Thunder Knocking On the Door* by Keith Glover **1998:** *The Glory of Living* by Rebecca Gilman **1999:** *Lamarck* by Dan O'Brien **2000:** *Marked Tree* by Coby Goss **2001:** *Waiting to Be Invited* by S.M. Shephard-Massat **2002:** *Chagrin Falls* by Mia McCullough **2003:** *The Dinosaur Within* by John Walch **2004:** *The Intelligent Design of Jenny Chow* by Rolin Jones **2005:** *Madagascar* by J.T. Rogers **2006:** *American Fiesta* by Steven Tomlinson **2007** *Vestibular Sense* by Ken LaZebnik **2008:** *Gee's Bend* by Elyzabeth Wilder **2009:** *Our Enemies: Lively Scenes of Love and Combat* by Yusseff El Guindi **2010:** *Perfect Mendacity* by Jason Wells

AUDELCO Awards - The "VIVS"

Monday, November 15, 2010; Harlem Stages/Aaron Davis Hall – Marion Anderson Theatre; 38th annual. Presented for excellence in Black Theatre for the 2009–2010 season by the Audience Development Committee, created by Vivian Robinson. Co-Chairs: Starletta DuPois and Rajendra Ramoon Hahar; Co-hosts: Melba Moore and Ron Lucas; Music, Tevin Thomas

Outstanding Dramatic Production of the Year: *What Would Jesus Do?* (Billie Holiday Theatre)

Outstanding Revival: *Pecong* (Take Wing and Soar)

Outstanding Musical Production of the Year: *Langston in Harlem* (Urban Stages)

Outstanding Director/Dramatic Production: Dr. May Edward Chinn, *Imani* (Castillo Theatre)

Outstanding Director/Musical Production: Akin Babatunde, *Blind Lemon Blues* (York Theatre)

Outstanding Choreographer: Byron Easley, *Langston in Harlem* (Urban Stages)

Outstanding Playwright: Yvette Heyliger, *What Would Jesus Do?* (Billie Holiday Theatre)

Outstanding Lead Actor: Jerome Preston Bates, *What Would Jesus Do?* (Billie Holiday Theatre)

Outstanding Lead Actress: Yvonne Farrow, *What Would Jesus Do?* (Billie Holiday Theatre)

Outstanding Supporting Actor: Jamil A.C. Mangan, *What Would Jesus Do?* (Billie Holiday Theatre)

Outstanding Supporting Actress: Johnnie Mae, *What Would Jesus Do?* (Billie Holiday Theatre)

Outstanding Performance in a Musical/Female: Kenita Miller, *Langston in Harlem* (Urban Stages)

Outstanding Performance in a Musical/Male: Glenn Turner, *Langston in Harlem* (Urban Stages)

Outstanding Ensemble Performance: *August Wilson's Women* (Juneteenth Legacy Theatre)

Outstanding Solo Performance: Daniel Beaty, *Through the Night* (Westside Theatre/Produced by Daryl Roth)

Outstanding Set Design: Patrice Davidson, *What Would Jesus Do?* (Billie Holiday Theatre)

Outstanding Costume Design: David Withrow, *Pecong* (Take Wing and Soar)

Outstanding Lighting Design: James Carter, *Pecong* (Take Wing and Soar)

Outstanding Sound Design: David D. Wright, *Oshun, The Yoruba Dance Drama* (National Black Theatre)

Pioneer Award: Rhonda "Passion" Hansome

Outstanding Pioneer Award: Roger Paris

Board of Directors Awards: Fred & Barbara Powell; Fulton C. Hodges

Rising Star Honoree: Trey Rollins

Special Achievement Awards: Woodie King Jr. (for Outstanding Producer); Rev. Dr. Johnny Ray Youngblood

Special Award: Layon Gray & The Black Gents

Barrymore Awards

October 3, 2010; Walnut Street Theatre; 17th annual. Presented by the Theatre Alliance of Greater Philadelphia for excellence in theatre in the greater Philadelphia area for the 2010-2011 season.

Outstanding Production of a Play: *In the Next Room, or the vibrator play* (Wilma Theater)

Outstanding Production of a Musical: *The Flea and the Professor* (Arden Theatre Company)

Outstanding Direction of a Play: Blanka Zizka, *In the Next Room, or the vibrator play* (Wilma Theater)

Outstanding Direction of a Musical: Matthew Decker, *The 25th Annual Putnam County Spelling Bee* (Theatre Horizon)

Outstanding Musical Direction: (11th Hour Theatre Company)

Outstanding Leading Actor in a Play: Dan Hodge, *Around the World in 80 Days* (Delaware Theatre Company)

Outstanding Leading Actress in a Play: Anna Deavere Smith, *Let Me Down Easy* (Philadelphia Theatre Company)

Outstanding Leading Actor in a Musical: Rob McClure, *The Flea and the Professor* (Arden Theatre Company)

Outstanding Leading Actress in a Musical: Melinda Chua, *Miss Saigon* (Walnut Street Theatre,)

Outstanding Supporting Actor in a Play: James Ijames, *Superior Donuts* (Arden Theatre Company)

Outstanding Supporting Actress in a Play: Krista Apple, *In the Next Room, or the vibrator play* (Wilma Theater)

Outstanding Supporting Actor in a Musical: Michael Doherty, *The 25th Annual Putnam County Spelling Bee* (Theatre Horizon)

Outstanding Supporting Actress in a Musical: Rachel Camp, *The 25th Annual Putnam County Spelling Bee* (Theatre Horizon)

Outstanding Set Design: Alexis Distler, *In the Next Room, or the vibrator play* (Wilma Theater)

Outstanding Lighting Design: Thom Weaver, *In the Next Room, or the vibrator play* (Wilma Theater)

Outstanding Costume Design: Oana Botez-Ban, *In the Next Room, or the vibrator play* (Wilma Theater)

Outstanding Sound Design: Christopher Colucci, *In the Next Room, or the vibrator play* (Wilma Theater)

Outstanding Music Direction: Alex Bechtel, *My Way: A Musical Tribute to Frank Sinatra* (Walnut Street Theatre)

Outstanding Choreography/Movement: Waldo Warshaw & Aaron Cromie, *The Lieutenant of Inishmore* (Theatre Exile)

Outstanding New Play: *Ghost-Writer* (Arden Theatre Company)

Outstanding Ensemble in a Play: *In the Next Room, or the vibrator play* (Wilma Theater)

Outstanding Ensemble in a Musical: *The 25th Annual Putnam County Spelling Bee* (Theatre Horizon)

Ted & Stevie Wolf Award for New Approaches to Collaborations: Robert Smythe and the Chamber Orchestra of Philadelphia — Stravinsky's *l'Histoire du Soldat* — Kimmel Center for the Performing Arts

F. Otto Haas Award for Emerging Philadelphia Theatre Artist: James Ijames

Brown Martin Philadelphia Award: *Love and Communication* (Passage Theatre)

Excellence in Theatre Education and Community Service Award: Otis D. Hackney III — Principal, South Philadelphia High School — The Wilma Theater/1812 Productions/Philadelphia Young Playwrights

Lifetime Achievement Award: Harry Dietzler, Executive Director, Upper Darber Summer Stage

Barrymore Tribute for a Distinguished Artist in the Theatre: Terrence McNally

Bay Area Theatre Critics Circle Awards

April 4, 2011; Palace of the Fine Arts Theatre Lobby; 35th Annual. Presented by members of the print and electronic media for outstanding achievement in theatre in the San Francisco Bay Area for the 2010 calendar year.

Theatres Over 300 Seats: Drama

Entire Production: *Opus* (TheatreWorks)

Principal Performance, Female: (tie) Jannie Jones and Jessica Wortham, *Black Pearl Sings!* (San Jose Repertory Theatre)

Principal Performance, Male: Bill Irwin, *Scapin* (American Conservatory Theater)

Supporting Performance, Female: Margo Hall, *The Brother/Sister Plays Part 3: Marcus: or The Secret of Sweet* (America Conservatory Theatre)

Supporting Performance, Male: Jud Williford, *Scapin* (American Conservatory Theater)

Director: Meredith McDonough, *Opus* (TheatreWorks)

Set Design: John Iacovelli, *Black Pearl Sings!* (San Jose Repertory Theatre)

Costume Design: Beaver Bauer, *License to Kiss II: A Sweet Conspiracy* (Teatro ZinZanni)

Lighting Design: Chris Studley, *Opus* (TheatreWorks)

Sound Design: Cliff Caruthers, *Opus* (TheatreWorks)

Specialties: Emily DeCola, Daniel Fay and Eric Wright (Puppeteers) and Matt Acheson (Puppet Design), *Compulsion* (B erkeley Repertory Theatre); Jessica Grindstaff and Erik Sanko aka Phantom Limb (Puppet Design), *Lemony Snicket's The Composer Is Dead* (Berkeley Repertory Theatre)

Original Script: *The Pastures of Heaven* by Octavia Solis (California Shakespeare Theater)

Solo Performance: Geoff Hoyle, *Lemony Snicket's The Composer Is Dead* (Berkeley Repertory Theatre)

Ensemble: *Secret Order* (San Jose Repertory Theatre)

Theatres Over 300 Seats: Musicals

Entire Production: *The Tosca Project* (American Conservatory Theater)

Principal Performance, Female: Jessica Knudsen, *Oklahoma* (Contra Costa Musical Theatre)

Principal Performance, Male: Gabriel Hoffman, *A Christmas Memory* (TheatreWorks)

Supporting Performance, Female: Renee DeWeese, *A Chorus Line* Contra Costa Musical Theatre)

Supporting Performance, Male: Constantine Germanacos, *The Light in the Piazza* (Contra Costa Musical Theatre)

Director: Jennifer Perry, *A Chorus Line* (Contra Costa Musical Theatre)

Music Director: William Liberatore, *The Light in the Piazza* (TheatreWorks)

Set Design: Douglas W. Schmidt, *The Tosca Project* (American Conservatory Theater)

Costume Design: Fumiko Bielfeldt, *The Light in the Piazza* (TheatreWorks)

Lighting Design: Robert Wierzel, *The Tosca Project* (American Conservatory Theater)

Sound Design: Darron L West, *The Tosca Project* (American Conservatory Theater)

Original Script: *Girlfriend* by Todd Almond (Berkeley Repertory Theatre)

Specialties: Jennifer Perry (Choreography), *A Chorus Line* (Contra Costa Musical Theatre)

Solo Performance: No award presented this season

Ensemble: (tie) *Girlfriend* (Berkeley Repertory Theatre); *The Tosca Project* (American Conservatory Theater)

Touring Production: *West Side Story* (SHN Best of Broadway)

Theatres 100 – 300 Seats: Drama

Entire Production: *Trouble in Mind* (Aurora Theatre Company)
Principal Performance, Female: Margo Hall, *Trouble in Mind* (Aurora Theatre Company)

Principal Performance, Male: Tim Kniffin, *Trouble in Mind* (Aurora Theatre Company)

Supporting Performance, Female: Marie O'Donnell, *Anita Bryant Died for Your Sins* (New Conservatory Theatre Center)

Supporting Performance, Male: Rhonnie Washington, *Trouble in Mind* (Aurora Theatre Company)

Director: Jasson Minadakis, *Equivocation* (Marin Theatre Company)

Set Design: Kuo-Hao-Lo, *The Sugar Witch* (New Conservatory Theatre Center)

Costume Design: Callie Floor, *Trouble in Mind* (Aurora Theatre Company)

Lighting Design: York Kennedy, *The Brother/Sister Plays Part 1: In the Red and Brown Water* (Marin Theatre Company)

Sound Design: Cliff Caruthers, *Dracula* (Center Reperatory Company)

Specialties: Dave Maier (Fight Choreography), *Oedipus el Rey* (Magic Theatre)

Original Script: *The First Grade* by Joel Drake Johnson (Aurora Theatre Company)

Solo Performance: David Cale, *Palomino* (Aurora Theatre Company)

Ensemble: *Trouble in Mind* (Aurora Theatre Company)

Theatres 100 – 300 Seats: Musicals

Entire Production: She Loves Me (Center Repertory Company)

Principal Performance, Female: Velina Brown, *Posibilidad, or Death of the Worker* (San Francisco Mime Troupe)

Principal Performance, Male: Ryan Drummond, *She Loves Me* (Center Repertory Company)

Supporting Performance, Female: (tie) Molly Bell, *A Marvelous Party* (Center Repertory Company); Rena Wilson, *Lady, Be Good!* (42nd Street Moon)

Supporting Performance, Male: Noel Anthony, *She Loves Me* (Center Repertory Company)

Director: Robert Barry Fleming, *She Loves Me* (Center Repertory Company)

Musical Director: Brandon Adams, *She Loves Me* (Center Repertory Company)

Set Design: Bill Forrester, *A Marvelous Party* (Center Repertory Company)

Costume Design: Victoria Livingston-Hall, *She Loves Me* (Center Repertory Company)

Lighting Design: Kurt Landisman, *She Loves Me* (Center Repertory Company)

Sound Design: Ted Crimy, *Woody Guthrie's American Song* - Marin Theatre Company

Specialties: David Maier (Fight Choreography), *The Fantasticks* (San Francisco Playhouse)

Original Script: *Becoming Britney* by Molly Bell & Daya Curley (Center Repertory Company)

Solo Performance: (tie) Klea Blackhurst, *Everything the Traffic Will Allow* (42nd Street Moon); Leanne Borghesi, *Divalicious* (New Conservatory Theatre Center)

Ensemble: *A Marvelous Party* (Center Repertory Company)

Theatres Under 99 Seats: Drama

Entire Production: *…and jesus Moonwalks the Mississippi* (The Cutting Ball Theater)

Performance, Female: Dawn Scott, *Intimate Apparel* (Alter Theatre)

Performance, Male: Aldo Billingslea, *…and Jesus Moonwalks the Mississippi* (The Cutting Ball Theater)

Director: Terry McGovern, *Humble Boy* (Ken Bacon and Marin Actors' Workshop)

Original Script: (tie) *Loveland* by Ann Randolph (The Marsh); *1001* by Jason Grote (Just Theatre)

Solo Performance: Marga Gomez, *Marga Gomez Is Proud and Bothered* (New Conservatory Theatre Center)

Ensemble: (tie) *…and jesus Moonwalks the Mississippi* (The Cutting Ball Theater); *Becoming Julia Morgan* (The Julia Morgan Project)

Specialties: Bert van Aalsburg (Set Design), *How the Other Half Loves* (Off Broadway West Theatre Company)

Theatres Under 99 Seats: Musicals

Entire Production: *Baby* (Ray of Light Theatre)

Performance, Female: Sarah Kathleen Farrell, *Baby* (Ray of Light Theatre)

Performance, Male: Andrew Willis-Woodward, *Baby* (Ray of Light Theatre)

Director: Dylan McBride, *Baby* (Ray of Light Theatre)

Musical Director: Rona Siddiqui, *Baby* (Ray of Light Theatre)

Ensemble: *Baby* (Ray of Light Theatre)

Specialties: Carl Jordan (Choreography), *Pirates of Penzance* (Novato Theater Company)

Special Awards

Paine Knickerbocker Award: Central Works (Gary Graves and Jan Zvaifler, Co-Artistic Directors)

Jerry Friedman Award (former the Barbara Bladen Porter Award): Jerry Friedman (President of San Francisco Bay Area Theatre Critics Circle)

Gene Price Award: Mike Ward, Director/Choreographer/Writer/Actor/Designer/Producer

Bistro Awards

April 26, 2011; Gotham Comedy Club; 26th annual. Presented by *Back Stage* for outstanding achievement in the cabaret field; Winners selected by a committee consisting of Elizabeth Ahlfors (*Cabaret Scenes*), David Finkle (*Back Stage's* "Bistro Bits" columnist), Rob Lester (*Cabaret Scenes* & *TalkinBroadway.com*), Erv Raible (Executive/Artistic Director of the Cabaret Conference – Yale University), Roy Sander (former "Bistro Bits" columnist) and Sherry Eaker (*Back Stage* Editor at Large); Produced by Sherry Eaker; Originally created by the late *Back Stage* cabaret critic Bob Harrington.

Outstanding Vocalists: Carole J. Bufford (Metropolitan Room/Don't Tell Mama); Kevin Dozier (Laurie Beechman Theatre/Feinstein's at Loews Regency/Don't Tell Mama)

Outstanding Entertainer: Colleen McHugh (The Duplex)

Outstanding Musical Group: The Johnny Rodgers Band: Johnny Rodgers, Brian Glassman, Danny Mallon, Joe Ravo (Birdland/Iridium/Oak Room at the Algonquin/Joe's Pub)

Outstanding Cabaret Series: *Sondheim Unplugged* Written, directed, and hosted by Phil Geoffrey Bond (Laurie Beechman Theatre/Don't Tell Mama)

Outstanding Debut: Liz Lark Brown, *Tarnished* (Metropolitan Room)

Ira Eaker Special Achievement Award: Robbie and Paul Rescigno

Outstanding Major Engagement: Tyne Daly (Feinstein's at Loews Regency)

Outstanding Recording: Hilary Kole, "You Are There"

Outstanding Instrumentalist: Sean Harkness

Outstanding Theme Show: Anthony Cochran, *Elvis Lives* (Metropolitan Room)

Outstanding Tribute Show: Janice Hall, *Grand Illusions: The Music of Marlene Dietrich* (Metropolitan Room/Urban Stages)

Outstanding Musical Comedy: Fay Lane, *Faye Lane's Beauty Shop Stories* (Soho Playhouse)

Ongoing Achievement in Jazz: Allan Harris

Outstanding Musical Director: Nate Buccieri

Special Awards: Carol Channing, Michael Feinstein

Bob Harrington Lifetime Achievement Award: Dionne Warwick

Broadway.com Audience Choice Awards

May 15, 2011; Allen Room at Jazz at Lincoln Center; 12th annual. Host: Vanessa Williams. The Broadway.com Audience Awards give real theatergoers a chance to honor their favorite Broadway and Off-Broadway shows and performers.

Favorite Musical: *Sister Act*

Favorite Play: *War Horse*

Favorite Musical Revival: *How to Succeed in Business Without Really Trying*

Favorite Play Revival: *Driving Miss Daisy*

Favorite Actor in a Musical: Daniel Radcliffe, *How to Succeed in Business Without Really Trying*

Favorite Actress in a Musical: Sutton Foster, *Anything Goes*

Favorite Actor in a Play: Robin Williams, *Bengal Tiger at the Baghdad Zoo*

Favorite Actress in a Play: Judith Light, *Lombardi*

Favorite Diva Performance: Nick Adams, *Priscilla Queen of the Desert*

Favorite Funny Performance: John Larroquette, *How to Succeed in Business Without Really Trying*

Favorite Onstage Pair: John Larroquette & Daniel Radcliffe, *How to Succeed in Business Without Really Trying*

Ensemble Cast: *American Idiot*

Favorite Breakthrough Performance: Nick Adams, *Priscilla Queen of the Desert*

Breakthrough Performance (Female): Krysta Rodriguez, *The Addams Family*

Favorite Replacement: Billy Joe Armstrong, *American Idiot*

Favorite New Broadway Song: ""I Believe" from *The Book of Mormon*

Favorite Long-Running Broadway Show: *Wicked*

Favorite Tour: *Wicked*

Carbonell Awards

April 4, 2011; Broward Center for the Performing Arts – Amaturo Theatre; 35th annual. Presented for outstanding achievement in South Florida theater during the 2010 calendar year.

Best New Work *When the Sun Shone Brighter* by Christopher Demos-Brown (Florida Stage)

Best Production of a Play: *Blasted* (GableStage)

Best Director, Play: Joseph Adler, *Blasted* (GableStage)

Best Actor, Play: Gregg Weiner, *Fifty Words* (GableStage))

Best Actress, Play: Barbara Bradshaw, *Collected Stories* (Mosaic Theatre)

Best Supporting Actor, Play: Will Connolly, *Candida* (Palm Beach Dramaworks)

Best Supporting Actress, Play: Deborah L. Sherman, *Goldie, Max & Milk*, (Florida Stage)

Best Production of a Musical: *Mack and Mabel* (Broward Stage Door Theatre)

Best Director, Musical: David Arisco, *Miss Saigon* (Actors' Playhouse at the Miracle Theatre)

Best Actor, Musical: Herman Sebek, *Miss Saigon* (Actors' Playhouse at the Miracle Theatre)

Best Actress, Musical: Tari Kelly, *Anything Goes* (Maltz Jupiter Theatre)

Best Supporting Actor, Musical: Nick Duckart, *Dr. Radio* (Florida Stage)

Best Supporting Actress, Musical: Lisa Manuli, *Motherhood the Musical* (GFour Productions)

Best Musical Direction: Eric Alsford, *Miss Saigon* (Actors' Playhouse at the Miracle Theatre)

Best Choreography: Marcia Milgrom Dodge, *Anything Goes* (Maltz Jupiter Theatre)

Best Scenic Design, Play or Musical: Tim Connolly, *Blasted* (GableStage)

Best Lighting, Play or Musical: Jeff Quinn, *Blasted* (GableStage)

Best Costume Design, Play or Musical: Jose M. Rivera, *La Cage Aux Folles* (Maltz Jupiter Theatre)

Best Sound Design: Matt Corey, *Blasted* (GableStage)

Best Ensemble, Play or Musical: *12 Angry Men* (Maltz Jupiter Theatre)

Special Awards

George Abbott Award: Patrice Bailey, Dean of Theater at Miami's New World School of the Arts

Ruth Foreman Award: Broward Center for the Performing Arts

Carbonell Scholarship Winners: Abby Jaros, Boca Raton Community High School; Jennifer Jaroslavsky, American Heritage School of Boca/Delray; Kimberlee Johnson, JP Taravella High School; Valerie Novakoff, Pine Crest School; Mario Pavón, Boca Raton Community High School

Clive Barnes Award

November 9, 2010; Walter Reade Theatre; 1st Annual. Presented by the Clive Barnes Foundation in honor of the late theatre and dance critic who died in 2008, and who also served as a member of the Theatre World Awards Voting Committee for several years. Awarded to a young actor and a young dancer for outstanding achievement.

Award for Theatre: Nina Arianda, *Venus in Fur*

Award for Dance: Chase Finlay, New York City Ballet

Connecticut Critics' Circle Awards

June 12, 2011; 21st annual. Presented for outstanding achievement in Connecticut theater, selected by statewide reviews, feature writers, columnists, and broadcasters, for 2010–2011 season.

Outstanding Production of a Play: *The Piano Lesson* (Yale Repertory Theatre)

Outstanding Production of a Musical: *My One and Only* (Goodspeed Musicals)

Outstanding Actress in a Play: Francesca Choy-Kee, *Agnes Under the Big Top* (Long Wharf Theatre)

Outstanding Actor in a Play: LeRoy McClain, *The Piano Lesson* (Yale Rep)

Outstanding Actress in a Musical: Klea Blackhurst, *Everything the Traffic Will Allow* (Music Theatre of Conn.)

Outstanding Actor in a Musical: Tony Yazbeck, *My One and Only* (Goodspeed Musicals)

Outstanding Direction of a Play: Peter Lockyer, *One Flew Over the Cuckoo's Nest* (Ivoryton Playhouse)

Outstanding Direction of a Musical: Scott Thompson, (*Joseph and the Amazing Technicolor Dreamcoat* (Downtown Cabaret)

Outstanding Choreography: Kelli Barclay, *My One and Only* (Goodspeed Musicals)

Outstanding Set Design: John Ezell, *The Diary of Anne Frank* (Westport Country Playhouse)

Outstanding Lighting Design: Travis McHale, *The Diary of Anne Frank* (Westport Country Playhouse)

Outstanding Costume Design: Robin L. McGee, *My One and Only* (Goodspeed Musicals)

Outstanding Sound Design: Katie Down, *Agnes Under the Big Top* (Long Wharf Theatre)

Outstanding Ensemble Performance: Robert Eli, Steven French, Christina Pumariega, Noble Shropshire in Alfred Hitchcock's *The 39 Steps* (Hartford Stage)

Outstanding Debut Awards: Eshan Bay, *Agnes Under the Big Top* (Long Wharf Theatre); Evan Jonigkeit, *High* (TheaterWorks); Aaron Moss, *The Winter's Tale* (Elm Shakespeare)

Tom Killen Memorial Award: Music Theatre of Connecticut

Special Recognition: The 100th Anniversary of the Ivoryton Playhouse

Craig Noel Awards

January 10, 2011; Museum of Contemporary Art; 9th annual. Presented by the San Diego Theatre Critics Circle for outstanding achievement in the greater San Diego theatre in the 2010 calendar year.

Outstanding Resident Musical: (tie) *Sweeney Todd* (Cygnet Theatre); *Hairspray* (San Diego Repertory Theatre)

Outstanding Original Score: Duncan Sheik, *Whisper House* (The Old Globe)

Outstanding New Musical: *Limelight: The Story of Charlie Chaplin* (La Jolla Playhouse)

Outstanding Direction of a Musical: Sean Murray & James Vasquez, *Sweeney Todd* (Cygnet Theatre)

Outstanding Musical Direction: Charlie Reuter, *Sweeney Todd* (Cygnet Theatre)

Outstanding Music for a Play: Mark Bennett, *A Midsummer Night's Dream* (La Jolla Playhouse)

Outstanding Lead Performance in a Musical, Female: Deborah Gilmour Smyth, *Sweeney Todd* (Cygnet Theatre)

Outstanding Lead Performance in a Musical, Male: Rob McClure, *Limelight: The Story of Charlie Chaplin* (La Jolla Playhouse)

Outstanding Featured Performance in a Musical, Male: Steve Gunderson, *Hairspray* (San Diego Repertory Theatre)

Outstanding Featured Performance in a Musical, Female: Joy Yandell, *MiXtape* (Lamb's Players Theatre)

Outstanding Choreography: (tie) Javier Velasco, *Hairspray* (San Diego Repertory Theatre)Casey Nicholaw, *Robin and the 7 Hoods* (The Old Globe)

Outstanding Direction of a Play: Liesl Tommy, *Ruined* (La Jolla Playhouse)

Outstanding Sound Design: Broken Chord Collective, *Ruined* (La Jolla Playhouse)

Outstanding Costume Design: Gregg Barnes, *Robin and the 7 Hoods* (The Old Globe)

Outstanding Lighting Design: Eric Lotze, *Private Lives* (Cygnet Theatre)

Outstanding Set Design: (tie) Andrew Hull, *Private Lives* (Cygnet Theatre); *Ruined* (La Jolla Playhouse)

Outstanding Ensemble: (tie) *Hurlyburly* (Ion Theatre); *Ruined* (La Jolla Playhouse)

Outstanding Featured Performance in a Play, Female: Zainab Jah, *Ruined* (La Jolla Playhouse)

Outstanding Featured Performance in a Play, Male: Jay Whittaker (Old Globe Shakespeare Festival body of work)

Outstanding Lead Performance in a Play, Male: Miles Anderson, *The Madness of George III* (The Old Globe)

Outstanding Lead Performance in a Play, Female: (tie) Shana Wride, *Private Lives* (Cygnet Theatre); Tonye Patano, *Ruined* (La Jolla Playhouse)

Outstanding Performance in a Touring Production: (tie) Bill Camp, *Notes From Underground* (La Jolla Playhouse); Tovah Feldshuh, *Golda's Balcony* (The Old Globe)

Outstanding Touring Production: *Notes From Underground* (La Jolla Playhouse)

Outstanding Dramatic Production: *Ruined* (La Jolla Playhouse)

Outstanding New Play: *Oyster* by Ronald McCants (Baldwin New Play Festival, UCSD)

Outstanding Young Artist: Victoria Matthews, *Hairspray* (San Diego Repertory Theatre)

Special Awards

Producer of the Year: Ion Theatre, Claudio Raygoza & Glenn Paris

Actor of the Year: Steve Gunderson

Des McAnuff New Visions Award: Seema Sueko, Mo'olelo Performing Arts Company

Dramatist Guild Awards

November 1, 2010; Hudson Theatre. Established in 2000, these awards are presented by the Dramatists Guild of America to outstanding writers at the Dramatists Guild Annual Benefit and Awards Gala.

Elizabeth Hull-Kate Warriner Award (to the playwright whose work deals with social, political or religious mores of the time): Lynn Nottage, *Ruined*

Frederick Loewe Award for Dramatic Composition: John Kander, *The Scottsboro Boys*

Flora Roberts Award: Michael Weller

Lifetime Achievement: Jerry Bock & Sheldon Harnick; Terrence McNally

Ed Kleban Award

June 27, 2010; BMI; 21st annual. Presented by New Dramatists in honor of Edward Kleban; award is given annually to both a librettist and a lyricist ($100,000 to each recipient payable over two years); Board of Directors: Andre Bishop, Elliot H. Brown, Sheldon Harnick, Richard Maltby Jr., Francis Neuwirth (Treasurer), Alan J. Stein (Secretary), John Weidman, Maury Yeston (President). Judges: Stephen Flaherty, Michael Korie, and David Zippel.

2011 Winners: Adam Gwon (lyricist), Michelle Elliott (librettist)

Elliot Norton Awards

May 23, 2011; Paramount Theatre; 29th annual. Presented for outstanding contribution to the theater in Boston from April 2010 to March 2011; selected by a Boston Theater Critics Association selection committee comprising of Don Aucoin, Jared Bowen, Terry Byrne, Carolyn Clay, Iris Fanger, Louise Kennedy, Joyce Kullhawik, Sandy MacDonald, Robert Nesti, Ed Siegel and Caldwell Titcomb.

Visiting Production: Play: *August: Osage County* (Broadway Across America); Musical: *Hair* (Broadway Across America)

Outstanding Production, Large Company: *Ruined* (Huntington Theatre Company)

Outstanding Production, Midsized Company: *The Life and Adventures of Nicholas Nickleby, Parts I & II* (Lyric Stage Company of Boston)

Outstanding Production, Small Company: *The Aliens* (Company One)

Outstanding Production, Fringe Company: *Mrs. Grinchley's Christmas Carol* (The Gold Dust Orphans)

Outstanding Local Musical Production: *The Blue Flower* (American Repertory Theater)

Outstanding Ensemble: *The Hotel Nepenthe* (Actors' Shakespeare Project)

Outstanding New Script: John Kuntz, *The Hotel Nepenthe* (Actors' Shakespeare Project)

Outstanding Director, Large Company: Diane Paulus, *Hair* (Broadway Across America)/*Johnny Baseball* (American Repertory Theater)/*Prometheus Bound* (American Repertory Theater)

Outstanding Director, Midsized Company: Spiro Veloudos and Courtney O'Connor, *The Life and Adventures of Nicholas Nickleby, Parts I and II* (Lyric Stage Company of Boston)

Outstanding Director, Small/Fringe Company: Shawn LaCount, *The Aliens* (Company One)

Outstanding Choreography: Doug Elkins, *Fräulein Maria* (ArtsEmerson/Doug Elkins and Friends)

Outstanding Actor, Large Company: Thomas Derrah, *R. Buckminster Fuller: The History (and Mystery) of the Universe* (American Repertory Theater)

Outstanding Actor, Midsized Company: Johnny Lee Davenport, *Broke-ology* (Lyric Stage Company of Boston)

Outstanding Actor, Small/Fringe Company: Alex Pollock, *The Aliens* (Company One)

Outstanding Actress: Large Company: Kate MacCluggage, *The Merchant of Venice* (ArtsEmerson/Theatre for a New Audience)

Outstanding Actress, Midsized Company: Anne Gottlieb, *Frankie and Johnny in the Claire de Lune* (New Repertory Theatre)/*In the Next Room, or the vibrator play* (SpeakEasy Stage Company)

Outstanding Actress, Small/Fringe Company: Stacy Fischer, *Hysteria, or Fragments of an Analysis of an Obsessional Neurosis* (Nora Theatre)

Outstanding Musical Performance: Uzo Aduba, *Prometheus Bound* (American Repertory Theater)

Outstanding Design, Large Company: *The Blue Flower* (American Repertory Theater): Marsha Ginsberg [set], Carol Bailey [costumes], Justin Townsend [lighting], Clive Goodwin [sound], Jim and Ruth Bauer [videography]

Outstanding Design, Small/Midsize Company: *The Aliens* (Company One): Cristina Todesco [sets], Bobby Frederick Tilley II [costumes], Aaron Mack [sound], Benjamin Williams [lighting]

Norton Prize for Sustained Excellence: Scott Edmiston

Special Citation: Wheelock Family Theatre 30th Anniversary

The Equity Awards

St. Clair Bayfield Award Established in 1973 in memory of Equity member St. Clair Bayfield, the Award honors the best performance by an actor in a Shakespearean play in the New York metropolitan area. **2010 Winner:** Charles Kimbrough, *The Merchant of Venice* (The Public Theater)

Joe A. Callaway Award Established by Equity member Joe A. Callaway in 1989 to encourage participation in the classics and non-profit theatre. **2010 Winners:** Lily Rabe, *The Merchant of Venice* (The Public Theater); Matthew Rauch, *The Duchess of Malfi* (Red Bull Theate)

Clarence Derwent Awards 67th annual; Presented to honor the most promising female and male performers on the New York metropolitan scene. **2011 Winners:** Tracee Chimo, *Bachelorette* (Second Stage); Santino Fontana, *The Importance of Being Earnest* (Roundabout Theatre)

Alan Eisenberg Award 4th and 5th annual; created by former AEA Executive Director, this award is presented to an outstanding graduating senior of the University of Michigan Musical Theatre program, Mr. Eisenberg's alma mater. **2010 Winner:** Kent Overshown, Class of 2010; **2011 Winner:** Desiree Oakley, Class of 2011

Lucy Jordan Award Established in 1992 to honor the legacy of Lucy Finney Jordan, a former ballerina and chorus "gypsy" who, for many years, was the "face" of Actors' Equity in the Western Region as the Union's Outside Field Rep. The award is given to those who demonstrate a lifetime commitment to the theatre and especially, helping other theatre artists. **2011 Winner:** Lynn Soffer (actress, acting coach, teacher, and dialect coach)

Rosetta LeNoire Award Established in 1988, the award was named in honor of the actress Rosetta LeNoire, who was also the first recipient, not only because of her body of work in the theatre - and her work with the then titled Actors' Equity Association's Ethnic Minorities Committee - but also for founding the AMAS Repertory Theatre Company. **2011 Winners:** Shakespeare Center of Los Angles (Ben Donenberg, Founder and Executive Director)

Paul Robeson Award Established in 1974 to recognize a person who best exemplified the principles by which Mr. Robeson lived. It was created by donations from members of the acting profession. **2010 Winner:** Charles Randolph-Wright (actor, director, writer, producer)

Richard Seff Award Established in 2003, this annual award is given to a male and female character actor who is 50 years old or older and who has been a member of the Actors' Equity for 25 years or longer, for the best performance in a featured or unfeatured supporting role in a Broadway or Off-Broadway production. **2011 Winners:** Deirdre O;Connell, *In the Wake* (The Public Theater); Reed Birney, *A Small Fire* (Playwrights Horizons)

Roger Sturtevant Musical Theatre Award 7th annual; established in 2005 in memory of Roger Sturtevant, a beloved box office treasurer and part-time casting director. This award is presented to Equity Membership Candidates who have demonstrated outstanding abilities in the musical theatre field. **2011 Winners:** Dayna Dantzler, Edward Miskie

ACCA Award 4th annual; Presented to an outstanding Broadway chorus. **2010 Winner:** *Fela!*

Diversity on Broadway Award Presented by AEA's Equal Employment Opportunity Committee for extraordinary excellence in diversity on Broadway. **2010 Winner:** Tom Hulce and Ira Pittelman, *American Idiot*

Fred Ebb Award

November 29, 2010; American Airlines Theatre Penthouse Lounge; 6th annual. The Fred Ebb Award recognizes excellence in musical theatre songwriting, by a lyricist, composer, or songwriting team that has not yet achieved significant commercial success. The award is meant to encourage and support aspiring songwriters to create new works for the musical theatre. The selection panel includes Mitchell S. Bernard, Sheldon Harnick, David Loud, Marin Mazzie, Tim Pinckney and Arthur Whitelaw. Presenter, Eric Schaeffer; The prize includes a $50,000 award.

2010 Winner: Douglas J. Cohen

Past Recipients: 2005: John Bucchino **2006:** Robert L. Freedman and Steven Lutvak **2007:** Peter Mills **2008:** Adam Gwon **2009:** Marcy Heisler and Zina Goldrich

George Freedley Memorial Award

Established in 1968 to honor the late George Freedley, theatre historian, critic, author, and first curator of the New York Public Library Theatre Collection, this award honors a work about live theatre published in or distributed in the United States during the previous year. Presented by authors, publishers and members of the Theatre Library Association.

2010 Winner: Andrew McConnell Stott, *The Pantomime Life of Joseph Grimaldi: Laughter, Madness, and the Story of Britain's Greatest Comedian* (Canongate, 2009); Special Jury Prize: Marc Robinson, *The American Play: 1787-2000* (Yale University Press, 2009)

George Jean Nathan Award

With his preamble "it is my object and desire to encourage and assist in developing the art of drama criticism and the stimulation of intelligent playgoing," the late George Jean Nathan provided in his will for a prize known as the George Jean Nathan Award for Dramatic Criticism. The prize consists of the annual net income of half of Mr. Nathan's estate, which "shall be paid to the American who has written the best piece of drama criticism during the theatrical year (July 1 to June 30), whether it is an article, an essay, treatise, or book. The award now amounts to $10,000 and in addition, the winner receives a trophy symbolic of, and attesting to, the award. **2011 Winner for 2009-2010:** Charles McNulty, Chief Theatre Critic for the Los Angeles Times

GLAAD Media Awards

New York: March 19, 2011 at the Marriott Marquis; Los Angeles: April 10, 2011 at the Westin Bonaventure Hotel; 22nd annual. Presented by the Gay and Lesbian Alliance Against Defamation for fair, accurate and inclusive representations of gay individuals in the media as a means of eliminating homophobia and discrimination based on gender identity and sexual orientation.

2011 Winners in Theater: New York Theater – Broadway & Off-Broadway: *When Last We Flew* by Harrison David Rivers; Los Angeles Theater: *Something Happened* by L. Trey Wilson

Grammy Awards

February 13, 2011; Staples Center, Los Angeles; 53rd annual. Presented by the Recording Academy for excellence in the recording industry for albums released October 1, 2009–September 30, 2010.

Best Musical Show Album: *American Idiot*, Billie Joe Armsrong, producer; Music and lyrics by Green Day (Reprise Records); featuring John Gallagher Jr, Michael Esper, Rebecca Naomi Jones, Mary Faber, and Stark Stands

Nominees: *A Little Night Music* (Nonesuch); *Fela!* (Knitting Factory); *Promises, Promises* (Sony Masterworks); *Sondheim on Sondheim* (PS Classics)

Helen Hayes Awards

April 25, 2011; The Warner Theatre; 27th annual. Presented by the Washington Theatre Awards Society in recognition of excellence in Washington, D.C. for the 2010 season; Witten by Renee Calarco; Director, Jerry Whiddon; Producer/Design, Daniel MacLean Wagner; Music Director, George Hummel; Choreography, Michael J. Bobbitt; Scenic Design, Carl Gudenius; Sound, Alan H. Perry; PSM, Martha Knight; Visual Media Producer, Jack Stillwell.

Outstanding Resident Play: (tie) *Clybourne Park* (Woolly Mammoth Theatre Company); *Hamlet* (Folger Theatre)

Outstanding Resident Musical: (tie) *Candide* (Shakespeare Theatre Company); *Oklahoma!* (Arena Stage)

Outstanding Lead Actress, Resident Musical: Lauren Molina, *Candide* (Shakespeare Theatre Company)

Outstanding Lead Actor, Resident Musical: (tie) Geoff Packard, *Candide* (Shakespeare Theatre Company); Nicholas Rodriguez, *Oklahoma!* (Arena Stage)

Outstanding Lead Actress, Resident Play: Erika Rose, *In Darfur* (Theater J)

Outstanding Lead Actor, Resident Play: Johnny Ramey, *Superior Donuts* (The Studio Theatre)

Outstanding Supporting Actress, Resident Musical: Hollis Resnik, *Candide* (Shakespeare Theatre Company)

Outstanding Supporting Actor, Resident Musical: Ed Dixon, *Sunset Boulevard* (Signature Theatre)

Outstanding Supporting Actress, Resident Play: Naomi Jacobson, *Richard II* (Shakespeare Theatre Company)

Outstanding Supporting Actor, Resident Play: Louis Butelli, *Henry VIII* (Folger Theatre)

Outstanding Director, Resident Play: (tie) Howard Shalwitz, *Clybourne Park* (Woolly Mammoth Theatre Company); Paata Tsikurishvili, *Othello* (Synetic Theater)

Outstanding Director, Resident Musical: Mary Zimmerman, *Candide* (Shakespeare Theatre Company)

Outstanding Set Design, Resident Production: Daniel Ostling, *Candide* (Shakespeare Theatre Company)

Outstanding Costume Design, Resident Production: Anastasia Ryurikov Simes, *Othello* (Synetic Theater)

Outstanding Lighting Design, Resident Production: Colin K. Bills, *The Master and Margarita* (Synetic Theater)

Outstanding Sound Design, Resident Production: Tom Teasley, *The Ramayana* (Constellation Theatre Company)

Outstanding Musical Direction, Resident Production: George Fulginiti-Shakar, *Oklahoma!* (Arena Stage)

Outstanding Choreography: Parker Esse, *Oklahoma!*, (Arena Stage)

Outstanding Ensemble, Resident Musical: *Sycamore Trees* (Signature Theatre)

Outstanding Ensemble, Resident Play: *Othello* (Synetic Theater)

Outstanding Non-Resident Production: *Thurgood* (The Kennedy Center)

Outstanding Production, Theatre for Young Audiences: *If You Give a Pig a Pancake* (Adventure Theatre)

Outstanding Lead Actress, Non-Resident: Caroline Sheen, *Mary Poppins* (The Kennedy Center)

Outstanding Lead Actor, Non-Resident: Laurence Fishburne, *Thurgood* (The Kennedy Center)

Outstanding Supporting Performer, Non-Resident: Josh Lamon, *Hair* (The Kennedy Center)

Charles MacArthur Award for Outstanding New Play or Musical: *The Liar* by David Ives, translated and adapted from the verse comedy by Pierre Corneille (Shakespeare Theatre Company)

John Aniello Award for Outstanding Emerging Theatre Company: No Rules Theatre Company; Factory 449: a theatre collective

Helen Hayes Tribute: Tommy Tune

Washington Post Award for Innovative Leadership in the Theatre Community: Ford's Theatre for their "History on Stage" and "History on Foot" programs

Henry Hewes Design Awards

November 2010; Sardi's Restaurant; 46th annual. Sponsored by the American Theatre Wing, these awards are presented for outstanding design originating in the U.S. for the 2009–2010 theatre season. The award (formerly known as the Maharam Theatre Design Award up until 1999) is named after the former theatre critic for the *Saturday Review* who passed away July 20, 2006. The awards are selected by a committee comprising of Jeffrey Eric Jenkins (chair), Dan Bacalzo, David Barbour, David Cote, Glenda Frank, Mario Fratti, and Joan Ungaro.

Scenic Design: Donayle Werle, *Bloody Bloody Andrew Jackson* (Public Theater)

Lighting Design: Kevin Adams, *American Idiot* (Broadway)

Costume Design: Martin Pakledinaz, *Lend Me A Tenor* (Broadway)

Notable Effects/Production Design: *The Orphans' Home Cycle* (Signature Theatre): Jeff Cowie and David M. Barber (scenery), David C. Woolard (costumes), Rui Rita (lighting), Jan Hartley (projections), John Gromada (sound)

IRNE Awards

April 25, 2011; Boston Center for the Arts. Founded in 1997 by Beverly Creasey and Larry Stark. Presented by The Independent Reviewers of New England for extraordinary theatre in the Boston area during the 2010 calendar year.

Large Theatre

Best New Play: *Stick Fly* by Lydia R. Diamond (Huntington Theatre)

Best Play: *Stick Fly* (Huntington Theatre)

Best Musical: *The Blue Flower* (American Repertory Theater)

Best Director, Play: Kenny Leon, *Stick Fly* (Huntington Theatre)

Best Director, Musical: Stacey Stephens, *Into the Woods* (Reagle Music Theatre)

Best Music Director: Mark Rubenstein, *The Blue Flower* (American Repertory Theater)

Best Choreography: Todd Michael Smith & Judine Sommerville, *Hairspray* (Reagle Music Theatre)

Best Solo Performance: Karen MacDonald, *The Blonde, The Brunette, and the Vengeful Redhead* (Merrimack Repertory Company)

Best Ensemble: *Cabaret* (American Repertory Theater)

Best Actress, Play: Karen Macdonald, *All My Sons* (Huntington Theatre)

Best Actor, Play: Will Lyman, *All My Sons* (Huntington Theatre)

Best Supporting Actress, Play: Ronette Levenson, *Bus Stop* (Huntington Theatre)

Best Supporting Actor, Play: Stephen Lee Anderson, *Bus Stop* (Huntington Theatre)

Best Actress, Musical: Rachel York, *Into the Woods* (Reagle Music Theatre)

Best Actor, Musical: Daniel Jenkins, *The Blue Flower* (American Repertory Theater)

Best Supporting Actress, Musical: Meghan McGeary, *The Blue Flower* (American Repertory Theatre)

Best Supporting Actor, Musical: Thomas Derrah, *Cabaret* (American Repertory Theater)

Best Set Design: Eugene Lee, *Vengeance is the Lord's* (Huntington Theatre Company)

Best Lighting Design: Justin Townsend, *The Blue Flower* (American Repertory Theater)

Best Costume Design: Stacey Stephens, *Into the Woods* (Reagle Music Theatre)

Best Sound Design: Clive Goodwin, *The Blue Flower* (American Repertory Theatre)

Most Promising Performance by a Young Performer: Sarah Safer, *Gypsy* (North Shore Music Theatre)

Best Visiting Production: *August: Osage County* (Broadway Across America)

Best Visiting Performer: Estelle Parsons, *August: Osage County* (Broadway Across America)

Midsize-Small Theatre

Best New Play: *From Orchids to Octopi* by Melinda Lopez (Underground Railway Theatre)

Best Play: *Nicholas Nickleby* (SpeakEasy Stage Company)

Best Musical: *The Adding Machine* (SpeakEasy Stage Company)

Best Small Production: *Ted Hughes' Tales From Ovid* (Whistler in the Dark)

Best Director, Play: Spiro Veloudos, *Nicholas Nickleby* (Lyric Stage Company of Boston)

Best Director, Musical: Jessie Strachman & Jennifer Condon, *Once on This Island* (Blue Spruce Theatre)

Best Music Director: Dan Rodriguez, *Once on This Island* (Blue Spruce Theatre)

Best Choreography: Kelli Edwards, *The Hot Mikado* (New Repertory Theatre)

Best Solo Performance: Gabriel Kuttner, *Fully Committed* (Herter Park)

Best Ensemble: *Nicholas Nickleby* (Lyric Stage Company of Boston)

Best Actress, Play: Anne Gottlieb, *Frankie and Johnny in the Claire de Lune* (New Repertory Theatre)

Best Actor, Play: Victor Shopov, *Enron* (Zeitgeist Stage Company)

Best Supporting Actress, Play: Becca A. Lewis, *Grimm* (Company One)

Best Supporting Actor, Play: Jason Powers, *Nicholas Nickleby* (Lyric Stage Company of Boston)

Best Actress, Musical: Tracy Nygard, *A Little Night Music* (Metro Stage Company)

Best Actor, Musical: James Fitzpatrick, *A Little Night Music* (Metro Stage Company)

Best Supporting Actress, Musical: Shana Dirik, *A Little Night Music* (Metro Stage Company)

Best Supporting Actor, Musical: Robert Case, *A Little Night Music* (Metro Stage Company)

Best Set Design: Susan Zeeman Rogers, *The Adding Machine* (SpeakEasy Stage Company)

Best Lighting Design: Scott Clyve, *Nicholas Nickleby* (Lyric Stage Company of Boston)

Best Costume Design: Stacey Stephens, *My Fair Lady* (Stoneham Theatre)

Best Sound Design: Nathan Leigh, *The Hound of the Baskervilles* (Central Square Theater)

Best Promising Performance by a Young Performer: Patrick Maloney, *Buddy* (Turtle Lane Playhouse)

Best Visiting Production: *Seth Rudetsky's Deconstructing Broadway* (SpeakEasy Stage Company)

Special Recognition

Kenneth A. MacDonald Award for Theater Excellence: Small Theatre Alliance of Boston

ITBA Awards – Patrick Lee Theater Blogger Awards

3rd Season; Founded by Ken Davenport, the Independent Theater Bloggers Association was created to provide structure to the quickly growing theatrical blogosphere, and give the new media voices a chance to recognize excellence for Broadway, Off-Broadway, and Off-Off Broadway productions. The Award was renamed the Patrick Lee Theater Blogger Award in honor of Patrick Lee who passed away in June 2010.

Outstanding New Broadway Play: *Jerusalem*

Outstanding Broadway Play Revival: *The Normal Heart*

Outstanding New Broadway Musical: *Bloody Bloody Andrew Jackson*

Outstanding Broadway Musical Revival: *Anything Goes*

Outstanding New Off-Broadway Play: *The Elaborate Entrance of Chad Deity*

Outstanding New Off-Broadway Musical: *The Kid*

Outstanding Off-Broadway Revival (Musical or Play): *Angels in America Part 1: Millennium Approaches*

Outstanding Off-Off Broadway Unique Theatrical Experience: *Sleep No More*

Outstanding Solo Show: Michael Shannon, *Mistakes Were Made*

Outstanding Ensemble Performance: *The Scottsboro Boys*

Citations for Outstanding Off-Off Broadway Show: *Feeder: A Love Story*; *Invasion!*; *The Caucasian Chalk Circle*; *Belarus Free Theater's Discover Love*; *Black Watch*; *ReWrite*

Citation for Excellence in Off-Off Broadway Theatre: LaMama E.S.T

Citations for Excellence by Individual Performances: Nina Arianda, *Born Yesterday*; Laura Benanti, *Women on the Verge of a Nervous Breakdown*; Reed Birney, *A Small Fire*; Christian Borle, *Peter and the Starcatcher*; Norbert Leo Butz, *Catch Me If You Can*; Bobby Canavale, *The Motherf**ker with the Hat*; Colman Domingo, *The Scottsboro Boys*; Sutton Foster, *Anything Goes*; Josh Gad, *The Book of Mormon*; Hamish Linklater, *School for Lies*; Joe Mantello, *The Normal Heart*; Arian Moayed, *Bengal Tiger at the Baghdad Zoo*; Lily Rabe, *The Merchant of Venice*; Mark Rylance, *Jerusalem*; Michael Shannon, *Mistakes Were Made*; Benjamin Walker, *Bloody Bloody Andrew Jackson*

Jonathan Larson Performing Arts Foundation Awards

March 29, 2011; B.B. Kings. Jonathan Larson's dream was to infuse musical theatre with a contemporary, joyful urban vitality. After 12 years of struggle as a classic "starving artist," his dream came true with the phenomenal success of *Rent*. To celebrate his creative spirit and honor his memory, Jonathan's family and friends created the Jonathan Larson Performing Arts Foundation. The mission of the Foundation is to provide financial support and encouragement to a new generation of musical theatre composers, lyricists and bookwriters, as well as nonprofit theatre companies that develop and produce their work.

2011 Recipients: Joshua Cohen (book/lyrics) and Marisa Michelson (composer), *Tamar and the River*, Michelle Elliott (book/co-lyricist) and Danny Larsen (composer/co-lyricist), *Cloaked*; Jack Lechner (lyrics), Andy Monroe (composer), and Michael Zam (book), *The Kid*

Joseph Jefferson Awards

Equity Wing Awards

October 26, 2010; Drury Lane Oakbrook; 42nd annual. Presented for achievement in Chicago Equity theater from August 1, 2009–July 31, 2010; given by the Jefferson Awards Committee. Director, Michael Weber; Producer, Diane Hires; Hosts, Deanna Dunagan and Felicia P. Fields.

Production – Play – Large: *The Elaborate Entrance of Chad Deity* (Victory Gardens in association with Teatro Vista)

Production – Play – Midsize: *The Farnsworth Invention* (TimeLine Theatre Company)

Production – Musical – Large: *Ragtime* (Drury Lane Productions)

Production – Revue: *Oh Coward!* (Writers' Theatre)

Ensemble: *The Brother/Sister Plays* (Steppenwolf Theatre Company)

Director – Play: Edward Torres, *The Elaborate Entrance of Chad Deity* (Victory Gardens in association with Teatro Vista)

Director – Musical: Rachel Rockwell, *Ragtime* (Drury Lane Productions)

Director – Revue: *Oh Coward!* (Writers' Theatre)

New Work – Play: Kristoffer Diaz, *The Elaborate Entrance of Chad Deity* (Victory Gardens in association with Teatro Vista)

Solo Performance: Mary Beth Fisher, *The Year of Magical Thinking* (Court Theatre)

Actress in a Principal Role – Play: Natasha Lowe, *A Streetcar Named Desire* (Writers' Theatre)

Actor in a Principal Role – Play: Desmin Borges, *The Elaborate Entrance of Chad Deity* (Victory Gardens in association with Teatro Vista)

Actress in a Supporting Role – Play: Natalie West, *Abigail's Party* (A Red Orchid Theatre)

Actor in a Supporting Role – Play: Francis Guinan, *A Guide for the Perplexed* (Victory Gardens Theatre)

Actress in a Principal Role – Musical: Cory Goodrich, *Ragtime* (Drury Lane Productions)

Actor in a Principal Role – Musical: Quentin Earl Darrington, *Ragtime* (Drury Lane Productions)

Actress in a Supporting Role – Musical: Valisia LeKae, *Ragtime* (Drury Lane Productions)

Actor in a Supporting Role – Musical: Francis Guinan, *A Guide for the Perplexed* (Victory Gardens Theater)

Actress in a Revue: Kate Fry, *Oh Coward!* (Writers' Theatre)

Actor in a Revue: Rob Lindley, *Oh Coward!* (Writers' Theatre)

Scenic Design – Large: Walt Spangler, *A True History of the Johnstown Flood* (Goodman Theatre)

Scenic Design – Midsize: James Leaming, *Tobacco Road* (American Blues Theater)

Costume Design – Large: Alison Siple, *The Mystery of Irma Vep* (Court Theatre)

Costume Design – Midsize: Sarah E. Ross & Kristin DeiTos, *Tobacco Road* (American Blues Theater)

Lighting Design – Large: John Culbert, *The Illusion* (Court Theatre)

Lighting Design – Midsize: Tammy Mader, *Thoroughly Modern Millie* (Drury Lane Productions)

Sound Design – Large: Ray Nardelli, *Hephaestus: A Greek Mythology Circus Tale* (Lookingglass Theatre Company and Silverguy Entertainment)

Sound Design – Midsize: Victoria Delorio, *Mary's Wedding* (Rivendell Theatre Ensemble)

Choreography: Tammy Mader, *Thoroughly Modern Millie* (Drury Lane Productions)

Original Incidental Music: Ray Nardelli, Andre Pluess, Josh Horvath and Kevin O'Donnell, *Hephaestus: A Greek Mythology Circus Tale* (Lookingglass Theatre Company and Silverguy Entertainment)

Musical Direction: Roberta Duchak, *Ragtime* (Drury Lane Productions)

Artistic Specialization: Bridges Media (Multimedia), *Trust* (Lookingglass Theatre Company); David Woolley (Fight Choreography), *The Elaborate Entrance of Chad Deity* (Victory Gardens in association with Teatro Vista)

Non-Equity Awards

June 6, 2011; Park West; 38th annual. Formerly called the Citations, the Non-Equity Awards are for outstanding achievement in professional productions which played at Chicago theaters not operating under union contracts from April 1, 2010–March 31, 2011; given by the Jefferson Awards Committee.

Production – Play: *Man from Nebraska* (Redtwist Theatre)

Production – Musical or Revue: *Cabaret* (The Hypocrites)

Ensemble: *Shakespeare's King Phycus* (The Strange Tree Group with The Lord Chamberlain's Men)

Director – Play: (tie) Jimmy McDermott, *The Three Faces of Dr. Crippen* (The Strange Tree Group); James Palmer, *The Love of the Nightingale* (Red Tape Theatre)

Director – Musical or Revue: Matt Hawkins, *Cabaret* (The Hypocrites)

New Work: *The Three Faces of Dr. Crippen* by Emily Schwartz (The Strange Tree Group)

New Adaptation: Robert Kauzlaric, *Neverwhere* (Lifeline Theatre)

Actress in a Principal Role – Play: (tie) Caroline Neff, *The Brief History of Helen of Troy* (Steep Theatre Company); Nicole Wiesner, *The First Ladies* (Trap Door Theatre)

Actor in a Principal Role – Play: Chuck Spencer, *Man from Nebraska* (Redtwist Theatre)

Actress in a Supporting Role – Play: Sara Pavlak, *Agnes of God* (Hubris Productions)

Actor in a Supporting Role – Play: Brian Parry, *Shining City* (Redtwist Theatre)

Actress in a Principal Role – Musical or Revue: Jessie Fisher, *Cabaret* (The Hypocrites)

Actor in a Principal Role – Musical or Revue: Andrew Mueller, *Big River* (Bohemian Theatre Ensemble)

Actress in a Supporting Role – Musical or Revue: Kate Harris, *Cabaret* (The Hypocrites)

Actor In a Supporting Role – Musical or Revue: Courtney Crouse, *Big River* (Bohemian Theatre Ensemble)

Scenic Design: Alan Donahue, *Neverwhere* (Lifeline Theatre)

Lighting Design: Jared Moore, *No Exit* (The Hypocrites)

Costume Design: (tie) Matt Guthier, *Cats* (Theo Ubique Cabaret Theatre with Michael James); Alison Siple, *Cabaret* (The Hypocrites)

Sound Design: Mikhail Fiksel, *Neverwhere* (Lifeline Theatre)

Choreography: Brenda Didier, *Cats* (Theo Ubique Cabaret Theatre with Michael James)

Original Incidental Music: Chris Gingrich, Henry Riggs, Thea Lux, and Tara Sissom, *That Sordid Little Story* (The New Colony)

Musical Direction: Austin Cook, *Some Enchanted Evening* (Theo Ubique Cabaret Theatre with Michael James)

Artistic Specialization: Glen Aduikas, Rick Buesing, Mike Fletcher, Salvador Garcia, Stuart Hecht, David Hyman, Terry Jackson, Don Kerste, Bruce Phillips, Al Schilling, Lisi Stoessel, and Eddy Wright (Robot design and engineering), *Heddatron* (Sideshow Theatre Company); Izumi Inaba (Makeup design), *Cats* (Theo Ubique Cabaret Theatre with Michael James)

Kennedy Center

Honors 33rd annual; December 5, 2010 (broadcast on CBS December 27, 2010); for distinguished achievement by individuals who have made significant contributions to American culture through the arts: Merle Haggard, Jerry Herman, Bill T. Jones, Paul McCartney, Oprah Winfrey

Mark Twain Prize 13th annual; November 9, 2010 (Broadcast on PBS November 14, 2010); for American humor: Tina Fey

Kevin Kline Awards

March 28, 2011; Loretto-Hilton Center for the Performing Arts; 6th annual. Presented for outstanding achievement in professional theatre in the Greater St. Louis area for the 2010 calendar year; produced by The Professional Theatre Awards Council (Steve Isom, Executive Director); Winners were selected by a floating pool of 45 judges.

Outstanding Production of a Play: *Hamlet* (Shakespeare Festival St. Louis)

Outstanding Director of a Play: Philip Boehm, *Outlying Islands* (Upstream Theater)

Outstanding Production of a Musical: *Show Boat* (The Muny)

Outstanding Director of a Musical: Michael Hamilton, *Promises, Promises* (Stages St. Louis)

Outstanding Lead Actress in a Play: Kari Ely, *Long Day's Journey Into Night* (Muddy Waters)

Outstanding Lead Actor in a Play: Jim Butz, *Hamlet* (Shakespeare Festival St. Louis)

Outstanding Lead Actress in a Musical: Ashley Brown, *The Sound of Music* (The Muny)

Outstanding Lead Actor in a Musical: Ben Nordstrom, *Promises, Promises* (Stages St. Louis)

Outstanding Supporting Actress in a Play: Kari Ely, *Why Torture is Wrong, and the People Who Love Them* (HotCity Theatre)

Outstanding Supporting Actor in a Play: Michael Jonigkeit, *High* (Repertory Theatre of St. Louis)

Outstanding Supporting Actress in a Musical: Brandi Wooten, *Promises, Promises* (Stages St. Louis)

Outstanding Supporting Actor in a Musical: Michel Bell, *Show Boat* (The Muny)

Outstanding Musical Direction: Charles Creath, *Five Guys Named Moe* (The Black Rep)

Outstanding Choreography: Mary MacLeod, *Damn Yankees* (The Muny)

Outstanding Costume Design: John Inchiostro, *The Aristocats* (Stages St. Louis)

Outstanding Lighting Design: John Lasiter, (Repertory Theatre of St. Louis)

Outstanding Set Design: David Gallo, *High* (Repertory Theatre of St. Louis)

Outstanding Sound Design: (tie) Josh Limpert, *Outlying Islands* (Upstream Theater); Ann Slayton and Robin Weatherall, *Hamlet* (Shakespeare Festival St. Louis); Matthew Koch, *Slasher* (HotCity Theatre)

Outstanding Ensemble in a Play: *The Chosen* (Mustard Seed Theatre)

Outstanding Ensemble in a Musical: *Five Guys Named Moe* (The Black Rep)

Production for Young Audiences: (tie) *Delilah's Wish* (Metro Theatre Company); *The Aristocats* (Stages St. Louis)

Outstanding New Play or Musical: David Slavitt (translator), *Oedipus King* (Upstream Theater)

Los Angeles Drama Critics Circle

March 14, 2011; Colony Theatre; 42nd annual. Presented for excellence in theatre in the Los Angeles and Orange County during the 2010 calendar year.

Productions: *Four Places* (John Perrin Flynn, Matthew Elkins and Deborah Puette for Rogue Machine Theatre at Theatre/Theater); *King Lear* (The Antaeus Company at Deaf West Theatre); *The Ballad Of Emmett Till* (Stephen Sachs and Deborah Lawler at the Fountain Theatre) *Yellow*, Louise Beard, Emerson Collins, Del Shores and Jason Dottley for JD3atrical Productions

T.H. McCulloh Award for Best Revival: *South Pacific* (Center Theatre Group at the Ahmanson Theatre)

Direction: Bart DeLorenzo, *King Lear* (The Antaeus Company at Deaf West Theatre); Shirley Jo Finney, *The Ballad Of Emmett Till* (The Fountain Theatre); Michael Michetti, *The Twentieth-Century Way* (The Theatre @ Boston Court)

Writing: Michael Hollinger, *Opus* (The Fountain Theatre)

Adaptation: Jeffrey Hatcher, *Cousin Bette* (The Antaeus Company at Deaf West)

Musical Direction: Eric Heinly, *A Wither's Tale* (Troubadour Theater Company at the Falcon Theatre); David O, *See What I Wanna See* (Blank Theatre)

Musical Score: Lin-Manuel Miranda, *In the Heights* (Broadway/L.A. at the Pantages Theatre)

Choreography: Andy Blankenbuehler, *In the Heights* (Broadway/L.A. at the Pantages Theatre)

Lead Performance: Lorenz Arnell, *The Ballad Of Emmett Till* (The Fountain Theatre); Anne Gee Byrd, *Four Places* (Rogue Machine Theatre at Theatre/Theater); Harry Groener, *King Lear* (The Antaeus Company at Deaf West Theatre); Nan McNamara, *Wit* (Actors Co-op at Crossley Theatres); Chris Pine, *The Lieutenant Of Inishmore* (Center Theatre Group at the Mark Taper Forum)

Featured Performance: Gregory Itzin, *King Lear* (The Antaeus Company at Deaf West Theatre); Matthew Scott Montgomery, *Yellow* (Louise Beard, Emerson Collins, Del Shores and Jason Dottley for JD3atrical Productions); Agatha Nowicki, *Parasite Drag* (Elephant Theatre Company)

Ensemble Performance: *Four Places* (Rogue Machine Theatre at Theatre/Theater); *Opus* (The Fountain Theatre); *The Ballad of Emmett Till* (The Fountain Theatre)

Solo Performance: Ed Harris, *Wrecks* (The Geffen Playhouse)

Set Design: Brian Sidney Bembridge, *The Good Book of Pedantry and Wonder* (The Theatre @ Boston Court and Circle X Theatre Company)

Lighting Design: KC Wilkerson, *The Who's Tommy* (Chance Theater)

Costume Design: Naila Alladin Sanders, *Neighbors* (The Matrix Theatre Company)

Sound Design: Peter Bayne, *Opus* (The Fountain Theatre); Sean Kozma, *The Arsonists*; John Zalewski, *King Lear*

CGI/Video Design: KC Wilkerson, *The Who's Tommy* (Chance Theater)

Special Prosthetic Effects: Matthew W. Mungle, *The Lieutenant of Inishmore* (Center Theatre Group at the Mark Taper Forum)

Special Effects: Chris Bell, Absinthe, *Opium & Magic: 1920s Shanghai* (The Grand Guignolers); Waldo Warshaw, *The Lieutenant of Inishmore* (Center Theatre Group at the Mark Taper Forum)

Special Awards

Ted Schmitt Award (for the world premiere of an outstanding new play): Del Shores, *Yellow*

Margaret Harford Award (for Sustained Excellence in Theatre): City Garage Theatre

Polly Warfield Award (for outstanding single season by a small to mid-sized theatre): Antaeus Company

Angstrom Award (for career achievement in lighting design): Dan Weingarten

Joel Hirschhorn Award (for outstanding achievement in musical theatre): Matt Walker

Bob Z Award (for career achievement in set design): Francois-Pierre Couture

Milton Katseals Award (for career or special achievement in direction): Simon Levy

MAC Awards

May 10, 2011; B.B. King's; 25th annual. Presented by the Manhattan Association of Cabarets and Clubs to honor achievements in cabaret, comedy, jazz, and live entertainment in the previous year. Producer, Julie Miller; Director, Lennie Watts; Musical Director, Steven Ray Watkins; Host, Christine Pedi.

Female Vocalist: Sarah Rice, *Screen Gems: Songs of Old Hollywood* (Laurie Beechman Theatre)

Male Vocalist: Kevin Dozier, *Take Me to the World* (Feinstein's/Laurie Beechman/Don't Tell Mama)

Major Artist: Julie Reyburn, *Live at Feinstein's*; *Summer Night*; *So Many People...a Sondheim Show* (Feinstein's/Laurie Beechman/Urban Stages)

New York Debut–Female: Liz Lark Brown, *Tarnished* (Metropolitan Room)

New York Debut–Male: Sean Harkness (Metropolitan Room/Top of the Rock)

Celebrity Artist: Marilyn Maye, *Her Own Kind of Broadway*; *The Merriest*; *In Love Again* (Metropolitan Room/Yale Cabaret Series)

Comedy/Musical Comedy Performer–Female: Amy Wolk, *Amy Wolk Sings Divine Madness* (Don't Tell Mama)

Comedy/Musical Comedy Performer–Male: Adelmo Guidarelli, *Operation Adelmo–The Clown Prince of Opera*; *The Adelmo Guidarelli Christmas Special* (Duplex/Don't Tell Mama/Triad/Brook Arts Center)

Vocal Duo/Group: Scott Coulter, Steve Ray Watkins, and Lennie Watts, *3Play The 70s* (Don't Tell Mama)

Special Production: Faye Lane's *Beauty Shop Stories*, Created and performed by Faye Lane, directed by Jay Rogers, produced by Adam Magazine (LaMama ETC/Huron Club at Soho Playhouse)

Variety Production/Recurring Series: *Cabaret Cares*, Produced by Joseph Macchia (Laurie Beechman)

Open Mic: *Salon*, Created and hosted by Mark Janas, produced by Tanya Moberly (Etcetera Etcetera)

Host – Variety Show/Series or Open Mic: Raissa Katona Bennett, *The Concerts at Tudor City Greens* (Tudor City Greens)

Piano Bar/Restaurant Singing Entertainer: Kristine Zbornik (Don't Tel Mama)

Piano Bar/Restaurant Instrumentalist: Nate Buccieri (Don't Tell Mama/Brandy's)

Director: Lennie Watts for Julie Reyburn (Feinstein's/Laurie Beechman), Kevin Dozier (Feinstein's/Laurie Beechman/Don't Tell Mama), Liz Lark Brown (Metropolitan Room), Jackie Fornatale (Don't Tell Mama/Laurie Beechman)

Technical Director: David Colbert for Karen Finley, Sarah Rice, Coco Peru (Laurie Beechman)

Musical Director: Alex Rybeck for: *Liz & Ann Hampton Callaway: Boom!* (Town Hall), Todd Murray (Feinstein's/Metropolitan Room), Kevin Dozier (Feinstein's/Laurie Beechman/Don't Tell Mama), Liz Callaway: New Year's Eve (Metropolitan Room), Donna McKechnie (Laurie Beechman), and Faith Prince (Caramoor)

Recording: Karen Oberlin, *Live at the Algonquin—Songs of Frank Loesser*

Song: "Haunted" by Marcus Simeone (lyrics) and Tracy Stark (music)

Special Musical Material: "Christmas in Michigan" by Mary Liz McNamara

Hanson Award: Marianne Challis

Board of Directors Award: George Sanders

Lifetime Achievement Award: Annie Ross

Margo Jones Citizen of the Theater Medal

Presented by the Ohio State University Libraries and College of the Arts to a citizen of the theater who has made a lifetime commitment to the theater in the United States and has demonstrated an understanding and affirmation of the craft of playwriting. The Medal Committee is comprised of Deborah Robison for the family of Jerome Lawrence, Janet Waldo Lee and Lucy Lee for the family of Robert E. Lee, Alan Woods, Mary Taratino and Nena Couch (from the Jerome Lawrence Institute).

2010-2011 Winner: Anne Cattaneo

Past Recipients: 1961: Lucille Lortel **1962:** Michael Ellis **1963:** Judith Rutherford Marechal; George Savage (university award) **1964:** Richard Barr; Edward Albee; and Clinton Wilder; Richard A. Duprey (university award) **1965:** Wynn Handman; Marston Balch (university award) **1966:** Jon Jory; Arthur Ballet (university award) **1967:** Paul Baker; George C. White (workshop award) **1968:** Davey Marlin-Jones; Ellen Stewart (workshop award) **1969:** Adrian Hall; Edward Parone and Gordon Davidson (workshop award) **1970:** Joseph Papp **1971:** Zelda Fichandler **1972:** Jules Irving **1973:** Douglas Turner Ward **1974:** Paul Weidner **1975:** Robert Kalfin **1976:** Gordon Davidson **1977:** Marshall W. Mason **1978:** Jon Jory **1979:** Ellen Stewart **1980:** John Clark Donahue **1981:** Lynne Meadow **1982:** Andre Bishop **1983:** Bill Bushnell **1984:** Gregory Mosher **1985:** John Lion **1986:** Lloyd Richards **1987:** Gerald Chapman **1988:** no award **1989:** Margaret Goheen **1990:** Richard Coe **1991:** Otis L. Guernsey Jr. **1992:** Abbot Van Nostrand **1993:** Henry Hewes **1994:** Jane Alexander **1995:** Robert Whitehead **1996:** Al Hirschfield **1997:** George C. White **1998:** James Houghton **1999:** George Keathley **2000:** Eileen Heckart **2001:** Mel Gussow **2002:** Emilie

S. Kilgore **2003-2004:** Christopher Durang and Marsha Norman **2005-2006:** Jerome Lawrence and Robert E. Lee **2007-2008:** David Emmes and Martin Benson **2009:** Bill Rauch

National Arts Club Awards

Joseph Kesselring Fellowship and Honors

National Arts Club member Joseph Otto Kesselring was born in New York in 1902. He was an actor, author, producer, and playwright. Mr. Kesselring died in 1967, leaving his estate in a trust, which terminated in 1978 when the life beneficiary died. A bequest was made to the National Arts Club "on condition that said bequest be used to establish a fund to be known as the Joseph Kesselring Fund, the income and principal of which shall be used to give financial aid to playwrights, on such a basis of selection and to such as the National Arts Club may, in its sole discretion, determine." A committee appointed by the president and the governors of the National Arts Club administers the Kesselring Prizes. It approves monetary prizes annually to playwrights nominated by qualified production companies whose dramatic work has demonstrated the highest possible merit and promise and is deserving of greater recognition, but who as yet has not received prominent national notice or acclaim in the theater. The winners are chosen by a panel of judges who are independent of the Club. In addition to a cash prize, the first-prize winner also receives a staged reading of a work of his or her choice. In the fall of 2007, the Club redefined the award to consist of the Kesselring Fellowship, and created a new category called the Kesselring Honors. No awards were presented in the 2010 season.

Previous Fellowship Recipients: 1980: Susan Charlotte **1981:** Cheryl Hawkins **1982:** No Award **1983:** Lynn Alvarez **1984:** Philip Kan Gotanda **1985:** Bill Elverman **1986:** Marlane Meyer **1987:** Paul Schmidt **1988:** Diane Ney **1989:** Jo Carson **1990:** Elizabeth Egloff, Mel Shapiro **1991:** Tony Kushner **1992:** Marion Isaac McClinton **1993:** Anna Deavere Smith **1994:** Nicky Silver **1995:** Amy Freed, Doug Wright **1996:** Naomi Wallace **1997:** No Award **1998:** Kira Obolensky **1999:** Heather McDonald **2000:** David Auburn **2001:** David Lindsay-Abaire **2002:** Melissa James Gibson **2003:** Bridget Carpenter **2004:** Tracey Scott Wilson **2005:** Deb Margolin **2006:** Mark Schultz **2007:** Jordan Harrison **2009:** Rajiv Joseph, David Adjmi

Previous Honors Recipients (if year is missing none were presented): **1980:** Carol Lashof **1981:** William Hathaway **1983:** Constance Congdon **1985:** Laura Harrington **1986:** John Leicht **1987:** Januszz Glowacki **1988:** Jose Rivera, Frank Hogan **1989:** Keith Reddin **1990:** Howard Korder **1991:** Quincy Long, Scott McPherson **1992:** José Rivera **1993:** Han Ong **1996:** Nilo Cruz **1997:** Kira Obolensky, Edwin Sanchez **1998:** Erik Ehn **1999:** Steven Dietz **2000:** Jessica Hagedorn **2001:** Dael Orlandersmith **2002:** Lydia Diamond **2003:** Lynn Nottage **2004:** John Borello **2005:** Tanya Barfield **2006:** Bruce Norris **2007:** Will Eno, Rinne Groff, Marcus Gardley **2009:** Jenny Schwartz, Tarrel Alvin McCraney

National Medals of the Arts

March 2, 2011; East Room at the White House. Presented to individuals who and organizations that have made outstanding contributions to the excellence, growth, support, and availability of the arts in the United States, selected by the President of the United States from nominees presented by the National Endowment of the Arts. **2010 Individual Winners:** Robert Brustein, Theatrical Critic, Producer, Playwright & Educator (New York, NY); Van Cliburn, Pianist and Music Educator (Shreveport, LA); Mark di Suvero, Sculptor (Shanghai, China); Donald Hall, Poet (New Haven, CT); Quincy Jones, Musician and Music Producer (Chicago, IL); Harper Lee, Author (Monroeville, AL); Sonny Rollins, Jazz Musician (Harlem, NY); Meryl Streep, Actress (Summit, NJ); James Taylor, Singer Songwriter (Boston, MA)

2010 Organization Winner: Jacob's Pillow Dance Festival (Becket, MA)

New Dramatists Lifetime Achievement Award

May 17, 2011; Marriott Marquis; 62nd annual. Presented to an individual who has made an outstanding artistic contribution to the American theater. **2011 Winner:** Roger Berlind

New York Innovative Theatre Awards

September 20, 2010; Cooper Union Great Hall; 6th annual; Host: Lisa Kron. Presented to honor individuals and organizations who have achieved artistic excellence in Off-Off-Broadway theatre for the 2009-2010 season. The New York IT Awards committee recognizes the unique and essential role Off-Off-Broadway plays in contributing to American and global culture, and believes that publicly recognizing excellence in independent theatre will expand audience awareness and appreciation of the full New York theatre experience. Staff: Jason Bowcutt, Shay Gines, Nick Micozzi, Executive Directors; Awards Committee: Paul Adams (Emerging Artists Theatre), Dan Bacalzo (*TheatreMania.com*), Christopher Borg (Actor/Director), Jason Bowcutt (IT Awards), Tim Errickson (Boomerang Theatre Company), Thecla Farrell (Castillo Theatre), Constance Congdon (Playwright), Shay Gines (New York IT Awards), Ben Hodges (*Theatre World*), Leonard Jacobs (*Back Stage*), Ron Lasko (Spin Cycle P.R.), Blake Lawrence, Bob Lee, Nick Micozzi (IT Awards), Risa Shoup, (chashama), Nicky Paraiso (La MaMa E.T.C.), Jeff Riebe (The January Initiative), Akia Squiterri (Rising Sun Performance Company). Presenters: Geraldine Hughes, Michael Patrick Walker, Wendy Seyb, David Draper, Lucy Thurber, Jill BC DuBoff, Martin Pakledinaz, Christine Jones, Allen Lee Hughes, Basil Twist, Jessica Burr, Matt Opatrny, Dylan Baker, Becky Ann Baker, Christian Parker, David Caparelliotis, Theodora Skipitares, Igor Goldin, Judith Malina

Outstanding Ensemble: Marc Bovino, Joe Curnutte, Michael Dalto, Stephanie Wright Thompson, *Samuel and Alasdair: A Personal History of the Robot War* (The Mad Ones)

Outstanding Solo Performance: Jesse Zaritt, *Binding* (Theatre C & terraNOVA Collective's soloNOVA Festival)

Outstanding Actor in a Featured Role: Amir Darvish, *Psyche* (Cake Productions)

Outstanding Actress in a Featured Role: Jennifer Harder, *MilkMilkLemonade* (The Management/Horse Trade Theater Group)

Outstanding Actor in a Lead Role: Frank Anderson, *The Return of Peter Grimm* (Metropolitan Playhouse)

Outstanding Actress in a Lead Role: Elizabeth A. Davis, *Emily, An Amethyst Remembrance* (Firebone Theatre)

Outstanding Choreography/Movement: Jesse Zaritt, *Binding* (Theatre C & terraNOVA Collective's soloNOVA Festival)

Outstanding Director: Brian Smith, *Pink!* (Down Payment Productions)

Outstanding Set Design: Michael Kramer, *Children of Eden* (Astoria Performing Arts Center)

Outstanding Costume Design: Olivera Gajic, *Le Serpent Rouge* (Company XIV)

Outstanding Lighting Design: Charles Foster, *Fêtes de la Nuit* (WeildWorks)

Outstanding Sound Design: Stowe Nelson, *Samuel and Alasdair: A Personal History of the Robot War* (The Mad Ones)

Outstanding Innovative Design: C. Andrew Bauer, *Fêtes de la Nuit* (WeildWorks)

Outstanding Original Music: Mark Valdez, *Caucasian Chalk Circle* (Performance Lab 115)

Outstanding Original Full-Length Script: Crystal Skillman, *The Vigil or The Guided Cradle* (Impetuous Theater Group & The Brick)

Outstanding Original Short Script: Jonothon Lyons, *The Tenement* (The Associated Mask Ensemble)

Outstanding Stage Manager: Jaimie Van Dyke (Blessed Unrest)

Outstanding Performance Art Production: *Binding* (Theatre C & terraNOVA Collective's soloNOVA Festival)

Outstanding Actor in a Featured Role: Amir Darvish, *Psyche* (Cake Productions)

Outstanding Production of a Musical: *Children of Eden* (Astoria Performing Arts Center)

Outstanding Production of a Play: *Samuel and Alasdair: A Personal History of the Robot War* (The Mad Ones)

Artistic Achievement Award: Lanford Wilson

Stewardship Award: Dixon Place

Caffe Cino Fellowship Award ($1,000 grant): New York Neo-Futurists

Otto René Castillo Awards

May 22, 2011; Castillo Theatre All Stars Project; 13th annual. Presented to artists for and theatres from around the world in recognition for contributions to Political Theatre. The Otto Award is named for the Guatemalan poet and revolutionary Otto Rene Castillo, who was murdered by that country's military junta in 1968. **2011 Winners:** Wajahat Ali; Freedom Train Productions; Lorna C. Hill; Liz Lerman Dance Exchange

Ovation Awards

January 17, 2011; Thousand Oaks Civic Arts Plaza; 21st annual. Established in 1989, the L.A. Stage Alliance Ovation Awards are Southern California's premiere awards for excellence in theatre. Winners were selected by a 190 member voting pool of theatre professionals working in the Los Angeles theatre community for productions that played September 1, 2009–August 31, 2010.

Best Season: Fountain Theatre: *The Ballad of Emmett Till, Opus, Shining City*

Production of a Play–Intimate Theatre: *The Ballad of Emmett Till* (Fountain Theatre); *Four Places* (Rogue Machine)

Production of a Musical–Intimate Theatre (Franklin R. Levy Memorial Award): *The Women of Brewster Place* (Celebration Theatre)

Production of a Play–Large Theatre: *Equivocation* (Geffen Playhouse)

Production of a Musical–Large Theatre: *Oedipus the King, Mama!* (Troubadour Theater Company)

Playwrighting for an Original Play: L. Trey Wilson, *Something Happened* (Pacific Stages)

Book for an Original Musical: John Caird, *Daddy Long Legs* (Rubicon Theatre Company)

Lyrics/Music for an Original Musical: Paul Gordon, *Daddy Long Legs* (Rubicon Theatre Company)

Director of a Play: Shirley Jo Finney, *The Ballad of Emmett Till* (Fountain Theatre)

Director of a Musical: Matt Walker, *Oedipus the King, Mama!* (Troubadour Theater Company)

Musical Direction: John Glaudini, *Sweeney Todd* (Musical Theatre West)

Choreographer: Lee Martino, *Carousel* (Reprise Theatre Company)

Ensemble Performance: The Cast of *The Ballad of Emmett Till* (Fountain Theatre)

Lead Actor in a Play: Bruce French, *The Browning Version* (Pacific Resident Theatre); Alan Mandell, *No Man's Land* (Odyssey Theatre Ensemble); Daniel Beaty, *Through the Night* (Geffen Playhouse)

Lead Actress in a Play: Beth Grant, *Grace & Glorie* (The Colony Theatre Company); Anna Khaja, *SHAHEED – The Dream and Death of Benazir Bhutto* (Stephanie Feury Studio Theatre)

Lead Actor in a Musical: Josh Grisetti, *How to Succeed in Business Without Really Trying* (Reprise Theatre Company); Brendan Hunt, *Savin' Up for Saturday Night* (Sacred Fools Theatre Company); Robert J. Townsend, *The Story of My Life* (Havok Theatre Company)

Lead Actress in a Musical: Megan McGinnis, *Daddy Long Legs* (Rubicon Theatre Company)

Featured Actor in a Play: Harry Groener, *Equivocation* (Geffen Playhouse)

Featured Actress in a Play: Deirdre O'Connell, *The Wake* (Center Theatre Group at the Kirk Douglas Theatre)

Featured Actor in a Musical: David St. Louis, *Parade* (Center Theatre Group at the Mark Taper Forum)

Featured Actress in a Musical: Sally Struthers, *Cinderella* (Cabrillo Music Theatre)

Set Design–Intimate Theatre: Brian Sidney Bembridge, *The Good Book of Pedantry and Wonder* (The Theatre @ Boston Court and Circle X Theatre Company)

Set Design–Large Theatre: Jeff McLaughlin, *Grace & Glorie* (The Colony Theatre Company)

Costume Design–Intimate Theatre: Teresa Shea, *Project Wonderland* (Bootleg Theater)

Costume Design–Large Theatre: Christopher Oram, *Parade* (Center Theatre Group: Mark Taper Forum); Snezana Petrovic, *Songs and Dances of Imaginary Lands* (Overtone Industries)

Lighting Design–Intimate Theatre: Jeremy Pivnick, *Oedipus el Rey* (The Theatre @ Boston Court)

Lighting Design–Large Theatre: Scott Zielinski, *Equivocation* (Geffen Playhouse)

Sound Design–Intimate Theatre: Peter Bayne, *Opus* (Fountain Theatre)

Sound Design–Large Theatre: Lindsay Jones, *Through the Night* (Geffen Playhouse)

Ovation Honors

Video Design: KC Wilkerson, *The Who's Tommy* (The Chance Theater)

Music Composition for a Play: Ego Plum, *Gogol Project* (Bootleg Theater and Rogue Artists Ensemble)

Puppet Design: Lynn Jeffries, *Project Wonderland* (Bootleg Theater)

Fight Choreography: Edgar Landa, *Oedipus el Rey* (The Theatre @ Boston Court)

Pittsburgh Civic Light Opera's Richard Rodgers Award

Founded in 1988. Recognizes the lifetime contributions of outstanding talents in musical theatre; Presented by The Pittsburgh Civic Light Opera in conjunction with the families of Richard Rodgers and Oscar Hammerstein II. No award was presented this year.

Past Recipients: 1988: Mary Martin **1989:** Dame Julie Andrews **1991:** Harold

Prince **1992:** Sir Cameron Mackintosh **1993:** Stephen Sondheim **1996:** Lord Andrew Lloyd Webber **2000:** Gwen Verdon **2002:** Bernadette Peters **2007:** Shirley Jones **2008:** Rob Marshall and Kathleen Marshall **2009:** Stephen Schwartz

Princess Grace Awards

November 10, 2010; Cipriani on 42nd Street, New York; 25th annual. Presented by the Princess Grace Foundation – USA for excellence in theatre, dance, and film across the United States. 2010 Awards: ***Statue Award:*** Anna D. Shapiro (Director/Head of Graduate Directing Program at Northwestern); **Pierre Cardin Theater Award**: Virginia Grise (Playwrights' Arena–Theatre Fellowship); **Fabergé Theater Award**: Tom Gleeson (Arden Theatre Company–Theatre Fellowship); **Robert and Gloria Houseman Theater Award:** Shana Cooper (Oregon Shakespeare Festival–Theater Fellowship); **Gant Gaither Theater Award:** Andrea Assaf (Pangea World Theater–Theater Fellowship); **George C. Wolfe Award:** Charlotte Brathwaite (Yale School of Drama–Theatre Scholarship; **Grace Le Vine Theater Award:** Adam Pinti (Arizona State University–Theatre Scholarship); **Playwrighting Fellowship:** A. Rey Pamatmat (New Dramatists Inc.)

Richard Rodgers Awards

For staged readings of musicals in nonprofit theaters, administered by the American Academy of Arts and Letters and selected by a jury including Stephen Sondheim (chairman), Lynn Ahrens, John Guare, Sheldon Harnick, David Ives, Richard Maltby Jr., and Lin-Manuel Miranda.

2011 Winners: *Dogfight* by Benj Pasek and Justin Paul; *Gloryana* by Andrew Gerle

Robert Whitehead Award

March 15, 2011; The Glass House Tavern; Founded in 1993. Presented for outstanding achievement in commercial theatre producing, bestowed on a graduate of the fourteen-week Commercial Theatre Institute Program who has demonstrated a quality of production exemplified by the late producer, Robert Whitehead. The Commercial Theatre Institute (Jed Bernstein, Director) is the nation's only formal program that professionally trains commercial theatre producers. It is a joint project of the League of American Theatres and Producers, Inc., and Theatre Development Fund. **2011 Winner:** Jill Furman

Previous Recipients: 1993: Susan Quint Gallin; Benjamin Mordecai **1994:** Dennis Grimaldi **1995:** Kevin McCollum **1996:** Randall L. Wreghitt **1997:** Marc Routh **1998:** Liz Oliver **1999:** Eric Krebs **2000:** Anne Strickland Squadron **2001–2003:** No Award **2004:** David Binder **2005–2007:** No Award **2008:** Nick Scandalios **2009:** Dori Bernstein **2010:** Stuart Thompson

Stage Director and Choreographers (SDC) Foundation Awards

Mr. Abbot Award

Named in honor of the legendary director George Abbot, this award is presented exclusively for directors and choreographers in recognition of lifetime achievement in the American Theatre.

No award presented this season.

Previous Recipients: 1985: Harold Prince **1986:** Bob Fosse **1987:** Mike Nichols **1988:** Agnes de Mille **1989:** Michael Bennet **1990:** Gene Saks **1991:** Tommy Tune **1992:** Arvin Brown **1993:** Trevor Nunn **1994:** Jerry Zaks **1995:** Gordon Davidson **1996:** Lloyd Richards **1997:** Garson Kanin **1998:** Graciela

Daniele **1999:** Vinnette Carrol, Zelda Fichandler, Peter Gennaro, Gillian Lynne, Marshall W. Mason, Andrei Serban **2000:** Cy Feuer **2001:** Susan Stroman **2002:** Jack O'Brien **2003:** Lynne Meadow **2005:** Kathleen Marshall and Rob Marshall **2007:** Daniel Sullivan **2009:** Donald Saddler

Joe A. Callaway Awards

Also known as the "Joey," this award, created in 1989, is issued for excellence in the craft of direction and/or choreography for during the New York City theatre season from September 1, 2009 through August 31, 2010.

2010 Winners: Director: Ciarán O'Reilly, *The Emperor Jones* (Irish Repertory Theatre); Choreographer: Byron Easley, *Langston in Harlem* (Byron Easley)

Previous Winners: 1989: Gloria Muzio **1990:** Frank Galati **1991:** Susan Stroman **1992:** George C. Wolfe, Hope Clark **1993:** Harold Prince **1994:** Gerald Gutierrez **1995:** Joe Mantello, Scott Elliott **1996:** Julie Taymor **1997:** Moisés Kaufman **1998:** Frank Galati, Graciela Daniele **1999:** Trevor Nunn **2000:** Gabriel Barre, Mark Dendy **2001:** Jack O'Brien **2002:** Bartlett Sher **2003:** Devanand Janki, Doug Hughes **2004:** Daniel Sullivan **2005:** Doug Hughes, Christopher Gattelli **2006:** Bill T. Jones, Peter DuBois **2007:** Thomas Kail, Andy Blankenbuehler **2008:** Giovanna Sardelli, Lynne Taylor-Corbett **2009:** Garry Hynes, Martha Clarke

Steinberg Playwright Award

October 26, 2010; Vivian Beaumont Theatre; Premiere Year. Created by the Harold and Mimi Steinberg Charitable Trust, this award recognizes playwrights at various stages of their early careers whose profession works show great promise. This award is presented on alternate years with the Steinberg Distinguished Playwright Award which recognizes an established American playwright whose body of work has made significant contributions to the American theater. Nominating and Selection Committee: André Bishop (Artistic Director, Lincoln Center Theater), David Emmes (Producing Artistic Director, South Coast Repertory), Oskar Eustis (Artistic Director, The Public Theater), Polly K. Carl (Producing Artistic Director, Playwrights Center), Martha Lavey (Artistic Director, Steppenwolf Theatre Company), Eduardo Machado (playwright/Artistic Director, INTAR Theatre), and Marc Masterson (Artistic Director, Actors Theatre of Louisville). The winners receive 'The Mimi,' a statue designed by David Rockwell, and a cash prize (a share of $100,000 for playwrights in early stages of their careers and $200,000 for established playwrights), making the award the largest ever created to honor and encourage artistic achievement in the American Theatre.

2010 Recipients: Bruce Norris ($50,000), Tarell Alvin McCraney & David Adjmi ($25,000 each)

Previous Distinguished Recipient: 2009: Tony Kushner

Susan Smith Blackburn Prize

February 28, 2011; New York City; 32ʳᵈ annual; Presenter: Doug Hughes. Presented to women who have written works of outstanding quality for the English-speaking theater. The Prize is administered in Houston, London, and New York by a board of directors who choose six judges each year and submitted by various theatres. 2010–2011 Judges: Judith Ivey, Anne Kauffman, Helen McCrory, Georgina Brown, Stephen Unwin. The winner receives a $20,000 cash prize and a signed and numbered print by artist Willem de Kooning. The Special Commendation winner receives a $5,000 cash prize, and each finalist receives $1,000.

2011 Winner: Katori Hall, *Hurt Village* (Signature Theatre Company U. S.)

Special Commendation: Not presented this year

Finalists: Lisa D'Amour, *Detroit* (Steppenwolf Theatre Company U.S.); Sam Burns, *Not the Worst Place* (Paines Plough U.K.); Frances Ya-Chu Cowhig,

Lidless (Marin Theatre Company U.S.); Georgia Fitch, *Fit and Proper People* (The Royal Shakespeare Company U.K.); Lisa Kron, *In the Wake* (Berkeley Repertory Theatre U.S.); Tamsin Oglesby, *Really Old, Like* 45 (The Royal National Theatre U.K.); Anne Washburn, *Mr. Burns: A Post-Electric Play* (Woolly Mammoth Theatre Company U.S); Joy Wilkinson, *The Golden Age* (Everyman Playhouse Liverpool U.K.); Alexandra Wood, *The Andes* (Out of Joint U.K.)

Theatre Development Fund Awards

Fred and Adele Astaire Awards

May 15, 2011; Skirball Center; 29ᵗʰ Annual; Hosts: Bebe Neuwirth and Lee Roy Reams. Originally known as the Astaire Awards these awards were founded by the Anglo-American Contemporary Dance Foundation and have been administered by Theatre Development Fund since 1991. These awards recognize outstanding achievement in dance on Broadway and in film. 2011 Nominating Committee: Sylviane Gold – Chair (*Dance Magazine*), Anna Kisselgoff (former *New York Times* Chief Dance Critic), Wendy Perron (*Dance Magazine* Editor-in-Chief), Damian Woetzel (former principal dancer, New York City Ballet), Manny and Lani Azenberg, Donna McKechnie, Lee Roy Reams, Wendy Federman, Barbara & Buddy Freitag, Michael Riedel, Marge Champion, Margaret Selby, Melinda Atwod, Bryan Bantry, Adam Zotovich, Andy Sandberg, Bruce Michael. Chairman Emeritus, Douglas Watt; Honorary Chairs, Judith Jamison and Wendy Federman; Gala Co-Chairs, Carolyn Kendall Buchter, Seidenfeld Lyster, Bruce Michael; Benefit Co-Chairs, Sara Kaplan Johnson, Jamie Watkins; Executive Producer, Patricia Watt; Co-Producer, New York City Dance Alliance; Associate Producer, Bronwen Carson; Director, Joe Lanteri

Best Broadway Choreographer: Susan Stroman, *The Scottsboro Boys*

Excellence in Dance on Film: Graeme Murphy and Janet Verno, *Mao's Last Dancer*

Best Female Dancer: Sutton Foster, *Anything Goes*

Best Male Dancer: Norbert Leo Butz, *Catch Me If You Can*

Douglas Watt Lifetime Achievement Award: Jacques d'Amboise

Adele Astaire Scholarship: Corey Snide

Irene Sharaff Awards

April 8, 2011; Hudson Theatre; 16ᵗʰ annual. Founded in 1993, this award has become an occasion for the costume design community to come together to honor its own and pays tribute to the art of costume design. Named after the revered costume designer, the awards are decided upon by the TDF Costume Collection Advisory Committee (Kitty Leech–Chair, Gregg Barnes, Suzy Benzinger, Dean Brown, Stephen Cabral, Linda Fisher, Lana Fritz, Rodney Gordon, Desmond Heeley, Allen Lee Hughes, Holly Hynes, Carolyn Kostopoulous, Anna Louizos, Mimi Maxmen, David Murin, Sally Ann Parsons, Robert Perdziola, Gregory A. Poplyk Carrie Robbins, Tony Walton, Patrick Wiley, David Zinn).

Lifetime Achievement Award: Lewis Brown

Young Master Award: Olivera Gajic

Artisan Award: Michael-Jon Costumes

The Robert L.B. Tobin Award: Robin Wagner

Memorial Tribute: Charles LeMaire

The Theater Hall of Fame

January 24, 2011; Gershwin Theatre North Rotunda; 40ᵗʰ annual; Host: Pia Lindstrom. The Theater of Hall of Fame was created in 1971 to honor those who have made outstanding contributions to the American theater in a career spanning at least twenty-five years, with at least five major credits. Producer, Terry Hodge Taylor; Presenters: Hal Prince, Robert Falls, Alexander Gemignani, James Nicola, James Houghton, Roger Berlind, Andre Bishop, Brian Stokes Mitchell

2011 Inductees (for the year 2010)**:** Michael Blakemore, Joseph Chaikin, Caryl Churchill, Brian Dennehy, Paul Gemignani, James Lapine, Linda Lavin, Fritz Weaver

Previous Inductees: George Abbott, Maude Adams, Viola Adams, Stella Adler, Edward Albee, Theoni V. Aldredge, Ira Aldridge, Jane Alexander, Mary Alice, Winthrop Ames, Judith Anderson, Maxwell Anderson, Robert Anderson, Julie Andrews, Margaret Anglin, Jean Anouilh, Harold Arlen, George Arliss, Boris Aronson, Adele Astaire, Fred Astaire, Eileen Atkins, Brooks Atkinson, Alan Ayckbourn, Emanuel Azenberg, Lauren Bacall, Pearl Bailey, George Balanchine, William Ball, Anne Bancroft, Tallulah Bankhead, Richard Barr, Philip Barry, Ethel Barrymore, John Barrymore, Lionel Barrymore, Howard Bay, Nora Bayes, John Lee Beatty, Julian Beck, Samuel Beckett, Brian Bedford, S.N. Behrman, Barbara Bel Geddes, Norman Bel Geddes, David Belasco, Michael Bennett, Richard Bennett, Robert Russell Bennett, Eric Bentley, Irving Berlin, Roger Berlind, Sarah Bernhardt, Leonard Bernstein, Patricia Birch, Earl Blackwell, Kermit Bloomgarden, Jerry Bock, Ray Bolger, Edwin Booth, Roscoe Lee Brown, Junius Brutus Booth, Shirley Booth, Philip Bosco, Dion Boucicault, Alice Brady, Bertolt Brecht, Fannie Brice, Peter Brook, John Mason Brown, Robert Brustein, Billie Burke, Abe Burrows, Richard Burton, Mrs. Patrick Campbell, Zoe Caldwell, Eddie Cantor, Len Cariou, Morris Carnovsky, Mrs. Leslie Carter, Gower Champion, Frank Chanfrau, Carol Channing, Stockard Channing, Ruth Chatterton, Paddy Chayefsky, Anton Chekhov, Ina Claire, Bobby Clark, Harold Clurman, Lee. J. Cobb, Richard L. Coe, George M. Cohan, Alexander H. Cohen, Jack Cole, Cy Coleman, Constance Collier, Alvin Colt, Betty Comden, Marc Connelly, Barbara Cook, Thomas Abthorpe Cooper, Katherine Cornell, Noel Coward, Jane Cowl, Lotta Crabtree, Cheryl Crawford, Hume Cronyn, Rachel Crothers, Russel Crouse, John Cullum, Charlotte Cushman, Jim Dale, Jean Dalrymple, Augustin Daly, Graciela Daniele, E.L. Davenport, Gordon Davidson, Ossie Davis, Owen Davis, Ruby Dee, Alfred De Liagre Jr., Agnes DeMille, Colleen Dewhurst, Howard Dietz, Dudley Digges, Melvyn Douglas, Eddie Dowling, Alfred Drake, Marie Dressler, John Drew, Mrs. John Drew, William Dunlap, Mildred Dunnock, Charles Durning, Eleanora Duse, Jeanne Eagles, Richard Easton, Fred Ebb, Ben Edwards, Florence Eldridge, Lehman Engel, Maurice Evans, Abe Feder, Jose Ferber, Cy Feuer, Zelda Fichandler, Dorothy Fields, Herbert Fields, Lewis Fields, W.C. Fields, Harvey Fierstein, Jules Fisher, Minnie Maddern Fiske, Clyde Fitch, Geraldine Fitzgerald, Henry Fonda, Lynn Fontanne, Horton Foote, Edwin Forrest, Bob Fosse, Brian Friel, Rudolf Friml, Charles Frohman, Daniel Frohman, Robert Fryer, Athol Fugard, John Gassner, Larry Gelbart, Peter Gennaro, Grace George, George Gershwin, Ira Gershwin, Bernard Gersten, William Gibson, John Gielgud, W.S. Gilbert, Jack Gilford, William Gillette, Charles Gilpin, Lillian Gish, Susan Glaspell, John Golden, Max Gordon, Ruth Gordon, Adolph Green, Paul Green, Charlotte Greenwood, Jane Greenwood, Joel Grey, Tammy Grimes, George Grizzard, John Guare, Otis L. Guernsey Jr., A.R. Gurney, Mel Gussow, Tyrone Guthrie, Uta Hagen, Sir Peter Hall, Lewis Hallam, T. Edward Hambleton, Marvin Hamlisch, Oscar Hammerstein II, Walter Hampden, Otto Harbach, E.Y. Harburg, Sheldon Harnick, Edward Harrigan, Jed Harris, Julie Harris, Rosemary Harris, Sam H. Harris, Rex Harrison, Kitty Carlisle Hart, Lorenz Hart, Moss Hart, Tony Hart, June Havoc, Helen Hayes, Leland Hayward, George Hearn, Ben Hecht, Eileen Heckart, Theresa Helburn, Lillian Hellman, Katharine Hepburn, Victor Herbert, Jerry Herman, James A. Herne, Henry Hewes, Gregory Hines, Al Hirschfeld, Raymond Hitchcock, Hal Holbrook, Celeste Holm, Hanya Holm, Arthur Hopkins, De Wolf Hopper, John Houseman, Eugene Howard, Leslie Howard, Sidney Howard, Willie Howard, Barnard Hughes, Henry Hull, Josephine Hull, Walter Huston, Earle Hyman, Henrik Ibsen, William Inge, Dana Ivey, Bernard B. Jacobs, Elise Janis, Joseph Jefferson, Al Jolson, James Earl Jones, Margo Jones, Robert Edmond Jones, Tom Jones, Jon Jory, Raul Julia, Madeline Kahn, John Kander, Garson Kanin, George S. Kaufman, Danny Kaye, Elia Kazan, Gene Kelly, George Kelly, Fanny Kemble, Jerome Kern, Walter Kerr, Michael Kidd, Richard Kiley, Willa Kim, Sidney Kingsley, Kevin Kline, Florence Klotz, Joseph Wood Krutch, Bert Lahr, Burton Lane, Frank Langella, Lawrence Langner, Lillie Langtry, Angela Lansbury, Nathan Lane, Charles Laughton, Arthur Laurents, Gertrude Lawrence, Jerome Lawrence, Eva Le Gallienne, Canada Lee, Eugene Lee, Ming Cho Lee, Robert E. Lee, Lotte Lenya, Alan Jay Lerner, Sam Levene, Robert Lewis, Beatrice Lillie, Howard Lindsay, John Lithgow, Andrew Lloyd Webber, Frank Loesser, Frederick Loewe, Joshua Logan, William Ivey Long, Santo Loquasto, Pauline Lord, Lucille Lortel, Charles Ludlam, Dorothy Loudon, Alfred Lunt, Patti LuPone, Charles MacArthur, Steele MacKaye, Judith Malina, David Mamet, Rouben Mamoulian, Ted Mann, Richard Mansfield, Robert B. Mantell, Frederic March, Nancy Marchand, Julia Marlowe, Ernest H. Martin, Mary Martin, Raymond Massey, Elizabeth Ireland McCann, Ian McKellen, Siobhan McKenna, John McMartin, Terrence McNally, Sanford Meisner, Helen Menken, Burgess Meredith, Ethel Merman, David Merrick, Jo Mielziner, Arthur Miller, Marilyn Miller, Liza Minnelli, Helena Modjeska, Ferenc Molnar, Lola Montez, Victor Moore, Robert Morse, Zero Mostel, Anna Cora Mowatt, Paul Muni, Brian Murray, Tharon Musser, George Jean Nathan, Mildred Natwick, Alla Nazimova, Patricia Neal, James M. Nederlander, Mike Nichols, Elliot Norton, Jack O'Brien, Sean O'Casey, Clifford Odets, Donald Oenslager, Laurence Olivier, Eugene O'Neill, Jerry Orbach, Geraldine Page, Joseph Papp, Estelle Parsons, Osgood Perkins, Bernadette Peters, Molly Picon, Harold Pinter, Luigi Pirandello, Christopher Plummer, Cole Porter, Robert Preston, Harold Prince, Jose Quintero, Ellis Rabb, John Raitt, Tony Randall, Lynn Redgrave, Michael Redgrave, Ada Rehan, Elmer Rice, Lloyd Richards, Ralph Richardson, Chita Rivera, Jason Robards, Jerome Robbins, Paul Robeson, Richard Rodgers, Will Rogers, Sigmund Romberg, Harold Rome, Billy Rose, Lillian Russell, Donald Saddler, Gene Saks, Diana Sands, William Saroyan, Joseph Schildkraut, Harvey Schmidt, Alan Schneider, Gerald Shoenfeld, Arthur Schwartz, Maurice Schwartz, Stephen Schwartz, George C. Scott, Marian Seldes, Peter Shaffer, Irene Sharaff, George Bernard Shaw, Sam Shepard, Robert F. Sherwood, J.J. Shubert, Lee Shubert, Herman Shumlin, Neil Simon, Lee Simonson, Edmund Simpson, Otis Skinner, Lois Smith, Maggie Smith, Oliver Smith, Stephen Sondheim, E.H. Sothern, Kim Stanley, Jean Stapleton, Maureen Stapleton, Joseph Stein, Frances Sternhagen, Roger L. Stevens, Isabelle Stevenson, Ellen Stewart, Dorothy Stickney, Fred Stone, Peter Stone, Tom Stoppard, Lee Strasburg, August Strindberg, Elaine Stritch, Charles Strouse, Jule Styne, Margaret Sullivan, Arthur Sullivan, Jessica Tandy, Laurette Taylor, Ellen Terry, Sada Thompson, Cleon Throckmorton, Tommy Tune, Jonathan Tunick, Gwen Verdon, Robin Wagner, Nancy Walker, Eli Wallach, James Wallack, Lester Wallack, Tony Walton, Douglas Turner Ward, David Warfield, Wendy Wasserstein, Ethel Waters, Clifton Webb, Joseph Weber, Margaret Webster, Kurt Weill, Orson Welles, Mae West, Robert Whitehead, Richard Wilbur, Oscar Wilde, Thorton Wilder, Bert Williams, Tennessee Williams, August Wilson, Elizabeth Wilson, Lanford Wilson, P.G. Wodehouse, Peggy Wood, Alexander Woollcott, Irene Worth, Teresa Wright, Ed Wynn, Vincent Youmans, Stark Young, Florenz Ziegfeld, Patricia Zipprodt

Theater Hall of Fame Founders Award

Established in 1993 in honor of Earl Blackwell, James M. Nederlander, Gerald Oestreicher and Arnold Weissberger. The Theater Hall of Fame Founders Award is voted by the Hall's board of directors and is presented to an individual for his of her outstanding contribution to the theater.

Past Recipients: (if year is missing, no award was presented) **1993:** James M. Nederlander **1994:** Kitty Carlisle Hart **1995:** Harvey Sabinson **1996:** Henry Hewes **1997:** Otis L. Guernsey Jr. **1998:** Edward Colton **2000:** Gerard Oestreicher; Arnold Weissberger **2001:** Tom Dillon **2003:** Price Berkley **2004:** No Award **2005:** Donald Seawell **2007:** Roy Somlyo **2009:** Shirley Herz

William Inge Theatre Festival Awards

April 13-16, 2011; 30th annual. The Inge Festival brings some of the world's most beloved playwrights to America's heartland in Independence, Missouri. During the four-day festival, honorees are chosen for distinguished achievement in

American theater. Also, the festival selects a winner of the Otis Guernsey New Voices Playwriting Award, which recognizes contemporary playwrights whose voices are helping shape the American theater of today. It is named for the late Otis L. Guernsey Jr., beloved theater writer and editor who was a frequent guest at the William Inge Theatre Festival and a champion of exciting new plays.

2011 Honoree: Marsha Norman

19th Annual Otis Guernsey New Voices in Playwrighting Award: Dael Orlandersmith

Previous Festival Honorees: 1982: William Inge Celebration; **1983:** Jerome Lawrence **1984:** William Gibson **1985:** Robert Anderson **1986:** John Patrick **1987:** Garson Kanin **1988:** Sidney Kingsley (in Independence), Robert E. Lee (on the road) **1989:** Horton Foote **1990:** Betty Comden & Adolph Green **1991:** Edward Albee **1992**: Peter Shaffer **1993:** Wendy Wasserstein **1994:** Terrence McNally **1995:** Arthur Miller **1996:** August Wilson **1997:** Neil Simon **1998**: Stephen Sondheim **1999:** John Guare **2000:** A.R. Gurney **2001:** Lanford Wilson **2002:** John Kander & Fred Ebb **2003:** Romulus Linney **2004:** Arthur Laurents **2005:** 25th Anniversary retrospective **2007:** Jerry Bock & Sheldon Harnick **2008:** Christopher Durang **2009:** Tom Jones and Harvey Schmidt **2010:** Paula Vogel

Previous New Voices Recipients: 1993: Jason Milligan **1994:** Catherine Butterfield **1995:** Mary Hanes **1996:** Brian Burgess Cross **1997:** Joe DiPietro **1998:** David Ives **1999:** David Hirson **2000:** James Still **2001:** Mark St. Germain **2002:** Dana Yeaton **2003:** Theresa Rebeck **2004:** Mary Portser **2005:** Lynne Kaufman **2006:** Melanie Marnich **2007:** JT Rogers **2008:** Adam Bock **2009:** Carlos Murillo **2010:** Katori Hall

LONGEST-RUNNING SHOWS

Top: Christine Anderson, Suzi Winson, Marilyn Farina, Vicki Belmonte, and
Semina De Laurentis in Nunsense (photo by Stephen Aucoin)
Middle: Keith Carradine and the cast of The Will Rogers Follies
(photo by Martha Swope)
Bottom: Charlotte d'Amboise in the revival of Chicago (photo by Jeremy Daniel)

Broadway

The Phantom of the Opera*
9,723 performances
Opened January 26, 1988

Cats
7,485 performances
Opened October 7, 1982
Closed September 10, 2000

Les Misérables
6,680 performances
Opened March 12, 1987
Closed May 18, 2003

A Chorus Line
6,137 performances
Opened July 25, 1975
Closed April 28, 1990

Chicago* (revival)
6,040 performances
Opened November 19, 1996

Oh! Calcutta (revival)
5,959 performances
Opened September 24, 1976
Closed August 6, 1989

The Lion King*
5,672 performances
Opened November 13, 1997

Beauty and the Beast
5,464 performances
Opened April 18, 1994
Closed July 29, 2007

Rent
5,124 performances
Opened April 29, 1996
Closed September 7, 2008

Miss Saigon
4,097 performances
Opened April 11, 1991
Closed January 28, 2001

Mamma Mia!*
4,000 performances
Opened October 12, 2001

42nd Street
3,486 performances
Opened August 25, 1980
Closed January 8, 1989

Grease
3,388 performances
Opened February 14, 1972
Closed April 13, 1980

Fiddler on the Roof
3,242 performances
Opened September 22, 1964
Closed July 2, 1972

Life With Father
3,224 performances
Opened November 8, 1939
Closed July 12, 1947

Tobacco Road
3,182 performances
Opened December 4, 1933
Closed May 31, 1941

Wicked*
3,154 performances
Opened October 30, 2003

Hello, Dolly!
2,844 performances
Opened January 16, 1964
Closed December 27, 1970

My Fair Lady
2,717 performances
Opened March 15, 1956
Closed September 29, 1962

Hairspray
2,641 performances
Opened August 15, 2002
Closed January 4, 2009

Avenue Q
2,534 performances
Opened July 31, 2003
Closed September 13, 2009

The Producers
2,502 performances
Opened April 19, 2001
Closed April 22, 2007

Cabaret (1998 revival)
2,378 performances
Opened March 19, 1998
Closed January 4, 2004

Annie
2,377 performances
Opened April 21, 1977
Closed January 22, 1983

Man of La Mancha
2,328 performances
Opened November 22, 1965
Closed June 26, 1971

Abie's Irish Rose
2,327 performances
Opened May 23, 1922
Closed October 21, 1927

Jersey Boys*
2,299 performances
Opened November 6, 2006

Oklahoma!
2,212 performances
Opened March 31, 1943
Closed May 29, 1948

Smokey Joe's Café
2,036 performances
Opened March 2, 1995
Closed January 16, 2000

Jessica Tandy and Hume Cronyn in The Fourposter *(photo by Jean Dalrymple)*

Pippin
1,944 performances
Opened October 23, 1972
Closed June 12, 1977

South Pacific
1,925 performances
Opened April 7, 1949
Closed January 16, 1954

The Magic Show
1,920 performances
Opened May 28, 1974
Closed December 31, 1978

Mary Poppins*
1,889 performances
Opened November 16, 2006

Aida performances
1,852 performances
Opened March 23, 2000
Closed September 5, 2004

Gemini
1,819 performances
Opened May 21, 1977
Closed September 6, 1981

Deathtrap
1,793 performances
Opened February 26, 1978
Closed June 13, 1982

Harvey
1,775 performances
Opened November 1, 1944
Closed January 15, 1949

Dancin'
1,774 performances
Opened March 27, 1978
Closed June 27, 1982

La Cage aux Folles
1,761 performances
Opened August 21, 1983
Closed November 15, 1987

Hair
1,750 performances
Opened April 29, 1968
Closed July 1, 1972

The Wiz
1,672 performances
Opened January 5, 1975
Closed January 29, 1979

Born Yesterday
1,642 performances
Opened February 4, 1946
Closed December 31, 1949

The Best Little Whorehouse in Texas
1,639 performances
Opened June 19, 1978
Closed March 27, 1982

Crazy for You
1,622 performances
Opened February 19, 1992
Closed January 7, 1996

Ain't Misbehavin'
1,604 performances
Opened May 9, 1978
Closed February 21, 1982

Monty Python's Spamalot
1,574 performances
Opened March 17, 2005
Closed January 11, 2009

Mary, Mary
1,572 performances
Opened March 8, 1961
Closed December 12, 1964

Evita
1,567 performances
Opened September 25, 1979
Closed June 26, 1983

The Voice of the Turtle
1,557 performances
Opened December 8, 1943
Closed January 3, 1948

Mabel King in The Wiz *(photo by Martha Swope)*

Jekyll & Hyde
1,543 performances
Opened April 28, 1997
Closed January 7, 2001]

Barefoot in the Park
1,530 performances
Opened October 23, 1963
Closed June 25, 1967

Brighton Beach Memoirs
1,530 performances
Opened March 27, 1983
Closed May 11, 1986

42nd Street (revival)
1,524 performances
Opened May 2, 2001
Closed January 2, 2005

Dreamgirls
1,522 performances
Opened December 20, 1981
Closed August 11, 1985

Mame
1,508 performances
Opened May 24, 1966
Closed January 3, 1970

Grease (1994 revival)
1,505 performances
Opened May 11, 1994
Closed January 25, 1998

Same Time, Next Year
1,453 performances
Opened March 14, 1975
Closed September 3, 1978

Arsenic and Old Lace
1,444 performances
Opened January 10, 1941
Closed June 17, 1944

The Sound of Music
1,443 performances
Opened November 16, 1959
Closed June 15, 1963

Me and My Girl
1,420 performances
Opened August 10, 1986
Closed December 31, 1989

How to Succeed in Business Without Really Trying
1,417 performances
Opened October 14, 1961
Closed March 6, 1965

Hellzapoppin'
1,404 performances
Opened September 22, 1938
Closed December 17, 1941

The Music Man
1,375 performances
Opened December 19, 1957
Closed April 15, 1961

Funny Girl
1,348 performances
Opened March 26, 1964
Closed July 15, 1967

Mummenschanz
1,326 performances
Opened March 30, 1977
Closed April 20, 1980

Movin' Out
1,303 performances
Opened October 24, 2002
Closed December 11, 2005

Angel Street
1,295 performances
Opened December 5, 1941
Closed December 30, 1944

Lightnin'
1,291 performances
Opened August 26, 1918
Closed August 27, 1921

Promises, Promises
1,281 performances
Opened December 1, 1968
Closed January 1, 1972

The King and I
1,246 performances
Opened March 29, 1951
Closed March 20, 1954

Cactus Flower
1,234 performances
Opened December 8, 1965
Closed November 23, 1968

Sleuth
1,222 performances
Opened November 12, 1970
Closed October 13, 1973

Torch Song Trilogy
1,222 performances
Opened June 10, 1982
Closed May 19, 1985

1776
1,217 performances
Opened March 16, 1969
Closed February 13, 1972

Equus
1,209 performances
Opened October 24, 1974
Closed October 7, 1977

Sugar Babies
1,208 performances
Opened October 8, 1979
Closed August 28, 1982

Guys and Dolls
1,200 performances
Opened November 24, 1950
Closed November 28, 1953

In the Heights
1,184 performances
Opened March 9, 2008
Closed January 9, 2011

Amadeus
1,181 performances
Opened December 17, 1980
Closed October 16, 1983

Cabaret
1,165 performances
Opened November 20, 1966
Closed September 6, 1969

Mister Roberts
1,157 performances
Opened February 18, 1948
Closed January 6, 1951

Annie Get Your Gun
1,147 performances
Opened May 16, 1946
Closed February 12, 1949

Guys and Dolls (1992 revival)
1,144 performances
Opened April 14, 1992
Closed January 8, 1995

The Seven Year Itch
1,141 performances
Opened November 20, 1952
Closed August 13, 1955

The 25th Annual Putnam County Spelling Bee
1,136 performances
Opened May 2, 2005
Closed January 20, 2008

Bring in 'da Noise, Bring in 'da Funk
1,130 performances
Opened April 25, 1996
Closed January 19, 1999

Butterflies Are Free
1,128 performances
Opened October 21, 1969
Closed July 2, 1972

Pins and Needles
1,108 performances
Opened November 27, 1937
Closed June 22, 1940

Patti LuPone and Howard McGillan in 1987 revival of Anything Goes *(photo by Brigitte Lacombe)*

Plaza Suite
1,097 performances
Opened February 14, 1968
Closed October 3, 1970

Fosse
1,093 performances
Opened January 14, 1999
Closed August 25, 2001

They're Playing Our Song
1,082 performances
Opened February 11, 1979
Closed September 6, 1981

Grand Hotel (musical)
1,077 performances
Opened November 12, 1989
Closed April 25, 1992

Kiss Me, Kate
1,070 performances
Opened December 30, 1948
Closed July 25, 1951

Don't Bother Me, I Can't Cope
1,065 performances
Opened April 19, 1972
Closed October 27, 1974

The Pajama Game
1,063 performances
Opened May 13, 1954
November 24, 1956

Billy Elliot The Musical*
1,061 performances
Opened November 13, 2008

Shenandoah
1,050 performances
Opened January 7, 1975
Closed August 7, 1977

Annie Get Your Gun (1999 revival)
1,046 performances
Opened March 4, 1999
Closed September 1, 2001

The Teahouse of the August Moon
1,027 performances
Opened October 15, 1953
Closed March 24, 1956

Damn Yankees
1,019 performances
Opened May 5, 1955
Closed October 12, 1957

Contact
1,010 performances
Opened March 30, 2000
Closed September 1, 2002

Never Too Late
1,007 performances
Opened November 26, 1962
Closed April 24, 1965

Big River
1,005 performances
Opened April 25, 1985
Closed September 20, 1987

South Pacific (revival)
996 performances
Opened April 3, 2008
Closed August 22, 2010

The Will Rogers Follies
983 performances
Opened May 1, 1991
Closed September 5, 1993

Any Wednesday
982 performances
Opened February 18, 1964
Closed June 26, 1966

Sunset Boulevard
977 performances
Opened November 17, 1994
Closed March 22, 1997

Urinetown the Musical
965 performances
Opened September 20, 2001
Closed January 18, 2004

A Funny Thing Happened on the Way to the Forum
964 performances
Opened May 8, 1962
Closed August 29, 1964

The Odd Couple
964 performances
Opened March 10, 1965
Closed July 2, 1967

Anna Lucasta
957 performances
Opened August 30, 1944
Closed November 30, 1946

Kiss and Tell
956 performances
Opened March 17, 1943
Closed June 23, 1945

Show Boat (1994 revival)
949 performances
Opened October 2, 1994
Closed January 5, 1997

Rock of Ages*
948 performances
Opened April 7, 2009

Dracula (1977 revival)
925 performances
Opened October 20, 1977
Closed January 6, 1980

Bells Are Ringing
924 performances
Opened November 29, 1956
Closed March 7, 1959

The Moon Is Blue
924 performances
Opened March 8, 1951
Closed May 30, 1953

Beatlemania
920 performances
Opened May 31, 1977
Closed October 17, 1979

Proof
917 performances
Opened October 24, 2000
Closed January 5, 2003

The Elephant Man
916 performances
Opened April 19, 1979
Closed June 28, 1981

The Color Purple
910 performances
Opened December 1, 2005
Closed February 24, 2008

Kiss of the Spider Woman
906 performances
Opened May 3, 1993
Closed July 1, 1995

Thoroughly Modern Millie
904 performances
Opened April 18, 2002
Closed June 20, 2004

Luv
901 performances
Opened November 11, 1964
Closed January 7, 1967

The Who's Tommy
900 performances
Opened April 22, 1993
Closed June 17, 1995

Chicago
898 performances
Opened June 3, 1975
Closed August 27, 1977

Applause
896 performances
Opened March 30, 1970
Closed July 27, 1972

Can-Can
892 performances
Opened May 7, 1953
Closed June 25, 1955

Carousel
890 performances
Opened April 19, 1945
Closed May 24, 1947

I'm Not Rappaport
890 performances
Opened November 19, 1985
Closed January 17, 1988

Hats Off to Ice
889 performances
Opened June 22, 1944
Closed April 2, 1946

Fanny
888 performances
Opened November 4, 1954
Closed December 16, 1956

Children of a Lesser God
887 performances
Opened March 30, 1980
Closed May 16, 1982

Richard Dysart and Walter McGinn in That Championship Season *(photo by Friedman-Ableles)*

Follow the Girls
882 performances
Opened April 8, 1944
Closed May 18, 1946

Kiss Me, Kate (revival)
881 performances
Opened November 18, 1999
Closed December 30, 2001

City of Angels
878 performances
Opened December 11, 1989
Closed January 19, 1992

Camelot
873 performances
Opened December 3, 1960
Closed January 5, 1963

I Love My Wife
872 performances
Opened April 17, 1977
Closed May 20, 1979

The Bat
867 performances
Opened August 23, 1920
Closed Unknown closing date

My Sister Eileen
864 performances
Opened December 26, 1940
Closed January 16, 1943

No, No, Nanette (revival)
861 performances
Opened January 19, 1971
Closed February 3, 1973

Ragtime
861 performances
Opened January 18, 1998
Closed January 16, 2000

Song of Norway
860 performances
Opened August 21, 1944
Closed September 7, 1946

Spring Awakening
859 performances
Opened December 10, 2006
Closed January 18, 2009

Chapter Two
857 performances
Opened December 4, 1977
Closed December 9, 1979

A Streetcar Named Desire
855 performances
Opened December 3, 1947
Closed December 17, 1949

Barnum
854 performances
Opened April 30, 1980
Closed May 16, 1982

Comedy in Music
849 performances
Opened October 2, 1953
Closed January 21, 1956

Raisin
847 performances
Opened October 18, 1973
Closed December 7, 1975

Blood Brothers
839 performances
Opened April 25, 1993
Closed April 30, 1995

You Can't Take It With You
837 performances
Opened December 14, 1936
Unknown closing date

La Plume de Ma Tante
835 performances
Opened November 11, 1958
Closed December 17, 1960

Three Men on a Horse
835 performances
Opened January 30, 1935
Closed January 9, 1937

The Subject Was Roses
832 performances
Opened May 25, 1964
Closed May 21, 1966

Black and Blue
824 performances
Opened January 26, 1989
Closed January 20, 1991

The King and I (1996 revival)
807 performances
Opened April 11, 1996
Closed February 22, 1998

Inherit the Wind
806 performances
Opened April 21, 1955
Closed June 22, 1957

Anything Goes (1987 revival)
804 performances
Opened October 19, 1987
Closed September 3, 1989

Titanic
804 performances
Opened April 23, 1997
Closed March 21, 1999

No Time for Sergeants
796 performances
Opened October 20, 1955
Closed September 14, 1957

Fiorello!
795 performances
Opened November 23, 1959
Closed October 28, 1961

Nancy Snyder, Jonathan Hogan, Amy Wright, Joyce Reehling, Helen Stenborg, William Hurt, Danton Stone, and Jeff Daniels in Fifth of July
(photo by Ken Howard)

Where's Charley?
792 performances
Opened October 11, 1948
Closed September 9, 1950

The Ladder
789 performances
Opened October 22, 1926
Unknown closing date

Fiddler on the Roof (2004 revival)
781 performances
Opened February 26, 2004
Closed January 8, 2006

Forty Carats
780 performances
Opened December 26, 1968
Closed November 7, 1970

Lost in Yonkers
780 performances
Opened February 21, 1991
Closed January 3, 1993

The Prisoner of Second Avenue
780 performances
Opened November 11, 1971
Closed September 29, 1973

M. Butterfly
777 performances
Opened March 20, 1988
Closed January 27, 1990

The Tale of the Allergist's Wife
777 performances
Opened November 2, 2000
Closed September 15, 2002

Oliver!
774 performances
Opened January 6, 1963
Closed November 14, 1964

The Pirates of Penzance
(1981 revival)
772 performances
Opened January 8, 1981
Closed November 28, 1982

The 39 Steps
771 performances
Opened January 15, 2008
Closed January 10, 2010

The Full Monty
770 performances
Opened October 26, 2000
Closed September 1, 2002

Woman of the Year
770 performances
Opened March 29, 1981
Closed March 13, 1983

My One and Only
767 performances
Opened May 1, 1983
Closed March 3, 1985

Sophisticated Ladies
767 performances
Opened March 1, 1981
Closed January 2, 1983

Bubbling Brown Sugar
766 performances
Opened March 2, 1976
Closed December 31, 1977

Into the Woods
765 performances
Opened November 5, 1987
Closed September 3, 1989

State of the Union
765 performances
Opened November 14, 1945
Closed September 13, 1947

Starlight Express
761 performances
Opened March 15, 1987
Closed January 8, 1989

The First Year
760 performances
Opened October 20, 1920
Unknown closing date

A Chorus Line (revival)
759 performances
Opened October 5, 2006
Closed August 17, 2008

Broadway Bound
756 performances
Opened December 4, 1986
Closed September 25, 1988

You Know I Can't Hear You When the Water's Running
755 performances
Opened March 13, 1967
Closed January 4, 1969

Two for the Seesaw
750 performances
Opened January 16, 1958
Closed October 31, 1959

West Side Story (2009 revival)
748 performances
Opened March 19, 2009
Closed January 2, 2011

Joseph and the Amazing Technicolor Dreamcoat
747 performances
Opened January 27, 1982
Closed September 4, 1983

Death of a Salesman
742 performances
Opened February 10, 1949
Closed November 18, 1950

for colored girls who have considered suicide/when the rainbow is enuf
742 performances
Opened September 15, 1976
Closed July 16, 1978

Sons o' Fun
742 performances
Opened December 1, 1941
Closed August 29, 1943

Candide (1974 revival)
740 performances
Opened March 10, 1974
Closed January 4, 1976

Gentlemen Prefer Blondes
740 performances
Opened December 8, 1949
Closed September 15, 1951

The Man Who Came to Dinner
739 performances
Opened October 16, 1939
Closed July 12, 1941

Nine
739 performances
Opened May 9, 1982
Closed February 4, 1984

Call Me Mister
734 performances
Opened April 18, 1946
Closed January 10, 1948

Victor/Victoria
734 performances
Opened October 25, 1995
Closed July 27, 1997

Next to Normal
733 performances
Opened April 15, 2009
Closed January 16, 2011

West Side Story
732 performances
Opened September 26, 1957
Closed June 27, 1959

High Button Shoes
727 performances
Opened October 9, 1947
Closed July 2, 1949

Finian's Rainbow
725 performances
Opened January 10, 1947
Closed October 2, 1948

Claudia
722 performances
Opened February 12, 1941
Closed January 9, 1943

The Gold Diggers
720 performances
Opened September 30, 1919
Unknown closing date

Jesus Christ Superstar
720 performances
Opened October 12, 1971
Closed June 30, 1973

Carnival!
719 performances
Opened April 13, 1961
Closed January 5, 1963

The Miracle Worker
719 performances
Opened October 19, 1959
Closed July 1, 1961

The Diary of Anne Frank
717 performances
Opened October 5, 1955
Closed June 22, 1955

A Funny Thing Happened on the Way to the Forum (revival)
715 performances
Opened April 18, 1996
Closed January 4, 1998

I Remember Mama
714 performances
Opened October 19, 1944
Closed June 29, 1946

Tea and Sympathy
712 performances
Opened September 30, 1953
Closed June 18, 1955

Junior Miss
710 performances
Opened November 18, 1941
Closed July 24, 1943

Footloose
708 performances
Opened October 22, 1998
Closed July 2, 2000

Last of the Red Hot Lovers
706 performances
Opened December 28, 1969
Closed September 4, 1971

The Secret Garden
706 performances
Opened April 25, 1991
Closed January 3, 1993

Company
705 performances
Opened April 26, 1970
Closed January 1, 1972

Seventh Heaven
704 performances
Opened October 30, 1922
Unknown closing date

Gypsy
702 performances
Opened May 21, 1959
Closed March 25, 1961

That Championship Season
700 performances
Opened September 14, 1972
Closed April 21, 1974

The Music Man (2000 revival)
698 performances
Opened April 27, 2000
Closed December 30, 2001

Da
697 performances
Opened May 1, 1978
Closed January 1, 1980

Cat on a Hot Tin Roof
694 performances
Opened March 24, 1955
Closed November 17, 1956

Matthew Broderick in the 1995 revival of How to Succeed in Business Without Really Trying *(photo by Joan Marcus)*

John Lithgow and B.D. Wong in M. Butterfly (photo by Joan Marcus)

Li'l Abner
693 performances
Opened November 15, 1956
Closed July 12, 1958

The Children's Hour
691 performances
Opened November 20, 1934
Unknown closing date

Purlie
688 performances
Opened March 15, 1970
Closed November 6, 1971

Dead End
687 performances
Opened October 28, 1935
Closed June 12, 1937

The Lion and the Mouse
686 performances
Opened November 20, 1905
Unknown closing date

White Cargo
686 performances
Opened November 5, 1923
Unknown closing date

The Little Mermaid
685 performances
Opened January 10, 2008
Closed August 30, 2009

Dear Ruth
683 performances
Opened December 13, 1944
Closed July 27, 1946

East Is West
680 performances
Opened December 25, 1918
Unknown closing date

Come Blow Your Horn
677 performances
Opened February 22, 1961
Closed October 6, 1962

The Most Happy Fella
676 performances
Opened May 3, 1956
Closed December 14, 1957

Memphis*
675 performances
Opened October 19, 2009

The Drowsy Chaperone
672 performances
Opened May 1, 2006
Closed December 30, 2007

Defending the Caveman
671 performances
Opened March 26, 1995
Closed June 22, 1997

The Doughgirls
671 performances
Opened December 30, 1942
Closed July 29, 1944

The Impossible Years
670 performances
Opened October 13, 1965
Closed May 27, 1967

Irene
670 performances
Opened November 18, 1919
Unknown closing date

Boy Meets Girl
669 performances
Opened November 27, 1935
Unknown closing date

The Tap Dance Kid
669 performances
Opened December 21, 1983
Closed August 11, 1985

Beyond the Fringe
667 performances
Opened October 27, 1962
Closed May 30, 1964

Who's Afraid of Virginia Woolf?
664 performances
Opened October 13, 1962
Closed May 16, 1964

Blithe Spirit
657 performances
Opened November 5, 1941
Closed June 5, 1943

A Trip to Chinatown
657 performances
Opened November 9, 1891
Unknown closing date

The Women
657 performances
Opened December 26, 1936
Unknown closing date

Bloomer Girl
654 performances
Opened October 5, 1944
Closed April 27, 1946

The Fifth Season
654 performances
Opened January 23, 1953
Closed October 23, 1954

August: Osage County
648 performances
Opened December 4, 2007
Closed June 28, 2009

Rain
648 performances
Opened September 1, 1924
Unknown closing date

Witness for the Prosecution
645 performances
Opened December 16, 1954
Closed June 30, 1956

Call Me Madam
644 performances
Opened October 12, 1950
Closed May 3, 1952

Janie
642 performances
Opened September 10, 1942
Closed January 16, 1944

The Green Pastures
640 performances
Opened February 26, 1930
Closed August 29, 1931

Auntie Mame
639 performances
Opened October 31, 1956
Closed June 28, 1958

A Man for All Seasons
637 performances
Opened November 22, 1961
Closed June 1, 1963

Jerome Robbins' Broadway
634 performances
Opened February 26, 1989
Closed September 1, 1990

The Fourposter
632 performances
Opened October 24, 1951
Closed May 2, 1953

Dirty Rotten Scoundrels
627 performances
Opened March 3, 2005
Closed September 3, 2006

The Music Master
627 performances
Opened September 26, 1904
Unknown closing date

Two Gentlemen of Verona
(musical)
627 performances
Opened December 1, 1971
Closed May 20, 1973

The Tenth Man
623 performances
Opened November 5, 1959
Closed May 13, 1961

The Heidi Chronicles
621 performances
Opened March 9, 1989
Closed September 1, 1990

Is Zat So?
618 performances
Opened January 5, 1925
Closed July 1926

Anniversary Waltz
615 performances
Opened April 7, 1954
Closed September 24, 1955

The Happy Time (play)
614 performances
Opened January 24, 1950
Closed July 14, 1951

Separate Rooms
613 performances
Opened March 23, 1940
Closed September 6, 1941

Affairs of State
610 performances
Opened September 25, 1950
Closed March 8, 1952

Oh! Calcutta!
610 performances
Opened June 17, 1969
Closed August 12, 1972

Star and Garter
609 performances
Opened June 24, 1942
Closed December 4, 1943

The Mystery of Edwin Drood
608 performances
Opened December 2, 1985
Closed May 16, 1987

The Student Prince
608 performances
Opened December 2, 1924
Unknown closing date

Sweet Charity
608 performances
Opened January 29, 1966
Closed July 15, 1967

Bye Bye Birdie
607 performances
Opened April 14, 1960
Closed October 7, 1961

Riverdance on Broadway
605 performances
Opened March 16, 2000
Closed August 26, 2001

Irene (revival)
604 performances
Opened March 13, 1973
Closed September 8, 1974

Sunday in the Park With George
604 performances
Opened May 2, 1984
Closed October 13, 1985

Adonis
603 performances
Opened 1884
Unknown closing date

Broadway
603 performances
Opened September 16, 1926
Unknown closing date

Peg o' My Heart
603 performances
Opened December 20, 1912
Unknown closing date

Master Class
601 performances
Opened November 5, 1995
Closed June 29, 1997

Street Scene (play)
601 performances
Opened January 10, 1929
Unknown closing date

Flower Drum Song
600 performances
Opened December 1, 1958
Closed May 7, 1960

Kiki
600 performances
Opened November 29, 1921
Unknown closing date

A Little Night Music
600 performances
Opened February 25, 1973
Closed August 3, 1974

Art
600 performances
Opened March 1, 1998
Closed August 8, 1999

Agnes of God
599 performances
Opened March 30, 1982
Closed September 4, 1983

Don't Drink the Water
598 performances
Opened November 17, 1966
Closed April 20, 1968

Wish You Were Here
598 performances
Opened June 25, 1952
Closed November 28, 1958

Sarafina!
597 performances
Opened January 28, 1988
Closed July 2, 1989

A Society Circus
596 performances
Opened December 13, 1905
Closed November 24, 1906

Legally Blonde
595 performances
Opened April 29, 2007
Closed October 19, 2008

Absurd Person Singular
592 performances
Opened October 8, 1974
Closed March 6, 1976

A Day in Hollywood/A Night in the Ukraine
588 performances
Opened May 1, 1980
Closed September 27, 1981

The Me Nobody Knows
586 performances
Opened December 18, 1970
Closed November 21, 1971

w
The Two Mrs. Carrolls
585 performances
Opened August 3, 1943
Closed February 3, 1945

Kismet (musical)
583 performances
Opened December 3, 1953
Closed April 23, 1955

Gypsy (1989 revival)
582 performances
Opened November 16, 1989
Closed July 28, 1991

Brigadoon
581 performances
Opened March 13, 1947
Closed July 31, 1948

Detective Story
581 performances
Opened March 23, 1949
Closed August 12, 1950

No Strings
580 performances
Opened March 14, 1962
Closed August 3, 1963

Brother Rat
577 performances
Opened December 16, 1936
Unknown closing date

Blossom Time
576 performances
Opened September 29, 1921
Unknown closing date

Pump Boys and Dinettes
573 performances
Opened February 4, 1982
Closed June 18, 1983

Show Boat
572 performances
Opened December 27, 1927
Closed May 4, 1929

The Show-Off
571 performances
Opened February 5, 1924
Unknown closing date

Sally
570 performances
Opened December 21, 1920
Closed April 22, 1922

Jelly's Last Jam
569 performances
Opened April 26, 1992
Closed September 5, 1993

Golden Boy (musical)
568 performances
Opened October 20, 1964
Closed March 5, 1966

One Touch of Venus
567 performances
Opened October 7, 1943
Closed February 10, 1945

The Real Thing
566 performances
Opened January 5, 1984
Closed May 12, 1985

Happy Birthday
564 performances
Opened October 31, 1946
Closed March 13, 1948

Look Homeward, Angel
564 performances
Opened November 28, 1957
Closed April 4, 1959

Morning's at Seven (revival)
564 performances
Opened April 10, 1980
Closed August 16, 1981

The Glass Menagerie
561 performances
Opened March 31, 1945
Closed August 3, 1946

I Do! I Do!
560 performances
Opened December 5, 1966
Closed June 15, 1968

Wonderful Town
559 performances
Opened February 25, 1953
Closed July 3, 1954

The Last Night of Ballyhoo
557 performances
Opened February 27, 1997
Closed June 28, 1998

Rose Marie
557 performances
Opened September 2, 1924
Unknown closing date

Strictly Dishonorable
557 performances
Opened September 18, 1929
Unknown closing date

Sweeney Todd, the Demon Barber of Fleet Street
557 performances
Opened March 1, 1979
Closed June 29, 1980

The Great White Hope
556 performances
Opened October 3, 1968
Closed January 31, 1970

A Majority of One
556 performances
Opened February 16, 1959
Closed June 25, 1960

The Sisters Rosensweig
556 performances
Opened March 18, 1993
Closed July 16, 1994

Sunrise at Campobello
556 performances
Opened January 30, 1958
Closed May 30, 1959

Toys in the Attic
556 performances
Opened February 25, 1960
Closed April 8, 1961

Jamaica
555 performances
Opened October 31, 1957
Closed April 11, 1959

Stop the World—
I Want to Get Off
555 performances
Opened October 3, 1962
Closed February 1, 1964

Grease (2007 revival)
554 performances
Opened August 19, 2007
Closed January 4, 2009

Florodora
553 performances
Opened November 10, 1900
Closed January 25, 1902

Noises Off
553 performances
Opened December 11, 1983
Closed April 6, 1985

Ziegfeld Follies (1943)
553 performances
Opened April 1, 1943
Closed July 22, 1944

Dial "M" for Murder
552 performances
Opened October 29, 1952
Closed February 27, 1954

Good News
551 performances
Opened September 6, 1927
Unknown closing date

Peter Pan (revival)
551 performances
Opened September 6, 1979
Closed January 4, 1981

How to Succeed in Business
Without Really Trying (revival)
548 performances
Opened March 23, 1995
Closed July 14, 1996

Let's Face It
547 performances
Opened October 29, 1941
Closed March 20, 1943

Milk and Honey
543 performances
Opened October 10, 1961
Closed January 26, 1963

Within the Law
541 performances
Opened September 11, 1912
Unknown closing date

Pal Joey (revival)
540 performances
Opened January 3, 1952
Closed April 18, 1953

The Sound of Music (revival)
540 performances
Opened March 12, 1998
Closed June 20, 1999

What Makes Sammy Run?
540 performances
Opened February 27, 1964
Closed June 12, 1965

The Sunshine Boys
538 performances
Opened December 20, 1972
Closed April 21, 1974

What a Life
538 performances
Opened April 13, 1930
Closed July 8, 1939

Crimes of the Heart
535 performances
Opened November 4, 1981
Closed February 13, 1983

Damn Yankees (revival)
533 performances
Opened March 3, 1994
Closed August 6, 1995

The Unsinkable Molly Brown
532 performances
Opened November 3, 1960
Closed February 10, 1962

The Red Mill (revival)
531 performances
Opened October 16, 1945
Closed January 18, 1947

Rumors
531 performances
Opened November 17, 1988
Closed February 24, 1990

A Raisin in the Sun
530 performances
Opened March 11, 1959
Closed June 25, 1960

Godspell
527 performances
Opened June 22, 1976
Closed September 4, 1977

Fences
526 performances
Opened March 26, 1987
Closed June 26, 1988

The Solid Gold Cadillac
526 performances
Opened November 5, 1953
Closed February 12, 1955

Doubt
525 performances
Opened March 9, 2005
Closed July 2, 2006

Biloxi Blues
524 performances
Opened March 28, 1985
Closed June 28, 1986

Irma La Douce
524 performances
Opened September 29, 1960
Closed December 31, 1961

The Boomerang
522 performances
Opened August 10, 1915
Unknown closing date

Follies
521 performances
Opened April 4, 1971
Closed July 1, 1972

Rosalinda
521 performances
Opened October 28, 1942
Closed January 22, 1944

The Best Man
520 performances
Opened March 31, 1960
Closed July 8, 1961

Chauve-Souris
520 performances
Opened February 4, 1922
Unknown closing date

Hair (revivial)
519 performances
Opened March 31, 2009
Closed June 27, 2010

Blackbirds of 1928
518 performances
Opened May 9, 1928
Unknown closing date

The Gin Game
517 performances
Opened October 6, 1977
Closed December 31, 1978

Side Man
517 performances
Opened June 25, 1988
Closed October 31, 1999

Sunny
517 performances
Opened September 22, 1925
Closed December 11, 1926

Victoria Regina
517 performances
Opened December 26, 1935
Unknown closing date

Xanadu
512 performances
Opened July 10, 2007
Closed September 28, 2008

Curtains
511 performances
Opened March 22, 2007
Closed June 29, 2008

Fifth of July
511 performances
Opened November 5, 1980
Closed January 24, 1982

Half a Sixpence
511 performances
Opened April 25, 1965
Closed July 16, 1966

The Vagabond King
511 performances
Opened September 21, 1925
Closed December 4, 1926

The New Moon
509 performances
Opened September 19, 1928
Closed December 14, 1929

The World of Suzie Wong
508 performances
Opened October 14, 1958
Closed January 2, 1960

The Rothschilds
507 performances
Opened October 19, 1970
Closed January 1, 1972

On Your Toes (revival)
505 performances
Opened March 6, 1983
Closed May 20, 1984

Sugar
505 performances
Opened April 9, 1972
Closed June 23, 1973

The Light in the Piazza
504 performances
Opened March 17, 2005
Closed July 2, 2006

Shuffle Along
504 performances
Opened May 23, 1921
Closed July 15, 1922

Up in Central Park
504 performances
Opened January 27, 1945
Closed January 13, 1946

Carmen Jones
503 performances
Opened December 2, 1943
Closed February 10, 1945

Saturday Night Fever
502 performances
Closed Opened October 21, 1999
December 30, 2000

The Member of the Wedding
501 performances
Opened January 5, 1950
Closed March 17, 1951

Panama Hattie
501 performances
Opened October 30, 1940
Closed January 13, 1942

Personal Appearance
501 performances
Opened October 17, 1934
Unknown closing date

Bird in Hand
500 performances
Opened April 4, 1929
Unknown closing date

Room Service
500 performances
Opened May 19, 1937
Unknown closing date

Sailor, Beware!
500 performances
Opened September 28, 1933
Unknown closing date

Tomorrow the World
500 performances
Opened April 14, 1943
Closed June 17, 1944

Off-Broadway

The Fantasticks
17,162 performances
Opened May 3, 1960
Closed January 13, 2002

Blue Man Group*
10,600 performances
Opened November 17, 1991

Perfect Crime*
9,865 performances
Opened April 18, 1987

Stomp*
7,284 performances
Opened February 27, 1994

Tony 'n' Tina's Wedding
5,901 performances
Opened February 6, 1988
Closed June 2, 2011

I Love You, You're Perfect, Now Change
5,003 performances
Opened August 1, 1996
Closed July 29, 2008

Nunsense
3,672 performances
Opened December 12, 1985
Closed October 16, 1994

Naked Boys Singing*
3,000 performances
Opened July 22, 1999

The Threepenny Opera
2,611 performances
Opened September 20, 1955
Closed December 17, 1961

De La Guarda
2,475 performances
Opened June 16, 1998
Closed September 12, 2004

Forbidden Broadway (original)
2,332 performances
Opened January 15, 1982
Closed August 30, 1987

Little Shop of Horrors
2,209 performances
Opened July 27, 1982
Closed November 1, 1987

Godspell
2,124 performances
Opened May 17, 1971
Closed June 13, 1976

Altar Boyz
2,032 performances
Opened March 1, 2005
Closed January 10, 2010

Vampire Lesbians of Sodom
2,024 performances
Opened June 19, 1985
Closed May 27, 1990

The Fantasticks* (revival)
1,888 performances
Opened August 23, 2006

Jacques Brel is Alive and Well and Living in Paris
1,847 performances
Opened January 22, 1968
Closed July 2, 1972

Forever Plaid
1,811 performances
Opened May 20, 1990
Closed June 12, 1994

Vanities
1,785 performances
Opened March 22, 1976
Closed August 3, 1980

The Donkey Show
1,717 performances
Opened August 18, 1999
Closed July 16, 2005

Menopause the Musical
1,712 performances
Opened April 4, 2002
Closed May 14, 2006

The Gazillion Bubble Show*
1,700 performances
Opened February 15, 2007

You're A Good Man, Charlie Brown
1,597 performances
Opened March 7, 1967
Closed February 14, 1971

The Blacks
1,408 performances
Opened May 4, 1961
Closed September 27, 1964

The Vagina Monologues
1,381 performances
Opened October 3, 1999
Closed January 26, 2003

One Mo' Time
1,372 performances
Opened October 22, 1979
Closed 1982–83 season

Grandma Sylvia's Funeral
1,360 performances
Opened October 9, 1994
Closed June 20, 1998

Let My People Come
1,327 performances
Opened January 8, 1974
Closed July 5, 1976

Fuerza Bruta: Look Up*
1,269 performances
Opened October 24, 2007

Late Nite Catechism
1,268 performances
Opened October 4, 1995
Closed May 18, 2003

Driving Miss Daisy
1,195 performances
Opened April 15, 1987
Closed June 3, 1990

The Hot L Baltimore
1,166 performances
Opened September 8, 1973
Closed January 4, 1976

Gretchen Cryer in
I'm Getting My Act Together
and Taking It on the Road
(photo by George E. Joseph)

I'm Getting My Act Together and Taking It on the Road
1,165 performances
Opened May 16, 1987
Closed March 15, 1981

Little Mary Sunshine
1,143 performances
Opened November 18, 1959
Closed September 2, 1962

Steel Magnolias
1,126 performances
Opened November 17, 1987
Closed February 25, 1990

El Grande de Coca-Cola
1,114 performances
Opened February 13, 1973
Closed April 13, 1975

The Proposition
1,109 performances
Opened March 24, 1971
Closed April 14, 1974

Our Sinatra
1,096 performances
Opened December 8, 1999
Closed July 28, 2002

Beau Jest
1,069 performances
Opened October 10, 1991
Closed May 1, 1994

Jewtopia
1,052 performances
Opened October 21, 2004
Closed April 29, 2007

Tamara
1,036 performances
Opened November 9, 1989
Closed July 15, 1990

One Flew Over the Cuckoo's Nest (revival)
1,025 performances
Opened March 23, 1971
Closed September 16, 1973

Slava's Snowshow
1,004 performances
Opened September 8, 2004
Closed January 14, 2007

The Boys in the Band
1,000 performances
Opened April 14, 1968
Closed September 29, 1985

Fool For Love
1,000 performances
Opened November 27, 1983
Closed September 29, 1985

Forbidden Broadway: 20th Anniversary Celebration
994 performances
Opened March 20, 2002
Closed July 4, 2004

Other People's Money
990 performances
Opened February 7, 1989
Closed July 4, 1991

Cloud 9
971 performances
Opened May 18, 1981
Closed September 4, 1983

Secrets Every Smart Traveler Should Know
953 performances
Opened October 30, 1997
Closed February 21, 2000

Sister Mary Ignatius Explains It All for You &
The Actor's Nightmare
947 performances
Opened October 21, 1981
Closed January 29, 1984

Your Own Thing
933 performances
Opened January 13, 1968
Closed April 5, 1970

Curley McDimple
931 performances
Opened November 22, 1967
Closed January 25, 1970

Leave It to Jane (revival)
928 performances
Opened May 29, 1959
Closed 1961–62 season

The Mad Show
871 performances
Opened January 9, 1966
Closed September 10, 1967

Hedwig and the Angry Inch
857 performances
Opened February 14, 1998
Closed April 9, 2000

Forbidden Broadway Strikes Back
850 performances
Opened October 17, 1996
Closed September 20, 1998

When Pigs Fly
840 performances
Opened August 14, 1996
Closed August 15, 1998

Scrambled Feet
831 performances
Opened June 11, 1979
Closed June 7, 1981

The Effect of Gamma Rays on Man-in-the-Moon Marigolds
819 performances
Opened April 7, 1970
Closed June 1, 1973

Michael Cerveris and Miriam Shor in Hedwig and the Angry Inch *(photo by Carol Rosegg)*

Forbidden Broadway SVU
816 performances
Opened December 16, 2004
Closed April 15, 2007

Over the River and Through the Woods
800 performances
Opened October 5, 1998
Closed September 3, 2000

A View from the Bridge (revival)
780 performances
Opened January 28, 1965
Closed December 11, 1966

The Boy Friend (revival)
763 performances
Opened January 25, 1958
Closed 1961–62 season

True West
762 performances
Opened December 23, 1980
Closed January 11, 1981

Forbidden Broadway Cleans Up Its Act!
754 performances
Opened November 17, 1998
Closed August 30, 2000

Isn't It Romantic
733 performances
Opened December 15, 1983
Closed September 1, 1985

Dime a Dozen
728 performances
Opened June 13, 1962
Closed 1963–64 season

The Pocket Watch
725 performances
Opened November 14, 1966
Closed June 18, 1967

The Connection
722 performances
Opened June 9, 1959
Closed June 4, 1961

The Passion of Dracula
714 performances
Opened September 28, 1977
Closed July 14, 1979

Love, Janis
713 performances
Opened April 22, 2001
Closed January 5, 2003

Adaptation & Next
707 performances
Opened February 10, 1969
Closed October 18, 1970

Oh! Calcutta!
704 performances
Opened June 17, 1969
Closed August 12, 1972

Scuba Duba
692 performances
Opened November 11, 1967
Closed June 8, 1969

The Foreigner
686 performances
Opened November 2, 1984
Closed June 8, 1986

The Knack
685 performances
Opened January 14, 1964
Closed January 9, 1966

My Mother's Italian, My Father's Jewish & I'm in Therapy
684 performances
Opened December 8, 2006
Closed August 24, 2008

Love, Loss, and What I Wore*
681 performances
Opened October 1, 2009

Fully Committed
675 performances
Opened December 14, 1999
Closed May 27, 2001

Frances Sternhagen and Morgan Freeman in Driving Miss Daisy *(photo by Carol Rosegg)*

The Club
674 performances
Opened October 14, 1976
Closed May 21, 1978

Avenue Q (transfer from Broadway)
672 performances
Closed Opened October 9, 2009

The Balcony
672 performances
Opened March 3, 1960
Closed December 21, 1961

Penn & Teller
666 performances
Opened July 30, 1985
Closed January 19, 1992

Dinner With Friends
654 performances
Opened November 4, 1999
Closed May 27, 2000

Our Town (revival)
644 performances
Opened February 26, 2009
Closed September 12, 2010

America Hurrah
634 performances
Opened November 7, 1966
Closed May 5, 1968

Cookin'
632 performances
Opened July 7, 2004
Closed August 7, 2005

Oil City Symphony
626 performances
Opened November 5, 1987
Closed May 7, 1989

The Countess
618 performances
Opened September 28, 1999
Closed December 30, 2000

The Exonerated
608 performances
Opened October 10, 2002
Closed March 7, 2004

The Dining Room
607 performances
Opened February 11, 1982
Closed July 17, 1983

Hogan's Goat
607 performances
Opened March 6, 1965
Closed April 23, 1967

Drumstruck
607 performances
Opened June 16, 2005
Closed November 16, 2006

Beehive
600 performances
Opened March 30, 1986
Closed August 23, 1987

Criss Angel Mindfreak
600 performances
Opened November 20, 2001
Closed January 5, 2003

The Trojan Women
600 performances
Opened December 23, 1963
Closed May 30, 1965

The Syringa Tree
586 performances
Opened September 14, 2000
Closed June 2, 2002

The Musical of Musicals (The Musical!)
583 performances
Opened December 16, 2003
Closed November 13, 2005

Krapp's Last Tape & The Zoo Story
582 performances
Opened August 29, 1960
Closed May 21, 1961

Three Tall Women
582 performances
Opened April 13, 1994
Closed August 26, 1995

The Dumbwaiter & The Collection
578 performances
Opened January 21, 1962
Closed April 12, 1964

Forbidden Broadway 1990
576 performances
Opened January 23, 1990
Closed June 9, 1991

Dames at Sea
575 performances
Opened April 22, 1969
Closed May 10, 1970

The Crucible (revival)
571 performances
Opened 1956-57 Season
Closed 1957-58 Season

The Iceman Cometh (revival)
565 performances
Opened May 8, 1956
Closed February 23, 1958

Forbidden Broadway 2001: A Spoof Odyssey
552 performances
Opened December 6, 2000
Closed February 6, 2002

The Hostage (revival)
545 performances
Opened October 16, 1972
Closed October 8, 1973

The Marvelous Wonderettes
545 performances
Opened September 14, 2008
Closed January 3, 2010

Quantum Eye
545 performances
Opened February 9, 2007

Wit
545 performances
Opened October 6, 1998
Closed April 9, 2000

What's a Nice Country Like You Doing in a State Like This?
543 performances
Opened July 31, 1985
Closed February 9, 1987

Forbidden Broadway 1988
534 performances
Opened September 15, 1988
Closed December 24, 1989

Gross Indecency: The Three Trials of Oscar Wilde
534 performances
Opened September 5, 1997
Closed September 13, 1998

Frankie and Johnny in the Claire de Lune
533 performances
Opened December 4, 1987
Closed March 12, 1989

Six Characters in Search of an Author (revival)
529 performances
Opened March 8, 1963
Closed June 28, 1964

All in the Timing
526 performances
Opened November 24, 1993
Closed February 13, 1994

Oleanna
513 performances
Opened October 3, 1992
Closed January 16, 1994

Making Porn
511 performances
Opened June 12, 1996
Closed September 14, 1997

The Dirtiest Show in Town
509 performances
Opened June 26, 1970
Closed September 17, 1971

Happy Ending & Day of Absence
504 performances
Opened June 13, 1965
Closed January 29, 1967

Greater Tuna
501 performances
Opened October 21, 1982
Closed December 31, 1983

A Shayna Maidel
501 performances
Opened October 29, 1987
Closed January 8, 1989

The Boys from Syracuse (revival)
500 performances
Opened April 15, 1963
Closed June 28, 1964

* Production is still running as of May 31, 2011; count includes performances up to and including that date. Performance counts do not include previews.

OBITUARIES

The Lights Dim On Broadway

Broadway dimmed the marquee lights upon the deaths of the following theatre luminaries, and did so on the following dates:

John Willis, editor in chief of *Theatre World* for over forty years: June 30, 2010

Patricia Neal, actress: August 17, 2010

Joseph Stein, librettist/playwright: October 28, 2010

Jerry Bock, composer: November 4, 2010

Jill Clayburgh, actress: November 9, 2010

Romulus Linney, playwright: January 19, 2011

Ellen Stewart, producer: January 19, 2011

Theoni V. Aldredge, costumer designer: January 25, 2011

Beverly Randolph, stage manager: March 16, 2011

Elizabeth Taylor, actress: March 25, 2011

Lanford Wilson, playwright: March 30, 2011

Arthur Laurents, playwright, librettis, and director: May 6, 2011

THEONI V. ALDREDGE (Theoni Athanasiou Vachliotis) Aldredge, 88, Salonika, Greece-born costume designer, died Jan. 21, 2011, in Stamford, CT, of cardiac arrest. A Tony-winner for her work on *Annie*, *Barnum*, and *La Cage aux Folles*, her numerous other Broadway credits include *Sweet Bird of Youth*; *The Nervous Set*; *Flowering Cherry*; *Silent Night, Lonely Night*; *A Distant Bell*; *The Best Man*; *Mary, Mary*; *The Devil's Advocate* (Tony nomination); *First Love*; *I Can Get It for You Wholesale*; *Who's Afraid of Virginia Woolf?*; *Mr. President*; *Tchin-Tchin*; *Strange Interlude*; *Any Wednesday*; *Anyone Can Whistle*; *The Three Sisters*; *Luv*; *P.S. I Love You*; *Poor Richard*; *Ready When You Are, C.B.!*; *Minor Miracle*; *Skyscraper*; *The Playroom*; *Cactus Flower*; *UTBU*; *First One Asleep, Whistle*; *Happily Never After*; *A Time for Singing*; *A Delicate Balance*; *You Know I Can't Hear You When the Water's Running*; *That Summer-That Fall*; *Illya Darling*; *Little Murders*; *Daphne in Cottage D*; *The Trial of Lee Harvey Oswald*; *Before You Go*; *I Never Sang for My Father*; *Portrait of a Queen*; *Weekend*; *The Only Game in Town*; *King Lear*; *A Way of Life*; *Billy*; *The Gingham Dog*; *The Incomparable Max*; *Two Gentleman of Verona* (Tony nomination; Drama Desk Award); *The Sign in Sidney Brustein's Window*; *Sticks and Bones*; *Voices*; *That Championship Season*; *Much Ado About Nothing* (Tony nomination); *No Hard Feelings*; *Nash at Nine*; *Boom Boom Room*; *Find Your Way Home*; *The au Pair Man* (Tony nomination); *Dance of Death*; *An American Millionaire*; *Short Eyes*; *Mert & Phil*; *In Praise of Love*; *A Doll's House*; *Little Black Sheep*; *A Chorus Line* (Tony nomination); *Trelawny of the Wells* (Drama Desk nomination); *Mrs. Warren's Profession*; *The Belle of Amherst*; *Threepenny Opera* (Tony nomination); *The Eccentricities of a Nightingale*; *Ballroom* (Tony nomination); *The Grand Tour*; *Break a Leg*; *I Remember Mama*; *The Madwoman of Central Park West*; *Clothes for a Summer Hotel*; *42nd Street* (Tony nomination); *Onward Victoria* (Drama Desk nomination); *Woman of the Year*; *Dreamgirls* (Drama Desk Award; Tony nomination); *Ghosts*; *A Little Family Business*; *Merlin*; *Private Lives*; *The Corn Is Green*; *The Rink*; *Blithe Spirit*; *Teddy & Alice*; *Chess*; *Gypsy* (Tony nomination); *Oh, Kay!*; *The Secret Garden* (Tony nomination); *Nick & Nora*; *The High Rollers Social and Pleasure Club*; *The Flowering Peach*; *The School for Scandal*; *Taking Sides*; *The Three Sisters*; *Annie* (1997); *Gore Vidal's The Best Man*; *Follies* (2001, Tony nomination); and *A Chorus Line* (2006). Her Off-Broadway credits include *Rosemary and The Alligators*; *Under the Milk Wood*; *Smiling the Boy Fell Dead*; *The Merchant of Venice*; *King Lear*; *Macbeth*; *The Blue Boy in Black*; *Twelfth Night*; *The Trojan Women*; *The Knack*; *Hamlet*; *Othello*; *Electra*; *Lover's Labor's Lost*; *Troilus and Cressida*; *Hair*; *Ergo*; *The Memorandum*; *Henry IV Part 1*; *Henry IV Part 2*; *Romeo and Juliet*; *Huui Huui*, *Ballad for a Firing Squad*; *Invitation to a Beheading*; *Peer Gynt* (Drama Desk Award); *Colette*; *Richard III*; *The Happiness Cage*; *Trelawny of the Wells*; *Jack MacGowran in the Works of Samuel Beckett*; *Subject to Fits*; *Blood*; *Underground*; *The Basic Training of Pavlo Hummel*; *Timon of Athens*; *Two Gentlemen of Verona*; *The Tale of Cymbeline*; *Sticks and Bones*; *Wedding of Iphigenia and Iphigenia in Concert*; *That Championship Season*; *The Corner*; *Ti-Jean and His Brothers*; *Much Ado About Nothing* (Drama Desk Award); *Wedding Band*; *The Children*; *The Cherry Orchard*; *The Orphan*; *As You Like It*; *King Lear*; *The Kildeer*; *Kid Champion*; *A Chorus Line*; *Rich and Famous*; *Marco Polo Sings a Solo*; *The Threepenny Opera*; *Alice in Concert*; *Buried Inside Extra*; *The Nest of the Wood Grouse*; *Richard II*; *Putting It Together*; *The Radical Mystique*; *The Time of the Cuckoo*; *Neil Simon's "Hotel Suite"*; and *The Spitfire Grill*. An Academy Award-winner for *The Great Gatsby*, her other film credits include *Network*, *Eyes of Laura Mars*; *Rich and Famous*; *Semi-tough*; *Moonstruck*; *Ghostbusters*; and *Addams Family Values*. Her credits also include numerous television, opera, and ballet productions. She studied at the Goodman School in Chicago, IL, and made her debut as a costume designer with *The Distaff Side* at the Goodman Theatre, where she also taught design at the theatre's school. First working with Joseph Papp in 1960 on *Measure for Measure*, she became the Public Theater's head designer for twenty years, eventually designing over eighty productions at The Public. She also designed a line of ready-to-wear known as Jane Fonda Workout Gear, and her designs for *The Great Gatsby* were adapted into a clothing line sold at Bloomingdale's. She was the recipient of the Irene Sharaff Lifetime Achievement Award from the Theatre Development Fund. The marquee lights on Broadway were dimmed in her honor on January 25, 2011. Her husband of over fifty years, actor Tom Aldredge, survives her.

MICHAEL ALLINSON, London, England-born actor, died Dec. 30, 2010, in Los Angeles, CA. His Broadway credits include *My Fair Lady* (and 1981 revival); *Hostile Witness*; *Come Live With Me*; *Coco*; *Sleuth*; *Angel Street*; *Oliver!* (1984); *Shadowlands*, and *An Ideal Husband*. His numerous film credits include *The Girl in the Watermelon*; *Man of the Century*; *Plan B*; and *Syriana*, and his numerous television credits include *Three Crooked Men*; *Adventures in Paradise*; *Hallmark Hall of Fame*; *Detective*; *Family Affair*; *Love of Life*; *George Washington*; and *Another* World. He attended Ryeford Hall, Wycliffe College in Gloucestireshire, and the University of Lausanne, as well as the Royal Academy of Dramatic Art. He was a veteran of W.W. II.

CLAUDIA ASBURY, 58, Houston, TX-born actress/singer/dancer, died May 29, 2011, in Altamonte Springs, FL, of lymphoma. Her Broadway credits include *Mack and Mabel*; *So Long, 174th Street*; *The Act*; *Evita*; and *Sophisticated Ladies*. She co-choreographed the 1984 Summer Olympics, the 1986 Academy Awards, and the first joint U.S.-Soviet musical theatre production of *Sophisticated Ladies*. Also a teacher at the American Musical and Dramatic Academy in New York City, she eventually relocated to Florida, where she served as choreographer for the Orlando Gay Chorus and directed and choreographed Orlando, FL's *Come Out With Pride* celebrations. Survivors include her life partner, Joyce Ducas; children, Jacob Wychulis of Gainseville, FL; and Mariel Fraunheim, of Jacksonville, FL; sister, Sandra Asbury Johnson, of Los Angeles, CA; and brother, Cleve Bloomfield, of Bloomfield, NJ.

LESLIE BARRETT (Leslie Klein), 90, Staten Island, NY-born actor/director/stage manager, died June 8, 2010. His Broadway credits include *The Primrose Path*; *Rhinoceros*; *The Dresser*; *Arms and the Girl*; *Wonderful Town*; *Once Upon a Mattress*; and *Passionate Ladies*. His regional credits include *Much Ado About Nothing* and *As You Like It* at the Westport Country Playhouse and *The Taming of the Shrew* at the Walnut Street Theatre. He was also the veteran of many television shows.

FRANK BAYER, 74, Brazil, IN-born actor/stage manager/theatrical production manager, died Sept. 22, 2010, in Englewood, NJ. His numerous Broadway credits include *Danton's Death*; *The Country Wife*; *The Little Foxes*; *A Cry of Players*; *The Miser*; *In the Matter of J. Robert Oppenheimer*; *The Playboy of the Western World*; *Enemies*; *The Plough and the Stars*; *The Merchant of Venice*; *A Streetcar Named Desire*; *Dance of Death*; *Sherlock Holmes*; *Habeas Corpus*; *Stand-Up Tragedy*; and *QED*. Beginning his career as an actor at the San Francisco Actor's Workshop founded by Jules Irving and Herbert Blau, Bayer accompanied Irving and Blau when they left to head the Vivian Beaumont Theater at Lincoln Center. From 1980 to 2005 he joined the Center Theatre Group in Los Angeles, CA, and was production supervisor for the Center Theatre Group Ahmanson Theatre for ten years.

JERRY BOCK (Jerrold Lewis Bock), 81, New Haven, CT-born composer, died Nov. 3, 2010, in Mount Kisco, NY, of heart failure. A Pulitzer Prize and Tony-winner in 1960 for *Fiorello!* and a Tony-winner for his music for *Fiddler on the Roof* in 1964, his other Broadway credits include *Mr. Wonderful; The Body Beautiful; Tenderloin; Never Too Late; Man in the Moon; She Loves Me* (Tony nomination, and 1993 revival); *Baker Street; Generation; The Apple Tree* (Tony nomination, and 2006 revival); *The Rothschilds* (Tony nomination); *Fiddler on the Roof* (1981, 1990, 2004 revivals); *The Madwoman of Central Park West; Barbara Cook: A Concert for the Theatre; Jerome Robbins' Broadway; Mostly Sondheim; Barbara Cook's Broadway; Chita Rivera: The Dancer's Life*, as well as the benefit *Back From Broadway*. His death occurred ten days after that of Joseph Stein, his partner on *Fiddler on the Roof*. He also won an Emmy Award for the original children's song *A Fiddler Crab Am I*. A graduate of the University of Wisconsin, he also wrote for television, including *The Admiral Broadway Revue*, which later evolved into Sid Caeser's *Your Show of Shows*. The marquee lights on Broadway were dimmed in his honor on Nov. 4, 2010. His wife of over fifty years, Patricia Faggan; son, George; daughter, Portia Bock; and a granddaughter survive him.

GERALD BORDMAN, 79, Bala Cynwyd, PA-born theatre scholar/author, died May 9, 2011, in Wynnewood, PA, of cancer. His numerous works include *The American Musical Theater; The Oxford Companion to American Theater; American Musical Comedy; American Musical Revue;* and biographies of Jerome Kern and Vincent Youmans. He was a graduate of Lafayette College and earned a master's degree and a doctorate in medieval literature at the University of Pennsylvania.

TOM BOSLEY, 83, Chicago, IL-born actor/singer, died Oct. 19, 2010, near his home in Palm Springs, CA, of heart failure. A Tony Award winner as Best Supporting Actor in a Musical for his Broadway debut in *Fiorello!* in 1959, his other Broadway credits include *The Power and the Glory; The Beaux Stratagem; Nowhere to Go But Up; Natural Affection; A Murderer Among Us; Catch Me If You Can; The Education of H*Y*M*A*N*K*A*P*L*A*N*; Beauty and the Beast;* and *Cabaret* (1998). His

film credits include *Love with the Proper Stranger; The World of Henry Orient; Divorce American Style; The Secret War of Harry Frigg; Yours Mine and Ours* (1968); *To Find a Man; Gus; Million Dollar Mystery;* and *The Backup Plan*. He is perhaps best known for his role as the patriarch Howard Cunningham on the hit sitcom *Happy Days*, from 1974 to 1984. He also appeared for several years in the *Father Dowling Mysteries* on television. He attended DePaul University. His second wife, Patricia Carr; a daughter from his first marriage; and three grandchildren survive him.

OSCAR BROCKETT, 87, Tennessee-born theatre historian, died Nov. 7, 2010, in Austin, TX, of complications of a stroke. One of America's foremost theatre historians, his publications include 1968's *A History of the Theatre; The Essential Theatre; Modern Theatre: Realism and Naturalism to the Present; The Theatre: An Introduction;* and *Making the Scene: A History of Stage Design and Technology in Europe and the United States* (with Margaret Mitchell and Linda Hardberger). He earned a doctorate in theatre at Stanford University, and taught in various locations in Iowa, Indiana, California, and Florida, before becoming the dean of the University of Texas' College of Fine Arts, where he was instrumental in overseeing the performing arts center there, as well as the Blanton Museum of Art. He was a veteran of W.W. II. His daughter, Francesca Brockett, and her husband, James Pedicano, of Austin, TX survive him.

ALAN CHAMPION, 55, Tulsa, OK-born Broadway sign language interpreter for over thirty years, died Apr. 22, 2010, in Ramona, OK, of appendix cancer. His first Broadway production was *The Elephant Man* in 1980, and one of his last was the 2009 revival of *West Side Story*. His other numerous Broadway credits include *A

Chorus Line; 'night Mother; and *Promises, Promises*. He also has interpreted for the State of New Jersey. His sister, Alice Burnett; and two brothers, Harold and Jerry survive him.

HELEN KRICH CHINOY, 87, Newark, NJ-born theatre historian and educator, died May 24, 2011, in Turner Falls, MA, of pneumonia complicated by Alzheimer's Disease. She taught at Smith College in Northampton, MA, for nearly three decades, and was the chairwoman of the theatre department from 1968-1971. Her numerous and influential publications include *Actors on Acting* (1949); *Directors on Directing* (1953); *Women in the American Theater* (1981, with Linda Walsh Jenkins); and *Reunion: A Self-Portrait of the Group Theater* (1976). She earned a bachelor's and a master's degree in English from New York University and taught at Rutgers and Queens College before teaching at Smith College, where she taught theatre from 1956-1987, only taking five years during the 1960s to complete her PhD. in English at Columbia University as well as to teach at University of Leicester in England. Her husband, sociologist Ely Chinoy; daughter, Claire, of Madrid; son, Mike, of Los Angeles, CA; and three grandchildren survive her.

JILL CLAYBURGH, 66, New York, NY-born actress, died Nov. 5, 2010, at her home in Lakeville, CT, after a long battle with chronic lymphocytic leukemia. Her Broadway credits include *The Sudden and Accidental Re-Education of Horse Johnson*, followed by *The Rothschilds; Pippin; Jumpers;* and *Design for Living*. Her Off-Broadway credits include *It's Called the Sugar Plum, Calling in Crazy,* and *The Nest*. Her numerous film credits include *An Unmarried Woman* (Academy Award nomination); *Portnoy's Complaint; The Thief Who Came to Dinner; The Terminal Man; Gable and Lombard; Silver Streak; Semi-Tough; Luna; Starting*

Over (Academy Award nomination); *It's My Turn; First Monday in October; I'm Dancing as Fast as I Can; Hanna K.; Whispers in the Dark; Rich in Love; Naked in New York; Going All the Way; Running with Scissors; Love and Other Drugs;* and *The Bridesmaids*. The marquee lights on Broadway were dimmed in her honor on Nov. 9, 2010. Her husband, playwright David Rabe; daughter, actress Lily Rabe; and one stepson survive her.

BLAKE EDWARDS (William Blake Crump), 88, Tulsa, OK-born director/writer, died Dec. 15, 2010, in Santa Monica, CA, from complications of pneumonia. With his sole Broadway producer credit of *Victor/Victoria* in 1995, he received an Academy Award-nomination for his screenplay of the film version. As a writer, his film credits include *All Ashore; Drive a Crooked Road; My Sister Eileen* (1955); *Operation Mad Ball; The Notorious Landlady;* and *Soldier in the Rain* (also producer); while his movies as

director include *Operation Petticoat; High Time; Experiment in Terror* (also producer); *Days of Wine and Roses; The Carey Treatment;* and *Micki + Maude*. Among his films as director-writer are *The Pink Panther; A Shot in the Dark; The Great Race; What Did You Do in the War Daddy?; The Party; Darling Lili; Wild Rovers; The Tamarind Seed; The Return of the Pink Panther; 10; S.O.B.; The Man Who Loved Women* (1983); *That's Life!; Skin Deep;* and *Switch* and *Son of the Pink Panther*. In 2004 he was given a Special Academy Award for his body of work. His second wife, actress-singer Julie Andrews; a daughter, Jennifer; son, Geoffrey, from his first marriage; two daughters with Ms. Andrews, Amy and Joanna; a stepdaughter, Emma—Ms. Andrews' daughter from her marriage to Broadway designer Tony Walton—and several grandchildren survive him.

HILLARD ELKINS, 81, Brooklyn, NY-born producer, died Dec. 1, 2010, in Los Angeles, CA, of a heart attack. Working his way up from the mailroom at the William Morris Agency, he became head of the company's theatrical division. He eventually opened his own talent agency, Hillard Elkins Management in 1953, and in 1960 formed Elkins Productions International production company. His clients eventually included the likes of Steve McQueen, James Coburn, and Mel Brooks. Also becoming a major Broadway producer, he was a Tony Award nominee for his productions of *Golden Boy*, *The Rothschilds*, and *The Island* (Drama Desk nomination). His other Broadway productions include *Come on Strong; The Best Laid Plans; A Doll's House; Hedda Gabler; An Evening with Richard Nixon and…; Sizwe Banzi Is Dead* (Drama Desk nomination)*;* and both the 1969 and 1976 productions of the groundbreaking *Oh, Calcutta!*, which became one of the longest-running and most successful productions in Broadway history and broke the nudity barrier onstage. He also produced the films *Alice's Restaurant; A New Leaf; A Doll's House;* and *Richard Pryor: Live In Concert*. He won an Emmy Award for Outstanding Children's Special for *In His Father's Shoes*. He was also a veteran of W.W. II. A marriage to actress Claire Bloom ended in divorce. His wife, Sandi Love; two sons, Daniel and John, both of Los Angeles, CA; and one grandchild survive him.

ROBERT ELLENSTEIN, 87, Newark, NJ-born actor/artistic director, died at his home in West Los Angeles, CA. Beginning his career with the Cleveland Play House in 1947, he was the first artistic director of the Company of Angels and artistic director of the Los Angeles Repertory Company, as well as a founding member of Theatre West in Hollywood. His Regional credits include *King Lear* at the Los Angeles Repertory Company, and touring credits include *Irma La Douce* with Juliet Prowse. His numerous television credits as an actor include *The Philco-Goodyear Television Playhouse; Robert Montgomery Presents;* and *The Lawless Years*, and numerous television directing credits, include *Love on a Rooftop*. His film credits include *North By Northwest* and *Star Trek IV*. A graduate of the University of Iowa, he was also a veteran of W.W. II, earning a Purple Heart Award for his service. His wife of fifty-eight years, Lois; sons, David, artistic director of North Coast Repertory Theater; Peter, artistic director of the William Inge Center for Arts in Kansas; daughter, Jan Ellenstein-Keeva, of Evanston, IL; and four grandchildren survive him.

JAMES GAMMON, 70, Newman, IL-born actor, died July 16, 2010, at his home in Costa Mesa, CA, of cancer of the adrenal glands and liver. He made his Broadway debut in *Buried Child* (1976). His Off-Broadway credits include *Curse of the Starving Class; Lie of the Mind; Simpatico;* and *That Championship Season*. He was also seen in such films as *Cool Hand Luke; A Man Called Horse; Macon County Line; Urban Cowboy; Silverado; Made in Heaven; Ironweed; The Milagro Beanfield War; Major League; Coup de Ville; I Love You to Death; Leaving Normal; The*

Adventures of Huck Finn; Cabin Boy; Wyatt Earp; Wild Bill; The Iron Giant (voice); *The Cell; Cold Mountain; Silver City;* and *Appaloosa*. His second wife; a brother; a sister; two daughters; and two grandchildren survive him.

JAY GARNER, 82, Sewanee, TN-born actor, died Jan. 21, 2011, in New York, NY, of respiratory failure as the result of pneumonia. His Broadway credits include *Red, White, and Maddox; 1776; Beggar on Horseback; Captain Brassbound's Conversion; Goodtime Charley; The Best Little Whorehouse in Texas; La Cage aux Folles; Me and My Girl;* and *Hello, Dolly!* His regional and touring credits include *The Secret Garden* and his numerous television credits include *Buck Rogers in the 25th Century* and *Three's Company*. His film credits include *Pennies From Heaven*.

BETTY GARRETT, 91, St. Joseph, MO-born actress, died Feb. 21st, 2011, in Los Angeles, CA, of an aortic aneurysm. Her Broadway credits include *Of V We Sing; Let Freedom Sing; Something for the Boys; Jackpot; Laffing Room Only; Call Me Mister; Bells Are Ringing; Beg, Borrow, or Steal; Spoon River Anthology; A Girl Could Get Lucky; The Supporting Cast; Meet Me in St. Louis;* and *Follies* (2001).

She was perhaps best recognized as Irene Lorenzo, Archie and Edith Bunker's neighbor in *All in the Family*, or as Edna Babish, the landlady in *Laverne & Shirley*. Her film credits include *Danton's Death; Words in Music; Take Me Out to the Ballgame; Neptune's Daughter;* and Brundhilde Esterhazy in *On the Town*. She studied at the Neighborhood Playhouse and performed at the 1939 World's Fair and on some Catskills stages. Her husband, actor Larry Parks, with whom she often worked regionally, died in 1975. She also performed *Waiting in the Wings* in Los Angeles in 2007. Her sons, Andrew and Garrett; and one grandchild survive her.

PAM GEMS (Iris Pamela Price), 85, Bransgore, Hampshire, England-born playwright, died May 13, 2011, in London, England. A Tony Award nominee for Best Play for *Stanley* and Best Book of a Musical in 1999 for *Marlene* starring Siân Phillips as Marlene Deitrich, her other plays include *Dusa, Fish, Stas, and Vi; Betty's Wonderful Christmas;* the monologues *My Warren* and *After Birthday; The Amiable Courtship of Miz Venus and Wild Bill; Go West, Young Woman;* and the Royal Shakespeare Company productions of *Queen Christina; Camille* (1984)*; The Danton Affair* (1986)*;* and *The Blue Angel* (1991); with *Piaf* being produced by the Royal Shakespeare Theatre at Stratford-on-Avon in 1978. York Theater Royal produced her *Mrs. Pat* in 2006. *Stanley* won two Olivier Awards in Britain, including Best New Play, before transferring to Broadway. She earned a psychology degree. Her husband, Keith Gems; children, Jonathan, Sara, David, and Lala; four grandchildren; and a brother, Mickey Price, survive her.

CARL GORDON (Rufus Carl Gordon Jr.), 78, Goochland, VA-born actor, died July 23, 2010, in Jetersville, VA, of non-Hodgkins lymphoma. His Broadway credits include *The Great White Hope; Ain't Supposed to Die a Natural Death; The Piano Lesson;* and *Ma Rainey's Black Bottom*. Perhaps best known for the role of Charles S. Dutton's father on the 1990s sitcom *Roc*, he also appeared in the television shows *ER* and *Law & Order* and in the film *The Brother From Another Planet*. His national tours include *Happy Ending/Day of Absence*. He also appeared in over thirty roles at the Negro Ensemble Company, and was a veteran of the U.S. Air Force. His third wife, Jacqueline Alston-Gordon; five daughters; a son; nine grandchildren; and five great-grandchildren survive him.

MARK GORDON, 84, actor, died Aug. 12, 2010, in New York, NY, of lung cancer. His Broadway credits include *Desire Under the Elms; Compulsion; The Moon Besieged; The Devils; The Sign in Sidney Brustein's Window;* and *Of Mice and Men*. His film credits include *Take the Money and Run; Don't Drink the Water;* and *Sleeper*. A member of the Chicago, IL-based Compass Players, an improvisational group and forerunner of Second City, he collaborated with Mike Nichols, Elaine May, and Barbara Harris, before relocating to New York and working with Elaine May, Louise Lasser, and Peter Boyle, among others, at the Premise, a similar improvisational troupe. He appeared Off-Broadway in May's *Adaptation/Next*. His film credits include *A New Leaf; The Nickel Ride;* and *The Ninth Configuration*. His numerous television credits include *The Mary Tyler Moore Show*, and he also taught at Carnegie-Mellon University; Finch College; Columbia University; and was an acting coach at the Guthrie Theater in Minneapolis, and taught privately for over twenty years. His wife of fifty-two years, Barbara Glenn Gordon, predeceased him. His son, director/writer Keith Gordon; and sister, Rose Gordon Vachio survive him.

MICHAEL GOUGH, 94, Kuala-Lumpur, Malaya (now Malaysia)-born actor, died Mar. 17, 2011, in London, England. A Best Supporting Actor Tony winner for *Bedroom Farce*, he is perhaps best known as Alfred Pennyworth in all four movies of the Burton/Schumacher *Batman* franchise. His other Broadway credits include *The Fighting Cock* and *Breaking the Code* (Tony nomination). His numerous film credits include *Blanche Fury; Dracula; Horrors of the Black Museum; The Corpse; Satan's Slave; Anna Karenina; Saraband for Dead Lovers; The Small Back Room;*

Blackmailed; The Man in the White Suit; Twice Upon a Time; The Sword and the Rose; Rob Roy; The Highland Rogue; Richard III; Reach for the Sky; Ill Met by Moonlight; Dracula; The Horse's Mouth; Model for Murder; What a Carve Up!; Konga; The Phantom of the Opera; Black Zoo; Tamahine; Dr. Terror's House of Horrors; The Skull; Alice in Wonderland; Doctor Who: The Celestial Toymaker; Berserk!; Curse of the Crimson Altar; Women in Love; A Walk with Love and Death; Julius Caesar; Trog; The Go-Between (BAFTA film nomination); *Henry VIII and His Six Wives; Savage Messiah; Horror Hospital; The Legend of Hell House; The Boys from Brazil; Venom; Smiley's People; Doctor Who: Arc of Infinity; The Dresser; Oxford Blues; Top Secret!; A Christmas Carol; Out of Africa; Caravaggio; Inspector Morse: The Silent World of Nicholas Quinn; The Fourth Protocol; The Serpent and the Rainbow; Strapless; Batman; Batman: The Lazarus Syndrome; Let Him Have It; The Young Indiana Jones Chronicles: Russia 1910; Batman Returns; The Age of Innocence; The Hour of the Pig; Wittgenstein; Batman Forever; Batman and Robin; St. Ives; The Cherry Orchard; Sleepy Hollow;* and *Corpse Bride*. His numerous television credits include *Doctor Who; The Celestial Toymaker; Suez 1956; Colditz; Arc of Infinity;* and *The Avengers*. His fourth wife, Henrietta; daughter, Emma; and sons, Simon and Jasper survive him.

FARLEY GRANGER, 85, San José, CA-born actor, died Mar. 26, 2011, in New York, NY, of natural causes. He made his Broadway debut in 1959 in *First Impressions*, followed by *The Warm Peninsula; Advise and Consent; The King and I* (City Center); *Brigadoon* (City Center); *The Seagull; The Crucible;* and *Deathtrap*. His Off-Broadway credits include *The Carefree Tree; A Month in the Country; Sailing; Outward Bound;* and *Tally and Son,* for which he won an Obie Award. His numerous film credits include *The North Star; The Purple Heart; Rope; Strangers on a Train; Senso;*

and *Edge of Doom*. His television credits include *The Heiress,* and he appeared frequently on shows such as *Kraft Television Theater* and *Playhouse 90*. His 2007 autobiography was entitled *Include Me Out: My Life From Goldwyn to Broadway*. His longtime partner, Robert Calhoun, died in 2008. He leaves no immediate survivors.

SUZANNE GROSSMAN, 72, Basle, Switzerland-born actress/writer, died Aug. 19, 2010, in Los Angeles, CA, of chronic obstructive pulmonary disease. Her Broadway credits as an actress include *The Lion in Winter; Cyrano de Bergerac; The Show Off; Private Lives; There's One in Every Marriage;* and as an adaptor, *Chemin de Fer,* with Paxton Whitehead. She also wrote for the television series *Ryan's Hope*. Her husband, Robert Scales survives her.

ISRAEL HICKS, 66, Orangeburg, SC-born director, died July 3, 2011, in Sleepy Hollow, NY, of cancer. In 2009 he completed a twenty-year project directing August Wilson's entire decade-by-decade cycle of plays (*Joe Turner's Come and Gone* [1991]; *The Piano Lesson* [1993]; *Ma Rainey's Black Bottom* [1994]; *Two Trains Running* [1996]; *Seven Guitars* [1997]; *Jitney* [2002]; *King Headley II* (2003]; *Gem of the Ocean* [2006]; and *Radio Golf* [2010]). His other regional theatre credits included those at the Guthrie Theater; Cleveland Play House; Pittsburgh Public Theater; American Conservatory Theater; Pasadena Playhouse; and especially at the Denver Theater Center. His New York credits include those at Primary Stages. A graduate of Boston University's College of Fine Arts, he received an M.F.A. from New York University. He also taught acting at Carnegie Mellon University, served as the dean of the Conservatory Theater Arts at Purchase College, State University of New York, and since 2001 was chairman and artistic director of the theater arts department at Mason Gross School of the Arts at Rutgers University in New Jersey. He was also the artistic director of the Ebony Repertory Theater in Los Angeles, CA. His wife, Renée Harriston Hicks survives him.

PETER HOBBS, 92, Etretat, France-born actor, died Jan. 2, 2011, in Santa Monica, CA. His Broadway credits include *Under This Roof; The Life of Reilly; Comes the Revelation; The Russian People; Truckline People; Joan of Lorraine;*

Clutterbuck; and *The Teahouse of the August Moon*. His television credits include *Secret Storm; Perry Mason; The Dick Van Dyke Show; The Andy Griffith Show; Bonanza; All in the Family; The Odd Couple; Streets of San Francisco; Happy Days; Barney Miller; Lou Grant; M*A*S*H*; Knots Landing;* and *L.A. Law* among many others. His film credits include *Sleeper; The Man with Two Brains; 9 to 5; Any Which Way You Can; Andromeda Strain; In the Mood;* and *The Lady in Red*. Raised in New York City, he was a graduate of Solebury School in Pennsylvania and Bard College in Manhattan, and was a veteran of W.W. II. His wife of twenty-eight years, Carolyn Adams Hobbs, of New York City; two stepsons, Mark and Adam Richards of Santa Monica, CA; six grandchildren; and two great-grandchildren survive him.

JUDD JONES, 79, Montgomery, AL-born actor/singer/dancer, died Mar. 9, 2011, in Manhattan. His Broadway credits include *Tambourines to Glory; The Royal Hunt of the Sun; Nöel Coward's Sweet Potato;* and *My One and Only*. Other theatre credits include *The Fantasticks; Finian's Rainbow; Kiss Me, Kate;* and *King Lear*. His touring credits include five years of *West Side Story*, and his one-man shows were based on Paul Robeson and Bert Williams. His Off-Broadway credits include *Two Gentleman of Verona*. He was a veteran of the U.S. Army. His brother, Edward Jones, of Huntsville, AL, survives him.

DONALD H. JOSEPHSON, 82, Elizabeth, NJ-born theatrical advertising executive, died Dec. 8, 2010, in New York, NY. Working at theatrical advertising companies Abraham & Strauss and Blaine-Thompson, where he worked his way up to vice-president, in 1978 he moved to Ash/Ledonne and was there for six years. In 1984 he formed The Golden Group as the theatrical advertising division of the film agency Diener/Hauser/Bates. His Broadway and Off-Broadway credits include over 500 productions, including *Who's Afraid of Virginia Woolf?; A Delicate Balance; That Championship Season; Two Gentlemen of Verona; The Fantasticks; Dancin' Deathtrap; Glengarry Glen Ross;* and *Driving Miss Daisy*. His longtime companion, Beryl Seidenberg, of Manhattan; sister, Ann Kranich of Harrisburg, PA; nieces, Betsy Kranich of Venice, CA; and Nancy Kranich McElroy, of Marblehead, MA; nephew Laurence Kranich, of Albany, NY; and six great nephews and nieces survive him.

GEORGE KEATHLEY, 85, artistic director of Kansas City Repertory Theatre from 1985-2000, died Sept. 12, 2010, in Fort Lauderdale, FL. He directed forty-nine plays at Kansas City Rep. including *Three Tall Women; A Delicate Balance; The Deputy; M. Butterfly; Of Mice and Men; The Seagull;* and *A Christmas Carol*. His New York credits as a director or producer include *The Square Root of Wonderful; The Glass Menagerie* (20th anniversary production, which also gave a command performance at The White House)*; Status Quo Vadis;* and *The Heiress*. Regional credits include *Night of the Iguana; Long Day's Journey into Night;* and *The Rake's Progress* at the Lyric Opera of Chicago, as well as *Desire Under the Elms* at the Guthrie Theater; *Cause Celebre* with Anne Baxter and Dorothy McGuire at the Ahmanson Theatre in Los Angeles; *Wait Until Dark* with Betsy Palmer at the Beverly Music Theatre; and *The Heiress* starring Jane Alexander and Richard Kiley at the Kennedy Center in Washington, D.C. He also directed several soap operas including *One Life To Live,* for which he won an Emmy Award for Best Direction. Prior to his work in Kansas City, he directed the first two-act version of Arthur Miller's *A View From the Bridge* for the Studebaker Theatre Company in Chicago, IL, as well as helmed the Ivanhoe dinner theatre in Chicago in the 1970s, where, among other works, he helmed *The Rose Tattoo,* starring Rita Moreno, and *Out Cry,* working with Tennessee Williams.

LARRY KEITH (Lawrence Jay Korn), 79, Brooklyn, NY-born actor/singer, died July 17, 2010, in Manhattan, of cancer. His Broadway credits include *My Fair Lady* (in which he was the first American to play the role of Henry Higgins)*; High Spirits; I Had a Ball; The Best Laid Plans; Gigi; Titanic; Cabaret* and *Caroline, or Change*. He founded the Actors Company Theater Off-Broadway in 1992, and was a prolific television actor, appearing in *All My Children; Law & Order* and *Damages,* among other television shows. His wife, the former Mina Wagman; daughter, Lisa Korn; brother, Alvin Korn; and a grandchild survive him.

BOB KELLY, 87, Brooklyn, NY-born makeup artists and wigmaker, died Apr. 18, 2011. With many Broadway shows under his belt, his credits include *Kwamina;*

A Funny Thing Happened on the Way to the Forum; Tovarich; High Spirits; The Rothschilds; King Richard III; Goodbye Fidel; Onward Victoria; and Say Goodnight, Gracie. He was a makeup artist on television for The Phil Silvers Show and Captain Kangaroo, and had the distinction of doing the makeup for the Beatles' first live television appearance on The Ed Sullivan Show. In 1970 he created Bob Kelly Cosmetics Company, a theatrical cosmetics company that was in business until 2003. He retired in 2008. He was a veteran of W.W. II, and received an AP Theater Ribbon and a two Bronze service stars for his service. His daughter, makeup artist Barbara Kelly; three other children; and three grandchildren survive him.

ARON KINCAID (Norman Neale Williams II), 70, Los Angeles, CA-born actor, died Jan. 6, 2011, in Los Angeles, CA, of heart-related problems. His many film credits include The Girls on the Beach; The Ghosts in the Invisible Bikini; Beach Ball; Ski Party; Doctor Goldfoot and the Bikini Machine; The Happiest Millionaire; and The Proud and the Damned, as well as many voiceover credits, including those in Smurfs; Johnny Quest; and The Transformers on television. His television credits as an actor include Bachelor Father; The Beverly Hillbillies; and Get Smart. He was a graduate of

UCLA and a veteran of the Coast Guard Reserve. He sold his seascapes and landscapes through galleries in Laguna Beach, CA, under the name N.N. Williams. He also was known for his caricatures of famous celebrities, usually under the name Aron Kincaid.

HARRIS LASKAWY (Harris Gerson Laskawy), 67, Bronx, NY-born actor/artistic director and co-founder of CSC Repertory Theatre in New York, died July 4, 2010, in Valley Village, CA. For seven seasons at CSC he appeared in forty roles, including Vanya; Claudius; Mendoze; the Devil; Marquis de Sade; Brutus; Titus; Ahab in Moby Dick; and Solness in The Master Builder. His Broadway credits include The World of Sholom Aleichem; The Guys in the Truck; Hurlyburly; and The Iceman Cometh. His Off-Broadway credits also include We Won't Pay We Won't Pay. An Obie Award-winner for Distinguished Performance as Uncle Vanya in Uncle Vanya, he also received a Drama-Logue Award nomination for Outstanding Achievement as Grumio in The Taming of the Shrew at the California Shakespeare Theatre. His wife, Jennifer Reed survives him.

MICHAEL LANGHAM (Michael Seymour Langham), 91, Somerset, England-born actor/artistic director, died Jan. 15, 2011, in Cranbrook, Kent, England, of a chest infection. His many Broadway credits include Two Gentlemen of Verona; The Broken Jug; Andorra; The Prime of Miss Jean Brodie; The Seagull; Saint Joan; Three Men on a Horse; Timon of Athens (Tony nomination); The Government Inspector; The Flowering Peach; The Molière Comedies; and Waiting in the Wings. He was the second artistic director of the Stratford Festival in Canada from 1956-1967, and was artistic director at the Guthrie Theater from 1971-1977, where his credits include Oedipus the King; Cyrano de Bergerac; and She Stoops to Conquer, and where he was largely credited with restoring the theatre to financial viability. He was also the director of the Juilliard School from 1979-1982 and again from 1987-1992, and served as an artistic advisor to Tony Randall's National Actors Theater. His credits as a director in England include those at Stratford-on-Avon; Birmingham Repertory Theater; The Old Vic in London; and he also worked in Australia; Belgium; The Netherlands; and Scotland. He had long associations with actors Christopher Plummer and Brian Bedford, both of whom considered him instrumental in their careers. He was educated at Radley College before spending five years as a prisoner of war in W.W. II, where he wrote and directed for other prisoners. His wife, actress Helen Burns; son, Chris Langham; five grandchildren; and half-sister, Susan Burnett survive him.

ARTHUR LAURENTS, 93, Brooklyn, NY-born playwright/director/librettist/screenwriter, died May 5, 2011, in New York, NY, of complications from pneumonia. One of the most prolific and celebrated artists of the twentieth century American theatre, he was responsible for creating many iconic theatre figures in films and onstage, and spared no punches in commenting on his contemporaries offstage. His many Broadway credits include Home of the Brave

(playwright); The Bird Cage (playwright); The Time of the Cuckoo (playwright); A Clearing in the Woods (playwright); I Can Get It For You Wholesale (director); West Side Story (book writer, 1957, 1960, 1964, 2009 [director]); Gypsy (1959, 1974 [director, Tony Award], 1989, 2003, 2008 [director, Tony nomination], book writer); Invitation to a March (writer/director); Anyone Can Whistle (director/book writer); Do I Hear A Waltz? (book writer); Hallelujah, Baby! (Tony Award; book writer); The Madwoman of Central Park West (director/book writer); La Cage aux Folles (1983, director, Tony Award); Jerome Robbins' Broadway (additional text); Nick & Nora (director/book writer); and the benefit, Angela Lansbury—A Celebration (writer). His other plays include The Radical Mystique; Jolson Sings Again; Attacks on the Heart; New Year's Eve; and Come Back, Come Back, Wherever You Are. His screenplays include Rope; Anna Lucasta (with Philip Yordan); The Turning Point; Anastasia; and The Way We Were (based on his novel of the same name). His memoirs were Original Story By in 2000, and in 2009, Mainly on Directing: Gypsy, West Side Story, and Other Musicals. He was a graduate of Cornell University and wrote for radio and also worked as a war correspondent while serving in W.W. II. He was also blacklisted for several years in the 1940s, labeled as a "subversive." He is godfather to composer Adam Guettel, and his longtime partner, Tom Thatcher, died in 2006. The marquee lights on Broadway were dimmed in his honor on May 7, 2011.

DOUGLAS B. LEEDS, 63, New York, NY-born advertising executive and longtime board member of the American Theatre Wing, died May 9, 2011, in New York, NY, of cancer. A board member of the American Theatre Wing for twenty-one years, he served alternately as secretary-treasurer, vice-chairman, and president—the capacity in which he was serving at the time of his death. He was president and CEO of Thomson-Leeds Co., and subsequently was founder and CEO of Storeboard Media. He also served on the board of the American Museum of American Art and on the council of the Frick Museum. He produced the Broadway show Street Heat in 1980 and co-produced Sleight of Hand in 1987. His wife, Anki; daughter; mother; and sister survive him.

MARCIA LEWIS (Marcia Bernice Lewis), 72, Melrose, MA-born actress/singer, died Dec. 21, 2010, in Nashville, TN, of lung cancer. Her Broadway credits include Hello, Dolly!; The Time of Your Life; Annie; Rags (Drama Desk nomination); Roza; Orpheus Descending; Fiddler on the Roof; Grease (1994, Tony nomination); Chicago (1997, Tony nomination, Drama Desk nomination); as well as the Funny Girl benefit in 2002. She was also a veteran of many television shows, including Baretta; The Bob Newhart Show; Happy Days; Kate & Allie; Mr. Belvedere; Goodtime Girls; and the mini-series Rich Man, Poor Man. Also a cabaret singer, she recorded the album Nowadays in 1998. She attended the University of Cincinnati and was a registered nurse. She is survived by her husband, Fred Bryan; brother, Edwin Parker Lewis, known as "Pete," of Milford, Ohio; Mary Fortin, of Memphis, TN; Margaret Hakimian, of Melrose, MA; William Felix Bryan, known as Felix, of Chapel Hill, TN; and six step-grandchildren.

DON LIBERTO, 92, actor/singer/dancer, died Aug. 8, 2010, in New York, NY, of a heart attack. His Broadway credits include Babes in Arms; DuBarry Was a Lady; By Jupiter; Jackpot; Annie Get Your Gun; and Look, Ma, I'm Dancin! Generations of nieces, nephews, and cousins survive him.

ROMULUS LINNEY (Romulus Zacharias Linney IV), 80, Philadelphia, PA-born playwright/professor, died Jan. 15, 2011, in Germantown, NY, of lung cancer. He also lived in New York. His sole Broadway credit was The Love Suicide at Shofield Barracks. But most of his plays were produced Off-Broadway or beyond. The author of more than thirty plays, they include: True Crimes; Childe Byron; The Sorrows of Frederick; Unchanging Love; Heathen Valley; Holy Ghosts; Love Drunk; and an adaption of A Christmas Carol. He had the distinction of being the first playwright to whom the Signature Theatre devoted their entire season, doing so in 1991. A graduate of Oberlin College and Yale School of Drama, he also received fellowships from the National Endowment of the Arts, and grants from the Guggenheim Foundation; National Endowment of the Arts; and New York Foundation of the Arts. He had been chair of the MFA Playwriting program at Columbia University's School of the Arts and professor of playwriting in the Actors Studio MFA program at The New School in New York. He also spent many years teaching at Princeton University;

the University of Pennsylvania; Hunter College; and Brooklyn College. He earned honorary doctorates from Oberlin College and Appalachian State University. He was a member of Ensemble Studio Theatre, the Fellowship of Southern Writers; National Theatre Conference; College of Fellows of the American Theatre; American Academy of Arts and Sciences; American Academy of Arts and Letters; and the Corporation of Yaddo. His novels include *Heathen Valley* and *Slowly by Thy Hand Unfurled*. His collection of stories, *Jesus Tales*, was a published in 1980. The marquee lights on Broadway were dimmed in his honor on Jan. 19, 2011. His first two marriages, to Ann Leggett and Margaret Jane Andrews, ended in divorce. His wife, Laura Callanan; daughters, actress Laura Linney and Susan Linney, of New York survive him.

SIDNEY LUMET, 86, Philadelphia, PA-born actor/director, died in New York, NY, of lymphoma. One of the most celebrated film directors of the twentieth century, he began his career as an actor with Broadway credits that include *Dead End; The Eternal Road; Sunup to Sundown; Schoolhouse on the Lot; My Heart's in the Highlands; Christmas Eve; Morning Star; Journey to Jerusalem; Brooklyn, U.S.A.; Seeds in the Wind;* and Broadway directing credits that include *Night of the Auk; Caligula;* and *Nowhere to Go But Up.* His Off-Broadway credits as a director include *The Shawl.* He was also a television director, with credits including many episodes of *Danger; Mama;* and *You Are There; Playhouse 90; Kraft Television Theatre;* and *Studio One.* His many iconic films include *12 Angry Men* (Academy Award nomination); *Stage Struck; That Kind of Woman; The Fugitive Kind; A View from the Bridge; Long Day's Journey Into Night; The Pawnbroker; Fail-Safe; The Hill; The Group; The Deadly Affair; Bye Bye Braverman; The Sea Gull; The Appointment; King: A Filmed Record…Montogmery to Memphis; Last of the Mobile Hot Shots; The Anderson Tapes; Child's Play; The Offence; Serpico; Lovin' Molly; Murder on the Orient Express; Dog Day Afternoon* (Academy Award nomination); *Network* (Academy Award nomination); *Equus; The Wiz; Just Tell Me What You Want; Prince of the City; Deathtrap; The Verdict* (Academy Award nomination); *Daniel; Garbo Talks; Power; The Morning After; Running on Empty; Family Business; Q&A; A Stranger Among Us; Guilty as Sin; Night Falls on Manhattan; Critical Care; Gloria; Strip Search; Find Me Guilty;* and *Before the Devil Knows You're Dead.* He was awarded a Special Academy Award, and was a veteran of W.W. II. Married four times. The first was to actress Rita Gamm, from 1949-1955; the second to Gloria Vanderbilt from 1956-1963; the third was Lena Horne's daughter Gail Jones from 1963-1978; and the fourth and final was to Mary Gimbel, who survives him, as do daughters, Amy, from marriage to Gail Jones; and actress/screenwriter Jenny, who wrote the screenplay for the 2008 film *Rachel Getting Married.*

JAMES MacARTHUR, 72, Los Angeles, CA-born actor, best known for playing Detective Danny "Danno" Williams on the long-running series *Hawaii Five-O,* died on Oct. 28, 2010, in Florida, of natural causes. His Broadway credits include *Invitation to a March,* for which he received a Theatre World Award. Following his movie debut in *The Young Stranger,* he was seen in such movies as *The Light in the Forest; Third Man on the Mountain; Kidnapped* (1960); *Swiss Family Robinson* (1960); *The Interns;*

Spencer's Mountain; Cry of Battle; Battle of the Bulge; The Love-Ins; and *Hang 'em High.* The adopted son of actress Helen Hayes and playwright Charles MacArthur, his third wife; four children; and seven grandchildren survive him.

KENNETH MARS, 75, Chicago, IL-born actor, died Feb. 13, 2011, in Grenada Hill, CA, of pancreatic cancer. His Broadway credits include *The Affair; The Best Laid Plans;* and *Any Wednesday.* His television roles include those in *Gunsmoke; Get Smart; Columbo; Murder, She Wrote; Star Trek: Deep Space Nine;* and *Malcolm in the Middle.* His film roles include Franz Liebkind in *The Producers;* the police inspector in *Young Frankenstein;* and roles in *Butch Cassidy and the Sundance Kid; What's Up, Doc?; Radio Days;* and *Shadows and Fog.* His daughters, Susannah Mars and Rebecca Tipton Mars; and six grandchildren survive him.

HUGH MARTIN, 96, Birmingham, AL-born actor/composer/musical arranger/ musical supervisor/vocal coach/playwright, died Mar. 11, 2006, in Encinitas, CA. His Broadway credits in any number of those capacities are *Hooray for What!; Where Do We Go From Here?; The Boys from Syracuse; One For The Money; Streets of Paris; Too Many Girls; Du Barry Was A Lady; Louisiana Purchase; Cabin in the Sky; Best Foot Forward; The Lady Comes Across; Barefoot Boy With Cheek; Look Ma, I'm Dancin!; Heaven on Earth; As the Girls Go; Gentleman Prefer Blondes; Make a Wish; Judy Garland at the Palace—Two A Day; Top Banana; Hazel Flagg; High Spirits* (Tony nomination); *Lorelei; Good News; Sugar Babies; Jerome Robbins' Broadway; Meet Me in St. Louis* (Tony nomination); and *Mostly Sondheim.* His film credits include songs for *Athena; The Girl Most Likely;* and the film version of *Meet Me In St. Louis* (Academy Award nomination). He also received an Academy Award nomination for *Good News.* He released an album with his songwriting partner, Ralph Blane, entitled *Martin and Blane Sing Martin and Blane.*

KEVIN McCARTHY, 96, Seattle, WA-born actor, died Sept. 11, 2010, in Hyannis, MA. He lived in Sherman Oaks, CA. His Broadway credits include *Abe Lincoln in Illinois; Flight to the West; Winged Victory* (as Sgt. Kevin McCarthy); *Truckline Café; Joan of Lorraine; The Survivors; Bravo!; Anna Christie; Love's Labour's Lost; Red Roses for Me; The Day the Money Stopped; Advise and Consent; Something About a Soldier; The Three Sisters; Cactus Flower; A Warm Body; Happy Birthday, Wanda June; Poor Murdered;* and *Alone Together.* His many film credits include the role of Biff in *Death of A Salesman* that was

based on his London stage portrayal, and for which he received an Academy Award nomination. His other film roles include those in *Winged Victory* (as Sgt. Kevin McCarthy); *Drive a Crooked Road; The Gambler from Natchez; Strange on Horseback; An Annapolis Story; Nightmare* (1957); *The Misfits; 40 Pounds of Trouble; A Gathering of Eagles; The Prize; The Best Man* (1964); *Mirage; A Big Hand for the Little Lady; Hotel; Ace High; Kansas City Bomber; Buffalo Bill and the Indians; Invasion of the Body Snatchers* (1978 remake); *Hero at Large; Those Lips Those Eyes; My Tutor; Innerspace; The Distinguished Gentleman; Matinee; Just Cause;* and *Steal Big Steal Little.* His television credits include *Flamingo Road.* A marriage to actress Augusta Dabney ended in divorce. His second marriage was to Kate Crane, and she, three daughters, Lillah, of Los Angeles, CA; Mary Dabney McCarthy, of Cape Cod; and Tess McCarthy, of New York City; and two sons, James Kevin McCarthy, of San Diego, CA; and Patrick McCarthy, of Portland, OR; stepdaughter, Kara Lichtman, of Boston, MA; brother, Preston; and three grandchildren survive him. His sister was the celebrated author Mary McCarthy. He toured the U.S. in *Give 'Em Hell, Harry,* a one-man show based on Harry S. Truman, for over two decades. Following his service in W.W. II, he became a member of the Actors Studio in New York. His daughter, Lillah McCarthy survives him.

RUE MCCLANAHAN (Eddi-Rue McClanahan), 76, Healdton, OK-born actress, died June 3, 2010, in New York, NY, of a brain hemorrhage. Her Broadway credits include her debut in 1965 in *Best Laid Plans*, followed by *Jimmy Shine*; *Father's Day*; *Sticks and Bone*; and *California Suite*. Her Off-Broadway credits include *The Secret Life of Walter Mitty*; *Big Man*; *MacBird*; *Tonight in Living Color*; *Who's Happy Now?* (Obie Award); *Dark of the Moon*; *God Says There Is No Peter Ott*; *Dylan*; *Crystal and Fox*; *After Play*; and *Oscar*. Perhaps best known for

her Emmy-winning role as Blanche Devereaux on the sitcom *The Golden Girls*, she also appeared on television opposite her *Golden Girls* co-star Bea Arthur in the 1970s sitcom *Maude*; as well as *All in the Family*; *The Golden Palace*; and *Mama's Family*. She appeared in such movies as *Five Minutes to Live* (*Door-to-Door Maniac*); *The People Next Door*; *The Pursuit of Happiness*; *They Might Be Giants*; *Modern Love, Dear God*; *Out to Sea*; *Starship Troopers*; and *The Fighting Temptations*. She was a 1956 graduate of University of Tulsa, and she also performed regionally at the Erie Playhouse and the Pasadena Playhouse. Her autobiography is entitled *My First Five Husbands…And the Ones Who Got Away*, and she also occasionally delivered a lecture entitled *Aging Gracefully*, as well as campaigned for animal rights. Her sixth husband, Morrow Wilson; son, Mark T. Bish; and sister, Dr. Melinda Lou McClanahan survive her.

JAMES MCCLURE (James Miller McClure Jr.), 59, Alexandria, LA-born playwright, died Feb. 17, 2011, in Marina del Rey, CA, of cancer. His Broadway credit is two one-act plays that are comprised of *Lone Star* and *Pvt. Wars*, and his other plays include *Laundry and Bourbon*; *Wild Oats*; and *The Day They Shot John Lennon*. He graduated from Southern Methodist University and his sister, Jenny Schroeder survives him.

MARIAN MERCER (Marian Ethel Mercer), 75, Akron, OH-born actress, died Apr. 27, 2011, in Newbury Park, CA, and she was a resident of the Motion Picture & Television Country House and Hospital in Woodland Hills, LA, where she had been suffering from Alzheimer's Disease. Her Broadway credits include *Greenwillow* in 1960, followed by *Fiorello!*; *Promises, Promises* (for which she received a Theatre World Award, a Drama Desk Award, and a Tony Award); *A Place for Polly*; *Hay Fever*; *Stop the World, I Want to Get Off*; and *Bosoms of Neglect*. Her Off-

Broadway credits include *Sancocho*; and *People in Show Business Make Long Goodbyes*. Her other stage credits include *New Faces of 1962*. Her television credits include being a regular on *The Dom Deluise Show*; *The Wacky World of Jonathan Winters*; *The Sandy Duncan Show*; *The Andy Williams Show*; *It's a Living*; *Mary Hartman, Mary Hartman*; *Forever Fernwood*; *St. Elsewhere*; *Empty Nest*; *Love, American Style*; *Archie Bunker's Place*; *Mama's Family*; *Benson*; *The Golden Girls*; *Murder, She Wrote*; *Touched by an Angel*; and *Suddenly Susan*, among many others. Her screen credits include *The Cracker Factory* and *9 to 5*. She was a graduate of University of Michigan. Her first marriage, to actor Martin Cassidy, ended in divorce. Her husband of thirty-one years, Patrick Hogan; her sister, Marjorie Keith; and daughter, Deidre Whitaker survive her.

SIDNEY MICHAELS (Sidney Ramon Michaels), 83, New York, NY-born playwright/lyricist, died Apr. 22, 2011, in Westport, CT, from complications of Alzheimer's Disease. His Broadway credits as a playwright include *Tchin-Tchin*

(Tony nomination); *Dylan* (Tony nomination); *Ben Franklin in Paris* (and lyrics, Tony nomination); *Goodtime Charley*; and *Tricks of the Trade*. His film credits include *The Night They Raided Minsky's*, as well as several television credits. His wife of over fifty years, Louisette; sister, Meryle Ober, of Newton, MA; son, Cotter, and daughter-in-law, Jennifer Jennings, of Fairfield, CT; daughter, Candia Steen, of New York City, and six grandchildren survive him.

PATRICIA NEAL (Patsy Louise Neal), 84, Packard, Whitley County, KY-born actress, who grew up in Knoxville, TN, died Aug. 8, 2010, in Edgarton, MA, on Martha's Vineyard, of lung cancer. A Theatre World Award and Tony Award winner for her role in *Another Part of the Forest*, her other Broadway credits include *The Children's Hour*; *A Roomful of Roses*; and *The Miracle Worker*. An Academy Award-winner for her role as the wearied housekeeper Alma in the classic 1963 film *Hud*, she made her film debut in 1948 in *John Loves Mary*, and was seen in such films as *The Hasty Heart*; *The*

Fountainhead; *Bright Leaf*; *The Breaking Point*; *Three Secrets*; *Operation Pacific*; *Raton Pass*; *The Day the Earth Stood Still*; *Something for the Birds*; *A Face in the Crowd*; *Breakfast at Tiffany's*; *Psyche 59*; *In Harm's Way*; *The Subject was Roses* (Oscar nomination); *Baxter!*; *Happy Mother's Day–Love George*; *Ghost Story*; *An Unremarkable Life*; and *Cookie's Fortune*. She attended the University of Tennessee and Northwestern University before working at the Barter Theatre and touring in *Voice of the Turtle*. Her television credits include those on *Little House on the Prairie* and *Murder, She Wrote*. She put much time into raising money for children and adults with brain injuries and she established the Patricia Neal Rehabilitation Center in Knoxville, TN, having suffered a series of life-threatening and debilitating strokes herself in the 1960s. Her two autobiographies are entitled *As I Am* and *An Unquiet Life*. She was divorced from her first husband, author Roald Dahl, who died in 1990. The marquee lights on Broadway were dimmed in her honor on Aug. 17, 2010. Her sister, Margaret Ann VanDeNoord; her brother, Pete Neal; children, Tessa, Ophelia, Theo, and Lucy; ten grandchildren and step-grandchildren; and a great-grandchild survive her.

JIM NEU (James A. Neu), 66, Brooklyn, NY-born playwright, July 19, 2010, died at his home in Carroll Gardens, Brooklyn, NY, of lung cancer. A staple of Off-Off-Broadway, his plays include *Doomed Love*; *The Big Blue*; *The Floatones*; *Mondo Beyondo*; *Undercurrent Incorporated*; *Gang of Seven*; and *Live Witness*. His productions were mainly performed at La MaMa Experimental Theatre Club. He was a graduate of the State University of New York, Oneonta (now SUNY College at Oneonta), and was a veteran of the Vietnam War, stationed in Korea. His wife, lighting designer Carol Mullins survives him.

EVELYN PAGE, 90, Nebraska-born actress, died Feb. 6, 2011, in New York, NY. Her Broadway credits include *Tattle Tales*; *Hold Your Horses*; *Wonderful Town*; *Little Me*; *On a Clear Day You Can See Forever*; and *Canterbury Tales*. Her touring credits include *Canterbury Tales*; *Stop the World—I Want to Get Off*; *Me and My Girl*; and *Anything Goes*. Her Off-Broadway credits include *Anything Goes* and *Waste*. She performed regularly with American Repertory Theatre in Cambridge, MA.

NEVA PATTERSON, 90, Nevada, IA-born actress, died Dec. 14, 2010, at her home in Brentwood, CA, of complications of a broken hip. She made her Broadway debut in 1947 in *The Druid Circle*, followed by *The Ivy Green*; *Ring Round the Moon*; *The Long Days*; *Lace on Her Petticoat*; *Seven Year Itch*; *Speaking of Murder*; *Double in Hearts*; *Make a Million*; and *Romantic Comedy*. Her film roles include those in *Taxi* (1953); *Desk Set*; *An Affair to Remember*; *Too Much Too Soon*; *The Spiral Road*; *David and Lisa*;

Dear Heart; Skin Game; All the President's Men; The Buddy Holly Story; Star 80; and *All of Me.* Her television roles include *The Governor and J.J.; Nichols; V;* and *V: The Final Battle.* Her husband, actor/writer James Lee, died in 2002. Survivors include her daughter, Megan Lee, of Brentwood, CA; and son, Filippo Quaretti-Lee, of Florida; six grandchildren; and two great-grandchildren.

ARTHUR PENN, 88, Philadelphia, PA-born director, died Sept. 28, 2010, in New York City, of congestive failure. A Tony Award winner for his direction of *The Miracle Worker*, his other Broadway credits include *The Lovers; Two for the Seesaw* (Tony Award nominee)*; Toys in the Attic; An Evening With Mike Nichols and Elaine May; All the Way Home* (Tony Award nomination)*; In the Counting House; Lorenzo; Golden Boy; Wait Until Dark; Sly Fox* (1976 and 2004)*; Golda; Monday After the Miracle;*

and *Fortune's Fool.* An Academy Award nominee for *Bonnie and Clyde;* his other films include *The Left-Handed Gun; The Miracle Worker* (Academy Award nomination)*; Mickey One* (and producer)*; The Chase* (1966)*; Alice's Restaurant* (also co-writer; Academy Award nomination for directing)*; Little Big Man; Night Moves; The Missouri Breaks; Four Friends* (and producer)*; Target; Dead of Winter;* and *Penn & Teller Get Killed* (also producer). A veteran of W.W. II., he joined Josh Logan's Soldier's Show Company, and he was first stage manager for a production of *Golden Boy.* He also attended Black Mountain College in North Carolina, University of Perugia and the University of Florence in Italy. He began a career in television as floor manager on NBC's *The Colgate Comedy Hour,* working his way up to assistant director. He eventually directed NBC's live dramatic anthology *Gulf Playhouse: 1st Person,* as well as *Goodyear TV Playhouse; Philco TV Playhouse;* and *Playhouse 90.* He was also a past president of the Actors Studio in New York. His wife of fifty-five years, former actress Peggy Maurer; two children, Matthew and Molly; and four grandchildren survive him.

WALLY PETERSON, 93, Boston, MA-born performer/stage manager; died Mar. 30, 2011, in New York City, of natural causes. His Broadway credits as a performer include *A Passage to India; Dinner at Eight* (1966)*; A Touch of the Poet;* and *The Kingfisher.* As a stage manager his Broadway credits include *Dinner at Eight; Never Too Late; Mating Dance; All the Girls Came Out to Play; Brief Lives; Dirty Linen and New-Found-Land; The Kingfisher; American Buffalo; Arsenic and Old Lace; The Circle;* and *The Shadowlands.* A veteran of W.W. II, he was also a member of the Barter Theatre in the 1930s and appeared in a number or operettas such as *The Student Prince; Lady Baltimore;* and *Rose Marie.* He also performed in the London, England production of *Oklahoma!,* forging a friendship with fellow castmates Elliot Martin and Marjorie Austin, who later became producers and with whom he worked for decades. He worked in London again in *South Pacific* and toured America in *Sunrise at Campobello* with Howard Keel. His one-man show was *Tin Pan Alley and the Silver Screen,* which he toured on the university circuit and performed at the London Arts Theater in 1992. Two daughters and a son survive him.

ADDISON POWELL (Addison Powell Shelburne), 89, Belmont, MA-born actor, died on Nov. 8, 2010. His Broadway credits include *The Shrike; Fragile Fox; Big Fish, Little Fish; The Enemy Is Dead;* and *Coastal Disturbances.* His Off-Broadway credits include *The Iceman Cometh* at Circle in the Square (Obie Award). His film roles include *Three Days of the Condor; The Thomas Crown Affair; MacArthur; Contract on Cherry Street;* and his television roles include *Gunsmoke; The Bob Newhart Show; Law and Order; The Mod Squad;* and *Dark Shadows.* He was a veteran of W.W. II. and a graduate of Yale Drama School. His three children and their spouses, Mary Powell and Mark Brooks of South Hero, VT; Julie and Richard Elmore of Westford, VT; and Michael Powell and Evelyn Intondi of Brooklyn, NY; his younger and beloved brother, Edward; eight grandchildren, Katie, Anthony, Michael, Nicholas, Tony, Aidan, Calvin, and Alexandra survive him.

JAMES T. PRICHETT, 88, died Mar. 15, 2011, in New York, NY. His Broadway credits include *King Lear; Two for the Seesaw; Sail Away;* and *Summer and*

Smoke. His national tours include *Mame* and *Other People's Money.* A Best Actor Emmy-winner for his role of Dr. Matt Powers on *The Doctors* from 1963-1982, his other television credits include *The Secret Storm* and *As The World Turns.* He was a veteran of W.W. II. His wife, Cynthia; daughter, Laura; son-in-law, Priest Dimitri; daughter, Shelley; son, Kyle; daughter-in-law, Claudia; and grandchildren Yevgraf, Vassily, and Theodora survive him.

BEVERLEY RANDOLPH, 59, Norristown, PA-born stage manager, died Mar. 15, 2011, at her home in Bloomingdale, NJ, from cancer. Her Broadway credits include *The Addams Family; Evita; Jerome Robbins' Broadway; Kiss of the Spiderwoman; Passion; Into the Woods;* and *Curtains.* She was a graduate of Ithaca College, and the marquee lights on Broadway were dimmed in her honor on Mar. 16, 2011. Her husband, theatrical production electrician James Eisner; mother, Sarah DaCosta; sister, Carolyn Borlo; brother-in-law, Joseph Barlo; and niece, Sarah Randolph Barlo survive her.

DAN RESIN, South Bend, IA-born actor, died July 31, 2010, from complications of Parkinson's Disease. He lived in Secaucus, NJ. His Broadway credits include *A Month of Sundays* and *Once Upon a Mattress; The Young Abe Lincoln; Fade Out-Fade In; On a Clear Day You Can See Forever;* and *Don't Drink the Water.* His Off-Broadway productions include *On Our Town; Edge of Night; Lovers and Friends; David Frost Review; Go U.S.A.; Captain Kangaroo;* and *Madhouse Brigade.* He is a graduate of Indiana University. His wife of fifty-five years, Margaret; and daughter, Elizabeth Olynick survive him.

PHILIP ROSE (Philip Rosenberg), 89, producer/writer, died May 31, 2011, at the Lillian Booth Actors Home of the Actors Fund in Englewood, NJ, after suffering a stroke. A Tony winner for his book of *Shenandoah* in 1975, his other Broadway credits include *A Raisin in the Sun* (Tony nomination)*; Semi-Detached; Purlie Victorious; Bravo Giovanni; The Heroine; Nobody Loves an Albatross; Café Crown; The Owl and the Pussycat; Nathan Weinstein, Mystic, Connecticut; The Ninety Day Mistress* (and director)*; Does a Tiger Wear a Necktie?; Purlie* (1970 Tony nominations as book writer and book writer; and 1972)*; Kings; The Trip Back Down; Angel* (and director)*; Checkmates; Truly Blessed;* and *The Cemetery Club.* As a director, his Broadway credits include *My Old Friends* and *Late Nite Comic.* He was a pioneer in the production of African-American playwrights (he produced Lorraine Hansbury's *A Raisin in the Sun,* the first Broadway play written by an African-American woman, with whom he had worked in a summer camp in the Catskills), and the play was also the first with an African-American director (Lloyd Richards). He was also a pioneer in nontraditional casting, pairing Caucasian Alan Alda with African-American Diana Sands in *The Owl and the Pussycat,* creating much controversy. He also worked as a record executive and founded an R&B music label, *Glory Records.* His memoir is entitled *You Can't Do That On Broadway!* His wife, actress Doris Belack; brother, Jack Rosenberg; and sisters Sylvia Smolkin, Pearl Yabroff, and Rose Diamond, all of Washington, D.C. area survive him.

PAUL RYAN RUDD, 70, Boston, MA-born actor/director/playwright, died Aug. 12, 2010, in Greenwich, CT, of pancreatic cancer. His Broadway credits include *The Changing Room* (1973)*; The National Health; The Glass Menagerie; Ah, Wilderness!; Romeo and Juliet;* and *Bosoms and Neglect.* His Off-Broadway credits include *Henry IV,* followed by *King Lear; A Cry of Players; A Midsummer Night's Dream; An Evening with Merlin Finch; In the Matter of J. Robert Oppenheimer; Elagabalus; Streamers;*

Henry V; Boys in the Band; Da; The Show-Off; and *The Lady and the Clarinet.* He performed the title role of Henry V with the New York Shakespeare Festival and other stage credits include *Romeo in Romeo and Juliet, Bosoms and Neglect;* and *Oberon and Theseus* in *A Midsummer Night's Dream.* His television credits include those in *Johnny, We Hardly Knew Ye; Hart to Hart; Moonlighting; Knots Landing;* and *Murder, She Wrote,* and his film credits include *The Betsy.* A teacher in middle and high schools occasionally, he was also on the staff of Sarah Lawrence College from 1999-2006. From 2004 until his death he was a faculty member and associate director of the MFA drama program at the New School for Drama. His wife, the former Martha Bannerman; and three children, Graeme, Kathryn, and Eliza survive him.

H. JAMES SCHLADER, 96, co-founder and producer of Woodminster Summer Musicals for forty-three years, died May 8, 2010, in Oakland, CA, after suffering a stroke two weeks earlier. During his tenure at Woodminster, he produced about 150 musicals, directing his last show, *Beauty and the Beast*, at age ninety-two, in 2006. His Broadway credits prior to relocating to California include *Brigadoon; The Girl in Tights; Hit the Trail; Plain and Fancy;* and *The Most Happy Fella* (1956 and 1959). Prior to co-founding Woodminster, he had been staging musicals at the WPA-built Woodminster Amphitheater in Oakland's Joaquin Miller Park, where he oversaw many improvements to the facility. He was a veteran of W.W. II and a graduate of Chicago Music College. His wife of over fifty years, Harriet; daughter Jody Jaron, and her husband Steve and daughter Megan; son Kim, and his wife Michelle and daughter Kristen; son Todd; and son Joel, his wife Anne and children Madison and Peyton survive him.

TOM SIGNORELLI, 74, actor, died July 6, 2010. His Broadway credits include *General Seeger; Borstal Boy; Lampost Reunion* (Drama Desk nomination); and *Death of a Salesman*.

WALTER STANE, 81, actor/stage manager, died Jan. 27, 2011. His Broadway credits as a performer include *Lady in the Dark; Lute Song; Look Ma, I'm Dancin!* (and stage manager); *Ballet Ballads; Along 5th Avenue; Regina;* and *Top Banana.* He was a resident of Jamaica, NY.

JOSEPH STEIN, 98, Bronx, NY-born producer/writer, died Oct. 24, 2010, in New York, NY, following a fall. Beginning his career as a radio writer for personalities such as Zero Mostel and Tallulah Bankhead, he eventually wrote for Sid Caesar's *Your Show of Shows.* A Tony Award and New York Drama Critics Circle Award winner for his book of *Fiddler on the Roof*, his other Broadway credits include *Lend an Ear; Mrs. Gibbons' Boys; Alive and Kicking; Plain and Fancy; Mr. Wonderful; The Body Beautiful; Juno; Take Me Along; Enter Laughing;* the revivals of *Fiddler on the Roof* (1976, 1981, 1990, 2004); *We Bombed in New Haven; Zorba* (Tony nomination, 1968; 1983) *Irene; So Long, 174th Street; King of Hearts; Carmelina; Rags* (Tony nomination); and *Jerome Robbins' Broadway.* He also wrote screenplays for three of his musicals—*Fiddler on the Roof; Enter Laughing;* and *Mrs. Gibbons' Boys.* In 2007 Westport Country Playhouse produced his *All About Us* and in 2008 Encores! presented a revival of *Juno.* His first marriage, to Sadie Singer, ended in her death in 1974. His second wife, Elisa Loti; three sons from his first marriage, Daniel, Harry, and Joshua Stein; stepson, John Bader; stepdaughter, playwright Jenny Lyn Bader; and six grandchildren survive him.

HELEN STENBORG, 86, Minneapolis, MN-born actress, died Mar. 22, 2011, in New York, NY. Her Broadway credits include *Sheep on the Runway; The Trial of the Cantonsville 9; A Doll's House; A Life; A Month in the Country; Waiting in the Wings* (Tony nomination); and *The Crucible* (2002). As a longtime member of the Circle Repertory Company, she appeared in the original productions of Lanford Wilson's *The Hot L Baltimore; The Fifth of July;* and *Talley and Son* (Obie Award). Her other Off-Broadway credits include *A Doll's House; Say Nothing; Romersholm; Rimers of Eldritch; Pericles; Elephant in the House; A Tribute to*

Lili Lamont; Museum; In the Recovery Lounge; The Chisholm Trial; Time Framed; Leviation; Enter a Free Man; Tomorrow's Monday; Niedecker; Heaven on Earth; Daytrips; A Perfect Ganesh; Wit; and *Vigil.* Her national tours include *Da*, with her husband, actor Barnard Hughes. Her television work includes *Another World*, from 1977-1978, and her film roles include *Her Mother Dreams; On the Hook;*

Three Days of the Condor; Starting Over; Enchanted; and *Doubt.* She attended Hunter College. Her husband, to whom she was married for over fifty years, died in 2006. Her son, director Doug Hughes and his partner, Kate Jennings Grant; daughter, actress Laura Hughes and her partner, actor/director/producer John Gould Rubin; and grandson, Sam Hughes Rubin survive her.

MARGOT STEVENSON (Margaret Helen Stevenson), 99, New York, NY-born actress, died Jan. 7, 2011, in New York, NY. Her Broadway credits include *Firebird; Evensong; A Party; The Barretts of Wimpole Street; Symphony; Truly Valiant; Call It A Day; Stage Door; You Can't Take It With You; Golden Wings; Little Women; The Rugged Path; The Leading Lady; The Young and Beautiful; Triple Play; Big Fish, Little Fish; One by One; Hostile Witness;* and *The Royal Family.* Having played opposite Orson Welles in *The Shadow* on radio, she also appeared in numerous regional productions and in London, England. Her movie credits include *Smashing the Money Ring* with Ronald Reagan. Her daughter, Margot Avery survives her.

HAILA STODDARD, 97, Great Fall, MT-born actress/producer, died Feb. 21, 2011, in Weston, CT, of cardiopulmonary arrest. As a performer, her Broadway credits include *A Woman's a Fool—to Be Clever; I Know What It's Like; Kindred; Yes, My Darling Daughter; Susannah and the Elders; The Rivals; The Moon Vine; Blithe Spirit; Dream Girl; The Secret Room; Dr. Social; Glad Tidings; The Frogs of Spring; One Eye Closed; Lunatics and Lovers; Patate;* and *Who's Afraid of Virginia Woolf.* Her Broadway credits as a producer include *A Thurber*

Carnival; Sail Away (Tony nomination); *The Affair; The Hollow Crown; The Beast in Me; The Birthday Party;* and *The Gingham Dog.* Her Off-Broadway credits include *Private Lives; Lemon Sky;* and *Love.* She toured the South Pacific in *The Man Who Came to Dinner*, and her other touring and regional credits include *Merrily We Roll Along* and *Tobacco Road.* She spent sixteen years portraying Aunt Pauline on *The Secret Storm*, from 1954-1970. She was also a graduate of the University of Southern California and a founding member of the Bucks County Playhouse in Pennsylvania, where she appeared in *Springtime for Henry* and *Dead Pigeons.* Her son, Christopher Kirkland, of Denver, CO; daughter, Robin Kirkland MacDonald, of Manhattan; stepdaughter, Erin Connor, of Los Angeles, CA; seven grandchildren; and six great-grandchildren survive her.

ELLEN STEWART, 91, Chicago, IL-born founder, artistic director, and producer of La MaMa Experimental Theater, died Jan. 13, 2011, in Manhattan, of heart trouble. Founding La MaMa in a basement apartment in 1961, it (and she) became central figures of the Off-Off-Broadway movement. Actors who worked at La Mama over the years include Al Pacino; Robert De Niro; Harvey Keitel; Bette Midler; Richard Dreyfuss; and Diane Lane. Directors who worked at La MaMa include Robert Wilson; Tom O'Horgan; Joseph Chaikin of the Open Theater;

and Joseph Papp (pre-Public Theater). Among the plays that originated at La MaMa include *Godspell* and *Torch Song Trilogy*, among over 3,000 productions produced there. She also created site-specific works all over the world, including those in Lebanon, Japan, and Italy. In 1969 the theatre moved into a former meatpacking plant at 74A East Fourth Street, which created two 99-seat theatres. Later, she opened the Annex, a 295-seat theatre in November 2009, which is now called the Ellen Stewart Theater. La Mama also now houses an art gallery, a six-story rehearsal space, and studio building nearby, as well as extensive archive on the history of Off-Off-Broadway theatre. The marquee lights on Broadway were dimmed in her honor on Jan. 19, 2011.

JAMES STOVALL, 52, Baltimore, MD-born actor/singer/dancer/writer, died Sept. 26, 2010, in New York NY, of heart failure. His Broadway credits include *Big Deal; Sweet Charity; Once on This Island; The Life; Ragtime; The Rocky Horror Show; Finian's Rainbow;* and the *Dreamgirls* benefit in 2001. His Off-Broadway credits include *Dessa Rose; Stars in Your Eyes; Sugar Hill;* and *Romance in Hard Times.* His national tours include *Once on This Island* and *Joseph and the Amazing Technicolor Dreamcoat.* A graduate of Morehouse College, as a writer he wrote *Nativity: A Life Story,* with Hattie Winston, which was regularly performed at the Reverend Ike's United Palace Theater in Washington Heights, Manhattan, where he was the executive director of ministry of arts and culture. Survivors include his father, Reverend James Stovall, Sr.

JACK SYDOW, 88, Rockford, IL-born actor/director/playwright/professor, died May 28, 2010, in Los Angeles, CA. His Broadway credit as an assistant director was *Once Upon a Mattress* before becoming a director himself, with Broadway credits in that capacity including *Sophie; The Crucible* (1964)*; Annie Get Your Gun* (1968, Tony nomination)*; The Imaginary Invalid; A Touch of the Poet; Tonight at 8:30;* and *The National Theater of the Deaf.* His Off-Broadway credits include *The Brothers Karamazov* (Obie Award)*; The Idiot;* and *The Giants' Dance.* He also directed the national tour of *Once Upon a Mattress* and his regional credits include *Mary Stuart; Elizabeth the Queen; Ring Round the Moon;* and *The Crucible.* Television credits include appearances on *Frasier; Touched By An Angel;* and *Brothers and Sisters.* He also headed the directing program of the University of Washington for sixteen years.

CLARICE TAYLOR, 93, Buckingham, VA-born actress, died May 30, 2011, at her home in Englewood, NJ, of congestive heart failure. Perhaps best known as Anna Huxtable, Dr. Heathcliff Huxtable's mother on NBC's *The Cosby Show* in the 1980s, her Broadway credits include *The Wiz.* An Obie Award winner for her role as Moms Mabley in *Moms,* her other Off-Broadway credits include *Kongi's Harvest; Daddy Goodness; god is a (Guess What?); An Evening of One Acts; Man Better Man; Five on the Black Hand Side; Akokawe; Rosalee Pritchett; The*

Sty of the Blind Pig; Wedding Band; and *Man, Woman, Dinosaur.* She began her career in New York with the American Negro Theater in Harlem, and was a founding member of the American Negro Theater in the East Village. Her films include *Change of Mind; Tell Me That You Love Me; Junie Moon; Play Misty for Me;* and *Five on the Blackhand Side* . Her two sons, William and James survive her. She also appeared as Harriet the grandmother on *Sesame Street.*

ELIZABETH TAYLOR (Elizabeth Rosemond Taylor), 79, London, England-born actress, died Mar. 23, 2011, in Los Angeles, CA, of congestive heart failure. A Special Theatre World Award winner in 1981 for her role in *The Little Foxes* with Maureen Stapleton, her other Broadway credits include *Private Lives* as an actress, and *The Corn Is Green* as a producer. Considered one of the greatest film stars of all time, she won Academy Awards for Best Actress in *BUtterfield 8* in 1961, and *Who's Afraid of Virginia Woolf?* in 1966. Her other film roles include *There's One Born Every Minute; Lassie Come Home; Jane Eyre; The White Cliffs of Dover; National Velvet; Courage of Lassie; Life with Father; Cynthia; A Date with Judy; Julia Misbehaves; Little Women; Conspirator; The Big Hangover; Father of the Bride; Father's Little Dividend; A Place in the Sun; Quo Vadis; Love Is Better Than Ever; Ivanhoe; The Girl Who Had Everything; Rhapsody; Elephant Walk; Beau Brummell; The Last Time I Saw Paris; Giant; Raintree County; Cat on a Hot Tin Roof; Suddenly, Last Summer; The V.I.P.s; Cleopatra; Becket; The Sandpiper; The Taming of the Shrew; Doctor Faustus; Reflections in a Golden Eye; The Comedians; Boom!; Secret Ceremony; The Only Game in Town; X, Y, and Zee; Under Milk Wood; Hammersmith Is Out; Ash Wednesday; The Drivers' seat; The Blue Bird; A Little Night Music; Winter Kills; The Mirror Crack'd; Young Toscanini;* and *The Flintstones.* Her numerous television appearances include *Victory at Entebbe; Hallmark Hall of Fame; General Hospital; Between Friends; All My Children; Hotel; Malice in Wonderland; There Must Be a Phony; Poker*

Alice; Sweet Bird of Youth; Captain Planet and the Planateers; The Simpsons; These Old Broads; and *God, the Devil and Bob.* She also received a 1992 Jean Herscholt Humanitarian Award for her work for AIDS; a 1997 Screen Actors Guild for Lifetime Achievement; a 1985 Cecil B. DeMille Award; a Kennedy Center Honor; and an American Film Institute Lifetime Achievement Award, among many other awards and honors. Although the subject of many books, she, herself, published *Nibbles and Me; My Love Affair with Jewelry; Elizabeth Taylor;* and *Elizabeth Takes Off: On Weight Gain, Weight Loss, Self-Image and Self-Esteem.* She received the French Legion of Honor in 1987, and in 2000 was named a Dame Commander of the Order of the British Empire. In 2001 she also received a Presidential Citizens Medal for her humanitarian work. (She raised more than $200 million for AIDS charity work.) Married and divorced eight times, her husbands were: Conrad "Nicky" Hilton; Michael Wilding; Michael Todd; Eddie Fisher; Richard Burton (twice); Senator John Warner; and Larry Fortensky. The marquee lights on Broadway were dimmed in her honor on March 25, 2011. Her sons, Michael Howard Wilding and Christopher Edward Wilding, from her marriage to Michael Wilding; and daughters, Elizabeth Frances "Liza" Todd and Maria, both later adopted by Richard Burton survive her.

NOEL TAYLOR (Harold Alexander Taylor), 97, Youngstown, OH-born costume designer, died Nov. 5, 2010, in Los Angeles, CA. His prolific Broadway theatre career includes design for *The Haven; Alice in Wonderland; Stalag 17; The Wild Duck; One Bright Day; The Male Animal; Tovarich; First Lady; Bernardine; Dial "M" for Murder; The Grey-Eyed People; The Teahouse of the August Moon; The Ladies of the Corridor; In the Summer House; The Burning Glass; Festival; No Time for Sergeants; Time Limit!; The Apple Cart; Auntie Mame; Good as Gold; The Square Root of Wonderful; The Body Beautiful; Comes a Day; Tall Story; The Wall; Little Moon of Alban; Everybody Loves Opal; A Shot in the Dark; Write Me a Murder; The Night of the Iguana* (1961, 1976)*; General Seeger; Great Day in the Morning; The Riot Act; Strange Interlude; One Flew Over the Cuckoo's Nest* (1963)*; Marathon '33; What Makes Sammy Run?; Hughie; And Things That Go Bump in the Night; The Great Indoors; Slapstick Tragedy; The Loves of Cass McGuire; We Have Always Lived in the Castle; Dr. Cook's Garden; Song of the Grasshopper; Lovers; We Bombed in New Haven; The Mundy Scheme; Brightower; Ovid's Metamorphoses; A Funny Thing Happened on the Way to the Forum* (1972)*; Mourning Becomes Electra* (1972)*; The Last of Mrs. Lincoln; The Norman Conquests; Chapter Two; Paul Robeson; Diversions and Delights; Mixed Couples; Lucifer's Child; The Glass Menagerie* (1994)*; The Gin Game* (1997)*;* and *The Sunshine Boys* (1997). For his work in television he was nominated for four Emmys, winning for *Actor: The Paul Muni Story,* and he received a Lifetime Achievement Award from the Designers Guild in 2004 for his contributions to television. He worked for Hallmark Hall of Fame for seventeen years in that medium. He was also a veteran of the Coast Guard during W.W. II. His nephew, Marshall C. Taylor, Jr. survives him.

SADA THOMPSON, 83, Des Moines, IA-born actress, died May 4, 2011, in Danbury, CT, of lung disease. Perhaps best known for her role as matriarch Kate Lawrence on *Family,* from 1976-1980, her Broadway credits include *The Carefree Tree; Juno; Tartuffe; Johnny No-Trump; The Death of Bessie Smith/The American Dream; Happy Days; Twigs* (Tony Award, Drama Desk Award)*; Saturday Sunday Monday;* and *Any Given Day.* Her Off-Broadway credits include *The Carefree Tree; The Misanthrope* (Drama Desk Award)*; U.S.A.; The River Line; Under Milk Wood; Save Me a Place at Forest Lawn/The Last Minstrel; Othello; An Evening for Merlin Finch; The Effect of Gamma Rays on*

Man-in-the-Moon Marigolds (Drama Desk Award); and *Real Estate*. Nominated for an Emmy Award nine times, she won for *Family* in 1978. Her other television credits include *Owen Marshall: Counselor at Law; The Love Boat; Father Downling Mysteries; André's Mother; Cheers; Indictment: The McMartin Trial;* and *Law & Order*. Her films include *The Pursuit of Happiness; Desperate Characters;* and *Pollock*. Her regional credits include *The Seagull; Pygmalion; Our Town; Arms and the Man;* and *Blithe Spirit*. She is a graduate of Carnegie Tech. and received training at Pittsburgh Playhouse, where she also performed. Her husband, Donald E. Stewart, of Southbury, CT; and daughter, costume designer Liza Stewart survives her.

MICHAEL TOLAN (Seymour Tuchow), 85, Detroit, MI-born actor and founder of the American Place Theatre in New York, died Jan. 31, 2011, in Hudson, NY, of heart disease and renal failure. He lived in Ancram, NY. He made his Broadway debut in 1955 in *Will Success Spoil Rock Hunter?;* followed by *A Hatful of Rain; The Genius and the Goddess; Romanoff and Juliet; A Majority of One; A Far Country;* and *Unlikely Heroes*. His Off-Broadway credits include *Coriolanus; Journey of the 5th Horse; Close Relations; Faces of Love/Portrait of America; A Step Out of Line; Bedroom Farce; American Voices; The Enforcer;* and *George Washington Slept Here*. His film roles include *Fort Worth* and *Romanoff and Juliet*. His television credits include *The Doctors and the Nurses; The Senator;* and *The Mary Tyler Moore Show*. The American Place Theatre was first located on W. 46th Street, and is now located at 9th Avenue between 44th and 45th Streets, in New York City. He was a graduate of Wayne State University. His partner, Donna Peck; brother, Gerald Tuchow, of Detroit; daughter, Alexandra, of Watertown, MA, from his first marriage to the actress Rosemary Forsyth; and two daughters, Jenny and Emilie, both of New York, from his marriage to Carol Hume survive him.

RUSSELL WARNER, 74, orchestrator/composer/music director/dance arranger died Apr. 26, 2011, in Seattle, WA, from lung fibrosis associated with rheumatoid arthritis. His Broadway credits include *Shenandoah; Very Good Eddie; Going Up; The American Dance Machine; Whoopee!; The Utter Glory of Morrissey Hall; The Five O'Clock Girl;* and *Little Johnny Jones*. His many regional arrangement credits include *Animal Crackers* and *The Cocoanuts* at Arena Stage; *Sunny; El Capitan; Tip Toes; Good News;* and *Sweet Adeline*, among others at Goodspeed Opera House. He also worked for four years on the radio show *A Prairie Home Companion*. His brother, Irving Warner; and cousin, Susan Warner survive him.

GEORGE DAVID WEISS, 89, New York, NY-born composer/writer/lyricist, died Aug. 22, 2010, in Oldwick, NJ. His Broadway credits include *Mr. Wonderful; First Impressions; Send Me No Flowers; Maggie Flynn;* and *All Shook Up*. He contributed to film scores including *Murder, Inc.; Gidget Goes to Rome; Mediterranean Holiday;* and *Mademoiselle*. was a former president of the Songwriters Guild of America.

DOLORES WILSON (Dolores Mae Wilson), 82, Philadelphia, PA-born actress/opera singer, died Sept. 28, 2010, at the Lillian Booth Actors Fund Home in Englewood, NJ. She made her Broadway debut in 1965 in *The Yearling;* followed by *Fiddler on the Roof; Cry for Us All; I Remember Mama; Annie;* and *The Ritz*. An opera coloratura, she had twenty-six shows at the Metropolitan Opera, including those with its touring companies. Making her debut there in 1954, her career there ranged in roles from those

in *Lucia di Lammermoor;* Rosa in *Il Barbiere di Siviglia;* Susanna in *Le Nozze di Figaro;* and Zerlina in *Don Giovanni*. Her last performance was at the Met in a 1959 revival of *Lucia*.

DORIC WILSON (Alan Doric Wilson), Los Angeles, CA-born playwright/director/producer/gay activist, died May 7, 2011, at his home in New York, NY, of natural causes. One of the first resident playwrights at Joe Cino's Caffé Cino, he was, along with Lanford Wilson, Robert Patrick, and others, one of the pioneers of the Off-Off-Broadway movement. His plays staged at the Cino include *And He Made a Her* and *Now She Dances*. He later co-founded TOSOS (The Other Side

of Silence) Theatre Company in 1974, with Billy Blackwell, Peter del Valle, and John McSpadden, which was the first professional theatre company to deal with the openly gay experience. Productions staged there include his *Street Theater* and *The West Street Gang*. He was also a founding member of Circle Repertory Theatre. In 2007 he was presented with an Honorary Award for Artistic Achievement by the New York Innovative Theatre Foundation.

LANFORD WILSON (Lanford Eugene Wilson), 73, Lebanon, MO-born Pulitzer Prize-winning playwright, died Mar. 23, 2011, of complications from pneumonia. His Broadway credits as a writer include *The Gingham Dog; Talley's Folly* (Tony nomination); *Fifth of July* (Tony nomination, Drama Desk nomination); *Burn This; Angels Fall* (Tony nomination); Redwood *Curtain;* and *The Three Sisters* (1997, translator). Broadway credits as a producer with Circle Rep include *Knock Knock; Gemini; The Musical Comedy Murders of 1940; Prelude to a Kiss;* and *Master Class*. Beginning his career in Chicago, he spent six years there before relocating to New York, where he was one of the first playwrights, with Doric Wilson, Robert Patrick, and others, who helped form the basis of the Off-Off-Broadway theatre movement in the 1960s at Joe Cino's Caffé Cino in the West Village. He then was one of the founders of Circle Rep in 1969, where many of his works would be performed, including *The Hot L Baltimore; Balm in Gilead;* and his *Talley's Folly,* for which he received a Pulitzer Prize, part of the *Talley Trilogy*. In 2001 he was elected into the Theatre Hall of Fame and in 2004 he was elected to the American Academy of Arts and Letters. The marquee lights on Broadway were dimmed in his honor on Mar. 30, 2011.

RANDALL WREGHITT (Randal Lloyd Francis Wreghitt), 55, producer, died May 18, 2011, of carbon monoxide poisoning. His Broadway credits include *The Beauty Queen of Leenane* (Drama Desk Award, Tony nomination); *Electra* (Tony nomination); *Band in Berlin; The Lonesome West* (Tony nomination); *The Real Thing* (2000); *One Flew Over the Cuckoo's Nest* (2001, Tony Award; Drama Desk nomination); *Hedda Gabler* (2001); *Metamorphoses* (Drama Desk Award, Tony nomination); *Golda's Balcony; Little Women; The Lieutenant of Inishmore* (Tony nomination, Drama Desk nomination); *Grey Gardens* (Tony nomination); *Impressionism;* and *The Miracle Worker* (2010). His Off-Broadway credits include *Waverly Gallery; As Bees in Honey Drown* (Drama Desk nomination); *The Boys in the Band* (revival); *The Food Chain;* and *Camping with Henry and Tom*. His Off-Broadway credits include *Electra* (Drama Desk nomination). His London's West End credits include *The Lobby Hero* and *The Boys in the Band*. A graduate of Iowa State University, he began his professional career as a marketing representative at Disney World from 1987-1990, before also working at the Big Apple Circus. His production company was called Iowa Boy Productions. In 1996, he won the Robert Whitehead Award for Outstanding Achievement in Commercial Theatrical Producing from the Commercial Theater Institute. His mother, Leona Wreghitt; and sister, Sheri Wreghitt survive him.

JOHN ALVIN WILLIS, 93, Morristown, TN-born editor in chief of *Theatre World* for over forty years and an employee since its inception in 1944, and widely regarded as one of the most important and influential theatre and film historians in America, died June 25, 2010, at his home in Manhattan, of complications from lung cancer. Having succeeded founder Daniel Blum upon his death in 1965 as editor of *Theatre World* (now in its sixty-seventh year and the oldest, most current, annual pictorial and statistical record of the American theatre), Mr. Willis meticulously chronicled the seasons of Broadway, regional theatre, summer stock, touring companies, actors' biographies, obituaries, major theatrical awards, and as they came into existence, Off-Broadway and Off-Off-Broadway. Mr. Willis also edited *Screen World*, which began publication in 1950, and as the companion volume to *Theatre World* is the annual record of foreign and domestic film releases. Both publications are now considered the definitive references in their respective fields, consulted daily by industry professionals, students, historians, as well as by theatre and film fans worldwide. Both volumes are currently published by Theatre World Media and are distributed by Applause Theatre and Cinema Books, a subsidiary of the Hal Leonard Corporation. *Screen World* is currently edited by Barry

Monush. Mr. Willis was hired as a typist for $1 an hour in 1945 for the inaugural edition of *Theatre World*, founded by producer Daniel Blum and director Norman MacDonald. Mr. MacDonald, however, eventually departed for Los Angeles to become house manager for the Dorothy Chandler Pavilion and would also co-found of the Los Angeles County Music Archives. Mr. Willis's *Dance World* annual was published for thirteen years, from 1966-1979. The annual *Opera World* Mr. Blum had founded and on which Mr. Willis assisted, was short-lived, published from 1952-54. In conjunction with the release in 1945 of the first *Theatre World* was the presentation of the first annual Theatre World Awards. The Theatre World Awards are now—along with the Clarence Derwent Awards—tied as the oldest awards for Broadway and Off-Broadway debut performances, as well as one of the oldest awards bestowed on New York stage actors. The first Theatre World Awards (then called *Promising Personalities*) were presented in 1945 by Daniel Blum in his West Village apartment and consisted of framed parchment paper. Recipients of the Theatre World Award in its inaugural year included Judy Holliday and John Raitt, followed the next year by such future stars as Barbara Bel Geddes and Burt Lancaster. Originally chosen by Mr. Blum and then also by Mr. Willis upon his assumption of the job in 1965, Mr. Willis personally sought out and vetted up and coming New York talent for the Theatre World Award, bestowing upon six actors and six actresses what was usually their first professional recognition. Awardees were selected for their talent regardless of the ultimate success of the productions in which the recipients appeared, and many Theatre World Award winners were selected from otherwise undistinguished productions. As a purveyor of new talent, Willis became instrumental in helping launch the careers of luminaries from Alan Alda to Bernadette Peters to Laura Linney. Dorothy Loudon, who won a 1977 Tony Award as Miss Hannigan in *Annie*, would regularly recall at Theatre World Awards ceremonies that Mr. Willis had presented her, in 1962, with an award from *Nowhere to Go But Up* (a show that had lasted only one week). Ms. Loudon would then illustrate the obscurity of the production by joking that hers were "the only producers in history to picket the theatre on opening night." The embellished anecdote nonetheless illustrates the extent to which Mr. Willis would buck the trend of jumping on the bandwagon of *buzz* surrounding performers and productions, instead favoring the hard work associated with seeing as many shows as possible in seeking out those deserving of an award for an *Outstanding Debut Performance*. With Mr. Willis's aversion to press and media attention and intention on providing those winners who had gone on to fame a place where they could avoid the media circus, for over fifty years invitees to the Theatre World Awards consisted only of previous and current winners and their guests. With no nominees and presented by previous recipients to six men and six women at an intimate and exclusive affair, the Theatre World Awards—more a recognition than competition—became a favorite award and ceremony of performers through the years. Mr. Willis presided solely over the administration of the awards ceremony until 2002, when Peter Filichia, theatre critic and writer for Theatermania.com became host of the ceremony, and Ben Hodges, current editor in chief of *Theatre World* and president of Theatre World Publications, became executive producer until 2007. The Theatre World Awards were incorporated into a 501 (c) 3 nonprofit organization in 1998. The Theatre World Awards are now voted on by a committee of New York drama critics and presented each spring and administered by a board of directors. For years Mr. Willis, confirmedly averse to the spotlight which he cast so readily on others, would goodheartedly preliminarily admonish the winners during his introduction to the ceremony by instructing them that "There is no need for a long speech," and that "were it most likely not for luck, looks, and supportive

parents you probably wouldn't be here," ending with the advice for them when accepting their awards, to "Be brief, be beautiful for our photographers, and be off." This curmudgeonly demeanor was taken by those in the know as an inside joke for the act that it most definitely was. Known as *Big Daddy* to many of recipients of the Theatre World Award and having no children of his own, Willis considered the over five hundred recipients of the Theatre World Award indeed all his *children,* keeping close relationships with many winners over the years. For over forty years he sent each and every one of the hundreds of winners an annual birthday card, only ceasing when he permanently misplaced his address book in the late 1990s. The parties thrown at Mr. Willis's Riverside Drive home following the Theatre World Awards from the '60s through the '80s were the stuff of legend, the space large enough to accommodate a salon of exuberant current and previous winners. Regular fixtures were Carol Channing, Colleen Dewhurst, Ms. Loudon, Bob Fosse's first wife and dance partner, Marianne Niles, and Maureen Stapleton, among many (occasionally bawdy) others. A jovial and trusted companion as well as obsessively discreet, Mr. Willis became a favorite confidante of many celebrities in the twilight of their years, becoming a close friend and companion to many, including Joan Crawford, with whom he was regularly seen prior to the end of her life. John Alvin Willis was born in Morristown, Tennessee, on October 16, 1916, to John Bradford Willis, a pharmacist, and Georgia Ann Meyers, the daughter of a wealthy landowner. He graduated cum laude from Milligan College in Johnson City, Tennessee, in 1938, and received a masters of arts from the University of Tennessee in 1941, along with having performed postgraduate work at Harvard and Indiana Universities. Enlisting in the United States Navy in 1941, he served a two-year stint in the Gilbert and Marshall Islands, becoming a part of the U.S. Naval Reserves until 1945. Moving to New York City in 1945 to become an actor, he was participating in summer stock in Cedarhurst, Long Island when Norman MacDonald, director of the production, mentioned that he and *Theatre World* co-founder Daniel Blum were looking for a typist to type the entries for the annual series. Having been the assistant typing teacher at alma mater Milligan College in Tennessee, Mr. Willis put in for the job, and got it. Working as an assistant on *Theatre World* and *Screen World* from 1945 and 1950, respectively, and until Mr. Blum's death in 1965, Mr. Willis also served as assistant editor to Daniel Blum on *Great Stars of the American Stage; Great Stars of Film; A Pictorial History of the Talkies; A Pictorial History of Television; A Pictorial Treasury of Opera in America;* and *A Pictorial History of the Silent Screen.* Mr. Willis updated and edited Daniel Blum's landmark *A Pictorial History of the American Theatre* 1860-1960 every five years thereafter through 1985. Willis' thoroughly researched and spot-on digests of each theatrical season complete with statistics and "Random Notes" of the previous Broadway and Off-Broadway seasons appeared in *Theatre World* until the 1990s, citing many occurrences through the seasons that might have gone unnoticed by others in the press, such as the intervening amount of time between a an actor's appearance on Broadway, or the closing of an Off-Broadway theatre. It was not atypical if a seasons was particularly lean, for his "Review of the Season," to begin thusly: "This past season on Broadway was the most dreary in years." No one could accuse him of not knowing that about which he spoke, however. The seasonal overviews have been restored to current editions provided respectively by seasoned theatre journalists and professionals, although less critical and more evaluative in scope. Prior to his falling and breaking his hip on his way to see *Surviving Grace* at the Union Square Theatre on Feb. 21, 2002, Mr. Willis had (and still has) an unofficial record of seeing more Broadway, Off-Broadway, and Off-Off-Broadway shows than any other person—alive or dead, having attended—with the exception of a two week vacation in June of every year—between seven and nine shows a week for over fifty-eight years. Exploration of the required official proof of Mr. Willis's attendance through the Guinness Book of World Records resulted in the realization that it would have required the prohibitive task of combing the massive *Theatre World* archive for ticket stubs to submit as proof, and as meticulous as Mr. Willis's record keeping was, ticket stubs were not necessarily one of the articles of memorabilia that made it into a theatre production's file. Attendance was a responsibility that he took extremely seriously, believing that "If producers can provide a seat for me, then the least I can do is to sit through the show–no matter what." In fact, until his illness, Mr. Willis missed only two second acts in his lifetime—one due to one of the city-wide blackout of 1977, and the other when an inebriated friend was thrown out of the theatre and he felt obliged to follow to ensure his safety. In his later years he became a grandfather-like figure to many press agents and publicists, as they advanced from interns to full-fledged publicists and press agents–eventually many helming their own firms. On behalf of *Theatre World*, Mr. Willis received a 2001 Tony Honor for Excellence in the Theatre; the 2003 Broadway Theater Institute Lifetime Achievement Award; a 1994 special Drama Desk Award; and in 1993, the first Outstanding Special Lucille Lortel Award. On behalf of *Screen World*, he received the 1998 National Board of Review Wiliam K. Everson Award for Film History. He also received a professional excellence award from his alma mater, Milligan College. In 1993, the auditorium in which he had performed as a high school student was renovated and christened the John Willis Performing Arts Center at Morristown-Hamblen High School East in Morristown, Tennessee, and in 2007 a classroom in his collegiate alma mater Milligan College was named the John Willis Classroom. Mr. Willis served on the Tony Award nominating committee; the New York University Musical Hall of Fame selection committee; the national board of directors for the Clarence Brown Theatre at the University of Tennessee in Knoxville, Tennessee; and was on the past board of directors of the National Board of Review. In 1996 he received a caricature on the wall of Sardi's. In addition, Mr. Willis was retired from the New York public school system with over twenty years of service, unfathomably and simultaneously combing full-time teaching with his book editing and production of the Theatre World Awards. He had also taught briefly at the University of Tennessee at Knoxville. Always understated as well as grammatically acute, Mr. Willis announced his resignation on his first day of eligibility as a retiree from public high school teaching in 1976 by slipping a note in his principal's message box that read, "I will not be in tomorrow, nor ever." Having compiled obituaries annually for *Theatre World* for over fifty years, Mr. Willis was known to express dismay when causes of death, (especially of older celebrities) were not cited. He was fond of saying: "Everyone dies of something. I don't understand why they say *natural causes*, when all causes are natural unless you're murdered or die in an accident, so they should print what it was that killed them!" He would then add that "When *I* go, please mention what killed me." for the record, Mr. Willis succumbed to complications from lung cancer. There are no immediate survivors. Marriages to Claire Olivier, in 1960, and Marina Sarda, in 1978, ended in divorce.

Bernadette Peters, Brenda Smiley, and Alice Playten, on June 30, 2010, as the Broadway marquee lights dimmed in honor of the passing of longtime Theatre World *editor John Willis. They hold a copy of* Theatre World Volume 24: 1967-68, *in which they all three appeared as* Theatre World Award *winners during that season.*

West 44th Street in New York City, at sundown on June 30, 2010, as the Broadway marquee lights dimmed in honor of the passing of longtime Theatre World *editor John Willis.*

Index

Ben Hodges (President and Publisher, Theatre World Media; Editor in Chief, Theatre World) served as an editorial assistant for seven years on the 2001 Special Tony Honor Award-winning *Theatre World*, becoming the associate editor to John Willis in 1998 and editor in chief in 2008. *Theatre World*–at sixty-seven–is the most current and complete annual pictorial and statistical record of the American theatre, including Broadway, Off-Broadway, Off-Off-Broadway, and regional theatre productions, and is referenced daily by students, historians, and industry professionals worldwide.

In 2011, Ben founded Theatre World Media, which publishes both *Theatre World* and its sister publication, *Screen World*—the oldest pictorial annual record of the foreign and domestic film seasons, edited by Barry Monush.

Also an assistant for seven years to John Willis for the prestigious Theatre World Awards given for Broadway and Off-Broadway debut performances, Ben was elected to the Theatre World Awards board of directors in 2002 and served as executive producer for the annual ceremony from 2002-2007. In 2003 he was presented with a Special Theatre World Award in recognition of his ongoing stewardship of the event. He also served as executive producer for the 2005 LAMBDA Literary Foundation "Lammy" Awards, given for excellence in LGBT publishing.

The Commercial Theater Institute Guide to Producing Plays and Musicals, which Hodges co-edited with late Commercial Theater Institute director Frederic B. Vogel, was released by Applause Theatre and Cinema Books in 2007, and with contributions by twenty-eight Broadway producers, general managers, attorneys, and publicists, has had multiple printings and has become the definitive resource in its field. It has also been adopted as a course book by North Carolina School for the Arts, among other colleges and universities.

Forbidden Acts, the acclaimed first collected anthology of gay and lesbian plays from the span of the twentieth century, edited and with an introduction by Hodges, was published by Applause Theatre and Cinema Books in 2003 and became a finalist for the 2003 LAMBDA Literary Award for Drama, and has had multiple printings. New York University, Cornell University, Salisbury University, University of Las Vegas, and University of Louisville have adopted it as a course book, among other high schools, colleges and universities.

His *Out Plays: Landmark Gay and Lesbian Plays from the Twentieth Century*, edited and with an introduction by Hodges, featuring a foreword by Harvey Fierstein as well as a new introduction to *The Boys in the Band* by Mart Crowley, was released by Alyson Books in spring 2008. With *Out Plays*, Hodges became the most prolific single anthologist of published gay and lesbian American plays either in or out-of-print.

His highly acclaimed *The American Theatre Wing Presents The Play That Changed My Life: America's Foremost Playwrights on the Plays That Influenced Them*, with essays and interviews by nineteen of America's foremost American playwrights including David Auburn, Christopher Durang, Lynn Nottage, and John Patrick Shanley, was released by Applause Theatre and Cinema Books in fall 2009 and has had numerous printings.

As an actor, director, and/or producer, Ben has appeared in New York with The Barrow Group Theater Company, Origin Theater Company, Daedalus Theater Company, Monday Morning Productions, the Strawberry One-Act Festival, Coyote Girls Productions, Jet Productions, New York Actors' Alliance, and Outcast Productions. Additionally, he has appeared in numerous productions presented by theatre companies that he founded, including the Tuesday Group and Visionary Works. On film, he can be seen in *Macbeth: The Comedy*.

In 2001, Ben became director of development and then served as executive director for Fat Chance Productions Inc. and the Ground Floor Theatre, a New York-based nonprofit theatre and film production company. *Fat Chance developed Prey for Rock and Roll* from their stage production (the first legit production to play CBGBs) into a critically acclaimed feature film starring Gina Gershon and *The Sopranos'* Emmy winner Drea de Matteo. *Prey for Rock and Roll* debuted at the Sundance Film Festival in 2003 and won Best Feature at the 2003 Santa Cruz Film Festival. Additionally, Fat Chance produced the American premiere of award-winning Irish playwright Enda Walsh's *Misterman* Off-Broadway, and a host of readings, workshops, and productions in their Ground Floor Theatre, their mission statement being to present new works by new artists.

In 2003, frustrated with the increasingly daunting economic prospects involved in producing theatre on a small scale in New York, Ben organized NOOBA, the New Off-Off Broadway Association, an advocacy group dedicated to representing the concerns of expressly Off-Off-Broadway producers in the public forum and in negotiations with other local professional arts organizations; their chief objective the reformation of the Actors' Equity Basic Showcase Code.

He also serves on the New York Innovative Theatre Awards Committee, selecting outstanding individuals for recognition Off-Off-Broadway, and as vice-president of Summer Stage New York, a professional summer theatre program in Fayetteville, New York, and as executive producer of the annual Fire Island Pines Literary Weekend.

In 2005 Ben founded and served for two years as executive director of The Learning Theatre Inc., a 501(c)(3) nonprofit organization incorporating theatre into the development and lives of learning disabled and autistic children. He currently serves on the board of directors.

In support of his projects and publications, Ben has appeared on nationwide radio on *The Joey Reynolds Show*; *The Michael Dresser Show*; *Stage and Screen with Mark Gordon*; and on television on New York 1 and *Philly Live* in Philadelphia, PA–the only live televised LGBT call-in show in the United States. Reviews and articles on Ben, his projects, or publications have appeared in the *New York Times*; *New Yorker*; *GQ*, *Elle*; *Genre*; *Back Stage*; *Time Out New York*; *Playbill*; *Next*; *New York Blade*; *Library Journal*; *The Advocate*; *Chicago Free Press*; *Philadelphia Gay News*; *Houston Voice*; *Stage Directions*; *Between the Lines*; *The Flint Journal*; and *Citizen Tribune*; as well as the web sites Broadwayworld.com; CurtainUp.com; Playbill.com; and in Peter Filichia's Diary on Theatermania.com. He has made guest appearances in support of his publications at the Nadine's in the West Village; Good Beans Café in Flint, Michigan; Common Language Bookstore in Ann Arbor, Michigan, A Different Light in both Los Angeles and San Francisco; Michigan Design Center in Birmingham, Michigan; The Open Book in Sacramento; and at Giovanni's Room In Philadelphia, as well as at the DR2 Theatre D-2 Lounge, Barnes and Noble Lincoln Center, and the Drama Book Shop, in New York City.

He holds a BFA in Theatre Acting and Directing from Otterbein College in Westerville, Ohio, is an alumnus of the Commercial Theater Institute, and will receive his Juris Doctorate in May 2012 from Seton Hall University School of Law in Newark, New Jersey. He lives in Jersey City, New Jersey. For more information or to schedule speaking engagements, please visit benhodges.com, or e-mail benjaminahodges@gmail.com.

Scott Denny (Coeditor) is an actor and singer who has worked professionally for over twenty years. Originally from Terre Haute, Indiana, he attended Western Kentucky University in Bowling Green, Kentucky and holds a degree in performing arts.

Most recently he appeared in the Irish Repertory Theatre's gala *Brigadoon* concert at the Shubert Theatre in June 2010 and at the 2010 MAC Awards.

His professional theatrical credits include Richard Henry Lee in the Big League Theatricals national tour of *1776*, Uncle Wes in the Las Vegas and national touring production of *Footloose*, and the assistant company manager and swing on the 2001-2002 national tour of Susan Stroman's production of *The Music Man*. While on tour he arranged several cast benefit cabarets for local charities.

Regionally he has appeared in *Evita*, *The Wizard of Oz*, and *The King and I* at Houston's Theatre Under the Stars, *The Mikado* starring Eric Idle at Houston Grand Opera, and in the regional premieres of *Silver Dollar* and *Paper Moon* at Stage One in Wichita,

Kansas. He performed frequently at the Broadway Palm Dinner Theatre in Fort Myers, Florida, as well as Beef and Boards Dinner Theatre (Indianapolis, Indiana),

Fireside Theatre (Fort Atkinson, Wisconsin), Miami Valley Dinner Theatre (Springboro, Ohio), Dutch Apple Dinner Theatre (Lancaster, Pennsylvania), Circa 21 (Rock Island, Illinois), and the Crown Uptown (Wichita, Kansas). He worked six summers the Galveston Island Outdoor Musicals and at Sullivan Illinois' historic Little Theatre on the Square. Credits at those theatres include *Me and My Girl*, *Gypsy*, *She Loves Me*, *The Best Little Whorehouse in Texas*, *The Music Man*, *Some Like It Hot*, *Man of La Mancha*, *The Odd Couple*, *South Pacific*, *Oklahoma*, *Grease*, *Wonderful Life! The Musical*, *How to Succeed...*, among several others

In New York he has appeared Off-Off-Broadway in *Election Day The Musical*, *Like You Like It*, *Vanity Fair*, and in several readings, workshops, and cabaret shows. He screen credits include the independent films *Red Hook*, *Clear Blue Tuesday*, and *Illegally Yours*.

Scott worked as an assistant editor on *Theatre World* Volume 60, and has been an associate editor on Volumes 61-65. In the fall of 2006 Scott served as Treasurer on the Board of Directors of the Theatre World Awards and was the associate producer for the 2006 Awards and co-producer for the 2007, 2008, and 2009 Awards.

Seasonally Scott works for the Macy's Thanksgiving Day Parade and Macy's Annual Events in the production office, and spent one season in the costume operations for the Parade. Since 2003 Scott has also worked as an outside group sales manager specializing in incentive groups for Cruise Everything, a travel agency located in Fort Myers, Florida. He coordinated the entertainment and sales operations for four cruises with two of QVC's most known and loved personalities, the Quacker Factory host Jeanne Bice, and Jenniefer Kirk of Kirks Folly Jewelry, as well as three New York Theatre vacations. In addition to his other many hats, he bartends at the Duplex Cabaret and Piano Bar.

He is honored to help continue the astounding work of the late John Willis, and would like to thank his high school drama teacher Jean Shutt for introducing him to the wonderful theatre world, as well as the former theatre faculties of Western Kentucky University and Indiana State University: Bill Leonard, Jackson Kessler, Beverly Veenker, Steve Probus, Jim Brown, Larry Ruff, Lew Hackleman, Gary Stewart, Glenn and Patti Harbaugh, Don Nigro, David DelColletti, and the late Whit Combs.

Shay Gines (Associate Off-Off-Broadway Editor) graduated from the Actors Training Program at the University of Utah. Since then she has done everything from spackling walls at the Pasadena Playhouse and running follow-spot for the Pioneer Theatre Company to serving as the Artist in Residence for Touchstone Theatre. She has performed in theatres of all sizes from 30 to 1,000 seats and across the country, from Los Angeles to New York City. She is an award-winning producer whose Off and Off-Off-Broadway shows include: *Home Again Home Again Jiggity Jig*, *What the F**k?!*, *Hamlet*, and *Muse of Fire*. She was a founding member and the Producing Director for Esperance Theatre Company, served for five years as the Managing Director for Emerging Artists Theatre Company, and is an Executive Director for the Innovative Theatre Foundation.

Raj Autencio (Associate Regional Editor) Rommel "Raj" Autencio is a native of Manila, Phillipines, where he graduated with a Bachelor of Arts in Organizational Communication from the University of Phillipines, Manila, in 2000. As a professional singer, he performed in various show bands that travelled throughout the Middle East and Asia, including performances in Hong Kong and Bahrain. In New York, he has studied photography at the International Center of Photography, and has served as a staff photographer for *Theatre World* and the Theatre World Awards and the Fire Island Pines Literary Theater Festival in Pines, New York. His first group photography exhibit was held in New York in November 2011, in collaboration with the ElevenEleven Collective. Autencio was a close friend to longtime *Theatre World* editor John Willis, and served as his primary caretaker for over three years and until his death in 2010. He lives in Brooklyn, New York.

Heath McCormack (Associate Editor) is a classically trained former dance whose lifelong passion for ballet and musical theatre has taken him on an amazing journey across the United States. In addition to dancing for three consecutive seasons in the largest outdoor drama in America, *Texas! The Musical Drama*, Heath has also had the opportunity to be seen performing alongside a very eclectic group of entertainers, among them, the Lightcrust Doughboys, the country's oldest Western swing band, the Jim Cullum Jazz band, Canadian illusionist Brian Glow, and countless productions *The Nutcracker*, his favorite being one of the most opulently executed under the direction and original choreography of Mr. Neil Hess with Lone Star Ballet. In recent years Heath has taken his love of entertaining to the friendly skies and can be seen by hundreds of people coast to coast, non-stop, daily.

Kelley Murphy Perlstein (Assistant Editor) has been working professionally in the theatre for over 20 years. She has her B.A. in Theatre from the University of Science and Arts of Oklahoma and an M.F.A. in Music Theatre Performance from Roosevelt University in Chicago. From 2000-2007, she was the Development Director and eventually Managing Director of Praxis Theatre Project, an Off-Off Broadway company in New York City. She currently resides in Dallas, TX.

Adam Feldman (Contributing Editor: Broadway Review) is the associate theater editor at *Time Out New York*, where he is also cabaret editor. Since 2005, he has served as president of the New York Drama Critics' Circle, making him both the youngest and the longest-serving president in the group's seventy-five-year history. His essays and reviews have appeared in Canada's *Globe and Mail* and *National Post*, as well as Broadway.com, *Time Out London*, *Time Out New York Kids* and the *Gay & Lesbian Review*. He is a frequent commentator on New York's NPR station, WNYC, and has been interviewed on ABC's Nightline, CNN and CBS News. He has hosted panel events at the 92nd Street Y, the Brooklyn Academy of Music, the Public Theater and Theater Row, among others. He is a graduate of Harvard University, where he received the Helen Choate Bell prize for essays on American literature.

Linda Buchwald (Contributing Editor: Off-Broadway Review) writes monthly features for *TDF Stages* and is the associate editor of *Scholastic MATH Magazine*. She contributes to *StageGrade* and has freelanced for various publications, including the *Village Voice* online, the *Sondheim Review*, and *Broadway Direct*. She also runs a (mostly) theater blog, Pataphysical Science, and is a member of the Independent Theater Bloggers Association (ITBA). She is a graduate of the Goldring Arts Journalism Program at Syracuse University. You can follow her on Twitter @PataphysicalSci.

Rob Weinert-Kendt (Contributing Editor: Regional Review) is associate editor at *American Theatre* magazine. He has written features and criticism for the *New York Times*, the *Los Angeles Times*, *Variety*, the *Sondheim Review*, and *Time Out NY*, among others. He was the founding editor of *Back Stage West*.